COMMON LISP

THE LANGUAGE

SECOND EDITION

Would it be wonderful if, under the pressure of all these difficulties, the Convention should have been forced into some deviations from that artificial structure and regular symmetry which an abstract view of the subject might lead an ingenious theorist to bestow on a constitution planned in his closet or in his imagination?

—*James Madison, The Federalist No. 37, January 11, 1788*

COMMON LISP

THE LANGUAGE

SECOND EDITION

GUY L. STEELE JR.

with contributions by
SCOTT E. FAHLMAN
RICHARD P. GABRIEL
DAVID A. MOON
DANIEL L. WEINREB

and with contributions to the second edition by
DANIEL G. BOBROW
LINDA G. DEMICHIEL
RICHARD P. GABRIEL
SONYA E. KEENE
GREGOR KICZALES
DAVID A. MOON
CRISPIN PERDUE
KENT M. PITMAN
RICHARD C. WATERS
JON L WHITE

Digital Press

9 8 7 6 5 4 3 2

Printed in the United States of America.

ADA used to be a registered trademark of the U.S. Government Ada Joint Program Office, but is no longer a trademark. Chevrolet is a registered trademark of General Motors. DEC, PDP, VAX, and VMS are trademarks of Digital Equipment Corporation. Hostess Twinkies is a registered trademark of Continental Baking Company. IBM is a registered trademark of International Business Machines Corporation. Macintosh is a registered trademark of Apple Computer, Inc. Multics is a registered trademark of Honeywell Inc. PostScript is a registered trademark of Adobe Systems Incorporated. Rolo is a registered trademark of Hershey Foods Corporation. SPAM is a registered trademark of Geo. A. Hormel & Co. Tang is a brand name of General Foods Corporation. Teenage Mutant Ninja Turtles is a registered trademark, and Donatello, Krang, Leonardo, Michaelangelo, Raphael, and Shredder are trademarks of Mirage Studios, USA. Teflon is a registered trademark of Du Pont. T_EX is a trademark of the American Mathematical Society. UNIX is a trademark of Bell Laboratories. ZETALISP is a registered trademark of Symbolics, Inc. All other trademarks are the property of their respective owners.

Design: David Ford
Copyediting: Alice Cheyer and Kate Schmit
Index: Marilyn Rowland
Composition: Guy L. Steele Jr. (See Colophon.)
Camera-ready copy: Advanced Computer Graphics
Production: Editorial Inc.
Printer: Hamilton Printing Company

Library of Congress Cataloging-in-Publication Data

Steele, Guy.
   COMMON LISP.

   Includes bibliography references (p.   )
   1. COMMON LISP (Computer program language) I. Title.
QA76.73.L23S73 1990 005.13′3 89-26016

Paperback order number EY-C187E-DP   ISBN 1-55558-041-6

Contents

Preface

SECOND EDITION

Common Lisp has succeeded. Since publication of the first edition of this book in 1984, many implementors have used it as a *de facto* standard for Lisp implementation. As a result, it is now much easier to port large Lisp programs from one implementation to another. Common Lisp has proved to be a useful and stable platform for rapid prototyping and systems delivery in artificial intelligence and other areas. With experience gained in using Common Lisp for so many applications, implementors found no shortage of opportunities for innovation. One of the important characteristics of Lisp is its good support for experimental extension of the language; while Common Lisp has been stable, it has not stagnated.

The 1984 definition of Common Lisp was imperfect and incomplete. In some cases this was inadvertent: some odd boundary situation was overlooked and its consequences not specified, or different passages were in conflict, or some property of Lisp was so well-known and traditionally relied upon that I forgot to write it down. In other cases the informal committee that was defining Common Lisp could not settle on a solution, and therefore agreed to leave some important aspect of the language unspecified rather than choose a less than satisfactory definition. An example is error handling; 1984 Common Lisp had plenty of ways to signal errors but no way for a program to trap or process them.

Over the next year I collected reports of errors in the book and gaps in the language. In December 1985, a group of implementors and users met in Boston to discuss the state of Common Lisp. I prepared two lists for this meeting, one of errata and clarifications that I thought would be relatively uncontroversial (boy, was I wrong!) and one of more substantial changes I thought should be considered and perhaps voted upon. Others also brought proposals to discuss. It became clear to everyone that there was now enough interest in Common Lisp, and dependence on its stability, that a more formal mechanism was needed for managing changes to the language.

This realization led to the formation of X3J13, a subcommittee of ANSI committee X3, to produce a formal American National Standard for Common Lisp.

That process is nearing completion. X3J13 has completed the bulk of its technical work in rectifying the 1984 definition and codifying extensions to that definition that have received widespread use and approval. A draft standard is now being prepared; it will probably be available in 1990. There will then be a period (required by ANSI) for public review. X3J13 must then consider the comments it receives and respond appropriately. If the comments result in substantial changes to the draft standard, multiple public review periods may be required before the draft can be approved as an American National Standard.

Fortunately, X3J13 has done an outstanding job of documenting its work. For every change that came to a formal vote, a document was prepared that described the problem to be solved and one or more solutions. For each solution there is a detailed proposal for changing the language; a rationale; test cases that distinguish the proposal from the status quo or from other proposals for solving that problem; discussions of current practice, cost to implementors, cost to users, cost of not adopting the proposal, benefits of adoption, aesthetic criteria; and any relevant informal discussion that may have preceded creation of the formal proposal. All of these proposal documents were made available on-line as well as in paper form. By my count, by June 1989 some 186 such proposals were approved as language changes. (This count does not include many proposals that came before the committee but were rejected.)

The purpose of this second edition is to bridge the gap between the first edition and the forthcoming ANSI standard for Common Lisp. Because of the requirement for formal public review, it will be some time yet before the ANSI standard is final. This book in no way resembles the forthcoming standard (which is being written independently by Kathy Chapman of Digital Equipment Corporation with assistance from the X3J13 Drafting Subcommittee).

I have incorporated into this second edition a great deal of material based on the votes of X3J13, in order to give the reader a picture of where the language is heading. My purpose here is not simply to quote the X3J13 documents verbatim but to paraphrase them and relate them to the structure of the first edition. A single vote by X3J13 may be discussed in many parts of this book, and a single passage of this book may be affected by many of the votes.

I wish to be very clear: this book is not an official document of X3J13, though it is based on publicly available material produced by X3J13. In no way does this book constitute a definitive description of the forthcoming ANSI standard. The committee's decisions have been remarkably stable (it has rescinded earlier decisions only two or three times), and I do not expect radical changes in direction. Nevertheless, it is quite probable that the draft standard will be substantively revised in response to editorial review or public comment. I have therefore reported here on the actions of X3J13 not to inscribe them in stone, but to make clear how the language of the first edition is likely to change. I have tried to be careful in my wording to avoid saying "the language has been changed" and to state simply that "X3J13 voted at such-and-so time to make the following change."

Until the day when an official ANSI Common Lisp standard emerges, it is likely that the 1984 definition of Common Lisp will continue to be used widely. This book has been designed to be used as a reference both to the 1984 definition and to the language as modified by the actions of X3J13.

It contains the entire text of the first edition of *Common Lisp: The Language*, with corrections and minor editorial changes; however, more than half of the material in this edition is new. All new material is identified by solid lines in the left margin. Dotted lines in the left margin indicate material from the first edition that applies to the 1984 definition but that has been modified by a vote of X3J13. Modifications to these outmoded passages are explained by preceding or following text (which will have a solid line in the margin). In summary:

- To use the 1984 language definition, read all material that does not have a solid line in the margin.

- To use the updated language definition, read everything, but be wary of material with a dotted line in the margin.

At the end of the book is an index of the X3J13 votes, ordered by the committee's internal code names (included to ease cross-reference to the X3J13 documents, which may be useful during the public review periods). References to this list of votes appear as numbers in angle brackets; thus "⟨14⟩" refers to the vote on issue number 14, whereas "[14]" refers to reference 14 in the bibliography.

I have kept changes to the wording of the first-edition material to a minimum. Obvious spelling and typographical errors have been corrected, and the entire text has been edited to a uniform style of spelling and punctuation. (Note in particular that the first edition used the spelling "signalling" but this edition, in deference to the style decision of the X3J13 Drafting Subcommittee, uses "signaling.") A few minor changes were made to accommodate typographical or layout constraints. (For example, the word "also" has been deleted from the first sentence of chapter 1, partly to make that paragraph look better and partly to allow a better page break at the bottom of page 2.) In a very few cases the first edition contained substantive errors that I could not in good conscience correct silently; these have been flagged by paragraphs beginning with the phrase *Notice of correction*.

The chapter and section numbering of this edition matches that of the first edition, with the exception that a new section 7.9 has been interpolated. Four new chapters (26–29) describe substantial changes approved by X3J13: an extended loop macro, a pretty printer interface, the Common Lisp Object System, and the Common Lisp Condition System.

X3J13, in the course of its work, formed a subcommittee to study whether additional means of iteration should be standardized for use in Common Lisp, for a great deal of existing practice in this area was not included in the first edition because of lack of agreement in 1984. The X3J13 Iteration Subcommittee produced reports on three possible facilities. One (loop) was approved for inclusion in the forthcoming draft standard and is described in chapter 26.

X3J13 expressed interest in the other two approaches (series and generators), but the consensus as of January 1989 was that these other approaches were not yet sufficiently mature or in sufficiently widespread use to warrant inclusion in the draft Common Lisp standard at that time. However, the subcommittee was directed to continue work on these approaches and X3J13 is open to the possibility of standardizing them at a later date. Please note that I do not wish to prejudge the question of whether X3J13 will ever choose to make the other two proposals the subject of standardization. Nevertheless, I have chosen to include them in the second edition, in cooperation with Dr. Richard C. Waters, as appendixes A and B, in order to make these ideas available to the Lisp community. In my judgment these proposals address an area of language design not otherwise covered by Common Lisp and are likely to have practical value even if they are never adopted as part of a formal standard.

Some new material in this book has nothing to do with the work of X3J13. In many places I have added explanations, clarifications, new examples, warnings, and tips on writing portable code. Appendix C contains a piece of code that may help in understanding the backquote syntax.

This second edition, unlike the first edition, also includes a few diagrams to pep up the text. However, there are absolutely no new jokes, and very few outright lies.

Acknowledgments

SECOND EDITION

First and foremost, I must thank the many people in the Lisp community who have worked so hard to specify, implement, and use Common Lisp. Some of these have volunteered many hours of effort as members of ANSI committee X3J13. Others have made presentations or proposals to X3J13, and yet others have sent suggestions and corrections to the first edition directly to me. This book builds on their efforts as well as mine.

An early draft of this book was made available to all members of X3J13 for their criticism. I have also worked with the many public documents that have been written during the course of the committee's work (which is not over yet). It is my hope that this book is an accurate reflection of the committee's actions as of October 1989. Nevertheless, any errors or inconsistencies are my responsibility. The fact that I have made a draft available to certain persons, received feedback from them, or thanked them in these acknowledgments does not necessarily imply that any one of them or any of the institutions with which they are affiliated endorse this book or anything of its contents.

Digital Press and I gave permission to X3J13 to use any or all parts of the first edition in the production of an ANSI Common Lisp standard. Conversely, in writing this book I have worked with publicly available documents produced by X3J13 in the course of its work, and in some cases as a courtesy have obtained the consent of the authors of those documents to quote them extensively. This common ancestry will result in similarities between this book and the emerging ANSI Common Lisp standard (that is the purpose, after all). Nevertheless, this second edition has no official connection whatsoever with X3J13 or ANSI, nor is it endorsed by either of those institutions.

The following persons have been members of X3J13 or involved in its activities at one time or another: Jim Allard, Dave Andre, Jim Antonisse, William Arbaugh, John Aspinall, Bob Balzer, Gerald Barber, Richard Barber, Kim Barrett, David Bartley, Roger Bate, Alan Bawden, Michael Beckerle, Paul Beiser, Eric Benson, Daniel Bobrow, Mary Boelk, Skona Brittain, Gary Brown, Tom Bucken, Robert

Buckley, Gary Byers, Dan Carnese, Bob Cassels, Jérôme Chailloux, Kathy Chapman, Thomas Christaller, Will Clinger, Peter Coffee, John Cugini, Pavel Curtis, Doug Cutting, Christopher Dabrowski, Jeff Dalton, Linda DeMichiel, Fred Discenzo, Jerry Duggan, Patrick Dussud, Susan Ennis, Scott Fahlman, Jogn Fitch, John Foderaro, Richard Gabriel, Steven Gadol, Nick Gall, Oscar Garcia, Robert Giansiracusa, Brad Goldstein, David Gray, Richard Greenblatt, George Hadden, Steve Haflich, Dave Henderson, Carl Hewitt, Carl Hoffman, Cheng Hu, Masayuki Ida, Takayasu Ito, Sonya Keene, James Kempf, Gregory Jennings, Robert Kerns, Gregor Kiczales, Kerry Kimbrough, Dieter Kolb, Timothy Koschmann, Ed Krall, Fritz Kunze, Aaron Larson, Joachim Laubsch, Kevin Layer, Michael Levin, Ray Lim, Thom Linden, David Loeffler, Sandra Loosemore, Barry Margolin, Larry Masinter, David Matthews, Robert Mathis, John McCarthy, Chris McConnell, Rob McLachlan, Jay Mendelsohn, Martin Mikelsons, Tracey Miles, Richard Mlyarnik, David Moon, Jarl Nilsson, Leo Noordhulsen, Ronald Ohlander, Julian Padget, Jeff Peck, Jan Pedersen, Bob Pellegrino, Crispin Perdue, Dan Pierson, Kent Pitman, Dexter Pratt, Christian Quiennec, B. Raghavan, Douglas Rand, Jonathan Rees, Chris Richardson, Jeff Rininger, Walter van Roggen, Jeffrey Rosenking, Don Sakahara, William Scherlis, David Slater, James Smith, Alan Snyder, Angela Sodan, Richard Soley, S. Sridhar, Bill St. Clair, Philip Stanhope, Guy Steele, Herbert Stoyan, Hiroshi Torii, Dave Touretzky, Paul Tucker, Rick Tucker, Thomas Turba, David Unietis, Mary Van Deusen, Ellen Waldrum, Richard Waters, Allen Wechsler, Mark Wegman, Jon L White, Skef Wholey, Alexis Wieland, Martin Yonke, Bill York, Taiichi Yuasa, Gail Zacharias, and Jan Zubkoff.

I must express particular gratitude and appreciation to a number of people for their exceptional efforts:

Larry Masinter, chairman of the X3J13 Cleanup Subcommittee, developed the standard format for documenting all proposals to be voted upon. The result has been an outstanding technical and historical record of all the actions taken by X3J13 to rectify and improve Common Lisp.

Sandra Loosemore, chairwoman of the X3J13 Compiler Subcommittee, produced many proposals for clarifying the semantics of the compilation process. She has been a diligent stickler for detail and has helped to clarify many parts of Common Lisp left vague in the first edition.

Jon L White, chairman of the X3J13 Iteration Subcommittee, supervised the consideration of several controversial proposals, one of which (loop) was eventually adopted by X3J13.

Thom Linden, chairman of the X3J13 Character Subcommittee, led a team in grappling with the difficult problem of accommodating various character sets in Common Lisp. One result is that Common Lisp will be more attractive for international use.

Kent Pitman, chairman of the X3J13 Error Handling Subcommittee, plugged the biggest outstanding hole in Common Lisp as described by the first edition.

Kathy Chapman, chairwoman of the X3J13 Drafting Subcommittee, and principal author of the draft standard, has not only written a great deal of text but also insisted on coherent and consistent terminology and pushed the rest of the committee forward when necessary.

Robert Mathis, chairman of X3J13, has kept administrative matters flowing smoothly during technical controversies.

Mary Van Deusen, secretary of X3J13, kept excellent minutes that were a tremendous aid to me in tracing the history of a number of complex discussions.

Jan Zubkoff, X3J13 meeting and mailing organizer, knows what's going on, as always. She is a master of organization and of physical arrangements. Moreover, she once again pulled me out of the fire at the last minute.

Dick Gabriel, international representative for X3J13, has kept information flowing smoothly between Europe, Japan, and the United States. He provided a great deal of the energy and drive for the completion of the Common Lisp Object System specification. He has also provided me with a great deal of valuable advice and has been on call for last-minute consultation at all hours during the final stages of preparation for this book.

David Moon has consistently been a source of reason, expert knowledge, and careful scrutiny. He has read the first edition and the X3J13 proposals perhaps more carefully than anyone else.

David Moon, Jon L White, Gregor Kiczales, Robert Mathis, and Mary Boelk provided extensive feedback on an early draft of this book. I thank them as well as the many others who commented in one way or another on the draft.

I wish to thank the authors of large proposals to X3J13 that have made material available for more or less wholesale inclusion in this book as distinct chapters. This material was produced primarily for the use of X3J13 in its work. It has been included here on a non-exclusive basis with the consent of the authors.

The author of the chapter on loop (Jon L White) notes that the chapter is based on documentation written at Lucid, Inc., by Molly M. Miller, Sonia Orin Lyris, and Kris Dinkel. Glenn Burke, Scott Fahlman, Colin Meldrum, David Moon, Cris Perdue, and Dick Waters contributed to the design of the loop macro.

The authors of the Common Lisp Object System specification (Daniel G. Bobrow, Linda G. DeMichiel, Richard P. Gabriel, Sonya E. Keene, Gregor Kiczales, and David A. Moon) wish to thank Patrick Dussud, Kenneth Kahn, Jim Kempf, Larry Masinter, Mark Stefik, Daniel L. Weinreb, and Jon L White for their contributions.

The author of the chapter on Conditions (Kent M. Pitman) notes that there is a paper [38] containing background information about the design of the condition system, which is based on the condition system of the Symbolics Lisp Machines

[49]. The members of the X3J13 Error Handling Subcommittee were Andy Daniels and Kent Pitman. Richard Mlynarik and David A. Moon made major design contributions. Useful comments, questions, suggestions, and criticisms were provided by Paul Anagnostopoulos, Alan Bawden, William Chiles, Pavel Curtis, Mary Fontana, Dick Gabriel, Dick King, Susan Lander, David D. Loeffler, Ken Olum, David C. Plummer, Alan Snyder, Eric Weaver, and Daniel L. Weinreb. The Condition System was designed specifically to accommodate the needs of Common Lisp. The design is, however, most directly based on the "New Error System" (NES) developed at Symbolics by David L. Andre, Bernard S. Greenberg, Mike McMahon, David A. Moon, and Daniel L. Weinreb. The NES was in turn based on experiences with the original Lisp Machine error system (developed at MIT), which was found to be inadequate for the needs of the modern Lisp Machine environments. Many aspects of the NES were inspired by the (PL/I) condition system used by the Honeywell Multics operating system. Henry Lieberman provided conceptual guidance and encouragement in the design of the NES. A reimplementation of the NES for non-Symbolics Lisp Machine dialects (MIT, LMI, and TI) was done at MIT by Richard M. Stallman. During the process of that reimplementation, some conceptual changes were made which have significantly influenced the Common Lisp Condition System.

As for the smaller but no less important proposals, Larry Masinter deserves recognition as an author of over half of them. He has worked indefatigably to write up proposals and to polish drafts by other authors. Kent Pitman, David Moon, and Sandra Loosemore have also been notably prolific, as well as Jon L White, Dan Pierson, Walter van Roggen, Skona Brittain, Scott Fahlman, and myself. Other authors of proposals include David Andre, John Aspinall, Kim Barrett, Eric Benson, Daniel Bobrow, Bob Cassels, Kathy Chapman, William Clinger, Pavel Curtis, Doug Cutting, Jeff Dalton, Linda DiMichiel, Richard Gabriel, Steven Haflich, Sonya Keene, James Kempf, Gregor Kiczales, Dieter Kolb, Barry Margolin, Chris McConnell, Jeff Peck, Jan Pedersen, Crispin Perdue, Jonathan Rees, Don Sakahara, David Touretzky, Richard Waters, and Gail Zacharias.

I am grateful to Donald E. Knuth and his colleagues for producing the TEX text formatting system [28], which was used to produce and typeset the manuscript. Knuth did an especially good job of publishing the program for TEX [29]; I had to consult the code about eight times while debugging particularly complicated macros. Thanks to the extensive indexing and cross-references, in each case it took me less than five minutes to find the relevant fragment of that 500-page program.

I also owe a debt to Leslie Lamport, author of the LATEX macro package [30] for TEX, within which I implemented the document style for this book.

Blue Sky Research sells and supports Textures, an implementation of TEX for

Apple Macintosh computers; Gayla Groom and Barry Smith of Blue Sky Research provided excellent technical support when I needed it. Other software tools that were invaluable in preparing this book were QuicKeys (sold by CE Software, Inc.), which provides keyboard macros; Gōfer (sold by Microlytics, Inc.), which performs rapid text searches in multiple files; Symantec Utilities for Macintosh (sold by Symantec Corporation), which saved me from more than one disk crash; and the PostScript language and compatible fonts (sold by Adobe Systems Incorporated).

Some of this software (such as LATEX) I obtained for free and some I bought, but all have proved to be useful tools of excellent quality. I am grateful to these developers for creating them.

Electronic mail has been indispensable to the writing of this book, as well as to the work of X3J13. (It is a humbling experience to publish a book and then for the next five years to receive at least one electronic mail message a week, if not twenty, pointing out some mistake or defect.) Kudos to those who develop and maintain the Internet, which arose from the Arpanet and other networks.

Chase Duffy, George Horesta, and Will Buddenhagen of Digital Press have given me much encouragement and support. David Ford designed the book and provided specifications that I could code into TEX. Alice Cheyer and Kate Schmit edited the copy for style and puzzled over the more obscure jokes with great patience. Marilyn Rowland created the index; Tim Evans and I did some polishing. Laura Fillmore and her colleagues at Editorial Inc. have tirelessly and meticulously checked one draft after another and have kept the paperwork flowing smoothly during the last hectic weeks of proofreading, page makeup, and typesetting.

Thinking Machines Corporation has supported all my work with X3J13. I thank all my colleagues there for their encouragement and help.

Others who provided indispensible encouragement and support include Guy and Nalora Steele; David Steele; Cordon and Ruth Kerns; David, Patricia, Tavis, Jacob, Nicholas, and Daniel Auwerda; Donald and Denise Kerns; and David, Joyce, and Christine Kerns.

Most of the writing of this book took place between 10 P.M. and 3 A.M. (I'm not as young as I used to be). I am grateful to Barbara, Julia, Peter, and Matthew for putting up with it, and for their love.

Guy L. Steele Jr.
Lexington, Massachusetts
All Saints' Day, 1989

Acknowledgments

FIRST EDITION (1984)

Common Lisp was designed by a diverse group of people affiliated with many institutions.

Contributors to the design and implementation of Common Lisp and to the polishing of this book are hereby gratefully acknowledged:

Paul Anagnostopoulos	Digital Equipment Corporation
Dan Aronson	Carnegie-Mellon University
Alan Bawden	Massachusetts Institute of Technology
Eric Benson	University of Utah, Stanford University, and Symbolics, Incorporated
Jon Bentley	Carnegie-Mellon University and Bell Laboratories
Jerry Boetje	Digital Equipment Corporation
Gary Brooks	Texas Instruments
Rodney A. Brooks	Stanford University
Gary L. Brown	Digital Equipment Corporation
Richard L. Bryan	Symbolics, Incorporated
Glenn S. Burke	Massachusetts Institute of Technology
Howard I. Cannon	Symbolics, Incorporated
George J. Carrette	Massachusetts Institute of Technology
Robert Cassels	Symbolics, Incorporated
Monica Cellio	Carnegie-Mellon University
David Dill	Carnegie-Mellon University
Scott E. Fahlman	Carnegie-Mellon University
Richard J. Fateman	University of California, Berkeley
Neal Feinberg	Carnegie-Mellon University
Ron Fischer	Rutgers University
John Foderaro	University of California, Berkeley
Steve Ford	Texas Instruments

Richard P. Gabriel	Stanford University and Lawrence Livermore National Laboratory
Joseph Ginder	Carnegie-Mellon University and Perq Systems Corp.
Bernard S. Greenberg	Symbolics, Incorporated
Richard Greenblatt	Lisp Machines Incorporated (LMI)
Martin L. Griss	University of Utah and Hewlett-Packard Incorporated
Steven Handerson	Carnegie-Mellon University
Charles L. Hedrick	Rutgers University
Gail Kaiser	Carnegie-Mellon University
Earl A. Killian	Lawrence Livermore National Laboratory
Steve Krueger	Texas Instruments
John L. Kulp	Symbolics, Incorporated
Jim Large	Carnegie-Mellon University
Rob Maclachlan	Carnegie-Mellon University
William Maddox	Carnegie-Mellon University
Larry M. Masinter	Xerox Corporation, Palo Alto Research Center
John McCarthy	Stanford University
Michael E. McMahon	Symbolics, Incorporated
Brian Milnes	Carnegie-Mellon University
David A. Moon	Symbolics, Incorporated
Beryl Morrison	Digital Equipment Corporation
Don Morrison	University of Utah
Dan Pierson	Digital Equipment Corporation
Kent M. Pitman	Massachusetts Institute of Technology
Jonathan Rees	Yale University
Walter van Roggen	Digital Equipment Corporation
Susan Rosenbaum	Texas Instruments
William L. Scherlis	Carnegie-Mellon University
Lee Schumacher	Carnegie-Mellon University
Richard M. Stallman	Massachusetts Institute of Technology
Barbara K. Steele	Carnegie-Mellon University
Guy L. Steele Jr.	Carnegie-Mellon University and Tartan Laboratories Incorporated
Peter Szolovits	Massachusetts Institute of Technology
William vanMelle	Xerox Corporation, Palo Alto Research Center
Ellen Waldrum	Texas Instruments
Allan C. Wechsler	Symbolics, Incorporated
Daniel L. Weinreb	Symbolics, Incorporated
Jon L White	Xerox Corporation, Palo Alto Research Center
Skef Wholey	Carnegie-Mellon University

| Richard Zippel | Massachusetts Institute of Technology |
| Leonard Zubkoff | Carnegie-Mellon University and Tartan Laboratories Incorporated |

Some contributions were relatively small; others involved enormous expenditures of effort and great dedication. A few of the contributors served more as worthy adversaries than as benefactors (and do not necessarily endorse the final design reported here), but their pointed criticisms were just as important to the polishing of Common Lisp as all the positively phrased suggestions. All of the people named above were helpful in one way or another, and I am grateful for the interest and spirit of cooperation that allowed most decisions to be made by consensus after due discussion.

Considerable encouragement and moral support were also provided by:

Norma Abel	Digital Equipment Corporation
Roger Bate	Texas Instruments
Harvey Cragon	Texas Instruments
Dennis Duncan	Digital Equipment Corporation
Sam Fuller	Digital Equipment Corporation
A. Nico Habermann	Carnegie-Mellon University
Berthold K. P. Horn	Massachusetts Institute of Technology
Gene Kromer	Texas Instruments
Gene Matthews	Texas Instruments
Allan Newell	Carnegie-Mellon University
Dana Scott	Carnegie-Mellon University
Harry Tennant	Texas Instruments
Patrick H. Winston	Massachusetts Institute of Technology
Lowell Wood	Lawrence Livermore National Laboratory
William A. Wulf	Carnegie-Mellon University and Tartan Laboratories Incorporated

I am very grateful to each of them.

Jan Zubkoff of Carnegie-Mellon University provided a great deal of organization, secretarial support, and unfailing good cheer in the face of adversity.

The development of Common Lisp would most probably not have been possible without the electronic message system provided by the ARPANET. Design decisions were made on several hundred distinct points, for the most part by consensus, and by simple majority vote when necessary. Except for two one-day face-to-face meetings, all of the language design and discussion was done through the ARPANET message system, which permitted effortless dissemination of messages to dozens of people, and several interchanges per day. The message system also provided automatic archiving of the entire discussion, which has proved invaluable in the preparation of this reference manual. Over the course of thirty months, approximately 3000 messages were sent (an average of three per day), ranging in length from one line to twenty pages. Assuming 5000 characters per printed page of text, the entire discussion totaled about 1100 pages. It would have been substantially more difficult to have conducted this discussion by any other means, and would have required much more time.

The ideas in Common Lisp have come from many sources and been polished by much discussion. I am responsible for the form of this book, and for any errors or inconsistencies that may remain; but the credit for the design and support of Common Lisp lies with the individuals named above, each of whom has made significant contributions.

The organization and content of this book were inspired in large part by the *MacLISP Reference Manual* by David A. Moon and others [33], and by the *LISP Machine Manual* (fourth edition) by Daniel Weinreb and David Moon [55], which in turn acknowledges the efforts of Richard Stallman, Mike McMahon, Alan Bawden, Glenn Burke, and "many people too numerous to list."

I thank Phyllis Keenan, Chase Duffy, Virginia Anderson, John Osborn, and Jonathan Baker of Digital Press for their help in preparing this book for publication. Jane Blake did an admirable job of copy-editing. James Gibson and Katherine Downs of Waldman Graphics were most cooperative in typesetting this book from my on-line manuscript files.

I am grateful to Carnegie-Mellon University and to Tartan Laboratories Incorporated for supporting me in the writing of this book over the last three years.

Part of the work on this book was done in conjunction with the Carnegie-Mellon University Spice Project, an effort to construct an advanced scientific software development environment for personal computers. The Spice Project is supported by the Defense Advanced Research Projects Agency, Department of Defense, ARPA Order 3597, monitored by the Air Force Avionics Laboratory under contract F33615-78-C-1551. The views and conclusions contained in this book are those of the author and should not be interpreted as representing the official policies, either expressed or implied, of the Defense Advanced Research Projects Agency or the U.S. Government.

Most of the writing of this book took place between midnight and 5 A.M. I am grateful to Barbara, Julia, and Peter for putting up with it, and for their love.

Guy L. Steele Jr.
Pittsburgh, Pennsylvania
March 1984

1

Introduction

Common Lisp is a new dialect of Lisp, a successor to MacLisp [33, 37], influenced strongly by Zetalisp [55, 34] and to some extent by Scheme [46] and Interlisp [50].

1.1. Purpose

Common Lisp is intended to meet these goals:

Commonality

Common Lisp originated in an attempt to focus the work of several implementation groups, each of which was constructing successor implementations of MacLisp for different computers. These implementations had begun to diverge because of the differences in the implementation environments: microcoded personal computers (Zetalisp, Spice Lisp), commercial timeshared computers (NIL—the "New Implementation of Lisp"), and supercomputers (S-1 Lisp). While the differences among the several implementation environments of necessity will continue to force certain incompatibilities among the implementations, Common Lisp serves as a common dialect to which each implementation makes any necessary extensions.

Portability

Common Lisp intentionally excludes features that cannot be implemented easily on a broad class of machines. On the one hand, features that are difficult or expensive to implement on hardware without special microcode are avoided or provided in a more abstract and efficiently implementable form. (Examples of this are the invisible forwarding pointers and locatives of Zetalisp. Some of the problems that they solve are addressed in different ways in Common Lisp.) On the other hand, features that are useful only on certain "ordinary" or "commercial" processors are avoided or made optional. (An example of this is the type declaration facility, which is useful in some implementations and completely ignored in others. Type declarations are completely optional and for correct pro-grams affect only efficiency, not semantics.) Common Lisp is designed to make it easy to write programs that depend as little as possible on machine-specific char-acteristics, such as word length, while allowing some variety of implementation techniques.

Consistency

Most Lisp implementations are internally inconsistent in that by default the in-terpreter and compiler may assign different semantics to correct programs. This semantic difference stems primarily from the fact that the interpreter assumes all variables to be dynamically scoped, whereas the compiler assumes all variables to be local unless explicitly directed otherwise. This difference has been the usual practice in Lisp for the sake of convenience and efficiency but can lead to very subtle bugs. The definition of Common Lisp avoids such anomalies by explic-itly requiring the interpreter and compiler to impose identical semantics on correct programs so far as possible.

Expressiveness

Common Lisp culls what experience has shown to be the most useful and under-standable constructs from not only MacLisp but also Interlisp, other Lisp dialects, and other programming languages. Constructs judged to be awkward or less useful have been excluded. (An example is the store construct of MacLisp.)

Compatibility

Unless there is a good reason to the contrary, Common Lisp strives to be compatible with Lisp Machine Lisp, MacLisp, and Interlisp, roughly in that order.

Efficiency

Common Lisp has a number of features designed to facilitate the production of high-quality compiled code in those implementations whose developers care to invest effort in an optimizing compiler. One implementation of Common Lisp, namely S-1 Lisp, already has a compiler that produces code for numerical computations that is competitive in execution speed to that produced by a Fortran compiler [11]. The S-1 Lisp compiler extends the work done in MacLisp to produce extremely efficient numerical code [19].

Power

Common Lisp is a descendant of MacLisp, which has traditionally placed emphasis on providing system-building tools. Such tools may in turn be used to build the user-level packages such as Interlisp provides; these packages are not, however, part of the Common Lisp core specification. It is expected such packages will be built on top of the Common Lisp core.

Stability

It is intended that Common Lisp will change only slowly and with due deliberation. The various dialects that are supersets of Common Lisp may serve as laboratories within which to test language extensions, but such extensions will be added to Common Lisp only after careful examination and experimentation.

The goals of Common Lisp are thus very close to those of Standard Lisp [31] and Portable Standard Lisp [51]. Common Lisp differs from Standard Lisp primarily in incorporating more features, including a richer and more complicated set of data types and more complex control structures.

This book is intended to be a language specification rather than an implementation specification (although implementation notes are scattered throughout the text). It defines a set of standard language concepts and constructs that may be used for communication of data structures and algorithms in the Common Lisp dialect. This set of concepts and constructs is sometimes referred to as the "core Common Lisp language" because it contains conceptually necessary or important features. It is not necessarily implementationally minimal. While many features could be defined in terms of others by writing Lisp code, and indeed may be implemented that way, it was felt that these features should be conceptually primitive so that there might be agreement among all users as to their usage. (For example, bignums and rational numbers could be implemented as Lisp code given operations on fixnums. However, it is important to the conceptual integrity of the language that they be regarded by the user as primitive, and they are useful enough to warrant a standard definition.)

For the most part, this book defines a programming language, not a programming environment. A few interfaces are defined for invoking such standard programming tools as a compiler, an editor, a program trace facility, and a debugger, but very little is said about their nature or operation. It is expected that one or more extensive programming environments will be built using Common Lisp as a foundation, and will be documented separately.

There are now many implementations of Common Lisp, some programmed by research groups in universities and some by companies that sell them commercially, and a number of useful programming environments have indeed grown up around these implementations. What is more, all the goals stated above have been achieved, most notably that of portability. Moving large bodies of Lisp code from one computer to another is now routine.

1.2. Notational Conventions

A number of special notational conventions are used throughout this book for the sake of conciseness.

1.2.1. Decimal Numbers

All numbers in this book are in decimal notation unless there is an explicit indication to the contrary. (Decimal notation is normally taken for granted, of course. Unfortunately, for certain other dialects of Lisp, MacLisp in particular, the default notation for numbers is octal (base 8) rather than decimal, and so the use of decimal notation for describing Common Lisp is, taken in its historical context, a bit unusual!)

1.2.2. Nil, False, and the Empty List

In Common Lisp, as in most Lisp dialects, the symbol nil is used to represent both the empty list and the "false" value for Boolean tests. An empty list may, of course, also be written (); this normally denotes the same object as nil. (It is possible, by extremely perverse manipulation of the package system, to cause the sequence of letters nil to be recognized not as the symbol that represents the empty list but as another symbol with the same name. This obscure possibility will be ignored in this book.) These two notations may be used interchangeably as far as the Lisp system is concerned. However, as a matter of style, this book uses the notation () when it is desirable to emphasize the use of an empty list, and uses the notation nil when it is desirable to emphasize the use of the Boolean "false". The notation ´nil (note the explicit quotation mark) is used to emphasize the use of a symbol. For example:

```
(defun three () 3)          ;Emphasize empty parameter list
(append ´() ´()) ⇒ ()        ;Emphasize use of empty lists
(not nil) ⇒ t               ;Emphasize use as Boolean "false"
(get ´nil ´color)           ;Emphasize use as a symbol
```

Any data object other than nil is construed to be Boolean "not false", that is, "true". The symbol t is conventionally used to mean "true" when no other value is more appropriate. When a function is said to "return *false*" or to "be *false*" in some circumstance, this means that it returns nil. However, when a function is said to "return *true*" or to "be *true*" in some circumstance, this means that it returns some value other than nil, but not necessarily t.

1.2.3. Evaluation, Expansion, and Equivalence

Execution of code in Lisp is called *evaluation* because executing a piece of code normally results in a data object called the *value* produced by the code. The symbol ⇒ is used in examples to indicate evaluation. For example,

```
(+ 4 5) ⇒ 9
```

means "the result of evaluating the code (+ 4 5) is (or would be, or would have been) 9."

The symbol → is used in examples to indicate macro expansion. For example,

```
(push x v) → (setf v (cons x v))
```

means "the result of expanding the macro-call form (push x v) is (setf v (cons x v))." This implies that the two pieces of code do the same thing; the second piece of code is the definition of what the first does.

The symbol ≡ is used in examples to indicate code equivalence. For example,

```
(gcd x (gcd y z)) ≡ (gcd (gcd x y) z)
```

means "the value and effects of evaluating the form (gcd x (gcd y z)) are always the same as the value and effects of (gcd (gcd x y) z) for any values of the variables x, y, and z." This implies that the two pieces of code do the same thing; however, neither directly defines the other in the way macro expansion does.

1.2.4. Errors

When this book specifies that it "is an error" for some situation to occur, this means that:

- No valid Common Lisp program should cause this situation to occur.

- If this situation occurs, the effects and results are completely undefined as far as adherence to the Common Lisp specification is concerned.

- No Common Lisp implementation is required to detect such an error. Of course, implementors are encouraged to provide for detection of such errors wherever reasonable.

This is not to say that some particular implementation might not define the effects and results for such a situation; the point is that no program conforming to the Common Lisp specification may correctly depend on such effects or results.

On the other hand, if it is specified in this book that in some situation "an error is *signaled*," this means that:

- If this situation occurs, an error will be signaled (see `error` and `cerror`).

- Valid Common Lisp programs may rely on the fact that an error will be signaled.

- Every Common Lisp implementation is required to detect such an error.

In places where it is stated that so-and-so "must" or "must not" or "may not" be the case, then it "is an error" if the stated requirement is not met. For example, if an argument "must be a symbol," then it "is an error" if the argument is not a symbol. In all cases where an error is to be *signaled*, the word "signaled" is always used explicitly in this book.

X3J13 has adopted a more elaborate terminology for errors, and has made some effort to specify the type of error to be signaled in situations where signaling is appropriate. This effort was not complete as of September 1989, and I have made little attempt to incorporate the new error terminology or error type specifications in this book. However, the new terminology is described and used in the specification of the Common Lisp Object System appearing in chapter 28; this gives the flavor of how erroneous situations will be described, and appropriate actions prescribed, in the forthcoming ANSI Common Lisp standard.

1.2.5. Descriptions of Functions and Other Entities

Functions, variables, named constants, special forms, and macros are described using a distinctive typographical format. Table 1-1 illustrates the manner in which Common Lisp functions are documented. The first line specifies the name of the function, the manner in which it accepts arguments, and the fact that it is a function. If the function takes many arguments, then the names of the arguments may spill across two or three lines. The paragraphs following this standard header explain the definition and uses of the function and often present examples or related functions.

Sometimes two or more related functions are explained in a single combined description. In this situation the headers for all the functions appear together, followed by the combined description.

In general, actual code (including actual names of functions) appears in this typeface: (`cons a b`). Names that stand for pieces of code (metavariables) are written in *italics*. In a function description, the names of the parameters appear in italics for expository purposes. The word `&optional` in the list of parameters indicates that all arguments past that point are optional; the default values for the parameters are described in the text. Parameter lists may also contain `&rest`, indicating that an indefinite number of arguments may appear, or `&key`, indicating that keyword arguments are accepted. (The `&optional`/`&rest`/`&key` syntax is actually used in Common Lisp function definitions for these purposes.)

Table 1-1: Sample Function Description

sample-function *arg1 arg2* &optional *arg3 arg4* [*Function*]

The function sample-function adds together *arg1* and *arg2*, and then multiplies the result by *arg3*. If *arg3* is not provided or is nil, the multiplication isn't done. sample-function then returns a list whose first element is this result and whose second element is *arg4* (which defaults to the symbol foo). For example:

```
(sample-function 3 4) ⇒ (7 foo)
(sample-function 1 2 2 'bar) ⇒ (6 bar)
```

In general, (sample-function *x y*) ≡ (list (+ *x y*) 'foo).

Table 1-2: Sample Variable Description

sample-variable [*Variable*]

The variable *sample-variable* specifies how many times the special form sample-special-form should iterate. The value should always be a non-negative integer or nil (which means iterate indefinitely many times). The initial value is 0 (meaning no iterations).

Table 1-3: Sample Constant Description

sample-constant [*Constant*]

The named constant sample-constant has as its value the height of the terminal screen in furlongs times the base-2 logarithm of the implementation's total disk capacity in bytes, as a floating-point number.

Table 1-2 illustrates the manner in which a global variable is documented. The first line specifies the name of the variable and the fact that it is a variable. Purely as a matter of convention, all global variables used by Common Lisp have names beginning and ending with an asterisk.

Table 1-3 illustrates the manner in which a named constant is documented. The first line specifies the name of the constant and the fact that it is a constant. (A constant is just like a global variable, except that it is an error ever to alter its value or to bind it to a new value.)

Table 1-4: Sample Special Form Description

```
sample-special-form [name] ( {var}* ) {form}+                [Special form]
```

This evaluates each form in sequence as an implicit progn, and does this as many times as specified by the global variable *sample-variable*. Each variable *var* is bound and initialized to 43 before the first iteration, and unbound after the last iteration. The name *name*, if supplied, may be used in a return-from form to exit from the loop prematurely. If the loop ends normally, sample-special-form returns nil. For example:

```
(setq *sample-variable* 3)
(sample-special-form () form1 form2)
```

This evaluates *form1*, *form2*, *form1*, *form2*, *form1*, *form2* in that order.

Table 1-5: Sample Macro Description

```
sample-macro var [[ declaration* | doc-string ]] {tag | statement}*      [Macro]
```

This evaluates the statements as a prog body, with the variable *var* bound to 43.

```
(sample-macro x (return (+ x x))) ⇒ 86
(sample-macro var . body) → (prog ((var 43)) . body)
```

Tables 1-4 and 1-5 illustrate the documentation of special forms and macros, which are closely related in purpose. These are very different from functions. Functions are called according to a single, specific, consistent syntax; the &optional/&rest/&key syntax specifies how the function uses its arguments internally but does not affect the syntax of a call. In contrast, each special form or macro can have its own idiosyncratic syntax. It is by special forms and macros that the syntax of Common Lisp is defined and extended.

In the description of a special form or macro, an italicized word names a corresponding part of the form that invokes the special form or macro. Parentheses stand for themselves and should be written as such when invoking the special form or macro. Brackets, braces, stars, plus signs, and vertical bars are metasyntactic marks. Brackets, [and], indicate that what they enclose is optional (may appear zero times or one time in that place); the square brackets should not be written in code. Braces, { and }, simply parenthesize what they enclose but may be followed by a star, *, or a plus sign, ⁺; a star indicates that what the braces enclose may appear any number of times (including zero, that is, not at all), whereas a plus sign indicates that what the braces enclose may appear any non-zero number of times (that is, must appear at least once). Within braces or brackets, a vertical bar, |, separates mutually exclusive choices. In summary, the notation $\{x\}^*$ means zero or more occurrences of x, the notation $\{x\}^+$ means one or more occurrences of x, and the notation $[x]$ means zero or one occurrence of x. These notations are also used for syntactic descriptions expressed as BNF-like productions, as in table 22-2.

Double brackets, ⟦ and ⟧, indicate that any number of the alternatives enclosed may be used, and those used may occur in any order, but each alternative may be used at most once unless followed by a star. For example,

$$p \; ⟦ \, x \mid \{y\}^* \mid z \, ⟧ \; q$$

means that at most one x, any number of y's, and at most one z may appear between the mandatory occurrences of p and q, and those that appear may be in any order.

A downward arrow, ↓, indicates a form of syntactic indirection that helps to make ⟦ ⟧ notation more readable. If X is some non-terminal symbol occurring on the left-hand side of some BNF production, then the right-hand side of that production is to be textually substituted for any occurrence of ↓X. Thus the two fragments

$$p \; ⟦ \, ↓xyz\text{-}mixture \, ⟧ \; q$$
$$xyz\text{-}mixture ::= x \mid \{y\}^* \mid z$$

are together equivalent to the previous example.

In the last example in table 1-5, notice the use of dot notation. The dot appearing in the expression (`sample-macro` *var* . *body*) means that the name *body* stands for a list of forms, not just a single form, at the end of a list. This notation is often used in examples.

In the heading line in table 1-5, notice the use of ⟦ ⟧ notation to indicate that any number of declarations may appear but at most one documentation string (which may appear before, after, or somewhere in the middle of any declarations).

1.2.6. The Lisp Reader

The term "Lisp reader" refers not to you, the reader of this book, nor to some person reading Lisp code, but specifically to a Lisp procedure, namely the function `read`, which reads characters from an input stream and interprets them by parsing as representations of Lisp objects.

1.2.7. Overview of Syntax

Certain characters are used in special ways in the syntax of Common Lisp. The complete syntax is explained in detail in chapter 22, but a quick summary here may be useful:

(A left parenthesis begins a list of items. The list may contain any number of items, including zero. Lists may be nested. For example, `(cons (car x) (cdr y))` is a list of three things, of which the last two are themselves lists.

)   A right parenthesis ends a list of items.

´   An acute accent (also called single quote or apostrophe) followed by an expression *form* is an abbreviation for (`quote` *form*). Thus ´foo means (`quote foo`) and ´(cons ´a ´b) means (`quote (cons (quote a) (quote b)))`.

;   Semicolon is the comment character. It and all characters up to the end of the line are discarded.

"   Double quotes surround character strings:
`"This is a thirty-nine-character string."`

\   Backslash is an escape character. It causes the next character to be treated as a letter rather than for its usual syntactic purpose. For example, `A\(B` denotes a symbol whose name consists of the three characters A, (, and B. Similarly, `"\""` denotes a character string containing one character, a double quote, because the first and third double quotes serve to delimit the string, and the second double quote serves as the contents of the string. The backslash causes the second double quote to be taken literally and prevents it from being interpreted as the terminating delimiter of the string.

| Vertical bars are used in pairs to surround the name (or part of the name) of a symbol that has many special characters in it. It is roughly equivalent to putting a backslash in front of every character so surrounded. For example, `|A(B)|`, `A|(|B|)|`, and `A\(B\)` all mean the symbol whose name consists of the four characters A, (, B, and).

\#   The number sign signals the beginning of a complicated syntactic structure. The next character designates the precise syntax to follow. For example, `#o105` means 105_8 (105 in octal notation); `#x105` means 105_{16} (105 in hexadecimal notation); `#b1011` means 1011_2 (1011 in binary notation); `#\L` denotes a character object for the character L; and `#(a b c)` denotes a vector of three elements a, b, and c. A particularly important case is that `#´fn` means (`function` *fn*), in a manner analogous to ´*form* meaning (`quote` *form*).

` Grave accent ("backquote") signals that the next expression is a template that may contain commas. The backquote syntax represents a program that will construct a data structure according to the template.

, Commas are used within the backquote syntax.

: Colon is used to indicate which package a symbol belongs to. For example, `network:reset` denotes the symbol named `reset` in the package named `network`. A leading colon indicates a *keyword*, a symbol that always evaluates to itself. The colon character is not actually part of the print name of the symbol. This is all explained in chapter 11; until you read that, just keep in mind that a symbol notated with a leading colon is in effect a constant that evaluates to itself.

Notice of correction. In the first edition, the characters "," and ":" at the left margin above were inadvertently omitted.

Brackets, braces, question mark, and exclamation point (that is, [,], {, }, ?, and !) are not used for any purpose in standard Common Lisp syntax. These characters are explicitly reserved to the user, primarily for use as *macro characters* for user-defined lexical syntax extensions (see section 22.1.3).

All code in this book is written using lowercase letters. Common Lisp is generally insensitive to the case in which code is written. Internally, names of symbols are ordinarily converted to and stored in uppercase form. There are ways to force case conversion on output if desired; see `*print-case*`. In this book, wherever an interactive exchange between a user and the Lisp system is shown, the input is exhibited with lowercase letters and the output with uppercase letters.

X3J13 voted in June 1989 ⟨150⟩ to introduce `readtable-case`. Certain settings allow the names of symbols to be case-sensitive. The default behavior, however, is as described in the previous paragraph. In any event, only uppercase letters appear in the internal print names of symbols naming the standard Common Lisp facilities described in this book.

2

Data Types

Common Lisp provides a variety of types of data objects. It is important to note that in Lisp it is data objects that are typed, not variables. Any variable can have any Lisp object as its value. (It is possible to make an explicit declaration that a variable will in fact take on one of only a limited set of values. However, such a declaration may always be omitted, and the program will still run correctly. Such a declaration merely constitutes advice from the user that may be useful in gaining efficiency. See `declare`.)

In Common Lisp, a data type is a (possibly infinite) set of Lisp objects. Many Lisp objects belong to more than one such set, and so it doesn't always make sense to ask what is *the* type of an object; instead, one usually asks only whether an object belongs to a given type. The predicate `typep` may be used to ask whether an object belongs to a given type, and the function `type-of` returns *a* type to which a given object belongs.

The data types defined in Common Lisp are arranged into a hierarchy (actually a partial order) defined by the subset relationship. Certain sets of objects, such as the set of numbers or the set of strings, are interesting enough to deserve labels. Symbols are used for most such labels (here, and throughout this book, the word "symbol" refers to atomic symbols, one kind of Lisp object, elsewhere known as literal atoms). See chapter 4 for a complete description of type specifiers.

The set of all objects is specified by the symbol `t`. The empty data type, which contains no objects, is denoted by `nil`.

A type called `common` encompasses all the data objects required by the Common Lisp language. A Common Lisp implementation is free to provide other data types that are not subtypes of `common`.

X3J13 voted in March 1989 ⟨17⟩ to remove the type `common` (and the predicate `commonp`) from the language, on the grounds that it has not proved to be useful in practice and that it could be difficult to redefine in the face of other changes to the Common Lisp type system (such as the introduction of CLOS classes).

The following categories of Common Lisp objects are of particular interest: numbers, characters, symbols, lists, arrays, structures, and functions. There are others as well. Some of these categories have many subdivisions. There are also standard types defined to be the union of two or more of these categories. The categories listed above, while they are data types, are neither more nor less "real" than other data types; they simply constitute a particularly useful slice across the type hierarchy for expository purposes.

Here are brief descriptions of various Common Lisp data types. The remaining sections of this chapter go into more detail and also describe notations for objects of each type. Descriptions of Lisp functions that operate on data objects of each type appear in later chapters.

- *Numbers* are provided in various forms and representations. Common Lisp provides a true integer data type: any integer, positive or negative, has in principle a representation as a Common Lisp data object, subject only to total memory limitations (rather than machine word width). A true rational data type is provided: the quotient of two integers, if not an integer, is a ratio. Floating-point numbers of various ranges and precisions are also provided, as well as Cartesian complex numbers.

- *Characters* represent printed glyphs such as letters or text formatting operations. Strings are one-dimensional arrays of characters. Common Lisp provides for a rich character set, including ways to represent characters of various type styles.

- *Symbols* (sometimes called *atomic symbols* for emphasis or clarity) are named data objects. Lisp provides machinery for locating a symbol object, given its name (in the form of a string). Symbols have *property lists*, which in effect allow symbols to be treated as record structures with an extensible set of named components, each of which may be any Lisp object. Symbols also serve to name functions and variables within programs.

- *Lists* are sequences represented in the form of linked cells called *conses*. There is a special object (the symbol nil) that is the empty list. All other lists are built recursively by adding a new element to the front of an existing list. This is done by creating a new *cons*, which is an object having two components called the *car* and the *cdr*. The car may hold anything, and the *cdr* is made to point to the previously existing list. (Conses may actually be used completely generally as two-element record structures, but their most important use is to represent lists.)

- *Arrays* are dimensioned collections of objects. An array can have any non-negative number of dimensions and is indexed by a sequence of integers. A general array can have any Lisp object as a component; other types of arrays are specialized for efficiency and can hold only certain types of Lisp objects. It is possible for two arrays, possibly with differing dimension information, to share the same set of elements (such that modifying one array modifies the other also) by causing one to be *displaced* to the other. One-dimensional arrays of any kind are called *vectors*. One-dimensional arrays of characters are called *strings*. One-dimensional arrays of bits (that is, of integers whose values are 0 or 1) are called *bit-vectors*.

- *Hash tables* provide an efficient way of mapping any Lisp object (a *key*) to an associated object.

- *Readtables* are used to control the built-in expression parser `read`.

- *Packages* are collections of symbols that serve as name spaces. The parser recognizes symbols by looking up character sequences in the current package.

- *Pathnames* represent names of files in a fairly implementation-independent manner. They are used to interface to the external file system.

- *Streams* represent sources or sinks of data, typically characters or bytes. They are used to perform I/O, as well as for internal purposes such as parsing strings.

- *Random-states* are data structures used to encapsulate the state of the built-in random-number generator.

- *Structures* are user-defined record structures, objects that have named components. The `defstruct` facility is used to define new structure types. Some Common Lisp implementations may choose to implement certain system-supplied data types, such as *bignums*, *readtables*, *streams*, *hash tables*, and *pathnames*, as structures, but this fact will be invisible to the user.

- *Functions* are objects that can be invoked as procedures; these may take arguments and return values. (All Lisp procedures can be construed to return values and therefore every procedure is a function.) Such objects include *compiled-functions* (compiled code objects). Some functions are represented as a list whose *car* is a particular symbol such as `lambda`. Symbols may also be used as functions.

X3J13 voted in June 1988 ⟨90⟩ to specify that symbols are not of type `function`, but are automatically coerced to functions in certain situations (see section 2.13).

X3J13 voted in June 1988 ⟨30⟩ to adopt the Common Lisp Condition System, thereby introducing a new category of data objects:

- *Conditions* are objects used to affect control flow in certain conventional ways by means of signals and handlers that intercept those signals. In particular, errors are signaled by raising particular conditions, and errors may be trapped by establishing handlers for those conditions.

X3J13 voted in June 1988 ⟨12⟩ to adopt the Common Lisp Object System, thereby introducing additional categories of data objects:

- *Classes* determine the structure and behavior of other objects, their *instances*. Every Common Lisp data object belongs to some class. (In some ways the CLOS class system is a generalization of the system of type specifiers of the first edition of this book, but the class system augments the type system rather than supplanting it.)

- *Methods* are chunks of code that operate on arguments satisfying a particular pattern of classes. Methods are not functions; they are not invoked directly on arguments but instead are bundled into generic functions.

- *Generic functions* are functions that contain, among other information, a set of methods. When invoked, a generic function executes a subset of its methods. The subset chosen for execution depends in a specific way on the classes or identities of the arguments to which it is applied.

These categories are not always mutually exclusive. The required relationships among the various data types are explained in more detail in section 2.15.

2.1. Numbers

Several kinds of numbers are defined in Common Lisp. They are divided into *integers*; *ratios*; *floating-point numbers*, with names provided for up to four different floating-point representations; and *complex numbers*.

X3J13 voted in March 1989 ⟨151⟩ to add the type real.

The number data type encompasses all kinds of numbers. For convenience, there are names for some subclasses of numbers as well. Integers and ratios are of type rational. Rational numbers and floating-point numbers are of type real. Real numbers and complex numbers are of type number.

Although the names of these types were chosen with the terminology of mathematics in mind, the correspondences are not always exact. Integers and ratios model the corresponding mathematical concepts directly. Numbers of type float may be used to approximate real numbers, both rational and irrational. The real type includes all Common Lisp numbers that represent mathematical real numbers, though there are mathematical real numbers (irrational numbers) that do not have an exact Common Lisp representation. Only real numbers may be ordered using the <, >, <=, and >= functions.

Compatibility note: The Fortran 77 standard defines the term *real datum* to mean "a processor approximation to the value of a real number." In practice the Fortran *basic real* type is the floating-point data type that Common Lisp calls `single-float`. The Fortran *double precision* type is Common Lisp's `double-float`. The Pascal `real` data type is an "implementation-defined subset of the real numbers." In practice this is usually a floating-point type, often what Common Lisp calls `double-float`.

A translation of an algorithm written in Fortran or Pascal that uses `real` data usually will use some appropriate precision of Common Lisp's `float` type. Some algorithms may gain accuracy or flexibility by using Common Lisp's `rational` or `real` type instead.

2.1.1. Integers

The `integer` data type is intended to represent mathematical integers. Unlike most programming languages, Common Lisp in principle imposes no limit on the magnitude of an integer; storage is automatically allocated as necessary to represent large integers.

In every Common Lisp implementation there is a range of integers that are represented more efficiently than others; each such integer is called a *fixnum*, and an integer that is not a fixnum is called a *bignum*. Common Lisp is designed to hide this distinction as much as possible; the distinction between fixnums and bignums is visible to the user in only a few places where the efficiency of representation is important. Exactly which integers are fixnums is implementation-dependent; typically they will be those integers in the range -2^n to $2^n - 1$, inclusive, for some n not less than 15. See `most-positive-fixnum` and `most-negative-fixnum`.

X3J13 voted in January 1989 ⟨76⟩ to specify that `fixnum` must be a supertype of the type (`signed-byte 16`), and additionally that the value of `array-dimension-limit` must be a fixnum (implying that the implementor should choose the range of fixnums to be large enough to accommodate the largest size of array to be supported).

Rationale: This specification allows programmers to declare variables in portable code to be of type `fixnum` for efficiency. Fixnums are guaranteed to encompass at least the set of 16-bit signed integers (compare this to the data type `short int` in the C programming language). In addition, any valid array index must be a fixnum, and therefore variables used to hold array indices (such as a `dotimes` variable) may be declared `fixnum` in portable code.

Integers are ordinarily written in decimal notation, as a sequence of decimal digits, optionally preceded by a sign and optionally followed by a decimal point. For example:

0	;Zero
-0	;This *always* means the same as 0
+6	;The first perfect number
28	;The second perfect number
1024.	;Two to the tenth power
-1	;$e^{\pi i}$
15511210043330985984000000.	;25 factorial (25!), probably a bignum

Compatibility note: MacLisp and Lisp Machine Lisp normally assume that integers are written in octal (radix-8) notation unless a decimal point is present. Interlisp assumes integers are written in decimal notation and uses a trailing Q to indicate octal radix; however, a decimal point, even in trailing position, *always* indicates a floating-point number. This is of course consistent with Fortran. Ada does not permit trailing decimal points but instead requires them to be embedded. In Common Lisp, integers written as described above are always construed to be in decimal notation, whether or not the decimal point is present; allowing the decimal point to be present permits compatibility with MacLisp.

Integers may be notated in radices other than ten. The notation

#nnrddddd or *#nnRddddd*

means the integer in radix-*nn* notation denoted by the digits *ddddd*. More precisely, one may write #, a non-empty sequence of decimal digits representing an unsigned decimal integer *n*, r (or R), an optional sign, and a sequence of radix-*n* digits, to indicate an integer written in radix *n* (which must be between 2 and 36, inclusive). Only legal digits for the specified radix may be used; for example, an octal number may contain only the digits 0 through 7. For digits above 9, letters of the alphabet of either case may be used in order. Binary, octal, and hexadecimal radices are useful enough to warrant the special abbreviations #b for #2r, #o for #8r, and #x for #16r. For example:

#2r11010101	;Another way of writing 213 decimal
#b11010101	;Ditto
#b+11010101	;Ditto
#o325	;Ditto, in octal radix
#xD5	;Ditto, in hexadecimal radix
#16r+D5	;Ditto
#o-300	;Decimal −192, written in base 8
#3r-21010	;Same thing in base 3
#25R-7H	;Same thing in base 25
#xACCEDED	;181202413, in hexadecimal radix

2.1.2. Ratios

A *ratio* is a number representing the mathematical ratio of two integers. Integers and ratios collectively constitute the type rational. The canonical representation of a rational number is as an integer if its value is integral, and otherwise as the ratio of two integers, the *numerator* and *denominator*, whose greatest common divisor is 1, and of which the denominator is positive (and in fact greater than 1, or else the value would be integral). A ratio is notated with / as a separator, thus: 3/5. It is possible to notate ratios in non-canonical (unreduced) forms, such as 4/6, but the Lisp function prin1 always prints the canonical form for a ratio.

If any computation produces a result that is a ratio of two integers such that the denominator evenly divides the numerator, then the result is immediately converted to the equivalent integer. This is called the rule of *rational canonicalization*.

Rational numbers may be written as the possibly signed quotient of decimal numerals: an optional sign followed by two non-empty sequences of digits separated by a /. This syntax may be described as follows:

ratio ::= [*sign*] {*digit*}$^+$ / {*digit*}$^+$

The second sequence may not consist entirely of zeros. For example:

2/3	;This is in canonical form
4/6	;A non-canonical form for the same number
-17/23	;A not very interesting ratio
-30517578125/32768	;This is $(-5/2)^{15}$
10/5	;The canonical form for this is 2

To notate rational numbers in radices other than ten, one uses the same radix specifiers (one of #*nn*R, #O, #B, or #X) as for integers. For example:

#o-101/75	;Octal notation for -65/61
#3r120/21	;Ternary notation for 15/7
#Xbc/ad	;Hexadecimal notation for 188/173
#xFADED/FACADE	;Hexadecimal notation for 1027565/16435934

2.1.3. Floating-Point Numbers

Common Lisp allows an implementation to provide one or more kinds of floating-point number, which collectively make up the type float. Now a floating-point number is a (mathematical) rational number of the form $s \cdot f \cdot b^{e-p}$, where s is +1 or −1, the *sign*; b is an integer greater than 1, the *base* or *radix* of the representation; p is a positive integer, the *precision* (in base-b digits) of the floating-point number;

f is a positive integer between b^{p-1} and $b^p - 1$ (inclusive), the *significand*; and e is an integer, the *exponent*. The value of p and the range of e depends on the implementation and on the type of floating-point number within that implementation. In addition, there is a floating-point zero; depending on the implementation, there may also be a "minus zero." If there is no minus zero, then 0.0 and -0.0 are both interpreted as simply a floating-point zero.

Implementation note: The form of the above description should not be construed to require the internal representation to be in sign-magnitude form. Two's-complement and other representations are also acceptable. Note that the radix of the internal representation may be other than 2, as on the IBM 360 and 370, which use radix 16; see `float-radix`.

Floating-point numbers may be provided in a variety of precisions and sizes, depending on the implementation. High-quality floating-point software tends to depend critically on the precise nature of the floating-point arithmetic and so may not always be completely portable. As an aid in writing programs that are moderately portable, however, certain definitions are made here:

- A *short* floating-point number (type `short-float`) is of the representation of smallest fixed precision provided by an implementation.

- A *long* floating-point number (type `long-float`) is of the representation of the largest fixed precision provided by an implementation.

- Intermediate between short and long formats are two others, arbitrarily called *single* and *double* (types `single-float` and `double-float`).

The precise definition of these categories is implementation-dependent. However, the rough intent is that short floating-point numbers be precise to at least four decimal places (but also have a space-efficient representation); single floating-point numbers, to at least seven decimal places; and double floating-point numbers, to at least fourteen decimal places. It is suggested that the precision (measured in bits, computed as $p \log_2 b$) and the exponent size (also measured in bits, computed as the base-2 logarithm of 1 plus the maximum exponent value) be at least as great as the values in table 2-1.

Floating-point numbers are written in either decimal fraction or computerized scientific notation: an optional sign, then a non-empty sequence of digits with an embedded decimal point, then an optional decimal exponent specification. If there is no exponent specifier, then the decimal point is required, and there must be digits after it. The exponent specifier consists of an exponent marker, an optional sign, and a non-empty sequence of digits. For preciseness, here is a modified-BNF description of floating-point notation.

Table 2-1: Recommended Minimum Floating-Point Precision and Exponent Size

Format	Minimum Precision	Minimum Exponent Size
Short	13 bits	5 bits
Single	24 bits	8 bits
Double	50 bits	8 bits
Long	50 bits	8 bits

floating-point-number ::= [*sign*] {*digit*}* *decimal-point* {*digit*}+ [*exponent*]
        | [*sign*] {*digit*}+ [*decimal-point* {*digit*}*] *exponent*
sign ::= + | -
decimal-point ::= .
digit ::= 0 | 1 | 2 | 3 | 4 | 5 | 6 | 7 | 8 | 9
exponent ::= *exponent-marker* [*sign*] {*digit*}+
exponent-marker ::= e | s | f | d | l | E | S | F | D | L

If no exponent specifier is present, or if the exponent marker e (or E) is used, then the precise format to be used is not specified. When such a representation is read and converted to an internal floating-point data object, the format specified by the variable `*read-default-float-format*` is used; the initial value of this variable is `single-float`.

The letters s, f, d, and l (or their respective uppercase equivalents) explicitly specify the use of *short*, *single*, *double*, and *long* format, respectively.

Examples of floating-point numbers:

```
0.0                            ; Floating-point zero in default format
0E0                            ; Also floating-point zero in default format
-.0                            ; This may be a zero or a minus zero,
                               ;   depending on the implementation
0.                             ; The integer zero, not a floating-point zero!
0.0s0                          ; A floating-point zero in short format
0s0                            ; Also a floating-point zero in short format
3.14159265358979323846d0       ; A double-format approximation to π
6.02E+23                       ; Avogadro's number, in default format
602E+21                        ; Also Avogadro's number, in default format
3.010299957f-1                 ; log₁₀ 2, in single format
-0.000000001s9                 ; eᵖⁱ in short format, the hard way
```

; A *double*-format approximation to π
; $\log_{10} 2$, in *single* format
; $e^{\pi i}$ in *short* format, the hard way

Notice of correction. The first edition unfortunately listed an incorrect value (3.1010299957f-1) for the base-10 logarithm of 2.

The internal format used for an external representation depends only on the exponent marker and not on the number of decimal digits in the external representation.

While Common Lisp provides terminology and notation sufficient to accommodate four distinct floating-point formats, not all implementations will have the means to support that many distinct formats. An implementation is therefore permitted to provide fewer than four distinct internal floating-point formats, in which case at least one of them will be "shared" by more than one of the external format names *short*, *single*, *double*, and *long* according to the following rules:

- If one internal format is provided, then it is considered to be *single*, but serves also as *short*, *double*, and *long*. The data types short-float, single-float, double-float, and long-float are considered to be identical. An expression such as (eql 1.0s0 1.0d0) will be true in such an implementation because the two numbers 1.0s0 and 1.0d0 will be converted into the same internal format and therefore be considered to have the same data type, despite the differing external syntax. Similarly, (typep 1.0L0 'short-float) will be true in such an implementation. For output purposes all floating-point numbers are assumed to be of *single* format and thus will print using the exponent letter E or F.

- If two internal formats are provided, then either of two correspondences may be used, depending on which is the more appropriate:

  – One format is *short*; the other is *single* and serves also as *double* and *long*. The data types single-float, double-float, and long-float are considered to be identical, but short-float is distinct. An expression such as (eql 1.0s0 1.0d0) will be false, but (eql 1.0f0 1.0d0) will be true. Similarly, (typep 1.0L0 'short-float) will be false, but (typep 1.0L0 'single-float) will be true. For output purposes all floating-point numbers are assumed to be of *short* or *single* format.

  – One format is *single* and serves also as *short*; the other is *double* and serves also as *long*. The data types short-float and single-float are considered to be identical, and the data types double-float and long-float are considered to be identical. An expression such as (eql 1.0s0 1.0d0) will be false, as will (eql 1.0f0 1.0d0); but (eql 1.0d0 1.0L0) will be true. Similarly, (typep 1.0L0 'short-float) will be false, but (typep 1.0L0 'double-float) will be true. For output purposes all floating-point numbers are assumed to be of *single* or *double* format.

- If three internal formats are provided, then either of two correspondences may be used, depending on which is the more appropriate:

- One format is *short*; another format is *single*; and the third format is *double* and serves also as *long*. Similar constraints apply.

- One format is *single* and serves also as *short*; another is *double*; and the third format is *long*.

Implementation note: It is recommended that an implementation provide as many distinct floating-point formats as feasible, using table 2-1 as a guideline. Ideally, short-format floating-point numbers should have an "immediate" representation that does not require heap allocation; single-format floating-point numbers should approximate IEEE proposed standard single-format floating-point numbers; and double-format floating-point numbers should approximate IEEE proposed standard double-format floating-point numbers [23, 17, 16].

2.1.4. Complex Numbers

Complex numbers (type `complex`) are represented in Cartesian form, with a real part and an imaginary part, each of which is a non-complex number (integer, ratio, or floating-point number). It should be emphasized that the parts of a complex number are not necessarily floating-point numbers; in this, Common Lisp is like PL/I and differs from Fortran. However, both parts must be of the same type: either both are rational, or both are of the same floating-point format.

Complex numbers may be notated by writing the characters `#C` followed by a list of the real and imaginary parts. If the two parts as notated are not of the same type, then they are converted according to the rules of floating-point contagion as described in chapter 12. (Indeed, `#C(`*a b*`)` is equivalent to `#,(complex `*a b*`)`; see the description of the function `complex`.) For example:

```
#C(3.0s1 2.0s-1)    ;Real and imaginary parts are short format
#C(5 -3)            ;A Gaussian integer
#C(5/3 7.0)         ;Will be converted internally to #C(1.66666 7.0)
#C(0 1)             ;The imaginary unit, that is, i
```

The type of a specific complex number is indicated by a list of the word `complex` and the type of the components; for example, a specialized representation for complex numbers with short floating-point parts would be of type `(complex short-float)`. The type `complex` encompasses all complex representations.

A complex number of type `(complex rational)`, that is, one whose components are rational, can never have a zero imaginary part. If the result of a computation would be a complex rational with a zero imaginary part, the result is immediately converted to a non-complex rational number by taking the real part.

This is called the rule of *complex canonicalization*. This rule does not apply to floating-point complex numbers; #C(5.0 0.0) and 5.0 are different.

2.2. Characters

Characters are represented as data objects of type character.

There are two subtypes of interest, called standard-char and string-char.

X3J13 voted in March 1989 ⟨11⟩ to remove the type string-char.

A character object can be notated by writing #\ followed by the character itself. For example, #\g means the character object for a lowercase g. This works well enough for printing characters. Non-printing characters have names, and can be notated by writing #\ and then the name; for example, #\Space (or #\SPACE or #\space or #\sPaCE) means the space character. The syntax for character names after #\ is the same as that for symbols. However, only character names that are known to the particular implementation may be used.

2.2.1. Standard Characters

Common Lisp defines a standard character set (subtype standard-char) for two purposes. Common Lisp programs that are *written* in the standard character set can be read by any Common Lisp implementation; and Common Lisp programs that *use* only standard characters as data objects are most likely to be portable. The Common Lisp character set consists of a space character #\Space, a newline character #\Newline, and the following ninety-four non-blank printing characters or their equivalents:

```
! " # $ % & ' ( ) * + , - . / 0 1 2 3 4 5 6 7 8 9 : ; < = > ?
@ A B C D E F G H I J K L M N O P Q R S T U V W X Y Z [ \ ] ^ _
` a b c d e f g h i j k l m n o p q r s t u v w x y z { | } ~
```

The Common Lisp standard character set is apparently equivalent to the ninety-five standard ASCII printing characters plus a newline character. Nevertheless, Common Lisp is designed to be relatively independent of the ASCII character encoding. For example, the collating sequence is not specified except to say that digits must be properly ordered, the uppercase letters must be properly ordered, and the lowercase letters must be properly ordered (see char< for a precise specification). Other character encodings, particularly EBCDIC, should be easily accommodated (with a suitable mapping of printing characters).

Of the ninety-four non-blank printing characters, the following are used in only limited ways in the syntax of Common Lisp programs:

[   ]   {   }   ?   !   ^   _   ~ $ %

All of these characters except ! and _ are used within format strings as formatting directives. Except for this, [,], {, }, ?, and ! are not used in Common Lisp and are reserved to the user for syntactic extensions; ^ and _ are not yet used in Common Lisp but are part of the syntax of reserved tokens and are reserved to implementors; ~ is not yet used in Common Lisp and is reserved to implementors; and $ and % are normally regarded as alphabetic characters but are not used in the names of any standard Common Lisp functions, variables, or other entities.

X3J13 voted in June 1989 ⟨139⟩ to add a format directive ~_ (see chapter 27). The following characters are called *semi-standard*:

#\Backspace   #\Tab   #\Linefeed   #\Page   #\Return   #\Rubout

Not all implementations of Common Lisp need to support them; but those implementations that use the standard ASCII character set should support them, treating them as corresponding respectively to the ASCII characters BS (octal code 010), HT (011), LF (012), FF (014), CR (015), and DEL (177). These characters are not members of the subtype standard-char unless synonymous with one of the standard characters specified above. For example, in a given implementation it might be sensible for the implementor to define #\Linefeed or #\Return to be synonymous with #\Newline, or #\Tab to be synonymous with #\Space.

2.2.2. Line Divisions

The treatment of line divisions is one of the most difficult issues in designing portable software, simply because there is so little agreement among operating systems. Some use a single character to delimit lines; the recommended ASCII character for this purpose is the line feed character LF (also called the new line character, NL), but some systems use the carriage return character CR. Much more common is the two-character sequence CR followed by LF. Frequently line divisions have no representation as a character but are implicit in the structuring of a file into records, each record containing a line of text. A deck of punched cards has this structure, for example.

Common Lisp provides an abstract interface by requiring that there be a single character, #\Newline, that within the language serves as a line delimiter. (The language C has a similar requirement.) An implementation of Common Lisp must translate between this internal single-character representation and whatever external representation(s) may be used.

Implementation note: How the character called #\Newline is represented internally is not specified here, but it is strongly suggested that the ASCII LF character be used in Common Lisp implementations that use the ASCII character encoding. The ASCII CR character is a workable, but in most cases inferior, alternative.

When the first edition was written it was not yet clear that UNIX would become so widely accepted. The decision to represent the line delimiter as a single character has proved to be a good one.

The requirement that a line division be represented as a single character has certain consequences. A character string written in the middle of a program in such a way as to span more than one line must contain exactly one character to represent each line division. Consider this code fragment:

```
(setq a-string "This string
contains
forty-two characters.")
```

Between g and c there must be exactly one character, #\Newline; a two-character sequence, such as #\Return and then #\Newline, is not acceptable, nor is the absence of a character. The same is true between s and f.

When the character #\Newline is written to an output file, the Common Lisp implementation must take the appropriate action to produce a line division. This might involve writing out a record or translating #\Newline to a CR/LF sequence.

Implementation note: If an implementation uses the ASCII character encoding, uses the CR/LF sequence externally to delimit lines, uses LF to represent #\Newline internally, and supports #\Return as a data object corresponding to the ASCII character CR, the question arises as to what action to take when the program writes out #\Return followed by #\Newline. It should first be noted that #\Return is not a standard Common Lisp character, and the action to be taken when #\Return is written out is therefore not defined by the Common Lisp language. A plausible approach is to buffer the #\Return character and suppress it if and only if the next character is #\Newline (the net effect is to generate a CR/LF sequence). Another plausible approach is simply to ignore the difficulty and declare that writing #\Return and then #\Newline results in the sequence CR/CR/LF in the output.

2.2.3. Non-standard Characters

Any implementation may provide additional characters, whether printing characters or named characters. Some plausible examples:

```
#\π   #\α   #\Break   #\Home-Up   #\Escape
```

The use of such characters may render Common Lisp programs non-portable.

2.2.4. Character Attributes

Every object of type `character` has three attributes: *code*, *bits*, and *font*. The code attribute is intended to distinguish among the printed glyphs and formatting functions for characters; it is a numerical encoding of the character proper. The bits attribute allows extra flags to be associated with a character. The font attribute permits a specification of the style of the glyphs (such as italics). Each of these attributes may be understood to be a non-negative integer.

The font attribute may be notated in unsigned decimal notation between the # and the \. For example, #3\a means the letter a in font 3. This might mean the same thing as #\α if font 3 were used to represent Greek letters. Note that not all Common Lisp implementations provide for non-zero font attributes; see `char-font-limit`.

The bits attribute may be notated by preceding the name of the character by the names or initials of the bits, separated by hyphens. The character itself may be written instead of the name, preceded if necessary by \. For example:

```
#\Control-Meta-Return          #\Meta-Control-Q
#\Hyper-Space                  #\Meta-\a
#\Control-A                    #\Meta-Hyper-\:
#\C-M-Return                   #\Hyper-\π
```

Note that not all Common Lisp implementations provide for non-zero bits attributes; see `char-bits-limit`.

X3J13 voted in March 1989 ⟨11⟩ to replace the notion of bits and font attributes with that of implementation-defined attributes.

2.2.5. String Characters

Any character whose bits and font attributes are zero may be contained in strings. All such characters together constitute a subtype of the characters; this subtype is called `string-char`.

X3J13 voted in March 1989 ⟨11⟩ to eliminate the type `string-char`. Two new subtypes of `character` are `base-character`, defined to be equivalent to the result of the function call

```
(upgraded-array-element-type 'standard-char)
```

and `extended-character`, defined to be equivalent to the type specifier

```
(and character (not base-character))
```

An implementation may support additional subtypes of `character` that may or may not be supertypes of `base-character`. In addition, an implementation may define `base-character` to be equivalent to `character`. The choice of any base characters that are not standard characters is implementation-defined. Only base characters can be elements of a base string. No upper bound is specified for the number of distinct characters of type `base-character`—that is implementation-dependent—but the lower bound is 96, the number of standard Common Lisp characters.

2.3. Symbols

Symbols are Lisp data objects that serve several purposes and have several interesting characteristics. Every object of type `symbol` has a name, called its *print name*. Given a symbol, one can obtain its name in the form of a string. Conversely, given the name of a symbol as a string, one can obtain the symbol itself. (More precisely, symbols are organized into *packages*, and all the symbols in a package are uniquely identified by name. See chapter 11.)

Symbols have a component called the *property list*, or *plist*. By convention this is always a list whose even-numbered components (calling the first component zero) are symbols, here functioning as property names, and whose odd-numbered components are associated property values. Functions are provided for manipulating this property list; in effect, these allow a symbol to be treated as an extensible record structure.

Symbols are also used to represent certain kinds of variables in Lisp programs, and there are functions for dealing with the values associated with symbols in this role.

A symbol can be notated simply by writing its name. If its name is not empty, and if the name consists only of uppercase alphabetic, numeric, or certain pseudo-alphabetic special characters (but not delimiter characters such as parentheses or space), and if the name of the symbol cannot be mistaken for a number, then the symbol can be notated by the sequence of characters in its name. Any uppercase letters that appear in the (internal) name may be written in either case in the external notation (more on this below). For example:

```
FROBBOZ              ;The symbol whose name is FROBBOZ
frobboz              ;Another way to notate the same symbol
fRObBoz              ;Yet another way to notate it
```

`unwind-protect`	; A symbol with a - in its name
`+$`	; The symbol named +$
`1+`	; The symbol named 1+
`+1`	; This is the integer 1, not a symbol
`pascal_style`	; This symbol has an underscore in its name
`b^2-4*a*c`	; This is a single symbol!
	; It has several special characters in its name
`file.rel.43`	; This symbol has periods in its name
`/usr/games/zork`	; This symbol has slashes in its name

In addition to letters and numbers, the following characters are normally considered to be alphabetic for the purposes of notating symbols:

```
+  -  *  /  @  $  %  ^  &  _  =  <  >  ~  .
```

Some of these characters have conventional purposes for naming things; for example, symbols that name special variables generally have names beginning and ending with *. The last character listed above, the period, is considered alphabetic *provided* that a token does not consist entirely of periods. A single period standing by itself is used in the notation of conses and dotted lists; a token consisting of two or more periods is syntactically illegal. (The period also serves as the decimal point in the notation of numbers.)

The following characters are also alphabetic by default but are explicitly reserved to the user for definition as reader macro characters (see section 22.1.3) or any other desired purpose and therefore should not be used routinely in names of symbols:

```
?  !  [  ]  {  }
```

A symbol may have uppercase letters, lowercase letters, or both in its print name. However, the Lisp reader normally converts lowercase letters to the corresponding uppercase letters when reading symbols. The net effect is that most of the time case makes no difference when *notating* symbols. Case *does* make a difference internally and when printing a symbol. Internally the symbols that name all standard Common Lisp functions, variables, and keywords have uppercase names; their names appear in lowercase in this book for readability. Typing such names with lowercase letters works because the function `read` will convert lowercase letters to the equivalent uppercase letters.

X3J13 voted in June 1989 ⟨150⟩ to introduce `readtable-case`, which controls whether `read` will alter the case of letters read as part of the name of a symbol.

If a symbol cannot be simply notated by the characters of its name because the (internal) name contains special characters or lowercase letters, then there are two "escape" conventions for notating them. Writing a \ character before any character causes the character to be treated itself as an ordinary character for use in a symbol name; in particular, it suppresses internal conversion of lowercase letters to their uppercase equivalents. If any character in a notation is preceded by \, then that notation can never be interpreted as a number. For example:

```
\(                      ;The symbol whose name is (
\+1                     ;The symbol whose name is +1
+\1                     ;Also the symbol whose name is +1
\frobboz                ;The symbol whose name is fROBBOZ
3.14159265\s0           ;The symbol whose name is 3.14159265s0
3.14159265\S0           ;A different symbol, whose name is 3.14159265S0
3.14159265s0            ;A short-format floating-point approximation to π
APL\\360                ;The symbol whose name is APL\360
apl\\360                ;Also the symbol whose name is APL\360
\(b^2\)\ -\ 4*a*c       ;The name is (B^2) - 4*A*C;
                        ;  it has parentheses and two spaces in it
\(\b^2\)\ -\ 4*\a*\c    ;The name is (b^2) - 4*a*c;
                        ;  the letters are explicitly lowercase
```

It may be tedious to insert a \ before *every* delimiter character in the name of a symbol if there are many of them. An alternative convention is to surround the name of a symbol with vertical bars; these cause every character between them to be taken as part of the symbol's name, as if \ had been written before each one, excepting only | itself and \, which must nevertheless be preceded by \. For example:

```
|"|                     ;The same as writing \"
|(b^2) - 4*a*c|         ;The name is (b^2) - 4*a*c
|frobboz|               ;The name is frobboz, not FROBBOZ
|APL\360|               ;The name is APL360, because the \ quotes the 3
|APL\\360|              ;The name is APL\360
|apl\\360|              ;The name is apl\360
|\|\||                  ;Same as \|\|: the name is ||
|(B^2) - 4*A*C|         ;The name is (B^2) - 4*A*C;
                        ;  it has parentheses and two spaces in it
|(b^2) - 4*a*c|         ;The name is (b^2) - 4*a*c
```

2.4. Lists and Conses

A cons is a record structure containing two components called the *car* and the *cdr*. Conses are used primarily to represent lists.

A *list* is recursively defined to be either the empty list or a cons whose *cdr* component is a list. A list is therefore a chain of conses linked by their *cdr* components and terminated by nil, the empty list. The *car* components of the conses are called the *elements* of the list. For each element of the list there is a cons. The empty list has no elements at all.

A list is notated by writing the elements of the list in order, separated by blank space (space, tab, or return characters) and surrounded by parentheses.

```
(a b c)             ;A list of three symbols
(2.0s0 (a 1) #\*)   ;A list of three things: a short floating-point
                    ; number, another list, and a character object
```

The empty list nil therefore can be written as (), because it is a list with no elements.

A *dotted list* is one whose last cons does not have nil for its *cdr*, rather some other data object (which is also not a cons, or the first-mentioned cons would not be the last cons of the list). Such a list is called "dotted" because of the special notation used for it: the elements of the list are written between parentheses as before, but after the last element and before the right parenthesis are written a dot (surrounded by blank space) and then the *cdr* of the last cons. As a special case, a single cons is notated by writing the *car* and the *cdr* between parentheses and separated by a space-surrounded dot. For example:

```
(a . 4)        ;A cons whose car is a symbol
               ; and whose cdr is an integer
(a b c . d)    ;A dotted list with three elements whose last cons
               ; has the symbol d in its cdr
```

Compatibility note: In MacLisp, the dot in dotted-list notation need not be surrounded by white space or other delimiters. The dot is required to be delimited in Common Lisp, as in Lisp Machine Lisp.

It is legitimate to write something like (a b . (c d)); this means the same as (a b c d). The standard Lisp output routines will never print a list in the first form, however; they will avoid dot notation wherever possible.

Often the term *list* is used to refer either to true lists or to dotted lists. When the distinction is important, the term "true list" will be used to refer to a list terminated by nil. Most functions advertised to operate on lists expect to be given true lists. Throughout this book, unless otherwise specified, it is an error to pass a dotted list to a function that is specified to require a list as an argument.

Implementation note: Implementors are encouraged to use the equivalent of the predicate endp wherever it is necessary to test for the end of a list. Whenever feasible, this test should explicitly signal an error if a list is found to be terminated by a non-nil atom. However, such an explicit error signal is not required, because some such tests occur in important loops where efficiency is important. In such cases, the predicate atom may be used to test for the end of the list, quietly treating any non-nil list-terminating atom as if it were nil.

Sometimes the term *tree* is used to refer to some cons and all the other conses transitively accessible to it through *car* and *cdr* links until non-conses are reached; these non-conses are called the *leaves* of the tree.

Lists, dotted lists, and trees are not mutually exclusive data types; they are simply useful points of view about structures of conses. There are yet other terms, such as *association list*. None of these are true Lisp data types. Conses are a data type, and nil is the sole object of type null. The Lisp data type list is taken to mean the union of the cons and null data types, and therefore encompasses both true lists and dotted lists.

2.5. Arrays

An array is an object with components arranged according to a Cartesian coordinate system. In general, these components may be any Lisp data objects.

The number of dimensions of an array is called its *rank* (this terminology is borrowed from APL); the rank is a non-negative integer. Likewise, each dimension is itself a non-negative integer. The total number of elements in the array is the product of all the dimensions.

An implementation of Common Lisp may impose a limit on the rank of an array, but this limit may not be smaller than 7. Therefore, any Common Lisp program may assume the use of arrays of rank 7 or less. (A program may determine the actual limit on array ranks for a given implementation by examining the constant array-rank-limit.)

It is permissible for a dimension to be zero. In this case, the array has no elements, and any attempt to access an element is in error. However, other properties of the array, such as the dimensions themselves, may be used. If the rank is zero, then there are no dimensions, and the product of the dimensions is then by definition 1. A zero-rank array therefore has a single element.

An array element is specified by a sequence of indices. The length of the sequence must equal the rank of the array. Each index must be a non-negative integer strictly less than the corresponding array dimension. Array indexing is therefore zero-origin, not one-origin as in (the default case of) Fortran.

As an example, suppose that the variable `foo` names a 3-by-5 array. Then the first index may be 0, 1, or 2, and the second index may be 0, 1, 2, 3, or 4. One may refer to array elements using the function `aref`; for example, (`aref foo 2 1`) refers to element (2, 1) of the array. Note that `aref` takes a variable number of arguments: an array, and as many indices as the array has dimensions. A zero-rank array has no dimensions, and therefore `aref` would take such an array and no indices, and return the sole element of the array.

In general, arrays can be multidimensional, can share their contents with other array objects, and can have their size altered dynamically (either enlarging or shrinking) after creation. A one-dimensional array may also have a *fill pointer*.

Multidimensional arrays store their components in row-major order; that is, internally a multidimensional array is stored as a one-dimensional array, with the multidimensional index sets ordered lexicographically, last index varying fastest. This is important in two situations: (1) when arrays with different dimensions share their contents, and (2) when accessing very large arrays in a virtual-memory implementation. (The first situation is a matter of semantics; the second, a matter of efficiency.)

An array that is not displaced to another array, has no fill pointer, and is not to have its size adjusted dynamically after creation is called a *simple* array. The user may provide declarations that certain arrays will be simple. Some implementations can handle simple arrays in an especially efficient manner; for example, simple arrays may have a more compact representation than non-simple arrays.

X3J13 voted in June 1989 ⟨3⟩ to clarify that if one or more of the `:adjustable`, `:fill-pointer`, and `:displaced-to` arguments is true when `make-array` is called, then whether the resulting array is simple is unspecified; but if all three arguments are false, then the resulting array is guaranteed to be simple.

2.5.1. Vectors

One-dimensional arrays are called *vectors* in Common Lisp and constitute the type `vector` (which is therefore a subtype of `array`). Vectors and lists are collectively considered to be *sequences*. They differ in that any component of a one-dimensional array can be accessed in constant time, whereas the average component access time for a list is linear in the length of the list; on the other hand, adding a new element to the front of a list takes constant time, whereas the same operation on an array takes time linear in the length of the array.

A general vector (a one-dimensional array that can have any data object as an element but that has no additional paraphernalia) can be notated by notating the components in order, separated by whitespace and surrounded by #(and). For example:

```
#(a  b  c)                    ;A vector of length 3
#()                           ;An empty vector
#(2  3  5  7  11  13  17  19  23  29  31  37  41  43  47)
                              ;A vector containing the primes below 50
```

Note that when the function `read` parses this syntax, it always constructs a *simple* general vector.

Rationale: Many people have suggested that brackets be used to notate vectors, as [a b c] instead of #(a b c). This notation would be shorter, perhaps more readable, and certainly in accord with cultural conventions in other parts of computer science and mathematics. However, to preserve the usefulness of the user-definable macro-character feature of the function `read`, it is necessary to leave some characters to the user for this purpose. Experience in MacLisp has shown that users, especially implementors of languages for use in artificial intelligence research, often want to define special kinds of brackets. Therefore Common Lisp avoids using brackets and braces for any syntactic purpose.

Implementations may provide certain specialized representations of arrays for efficiency in the case where all the components are of the same specialized (typically numeric) type. All implementations provide specialized arrays for the cases when the components are characters (or rather, a special subset of the characters); the one-dimensional instances of this specialization are called *strings*. All implementations are also required to provide specialized arrays of bits, that is, arrays of type `(array bit)`; the one-dimensional instances of this specialization are called *bit-vectors*.

2.5.2. Strings

A string is simply a vector of characters. More precisely, a string is a specialized vector whose elements are of type `string-char`.

X3J13 voted in March 1989 ⟨11⟩ to eliminate the type `string-char` and to redefine the type `string` to be the union of one or more specialized vector types, the types of whose elements are subtypes of the type `character`. Subtypes of `string` include `simple-string`, `base-string`, and `simple-base-string`.

```
base-string ≡ (vector base-character)
simple-base-string ≡ (simple-array base-character (*))
```

An implementation may support other string subtypes as well. All Common Lisp functions that operate on strings treat all strings uniformly; note, however, that it is an error to attempt to insert an extended character into a base string.

The type string is therefore a subtype of the type vector.

A string can be written as the sequence of characters contained in the string, preceded and followed by a " (double quote) character. Any " or \ character in the sequence must additionally have a \ character before it.

For example:

```
"Foo"                        ;A string with three characters in it
""                           ;An empty string
"\"APL\\360?\" he cried."    ;A string with twenty characters
"|x| = |-x|"                 ;A ten-character string
```

Notice that any vertical bar | in a string need not be preceded by a \. Similarly, any double quote in the name of a symbol written using vertical-bar notation need not be preceded by a \. The double-quote and vertical-bar notations are similar but distinct: double quotes indicate a character string containing the sequence of characters, whereas vertical bars indicate a symbol whose name is the contained sequence of characters.

The characters contained by the double quotes, taken from left to right, occupy locations within the string with increasing indices. The leftmost character is string element number 0, the next one is element number 1, the next one is element number 2, and so on.

Note that the function prin1 will print any character vector (not just a simple one) using this syntax, but the function read will always construct a simple string when it reads this syntax.

2.5.3. Bit-Vectors

A bit-vector can be written as the sequence of bits contained in the string, preceded by #*; any delimiter character, such as whitespace, will terminate the bit-vector syntax. For example:

```
#*10110      ;A five-bit bit-vector; bit 0 is a 1
#*           ;An empty bit-vector
```

The bits notated following the #*, taken from left to right, occupy locations within the bit-vector with increasing indices. The leftmost notated bit is bit-vector element number 0, the next one is element number 1, and so on.

The function prin1 will print any bit-vector (not just a simple one) using this syntax, but the function read will always construct a simple bit-vector when it reads this syntax.

2.6. Hash Tables

Hash tables provide an efficient way of mapping any Lisp object (a *key*) to an associated object. They are provided as primitives of Common Lisp because some implementations may need to use internal storage management strategies that would make it very difficult for the user to implement hash tables in a portable fashion. Hash tables are described in chapter 16.

2.7. Readtables

A readtable is a data structure that maps characters into syntax types for the Lisp expression parser. In particular, a readtable indicates for each character with syntax *macro character* what its macro definition is. This is a mechanism by which the user may reprogram the parser to a limited but useful extent. See section 22.1.5.

2.8. Packages

Packages are collections of symbols that serve as name spaces. The parser recognizes symbols by looking up character sequences in the current package. Packages can be used to hide names internal to a module from other code. Mechanisms are provided for exporting symbols from a given package to the primary "user" package. See chapter 11.

2.9. Pathnames

Pathnames are the means by which a Common Lisp program can interface to an external file system in a reasonably implementation-independent manner. See section 23.1.1.

2.10. Streams

A stream is a source or sink of data, typically characters or bytes. Nearly all functions that perform I/O do so with respect to a specified stream. The function open takes a pathname and returns a stream connected to the file specified by the pathname. There are a number of standard streams that are used by default for various purposes. See chapter 21.

   X3J13 voted in January 1989 ⟨167⟩ to introduce subtypes of type stream: broadcast-stream, concatenated-stream, echo-stream, synonym-stream, string-stream, file-stream, and two-way-stream are disjoint subtypes of stream. Note particularly that a synonym stream is always and only of type synonym-stream, regardless of the type of the stream for which it is a synonym.

2.11. Random-States

An object of type random-state is used to encapsulate state information used by the pseudo-random number generator. For more information about random-state objects, see section 12.9.

2.12. Structures

Structures are instances of user-defined data types that have a fixed number of named components. They are analogous to records in Pascal. Structures are declared using the defstruct construct; defstruct automatically defines access and constructor functions for the new data type.

Different structures may print out in different ways; the definition of a structure type may specify a print procedure to use for objects of that type (see the :print-function option to defstruct). The default notation for structures is

#S(*structure-name*
        slot-name-1 slot-value-1
        slot-name-2 slot-value-2
            ...)

where #S indicates structure syntax, *structure-name* is the name (a symbol) of the structure type, each *slot-name* is the name (also a symbol) of a component, and each corresponding *slot-value* is the representation of the Lisp object in that slot.

2.13. Functions

A *function* is anything that may be correctly given to the funcall or apply function, and is to be executed as code when arguments are supplied.

A *compiled-function* is a compiled code object.

A lambda-expression (a list whose *car* is the symbol lambda) may serve as a function. Depending on the implementation, it may be possible for other lists to serve as functions. For example, an implementation might choose to represent a "lexical closure" as a list whose *car* contains some special marker.

A symbol may serve as a function; an attempt to invoke a symbol as a function causes the contents of the symbol's function cell to be used. See symbol-function and defun.

The result of evaluating a function special form will always be a function.

X3J13 voted in June 1988 ⟨90⟩ to revise these specifications. The type function is to be disjoint from cons and symbol, and so a list whose *car* is lambda is not, properly speaking, of type function, nor is any symbol. However, standard Common Lisp functions that accept functional arguments will accept a symbol or a list whose *car* is lambda and automatically coerce it to be a function; such standard functions include funcall, apply, and mapcar. Such functions do not, however, accept a lambda-expression as a functional argument; therefore one may not write

(mapcar '(lambda (x y) (sqrt (* x y))) p q)

but instead one must write something like

(mapcar #'(lambda (x y) (sqrt (* x y))) p q)

This change makes it impermissible to represent a lexical closure as a list whose *car* is some special marker.

The value of a function special form will always be of type function.

2.14. Unreadable Data Objects

Some objects may print in implementation-dependent ways. Such objects cannot necessarily be reliably reconstructed from a printed representation, and so they are usually printed in a format informative to the user but not acceptable to the read function: #<*useful information*>. The Lisp reader will signal an error on encountering #<.

As a hypothetical example, an implementation might print

#<stack-pointer si:rename-within-new-definition-maybe #o311037552>

for an implementation-specific "internal stack pointer" data type whose printed representation includes the name of the type, some information about the stack slot pointed to, and the machine address (in octal) of the stack slot.

See print-unreadable-object, a macro that prints an object using #< syntax.

2.15. Overlap, Inclusion, and Disjointness of Types

The Common Lisp data type hierarchy is tangled and purposely left somewhat open-ended so that implementors may experiment with new data types as extensions to the language. This section explicitly states all the defined relationships between types, including subtype/supertype relationships, disjointness, and exhaustive partitioning. The user of Common Lisp should not depend on any relationships not explicitly stated here. For example, it is not valid to assume that because a number is not complex and not rational that it must be a float, because implementations are permitted to provide yet other kinds of numbers.

First we need some terminology. If x is a supertype of y, then any object of type y is also of type x, and y is said to be a subtype of x. If types x and y are disjoint, then no object (in any implementation) may be both of type x and of type y. Types a_1 through a_n are an *exhaustive union* of type x if each a_j is a subtype of x, and any object of type x is necessarily of at least one of the types a_j; a_1 through a_n are furthermore an *exhaustive partition* if they are also pairwise disjoint.

- The type t is a supertype of every type whatsoever. Every object is of type t.

- The type nil is a subtype of every type whatsoever. No object is of type nil.

- The types cons, symbol, array, number, and character are pairwise disjoint.

X3J13 voted in June 1988 ⟨41⟩ to extend the preceding paragraph as follows.

- The types cons, symbol, array, number, character, hash-table, readtable, package, pathname, stream, random-state, and any single other type created by defstruct or defclass are pairwise disjoint.

The wording of the first edition was intended to allow implementors to use the defstruct facility to define the built-in types hash-table, readtable, package, pathname, stream, random-state. The change still permits this implementation strategy but forbids these built-in types from including, or being included in, other types (in the sense of the defstruct :include option).

X3J13 voted in June 1988 ⟨90⟩ to specify that the type function is disjoint from the types cons, symbol, array, number, and character. The type compiled-function is a subtype of function; implementations are free to define other subtypes of function.

- The types rational, float, and complex are pairwise disjoint subtypes of number.

X3J13 voted in March 1989 ⟨151⟩ to rewrite the preceding item as follows.

- The types real and complex are pairwise disjoint subtypes of number.

Rationale: It might be thought that real and complex should form an exhaustive partition of the type number. This is purposely avoided here in order to permit compatible experimentation with extensions to the Common Lisp number system.

- The types rational and float are pairwise disjoint subtypes of real.

Rationale: It might be thought that rational and float should form an exhaustive partition of the type real. This is purposely avoided here in order to permit compatible experimentation with extensions to the Common Lisp number system.

• The types integer and ratio are disjoint subtypes of rational.

Rationale: It might be thought that integer and ratio should form an exhaustive partition of the type rational. This is purposely avoided here in order to permit compatible experimentation with extensions to the Common Lisp rational number system.

• The types fixnum and bignum are disjoint subtypes of integer.

Rationale: It might be thought that fixnum and bignum should form an exhaustive partition of the type integer. This is purposely avoided here in order to permit compatible experimentation with extensions to the Common Lisp integer number system, such as the idea of adding explicit representations of infinity or of positive and negative infinity.

X3J13 voted in January 1989 ⟨76⟩ to specify that the types fixnum and bignum do in fact form an exhaustive partition of the type integer; more precisely, they voted to specify that the type bignum is by definition equivalent to (and integer (not fixnum)). This is consistent with the first edition text in section 2.1.1.

I interpret this to mean that implementators could still experiment with such extensions as adding explicit representations of infinity, but such infinities would necessarily be of type bignum.

• The types short-float, single-float, double-float, and long-float are subtypes of float. Any two of them must be either disjoint or identical; if identical, then any other types between them in the above ordering must also be identical to them (for example, if single-float and long-float are identical types, then double-float must be identical to them also).

• The type null is a subtype of symbol; the only object of type null is nil.

• The types cons and null form an exhaustive partition of the type list.

• The type standard-char is a subtype of string-char; string-char is a subtype of character.

X3J13 voted in March 1989 ⟨11⟩ to remove the type string-char. The preceding item is replaced by the following.

• The type standard-char is a subtype of base-character. The types base-character and extended-character form an exhaustive partition of character.

• The type string is a subtype of vector, for string means (vector string-char).

X3J13 voted in March 1989 ⟨11⟩ to remove the type string-char. The preceding item is replaced by the following.

- The type string is a subtype of vector; it is the union of all types (vector c) such that c is a subtype of character.

- The type bit-vector is a subtype of vector, for bit-vector means (vector bit).

- The types (vector t), string, and bit-vector are disjoint.

- The type vector is a subtype of array; for all types x, the type (vector x) is the same as the type (array x (*)).

- The type simple-array is a subtype of array.

- The types simple-vector, simple-string, and simple-bit-vector are disjoint subtypes of simple-array, for they respectively mean (simple-array t (*)), (simple-array string-char (*)), and (simple-array bit (*)).

X3J13 voted in March 1989 ⟨11⟩ to remove the type string-char. The preceding item is replaced by the following.

- The types simple-vector, simple-string, and simple-bit-vector are disjoint subtypes of simple-array, for they mean (simple-array t (*)), the union of all types (simple-array c (*)) such that c is a subtype of character, and (simple-array bit (*)), respectively.

- The type simple-vector is a subtype of vector and indeed is a subtype of (vector t).

- The type simple-string is a subtype of string. (Note that although string is a subtype of vector, simple-string is not a subtype of simple-vector.)

Rationale: The hypothetical name simple-general-vector would have been more accurate than simple-vector, but in this instance euphony and user convenience were deemed more important to the design of Common Lisp than a rigid symmetry.

- The type simple-bit-vector is a subtype of bit-vector. (Note that although bit-vector is a subtype of vector, simple-bit-vector is not a subtype of simple-vector.)

- The types vector and list are disjoint subtypes of sequence.

- The types random-state, readtable, package, pathname, stream, and hash-table are pairwise disjoint.

X3J13 voted in June 1988 ⟨41⟩ to make random-state, readtable, package, pathname, stream, and hash-table pairwise disjoint from a number of other types as well; see note above.

X3J13 voted in January 1989 ⟨167⟩ to introduce subtypes of type stream.

- The types two-way-stream, echo-stream, broadcast-stream, file-stream, synonym-stream, string-stream, and concatenated-stream are disjoint subtypes of stream.

- Any two types created by defstruct are disjoint unless one is a supertype of the other by virtue of the :include option.

- An exhaustive union for the type common is formed by the types cons, symbol, (array x) where x is either t or a subtype of common, string, fixnum, bignum, ratio, short-float, single-float, double-float, long-float, (complex x) where x is a subtype of common, standard-char, hash-table, readtable, package, pathname, stream, random-state, and all types created by the user via defstruct. An implementation may not unilaterally add subtypes to common; however, future revisions to the Common Lisp standard may extend the definition of the common data type. Note that a type such as number or array may or may not be a subtype of common, depending on whether or not the given implementation has extended the set of objects of that type.

X3J13 voted in March 1989 ⟨17⟩ to remove the type common from the language.

3

Scope and Extent

In describing various features of the Common Lisp language, the notions of *scope* and *extent* are frequently useful. These notions arise when some object or construct must be referred to from some distant part of a program. *Scope* refers to the spatial or textual region of the program within which references may occur. *Extent* refers to the interval of time during which references may occur.

As a simple example, consider this program:

```
(defun copy-cell (x) (cons (car x) (cdr x)))
```

The scope of the parameter named x is the body of the defun form. There is no way to refer to this parameter from any other place but within the body of the defun. Similarly, the extent of the parameter x (for any particular call to copy-cell) is the interval from the time the function is invoked to the time it is exited. (In the general case, the extent of a parameter may last beyond the time of function exit, but that cannot occur in this simple case.)

Within Common Lisp, a referenceable entity is *established* by the execution of some language construct, and the scope and extent of the entity are described relative to the construct and the time (during execution of the construct) at which the entity is established. For the purposes of this discussion, the term "entity" refers not only to Common Lisp data objects, such as symbols and conses, but also to variable bindings (both ordinary and special), catchers, and go targets. It is important to distinguish between an entity and a name for the entity. In a function definition such as

```
(defun foo (x y) (* x (+ y 1)))
```

there is a single name, x, used to refer to the first parameter of the procedure whenever it is invoked; however, a new binding is established on every invocation. A *binding* is a particular parameter instance. The value of a reference to the name x depends not only on the scope within which it occurs (the one in the body of foo in the example occurs in the scope of the function definition's parameters) but also on the particular binding or instance involved. (In this case, it depends on the invocation during which the reference is made). More complicated examples appear at the end of this chapter.

There are a few kinds of scope and extent that are particularly useful in describing Common Lisp:

- *Lexical scope.* Here references to the established entity can occur only within certain program portions that are lexically (that is, textually) contained within the establishing construct. Typically the construct will have a part designated the *body*, and the scope of all entities established will be (or include) the body.

  Example: the names of parameters to a function normally are lexically scoped.

- *Indefinite scope.* References may occur anywhere, in any program.

- *Dynamic extent.* References may occur at any time in the interval between establishment of the entity and the explicit disestablishment of the entity. As a rule, the entity is disestablished when execution of the establishing construct completes or is otherwise terminated. Therefore entities with dynamic extent obey a stack-like discipline, paralleling the nested executions of their establishing constructs.

  Example: the `with-open-file` construct opens a connection to a file and creates a stream object to represent the connection. The stream object has indefinite extent, but the connection to the open file has dynamic extent: when control exits the `with-open-file` construct, either normally or abnormally, the stream is automatically closed.

  Example: the binding of a "special" variable has dynamic extent.

- *Indefinite extent.* The entity continues to exist as long as the possibility of reference remains. (An implementation is free to destroy the entity if it can prove that reference to it is no longer possible. Garbage collection strategies implicitly employ such proofs.)

  Example: most Common Lisp data objects have indefinite extent.

  Example: the bindings of lexically scoped parameters of a function have indefinite extent. (By contrast, in Algol the bindings of lexically scoped parameters of a procedure have dynamic extent.) The function definition

```
(defun compose (f g)
  #'(lambda (x)
      (funcall f (funcall g x))))
```

when given two arguments, immediately returns a function as its value. The parameter bindings for f and g do not disappear because the returned function, when called, could still refer to those bindings. Therefore

```
(funcall (compose #'sqrt #'abs) -9.0)
```

produces the value 3.0. (An analogous procedure would not necessarily work correctly in typical Algol implementations or, for that matter, in most Lisp dialects.)

In addition to the above terms, it is convenient to define *dynamic scope* to mean *indefinite scope and dynamic extent*. Thus we speak of "special" variables as having dynamic scope, or being dynamically scoped, because they have indefinite scope and dynamic extent: a special variable can be referred to anywhere as long as its binding is currently in effect.

The term "dynamic scope" is a misnomer. Nevertheless it is both traditional and useful.

The above definitions do not take into account the possibility of *shadowing*. Remote reference of entities is accomplished by using *names* of one kind or another. If two entities have the same name, then the second may shadow the first, in which case an occurrence of the name will refer to the second and cannot refer to the first.

In the case of lexical scope, if two constructs that establish entities with the same name are textually nested, then references within the inner construct refer to the entity established by the inner one; the inner one shadows the outer one. Outside the inner construct but inside the outer one, references refer to the entity established by the outer construct. For example:

```
(defun test (x z)
  (let ((z (* x 2))) (print z))
  z)
```

The binding of the variable z by the let construct shadows the parameter binding for the function test. The reference to the variable z in the print form refers to the let binding. The reference to z at the end of the function refers to the parameter named z.

In the case of dynamic extent, if the time intervals of two entities overlap, then one interval will necessarily be nested within the other one. This is a property of the design of Common Lisp.

Implementation note: Behind the assertion that dynamic extents nest properly is the assumption that there is only a single program or process. Common Lisp does not address the problems of multiprogramming (timesharing) or multiprocessing (more than one active processor) within a single Lisp environment. The documentation for implementations that extend Common Lisp for multiprogramming or multiprocessing should be very clear on what modifications are induced by such extensions to the rules of extent and scope. Implementors should note that Common Lisp has been carefully designed to allow special variables to be implemented using either the "deep binding" technique or the "shallow binding" technique, but the two techniques have different semantic and performance implications for multiprogramming and multiprocessing.

A reference by name to an entity with dynamic extent will always refer to the entity of that name that has been most recently established that has not yet been disestablished. For example:

```
(defun fun1 (x)
   (catch 'trap (+ 3 (fun2 x))))

(defun fun2 (y)
   (catch 'trap (* 5 (fun3 y))))

(defun fun3 (z)
   (throw 'trap z))
```

Consider the call (fun1 7). The result will be 10. At the time the throw is executed, there are two outstanding catchers with the name trap: one established within procedure fun1, and the other within procedure fun2. The latter is the more recent, and so the value 7 is returned from the catch form in fun2. Viewed from within fun3, the catch in fun2 shadows the one in fun1. Had fun2 been defined as

```
(defun fun2 (y)
   (catch 'snare (* 5 (fun3 y))))
```

then the two catchers would have different names, and therefore the one in fun1 would not be shadowed. The result would then have been 7.

As a rule, this book simply speaks of the scope or extent of an entity; the possibility of shadowing is left implicit.

The important scope and extent rules in Common Lisp follow:

- Variable bindings normally have lexical scope and indefinite extent.

- Variable bindings for which there is a dynamic-extent declaration also have lexical scope and indefinite extent, but objects that are the values of such bindings may have dynamic extent. (The declaration is the programmer's guarantee that the program will behave correctly even if certain of the data objects have only dynamic extent rather than the usual indefinite extent.)

- Bindings of variable names to symbol macros by `symbol-macrolet` have lexical scope and indefinite extent.

- Variable bindings that are declared to be `special` have dynamic scope (indefinite scope and dynamic extent).

- Bindings of function names established, for example, by `flet` and `labels` have lexical scope and indefinite extent.

- Bindings of function names for which there is a `dynamic-extent` declaration also have lexical scope and indefinite extent, but function objects that are the values of such bindings may have dynamic extent.

- Bindings of function names to macros as established by `macrolet` have lexical scope and indefinite extent.

- Condition handlers and restarts have dynamic scope (see chapter 29).

- A catcher established by a `catch` or `unwind-protect` special form has dynamic scope.

- An exit point established by a `block` construct has lexical scope and dynamic extent. (Such exit points are also established by `do`, `prog`, and other iteration constructs.)

- The `go` targets established by a `tagbody`, named by the tags in the `tagbody`, and referred to by `go` have lexical scope and dynamic extent. (Such `go` targets may also appear as tags in the bodies of `do`, `prog`, and other iteration constructs.)

- Named constants such as `nil` and `pi` have indefinite scope and indefinite extent.

The rules of lexical scoping imply that lambda-expressions appearing in the `function` construct will, in general, result in "closures" over those non-special variables visible to the lambda-expression. That is, the function represented by a lambda-expression may refer to any lexically apparent non-special variable and get the correct value, even if the construct that established the binding has been exited in the course of execution. The `compose` example shown earlier in this chapter provides one illustration of this. The rules also imply that special variable bindings are not "closed over" as they may be in certain other dialects of Lisp.

Constructs that use lexical scope effectively generate a new name for each established entity on each execution. Therefore dynamic shadowing cannot occur (though lexical shadowing may). This is of particular importance when dynamic extent is involved. For example:

```
(defun contorted-example (f g x)
  (if (= x 0)
      (funcall f)
      (block here
        (+ 5 (contorted-example g
                                #'(lambda ()
                                    (return-from here 4))
                                (- x 1)))))))
```

Consider the call (contorted-example nil nil 2). This produces the result 4. During the course of execution, there are three calls on contorted-example, interleaved with two establishments of blocks:

```
(contorted-example nil nil 2)

  (block here₁ ...)

    (contorted-example nil #'(lambda () (return-from here₁ 4)) 1)

      (block here₂ ...)

        (contorted-example #'(lambda () (return-from here₁ 4))
                           #'(lambda () (return-from here₂ 4))
                           0)
          (funcall f)
                where f ⇒ #'(lambda () (return-from here₁ 4))

          (return-from here₁ 4)
```

At the time the funcall is executed there are two block exit points outstanding, each apparently named here. In the trace above, these exit points are distinguished for expository purposes by subscripts. The return-from form executed as a result of the funcall operation refers to the *outer* outstanding exit point (here₁), not the inner one (here₂). This is a consequence of the rules of lexical scoping: it refers to that exit point textually visible at the point of execution of the function construct (here abbreviated by the #´ syntax) that resulted in creation of the function object actually invoked by the funcall.

If, in this example, one were to change the form (funcall f) to (funcall g), then the value of the call (contorted-example nil nil 2) would be 9. The value would change because the funcall would cause the execution of (return-from here₂ 4), thereby causing a return from the inner exit point (here₂). When that occurs, the value 4 is returned from the middle invocation of `contorted-example`, 5 is added to that to get 9, and that value is returned from the outer block and the outermost call to `contorted-example`. The point is that the choice of exit point returned from has nothing to do with its being innermost or outermost; rather, it depends on the lexical scoping information that is effectively packaged up with a lambda-expression when the `function` construct is executed.

This function `contorted-example` works only because the function named by `f` is invoked during the extent of the exit point. Block exit points are like non-special variable bindings in having lexical scope, but they differ in having dynamic extent rather than indefinite extent. Once the flow of execution has left the block construct, the exit point is disestablished. For example:

```
(defun illegal-example ()
  (let ((y (block here #'(lambda (z) (return-from here z)))))
    (if (numberp y) y (funcall y 5))))
```

One might expect the call `(illegal-example)` to produce 5 by the following incorrect reasoning: the `let` statement binds the variable `y` to the value of the `block` construct; this value is a function resulting from the lambda-expression. Because `y` is not a number, it is invoked on the value 5. The `return-from` should then return this value from the exit point named `here`, thereby exiting from the block *again* and giving `y` the value 5 which, being a number, is then returned as the value of the call to `illegal-example`.

The argument fails only because exit points are defined in Common Lisp to have dynamic extent. The argument is correct up to the execution of the `return-from`. The execution of the `return-from` is an error, however, *not* because it cannot refer to the exit point, but because it does correctly refer to an exit point *and* that exit point has been disestablished.

4

Type Specifiers

In Common Lisp, types are named by Lisp objects, specifically symbols and lists, called *type specifiers*. Symbols name predefined classes of objects, whereas lists usually indicate combinations or specializations of simpler types. Symbols or lists may also be abbreviations for types that could be specified in other ways.

4.1. Type Specifier Symbols

The type symbols defined by the system include those shown in table 4-1. In addition, when a structure type is defined using `defstruct`, the name of the structure type becomes a valid type symbol.

Notice of correction. In the first edition, the type specifiers `signed-byte` and `unsigned-byte` were inadvertently omitted from table 4-1.

X3J13 voted in March 1989 ⟨17⟩ to eliminate the type `common`; this fact is indicated by the brackets around the `common` type specifier in the table.

X3J13 voted in March 1989 ⟨11⟩ to eliminate the type `string-char`; this fact is indicated by the brackets around the `string-char` type specifier in the table.

X3J13 voted in March 1989 ⟨11⟩ to add the type `extended-character` and the type `base-character`.

X3J13 voted in March 1989 ⟨151⟩ to add the type specifier `real`.

X3J13 votes have also implicitly added many other type specifiers as names of classes (see chapter 28) or of conditions (see chapter 29).

4.2. Type Specifier Lists

If a type specifier is a list, the *car* of the list is a symbol, and the rest of the list is subsidiary type information. In many cases a subsidiary item may be *unspecified*. The unspecified subsidiary item is indicated by writing *. For example, to completely specify a vector type, one must mention the type of the elements and the length of the vector, as for example

49

Table 4-1: Standard Type Specifier Symbols

array	fixnum	package	simple-string
atom	float	pathname	simple-vector
bignum	function	random-state	single-float
bit	hash-table	ratio	standard-char
bit-vector	integer	rational	stream
character	keyword	readtable	string
[common]	list	sequence	[string-char]
compiled-function	long-float	short-float	symbol
complex	nil	signed-byte	t
cons	null	simple-array	unsigned-byte
double-float	number	simple-bit-vector	vector

X3J13 voted in March 1989 ⟨17⟩ to remove the type common.
X3J13 voted in March 1989 ⟨11⟩ to remove the type string-char.
X3J13 voted in March 1989 ⟨11⟩ to add base-character and extended-character.
X3J13 voted in March 1989 ⟨151⟩ to add the type real.

```
(vector double-float 100)
```

To leave the length unspecified, one would write

```
(vector double-float *)
```

To leave the element type unspecified, one would write

```
(vector * 100)
```

One may also leave both length and element type unspecified:

```
(vector * *)
```

Suppose that two type specifiers are the same except that the first has a * where the second has a more explicit specification. Then the second denotes a subtype of the type denoted by the first.

As a convenience, if a list has one or more unspecified items at the end, such items may simply be dropped rather than writing an explicit * for each one. If dropping all occurrences of * results in a singleton list, then the parentheses may be dropped as well (the list may be replaced by the symbol in its *car*). For example, (vector double-float *) may be abbreviated to (vector double-float), and (vector * *) may be abbreviated to (vector) and then to simply vector.

4.3. Predicating Type Specifiers

A type specifier list (satisfies *predicate-name*) denotes the set of all objects that satisfy the predicate named by *predicate-name*, which must be a symbol whose global function definition is a one-argument predicate. (A name is required; lambda-expressions are disallowed in order to avoid scoping problems.) For example, the type (satisfies numberp) is the same as the type number. The call (typep x '(satisfies p)) results in applying p to x and returning t if the result is true and nil if the result is false.

As an example, the type string-char could be defined as

```
(deftype string-char ()
  '(and character (satisfies string-char-p)))
```

See deftype.

X3J13 voted in March 1989 ⟨17⟩ to remove the type string-char and the function string-char-p from the language.

It is not a good idea for a predicate appearing in a satisfies type specifier to cause any side effects when invoked.

4.4. Type Specifiers That Combine

The following type specifier lists define a type in terms of other types or objects.

(member *object1 object2* ...)

This denotes the set containing precisely those objects named. An object is of this type if and only if it is eql to one of the specified objects.

Compatibility note: This is roughly equivalent to the Interlisp DECL package's memq.

(eql *object*)

X3J13 voted in June 1988 ⟨12⟩ to add the eql type specifier. It may be used as a parameter specializer for CLOS methods (see section 28.1.6.2 and find-method). It denotes the set of the one object named; an object is of this type if and only if it is eql to *object*. While (eql *object*) denotes the same type as (member *object*), only (eql *object*) may be used as a CLOS parameter specializer.

(not *type*)

This denotes the set of all those objects that are *not* of the specified type.

(and *type1* *type2* ...)
This denotes the intersection of the specified types.

Compatibility note: This is roughly equivalent to the Interlisp DECL package's `allof`.

When `typep` processes an `and` type specifier, it always tests each of the component types in order from left to right and stops processing as soon as one component of the intersection has been found to which the object in question does not belong. In this respect an `and` type specifier is similar to an executable `and` form. The purpose of this similarity is to allow a `satisfies` type specifier to depend on filtering by previous type specifiers. For example, suppose there were a function `primep` that takes an integer and says whether it is prime. Suppose also that it is an error to give any object other than an integer to `primep`. Then the type specifier

```
(and integer (satisfies primep))
```

is guaranteed never to result in an error because the function `primep` will not be invoked unless the object in question has already been determined to be an integer.

(or *type1* *type2* ...)
This denotes the union of the specified types. For example, the type `list` by definition is the same as (or `null` `cons`). Also, the value returned by the function `position` is always of type (or `null` (`integer` 0 *)) (either `nil` or a non-negative integer).

Compatibility note: This is roughly equivalent to the Interlisp DECL package's `oneof`.

As for `and`, when `typep` processes an `or` type specifier, it always tests each of the component types in order from left to right and stops processing as soon as one component of the union has been found to which the object in question belongs.

4.5. Type Specifiers That Specialize

Some type specifier lists denote *specializations* of data types named by symbols. These specializations may be reflected by more efficient representations in the underlying implementation. As an example, consider the type (`array` `short-float`). Implementation A may choose to provide a specialized representation for arrays of short floating-point numbers, and implementation B may choose not to.

If you should want to create an array for the express purpose of holding only short-float objects, you may optionally specify to make-array the element type short-float. This does not *require* make-array to create an object of type (array short-float); it merely *permits* it. The request is construed to mean "Produce the most specialized array representation capable of holding short-floats that the implementation can provide." Implementation A will then produce a specialized array of type (array short-float), and implementation B will produce an ordinary array of type (array t).

If one were then to ask whether the array were actually of type (array short-float), implementation A would say "yes," but implementation B would say "no." This is a property of make-array and similar functions: what you ask for is not necessarily what you get.

Types can therefore be used for two different purposes: *declaration* and *discrimination*. Declaring to make-array that elements will always be of type short-float permits optimization. Similarly, declaring that a variable takes on values of type (array short-float) amounts to saying that the variable will take on values that might be produced by specifying element type short-float to make-array. On the other hand, if the predicate typep is used to test whether an object is of type (array short-float), only objects actually of that specialized type can satisfy the test; in implementation B no object can pass that test.

X3J13 voted in January 1989 ⟨8⟩ to eliminate the differing treatment of types when used "for discrimination" rather than "for declaration" on the grounds that implementors have not treated the distinction consistently and (which is more important) users have found the distinction confusing.

As a consequence of this change, the behavior of typep and subtypep on array and complex type specifiers must be modified. See the descriptions of those functions. In particular, under their new behavior, implementation B would say "yes," agreeing with implementation A, in the discussion above.

Note that the distinction between declaration and discrimination remains useful, if only so that we may remark that the specialized (list) form of the function type specifier may still be used only for declaration and not for discrimination.

X3J13 voted in June 1988 ⟨90⟩ to clarify that while the specialized form of the function type specifier (a list of the symbol function possibly followed by argument and value type specifiers) may be used only for declaration, the symbol form (simply the name function) may be used for discrimination.

The valid list-format names for data types are as follows:

(array *element-type dimensions*)
This denotes the set of specialized arrays whose elements are all members of the type *element-type* and whose dimensions match *dimensions*. For declaration

purposes, this type encompasses those arrays that can result by specifying *element-type* as the element type to the function make-array; this may be different from what the type means for discrimination purposes. *element-type* must be a valid type specifier or unspecified. *dimensions* may be a non-negative integer, which is the number of dimensions, or it may be a list of non-negative integers representing the length of each dimension (any dimension may be unspecified instead), or it may be unspecified. For example:

```
(array integer 3)              ;Three-dimensional arrays of integers
(array integer (* * *))        ;Three-dimensional arrays of integers
(array * (4 5 6))              ;4-by-5-by-6 arrays
(array character (3 *))        ;Two-dimensional arrays of characters
                               ; that have exactly three rows
(array short-float ())         ;Zero-rank arrays of short-format
                               ; floating-point numbers
```

Note that (array t) is a proper subset of (array *). The reason is that (array t) is the set of arrays that can hold any Common Lisp object (the elements are of type t, which includes all objects). On the other hand, (array *) is the set of all arrays whatsoever, including, for example, arrays that can hold only characters. Now (array character) is not a subset of (array t); the two sets are in fact disjoint because (array character) is not the set of all arrays that can hold characters but rather the set of arrays that are specialized to hold precisely characters and no other objects. To test whether an array foo can hold a character, one should not use

```
(typep foo '(array character))
```

but rather

```
(subtypep 'character (array-element-type foo))
```

See array-element-type.

X3J13 voted in January 1989 ⟨8⟩ to change typep and subtypep so that the specialized array type specifier means the same thing for discrimination as for declaration: it encompasses those arrays that can result by specifying *element-type* as the element type to the function make-array. Under this interpretation (array character) might be the same type as (array t) (although it also might not be the same). See upgraded-array-element-type. However,

```
(typep foo '(array character))
```

is still not a legitimate test of whether the array `foo` can hold a character; one must still say

```
(subtypep 'character (array-element-type foo))
```

to determine that question.

X3J13 also voted in January 1989 ⟨43⟩ to specify that within the lexical scope of an array type declaration, it is an error for an array element, when referenced, not to be of the exact declared element type. A compiler may, for example, treat every reference to an element of a declared array as if the reference were surrounded by a `the` form mentioning the declared array element type (*not* the upgraded array element type). Thus

```
(defun snarf-hex-digits (the-array)
  (declare (type (array (unsigned-byte 4) 1) the-array))
  (do ((j (- (length array) 1) (- j 1))
       (val 0 (logior (ash val 4)
                      (aref the-array j))))
      ((< j 0) val)))
```

may be treated as

```
(defun snarf-hex-digits (the-array)
  (declare (type (array (unsigned-byte 4) 1) the-array))
  (do ((j (- (length array) 1) (- j 1))
       (val 0 (logior (ash val 4)
                      (the (unsigned-byte 4)
                           (aref the-array j)))))
      ((< j 0) val)))
```

The declaration amounts to a promise by the user that the `aref` will never produce a value outside the interval 0 to 15, even if in that particular implementation the array element type (`unsigned-byte 4`) is upgraded to, say, (`unsigned-byte 8`). If such upgrading does occur, then values outside that range may in fact be stored in the-array, as long as the code in `snarf-hex-digits` never sees them.

As a general rule, a compiler would be justified in transforming

```
(aref (the (array elt-type ...) a) ...)
```

into

```
(the elt-type (aref (the (array elt-type ...) a) ...)
```

It may also make inferences involving more complex functions, such as position or find. For example, find applied to an array always returns either nil or an object whose type is the element type of the array.

```
(simple-array element-type dimensions)
```

This is equivalent to (array element-type dimensions) except that it additionally specifies that objects of the type are *simple* arrays (see section 2.5).

```
(vector element-type size)
```

This denotes the set of specialized one-dimensional arrays whose elements are all of type *element-type* and whose lengths match *size*. This is entirely equivalent to (array element-type (size)). For example:

```
(vector double-float)      ; Vectors of double-format
                           ;  floating-point numbers
(vector * 5)               ; Vectors of length 5
(vector t 5)               ; General vectors of length 5
(vector (mod 32) *)        ; Vectors of integers between 0 and 31
```

The specialized types (vector string-char) and (vector bit) are so useful that they have the special names string and bit-vector. Every implementation of Common Lisp must provide distinct representations for these as distinct specialized data types.

X3J13 voted in March 1989 ⟨11⟩ to eliminate the type string-char and to redefine the type string to be the union of one or more specialized vector types, the types of whose elements are subtypes of the type character.

```
(simple-vector size)
```

This is the same as (vector t size) except that it additionally specifies that its elements are *simple* general vectors.

```
(complex type)
```

Every element of this type is a complex number whose real part and imaginary part are each of type *type*. For declaration purposes, this type encompasses those complex numbers that can result by giving numbers of the specified type to the function complex; this may be different from what the type means for discrimination purposes. As an example, Gaussian integers might be described as (complex integer), even in implementations where giving two integers to the function complex results in an object of type (complex rational).

X3J13 voted in January 1989 ⟨8⟩ to change typep and subtypep so that the specialized complex type specifier means the same thing for discrimination purposes as for declaration purposes. See upgraded-complex-part-type.

(function (*arg1-type arg2-type* ...) *value-type*)

This type may be used only for declaration and not for discrimination; typep will signal an error if it encounters a specifier of this form. Every element of this type is a function that accepts arguments at *least* of the types specified by the *argj-type* forms and returns a value that is a member of the types specified by the *value-type* form. The &optional, &rest, and &key markers may appear in the list of argument types. The *value-type* may be a values type specifier in order to indicate the types of multiple values.

X3J13 voted in January 1989 ⟨93⟩ to specify that the *arg-type* that follows a &rest marker indicates the type of each actual argument that would be gathered into the list for a &rest parameter, and not the type of the &rest parameter itself (which is always list). Thus one might declare the function gcd to be of type (function (&rest integer) integer), or the function aref to be of type (function (array &rest fixnum) t).

X3J13 voted in March 1988 ⟨92⟩ to specify that, in a function type specifier, an argument type specifier following &key must be a list of two items, a keyword and a type specifier. The keyword must be a valid keyword-name symbol that may be supplied in the actual arguments of a call to the function, and the type specifier indicates the permitted type of the corresponding argument value. (The keyword-name symbol is typically a keyword, but another X3J13 vote ⟨105⟩ allows it to be any symbol.) Furthermore, if &allow-other-keys is not present, the set of keyword-names mentioned in the function type specifier may be assumed to be exhaustive; for example, a compiler would be justified in issuing a warning for a function call using a keyword argument name not mentioned in the type declaration for the function being called. If &allow-other-keys is present in the function type specifier, other keyword arguments may be supplied when calling a function of the indicated type, and if supplied such arguments may possibly be used.

As an example, the function cons is of type (function (t t) cons), because it can accept any two arguments and always returns a cons. The function cons is also of type (function (float string) list), because it can certainly accept a floating-point number and a string (among other things), and its result is always of type list (in fact a cons is never null, but that does not matter for this type declaration). The function truncate is of type (function (number number) (values number number)), as well as of type (function (integer (mod 8)) integer).

X3J13 voted in January 1989 ⟨91⟩ to alter the meaning of the function type specifier when used in type and ftype declarations. While the preceding formulation may be theoretically elegant, they have found that it is not useful to compiler implementors and that it is not the interpretation that users expect. X3J13 prescribed instead the following interpretation of declarations.

A declaration specifier of the form

(ftype (function (*arg1-type arg2-type* ... *argn-type*) *value-type*) *fname*)

implies that any function call of the form

(*fname arg1 arg2* ...)

within the scope of the declaration can be treated as if it were rewritten to use the-forms in the following manner:

(the *value-type*
    (*fname* (the *arg1-type arg1*)
        (the *arg2-type arg2*)
        ...
        (the *argn-type argn*)))

That is, it is an error for any of the actual arguments not to be of its specified type *arg-type* or for the result not to be of the specified type *value-type*. (In particular, if any argument is not of its specified type, then the result is not guaranteed to be of the specified type—if indeed a result is returned at all.)

Similarly, a declaration specifier of the form

(type (function (*arg1-type arg2-type* ... *argn-type*) *value-type*) *var*)

is interpreted to mean that any reference to the variable *var* will find that its value is a function, and that it is an error to call this function with any actual argument not of its specified type *arg-type*. Also, it is an error for the result not to be of the specified type *value-type*. For example, a function call of the form

(funcall *var arg1 arg2* ...)

could be rewritten to use the-forms as well. If any argument is not of its specified type, then the result is not guaranteed to be of the specified type—if indeed a result is returned at all.

Thus, a `type` or `ftype` declaration specifier describes type requirements imposed on calls to a function as opposed to requirements imposed on the definition of the function. This is analogous to the treatment of type declarations of variables as imposing type requirements on references to variables, rather than on the contents of variables. See the vote of X3J13 on `type` declaration specifiers in general, discussed in section 9.2.

In the same manner as for variable type declarations in general, if two or more of these declarations apply to the same function call (which can occur if declaration scopes are suitably nested), then they all apply; in effect, the types for each argument or result are intersected. For example, the code fragment

```
(locally (declare (ftype (function (biped) digit)
                         butcher-fudge))
  (locally (declare (ftype (function (featherless) opposable)
                           butcher-fudge))
    (butcher-fudge sam)))
```

may be regarded as equivalent to

```
(the opposable
     (the digit (butcher-fudge (the featherless
                                    (the biped sam)))))
```

or to

```
(the (and opposable digit)
     (butcher-fudge (the (and featherless biped) sam)))
```

That is, `sam` had better be both `featherless` and a `biped`, and the result of `butcher-fudge` had better be both `opposable` and a `digit`; otherwise the code is in error. Therefore a compiler may generate code that relies on these type assumptions, for example.

(values *value1-type value2-type* ...)

This type specifier is extremely restricted: it may be used *only* as the *value-type* in a `function` type specifier or in a `the` special form. It is used to specify individual types when multiple values are involved. The `&optional`, `&rest`, and `&key` markers may appear in the *value-type* list; they thereby indicate the parameter list of a function that, when given to `multiple-value-call` along with the values, would be suitable for receiving those values.

4.6. Type Specifiers That Abbreviate

The following type specifiers are, for the most part, abbreviations for other type specifiers that would be far too verbose to write out explicitly (using, for example, member).

(integer *low high*)

Denotes the integers between *low* and *high*. The limits *low* and *high* must each be an integer, a list of an integer, or unspecified. An integer is an inclusive limit, a list of an integer is an exclusive limit, and * means that a limit does not exist and so effectively denotes minus or plus infinity, respectively. The type fixnum is simply a name for (integer *smallest largest*) for implementation-dependent values of *smallest* and *largest* (see most-negative-fixnum and most-positive-fixnum). The type (integer 0 1) is so useful that it has the special name bit.

(mod *n*)

Denotes the set of non-negative integers less than *n*. This is equivalent to (integer 0 *n*–1) or to (integer 0 (*n*)).

(signed-byte *s*)

Denotes the set of integers that can be represented in two's-complement form in a byte of *s* bits. This is equivalent to (integer -2^{s-1} $2^{s-1}-1$). Simply signed-byte or (signed-byte *) is the same as integer.

(unsigned-byte *s*)

Denotes the set of non-negative integers that can be represented in a byte of *s* bits. This is equivalent to (mod 2^s), that is, (integer 0 2^s-1). Simply unsigned-byte or (unsigned-byte *) is the same as (integer 0 *), the set of non-negative integers.

(rational *low high*)

Denotes the rationals between *low* and *high*. The limits *low* and *high* must each be a rational, a list of a rational, or unspecified. A rational is an inclusive limit, a list of a rational is an exclusive limit, and * means that a limit does not exist and so effectively denotes minus or plus infinity, respectively.

(float *low high*)

Denotes the set of floating-point numbers between *low* and *high*. The limits *low* and *high* must each be a floating-point number, a list of a floating-point number, or unspecified; a floating-point number is an inclusive limit, a list of a floating-point number is an exclusive limit, and * means that a limit does not exist and so effectively denotes minus or plus infinity, respectively.

In a similar manner, one may use:

```
(short-float low high)
(single-float low high)
(double-float low high)
(long-float low high)
```

In this case, if a limit is a floating-point number (or a list of one), it must be one of the appropriate format.

X3J13 voted in March 1989 ⟨151⟩ to add a list form of the real type specifier to denote an interval of real numbers.

(real *low* *high*)

Denotes the real numbers between *low* and *high*. The limits *low* and *high* must each be a real, a list of a real, or unspecified. A real is an inclusive limit, a list of a real is an exclusive limit, and * means that a limit does not exist and so effectively denotes minus or plus infinity, respectively.

(string *size*)

Means the same as (array string-char (*size*)): the set of strings of the indicated size.

(simple-string *size*)

Means the same as (simple-array string-char (*size*)): the set of simple strings of the indicated size.

X3J13 voted in March 1989 ⟨11⟩ to eliminate the type string-char and to redefine the type string to be the union of one or more specialized vector types, the types of whose elements are subtypes of the type character. Similarly, the type simple-string is redefined to be the union of one or more specialized simple vector types, the types of whose elements are subtypes of the type character.

(base-string *size*)

Means the same as (vector base-character *size*): the set of base strings of the indicated size.

```
(simple-base-string size)
```
Means the same as (simple-array base-character (*size*)): the set of simple base strings of the indicated size.

```
(bit-vector size)
```
Means the same as (array bit (*size*)): the set of bit-vectors of the indicated size.

```
(simple-bit-vector size)
```
This means the same as (simple-array bit (*size*)): the set of bit-vectors of the indicated size.

4.7. Defining New Type Specifiers

New type specifiers can come into existence in two ways. First, defining a new structure type with defstruct automatically causes the name of the structure to be a new type specifier symbol. Second, the deftype special form can be used to define new type-specifier abbreviations.

deftype *name lambda-list* ⟦ {*declaration*}* | *doc-string* ⟧ {*form*}*   [*Macro*]

This is very similar to a defmacro form: *name* is the symbol that identifies the type specifier being defined, *lambda-list* is a lambda-list (and may contain &optional and &rest markers), and the *forms* constitute the body of the expander function. If we view a type specifier list as a list containing the type specifier name and some argument forms, the argument forms (unevaluated) are bound to the corresponding parameters in *lambda-list*. Then the body forms are evaluated as an implicit progn, and the value of the last form is interpreted as a new type specifier for which the original specifier was an abbreviation. The *name* is returned as the value of the deftype form.

deftype differs from defmacro in that if no *initform* is specified for an &optional parameter, the default value is *, not nil.

If the optional documentation string *doc-string* is present, then it is attached to the *name* as a documentation string of type type; see documentation.

Here are some examples of the use of deftype:

```
(deftype mod (n) `(integer 0 (,n)))
```

```
(deftype list () '(or null cons))
```

```
(deftype square-matrix (&optional type size)
  "SQUARE-MATRIX includes all square two-dimensional arrays."
  `(array ,type (,size ,size)))
```

```
(square-matrix short-float 7) means (array short-float (7 7))
```

```
(square-matrix bit) means (array bit (* *))
```

If the type name defined by deftype is used simply as a type specifier symbol,
it is interpreted as a type specifier list with no argument forms. Thus, in the
example above, square-matrix would mean (array * (* *)), the set of two-
dimensional arrays. This would unfortunately fail to convey the constraint that the
two dimensions be the same; (square-matrix bit) has the same problem. A
better definition is

```
(defun equidimensional (a)
  (or (< (array-rank a) 2)
      (apply #´= (array-dimensions a))))
```

```
(deftype square-matrix (&optional type size)
  `(and (array ,type (,size ,size))
        (satisfies equidimensional)))
```

X3J13 voted in March 1988 ⟨78⟩ to specify that the body of the expander function
defined by deftype is implicitly enclosed in a block construct whose name is the
same as the *name* of the defined type. Therefore return-from may be used to
exit from the function.

X3J13 voted in March 1989 ⟨50⟩ to clarify that, while defining forms normally appear at top level, it is meaningful to place them in non-top-level contexts;
deftype must define the expander function within the enclosing lexical environment, not within the global environment.

4.8. Type Conversion Function

The following function may be used to convert an object to an equivalent object
of another type.

coerce *object result-type*   [*Function*]

The *result-type* must be a type specifier; the *object* is converted to an "equivalent"
object of the specified type. If the coercion cannot be performed, then an error

is signaled. In particular, (coerce x 'nil) always signals an error. If *object* is already of the specified type, as determined by typep, then it is simply returned. It is not generally possible to convert any object to be of any type whatsoever; only certain conversions are permitted:

- Any sequence type may be converted to any other sequence type, provided the new sequence can contain all actual elements of the old sequence (it is an error if it cannot). If the *result-type* is specified as simply array, for example, then (array t) is assumed. A specialized type such as string or (vector (complex short-float)) may be specified; of course, the result may be of either that type or some more general type, as determined by the implementation. Elements of the new sequence will be eql to corresponding elements of the old sequence. If the *sequence* is already of the specified type, it may be returned without copying it; in this, (coerce *sequence type*) differs from (concatenate *type sequence*), for the latter is required to copy the argument *sequence*. In particular, if one specifies sequence, then the argument may simply be returned if it already is a sequence.

  (coerce '(a b c) 'vector) ⇒ #(a b c)

  X3J13 voted in June 1989 ⟨158⟩ to specify that coerce should signal an error if the new sequence type specifies the number of elements and the old sequence has a different length.
  X3J13 voted in March 1989 ⟨11⟩ to specify that if the *result-type* is string then it is understood to mean (vector character), and simple-string is understood to mean (simple-array character (*)).

- Some strings, symbols, and integers may be converted to characters. If *object* is a string of length 1, then the sole element of the string is returned. If *object* is a symbol whose print name is of length 1, then the sole element of the print name is returned. If *object* is an integer *n*, then (int-char *n*) is returned. See character.

  (coerce "a" 'character) ⇒ #\a

  X3J13 voted in March 1989 ⟨11⟩ to eliminate int-char from Common Lisp. Presumably this eliminates the possibility of coercing an integer to a character, although the vote did not address this question directly.

- Any non-complex number can be converted to a short-float, single-float, double-float, or long-float. If simply float is specified, and *object* is not already a float of some kind, then the object is converted to a single-float.

  (coerce 0 'short-float) ⇒ 0.0S0

```
(coerce 3.5L0 'float) ⇒ 3.5L0
(coerce 7/2 'float) ⇒ 3.5
```

- Any number can be converted to a complex number. If the number is not already complex, then a zero imaginary part is provided by coercing the integer zero to the type of the given real part. (If the given real part is rational, however, then the rule of canonical representation for complex rationals will result in the immediate re-conversion of the result from type `complex` back to type `rational`.)

```
(coerce 4.5s0 'complex) ⇒ #C(4.5S0 0.0S0)
(coerce 7/2 'complex) ⇒ 7/2
(coerce #C(7/2 0) '(complex double-float))
    ⇒ #C(3.5D0 0.0D0)
```

- Any object may be coerced to type t.

```
(coerce x 't) ≡ (identity x) ≡ x
```

X3J13 voted in June 1988 ⟨90⟩ to allow coercion of certain objects to the type `function`:

- A symbol or lambda-expression can be converted to a function. A symbol is coerced to type `function` as if by applying `symbol-function` to the symbol; an error is signaled if the predicate `fboundp` is not true of the symbol or if the symbol names a macro or special form. A list *x* whose *car* is the symbol `lambda` is coerced to a function as if by execution of (`eval` `#'`,*x*), that is, of (`eval` (`list` 'function *x*)).

Coercions from floating-point numbers to rationals and from ratios to integers are purposely *not* provided because of rounding problems. The functions `rational`, `rationalize`, `floor`, `ceiling`, `truncate`, and `round` may be used for such purposes. Similarly, coercions from characters to integers are purposely not provided; `char-code` or `char-int` may be used explicitly to perform such conversions.

4.9. Determining the Type of an Object

The following function may be used to obtain a type specifier describing the type of a given object.

type-of *object* [*Function*]

(`type-of` *object*) returns an implementation-dependent result: some *type* of which the *object* is a member. Implementors are encouraged to arrange for `type-of` to return the most specific type that can be conveniently computed and is likely to be useful to the user. If the argument is a user-defined named structure created by defstruct, then type-of will return the type name of that structure. Because the result is implementation-dependent, it is usually better to use type-of primarily for debugging purposes; however, in a few situations portable code requires the use of type-of, such as when the result is to be given to the coerce or map function. On the other hand, often the typep function or the typecase construct is more appropriate than type-of.

Compatibility note: In MacLisp the function type-of is called typep, and anomalously so, for it is not a predicate.

Many have observed (and rightly so) that this specification is totally wimpy and therefore nearly useless. X3J13 voted in June 1989 ⟨179⟩ to place the following constraints on type-of:

- Let *x* be an object such that (typep *x* *type*) is true and *type* is one of the following:

array	float	package	sequence
bit-vector	function	pathname	short-float
character	hash-table	random-state	single-float
complex	integer	ratio	stream
condition	long-float	rational	string
cons	null	readtable	symbol
double-float	number	restart	vector

  Then (subtypep (type-of *x*) *type*)) must return the values t and t; that is, type-of applied to *x* must return either *type* itself or a subtype of *type* that subtypep can recognize in that implementation.

- For any object *x*, (subtypep (type-of *x*) (class-of *x*)) must produce the values t and t.

- For every object *x*, (typep *x* (type-of *x*)) must be true. (This implies that type-of can never return nil, for no object is of type nil.)

- type-of never returns t and never uses a satisfies, and, or, not, or values type specifier in its result.

- For objects of CLOS metaclass structure-class or of standard-class, type-of returns the proper name of the class returned by class-of if it has a proper name, and otherwise returns the class itself. In particular, for any object created by a `defstruct` constructor function, where the `defstruct` had the name *name* and no `:type` option, `type-of` will return *name*.

As an example, (`type-of "acetylcholinesterase"`) may return `string` or `simple-string` or (`simple-string 20`), but not `array` or `simple-vector`. As another example, it is permitted for (`type-of 1729`) to return `integer` or `fixnum` (if it is indeed a fixnum) or (`signed-byte 16`) or (`integer 1729 1729`) or (`integer 1685 1750`) or even (`mod 1730`), but not `rational` or `number`, because

```
(typep (+ (expt 9 3) (expt 10 3)) 'integer)
```

is true, `integer` is in the list of types mentioned above, and

```
(subtypep (type-of (+ (expt 1 3) (expt 12 3))) 'integer)
```

would be false if `type-of` were to return `rational` or `number`.

4.10. Type Upgrading

X3J13 voted in January 1989 ⟨8⟩ to add new functions by which a program can determine, in a given Common Lisp implementation, how that implementation will *upgrade* a type when constructing an array specialized to contain elements of that type, or a complex number specialized to contain parts of that type.

`upgraded-array-element-type` *type*   [*Function*]

A type specifier is returned, indicating the element type of the most specialized array representation capable of holding items of the specified argument *type*. The result is necessarily a supertype of the given *type*. Furthermore, if a type *A* is a subtype of type *B*, then (`upgraded-array-element-type` *A*) is a subtype of (`upgraded-array-element-type` *B*).

The manner in which an array element type is upgraded depends only on the element type as such and not on any other property of the array such as size, rank, adjustability, presence or absence of a fill pointer, or displacement.

Rationale: If upgrading were allowed to depend on any of these properties, all of which can be referred to, directly or indirectly, in the language of type specifiers, then it would not be possible to displace an array in a consistent and dependable manner to another array created with the same `:element-type` argument but differing in one of these properties.

Note that `upgraded-array-element-type` could be defined as

```
(defun upgraded-array-element-type (type)
  (array-element-type (make-array 0 :element-type type)))
```

but this definition has the disadvantage of allocating an array and then immediately discarding it. The clever implementor surely can conjure up a more practical approach.

upgraded-complex-part-type *type*   [*Function*]

A type specifier is returned, indicating the element type of the most specialized complex number representation capable of having parts of the specified argument *type*. The result is necessarily a supertype of the given *type*. Furthermore, if a type *A* is a subtype of type *B*, then (upgraded-complex-part-type *A*) is a subtype of (upgraded-complex-part-type *B*).

5

Program Structure

In chapter 2 the syntax was sketched for notating data objects in Common Lisp. The same syntax is used for notating programs because all Common Lisp programs have a representation as Common Lisp data objects.

Lisp programs are organized as forms and functions. Forms are *evaluated* (relative to some context) to produce values and side effects. Functions are invoked by *applying* them to arguments. The most important kind of form performs a function call; conversely, a function performs computation by evaluating forms.

In this chapter, forms are discussed first and then functions. Finally, certain "top level" special forms are discussed; the most important of these is defun, whose purpose is to define a named function.

5.1. Forms

The standard unit of interaction with a Common Lisp implementation is the *form*, which is simply a data object meant to be *evaluated* as a program to produce one or more *values* (which are also data objects). One may request evaluation of *any* data object, but only certain ones are meaningful. For instance, symbols and lists are meaningful forms, while arrays normally are not. Examples of meaningful forms are 3, whose value is 3, and (+ 3 4), whose value is 7. We write 3 ⇒ 3 and (+ 3 4) ⇒ 7 to indicate these facts. (⇒ means "evaluates to.")

Meaningful forms may be divided into three categories: self-evaluating forms, such as numbers; symbols, which stand for variables; and lists. The lists in turn may be divided into three categories: special forms, macro calls, and function calls.

Any Common Lisp data object not explicitly defined here to be a valid form is not a valid form. It is an error to evaluate anything but a valid form.

Implementation note: An implementation is free to make implementation-dependent extensions to the evaluator but is strongly encouraged to signal an error on any attempt to evaluate anything but a valid form or an object for which a meaningful evaluation extension has been purposely defined.

X3J13 voted in October 1988 ⟨72⟩ to specify that *all* standard Common Lisp data objects other than symbols and lists (including `defstruct` structures defined without the `:type` option) are self-evaluating.

5.1.1. Self-Evaluating Forms

All numbers, characters, strings, and bit-vectors are *self-evaluating* forms. When such an object is evaluated, that object (or possibly a copy in the case of numbers or characters) is returned as the value of the form. The empty list (), which is also the false value `nil`, is also a self-evaluating form: the value of `nil` is `nil`. Keywords (symbols written with a leading colon) also evaluate to themselves: the value of `:start` is `:start`.

X3J13 voted in January 1989 ⟨36⟩ to clarify that it is an error to destructively modify any object that appears as a constant in executable code, whether as a self-evaluating form or within a `quote` special form.

5.1.2. Variables

Symbols are used as names of variables in Common Lisp programs. When a symbol is evaluated as a form, the value of the variable it names is produced. For example, after doing (`setq items 3`), which assigns the value 3 to the variable named `items`, then `items` ⇒ 3. Variables can be *assigned* to, as by `setq`, or *bound*, as by `let`. Any program construct that binds a variable effectively saves the old value of the variable and causes it to have a new value, and on exit from the construct the old value is reinstated.

There are actually two kinds of variables in Common Lisp, called *lexical* (or *static*) variables and *special* (or *dynamic*) variables. At any given time either or both kinds of variable with the same name may have a current value. Which of the two kinds of variable is referred to when a symbol is evaluated depends on the context of the evaluation. The general rule is that if the symbol occurs textually within a program construct that creates a *binding* for a variable of the same name, then the reference is to the variable specified by the binding; if no such program construct textually contains the reference, then it is taken to refer to the special variable of that name.

The distinction between the two kinds of variable is one of scope and extent. A lexically bound variable can be referred to *only* by forms occurring at any *place* textually within the program construct that binds the variable. A dynamically bound (special) variable can be referred to at any *time* from the time the binding is made until the time evaluation of the construct that binds the variable terminates. Therefore lexical binding of variables imposes a spatial limitation on occurrences of references (but no temporal limitation, for the binding continues to exist as long as the possibility of reference remains). Conversely, dynamic binding of variables imposes a temporal limitation on occurrences of references (but no spatial limitation). For more information on scope and extent, see chapter 3.

The value a special variable has when there are currently no bindings of that variable is called the *global* value of the (special) variable. A global value can be given to a variable only by assignment, because a value given by binding is by definition not global.

It is possible for a special variable to have no value at all, in which case it is said to be *unbound*. By default, every global variable is unbound unless and until explicitly assigned a value, except for those global variables defined in this book or by the implementation already to have values when the Lisp system is first started. It is also possible to establish a binding of a special variable and then cause that binding to be valueless by using the function makunbound. In this situation the variable is also said to be "unbound," although this is a misnomer; precisely speaking, it is bound but valueless. It is an error to refer to a variable that is unbound.

X3J13 voted in June 1989 ⟨180⟩ to specify more precisely the effects of referring to an unbound variable.

Reading an unbound variable or an undefined function must be detected in the highest safety setting (see the safety quality of the optimize declaration specifier) but the effect is undefined in any other safety setting. That is, reading an unbound variable should signal an error and reading an undefined function should signal an error. ("Reading a function" includes both references to the function using the function special form, such as f in (function f), and references to the function in a call, such as f in (f x y).)

For the case of inline functions (in implementations where they are supported), a permitted point of view is that performing the inlining constitutes the read of the function, so that an fboundp check need not be done at execution time. Put another way, the effect of the application of fmakunbound to a function name on potentially inlined references to that function is undefined.

When an unbound variable is detected an error of type unbound-variable is signaled, and the name slot of the unbound-variable condition is initialized to the name of the offending variable.

When an undefined function is detected an error of type undefined-function is signaled, and the name slot of the undefined-function condition is initialized to the name of the offending function.

The condition type unbound-slot, which inherits from cell-error, has an additional slot instance, which can be initialized using the :instance keyword to make-condition. The function unbound-slot-instance accesses this slot.

The type of error signaled by the default primary method for the CLOS slot-unbound generic function is unbound-slot. The instance slot of the unbound-slot condition is initialized to the offending instance and the name slot is initialized to the name of the offending variable.

Certain global variables are reserved as "named constants." They have a global value and may not be bound or assigned to. For example, the symbols t and nil are reserved. One may not assign a value to t or nil, and one may not bind t or nil. The global value of t is always t, and the global value of nil is always nil. Constant symbols defined by defconstant also become reserved and may not be further assigned to or bound (although they may be redefined, if necessary, by using defconstant again). Keyword symbols, which are notated with a leading colon, are reserved and may never be assigned to or bound; a keyword always evaluates to itself.

5.1.3. Special Forms

If a list is to be evaluated as a form, the first step is to examine the first element of the list. If the first element is one of the symbols appearing in table 5-1, then the list is called a *special form*. (This use of the word "special" is unrelated to its use in the phrase "special variable.")

Special forms are generally environment and control constructs. Every special form has its own idiosyncratic syntax. An example is the if special form: (if p (+ x 4) 5) in Common Lisp means what "**if** p **then** $x+4$ **else** 5" means in Algol.

The evaluation of a special form normally produces a value or values, but the evaluation may instead call for a non-local exit; see return-from, go, and throw.

The set of special forms is fixed in Common Lisp; no way is provided for the user to define more. The user can create new syntactic constructs, however, by defining macros.

The set of special forms in Common Lisp is purposely kept very small because any program-analyzing program must have special knowledge about every type of special form. Such a program needs no special knowledge about macros because it is simple to expand the macro and operate on the resulting expansion. (This is not to say that many such programs, particularly compilers, will not have such special knowledge. A compiler may be able to produce much better code if it recognizes such constructs as typecase and multiple-value-bind and gives them customized treatment.)

Table 5-1: Names of All Common Lisp Special Forms

block	if	progv
catch	labels	quote
[compiler-let]	let	return-from
declare	let*	setq
eval-when	macrolet	tagbody
flet	multiple-value-call	the
function	multiple-value-prog1	throw
go	progn	unwind-protect

X3J13 voted in June 1989 ⟨25⟩ to remove compiler-let from the language.
X3J13 voted in June 1988 ⟨12⟩ to add the special forms generic-flet, generic-labels, symbol-macrolet, and with-added-methods.
X3J13 voted in March 1989 ⟨113⟩ to make locally a special form rather than a macro.
X3J13 voted in March 1989 ⟨111⟩ to add the special form load-time-eval.

An implementation is free to implement as a macro any construct described herein as a special form. Conversely, an implementation is free to implement as a special form any construct described herein as a macro if an equivalent macro definition is also provided. The practical consequence is that the predicates macro-function and special-form-p may both be true of the same symbol. It is recommended that a program-analyzing program process a form that is a list whose *car* is a symbol as follows:

1. If the program has particular knowledge about the symbol, process the form using special-purpose code. All of the symbols listed in table 5-1 should fall into this category.

2. Otherwise, if macro-function is true of the symbol, apply either macroexpand or macroexpand-1, as appropriate, to the entire form and then start over.

3. Otherwise, assume it is a function call.

5.1.4. Macros

If a form is a list and the first element is not the name of a special form, it may be the name of a *macro*; if so, the form is said to be a *macro call*. A macro is essentially a function from forms to forms that will, given a call to that macro, compute a new form to be evaluated in place of the macro call. (This computation is sometimes referred to as *macro expansion*.) For example, the macro named return will take a form such as (return x) and from that form compute a new form (return-from nil x). We say that the old form *expands* into the new form. The new form is then evaluated in place of the original form; the value of the new form is returned as the value of the original form.

X3J13 voted in January 1989 ⟨67⟩ to clarify that macro calls, and subforms of macro calls, need not be proper lists, but that use of dotted forms requires the macro definition to use ". *var*" or "&rest *var*" in order to match them properly. It is then the responsibility of the macro definition to recognize and appropriately handle such dotted forms or subforms.

There are a number of standard macros in Common Lisp, and the user can define more by using defmacro.

Macros provided by a Common Lisp implementation as described herein may expand into code that is not portable among differing implementations. That is, a macro call may be implementation-independent because the macro is defined in this book, but the expansion need not be.

Implementation note: Implementors are encouraged to implement the macros defined in this book, as far as is possible, in such a way that the expansion will not contain any implementation-dependent special forms, nor contain as forms data objects that are not considered to be forms in Common Lisp. The purpose of this restriction is to ensure that the expansion can be processed by a program-analyzing program in an implementation-independent manner. There is no problem with a macro expansion containing calls to implementation-dependent functions. This restriction is not a requirement of Common Lisp; it is recognized that certain complex macros may be able to expand into significantly more efficient code in certain implementations by using implementation-dependent special forms in the macro expansion.

5.1.5. Function Calls

If a list is to be evaluated as a form and the first element is not a symbol that names a special form or macro, then the list is assumed to be a *function call*. The first element of the list is taken to name a function. Any and all remaining elements of the list are forms to be evaluated; one value is obtained from each form, and these values become the *arguments* to the function. The function is then *applied* to the arguments. The functional computation normally produces a value, but it may instead call for a non-local exit; see throw. A function that does return may produce no value or several values; see values. If and when the function returns, whatever values it returns become the values of the function-call form.

For example, consider the evaluation of the form (+ 3 (* 4 5)). The symbol + names the addition function, not a special form or macro. Therefore the two forms 3 and (* 4 5) are evaluated to produce arguments. The form 3 evaluates to 3, and the form (* 4 5) is a function call (to the multiplication function). Therefore the forms 4 and 5 are evaluated, producing arguments 4 and 5 for the multiplication. The multiplication function calculates the number 20 and returns it. The values 3 and 20 are then given as arguments to the addition function, which calculates and returns the number 23. Therefore we say (+ 3 (* 4 5)) ⇒ 23.

X3J13 voted in October 1988 ⟨86⟩ to clarify that while the arguments in a function call are always evaluated in strict left-to-right order, whether the function to be called is determined before or after argument evaluation is unspecified. Programs are in error that rely on a particular order of evaluation of the first element of a function call relative to the argument forms.

5.2. Functions

There are two ways to indicate a function to be used in a function-call form. One is to use a symbol that names the function. This use of symbols to name functions is completely independent of their use in naming special and lexical variables. The other way is to use a *lambda-expression*, which is a list whose first element is the symbol lambda. A lambda-expression is *not* a form; it cannot be meaningfully evaluated. Lambda-expressions and symbols, when used in programs as names of functions, can appear only as the first element of a function-call form, or as the second element of the function special form. Note that symbols and lambda-expressions are treated as *names* of functions in these two contexts. This should be distinguished from the treatment of symbols and lambda-expressions as *function objects*, that is, objects that satisfy the predicate functionp, as when giving such an object to apply or funcall to be invoked.

5.2.1. Named Functions

A name can be given to a function in one of two ways. A *global name* can be given to a function by using the defun construct. A *local name* can be given to a function by using the flet or labels special form. When a function is named, a lambda-expression is effectively associated with that name along with information about the entities that are lexically apparent at that point. If a symbol appears as the first element of a function-call form, then it refers to the definition established by the innermost flet or labels construct that textually contains the reference, or to the global definition (if any) if there is no such containing construct.

5.2.2. Lambda-Expressions

A *lambda-expression* is a list with the following syntax:

(lambda *lambda-list* . *body*)

The first element must be the symbol lambda. The second element must be a list. It is called the *lambda-list*, and specifies names for the *parameters* of the function. When the function denoted by the lambda-expression is applied to arguments, the arguments are matched with the parameters specified by the lambda-list. The *body* may then refer to the arguments by using the parameter names. The *body* consists of any number of forms (possibly zero). These forms are evaluated in sequence, and the results of the *last* form only are returned as the results of the application (the value nil is returned if there are zero forms in the body). The complete syntax of a lambda-expression is:

(lambda ({*var*}*
              [&optional {*var* | (*var* [*initform* [*svar*]])}*]
              [&rest *var*]
              [&key {*var* | ({*var* | (*keyword var*)} [*initform* [*svar*]])}*]
              [&aux {*var* | (*var* [*initform*])}*])
    ⟦ {*declaration*}* | *documentation-string* ⟧
    {*form*}*)

Each element of a lambda-list is either a *parameter specifier* or a *lambda-list keyword*; lambda-list keywords begin with &. (Note that lambda-list keywords are not keywords in the usual sense; they do not belong to the keyword package. They are ordinary symbols each of whose names begins with an ampersand. This terminology is unfortunately confusing but is retained for historical reasons.)

In all cases a *var* or *svar* must be a symbol, the name of a variable; each *keyword* must be a keyword symbol, such as :start. An *initform* may be any form.

X3J13 voted in March 1988 ⟨105⟩ to allow a *keyword* in the preceding specification of a lambda-list to be any symbol whatsoever, not just a keyword symbol in the keyword package. See below.

A lambda-list has five parts, any or all of which may be empty:

- Specifiers for the *required* parameters. These are all the parameter specifiers up to the first lambda-list keyword; if there is no such lambda-list keyword, then all the specifiers are for required parameters.

- Specifiers for *optional* parameters. If the lambda-list keyword &optional is present, the *optional* parameter specifiers are those following the lambda-list keyword &optional up to the next lambda-list keyword or the end of the list.

- A specifier for a *rest* parameter. The lambda-list keyword &rest, if present, must be followed by a single *rest* parameter specifier, which in turn must be followed by another lambda-list keyword or the end of the lambda-list.

- Specifiers for *keyword* parameters. If the lambda-list keyword &key is present, all specifiers up to the next lambda-list keyword or the end of the list are *keyword* parameter specifiers. The keyword parameter specifiers may optionally be followed by the lambda-list keyword &allow-other-keys.

- Specifiers for *aux* variables. These are not really parameters. If the lambda-list keyword &key is present, all specifiers after it are *auxiliary variable* specifiers.

When the function represented by the lambda-expression is applied to arguments, the arguments and parameters are processed in order from left to right. In the simplest case, only required parameters are present in the lambda-list; each is specified simply by a name *var* for the parameter variable. When the function is applied, there must be exactly as many arguments as there are parameters, and each parameter is bound to one argument. Here, and in general, the parameter is bound as a lexical variable unless a declaration has been made that it should be a special binding; see defvar, proclaim, and declare.

In the more general case, if there are *n* required parameters (*n* may be zero), there must be at least *n* arguments, and the required parameters are bound to the first *n* arguments. The other parameters are then processed using any remaining arguments.

If *optional* parameters are specified, then each one is processed as follows. If any unprocessed arguments remain, then the parameter variable *var* is bound to the next remaining argument, just as for a required parameter. If no arguments remain, however, then the *initform* part of the parameter specifier is evaluated, and the parameter variable is bound to the resulting value (or to nil if no *initform* appears in the parameter specifier). If another variable name *svar* appears in the specifier, it is bound to *true* if an argument was available, and to *false* if no argument remained (and therefore *initform* had to be evaluated). The variable *svar* is called a *supplied-p* parameter; it is bound not to an argument but to a value indicating whether or not an argument had been supplied for another parameter.

After all *optional* parameter specifiers have been processed, then there may or may not be a *rest* parameter. If there is a *rest* parameter, it is bound to a list of all as-yet-unprocessed arguments. (If no unprocessed arguments remain, the *rest* parameter is bound to the empty list.) If there is no *rest* parameter and there are no *keyword* parameters, then there should be no unprocessed arguments (it is an error if there are).

X3J13 voted in January 1989 ⟨155⟩ to clarify that if a function has a *rest* parameter and is called using apply, then the list to which the *rest* parameter is bound is permitted, but not required, to share top-level list structure with the list that was the last argument to apply. Programmers should be careful about performing side effects on the top-level list structure of a *rest* parameter.

This was the result of a rather long discussion within X3J13 and the wider Lisp community. To set it in its historical context, I must remark that in Lisp Machine Lisp the list to which a *rest* parameter was bound had only dynamic extent; this in conjunction with the technique of "cdr-coding" permitted a clever stack-allocation technique with very low overhead. However, the early designers of Common Lisp, after a great deal of debate, concluded that it was dangerous for cons cells to have dynamic extent; as an example, the "obvious" definition of the function list

```
(defun list (&rest x) x)
```

could fail catastrophically. Therefore the first edition simply implied that the list for a *rest* parameter, like all other lists, would have indefinite extent. This still left open the flip side of the question, namely, Is the list for a *rest* parameter guaranteed fresh? This is the question addressed by the X3J13 vote. If it is always freshly consed, then it is permissible to destroy it, for example by giving it to nconc. However, the requirement always to cons fresh lists could impose an unacceptable overhead in many implementations. The clarification approved by X3J13 specifies that the programmer may not rely on the list being fresh; if the function was called using apply, there is no way to know where the list came from.

Next, any *keyword* parameters are processed. For this purpose the same arguments are processed that would be made into a list for a *rest* parameter. (Indeed, it is permitted to specify both &rest and &key. In this case the remaining arguments are used for both purposes; that is, all remaining arguments are made into a list for the &rest parameter and are also processed for the &key parameters. This is the only situation in which an argument is used in the processing of more than one parameter specifier.) If &key is specified, there must remain an even number of arguments; these are considered as pairs, the first argument in each pair being interpreted as a keyword name and the second as the corresponding value.

It is an error for the first object of each pair to be anything but a keyword.

Rationale: This last restriction is imposed so that a compiler may issue warnings about certain malformed calls to functions that take keyword arguments. It must be remembered that the arguments in a function call that evaluate to keywords are just like any other arguments and may be any evaluable forms. A compiler could not, without additional context, issue a warning about the call

```
(fill seq item x y)
```

because in principle the variable x might have as its value a keyword such as :start. However, a compiler would be justified in issuing a warning about the call

```
(fill seq item 0 10)
```

because the constant 0 is definitely not a keyword. Similarly, if in the first case the variable x had been declared to be of type `integer`, then type analysis could enable the compiler to justify a warning.

X3J13 voted in March 1988 ⟨105⟩ to allow a *keyword* in a lambda-list to be any symbol whatsoever, not just a keyword symbol in the `keyword` package. If, after `&key`, a variable appears alone or within only one set of parentheses (possibly with an *initform* and a *svar*), then the behavior is as before: a keyword symbol with the same name as the variable is used as the keyword-name when matching arguments to parameter specifiers. Only a parameter specifier of the form ((*keyword var*) ...) can cause the keyword-name not to be a keyword symbol, by specifying a symbol not in the `keyword` package as the *keyword*. For example:

```
(defun wager (&key ((secret password) nil) amount)
   (format nil "You ~A $~D"
             (if (eq password 'joe-sent-me) "win" "lose")
             amount))
```

```
(wager :amount 100) ⇒ "You lose $100"
(wager :amount 100 'secret 'joe-sent-me) ⇒ "You win $100"
```

The `secret` word could be made even more secret in this example by placing it in some other `obscure` package, so that one would have to write

```
(wager :amount 100 'obscure:secret 'joe-sent-me) ⇒ "You win $100"
```

to win anything.

In each keyword parameter specifier must be a name *var* for the parameter variable. If an explicit *keyword* is specified, then that is the keyword name for the parameter. Otherwise the name *var* serves to indicate the keyword name, in that a keyword with the same name (in the `keyword` package) is used as the keyword. Thus

```
(defun foo (&key radix (type 'integer)) ...)
```

means exactly the same as

```
(defun foo (&key ((:radix radix)) ((:type type) 'integer)) ...)
```

The keyword parameter specifiers are, like all parameter specifiers, effectively processed from left to right. For each keyword parameter specifier, if there is an argument pair whose keyword name matches that specifier's keyword name (that is, the names are eq), then the parameter variable for that specifier is bound to the second item (the value) of that argument pair. If more than one such argument pair matches, it is not an error; the leftmost argument pair is used. If no such argument pair exists, then the *initform* for that specifier is evaluated and the parameter variable is bound to that value (or to nil if no *initform* was specified). The variable *svar* is treated as for ordinary *optional* parameters: it is bound to *true* if there was a matching argument pair, and to *false* otherwise.

It is an error if an argument pair has a keyword name not matched by any parameter specifier, unless at least one of the following two conditions is met:

• &allow-other-keys was specified in the lambda-list.

• Somewhere among the keyword argument pairs is a pair whose keyword is :allow-other-keys and whose value is not nil.

If either condition obtains, then it is not an error for an argument pair to match no parameter specified, and the argument pair is simply ignored (but such an argument pair is accessible through the &rest parameter if one was specified). The purpose of these mechanisms is to allow sharing of argument lists among several functions and to allow either the caller or the called function to specify that such sharing may be taking place.

After all parameter specifiers have been processed, the auxiliary variable specifiers (those following the lambda-list keyword &aux) are processed from left to right. For each one, the *initform* is evaluated and the variable *var* bound to that value (or to nil if no *initform* was specified). Nothing can be done with &aux variables that cannot be done with the special form let*:

```
(lambda (x y &aux (a (car x)) (b 2) c) ...)
   ≡ (lambda (x y) (let* ((a (car x)) (b 2) c) ...))
```

Which to use is purely a matter of style.

Whenever any *initform* is evaluated for any parameter specifier, that form may refer to any parameter variable to the left of the specifier in which the *initform* appears, including any supplied-p variables, and may rely on the fact that no other parameter variable has yet been bound (including its own parameter variable).

Once the lambda-list has been processed, the forms in the body of the lambda-expression are executed. These forms may refer to the arguments to the function by using the names of the parameters. On exit from the function, either by a normal return of the function's value(s) or by a non-local exit, the parameter bindings, whether lexical or special, are no longer in effect. (The bindings are not necessarily permanently discarded, for a lexical binding can later be reinstated if a "closure" over that binding was created, perhaps by using function, and saved before the exit occurred.)

Examples of &optional and &rest parameters:

```
((lambda (a b) (+ a (* b 3))) 4 5) ⇒ 19
((lambda (a &optional (b 2)) (+ a (* b 3))) 4 5) ⇒ 19
((lambda (a &optional (b 2)) (+ a (* b 3))) 4) ⇒ 10
((lambda (&optional (a 2 b) (c 3 d) &rest x) (list a b c d x)))
   ⇒ (2 nil 3 nil nil)
((lambda (&optional (a 2 b) (c 3 d) &rest x) (list a b c d x))
 6)
   ⇒ (6 t 3 nil nil)
((lambda (&optional (a 2 b) (c 3 d) &rest x) (list a b c d x))
 6 3)
   ⇒ (6 t 3 t nil)
((lambda (&optional (a 2 b) (c 3 d) &rest x) (list a b c d x))
 6 3 8)
   ⇒ (6 t 3 t (8))
((lambda (&optional (a 2 b) (c 3 d) &rest x) (list a b c d x))
 6 3 8 9 10 11)
   ⇒ (6 t 3 t (8 9 10 11))
```

Examples of &key parameters:

```
((lambda (a b &key c d) (list a b c d)) 1 2)
   ⇒ (1 2 nil nil)
((lambda (a b &key c d) (list a b c d)) 1 2 :c 6)
   ⇒ (1 2 6 nil)
((lambda (a b &key c d) (list a b c d)) 1 2 :d 8)
   ⇒ (1 2 nil 8)
((lambda (a b &key c d) (list a b c d)) 1 2 :c 6 :d 8)
   ⇒ (1 2 6 8)
((lambda (a b &key c d) (list a b c d)) 1 2 :d 8 :c 6)
   ⇒ (1 2 6 8)
((lambda (a b &key c d) (list a b c d)) :a 1 :d 8 :c 6)
   ⇒ (:a 1 6 8)
((lambda (a b &key c d) (list a b c d)) :a :b :c :d)
   ⇒ (:a :b :d nil)
```

Examples of mixtures:

```
((lambda (a &optional (b 3) &rest x &key c (d a))
   (list a b c d x))
 1) ⇒ (1 3 nil 1 ())
```

```
((lambda (a &optional (b 3) &rest x &key c (d a))
   (list a b c d x))
 1 2) ⇒ (1 2 nil 1 ())

((lambda (a &optional (b 3) &rest x &key c (d a))
   (list a b c d x))
 :c 7) ⇒ (:c 7 nil :c ())

((lambda (a &optional (b 3) &rest x &key c (d a))
   (list a b c d x))
 1 6 :c 7) ⇒ (1 6 7 1 (:c 7))

((lambda (a &optional (b 3) &rest x &key c (d a))
   (list a b c d x))
 1 6 :d 8) ⇒ (1 6 nil 8 (:d 8))

((lambda (a &optional (b 3) &rest x &key c (d a))
   (list a b c d x))
 1 6 :d 8 :c 9 :d 10) ⇒ (1 6 9 8 (:d 8 :c 9 :d 10))
```

All lambda-list keywords are permitted, but not terribly useful, in lambda-expressions appearing explicitly as the first element of a function-call form. They are extremely useful, however, in functions given global names by defun.

All symbols whose names begin with & are conventionally reserved for use as lambda-list keywords and should not be used as variable names. Implementations of Common Lisp are free to provide additional lambda-list keywords.

lambda-list-keywords   [*Constant*]

The value of lambda-list-keywords is a list of all the lambda-list keywords used in the implementation, including the additional ones used only by defmacro. This list must contain at least the symbols &optional, &rest, &key, &allow-other-keys, &aux, &body, &whole, and &environment.

As an example of the use of &allow-other-keys and :allow-other-keys, consider a function that takes two keyword arguments of its own and also accepts additional keyword arguments to be passed to make-array:

```
(defun array-of-strings (str dims &rest keyword-pairs
                         &key (start 0) end &allow-other-keys)
  (apply #'make-array dims
         :initial-element (subseq str start end)
```

```
        :allow-other-keys t
        keyword-pairs))
```

This function takes a string and dimensioning information and returns an array of the specified dimensions, each of whose elements is the specified string. However, `:start` and `:end` keyword arguments may be used in the usual manner (see chapter 14) to specify that a substring of the given string should be used. In addition, the presence of `&allow-other-keys` in the lambda-list indicates that the caller may specify additional keyword arguments; the `&rest` argument provides access to them. These additional keyword arguments are fed to `make-array`. Now, `make-array` normally does not allow the keywords `:start` and `:end` to be used, and it would be an error to specify such keyword arguments to `make-array`. However, the presence in the call to `make-array` of the keyword argument `:allow-other-keys` with a non-nil value causes any extraneous keyword arguments, including `:start` and `:end`, to be acceptable and ignored.

`lambda-parameters-limit`   [*Constant*]

The value of `lambda-parameters-limit` is a positive integer that is the upper exclusive bound on the number of distinct parameter names that may appear in a single lambda-list. This bound depends on the implementation but will not be smaller than 50. Implementors are encouraged to make this limit as large as practicable without sacrificing performance. See `call-arguments-limit`.

5.3. Top-Level Forms

The standard way for the user to interact with a Common Lisp implementation is via a *read-eval-print loop*: the system repeatedly reads a form from some input source (such as a keyboard or a disk file), evaluates it, and then prints the value(s) to some output sink (such as a display screen or another disk file). Any form (evaluable data object) is acceptable; however, certain special forms are specifically designed to be convenient for use as *top-level* forms, rather than as forms embedded within other forms in the way that `(+ 3 4)` is embedded within `(if p (+ 3 4) 6)`. These top-level special forms may be used to define globally named functions, to define macros, to make declarations, and to define global values for special variables.

It is not illegal to use these forms at other than top level, but whether it is meaningful to do so depends on context. Compilers, for example, may not recognize these forms properly in other than top-level contexts. (As a special case, however, if a `progn` form appears at top level, then all forms within that `progn` are considered by the compiler to be top-level forms.)

X3J13 voted in March 1989 ⟨50⟩ to clarify that, while defining forms normally appear at top level, it is meaningful to place them in non-top-level contexts. All defining forms that create functional objects from code appearing as argument forms must ensure that such argument forms refer to the enclosing lexical environment. Compilers must handle defining forms properly in all situations, not just top-level contexts. However, certain compile-time side effects of these defining forms are performed only when the defining forms occur at top level (see section 25.1).

Compatibility note: In MacLisp, a top-level `progn` is considered to contain top-level forms only if the first form is (`quote compile`). This odd marker is unnecessary in Common Lisp.

Macros are usually defined by using the special form `defmacro`. This facility is fairly complicated; it is described in chapter 8.

5.3.1. Defining Named Functions

The `defun` special form is the usual means of defining named functions.

`defun` *name lambda-list* ⟦ {*declaration*}* | *doc-string* ⟧ {*form*}*   [*Macro*]

Evaluating a `defun` form causes the symbol *name* to be a global name for the function specified by the lambda-expression

(`lambda` *lambda-list* {*declaration* | *doc-string*}* {*form*}*)

defined in the lexical environment in which the `defun` form was executed. Because `defun` forms normally appear at top level, this is normally the null lexical environment.

X3J13 voted in March 1989 ⟨50⟩ to clarify that, while defining forms normally appear at top level, it is meaningful to place them in non-top-level contexts; `defun` must define the function within the enclosing lexical environment, not within the null lexical environment.

X3J13 voted in March 1989 ⟨89⟩ to extend `defun` to accept any function-name (a symbol or a list whose *car* is `setf`—see section 7.1) as a *name*. Thus one may write

(`defun` (`setf cadr`) ...)

to define a `setf` expansion function for `cadr` (although it may be much more convenient to use `defsetf` or `define-modify-macro`).

If the optional documentation string *doc-string* is present, then it is attached to the *name* as a documentation string of type `function`; see `documentation`. If *doc-string* is not followed by a declaration, it may be present only if at least one *form* is also specified, as it is otherwise taken to be a *form*. It is an error if more than one *doc-string* is present.

The *forms* constitute the body of the defined function; they are executed as an implicit `progn`.

The body of the defined function is implicitly enclosed in a `block` construct whose name is the same as the *name* of the function. Therefore `return-from` may be used to exit from the function.

Other implementation-dependent bookkeeping actions may be taken as well by `defun`. The *name* is returned as the value of the `defun` form. For example:

```
(defun discriminant (a b c)
  (declare (number a b c))
  "Compute the discriminant for a quadratic equation.
   Given a, b, and c, the value b^2-4*a*c is calculated.
   The quadratic equation a*x^2+b*x+c=0 has real, multiple,
   or complex roots depending on whether this calculated
   value is positive, zero, or negative, respectively."
  (- (* b b) (* 4 a c)))
  ⇒ discriminant
and now (discriminant 1 2/3 -2) ⇒ 76/9
```

The documentation string in this example neglects to mention that the coefficients a, b, and c must be real for the discrimination criterion to hold. Here is an improved version:

```
  "Compute the discriminant for a quadratic equation.
   Given a, b, and c, the value b^2-4*a*c is calculated.
   If the coefficients a, b, and c are all real (that is,
   not complex), then the quadratic equation a*x^2+b*x+c=0
   has real, multiple, or complex roots depending on
   whether this calculated value is positive, zero, or
   negative, respectively."
```

It is permissible to use `defun` to redefine a function, to install a corrected version of an incorrect definition, for example. It is permissible to redefine a macro as a function. It is an error to attempt to redefine the name of a special form (see table 5-1) as a function.

5.3.2. Declaring Global Variables and Named Constants

The defvar and defparameter special forms are the usual means of specifying globally defined variables. The defconstant special form is used for defining named constants.

defvar *name* [*initial-value* [*documentation*]]	[*Macro*]
defparameter *name* *initial-value* [*documentation*]	[*Macro*]
defconstant *name* *initial-value* [*documentation*]	[*Macro*]

defvar is the recommended way to declare the use of a special variable in a program.

(defvar *variable*)

proclaims *variable* to be special (see proclaim), and may perform other system-dependent bookkeeping actions.

X3J13 voted in June 1987 ⟨61⟩ to clarify that if no *initial-value* form is provided, defvar does not change the value of the *variable*; if no *initial-value* form is provided and the variable has no value, defvar does not give it a value.

If a second argument form is supplied,

(defvar *variable initial-value*)

then *variable* is initialized to the result of evaluating the form *initial-value* unless it already has a value. The *initial-value* form is not evaluated unless it is used; this fact is useful if evaluation of the *initial-value* form does something expensive like creating a large data structure.

X3J13 voted in June 1987 ⟨60⟩ to clarify that evaluation of the *initial-value* and the initialization of the variable occur, if at all, at the time the defvar form is executed, and that the *initial-value* form is evaluated if and only if the *variable* does not already have a value.

The initialization is performed by assignment and thus assigns a global value to the variable unless there are currently special bindings of that variable. Normally there should not be any such special bindings.

defvar also provides a good place to put a comment describing the meaning of the variable, whereas an ordinary special proclamation offers the temptation to declare several variables at once and not have room to describe them all.

```
(defvar *visible-windows* 0
  "Number of windows at least partially visible on the screen")
```

defparameter is similar to defvar, but defparameter requires an *initial-value* form, always evaluates the form, and assigns the result to the variable. The semantic distinction is that defvar is intended to declare a variable changed by the program, whereas defparameter is intended to declare a variable that is normally constant but can be changed (possibly at run time), where such a change is considered a change *to* the program. defparameter therefore does not indicate that the quantity *never* changes; in particular, it does not license the compiler to build assumptions about the value into programs being compiled.

defconstant is like defparameter but *does* assert that the value of the variable *name* is fixed and does license the compiler to build assumptions about the value into programs being compiled. (However, if the compiler chooses to replace references to the name of the constant by the value of the constant in code to be compiled, perhaps in order to allow further optimization, the compiler must take care that such "copies" appear to be eql to the object that is the actual value of the constant. For example, the compiler may freely make copies of numbers but must exercise care when the value is a list.)

It is an error if there are any special bindings of the variable at the time the defconstant form is executed (but implementations may or may not check for this).

Once a name has been declared by defconstant to be constant, any further assignment to or binding of that special variable is an error. This is the case for such system-supplied constants as t and most-positive-fixnum. A compiler may also choose to issue warnings about bindings of the lexical variable of the same name.

X3J13 voted in January 1989 ⟨48⟩ to clarify the preceding paragraph by specifying that it is an error to rebind constant symbols as either lexical or special variables. Consequently, a valid reference to a symbol declared with defconstant always refers to its global value. (Unfortunately, this violates the principle of referential transparency, for one cannot always choose names for lexical variables without regard to surrounding context.)

For any of these constructs, the documentation should be a string. The string is attached to the name of the variable, parameter, or constant under the variable documentation type; see the documentation function.

X3J13 voted in March 1988 ⟨59⟩ to clarify that the *documentation-string* is not evaluated but must appear as a literal string when the defvar, defparameter, or defconstant form is evaluated.

For example, the form

```
(defvar *avoid-registers* nil "Compilation control switch #43")
```

is legitimate, but

```
(defvar *avoid-registers* nil
   (format nil "Compilation control switch #~D"
           (incf *compiler-switch-number*)))
```

is erroneous because the call to format is not a literal string.
(On the other hand, the form

```
(defvar *avoid-registers* nil
   #.(format nil "Compilation control switch #~D"
             (incf *compiler-switch-number*)))
```

might be used to accomplish the same purpose, because the call to format is evaluated at read time; when the defvar form is evaluated, only the result of the call to format, a string, appears in the defvar form.)

These constructs are normally used only as top-level forms. The value returned by each of these constructs is the *name* declared.

5.3.3. Control of Time of Evaluation

The eval-when special form allows pieces of code to be executed only at compile time, only at load time, or when interpreted but not compiled. Its uses are relatively esoteric.

eval-when ({*situation*}*) {*form*}*   [*Special form*]

The body of an eval-when form is processed as an implicit progn, but only in the situations listed. Each *situation* must be a symbol, either compile, load, or eval.

eval specifies that the interpreter should process the body. compile specifies that the compiler should evaluate the body at compile time in the compilation context. load specifies that the compiler should arrange to evaluate the forms in the body when the compiled file containing the eval-when form is loaded.

The eval-when construct may be more precisely understood in terms of a model of how the compiler processes forms in a file to be compiled. Successive forms are read from the file using the function read. These top-level forms are normally processed in what we shall call *not-compile-time* mode. There is another mode called *compile-time-too* mode. The eval-when special form controls which of these two modes to use.

Every form is processed as follows:

• If the form is an eval-when form:

  – If the situation load is specified:

If the situation compile is specified, *or* if the current processing mode is *compile-time-too* and the situation eval is specified, then process each of the forms in the body in *compile-time-too* mode.

Otherwise, process each of the forms in the body in *not-compile-time* mode.

- If the situation load is not specified:

    If the situation compile is specified, *or* if the current processing mode is *compile-time-too* and the situation eval is specified, then evaluate each of the forms in the body in the compiler's executing environment.

    Otherwise, ignore the eval-when form entirely.

- If the form is not an eval-when form, then do two things. First, if the current processing mode is *compile-time-too* mode, evaluate the form in the compiler's executing environment. Second, perform normal compiler processing of the form (compiling functions defined by defun forms, and so on).

One example of the use of eval-when is that if the compiler is to be able to properly read a file that uses user-defined reader macro characters, it is necessary to write

```
(eval-when (compile load eval)
  (set-macro-character #\$ #'(lambda (stream char)
                              (declare (ignore char))
                              (list 'dollar (read stream)))))
```

This causes the call to set-macro-character to be executed in the compiler's execution environment, thereby modifying its reader syntax table.

X3J13 voted in March 1989 ⟨73⟩ to completely redesign the eval-when construct to solve some problems concerning its treatment in other than top-level contexts. The new definition is upward compatible with the old definition, but the old keywords are deprecated.

eval-when ({*situation*}*) {*form*}*   [*Special form*]

The body of an eval-when form is processed as an implicit progn, but only in the situations listed. Each *situation* must be a symbol, either :compile-toplevel, :load-toplevel, or :execute.
   The use of :compile-toplevel and :load-toplevel controls whether and when processing occurs for top-level forms. The use of :execute controls whether processing occurs for non-top-level forms.

The eval-when construct may be more precisely understood in terms of a model of how the file compiler, compile-file, processes forms in a file to be compiled.

Successive forms are read from the file by the file compiler using read. These top-level forms are normally processed in what we call "not-compile-time" mode. There is one other mode, called "compile-time-too" mode, which can come into play for top-level forms. The eval-when special form is used to annotate a program in a way that allows the program doing the processing to select the appropriate mode.

Processing of top-level forms in the file compiler works as follows:

- If the form is a macro call, it is expanded and the result is processed as a top-level form in the same processing mode (compile-time-too or not-compile-time).

- If the form is a progn (or locally ⟨113⟩) form, each of its body forms is sequentially processed as top-level forms in the same processing mode.

- If the form is a compiler-let, macrolet, or symbol-macrolet, the file compiler makes the appropriate bindings and recursively processes the body forms as an implicit top-level progn with those bindings in effect, in the same processing mode.

- If the form is an eval-when form, it is handled according to the following table:

LT	CT	EX	CTTM	Action
yes	yes	–	–	process body in compile-time-too mode
yes	no	yes	yes	process body in compile-time-too mode
yes	no	–	no	process body in not-compile-time mode
yes	no	no	–	process body in not-compile-time mode
no	yes	–	–	evaluate body
no	no	yes	yes	evaluate body
no	no	–	no	do nothing
no	no	no	–	do nothing

In the preceding table the column LT asks whether :load-toplevel is one of the situations specified in the eval-when form; CT similarly refers to :compile-toplevel and EX to :execute. The column CTTM asks whether the eval-when form was encountered while in compile-time-too mode. The phrase "process body" means to process the body as an implicit top-level progn in the indicated mode, and "evaluate body" means to evaluate the body forms sequentially as an implicit progn in the dynamic execution context of the compiler and in the lexical environment in which the eval-when appears.

- Otherwise, the form is a top-level form that is not one of the special cases. If in compile-time-too mode, the compiler first evaluates the form and then performs normal compiler processing on it. If in not-compile-time mode, only normal compiler processing is performed (see section 25.1). Any subforms are treated as non-top-level forms.

Note that top-level forms are guaranteed to be processed in the order in which they textually appear in the file, and that each top-level form read by the compiler is processed before the next is read. However, the order of processing (including, in particular, macro expansion) of subforms that are not top-level forms is unspecified.

For an eval-when form that is not a top-level form in the file compiler (that is, either in the interpreter, in compile, or in the file compiler but not at top level), if the :execute situation is specified, its body is treated as an implicit progn. Otherwise, the body is ignored and the eval-when form has the value nil.

For the sake of backward compatibility, a *situation* may also be compile, load, or eval. Within a top-level eval-when form these have the same meaning as :compile-toplevel, :load-toplevel, and :execute, respectively; but their effect is undefined when used in an eval-when form that is not at top level.

The following effects are logical consequences of the preceding specification:

- It is never the case that the execution of a single eval-when expression will execute the body code more than once.

- The old keyword eval was a misnomer because execution of the body need not be done by eval. For example, when the function definition

```
(defun foo () (eval-when (:execute) (print 'foo)))
```

is compiled the call to print should be compiled, not evaluated at compile time.

- Macros intended for use in top-level forms should arrange for all side-effects to be done by the forms in the macro expansion. The macro-expander itself should not perform the side-effects.

```
(defmacro foo ()
  (really-foo)                              ;Wrong
  `(really-foo))

(defmacro foo ()
  `(eval-when (:compile-toplevel
               :load-toplevel :execute)     ;Right
     (really-foo)))
```

Adherence to this convention will mean that such macros will behave intuitively when called in non-top-level positions.

- Placing a variable binding around an eval-when reliably captures the binding because the "compile-time-too" mode cannot occur (because the eval-when could not be a top-level form). For example,

```
(let ((x 3))
  (eval-when (:compile-toplevel :load-toplevel :execute)
    (print x)))
```

will print 3 at execution (that is, load) time and will not print anything at compile time. This is important so that expansions of defun and defmacro can be done in terms of eval-when and can correctly capture the lexical environment. For example, an implementation might expand a defun form such as

```
(defun bar (x) (defun foo () (+ x 3)))
```

into

```
(progn (eval-when (:compile-toplevel)
         (compiler::notice-function 'bar '(x)))
       (eval-when (:load-toplevel :execute)
         (setf (symbol-function 'bar)
               #'(lambda (x)
                   (progn (eval-when (:compile-toplevel)
                            (compiler::notice-function 'foo
                                                       '()))
                          (eval-when (:load-toplevel :execute)
                            (setf (symbol-function 'foo)
                                  #'(lambda () (+ x 3)))))))))
```

which by the preceding rules would be treated the same as

```
(progn (eval-when (:compile-toplevel)
         (compiler::notice-function 'bar '(x)))
       (eval-when (:load-toplevel :execute)
         (setf (symbol-function 'bar)
               #'(lambda (x)
                   (progn (eval-when (:load-toplevel :execute)
                            (setf (symbol-function 'foo)
                                  #'(lambda () (+ x 3)))))))))
```

Here are some additional examples.

```
(let ((x 1))
   (eval-when (:execute :load-toplevel :compile-toplevel)
     (setf (symbol-function 'foo1) #'(lambda () x))))
```

The eval-when in the preceding expression is not at top level, so only the
:execute keyword is considered. At compile time, this has no effect. At load
time (if the let is at top level), or at execution time (if the let is embedded in
some other form which does not execute until later), this sets (symbol-function
'foo1) to a function that returns 1.

```
(eval-when (:execute :load-toplevel :compile-toplevel)
   (let ((x 2))
     (eval-when (:execute :load-toplevel :compile-toplevel)
       (setf (symbol-function 'foo2) #'(lambda () x)))))
```

If the preceding expression occurs at the top level of a file to be compiled, it has
both a compile time *and* a load-time effect of setting (symbol-function 'foo2)
to a function that returns 2.

```
(eval-when (:execute :load-toplevel :compile-toplevel)
   (setf (symbol-function 'foo3) #'(lambda () 3)))
```

If the preceding expression occurs at the top level of a file to be compiled, it has
both a compile time *and* a load-time effect of setting the function cell of foo3 to
a function that returns 3.

```
(eval-when (:compile-toplevel)
   (eval-when (:compile-toplevel)
     (print 'foo4)))
```

The preceding expression always does nothing; it simply returns nil.

```
(eval-when (:compile-toplevel)
   (eval-when (:execute)
     (print 'foo5)))
```

If the preceding form occurs at the top level of a file to be compiled, foo5 is
printed at compile time. If this form occurs in a non-top-level position, nothing
is printed at compile time. Regardless of context, nothing is ever printed at load
time or execution time.

```
(eval-when (:execute :load-toplevel)
   (eval-when (:compile-toplevel)
     (print 'foo6)))
```

If the preceding form occurs at the top level of a file to be compiled, foo6 is printed at compile time. If this form occurs in a non-top-level position, nothing is printed at compile time. Regardless of context, nothing is ever printed at load time or execution time.

6

Predicates

A *predicate* is a function that tests for some condition involving its arguments and returns nil if the condition is false, or some non-nil value if the condition is true. One may think of a predicate as producing a Boolean value, where nil stands for *false* and anything else stands for *true*. Conditional control structures such as cond, if, when, and unless test such Boolean values. We say that a predicate *is true* when it returns a non-nil value, and *is false* when it returns nil; that is, it is true or false according to whether the condition being tested is true or false.

By convention, the names of predicates usually end in the letter p (which stands for "predicate"). Common Lisp uses a uniform convention in hyphenating names of predicates. If the name of the predicate is formed by adding a p to an existing name, such as the name of a data type, a hyphen is placed before the final p if and only if there is a hyphen in the existing name. For example, number begets numberp but standard-char begets standard-char-p. On the other hand, if the name of a predicate is formed by adding a prefixing qualifier to the front of an existing predicate name, the two names are joined with a hyphen and the presence or absence of a hyphen before the final p is not changed. For example, the predicate string-lessp has no hyphen before the p because it is the string version of lessp (a MacLisp function that has been renamed < in Common Lisp). The name string-less-p would incorrectly imply that it is a predicate that tests for a kind of object called a string-less, and the name stringlessp would connote a predicate that tests whether something has no strings (is "stringless")!

The control structures that test Boolean values only test for whether or not the value is nil, which is considered to be false. Any other value is considered to be true. Often a predicate will return nil if it "fails" and some *useful* value if it "succeeds"; such a function can be used not only as a test but also for the useful value provided in case of success. An example is member.

If no better non-nil value is available for the purpose of indicating success, by convention the symbol t is used as the "standard" true value.

6.1. Logical Values

The names nil and t are constants in Common Lisp. Although they are symbols like any other symbols, and appear to be treated as variables when evaluated, it is not permitted to modify their values. See defconstant.

nil   [*Constant*]

The value of nil is always nil. This object represents the logical *false* value and also the empty list. It can also be written ( ).

t   [*Constant*]

The value of t is always t.

6.2. Data Type Predicates

Perhaps the most important predicates in Lisp are those that deal with data types; that is, given a data object one can determine whether or not it belongs to a given type, or one can compare two type specifiers.

6.2.1. General Type Predicates

If a data type is viewed as the set of all objects belonging to the type, then the typep function is a set membership test, while subtypep is a subset test.

typep *object type*   [*Function*]

typep is a predicate that is true if *object* is of type *type*, and is false otherwise. Note that an object can be "of" more than one type, since one type can include another. The *type* may be any of the type specifiers mentioned in chapter 4 *except* that it may not be or contain a type specifier list whose first element is function or values. A specifier of the form (satisfies *fn*) is handled simply by applying the function *fn* to *object* (see funcall); the *object* is considered to be of the specified type if the result is not nil.

X3J13 voted in January 1989 ⟨8⟩ to change typep to give specialized array and complex type specifiers the same meaning for purposes of type discrimination as they have for declaration purposes. Of course, this also applies to such type specifiers as vector and simple-array (see section 4.5). Thus

```
(typep foo '(array bignum))
```

in the first edition asked the question, Is foo an array specialized to hold bignums? but under the new interpretation asks the question, Could the array foo have resulted from giving bignum as the :element-type argument to make-array?

subtypep *type1* *type2*   [*Function*]

The arguments must be type specifiers that are acceptable to typep. The two type specifiers are compared; this predicate is true if *type1* is definitely a (not necessarily proper) subtype of *type2*. If the result is nil, however, then *type1* may or may not be a subtype of *type2* (sometimes it is impossible to tell, especially when satisfies type specifiers are involved). A second returned value indicates the certainty of the result; if it is true, then the first value is an accurate indication of the subtype relationship. Thus there are three possible result combinations:

t   t   *type1* is definitely a subtype of *type2*
nil t   *type1* is definitely not a subtype of *type2*
nil nil subtypep could not determine the relationship

X3J13 voted in January 1989 ⟨171⟩ to place certain requirements upon the implementation of subtypep, for it noted that implementations in many cases simply "give up" and return the two values nil and nil when in fact it would have been possible to determine the relationship between the given types. The requirements are as follows, where it is understood that a type specifier *s* *involves* a type specifier *u* if either *s* contains an occurrence of *u* directly or *s* contains a type specifier *w* defined by deftype whose expansion involves *u*.

• subtypep is not permitted to return a second value of nil unless one or both of its arguments involves satisfies, and, or, not, or member.

• subtypep should signal an error when one or both of its arguments involves values or the list form of the function type specifier.

• subtypep must always return the two values t and t in the case where its arguments, after expansion of specifiers defined by deftype, are equal.

In addition, X3J13 voted to clarify that in some cases the relationships between types as reflected by subtypep may be implementation-specific. For example, in an implementation supporting only one type of floating-point number, (subtypep 'float 'long-float) would return t and t, since the two types would be identical.

Note that satisfies is an exception because relationships between types involving satisfies are undecidable in general, but (as X3J13 noted) and, or, not, and `member` are merely very messy to deal with. In all likelihood these will not be addressed unless and until someone is willing to write a careful specification that covers all the cases for the processing of these type specifiers by `subtypep`. The requirements stated above were easy to state and probably suffice for most cases of interest.

X3J13 voted in January 1989 ⟨8⟩ to change `subtypep` to give specialized `array` and `complex` type specifiers the same meaning for purposes of type discrimination as they have for declaration purposes. Of course, this also applies to such type specifiers as `vector` and `simple-array` (see section 4.5).

If *A* and *B* are type specifiers (other than `*`, which technically is not a type specifier anyway), then `(array A)` and `(array B)` represent the same type in a given implementation if and only if they denote arrays of the same specialized representation in that implementation; otherwise they are disjoint. To put it another way, they represent the same type if and only if `(upgraded-array-element-type 'A)` and `(upgraded-array-element-type 'B)` are the same type. Therefore

```
(subtypep '(array A) '(array B))
```

is true if and only if `(upgraded-array-element-type 'A)` is the same type as `(upgraded-array-element-type 'B)`.

The `complex` type specifier is treated in a similar but subtly different manner. If *A* and *B* are two type specifiers (but not `*`, which technically is not a type specifier anyway), then `(complex A)` and `(complex B)` represent the same type in a given implementation if and only if they refer to complex numbers of the same specialized representation in that implementation; otherwise they are disjoint. Note, however, that there is no function called `make-complex` that allows one to specify a particular element type (then to be upgraded); instead, one must describe specialized complex numbers in terms of the actual types of the parts from which they were constructed. There is no number of type (or rather, *representation*) `float` as such; there are only numbers of type `single-float`, numbers of type `double-float`, and so on. Therefore we want `(complex single-float)` to be a subtype of `(complex float)`.

The rule, then, is that `(complex A)` and `(complex B)` represent the same type (and otherwise are disjoint) in a given implementation if and only if *either* the type *A* is a subtype of *B*, or `(upgraded-complex-part-type 'A)` and `(upgraded-complex-part-type 'B)` are the same type. In the latter case `(complex A)` and `(complex B)` in fact refer to the same specialized representation. Therefore

```
(subtypep '(complex A) '(complex B))
```

is true if and only if the results of (upgraded-complex-part-type ´A) and (upgraded-complex-part-type ´B) are the same type.

   Under this interpretation

(subtypep ´(complex single-float) ´(complex float))

must be true in all implementations; but

(subtypep ´(array single-float) ´(array float))

is true only in implementations that do not have a specialized array representation for single-float elements distinct from that for float elements in general.

6.2.2. Specific Data Type Predicates

The following predicates test for individual data types.

null *object*   [*Function*]

null is true if its argument is (), and otherwise is false. This is the same operation performed by the function not; however, not is normally used to invert a Boolean value, whereas null is normally used to test for an empty list. The programmer can therefore express *intent* by the choice of function name.

(null x) ≡ (typep x ´null) ≡ (eq x ´())

symbolp *object*   [*Function*]

symbolp is true if its argument is a symbol, and otherwise is false.

(symbolp x) ≡ (typep x ´symbol)

Compatibility note: The Interlisp equivalent of symbolp is called litatom.

---

atom *object*   [*Function*]

The predicate atom is true if its argument is not a cons, and otherwise is false. Note that (atom ´()) is true, because () ≡ nil.

(atom x) ≡ (typep x ´atom) ≡ (not (typep x ´cons))

consp *object*   [*Function*]

The predicate consp is true if its argument is a cons, and otherwise is false. Note that the empty list is not a cons, so (consp ´()) ≡ (consp ´nil) ⇒ nil.

(consp x) ≡ (typep x ´cons) ≡ (not (typep x ´atom))

listp *object*   [*Function*]

listp is true if its argument is a cons or the empty list ( ), and otherwise is false. It does not check for whether the list is a "true list" (one terminated by nil) or a "dotted list" (one terminated by a non-null atom).

(listp x) ≡ (typep x ´list) ≡ (typep x ´(or cons null))

numberp *object*   [*Function*]

numberp is true if its argument is any kind of number, and otherwise is false.

(numberp x) ≡ (typep x ´number)

integerp *object*   [*Function*]

integerp is true if its argument is an integer, and otherwise is false.

(integerp x) ≡ (typep x ´integer)

rationalp *object*   [*Function*]

rationalp is true if its argument is a rational number (a ratio or an integer), and
otherwise is false.

(rationalp x) ≡ (typep x 'rational)

floatp *object*   [*Function*]

floatp is true if its argument is a floating-point number, and otherwise is false.

(floatp x) ≡ (typep x 'float)

realp *object*   [*Function*]

X3J13 voted in March 1989 ⟨151⟩ to add the function realp. realp is true if its
argument is a real number, and otherwise is false.

(realp x) ≡ (typep x 'real)

complexp *object*   [*Function*]

complexp is true if its argument is a complex number, and otherwise is false.

(complexp x) ≡ (typep x 'complex)

characterp *object*   [*Function*]

characterp is true if its argument is a character, and otherwise is false.

(characterp x) ≡ (typep x 'character)

stringp *object*   [*Function*]

stringp is true if its argument is a string, and otherwise is false.

(stringp x) ≡ (typep x 'string)

bit-vector-p *object*   [*Function*]

bit-vector-p is true if its argument is a bit-vector, and otherwise is false.

(bit-vector-p x) ≡ (typep x 'bit-vector)

vectorp *object*   [*Function*]

vectorp is true if its argument is a vector, and otherwise is false.

(vectorp x) ≡ (typep x ´vector)

simple-vector-p *object*   [*Function*]

vectorp is true if its argument is a simple general vector, and otherwise is false.

(simple-vector-p x) ≡ (typep x ´simple-vector)

simple-string-p *object*   [*Function*]

simple-string-p is true if its argument is a simple string, and otherwise is false.

(simple-string-p x) ≡ (typep x ´simple-string)

simple-bit-vector-p *object*   [*Function*]

simple-bit-vector-p is true if its argument is a simple bit-vector, and otherwise
is false.

(simple-bit-vector-p x) ≡ (typep x ´simple-bit-vector)

arrayp *object*   [*Function*]

arrayp is true if its argument is an array, and otherwise is false.

(arrayp x) ≡ (typep x ´array)

packagep *object*   [*Function*]

packagep is true if its argument is a package, and otherwise is false.

(packagep x) ≡ (typep x ´package)

functionp *object*   [*Function*]

   functionp is true if its argument is suitable for applying to arguments, using
for example the funcall or apply function. Otherwise functionp is false.
   functionp is always true of symbols, lists whose *car* is the symbol lambda,
any value returned by the function special form, and any values returned by the
function compile when the first argument is nil.
   X3J13 voted in June 1988 ⟨90⟩ to define

(functionp x) ≡ (typep x ´function)

Because the vote also specifies that types cons and symbol are disjoint from the type function, this is an incompatible change; now functionp is in fact always false of symbols and lists.

compiled-function-p *object*   [*Function*]

compiled-function-p is true if its argument is any compiled code object, and otherwise is false.

(compiled-function-p x) ≡ (typep x ´compiled-function)

commonp *object*   [*Function*]

commonp is true if its argument is any standard Common Lisp data type, and otherwise is false.

(commonp x) ≡ (typep x ´common)

X3J13 voted in March 1989 ⟨17⟩ to remove the predicate commonp (and the type common) from the language.

See also standard-char-p, string-char-p, streamp, random-state-p, readtablep, hash-table-p, and pathnamep.

6.3. Equality Predicates

Common Lisp provides a spectrum of predicates for testing for equality of two objects: eq (the most specific), eql, equal, and equalp (the most general). eq and equal have the meanings traditional in Lisp. eql was added because it is frequently needed, and equalp was added primarily in order to have a version of equal that would ignore type differences when comparing numbers and case differences when comparing characters. If two objects satisfy any one of these equality predicates, then they also satisfy all those that are more general.

eq *x y*   [*Function*]

(eq *x y*) is true if and only if *x* and *y* are the same identical object. (Implementationally, *x* and *y* are usually eq if and only if they address the same identical memory location.)

It should be noted that things that print the same are not necessarily eq to each other. Symbols with the same print name usually are eq to each other because of the use of the intern function. However, numbers with the same value need not be eq, and two similar lists are usually not eq. For example:

```
(eq 'a 'b) is false.
(eq 'a 'a) is true.
(eq 3 3) might be true or false, depending on the implementation.
(eq 3 3.0) is false.
(eq 3.0 3.0) might be true or false, depending on the implementation.
(eq #c(3 -4) #c(3 -4))
    might be true or false, depending on the implementation.
(eq #c(3 -4.0) #c(3 -4)) is false.
(eq (cons 'a 'b) (cons 'a 'c)) is false.
(eq (cons 'a 'b) (cons 'a 'b)) is false.
(eq '(a . b) '(a . b)) might be true or false.
(progn (setq x (cons 'a 'b)) (eq x x)) is true.
(progn (setq x '(a . b)) (eq x x)) is true.
(eq #\A #\A) might be true or false, depending on the implementation.
(eq "Foo" "Foo") might be true or false.
(eq "Foo" (copy-seq "Foo")) is false.
(eq "FOO" "foo") is false.
```

In Common Lisp, unlike some other Lisp dialects, the implementation is permitted to make "copies" of characters and numbers at any time. (This permission is granted because it allows tremendous performance improvements in many common situations.) The net effect is that Common Lisp makes no guarantee that eq will be true even when both its arguments are "the same thing" if that thing is a character or number. For example:

```
(let ((x 5)) (eq x x)) might be true or false.
```

The predicate eql is the same as eq, except that if the arguments are characters or numbers of the same type then their values are compared. Thus eql tells whether two objects are *conceptually* the same, whereas eq tells whether two objects are *implementationally* identical. It is for this reason that eql, not eq, is the default comparison predicate for the sequence functions defined in chapter 14.

Implementation note: eq simply compares the two given pointers, so any kind of object that is represented in an "immediate" fashion will indeed have like-valued instances satisfy eq. In some implementations, for example, fixnums and characters happen to "work." However, no program should depend on this, as other implementations of Common Lisp might not use an immediate representation for these data types.

An additional problem with eq is that the implementation is permitted to "collapse" constants (or portions thereof) appearing in code to be compiled if they are equal. An object is considered to be a constant in code to be compiled if it is a self-evaluating form or is contained in a quote form. This is why (eq "Foo" "Foo") might be true or false; in interpreted code it would normally be false, because reading in the form (eq "Foo" "Foo") would construct distinct strings for the two arguments to eq, but the compiler might choose to use the same identical string or two distinct copies as the two arguments in the call to eq. Similarly, (eq '(a . b) '(a . b)) might be true or false, depending on whether the constant conses appearing in the quote forms were collapsed by the compiler. However, (eq (cons 'a 'b) (cons 'a 'b)) is always false, because every distinct call to the cons function necessarily produces a new and distinct cons.

X3J13 voted in March 1989 ⟨147⟩ to clarify that eval and compile are not permitted either to copy or to coalesce ("collapse") constants (see eq) appearing in the code they process; the resulting program behavior must refer to objects that are eql to the corresponding objects in the source code. Only the compile-file/load process is permitted to copy or coalesce constants (see section 25.1).

---

eql *x y*   [*Function*]

The eql predicate is true if its arguments are eq, or if they are numbers of the same type with the same value, or if they are character objects that represent the same character. For example:

```
(eql 'a 'b) is false.
(eql 'a 'a) is true.
(eql 3 3) is true.
(eql 3 3.0) is false.
(eql 3.0 3.0) is true.
(eql #c(3 -4) #c(3 -4)) is true.
(eql #c(3 -4.0) #c(3 -4)) is false.
(eql (cons 'a 'b) (cons 'a 'c)) is false.
(eql (cons 'a 'b) (cons 'a 'b)) is false.
(eql '(a . b) '(a . b)) might be true or false.
(progn (setq x (cons 'a 'b)) (eql x x)) is true.
(progn (setq x '(a . b)) (eql x x)) is true.
(eql #\A #\A) is true.
```

(eql "Foo" "Foo") might be true or false.
(eql "Foo" (copy-seq "Foo")) is false.
(eql "FOO" "foo") is false.

Normally (eql 1.0s0 1.0d0) would be false, under the assumption that 1.0s0 and 1.0d0 are of distinct data types. However, implementations that do not provide four distinct floating-point formats are permitted to "collapse" the four formats into some smaller number of them; in such an implementation (eql 1.0s0 1.0d0) might be true. The predicate = will compare the values of two numbers even if the numbers are of different types.

If an implementation supports positive and negative zeros as distinct values (as in the IEEE proposed standard floating-point format), then (eql 0.0 -0.0) will be false. Otherwise, when the syntax -0.0 is read it will be interpreted as the value 0.0, and so (eql 0.0 -0.0) will be true. The predicate = differs from eql in that (= 0.0 -0.0) will always be true, because = compares the mathematical values of its operands, whereas eql compares the representational values, so to speak.

Two complex numbers are considered to be eql if their real parts are eql and their imaginary parts are eql. For example, (eql #C(4 5) #C(4 5)) is true and (eql #C(4 5) #C(4.0 5.0)) is false. Note that while (eql #C(5.0 0.0) 5.0) is false, (eql #C(5 0) 5) is true. In the case of (eql #C(5.0 0.0) 5.0) the two arguments are of different types and so cannot satisfy eql; that's all there is to it. In the case of (eql #C(5 0) 5), however, #C(5 0) is not a complex number but is always automatically reduced by the rule of complex canonicalization to the integer 5, just as the apparent ratio 20/4 is always simplified to 5.

The case of (eql "Foo" "Foo") is discussed above in the description of eq. While eql compares the values of numbers and characters, it does not compare the contents of strings. To compare the characters of two strings, one should use equal, equalp, string=, or string-equal.

Compatibility note: The Common Lisp function eql is similar to the Interlisp function eqp. However, eql considers 3 and 3.0 to be different, whereas eqp considers them to be the same; eqp behaves like the Common Lisp = function, not like eql, when both arguments are numbers.

---

equal *x y*   [*Function*]

The equal predicate is true if its arguments are structurally similar (isomorphic) objects. A rough rule of thumb is that two objects are equal if and only if their printed representations are the same.

Numbers and characters are compared as for eql. Symbols are compared as for eq. This method of comparing symbols can violate the rule of thumb for equal and printed representations, but only in the infrequently occurring case of two distinct symbols with the same print name.

Certain objects that have components are equal if they are of the same type and corresponding components are equal. This test is implemented in a recursive manner and may fail to terminate for circular structures.

For conses, equal is defined recursively as the two *car*'s being equal and the two *cdr*'s being equal.

Two arrays are equal only if they are eq, with one exception: strings and bit-vectors are compared element-by-element. If either argument has a fill pointer, the fill pointer limits the number of elements examined by equal. Uppercase and lowercase letters in strings are considered by equal to be distinct. (In contrast, equalp ignores case distinctions in strings.)

Compatibility note: In Lisp Machine Lisp, equal ignores the difference between uppercase and lowercase letters in strings. This violates the rule of thumb about printed representations, however, which is very useful, especially to novices. It is also inconsistent with the treatment of single characters, which in Lisp Machine Lisp are represented as fixnums.

Two pathname objects are equal if and only if all the corresponding components (host, device, and so on) are equivalent. (Whether or not uppercase and lowercase letters are considered equivalent in strings appearing in components depends on the file name conventions of the file system.) Pathnames that are equal should be functionally equivalent.

X3J13 voted in June 1989 ⟨71⟩ to clarify that equal never recursively descends any structure or data type other than the ones explicitly described above: conses, bit-vectors, strings, and pathnames. Numbers and characters are compared as if by eql, and all other data objects are compared as if by eq.

```
(equal 'a 'b) is false.
(equal 'a 'a) is true.
(equal 3 3) is true.
(equal 3 3.0) is false.
(equal 3.0 3.0) is true.
(equal #c(3 -4) #c(3 -4)) is true.
(equal #c(3 -4.0) #c(3 -4)) is false.
(equal (cons 'a 'b) (cons 'a 'c)) is false.
(equal (cons 'a 'b) (cons 'a 'b)) is true.
(equal '(a . b) '(a . b)) is true.
```

```
(progn (setq x (cons 'a 'b)) (equal x x)) is true.
(progn (setq x '(a . b)) (equal x x)) is true.
(equal #\A #\A) is true.
(equal "Foo" "Foo") is true.
(equal "Foo" (copy-seq "Foo")) is true.
(equal "FOO" "foo") is false.
```

To compare a tree of conses using eql (or any other desired predicate) on the leaves, use tree-equal.

equalp *x y*   [*Function*]

Two objects are equalp if they are equal; if they are characters and satisfy char-equal, which ignores alphabetic case and certain other attributes of characters; if they are numbers and have the same numerical value, even if they are of different types; or if they have components that are all equalp.

Objects that have components are equalp if they are of the same type and corresponding components are equalp. This test is implemented in a recursive manner and may fail to terminate for circular structures. For conses, equalp is defined recursively as the two *car*'s being equalp and the two *cdr*'s being equalp.

Two arrays are equalp if and only if they have the same number of dimensions, the dimensions match, and the corresponding components are equalp. The specializations need not match; for example, a string and a general array that happens to contain the same characters will be equalp (though definitely not equal). If either argument has a fill pointer, the fill pointer limits the number of elements examined by equalp. Because equalp performs element-by-element comparisons of strings and ignores the alphabetic case of characters, case distinctions are therefore also ignored when equalp compares strings.

Two symbols can be equalp only if they are eq, that is, the same identical object.

X3J13 voted in June 1989 ⟨71⟩ to specify that equalp compares components of hash tables (see below), and to clarify that otherwise equalp never recursively descends any structure or data type other than the ones explicitly described above: conses, arrays (including bit-vectors and strings), and pathnames. Numbers are compared for numerical equality (see =), characters are compared as if by char-equal, and all other data objects are compared as if by eq.

Two hash tables are considered the same by equalp if and only if they satisfy a four-part test:

• They must be of the same kind; that is, equivalent :test arguments were given to make-hash-table when the two hash tables were created.

- They must have the same number of entries (see hash-table-count).

- For every entry (*key1*, *value1*) in one hash table there must be a corresponding entry (*key2*, *value2*) in the other, such that *key1* and *key2* are considered to be the same by the :test function associated with the hash tables.

- For every entry (*key1*, *value1*) in one hash table and its corresponding entry (*key2*, *value2*) in the other, such that *key1* and *key2* are the same, equalp must be true of *value1* and *value2*.

The four parts of this test are carried out in the order shown, and if some part of the test fails, equalp returns nil and the other parts of the test are not attempted.

If equalp must compare two structures and the defstruct definition for one used the :type option and the other did not, then equalp returns nil.

If equalp must compare two structures and neither defstruct definition used the :type option, then equalp returns t if and only if the structures have the same type (that is, the same defstruct name) and the values of all corresponding slots (slots having the same name) are equalp.

As part of the X3J13 discussion of this issue the following observations were made. Object equality is not a concept for which there is a uniquely determined correct algorithm. The appropriateness of an equality predicate can be judged only in the context of the needs of some particular program. Although these functions take any type of argument and their names sound very generic, equal and equalp are not appropriate for every application. Any decision to use or not use them should be determined by what they are documented to do rather than by any abstract characterization of their function. If neither equal nor equalp is found to be appropriate in a particular situation, programmers are encouraged to create another operator that is appropriate rather than blame equal or equalp for "doing the wrong thing."

Note that one consequence of the vote to change the rules of floating-point contagion ⟨37⟩ (described in section 12.1) is to make equalp a true equivalence relation on numbers.

```
(equalp 'a 'b) is false.
(equalp 'a 'a) is true.
(equalp 3 3) is true.
(equalp 3 3.0) is true.
(equalp 3.0 3.0) is true.
(equalp #c(3 -4) #c(3 -4)) is true.
(equalp #c(3 -4.0) #c(3 -4)) is true.
(equalp (cons 'a 'b) (cons 'a 'c)) is false.
(equalp (cons 'a 'b) (cons 'a 'b)) is true.
```

```
(equalp '(a . b) '(a . b)) is true.
(progn (setq x (cons 'a 'b)) (equalp x x)) is true.
(progn (setq x '(a . b)) (equalp x x)) is true.
(equalp #\A #\A) is true.
(equalp "Foo" "Foo") is true.
(equalp "Foo" (copy-seq "Foo")) is true.
(equalp "FOO" "foo") is true.
```

6.4. Logical Operators

Common Lisp provides three operators on Boolean values: and, or, and not. Of these, and and or are also control structures because their arguments are evaluated conditionally. The function not necessarily examines its single argument, and so is a simple function.

---

not *x*   [*Function*]

not returns t if *x* is nil, and otherwise returns nil. It therefore inverts its argument considered as a Boolean value.

   null is the same as not; both functions are included for the sake of clarity. As a matter of style, it is customary to use null to check whether something is the empty list and to use not to invert the sense of a logical value.

---

and {*form*}*   [*Macro*]

(and *form1 form2* ...) evaluates each *form*, one at a time, from left to right. If any *form* evaluates to nil, the value nil is immediately returned without evaluating the remaining *forms*. If every *form* but the last evaluates to a non-nil value, and returns whatever the last *form* returns. Therefore in general and can be used both for logical operations, where nil stands for *false* and non-nil values stand for *true*, and as a conditional expression. An example follows.

```
(if (and (>= n 0)
         (< n (length a-simple-vector))
         (eq (elt a-simple-vector n) 'foo))
    (princ "Foo!"))
```

The above expression prints Foo! if element n of a-simple-vector is the symbol foo, provided also that n is indeed a valid index for a-simple-vector. Because and guarantees left-to-right testing of its parts, elt is not called if n is out of range.

To put it another way, the and special form does *short-circuit* Boolean evaluation, like the **and then** operator in Ada and what in some Pascal-like languages is called **cand** (for "conditional and"); the Lisp and special form is unlike the Pascal or Ada **and** operator, which always evaluates both arguments.

In the previous example writing

```
(and (>= n 0)
     (< n (length a-simple-vector))
     (eq (elt a-simple-vector n) 'foo)
     (princ "Foo!"))
```

would accomplish the same thing. The difference is purely stylistic. Some programmers never use expressions containing side effects within and, preferring to use if or when for that purpose.

From the general definition, one can deduce that (and x) $\equiv x$. Also, (and) evaluates to t, which is an identity for this operation.

One can define and in terms of cond in this way:

```
(and x y z ... w) ≡ (cond ((not x) nil)
                          ((not y) nil)
                          ((not z) nil)
                          ...
                          (t w))
```

See if and when, which are sometimes stylistically more appropriate than and for conditional purposes. If it is necessary to test whether a predicate is true of all elements of a list or vector (element 0 *and* element 1 *and* element 2 *and* ...), then the function every may be useful.

---

or {*form*}*   [*Macro*]

(or *form1 form2* ...) evaluates each *form*, one at a time, from left to right. If any *form* other than the last evaluates to something other than nil, or immediately returns that non-nil value without evaluating the remaining *forms*. If every *form* but the last evaluates to nil, or returns whatever evaluation of the last of the *forms* returns. Therefore in general or can be used both for logical operations, where nil stands for *false* and non-nil values stand for *true*, and as a conditional expression.

To put it another way, the or special form does *short-circuit* Boolean evaluation, like the **or else** operator in Ada and what in some Pascal-like languages is called **cor** (for "conditional or"); the Lisp or special form is unlike the Pascal or Ada **or** operator, which always evaluates both arguments.

From the general definition, one can deduce that $(or\ x) \equiv x$. Also, (or) evaluates to nil, which is the identity for this operation.

One can define or in terms of cond in this way:

$$(or\ x\ y\ z\ \ldots\ w) \equiv (cond\ (x)\ (y)\ (z)\ \ldots\ (t\ w))$$

See if and unless, which are sometimes stylistically more appropriate than or for conditional purposes. If it is necessary to test whether a predicate is true of one or more elements of a list or vector (element 0 *or* element 1 *or* element 2 *or* ...), then the function some may be useful.

7

Control Structure

Common Lisp provides a variety of special structures for organizing programs. Some have to do with flow of control (control structures), while others control access to variables (environment structures). Some of these features are implemented as special forms; others are implemented as macros, which typically expand into complex program fragments expressed in terms of special forms or other macros.

Function application is the primary method for construction of Lisp programs. Operations are written as the application of a function to its arguments. Usually, Lisp programs are written as a large collection of small functions, each of which implements a simple operation. These functions operate by calling one another, and so larger operations are defined in terms of smaller ones. Lisp functions may call upon themselves recursively, either directly or indirectly.

Locally defined functions (flet, labels) and macros (macrolet) are quite versatile. The new symbol macro facility allows even more syntactic flexibility.

While the Lisp language is more applicative in style than statement-oriented, it nevertheless provides many operations that produce side effects and consequently requires constructs for controlling the sequencing of side effects. The construct progn, which is roughly equivalent to an Algol **begin-end** block with all its semi-colons, executes a number of forms sequentially, discarding the values of all but the last. Many Lisp control constructs include sequencing implicitly, in which case they are said to provide an "implicit progn." Other sequencing constructs include prog1 and prog2.

For looping, Common Lisp provides the general iteration facility do as well as a variety of special-purpose iteration facilities for iterating or mapping over various data structures.

Common Lisp provides the simple one-way conditionals when and unless, the simple two-way conditional if, and the more general multi-way conditionals such as cond and case. The choice of which form to use in any particular situation is a matter of taste and style.

Constructs for performing non-local exits with various scoping disciplines are provided: block, return, return-from, catch, and throw.

The multiple-value constructs provide an efficient way for a function to return more than one value; see values.

7.1. Constants and Variables

Because some Lisp data objects are used to represent programs, one cannot always notate a constant data object in a program simply by writing the notation for the object unadorned; it would be ambiguous whether a constant object or a program fragment was intended. The quote special form resolves this ambiguity.

There are two kinds of variables in Common Lisp, in effect: ordinary variables and function names. There are some similarities between the two kinds, and in a few cases there are similar functions for dealing with them, for example boundp and fboundp. However, for the most part the two kinds of variables are used for very different purposes: one to name defined functions, macros, and special forms, and the other to name data objects.

X3J13 voted in March 1989 ⟨89⟩ to introduce the concept of a *function-name*, which may be either a symbol or a two-element list whose first element is the symbol setf and whose second element is a symbol. The primary purpose of this is to allow setf expander functions to be CLOS generic functions with user-defined methods. Many places in Common Lisp that used to require a symbol for a function name are changed to allow 2-lists as well; for example, defun is changed so that one may write (defun (setf foo) ...), and the function special form is changed to accept any function-name. See also fdefinition.

By convention, any function named (setf *f*) should return its first argument as its only value, in order to preserve the specification that setf returns its *newvalue*. See setf.

Implementations are free to extend the syntax of function-names to include lists beginning with additional symbols other than setf or lambda.

7.1.1. Reference

The value of an ordinary variable may be obtained simply by writing the name of the variable as a form to be executed. Whether this is treated as the name of a special variable or a lexical variable is determined by the presence or absence of an applicable special declaration; see chapter 9.

The following functions and special forms allow reference to the values of constants and variables in other ways.

quote *object*   [*Special form*]

(quote *x*) simply returns *x*. The *object* is not evaluated and may be any Lisp object whatsoever. This construct allows any Lisp object to be written as a constant value in a program. For example:

```
(setq a 43)
(list a (cons a 3)) ⇒ (43 (43 . 3))
(list ´(quote a) (quote (cons a 3)) ⇒ (a (cons a 3))
```

Since quote forms are so frequently useful but somewhat cumbersome to type, a standard abbreviation is defined for them: any form *f* preceded by a single quote (´) character is assumed to have (quote   ) wrapped around it to make (quote *f*). For example:

```
(setq x ´(the magic quote hack))
```

is normally interpreted by read to mean

```
(setq x (quote (the magic quote hack)))
```

See section 22.1.3.

X3J13 voted in January 1989 ⟨36⟩ to clarify that it is an error to destructively modify any object that appears as a constant in executable code, whether within a quote special form or as a self-evaluating form.

See section 25.1 for a discussion of how quoted constants are treated by the compiler.

X3J13 voted in March 1989 ⟨147⟩ to clarify that eval and compile are not permitted either to copy or to coalesce ("collapse") constants (see eq) appearing in the code they process; the resulting program behavior must refer to objects that are eql to the corresponding objects in the source code. Moreover, the constraints introduced by the votes on issues ⟨34⟩ and ⟨32⟩ on what kinds of objects may appear as constants apply only to compile-file (see section 25.1).

function *fn*   [*Special form*]

The value of function is always the functional interpretation of *fn*; *fn* is interpreted as if it had appeared in the functional position of a function invocation. In particular, if *fn* is a symbol, the functional definition associated with that symbol is returned; see symbol-function. If *fn* is a lambda-expression, then a "lexical closure" is returned, that is, a function that when invoked will execute the body of the lambda-expression in such a way as to observe the rules of lexical scoping properly.

X3J13 voted in June 1988 ⟨90⟩ to specify that the result of a function special form is always of type function. This implies that a form (function *fn*) may be interpreted as (the (function *fn*)).

It is an error to use the function special form on a symbol that does not denote a function in the lexical or global environment in which the special form appears. Specifically, it is an error to use the function special form on a symbol that denotes a macro or special form. Some implementations may choose not to signal this error for performance reasons, but implementations are forbidden to extend the semantics of function in this respect; that is, an implementation is not allowed to define the failure to signal an error to be a "useful" behavior.

X3J13 voted in March 1989 ⟨89⟩ to extend function to accept any function-name (a symbol or a list whose *car* is setf—see section 7.1) as well as lambda-expressions. Thus one may write (function (setf cadr)) to refer to the setf expansion function for cadr.

For example:

```
(defun adder (x) (function (lambda (y) (+ x y))))
```

The result of (adder 3) is a function that will add 3 to its argument:

```
(setq add3 (adder 3))
(funcall add3 5) ⇒ 8
```

This works because function creates a closure of the inner lambda-expression that is able to refer to the value 3 of the variable x even after control has returned from the function adder.

More generally, a lexical closure in effect retains the ability to refer to lexically visible *bindings*, not just values. Consider this code:

```
(defun two-funs (x)
  (list (function (lambda () x))
        (function (lambda (y) (setq x y)))))
(setq funs (two-funs 6))
(funcall (car funs)) ⇒ 6
(funcall (cadr funs) 43) ⇒ 43
(funcall (car funs)) ⇒ 43
```

The function two-funs returns a list of two functions, each of which refers to the *binding* of the variable x created on entry to the function two-funs when it was called with argument 6. This binding has the value 6 initially, but setq can alter a binding. The lexical closure created for the first lambda-expression does not "snapshot" the value 6 for x when the closure is created. The second function can be used to alter the binding (to 43, in the example), and this altered value then becomes accessible to the first function.

In situations where a closure of a lambda-expression over the same set of bindings may be produced more than once, the various resulting closures may or may not be eq, at the discretion of the implementation. For example:

```
(let ((x 5) (funs '()))
  (dotimes (j 10)
    (push #'(lambda (z)
              (if (null z) (setq x 0) (+ x z)))
          funs))
  funs)
```

The result of the above expression is a list of ten closures. Each logically requires only the binding of x. It is the same binding in each case, so the ten closures may or may not be the same identical (eq) object. On the other hand, the result of the expression

```
(let ((funs '()))
  (dotimes (j 10)
    (let ((x 5))
      (push (function (lambda (z)
                        (if (null z) (setq x 0) (+ x z))))
            funs)))
  funs)
```

is also a list of ten closures. However, in this case no two of the closures may be eq, because each closure is over a distinct binding of x, and these bindings can be behaviorally distinguished because of the use of setq.

The question of distinguishable behavior is important; the result of the simpler expression

```
(let ((funs '()))
  (dotimes (j 10)
    (let ((x 5))
      (push (function (lambda (z) (+ x z)))
            funs)))
  funs)
```

is a list of ten closures that *may* be pairwise eq. Although one might think that a different binding of x is involved for each closure (which is indeed the case), the bindings cannot be distinguished because their values are identical and immutable, there being no occurrence of setq on x. A compiler would therefore be justified in transforming the expression to

```
(let ((funs '()))
  (dotimes (j 10)
    (push (function (lambda (z) (+ 5 z)))
          funs))
  funs)
```

where clearly the closures may be the same after all. The general rule, then, is that the implementation is free to have two distinct evaluations of the same function form produce identical (eq) closures if it can prove that the two conceptually distinct resulting closures must in fact be behaviorally identical with respect to invocation. This is merely a permitted optimization; a perfectly valid implementation might simply cause every distinct evaluation of a function form to produce a new closure object not eq to any other.

Frequently a compiler can deduce that a closure in fact does not need to close over any variable bindings. For example, in the code fragment

```
(mapcar (function (lambda (x) (+ x 2))) y)
```

the function (lambda (x) (+ x 2)) contains no references to any outside entity. In this important special case, the same "closure" may be used as the value for all evaluations of the function special form. Indeed, this value need not be a closure object at all; it may be a simple compiled function containing no environment information. This example is simply a special case of the foregoing discussion and is included as a hint to implementors familiar with previous methods of implementing Lisp. The distinction between closures and other kinds of functions is somewhat pointless, actually, as Common Lisp defines no particular representation for closures and no way to distinguish between closures and non-closure functions. All that matters is that the rules of lexical scoping be obeyed.

Since function forms are so frequently useful but somewhat cumbersome to type, a standard abbreviation is defined for them: any form f preceded by #´ (# followed by an apostrophe) is assumed to have (function) wrapped around it to make (function f). For example,

```
(remove-if #'numberp '(1 a b 3))
```

is normally interpreted by read to mean

```
(remove-if (function numberp) '(1 a b 3))
```

See section 22.1.4.

symbol-value *symbol* [*Function*]

symbol-value returns the current value of the dynamic (special) variable named by *symbol*. An error occurs if the symbol has no value; see boundp and makunbound. Note that constant symbols are really variables that cannot be changed, and so symbol-value may be used to get the value of a named constant. In particular, symbol-value of a keyword will return that keyword.

symbol-value cannot access the value of a lexical variable.

This function is particularly useful for implementing interpreters for languages embedded in Lisp. The corresponding assignment primitive is set; alternatively, symbol-value may be used with setf.

symbol-function *symbol* [*Function*]

symbol-function returns the current global function definition named by *symbol*. An error is signalled if the symbol has no function definition; see fboundp. Note that the definition may be a function or may be an object representing a special form or macro. In the latter case, however, it is an error to attempt to invoke the object as a function. If it is desired to process macros, special forms, and functions equally well, as when writing an interpreter, it is best first to test the symbol with macro-function and special-form-p and then to invoke the functional value only if these two tests both yield false.

This function is particularly useful for implementing interpreters for languages embedded in Lisp.

symbol-function cannot access the value of a lexical function name produced by flet or labels; it can access only the global function value.

The global function definition of a symbol may be altered by using setf with symbol-function. Performing this operation causes the symbol to have *only* the specified definition as its global function definition; any previous definition, whether as a macro or as a function, is lost. It is an error to attempt to redefine the name of a special form (see table 5-1).

X3J13 voted in June 1988 ⟨90⟩ to clarify the behavior of symbol-function in the light of the redefinition of the type function.

• It is permissible to call symbol-function on any symbol for which fboundp returns true. Note that fboundp must return true for a symbol naming a macro or a special form.

• If fboundp returns true for a symbol but the symbol denotes a macro or special form, then the value returned by symbol-function is not well-defined but symbol-function will not signal an error.

• When `symbol-function` is used with `setf` the new value must be of type `function`. It is an error to set the `symbol-function` of a symbol to a symbol, a list, or the value returned by `symbol-function` on the name of a macro or a special form.

`fdefinition` *function-name*   [*Function*]

X3J13 voted in March 1989 ⟨89⟩ to add the function `fdefinition` to the language. It is exactly like `symbol-function` except that its argument may be any function-name (a symbol or a list whose *car* is `setf`—see section 7.1); it returns the current global function definition named by the argument *function-name*. One may use `fdefinition` with `setf` to change the current global function definition associated with a function-name.

`boundp` *symbol*   [*Function*]

`boundp` is true if the dynamic (special) variable named by *symbol* has a value; otherwise, it returns `nil`.
    See also `set` and `makunbound`.

`fboundp` *symbol*   [*Function*]

`fboundp` is true if the symbol has a global function definition. Note that `fboundp` is true when the symbol names a special form or macro. `macro-function` and `special-form-p` may be used to test for these cases.
    X3J13 voted in June 1988 ⟨90⟩ to emphasize that, despite the tightening of the definition of the type `function`, `fboundp` must return true when the argument names a special form or macro.
    See also `symbol-function` and `fmakunbound`.
    X3J13 voted in March 1989 ⟨89⟩ to extend `fboundp` to accept any function-name (a symbol or a list whose *car* is `setf`—see section 7.1). Thus one may write `(fboundp ´(setf cadr))` to determine whether a `setf` expansion function has been globally defined for `cadr`.

`special-form-p` *symbol*   [*Function*]

The function `special-form-p` takes a symbol. If the symbol globally names a special form, then a non-`nil` value is returned; otherwise `nil` is returned. A returned non-`nil` value is typically a function of implementation-dependent nature that can be used to interpret (evaluate) the special form.

It is possible for *both* special-form-p and macro-function to be true of a symbol. This is possible because an implementation is permitted to implement any macro also as a special form for speed. On the other hand, the macro definition must be available for use by programs that understand only the standard special forms listed in table 5-1.

7.1.2. Assignment

The following facilities allow the value of a variable (more specifically, the value associated with the current binding of the variable) to be altered. Such alteration is different from establishing a new binding. Constructs for establishing new bindings of variables are described in section 7.5.

setq {*var form*}*   [*Special form*]

The special form (setq *var1 form1 var2 form2* ...) is the "simple variable assignment statement" of Lisp. First *form1* is evaluated and the result is stored in the variable *var1*, then *form2* is evaluated and the result stored in *var2*, and so forth. The variables are represented as symbols, of course, and are interpreted as referring to static or dynamic instances according to the usual rules. Therefore setq may be used for assignment of both lexical and special variables.

   setq returns the last value assigned, that is, the result of the evaluation of its last argument. As a boundary case, the form (setq) is legal and returns nil. There must be an even number of argument forms. For example, in

(setq x (+ 3 2 1) y (cons x nil))

x is set to 6, y is set to (6), and the setq returns (6). Note that the first assignment is performed before the second form is evaluated, allowing that form to use the new value of x.

   See also the description of setf, the Common Lisp "general assignment statement" that is capable of assigning to variables, array elements, and other locations.

   Some programmers choose to avoid setq as a matter of style, always using setf for any kind of structure modification. Others use setq with simple variable names and setf with all other generalized variables.

   X3J13 voted in March 1989 ⟨173⟩ to specify that if any *var* refers not to an ordinary variable but to a binding made by symbol-macrolet, then that *var* is handled as if setf had been used instead of setq.

psetq {*var form*}*   [*Macro*]

A psetq form is just like a setq form, except that the assignments happen in parallel. First all of the forms are evaluated, and then the variables are set to the resulting values. The value of the psetq form is nil. For example:

```
(setq a 1)
(setq b 2)
(psetq a b b a)
a ⇒ 2
b ⇒ 1
```

In this example, the values of a and b are exchanged by using parallel assignment. (If several variables are to be assigned in parallel in the context of a loop, the do construct may be appropriate.)

See also the description of psetf, the Common Lisp "general parallel assignment statement" that is capable of assigning to variables, array elements, and other locations.

X3J13 voted in March 1989 ⟨173⟩ to specify that if any *var* refers not to an ordinary variable but to a binding made by symbol-macrolet, then that *var* is handled as if psetf had been used instead of psetq.

set *symbol value*   [*Function*]

set allows alteration of the value of a dynamic (special) variable. set causes the dynamic variable named by *symbol* to take on *value* as its value.

X3J13 voted in January 1989 ⟨7⟩ to clarify that the *value* may be any Lisp datum whatsoever.

Only the value of the current dynamic binding is altered; if there are no bindings in effect, the most global value is altered. For example,

```
(set (if (eq a b) ´c ´d) ´foo)
```

will either set c to foo or set d to foo, depending on the outcome of the test (eq a b).

set returns *value* as its result.

set cannot alter the value of a local (lexically bound) variable. The special form setq is usually used for altering the values of variables (lexical or dynamic) in programs. set is particularly useful for implementing interpreters for languages embedded in Lisp. See also progv, a construct that performs binding rather than assignment of dynamic variables.

makunbound *symbol*   [*Function*]
fmakunbound *symbol*   [*Function*]

makunbound causes the dynamic (special) variable named by *symbol* to become
unbound (have no value). fmakunbound does the analogous thing for the global
function definition named by *symbol*. For example:

```
(setq a 1)
a ⇒ 1
(makunbound 'a)
a ⇒ causes an error
```

```
(defun foo (x) (+ x 1))
(foo 4) ⇒ 5
(fmakunbound 'foo)
(foo 4) ⇒ causes an error
```

Both functions return *symbol* as the result value.

X3J13 voted in March 1989 ⟨89⟩ to extend fmakunbound to accept any function-
name (a symbol or a list whose *car* is setf—see section 7.1). Thus one may
write (fmakunbound '(setf cadr)) to remove any global definition of a setf
expansion function for cadr.

7.2. Generalized Variables

In Lisp, a variable can remember one piece of data, that is, one Lisp object. The
main operations on a variable are to recover that object and to alter the variable
to remember a new object; these operations are often called *access* and *update*
operations. The concept of variables named by symbols can be generalized to any
storage location that can remember one piece of data, no matter how that location is
named. Examples of such storage locations are the *car* and *cdr* of a cons, elements
of an array, and components of a structure.

For each kind of generalized variable, typically there are two functions that
implement the conceptual *access* and *update* operations. For a variable, merely
mentioning the name of the variable accesses it, while the setq special form can
be used to update it. The function car accesses the *car* of a cons, and the function
rplaca updates it. The function symbol-value accesses the dynamic value of a
variable named by a given symbol, and the function set updates it.

Rather than thinking about two distinct functions that respectively access and
update a storage location somehow deduced from their arguments, we can instead
simply think of a call to the access function with given arguments as a *name* for the

storage location. Thus, just as x may be considered a name for a storage location
(a variable), so (car x) is a name for the *car* of some cons (which is in turn
named by x). Now, rather than having to remember two functions for each kind of
generalized variable (having to remember, for example, that rplaca corresponds
to car), we adopt a uniform syntax for updating storage locations named in this
way, using the setf macro. This is analogous to the way we use the setq special
form to convert the name of a variable (which is also a form that accesses it) into a
form that updates it. The uniformity of this approach is illustrated in the following
table.

Access Function	Update Function	Update Using setf
x	(setq x datum)	(setf x datum)
(car x)	(rplaca x datum)	(setf (car x) datum)
(symbol-value x)	(set x datum)	(setf (symbol-value x) datum)

setf is actually a macro that examines an access form and produces a call to the
corresponding update function.

Given the existence of setf in Common Lisp, it is not necessary to have setq,
rplaca, and set; they are redundant. They are retained in Common Lisp because
of their historical importance in Lisp. However, most other update functions (such
as putprop, the update function for get) have been eliminated from Common Lisp
in the expectation that setf will be uniformly used in their place.

setf {*place newvalue*}*   [*Macro*]

(setf *place newvalue*) takes a form *place* that when evaluated *accesses* a data
object in some location and "inverts" it to produce a corresponding form to *update*
the location. A call to the setf macro therefore expands into an update form that
stores the result of evaluating the form *newvalue* into the place referred to by the
access form.

If more than one *place-newvalue* pair is specified, the pairs are processed sequentially; that is,

(setf *place1 newvalue1*
        place2 newvalue2)
        . . .
        placen newvaluen)

is precisely equivalent to

(progn (setf *place1 newvalue1*)
         (setf *place2 newvalue2*)

```
    ...
  (setf placen newvaluen))
```

For consistency, it is legal to write (setf), which simply returns nil.
  The form *place* may be any one of the following:

- The name of a variable (either lexical or dynamic).

- A function call form whose first element is the name of any one of the following functions:

aref	car	svref	
nth	cdr	get	
elt	caar	getf	symbol-value
rest	cadr	gethash	symbol-function
first	cdar	documentation	symbol-plist
second	cddr	fill-pointer	macro-function
third	caaar	caaaar	cdaaar
fourth	caadr	caaadr	cdaadr
fifth	cadar	caadar	cdadar
sixth	caddr	caaddr	cdaddr
seventh	cdaar	cadaar	cddaar
eighth	cdadr	cadadr	cddadr
ninth	cddar	caddar	cdddar
tenth	cdddr	cadddr	cddddr

X3J13 voted in March 1988 ⟨6⟩ to add row-major-aref to this list.

X3J13 voted in June 1989 ⟨49⟩ to add compiler-macro-function to this list.

X3J13 voted in March 1989 ⟨89⟩ to clarify that this rule applies only when the function name refers to a global function definition and not to a locally defined function or macro.

- A function call form whose first element is the name of a selector function constructed by defstruct.

X3J13 voted in March 1989 ⟨89⟩ to clarify that this rule applies only when the function name refers to a global function definition and not to a locally defined function or macro.

- A function call form whose first element is the name of any one of the following functions, provided that the new value is of the specified type so that it can be used to replace the specified "location" (which is in each of these cases not truly a generalized variable):

Function Name	Required Type
char	string-char
schar	string-char
bit	bit
sbit	bit
subseq	sequence

X3J13 voted in March 1989 ⟨11⟩ to eliminate the type string-char and to redefine string to be the union of one or more specialized vector types, the types of whose elements are subtypes of the type character. In the preceding table, the type string-char should be replaced by some such phrase as "the element-type of the argument vector."

X3J13 voted in March 1989 ⟨89⟩ to clarify that this rule applies only when the function name refers to a global function definition and not to a locally defined function or macro.

In the case of subseq, the replacement value must be a sequence whose elements may be contained by the sequence argument to subseq. (Note that this is not so stringent as to require that the replacement value be a sequence of the same type as the sequence of which the subsequence is specified.) If the length of the replacement value does not equal the length of the subsequence to be replaced, then the shorter length determines the number of elements to be stored, as for the function replace.

· A function call form whose first element is the name of any one of the following functions, provided that the specified argument to that function is in turn a *place* form; in this case the new *place* has stored back into it the result of applying the specified "update" function (which is in each of these cases not a true update function):

Function Name	Argument That Is a *place*	Update Function Used
char-bit	first	set-char-bit
ldb	second	dpb
mask-field	second	deposit-field

X3J13 voted in March 1989 ⟨11⟩ to eliminate char-bit and set-char-bit.

X3J13 voted in March 1989 ⟨89⟩ to clarify that this rule applies only when the function name refers to a global function definition and not to a locally defined function or macro.

- A the type declaration form, in which case the declaration is transferred to the *newvalue* form, and the resulting `setf` form is analyzed. For example,

```
(setf (the integer (cadr x)) (+ y 3))
```

is processed as if it were

```
(setf (cadr x) (the integer (+ y 3)))
```

- A call to `apply` where the first argument form is of the form #´*name*, that is, (`function` *name*), where *name* is the name of a function, calls to which are recognized as places by `setf`. Suppose that the use of `setf` with `apply` looks like this:

```
(setf (apply #´name x1 x2 ... xn rest) x0)
```

The `setf` method for the function *name* must be such that

```
(setf (name z1 z2 ... zm) z0)
```

expands into a store form

$$(\mathit{storefn}\ zi_1\ zi_2\ \ldots\ zi_k\ zm)$$

That is, it must expand into a function call such that all arguments but the last may be any permutation or subset of the new value *z0* and the arguments of the access form, but the *last* argument of the storing call must be the same as the last argument of the access call. See `define-setf-method` for more details on accessing and storing forms.

Given this, the `setf-of-apply` form shown above expands into

$$(\texttt{apply}\ \#´\mathit{storefn}\ xi_1\ xi_2\ \ldots\ xi_k\ \mathit{rest})$$

As an example, suppose that the variable `indexes` contains a list of subscripts for a multidimensional array *foo* whose rank is not known until run time. One may access the indicated element of the array by writing

```
(apply #´aref foo indexes)
```

and one may alter the value of the indicated element to that of `newvalue` by writing

```
(setf (apply #´aref foo indexes) newvalue)
```

X3J13 voted in March 1989 ⟨89⟩ to clarify that this rule applies only when the function name `apply` refers to the global function definition and not to a locally defined function or macro named `apply`.

- A macro call, in which case `setf` expands the macro call and then analyzes the resulting form.

X3J13 voted in March 1989 ⟨89⟩ to clarify that this step uses `macroexpand-1`, not `macroexpand`. This allows the chance to apply any of the rules preceding this one to any of the intermediate expansions.

- Any form for which a `defsetf` or `define-setf-method` declaration has been made.

X3J13 voted in March 1989 ⟨89⟩ to clarify that this rule applies only when the function name in the form refers to a global function definition and not to a locally defined function or macro.

X3J13 voted in March 1989 ⟨89⟩ to add one more rule to the preceding list, coming after all those listed above:

- Any other list whose first element is a symbol (call it f). In this case, the call to `setf` expands into a call to the function named by the list (`setf` f) (see section 7.1). The first argument is the new value and the remaining arguments are the values of the remaining elements of *place*. This expansion occurs regardless of whether either f or (`setf` f) is defined as a function locally, globally, or not at all. For example,

```
(setf (f arg1 arg2 ...) newvalue)
```

expands into a form with the same effect and value as

```
(let ((#:temp1 arg1)        ;Force correct order of evaluation
      (#:temp2 arg2)
      ...
      (#:temp0 newvalue))
  (funcall (function (setf f))
           #:temp0
           #:temp1
           #:temp2 ...))
```

By convention, any function named (`setf` f) should return its first argument as its only value, in order to preserve the specification that `setf` returns its *newvalue*.

X3J13 voted in March 1989 ⟨173⟩ to add this case as well:

- A variable reference that refers to a symbol macro definition made by `symbol-macrolet`, in which case `setf` expands the reference and then analyzes the resulting form.

setf carefully arranges to preserve the usual left-to-right order in which the various subforms are evaluated. On the other hand, the exact expansion for any particular form is not guaranteed and may even be implementation-dependent; all that is guaranteed is that the expansion of a setf form will be an update form that works for that particular implementation, and that the left-to-right evaluation of subforms is preserved.

The ultimate result of evaluating a setf form is the value of *newvalue*. Therefore (setf (car x) y) does not expand into precisely (rplaca x y), but into something more like

```
(let ((G1 x) (G2 y)) (rplaca G1 G2) G2)
```

the precise expansion being implementation-dependent.

The user can define new setf expansions by using defsetf.

X3J13 voted in June 1989 ⟨159⟩ to extend the specification of setf to allow a *place* whose setf method has more than one store variable (see define-setf-method). In such a case as many values are accepted from the *newvalue* form as there are store variables; extra values are ignored and missing values default to nil, as is usual in situations involving multiple values.

A proposal was submitted to X3J13 in September 1989 to add a setf method for values so that one could in fact write, for example,

```
(setf (values quotient remainder)
      (truncate linewidth tabstop))
```

but unless this proposal is accepted users will have to define a setf method for values themselves (not a difficult task).

---

psetf {*place newvalue*}*   [*Macro*]

psetf is like setf except that if more than one *place-newvalue* pair is specified, then the assignments of new values to places are done in parallel. More precisely, all subforms that are to be evaluated are evaluated from left to right; after all evaluations have been performed, all of the assignments are performed in an unpredictable order. (The unpredictability matters only if more than one *place* form refers to the same place.) psetf always returns nil.

X3J13 voted in June 1989 ⟨159⟩ to extend the specification of psetf to allow a *place* whose setf method has more than one store variable (see define-setf-method). In such a case as many values are accepted from the *newvalue* form as there are store variables; extra values are ignored and missing values default to nil, as is usual in situations involving multiple values.

shiftf {*place*}⁺ *newvalue*   [*Macro*]

Each *place* form may be any form acceptable as a generalized variable to setf.
In the form (shiftf *place1 place2* ... *placen newvalue*), the values in *place1*
through *placen* are accessed and saved, and *newvalue* is evaluated, for a total of
$n + 1$ values in all. Values 2 through $n + 1$ are then stored into *place1* through
placen, and value 1 (the original value of *place1*) is returned. It is as if all the
places form a shift register; the *newvalue* is shifted in from the right, all values
shift over to the left one place, and the value shifted out of *place1* is returned. For
example:

(setq x (list 'a 'b 'c)) ⇒ (a b c)

(shiftf (cadr x) 'z) ⇒ b
     and now x ⇒ (a z c)

(shiftf (cadr x) (cddr x) 'q) ⇒ z
     and now x ⇒ (a (c) . q)

The effect of (shiftf *place1 place2* ... *placen newvalue*) is equivalent to

(let ((*var1 place1*)
       (*var2 place2*)
       ...
       (*varn placen*))
   (setf *place1 var2*)
   (setf *place2 var3*)
   ...
   (setf *placen newvalue*)
   var1)

except that the latter would evaluate any subforms of each *place* twice, whereas
shiftf takes care to evaluate them only once. For example:

(setq n 0)
(setq x '(a b c d))
(shiftf (nth (setq n (+ n 1)) x) 'z) ⇒ b
     and now x ⇒ (a z c d)

but

(setq n 0)
(setq x '(a b c d))

```
(prog1 (nth (setq n (+ n 1)) x)
       (setf (nth (setq n (+ n 1)) x) 'z)) ⇒ b
   and now x ⇒ (a b z d)
```

Moreover, for certain *place* forms `shiftf` may be significantly more efficient than the `prog1` version.

X3J13 voted in June 1989 ⟨159⟩ to extend the specification of `shiftf` to allow a *place* whose `setf` method has more than one store variable (see `define-setf-method`). In such a case as many values are accepted from the *newvalue* form as there are store variables; extra values are ignored and missing values default to `nil`, as is usual in situations involving multiple values.

Rationale: `shiftf` and `rotatef` have been included in Common Lisp as generalizations of two-argument versions formerly called `swapf` and `exchf`. The two-argument versions have been found to be very useful, but the names were easily confused. The generalization to many argument forms and the change of names were both inspired by the work of Suzuki [47], which indicates that use of these primitives can make certain complex pointer-manipulation programs clearer and easier to prove correct.

`rotatef` {*place*}*   [*Macro*]

Each *place* form may be any form acceptable as a generalized variable to `setf`. In the form (`rotatef` *place1 place2* ... *placen*), the values in *place1* through *placen* are accessed and saved. Values 2 through *n* and value 1 are then stored into *place1* through *placen*. It is as if all the places form an end-around shift register that is rotated one place to the left, with the value of *place1* being shifted around the end to *placen*. Note that (`rotatef` *place1 place2*) exchanges the contents of *place1* and *place2*.

The effect of (`rotatef` *place1 place2* ... *placen*) is roughly equivalent to

```
(psetf place1 place2
       place2 place3
         ...
       placen place1)
```

except that the latter would evaluate any subforms of each *place* twice, whereas `rotatef` takes care to evaluate them only once. Moreover, for certain *place* forms `rotatef` may be significantly more efficient.

`rotatef` always returns `nil`.

X3J13 voted in June 1989 ⟨159⟩ to extend the specification of `rotatef` to allow a *place* whose `setf` method has more than one store variable (see define-setf-method). In such a case as many values are accepted from the *newvalue* form as there are store variables; extra values are ignored and missing values default to nil, as is usual in situations involving multiple values.

Other macros that manipulate generalized variables include getf, remf, incf, decf, push, pop, assert, ctypecase, and ccase.

Macros that manipulate generalized variables must guarantee the "obvious" semantics: subforms of generalized-variable references are evaluated exactly as many times as they appear in the source program, and they are evaluated in exactly the same order as they appear in the source program.

In generalized-variable references such as shiftf, incf, push, and setf of ldb, the generalized variables are both read and written in the same reference. Preserving the source program order of evaluation and the number of evaluations is particularly important.

As an example of these semantic rules, in the generalized-variable reference (setf *reference value*) the *value* form must be evaluated *after* all the subforms of the reference because the *value* form appears to the right of them.

The expansion of these macros must consist of code that follows these rules or has the same effect as such code. This is accomplished by introducing temporary variables bound to the subforms of the reference. As an optimization in the implementation, temporary variables may be eliminated whenever it can be proved that removing them has no effect on the semantics of the program. For example, a constant need never be saved in a temporary variable. A variable, or for that matter any form that does not have side effects, need not be saved in a temporary variable if it can be proved that its value will not change within the scope of the generalized-variable reference.

Common Lisp provides built-in facilities to take care of these semantic complications and optimizations. Since the required semantics can be guaranteed by these facilities, the user does not have to worry about writing correct code for them, especially in complex cases. Even experts can become confused and make mistakes while writing this sort of code.

X3J13 voted in March 1988 ⟨146⟩ to clarify the preceding discussion about the order of evaluation of subforms in calls to setf and related macros. The general intent is clear: evaluation proceeds from left to right whenever possible. However, the left-to-right rule does not remove the obligation on writers of macros and define-setf-method to work to ensure left-to-right order of evaluation.

Let it be emphasized that, in the following discussion, a *form* is something whose syntactic use is such that it will be evaluated. A *subform* means a form that is nested inside another form, not merely any Lisp object nested inside a form regardless of syntactic context.

The evaluation ordering of subforms within a generalized variable reference is determined by the order specified by the second value returned by get-setf-method. For all predefined generalized variable references (getf, 1db), this order of evaluation is exactly left-to-right. When a generalized variable reference is derived from a macro expansion, this rule is applied *after* the macro is expanded to find the appropriate generalized variable reference.

This is intended to make it clear that if the user writes a defmacro or define-setf-method macro that doesn't preserve left-to-right evaluation order, the order specified in the user's code holds. For example, given

```
(defmacro wrong-order (x y) `(getf ,y ,x))
```

then

```
(push value (wrong-order place1 place2))
```

will evaluate *place2* first and then *place1* because that is the order they are evaluated in the macro expansion.

For the macros that manipulate generalized variables (push, pushnew, getf, remf, incf, decf, shiftf, rotatef, psetf, setf, pop, and those defined with define-modify-macro) the subforms of the macro call are evaluated exactly once in left-to-right order, with the subforms of the generalized variable references evaluated in the order specified above.

Each of push, pushnew, getf, remf, incf, decf, shiftf, rotatef, psetf, and pop evaluates all subforms before modifying any of the generalized variable locations. Moreover, setf itself, in the case when a call on it has more than two arguments, performs its operation on each pair in sequence. That is, in

```
(setf place1 value1 place2 value2 ...)
```

the subforms of *place1* and *value1* are evaluated, the location specified by *place1* is modified to contain the value returned by *value1*, and then the rest of the setf form is processed in a like manner.

For the macros check-type, ctypecase, and ccase, subforms of the generalized variable reference are evaluated once per test of a generalized variable, but they may be evaluated again if the type check fails (in the case of check-type) or if none of the cases holds (in ctypecase or ccase).

For the macro assert, the order of evaluation of the generalized variable references is not specified.

Another reason for building in these functions is that the appropriate optimizations will differ from implementation to implementation. In some implementations most of the optimization is performed by the compiler, while in others a simpler compiler is used and most of the optimization is performed in the macros. The cost of binding a temporary variable relative to the cost of other Lisp operations may differ greatly between one implementation and another, and some implementations may find it best never to remove temporary variables except in the simplest cases.

A good example of the issues involved can be seen in the following generalized-variable reference:

```
(incf (ldb byte-field variable))
```

This ought to expand into something like

```
(setq variable
      (dpb (1+ (ldb byte-field variable))
           byte-field
           variable))
```

In this expansion example we have ignored the further complexity of returning the correct value, which is the incremented byte, not the new value of variable. Note that the variable byte-field is evaluated twice, and the variable variable is referred to three times: once as the location in which to store a value, and twice during the computation of that value.

Now consider this expression:

```
(incf (ldb (aref byte-fields (incf i))
           (aref (determine-words-array) i)))
```

It ought to expand into something like this:

```
(let ((temp1 (aref byte-fields (incf i)))
      (temp2 (determine-words-array)))
  (setf (aref temp2 i)
        (dpb (1+ (ldb temp1 (aref temp2 i)))
             temp1
             (aref temp2 i))))
```

Again we have ignored the complexity of returning the correct value. What is important here is that the expressions (incf i) and (determine-words-array) must not be duplicated because each may have a side effect or be affected by side effects.

X3J13 voted in January 1989 ⟨160⟩ to specify more precisely the order of evaluation of subforms when setf is used with an access function that itself takes a *place* as an argument, for example, ldb, mask-field, and getf. (The vote also discussed the function char-bit, but another vote ⟨11⟩ removed that function from the language.) The `setf` methods for such accessors produce expansions that effectively require explicit calls to `get-setf-method`.

The code produced as the macro expansion of a `setf` form that itself admits a generalized variable as an argument must essentially do the following major steps:

- It evaluates the value-producing subforms, in left-to-right order, and binds the temporary variables to them; this is called *binding the temporaries.*

- It reads the value from the generalized variable, using the supplied accessing form, to get the old value; this is called *doing the access.* Note that this is done after all the evaluations of the preceding step, including any side effects they may have.

- It binds the store variable to a new value, and then installs this new value into the generalized variable using the supplied storing form; this is called *doing the store.*

Doing the access for a generalized variable reference is not part of the series of evaluations that must be done in left-to-right order.

The place-specifier forms `ldb`, `mask-field`, and `getf` admit (other) *place* specifiers as arguments. During the `setf` expansion of these forms, it is necessary to call `get-setf-method` to determine how the inner, nested generalized variable must be treated.

In a form such as

(`setf` (`ldb` *byte-spec place-form*) *newvalue-form*)

the place referred to by the *place-form* must always be both accessed and updated; note that the update is to the generalized variable specified by *place-form*, not to any object of type `integer`.

Thus this call to `setf` should generate code to do the following:

- Evaluate *byte-spec* and bind into a temporary

- Bind the temporaries for *place-form*

- Evaluate *newvalue-form* and bind into the store variable

- Do the access to *place-form*

- Do the store into *place-form* with the given bit-field of the accessed integer replaced with the value in the store variable

If the evaluation of *newvalue-form* alters what is found in the given *place*—such as setting a different bit-field of the integer—then the change of the bit-field denoted by *byte-spec* will be to that altered integer, because the access step must be done after the *newvalue-form* evaluation. Nevertheless, the evaluations required for binding the temporaries are done before the evaluation of the *newvalue-form*, thereby preserving the required left-to-right evaluation order.

The treatment of `mask-field` is similar to that of `ldb`.

In a form such as:

```
(setf (getf place-form ind-form) newvalue-form)
```

the place referred to by the *place-form* must always be both accessed and updated; note that the update is to the generalized variable specified by *place-form*, not necessarily to the particular list which is the property list in question.

Thus this call to `setf` should generate code to do the following:

- Bind the temporaries for *place-form*

- Evaluate *ind-form* and bind into a temporary

- Evaluate the *newvalue-form* and bind into the store variable

- Do the access to *place-form*

- Do the store into *place-form* with a possibly new property list obtained by combining the results of the evaluations and the access

If the evaluation of *newvalue-form* alters what is found in the given *place*—such as setting a different named property in the list—then the change of the property denoted by *ind-form* will be to that altered list, because the access step is done after the *newvalue-form* evaluation. Nevertheless, the evaluations required for binding the temporaries are done before the evaluation of the *newvalue-form*, thereby preserving the required left-to-right evaluation order.

Note that the phrase "possibly new property list" treats the implementation of property lists as a "black box"; it can mean that the former property list is somehow destructively re-used, or it can mean partial or full copying of it. A side effect may or may not occur; therefore `setf` must proceed as if the resultant property list were a different copy needing to be stored back into the generalized variable.

The Common Lisp facilities provided to deal with these semantic issues include:

- Built-in macros such as `setf` and `push` that follow the semantic rules.

- The `define-modify-macro` macro, which allows new generalized-variable manipulating macros (of a certain restricted kind) to be defined easily. It takes care of the semantic rules automatically.

- The `defsetf` macro, which allows new types of generalized-variable references to be defined easily. It takes care of the semantic rules automatically.

- The `define-setf-method` macro and the `get-setf-method` function, which provide access to the internal mechanisms when it is necessary to define a complicated new type of generalized-variable reference or generalized-variable-manipulating macro.

Also important are the changes that allow lexical environments to be used in appropriate ways in `setf` methods.

`define-modify-macro` *name lambda-list function* [*doc-string*]　　　　[*Macro*]

This macro defines a read-modify-write macro named *name*. An example of such a macro is `incf`. The first subform of the macro will be a generalized-variable reference. The *function* is literally the function to apply to the old contents of the generalized-variable to get the new contents; it is not evaluated. *lambda-list* describes the remaining arguments for the *function*; these arguments come from the remaining subforms of the macro after the generalized-variable reference. *lambda-list* may contain &optional and &rest markers. (The &key marker is not permitted here; &rest suffices for the purposes of `define-modify-macro`.) *doc-string* is documentation for the macro *name* being defined.

The expansion of a `define-modify-macro` is equivalent to the following, except that it generates code that follows the semantic rules outlined above.

```
(defmacro name (reference . lambda-list)
  doc-string
  `(setf ,reference
         (function ,reference ,arg1 ,arg2 ...)))
```

where *arg1*, *arg2*, ..., are the parameters appearing in *lambda-list*; appropriate provision is made for a &rest parameter.

As an example, `incf` could have been defined by:

```
(define-modify-macro incf (&optional (delta 1)) +)
```

An example of a possibly useful macro not predefined in Common Lisp is

```
(define-modify-macro unionf (other-set &rest keywords) union)
```

X3J13 voted in March 1988 ⟨96⟩ to specify that `define-modify-macro` creates macros that take &environment arguments and perform the equivalent of correctly passing such lexical environments to `get-setf-method` in order to correctly maintain lexical references.

defsetf *access-fn* {*update-fn* [*doc-string*] | *[Macro]*
         lambda-list (*store-variable*)
         ⟦ {*declaration*}* | *doc-string* ⟧ {*form*}* }

This defines how to `setf` a generalized-variable reference of the form (*access-fn*
...). The value of a generalized-variable reference can always be obtained simply
by evaluating it, so *access-fn* should be the name of a function or a macro.

The user of `defsetf` provides a description of how to store into the generalized-
variable reference and return the value that was stored (because `setf` is defined
to return this value). The implementation of `defsetf` takes care of ensuring that
subforms of the reference are evaluated exactly once and in the proper left-to-
right order. In order to do this, `defsetf` requires that *access-fn* be a function
or a macro that evaluates its arguments, behaving like a function. Furthermore,
a `setf` of a call on *access-fn* will also evaluate all of *access-fn*'s arguments; it
cannot treat any of them specially. This means that `defsetf` cannot be used to
describe how to store into a generalized variable that is a byte, such as (`ldb`
`field reference`). To handle situations that do not fit the restrictions imposed
by `defsetf`, use `define-setf-method`, which gives the user additional control at
the cost of increased complexity.

A `defsetf` declaration may take one of two forms. The simple form is

(`defsetf` *access-fn* *update-fn* [*doc-string*])

The *update-fn* must name a function (or macro) that takes one more argument than
access-fn takes. When `setf` is given a *place* that is a call on *access-fn*, it expands
into a call on *update-fn* that is given all the arguments to *access-fn* and also, as its
last argument, the new value (which must be returned by *update-fn* as its value).
For example, the effect of

(`defsetf` `symbol-value` `set`)

is built into the Common Lisp system. This causes the expansion

(`setf` (`symbol-value` `foo`) `fu`) → (`set` `foo` `fu`)

for example. Note that

(`defsetf` `car` `rplaca`)

would be incorrect because `rplaca` does not return its last argument.

The complex form of `defsetf` looks like

(`defsetf` *access-fn* *lambda-list* (*store-variable*) . *body*) and resembles defmacro. The *body* must compute the expansion of a setf of a call on *access-fn*.

The *lambda-list* describes the arguments of *access-fn*. &optional, &rest, and &key markers are permitted in *lambda-list*. Optional arguments may have defaults and "supplied-p" flags. The *store-variable* describes the value to be stored into the generalized-variable reference.

Rationale: The *store-variable* is enclosed in parentheses to provide for an extension to multiple store variables that would receive multiple values from the second subform of setf. The rules given below for coding setf methods discuss the proper handling of multiple store variables to allow for the possibility that this extension may be incorporated into Common Lisp in the future.

The *body* forms can be written as if the variables in the *lambda-list* were bound to subforms of the call on *access-fn* and the *store-variable* were bound to the second subform of setf. However, this is not actually the case. During the evaluation of the *body* forms, these variables are bound to names of temporary variables, generated as if by gensym or gentemp, that will be bound by the expansion of setf to the values of those subforms. This binding permits the *body* forms to be written without regard for order-of-evaluation issues. defsetf arranges for the temporary variables to be optimized out of the final result in cases where that is possible. In other words, an attempt is made by defsetf to generate the best code possible in a particular implementation.

Note that the code generated by the *body* forms must include provision for returning the correct value (the value of *store-variable*). This is handled by the *body* forms rather than by defsetf because in many cases this value can be returned at no extra cost, by calling a function that simultaneously stores into the generalized variable and returns the correct value.

An example of the use of the complex form of defsetf:

```
(defsetf subseq (sequence start &optional end) (new-sequence)
  `(progn (replace ,sequence ,new-sequence
                   :start1 ,start :end1 ,end)
          ,new-sequence))
```

X3J13 voted in March 1988 ⟨78⟩ to specify that the body of the expander function defined by the complex form of defsetf is implicitly enclosed in a block construct whose name is the same as the *name* of the *access-fn*. Therefore return-from may be used to exit from the function.

X3J13 voted in March 1989 ⟨50⟩ to clarify that, while defining forms normally appear at top level, it is meaningful to place them in non-top-level contexts; the complex form of defsetf must define the expander function within the enclosing lexical environment, not within the global environment.

The underlying theory by which setf and related macros arrange to conform to the semantic rules given above is that from any generalized-variable reference one may derive its "setf method," which describes how to store into that reference and which subforms of it are evaluated.

Compatibility note: To avoid confusion, it should be noted that the use of the word "method" here in connection with setf has nothing to do with its use in Lisp Machine Lisp in connection with message-passing and the Lisp Machine Lisp "flavor system."

And of course it also has nothing to do with the methods in the Common Lisp Object System ⟨12⟩.

Given knowledge of the subforms of the reference, it is possible to avoid evaluating them multiple times or in the wrong order. A setf method for a given access form can be expressed as five values:

- A list of *temporary variables*

- A list of *value forms* (subforms of the given form) to whose values the temporary variables are to be bound

- A second list of temporary variables, called *store variables*

- A *storing form*

- An *accessing form*

The temporary variables will be bound to the values of the value forms as if by let*; that is, the value forms will be evaluated in the order given and may refer to the values of earlier value forms by using the corresponding variables.

The store variables are to be bound to the values of the *newvalue* form, that is, the values to be stored into the generalized variable. In almost all cases only a single value is to be stored, and there is only one store variable.

The storing form and the accessing form may contain references to the temporary variables (and also, in the case of the storing form, to the store variables). The accessing form returns the value of the generalized variable. The storing form modifies the value of the generalized variable and guarantees to return the values of the store variables as its values; these are the correct values for setf to return. (Again, in most cases there is a single store variable and thus a single value to be returned.) The value returned by the accessing form is, of course, affected by execution of the storing form, but either of these forms may be evaluated any number of times and therefore should be free of side effects (other than the storing action of the storing form).

The temporary variables and the store variables are generated names, as if by gensym or gentemp, so that there is never any problem of name clashes among them, or between them and other variables in the program. This is necessary to make the special forms that do more than one setf in parallel work properly; these are psetf, shiftf, and rotatef. Computation of the setf method must always create new variable names; it may not return the same ones every time.

Some examples of setf methods for particular forms:

- For a variable x:

```
()
()
(g0001)
(setq x g0001)
x
```

- For (car *exp*):

```
(g0002)
(exp)
(g0003)
(progn (rplaca g0002 g0003) g0003)
(car g0002)
```

- For (subseq *seq s e*):

```
(g0004 g0005 g0006)
(seq s e)
(g0007)
(progn (replace g0004 g0007 :start1 g0005 :end1 g0006)
       g0007)
(subseq g0004 g0005 g0006)
```

---

define-setf-method *access-fn lambda-list*   [*Macro*]
        ⟦ {*declaration*}* | *doc-string* ⟧ {*form*}*

This defines how to setf a generalized-variable reference that is of the form (*access-fn*...). The value of a generalized-variable reference can always be obtained simply by evaluating it, so *access-fn* should be the name of a function or a macro.

The *lambda-list* describes the subforms of the generalized-variable reference, as with defmacro. The result of evaluating the *forms* in the body must be five values representing the setf method, as described above. Note that define-setf-method differs from the complex form of defsetf in that while the body is being executed the variables in *lambda-list* are bound to parts of the generalized-variable reference, not to temporary variables that will be bound to the values of such parts. In addition, define-setf-method does not have defsetf's restriction that *access-fn* must be a function or a function-like macro; an arbitrary defmacro destructuring pattern is permitted in *lambda-list*.

By definition there are no good small examples of define-setf-method because the easy cases can all be handled by defsetf. A typical use is to define the setf method for ldb:

```
;;; SETF method for the form (LDB bytespec int).
;;; Recall that the int form must itself be suitable for SETF.
(define-setf-method ldb (bytespec int)
  (multiple-value-bind (temps vals stores
                        store-form access-form)
      (get-setf-method int)          ;Get SETF method for int
    (let ((btemp (gensym))           ;Temp var for byte specifier
          (store (gensym))           ;Temp var for byte to store
          (stemp (first stores)))    ;Temp var for int to store
      ;; Return the SETF method for LDB as five values.
      (values (cons btemp temps)     ;Temporary variables
              (cons bytespec vals)   ;Value forms
              (list store)           ;Store variables
              `(let ((,stemp (dpb ,store ,btemp ,access-form)))
                 ,store-form
                 ,store)             ;Storing form
              `(ldb ,btemp ,access-form)   ;Accessing form
              ))))
```

X3J13 voted in March 1988 ⟨96⟩ to specify that the &environment lambda-list keyword may appear in the *lambda-list* in the same manner as for defmacro in order to obtain the lexical environment of the call to the setf macro. The preceding example should be modified to take advantage of this new feature. The setf method must accept an &environment parameter, which will receive the lexical environment of the call to setf; this environment must then be given to get-setf-method in order that it may correctly use any locally bound setf method that might be applicable to the *place* form that appears as the second argument to ldb in the call to setf.

```
;;; SETF method for the form (LDB bytespec int).
;;; Recall that the int form must itself be suitable for SETF.
;;; Note the use of an &environment parameter to receive the
;;; lexical environment of the call for use with GET-SETF-METHOD.
(define-setf-method ldb (bytespec int &environment env)
  (multiple-value-bind (temps vals stores
                        store-form access-form)
      (get-setf-method int env)      ;Get SETF method for int
    (let ((btemp (gensym))           ;Temp var for byte specifier
          (store (gensym))           ;Temp var for byte to store
          (stemp (first stores)))    ;Temp var for int to store
      ;; Return the SETF method for LDB as five values.
      (values (cons btemp temps)     ;Temporary variables
              (cons bytespec vals)   ;Value forms
              (list store)           ;Store variables
              `(let ((,stemp (dpb ,store ,btemp ,access-form)))
                 ,store-form
                 ,store)             ;Storing form
              `(ldb ,btemp ,access-form)   ;Accessing form
              ))))
```

X3J13 voted in March 1988 ⟨78⟩ to specify that the body of the expander function defined by define-setf-method is implicitly enclosed in a block construct whose name is the same as the *name* of the *access-fn*. Therefore return-from may be used to exit from the function.

X3J13 voted in March 1989 ⟨50⟩ to clarify that, while defining forms normally appear at top level, it is meaningful to place them in non-top-level contexts; define-setf-method must define the expander function within the enclosing lexical environment, not within the global environment.

get-setf-method *form*   [*Function*]

get-setf-method returns five values constituting the setf method for *form*. The *form* must be a generalized-variable reference. get-setf-method takes care of error-checking and macro expansion and guarantees to return exactly one store variable.

As an example, an extremely simplified version of setf, allowing no more and no fewer than two subforms, containing no optimization to remove unnecessary variables, and not allowing storing of multiple values, could be defined by:

```
(defmacro setf (reference value)
  (multiple-value-bind (vars vals stores store-form access-form)
      (get-setf-method reference)
    (declare (ignore access-form))
    `(let* ,(mapcar #'list
                    (append vars stores)
                    (append vals (list value)))
       ,store-form)))
```

X3J13 voted in March 1988 ⟨96⟩ to add an optional environment argument to get-setf-method. The revised definition and example are as follows.

get-setf-method *form* &optional *env*   [*Function*]

get-setf-method returns five values constituting the setf method for *form*. The *form* must be a generalized-variable reference. The *env* must be an environment of the sort obtained through the &environment lambda-list keyword; if *env* is nil or omitted, the null lexical environment is assumed. get-setf-method takes care of error checking and macro expansion and guarantees to return exactly one store variable.

As an example, an extremely simplified version of setf, allowing no more and no fewer than two subforms, containing no optimization to remove unnecessary variables, and not allowing storing of multiple values, could be defined by:

```
(defmacro setf (reference value &environment env)
  (multiple-value-bind (vars vals stores store-form access-form)
      (get-setf-method reference env)        ;Note use of environment
    (declare (ignore access-form))
    `(let* ,(mapcar #'list
                    (append vars stores)
                    (append vals (list value)))
       ,store-form)))
```

get-setf-method-multiple-value *form*   [*Function*]

get-setf-method-multiple-value returns five values constituting the setf method for *form*. The *form* must be a generalized-variable reference. This is the same as get-setf-method except that it does not check the number of store variables; use this in cases that allow storing multiple values into a generalized variable. There are no such cases in standard Common Lisp, but this function is provided to allow for possible extensions.

X3J13 voted in March 1988 ⟨96⟩ to add an optional environment argument to get-setf-method. The revised definition is as follows.

get-setf-method-multiple-value *form* &optional *env*   [*Function*]

get-setf-method-multiple-value returns five values constituting the setf method for *form*. The *form* must be a generalized-variable reference. The *env* must be an environment of the sort obtained through the &environment lambda-list keyword; if *env* is nil or omitted, the null lexical environment is assumed.

This is the same as get-setf-method except that it does not check the number of store variables; use this in cases that allow storing multiple values into a generalized variable. There are no such cases in standard Common Lisp, but this function is provided to allow for possible extensions.

X3J13 voted in March 1988 ⟨96⟩ to clarify that a setf method for a functional name is applicable only when the global binding of that name is lexically visible. If such a name has a local binding introduced by flet, labels, or macrolet, then global definitions of setf methods for that name do not apply and are not visible. All of the standard Common Lisp macros that modify a setf *place* (for example, incf, decf, pop, and rotatef) obey this convention.

7.3. Function Invocation

The most primitive form for function invocation in Lisp of course has no name; any list that has no other interpretation as a macro call or special form is taken to be a function call. Other constructs are provided for less common but nevertheless frequently useful situations.

apply *function arg* &rest *more-args*   [*Function*]

This applies *function* to a list of arguments.

The *function* may be a compiled-code object, or a lambda-expression, or a symbol; in the latter case the global functional value of that symbol is used (but it is illegal for the symbol to be the name of a macro or special form).

X3J13 voted in June 1988 ⟨90⟩ to allow the *function* to be only of type symbol or function; a lambda-expression is no longer acceptable as a functional argument. One must use the function special form or the abbreviation #´ before a lambda-expression that appears as an explicit argument form.

The arguments for the *function* consist of the last argument to apply appended to the end of a list of all the other arguments to apply but the *function* itself; it is as if all the arguments to apply except the *function* were given to list* to create the argument list. For example:

```
(setq f '+) (apply f '(1 2)) ⇒ 3
(setq f #'-) (apply f '(1 2)) ⇒ -1
(apply #'max 3 5 '(2 7 3)) ⇒ 7
(apply 'cons '((+ 2 3) 4)) ⇒
        ((+ 2 3) . 4) not (5 . 4)
(apply #'+ '()) ⇒ 0
```

Note that if the function takes keyword arguments, the keywords as well as the corresponding values must appear in the argument list:

```
(apply #'(lambda (&key a b) (list a b)) '(:b 3)) ⇒ (nil 3)
```

This can be very useful in conjunction with the &allow-other-keys feature:

```
(defun foo (size &rest keys &key double &allow-other-keys)
   (let ((v (apply #'make-array size :allow-other-keys t keys)))
      (if double (concatenate (type-of v) v v) v)))

(foo 4 :initial-contents '(a b c d) :double t)
   ⇒ #(a b c d a b c d)
```

funcall *fn* &rest *arguments*   [*Function*]

(funcall *fn* *a1* *a2* ... *an*) applies the function *fn* to the arguments *a1, a2, ..., an*. The *fn* may not be a special form or a macro; this would not be meaningful.

X3J13 voted in June 1988 ⟨90⟩ to allow the *fn* to be only of type symbol or function; a lambda-expression is no longer acceptable as a functional argument. One must use the function special form or the abbreviation #' before a lambda-expression that appears as an explicit argument form.

For example:

```
(cons 1 2) ⇒ (1 . 2)
(setq cons (symbol-function '+))
(funcall cons 1 2) ⇒ 3
```

The difference between funcall and an ordinary function call is that the function is obtained by ordinary Lisp evaluation rather than by the special interpretation of the function position that normally occurs.

Compatibility note: The Common Lisp function `funcall` corresponds roughly to the Interlisp primitive `apply*`.

`call-arguments-limit` *[Constant]*

The value of `call-arguments-limit` is a positive integer that is the upper exclusive bound on the number of arguments that may be passed to a function. This bound depends on the implementation but will not be smaller than 50. (Implementors are encouraged to make this limit as large as practicable without sacrificing performance.) The value of `call-arguments-limit` must be at least as great as that of `lambda-parameters-limit`. See also `multiple-values-limit`.

7.4. Simple Sequencing

Each of the constructs in this section simply evaluates all the argument forms in order. They differ only in what results are returned.

`progn` {*form*}* *[Special form]*

The `progn` construct takes a number of forms and evaluates them sequentially, in order, from left to right. The values of all the forms but the last are discarded; whatever the last form returns is returned by the `progn` form. One says that all the forms but the last are evaluated for *effect*, because their execution is useful only for the side effects caused, but the last form is executed for *value*.

  `progn` is the primitive control structure construct for "compound statements," such as **begin**-**end** blocks in Algol-like languages. Many Lisp constructs are "implicit `progn`" forms: as part of their syntax each allows many forms to be written that are to be evaluated sequentially, discarding the results of all forms but the last and returning the results of the last form.

  If the last form of the `progn` returns multiple values, then those multiple values are returned by the `progn` form. If there are no forms for the `progn`, then the result is `nil`. These rules generally hold for implicit `progn` forms as well.

`prog1` *first* {*form*}* *[Macro]*

`prog1` is similar to `progn`, but it returns the value of its *first* form. All the argument forms are executed sequentially; the value of the first form is saved while all the others are executed and is then returned.

  `prog1` is most commonly used to evaluate an expression with side effects and to return a value that must be computed *before* the side effects happen. For example:

```
(prog1 (car x) (rplaca x 'foo))
```

alters the *car* of x to be foo and returns the old *car* of x.

prog1 always returns a single value, even if the first form tries to return multiple values. As a consequence, (prog1 x) and (progn x) may behave differently if x can produce multiple values. See multiple-value-prog1. A point of style: although prog1 can be used to force exactly a single value to be returned, it is conventional to use the function values for this purpose.

prog2 *first second* {*form*}*   [*Macro*]

prog2 is similar to prog1, but it returns the value of its *second* form. All the argument forms are executed sequentially; the value of the second form is saved while all the other forms are executed and is then returned. prog2 is provided mostly for historical compatibility.

(prog2 *a b c* ... *z*) ≡ (progn *a* (prog1 *b c* ... *z*))

Occasionally it is desirable to perform one side effect, then a value-producing operation, then another side effect. In such a peculiar case, prog2 is fairly perspicuous. For example:

```
(prog2 (open-a-file) (process-the-file) (close-the-file))
                              ;value is that of process-the-file
```

prog2, like prog1, always returns a single value, even if the second form tries to return multiple values. As a consequence of this, (prog2 x y) and (progn x y) may behave differently if y can produce multiple values.

7.5. Establishing New Variable Bindings

During the invocation of a function represented by a lambda-expression (or a closure of a lambda-expression, as produced by function), new bindings are established for the variables that are the parameters of the lambda-expression. These bindings initially have values determined by the parameter-binding protocol discussed in section 5.2.2.

The following constructs may also be used to establish bindings of variables, both ordinary and functional.

let ({*var* | (*var value*)}*) {*declaration*}* {*form*}*   [*Special form*]

A let form can be used to execute a series of forms with specified variables bound to specified values.

More precisely, the form

```
(let ((var1  value1)
      (var2  value2)
       ...
      (varm  valuem))
  declaration1
  declaration2
   ...
  declarationp
  body1
  body2
   ...
  bodyn)
```

first evaluates the expressions *value1*, *value2*, and so on, in that order, saving the resulting values. Then all of the variables *varj* are bound to the corresponding values in parallel; each binding will be a lexical binding unless there is a special declaration to the contrary. The expressions *bodyk* are then evaluated in order; the values of all but the last are discarded (that is, the body of a let form is an implicit progn). The let form returns what evaluating *bodyn* produces (if the body is empty, which is fairly useless, let returns nil as its value). The bindings of the variables have lexical scope and indefinite extent.

Instead of a list (*varj* *valuej*), one may write simply *varj*. In this case *varj* is initialized to nil. As a matter of style, it is recommended that *varj* be written only when that variable will be stored into (such as by setq) before its first use. If it is important that the initial value be nil rather than some undefined value, then it is clearer to write out (*varj* nil) if the initial value is intended to mean "false," or (*varj* ´()) if the initial value is intended to be an empty list. Note that the code

```
(let (x)
  (declare (integer x))
  (setq x (gcd y z))
  ...)
```

is incorrect; although x is indeed set before it is used, and is set to a value of the declared type integer, nevertheless x momentarily takes on the value nil in violation of the type declaration.

Declarations may appear at the beginning of the body of a let. See declare. See also destructuring-bind.

X3J13 voted in January 1989 ⟨182⟩ to regularize the binding formats for do, do*, let, let*, prog, prog*, and compiler-let. The new syntactic definition for let makes the *value* optional:

let ({*var* | (*var* [*value*])}*) {*declaration*}* {*form*}*   [*Special form*]

This changes let to allow a list (*var*) to appear, meaning the same as simply *var*.

let* ({*var* | (*var value*)}*) {*declaration*}* {*form*}*   [*Special form*]

let* is similar to let, but the bindings of variables are performed sequentially rather than in parallel. This allows the expression for the value of a variable to refer to variables previously bound in the let* form.
    More precisely, the form

```
(let* ((var1  value1)
       (var2  value2)
        . . .
       (varm  valuem))
   declaration1
   declaration2
    . . .
   declarationp
   body1
   body2
    . . .
   bodyn)
```

first evaluates the expression *value1*, then binds the variable *var1* to that value; then it evaluates *value2* and binds *var2*; and so on. The expressions *bodyj* are then evaluated in order; the values of all but the last are discarded (that is, the body of a let* form is an implicit progn). The let* form returns the results of evaluating *bodyn* (if the body is empty, which is fairly useless, let* returns nil as its value). The bindings of the variables have lexical scope and indefinite extent.
    Instead of a list (*varj valuej*), one may write simply *varj*. In this case *varj* is initialized to nil. As a matter of style, it is recommended that *varj* be written only when that variable will be stored into (such as by setq) before its first use. If it is important that the initial value be nil rather than some undefined value, then it is clearer to write out (*varj* nil) if the initial value is intended to mean "false," or (*varj* ´()) if the initial value is intended to be an empty list.
    Declarations may appear at the beginning of the body of a let*. See declare.

X3J13 voted in January 1989 ⟨182⟩ to regularize the binding formats for do, do*, let, let*, prog, prog*, and compiler-let. The new syntactic definition for let* makes the *value* optional:

let* ({*var* | (*var* [*value*])}*) {*declaration*}* {*form*}*   [*Special form*]

This changes let* to allow a list (*var*) to appear, meaning the same as simply *var*.

compiler-let ({*var* | (*var value*)}*) {*form*}*   [*Special form*]

When executed by the Lisp interpreter, compiler-let behaves exactly like let with all the variable bindings implicitly declared special. When the compiler processes this form, however, no code is compiled for the bindings; instead, the processing of the body by the compiler (including, in particular, the expansion of any macro calls within the body) is done with the special variables bound to the indicated values *in the execution context of the compiler*. This is primarily useful for communication among complicated macros.

Declarations may *not* appear at the beginning of the body of a compiler-let.

Rationale: Because of the unorthodox handling by compiler-let of its variable bindings, it would be complicated and confusing to permit declarations that apparently referred to the variables bound by compiler-let. Disallowing declarations eliminates the problem.

X3J13 voted in January 1989 ⟨182⟩ to regularize the binding formats for do, do*, let, let*, prog, prog*, and compiler-let. The new syntactic definition for compiler-let makes the *value* optional:

compiler-let ({*var* | (*var* [*value*])}*) {*form*}*   [*Special form*]

This changes compiler-let to allow a list (*var*) to appear, meaning the same as simply *var*.

X3J13 voted in June 1989 ⟨25⟩ to remove compiler-let from the language. Many uses of compiler-let can be replaced with more portable code that uses macrolet or symbol-macrolet.

`progv` *symbols values* {*form*}*   [*Special form*]

`progv` is a special form that allows binding one or more dynamic variables whose
names may be determined at run time. The sequence of forms (an implicit `progn`)
is evaluated with the dynamic variables whose names are in the list *symbols* bound
to corresponding values from the list *values*. (If too few values are supplied, the
remaining symbols are bound and then made to have no value; see `makunbound`.
If too many values are supplied, the excess values are ignored.) The results of
the `progv` form are those of the last *form*. The bindings of the dynamic variables
are undone on exit from the `progv` form. The lists of symbols and values are
computed quantities; this is what makes `progv` different from, for example, `let`,
where the variable names are stated explicitly in the program text.

   `progv` is particularly useful for writing interpreters for languages embedded in
Lisp; it provides a handle on the mechanism for binding dynamic variables.

`flet` ({(*name lambda-list*   [*Special form*]
            ⟦ {*declaration*}* | *doc-string* ⟧ {*form*}*)}*)
         {*form*}*
`labels` ({(*name lambda-list*   [*Special form*]
            ⟦ {*declaration*}* | *doc-string* ⟧ {*form*}*)}*)
         {*form*}*
`macrolet` ({(*name varlist*   [*Special form*]
            ⟦ {*declaration*}* | *doc-string* ⟧ {*form*}*)}*)
           {*form*}*

`flet` may be used to define locally named functions. Within the body of the
`flet` form, function names matching those defined by the `flet` refer to the locally
defined functions rather than to the global function definitions of the same name.

   Any number of functions may be simultaneously defined. Each definition is
similar in format to a `defun` form: first a name, then a parameter list (which may
contain &optional, &rest, or &key parameters), then optional declarations and
documentation string, and finally a body.

```
(flet ((safesqrt (x) (sqrt (abs x))))
  ;; The safesqrt function is used in two places.
  (safesqrt (apply #'+ (map 'list #'safesqrt longlist))))
```

   The `labels` construct is identical in form to the `flet` construct. These constructs
differ in that the scope of the defined function names for `flet` encompasses only
the body, whereas for `labels` it encompasses the function definitions themselves.
That is, `labels` can be used to define mutually recursive functions, but `flet`

cannot. This distinction is useful. Using flet one can locally redefine a global function name, and the new definition can refer to the global definition; the same construction using labels would not have that effect.

```
(defun integer-power (n k)        ;A highly "bummed" integer
  (declare (integer n))           ; exponentiation routine
  (declare (type (integer 0 *) k))
  (labels ((expt0 (x k a)
              (declare (integer x a) (type (integer 0 *) k))
              (cond ((zerop k) a)
                    ((evenp k) (expt1 (* x x) (floor k 2) a))
                    (t (expt0 (* x x) (floor k 2) (* x a)))))
           (expt1 (x k a)
              (declare (integer x a) (type (integer 1 *) k))
              (cond ((evenp k) (expt1 (* x x) (floor k 2) a))
                    (t (expt0 (* x x) (floor k 2) (* x a))))))
    (expt0 n k 1)))
```

macrolet is similar in form to flet but defines local macros, using the same format used by defmacro. The names established by macrolet as names for macros are lexically scoped.

I have observed that, while most Common Lisp users pronounce macrolet to rhyme with "silhouette," a small but vocal minority pronounce it to rhyme with "Chevrolet." A very few extremists furthermore adjust their pronunciation of flet similarly: they say "flay." Hey, hey! *Très outré.*

Macros often must be expanded at "compile time" (more generally, at a time before the program itself is executed), and so the run-time values of variables are not available to macros defined by macrolet.

The precise rule is that the macro-expansion functions defined by macrolet are defined in the *global* environment; lexically scoped entities that would ordinarily be lexically apparent are not visible within the expansion functions.

X3J13 voted in March 1989 ⟨50⟩ to retract the previous sentence and specify that the macro-expansion functions created by macrolet are defined in the lexical environment in which the macrolet form appears, not in the null lexical environment. Declarations, macrolet definitions, and symbol-macrolet definitions affect code within the expansion functions in a macrolet, but the consequences are undefined if such code attempts to refer to any local variable or function bindings that are visible in that lexical environment.

However, lexically scoped entities *are* visible within the body of the macrolet form and *are* visible to the code that is the expansion of a macro call. The following example should make this clear:

```
;;; Example of scoping in macrolet.

(defun foo (x flag)
  (macrolet ((fudge (z)
                  ;;The parameters x and flag are not accessible
                  ;; at this point; a reference to flag would be to
                  ;; the global variable of that name.
                  `(if flag
                      (* ,z ,z)
                      ,z)))
    ;;The parameters x and flag are accessible here.
    (+ x
       (fudge x)
       (fudge (+ x 1)))))
```

The body of the `macrolet` becomes

```
(+ x
   (if flag
       (* x x)
       x))
   (if flag
       (* (+ x 1) (+ x 1))
       (+ x 1)))
```

after macro expansion. The occurrences of x and flag legitimately refer to the parameters of the function foo because those parameters are visible at the site of the macro call which produced the expansion.

X3J13 voted in March 1988 ⟨78⟩ to specify that the body of each function or expander function defined by flet, labels, or macrolet is implicitly enclosed in a block construct whose name is the same as the *name* of the function. Therefore return-from may be used to exit from the function.

X3J13 voted in March 1989 ⟨89⟩ to extend flet and labels to accept any function-name (a symbol or a list whose *car* is setf—see section 7.1) as a *name* for a function to be locally defined. In this way one can create local definitions for setf expansion functions. (X3J13 explicitly declined to extend macrolet in the same manner.)

X3J13 voted in March 1988 ⟨77⟩ to change flet, labels, and macrolet to allow declarations to appear before the body. The new descriptions are therefore as follows:

```
flet ( {(name lambda-list                           [Special form]
        ⟦ {declaration}* | doc-string ⟧  {form}* )}* )
     {declaration}*  {form}*
labels ( {(name lambda-list                         [Special form]
          ⟦ {declaration}* | doc-string ⟧  {form}* )}* )
       {declaration}*  {form}*
macrolet ( {(name varlist                           [Special form]
            ⟦ {declaration}* | doc-string ⟧  {form}* )}* )
         {declaration}*  {form}*
```

These are now syntactically more similar to such other binding forms as let.

For flet and labels, the bodies of the locally defined functions are part of the scope of pervasive declarations appearing before the main body. (This is consistent with the treatment of initialization forms in let.) For macrolet, however, the bodies of the locally defined macro expander functions are *not* included in the scope of pervasive declarations appearing before the main body. (This is consistent with the rule, stated below, that the bodies of macro expander functions are in the global environment, not the local lexical environment.) Here is an example:

```
(flet ((stretch (x) (* x *stretch-factor*))
       (chop (x) (- x *chop-margin*)))
   (declare (inline stretch chop))     ;Illegal in original Common Lisp
   (if (> x *chop-margin*) (stretch (chop x)) (chop (stretch x))))
```

X3J13 voted to permit declarations of the sort noted above.

```
symbol-macrolet ( {(var expansion)}* )              [Special form]
                {declaration}*  {form}*
```

X3J13 voted in June 1988 ⟨12⟩ to adopt the Common Lisp Object System. Part of this proposal is a general mechanism, symbol-macrolet, for treating certain variable names as if they were parameterless macro calls. This facility may be useful independent of CLOS. X3J13 voted in March 1989 ⟨173⟩ to modify the definition of symbol-macrolet substantially and also voted ⟨172⟩ to allow declarations before the body of symbol-macrolet but with peculiar treatment of special and type declarations.

The *forms* are executed as an implicit progn in a lexical environment that causes every reference to any defined *var* to be replaced by the corresponding *expansion*. It is as if the reference to the *var* were a parameterless macro call; the *expansion* is evaluated or otherwise processed in place of the reference (in particular, the expansion form is itself subject to further expansion—this is one of the changes ⟨173⟩ from the original definition in the CLOS proposal). Note, however, that the names of such symbol macros occupy the name space of variables, not the name space of functions; just as one may have a function (or macro, or special form) and a variable with the same name without interference, so one may have an ordinary macro (or function, or special form) and a symbol macro with the same name. The use of symbol-macrolet can therefore be shadowed by let or other constructs that bind variables; symbol-macrolet does not substitute for all occurrences of a *var* as a variable but only for those occurrences that would be construed as references in the scope of a lexical binding of *var* as a variable. For example:

```
(symbol-macrolet ((pollyanna 'goody))
  (list pollyanna (let ((pollyanna 'two-shoes)) pollyanna)))
⇒ (goody two-shoes), not (goody goody)
```

One might think that 'goody simply replaces all occurrences of pollyanna, and so the value of the let would be goody; but this is not so. A little reflection shows that under this incorrect interpretation the body in expanded form would be

```
(list 'goody (let (('goody 'two-shoes)) 'goody))
```

which is syntactically malformed. The correct expanded form is

```
(list 'goody (let ((pollyanna 'two-shoes)) pollyanna))
```

because the rebinding of pollyanna by the let form shadows the symbol macro definition.

The *expansion* for each *var* is not evaluated at binding time but only after it has replaced a reference to the *var*. The setf macro allows a symbol macro to be used as a *place*, in which case its expansion is used; moreover, setq of a variable that is really a symbol macro will be treated as if setf had been used. The values of the last form are returned, or nil if there is no value.

See macroexpand and macroexpand-1; they will expand symbol macros as well as ordinary macros.

Certain *declarations* before the body are handled in a peculiar manner; see section 9.1.

7.6. Conditionals

The traditional conditional construct in Lisp is cond. However, if is much simpler and is directly comparable to conditional constructs in other programming languages, so it is considered to be primitive in Common Lisp and is described first. Common Lisp also provides the dispatching constructs case and typecase, which are often more convenient than cond.

if *test then* [*else*]   [*Special form*]

The if special form corresponds to the **if-then-else** construct found in most algebraic programming languages. First the form *test* is evaluated. If the result is not nil, then the form *then* is selected; otherwise the form *else* is selected. Whichever form is selected is then evaluated, and if returns whatever is returned by evaluation of the selected form.

(if *test then else*) ≡ (cond (*test then*) (t *else*))

but if is considered more readable in some situations.

The *else* form may be omitted, in which case if the value of *test* is nil then nothing is done and the value of the if form is nil. If the value of the if form is important in this situation, then the and construct may be stylistically preferable, depending on the context. If the value is not important, but only the effect, then the when construct may be stylistically preferable.

when *test* {*form*}*   [*Macro*]

(when *test form1 form2* ...) first evaluates *test*. If the result is nil, then no *form* is evaluated, and nil is returned. Otherwise the *form*s constitute an implicit progn and are evaluated sequentially from left to right, and the value of the last one is returned.

(when *p a b c*) ≡ (and *p* (progn *a b c*))
(when *p a b c*) ≡ (cond (*p a b c*))
(when *p a b c*) ≡ (if *p* (progn *a b c*) nil)
(when *p a b c*) ≡ (unless (not *p*) *a b c*)

As a matter of style, when is normally used to conditionally produce some side effects, and the value of the when form is normally not used. If the value is relevant, then it may be stylistically more appropriate to use and or if.

unless *test* {*form*}*   [*Macro*]

(unless *test form1 form2* ...) first evaluates *test*. If the result is *not* nil, then the *form*s are not evaluated, and nil is returned. Otherwise the *form*s constitute an implicit progn and are evaluated sequentially from left to right, and the value of the last one is returned.

```
(unless p a b c) ≡ (cond ((not p) a b c))
(unless p a b c) ≡ (if p nil (progn a b c))
(unless p a b c) ≡ (when (not p) a b c)
```

As a matter of style, unless is normally used to conditionally produce some side effects, and the value of the unless form is normally not used. If the value is relevant, then it may be stylistically more appropriate to use if.

cond {(*test* {*form*}*)}*   [*Macro*]

A cond form has a number (possibly zero) of *clauses*, which are lists of forms. Each clause consists of a *test* followed by zero or more *consequents*. For example:

```
(cond (test-1 consequent-1-1 consequent-1-2 ...)
      (test-2)
      (test-3 consequent-3-1 ...)
      ... )
```

The first clause whose *test* evaluates to non-nil is selected; all other clauses are ignored, and the consequents of the selected clause are evaluated in order (as an implicit progn).

More specifically, cond processes its clauses in order from left to right. For each clause, the *test* is evaluated. If the result is nil, cond advances to the next clause. Otherwise, the *cdr* of the clause is treated as a list of forms, or consequents; these forms are evaluated in order from left to right, as an implicit progn. After evaluating the consequents, cond returns without inspecting any remaining clauses. The cond special form returns the results of evaluating the last of the selected consequents; if there were no consequents in the selected clause, then the single (and necessarily non-null) value of the *test* is returned. If cond runs out of clauses (every test produced nil, and therefore no clause was selected), the value of the cond form is nil.

If it is desired to select the last clause unconditionally if all others fail, the standard convention is to use t for the *test*. As a matter of style, it is desirable to write a last clause (t nil) if the value of the cond form is to be used for something. Similarly, it is in questionable taste to let the last clause of a cond be a "singleton clause"; an explicit t should be provided. (Note moreover that (cond ... (x)) may behave differently from (cond ... (t x)) if x might produce multiple values; the former always returns a single value, whereas the latter returns whatever values x returns. However, as a matter of style it is preferable to obtain this behavior by writing (cond ... (t (values x))), using the values function explicitly to indicate the discarding of any excess values.) For example:

```
(setq z (cond (a 'foo) (b 'bar)))              ;Possibly confusing
(setq z (cond (a 'foo) (b 'bar) (t nil)))      ;Better
(cond (a b) (c d) (e))                         ;Possibly confusing
(cond (a b) (c d) (t e))                       ;Better
(cond (a b) (c d) (t (values e)))              ;Better (if one value
                                               ;  needed)
(cond (a b) (c))                               ;Possibly confusing
(cond (a b) (t c))                             ;Better
(if a b c)                                     ;Also better
```

A Lisp cond form may be compared to a continued **if-then-else** as found in many algebraic programming languages:

`(cond (p ...)`		**if** p **then** ...
`(q ...)`	roughly	**else if** q **then** ...
`(r ...)`	corresponds	**else if** r **then** ...
`...`	to	...
`(t ...))`		**else** ...

case *keyform* {({({*key*}*) | *key*} {*form*}*)}*   [*Macro*]

case is a conditional that chooses one of its clauses to execute by comparing a value to various constants, which are typically keyword symbols, integers, or characters (but may be any objects). Its form is as follows:

```
(case keyform
    (keylist-1 consequent-1-1 consequent-1-2 ...)
    (keylist-2 consequent-2-1 ...)
    (keylist-3 consequent-3-1 ...)
    ...)
```

Structurally case is much like cond, and it behaves like cond in selecting one clause and then executing all consequents of that clause. However, case differs in the mechanism of clause selection.

The first thing case does is to evaluate the form *keyform* to produce an object called the *key object*. Then case considers each of the clauses in turn. If *key* is in the *keylist* (that is, is eql to any item in the *keylist*) of a clause, the consequents of that clause are evaluated as an implicit progn; case returns what was returned by the last consequent (or nil if there are no consequents in that clause). If no clause is satisfied, case returns nil.

The keys in the keylists are *not* evaluated; literal key values must appear in the keylists. It is an error for the same key to appear in more than one clause;

a consequence is that the order of the clauses does not affect the behavior of the case construct.

Instead of a *keylist*, one may write one of the symbols t and otherwise. A clause with such a symbol always succeeds and must be the last clause (this is an exception to the order-independence of clauses). See also ecase and ccase, each of which provides an implicit otherwise clause to signal an error if no clause is satisfied.

If there is only one key for a clause, then that key may be written in place of a list of that key, provided that no ambiguity results. Such a "singleton key" may not be nil (which is confusable with ( ), a list of no keys), t, otherwise, or a cons.

Compatibility note: The Lisp Machine Lisp caseq construct uses eq for the comparison. In Lisp Machine Lisp caseq therefore works for fixnums but not bignums. The MacLisp caseq construct simply prohibits the use of bignums; indeed, it permits only fixnums and symbols as clause keys. In the interest of hiding the fixnum-bignum distinction, and for general language consistency, case uses eql in Common Lisp.

The Interlisp selectq construct is similar to case.

---

typecase *keyform* {(*type* {*form*}*)}*   [*Macro*]

typecase is a conditional that chooses one of its clauses by examining the type of an object. Its form is as follows:

```
(typecase keyform
   (type-1 consequent-1-1 consequent-1-2 ...)
   (type-2 consequent-2-1 ...)
   (type-3 consequent-3-1 ...)
   ...)
```

Structurally typecase is much like cond or case, and it behaves like them in selecting one clause and then executing all consequents of that clause. It differs in the mechanism of clause selection.

The first thing typecase does is to evaluate the form *keyform* to produce an object called the key object. Then typecase considers each of the clauses in turn. The *type* that appears in each clause is a type specifier; it is not evaluated but is a literal type specifier. The first clause for which the key is of that clause's specified *type* is selected, the consequents of this clause are evaluated as an implicit progn, and typecase returns what was returned by the last consequent (or nil if there are no consequents in that clause). If no clause is satisfied, typecase returns nil.

As for case, the symbol t or otherwise may be written for *type* to indicate that the clause should always be selected. See also etypecase and ctypecase, each of which provides an implicit otherwise clause to signal an error if no clause is satisfied.

It is permissible for more than one clause to specify a given type, particularly if one is a subtype of another; the earliest applicable clause is chosen. Thus for typecase, unlike case, the order of the clauses may affect the behavior of the construct. For example:

```
(typecase an-object
    (string ...)              ;This clause handles strings
    ((array t) ...)           ;This clause handles general arrays
    ((array bit) ...)         ;This clause handles bit arrays
    (array ...)               ;This handles all other arrays
    ((or list number) ...)    ;This handles lists and numbers
    (t ...))                  ;This handles all other objects
```

A Common Lisp compiler may choose to issue a warning if a clause cannot be selected because it is completely shadowed by earlier clauses.

7.7. Blocks and Exits

The block and return-from constructs provide a structured lexical non-local exit facility. At any point lexically within a block construct, a return-from with the same name may be used to perform an immediate transfer of control that exits from the block. In the most common cases this mechanism is more efficient than the dynamic non-local exit facility provided by catch and throw, described in section 7.11.

block *name* {*form*}*   [*Special form*]

The block construct executes each *form* from left to right, returning whatever is returned by the last *form*. If, however, a return or return-from form that specifies the same *name* is executed during the execution of some *form*, then the results specified by the return or return-from are immediately returned as the value of the block construct, and execution proceeds as if the block had terminated normally. In this, block differs from progn; the progn construct has nothing to do with return.

The *name* is not evaluated; it must be a symbol. The scope of the *name* is lexical; only a return or return-from textually contained in some *form* can exit from the block. The extent of the name is dynamic. Therefore it is only possible to exit from a given run-time incarnation of a block once, either normally or by explicit return.

The defun form implicitly puts a block around the body of the function defined; the block has the same name as the function. Therefore one may use return-from to return prematurely from a function defined by defun.

The lexical scoping of the block name is fully general and has consequences that may be surprising to users and implementors of other Lisp systems. For example, the return-from in the following example actually does work in Common Lisp as one might expect:

```
(block loser
    (catch 'stuff
        (mapcar #'(lambda (x) (if (numberp x)
                                  (hairyfun x)
                                  (return-from loser nil)))
                items)))
```

Depending on the situation, a return in Common Lisp may not be simple. A return can break up catchers if necessary to get to the block in question. It is possible for a "closure" created by function for a lambda-expression to refer to a block name as long as the name is lexically apparent.

return-from *name* [*result*]   [*Special form*]

return-from is used to return from a block or from such constructs as do and prog that implicitly establish a block. The *name* is not evaluated and must be a symbol. A block construct with the same name must lexically enclose the occurrence of return-from; whatever the evaluation of *result* produces is immediately returned from the block. (If the *result* form is omitted, it defaults to nil. As a matter of style, this form ought to be used to indicate that the particular value returned doesn't matter.)

The return-from form itself never returns and cannot have a value; it causes results to be returned from a block construct. If the evaluation of *result* produces multiple values, those multiple values are returned by the construct exited.

return [*result*]   [*Macro*]

(return *form*) is identical in meaning to (return-from nil *form*); it returns from a block named nil. Blocks established implicitly by iteration constructs such as do are named nil, so that return will exit properly from such a construct.

7.8. Iteration

Common Lisp provides a number of iteration constructs. The loop construct provides a trivial iteration facility; it is little more than a progn with a branch from the bottom back to the top. The do and do* constructs provide a general iteration facility for controlling the variation of several variables on each cycle. For specialized iterations over the elements of a list or *n* consecutive integers, dolist and dotimes are provided. The tagbody construct is the most general, permitting arbitrary go statements within it. (The traditional prog construct is a synthesis of tagbody, block, and let.) Most of the iteration constructs permit statically defined non-local exits (see return-from and return).

7.8.1. Indefinite Iteration

The loop construct is the simplest iteration facility. It controls no variables, and simply executes its body repeatedly.

loop {*form*}*   [*Macro*]

Each *form* is evaluated in turn from left to right. When the last *form* has been evaluated, then the first *form* is evaluated again, and so on, in a never-ending cycle. The loop construct never returns a value. Its execution must be terminated explicitly, using return or throw, for example.

loop, like most iteration constructs, establishes an implicit block named nil. Thus return may be used to exit from a loop with specified results.

A loop construct has this meaning only if every *form* is non-atomic (a list). The case where some *form* is atomic is reserved for future extensions.

Implementation note: There have been several proposals for a powerful iteration mechanism to be called loop. One version is provided in Lisp Machine Lisp. Implementors are encouraged to experiment with extensions to the loop syntax, but users should be advised that in all likelihood some specific set of extensions to loop will be adopted in a future revision of Common Lisp.

X3J13 voted in January 1989 ⟨115⟩ to include just such an extension of loop. See chapter 26.

7.8.2. General Iteration

In contrast to loop, do and do* provide a powerful and general mechanism for repetitively recalculating many variables.

```
do ( {(var [init [step]] )}* )                                    [Macro]
    (end-test {result}* )
    {declaration}*  {tag | statement}*
do* ( {(var [init [step]] )}* )                                   [Macro]
    (end-test {result}* )
    {declaration}*  {tag | statement}*
```

The do special form provides a generalized iteration facility, with an arbitrary number of "index variables." These variables are bound within the iteration and stepped in parallel in specified ways. They may be used both to generate successive values of interest (such as successive integers) or to accumulate results. When an end condition is met, the iteration terminates with a specified value.

In general, a do loop looks like this:

```
(do ((var1 init1 step1)
     (var2 init2 step2)
     . . .
     (varn initn stepn))
    (end-test . result)
   {declaration}*
   . tagbody)
```

A do* loop looks exactly the same except that the name do is replaced by do*.

The first item in the form is a list of zero or more index-variable specifiers. Each index-variable specifier is a list of the name of a variable var, an initial value init, and a stepping form step. If init is omitted, it defaults to nil. If step is omitted, the var is not changed by the do construct between repetitions (though code within the do is free to alter the value of the variable by using setq).

An index-variable specifier can also be just the name of a variable. In this case, the variable has an initial value of nil and is not changed between repetitions. As a matter of style, it is recommended that an unadorned variable name be written only when that variable will be stored into (such as by setq) before its first use. If it is important that the initial value be nil rather than some undefined value, then it is clearer to write out (varj nil) if the initial value is intended to mean "false," or (varj '()) if the initial value is intended to be an empty list.

X3J13 voted in January 1989 ⟨182⟩ to regularize the binding formats for do, do*, let, let*, prog, prog*, and compiler-let. In the case of do and do* the first edition was inconsistent; the formal syntax fails to reflect the fact that a simple variable name may appear, as described in the preceding paragraph. The definitions should read

do ({*var* | (*var* [*init* [*step*]])}*)   [*Macro*]
    (*end-test* {*result*}*)
    {*declaration*}* {*tag* | *statement*}*
do* ({*var* | (*var* [*init* [*step*]])}*)   [*Macro*]
    (*end-test* {*result*}*)
    {*declaration*}* {*tag* | *statement*}*

for consistency with the reading of the first edition and the X3J13 vote.

Before the first iteration, all the *init* forms are evaluated, and each *var* is bound to the value of its respective *init*. This is a binding, not an assignment; when the loop terminates, the old values of those variables will be restored. For do, *all* of the *init* forms are evaluated *before* any *var* is bound; hence all the *init* forms may refer to the old bindings of all the variables (that is, to the values visible before beginning execution of the do construct). For do*, the first *init* form is evaluated, then the first *var* is bound to that value, then the second *init* form is evaluated, then the second *var* is bound, and so on; in general, the *initj* form can refer to the *new* binding *vark* if $k < j$, and otherwise to the *old* binding of *vark*.

The second element of the loop is a list of an end-testing predicate form *end-test* and zero or more *result* forms. This resembles a cond clause. At the beginning of each iteration, after processing the variables, the *end-test* is evaluated. If the result is nil, execution proceeds with the body of the do (or do*) form. If the result is not nil, the *result* forms are evaluated in order as an implicit progn, and then do returns. do returns the results of evaluating the last *result* form. If there are no *result* forms, the value of do is nil. Note that this is not quite analogous to the treatment of clauses in a cond form, because a cond clause with no *result* forms returns the (non-nil) result of the test.

At the beginning of each iteration other than the first, the index variables are updated as follows. All the *step* forms are evaluated, from left to right, and the resulting values are assigned to the respective index variables. Any variable that has no associated *step* form is not assigned to. For do, all the *step* forms are evaluated before any variable is updated; the assignment of values to variables is done in parallel, as if by psetq. Because *all* of the *step* forms are evaluated before *any* of the variables are altered, a *step* form when evaluated always has access to the *old* values of *all* the index variables, even if other *step* forms precede it. For do*, the first *step* form is evaluated, then the value is assigned to the first *var*, then the second *step* form is evaluated, then the value is assigned to the second *var*, and so on; the assignment of values to variables is done sequentially, as if by setq. For either do or do*, after the variables have been updated, the *end-test* is evaluated as described above, and the iteration continues.

If the *end-test* of a do form is nil, the test will never succeed. Therefore this provides an idiom for "do forever": the *body* of the do is executed repeatedly, stepping variables as usual. (The loop construct performs a "do forever" that steps no variables.) The infinite loop can be terminated by the use of return, return-from, go to an outer level, or throw. For example:

```
(do ((j 0 (+ j 1)))
    (nil)                          ;Do forever
  (format t "~%Input ~D:" j)
  (let ((item (read)))
    (if (null item) (return)       ;Process items until nil seen
        (format t "~&Output ~D: ~S" j (process item)))))
```

The remainder of the do form constitutes an implicit tagbody. Tags may appear within the body of a do loop for use by go statements appearing in the body (but such go statements may not appear in the variable specifiers, the *end-test*, or the *result* forms). When the end of a do body is reached, the next iteration cycle (beginning with the evaluation of *step* forms) occurs.

An implicit block named nil surrounds the entire do form. A return statement may be used at any point to exit the loop immediately.

declare forms may appear at the beginning of a do body. They apply to code in the do body, to the bindings of the do variables, to the *init* forms, to the *step* forms, to the *end-test*, and to the *result* forms.

Compatibility note: "Old-style" MacLisp do loops, that is, those of the form (do *var init step end-test . body*), are not supported in Common Lisp. Such old-style loops are considered obsolete and in any case are easily converted to a new-style do with the insertion of three pairs of parentheses. In practice the compiler can catch nearly all instances of old-style do loops because they will not have a legal format anyway.

Here are some examples of the use of do:

```
(do ((i 0 (+ i 1))          ;Sets every null element of a-vector to zero
     (n (length a-vector)))
    ((= i n))
  (when (null (aref a-vector i))
    (setf (aref a-vector i) 0)))
```

The construction

```
(do ((x e (cdr x))
     (oldx x x))
    ((null x))
   body)
```

exploits parallel assignment to index variables. On the first iteration, the value of oldx is whatever value x had before the do was entered. On succeeding iterations, oldx contains the value that x had on the previous iteration.

Very often an iterative algorithm can be most clearly expressed entirely in the *step* forms of a do, and the *body* is empty. For example,

```
(do ((x foo (cdr x))
     (y bar (cdr y))
     (z '() (cons (f (car x) (car y)) z)))
    ((or (null x) (null y))
     (nreverse z)))
```

does the same thing as (mapcar #'f foo bar). Note that the *step* computation for z exploits the fact that variables are stepped in parallel. Also, the body of the loop is empty. Finally, the use of nreverse to put an accumulated do loop result into the correct order is a standard idiom. Another example:

```
(defun list-reverse (list)
       (do ((x list (cdr x))
            (y '() (cons (car x) y)))
           ((endp x) y)))
```

Note the use of endp rather than null or atom to test for the end of a list; this may result in more robust code.

As an example of nested loops, suppose that env holds a list of conses. The *car* of each cons is a list of symbols, and the *cdr* of each cons is a list of equal length containing corresponding values. Such a data structure is similar to an association list but is divided into "frames"; the overall structure resembles a rib cage. A lookup function on such a data structure might be

```
(defun ribcage-lookup (sym ribcage)
       (do ((r ribcage (cdr r)))
           ((null r) nil)
         (do ((s (caar r) (cdr s))
              (v (cdar r) (cdr v)))
             ((null s))
```

```
(when (eq (car s) sym)
       (return-from ribcage-lookup (car v))))))
```

(Notice the use of indentation in the above example to set off the bodies of the do loops.)

A do loop may be explained in terms of the more primitive constructs block, return, let, loop, tagbody, and psetq as follows:

```
(block nil
  (let ((var1 init1)
        (var2 init2)
        . . .
        (varn initn))
    {declaration}*
    (loop (when end-test (return (progn . result)))
          (tagbody . tagbody)
          (psetq var1 step1
                 var2 step2
                 . . .
                 varn stepn))))
```

do* is exactly like do except that the bindings and steppings of the variables are performed sequentially rather than in parallel. It is as if, in the above explanation, let were replaced by let* and psetq were replaced by setq.

7.8.3. Simple Iteration Constructs

The constructs dolist and dotimes execute a body of code once for each value taken by a single variable. They are expressible in terms of do, but capture very common patterns of use.

Both dolist and dotimes perform a body of statements repeatedly. On each iteration a specified variable is bound to an element of interest that the body may examine. dolist examines successive elements of a list, and dotimes examines integers from 0 to $n - 1$ for some specified positive integer n.

The value of any of these constructs may be specified by an optional result form, which if omitted defaults to the value nil.

The return statement may be used to return immediately from a dolist or dotimes form, discarding any following iterations that might have been performed; in effect, a block named nil surrounds the construct. The body of the loop is implicitly a tagbody construct; it may contain tags to serve as the targets of go statements. Declarations may appear before the body of the loop.

dolist (*var listform* [*resultform*]) [*Macro*]
    {*declaration*}* {*tag* | *statement*}*

dolist provides straightforward iteration over the elements of a list. First dolist evaluates the form *listform*, which should produce a list. It then executes the body once for each element in the list, in order, with the variable *var* bound to the element. Then *resultform* (a single form, *not* an implicit progn) is evaluated, and the result is the value of the dolist form. (When the *resultform* is evaluated, the control variable *var* is still bound and has the value nil.) If *resultform* is omitted, the result is nil.

```
(dolist (x '(a b c d)) (prin1 x) (princ " ")) ⇒ nil
    after printing "a b c d " (note the trailing space)
```

An explicit return statement may be used to terminate the loop and return a specified value.

| X3J13 voted in January 1989 ⟨121⟩ to restrict user side effects; see section 7.9.

dotimes (*var countform* [*resultform*]) [*Macro*]
    {*declaration*}* {*tag* | *statement*}*

dotimes provides straightforward iteration over a sequence of integers. The expression (dotimes (*var countform resultform*) . *progbody*) evaluates the form *countform*, which should produce an integer. It then performs *progbody* once for each integer from zero (inclusive) to *count* (exclusive), in order, with the variable *var* bound to the integer; if the value of *countform* is zero or negative, then the *progbody* is performed zero times. Finally, *resultform* (a single form, *not* an implicit progn) is evaluated, and the result is the value of the dotimes form. (When the *resultform* is evaluated, the control variable *var* is still bound and has as its value the number of times the body was executed.) If *resultform* is omitted, the result is nil.

An explicit return statement may be used to terminate the loop and return a specified value.

Here is an example of the use of dotimes in processing strings:

```
;;; True if the specified subsequence of the string is a
;;; palindrome (reads the same forwards and backwards).

(defun palindromep (string &optional
                    (start 0)
                    (end (length string)))
```

```
(dotimes (k (floor (- end start) 2) t)
  (unless (char-equal (char string (+ start k))
                      (char string (- end k 1)))
    (return nil))))
```

(palindromep "Able was I ere I saw Elba") ⇒ t

(palindromep "A man, a plan, a canal--Panama!") ⇒ nil

(remove-if-not #´alpha-char-p   ;Remove punctuation
              "A man, a plan, a canal--Panama!")
  ⇒ "AmanaplanacanalPanama"

```
(palindromep
 (remove-if-not #´alpha-char-p
                "A man, a plan, a canal--Panama!")) ⇒ t
```

```
(palindromep
 (remove-if-not
   #´alpha-char-p
   "Unremarkable was I ere I saw Elba Kramer, nu?")) ⇒ t
```

```
(palindromep
 (remove-if-not
   #´alpha-char-p
   "A man, a plan, a cat, a ham, a yak,
              a yam, a hat, a canal--Panama!")) ⇒ t
(palindromep
 (remove-if-not
   #´alpha-char-p
   "Ja-da, ja-da, ja-da ja-da jing jing jing")) ⇒ nil
```

Altering the value of *var* in the body of the loop (by using setq, for example) will have unpredictable, possibly implementation-dependent results. A Common Lisp compiler may choose to issue a warning if such a variable appears in a setq.

Compatibility note: The dotimes construct is the closest thing in Common Lisp to the Interlisp rptq construct.

See also do-symbols, do-external-symbols, and do-all-symbols.

7.8.4. Mapping

Mapping is a type of iteration in which a function is successively applied to pieces of one or more sequences. The result of the iteration is a sequence containing the respective results of the function applications. There are several options for the way in which the pieces of the list are chosen and for what is done with the results returned by the applications of the function.

The function map may be used to map over any kind of sequence. The following functions operate only on lists.

mapcar *function list* &rest *more-lists*	[*Function*]
maplist *function list* &rest *more-lists*	[*Function*]
mapc *function list* &rest *more-lists*	[*Function*]
mapl *function list* &rest *more-lists*	[*Function*]
mapcan *function list* &rest *more-lists*	[*Function*]
mapcon *function list* &rest *more-lists*	[*Function*]

For each of these mapping functions, the first argument is a function and the rest must be lists. The function must take as many arguments as there are lists.

mapcar operates on successive elements of the lists. First the function is applied to the *car* of each list, then to the *cadr* of each list, and so on. (Ideally all the lists are the same length; if not, the iteration terminates when the shortest list runs out, and excess elements in other lists are ignored.) The value returned by mapcar is a list of the results of the successive calls to the function. For example:

```
(mapcar #'abs '(3 -4 2 -5 -6)) ⇒ (3 4 2 5 6)
(mapcar #'cons '(a b c) '(1 2 3)) ⇒ ((a . 1) (b . 2) (c . 3))
```

maplist is like mapcar except that the function is applied to the lists and successive *cdr*'s of those lists rather than to successive elements of the lists. For example:

```
(maplist #'(lambda (x) (cons 'foo x))
         '(a b c d))
   ⇒ ((foo a b c d) (foo b c d) (foo c d) (foo d))

(maplist #'(lambda (x) (if (member (car x) (cdr x)) 0 1)))
         '(a b a c d b c))
   ⇒ (0 0 1 0 1 1 1)
   ;An entry is 1 if the corresponding element of the input
   ; list was the last instance of that element in the input list.
```

mapl and mapc are like maplist and mapcar, respectively, except that they do not accumulate the results of calling the function.

Compatibility note: In all Lisp systems since Lisp 1.5, mapl has been called map. In the chapter on sequences it is explained why this was a bad choice. Here the name map is used for the far more useful generic sequence mapper, in closer accordance with the computer science literature, especially the growing body of papers on functional programming.

Note that this remark, predating the design of the Common Lisp Object System, uses the term "generic" in a generic sense and not necessarily in the technical sense used by CLOS (see chapter 2).

These functions are used when the function is being called merely for its side effects rather than for its returned values. The value returned by mapl or mapc is the second argument, that is, the first sequence argument.

mapcan and mapcon are like mapcar and maplist, respectively, except that they combine the results of the function using nconc instead of list. That is,

```
(mapcon f x1 ... xn)
   ≡ (apply #'nconc (maplist f x1 ... xn))
```

and similarly for the relationship between mapcan and mapcar. Conceptually, these functions allow the mapped function to return a variable number of items to be put into the output list. This is particularly useful for effectively returning zero or one item:

```
(mapcan #'(lambda (x) (and (numberp x) (list x)))
        '(a 1 b c 3 4 d 5))
   ⇒ (1 3 4 5)
```

In this case the function serves as a filter; this is a standard Lisp idiom using mapcan. (The function remove-if-not might have been useful in this particular context, however.) Remember that nconc is a destructive operation, and therefore so are mapcan and mapcon; the lists returned by the *function* are altered in order to concatenate them.

Sometimes a do or a straightforward recursion is preferable to a mapping operation; however, the mapping functions should be used wherever they naturally apply because this increases the clarity of the code.

The functional argument to a mapping function must be acceptable to apply; it cannot be a macro or the name of a special form. Of course, there is nothing wrong with using a function that has &optional and &rest parameters as the functional argument.

X3J13 voted in June 1988 ⟨90⟩ to allow the *function* to be only of type symbol or function; a lambda-expression is no longer acceptable as a functional argument. One must use the function special form or the abbreviation #´ before a lambda-expression that appears as an explicit argument form.

X3J13 voted in January 1989 ⟨121⟩ to restrict user side effects; see section 7.9.

7.8.5. The "Program Feature"

Lisp implementations since Lisp 1.5 have had what was originally called "the program feature," as if it were impossible to write programs without it! The prog construct allows one to write in an Algol-like or Fortran-like statement-oriented style, using go statements that can refer to tags in the body of the prog. Modern Lisp programming style tends to use prog rather infrequently. The various iteration constructs, such as do, have bodies with the characteristics of a prog. (However, the ability to use go statements within iteration constructs is very seldom called upon in practice.)

Three distinct operations are performed by prog: it binds local variables, it permits use of the return statement, and it permits use of the go statement. In Common Lisp, these three operations have been separated into three distinct constructs: let, block, and tagbody. These three constructs may be used independently as building blocks for other types of constructs.

---

tagbody {*tag* | *statement*}*   [*Special form*]

The part of a tagbody after the variable list is called the *body*. An item in the body may be a symbol or an integer, in which case it is called a *tag*, or an item in the body may be a list, in which case it is called a *statement*.

Each element of the body is processed from left to right. A *tag* is ignored; a *statement* is evaluated, and its results are discarded. If the end of the body is reached, the tagbody returns nil.

If (go *tag*) is evaluated, control jumps to the part of the body labelled with the *tag*.

Compatibility note: The "computed go" feature of MacLisp is not supported. The syntax of a computed go is idiosyncratic, and the feature is not supported by Lisp Machine Lisp, NIL (New Implementation of Lisp), or Interlisp. The computed go has been infrequently used in MacLisp anyway and is easily simulated with no loss of efficiency by using a case statement each of whose clauses performs a (non-computed) go.

The scope of the tags established by a tagbody is lexical, and the extent is dynamic. Once a tagbody construct has been exited, it is no longer legal to go to a *tag* in its body. It is permissible for a go to jump to a tagbody that is not the innermost tagbody construct containing that go; the tags established by a tagbody will only shadow other tags of like name.

The lexical scoping of the go targets named by tags is fully general and has consequences that may be surprising to users and implementors of other Lisp systems. For example, the go in the following example actually does work in Common Lisp as one might expect:

```
(tagbody
   (catch 'stuff
      (mapcar #'(lambda (x) (if (numberp x)
                                (hairyfun x)
                                (go lose)))
              items))
   (return)
 lose
   (error "I lost big!")))
```

Depending on the situation, a go in Common Lisp does not necessarily correspond to a simple machine "jump" instruction. A go can break up catchers if necessary to get to the target. It is possible for a "closure" created by function for a lambda-expression to refer to a go target as long as the tag is lexically apparent. See chapter 3 for an elaborate example of this.

There are some holes in this specification (and that of go) that leave some room for interpretation. For example, there is no explicit prohibition against the same tag appearing more than once in the same tagbody body. Every implementation I know of will complain in the compiler, if not in the interpreter, if there is a go to such a duplicated tag; but some implementors take the position that duplicate tags are permitted provided there is no go to such a tag. ("If a tree falls in the forest, and there is no one there to hear it, then no one needs to yell 'Timber!'") Also, some implementations allow objects other than symbols, integers, and lists in the body and typically ignore them. Consequently, some programmers use redundant tags such as --- for formatting purposes, and strings as comments:

```
(defun dining-philosopher (j)
   (tagbody ---
    think    (unless (hungry) (go think))
             ---
```

```
                   "Can't eat without chopsticks."
                   (snatch (chopstick j))
                   (snatch (chopstick (mod (+ j 1) 5)))
                   ---
     eat           (when (hungry)
                     (mapc #'gobble-down
                           '(twice-cooked-pork kung-pao-chi-ding
                             wu-dip-har orange-flavor-beef
                             two-side-yellow-noodles twinkies))
                     (go eat))
                   ---
                   "Can't think with my neighbors' stomachs rumbling."
                   (relinquish (chopstick j))
                   (relinquish (chopstick (mod (+ j 1) 5)))
                   ---
                   (if (happy) (go think)
                       (become insurance-salesman))))
```

In certain implementations of Common Lisp they get away with it. Others abhor
what they view as an abuse of unintended ambiguity in the language specification.
For maximum portability, I advise users to steer clear of these issues. Similarly,
it is best to avoid using nil as a tag, even though it is a symbol, because a few
implementations treat nil as a list to be executed. To be extra careful, avoid
calling from within a tagbody a macro whose expansion might not be a non-nil
list; wrap such a call in (progn ...), or rewrite the macro to return (progn ...)
if possible.

prog ({var | (var [init])}*) {declaration}* {tag | statement}*   [Macro]
prog* ({var | (var [init])}*) {declaration}* {tag | statement}*   [Macro]

The prog construct is a synthesis of let, block, and tagbody, allowing bound
variables and the use of return and go within a single construct. A typical prog
construct looks like this:

```
(prog (var1 var2 (var3 init3) var4 (var5 init5))
      {declaration}*
      statement1
  tag1
      statement2
      statement3
      statement4
```

    tag2

       statement5

       . . .

)

The list after the keyword prog is a set of specifications for binding *var1*, *var2*, etc., which are temporary variables bound locally to the prog. This list is processed exactly as the list in a let statement: first all the *init* forms are evaluated from left to right (where nil is used for any omitted *init* form), and then the variables are all bound in parallel to the respective results. Any *declaration* appearing in the prog is used as if appearing at the top of the let body.

    The body of the prog is executed as if it were a tagbody construct; the go statement may be used to transfer control to a *tag*.

    A prog implicitly establishes a block named nil around the entire prog construct, so that return may be used at any time to exit from the prog construct.

    Here is a fine example of what can be done with prog:

```
(defun king-of-confusion (w)
  "Take a cons of two lists and make a list of conses.
   Think of this function as being like a zipper."
  (prog (x y z)        ;Initialize x, y, z to nil
        (setq y (car w) z (cdr w))
   loop
        (cond ((null y) (return x))
              ((null z) (go err)))
   rejoin
        (setq x (cons (cons (car y) (car z)) x))
        (setq y (cdr y) z (cdr z))
        (go loop)
   err
        (cerror "Will self-pair extraneous items"
                "Mismatch - gleep!  S" y)
        (setq z y)
        (go rejoin)))
```

which is accomplished somewhat more perspicuously by

```
(defun prince-of-clarity (w)
  "Take a cons of two lists and make a list of conses.
   Think of this function as being like a zipper."
  (do ((y (car w) (cdr y))
```

```
          (z (cdr w) (cdr z))
          (x '() (cons (cons (car y) (car z)) x)))
        ((null y) x)
      (when (null z)
        (cerror "Will self-pair extraneous items"
                "Mismatch - gleep!  S" y)
        (setq z y))))
```

The prog construct may be explained in terms of the simpler constructs block, let, and tagbody as follows:

(prog *variable-list* {*declaration*}* . *body*)
    ≡ (block nil (let *variable-list* {*declaration*}* (tagbody . *body*)))

The prog* special form is almost the same as prog. The only difference is that the binding and initialization of the temporary variables is done *sequentially*, so that the *init* form for each one can use the values of previous ones. Therefore prog* is to prog as let* is to let. For example,

(prog* ((y z) (x (car y)))
        (return x))

returns the *car* of the value of z.

I haven't seen prog used very much in the last several years. Apparently splitting it into functional constituents (let, block, tagbody) has been a success. Common Lisp programmers now tend to use whichever specific construct is appropriate.

go *tag*   [*Special form*]

The (go *tag*) special form is used to do a "go to" within a tagbody construct. The *tag* must be a symbol or an integer; the *tag* is not evaluated. go transfers control to the point in the body labelled by a tag eql to the one given. If there is no such tag in the body, the bodies of lexically containing tagbody constructs (if any) are examined as well. It is an error if there is no matching tag lexically visible to the point of the go.

The go form does not ever return a value.

As a matter of style, it is recommended that the user think twice before using a go. Most purposes of go can be accomplished with one of the iteration primitives, nested conditional forms, or return-from. If the use of go seems to be unavoidable, perhaps the control structure implemented by go should be packaged as a macro definition.

7.9. Structure Traversal and Side Effects

X3J13 voted in January 1989 ⟨121⟩ to restrict side effects during the course of a built-in operation that can execute user-supplied code while traversing a data structure.

Consider the following example:

```
(let ((x '(apples peaches pumpkin pie)))
  (dolist (z x)
    (when (eq z 'peaches)
      (setf (cddr x) '(mango kumquat)))
    (format t " S " (car z))))
```

Depending on the details of the implementation of dolist, this bit of code could easily print

```
apples peaches mango kumquat
```

(which is perhaps what was intended), but it might as easily print

```
apples peaches pumpkin pie
```

Here is a plausible implementation of dolist that produces the first result:

```
(defmacro dolist ((var listform &optional (resultform ''nil))
                  &body body)
  (let ((tailvar (gensym "DOLIST")))
    `(do ((,tailvar ,listform (cdr ,tailvar)))
         ((null ,tailvar) ,resultform)
       (let ((,var (car ,tailvar))) ,@body))))
```

But here is a plausible implementation of dolist that produces the second result:

```
(defmacro dolist ((var listform &optional (resultform ''nil))
                  &body body)
  (let ((tailvar (gensym "DOLIST")))
    `(do ((,tailvar ,listform))
         ((null ,tailvar) ,resultform)
       (let ((,var (pop ,tailvar))) ,@body))))
```

The X3J13 recognizes and legitimizes varying implementation practices: in general it is an error for code executed during a "structure-traversing" operation to destructively modify the structure in a way that might affect the ongoing traversal operation. The committee identified in particular the following special cases.

For list traversal operations, the *cdr* chain may not be destructively modified.

For array traversal operations, the array may not be adjusted (see `adjust-array`) and its fill pointer, if any, may not be modified.

For hash table operations (such as `with-hash-table-iterator` and `maphash`), new entries may not be added or deleted, *except* that the very entry being processed by user code may be changed or deleted.

For package symbol operations (for example, `with-package-iterator` and `do-symbols`), new symbols may not be interned in, nor symbols uninterned from, the packages being traversed or any packages they use, *except* that the very symbol being processed by user code may be uninterned.

X3J13 noted that this vote is intended to clarify restrictions on the use of structure traversal operations that are not themselves inherently destructive; for example, it applies to `map` and `dolist`. Destructive operators such as `delete` require even more complicated restrictions and are addressed by a separate proposal.

The X3J13 vote did not specify a complete list of the operations to which these restrictions apply. Table 7-1 shows what I believe to be a complete list of operations that traverse structures and take user code as a body (in the case of macros) or as a functional argument (in the case of functions).

In addition, note that user code should not modify list structure that might be undergoing interpretation by the evaluator, whether explicitly invoked via `eval` or implicitly invoked, for example as in the case of a hook function (a `defstruct` print function, the value of `*evalhook*` or `*applyhook*`, etc.) that happens to be a closure of interpreted code. Similarly, `defstruct` print functions and other hooks should not perform side effects on data structures being printed or being processed by `format`, or on a string given to `make-string-input-stream`. You get the idea; be sensible.

Note that an operation such as `mapcar` or `dolist` traverses not only *cdr* pointers (in order to chase down the list) but also *car* pointers (in order to obtain the elements themselves). The restriction against modification appears to apply to all these pointers.

7.10. Multiple Values

Ordinarily the result of calling a Lisp function is a single Lisp object. Sometimes, however, it is convenient for a function to compute several objects and return them. Common Lisp provides a mechanism for handling multiple values directly. This mechanism is cleaner and more efficient than the usual tricks involving returning a list of results or stashing results in global variables.

Table 7-1: Structure Traversal Operations Subject to Side Effect Restrictions

adjoin	maphash	reduce
assoc	mapl	remove
assoc-if	maplist	remove-duplicates
assoc-if-not	member	remove-if
count	member-if	remove-if-not
count-if	member-if-not	search
count-if-not	merge	set-difference
delete	mismatch	set-exclusive-or
delete-duplicates	nintersection	some
delete-if	notany	sort
delete-if-not	notevery	stable-sort
do-all-symbols	nset-difference	sublis
do-external-symbols	nset-exclusive-or	subsetp
do-symbols	nsublis	subst
dolist	nsubst	subst-if
eval	nsubst-if	subst-if-not
every	nsubst-if-not	substitute
find	nsubstitute	substitute-if
find-if	nsubstitute-if	substitute-if-not
find-if-not	nsubstitute-if-not	tree-equal
intersection	nunion	union
certain loop clauses	position	with-hash-table-iterator
map	position-if	with-input-from-string
mapc	position-if-not	with-output-to-string
mapcan	rassoc	with-package-iterator
mapcar	rassoc-if	
mapcon	rassoc-if-not	

7.10.1. Constructs for Handling Multiple Values

Normally multiple values are not used. Special forms are required both to *produce* multiple values and to *receive* them. If the caller of a function does not request multiple values, but the called function produces multiple values, then the first value is given to the caller and all others are discarded; if the called function produces zero values, then the caller gets nil as a value.

The primary primitive for producing multiple values is values, which takes any number of arguments and returns that many values. If the last form in the body of a function is a values with three arguments, then a call to that function will return three values. Other special forms also produce multiple values, but they can be described in terms of values. Some built-in Common Lisp functions, such as floor, return multiple values; those that do are so documented.

The special forms and macros for receiving multiple values are as follows:

```
multiple-value-list
multiple-value-call
multiple-value-prog1
multiple-value-bind
multiple-value-setq
```

These specify a form to evaluate and an indication of where to put the values returned by that form.

values &rest *args*   [*Function*]

All of the arguments are returned, in order, as values. For example:

```
(defun polar (x y)
  (values (sqrt (+ (* x x) (* y y))) (atan y x)))

(multiple-value-bind (r theta) (polar 3.0 4.0)
  (vector r theta))
  ⇒ #(5.0 0.9272952)
```

The expression (values) returns zero values. This is the standard idiom for returning no values from a function.

Sometimes it is desirable to indicate explicitly that a function will return exactly one value. For example, the function

```
(defun foo (x y)
  (floor (+ x y) y))
```

will return two values because floor returns two values. It may be that the second value makes no sense, or that for efficiency reasons it is desired not to compute the second value. The values function is the standard idiom for indicating that only one value is to be returned, as shown in the following example.

```
(defun foo (x y)
  (values (floor (+ x y) y)))
```

This works because values returns exactly *one* value for each of its argument forms; as for any function call, if any argument form to values produces more than one value, all but the first are discarded.

There is absolutely no way in Common Lisp for a caller to distinguish between returning a single value in the ordinary manner and returning exactly one "multiple value." For example, the values returned by the expressions (+ 1 2) and (values (+ 1 2)) are identical in every respect: the single value 3.

multiple-values-limit   [*Constant*]

The value of multiple-values-limit is a positive integer that is the upper exclusive bound on the number of values that may be returned from a function. This bound depends on the implementation but will not be smaller than 20. (Implementors are encouraged to make this limit as large as practicable without sacrificing performance.) See lambda-parameters-limit and call-arguments-limit.

values-list *list*   [*Function*]

All of the elements of *list* are returned as multiple values. For example:

(values-list (list a b c)) ≡ (values a b c)

In general,

(values-list *list*) ≡ (apply #´values *list*)

but values-list may be clearer or more efficient.

multiple-value-list *form*   [*Macro*]

multiple-value-list evaluates *form* and returns a list of the multiple values it returned. For example:

(multiple-value-list (floor -3 4)) ⇒ (-1 1)

multiple-value-list and values-list are therefore inverses of each other.

multiple-value-call *function* {*form*}*   [*Special form*]

multiple-value-call first evaluates *function* to obtain a function and then evaluates all of the *forms*. All the values of the *forms* are gathered together (not just one value from each) and are all given as arguments to the function. The result of multiple-value-call is whatever is returned by the function. For example:

```
(+ (floor 5 3) (floor 19 4))
   ≡ (+ 1 4) ⇒ 5
(multiple-value-call #´+ (floor 5 3) (floor 19 4))
   ≡ (+ 1 2 4 3) ⇒ 10
(multiple-value-list form) ≡ (multiple-value-call #´list form)
```

multiple-value-prog1 *form* {*form*}*   [*Special form*]

multiple-value-prog1 evaluates the first *form* and saves all the values produced by that form. It then evaluates the other *form*s from left to right, discarding their values. The values produced by the first *form* are returned by
multiple-value-prog1. See prog1, which always returns a single value.

multiple-value-bind ({*var*}*) *values-form*   [*Macro*]
                    {*declaration*}* {*form*}*

The *values-form* is evaluated, and each of the variables *var* is bound to the respective value returned by that form. If there are more variables than values returned,
extra values of nil are given to the remaining variables. If there are more values
than variables, the excess values are simply discarded. The variables are bound to
the values over the execution of the forms, which make up an implicit progn. For
example:

```
(multiple-value-bind (x) (floor 5 3) (list x)) ⇒ (1)
(multiple-value-bind (x y) (floor 5 3) (list x y)) ⇒ (1 2)
(multiple-value-bind (x y z) (floor 5 3) (list x y z))
   ⇒ (1 2 nil)
```

multiple-value-setq *variables form*   [*Macro*]

The *variables* must be a list of variables. The *form* is evaluated, and the variables
are *set* (not bound) to the values returned by that form. If there are more variables
than values returned, extra values of nil are assigned to the remaining variables.
If there are more values than variables, the excess values are simply discarded.

Compatibility note: In Lisp Machine Lisp this is called multiple-value. The added clarity
of the name multiple-value-setq in Common Lisp was deemed worth the incompatibility
with Lisp Machine Lisp.

`multiple-value-setq` always returns a single value, which is the first value returned by *form*, or `nil` if *form* produces zero values.

X3J13 voted in March 1989 ⟨173⟩ to specify that if any *var* refers not to an ordinary variable but to a binding made by `symbol-macrolet`, then that *var* is handled as if `setq` were used to assign the appropriate value to it.

`nth-value` *n form*   [*Macro*]

X3J13 voted in January 1989 ⟨123⟩ to add a new macro named `nth-value`. The argument forms *n* and *form* are both evaluated. The value of *n* must be a non-negative integer, and the *form* may produce any number of values. The integer *n* is used as a zero-based index into the list of values. Value *n* of the *form* is returned as the single value of the `nth-value` form; `nil` is returned if the *form* produces no more than *n* values.

As an example, mod could be defined as

```
(defun mod (number divisor)
  (nth-value 1 (floor number divisor)))
```

Value number 1 is the *second* value returned by `floor`, the first value being value number 0.

One could define `nth-value` simply as

```
(defmacro nth-value (n form)
  `(nth ,n (multiple-value-list ,form)))
```

but the clever implementor will doubtless find an implementation technique for `nth-value` that avoids constructing an intermediate list of all the values of the *form*.

7.10.2. Rules Governing the Passing of Multiple Values

It is often the case that the value of a special form or macro call is defined to be the value of one of its subforms. For example, the value of a `cond` is the value of the last form in the selected clause.

In most such cases, if the subform produces multiple values, then the original form will also produce all of those values. This *passing back* of multiple values of course has no effect unless eventually one of the special forms for receiving multiple values is reached.

To be explicit, multiple values can result from a special form under precisely these circumstances:

Evaluation and application

- `eval` returns multiple values if the form given it to evaluate produces multiple values.

- `apply`, `funcall`, and `multiple-value-call` pass back multiple values from the function applied or called.

Implicit `progn` *contexts*

- The special form `progn` passes back multiple values resulting from evaluation of the last subform. Other situations referred to as "implicit `progn`," where several forms are evaluated and the results of all but the last form are discarded, also pass back multiple values from the last form. These situations include the body of a lambda-expression, in particular those constructed by `defun`, `defmacro`, and `deftype`. Also included are bodies of the constructs `eval-when`, `progv`, `let`, `let*`, `when`, `unless`, `block`, `multiple-value-bind`, and `catch`, as well as clauses in such conditional constructs as `case`, `typecase`, `ecase`, `etypecase`, `ccase`, and `ctypecase`.

X3J13 has voted to add many new constructs to the language that contain implicit `progn` contexts. I won't attempt to list them all here. Of particular interest, however, is `locally`, which may be regarded as simply a version of `progn` that permits declarations before its body. This provides a useful building block for constructing macros that permit declarations (but not documentation strings) before their bodies and pass back any multiple values produced by the last sub-form of a body. (If a body can contain a documentation string, most likely `lambda` is the correct building block to use.)

Conditional constructs

- `if` passes back multiple values from whichever subform is selected (the *then* form or the *else* form).

- `and` and `or` pass back multiple values from the last subform but not from sub-forms other than the last.

- `cond` passes back multiple values from the last subform of the implicit `progn` of the selected clause. If, however, the clause selected is a singleton clause, then only a single value (the non-`nil` predicate value) is returned. This is true even if the singleton clause is the last clause of the `cond`. It is *not* permitted to treat a final clause `(x)` as being the same as `(t x)` for this reason; the latter passes back multiple values from the form x.

Returning from a block

- The `block` construct passes back multiple values from its last subform when it exits normally. If `return-from` (or `return`) is used to terminate the `block` prematurely, then `return-from` passes back multiple values from its subform as the values of the terminated `block`. Other constructs that create implicit blocks, such as `do`, `dolist`, `dotimes`, `prog`, and `prog*`, also pass back multiple values specified by `return-from` (or `return`).

- `do` passes back multiple values from the last form of the exit clause, exactly as if the exit clause were a `cond` clause. Similarly, `dolist` and `dotimes` pass back multiple values from the *resultform* if that is executed. These situations are all examples of implicit uses of `return-from`.

Throwing out of a catch

- The `catch` construct returns multiple values if the result form in a `throw` exiting from such a catch produces multiple values.

Miscellaneous situations

- `multiple-value-prog1` passes back multiple values from its first subform. However, `prog1` always returns a single value.

- `unwind-protect` returns multiple values if the form it protects returns multiple values.

- `the` returns multiple values if the form it contains returns multiple values.

Among special forms that *never* pass back multiple values are `prog1`, `prog2`, `setq`, and `multiple-value-setq`. The conventional way to force only one value to be returned from a form x is to write (`values` x).

The most important rule about multiple values is: **No matter how many values a form produces, if the form is an argument form in a function call, then exactly one value (the first one) is used.**

For example, if you write (`cons` (`floor` x)), then `cons` will always receive *exactly* one argument (which is of course an error), even though `floor` returns two values. To pass both values from `floor` to `cons`, one must write something like (`multiple-value-call` #´`cons` (`floor` x)). In an ordinary function call, each argument form produces exactly *one* argument; if such a form returns zero values, `nil` is used for the argument, and if more than one value, all but the first are discarded. Similarly, conditional constructs such as `if` that test the value of a form will use exactly one value, the first one, from that form and discard the rest; such constructs will use `nil` as the test value if zero values are returned.

7.11. Dynamic Non-Local Exits

Common Lisp provides a facility for exiting from a complex process in a non-local, dynamically scoped manner. There are two classes of special forms for this purpose, called *catch* forms and *throw* forms, or simply *catches* and *throws*. A catch form evaluates some subforms in such a way that, if a throw form is executed during such evaluation, the evaluation is aborted at that point and the catch form immediately returns a value specified by the throw. Unlike `block` and `return` (section 7.7), which allow for exiting a `block` form from any point lexically within the body of the `block`, the catch/throw mechanism works even if the throw form is not textually within the body of the catch form. The throw need only occur within the extent (time span) of the evaluation of the body of the catch. This is analogous to the distinction between dynamically bound (special) variables and lexically bound (local) variables.

`catch` *tag* {*form*}*   [*Special form*]

The `catch` special form serves as a target for transfer of control by `throw`. The form *tag* is evaluated first to produce an object that names the catch; it may be any Lisp object. A catcher is then established with the object as the tag. The *form*s are evaluated as an implicit `progn`, and the results of the last form are returned, except that if during the evaluation of the *form*s a throw should be executed such that the tag of the throw matches (is eq to) the tag of the `catch` and the catcher is the most recent outstanding catcher with that tag, then the evaluation of the *form*s is aborted and the results specified by the throw are immediately returned from the `catch` expression. The catcher established by the `catch` expression is disestablished just before the results are returned.

The tag is used to match throws with catches. (`catch` ´foo *form*) will catch a (`throw` ´foo *form*) but not a (`throw` ´bar *form*). It is an error if throw is done when there is no suitable `catch` ready to catch it.

Catch tags are compared using eq, not eql; therefore numbers and characters should not be used as catch tags.

Compatibility note: The name `catch` comes from MacLisp, but the syntax of `catch` in Common Lisp is different. The MacLisp syntax was (`catch` *form* *tag*), where the *tag* was not evaluated.

unwind-protect *protected-form* {*cleanup-form*}*   [*Special form*]

Sometimes it is necessary to evaluate a form and make sure that certain side effects take place after the form is evaluated; a typical example is

```
(progn (start-motor)
       (drill-hole)
       (stop-motor))
```

The non-local exit facility of Common Lisp creates a situation in which the above code won't work, however: if drill-hole should do a throw to a catch that is outside of the progn form (perhaps because the drill bit broke), then (stop-motor) will never be evaluated (and the motor will presumably be left running). This is particularly likely if drill-hole causes a Lisp error and the user tells the error-handler to give up and abort the computation. (A possibly more practical example might be

```
(prog2 (open-a-file)
       (process-file)
       (close-the-file))
```

where it is desired always to close the file when the computation is terminated for whatever reason. This case is so important that Common Lisp provides the special form with-open-file for this purpose.)

   In order to allow the example hole-drilling program to work, it can be rewritten using unwind-protect as follows:

```
;; Stop the motor no matter what (even if it failed to start).

(unwind-protect
  (progn (start-motor)
         (drill-hole))
  (stop-motor))
```

If drill-hole does a throw that attempts to quit out of the unwind-protect, then (stop-motor) will be executed.

   This example assumes that it is correct to call stop-motor even if the motor has not yet been started. Remember that an error or interrupt may cause an exit even before any initialization forms have been executed. Any state restoration code should operate correctly no matter where in the protected code an exit occurred. For example, the following code is not correct:

```
(unwind-protect
  (progn (incf *access-count*)
         (perform-access))
  (decf *access-count*))
```

If an exit occurs before completion of the `incf` operation the `decf` operation will be executed anyway, resulting in an incorrect value for `*access-count*`. The correct way to code this is as follows:

```
(let ((old-count *access-count*))
  (unwind-protect
    (progn (incf *access-count*)
           (perform-access))
    (setq *access-count* old-count)))
```

As a general rule, `unwind-protect` guarantees to execute the *cleanup-forms* before exiting, whether it terminates normally or is aborted by a throw of some kind. (If, however, an exit occurs during execution of the *cleanup-forms*, no special action is taken. The *cleanup-forms* of an `unwind-protect` are not protected by that `unwind-protect`, though they may be protected if that `unwind-protect` occurs within the protected form of another `unwind-protect`.) `unwind-protect` returns whatever results from evaluation of the *protected-form* and discards all the results from the *cleanup-forms*.

It should be emphasized that `unwind-protect` protects against *all* attempts to exit from the protected form, including not only "dynamic exit" facilities such as `throw` but also "lexical exit" facilities such as `go` and `return-from`. Consider this situation:

```
(tagbody
  (let ((x 3))
    (unwind-protect
      (if (numberp x) (go out))
      (print x)))
 out
  ...)
```

When the `go` is executed, the call to `print` is executed first, and then the transfer of control to the tag `out` is completed.

X3J13 voted in March 1989 ⟨74⟩ to clarify the interaction of `unwind-protect` with constructs that perform exits.

Let an *exit* be a point out of which control can be transferred. For a `throw` the exit is the matching `catch`; for a `return-from` the exit is the corresponding block. For a go the exit is the statement within the tagbody (the one to which the target tag belongs) which is being executed at the time the go is performed.

The extent of an exit is dynamic; it is not indefinite. The extent of an exit begins when the corresponding form (catch, block, or tagbody statement) is entered. When the extent of an exit has ended, it is no longer legal to return from it.

Note that the extent of an exit is not the same thing as the scope or extent of the designator by which the exit is identified. For example, a block name has lexical scope but the extent of its exit is dynamic. The extent of a catch tag could differ from the extent of the exit associated with the catch (which is exactly what is at issue here). The difference matters when there are transfers of control from the cleanup clauses of an unwind-protect.

When a transfer of control out of an exit is initiated by throw, return-from, or go, a variety of events occur before the transfer of control is complete:

- The cleanup clauses of any intervening unwind-protect clauses are evaluated.

- Intervening dynamic bindings of special variables and catch tags are undone.

- Intervening exits are *abandoned*, that is, their extent ends and it is no longer legal to attempt to transfer control from them.

- The extent of the exit being invoked ends.

- Control is finally passed to the target.

The first edition left the order of these events in some doubt. The implementation note for throw hinted that the first two processes are interwoven, but it was unclear whether it is permissible for an implementation to abandon all intervening exits before processing any intervening unwind-protect cleanup clauses.

The clarification adopted by X3J13 is as follows. Intervening exits are abandoned as soon as the transfer of control is initiated; in the case of a throw, this occurs at the beginning of the "second pass" mentioned in the implementation note. It is an error to attempt a transfer of control to an exit whose dynamic extent has ended.

Next the evaluation of unwind-protect cleanup clauses and the undoing of dynamic bindings and catch tags are performed together, in the order corresponding to the reverse of the order in which they were established. The effect of this is that the cleanup clauses of an unwind-protect will see the same dynamic bindings of variables and catch tags as were visible when the unwind-protect was entered. (However, some of those catch tags may not be useable because they correspond to abandoned exit points.)

Finally control is transferred to the originally invoked exit and simultaneously that exit is abandoned.

The effect of this specification is that once a program has attempted to transfer
control to a particular exit, an unwind-protect cleanup form cannot step in and
decide to transfer control to a more recent (nested) exit, blithely forgetting the
original exit request. However, a cleanup form may restate the request to transfer
to the same exit that started the cleanup process.

Here is an example based on a nautical metaphor. The function gently moves
an oar in the water with low force, but if an oar gets stuck, the caller will catch
a crab. The function row takes a boat, an oar-stroking function, a stream, and a
count; an oar is constructed for the boat and stream and the oar-stroking function
is called :count times. The function life rows a particular boat. Merriment
follows, except that if the oarsman is winded he must stop to catch his breath.

```
(defun gently (oar)
  (stroke oar :force 0.5)
  (when (stuck oar)
    (throw 'crab nil)))

(defun row (boat stroke-fn stream &key count)
  (let ((oar (make-oar boat stream)))
    (loop repeat count do (funcall stroke-fn oar))))

(defun life ()
  (catch 'crab
    (catch 'breath
      (unwind-protect
          (row *your-boat* #'gently *query-io* :count 3))
        (when (winded) (throw 'breath nil)))
      (loop repeat 4 (set-mode :merry))
      (dream))))
```

Suppose that the oar gets stuck, causing gently to call throw with the tag crab.
The program is then committed to exiting from the outer catch (the one with the
tag crab). As control breaks out of the unwind-protect form, the winded test is
executed. Suppose it is true; then another call to throw occurs, this time with the
tag breath. The inner catch (the one with the tag breath) has been abandoned
as a result of the first throw operation (still in progress). The clarification voted
by X3J13 specifies that the program is in error for attempting to transfer control to
an abandoned exit point. To put it in terms of the example: once you have begun
to catch a crab, you cannot rely on being able to catch your breath.

Implementations may support longer extents for exits than is required by this
specification, but portable programs may not rely on such extended extents.

(This specification is somewhat controversial. An alternative proposal was that the abandoning of exits should be lumped in with the evaluation of unwind-protect cleanup clauses and the undoing of dynamic bindings and catch tags, performing all in reverse order of establishment. X3J13 agreed that this approach is theoretically cleaner and more elegant but also more stringent and of little additional practical use. There was some concern that a more stringent specification might be a great added burden to some implementors and would achieve only a small gain for users.)

throw *tag result*   [*Special form*]

The throw special form transfers control to a matching catch construct. The *tag* is evaluated first to produce an object called the throw tag; then the *result* form is evaluated, and its results are saved (if the *result* form produces multiple values, then *all* the values are saved). The most recent outstanding catch whose tag matches the throw tag is exited; the saved results are returned as the value(s) of the catch. A catch matches only if the catch tag is eq to the throw tag.

In the process, dynamic variable bindings are undone back to the point of the catch, and any intervening unwind-protect cleanup code is executed. The *result* form is evaluated before the unwinding process commences, and whatever results it produces are returned from the catch.

If there is no outstanding catcher whose tag matches the throw tag, no unwinding of the stack is performed, and an error is signalled. When the error is signalled, the outstanding catchers and the dynamic variable bindings are those in force at the point of the throw.

Implementation note: These requirements imply that throwing should typically make two passes over the control stack. In the first pass it simply searches for a matching catch. In this search every catch must be considered, but every unwind-protect should be ignored. On the second pass the stack is actually unwound, one frame at a time, undoing dynamic bindings and outstanding unwind-protect constructs in reverse order of creation until the matching catch is reached.

Compatibility note: The name throw comes from MacLisp, but the syntax of throw in Common Lisp is different. The MacLisp syntax was (throw *form tag*), where the *tag* was not evaluated.

8

Macros

The Common Lisp macro facility allows the user to define arbitrary functions that convert certain Lisp forms into different forms before evaluating or compiling them. This is done at the expression level, not at the character-string level as in most other languages. Macros are important in the writing of good code: they make it possible to write code that is clear and elegant at the user level but that is converted to a more complex or more efficient internal form for execution.

When `eval` is given a list whose *car* is a symbol, it looks for local definitions of that symbol (by `flet`, `labels`, and `macrolet`); if that fails, it looks for a global definition. If the definition is a macro definition, then the original list is said to be a *macro call*. Associated with the definition will be a function of two arguments, called the *expansion function*. This function is called with the entire macro call as its first argument (the second argument is a lexical environment); it must return some new Lisp form, called the *expansion* of the macro call. (Actually, a more general mechanism is involved; see `macroexpand`.) This expansion is then evaluated in place of the original form.

When a function is being compiled, any macros it contains are expanded at compilation time. This means that a macro definition must be seen by the compiler before the first use of the macro.

More generally, an implementation of Common Lisp has great latitude in deciding exactly when to expand macro calls within a program. For example, it is acceptable for the `defun` special form to expand all macro calls within its body at the time the `defun` form is executed and record the fully expanded body as the body of the function being defined. (An implementation might even choose always to compile functions defined by `defun`, even when operating in an "interpretive" mode.)

Macros should be written so as to depend as little as possible on the execution environment to produce a correct expansion. To ensure consistent behavior, it is best to ensure that all macro definitions are available, whether to the interpreter or compiler, before any code containing calls to those macros is introduced.

In Common Lisp, macros are not functions. In particular, macros cannot be used as functional arguments to such functions as `apply`, `funcall`, or `map`; in such situations, the list representing the "original macro call" does not exist, and cannot exist, because in some sense the arguments have already been evaluated.

8.1. Macro Definition

The function `macro-function` determines whether a given symbol is the name of a macro. The `defmacro` construct provides a convenient way to define new macros.

`macro-function` *symbol*   [*Function*]

The argument must be a symbol. If the symbol has a global function definition that is a macro definition, then the expansion function (a function of two arguments, the macro-call form and an environment) is returned. If the symbol has no global function definition, or has a definition as an ordinary function or as a special form but not as a macro, then `nil` is returned. The function `macroexpand` is the best way to invoke the expansion function.

It is possible for *both* `macro-function` and `special-form-p` to be true of a symbol. This is possible because an implementation is permitted to implement any macro also as a special form for speed. On the other hand, the macro definition must be available for use by programs that understand only the standard special forms listed in table 5-1.

`macro-function` cannot be used to determine whether a symbol names a locally defined macro established by `macrolet`; `macro-function` can examine only global definitions.

`setf` may be used with `macro-function` to install a macro as a symbol's global function definition:

`(setf (macro-function `*symbol*`) `*fn*`)`

The value installed must be a function that accepts two arguments, an entire macro call and an environment, and computes the expansion for that call. Performing this operation causes the symbol to have *only* that macro definition as its global function definition; any previous definition, whether as a macro or as a function, is lost. It is an error to attempt to redefine the name of a special form.

X3J13 voted in March 1988 ⟨118⟩ to add an optional environment argument to `macro-function`.

`macro-function` *symbol* &optional *env*   [*Function*]

The first argument must be a symbol. If the symbol has a function definition that is a macro definition, whether a local one established in the environment *env* by `macrolet` or a global one established as if by `defmacro`, then the expansion function (a function of two arguments, the macro-call form and an environment) is returned. If the symbol has no function definition, or has a definition as an ordinary function or as a special form but not as a macro, then `nil` is returned. The function `macroexpand` or `macroexpand-1` is the best way to invoke the expansion function.

It is possible for *both* `macro-function` and `special-form-p` to be true of a symbol. This is possible because an implementation is permitted to implement any macro also as a special form for speed. On the other hand, the macro definition must be available for use by programs that understand only the standard special forms listed in table 5-1.

`setf` may be used with `macro-function` to install a macro as a symbol's global function definition:

`(setf (macro-function` *symbol*`)` *fn*`)`

The value installed must be a function that accepts two arguments, an entire macro call and an environment, and computes the expansion for that call. Performing this operation causes the symbol to have *only* that macro definition as its global function definition; any previous definition, whether as a macro or as a function, is lost. One cannot use `setf` to establish a local macro definition; it is an error to supply a second argument to `macro-function` when using it with `setf`. It is an error to attempt to redefine the name of a special form.

See also `compiler-macro-function`.

`defmacro` *name lambda-list* ⟦ {*declaration*}* | *doc-string* ⟧ {*form*}*   [*Macro*]

`defmacro` is a macro-defining macro that arranges to decompose the macro-call form in an elegant and useful way. `defmacro` has essentially the same syntax as `defun`: *name* is the symbol whose macro definition we are creating, *lambda-list* is similar in form to a lambda-list, and the *form*s constitute the body of the expander function. The `defmacro` construct arranges to install this expander function, as the global macro definition of *name*.

The expander function is effectively defined in the *global* environment; lexically scoped entities established outside the `defmacro` form that would ordinarily be lexically apparent are not visible within the body of the expansion function.

X3J13 voted in March 1989 ⟨50⟩ to clarify that, while defining forms normally appear at top level, it is meaningful to place them in non-top-level contexts.

Furthermore, defmacro should define the expander function within the enclosing lexical environment, not within the global environment.

X3J13 voted in March 1988 ⟨78⟩ to specify that the body of the expander function defined by defmacro is implicitly enclosed in a block construct whose name is the same as the *name* of the defined macro. Therefore return-from may be used to exit from the function.

The *name* is returned as the value of the defmacro form.

If we view the macro call as a list containing a function name and some argument forms, in effect the expander function and the list of (unevaluated) argument forms is given to apply. The parameter specifiers are processed as for any lambda-expression, using the macro-call argument forms as the arguments. Then the body forms are evaluated as an implicit progn, and the value of the last form is returned as the expansion of the macro call.

If the optional documentation string *doc-string* is present (if not followed by a declaration, it may be present only if at least one *form* is also specified, as it is otherwise taken to be a *form*), then it is attached to the *name* as a documentation string of type function; see documentation.

Like the lambda-list in a defun, a defmacro *lambda-list* may contain the lambda-list keywords &optional, &rest, &key, &allow-other-keys, and &aux. For &optional and &key parameters, initialization forms and supplied-p parameters may be specified, just as for defun. Three additional markers are allowed in defmacro variable lists only.

These three markers are now allowed in other constructs as well.

&body   This is identical in function to &rest, but it informs certain output-formatting and editing functions that the remainder of the form is treated as a body and should be indented accordingly. (Only one of &body or &rest may be used.)

&whole   This is followed by a single variable that is bound to the entire macro-call form; this is the value that the macro definition function receives as its single argument. &whole and the following variable should appear first in the lambda-list, before any other parameter or lambda-list keyword.

&environment This is followed by a single variable that is bound to an environment representing the lexical environment in which the macro call is to be interpreted. This environment may not be the complete lexical environment; it should be used only with the function macroexpand for the sake of any local macro definitions that the macrolet construct may have established within that lexical environment. This is useful primarily in the rare cases where a macro definition must explicitly expand any macros in a subform of the macro call before computing its own expansion.

See `lambda-list-keywords`.

Notice of correction. In the first edition, the symbol `&environment` at the left margin above was inadvertently omitted.

X3J13 voted in March 1989 ⟨117⟩ to specify that macro environment objects received with the `&environment` argument of a macro function have only dynamic extent. The consequences are undefined if such objects are referred to outside the dynamic extent of that particular invocation of the macro function. This allows implementations to use somewhat more efficient techniques for representing environment objects.

X3J13 voted in March 1989 ⟨51⟩ to clarify the permitted uses of `&body`, `&whole`, and `&environment`:

• `&body` may appear at any level of a `defmacro` lambda-list.

• `&whole` may appear at any level of a `defmacro` lambda-list. At inner levels a `&whole` variable is bound to that part of the argument that matches the sub-lambda-list in which `&whole` appears. No matter where `&whole` is used, other parameters or lambda-list keywords may follow it.

• `&environment` may occur only at the outermost level of a `defmacro` lambda-list, and it may occur at most once, but it may occur anywhere within that lambda-list, even before an occurrence of `&whole`.

`defmacro`, unlike any other Common Lisp construct that has a lambda-list as part of its syntax, provides an additional facility known as *destructuring*.

See `destructuring-bind`, which provides the destructuring facility separately.

Anywhere in the lambda-list where a parameter name may appear, and where ordinary lambda-list syntax (as described in section 5.2.2) does not otherwise allow a list, a lambda-list may appear in place of the parameter name. When this is done, then the argument form that would match the parameter is treated as a (possibly dotted) list, to be used as an argument forms list for satisfying the parameters in the embedded lambda-list. As an example, one could write the macro definition for `dolist` in this manner:

```
(defmacro dolist ((var listform &optional resultform)
                  &rest body)
   ...)
```

More examples of embedded lambda-lists in `defmacro` are shown below.

Another destructuring rule is that defmacro allows any lambda-list (whether top-level or embedded) to be dotted, ending in a parameter name. This situation is treated exactly as if the parameter name that ends the list had appeared preceded by &rest. For example, the definition skeleton for dolist shown above could instead have been written

```
(defmacro dolist ((var listform &optional resultform)
                  . body)
  ...)
```

If the compiler encounters a defmacro, the new macro is added to the compilation environment, and a compiled form of the expansion function is also added to the output file so that the new macro will be operative at run time. If this is not the desired effect, the defmacro form can be wrapped in an eval-when construct.

It is permissible to use defmacro to redefine a macro (for example, to install a corrected version of an incorrect definition), or to redefine a function as a macro. It is an error to attempt to redefine the name of a special form (see table 5-1) as a macro. See macrolet, which establishes macro definitions over a restricted lexical scope.

See also define-compiler-macro.

Suppose, for the sake of example, that it were desirable to implement a conditional construct analogous to the Fortran arithmetic IF statement. (This of course requires a certain stretching of the imagination and suspension of disbelief.) The construct should accept four forms: a *test-value*, a *neg-form*, a *zero-form*, and a *pos-form*. One of the last three forms is chosen to be executed according to whether the value of the *test-form* is positive, negative, or zero. Using defmacro, a definition for such a construct might look like this:

```
(defmacro arithmetic-if (test neg-form zero-form pos-form)
  (let ((var (gensym)))
    `(let ((,var ,test))
       (cond ((< ,var 0) ,neg-form)
             ((= ,var 0) ,zero-form)
             (t ,pos-form)))))
```

Note the use of the backquote facility in this definition (see section 22.1.3). Also note the use of gensym to generate a new variable name. This is necessary to avoid conflict with any variables that might be referred to in *neg-form*, *zero-form*, or *pos-form*.

If the form is executed by the interpreter, it will cause the function definition of the symbol arithmetic-if to be a macro associated with which is a two-argument expansion function roughly equivalent to

```
(lambda (calling-form environment)
  (declare (ignore environment))
  (let ((var (gensym)))
    (list 'let
          (list (list 'var (cadr calling-form)))
          (list 'cond
                (list (list '< var '0) (caddr calling-form))
                (list (list '= var '0) (cadddr calling-form))
                (list 't (fifth calling-form))))))
```

The lambda-expression is produced by the defmacro declaration. The calls to list are the (hypothetical) result of the backquote (`) macro character and its associated commas. The precise macro expansion function may depend on the implementation, for example providing some degree of explicit error checking on the number of argument forms in the macro call.

Now, if eval encounters

```
(arithmetic-if (- x 4.0)
               (- x)
               (error "Strange zero")
               x)
```

this will be expanded into something like

```
(let ((g407 (- x 4.0)))
  (cond ((< g407 0) (- x))
        ((= g407 0) (error "Strange zero"))
        (t x)))
```

and eval tries again on this new form. (It should be clear now that the backquote facility is very useful in writing macros, since the form to be returned is normally a complex list structure, typically consisting of a mostly constant template with a few evaluated forms here and there. The backquote template provides a "picture" of the resulting code, with places to be filled in indicated by preceding commas.)

To expand on this example, stretching credibility to its limit, we might allow the *pos-form* and *zero-form* to be omitted, allowing their values to default to nil, in much the same way that the *else* form of a Common Lisp if construct may be omitted:

```
(defmacro arithmetic-if (test neg-form
                              &optional zero-form pos-form)
   (let ((var (gensym)))
    `(let ((,var ,test))
       (cond ((< ,var 0) ,neg-form)
             ((= ,var 0) ,zero-form)
             (t ,pos-form)))))
```

Then one could write

```
(arithmetic-if (- x 4.0) (print x))
```

which would be expanded into something like

```
(let ((g408 (- x 4.0)))
  (cond ((< g408 0) (print x))
        ((= g408 0) nil)
        (t nil)))
```

The resulting code is correct but rather silly-looking. One might rewrite the macro definition to produce better code when *pos-form* and possibly *zero-form* are omitted, or one might simply rely on the Common Lisp implementation to provide a compiler smart enough to improve the code itself.

Destructuring is a very powerful facility that allows the defmacro lambda-list to express the structure of a complicated macro-call syntax. If no lambda-list keywords appear, then the defmacro lambda-list is simply a list, nested to some extent, containing parameter names at the leaves. The macro-call form must have the same list structure. For example, consider this macro definition:

```
(defmacro halibut ((mouth eye1 eye2)
                   ((fin1 length1) (fin2 length2))
                   tail)
  ...)
```

Now consider this macro call:

```
(halibut (m (car eyes) (cdr eyes))
         ((f1 (count-scales f1)) (f2 (count-scales f2)))
         my-favorite-tail)
```

This would cause the expansion function to receive the following values for its parameters:

Parameter	Value
mouth	m
eye1	(car eyes)
eye2	(cdr eyes)
fin1	f1
length1	(count-scales f1)
fin2	f2
length2	(count-scales f2)
tail	my-favorite-tail

The following macro call would be in error because there would be no argument form to match the parameter length1:

```
(halibut (m (car eyes) (cdr eyes))
         ((f1) (f2 (count-scales f2)))
         my-favorite-tail)
```

The following macro call would be in error because a symbol appears in the call where the structure of the lambda-list requires a list.

```
(halibut my-favorite-head
         ((f1 (count-scales f1)) (f2 (count-scales f2)))
         my-favorite-tail)
```

The fact that the value of the variable my-favorite-head might happen to be a list is irrelevant here. It is the macro call itself whose structure must match that of the defmacro lambda-list.

The use of lambda-list keywords adds even greater flexibility. For example, suppose it is convenient within the expansion function for halibut to be able to refer to the list whose components are called mouth, eye1, and eye2 as head. One may write this:

```
(defmacro halibut ((&whole head mouth eye1 eye2)
                   ((fin1 length1) (fin2 length2))
                   tail)
```

Now consider the same valid macro call as before:

```
(halibut (m (car eyes) (cdr eyes))
         ((f1 (count-scales f1)) (f2 (count-scales f2)))
         my-favorite-tail)
```

This would cause the expansion function to receive the same values for its parameters and also a value for the parameter head:

Parameter	Value
head	`(m (car eyes) (cdr eyes))`

The stipulation that an embedded lambda-list is permitted only where ordinary lambda-list syntax would permit a parameter name but not a list is made to prevent ambiguity. For example, one may not write

```
(defmacro loser (x &optional (a b &rest c) &rest z)
  ...)
```

because ordinary lambda-list syntax does permit a list following &optional; the list (a b &rest c) would be interpreted as describing an optional parameter named a whose default value is that of the form b, with a supplied-p parameter named &rest (not legal), and an extraneous symbol c in the list (also not legal). An almost correct way to express this is

```
(defmacro loser (x &optional ((a b &rest c)) &rest z)
  ...)
```

The extra set of parentheses removes the ambiguity. However, the definition is now incorrect because a macro call such as (loser (car pool)) would not provide any argument form for the lambda-list (a b &rest c), and so the default value against which to match the lambda-list would be nil because no explicit default value was specified. This is in error because nil is an empty list; it does not have forms to satisfy the parameters a and b. The fully correct definition would be either

```
(defmacro loser (x &optional ((a b &rest c) '(nil nil)) &rest z)
  ...)
```

or

```
(defmacro loser (x &optional ((&optional a b &rest c)) &rest z)
  ...)
```

These differ slightly: the first requires that if the macro call specifies a explicitly then it must also specify b explicitly, whereas the second does not have this requirement. For example,

```
(loser (car pool) ((+ x 1)))
```

would be a valid call for the second definition but not for the first.

8.2. Macro Expansion

The `macroexpand` function is the conventional means for expanding a macro call. A hook is provided for a user function to gain control during the expansion process.

`macroexpand` *form* &optional *env*	[*Function*]
`macroexpand-1` *form* &optional *env*	[*Function*]

If *form* is a macro call, then `macroexpand-1` will expand the macro call *once* and return two values: the expansion and t. If *form* is not a macro call, then the two values *form* and `nil` are returned.

A *form* is considered to be a macro call only if it is a cons whose *car* is a symbol that names a macro. The environment *env* is similar to that used within the evaluator (see `evalhook`); it defaults to a null environment. Any local macro definitions established within *env* by `macrolet` will be considered. If only *form* is given as an argument, then the environment is effectively null, and only global macro definitions (as established by `defmacro`) will be considered.

Macro expansion is carried out as follows. Once `macroexpand-1` has determined that a symbol names a macro, it obtains the expansion function for that macro. The value of the variable `*macroexpand-hook*` is then called as a function of three arguments: the expansion function, the *form*, and the environment *env*. The value returned from this call is taken to be the expansion of the macro call. The initial value of `*macroexpand-hook*` is `funcall`, and the net effect is to invoke the expansion function, giving it *form* and *env* as its two arguments.

X3J13 voted in June 1988 ⟨90⟩ to specify that the value of `*macroexpand-hook*` is first coerced to a function before being called as the expansion interface hook. Therefore its value may be a symbol, a lambda-expression, or any object of type `function`.

X3J13 voted in March 1989 ⟨117⟩ to specify that macro environment objects received by a `*macroexpand-hook*` function have only dynamic extent. The consequences are undefined if such objects are referred to outside the dynamic extent of that particular invocation of the hook function. This allows implementations to use somewhat more efficient techniques for representing environment objects.

(The purpose of `*macroexpand-hook*` is to facilitate various techniques for improving interpretation speed by caching macro expansions.)

X3J13 voted in June 1989 ⟨116⟩ to clarify that, while `*macroexpand-hook*` may be useful for debugging purposes, despite the original design intent there is currently no correct portable way to use it for caching macro expansions.

- Caching by displacement (performing a side effect on the macro-call form) won't work because the same (eq) macro-call form may appear in distinct lexical contexts. In addition, the macro-call form may be a read-only constant (see quote and also section 25.1).

- Caching by table lookup won't work because such a table would have to be keyed by both the macro-call form and the environment, but X3J13 voted in March 1989 ⟨117⟩ to permit macro environments to have only dynamic extent.

- Caching by storing macro-call forms and expansions within the environment object itself would work, but there are no portable primitives that would allow users to do this.

X3J13 also noted that, although there seems to be no correct portable way to use *macroexpand-hook* to cache macro expansions, there is no requirement that an implementation call the macro expansion function more than once for a given form and lexical environment.

X3J13 voted in March 1989 ⟨173⟩ to specify that macroexpand-1 will also expand symbol macros defined by symbol-macrolet; therefore a *form* may also be a macro call if it is a symbol. The vote did not address the interaction of this feature with the *macroexpand-hook* function. An obvious implementation choice is that the hook function is indeed called and given a special expansion function that, when applied to the *form* (a symbol) and *env*, will produce the expansion, just as for an ordinary macro; but this is only my suggestion.

The evaluator expands macro calls as if through the use of macroexpand-1; the point is that eval also uses *macroexpand-hook*.

macroexpand is similar to macroexpand-1, but repeatedly expands *form* until it is no longer a macro call. (In effect, macroexpand simply calls macroexpand-1 repeatedly until the second value returned is nil.) A second value of t or nil is returned as for macroexpand-1, indicating whether the original *form* was a macro call.

---

macroexpand-hook   [*Variable*]

The value of *macroexpand-hook* is used as the expansion interface hook by macroexpand-1.

8.3. Destructuring

X3J13 voted in March 1989 ⟨64⟩ to make the destructuring feature of defmacro available as a separate facility.

destructuring-bind *lambda-list expression* {*declaration*}* {*form*}* [*Macro*]

This macro binds the variables specified in *lambda-list* to the corresponding values in the tree structure resulting from evaluating the *expression*, then executes the *form*s as an implicit progn.

A destructuring-bind *lambda-list* may contain the lambda-list keywords &optional, &rest, &key, &allow-other-keys, and &aux; &body and &whole may also be used as they are in defmacro, but &environment may *not* be used. Nested and dotted lambda-lists are also permitted as for defmacro. The idea is that a destructuring-bind *lambda-list* has the same format as inner levels of a defmacro lambda-list.

If the result of evaluating the *expression* does not match the destructuring pattern, an error should be signaled.

8.4. Compiler Macros

X3J13 voted in June 1989 ⟨49⟩ to add a facility for defining *compiler macros* that take effect only when compiling code, not when interpreting it.

The purpose of this facility is to permit selective source-code transformations only when the compiler is processing the code. When the compiler is about to compile a non-atomic form, it first calls compiler-macroexpand-1 repeatedly until there is no more expansion (there might not be any to begin with). Then it continues its remaining processing, which may include calling macroexpand-1 and so on.

The compiler is required to expand compiler macros. It is unspecified whether the interpreter does so. The intention is that only the compiler will do so, but the range of possible "compiled-only" implementation strategies precludes any firm specification.

define-compiler-macro *name lambda-list*   [*Macro*]
                     {*declaration* | *doc-string*}* {*form*}*

This is just like defmacro except the definition is not stored in the symbol function cell of *name* and is not seen by macroexpand-1. It is, however, seen by compiler-macroexpand-1. As with defmacro, the *lambda-list* may include &environment and &whole and may include destructuring. The definition is global. (There is no provision for defining local compiler macros in the way that macrolet defines local macros.)

A top-level call to define-compiler-macro in a file being compiled by compile-file has an effect on the compilation environment similar to that of a call to defmacro, except it is noticed as a compiler macro (see section 25.1).

Note that compiler macro definitions do not appear in information returned by function-information; they are global, and their interaction with other lexical and global definitions can be reconstructed by compiler-macro-function. It is up to code-walking programs to decide whether to invoke compiler macro expansion.

X3J13 voted in March 1988 ⟨78⟩ to specify that the body of the expander function defined by defmacro is implicitly enclosed in a block construct whose name is the same as the *name* of the defined macro; presumably this applies also to define-compiler-macro. Therefore return-from may be used to exit from the function.

---

compiler-macro-function *name* &optional *env*   [*Function*]

The *name* must be a symbol. If it has been defined as a compiler macro, then compiler-macro-function returns the macro expansion function; otherwise it returns nil. The lexical environment *env* may override any global definition for *name* by defining a local function or local macro (such as by flet, labels, or macrolet) in which case nil is returned.

setf may be used with compiler-macro-function to install a function as the expansion function for the compiler macro *name*, in the same manner as for macro-function. Storing the value nil removes any existing compiler macro definition. As with macro-function, a non-nil stored value must be a function of two arguments, the entire macro call and the environment. The second argument to compiler-macro-function must be omitted when it is used with setf.

---

compiler-macroexpand *form* &optional *env*   [*Function*]
compiler-macroexpand-1 *form* &optional *env*   [*Function*]

These are just like macroexpand and macroexpand-1 except that the expander function is obtained as if by a call to compiler-macro-function on the *car* of the *form* rather than by a call to macro-function. Note that compiler-macroexpand performs repeated expansion but compiler-macroexpand-1 performs at most one expansion. Two values are returned, the expansion (or the original *form*) and a value that is true if any expansion occurred and nil otherwise.

There are three cases where no expansion happens:

• There is no compiler macro definition for the *car* of *form*.

• There is such a definition but there is also a notinline declaration, either globally or in the lexical environment *env*.

• A global compiler macro definition is shadowed by a local function or macro definition (such as by flet, labels, or macrolet).

Note that if there is no expansion, the original *form* is returned as the first value, and `nil` as the second value.

Any macro expansion performed by the function `compiler-macroexpand` or by the function `compiler-macroexpand-1` is carried out by calling the function that is the value of `*macroexpand-hook*`.

A compiler macro may decline to provide any expansion merely by returning the original form. This is useful when using the facility to put "compiler optimizers" on various function names. For example, here is a compiler macro that "optimizes" (one would hope) the zero-argument and one-argument cases of a function called `plus`:

```
(define-compiler-macro plus (&whole form &rest args)
  (case (length args)
    (0 0)
    (1 (car args))
    (t form)))
```

8.5. Environments

X3J13 voted in June 1989 ⟨174⟩ to add some facilities for obtaining information from environment objects of the kind received as arguments by macro expansion functions, `*macroexpand-hook*` functions, and `*evalhook*` functions. There is a minimal set of accessors (`variable-information`, `function-information`, and `declaration-information`) and a constructor (`augment-environment`) for environments.

All of the standard declaration specifiers, with the exception of `special`, can be defined fairly easily using `define-declaration`. It also seems to be able to handle most extended declarations.

The function `parse-macro` is provided so that users don't have to write their own code to destructure macro arguments. This function is not entirely necessary since X3J13 voted in March 1989 ⟨64⟩ to add `destructuring-bind` to the language. However, `parse-macro` is worth having anyway, since any program-analyzing program is going to need to define it, and the implementation isn't completely trivial even with `destructuring-bind` to build upon.

The function `enclose` allows expander functions to be defined in a non-null lexical environment, as required by the vote of X3J13 in March 1989 ⟨50⟩. It also provides a mechanism by which a program processing the body of an (`eval-when` (`:compile-toplevel`) `...`) form can execute it in the enclosing environment (see issue ⟨73⟩).

In all of these functions the argument named *env* is an environment object. (It is not required that implementations provide a distinguished representation for such objects.) Optional *env* arguments default to `nil`, which represents the local null lexical environment (containing only global definitions and proclamations that are present in the run-time environment). All of these functions should signal an error of type `type-error` if the value of an environment argument is not a syntactic environment object.

The accessor functions `variable-information`, `function-information`, and `declaration-information` retrieve information about declarations that are in effect in the environment. Since implementations are permitted to ignore declarations (except for `special` declarations and `optimize safety` declarations if they ever compile unsafe code), these accessors are required only to return information about declarations that were explicitly added to the environment using `augment-environment`. They might also return information about declarations recognized and added to the environment by the interpreter or the compiler, but that is at the discretion of the implementor. Implementations are also permitted to canonicalize declarations, so the information returned by the accessors might not be identical to the information that was passed to `augment-environment`.

`variable-information` *variable* `&optional` *env*   [*Function*]

This function returns information about the interpretation of the symbol *variable* when it appears as a variable within the lexical environment *env*. Three values are returned.

The first value indicates the type of definition or binding for *variable* in *env*:

`nil`   There is no apparent definition or binding for *variable*.

`:special`   The *variable* refers to a special variable, either declared or proclaimed.

`:lexical`   The *variable* refers to a lexical variable.

`:symbol-macro`   The *variable* refers to a `symbol-macrolet` binding.

`:constant`   Either the *variable* refers to a named constant defined by `defconstant` or the *variable* is a keyword symbol.

The second value indicates whether there is a local binding of the name. If the name is locally bound, the second value is true; otherwise, the second value is `nil`.

The third value is an a-list containing information about declarations that apply to the apparent binding of the *variable*. The keys in the a-list are symbols that name declaration specifiers, and the format of the corresponding value in the *cdr* of each pair depends on the particular declaration name involved. The standard declaration names that might appear as keys in this a-list are:

dynamic-extent   A non-nil value indicates that the *variable* has been declared dynamic-extent. If the value is nil, the pair might be omitted.

ignore   A non-nil value indicates that the *variable* has been declared ignore. If the value is nil, the pair might be omitted.

type   The value is a type specifier associated with the *variable* by a type declaration or an abbreviated declaration such as (fixnum *variable*). If no explicit association exists, either by proclaim or declare, then the type specifier is t. It is permissible for implementations to use a type specifier that is equivalent to or a supertype of the one appearing in the original declaration. If the value is t, the pair might be omitted.

If an implementation supports additional declaration specifiers that apply to variable bindings, those declaration names might also appear in the a-list. However, the corresponding key must not be a symbol that is external in any package defined in the standard or that is otherwise accessible in the common-lisp-user package.

The a-list might contain multiple entries for a given key. The consequences of destructively modifying the list structure of this a-list or its elements (except for values that appear in the a-list as a result of define-declaration) are undefined.

Note that the global binding might differ from the local one and can be retrieved by calling variable-information with a null lexical environment.

function-information *function* &optional *env*   [*Function*]

This function returns information about the interpretation of the function-name *function* when it appears in a functional position within lexical environment *env*. Three values are returned.

The first value indicates the type of definition or binding of the function-name which is apparent in *env*:

nil   There is no apparent definition for *function*.

:function   The *function* refers to a function.

:macro   The *function* refers to a macro.

:special-form   The *function* refers to a special form.

Some function-names can refer to both a global macro and a global special form. In such a case the macro takes precedence and :macro is returned as the first value.

The second value specifies whether the definition is local or global. If local, the second value is true; it is nil when the definition is global.

The third value is an a-list containing information about declarations that apply to the apparent binding of the function. The keys in the a-list are symbols that name declaration specifiers, and the format of the corresponding values in the *cdr* of each pair depends on the particular declaration name involved. The standard declaration names that might appear as keys in this a-list are:

dynamic-extent   A non-nil value indicates that the function has been declared dynamic-extent. If the value is nil, the pair might be omitted.

inline   The value is one of the symbols inline, notinline, or nil to indicate whether the function-name has been declared inline, declared notinline, or neither, respectively. If the value is nil, the pair might be omitted.

ftype   The value is the type specifier associated with the function-name in the environment, or the symbol function if there is no functional type declaration or proclamation associated with the function-name. This value might not include all the apparent ftype declarations for the function-name. It is permissible for implementations to use a type specifier that is equivalent to or a supertype of the one that appeared in the original declaration. If the value is function, the pair might be omitted.

If an implementation supports additional declaration specifiers that apply to function bindings, those declaration names might also appear in the a-list. However, the corresponding key must not be a symbol that is external in any package defined in the standard or that is otherwise accessible in the common-lisp-user package.

The a-list might contain multiple entries for a given key. In this case the value associated with the first entry has precedence. The consequences of destructively modifying the list structure of this a-list or its elements (except for values that appear in the a-list as a result of define-declaration) are undefined.

Note that the global binding might differ from the local one and can be retrieved by calling function-information with a null lexical environment.

declaration-information *decl-name* &optional *env*   [*Function*]

This function returns information about declarations named by the symbol *decl-*

name that are in force in the environment *env*. Only declarations that do not apply to function or variable bindings can be accessed with this function. The format of the information that is returned depends on the *decl-name* involved.

It is required that this function recognize `optimize` and `declaration` as *decl-names*. The values returned for these two cases are as follows:

optimize   A single value is returned, a list whose entries are of the form (*quality value*), where *quality* is one of the standard optimization qualities (`speed`, `safety`, `compilation-speed`, `space`, `debug`) or some implementation-specific optimization quality, and *value* is an integer in the range 0 to 3 (inclusive). The returned list always contains an entry for each of the standard qualities and for each of the implementation-specific qualities. In the absence of any previous declarations, the associated values are implementation-dependent. The list might contain multiple entries for a quality, in which case the first such entry specifies the current value. The consequences of destructively modifying this list or its elements are undefined.

declaration   A single value is returned, a list of the declaration names that have been proclaimed as valid through the use of the `declaration` proclamation. The consequences of destructively modifying this list or its elements are undefined.

If an implementation is extended to recognize additional declaration specifiers in `declare` or `proclaim`, it is required that either the `declaration-information` function should recognize those declarations also or the implementation should provide a similar accessor that is specialized for that declaration specifier. If `declaration-information` is used to return the information, the corresponding *decl-name* must not be a symbol that is external in any package defined in the standard or that is otherwise accessible in the `common-lisp-user` package.

augment-environment *env* &key :variable :symbol-macro   [*Function*]
                   :function :macro :declare

This function returns a new environment containing the information present in *env* augmented with the information provided by the keyword arguments. It is intended to be used by program analyzers that perform a code walk.

The arguments are supplied as follows.

:variable
The argument is a list of symbols that will be visible as bound variables in the

new environment. Whether each binding is to be interpreted as special or lexical depends on `special` declarations recorded in the environment or provided in the `:declare` argument.

`:symbol-macro`

The argument is a list of symbol macro definitions, each of the form (*name defini-tion*); that is, the argument is in the same format as the *cadr* of a `symbol-macrolet` special form. The new environment will have local symbol-macro bindings of each symbol to the corresponding expansion, so that `macroexpand` will be able to ex-pand them properly. A type declaration in the `:declare` argument that refers to a name in this list implicitly modifies the definition associated with the name. The effect is to wrap a `the` form mentioning the type around the definition.

`:function`

The argument is a list of function-names that will be visible as local function bindings in the new environment.

`:macro`

The argument is a list of local macro definitions, each of the form (*name def-inition*). Note that the argument is *not* in the same format as the *cadr* of a `macrolet` special form. Each *definition* must be a function of two arguments (a form and an environment). The new environment will have local macro bind-ings of each name to the corresponding expander function, which will be returned by `macro-function` and used by `macroexpand`.

`:declare`

The argument is a list of declaration specifiers. Information about these declarations can be retrieved from the resulting environment using `variable-information`, `function-information`, and `declaration-information`.

The consequences of subsequently destructively modifying the list structure of any of the arguments to this function are undefined.

An error is signaled if any of the symbols naming a symbol macro in the `:symbol-macro` argument is also included in the `:variable` argument. An error is signaled if any symbol naming a symbol macro in the `:symbol-macro` argument is also included in a `special` declaration specifier in the `:declare` argument. An error is signaled if any symbol naming a macro in the `:macro` argument is also included in the `:function` argument. The condition type of each of these errors is `program-error`.

The extent of the returned environment is the same as the extent of the argument environment *env*. The result might share structure with *env* but *env* is not modified.

While an environment argument received by an `*evalhook*` function is permitted to be used as the environment argument to `augment-environment`, the consequences are undefined if an attempt is made to use the result of `augment-environment` as the environment argument for `evalhook`. The environment returned by `augment-environment` can be used only for syntactic analysis, that is, as an argument to the functions defined in this section and functions such as `macroexpand`.

`define-declaration` *decl-name lambda-list* {*form*}*   [*Macro*]

This macro defines a handler for the named declaration. It is the mechanism by which `augment-environment` is extended to support additional declaration specifiers. The function defined by this macro will be called with two arguments, a declaration specifier whose *car* is *decl-name* and the *env* argument to `augment-environment`. This function must return two values. The first value must be one of the following keywords:

`:variable`   The declaration applies to variable bindings.

`:function`   The declaration applies to function bindings.

`:declare`   The declaration does not apply to bindings.

If the first value is `:variable` or `:function` then the second value must be a list, the elements of which are lists of the form (*binding-name key value*). If the corresponding information function (either `variable-information` or `function-information`) is applied to the *binding-name* and the augmented environment, the a-list returned by the information function as its third value will contain the *value* under the specified *key*.

If the first value is `:declare`, the second value must be a cons of the form (*key* . *value*). The function `declaration-information` will return *value* when applied to the *key* and the augmented environment.

`define-declaration` causes *decl-name* to be proclaimed to be a declaration; it is as if its expansion included a call (`proclaim` ´(`declaration` *decl-name*)). As is the case with standard declaration specifiers, the evaluator and compiler are permitted, but not required, to add information about declaration specifiers defined with `define-declaration` to the macro expansion and `*evalhook*` environments.

The consequences are undefined if *decl-name* is a symbol that can appear as the *car* of any standard declaration specifier.

The consequences are also undefined if the return value from a declaration handler defined with define-declaration includes a *key* name that is used by the corresponding accessor to return information about any standard declaration specifier. (For example, if the first return value from the handler is :variable, the second return value may not use the symbols dynamic-extent, ignore, or type as *key* names.)

The define-declaration macro does not have any special compile-time side effects (see section 25.1).

parse-macro *name lambda-list body* &optional *env*   [*Function*]

This function is used to process a macro definition in the same way as defmacro and macrolet. It returns a lambda-expression that accepts two arguments, a form and an environment. The *name*, *lambda-list*, and *body* arguments correspond to the parts of a defmacro or macrolet definition.

The *lambda-list* argument may include &environment and &whole and may include destructuring. The *name* argument is used to enclose the *body* in an implicit block and might also be used for implementation-dependent purposes (such as including the name of the macro in error messages if the form does not match the *lambda-list*).

enclose *lambda-expression* &optional *env*   [*Function*]

This function returns an object of type function that is equivalent to what would be obtained by evaluating `(function ,*lambda-expression*) in a syntactic environment *env*. The *lambda-expression* is permitted to reference only the parts of the environment argument *env* that are relevant only to syntactic processing, specifically declarations and the definitions of macros and symbol macros. The consequences are undefined if the *lambda-expression* contains any references to variable or function bindings that are lexically visible in *env*, any go to a tag that is lexically visible in *env*, or any return-from mentioning a block name that is lexically visible in *env*.

9

Declarations

Declarations allow you to specify extra information about your program to the Lisp system. With one exception, declarations are completely optional and correct declarations do not affect the meaning of a correct program. The exception is that `special` declarations *do* affect the interpretation of variable bindings and references and so *must* be specified where appropriate. All other declarations are of an advisory nature, and may be used by the Lisp system to aid the programmer by performing extra error checking or producing more efficient compiled code. Declarations are also a good way to add documentation to a program.

Note that it is considered an error for a program to violate a declaration (such as a `type` declaration), but an implementation is not required to detect such errors (though such detection, where feasible, is to be encouraged).

9.1. Declaration Syntax

The `declare` construct is used for embedding declarations within executable code. Global declarations and declarations that are computed by a program are established by the `proclaim` construct.

X3J13 voted in June 1989 ⟨144⟩ to introduce the new macro `declaim`, which is guaranteed to be recognized appropriately by the compiler and is often more convenient than `proclaim` for establishing global declarations.

declare {*decl-spec*}*   [*Special form*]

A `declare` form is known as a *declaration*. Declarations may occur only at the beginning of the bodies of certain special forms; that is, a declaration may occur only as a statement of such a special form, and all statements preceding it (if any) must also be `declare` forms (or possibly documentation strings, in some cases). Declarations may occur in lambda-expressions and in the forms listed here.

```
define-setf-method        labels
defmacro                  let
defsetf                   let*
deftype                   locally
defun                     macrolet
do                        multiple-value-bind
do*                       prog
do-all-symbols            prog*
do-external-symbols       with-input-from-string
do-symbols                with-open-file
dolist                    with-open-stream
dotimes                   with-output-to-string
flet
```

Notice of correction. In the first edition, the above list failed to mention the forms `define-setf-method`, `with-input-from-string`, `with-open-file`, `with-open-stream`, and `with-output-to-string`, even though their individual descriptions in the first edition specified that declarations may appear in those forms.

X3J13 voted in June 1989 ⟨31⟩ to add `with-condition-restarts` and also ⟨40⟩ to add `print-unreadable-object` and `with-standard-io-syntax`. The X3J13 vote left it unclear whether these macros permit declarations to appear at the heads of their bodies. I believe that was the intent, but this is only my interpretation.

X3J13 voted in June 1988 ⟨12⟩ to adopt the Common Lisp Object System, which includes the following additional forms in which declarations may occur:

```
defgeneric                  generic-function
define-method-combination   generic-labels
defmethod                   with-added-methods
generic-flet
```

Furthermore X3J13 voted in January 1989 ⟨172⟩ to allow declarations to occur before the bodies of these forms:

```
symbol-macrolet             with-slots
with-accessors
```

There are certain aspects peculiar to `symbol-macrolet` (and therefore also to `with-accessors` and `with-slots`, which expand into uses of `symbol-macrolet`). An error is signaled if a name defined by `symbol-macrolet` is declared `special`, and a type declaration of a name defined by `symbol-macrolet` is equivalent in effect to wrapping a the form mentioning that type around the expansion of the defined symbol.

It is an error to attempt to evaluate a declaration. Those special forms that permit declarations to appear perform explicit checks for their presence.

Compatibility note: In MacLisp, declare is a special form that does nothing but return the symbol declare as its result. The MacLisp interpreter knows nothing about declarations but just blindly evaluates them, effectively ignoring them. The MacLisp compiler recognizes declarations but processes them simply by evaluating the subforms of the declaration in the compilation context. In Common Lisp it is important that both the interpreter and compiler recognize declarations (especially special declarations) and treat them consistently, and so the rules about the structure and use of declarations have been made considerably more stringent. The odd tricks played in MacLisp by writing arbitrary forms to be evaluated within a declare form are better done in both MacLisp and Common Lisp by using eval-when.

It is permissible for a macro call to expand into a declaration and be recognized as such, provided that the macro call appears where a declaration may legitimately appear. (However, a macro call may not appear in place of a *decl-spec*.)

X3J13 voted in March 1988 ⟨45⟩ to eliminate the recognition of a declaration resulting from the expansion of a macro call. This feature proved to be seldom used and awkward to implement in interpreters, compilers, and other code-analyzing programs.

Under this change, a declaration is recognized only as such if it appears explicitly, as a list whose *car* is the symbol declare, in the body of a relevant special form. (Note, however, that it is still possible for a macro to expand into a call to the proclaim function.)

Each *decl-spec* is a list whose *car* is a symbol specifying the kind of declaration to be made. Declarations may be divided into two classes: those that concern the bindings of variables, and those that do not. (The special declaration is the sole exception: it effectively falls into both classes, as explained below.) Those that concern variable bindings apply only to the bindings made by the form at the head of whose body they appear. For example, in

```
(defun foo (x)
  (declare (type float x)) ...
  (let ((x 'a)) ...)
  ...)
```

the type declaration applies only to the outer binding of x, and not to the binding made in the let.

Compatibility note: This represents a difference from MacLisp, in which type declarations are pervasive.

Declarations that do not concern themselves with variable bindings are pervasive, affecting all code in the body of the special form. As an example of a pervasive declaration,

```
(defun foo (x y) (declare (notinline floor)) ...)
```

advises that everywhere within the body of foo the function floor should not be open-coded but called as an out-of-line subroutine.

Some special forms contain pieces of code that, properly speaking, are not part of the body of the special form. Examples of this are initialization forms that provide values for bound variables, and the result forms of iteration constructs. In all cases such additional code is within the scope of any pervasive declarations appearing before the body of the special form. Non-pervasive declarations have no effect on such code, except (of course) in those situations where the code is defined to be within the scope of the variables affected by such non-pervasive declarations. For example:

```
(defun few (x &optional (y *print-circle*))
  (declare (special *print-circle*))
  ...)
```

The reference to *print-circle* in the first line of this example is special because of the declaration in the second line.

```
(defun nonsense (k x z)
  (foo z x)                 ;First call to foo
  (let ((j (foo k x))       ;Second call to foo
        (x (* k k)))
    (declare (inline foo) (special x z))
    (foo x j z)))           ;Third call to foo
```

In this rather nonsensical example, the inline declaration applies to the second and third calls to foo, but not to the first one. The special declaration of x causes the let form to make a special binding for x and causes the reference to x in the body of the let to be a special reference. The reference to x in the second call to foo is also a special reference. The reference to x in the first call to foo is a local reference, not a special one. The special declaration of z causes the reference to z in the call to foo to be a special reference; it will not refer to the parameter to nonsense named z, because that parameter binding has not been declared to be special. (The special declaration of z does not appear in the body of the defun, but in an inner construct, and therefore does not affect the binding of the parameter.)

X3J13 voted in January 1989 ⟨42⟩ to replace the rules concerning the scope of declarations occurring at the head of a special form or lambda-expression:

• The scope of a declaration always includes the body forms, as well as any "stepper" or "result" forms (which are logically part of the body), of the special form or lambda-expression.

• If the declaration applies to a name binding, then the scope of the declaration also includes the scope of the name binding.

Note that the distinction between pervasive and non-pervasive declarations is eliminated. An important change from the first edition is that "initialization" forms are specifically *not* included as part of the body under the first rule; on the other hand, in many cases initialization forms may fall within the scope of certain declarations under the second rule.

X3J13 also voted in January 1989 ⟨46⟩ to change the interpretation of type declarations (see section 9.2).

These changes affect the interpretation of some of the examples from the first edition.

```
(defun foo (x)
  (declare (type float x)) ...
  (let ((x ´a)) ...)
  ...)
```

Under the interpretation approved by X3J13, the type declaration applies to *both* bindings of x. More accurately, the type declaration is considered to apply to variable references rather than bindings, and the type declaration refers to every reference in the body of foo to a variable named x, no matter to what binding it may refer.

```
(defun foo (x y) (declare (notinline floor)) ...)
```

This example of the use of notinline stands unchanged, but the following slight extension of it would change:

```
(defun foo (x &optional (y (floor x)))
  (declare (notinline floor)) ...)
```

Under first edition rules, the notinline declaration would be considered to apply to the call to floor in the initialization form for y. Under the interpretation approved by X3J13, the notinline would *not* apply to that particular call to floor. Instead the user must write something like

```
(defun foo (x &optional (y (locally (declare (notinline floor))
                                     (floor x))))
  (declare (notinline floor)) ...)
```

or perhaps

```
(locally (declare (notinline floor))
  (defun foo (x &optional (y (floor x))) ...))
```

Similarly, the special declaration in

```
(defun few (x &optional (y *print-circle*))
  (declare (special *print-circle*))
  ...)
```

is not considered to apply to the reference in the initialization form for y in few. As for the nonsense example,

```
(defun nonsense (k x z)
  (foo z x)                    ;First call to foo
  (let ((j (foo k x))          ;Second call to foo
        (x (* k k)))
    (declare (inline foo) (special x z))
    (foo x j z)))              ;Third call to foo
```

under the interpretation approved by X3J13, the inline declaration is no longer considered to apply to the second call to foo, because it is in an initialization form, which is no longer considered in the scope of the declaration. Similarly, the reference to x in that second call to foo is no longer taken to be a special reference, but a local reference to the second parameter of nonsense.

locally {*declaration*}* {*form*}*   [*Macro*]

This macro may be used to make local pervasive declarations where desired. It does not bind any variables and therefore cannot be used meaningfully for declarations of variable bindings. (Note that the special declaration may be used with locally to pervasively affect references to, rather than bindings of, variables.) For example:

```
(locally (declare (inline floor) (notinline car cdr))
         (declare (optimize space))
   (floor (car x) (cdr y)))
```

X3J13 voted in January 1989 ⟨156⟩ to specify that `locally` executes the *forms* as an implicit `progn` and returns the value(s) of the last *form*.

X3J13 voted in March 1989 ⟨113⟩ to make `locally` be a special form rather than a macro. It still has the same syntax.

`locally` {*declaration*}* {*form*}*   [*Special form*]

This change was made to accommodate the new compilation model for top-level forms in a file (see section 25.1). When a `locally` form appears at top level, the forms in its body are processed as top-level forms. This means that one may, for example, meaningfully use `locally` to wrap declarations around a `defun` or `defmacro` form:

```
(locally
   (declare (optimize (safety 3) (space 3) (debug 3) (speed 1)))
   (defun foo (x &optional (y (abs x)) (z (sqrt y)))
     (bar x y z)))
```

Without assurance that this works one must write something cumbersome such as

```
(defun foo (x &optional (y (locally
                             (declare (optimize (safety 3)
                                                (space 3)
                                                (debug 3)
                                                (speed 1)))
                             (abs x)))
                        (z (locally
                             (declare (optimize (safety 3)
                                                (space 3)
                                                (debug 3)
                                                (speed 1)))
                             (sqrt y))))
   (locally
     (declare (optimize (safety 3) (space 3) (debug 3) (speed 1)))
     (bar x y z)))
```

proclaim *decl-spec*   [*Function*]

The function `proclaim` takes a *decl-spec* as its argument and puts it into effect globally. (Such a global declaration is called a *proclamation*.) Because `proclaim` is a function, its argument is always evaluated. This allows a program to compute a declaration and then put it into effect by calling `proclaim`.

Any variable names mentioned are assumed to refer to the dynamic values of the variable. For example, the proclamation

```
(proclaim '(type float tolerance))
```

once executed, specifies that the dynamic value of `tolerance` should always be a floating-point number. Similarly, any function-names mentioned are assumed to refer to the global function definition.

A proclamation constitutes a universal declaration, always in force unless locally shadowed. For example,

```
(proclaim '(inline floor))
```

advises that `floor` should normally be open-coded in-line by the compiler (but in the situation

```
(defun foo (x y) (declare (notinline floor)) ...)
```

it will be compiled out-of-line anyway in the body of `foo`, because of the shadowing local declaration to that effect).

X3J13 voted in January 1989 ⟨164⟩ to clarify that such shadowing does not occur in the case of type declarations. If there is a local type declaration for a special variable and there is also a global proclamation for that same variable, then the value of the variable within the scope of the local declaration must be a member of the intersection of the two declared types. This is consistent with the treatment of nested local type declarations on which X3J13 also voted in January 1989 ⟨46⟩.

As a special case (so to speak), `proclaim` treats a `special` *decl-spec* as applying to all bindings as well as to all references of the mentioned variables.

Notice of correction. In the first edition, this sentence referred to a "`special` *declaration-form*." That was incorrect; `proclaim` accepts only a *decl-spec*, not a *declaration-form*.

For example, after

```
(proclaim '(special x))
```

in a function definition such as

```
(defun example (x) ...)
```

the parameter x will be bound as a special (dynamic) variable rather than as a lexical (static) variable. This facility should be used with caution. The usual way to define a globally special variable is with `defvar` or `defparameter`.

X3J13 voted in June 1989 ⟨144⟩ to clarify that the compiler is not required to treat calls to `proclaim` any differently from the way it treats any other function call. If a top-level call to `proclaim` is to take effect at compile time, it should be surrounded by an appropriate `eval-when` form. Better yet, the new macro `declaim` may be used instead.

declaim {*decl-spec*}*   [*Macro*]

This macro is syntactically like `declare` and semantically like `proclaim`. It is an executable form and may be used anywhere `proclaim` may be called. However, each *decl-spec* is not evaluated.

If a call to this macro appears at top level in a file being processed by the file compiler, the proclamations are also made at compile time. As with other defining macros, it is unspecified whether or not the compile-time side effects of a `declaim` persist after the file has been compiled (see section 25.1).

9.2. Declaration Specifiers

Here is a list of valid declaration specifiers for use in `declare`. A construct is said to be "affected" by a declaration if it occurs within the scope of a declaration.

special

(`special` *var1* *var2* ...) specifies that all of the variables named are to be considered *special*. This specifier affects variable bindings but also pervasively affects references. All variable bindings affected are made to be dynamic bindings, and affected variable references refer to the current dynamic binding rather than to the current local binding. For example:

```
(defun hack (thing *mod*)       ;The binding of the parameter
   (declare (special *mod*))     ; *mod* is visible to hack1,
   (hack1 (car thing)))          ; but not that of thing

(defun hack1 (arg)
   (declare (special *mod*))     ;Declare references to *mod*
                                 ; within hack1 to be special
   (if (atom arg) *mod*
       (cons (hack1 (car arg)) (hack1 (cdr arg)))))
```

Note that it is conventional, though not required, to give special variables names that begin and end with an asterisk.

A `special` declaration does *not* affect bindings pervasively. Inner bindings of a variable implicitly shadow a `special` declaration and must be explicitly re-declared to be special. (However, a `special` proclamation *does* pervasively affect bindings; this exception is made for reasons of convenience and compatibility with MacLisp.) For example:

```
(proclaim '(special x))        ;x is always special

(defun example (x y)
  (declare (special y))
  (let ((y 3) (x (* x 2)))
    (print (+ y (locally (declare (special y)) y)))
    (let ((y 4)) (declare (special y)) (foo x))))
```

In the contorted code above, the outermost and innermost bindings of y are special and therefore dynamically scoped, but the middle binding is lexically scoped. The two arguments to + are different, one being the value, which is 3, of the lexically bound variable y, and the other being the value of the special variable named y (a binding of which happens, coincidentally, to lexically surround it at an outer level). All the bindings of x and references to x are special, however, because of the proclamation that x is always `special`.

As a matter of style, use of `special` proclamations should be avoided. The `defvar` and `defparameter` macros are the conventional means for proclaiming special variables in a program.

type

(type *type var1 var2* ...) affects only variable bindings and specifies that the variables mentioned will take on values only of the specified type. In particu-lar, values assigned to the variables by `setq`, as well as the initial values of the variables, must be of the specified type.

X3J13 voted in January 1989 ⟨46⟩ to alter the interpretation of type declarations. They are not to be construed to affect "only variable bindings." The new rule for a declaration of a variable to have a specified type is threefold:

- It is an error if, during the execution of any reference to that variable within the scope of the declaration, the value of the variable is not of the declared type.

- It is an error if, during the execution of a `setq` of that variable within the scope of the declaration, the new value for the variable is not of the declared type.

• It is an error if, at any moment that execution enters the scope of the declaration, the value of the variable is not of the declared type.

One may think of a type declaration (declare (type face bodoni)) as implicitly changing every reference to bodoni within the scope of the declaration to (the face bodoni); changing every expression *exp* assigned to bodoni within the scope of the declaration to (the face *exp*); and implicitly executing (the face bodoni) every time execution enters the scope of the declaration.

These new rules make type declarations much more useful. Under first edition rules, a type declaration was useless if not associated with a variable binding; declarations such as in

```
(locally
  (declare (type (byte 8) x y))
  (+ x y))
```

at best had no effect and at worst were erroneous, depending on one's interpretation of the first edition. Under the interpretation approved by X3J13, such declarations have "the obvious natural interpretation."

X3J13 noted that if nested type declarations refer to the same variable, then all of them have effect; the value of the variable must be a member of the intersection of the declared types.

Nested type declarations could occur as a result of either macro expansion or carefully crafted code. There are three cases. First, the inner type might be a subtype of the outer one:

```
(defun compare (apples oranges)
  (declare (type number apples oranges))
  (cond ((typep apples 'fixnum)
         ;; The programmer happens to know that, thanks to
         ;; constraints imposed by the caller, if APPLES
         ;; is a fixnum, then ORANGES will be also, and
         ;; therefore wishes to avoid the unnecessary cost
         ;; of checking ORANGES.  Nevertheless the compiler
         ;; should be informed to allow it to optimize code.
         (locally (declare (type fixnum apples oranges)))
                  ;; Maybe the compiler could have figured
                  ;; out by flow analysis that APPLES must
                  ;; be a fixnum here, but it doesn't hurt
                  ;; to say it explicitly.
           (< apples oranges))))
```

```
((or (complex apples)
     (complex oranges))
 (error "Not yet implemented.   Sorry."))
 ...))
```

This is the case most likely to arise in code written completely by hand.

Second, the outer type might be a subtype of the inner one. In this case the inner declaration has no additional practical effect, but it is harmless. This is likely to occur if code declares a variable to be of a very specific type and then passes it to a macro that then declares it to be of a less specific type.

Third, the inner and outer declarations might be for types that overlap, neither being a subtype of the other. This is likely to occur only as a result of macro expansion. For example, user code might declare a variable to be of type integer, and a macro might later declare it to be of type (or fixnum package); in this case a compiler could intersect the two types to determine that in this instance the variable may hold only fixnums.

The reader should note that the following code fragment is, perhaps astonishingly, *not in error* under the interpretation approved by X3J13:

```
(let ((james .007)
      (maxwell 86))
  (flet ((spy-swap ()
           (rotatef james maxwell)))
    (locally (declare (integer maxwell))
      (spy-swap)
      (view-movie "The Sound of Music")
      (spy-swap)
      maxwell)))
⇒ 86   (after a couple of hours of Julie Andrews)
```

The variable maxwell is declared to be an integer over the *scope* of the type declaration, not over its *extent*. Indeed maxwell takes on the non-integer value .007 while the Trapp family make their escape, but because no reference to maxwell within the scope of the declaration ever produces a non-integer value, the code is correct.

Now the assignment to maxwell during the first call to spy-swap, and the reference to maxwell during the second call, *do* involve non-integer values, but they occur within the body of spy-swap, which is *not* in the scope of the type declaration! One could put the declaration in a different place so as to include spy-swap in the scope:

```
(let ((james .007)
      (maxwell 86))
  (locally (declare (integer maxwell))
    (flet ((spy-swap ()
             (rotatef james maxwell)))
      (spy-swap)                                           ;Bug!
      (view-movie "The Sound of Music")
      (spy-swap)
      maxwell))))
```

and then the code is indeed in error.

X3J13 also voted in January 1989 ⟨91⟩ to alter the meaning of the `function` type specifier when used in `type` declarations (see section 4.5).

type

(*type var1 var2* ...) is an abbreviation for (type *type var1 var2* ...), provided that *type* is one of the symbols appearing in table 4-1.

Observe that this covers the particularly common case of declaring numeric variables:

```
(declare (single-float mass dx dy dz)
         (double-float acceleration sum))
```

In many implementations there is also some advantage to declaring variables to have certain specialized vector types such as `base-string`.

ftype

(*ftype type function-name-1 function-name-2* ...) specifies that the named functions will be of the functional type *type*, an example of which follows. For example:

```
(declare (ftype (function (integer list) t) nth)
         (ftype (function (number) float) sin cos))
```

Note that rules of lexical scoping are observed; if one of the functions mentioned has a lexically apparent local definition (as made by `flet` or `labels`), then the declaration applies to that local definition and not to the global function definition.

X3J13 voted in March 1989 ⟨89⟩ to extend `ftype` declaration specifiers to accept any function-name (a symbol or a list whose *car* is `setf`—see section 7.1). Thus one may write

```
(declaim (ftype (function (list) t) (setf cadr)))
```

to indicate the type of the setf expansion function for cadr.

X3J13 voted in January 1989 ⟨91⟩ to alter the meaning of the function type specifier when used in ftype declarations (see section 4.5).

function

(function *name arglist result-type1 result-type2* ...) is entirely equivalent to

(ftype (function *arglist result-type1 result-type2* ...) *name*)

but may be more convenient for some purposes. For example:

```
(declare (function nth (integer list) t)
         (function sin (number) float)
         (function cos (number) float))
```

The syntax mildly resembles that of defun: a function-name, then an argument list, then a specification of results.

Note that rules of lexical scoping are observed; if one of the functions mentioned has a lexically apparent local definition (as made by flet or labels), then the declaration applies to that local definition and not to the global function definition.

X3J13 voted in January 1989 ⟨44⟩ to remove this interpretation of the function declaration specifier from the language. Instead, a declaration specifier

(function *var1 var2* ...)

is to be treated simply as an abbreviation for

(type function *var1 var2* ...)

just as for all other symbols appearing in table 4-1.

X3J13 noted that although function appears in table 4-1, the first edition also discussed it explicitly, with a different meaning, without noting whether the differing interpretation was to replace or augment the interpretation regarding table 4-1. Unfortunately there is an ambiguous case: the declaration

(declare (function foo nil string))

can be construed to abbreviate either

(declare (ftype (function () string) foo))

or

```
(declare (type function foo nil string))
```

The latter could perhaps be rejected on semantic grounds: it would be an error to declare nil, a constant, to be of type function. In any case, X3J13 determined that the ice was too thin here; the possibility of confusion is not worth the convenience of an abbreviation for ftype declarations. The change also makes the language more consistent.

inline

(inline *function1* *function2* ...) specifies that it is desirable for the compiler to open-code calls to the specified functions; that is, the code for a specified function should be integrated into the calling routine, appearing in-line in place of a procedure call. This may achieve extra speed at the expense of debuggability (calls to functions compiled in-line cannot be traced, for example). This declaration is pervasive. Remember that a compiler is free to ignore this declaration.

Note that rules of lexical scoping are observed; if one of the functions mentioned has a lexically apparent local definition (as established by flet or labels), then the declaration applies to that local definition and not to the global function definition.

X3J13 voted in October 1988 ⟨145⟩ to clarify that during compilation the inline declaration specifier serves two distinct purposes: it indicates not only that affected calls to the specified functions should be expanded in-line, but also that affected definitions of the specified functions must be recorded for possible use in performing such expansions.

Looking at it the other way, the compiler is not required to save function definitions against the possibility of future expansions unless the functions have already been proclaimed to be inline. If a function is proclaimed (or declaimed) inline before some call to that function but the current definition of that function was established before the proclamation was processed, it is implementation-dependent whether that call will be expanded in-line. (Of course, it is implementation-dependent anyway, because a compiler is always free to ignore inline declaration specifiers. However, the intent of the committee is clear: for best results, the user is advised to put any inline proclamation of a function before any definition of or call to that function.)

Consider these examples:

```
(defun huey (x) (+ x 100))          ;Compiler need not remember this
(declaim (inline huey dewey))
(defun dewey (y) (huey (sqrt y)))   ;Call to huey unlikely to be expanded
(defun louie (z) (dewey (/ z)))     ;Call to dewey likely to be expanded
```

X3J13 voted in March 1989 ⟨89⟩ to extend inline declaration specifiers to accept any function-name (a symbol or a list whose *car* is setf—see section 7.1). Thus one may write (declare (inline (setf cadr))) to indicate that the setf expansion function for cadr should be compiled in-line.

notinline

(notinline *function1* *function2* ...) specifies that it is *undesirable* to compile the specified functions in-line. This declaration is pervasive. A compiler is *not* free to ignore this declaration.

Note that rules of lexical scoping are observed; if one of the functions mentioned has a lexically apparent local definition (as made by flet or labels), then the declaration applies to that local definition and not to the global function definition.

X3J13 voted in March 1989 ⟨89⟩ to extend notinline declaration specifiers to accept any function-name (a symbol or a list whose *car* is setf—see section 7.1). Thus one may write (declare (notinline (setf cadr))) to indicate that the setf expansion function for cadr should not be compiled in-line.

X3J13 voted in January 1989 ⟨4⟩ to clarify that the proper way to define a function gnards that is not inline by default, but for which a local declaration (declare (inline gnards)) has half a chance of actually compiling gnards in-line, is as follows:

```
(declaim (inline gnards))

(defun gnards ...)

(declaim (notinline gnards))
```

The point is that the first declamation informs the compiler that the definition of gnards may be needed later for in-line expansion, and the second declamation prevents any expansions unless and until it is overridden.

While an implementation is never required to perform in-line expansion, many implementations that do support such expansion will not process inline requests successfully unless definitions are written with these proclamations in the manner shown above.

ignore

(ignore *var1* *var2* ... *varn*) affects only variable bindings and specifies that the bindings of the specified variables are never used. It is desirable for a compiler to issue a warning if a variable so declared is ever referred to or is also declared special, or if a variable is lexical, never referred to, and not declared to be ignored.

optimize

(optimize (*quality1* *value1*) (*quality2* *value2*)...) advises the compiler that each *quality* should be given attention according to the specified corresponding *value*. A quality is a symbol; standard qualities include speed (of the object code), space (both code size and run-time space), safety (run-time error checking), and compilation-speed (speed of the compilation process).

X3J13 voted in October 1988 ⟨124⟩ to add the standard quality debug (ease of debugging).

Other qualities may be recognized by particular implementations. A *value* should be a non-negative integer, normally in the range 0 to 3. The value 0 means that the quality is totally unimportant, and 3 that the quality is extremely important; 1 and 2 are intermediate values, with 1 the "normal" or "usual" value. One may abbreviate (*quality* 3) to simply *quality*. This declaration is pervasive. For example:

```
(defun often-used-subroutine (x y)
  (declare (optimize (safety 2)))
  (error-check x y)
  (hairy-setup x)
  (do ((i 0 (+ i 1))
       (z x (cdr z)))
      ((null z) i)
    ;; This inner loop really needs to burn.
    (declare (optimize speed))
    (declare (fixnum i))
    )))
```

declaration

(declaration *name1* *name2* ...) advises the compiler that each *namej* is a valid but non-standard declaration name. The purpose of this is to tell one compiler not to issue warnings for declarations meant for another compiler or other program processor.

This kind of declaration may be used only as a proclamation. For example:

```
(proclaim '(declaration author
                        target-language
                        target-machine))

(proclaim '(target-language ada))

(proclaim '(target-machine IBM-650))
```

```
(defun strangep (x)
  (declare (author "Harry Tweeker"))
  (member x '(strange weird odd peculiar)))
```

X3J13 voted in June 1989 ⟨144⟩ to introduce the new macro declaim, which is guaranteed to be recognized appropriately by the compiler and is often more convenient than proclaim for establishing global declarations.

The declaration declaration specifier may be used with declaim as well as proclaim. The preceding examples would be better written using declaim, to ensure that the compiler will process them properly.

```
(declaim (declaration author
                      target-language
                      target-machine))
```

```
(declaim (target-language ada)
         (target-machine IBM-650))
```

```
(defun strangep (x)
  (declare (author "Harry Tweeker"))
  (member x '(strange weird odd peculiar)))
```

X3J13 voted in March 1989 ⟨69⟩ to introduce a new declaration specifier dynamic-extent for variables, and voted in June 1989 ⟨70⟩ to extend it to handle function-names as well.

dynamic-extent

(dynamic-extent *item1 item2 ... itemn*) declares that certain variables or function-names refer to data objects whose extents may be regarded as dynamic; that is, the declaration may be construed as a guarantee on the part of the programmer that the program will behave correctly even if the data objects have only dynamic extent rather than the usual indefinite extent.

Each *item* may be either a variable name or (function *f*) where *f* is a function-name (see section 7.1). (Of course, (function *f*) may be abbreviated in the usual way as #'*f*.)

It is permissible for an implementation simply to ignore this declaration. In implementations that do not ignore it, the compiler (or interpreter) is free to make whatever optimizations are appropriate given this information; the most common optimization is to stack-allocate the initial value of the object. The data types that can be optimized in this manner may vary from implementation to implementation.

The meaning of this declaration can be stated more precisely. We say that object x is an *otherwise inaccessible part* of y if and only if making y inaccessible would make x inaccessible. (Note that every object is an otherwise inaccessible part of itself.) Now suppose that construct c contains a `dynamic-extent` declaration for variable (or function) v (which need not be bound by c). Consider the values $w_1, \ldots, w_n$ taken on by v during the course of some execution of c. The declaration asserts that if some object x is an otherwise inaccessible part of w_j whenever w_j becomes the value of v, then just after execution of c terminates x will be either inaccessible or still an otherwise inaccessible part of the value of v. If this assertion is ever violated, the consequences are undefined.

In some implementations, it is possible to allocate data structures in a way that will make them easier to reclaim than by general-purpose garbage collection (for example, on the stack or in some temporary area). The `dynamic-extent` declaration is designed to give the implementation the information necessary to exploit such techniques.

For example, in the code fragment

```
(let ((x (list 'a1 'b1 'c1))
      (y (cons 'a2 (cons 'b2 (cons 'c2 'd2)))))
  (declare (dynamic-extent x y))
  ...)
```

it is not difficult to prove that the otherwise inaccessible parts of x include the three conses constructed by `list`, and that the otherwise inaccessible parts of y include three other conses manufactured by the three calls to `cons`. Given the presence of the `dynamic-extent` declaration, a compiler would be justified in stack-allocating these six conses and reclaiming their storage on exit from the `let` form.

Since stack allocation of the initial value entails knowing at the object's creation time that the object can be stack-allocated, it is not generally useful to declare `dynamic-extent` for variables that have no lexically apparent initial value. For example,

```
(defun f ()
  (let ((x (list 1 2 3)))
    (declare (dynamic-extent x))
    ...))
```

would permit a compiler to stack-allocate the list in x. However,

```
(defun g (x) (declare (dynamic-extent x)) ...)
(defun f () (g (list 1 2 3)))
```

could not typically permit a similar optimization in f because of the possibility of later redefinition of g. Only an implementation careful enough to recompile f if the definition of g were to change incompatibly could stack-allocate the list argument to g in f.

Other interesting cases are

```
(declaim (inline g))
(defun g (x) (declare (dynamic-extent x)) ...)
(defun f () (g (list 1 2 3)))
```

and

```
(defun f ()
   (flet ((g (x) (declare (dynamic-extent x)) ...))
     (g (list 1 2 3))))
```

In each case some compilers might realize the optimization is possible and others might not.

An interesting variant of this is the so-called *stack-allocated rest list,* which can be achieved (in implementations supporting the optimization) by

```
(defun f (&rest x)
   (declare (dynamic-extent x))
   ...)
```

Note here that although the initial value of x is not explicitly present, nevertheless in the usual implementation strategy the function f is responsible for assembling the list for x from the passed arguments, so the f function can be optimized by a compiler to construct a stack-allocated list instead of a heap-allocated list.

Some Common Lisp functions take other functions as arguments; frequently the argument function is a so-called *downward funarg,* that is, a functional argument that is passed only downward and whose extent may therefore be dynamic.

```
(flet ((gd (x) (atan (sinh x))))
   (declare (dynamic-extent #'gd))        ;mapcar won't hang on to gd
   (mapcar #'gd my-list-of-numbers))
```

The following three examples are in error, since in each case the value of x is used outside of its extent.

```
(length (let ((x (list 1 2 3)))
          (declare (dynamic-extent x))
          x))                                          ;Wrong
```

The preceding code is obviously incorrect, because the cons cells making up the list in x might be deallocated (thanks to the declaration) before length is called.

```
(length (list (let ((x (list 1 2 3)))
                (declare (dynamic-extent x))
                x)))                                   ;Wrong
```

In this second case it is less obvious that the code is incorrect, because one might argue that the cons cells making up the list in x have no effect on the result to be computed by length. Nevertheless the code briefly violates the assertion implied by the declaration and is therefore incorrect. (It is not difficult to imagine a perfectly sensible implementation of a garbage collector that might become confused by a cons cell containing a dangling pointer to a list that was once stack-allocated but then deallocated.)

```
(progn (let ((x (list 1 2 3)))
         (declare (dynamic-extent x))
         x)                                            ;Wrong
       (print "Six dollars is your change have a nice day NEXT!"))
```

In this third case it is even less obvious that the code is incorrect, because the value of x returned from the let construct is discarded right away by the progn. Indeed it is, but "right away" isn't fast enough. The code briefly violates the assertion implied by the declaration and is therefore incorrect. (If the code is being interpreted, the interpreter might hang on to the value returned by the let for some time before it is eventually discarded.)

Here is one last example, one that has little practical import but is theoretically quite instructive.

```
(dotimes (j 10)
  (declare (dynamic-extent j))
  (setq foo 3)                  ;Correct
  (setq foo j))                 ;Erroneous—but why? (see text)
```

Since j is an integer by the definition of dotimes, but eq and eql are not necessarily equivalent for integers, what are the otherwise inaccessible parts of j, which this declaration requires the body of the dotimes not to "save"? If the value of j is 3, and the body does (setq foo 3), is that an error? The answer is no, but the interesting thing is that it depends on the implementation-dependent behavior of eq on numbers. In an implementation where eq and eql are equivalent for 3, then 3 is not an otherwise inaccessible part because (eq j (+ 2 1)) is true, and therefore there is another way to access the object besides going through j. On the other hand, in an implementation where eq and eql are not equivalent for 3, then the particular 3 that is the value of j is an otherwise inaccessible part, but any other 3 is not. Thus (setq foo 3) is valid but (setq foo j) is erroneous. Since (setq foo j) is erroneous in some implementations, it is erroneous in all portable programs, but some other implementations may not be able to detect the error. (If this conclusion seems strange, it may help to replace 3 everywhere in the preceding argument with some obvious bignum such as 375374638837424898243 and to replace 10 with some even larger bignum.)

The dynamic-extent declaration should be used with great care. It makes possible great performance improvements in some situations, but if the user mis-declares something and consequently the implementation returns a pointer into the stack (or stores it in the heap), an undefined situation may result and the integrity of the Lisp storage mechanism may be compromised. Debugging these situations may be tricky. Users who have asked for this feature have indicated a willingness to deal with such problems; nevertheless, I do not encourage casual users to use this declaration.

An implementation is free to support other (implementation-dependent) declaration specifiers as well. On the other hand, a Common Lisp compiler is free to ignore entire classes of declaration specifiers (for example, implementation-dependent declaration specifiers not supported by that compiler's implementation), except for the declaration declaration specifier. Compiler implementors are encouraged, however, to program the compiler to issue by default a warning if the compiler finds a declaration specifier of a kind it never uses. Such a warning is required in any case if a declaration specifier is not one of those defined above and has not been declared in a declaration declaration.

9.3. Type Declaration for Forms

Frequently it is useful to declare that the value produced by the evaluation of some form will be of a particular type. Using declare one can declare the type of the value held by a bound variable, but there is no easy way to declare the type of the value of an unnamed form. For this purpose the the special form is defined; (the type form) means that the value of *form* is declared to be of type *type*.

the *value-type form*   [*Special form*]

The *form* is evaluated; whatever it produces is returned by the the form. In addition, it is an error if what is produced by the *form* does not conform to the data type specified by *value-type* (which is not evaluated). (A given implementation may or may not actually check for this error. Implementations are encouraged to make an explicit error check when running interpretively.) In effect, this declares that the user undertakes to guarantee that the values of the form will always be of the specified type. For example:

```
(the string (copy-seq x))       ;The result will be a string
(the integer (+ x 3))           ;The result of + will be an integer
(+ (the integer x) 3)           ;The value of x will be an integer
(the (complex rational) (* z 3))
(the (unsigned-byte 8) (logand x mask))
```

The values type specifier may be used to indicate the types of multiple values:

```
(the (values integer integer) (floor x y))
(the (values string t)
     (gethash the-key the-string-table))
```

X3J13 voted in June 1989 ⟨177⟩ to clarify that *value-type* may be any valid type specifier whatsoever. The point is that a type specifier need not be one suitable for discrimination but only for declaration.

In the case that the *form* produces exactly one value and *value-type* is not a values type specifier, one may describe a the form as being entirely equivalent to

```
(let ((#1=#:temp form)) (declare (type value-type #1#)) #1#)
```

A more elaborate expression could be written to describe the case where *value-type* is a values type specifier.

Compatibility note: This construct is borrowed from the Interlisp DECL package; Interlisp, however, allows an implicit progn after the type specifier rather than just a single form. The MacLisp fixnum-identity and flonum-identity constructs can be expressed as (the fixnum *x*) and (the single-float *x*).

10

Symbols

A Lisp symbol is a data object that has three user-visible components:

- The *property list* is a list that effectively provides each symbol with many modifiable named components.

- The *print name* must be a string, which is the sequence of characters used to identify the symbol. Symbols are of great use because a symbol can be located once its name is given (typed, say, on a keyboard). One may ordinarily not alter a symbol's print name.

  X3J13 voted in March 1989 ⟨11⟩ to specify it is an error to alter a print name.

- The *package cell* must refer to a package object. A package is a data structure used to locate a symbol once given the symbol's name. A symbol is uniquely identified by its name only when considered relative to a package. A symbol may appear in many packages, but it can be *owned* by at most one package. The package cell points to the owner, if any. Package cells are discussed along with packages in chapter 11.

A symbol may actually have other components for use by the implementation. One of the more important uses of symbols is as names for program variables; it is frequently desirable for the implementor to use certain components of a symbol to implement the semantics of variables. See `symbol-value` and `symbol-function`. However, there are several possible implementation strategies, and so such possible components are not described here.

10.1. The Property List

Since its inception, Lisp has associated with each symbol a kind of tabular data structure called a *property list* (*plist* for short). A property list contains zero or more entries; each entry associates with a key (called the *indicator*), which is typically a symbol, an arbitrary Lisp object (called the *value* or, sometimes, the *property*). There are no duplications among the indicators; a property list may only have one property at a time with a given name. In this way, given a symbol and an indicator (another symbol), an associated value can be retrieved.

A property list is very similar in purpose to an association list. The difference is that a property list is an object with a unique identity; the operations for adding and removing property-list entries are destructive operations that alter the property list rather than making a new one. Association lists, on the other hand, are normally augmented non-destructively (without side effects) by adding new entries to the front (see `acons` and `pairlis`).

A property list is implemented as a memory cell containing a list with an even number (possibly zero) of elements. (Usually this memory cell is the property-list cell of a symbol, but any memory cell acceptable to `setf` can be used if `getf` and `remf` are used.) Each pair of elements in the list constitutes an entry; the first item is the indicator, and the second is the value. Because property-list functions are given the symbol and not the list itself, modifications to the property list can be recorded by storing back into the property-list cell of the symbol.

When a symbol is created, its property list is initially empty. Properties are created by using `get` within a `setf` form.

Common Lisp does not use a symbol's property list as extensively as earlier Lisp implementations did. Less-used data, such as compiler, debugging, and documentation information, is kept on property lists in Common Lisp.

Compatibility note: In older Lisp implementations, the print name, value, and function definition of a symbol were kept on its property list. The value cell was introduced into MacLisp and Interlisp to speed up access to variables; similarly for the print-name cell and function cell (MacLisp does not use a function cell). Recent Lisp implementations such as Spice Lisp, Lisp Machine Lisp, and NIL have introduced all of these cells plus the package cell. None of the MacLisp system property names (`expr`, `fexpr`, `macro`, `array`, `subr`, `lsubr`, `fsubr`, and in former times `value` and `pname`) exist in Common Lisp.

In Common Lisp, the notion of "disembodied property list" introduced in MacLisp is eliminated. It tended to be used for rather kludgy things, and in Lisp Machine Lisp is often associated with the use of locatives (to make it "off by one" for searching alternating keyword lists). In Common Lisp special `setf`-like property-list functions are introduced: `getf` and `remf`.

`get` *symbol indicator* &optional *default*   [*Function*]

`get` searches the property list of *symbol* for an indicator eq to *indicator*. The first argument must be a symbol. If one is found, then the corresponding value is returned; otherwise *default* is returned.

If *default* is not specified, then `nil` is used for *default*.

Note that there is no way to distinguish an absent property from one whose value is *default*.

```
(get x y) ≡ (getf (symbol-plist x) y)
```

Suppose that the property list of `foo` is `(bar t baz 3 hunoz "Huh?")`. Then, for example:

```
(get 'foo 'baz) ⇒ 3
(get 'foo 'hunoz) ⇒ "Huh?"
(get 'foo 'zoo) ⇒ nil
```

Compatibility note: In MacLisp, the first argument to `get` could be a list, in which case the *cdr* of the list was treated as a so-called "disembodied property list." The first argument to `get` could also be any other object, in which case `get` would always return `nil`. In Common Lisp, it is an error to give anything but a symbol as the first argument to `get`.

What Common Lisp calls `get`, Interlisp calls `getprop`.

What MacLisp and Interlisp call `putprop` is accomplished in Common Lisp by using `get` with `setf`.

`setf` may be used with `get` to create a new property-value pair, possibly replacing an old pair with the same property name. For example:

```
(get 'clyde 'species) ⇒ nil
(setf (get 'clyde 'species) 'elephant) ⇒ elephant
and now (get 'clyde 'species) ⇒ elephant
```

The *default* argument may be specified to `get` in this context; it is ignored by `setf` but may be useful in such macros as `push` that are related to `setf`:

```
(push item (get sym 'token-stack '(initial-item)))
```

means approximately the same as

```
(setf (get sym 'token-stack '(initial-item))
      (cons item (get sym 'token-stack '(initial-item))))
```

which in turn would be treated as simply

```
(setf (get sym 'token-stack)
      (cons item (get sym 'token-stack '(initial-item))))
```

X3J13 voted in March 1989 ⟨153⟩ to clarify the permissible side effects of certain operations; (setf (get *symbol indicator*) *newvalue*) is required to behave exactly the same as (setf (getf (symbol-plist *symbol*) *indicator*) *newvalue*).

remprop *symbol indicator*   [*Function*]

This removes from *symbol* the property with an indicator eq to *indicator*. The property indicator and the corresponding value are removed by destructively splicing the property list. It returns nil if no such property was found, or non-nil if a property was found.

(remprop x y) ≡ (remf (symbol-plist x) y)

For example, if the property list of foo is initially

(color blue height 6.3 near-to bar)

then the call

(remprop 'foo 'height)

returns a non-nil value after altering foo's property list to be

(color blue near-to bar)

X3J13 voted in March 1989 ⟨153⟩ to clarify the permissible side effects of certain operations; (remprop *symbol indicator*) is required to behave exactly the same as (remf (symbol-plist *symbol*) *indicator*).

symbol-plist *symbol*   [*Function*]

This returns the list that contains the property pairs of *symbol*; the contents of the property-list cell are extracted and returned.

Note that using get on the result of symbol-plist does *not* work. One must give the symbol itself to get or else use the function getf.

setf may be used with symbol-plist to destructively replace the entire property list of a symbol. This is a relatively dangerous operation, as it may destroy important information that the implementation may happen to store in property lists. Also, care must be taken that the new property list is in fact a list of even length.

Compatibility note: In MacLisp, this function is called plist; in Interlisp, it is called getproplist.

`getf` *place indicator* &optional *default*   [*Function*]

`getf` searches the property list stored in *place* for an indicator eq to *indicator*. If one is found, then the corresponding value is returned; otherwise *default* is returned. If *default* is not specified, then `nil` is used for *default*. Note that there is no way to distinguish an absent property from one whose value is *default*. Often *place* is computed from a generalized variable acceptable to `setf`.

`setf` may be used with `getf`, in which case the *place* must indeed be acceptable as a *place* to `setf`. The effect is to add a new property-value pair, or update an existing pair, in the property list kept in the *place*. The *default* argument may be specified to `getf` in this context; it is ignored by `setf` but may be useful in such macros as `push` that are related to `setf`. See the description of `get` for an example of this.

X3J13 voted in March 1989 ⟨153⟩ to clarify the permissible side effects of certain operations; `setf` used with `getf` is permitted to perform a `setf` on the *place* or on any part, *car* or *cdr*, of the top-level list structure held by that *place*.

X3J13 voted in March 1988 ⟨146⟩ to clarify order of evaluation (see section 7.2).

Compatibility note: The Interlisp function `listget` is similar to `getf`. The Interlisp function `listput` is similar to using `getf` with `setf`.

`remf` *place indicator*   [*Macro*]

This removes from the property list stored in *place* the property with an indicator eq to *indicator*. The property indicator and the corresponding value are removed by destructively splicing the property list. `remf` returns `nil` if no such property was found, or some non-`nil` value if a property was found. The form *place* may be any generalized variable acceptable to `setf`. See `remprop`.

X3J13 voted in March 1989 ⟨153⟩ to clarify the permissible side effects of certain operations; `remf` is permitted to perform a `setf` on the *place* or on any part, *car* or *cdr*, of the top-level list structure held by that *place*.

X3J13 voted in March 1988 ⟨146⟩ to clarify order of evaluation (see section 7.2).

`get-properties` *place indicator-list*   [*Function*]

`get-properties` is like `getf`, except that the second argument is a list of indicators. `get-properties` searches the property list stored in *place* for any of the indicators in *indicator-list* until it finds the first property in the property list whose indicator is one of the elements of *indicator-list*. Normally *place* is computed from a generalized variable acceptable to `setf`.

`get-properties` returns three values. If any property was found, then the first two values are the indicator and value for the first property whose indicator was in *indicator-list*, and the third is that tail of the property list whose *car* was the indicator (and whose *cadr* is therefore the value). If no property was found, all three values are `nil`. Thus the third value serves as a flag indicating success or failure and also allows the search to be restarted, if desired, after the property was found.

10.2. The Print Name

Every symbol has an associated string called the *print name*. This string is used as the external representation of the symbol: if the characters in the string are typed in to `read` (with suitable escape conventions for certain characters), it is interpreted as a reference to that symbol (if it is interned); and if the symbol is printed, `print` types out the print name. For more information, see the sections on the *reader* (section 22.1.1) and *printer* (section 22.1.6).

`symbol-name` *sym*   [*Function*]

This returns the print name of the symbol *sym*. For example:

`(symbol-name 'xyz)` ⇒ `"XYZ"`

It is an extremely bad idea to modify a string being used as the print name of a symbol. Such a modification may tremendously confuse the function `read` and the package system.

X3J13 voted in March 1989 ⟨11⟩ to specify that it is an error to modify a string being used as the print name of a symbol.

10.3. Creating Symbols

Symbols can be used in two rather different ways. An *interned* symbol is one that is indexed by its print name in a catalogue called a *package*. A request to locate a symbol with that print name results in the same (`eq`) symbol. Every time input is read with the function `read`, and that print name appears, it is read as the same symbol. This property of symbols makes them appropriate to use as names for things and as hooks on which to hang permanent data objects (using the property list, for example).

Interned symbols are normally created automatically; the first time something (such as the function `read`) asks the package system for a symbol with a given print name, that symbol is automatically created. The function used to ask for an interned symbol is `intern`, or one of the functions related to `intern`.

Although interned symbols are the most commonly used, they will not be discussed further here. For more information, see chapter 11.

An *uninterned* symbol is a symbol used simply as a data object, with no special cataloguing (it belongs to no particular package). An uninterned symbol is printed as `#:` followed by its print name. The following are some functions for creating uninterned symbols.

`make-symbol` *print-name*   [*Function*]

(`make-symbol` *print-name*) creates a new uninterned symbol, whose print name is the string *print-name*. The value and function bindings will be unbound and the property list will be empty.

The string actually installed in the symbol's print-name component may be the given string *print-name* or may be a copy of it, at the implementation's discretion. The user should not assume that (`symbol-name` (`make-symbol` x)) is eq to x, but also should not alter a string once it has been given as an argument to `make-symbol`.

Implementation note: An implementation might choose, for example, to copy the string to some read-only area, in the expectation that it will never be altered.

`copy-symbol` *sym* &optional *copy-props*   [*Function*]

This returns a new uninterned symbol with the same print name as *sym*.

X3J13 voted in March 1989 ⟨39⟩ that the print name of the new symbol is required to be the same only in the sense of `string=`; in other words, an implementation is permitted (but not required) to make a copy of the print name. User programs should not assume that the print names of the old and new symbols will be eq, although they may happen to be eq in some implementations.

If *copy-props* is non-`nil`, then the initial value and function definition of the new symbol will be the same as those of *sym*, and the property list of the new symbol will be a copy of *sym*'s.

X3J13 voted in March 1989 ⟨38⟩ to clarify that only the top-level conses of the property list are copied; it is as if (`copy-list` (`symbol-plist` *sym*)) were used as the property list of the new symbol.

If *copy-props* is `nil` (the default), then the new symbol will be unbound and undefined, and its property list will be empty.

gensym &optional *x*   [*Function*]

gensym invents a print name and creates a new symbol with that print name. It returns the new, uninterned symbol.

The invented print name consists of a prefix (which defaults to G), followed by the decimal representation of a number.

The number is increased by 1 every time gensym is called.

If the argument *x* is present and is an integer, then *x* must be non-negative, and the internal counter is set to *x* for future use; otherwise the internal counter is incremented. If *x* is a string, then that string is made the default prefix for this and future calls to gensym. After handling the argument, gensym creates a symbol as it would with no argument. For example:

```
(gensym) ⇒ G7
(gensym "FOO-") ⇒ FOO-8
(gensym 32) ⇒ FOO-32
(gensym) ⇒ FOO-33
(gensym "GARBAGE-") ⇒ GARBAGE-34
```

gensym is usually used to create a symbol that should not normally be seen by the user and whose print name is unimportant except to allow easy distinction by eye between two such symbols. The optional argument is rarely supplied. The name comes from "generate symbol," and the symbols produced by it are often called "gensyms."

Compatibility note: In earlier versions of Lisp, such as MacLisp and Interlisp, the print name of a gensym was of fixed length, consisting of a single letter and a fixed-length decimal representation with leading zeros if necessary, for example, G0007. This convention was motivated by an implementation consideration, namely that the name should fit into a single machine word, allowing a quick and clever implementation. Such considerations are less relevant in Common Lisp. The consistent use of mnemonic prefixes can make it easier for the programmer, when debugging, to determine what code generated a particular symbol. The elimination of the fixed-length decimal representation prevents the same name from being used twice unless the counter is explicitly reset.

If it is desirable for the generated symbols to be interned, and yet guaranteed to be symbols distinct from all others, then the function gentemp may be more appropriate to use.

X3J13 voted in March 1989 ⟨94⟩ to alter the specification of gensym so that supplying an optional argument (whether a string or a number) does *not* alter the internal state maintained by gensym. Instead, the internal counter is made explicitly available as a variable named *gensym-counter*.

If a string argument is given to gensym, that string is used as the prefix; otherwise "G" is used. If a number is provided, its decimal representation is used, but the internal counter is unaffected. X3J13 deprecates the use of a number as an argument.

---

gensym-counter   [*Variable*]

X3J13 voted in March 1989 ⟨94⟩ to add *gensym-counter*, which holds the state of the gensym counter; that is, gensym uses the decimal representation of its value as part of the generated name and then increments its value.

The initial value of this variable is implementation-dependent but will be a non-negative integer.

The user may assign to or bind this variable at any time, but its value must always be a non-negative integer.

---

gentemp &optional *prefix package*   [*Function*]

gentemp, like gensym, creates and returns a new symbol. gentemp differs from gensym in that it interns the symbol (see intern) in the *package* (which defaults to the current package; see *package*). gentemp guarantees the symbol will be a new one not already existing in the package. It does this by using a counter as gensym does, but if the generated symbol is not really new, then the process is repeated until a new one is created. There is no provision for resetting the gentemp counter. Also, the prefix for gentemp is not remembered from one call to the next; if *prefix* is omitted, the default prefix T is used.

---

symbol-package *sym*   [*Function*]

Given a symbol *sym*, symbol-package returns the contents of the package cell of that symbol. This will be a package object or nil.

---

keywordp *object*   [*Function*]

The argument may be any Lisp object. The predicate keywordp is true if the argument is a symbol and that symbol is a keyword (that is, belongs to the keyword package). Keywords are those symbols that are written with a leading colon. Every keyword is a constant, in the sense that it always evaluates to itself. See constantp.

11

Packages

One problem with earlier Lisp systems is the use of a single name space for all symbols. In large Lisp systems, with modules written by many different programmers, accidental name collisions become a serious problem. Common Lisp addresses this problem through the *package system*, derived from an earlier package system developed for Lisp Machine Lisp [55]. In addition to preventing name-space conflicts, the package system makes the modular structure of large Lisp systems more explicit.

A *package* is a data structure that establishes a mapping from print names (strings) to symbols. The package thus replaces the "oblist" or "obarray" machinery of earlier Lisp systems. At any given time one package is current, and this package is used by the Lisp reader in translating strings into symbols. The current package is, by definition, the one that is the value of the global variable *package*. It is possible to refer to symbols in packages other than the current one through the use of *package qualifiers* in the printed representation of the symbol. For example, foo:bar, when seen by the reader, refers to the symbol whose name is bar in the package whose name is foo. (Actually, this is true only if bar is an external symbol of foo, that is, a symbol that is supposed to be visible outside of foo. A reference to an internal symbol requires the intentionally clumsier syntax foo::bar.)

The string-to-symbol mappings available in a given package are divided into two classes, *external* and *internal*. We refer to the symbols accessible via these mappings as being *external* and *internal* symbols of the package in question, though really it is the mappings that are different and not the symbols themselves. Within a given package, a name refers to one symbol or to none; if it does refer to a symbol, then it is either external or internal in that package, but not both.

External symbols are part of the package's public interface to other packages. External symbols are supposed to be chosen with some care and are advertised to users of the package. Internal symbols are for internal use only, and these symbols are normally hidden from other packages. Most symbols are created as internal symbols; they become external only if they appear explicitly in an `export` command for the package.

A symbol may appear in many packages. It will always have the same name wherever it appears, but it may be external in some packages and internal in others. On the other hand, the same name (string) may refer to different symbols in different packages.

Normally, a symbol that appears in one or more packages will be *owned* by one particular package, called the *home package* of the symbol; that package is said to *own* the symbol. Every symbol has a component called the *package cell* that contains a pointer to its home package. A symbol that is owned by some package is said to be *interned*. Some symbols are not owned by any package; such a symbol is said to be *uninterned*, and its package cell contains `nil`.

Packages may be built up in layers. From the point of view of a package's user, the package is a single collection of mappings from strings into internal and external symbols. However, some of these mappings may be established within the package itself, while other mappings are inherited from other packages via the `use-package` construct. (The mechanisms responsible for this inheritance are described below.) In what follows, we will refer to a symbol as being *accessible* in a package if it can be referred to without a package qualifier when that package is current, regardless of whether the mapping occurs within that package or via inheritance. We will refer to a symbol as being *present* in a package if the mapping is in the package itself and is not inherited from somewhere else. Thus a symbol present in a package is accessible, but an accessible symbol is not necessarily present.

A symbol is said to be *interned in a package* if it is accessible in that package and also is owned (by either that package or some other package). Normally all the symbols accessible in a package will in fact be owned by some package, but the terminology is useful when discussing the pathological case of an accessible but unowned (uninterned) symbol.

As a verb, to *intern* a symbol in a package means to cause the symbol to be interned in the package if it was not already; this process is performed by the function `intern`. If the symbol was previously unowned, then the package it is being interned in becomes its owner (home package); but if the symbol was previously owned by another package, that other package continues to own the symbol.

To *unintern* a symbol from the package means to cause it to be not present in the package and, additionally, to cause the symbol to be uninterned if the package was the home package (owner) of the symbol. This process is performed by the function `unintern`.

11.1. Consistency Rules

Package-related bugs can be very subtle and confusing: things are not what they appear to be. The Common Lisp package system is designed with a number of safety features to prevent most of the common bugs that would otherwise occur in normal use. This may seem over-protective, but experience with earlier package systems has shown that such safety features are needed.

In dealing with the package system, it is useful to keep in mind the following consistency rules, which remain in force as long as the value of `*package*` is not changed by the user:

- *Read-read consistency:* Reading the same print name always results in the same (`eq`) symbol.

- *Print-read consistency:* An interned symbol always prints as a sequence of characters that, when read back in, yields the same (`eq`) symbol.

- *Print-print consistency:* If two interned symbols are not `eq`, then their printed representations will be different sequences of characters.

These consistency rules remain true in spite of any amount of implicit interning caused by typing in Lisp forms, loading files, etc. This has the important implication that, as long as the current package is not changed, results are reproducible regardless of the order of loading files or the exact history of what symbols were typed in when. The rules can only be violated by explicit action: changing the value of `*package*`, forcing some action by continuing from an error, or calling one of the "dangerous" functions `unintern`, `unexport`, `shadow`, `shadowing-import`, or `unuse-package`.

11.2. Package Names

Each package has a name (a string) and perhaps some nicknames. These are assigned when the package is created, though they can be changed later. A package's name should be something long and self-explanatory, like `editor`; there might be a nickname that is shorter and easier to type, such as `ed`.

There is a single name space for packages. The function `find-package` translates a package name or nickname into the associated package. The function `package-name` returns the name of a package. The function `package-nicknames` returns a list of all nicknames for a package. The function `rename-package` removes a package's current name and nicknames and replaces them with new ones specified by the user. Package renaming is occasionally useful when, for development purposes, it is desirable to load two versions of a package into the same

Lisp. One can load the first version, rename it, and then load the other version, without getting a lot of name conflicts.

When the Lisp reader sees a qualified symbol, it handles the package-name part in the same way as the symbol part with respect to capitalization. Lowercase characters in the package name are converted to corresponding uppercase characters unless preceded by the escape character \ or surrounded by | characters. The lookup done by the `find-package` function is case-sensitive, like that done for symbols. Note that `|Foo|:|Bar|` refers to a symbol whose name is `Bar` in a package whose name is `Foo`. By contrast, `|Foo:Bar|` refers to a seven-character symbol that has a colon in its name (as well as two uppercase letters and four lowercase letters) and is interned in the current package. Following the convention used in this book for symbols, we show ordinary package names using lowercase letters, even though the name string is internally represented with uppercase letters.

Most of the functions that require a package-name argument from the user accept either a symbol or a string. If a symbol is supplied, its print name will be used; the print name will already have undergone case-conversion by the usual rules. If a string is supplied, it must be so capitalized as to match exactly the string that names the package.

X3J13 voted in January 1989 ⟨127⟩ to clarify that one may use either a package object or a package name (symbol or string) in any of the following situations:

- the `:use` argument to `make-package`

- the first argument to `package-use-list`, `package-used-by-list`, `package-name`, `package-nicknames`, `in-package`, `find-package`, `rename-package`, or `delete-package`,

- the second argument to `intern`, `find-symbol`, `unintern`, `export`, `unexport`, `import`, `shadowing-import`, or `shadow`

- the first argument, or a member of the list that is the first argument, to `use-package` or `unuse-package`

- the value of the *package* given to `do-symbols`, `do-external-symbols`, or `do-all-symbols`

- a member of the *package-list* given to `with-package-iterator`

Note that the first argument to `make-package` must still be a package name and not an actual package; it makes no sense to create an already existing package. Similarly, package nicknames must always be expressed as package names and not as package objects. If `find-package` is given a package object instead of a name, it simply returns that package.

11.3. Translating Strings to Symbols

The value of the special variable `*package*` must always be a package object (not a name). Whatever package object is currently the value of `*package*` is referred to as the *current package*.

When the Lisp reader has, by parsing, obtained a string of characters thought to name a symbol, that name is looked up in the current package. This lookup may involve looking in other packages whose external symbols are inherited by the current package. If the name is found, the corresponding symbol is returned. If the name is not found (that is, there is no symbol of that name accessible in the current package), a new symbol is created for it and is placed in the current package as an internal symbol. Moreover, the current package becomes the owner (home package) of the symbol, and so the symbol becomes interned in the current package. If the name is later read again while this same package is current, the same symbol will then be found and returned.

Often it is desirable to refer to an external symbol in some package other than the current one. This is done through the use of a *qualified name*, consisting of a package name, then a colon, then the name of the symbol. This causes the symbol's name to be looked up in the specified package, rather than in the current one. For example, `editor:buffer` refers to the external symbol named `buffer` accessible in the package named `editor`, regardless of whether there is a symbol named `buffer` in the current package. If there is no package named `editor`, or if no symbol named `buffer` is accessible in `editor`, or if `buffer` is an internal symbol in `editor`, the Lisp reader will signal a correctable error to ask the user for instructions.

On rare occasions, a user may need to refer to an *internal* symbol of some package other than the current one. It is illegal to do this with the colon qualifier, since accessing an internal symbol of some other package is usually a mistake. However, this operation is legal if a doubled colon `::` is used as the separator in place of the usual single colon. If `editor::buffer` is seen, the effect is exactly the same as reading `buffer` with `*package*` temporarily rebound to the package whose name is `editor`. This special-purpose qualifier should be used with caution.

The package named `keyword` contains all keyword symbols used by the Lisp system itself and by user-written code. Such symbols must be easily accessible from any package, and name conflicts are not an issue because these symbols are used only as labels and never to carry package-specific values or properties. Because keyword symbols are used so frequently, Common Lisp provides a special reader syntax for them. Any symbol preceded by a colon but no package name (for example `:foo`) is added to (or looked up in) the `keyword` package as an *external* symbol. The keyword package is also treated specially in that whenever a symbol is added to the keyword package the symbol is always made external; the symbol is also automatically declared to be a constant (see defconstant) and made to have itself as its value. This is why every keyword evaluates to itself. As a matter of style, keywords should always be accessed using the leading-colon convention; the user should never import or inherit keywords into any other package. It is an error to try to apply use-package to the keyword package.

Each symbol contains a package cell that is used to record the home package of the symbol, or nil if the symbol is uninterned. This cell may be accessed by using the function symbol-package. When an interned symbol is printed, if it is a symbol in the keyword package, then it is printed with a preceding colon; otherwise, if it is accessible (directly or by inheritance) in the current package, it is printed without any qualification; otherwise, it is printed with the name of the home package as the qualifier, using : as the separator if the symbol is external and :: if not.

A symbol whose package slot contains nil (that is, has no home package) is printed preceded by #:. It is possible, by the use of import and unintern, to create a symbol that has no recorded home package but that in fact is accessible in some package. The system does not check for this pathological case, and such symbols will always be printed preceded by #:.

In summary, the following four uses of symbol qualifier syntax are defined.

foo:bar

When read, looks up BAR among the external symbols of the package named FOO. Printed when symbol bar is external in its home package foo and is not accessible in the current package.

foo::bar

When read, interns BAR as if FOO were the current package. Printed when symbol bar is internal in its home package foo and is not accessible in the current package.

:bar

When read, interns BAR as an external symbol in the keyword package and makes it evaluate to itself. Printed when the home package of symbol bar is keyword.

#:bar

When read, creates a new uninterned symbol named BAR. Printed when the symbol bar is uninterned (has no home package), even in the pathological case that bar is uninterned but nevertheless somehow accessible in the current package.

All other uses of colons within names of symbols are not defined by Common Lisp but are reserved for implementation-dependent use; this includes names that end in a colon, contain two or more colons, or consist of just a colon.

11.4. Exporting and Importing Symbols

Symbols from one package may be made accessible in another package in two ways.

First, any individual symbol may be added to a package by use of the function import. The form (import 'editor:buffer) takes the external symbol named buffer in the editor package (this symbol was located when the form was read by the Lisp reader) and adds it to the current package as an internal symbol. The symbol is then present in the current package. The imported symbol is not automatically exported from the current package, but if it is already present and external, then the fact that it is external is not changed. After the call to import it is possible to refer to buffer in the importing package without any qualifier. The status of buffer in the package named editor is unchanged, and editor remains the home package for this symbol. Once imported, a symbol is *present* in the importing package and can be removed only by calling unintern.

If the symbol is already present in the importing package, import has no effect. If a distinct symbol with the name buffer is accessible in the importing package (directly or by inheritance), then a correctable error is signaled, as described in section 11.5, because import avoids letting one symbol shadow another.

A symbol is said to be *shadowed* by another symbol in some package if the first symbol would be accessible by inheritance if not for the presence of the second symbol. To import a symbol without the possibility of getting an error because of shadowing, use the function shadowing-import. This inserts the symbol into the specified package as an internal symbol, regardless of whether another symbol of the same name will be shadowed by this action. If a different symbol of the same name is already present in the package, that symbol will first be uninterned from the package (see unintern). The new symbol is added to the package's shadowing-symbols list. shadowing-import should be used with caution. It changes the state of the package system in such a way that the consistency rules do not hold across the change.

The second mechanism is provided by the function use-package. This causes a package to inherit all of the external symbols of some other package. These symbols become accessible as *internal* symbols of the using package. That is, they can be referred to without a qualifier while this package is current, but they are not passed along to any other package that uses this package. Note that use-package, unlike import, does not cause any new symbols to be *present* in the current package but only makes them *accessible* by inheritance. use-package checks carefully for name conflicts between the newly imported symbols and those already accessible in the importing package. This is described in detail in section 11.5.

Typically a user, working by default in the user package, will load a number of packages into Lisp to provide an augmented working environment, and then call use-package on each of these packages to allow easy access to their external symbols. unuse-package undoes the effects of a previous use-package. The external symbols of the used package are no longer inherited. However, any symbols that have been imported into the using package continue to be present in that package.

There is no way to inherit the *internal* symbols of another package; to refer to an internal symbol, the user must either make that symbol's home package current, use a qualifier, or import that symbol into the current package.

The distinction between external and internal symbols is a primary means of hiding names so that one program does not tread on the namespace of another.

When intern or some other function wants to look up a symbol in a given package, it first looks for the symbol among the external and internal symbols of the package itself; then it looks through the external symbols of the used packages in some unspecified order. The order does not matter; according to the rules for handling name conflicts (see below), if conflicting symbols appear in two or more packages inherited by package X, a symbol of this name must also appear in X itself as a shadowing symbol. Of course, implementations are free to choose other, more efficient ways of implementing this search, as long as the user-visible behavior is equivalent to what is described here.

The function export takes a symbol that is accessible in some specified package (directly or by inheritance) and makes it an external symbol of that package. If the symbol is already accessible as an external symbol in the package, export has no effect. If the symbol is directly present in the package as an internal symbol, it is simply changed to external status. If it is accessible as an internal symbol via use-package, the symbol is first imported into the package, then exported. (The symbol is then present in the specified package whether or not the package continues to use the package through which the symbol was originally inherited.) If the symbol is not accessible at all in the specified package, a correctable error is signaled that, upon continuing, asks the user whether the symbol should be imported.

The function unexport is provided mainly as a way to undo erroneous calls to export. It works only on symbols directly present in the current package, switching them back to internal status. If unexport is given a symbol already accessible as an internal symbol in the current package, it does nothing; if it is given a symbol not accessible in the package at all, it signals an error.

11.5. Name Conflicts

A fundamental invariant of the package system is that within one package any particular name can refer to at most one symbol. A *name conflict* is said to occur when there is more than one candidate symbol and it is not obvious which one to choose. If the system does not always choose the same way, the read-read consistency rule would be violated. For example, some programs or data might have been read in under a certain mapping of the name to a symbol. If the mapping changes to a different symbol, and subsequently additional programs or data are read, then the two programs will not access the same symbol even though they use the same name. Even if the system did always choose the same way, a name conflict is likely to result in a mapping from names to symbols different from what was expected by the user, causing programs to execute incorrectly. Therefore, any time a name conflict is about to occur, an error is signaled. The user may continue from the error and tell the package system how to resolve the conflict.

It may be that the same symbol is accessible to a package through more than one path. For example, the symbol might be an external symbol of more than one used package, or the symbol might be directly present in a package and also inherited from another package. In such cases there is no name conflict. The same identical symbol cannot conflict with itself. Name conflicts occur only between distinct symbols with the same name.

The creator of a package can tell the system in advance how to resolve a name conflict through the use of *shadowing*. Every package has a list of shadowing symbols. A shadowing symbol takes precedence over any other symbol of the same name that would otherwise be accessible to the package. A name conflict involving a shadowing symbol is always resolved in favor of the shadowing symbol, without signaling an error (except for one instance involving import described below). The functions shadow and shadowing-import may be used to declare shadowing symbols.

Name conflicts are detected when they become possible, that is, when the package structure is altered. There is no need to check for name conflicts during every name lookup.

The functions use-package, import, and export check for name conflicts. use-package makes the external symbols of the package being used accessible to the using package; each of these symbols is checked for name conflicts with the symbols already accessible. import adds a single symbol to the internals of a package, checking for a name conflict with an existing symbol either present in the package or accessible to it. import signals a name conflict error even if the conflict is with a shadowing symbol, the rationale being that the user has given two explicit and inconsistent directives. export makes a single symbol accessible to all the packages that use the package from which the symbol is exported. All of these packages are checked for name conflicts: (export *s p*) does (find-symbol (symbol-name *s*) *q*) for each package *q* in (package-used-by-list *p*). Note that in the usual case of an export during the initial definition of a package, the result of package-used-by-list will be nil and the name-conflict checking will take negligible time.

The function intern, which is the one used most frequently by the Lisp reader for looking up names of symbols, does not need to do any name-conflict checking, because it never creates a new symbol if there is already an accessible symbol with the name given.

shadow and shadowing-import never signal a name-conflict error because the user, by calling these functions, has specified how any possible conflict is to be resolved. shadow does name-conflict checking to the extent that it checks whether a distinct existing symbol with the specified name is accessible and, if so, whether it is directly present in the package or inherited. In the latter case, a new symbol is created to shadow it. shadowing-import does name-conflict checking to the extent that it checks whether a distinct existing symbol with the same name is accessible; if so, it is shadowed by the new symbol, which implies that it must be uninterned if it was directly present in the package.

unuse-package, unexport, and unintern (when the symbol being uninterned is not a shadowing symbol) do not need to do any name-conflict checking because they only remove symbols from a package; they do not make any new symbols accessible.

Giving a shadowing symbol to unintern can uncover a name conflict that had previously been resolved by the shadowing. If package A uses packages B and C, A contains a shadowing symbol x, and B and C each contain external symbols named x, then removing the shadowing symbol x from A will reveal a name conflict between b:x and c:x if those two symbols are distinct. In this case unintern will signal an error.

Aborting from a name-conflict error leaves the original symbol accessible. Package functions always signal name-conflict errors before making any change to the package structure. When multiple changes are to be made, however, for example when export is given a list of symbols, it is permissible for the implementation to process each change separately, so that aborting from a name conflict caused by the second symbol in the list will not unexport the first symbol in the list. However, aborting from a name-conflict error caused by export of a single symbol will not leave that symbol accessible to some packages and inaccessible to others; with respect to each symbol processed, export behaves as if it were an atomic operation.

Continuing from a name-conflict error should offer the user a chance to resolve the name conflict in favor of either of the candidates. The package structure should be altered to reflect the resolution of the name conflict, via `shadowing-import`, `unintern`, or `unexport`.

A name conflict in `use-package` between a symbol directly present in the using package and an external symbol of the used package may be resolved in favor of the first symbol by making it a shadowing symbol, or in favor of the second symbol by uninterning the first symbol from the using package. The latter resolution is dangerous if the symbol to be uninterned is an external symbol of the using package, since it will cease to be an external symbol.

A name conflict in `use-package` between two external symbols inherited by the using package from other packages may be resolved in favor of either symbol by importing it into the using package and making it a shadowing symbol.

A name conflict in `export` between the symbol being exported and a symbol already present in a package that would inherit the newly exported symbol may be resolved in favor of the exported symbol by uninterning the other one, or in favor of the already-present symbol by making it a shadowing symbol.

A name conflict in `export` or `unintern` due to a package inheriting two distinct symbols with the same name from two other packages may be resolved in favor of either symbol by importing it into the using package and making it a shadowing symbol, just as with `use-package`.

A name conflict in `import` between the symbol being imported and a symbol inherited from some other package may be resolved in favor of the symbol being imported by making it a shadowing symbol, or in favor of the symbol already accessible by not doing the `import`. A name conflict in `import` with a symbol already present in the package may be resolved by uninterning that symbol, or by not doing the `import`.

Good user-interface style dictates that `use-package` and `export`, which can cause many name conflicts simultaneously, first check for all of the name conflicts before presenting any of them to the user. The user may then choose to resolve all of them wholesale or to resolve each of them individually, the latter requiring a lot of interaction but permitting different conflicts to be resolved different ways.

Implementations may offer other ways of resolving name conflicts. For instance, if the symbols that conflict are not being used as objects but only as names for functions, it may be possible to "merge" the two symbols by putting the function definition onto both symbols. References to either symbol for purposes of calling a function would be equivalent. A similar merging operation can be done for variable values and for things stored on the property list. In Lisp Machine Lisp, for example, one can also *forward* the value, function, and property cells so that future changes to either symbol will propagate to the other one. Some other implementations are able to do this with value cells but not with property lists. Only the user can know whether this way of resolving a name conflict is adequate, because it will work only if the use of two non-eq symbols with the same name will not prevent the correct operation of the program. The value of offering symbol merging as a way of resolving name conflicts is that it can avoid the need to throw away the whole Lisp world, correct the package-definition forms that caused the error, and start over from scratch.

11.6. Built-in Packages

The following packages, at least, are built into every Common Lisp system.

lisp

The package named lisp contains the primitives of the Common Lisp system. Its external symbols include all of the user-visible functions and global variables that are present in the Common Lisp system, such as car, cdr, and *package*. Almost all other packages will want to use lisp so that these symbols will be accessible without qualification.

user

The user package is, by default, the current package at the time a Common Lisp system starts up. This package uses the lisp package.

X3J13 voted in March 1989 ⟨108⟩ to specify that the forthcoming ANSI Common Lisp will use the package name common-lisp instead of lisp and the package name common-lisp-user instead of user. The purpose is to allow a single Lisp system to support both "old" Common Lisp and "new" ANSI Common Lisp simultaneously despite the fact that in some cases the two languages use the same names for incompatible purposes. (That's what packages are for!)

common-lisp

The package named common-lisp contains the primitives of the ANSI Common Lisp system (as opposed to a Common Lisp system based on the 1984 specification). Its external symbols include all of the user-visible functions and global variables that are present in the ANSI Common Lisp system, such as car, cdr, and *package*. Note, however, that the home package of such symbols is not necessarily the common-lisp package (this makes it easier for symbols such as t and lambda to be shared between the common-lisp package and another package, possibly one named lisp). Almost all other packages ought to use common-lisp so that these symbols will be accessible without qualification. This package has the nickname cl.

common-lisp-user

The common-lisp-user package is, by default, the current package at the time an ANSI Common Lisp system starts up. This package uses the common-lisp package and has the nickname cl-user. It may contain other implementation-dependent symbols and may use other implementation-specific packages.

keyword

This package contains all of the keywords used by built-in or user-defined Lisp functions. Printed symbol representations that start with a colon are interpreted as referring to symbols in this package, which are always external symbols. All symbols in this package are treated as constants that evaluate to themselves, so that the user can type :foo instead of ´:foo.

system

This package name is reserved to the implementation. Normally this is used to contain names of implementation-dependent system-interface functions. This package uses lisp and has the nickname sys.

X3J13 voted in January 1989 ⟨125⟩ to modify the requirements on the built-in packages so as to limit what may appear in the common-lisp package and to lift the requirement that every implementation have a package named system. The details are as follows.

Not only must the common-lisp package in any given implementation contain all the external symbols prescribed by the standard; the common-lisp package moreover may not contain any external symbol that is not prescribed by the standard. However, the common-lisp package may contain additional internal symbols, depending on the implementation.

An external symbol of the common-lisp package may not have a function, macro, or special form definition, or a top-level value, or a special proclamation, or a type definition, unless specifically permitted by the standard. Programmers may validly rely on this fact; for example, fboundp is guaranteed to be false for all external symbols of the common-lisp package except those explicitly specified in the standard to name functions, macros, and special forms. Similarly, boundp will be false of all such external symbols except those documented to be variables or constants.

Portable programs may use external symbols in the common-lisp package that are not documented to be constants or variables as names of local lexical variables with the presumption that the implementation has not proclaimed such variables to be special; this legitimizes the common practice of using such names as list and string as names for local variables.

A valid implementation may initially have properties on any symbol, or dynamically put new properties on symbols (even user-created symbols), as long as no property indicator used for this purpose is an external symbol of any package defined by the standard or a symbol that is accessible from the common-lisp-user package or any package defined by the user.

This vote eliminates the requirement that every implementation have a predefined package named system. An implementation may provide any number of predefined packages; these should be described in the documentation for that implementation.

The common-lisp-user package may contain symbols not described by the standard and may use other implementation-specific packages.

X3J13 voted in March 1989 ⟨109⟩ to restrict user programs from performing certain actions that might interfere with built-in facilities or interact badly with them. Except where explicitly allowed, the consequences are undefined if any of the following actions are performed on a symbol in the common-lisp package.

• binding or altering its value (lexically or dynamically)

• defining or binding it as a function

• defining or binding it as a macro

• defining it as a type specifier (defstruct, defclass, deftype)

• defining it as a structure (defstruct)

• defining it as a declaration

• dsing it as a symbol macro

• altering its print name

• altering its package

• tracing it

• declaring or proclaiming it special or lexical

• declaring or proclaiming its type or ftype

• removing it from the package common-lisp

X3J13 also voted in June 1989 ⟨49⟩ to add to this list the item

• defining it as a compiler macro

If such a symbol is not globally defined as a variable or a constant, a user program is allowed to lexically bind it and declare the type of that binding.

If such a symbol is not defined as a function, macro, or special form, a user program is allowed to (lexically) bind it as a function and to declare the `ftype` of that binding and to trace that binding.

If such a symbol is not defined as a function, macro, or special form, a user program is allowed to (lexically) bind it as a macro.

As an example, the behavior of the code fragment

```
(flet ((open (filename &key direction)
          (format t "~%OPEN was called.")
          (open filename :direction direction)))
   (with-open-file (x "frob" :direction ´:output)
     (format t "~%Was OPEN called?")))
```

is undefined. Even in a "reasonable" implementation, for example, the macro expansion of `with-open-file` might refer to the `open` function and might not. However, the preceding rules eliminate the burden of deciding whether an implementation is reasonable. The code fragment violates the rules; officially its behavior is therefore completely undefined, and that's that.

Note that "altering the property list" is not in the list of proscribed actions, so a user program *is* permitted to add properties to or remove properties from symbols in the `common-lisp` package.

11.7. Package System Functions and Variables

Some of the functions and variables in this section are described in previous sections but are included here for completeness.

It is up to each implementation's compiler to ensure that when a compiled file is loaded, all of the symbols in the file end up in the same packages that they would occupy if the Lisp source file were loaded. In most compilers, this will be accomplished by treating certain package operations as though they are surrounded by `(eval-when (compile load eval) ...)`; see `eval-when`. These operations are `make-package`, `in-package`, `shadow`, `shadowing-import`, `export`, `unexport`, `use-package`, `unuse-package`, and `import`. To guarantee proper compilation in all Common Lisp implementations, these functions should appear only at top level within a file. As a matter of style, it is suggested that each file contain only one package, and that all of the package setup forms appear near the start of the file. This is discussed in more detail, with examples, in section 11.9.

X3J13 voted in March 1989 ⟨103⟩ to cancel the specifications of the preceding paragraph in order to support a model of file compilation in which the compiler need never take special note of ordinary function calls; only special forms and macros are recognized as affecting the state of the compilation process. As part of this change in-package was changed to be a macro rather than a function and its functionality was restricted. The actions of shadow, shadowing-import, use-package, import, intern, and export for compilation purposes may be accomplished with the new macro defpackage.

Implementation note: In the past, some Lisp compilers have read the entire file into Lisp before processing any of the forms. Other compilers have arranged for the loader to do all of its intern operations before evaluating any of the top-level forms. Neither of these techniques will work in a straightforward way in Common Lisp because of the presence of multiple packages.

For the functions described here, all optional arguments named *package* default to the current value of *package*. Where a function takes an argument that is either a symbol or a list of symbols, an argument of nil is treated as an empty list of symbols. Any argument described as a package name may be either a string or a symbol. If a symbol is supplied, its print name will be used as the package name; if a string is supplied, the user must take care to specify the same capitalization used in the package name, normally all uppercase.

package   [*Variable*]

The value of this variable must be a package; this package is said to be the current package. The initial value of *package* is the user package.

X3J13 voted in March 1989 ⟨108⟩ to specify that the forthcoming ANSI Common Lisp will use the package name common-lisp-user instead of user.

The function load rebinds *package* to its current value. If some form in the file changes the value of *package* during loading, the old value will be restored when the loading is completed.

X3J13 voted in October 1988 ⟨21⟩ to require compile-file to rebind *package* to its current value.

make-package *package-name* &key :nicknames :use   [*Function*]

This creates and returns a new package with the specified package name. As described above, this argument may be either a string or a symbol. The :nicknames argument must be a list of strings to be used as alternative names for the package. Once again, the user may supply symbols in place of the strings, in which case the print names of the symbols are used. These names and nicknames must not conflict with any existing package names; if they do, a correctable error is signaled.

The :use argument is a list of packages or the names (strings or symbols) of packages whose external symbols are to be inherited by the new package. These packages must already exist. If not supplied, :use defaults to a list of one package, the lisp package.

X3J13 voted in March 1989 ⟨108⟩ to specify that the forthcoming ANSI Common Lisp will use the package name common-lisp instead of lisp.

X3J13 voted in January 1989 ⟨119⟩ to change the specification of make-package so that the default value for the :use argument is unspecified. Portable code should specify :use ´("COMMON-LISP") explicitly.

Rationale: Many existing implementations of Common Lisp happen to have violated the first edition specification, providing as the default not only the lisp package but also (or instead) a package containing implementation-dependent language extensions. This is for good reason: usually it is much more convenient to the user for the default :use list to be the entire, implementation-dependent, extended language rather than only the facilities specified in this book. The X3J13 vote simply legitimizes existing practice.

---

in-package *package-name* &key :nicknames :use   [*Function*]

The in-package function is intended to be placed at the start of a file containing a subsystem that is to be loaded into some package other than user.

If there is not already a package named *package-name*, this function is similar to make-package, except that after the new package is created, *package* is set to it. This binding will remain in force until changed by the user (perhaps with another in-package call) or until the *package* variable reverts to its old value at the completion of a load operation.

If there is an existing package whose name is *package-name*, the assumption is that the user is re-loading a file after making some changes. The existing package is augmented to reflect any new nicknames or new packages in the :use list (with the usual error checking), and *package* is then set to this package.

X3J13 voted in January 1989 ⟨156⟩ to specify that in-package returns the new package, that is, the value of *package* after the operation has been executed.

X3J13 voted in March 1989 ⟨108⟩ to specify that the forthcoming ANSI Common Lisp will use the package name common-lisp-user instead of user.

X3J13 voted in March 1989 ⟨103⟩ to restrict the functionality of in-package and to make it a macro. This is an incompatible change.

Making in-package a macro rather than a function means that there is no need to require compile-file to handle it specially. Since defpackage is also defined to have side effects on the compilation environment, there is no need to require any of the package functions to be treated specially by the compiler.

in-package *name*   [*Macro*]

This macro causes *package* to be set to the package named *name*, which must be a symbol or string. The *name* is not evaluated. An error is signaled if the package does not already exist. Everything this macro does is also performed at compile time if the call appears at top level.

find-package *name*   [*Function*]

The *name* must be a string that is the name or nickname for a package. This argument may also be a symbol, in which case the symbol's print name is used. The package with that name or nickname is returned; if no such package exists, find-package returns nil. The matching of names observes case (as in string=).
   X3J13 voted in January 1989 ⟨127⟩ to allow find-package to accept a package object, in which case the package is simply returned (see section 11.2).

package-name *package*   [*Function*]

The argument must be a package. This function returns the string that names that package.
   X3J13 voted in January 1989 ⟨127⟩ to allow package-name to accept a package name or nickname, in which case the primary name of the package so specified is returned (see section 11.2).
   X3J13 voted in January 1989 ⟨126⟩ to add a function to delete packages. One consequence of this vote is that package-name will return nil instead of a package name if applied to a deleted package object. See delete-package.

package-nicknames *package*   [*Function*]

The argument must be a package. This function returns the list of nickname strings for that package, not including the primary name.
   X3J13 voted in January 1989 ⟨127⟩ to allow package-nicknames to accept a package name or nickname, in which case the nicknames of the package so specified are returned (see section 11.2).

rename-package *package new-name* &optional *new-nicknames*   [*Function*]

The old name and all of the old nicknames of *package* are eliminated and are replaced by *new-name* and *new-nicknames*. The *new-name* argument is a string or symbol; the *new-nicknames* argument, which defaults to `nil`, is a list of strings or symbols.

X3J13 voted in January 1989 ⟨127⟩ to clarify that the *package* argument may be either a package object or a package name (see section 11.2).

X3J13 voted in January 1989 ⟨156⟩ to specify that `rename-package` returns *package*.

`package-use-list` *package*   [*Function*]

A list of other packages used by the argument package is returned.

X3J13 voted in January 1989 ⟨127⟩ to clarify that the *package* argument may be either a package object or a package name (see section 11.2).

`package-used-by-list` *package*   [*Function*]

A list of other packages that use the argument package is returned.

X3J13 voted in January 1989 ⟨127⟩ to clarify that the *package* argument may be either a package object or a package name (see section 11.2).

`package-shadowing-symbols` *package*   [*Function*]

A list is returned of symbols that have been declared as shadowing symbols in this package by `shadow` or `shadowing-import`. All symbols on this list are present in the specified package.

X3J13 voted in January 1989 ⟨127⟩ to clarify that the *package* argument may be either a package object or a package name (see section 11.2).

`list-all-packages`   [*Function*]

This function returns a list of all packages that currently exist in the Lisp system.

`delete-package` *package*   [*Function*]

X3J13 voted in January 1989 ⟨126⟩ to add the `delete-package` function, which deletes the specified *package* from all package system data structures. The *package* argument may be either a package or the name of a package.

If *package* is a name but there is currently no package of that name, a correctable error is signaled. Continuing from the error makes no deletion attempt but merely returns `nil` from the call to `delete-package`.

If *package* is a package object that has already been deleted, no error is signaled and no deletion is attempted; instead, `delete-package` immediately returns `nil`.

If the package specified for deletion is currently used by other packages, a correctable error is signaled. Continuing from this error, the effect of the function unuse-package is performed on all such other packages so as to remove their dependency on the specified package, after which delete-package proceeds to delete the specified package as if no other package had been using it.

If any symbol had the specified package as its home package before the call to delete-package, then its home package is unspecified (that is, the contents of its package cell are unspecified) after the delete-package operation has been completed. Symbols in the deleted package are not modified in any other way.

The name and nicknames of the *package* cease to be recognized package names. The package object is still a package, but anonymous; packagep will be true of it, but package-name applied to it will return nil.

The effect of any other package operation on a deleted package object is undefined. In particular, an attempt to locate a symbol within a deleted package (using intern or find-symbol, for example) will have unspecified results.

delete-package returns t if the deletion succeeds, and nil otherwise.

---

intern *string* &optional *package*   [*Function*]

The *package*, which defaults to the current package, is searched for a symbol with the name specified by the *string* argument. This search will include inherited symbols, as described in section 11.4. If a symbol with the specified name is found, it is returned. If no such symbol is found, one is created and is installed in the specified package as an internal symbol (as an external symbol if the package is the keyword package); the specified package becomes the home package of the created symbol.

X3J13 voted in March 1989 ⟨11⟩ to specify that intern may in effect perform the search using a copy of the argument string in which some or all of the implementation-defined attributes have been removed from the characters of the string. It is implementation-dependent which attributes are removed.

Two values are returned. The first is the symbol that was found or created. The second value is nil if no pre-existing symbol was found, and takes on one of three values if a symbol was found:

:internal   The symbol was directly present in the package as an internal symbol.

:external   The symbol was directly present as an external symbol.

:inherited   The symbol was inherited via use-package (which implies that the symbol is internal).

X3J13 voted in January 1989 ⟨127⟩ to clarify that the *package* argument may be either a package object or a package name (see section 11.2).

Compatibility note: Conceptually, intern translates a string to a symbol. In MacLisp and several other dialects of Lisp, intern can take either a string or a symbol as its argument; in the latter case, the symbol's print name is extracted and used as the string. However, this leads to some confusing issues about what to do if intern finds a symbol that is not eq to the argument symbol. To avoid such confusion, Common Lisp requires the argument to be a string.

---

find-symbol *string* &optional *package*   [*Function*]

This is identical to intern, but it never creates a new symbol. If a symbol with the specified name is found in the specified package, directly or by inheritance, the symbol found is returned as the first value and the second value is as specified for intern. If the symbol is not accessible in the specified package, both values are nil.

X3J13 voted in January 1989 ⟨127⟩ to clarify that the *package* argument may be either a package object or a package name (see section 11.2).

---

unintern *symbol* &optional *package*   [*Function*]

If the specified symbol is present in the specified *package*, it is removed from that package and also from the package's shadowing-symbols list if it is present there. Moreover, if the *package* is the home package for the symbol, the symbol is made to have no home package. Note that in some circumstances the symbol may continue to be accessible in the specified package by inheritance. unintern returns t if it actually removed a symbol, and nil otherwise.

unintern should be used with caution. It changes the state of the package system in such a way that the consistency rules do not hold across the change.

X3J13 voted in January 1989 ⟨127⟩ to clarify that the *package* argument may be either a package object or a package name (see section 11.2).

Compatibility note: The equivalent of this in MacLisp is remob.

---

export *symbols* &optional *package*   [*Function*]

The *symbols* argument should be a list of symbols, or possibly a single symbol. These symbols become accessible as external symbols in *package* (see section 11.4). export returns t.

By convention, a call to `export` listing all exported symbols is placed near the start of a file to advertise which of the symbols mentioned in the file are intended to be used by other programs.

X3J13 voted in January 1989 ⟨127⟩ to clarify that the *package* argument may be either a package object or a package name (see section 11.2).

---

unexport *symbols* &optional *package*   [*Function*]

The argument should be a list of symbols, or possibly a single symbol. These symbols become internal symbols in *package*. It is an error to unexport a symbol from the `keyword` package (see section 11.4). `unexport` returns t.

X3J13 voted in January 1989 ⟨127⟩ to clarify that the *package* argument may be either a package object or a package name (see section 11.2).

---

import *symbols* &optional *package*   [*Function*]

The argument should be a list of symbols, or possibly a single symbol. These symbols become internal symbols in *package* and can therefore be referred to without having to use qualified-name (colon) syntax. `import` signals a correctable error if any of the imported symbols has the same name as some distinct symbol already accessible in the package (see section 11.4). `import` returns t.

X3J13 voted in June 1987 ⟨102⟩ to clarify that if any symbol to be imported has no home package then `import` sets the home package of the symbol to the *package* to which the symbol is being imported.

X3J13 voted in January 1989 ⟨127⟩ to clarify that the *package* argument may be either a package object or a package name (see section 11.2).

---

shadowing-import *symbols* &optional *package*   [*Function*]

This is like `import`, but it does not signal an error even if the importation of a symbol would shadow some symbol already accessible in the package. In addition to being imported, the symbol is placed on the shadowing-symbols list of *package* (see section 11.5). `shadowing-import` returns t.

`shadowing-import` should be used with caution. It changes the state of the package system in such a way that the consistency rules do not hold across the change.

X3J13 voted in January 1989 ⟨127⟩ to clarify that the *package* argument may be either a package object or a package name (see section 11.2).

`shadow` *symbols* &optional *package*   [*Function*]

The argument should be a list of symbols, or possibly a single symbol. The print name of each symbol is extracted, and the specified *package* is searched for a symbol of that name. If such a symbol is present in this package (directly, not by inheritance), then nothing is done. Otherwise, a new symbol is created with this print name, and it is inserted in the *package* as an internal symbol. The symbol is also placed on the shadowing-symbols list of the *package* (see section 11.5). `shadow` returns `t`.

X3J13 voted in March 1988 ⟨161⟩ to change `shadow` to accept strings as well as well as symbols (a string in the *symbols* list being treated as a print name), and to clarify that if a symbol of specified name is already in the *package* but is not yet on the shadowing-symbols list for that *package*, then `shadow` does add it to the shadowing-symbols list rather than simply doing nothing.

`shadow` should be used with caution. It changes the state of the package system in such a way that the consistency rules do not hold across the change.

X3J13 voted in January 1989 ⟨127⟩ to clarify that the *package* argument may be either a package object or a package name (see section 11.2).

`use-package` *packages-to-use* &optional *package*   [*Function*]

The *packages-to-use* argument should be a list of packages or package names, or possibly a single package or package name. These packages are added to the use-list of *package* if they are not there already. All external symbols in the packages to use become accessible in *package* as internal symbols (see section 11.4). It is an error to try to use the `keyword` package. `use-package` returns `t`.

X3J13 voted in January 1989 ⟨127⟩ to clarify that the *package* argument may be either a package object or a package name (see section 11.2).

`unuse-package` *packages-to-unuse* &optional *package*   [*Function*]

The *packages-to-unuse* argument should be a list of packages or package names, or possibly a single package or package name. These packages are removed from the use-list of *package*. `unuse-package` returns `t`.

X3J13 voted in January 1989 ⟨127⟩ to clarify that the *package* argument may be either a package object or a package name (see section 11.2).

X3J13 voted in January 1989 ⟨52⟩ to add a macro `defpackage` to the language to make it easier to create new packages, alleviating the burden on the programmer to perform the various setup operations in exactly the correct sequence.

defpackage *defined-package-name* {*option*}*   [*Macro*]

This creates a new package, or modifies an existing one, whose name is *defined-package-name*. The *defined-package-name* may be a string or a symbol; if it is a symbol, only its print name matters, and not what package, if any, the symbol happens to be in. The newly created or modified package is returned as the value of the defpackage form.

Each standard *option* is a list of a keyword (the name of the option) and associated arguments. No part of a defpackage form is evaluated. Except for the :size option, more than one option of the same kind may occur within the same defpackage form.

The standard options for defpackage are as follows. In every case, any option argument called *package-name* or *symbol-name* may be a string or a symbol; if it is a symbol, only its print name matters, and not what package, if any, the symbol happens to be in.

(:size *integer*)

This specifies approximately the number of symbols expected to be in the package. This is purely an efficiency hint to the storage allocator, so that implementations using hash tables as part of the package data structure (the usual technique) will not have to incrementally expand the package as new symbols are added to it (for example, as a large file is read while "in" that package).

(:nicknames {*package-name*}*)

The specified names become nicknames of the package being defined. If any of the specified nicknames already refers to an existing package, a continuable error is signaled exactly as for the function make-package.

(:shadow {*symbol-name*}*)

Symbols with the specified names are created as shadows in the package being defined, just as with the function shadow.

(:shadowing-import-from *package-name* {*symbol-name*}*)

Symbols with the specified names are located in the specified package. These symbols are imported into the package being defined, shadowing other symbols if necessary, just as with the function shadowing-import. In no case will symbols be created in a package other than the one being defined; a continuable error is signaled if for any *symbol-name* there is no symbol of that name accessible in the package named *package-name*.

(:use *{package-name}**)

The package being defined is made to "use" (inherit from) the packages specified by this option, just as with the function use-package. If no :use option is supplied, then a default list is assumed as for make-package.

X3J13 voted in January 1989 ⟨119⟩ to change the specification of make-package so that the default value for the :use argument is unspecified. This change affects defpackage as well. Portable code should specify (:use ´("COMMON-LISP")) explicitly.

(:import-from *package-name* *{symbol-name}**)

Symbols with the specified names are located in the specified package. These symbols are imported into the package being defined, just as with the function import. In no case will symbols be created in a package other than the one being defined; a continuable error is signaled if for any *symbol-name* there is no symbol of that name accessible in the package named *package-name*.

(:intern *{symbol-name}**)

Symbols with the specified names are located or created in the package being defined, just as with the function intern. Note that the action of this option may be affected by a :use option, because an inherited symbol will be used in preference to creating a new one.

(:export *{symbol-name}**)

Symbols with the specified names are located or created in the package being defined and then exported, just as with the function export. Note that the action of this option may be affected by a :use, :import-from, or :shadowing-import-from option, because an inherited or imported symbol will be used in preference to creating a new one.

The order in which options appear in a defpackage form does not matter; part of the convenience of defpackage is that it sorts out the options into the correct order for processing. Options are processed in the following order:

1. :shadow and :shadowing-import-from
2. :use
3. :import-from and :intern
4. :export

Shadows are established first in order to avoid spurious name conflicts when use links are established. Use links must occur before importing and interning so that those operations may refer to normally inherited symbols rather than creating new ones. Exports are performed last so that symbols created by any of the other options, in particular, shadows and imported symbols, may be exported. Note that exporting an inherited symbol implicitly imports it first (see section 11.4).

If no package named *defined-package-name* already exists, defpackage creates it. If such a package does already exist, then no new package is created. The existing package is modified, if possible, to reflect the new definition. The results are undefined if the new definition is not consistent with the current state of the package.

An error is signaled if more than one :size option appears.

An error is signaled if the same symbol-name argument (in the sense of comparing names with string=) appears more than once among the arguments to all the :shadow, :shadowing-import-from, :import-from, and :intern options.

An error is signaled if the same symbol-name argument (in the sense of comparing names with string=) appears more than once among the arguments to all the :intern and :export options.

Other kinds of name conflicts are handled in the same manner that the underlying operations use-package, import, and export would handle them.

Implementations may support other defpackage options. Every implementation should signal an error on encountering a defpackage option it does not support.

The function compile-file should treat top-level defpackage forms in the same way it would treat top-level calls to package-affecting functions (as described at the beginning of section 11.7).

Here is an example of a call to defpackage that "plays it safe" by using only strings as names.

```
(cl:defpackage "MY-VERY-OWN-PACKAGE"
  (:size 496)
  (:nicknames "MY-PKG" "MYPKG" "MVOP")
  (:use "COMMON-LISP")
  (:shadow "CAR" "CDR")
  (:shadowing-import-from "BRAND-X-LISP" "CONS")
  (:import-from "BRAND-X-LISP" "GC" "BLINK-FRONT-PANEL-LIGHTS")
  (:export "EQ" "CONS" "MY-VERY-OWN-FUNCTION"))
```

The preceding defpackage example is designed to operate correctly even if the package current when the form is read happens not to "use" the common-lisp package. (Note the use in this example of the nickname cl for the common-lisp package.) Moreover, neither reading in nor evaluating this defpackage form will ever create any symbols in the current package. Note too the use of uppercase letters in the strings.

Here, for the sake of contrast, is a rather similar use of defpackage that "plays the whale" by using all sorts of permissible syntax.

```
(defpackage my-very-own-package
   (:export :EQ common-lisp:cons my-very-own-function)
   (:nicknames "MY-PKG" #:MyPkg)
   (:use "COMMON-LISP")
   (:shadow "CAR")
   (:size 496)
   (:nicknames mvop)
   (:import-from "BRAND-X-LISP" "GC" Blink-Front-Panel-Lights)
   (:shadow common-lisp::cdr)
   (:shadowing-import-from "BRAND-X-LISP" CONS))
```

This example has exactly the same effect on the newly created package but may create useless symbols in other packages. The use of explicit package tags is particularly confusing; for example, this defpackage form will cause the symbol cdr to be shadowed *in the new package*; it will not be shadowed in the package common-lisp. The fact that the name "CDR" was specified by a package-qualified reference to a symbol in the common-lisp package is a red herring. The moral is that the syntactic flexibility of defpackage, as in other parts of Common Lisp, yields considerable convenience when used with commonsense competence, but unutterable confusion when used with Malthusian profusion.

Implementation note: An implementation of defpackage might choose to transform all the *package-name* and *symbol-name* arguments into strings at macro expansion time, rather than at the time the resulting expansion is executed, so that even if source code is expressed in terms of strange symbols in the defpackage form, the binary file resulting from compiling the source code would contain only strings. The purpose of this is simply to minimize the creation of useless symbols in production code. This technique is permitted as an implementation strategy but is not a behavior required by the specification of defpackage.

Note that defpackage is not capable by itself of defining mutually recursive packages, for example two packages each of which uses the other. However, nothing prevents one from using defpackage to perform much of the initial setup and then using functions such as use-package, import, and export to complete the links.

The purpose of defpackage is to encourage the user to put the entire definition of a package and its relationships to other packages in a single place. It may also encourage the designer of a large system to place the definitions of all relevant packages into a single file (say) that can be loaded before loading or compiling any code that depends on those packages. Such a file, if carefully constructed, can simply be loaded into the `common-lisp-user` package.

Implementations and programming environments may also be better able to support the programming process (if only by providing better error checking) through global knowledge of the intended package setup.

`find-all-symbols` *string-or-symbol*   [*Function*]

`find-all-symbols` searches every package in the Lisp system to find every symbol whose print name is the specified string. A list of all such symbols found is returned. This search is case-sensitive. If the argument is a symbol, its print name supplies the string to be searched for.

`do-symbols` (*var* [*package* [*result-form*]])   [*Macro*]
        {*declaration*}* {*tag* | *statement*}*

`do-symbols` provides straightforward iteration over the symbols of a package. The body is performed once for each symbol accessible in the *package*, in no particular order, with the variable *var* bound to the symbol. Then *result-form* (a single form, *not* an implicit `progn`) is evaluated, and the result is the value of the `do-symbols` form. (When the *result-form* is evaluated, the control variable *var* is still bound and has the value `nil`.) If the *result-form* is omitted, the result is `nil`. `return` may be used to terminate the iteration prematurely. If execution of the body affects which symbols are contained in the *package*, other than possibly to remove the symbol currently the value of *var* by using `unintern`, the effects are unpredictable.

X3J13 voted in January 1989 ⟨127⟩ to clarify that the *package* argument may be either a package object or a package name (see section 11.2).

X3J13 voted in March 1988 ⟨66⟩ to specify that the body of a `do-symbols` form may be executed more than once for the same accessible symbol, and users should take care to allow for this possibility.

The point is that the same symbol might be accessible via more than one chain of inheritance, and it is implementationally costly to eliminate such duplicates. Here is an example:

```
(setq *a* (make-package 'a))        ;Implicitly uses package common-lisp
(setq *b* (make-package 'b))        ;Implicitly uses package common-lisp
(setq *c* (make-package 'c :use '(a b)))

(do-symbols (x *c*) (print x))      ;Symbols in package common-lisp
                                    ; might be printed once or twice here
```

X3J13 voted in January 1989 ⟨121⟩ to restrict user side effects; see section 7.9.

Note that the loop construct provides a kind of for clause that can iterate over the symbols of a package (see chapter 26).

---

do-external-symbols (*var* [*package* [*result*]])   [*Macro*]
          {*declaration*}* {*tag* | *statement*}*

do-external-symbols is just like do-symbols, except that only the external symbols of the specified package are scanned.

The clarification voted by X3J13 in March 1988 for do-symbols ⟨66⟩, regarding redundant executions of the body for the same symbol, applies also to do-external-symbols.

X3J13 voted in January 1989 ⟨127⟩ to clarify that the *package* argument may be either a package object or a package name (see section 11.2).

X3J13 voted in January 1989 ⟨121⟩ to restrict user side effects; see section 7.9.

---

do-all-symbols (*var* [*result-form*])   [*Macro*]
          {*declaration*}* {*tag* | *statement*}*

This is similar to do-symbols but executes the body once for every symbol contained in every package. (This will not process every symbol whatsoever, because a symbol not accessible in any package will not be processed. Normally, uninterned symbols are not accessible in any package.) It is *not* in general the case that each symbol is processed only once, because a symbol may appear in many packages.

The clarification voted by X3J13 in March 1988 for do-symbols ⟨66⟩, regarding redundant executions of the body for the same symbol, applies also to do-all-symbols.

X3J13 voted in January 1989 ⟨127⟩ to clarify that the *package* argument may be either a package object or a package name (see section 11.2).

X3J13 voted in January 1989 ⟨121⟩ to restrict user side effects; see section 7.9.

X3J13 voted in January 1989 ⟨98⟩ to add a new macro with-package-iterator to the language.

---

with-package-iterator (*mname package-list* {*symbol-type*}⁺)   [*Macro*]
          {*form*}*

The name *mname* is bound and defined as if by macrolet, with the body *form*s as its lexical scope, to be a "generator macro" such that each invocation of (*mname*) will return a symbol and that successive invocations will eventually deliver, one by one, all the symbols from the packages that are elements of the list that is the value of the expression *package-list* (which is evaluated exactly once).

Each element of the *package-list* value may be either a package or the name of a package. As a further convenience, if the *package-list* value is itself a package or the name of a package, it is treated as if a singleton list containing that value had been provided. If the *package-list* value is nil, it is considered to be an empty list of packages.

At each invocation of the generator macro, there are two possibilities. If there is yet another unprocessed symbol, then four values are returned: t, the symbol, a keyword indicating the accessibility of the symbol within the package (see below), and the package from which the symbol was accessed. If there are no more unprocessed symbols in the list of packages, then one value is returned: nil.

When the generator macro returns a symbol as its second value, the fourth value is always one of the packages present or named in the *package-list* value, and the third value is a keyword indicating accessibility: :internal means present in the package and not exported; :external means present and exported; and :inherited means not present (thus not shadowed) but inherited from some package used by the package that is the fourth value.

Each *symbol-type* in an invocation of with-package-iterator is not evaluated. More than one may be present; their order does not matter. They indicate the accessibility types of interest. A symbol is not returned by the generator macro unless its actual accessibility matches one of the *symbol-type* indicators. The standard *symbol-type* indicators are :internal, :external, and :inherited, but implementations are permitted to extend the syntax of with-package-iterator by recognizing additional symbol accessibility types. An error is signaled if no *symbol-type* is supplied, or if any supplied *symbol-type* is not recognized by the implementation.

The order in which symbols are produced by successive invocations of the generator macro is not necessarily correlated in any way with the order of the packages in the *package-list*. When more than one package is in the *package-list*, symbols accessible from more than one package may be produced once or more than once. Even when only one package is specified, symbols inherited in multiple ways via used packages may be produced once or more than once.

The implicit interior state of the iteration over the list of packages and the symbols within them has dynamic extent. It is an error to invoke the generator macro once the with-package-iterator form has been exited.

Any number of invocations of with-package-iterator and related macros may be nested, and the generator macro of an outer invocation may be called from within an inner invocation (provided, of course, that its name is visible or otherwise made available).

X3J13 voted in January 1989 ⟨121⟩ to restrict user side effects; see section 7.9.

Rationale: This facility is a bit more flexible in some ways than do-symbols and friends. In particular, it makes it possible to implement loop clauses for iterating over packages in a way that is both portable and efficient (see chapter 26).

11.8. Modules

A *module* is a Common Lisp subsystem that is loaded from one or more files. A module is normally loaded as a single unit, regardless of how many files are involved. A module may consist of one package or several packages. The file-loading process is necessarily implementation-dependent, but Common Lisp provides some very simple portable machinery for naming modules, for keeping track of which modules have been loaded, and for loading modules as a unit.

X3J13 voted in January 1989 ⟨154⟩ to eliminate the entire module facility from the language; that is, the variable *modules* and the functions provide and require are deleted. X3J13 commented that the file-loading feature of require is not portable, and that the remaining functionality is easily implemented by user code. (I will add that in any case the specification of require is so vague that different implementations are likely to have differing behavior.)

---

modules   [*Variable*]

The variable *modules* is a list of names of the modules that have been loaded into the Lisp system so far. This list is used by the functions provide and require.

---

provide *module-name*   [*Function*]
require *module-name* &optional *pathname*   [*Function*]

Each module has a unique name (a string). The provide and require functions accept either a string or a symbol as the *module-name* argument. If a symbol is provided, its print name is used as the module name. If the module consists of a single package, it is customary for the package and module names to be the same.

The provide function adds a new module name to the list of modules maintained in the variable *modules*, thereby indicating that the module in question has been loaded.

The require function tests whether a module is already present (using a case-sensitive comparison); if the module is not present, require proceeds to load the appropriate file or set of files. The *pathname* argument, if present, is a single pathname or a list of pathnames whose files are to be loaded in order, left to right. If the *pathname* argument is `nil` or is not provided, the system will attempt to determine, in some system-dependent manner, which files to load. This will typically involve some central registry of module names and the associated file lists.

X3J13 voted in March 1988 not to permit symbols as pathnames ⟨134⟩ and to specify exactly which streams may be used as pathnames ⟨132⟩ (see section 23.1.6). Of course, this is moot if `require` is not in the language.

X3J13 voted in January 1989 ⟨156⟩ to specify that the values returned by `provide` and `require` are implementation-dependent. Of course, this is moot if `provide` and `require` are not in the language.

Implementation note: One way to implement such a registry on many operating systems is simply to use a distinguished "library" directory within the file system, where the name of each file is the same as the module it contains.

11.9. An Example

Most users will want to load and use packages but will never need to build one. Often a user will load a number of packages into the `user` package whenever using Common Lisp. Typically an implementation might provide some sort of initialization file mechanism to make such setup automatic when the Lisp starts up. Table 11-1 shows such an initialization file, one that simply causes other facilities to be loaded.

X3J13 voted in March 1989 ⟨108⟩ to specify that the forthcoming ANSI Common Lisp will use the package name `common-lisp-user` instead of `user`.

When each of two files uses some symbols from the other, the author of those files must be careful to arrange the contents of the file in the proper order. Typically each file contains a single package that is a complete module. The contents of such a file should include the following items, in order:

1. A call to `provide` that announces the module name.

2. A call to `in-package` that establishes the package.

3. A call to `shadow` that establishes any local symbols that will shadow symbols that would otherwise be inherited from packages that this package will use.

4. A call to `export` that establishes all of this package's external symbols.

5. Any number of calls to `require` to load other modules that the contents of this file might want to use or refer to. (Because the calls to `require` follow the calls

Table 11-1: An Initialization File

```
;;;; Lisp init file for I. Newton.

;;; Set up the USER package the way I like it.

(require 'calculus)              ;I use CALCULUS a lot; load it.
(use-package 'calculus)         ;Get easy access to its
                                ; exported symbols.

(require 'newtonian-mechanics)   ;Same thing for NEWTONIAN-MECHANICS
(use-package 'newtonian-mechanics)

;;; I just want a few things from RELATIVITY,
;;; and other things conflict.
;;; Import only what I need into the USER package.

(require 'relativity)
(import '(relativity:speed-of-light
          relativity:ignore-small-errors))

;;; These are worth loading, but I will use qualified names,
;;; such as PHLOGISTON:MAKE-FIRE-BOTTLE, to get at any symbols
;;; I might need from these packages.

(require 'phlogiston)
(require 'alchemy)

;;; End of Lisp init file for I. Newton.
```

to in-package, shadow, and export, it is possible for the packages that may be loaded to refer to external symbols in this package.)

6. Any number of calls to use-package, to make external symbols from other packages accessible in this package.

7. Any number of calls to import, to make symbols from other packages present in this package.

8. Finally, the definitions making up the contents of this package/module.

The following mnemonic sentence may be helpful in remembering the proper order of these calls:

Put in seven extremely random user interface commands.

Each word of the sentence corresponds to one item in the above ordering:

Put	Provide
IN	IN-package
Seven	Shadow
EXtremely	EXport
Random	Require
USEr	USE-package
Interface	Import
COmmands	COntents of package/module

The sentence says what it helps you to do.

The most distressing aspect of the X3J13 vote to eliminate provide and require ⟨154⟩ is of course that it completely ruins the mnemonic sentence.

Now, suppose for the sake of example that the phlogiston and alchemy packages are single-file, single-package modules as described above. The phlogiston package needs to use the alchemy package, and the alchemy package needs to use several external symbols from the phlogiston package. The definitions in the alchemy and phlogiston files (see tables 11-2 and 11-3) allow a user to specify require statements for either of these modules, or for both of them in either order, and all relevant information will be loaded automatically and in the correct order.

For very large modules whose contents are spread over several files (the lisp package is an example), it is recommended that the user create the package and declare all of the shadows and external symbols in a separate file, so that this can be loaded before anything that might use symbols from this package.

Indeed, the defpackage macro approved by X3J13 in January 1989 ⟨52⟩ encourages the use of such a separate file. (By the way, X3J13 voted in March 1989 ⟨108⟩ to specify that the forthcoming ANSI Common Lisp will use the package name common-lisp instead of lisp.) Let's take a look at a revision of I. Newton's files using defpackage.

The new version of the initialization file avoids using require; instead, we assume that load will do the job (see table 11-4).

The other files have each been split into two parts, one that establishes the package and one that defines the contents. This example uses a simple convention that for any file named, say, "foo" the file named "foo-package" contains the necessary defpackage and/or other package-establishing code. The idiom

```
(unless (find-package "FOO")
  (load "foo-package"))
```

Table 11-2: File alchemy

```
;;;; Alchemy functions, written and maintained by Merlin, Inc.

(provide 'alchemy)              ;The module is named ALCHEMY.
(in-package 'alchemy)           ;So is the package.

;;; There is nothing to shadow.

;;; Here is the external interface.

(export '(lead-to-gold gold-to-lead
          antimony-to-zinc elixir-of-life))

;;; This package/module needs a function from
;;; the PHLOGISTON package/module.

(require 'phlogiston)

;;; We don't frequently need most of the external symbols from
;;; PHLOGISTON, so it's not worth doing a USE-PACKAGE on it.
;;; We'll just use qualified names as needed.  But we use
;;; one function, MAKE-FIRE-BOTTLE, a lot, so import it.
;;; It's external in PHLOGISTON and so can be referred to
;;; here using ":" qualified-name syntax.

(import '(phlogiston:make-fire-bottle))

;;; Now for the real contents of this file.

(defun lead-to-gold (x)
  "Takes a quantity of lead and returns gold."
  (when (> (phlogiston:heat-flow 5 x x)   ;Using a qualified symbol
           3)
    (make-fire-bottle x))                 ;Using an imported symbol
  (gild x))

;;; And so on ...
```

Table 11-3: File phlogiston

```
;;;; Phlogiston functions, by Thermofluidics, Ltd.

(provide 'phlogiston)            ;The module is named PHLOGISTON.
(in-package 'phlogiston)         ;So is the package.

;;; There is nothing to shadow.

;;; Here is the external interface.

(export '(heat-flow cold-flow mix-fluids separate-fluids
          burn make-fire-bottle))

;;; This file uses functions from the ALCHEMY package/module.

(require 'alchemy)

;;; We use alchemy functions a lot, so use the package.
;;; This will allow symbols exported from the ALCHEMY package
;;; to be referred to here without the need for qualified names.

(use-package 'alchemy)

;;; No calls to IMPORT are needed here.

;;; The real contents of this package/module.

(defvar *feeling-weak* nil)

(defun heat-flow (amount x y)
  "Make some amount of heat flow from x to y."
  (when *feeling-weak*
    (quaff (elixir-of-life)))      ;No qualifier is needed.
  (push-heat amount x y))

;;; And so on ...
```

Table 11-4: An Initialization File When `defpackage` Is Used

```
;;;; Lisp init file for I. Newton.

;;; Set up the USER package the way I like it.

(load "calculus")              ;I use CALCULUS a lot; load it.
(use-package 'calculus)        ;Get easy access to its
                               ; exported symbols.

(load "newtonian-mechanics")   ;Ditto for NEWTONIAN-MECHANICS
(use-package 'newtonian-mechanics)

;;; I just want a few things from RELATIVITY,
;;; and other things conflict.
;;; Import only what I need into the USER package.

(load "relativity")
(import '(relativity:speed-of-light
          relativity:ignore-small-errors))

;;; These are worth loading, but I will use qualified names,
;;; such as PHLOGISTON:MAKE-FIRE-BOTTLE, to get at any symbols
;;; I might need from these packages.

(load "phlogiston")
(load "alchemy")

;;; End of Lisp init file for I. Newton.
```

is conventionally used to load a package definition but only if the package has not already been defined. (This is a bit clumsy, and there are other ways to arrange things so that a package is defined no more than once.)

The file `alchemy-package` is shown in table 11-5. The tricky point here is that the `alchemy` and `phlogiston` packages contain mutual references (each imports from the other), and so `defpackage` alone cannot do the job. Therefore the `phlogiston` package is not mentioned in a `:use` option in the `defpackage` for the `alchemy` package. Instead, the function `use-package` is called explicitly, after the package definition for `phlogiston` has been loaded. Note that this file has been coded with excruciating care so as to operate correctly even if the package current when the file is loaded does not inherit from the common-lisp package. In particular, the standard load-package-definition idiom has been peppered with package qualifiers:

```
(cl:unless (cl:find-package "PHLOGISTON")
  (cl:load "phlogiston-package"))
```

Note the use of the nickname cl for the common-lisp package.

The alchemy file, shown in table 11-6, simply loads the alchemy package definition, makes that package current, and then defines the "real contents" of the package.

The file phlogiston-package is shown in table 11-7. This one is a little more straightforward than the file alchemy-package, because the latter bears the responsibility for breaking the circular package references. This file simply makes sure that the alchemy package is defined and then performs a defpackage for the phlogiston package.

The phlogiston file, shown in table 11-8, simply loads the phlogiston package definition, makes that package current, and then defines the "real contents" of the package.

Let's look at the question of package circularity in this example a little more closely. Suppose that the file alchemy-package is loaded first. It defines the alchemy package and then loads file phlogiston-package. That file in turn finds that the package alchemy has already been defined and therefore does not attempt to load file alchemy-package again; it merely defines package phlogiston. The file alchemy-package then has a chance to import phlogiston:make-fire-bottle and everything is fine.

On the other hand, suppose that the file phlogiston-package is loaded first. It finds that the package alchemy has *not* already been defined, and therefore it immediately loads file alchemy-package. That file in turn defines the alchemy package; then it finds that package phlogiston is not yet defined and so loads file phlogiston-package *again* (indeed, in nested fashion). This time file phlogiston-package *does* find that the package alchemy has already been defined, so it simply defines package phlogiston and terminates. The file alchemy-package then imports phlogiston:make-fire-bottle and terminates. Finally, the outer loading of file phlogiston-package *re-defines* package phlogiston. Oh, dear. Fortunately the two definitions of package phlogiston agree in every detail, so everything ought to be all right. Still, it looks a bit dicey; *I* certainly don't have the same warm, fuzzy feeling that I would if no package were defined more than once.

Table 11-5: File alchemy-package Using defpackage

```
;;;; Alchemy package, written and maintained by Merlin, Inc.

(cl:defpackage "ALCHEMY"
  (:export "LEAD-TO-GOLD" "GOLD-TO-LEAD"
           "ANTIMONY-TO-ZINC" "ELIXIR-OF-LIFE")
  )

;;; This package needs a function from the PHLOGISTON package.
;;; Load the definition of the PHLOGISTON package if necessary.

(cl:unless (cl:find-package "PHLOGISTON")
  (cl:load "phlogiston-package"))

;;; We don't frequently need most of the external symbols from
;;; PHLOGISTON, so it's not worth doing a USE-PACKAGE on it.
;;; We'll just use qualified names as needed. But we use
;;; one function, MAKE-FIRE-BOTTLE, a lot, so import it.
;;; It's external in PHLOGISTON and so can be referred to
;;; here using ":" qualified-name syntax.

(cl:import '(phlogiston:make-fire-bottle))
```

Table 11-6: File alchemy Using defpackage

```
;;;; Alchemy functions, written and maintained by Merlin, Inc.

(unless (find-package "ALCHEMY")
  (load "alchemy-package"))

(in-package 'alchemy)

(defun lead-to-gold (x)
  "Takes a quantity of lead and returns gold."
  (when (> (phlogiston:heat-flow 5 x x)   ;Using a qualified symbol
        3)
    (make-fire-bottle x))                 ;Using an imported symbol
  (gild x))

;;;; And so on ...
```

Table 11-7: File `phlogiston-package` Using `defpackage`

```
;;;; Phlogiston package definition, by Thermofluidics, Ltd.

;;; This package uses functions from the ALCHEMY package.

(cl:unless (cl:find-package "ALCHEMY")
  (cl:load "alchemy-package"))

(cl:defpackage "PHLOGISTON"
  (:use "COMMON-LISP" "ALCHEMY")
  (:export "HEAT-FLOW"
           "COLD-FLOW"
           "MIX-FLUIDS"
           "SEPARATE-FLUIDS"
           "BURN"
           "MAKE-FIRE-BOTTLE")
  )
```

Table 11-8: File `phlogiston` Using `defpackage`

```
;;;; Phlogiston functions, by Thermofluidics, Ltd.

(unless (find-package "PHLOGISTON")
  (load "phlogiston-package"))

(in-package 'phlogiston)

(defvar *feeling-weak* nil)

(defun heat-flow (amount x y)
  "Make some amount of heat flow from x to y."
  (when *feeling-weak*
    (quaff (elixir-of-life)))        ;No qualifier is needed.
  (push-heat amount x y))

;;; And so on ...
```

Conclusion: `defpackage` goes a long way, but it certainly doesn't solve all the possible problems of package and file management. Neither did `require` and `provide`. Perhaps further experimentation will yield facilities appropriate for future standardization.

12

Numbers

Common Lisp provides several different representations for numbers. These representations may be divided into four categories: integers, ratios, floating-point numbers, and complex numbers. Many numeric functions will accept any kind of number; they are *generic*. Other functions accept only certain kinds of numbers.

Note that this remark, predating the design of the Common Lisp Object System, uses the term "generic" in a generic sense and not necessarily in the technical sense used by CLOS (see chapter 2).

In general, numbers in Common Lisp are not true objects; eq cannot be counted upon to operate on them reliably. In particular, it is possible that the expression

```
(let ((x z) (y z)) (eq x y))
```

may be false rather than true if the value of z is a number.

Rationale: This odd breakdown of eq in the case of numbers allows the implementor enough design freedom to produce exceptionally efficient numerical code on conventional architectures. MacLisp requires this freedom, for example, in order to produce compiled numerical code equal in speed to Fortran. Common Lisp makes this same restriction, if not for this freedom, then at least for the sake of compatibility.

If two objects are to be compared for "identity," but either might be a number, then the predicate eql is probably appropriate; if both objects are known to be numbers, then = may be preferable.

12.1. Precision, Contagion, and Coercion

In general, computations with floating-point numbers are only approximate. The *precision* of a floating-point number is not necessarily correlated at all with the *accuracy* of that number. For instance, 3.1428571428571428571 is a more precise approximation to π than 3.14159, but the latter is more accurate. The precision refers to the number of bits retained in the representation. When an operation combines a short floating-point number with a long one, the result will be a long floating-point number. This rule is made to ensure that as much accuracy as possible is preserved; however, it is by no means a guarantee. Common Lisp numerical routines do assume, however, that the accuracy of an argument does not exceed its precision. Therefore when two small floating-point numbers are combined, the result will always be a small floating-point number. This assumption can be overridden by first explicitly converting a small floating-point number to a larger representation. (Common Lisp never converts automatically from a larger size to a smaller one.)

Rational computations cannot overflow in the usual sense (though of course there may not be enough storage to represent one), as integers and ratios may in principle be of any magnitude. Floating-point computations may get exponent overflow or underflow; this is an error.

X3J13 voted in June 1989 ⟨79⟩ to address certain problems relating to floating-point overflow and underflow, but certain parts of the proposed solution were not adopted, namely to add the macro without-floating-underflow-traps to the language and to require certain behavior of floating-point overflow and underflow. The committee agreed that this area of the language requires more discussion before a solution is standardized.

For the record, the proposal that was considered and rejected (for the nonce) introduced a macro without-floating-underflow-traps that would execute its body in such a way that, within its dynamic extent, a floating-point underflow must not signal an error but instead must produce either a denormalized number or zero as the result. The rejected proposal also specified the following treatment of overflow and underflow:

- A floating-point computation that overflows should signal an error of type floating-point-overflow.

- Unless the dynamic extent of a use of without-floating-underflow-traps, a floating-point computation that underflows should signal an error of type floating-point-underflow. A result that can be represented only in denormalized form must be considered an underflow in implementations that support denormalized floating-point numbers.

These points refer to conditions floating-point-overflow and floating-point-underflow that were approved by X3J13 and are described in section 29.5.

When rational and floating-point numbers are compared or combined by a numerical function, the rule of *floating-point contagion* is followed: when a rational meets a floating-point number, the rational is first converted to a floating-point number of the same format. For functions such as + that take more than two arguments, it may be that part of the operation is carried out exactly using rationals and then the rest is done using floating-point arithmetic.

X3J13 voted in January 1989 ⟨37⟩ to apply the rule of floating-point contagion stated above to the case of *combining* rational and floating-point numbers. For *comparing*, the following rule is to be used instead: When a rational number and a floating-point number are to be compared by a numerical function, in effect the floating-point number is first converted to a rational number as if by the function rational, and then an exact comparison of two rational numbers is performed. It is of course valid to use a more efficient implementation than actually calling the function rational, as long as the result of the comparison is the same. In the case of complex numbers, the real and imaginary parts are handled separately.

Rationale: In general, accuracy cannot be preserved in combining operations, but it can be preserved in comparisons, and preserving it makes that part of Common Lisp algebraically a bit more tractable. In particular, this change prevents the breakdown of transitivity. Let a be the result of (/ 10.0 single-float-epsilon), and let j be the result of (floor a). (Note that (= a (+ a 1.0)) is true, by the definition of single-float-epsilon.) Under the old rules, all of (<= a j), (< j (+ j 1)), and (<= (+ j 1) a) would be true; transitivity would then imply that (< a a) ought to be true, but of course it is false, and therefore transitivity fails. Under the new rule, however, (<= (+ j 1) a) is false.

For functions that are mathematically associative (and possibly commutative), a Common Lisp implementation may process the arguments in any manner consistent with associative (and possibly commutative) rearrangement. This does not affect the order in which the argument forms are evaluated, of course; that order is always left to right, as in all Common Lisp function calls. What is left loose is the order in which the argument values are processed. The point of all this is that implementations may differ in which automatic coercions are applied because of differing orders of argument processing. As an example, consider this expression:

```
(+ 1/3 2/3 1.0D0 1.0 1.0E-15)
```

One implementation might process the arguments from left to right, first adding 1/3 and 2/3 to get 1, then converting that to a double-precision floating-point number for combination with 1.0D0, then successively converting and adding 1.0 and 1.0E-15. Another implementation might process the arguments from right to left, first performing a single-precision floating-point addition of 1.0 and 1.0E-15 (and probably losing some accuracy in the process!), then converting the sum to double precision and adding 1.0D0, then converting 2/3 to double-precision floating-point and adding it, and then converting 1/3 and adding that. A third implementation might first scan all the arguments, process all the rationals first to keep that part of the computation exact, then find an argument of the largest floating-point format among all the arguments and add that, and then add in all other arguments, converting each in turn (all in a perhaps misguided attempt to make the computation as accurate as possible). In any case, all three strategies are legitimate. The user can of course control the order of processing explicitly by writing several calls; for example:

```
(+ (+ 1/3 2/3) (+ 1.0D0 1.0E-15) 1.0)
```

The user can also control all coercions simply by writing calls to coercion functions explicitly.

In general, then, the type of the result of a numerical function is a floating-point number of the largest format among all the floating-point arguments to the function; but if the arguments are all rational, then the result is rational (except for functions that can produce mathematically irrational results, in which case a single-format floating-point number may result).

There is a separate rule of complex contagion. As a rule, complex numbers never result from a numerical function unless one or more of the arguments is complex. (Exceptions to this rule occur among the irrational and transcendental functions, specifically `expt`, `log`, `sqrt`, `asin`, `acos`, `acosh`, and `atanh`; see section 12.5.) When a non-complex number meets a complex number, the non-complex number is in effect first converted to a complex number by providing an imaginary part of zero.

If any computation produces a result that is a ratio of two integers such that the denominator evenly divides the numerator, then the result is immediately converted to the equivalent integer. This is called the rule of *rational canonicalization*.

If the result of any computation would be a complex rational with a zero imaginary part, the result is immediately converted to a non-complex rational number by taking the real part. This is called the rule of *complex canonicalization*. Note that this rule does *not* apply to complex numbers whose components are floating-point numbers. Whereas `#C(5 0)` and 5 are not distinct values in Common Lisp (they are always `eql`), `#C(5.0 0.0)` and 5.0 are always distinct values in Common Lisp (they are never `eql`, although they are `equalp`).

12.2. Predicates on Numbers

Each of the following functions tests a single number for a specific property. Each function requires that its argument be a number; to call one with a non-number is an error.

zerop *number*   [*Function*]

This predicate is true if *number* is zero (the integer zero, a floating-point zero, or a complex zero), and is false otherwise. Regardless of whether an implementation provides distinct representations for positive and negative floating-point zeros, (zerop -0.0) is always true. It is an error if the argument *number* is not a number.

plusp *number*   [*Function*]

This predicate is true if *number* is strictly greater than zero, and is false otherwise. It is an error if the argument *number* is not a non-complex number.

minusp *number*   [*Function*]

This predicate is true if *number* is strictly less than zero, and is false otherwise. Regardless of whether an implementation provides distinct representations for positive and negative floating-point zeros, (minusp -0.0) is always false. (The function float-sign may be used to distinguish a negative zero.) It is an error if the argument *number* is not a non-complex number.

oddp *integer*   [*Function*]

This predicate is true if the argument *integer* is odd (not divisible by 2), and otherwise is false. It is an error if the argument is not an integer.

evenp *integer*   [*Function*]

This predicate is true if the argument *integer* is even (divisible by 2), and otherwise is false. It is an error if the argument is not an integer.

See also the data-type predicates integerp, rationalp, floatp, complexp, and numberp.

12.3. Comparisons on Numbers

Each of the functions in this section requires that its arguments all be numbers; to call one with a non-number is an error. Unless otherwise specified, each works on all types of numbers, automatically performing any required coercions when arguments are of different types.

= *number* &rest *more-numbers*	[*Function*]
/= *number* &rest *more-numbers*	[*Function*]
< *number* &rest *more-numbers*	[*Function*]
> *number* &rest *more-numbers*	[*Function*]
<= *number* &rest *more-numbers*	[*Function*]
>= *number* &rest *more-numbers*	[*Function*]

These functions each take one or more arguments. If the sequence of arguments satisfies a certain condition:

=	all the same
/=	all different
<	monotonically increasing
>	monotonically decreasing
<=	monotonically nondecreasing
>=	monotonically nonincreasing

then the predicate is true, and otherwise is false. Complex numbers may be compared using = and /=, but the others require non-complex arguments. Two complex numbers are considered equal by = if their real parts are equal and their imaginary parts are equal according to =. A complex number may be compared with a non-complex number with = or /=. For example:

(= 3 3) is true.	(/= 3 3) is false.
(= 3 5) is false.	(/= 3 5) is true.
(= 3 3 3 3) is true.	(/= 3 3 3 3) is false.
(= 3 3 5 3) is false.	(/= 3 3 5 3) is false.
(= 3 6 5 2) is false.	(/= 3 6 5 2) is true.
(= 3 2 3) is false.	(/= 3 2 3) is false.
(< 3 5) is true.	(<= 3 5) is true.
(< 3 -5) is false.	(<= 3 -5) is false.
(< 3 3) is false.	(<= 3 3) is true.
(< 0 3 4 6 7) is true.	(<= 0 3 4 6 7) is true.
(< 0 3 4 4 6) is false.	(<= 0 3 4 4 6) is true.
(> 4 3) is true.	(>= 4 3) is true.
(> 4 3 2 1 0) is true.	(>= 4 3 2 1 0) is true.
(> 4 3 3 2 0) is false.	(>= 4 3 3 2 0) is true.
(> 4 3 1 2 0) is false.	(>= 4 3 1 2 0) is false.
(= 3) is true.	(/= 3) is true.
(< 3) is true.	(<= 3) is true.
(= 3.0 #C(3.0 0.0)) is true.	(/= 3.0 #C(3.0 1.0)) is true.
(= 3 3.0) is true.	(= 3.0s0 3.0d0) is true.

(= 0.0 -0.0) is true.   (= 5/2 2.5) is true.
(> 0.0 -0.0) is false.   (= 0 -0.0) is true.

With two arguments, these functions perform the usual arithmetic comparison tests. With three or more arguments, they are useful for range checks, as shown in the following example:

```
(<= 0 x 9)                    ;true if x is between 0 and 9, inclusive
(< 0.0 x 1.0)                 ;true if x is between 0.0 and 1.0, exclusive
(< -1 j (length s))           ;true if j is a valid index for s
(<= 0 j k (- (length s) 1))   ;true if j and k are each valid
                              ; indices for s and j ≤ k
```

Rationale: The "unequality" relation is called /= rather than <> (the name used in Pascal) for two reasons. First, /= of more than two arguments is not the same as the or of < and > of those same arguments. Second, unequality is meaningful for complex numbers even though < and > are not. For both reasons it would be misleading to associate unequality with the names of < and >.

Compatibility note: In Common Lisp, the comparison operations perform "mixed-mode" comparisons: (= 3 3.0) is true. In MacLisp, there must be exactly two arguments, and they must be either both fixnums or both floating-point numbers. To compare two numbers for numerical equality and type equality, use eql.

---

max *number* &rest *more-numbers*   [*Function*]
min *number* &rest *more-numbers*   [*Function*]

The arguments may be any non-complex numbers. max returns the argument that is greatest (closest to positive infinity). min returns the argument that is least (closest to negative infinity).

For max, if the arguments are a mixture of rationals and floating-point numbers, and the largest argument is a rational, then the implementation is free to produce either that rational or its floating-point approximation; if the largest argument is a floating-point number of a smaller format than the largest format of any floating-point argument, then the implementation is free to return the argument in its given format or expanded to the larger format. More concisely, the implementation has the choice of returning the largest argument as is or applying the rules of floating-point contagion, taking all the arguments into consideration for contagion purposes. Also, if two or more of the arguments are equal, then any one of them may be chosen as the value to return. Similar remarks apply to min (replacing "largest argument" by "smallest argument").

```
(max 6 12) ⇒ 12                    (min 6 12) ⇒ 6
(max -6 -12) ⇒ -6                  (min -6 -12) ⇒ -12
(max 1 3 2 -7) ⇒ 3                 (min 1 3 2 -7) ⇒ -7
(max -2 3 0 7) ⇒ 7                 (min -2 3 0 7) ⇒ -2
(max 3) ⇒ 3                        (min 3) ⇒ 3
(max 5.0 2) ⇒ 5.0                  (min 5.0 2) ⇒ 2 or 2.0
(max 3.0 7 1) ⇒ 7 or 7.0          (min 3.0 7 1) ⇒ 1 or 1.0
(max 1.0s0 7.0d0) ⇒ 7.0d0
(min 1.0s0 7.0d0) ⇒ 1.0s0 or 1.0d0
(max 3 1 1.0s0 1.0d0) ⇒ 3 or 3.0d0
(min 3 1 1.0s0 1.0d0) ⇒ 1 or 1.0s0 or 1.0d0
```

12.4. Arithmetic Operations

Each of the functions in this section requires that its arguments all be numbers; to call one with a non-number is an error. Unless otherwise specified, each works on all types of numbers, automatically performing any required coercions when arguments are of different types.

+ &rest *numbers* [*Function*]

This returns the sum of the arguments. If there are no arguments, the result is 0, which is an identity for this operation.

Compatibility note: While + is compatible with its use in Lisp Machine Lisp, it is incompatible with MacLisp, which uses + for fixnum-only addition.

- *number* &rest *more-numbers* [*Function*]

The function -, when given one argument, returns the negative of that argument.

The function -, when given more than one argument, successively subtracts from the first argument all the others, and returns the result. For example, (- 3 4 5) ⇒ -6.

Compatibility note: While - is compatible with its use in Lisp Machine Lisp, it is incompatible with MacLisp, which uses - for fixnum-only subtraction. Also, - differs from difference as used in most Lisp systems in the case of one argument.

---

* &rest *numbers*   [*Function*]

This returns the product of the arguments. If there are no arguments, the result is 1, which is an identity for this operation.

Compatibility note: While * is compatible with its use in Lisp Machine Lisp, it is incompatible with MacLisp, which uses * for fixnum-only multiplication.

/ *number* &rest *more-numbers*   [*Function*]

The function /, when given more than one argument, successively divides the first argument by all the others and returns the result.

It is generally accepted that it is an error for any argument other than the first to be zero.

With one argument, / reciprocates the argument.

It is generally accepted that it is an error in this case for the argument to be zero.

/ will produce a ratio if the mathematical quotient of two integers is not an exact integer. For example:

```
(/ 12 4)  ⇒  3
(/ 13 4)  ⇒  13/4
(/ -8)  ⇒  -1/8
(/ 3 4 5)  ⇒  3/20
```

To divide one integer by another producing an integer result, use one of the functions floor, ceiling, truncate, or round.

If any argument is a floating-point number, then the rules of floating-point contagion apply.

Compatibility note: What / does is totally unlike what the usual // or quotient operator does. In most Lisp systems, quotient behaves like / except when dividing integers, in which case it behaves like truncate of two arguments; this behavior is mathematically intractable, leading to such anomalies as

(quotient 1.0 2.0) ⇒ 0.5 but (quotient 1 2) ⇒ 0

In contrast, the Common Lisp function / produces these results:

(/ 1.0 2.0) ⇒ 0.5 and (/ 1 2) ⇒ 1/2

In practice quotient is used only when one is sure that both arguments are integers, *or* when one is sure that at least one argument is a floating-point number. / is tractable for its purpose and works for *any* numbers.

1+ *number*   [*Function*]
1- *number*   [*Function*]

(1+ *x*) is the same as (+ *x* 1).

   (1- *x*) is the same as (- *x* 1). Note that the short name may be confusing:
(1- *x*) does *not* mean 1 − *x*; rather, it means *x* − 1.

Rationale: These are included primarily for compatibility with MacLisp and Lisp Machine
Lisp. Some programmers prefer always to write (+ x 1) and (- x 1) instead of (1+ x)
and (1- x).

Implementation note: Compiler writers are very strongly encouraged to ensure that (1+ x)
and (+ x 1) compile into identical code, and similarly for (1- x) and (- x 1), to avoid
pressure on a Lisp programmer to write possibly less clear code for the sake of efficiency.
This can easily be done as a source-language transformation.

---

incf *place* [*delta*]   [*Macro*]
decf *place* [*delta*]   [*Macro*]

The number produced by the form *delta* is added to (incf) or subtracted from
(decf) the number in the generalized variable named by *place*, and the sum is
stored back into *place* and returned. The form *place* may be any form acceptable
as a generalized variable to setf. If *delta* is not supplied, then the number in *place*
is changed by 1. For example:

```
(setq n 0)
(incf n) ⇒ 1          and now n ⇒ 1
(decf n 3) ⇒ -2       and now n ⇒ -2
(decf n -5) ⇒ 3       and now n ⇒ 3
(decf n) ⇒ 2          and now n ⇒ 2
```

The effect of (incf *place* *delta*) is roughly equivalent to

(setf *place* (+ *place* *delta*))

except that the latter would evaluate any subforms of *place* twice, whereas incf
takes care to evaluate them only once. Moreover, for certain *place* forms incf
may be significantly more efficient than the setf version.

   X3J13 voted in March 1988 ⟨146⟩ to clarify order of evaluation (see section 7.2).

conjugate *number* [*Function*]

This returns the complex conjugate of *number*. The conjugate of a non-complex number is itself. For a complex number z,

```
(conjugate z) ≡ (complex (realpart z) (- (imagpart z)))
```

For example:

```
(conjugate #C(3/5 4/5)) ⟹ #C(3/5 -4/5)
(conjugate #C(0.0D0 -1.0D0)) ⟹ #C(0.0D0 1.0D0)
(conjugate 3.7) ⟹ 3.7
```

gcd &rest *integers* [*Function*]

This returns the greatest common divisor of all the arguments, which must be integers. The result of gcd is always a non-negative integer. If one argument is given, its absolute value is returned. If no arguments are given, gcd returns 0, which is an identity for this operation. For three or more arguments,

```
(gcd a b c ... z) ≡ (gcd (gcd a b) c ... z)
```

Here are some examples of the use of gcd:

```
(gcd 91 -49) ⟹ 7
(gcd 63 -42 35) ⟹ 7
(gcd 5) ⟹ 5
(gcd -4) ⟹ 4
(gcd) ⟹ 0
```

lcm *integer* &rest *more-integers* [*Function*]

This returns the least common multiple of its arguments, which must be integers. The result of lcm is always a non-negative integer. For two arguments that are not both zero,

```
(lcm a b) ≡ (/ (abs (* a b)) (gcd a b))
```

If one or both arguments are zero,

```
(lcm a 0) ≡ (lcm 0 a) ≡ 0
```

For one argument, lcm returns the absolute value of that argument. For three or more arguments, (lcm *a b c* ... *z*) ≡ (lcm (lcm *a b*) *c* ... *z*)

Some examples:

(lcm 14 35) ⇒ 70
(lcm 0 5) ⇒ 0
(lcm 1 2 3 4 5 6) ⇒ 60

Mathematically, (lcm) should return infinity. Because Common Lisp does not have a representation for infinity, lcm, unlike gcd, always requires at least one argument.

X3J13 voted in January 1989 ⟨107⟩ to specify that (lcm) ⇒ 1.

This is one of my biggest boners. The identity for lcm is of course 1, not infinity, and so (lcm) ought to have been defined to return 1. Sorry about that, though in point of fact very few users have complained to me that this mistake in the first edition has cramped their programming style.

12.5. Irrational and Transcendental Functions

Common Lisp provides no data type that can accurately represent irrational numerical values. The functions in this section are described as if the results were mathematically accurate, but actually they all produce floating-point approximations to the true mathematical result in the general case. In some places mathematical identities are set forth that are intended to elucidate the meanings of the functions; however, two mathematically identical expressions may be computationally different because of errors inherent in the floating-point approximation process.

When the arguments to a function in this section are all rational and the true mathematical result is also (mathematically) rational, then unless otherwise noted an implementation is free to return either an accurate result of type rational or a single-precision floating-point approximation. If the arguments are all rational but the result cannot be expressed as a rational number, then a single-precision floating-point approximation is always returned.

X3J13 voted in March 1989 ⟨29⟩ to clarify that the provisions of the previous paragraph apply to complex numbers. If the arguments to a function are all of type (or rational (complex rational)) and the true mathematical result is (mathematically) a complex number with rational real and imaginary parts, then unless otherwise noted an implementation is free to return either an accurate result of type (or rational (complex rational)) or a single-precision floating-point approximation of type single-float (permissible only if the imaginary part of the true mathematical result is zero) or (complex single-float). If the arguments are all of type (or rational (complex rational)) but the result cannot be expressed as a rational or complex rational number, then the returned value will be of type single-float (permissible only if the imaginary part of the true mathematical result is zero) or (complex single-float).

The rules of floating-point contagion and complex contagion are effectively obeyed by all the functions in this section except expt, which treats some cases of rational exponents specially. When, possibly after contagious conversion, all of the arguments are of the same floating-point or complex floating-point type, then the result will be of that same type unless otherwise noted.

Implementation note: There is a "floating-point cookbook" by Cody and Waite [14] that may be a useful aid in implementing the functions defined in this section.

12.5.1. Exponential and Logarithmic Functions

Along with the usual one-argument and two-argument exponential and logarithm functions, sqrt is considered to be an exponential function, because it raises a number to the power 1/2.

exp *number*   [*Function*]

Returns *e* raised to the power *number*, where *e* is the base of the natural logarithms.

expt *base-number* *power-number*   [*Function*]

Returns *base-number* raised to the power *power-number*. If the *base-number* is of type rational and the *power-number* is an integer, the calculation will be exact and the result will be of type rational; otherwise a floating-point approximation may result.

X3J13 voted in March 1989 ⟨29⟩ to clarify that provisions similar to those of the previous paragraph apply to complex numbers. If the *base-number* is of type (complex rational) and the *power-number* is an integer, the calculation will also be exact and the result will be of type (or rational (complex rational)); otherwise a floating-point or complex floating-point approximation may result.

When *power-number* is 0 (a zero of type integer), then the result is always the value 1 in the type of *base-number*, even if the *base-number* is zero (of any type). That is:

```
(expt x 0) ≡ (coerce 1 (type-of x))
```

If the *power-number* is a zero of any other data type, then the result is also the value 1, in the type of the arguments after the application of the contagion rules, with one exception: it is an error if *base-number* is zero when the *power-number* is a zero not of type integer.

Implementations of expt are permitted to use different algorithms for the cases of a rational *power-number* and a floating-point *power-number*; the motivation is that in many cases greater accuracy can be achieved for the case of a rational *power-number*. For example, (expt pi 16) and (expt pi 16.0) may yield slightly different results if the first case is computed by repeated squaring and the second by the use of logarithms. Similarly, an implementation might choose to compute (expt x 3/2) as if it had been written (sqrt (expt x 3)), perhaps producing a more accurate result than would (expt x 1.5). It is left to the implementor to determine the best strategies.

X3J13 voted in January 1989 ⟨75⟩ to clarify that the preceding remark is in error, because (sqrt (expt x 3)) does not produce the same value as (expt x 3/2) in most cases, and to specify that the specification of the principal value of expt as given in section 12.5.3 should be regarded as definitive.

As an example of the difficulty, let $x = \text{cis} \frac{2\pi}{3} = -\frac{1}{2} + \frac{\sqrt{3}}{2}i$. Then $\sqrt{x^3} = \sqrt{1} = 1$, but $x^{3/2} = e^{(3/2)\log x} = e^{(3/2)(2\pi/3)i} = e^{\pi i} = -1$. Another example is $x = -1$; then $\sqrt{x^3} = \sqrt{-1} = i$, but $x^{3/2} = e^{(3/2)\log x} = e^{(3/2)\pi i} = -i$.

The result of expt can be a complex number, even when neither argument is complex, if *base-number* is negative and *power-number* is not an integer. The result is always the principal complex value. Note that (expt -8 1/3) is not permitted to return -2; while -2 is indeed one of the cube roots of -8, it is not the principal cube root, which is a complex number approximately equal to #C(1.0 1.73205).

Notice of correction. The first edition gave the incorrect value #C(0.5 1.73205) for the principal cube root of -8. The correct value is #C(1.0 1.73205), that is, $1 + \sqrt{3}i$. I simply don't know what I was thinking of!

---

log *number* &optional *base*   [*Function*]

Returns the logarithm of *number* in the base *base*, which defaults to *e*, the base of the natural logarithms. For example:

```
(log 8.0 2)   ⇒ 3.0
(log 100.0 10) ⇒ 2.0
```

The result of (log 8 2) may be either 3 or 3.0, depending on the implementation.

Note that log may return a complex result when given a non-complex argument if the argument is negative. For example:

```
(log -1.0) ≡ (complex 0.0 (float pi 0.0))
```

X3J13 voted in January 1989 ⟨101⟩ to specify certain floating-point behavior when minus zero is supported. As a part of that vote it approved a mathematical definition of complex logarithm in terms of real logarithm, absolute value, arc tangent of two real arguments, and the phase function as

Logarithm $\qquad\qquad \log|z| + i\, \text{phase}\, z$

This specifies the branch cuts precisely whether minus zero is supported or not; see phase and atan.

---

sqrt *number* $\qquad\qquad\qquad\qquad\qquad\qquad\qquad$ [*Function*]

Returns the principal square root of *number*. If the *number* is not complex but is negative, then the result will be a complex number. For example:

```
(sqrt 9.0) ⇒ 3.0
(sqrt -9.0) ⇒ #c(0.0 3.0)
```

The result of (sqrt 9) may be either 3 or 3.0, depending on the implementation. The result of (sqrt -9) may be either #c(0 3) or #c(0.0 3.0).

X3J13 voted in January 1989 ⟨101⟩ to specify certain floating-point behavior when minus zero is supported. As a part of that vote it approved a mathematical definition of complex square root in terms of complex logarithm and exponential functions as

Square root $\qquad\qquad e^{(\log z)/2}$

This specifies the branch cuts precisely whether minus zero is supported or not; see phase and atan.

---

isqrt *integer* $\qquad\qquad\qquad\qquad\qquad\qquad\qquad$ [*Function*]

Integer square root: the argument must be a non-negative integer, and the result is the greatest integer less than or equal to the exact positive square root of the argument. For example:

```
(isqrt 9) ⇒ 3
(isqrt 12) ⇒ 3
(isqrt 300) ⇒ 17
(isqrt 325) ⇒ 18
```

12.5.2. Trigonometric and Related Functions

Some of the functions in this section, such as abs and signum, are apparently unrelated to trigonometric functions when considered as functions of real numbers only. The way in which they are extended to operate on complex numbers makes the trigonometric connection clear.

abs *number*   [*Function*]

Returns the absolute value of the argument. For a non-complex number x,

```
(abs x) ≡ (if (minusp x) (- x) x)
```

and the result is always of the same type as the argument.

For a complex number z, the absolute value may be computed as

```
(sqrt (+ (expt (realpart z) 2) (expt (imagpart z) 2)))
```

Implementation note: The careful implementor will not use this formula directly for all complex numbers but will instead handle very large or very small components specially to avoid intermediate overflow or underflow.

For example:

```
(abs #c(3.0 -4.0)) ⇒ 5.0
```

The result of (abs #c(3 4)) may be either 5 or 5.0, depending on the implementation.

phase *number*   [*Function*]

The phase of a number is the angle part of its polar representation as a complex number. That is,

```
(phase z) ≡ (atan (imagpart z) (realpart z))
```

The result is in radians, in the range $-\pi$ (exclusive) to π (inclusive). The phase of a positive non-complex number is zero; that of a negative non-complex number is π. The phase of zero is arbitrarily defined to be zero.

X3J13 voted in January 1989 ⟨101⟩ to specify certain floating-point behavior when minus zero is supported; phase is still defined in terms of atan as above, but thanks to a change in atan the range of phase becomes $-\pi$ *inclusive* to π inclusive. The value $-\pi$ results from an argument whose real part is negative and whose imaginary part is minus zero. The phase function therefore has a branch cut along the negative real axis. The phase of $+0 + 0i$ is $+0$, of $+0 - 0i$ is -0, of $-0 + 0i$ is $+\pi$, and of $-0 - 0i$ is $-\pi$.

If the argument is a complex floating-point number, the result is a floating-point number of the same type as the components of the argument. If the argument is a floating-point number, the result is a floating-point number of the same type. If the argument is a rational number or complex rational number, the result is a single-format floating-point number.

---

signum *number*   [*Function*]

By definition,

```
(signum x) ≡ (if (zerop x) x (/ x (abs x)))
```

For a rational number, signum will return one of -1, 0, or 1 according to whether the number is negative, zero, or positive. For a floating-point number, the result will be a floating-point number of the same format whose value is -1, 0, or 1. For a complex number z, (signum z) is a complex number of the same phase but with unit magnitude, unless z is a complex zero, in which case the result is z. For example:

```
(signum 0) ⇒ 0
(signum -3.7L5) ⇒ -1.0L0
(signum 4/5) ⇒ 1
(signum #C(7.5 10.0)) ⇒ #C(0.6 0.8)
(signum #C(0.0 -14.7)) ⇒ #C(0.0 -1.0)
```

For non-complex rational numbers, signum is a rational function, but it may be irrational for complex arguments.

---

sin *radians*   [*Function*]
cos *radians*   [*Function*]
tan *radians*   [*Function*]

sin returns the sine of the argument, cos the cosine, and tan the tangent. The argument is in radians. The argument may be complex.

---

cis *radians*   [*Function*]

This computes $e^{i \cdot radians}$. The name cis means "cos $+ i$ sin," because $e^{i\theta} = \cos \theta + i \sin \theta$. The argument is in radians and may be any non-complex number. The result is a complex number whose real part is the cosine of the argument and whose imaginary part is the sine. Put another way, the result is a complex number whose phase is the equal to the argument (mod 2π) and whose magnitude is unity.

Implementation note: Often it is cheaper to calculate the sine and cosine of a single angle together than to perform two disjoint calculations.

---

asin *number*   [*Function*]
acos *number*   [*Function*]

asin returns the arc sine of the argument, and acos the arc cosine. The result is in radians. The argument may be complex.

The arc sine and arc cosine functions may be defined mathematically for an argument z as follows:

Arc sine $-i\log\left(iz + \sqrt{1 - z^2}\right)$

Arc cosine $-i\log\left(z + i\sqrt{1 - z^2}\right)$

Note that the result of asin or acos may be complex even if the argument is not complex; this occurs when the absolute value of the argument is greater than 1.

Kahan [25] suggests for acos the defining formula

Arc cosine $$\frac{2\log\left(\sqrt{\frac{1+z}{2}} + i\sqrt{\frac{1-z}{2}}\right)}{i}$$

or even the much simpler $(\pi/2) - \arcsin z$. Both equations are mathematically equivalent to the formula shown above.

Implementation note: These formulae are mathematically correct, assuming completely accurate computation. They may be terrible methods for floating-point computation. Implementors should consult a good text on numerical analysis. The formulae given above are not necessarily the simplest ones for real-valued computations, either; they are chosen to define the branch cuts in desirable ways for the complex case.

---

atan *y* &optional *x*   [*Function*]

An arc tangent is calculated and the result is returned in radians.

With two arguments y and x, neither argument may be complex. The result is the arc tangent of the quantity y/x. The signs of y and x are used to derive quadrant information; moreover, x may be zero provided y is not zero. The value of atan is always between $-\pi$ (exclusive) and π (inclusive). The following table details various special cases.

Condition		Cartesian Locus	Range of Result
$y = 0$	$x > 0$	Positive x-axis	0
$y > 0$	$x > 0$	Quadrant I	$0 < \text{result} < \pi/2$
$y > 0$	$x = 0$	Positive y-axis	$\pi/2$
$y > 0$	$x < 0$	Quadrant II	$\pi/2 < \text{result} < \pi$
$y = 0$	$x < 0$	Negative x-axis	π
$y < 0$	$x < 0$	Quadrant III	$-\pi < \text{result} < -\pi/2$
$y < 0$	$x = 0$	Negative y-axis	$-\pi/2$
$y < 0$	$x > 0$	Quadrant IV	$-\pi/2 < \text{result} < 0$
$y = 0$	$x = 0$	Origin	error

X3J13 voted in January 1989 ⟨101⟩ to specify certain floating-point behavior when minus zero is supported. When there is a minus zero, the preceding table must be modified slightly:

Condition		Cartesian Locus	Range of Result
$y = +0$	$x > 0$	Just above positive x-axis	$+0$
$y > 0$	$x > 0$	Quadrant I	$+0 < \text{result} < \pi/2$
$y > 0$	$x = \pm 0$	Positive y-axis	$\pi/2$
$y > 0$	$x < 0$	Quadrant II	$\pi/2 < \text{result} < \pi$
$y = +0$	$x < 0$	Just below negative x-axis	π
$y = -0$	$x < 0$	Just above negative x-axis	π
$y < 0$	$x < 0$	Quadrant III	$-\pi < \text{result} < -\pi/2$
$y < 0$	$x = \pm 0$	Negative y-axis	$-\pi/2$
$y < 0$	$x > 0$	Quadrant IV	$-\pi/2 < \text{result} < -0$
$y = -0$	$x > 0$	Just below positive x-axis	-0
$y = +0$	$x = +0$	Near origin	$+0$
$y = -0$	$x = +0$	Near origin	-0
$y = +0$	$x = -0$	Near origin	π
$y = -0$	$x = -0$	Near origin	$-\pi$

Note that the case $y = 0, x = 0$ is an error in the absence of minus zero, but the four cases $y = \pm 0, x = \pm 0$ are defined in the presence of minus zero.

With only one argument y, the argument may be complex. The result is the arc tangent of y, which may be defined by the following formula:

Arc tangent
$$-i \log \left((1 + iy) \sqrt{1/(1 + y^2)} \right)$$

Implementation note: This formula is mathematically correct, assuming completely accurate computation. It may be a terrible method for floating-point computation. Implementors should consult a good text on numerical analysis. The formula given above is not necessarily the simplest one for real-valued computations, either; it is chosen to define the branch cuts in desirable ways for the complex case.

X3J13 voted in January 1989 ⟨28⟩ to replace the preceding formula with the formula

Arc tangent
$$\frac{\log(1 + iy) - \log(1 - iy)}{2i}$$

This change alters the direction of continuity for the branch cuts, which alters the result returned by atan only for arguments on the imaginary axis that are of magnitude greater than 1. See section 12.5.3 for further details.

For a non-complex argument y, the result is non-complex and lies between $-\pi/2$ and $\pi/2$ (both exclusive).

Compatibility note: MacLisp has a function called atan whose range is from 0 to 2π. Almost every other programming language (ANSI Fortran, IBM PL/1, Interlisp) has a two-argument arc tangent function with range $-\pi$ to π. Lisp Machine Lisp provides two two-argument arc tangent functions, atan (compatible with MacLisp) and atan2 (compatible with all others).

Common Lisp makes two-argument atan the standard one with range $-\pi$ to π. Observe that this makes the one-argument and two-argument versions of atan compatible in the sense that the branch cuts do not fall in different places. The Interlisp one-argument function arctan has a range from 0 to π, while nearly every other programming language provides the range $-\pi/2$ to $\pi/2$ for one-argument arc tangent! Nevertheless, since Interlisp uses the standard two-argument version of arc tangent, its branch cuts are inconsistent anyway.

pi   [*Constant*]

This global variable has as its value the best possible approximation to π in *long* floating-point format. For example:

```
(defun sind (x)      ;The argument is in degrees
  (sin (* x (/ (float pi x) 180))))
```

An approximation to π in some other precision can be obtained by writing (float pi x), where x is a floating-point number of the desired precision, or by writing (coerce pi *type*), where *type* is the name of the desired type, such as short-float.

sinh *number*	[*Function*]
cosh *number*	[*Function*]
tanh *number*	[*Function*]
asinh *number*	[*Function*]
acosh *number*	[*Function*]
atanh *number*	[*Function*]

These functions compute the hyperbolic sine, cosine, tangent, arc sine, arc cosine, and arc tangent functions, which are mathematically defined for an argument z as follows:

Hyperbolic sine	$(e^z - e^{-z})/2$
Hyperbolic cosine	$(e^z + e^{-z})/2$
Hyperbolic tangent	$(e^z - e^{-z})/(e^z + e^{-z})$
Hyperbolic arc sine	$\log\left(z + \sqrt{1 + z^2}\right)$
Hyperbolic arc cosine	$\log\left(z + (z + 1)\sqrt{(z - 1)/(z + 1)}\right)$
Hyperbolic arc tangent	$\log\left((1 + z)\sqrt{1 - 1/z^2}\right)$ **WRONG!**

WARNING! *The formula shown above for hyperbolic arc tangent is incorrect.* It is not a matter of incorrect branch cuts; it simply does not compute anything like a hyperbolic arc tangent. This unfortunate error in the first edition was the result of mistranscribing a (correct) APL formula from Penfield's paper [36]. The formula should have been transcribed as

Hyperbolic arc tangent $\log\left((1 + z)\sqrt{1/(1 - z^2)}\right)$

A proposal was submitted to X3J13 in September 1989 to replace the formulae for acosh and atanh. See section 12.5.3 for further discussion.

Note that the result of acosh may be complex even if the argument is not complex; this occurs when the argument is less than 1. Also, the result of atanh may be complex even if the argument is not complex; this occurs when the absolute value of the argument is greater than 1.

Implementation note: These formulae are mathematically correct, assuming completely accurate computation. They may be terrible methods for floating-point computation. Implementors should consult a good text on numerical analysis. The formulae given above are not necessarily the simplest ones for real-valued computations, either; they are chosen to define the branch cuts in desirable ways for the complex case.

12.5.3. Branch Cuts, Principal Values, and Boundary Conditions in the Complex Plane

Many of the irrational and transcendental functions are multiply defined in the complex domain; for example, there are in general an infinite number of complex values for the logarithm function. In each such case, a principal value must be chosen for the function to return. In general, such values cannot be chosen so as to make the range continuous; lines in the domain called *branch cuts* must be defined, which in turn define the discontinuities in the range.

Common Lisp defines the branch cuts, principal values, and boundary conditions for the complex functions following a proposal for complex functions in APL [36]. The contents of this section are borrowed largely from that proposal.

Compatibility note: The branch cuts defined here differ in a few very minor respects from those advanced by W. Kahan, who considers not only the "usual" definitions but also the special modifications necessary for IEEE proposed floating-point arithmetic, which has infinities and minus zero as explicit computational objects. For example, he proposes that $\sqrt{-4 + 0i} = 2i$, but $\sqrt{-4 - 0i} = -2i$.

It may be that the differences between the APL proposal and Kahan's proposal will be ironed out. If so, Common Lisp may be changed as necessary to be compatible with these other groups. Any changes from the specification below are likely to be quite minor, probably concerning primarily questions of which side of a branch cut is continuous with the cut itself.

Indeed, X3J13 voted in January 1989 ⟨28⟩ to alter the direction of continuity for the branch cuts of `atan`, and also ⟨101⟩ to address the treatment of branch cuts in implementations that have a distinct floating-point minus zero.

The treatment of minus zero centers in two-argument `atan`. If there is no minus zero, then the branch cut runs just below the negative real axis as before, and the range of two-argument `atan` is $(-\pi, \pi]$. If there is a minus zero, however, then the branch cut runs precisely on the negative real axis, skittering between pairs of numbers of the form $-x \pm 0i$, and the range of two-argument `atan` is $[-\pi, \pi]$.

The treatment of minus zero by all other irrational and transcendental functions is then specified by defining those functions in terms of two-argument `atan`. First, `phase` is defined in terms of two-argument `atan`, and complex `abs` in terms of real `sqrt`; then complex `log` is defined in terms of `phase`, `abs`, and real `log`; then complex `sqrt` in terms of complex `log`; and finally all others are defined in terms of these.

Kahan [25] treats these matters in some detail and also suggests specific algorithms for implementing irrational and transcendental functions in IEEE standard floating-point arithmetic [23].

Remarks in the first edition about the direction of the continuity of branch cuts continue to hold in the absence of minus zero and may be ignored if minus zero is supported; since all branch cuts happen to run along the principal axes, they run *between* plus zero and minus zero, and so each sort of zero is associated with the obvious quadrant.

sqrt

The branch cut for square root lies along the negative real axis, continuous with quadrant II. The range consists of the right half-plane, including the non-negative imaginary axis and excluding the negative imaginary axis.

X3J13 voted in January 1989 ⟨101⟩ to specify certain floating-point behavior when minus zero is supported. As a part of that vote it approved a mathematical definition of complex square root:

$$\sqrt{z} = e^{(\log z)/2}$$

This defines the branch cuts precisely, whether minus zero is supported or not.

phase

The branch cut for the phase function lies along the negative real axis, continuous with quadrant II. The range consists of that portion of the real axis between $-\pi$ (exclusive) and π (inclusive).

X3J13 voted in January 1989 ⟨101⟩ to specify certain floating-point behavior when minus zero is supported. As a part of that vote it approved a mathematical definition of phase:

$$\text{phase } z = \arctan(\Im z, \Re z)$$

where $\Im z$ is the imaginary part of z and $\Re z$ the real part of z. This defines the branch cuts precisely, whether minus zero is supported or not.

log

The branch cut for the logarithm function of one argument (natural logarithm) lies along the negative real axis, continuous with quadrant II. The domain excludes the origin. For a complex number z, $\log z$ is defined to be

$$\log z = \left(\log |z|\right) + i(\text{phase } z)$$

Therefore the range of the one-argument logarithm function is that strip of the complex plane containing numbers with imaginary parts between $-\pi$ (exclusive) and π (inclusive).

The X3J13 vote on minus zero ⟨101⟩ would alter that exclusive bound of $-\pi$ to be inclusive if minus zero is supported.

The two-argument logarithm function is defined as $\log_b z = (\log z)/(\log b)$. This defines the principal values precisely. The range of the two-argument logarithm function is the entire complex plane. It is an error if z is zero. If z is non-zero and b is zero, the logarithm is taken to be zero.

exp

The simple exponential function has no branch cut.

expt

The two-argument exponential function is defined as $b^x = e^{x \log b}$. This defines the principal values precisely. The range of the two-argument exponential function is the entire complex plane. Regarded as a function of x, with b fixed, there is no branch cut. Regarded as a function of b, with x fixed, there is in general a branch cut along the negative real axis, continuous with quadrant II. The domain excludes the origin. By definition, $0^0 = 1$. If $b = 0$ and the real part of x is strictly positive, then $b^x = 0$. For all other values of x, 0^x is an error.

asin

The following definition for arc sine determines the range and branch cuts:

$$\arcsin z = -i \log \left(iz + \sqrt{1 - z^2} \right)$$

This is equivalent to the formula

$$\arcsin z = \frac{\operatorname{arcsinh} iz}{i}$$

recommended by Kahan [25].

The branch cut for the arc sine function is in two pieces: one along the negative real axis to the left of -1 (inclusive), continuous with quadrant II, and one along the positive real axis to the right of 1 (inclusive), continuous with quadrant IV. The range is that strip of the complex plane containing numbers whose real part is between $-\pi/2$ and $\pi/2$. A number with real part equal to $-\pi/2$ is in the range if and only if its imaginary part is non-negative; a number with real part equal to $\pi/2$ is in the range if and only if its imaginary part is non-positive.

acos

The following definition for arc cosine determines the range and branch cuts:

$$\arccos z = -i \log \left(z + i\sqrt{1 - z^2} \right)$$

or, which is equivalent,

$$\arccos z = \tfrac{\pi}{2} - \arcsin z$$

The branch cut for the arc cosine function is in two pieces: one along the negative real axis to the left of -1 (inclusive), continuous with quadrant II, and one along the positive real axis to the right of 1 (inclusive), continuous with quadrant IV. This is the same branch cut as for arc sine. The range is that strip of the complex plane containing numbers whose real part is between zero and π. A number with real part equal to zero is in the range if and only if its imaginary part is non-negative; a number with real part equal to π is in the range if and only if its imaginary part is non-positive.

atan

The following definition for (one-argument) arc tangent determines the range and branch cuts:

$$\arctan z = -i \log \left((1 + iz)\sqrt{1/(1 + z^2)} \right)$$

Beware of simplifying this formula; "obvious" simplifications are likely to alter the branch cuts or the values on the branch cuts incorrectly.

The branch cut for the arc tangent function is in two pieces: one along the positive imaginary axis above i (exclusive), continuous with quadrant II, and one along the negative imaginary axis below $-i$ (exclusive), continuous with quadrant IV. The points i and $-i$ are excluded from the domain. The range is that strip of the complex plane containing numbers whose real part is between $-\pi/2$ and $\pi/2$. A number with real part equal to $-\pi/2$ is in the range if and only if its imaginary part is strictly positive; a number with real part equal to $\pi/2$ is in the range if and only if its imaginary part is strictly negative. Thus the range of the arc tangent function is identical to that of the arc sine function with the points $-\pi/2$ and $\pi/2$ excluded.

X3J13 voted in January 1989 ⟨28⟩ to replace the formula shown above with the formula

$$\arctan z = \frac{\log(1 + iz) - \log(1 - iz)}{2i}$$

This is equivalent to the formula

$$\arctan z = \frac{\operatorname{arctanh} iz}{i}$$

recommended by Kahan [25]. It causes the upper branch cut to be continuous with quadrant I rather than quadrant II, and the lower branch cut to be continuous with quadrant III rather than quadrant IV; otherwise it agrees with the formula of the first edition. Therefore this change alters the result returned by atan only for arguments on the positive imaginary axis that are of magnitude greater than 1. The full description for this new formula is as follows.

The branch cut for the arc tangent function is in two pieces: one along the positive imaginary axis above i (exclusive), continuous with quadrant I, and one along the negative imaginary axis below $-i$ (exclusive), continuous with quadrant III. The points i and $-i$ are excluded from the domain. The range is that strip of the complex plane containing numbers whose real part is between $-\pi/2$ and $\pi/2$. A number with real part equal to $-\pi/2$ is in the range if and only if its imaginary part is strictly negative; a number with real part equal to $\pi/2$ is in the range if and only if its imaginary part is strictly positive. Thus the range of the arc tangent function is *not* identical to that of the arc sine function.

asinh

The following definition for the inverse hyperbolic sine determines the range and branch cuts:

$$\operatorname{arcsinh} z = \log\left(z + \sqrt{1 + z^2}\right)$$

The branch cut for the inverse hyperbolic sine function is in two pieces: one along the positive imaginary axis above i (inclusive), continuous with quadrant I, and one along the negative imaginary axis below $-i$ (inclusive), continuous with quadrant III. The range is that strip of the complex plane containing numbers whose imaginary part is between $-\pi/2$ and $\pi/2$. A number with imaginary part equal to $-\pi/2$ is in the range if and only if its real part is non-positive; a number with imaginary part equal to $\pi/2$ is in the range if and only if its real part is non-negative.

acosh

The following definition for the inverse hyperbolic cosine determines the range and branch cuts:

$$\operatorname{arccosh} z = \log\left(z + (z + 1)\sqrt{(z - 1)/(z + 1)}\right)$$

Kahan [25] suggests the formula

$$\text{arccosh } z = 2 \log \left(\sqrt{(z + 1)/2} + \sqrt{(z - 1)/2} \right)$$

pointing out that it yields the same principal value but eliminates a gratuitous removable singularity at $z = -1$. A proposal was submitted to X3J13 in September 1989 to replace the formula acosh with that recommended by Kahan. There is a good possibility that it will be adopted.

The branch cut for the inverse hyperbolic cosine function lies along the real axis to the left of 1 (inclusive), extending indefinitely along the negative real axis, continuous with quadrant II and (between 0 and 1) with quadrant I. The range is that half-strip of the complex plane containing numbers whose real part is non-negative and whose imaginary part is between $-\pi$ (exclusive) and π (inclusive). A number with real part zero is in the range if its imaginary part is between zero (inclusive) and π (inclusive).

atanh

The following definition for the inverse hyperbolic tangent determines the range and branch cuts:

$$\text{arctanh } z = \log \left((1 + z)\sqrt{1 - 1/z^2} \right) \qquad \textbf{WRONG!}$$

WARNING! *The formula shown above for hyperbolic arc tangent is incorrect.* It is not a matter of incorrect branch cuts; it simply does not compute anything like a hyperbolic arc tangent. This unfortunate error in the first edition was the result of mistranscribing a (correct) APL formula from Penfield's paper [36]. The formula should have been transcribed as

$$\text{arctanh } z = \log \left((1 + z)\sqrt{1/(1 - z^2)} \right)$$

Beware of simplifying this formula; "obvious" simplifications are likely to alter the branch cuts or the values on the branch cuts incorrectly.

The branch cut for the inverse hyperbolic tangent function is in two pieces: one along the negative real axis to the left of -1 (inclusive), continuous with quadrant III, and one along the positive real axis to the right of 1 (inclusive), continuous with quadrant I. The points -1 and 1 are excluded from the domain. The range is that strip of the complex plane containing numbers whose imaginary part is between $-\pi/2$ and $\pi/2$. A number with imaginary part equal to $-\pi/2$ is in the range if and only if its real part is strictly negative; a number with imaginary part equal to $\pi/2$ is in the range if and only if its real part is strictly positive. Thus the range of the inverse hyperbolic tangent function is identical to that of the inverse hyperbolic sine function with the points $-\pi i/2$ and $\pi i/2$ excluded.

A proposal was submitted to X3J13 in September 1989 to replace the formula atanh with that recommended by Kahan [25]:

$$\text{arctanh } z = \frac{\left(\log(1+z) - \log(1-z)\right)}{2}$$

There is a good possibility that it will be adopted. If it is, the complete description of the branch cuts of atanh will then be as follows.

The branch cut for the inverse hyperbolic tangent function is in two pieces: one along the negative real axis to the left of -1 (inclusive), continuous with quadrant II, and one along the positive real axis to the right of 1 (inclusive), continuous with quadrant IV. The points -1 and 1 are excluded from the domain. The range is that strip of the complex plane containing numbers whose imaginary part is between $-\pi/2$ and $\pi/2$. A number with imaginary part equal to $-\pi/2$ is in the range if and only if its real part is strictly positive; a number with imaginary part equal to $\pi/2$ is in the range if and only if its real part is strictly negative. Thus the range of the inverse hyperbolic tangent function is *not* the same as that of the inverse hyperbolic sine function.

With these definitions, the following useful identities are obeyed throughout the applicable portion of the complex domain, even on the branch cuts:

$\sin iz = i \sinh z$	$\sinh iz = i \sin z$	$\arctan iz = i \operatorname{arctanh} z$
$\cos iz = \cosh z$	$\cosh iz = \cos z$	$\operatorname{arcsinh} iz = i \arcsin z$
$\tan iz = i \tanh z$	$\arcsin iz = i \operatorname{arcsinh} z$	$\operatorname{arctanh} iz = i \arctan z$

I thought it would be useful to provide some graphs illustrating the behavior of the irrational and transcendental functions in the complex plane. It also provides an opportunity to show off the Common Lisp code that was used to generate them.

Imagine the complex plane to be decorated as follows. The real and imaginary axes are painted with thick lines. Parallels from the axes on both sides at distances of 1, 2, and 3 are painted with thin lines; these parallels are doubly infinite lines, as are the axes. Four annuli (rings) are painted in gradated shades of gray. Ring 1, the inner ring, consists of points whose radial distances from the origin lie in the range $[1/4, 1/2]$; ring 2 is in the radial range $[3/4, 1]$; ring 3, in the range $[\pi/2, 2]$; and ring 4, in the range $[3, \pi]$. Ring j is divided into 2^{j+1} equal sectors, with each sector painted a different shade of gray, darkening as one proceeds counterclockwise from the positive real axis.

We can illustrate the behavior of a numerical function f by considering how it maps the complex plane to itself. More specifically, consider each point z of the decorated plane. We decorate a new plane by coloring the point $f(z)$ with the same color that point z had in the original decorated plane. In other words, the newly decorated plane illustrates how the f maps the axes, other horizontal and vertical lines, and annuli.

In each figure we will show only a fragment of the complex plane, with the real axis horizontal in the usual manner ($-\infty$ to the left, $+\infty$ to the right) and the imaginary axis vertical ($-\infty i$ below, $+\infty i$ above). Each fragment shows a region containing points whose real and imaginary parts are in the range $[-4.1, 4.1]$. The axes of the new plane are shown as very thin lines, with large tick marks at integer coordinates and somewhat smaller tick marks at multiples of $\pi/2$.

Figure 12-1 shows the result of plotting the identity function (quite literally); the graph exhibits the decoration of the original plane.

Figures 12-2 through 12-20 show the graphs for the functions sqrt, exp, log, sin, asin, cos, acos, tan, atan, sinh, asinh, cosh, acosh, tanh, and atanh, and as a bonus, the graphs for the functions $\sqrt{1-z^2}$, $\sqrt{1+z^2}$, $(z-1)/(z+1)$, and $(1+z)/(1-z)$. All of these are related to the trigonometric functions in various ways. For example, if $f(z) = (z-1)/(z+1)$, then $\tanh z = f(e^{2z})$, and if $g(z) = \sqrt{1-z^2}$, then $\cos z = g(\sin z)$. It is instructive to examine the graph for $\sqrt{1-z^2}$ and try to visualize how it transforms the graph for sin into the graph for cos.

Each figure is accompanied by a commentary on what maps to what and other interesting features. None of this material is terribly new; much of it may be found in any good textbook on complex analysis. I believe that the particular form in which the graphs are presented is novel, as well as the fact that the graphs have been generated as PostScript [1] code by Common Lisp code. This PostScript code was then fed directly to the typesetting equipment that set the pages for this book. Samples of this PostScript code follow the figures themselves, after which the code for the entire program is presented.

In the commentaries that accompany the figures I sometimes speak of mapping the points $\pm\infty$ or $\pm\infty i$. When I say that function f maps $+\infty$ to a certain point z, I mean that

$$z = \lim_{x \to +\infty} f(x + 0i)$$

Similarly, when I say that f maps $-\infty i$ to z, I mean that

$$z = \lim_{y \to -\infty} f(0 + yi)$$

In other words, I am considering a limit as one travels out along one of the main axes. I also speak in a similar manner of mapping to one of these infinities.

Figure 12-1: Initial Decoration of the Complex Plane (Identity Function)

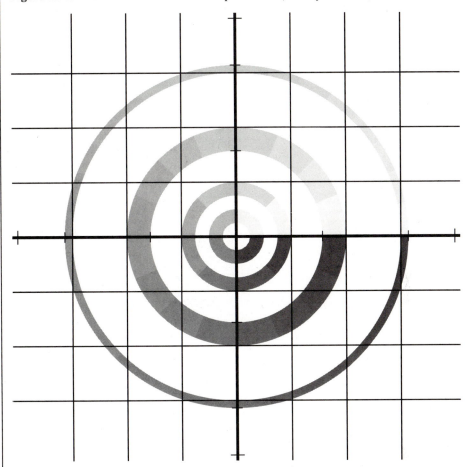

This figure was produced in exactly the same manner as succeeding figures, simply by plotting the function identity instead of a numerical function. Thus the first of these figures was produced by the last function of the first edition. I knew it would come in handy someday!

Figure 12-2: Illustration of the Range of the Square Root Function

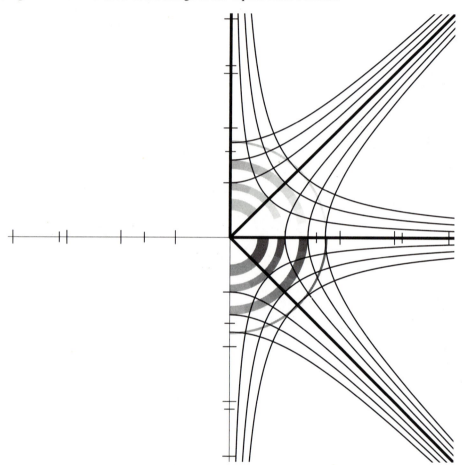

The sqrt function maps the complex plane into the right half of the plane by slitting it along the negative real axis and then sweeping it around as if half-closing a folding fan. The fan also shrinks, as if it were made of cotton and had gotten wetter at the periphery than at the center. The positive real axis is mapped onto itself. The negative real axis is mapped onto the positive imaginary axis (but if minus zero is supported, then $-x + 0i$ is mapped onto the positive imaginary axis and $-x - 0i$ onto the negative imaginary axis, assuming $x > 0$). The positive imaginary axis is mapped onto the northeast diagonal, and the negative imaginary axis onto the southeast diagonal. More generally, lines are mapped to rectangular hyperbolas (or fragments thereof) centered on the origin; lines through the origin are mapped to degenerate hyperbolas (perpendicular lines through the origin).

Figure 12-3: Illustration of the Range of the Exponential Function

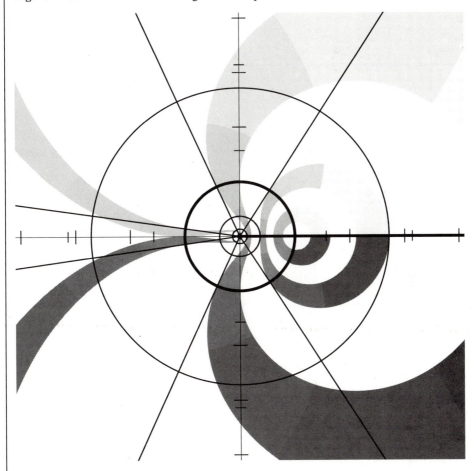

The exp function maps horizontal lines to radii and maps vertical lines to circles centered at the origin. The origin is mapped to 1. (It is instructive to compare this graph with those of other functions that map the origin to 1, for example $(1+z)/(1-z)$, $\cos z$, and $\sqrt{1-z^2}$.) The entire real axis is mapped to the positive real axis, with $-\infty$ mapping to the origin and $+\infty$ to itself. The imaginary axis is mapped to the unit circle with infinite multiplicity (period 2π); therefore the mapping of the imaginary infinities $\pm\infty i$ is indeterminate. It follows that the entire left half-plane is mapped to the interior of the unit circle, and the right half-plane is mapped to the exterior of the unit circle. A line at any angle other than horizontal or vertical is mapped to a logarithmic spiral (but this is not illustrated here).

Figure 12-4: Illustration of the Range of the Natural Logarithm Function

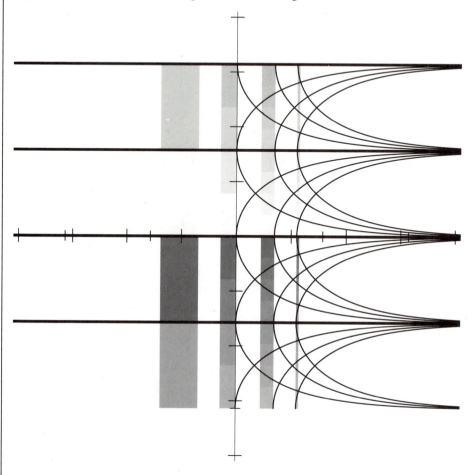

The log function, which is the inverse of exp, naturally maps radial lines to horizontal lines and circles centered at the origin to vertical lines. The interior of the unit circle is thus mapped to the entire left half-plane, and the exterior of the unit circle is mapped to the right half-plane. The positive real axis is mapped to the entire real axis, and the negative real axis to a horizontal line of height π. The positive and negative imaginary axes are mapped to horizontal lines of height $\pm\pi/2$. The origin is mapped to $-\infty$.

Figure 12-5: Illustration of the Range of the Function $(z-1)/(z+1)$

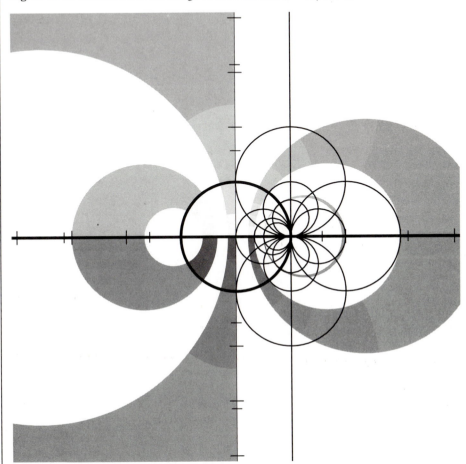

A line is a degenerate circle with infinite radius; when I say "circles" here I also mean lines. Then $(z-1)/(z+1)$ maps circles into circles. All circles through -1 become lines; all lines become circles through 1. The real axis is mapped onto itself: 1 to the origin, the origin to -1, -1 to infinity, and infinity to 1. The imaginary axis becomes the unit circle; i is mapped to itself, as is $-i$. Thus the entire right half-plane is mapped to the interior of the unit circle, the unit circle interior to the left half-plane, the left half-plane to the unit circle exterior, and the unit circle exterior to the right half-plane. Imagine the complex plane to be a vast sea. The Colossus of Rhodes straddles the origin, its left foot on i and its right foot on $-i$. It bends down and briefly paddles water between its legs so furiously that the water directly beneath is pushed out into the entire area behind it; much that was behind swirls forward to either side; and all that was before is sucked in to lie between its feet.

Figure 12-6: Illustration of the Range of the Function $(1 + z)/(1 - z)$

The function $h(z) = (1 + z)/(1 - z)$ is the inverse of $f(z) = (z - 1)/(z + 1)$; that is, $h(f(z)) = f(h(z)) = z$. At first glance, the graph of h appears to be that of f flipped left-to-right, or perhaps reflected in the origin, but careful consideration of the shaded annuli reveals that this is not so; something more subtle is going on. Note that $f(f(z)) = h(h(z)) = g(z) = -1/z$. The functions f, g, h, and the identity function thus form a group under composition, isomorphic to the group of the cyclic permutations of the points -1, 0, 1, and ∞, as indeed these functions accomplish the four possible cyclic permutations on those points. This function group is a subset of the group of bilinear transformations $(az + b)/(cz + d)$, all of which are conformal (angle-preserving) and map circles onto circles. Now, doesn't that tangle of circles through -1 look like something the cat got into?

Figure 12-7: Illustration of the Range of the Sine Function

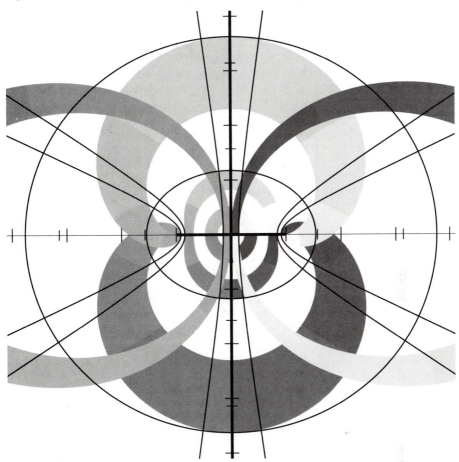

We are used to seeing s i n looking like a wiggly ocean wave, graphed vertically as a function of the real axis only. Here is a different view. The entire real axis is mapped to the segment $[-1, 1]$ of the real axis with infinite multiplicity (period 2π). The imaginary axis is mapped to itself as if by s i nh considered as a real function. The origin is mapped to itself. Horizontal lines are mapped to ellipses with foci at ± 1 (note that two horizontal lines equidistant from the real axis will map onto the same ellipse). Vertical lines are mapped to hyperbolas with the same foci. There is a curious accident: the ellipse for horizontal lines at distance ± 1 from the real axis appears to intercept the real axis at $\pm \pi/2 \approx \pm 1.57 \dots$ but this is not so; the intercepts are actually at $\pm(e + 1/e)/2 \approx \pm 1.54 \dots$.

Figure 12-8: Illustration of the Range of the Arc Sine Function

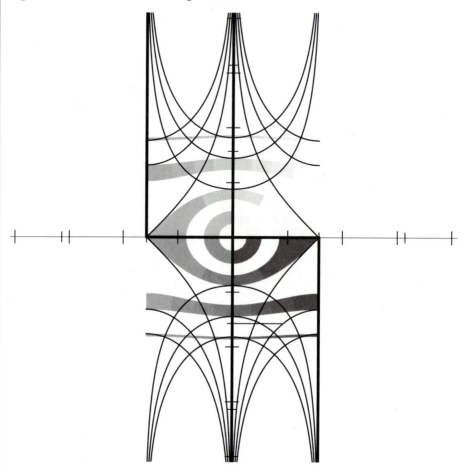

Just as sin grabs horizontal lines and bends them into elliptical loops around the origin, so its inverse asin takes annuli and yanks them more or less horizontally straight. Because sine is not injective, its inverse as a function cannot be surjective. This is just a highfalutin way of saying that the range of the asin function doesn't cover the entire plane but only a strip π wide; arc sine as a one-to-many relation would cover the plane with an infinite number of copies of this strip side by side, looking for all the world like the tail of a peacock with an infinite number of feathers. The imaginary axis is mapped to itself as if by asinh considered as a real function. The real axis is mapped to a bent path, turning corners at $\pm\pi/2$ (the points to which ±1 are mapped); $+\infty$ is mapped to $\pi/2 - \infty i$, and $-\infty$ to $-\pi/2 + \infty i$.

Figure 12-9: Illustration of the Range of the Cosine Function

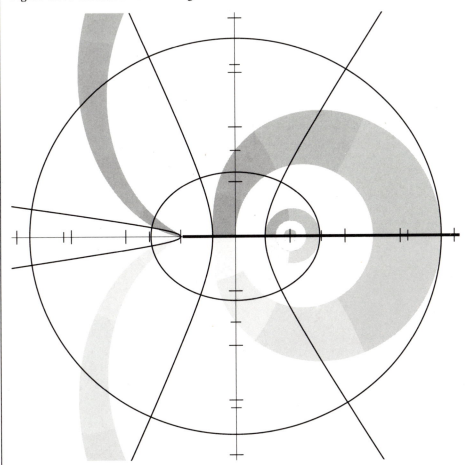

We are used to seeing cos looking exactly like sin, a wiggly ocean wave, only displaced. Indeed the complex mapping of cos is also similar to that of sin, with horizontal and vertical lines mapping to the same ellipses and hyperbolas with foci at ± 1, although mapping to them in a different manner, to be sure. The entire real axis is again mapped to the segment $[-1, 1]$ of the real axis, but each half of the imaginary axis is mapped to the real axis to the right of 1 (as if by cosh considered as a real function). Therefore $\pm\infty i$ both map to $+\infty$. The origin is mapped to 1. Whereas sin is an odd function, cos is an even function; as a result *two* points in each annulus, one the negative of the other, are mapped to the same shaded point in this graph; the shading shown here is taken from points in the original upper half-plane.

Figure 12-10: Illustration of the Range of the Arc Cosine Function

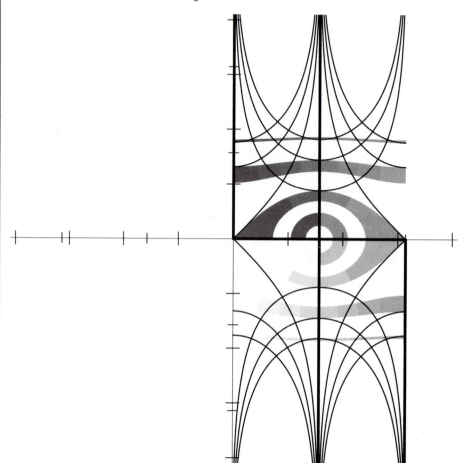

The graph of acos is very much like that of asin. One might think that our nervous peacock has shuffled half a step to the right, but the shading on the annuli shows that we have instead caught the bird exactly in mid-flight while doing a cartwheel. This is easily understood if we recall that $\arccos z = (\pi/2) - \arcsin z$; negating $\arcsin z$ rotates it upside down, and adding the result to $\pi/2$ translates it $\pi/2$ to the right. The imaginary axis is mapped upside down to the vertical line at $\pi/2$. The point $+1$ is mapped to the origin, and -1 to π. The image of the real axis is again cranky; $+\infty$ is mapped to $+\infty i$, and $-\infty$ to $\pi - \infty i$.

Figure 12-11: Illustration of the Range of the Tangent Function

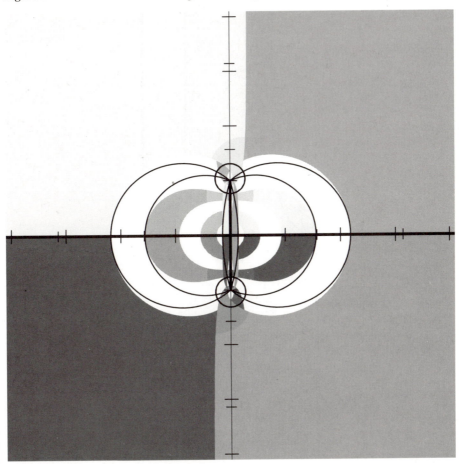

The usual graph of `tan` as a real function looks like an infinite chorus line of disco dancers, left hands pointed skyward and right hands to the floor. The `tan` function is the quotient of `sin` and `cos` but it doesn't much look like either except for having period 2π. This goes for the complex plane as well, although the swoopy loops produced from the annulus between $\pi/2$ and 2 look vaguely like those from the graph of `sin` inside out. The real axis is mapped onto itself with infinite multiplicity (period 2π). The imaginary axis is mapped backwards onto $[-i, i]$: $+\infty i$ is mapped to $-i$ and $-\infty i$ to $+i$. Horizontal lines below or above the real axis become circles surrounding $+i$ or $-i$, respectively. Vertical lines become circular arcs from $+i$ to $-i$; two vertical lines separated by $(2k + 1)\pi$ for integer k together become a complete circle. It seems that two arcs shown hit the real axis at $\pm\pi/2 = \pm 1.57\ldots$ but that is a coincidence; they really hit the axis at $\pm \tan 1 = 1.55\ldots$.

Figure 12-12: Illustration of the Range of the Arc Tangent Function

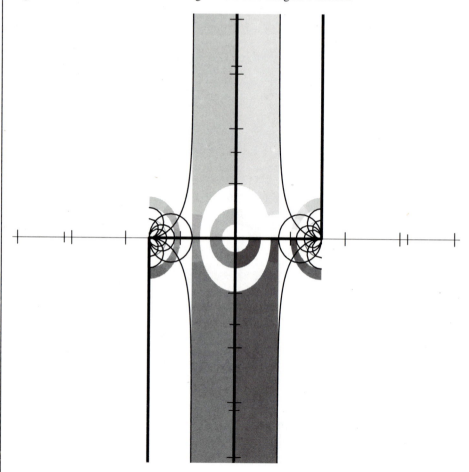

All I can say is that this peacock is a horse of another color. At first glance, the axes seem to map in the same way as for asin and acos, but look again: this time it's the imaginary axis doing weird things. All infinities map multiply to the points $(2k + 1)\pi/2$; within the strip of principal values we may say that the real axis is mapped to the interval $[-\pi/2, +\pi/2]$ and therefore $-\infty$ is mapped to $-\pi/2$ and $+\infty$ to $+\pi/2$. The point $+i$ is mapped to $+\infty i$, and $-i$ to $-\infty i$, and so the imaginary axis is mapped into three pieces: the segment $[-\infty i, -i]$ is mapped to $[\pi/2, \pi/2 - \infty i]$; the segment $[-i, i]$ is mapped to the imaginary axis $[-\infty i, +\infty i]$; and the segment $[+i, +\infty i]$ is mapped to $[-\pi/2 + \infty i, -\pi/2]$.

Figure 12-13: Illustration of the Range of the Hyperbolic Sine Function

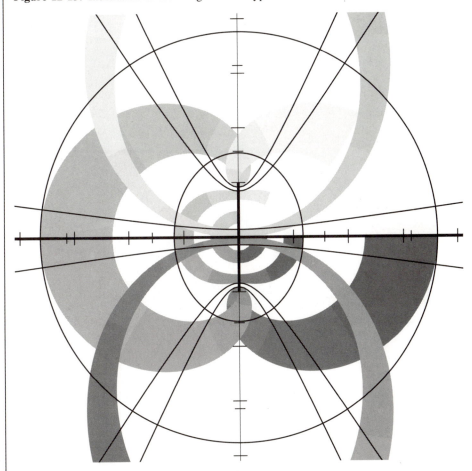

It would seem that the graph of sinh is merely that of sin rotated 90 degrees. If that were so, then we would have $\sinh z = i \sin z$. Careful inspection of the shading, however, reveals that this is not quite the case; in both graphs the lightest and darkest shades, which initially are adjacent to the positive real axis, remain adjacent to the positive real axis in both cases. To derive the graph of sinh from sin we must therefore first rotate the complex plane by -90 degrees, then apply sin, then rotate the result by 90 degrees. In other words, $\sinh z = i \sin(-i)z$; consistently replacing z with iz in this formula yields the familiar identity $\sinh iz = i \sin z$.

Figure 12-14: Illustration of the Range of the Hyperbolic Arc Sine Function

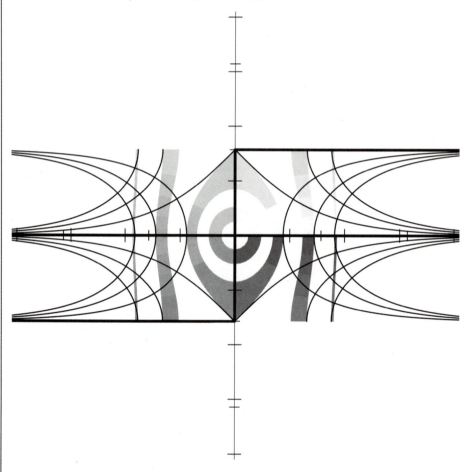

The peacock sleeps. Because arcsinh $iz = i$ arcsin z, the graph of asinh is related to that of asin by pre- and post-rotations of the complex plane in the same way as for sinh and sin.

Figure 12-15: Illustration of the Range of the Hyperbolic Cosine Function

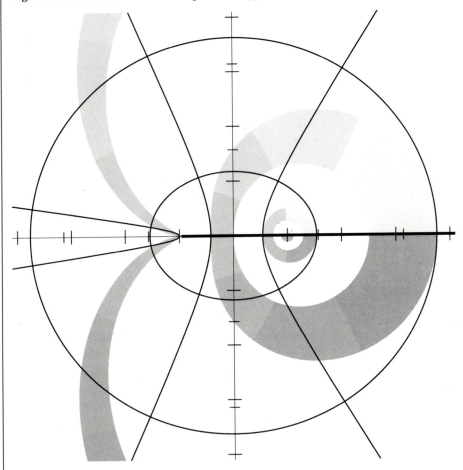

The graph of cosh does *not* look like that of cos rotated 90 degrees; instead it looks like that of cos unrotated. That is because cosh iz is not equal to $i \cos z$; rather, cosh $iz = \cos z$. Interpreted, that means that the shading is pre-rotated but there is no post-rotation.

Figure 12-16: Illustration of the Range of the Hyperbolic Arc Cosine Function

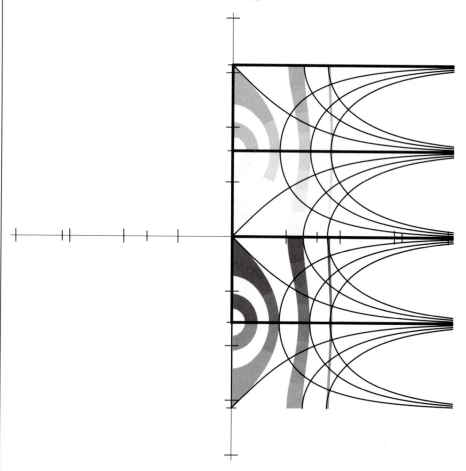

Hmm—I'd rather not say what happened to this peacock. This feather looks a bit mangled. Actually it is all right—the principal value for acosh is so chosen that its graph does not look simply like a rotated version of the graph of acos, but if all values were shown, the two graphs would fill the plane in repeating patterns related by a rotation.

Figure 12-17: Illustration of the Range of the Hyperbolic Tangent Function

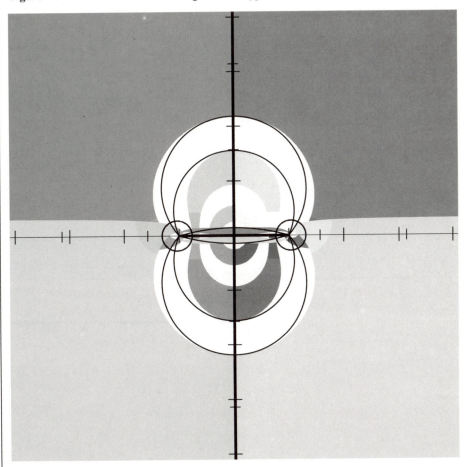

The diagram for tanh is simply that of tan turned on its ear: $i \tan z = \tanh iz$. The imaginary axis is mapped onto itself with infinite multiplicity (period 2π), and the real axis is mapped onto the segment $[-1, +1]$: $+\infty$ is mapped to $+1$, and $-\infty$ to -1. Vertical lines to the left or right of the real axis are mapped to circles surrounding -1 or 1, respectively. Horizontal lines are mapped to circular arcs anchored at -1 and $+1$; two horizontal lines separated by a distance $(2k+1)\pi$ for integer k are together mapped into a complete circle. How do we know these really are circles? Well, $\tanh z = ((\exp 2z) - 1)/((\exp 2z) + 1)$, which is the composition of the bilinear transform $(z - 1)/(z + 1)$, the exponential $\exp z$, and the magnification $2z$. Magnification maps lines to lines of the same slope; the exponential maps horizontal lines to circles and vertical lines to radial lines; and a bilinear transform maps generalized circles (including lines) to generalized circles. Q.E.D.

Figure 12-18: Illustration of the Range of the Hyperbolic Arc Tangent Function

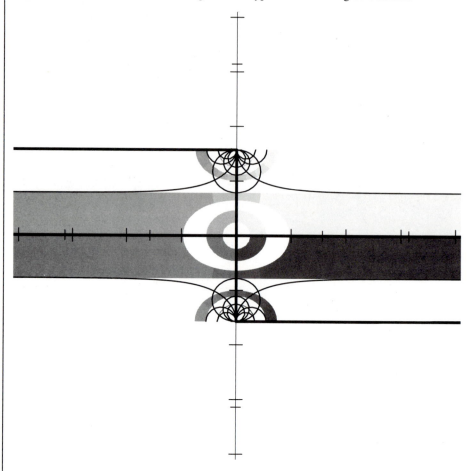

A sleeping peacock of another color: arctanh $iz = i$ arctan z.

Figure 12-19: Illustration of the Range of the Function $\sqrt{1-z^2}$

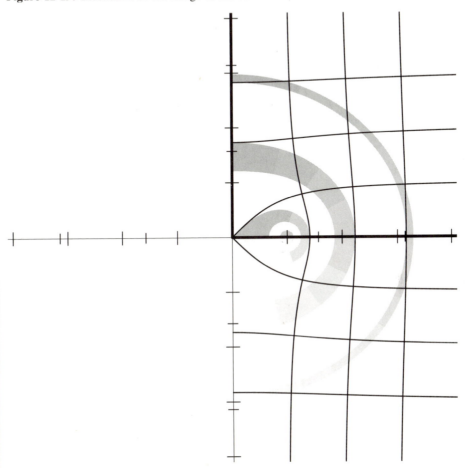

Here is a curious graph indeed for so simple a function! The origin is mapped to 1. The real axis segment $[0, 1]$ is mapped backwards (and non-linearly) into itself; the segment $[1, +\infty]$ is mapped non-linearly onto the positive imaginary axis. The negative real axis is mapped to the same points as the positive real axis. Both halves of the imaginary axis are mapped into $[1, +\infty]$ on the real axis. Horizontal lines become vaguely vertical, and vertical lines become vaguely horizontal. Circles centered at the origin are transformed into Cassinian (half-)ovals; the unit circle is mapped to a (half-)lemniscate of Bernoulli. The outermost annulus appears to have its *inner* edge at π on the real axis and its *outer* edge at 3 on the imaginary axis, but this is another accident; the intercept on the real axis, for example, is not really at $\pi \approx 3.14\ldots$ but at $\sqrt{1-(3i)^2} = \sqrt{10} \approx 3.16\ldots$.

Figure 12-20: Illustration of the Range of the Function $\sqrt{1+z^2}$

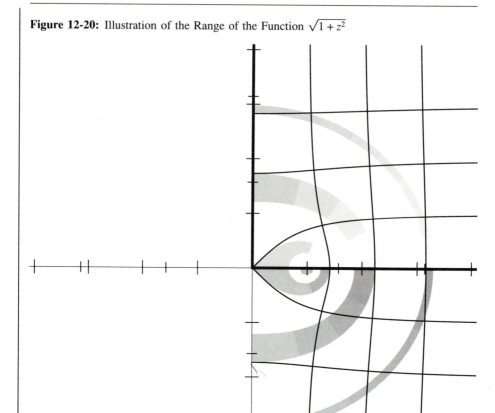

The graph of $q(z) = \sqrt{1+z^2}$ looks like that of $p(z) = \sqrt{1-z^2}$ except for the shading. You might not expect p and q to be related in the same way that cos and cosh are, but after a little reflection (or perhaps I should say, after turning it around in one's mind) one can see that $q(iz) = p(z)$. This formula is indeed of exactly the same form as $\cosh iz = \cos z$. The function $\sqrt{1+z^2}$ maps both halves of the real axis into $[1, +\infty]$ on the real axis. The segments $[0, i]$ and $[0, -i]$ of the imaginary axis are each mapped backwards onto segment $[0, 1]$ of the real axis; $[i, +\infty i]$ and $[-, -\infty i]$ are each mapped onto the positive imaginary axis (but if minus zero is supported then opposite sides of the imaginary axis map to opposite halves of the imaginary axis—for example, $q(+0 + 2i) = \sqrt{5}i$ but $q(-0 + 2i) = -\sqrt{5}i$).

Here is a sample of the PostScript code that generated figure 12-1, showing the initial scaling, translation, and clipping parameters; the code for one sector of the innermost annulus; and the code for the negative imaginary axis. Comment lines indicate how path or boundary segments were generated separately and then spliced (in order to allow for the places that a singularity might lurk, in which case the generating code can "inch up" to the problematical argument value).

The size of the entire PostScript file for the identity function was about 68 kilobytes (2757 lines, including comments). The smallest files were the plots for atan and atanh, about 65 kilobytes apiece; the largest were the plots for sin, cos, sinh, and cosh, about 138 kilobytes apiece.

```
% PostScript file for plot of function IDENTITY
% Plot is to fit in a region 4.666666666666667 inches square
%   showing axes extending 4.1 units from the origin.

40.97560975609756 40.97560975609756 scale
4.1 4.1 translate
newpath
    -4.1 -4.1 moveto
    4.1 -4.1 lineto
    4.1 4.1 lineto
    -4.1 4.1 lineto
    closepath
clip
% Moby grid for function IDENTITY
% Annulus 0.25 0.5 4 0.97 0.45
% Sector from 4.7124 to 6.2832 (quadrant 3)
newpath
    0.0 -0.25 moveto
    0.0 -0.375 lineto
    %middle radial
    0.0 -0.375 lineto
    0.0 -0.5 lineto
    %end radial
    0.0 -0.5 lineto
    0.092 -0.4915 lineto
    0.1843 -0.4648 lineto
    0.273 -0.4189 lineto
    0.3536 -0.3536 lineto
    %middle circumferential
    0.3536 -0.3536 lineto
    0.413 -0.2818 lineto
    0.4594 -0.1974 lineto
    0.4894 -0.1024 lineto
    0.5 0.0 lineto
```

```
     %end circumferential
     0.5 0.0 lineto
     0.375 0.0 lineto
     %middle radial
     0.375 0.0 lineto
     0.25 0.0 lineto
     %end radial
     0.25 0.0 lineto
     0.2297 -0.0987 lineto
     0.1768 -0.1768 lineto
     %middle circumferential
     0.1768 -0.1768 lineto
     0.0922 -0.2324 lineto
     0.0 -0.25 lineto
     %end circumferential
     closepath
currentgray   0.45 setgray   fill   setgray
```

[2598 lines omitted]

```
% Vertical line from (0.0, -0.5) to (0.0, 0.0)
newpath
   0.0 -0.5 moveto
   0.0 0.0 lineto
0.05 setlinewidth   1 setlinecap  stroke
% Vertical line from (0.0, -0.5) to (0.0, -1.0)
newpath
   0.0 -0.5 moveto
   0.0 -1.0 lineto
0.05 setlinewidth   1 setlinecap  stroke
% Vertical line from (0.0, -2.0) to (0.0, -1.0)
newpath
   0.0 -2.0 moveto
   0.0 -1.0 lineto
0.05 setlinewidth   1 setlinecap  stroke
% Vertical line from (0.0, -2.0) to (0.0, -1.1579208923731617E77)
newpath
   0.0 -2.0 moveto
   0.0 -6.3553 lineto
   0.0 -6.378103166302659 lineto
   0.0 -6.378103166302659 lineto
   0.0 -6.378103166302659 lineto
0.05 setlinewidth 1 setlinecap stroke
```

[84 lines omitted]

```
% End of PostScript file for plot of function IDENTITY
```

Here is the program that generated the PostScript code for the graphs shown in figures 12-1 through 12-20. It contains a mixture of fairly general mechanisms and *ad hoc* kludges for plotting functions of a single complex argument while gracefully handling extremely large and small values, branch cuts, singularities, and periodic behavior. The aim was to provide a simple user interface that would not require the caller to provide special advice for each function to be plotted. The file for figure 12-1, for example, was generated by the call (picture ´identity), which resulted in the writing of a file named identity-plot.ps.

The program assumes that any periodic behavior will have a period that is a multiple of 2π; that branch cuts will fall along the real or imaginary axis; and that singularities or very large or small values will occur only at the origin, at ± 1 or $\pm i$, or on the boundaries of the annuli (particularly those with radius $\pi/2$ or π). The central function is parametric-path, which accepts four arguments: two real numbers that are the endpoints of an interval of real numbers, a function that maps this interval into a path in the complex plane, and the function to be plotted; the task of parametric-path is to generate PostScript code (a series of lineto operations) that will plot an approximation to the image of the parametric path as transformed by the function to be plotted. Each of the functions hline, vline, -hline, -vline, radial, and circumferential takes appropriate parameters and returns a function suitable for use as the third argument to parametric-path. There is some code that defends against errors (by using ignore-errors) and against certain peculiarities of IEEE floating-point arithmetic (the code that checks for not-a-number (NaN) results).

The program is offered here without further comment or apology.

```
(defparameter units-to-show 4.1)
(defparameter text-width-in-picas 28.0)
(defparameter device-pixels-per-inch 300)
(defparameter pixels-per-unit
  (* (/ (/ text-width-in-picas 6)
        (* units-to-show 2))
     device-pixels-per-inch))

(defparameter big (sqrt (sqrt most-positive-single-float)))
(defparameter tiny (sqrt (sqrt least-positive-single-float)))

(defparameter path-really-losing 1000.0)
(defparameter path-outer-limit (* units-to-show (sqrt 2) 1.1))
(defparameter path-minimal-delta (/ 10 pixels-per-unit))
(defparameter path-outer-delta (* path-outer-limit 0.3))
(defparameter path-relative-closeness 0.00001)
(defparameter back-off-delta 0.0005)
```

```
(defun comment-line (stream &rest stuff)
  (format stream "~%% ")
  (apply #'format stream stuff)
  (format t "~%% ")
  (apply #'format t stuff))

(defun parametric-path (from to paramfn plotfn)
  (assert (and (plusp from) (plusp to)))
  (flet ((domainval (x) (funcall paramfn x))
         (rangeval (x) (funcall plotfn (funcall paramfn x)))
         (losing (x) (or (null x)
                         (/= (realpart x) (realpart x))   ;NaN?
                         (/= (imagpart x) (imagpart x))   ;NaN?
                         (> (abs (realpart x)) path-really-losing)
                         (> (abs (imagpart x)) path-really-losing))))
    (when (> to 1000.0)
      (let ((f0 (rangeval from))
            (f1 (rangeval (+ from 1)))
            (f2 (rangeval (+ from (* 2 pi))))
            (f3 (rangeval (+ from 1 (* 2 pi))))
            (f4 (rangeval (+ from (* 4 pi)))))
        (flet ((close (x y)
                 (or (< (careful-abs (- x y)) path-minimal-delta)
                     (< (careful-abs (- x y))
                        (* (+ (careful-abs x) (careful-abs y))
                           path-relative-closeness)))))
          (when (and (close f0 f2)
                     (close f2 f4)
                     (close f1 f3)
                     (or (and (close f0 f1)
                              (close f2 f3))
                         (and (not (close f0 f1))
                              (not (close f2 f3)))))
            (format t "~&Periodicity detected.")
            (setq to (+ from (* (signum (- to from)) 2 pi)))))))
    (let ((fromrange (ignore-errors (rangeval from)))
          (torange (ignore-errors (rangeval to))))
      (if (losing fromrange)
          (if (losing torange)
              '()
              (parametric-path (back-off from to) to paramfn plotfn))
          (if (losing torange)
              (parametric-path from (back-off to from) paramfn plotfn)
              (expand-path (refine-path (list from to) #'rangeval)
                           #'rangeval))))))
```

```
(defun back-off (point other)
  (if (or (> point 10.0) (< point 0.1))
      (let ((sp (sqrt point)))
        (if (or (> point sp other) (< point sp other))
            sp
            (* sp (sqrt other))))
      (+ point (* (signum (- other point)) back-off-delta))))

(defun careful-abs (z)
  (cond ((or (> (realpart z) big)
             (< (realpart z) (- big))
             (> (imagpart z) big)
             (< (imagpart z) (- big)))
         big)
        ((complexp z) (abs z))
        ((minusp z) (- z))
        (t z)))


(defparameter max-refinements 5000)

(defun refine-path (original-path rangevalfn)
  (flet ((rangeval (x) (funcall rangevalfn x)))
    (let ((path original-path))
      (do ((j 0 (+ j 1)))
          ((null (rest path)))
        (when (zerop (mod (+ j 1) max-refinements))
              (break "Runaway path"))
        (let* ((from (first path))
               (to (second path))
               (fromrange (rangeval from))
               (torange (rangeval to))
               (dist (careful-abs (- torange fromrange)))
               (mid (* (sqrt from) (sqrt to)))
               (midrange (rangeval mid)))
          (cond ((or (and (far-out fromrange) (far-out torange))
                     (and (< dist path-minimal-delta)
                          (< (abs (- midrange fromrange))
                             path-minimal-delta)
                          ;; Next test is intentionally asymmetric to
                          ;;   avoid problems with periodic functions.
                          (< (abs (- (rangeval (/ (+ to (* from 1.5))
                                                  2.5))
                                     fromrange))
                             path-minimal-delta)))
                 (pop path))
```

```
                ((= mid from) (pop path))
                ((= mid to) (pop path))
                (t (setf (rest path) (cons mid (rest path))))))))))
  original-path)

(defun expand-path (path rangevalfn)
  (flet ((rangeval (x) (funcall rangevalfn x)))
    (let ((final-path (list (rangeval (first path)))))
      (do ((p (rest path) (cdr p)))
          ((null p)
           (unless (rest final-path)
             (break "Singleton path"))
           (reverse final-path))
        (let ((v (rangeval (car p))))
          (cond ((and (rest final-path)
                      (not (far-out v))
                      (not (far-out (first final-path)))
                      (between v (first final-path)
                               (second final-path)))
                 (setf (first final-path) v))
                ((null (rest p))    ;Mustn't omit last point
                 (push v final-path))
                ((< (abs (- v (first final-path))) path-minimal-delta))
                ((far-out v)
                 (unless (and (far-out (first final-path))
                              (< (abs (- v (first final-path)))
                                 path-outer-delta))
                   (push (* 1.01 path-outer-limit (signum v))
                         final-path)))
                (t (push v final-path))))))))

(defun far-out (x)
  (> (careful-abs x) path-outer-limit))

(defparameter between-tolerance 0.000001)

(defun between (p q r)
  (let ((px (realpart p)) (py (imagpart p))
        (qx (realpart q)) (qy (imagpart q))
        (rx (realpart r)) (ry (imagpart r)))
    (and (or (<= px qx rx) (>= px qx rx))
         (or (<= py qy ry) (>= py qy ry))
         (< (abs (- (* (- qx px) (- ry qy))
                    (* (- rx qx) (- qy py))))
            between-tolerance))))
```

```
(defun circle (radius)
  #'(lambda (angle) (* radius (cis angle))))

(defun hline (imag)
  #'(lambda (real) (complex real imag)))

(defun vline (real)
  #'(lambda (imag) (complex real imag)))

(defun -hline (imag)
  #'(lambda (real) (complex (- real) imag)))

(defun -vline (real)
  #'(lambda (imag) (complex real (- imag))))

(defun radial (phi quadrant)
  #'(lambda (rho) (repair-quadrant (* rho (cis phi)) quadrant)))

(defun circumferential (rho quadrant)
  #'(lambda (phi) (repair-quadrant (* rho (cis phi)) quadrant)))

;;; Quadrant is 0, 1, 2, or 3, meaning I, II, III, or IV.

(defun repair-quadrant (z quadrant)
  (complex (* (+ (abs (realpart z)) tiny)
              (case quadrant (0 1.0) (1 -1.0) (2 -1.0) (3 1.0)))
           (* (+ (abs (imagpart z)) tiny)
              (case quadrant (0 1.0) (1 1.0) (2 -1.0) (3 -1.0)))))

(defun clamp-real (x)
  (if (far-out x)
      (* (signum x) path-outer-limit)
      (round-real x)))

(defun round-real (x)
  (/ (round (* x 10000.0)) 10000.0))

(defun round-point (z)
  (complex (round-real (realpart z)) (round-real (imagpart z))))

(defparameter hiringshade 0.97)
(defparameter loringshade 0.45)

(defparameter ticklength 0.12)
(defparameter smallticklength 0.09)
```

```
;;; This determines the pattern of lines and annuli to be drawn.
(defun moby-grid (&optional (fn 'sqrt) (stream t))
  (comment-line stream "Moby grid for function ~S" fn)
  (shaded-annulus 0.25 0.5 4 hiringshade loringshade fn stream)
  (shaded-annulus 0.75 1.0 8 hiringshade loringshade fn stream)
  (shaded-annulus (/ pi 2) 2.0 16 hiringshade loringshade fn stream)
  (shaded-annulus 3 pi 32 hiringshade loringshade fn stream)
  (moby-lines :horizontal 1.0 fn stream)
  (moby-lines :horizontal -1.0 fn stream)
  (moby-lines :vertical 1.0 fn stream)
  (moby-lines :vertical -1.0 fn stream)
  (let ((tickline 0.015)
        (axisline 0.008))
    (flet ((tick (n) (straight-line (complex n ticklength)
                                    (complex n (- ticklength))
                                    tickline
                                    stream))
           (smalltick (n) (straight-line (complex n smallticklength)
                                         (complex n (- smallticklength))
                                         tickline
                                         stream)))
      (comment-line stream "Real axis")
      (straight-line #c(-5 0) #c(5 0) axisline stream)
      (dotimes (j (floor units-to-show))
        (let ((q (+ j 1))) (tick q) (tick (- q))))
      (dotimes (j (floor units-to-show (/ pi 2)))
        (let ((q (* (/ pi 2) (+ j 1))))
          (smalltick q)
          (smalltick (- q)))))
    (flet ((tick (n) (straight-line (complex ticklength n)
                                    (complex (- ticklength) n)
                                    tickline
                                    stream))
           (smalltick (n) (straight-line (complex smallticklength n)
                                         (complex (- smallticklength) n)
                                         tickline
                                         stream)))
      (comment-line stream "Imaginary axis")
      (straight-line #c(0 -5) #c(0 5) axisline stream)
      (dotimes (j (floor units-to-show))
        (let ((q (+ j 1))) (tick q) (tick (- q))))
      (dotimes (j (floor units-to-show (/ pi 2)))
        (let ((q (* (/ pi 2) (+ j 1))))
          (smalltick q)
          (smalltick (- q)))))))
```

```
(defun straight-line (from to wid stream)
  (format stream
          "~%newpath  ~S ~S moveto  ~S ~S lineto  ~S ~
           setlinewidth  1  setlinecap  stroke"
          (realpart from)
          (imagpart from)
          (realpart to)
          (imagpart to)
          wid))


;;; This function draws the lines for the pattern.
(defun moby-lines (orientation signum plotfn stream)
  (let ((paramfn (ecase orientation
                   (:horizontal (if (< signum 0) #'-hline #'hline))
                   (:vertical (if (< signum 0) #'-vline #'vline)))))
    (flet ((foo (from to other wid)
             (ecase orientation
               (:horizontal
                (comment-line stream
                              "Horizontal line from (~S, ~S) to (~S, ~S)"
                              (round-real (* signum from))
                              (round-real other)
                              (round-real (* signum to))
                              (round-real other)))
               (:vertical
                (comment-line stream
                              "Vertical line from (~S, ~S) to (~S, ~S)"
                              (round-real other)
                              (round-real (* signum from))
                              (round-real other)
                              (round-real (* signum to)))))
             (postscript-path
               stream
               (parametric-path from
                                to
                                (funcall paramfn other)
                                plotfn))
             (postscript-penstroke stream wid)))
      (let* ((thick 0.05)
             (thin 0.02))
        ;; Main axis
        (foo 0.5 tiny 0.0 thick)
        (foo 0.5 1.0 0.0 thick)
        (foo 2.0 1.0 0.0 thick)
        (foo 2.0 big 0.0 thick)
```

```
            ;; Parallels at 1 and -1
            (foo 2.0 tiny 1.0 thin)
            (foo 2.0 big 1.0 thin)
            (foo 2.0 tiny -1.0 thin)
            (foo 2.0 big -1.0 thin)
            ;; Parallels at 2, 3, -2, -3
            (foo tiny big 2.0 thin)
            (foo tiny big -2.0 thin)
            (foo tiny big 3.0 thin)
            (foo tiny big -3.0 thin)))))

(defun splice (p q)
  (let ((v (car (last p)))
        (w (first q)))
    (and (far-out v)
         (far-out w)
         (>= (abs (- v w)) path-outer-delta)
         ;; Two far-apart far-out points.  Try to walk around
         ;;   outside the perimeter, in the shorter direction.
         (let* ((pdiff (phase (/ v w)))
                (npoints (floor (abs pdiff) (asin .2)))
                (delta (/ pdiff (+ npoints 1)))
                (incr (cis delta)))
           (do ((j 0 (+ j 1))
                (p (list w "end splice") (cons (* (car p) incr) p)))
               ((= j npoints) (cons "start splice" p)))))))



;;; This function draws the annuli for the pattern.
(defun shaded-annulus (inner outer sectors firstshade lastshade fn stream)
  (assert (zerop (mod sectors 4)))
  (comment-line stream "Annulus ~S ~S ~S ~S ~S"
                (round-real inner) (round-real outer)
                sectors firstshade lastshade)
  (dotimes (jj sectors)
    (let ((j (- sectors jj 1)))
      (let* ((lophase (+ tiny (* 2 pi (/ j sectors))))
             (hiphase (* 2 pi (/ (+ j 1) sectors)))
             (midphase (/ (+ lophase hiphase) 2.0))
             (midradius (/ (+ inner outer) 2.0))
             (quadrant (floor (* j 4) sectors)))
        (comment-line stream "Sector from ~S to ~S (quadrant ~S)"
                      (round-real lophase)
                      (round-real hiphase)
                      quadrant)
```

```
(let ((p0 (reverse (parametric-path midradius
                                    inner
                                    (radial lophase quadrant)
                                    fn)))
      (p1 (parametric-path midradius
                           outer
                           (radial lophase quadrant)
                           fn))
      (p2 (reverse (parametric-path midphase
                                    lophase
                                    (circumferential outer
                                                     quadrant)
                                    fn)))
      (p3 (parametric-path midphase
                           hiphase
                           (circumferential outer quadrant)
                           fn))
      (p4 (reverse (parametric-path midradius
                                    outer
                                    (radial hiphase quadrant)
                                    fn)))
      (p5 (parametric-path midradius
                           inner
                           (radial hiphase quadrant)
                           fn))
      (p6 (reverse (parametric-path midphase
                                    hiphase
                                    (circumferential inner
                                                     quadrant)
                                    fn)))
      (p7 (parametric-path midphase
                           lophase
                           (circumferential inner quadrant)
                           fn)))
  (postscript-closed-path stream
    (append
      p0 (splice p0 p1) '("middle radial")
      p1 (splice p1 p2) '("end radial")
      p2 (splice p2 p3) '("middle circumferential")
      p3 (splice p3 p4) '("end circumferential")
      p4 (splice p4 p5) '("middle radial")
      p5 (splice p5 p6) '("end radial")
      p6 (splice p6 p7) '("middle circumferential")
      p7 (splice p7 p0) '("end circumferential")
      )))
```

```
              (postscript-shade stream
                              (/ (+ (* firstshade (- (- sectors 1) j))
                                    (* lastshade j))
                                 (- sectors 1))))))))

(defun postscript-penstroke (stream wid)
  (format stream "~%~S setlinewidth   1 setlinecap   stroke"
          wid))

(defun postscript-shade (stream shade)
  (format stream "~%currentgray    ~S setgray    fill    setgray"
          shade))

(defun postscript-closed-path (stream path)
  (unless (every #'far-out (remove-if-not #'numberp path))
    (postscript-raw-path stream path)
    (format stream "~%  closepath")))

(defun postscript-path (stream path)
  (unless (every #'far-out (remove-if-not #'numberp path))
    (postscript-raw-path stream path)))

;;; Print a path as a series of PostScript "lineto" commands.
(defun postscript-raw-path (stream path)
  (format stream "~%newpath")
  (let ((fmt "~%  ~S ~S moveto"))
    (dolist (pt path)
      (cond ((stringp pt)
             (format stream "~%  %~A" pt))
            (t (format stream
                       fmt
                       (clamp-real (realpart pt))
                       (clamp-real (imagpart pt)))
               (setq fmt "~%  ~S ~S lineto"))))))

;;; Definitions of functions to be plotted that are not
;;; standard Common Lisp functions.

(defun one-plus-over-one-minus (x) (/ (+ 1 x) (- 1 x)))

(defun one-minus-over-one-plus (x) (/ (- 1 x) (+ 1 x)))

(defun sqrt-square-minus-one (x) (sqrt (- 1 (* x x))))

(defun sqrt-one-plus-square (x) (sqrt (+ 1 (* x x))))
```

```
;;; Because X3J13 voted for a new definition of the atan function,
;;; the following definition was used in place of the atan function
;;; provided by the Common Lisp implementation I was using.

(defun good-atan (x)
  (/ (- (log (+ 1 (* x #c(0 1))))
        (log (- 1 (* x #c(0 1)))))
     #c(0 2)))

;;; Because the first edition had an erroneous definition of atanh,
;;; the following definition was used in place of the atanh function
;;; provided by the Common Lisp implementation I was using.

(defun really-good-atanh (x)
  (/ (- (log (+ 1 x))
        (log (- 1 x)))
     2))

;;; This is the main procedure that is intended to be called by a user.
(defun picture (&optional (fn #'sqrt))
  (with-open-file (stream (concatenate 'string
                                       (string-downcase (string fn))
                                       "-plot.ps")
                          :direction :output)
    (format stream "% PostScript file for plot of function ~S~%" fn)
    (format stream "% Plot is to fit in a region ~S inches square~%"
            (/ text-width-in-picas 6.0))
    (format stream
            "%  showing axes extending ~S units from the origin.~%"
            units-to-show)
    (let ((scaling (/ (* text-width-in-picas 12) (* units-to-show 2))))
      (format stream "~%~S ~:*~S scale" scaling))
    (format stream "~%~S ~:*~S translate" units-to-show)
    (format stream "~%newpath")
    (format stream "~%  ~S ~S moveto" (- units-to-show) (- units-to-show))
    (format stream "~%  ~S ~S lineto" units-to-show (- units-to-show))
    (format stream "~%  ~S ~S lineto" units-to-show units-to-show)
    (format stream "~%  ~S ~S lineto" (- units-to-show) units-to-show)
    (format stream "~%  closepath")
    (format stream "~%clip")
    (moby-grid fn stream)
    (format stream
            "~%%% End of PostScript file for plot of function ~S"
            fn)
    (terpri stream)))
```

12.6. Type Conversions and Component Extractions on Numbers

While most arithmetic functions will operate on any kind of number, coercing types if necessary, the following functions are provided to allow specific conversions of data types to be forced when desired.

`float` *number* &optional *other*   [*Function*]

This converts any non-complex number to a floating-point number. With no second argument, if *number* is already a floating-point number, then *number* is returned; otherwise a single-float is produced. If the argument *other* is provided, then it must be a floating-point number, and *number* is converted to the same format as *other*. See also coerce.

`rational` *number*   [*Function*]
`rationalize` *number*   [*Function*]

Each of these functions converts any non-complex number to a rational number. If the argument is already rational, it is returned. The two functions differ in their treatment of floating-point numbers.

   rational assumes that the floating-point number is completely accurate and returns a rational number mathematically equal to the precise value of the floating-point number.

   rationalize assumes that the floating-point number is accurate only to the precision of the floating-point representation and may return any rational number for which the floating-point number is the best available approximation of its format; in doing this it attempts to keep both numerator and denominator small.

   It is always the case that

```
(float (rational x) x) ≡ x
```

and

```
(float (rationalize x) x) ≡ x
```

That is, rationalizing a floating-point number by either method and then converting it back to a floating-point number of the same format produces the original number. What distinguishes the two functions is that rational typically has a simple, inexpensive implementation, whereas rationalize goes to more trouble to produce a result that is more pleasant to view and simpler to compute with for some purposes.

numerator *rational*   [*Function*]
denominator *rational*   [*Function*]

These functions take a rational number (an integer or ratio) and return as an integer
the numerator or denominator of the canonical reduced form of the rational. The
numerator of an integer is that integer; the denominator of an integer is 1. Note
that

```
(gcd (numerator x) (denominator x)) ⇒ 1
```

The denominator will always be a strictly positive integer; the numerator may be
any integer. For example:

```
(numerator (/ 8 -6)) ⇒ -4
(denominator (/ 8 -6)) ⇒ 3
```

There is no `fix` function in Common Lisp because there are several interesting ways to convert non-integral values to integers. These are provided by the
functions below, which perform not only type conversion but also some non-trivial
calculations as well.

floor *number* &optional *divisor*   [*Function*]
ceiling *number* &optional *divisor*   [*Function*]
truncate *number* &optional *divisor*   [*Function*]
round *number* &optional *divisor*   [*Function*]

In the simple one-argument case, each of these functions converts its argument
number (which must not be complex) to an integer. If the argument is already an
integer, it is returned directly. If the argument is a ratio or floating-point number,
the functions use different algorithms for the conversion.

`floor` converts its argument by truncating toward negative infinity; that is, the
result is the largest integer that is not larger than the argument.

`ceiling` converts its argument by truncating toward positive infinity; that is, the
result is the smallest integer that is not smaller than the argument.

`truncate` converts its argument by truncating toward zero; that is, the result is
the integer of the same sign as the argument and which has the greatest integral
magnitude not greater than that of the argument.

`round` converts its argument by rounding to the nearest integer; if *number* is
exactly halfway between two integers (that is, of the form *integer* + 0.5), then it is
rounded to the one that is even (divisible by 2).

The following table shows what the four functions produce when given various
arguments.

Argument	floor	ceiling	truncate	round
2.6	2	3	2	3
2.5	2	3	2	2
2.4	2	3	2	2
0.7	0	1	0	1
0.3	0	1	0	0
-0.3	-1	0	0	0
-0.7	-1	0	0	-1
-2.4	-3	-2	-2	-2
-2.5	-3	-2	-2	-2
-2.6	-3	-2	-2	-3

If a second argument *divisor* is supplied, then the result is the appropriate type of rounding or truncation applied to the result of dividing the *number* by the *divisor*. For example, (floor 5 2) ≡ (floor (/ 5 2)) but is potentially more efficient.

This statement is not entirely accurate; one should instead say that (values (floor 5 2)) ≡ (values (floor (/ 5 2))), because there is a second value to consider, as discussed below. In other words, the first values returned by the two forms will be the same, but in general the second values will differ. Indeed, we have

```
(floor 5 2)      ⇒ 2 and 1
(floor (/ 5 2))  ⇒ 2 and 1/2
```

for this example.

The *divisor* may be any non-complex number.

It is generally accepted that it is an error for the *divisor* to be zero.

The one-argument case is exactly like the two-argument case where the second argument is 1.

In other words, the one-argument case returns an integer and fractional part for the *number*: (truncate 5.3) ⇒ 5.0 and 0.3, for example.

Each of the functions actually returns *two* values, whether given one or two arguments. The second result is the remainder and may be obtained using multiple-value-bind and related constructs. If any of these functions is given two arguments x and y and produces results q and r, then $q \cdot y + r = x$. The first result q is always an integer. The remainder r is an integer if both arguments are integers, is rational if both arguments are rational, and is floating-point if either argument is floating-point. One consequence is that in the one-argument case the remainder is always a number of the same type as the argument.

When only one argument is given, the two results are exact; the mathematical sum of the two results is always equal to the mathematical value of the argument.

Compatibility note: The names of the functions floor, ceiling, truncate, and round are more accurate than names like fix that have heretofore been used in various Lisp systems. The names used here are compatible with standard mathematical terminology (and with PL/1, as it happens). In Fortran ifix means truncate. Algol 68 provides round and uses entier to mean floor. In MacLisp, fix and ifix both mean floor (one is generic, the other flonum-in/fixnum-out). In Interlisp, fix means truncate. In Lisp Machine Lisp, fix means floor and fixr means round. Standard Lisp provides a fix function but does not specify precisely what it does. The existing usage of the name fix is so confused that it seemed best to avoid it altogether.

The names and definitions given here have recently been adopted by Lisp Machine Lisp, and MacLisp and NIL (New Implementation of Lisp) seem likely to follow suit.

mod *number divisor*   [*Function*]
rem *number divisor*   [*Function*]

mod performs the operation floor on its two arguments and returns the *second* result of floor as its only result. Similarly, rem performs the operation truncate on its arguments and returns the *second* result of truncate as its only result.

mod and rem are therefore the usual modulus and remainder functions when applied to two integer arguments. In general, however, the arguments may be integers or floating-point numbers.

```
(mod 13 4) ⇒ 1               (rem 13 4) ⇒ 1
(mod -13 4) ⇒ 3              (rem -13 4) ⇒ -1
(mod 13 -4) ⇒ -3            (rem 13 -4) ⇒ 1
(mod -13 -4) ⇒ -1          (rem -13 -4) ⇒ -1
(mod 13.4 1) ⇒ 0.4       (rem 13.4 1) ⇒ 0.4
(mod -13.4 1) ⇒ 0.6     (rem -13.4 1) ⇒ -0.4
```

Compatibility note: The Interlisp function remainder is essentially equivalent to the Common Lisp function rem. The MacLisp function remainder is like rem but accepts only integer arguments.

ffloor *number* &optional *divisor*   [*Function*]
fceiling *number* &optional *divisor*   [*Function*]
ftruncate *number* &optional *divisor*   [*Function*]
fround *number* &optional *divisor*   [*Function*]

These functions are just like floor, ceiling, truncate, and round, except that the result (the first result of two) is always a floating-point number rather than an integer. It is roughly as if ffloor gave its arguments to floor, and then applied float to the first result before passing them both back. In practice, however, ffloor may be implemented much more efficiently. Similar remarks apply to the other three functions. If the first argument is a floating-point number, and the second argument is not a floating-point number of longer format, then the first result will be a floating-point number of the same type as the first argument. For example:

```
(ffloor -4.7) ⇒ -5.0 and 0.3
(ffloor 3.5d0) ⇒ 3.0d0 and 0.5d0
```

decode-float *float*	[*Function*]
scale-float *float integer*	[*Function*]
float-radix *float*	[*Function*]
float-sign *float1* &optional *float2*	[*Function*]
float-digits *float*	[*Function*]
float-precision *float*	[*Function*]
integer-decode-float *float*	[*Function*]

The function decode-float takes a floating-point number and returns three values.

The first value is a new floating-point number of the same format representing the significand; the second value is an integer representing the exponent; and the third value is a floating-point number of same format indicating the sign (-1.0 or 1.0). Let b be the radix for the floating-point representation; then decode-float divides the argument by an integral power of b so as to bring its value between $1/b$ (inclusive) and 1 (exclusive) and returns the quotient as the first value. If the argument is zero, however, the result is equal to the absolute value of the argument (that is, if there is a negative zero, its significand is considered to be a positive zero).

The second value of decode-float is the integer exponent e to which b must be raised to produce the appropriate power for the division. If the argument is zero, any integer value may be returned, provided that the identity shown below for scale-float holds.

The third value of decode-float is a floating-point number, of the same format as the argument, whose absolute value is 1 and whose sign matches that of the argument.

The function scale-float takes a floating-point number f (not necessarily between $1/b$ and 1) and an integer k, and returns (* f (expt (float b f) k)). (The use of scale-float may be much more efficient than using exponentiation and multiplication and avoids intermediate overflow and underflow if the final result is representable.)

Note that

```
(multiple-value-bind (signif expon sign)
                     (decode-float f)
   (scale-float signif expon))
≡ (abs f)
```

and

```
(multiple-value-bind (signif expon sign)
                     (decode-float f)
   (* (scale-float signif expon) sign))
≡ f
```

The function `float-radix` returns (as an integer) the radix b of the floating-point argument.

The function `float-sign` returns a floating-point number z such that z and *float1* have the same sign and also such that z and *float2* have the same absolute value. The argument *float2* defaults to the value of (`float 1` *float1*); (`float-sign x`) therefore always produces a `1.0` or `-1.0` of appropriate format according to the sign of x. (Note that if an implementation has distinct representations for negative zero and positive zero, then (`float-sign -0.0`) $\Rightarrow$ `-1.0`.)

The function `float-digits` returns, as a non-negative integer, the number of radix-b digits used in the representation of its argument (including any implicit digits, such as a "hidden bit"). The function `float-precision` returns, as a non-negative integer, the number of significant radix-b digits present in the argument; if the argument is (a floating-point) zero, then the result is (an integer) zero. For normalized floating-point numbers, the results of `float-digits` and `float-precision` will be the same, but the precision will be less than the number of representation digits for a denormalized or zero number.

The function `integer-decode-float` is similar to `decode-float` but for its first value returns, as an `integer`, the significand scaled so as to be an integer. For an argument f, this integer will be strictly less than

```
(expt b (float-precision f))
```

but no less than

```
(expt b (- (float-precision f) 1))
```

except that if f is zero, then the integer value will be zero.

The second value bears the same relationship to the first value as for `decode-float`:

```
(multiple-value-bind (signif expon sign)
                     (integer-decode-float f)
  (scale-float (float signif f) expon))
≡ (abs f)
```

The third value of integer-decode-float will be 1 or -1.

Rationale: These functions allow the writing of machine-independent, or at least machine-parameterized, floating-point software of reasonable efficiency.

---

complex *realpart* &optional *imagpart*   [*Function*]

The arguments must be non-complex numbers; a number is returned that has *real-part* as its real part and *imagpart* as its imaginary part, possibly converted according to the rule of floating-point contagion (thus both components will be of the same type). If *imagpart* is not specified, then (coerce 0 (type-of *realpart*)) is effectively used. Note that if both the *realpart* and *imagpart* are rational and the *imagpart* is zero, then the result is just the *realpart* because of the rule of canonical representation for complex rationals. It follows that the result of complex is not always a complex number; it may be simply a rational.

realpart *number*   [*Function*]
imagpart *number*   [*Function*]

These return the real and imaginary parts of a complex number. If *number* is a non-complex number, then realpart returns its argument *number* and imagpart returns (* 0 *number*), which has the effect that the imaginary part of a rational is 0 and that of a floating-point number is a floating-point zero of the same format.

A clever way to multiply a complex number z by i is to write

```
(complex (- (imagpart z)) (realpart z))
```

instead of (* z #c(0 1)). This cleverness is not always gratuitous; it may be of particular importance in the presence of minus zero. For example, if we are using IEEE standard floating-point arithmetic and $z = 4+0i$, the result of the clever expression is $-0+4i$, a true 90° rotation of z, whereas the result of (* z #c(0 1)) is likely to be

$$(4 + 0i)(+0 + i) = ((4)(+0) - (+0)(1)) + ((4)(1) + (+0)(+0))i$$
$$= ((+0) - (+0)) + ((4) + (+0))i = +0 + 4i$$

which could land on the wrong side of a branch cut, for example.

12.7. Logical Operations on Numbers

The logical operations in this section require integers as arguments; it is an error
to supply a non-integer as an argument. The functions all treat integers as if they
were represented in two's-complement notation.

Implementation note: Internally, of course, an implementation of Common Lisp may or
may not use a two's-complement representation. All that is necessary is that the logical
operations perform calculations so as to give this appearance to the user.

The logical operations provide a convenient way to represent an infinite vector
of bits. Let such a conceptual vector be indexed by the non-negative integers.
Then bit j is assigned a "weight" 2^j. Assume that only a finite number of bits are
1's or only a finite number of bits are 0's. A vector with only a finite number of
one-bits is represented as the sum of the weights of the one-bits, a positive integer.
A vector with only a finite number of zero-bits is represented as -1 minus the sum
of the weights of the zero-bits, a negative integer.

This method of using integers to represent bit-vectors can in turn be used to
represent sets. Suppose that some (possibly countably infinite) universe of discourse
for sets is mapped into the non-negative integers. Then a set can be represented
as a bit vector; an element is in the set if the bit whose index corresponds to that
element is a one-bit. In this way all finite sets can be represented (by positive
integers), as well as all sets whose complements are finite (by negative integers).
The functions logior, logand, and logxor defined below then compute the union,
intersection, and symmetric difference operations on sets represented in this way.

logior &rest *integers*   [*Function*]

This returns the bit-wise logical *inclusive or* of its arguments. If no argument is
given, then the result is zero, which is an identity for this operation.

logxor &rest *integers*   [*Function*]

This returns the bit-wise logical *exclusive or* of its arguments. If no argument is
given, then the result is zero, which is an identity for this operation.

logand &rest *integers*   [*Function*]

This returns the bit-wise logical *and* of its arguments. If no argument is given,
then the result is -1, which is an identity for this operation.

`logeqv &rest` *integers*   [*Function*]

This returns the bit-wise logical *equivalence* (also known as *exclusive nor*) of its arguments. If no argument is given, then the result is -1, which is an identity for this operation.

`lognand` *integer1 integer2*   [*Function*]
`lognor` *integer1 integer2*   [*Function*]
`logandc1` *integer1 integer2*   [*Function*]
`logandc2` *integer1 integer2*   [*Function*]
`logorc1` *integer1 integer2*   [*Function*]
`logorc2` *integer1 integer2*   [*Function*]

These are the other six non-trivial bit-wise logical operations on two arguments. Because they are not associative, they take exactly two arguments rather than any non-negative number of arguments.

```
(lognand n1 n2) ≡ (lognot (logand n1 n2))
(lognor n1 n2) ≡ (lognot (logior n1 n2))
(logandc1 n1 n2) ≡ (logand (lognot n1) n2)
(logandc2 n1 n2) ≡ (logand n1 (lognot n2))
(logorc1 n1 n2) ≡ (logior (lognot n1) n2)
(logorc2 n1 n2) ≡ (logior n1 (lognot n2))
```

The ten bit-wise logical operations on two integers are summarized in the following table:

integer1	0	0	1	1	
integer2	0	1	0	1	Operation Name
logand	0	0	0	1	and
logior	0	1	1	1	inclusive or
logxor	0	1	1	0	exclusive or
logeqv	1	0	0	1	equivalence (exclusive nor)
lognand	1	1	1	0	not-and
lognor	1	0	0	0	not-or
logandc1	0	1	0	0	and complement of *integer1* with *integer2*
logandc2	0	0	1	0	and *integer1* with complement of *integer2*
logorc1	1	1	0	1	or complement of *integer1* with *integer2*
logorc2	1	0	1	1	or *integer1* with complement of *integer2*

`boole` *op integer1 integer2*	[*Function*]
`boole-clr`	[*Constant*]
`boole-set`	[*Constant*]
`boole-1`	[*Constant*]
`boole-2`	[*Constant*]
`boole-c1`	[*Constant*]
`boole-c2`	[*Constant*]
`boole-and`	[*Constant*]
`boole-ior`	[*Constant*]
`boole-xor`	[*Constant*]
`boole-eqv`	[*Constant*]
`boole-nand`	[*Constant*]
`boole-nor`	[*Constant*]
`boole-andc1`	[*Constant*]
`boole-andc2`	[*Constant*]
`boole-orc1`	[*Constant*]
`boole-orc2`	[*Constant*]

The function `boole` takes an operation *op* and two integers, and returns an integer produced by performing the logical operation specified by *op* on the two integers. The precise values of the sixteen constants are implementation-dependent, but they are suitable for use as the first argument to `boole`:

integer1	0	0	1	1	
integer2	0	1	0	1	Operation Performed
`boole-clr`	0	0	0	0	always 0
`boole-set`	1	1	1	1	always 1
`boole-1`	0	0	1	1	*integer1*
`boole-2`	0	1	0	1	*integer2*
`boole-c1`	1	1	0	0	complement of *integer1*
`boole-c2`	1	0	1	0	complement of *integer2*
`boole-and`	0	0	0	1	and
`boole-ior`	0	1	1	1	inclusive or
`boole-xor`	0	1	1	0	exclusive or
`boole-eqv`	1	0	0	1	equivalence (exclusive nor)
`boole-nand`	1	1	1	0	not-and
`boole-nor`	1	0	0	0	not-or
`boole-andc1`	0	1	0	0	and complement of *integer1* with *integer2*
`boole-andc2`	0	0	1	0	and *integer1* with complement of *integer2*
`boole-orc1`	1	1	0	1	or complement of *integer1* with *integer2*
`boole-orc2`	1	0	1	1	or *integer1* with complement of *integer2*

boole can therefore compute all sixteen logical functions on two arguments. In general,

```
(boole boole-and x y) ≡ (logand x y)
```

and the latter is more perspicuous. However, boole is useful when it is necessary to parameterize a procedure so that it can use one of several logical operations.

lognot *integer*   [*Function*]

This returns the bit-wise logical *not* of its argument. Every bit of the result is the complement of the corresponding bit in the argument.

```
(logbitp j (lognot x)) ≡ (not (logbitp j x))
```

logtest *integer1* *integer2*   [*Function*]

logtest is a predicate that is true if any of the bits designated by the 1's in *integer1* are 1's in *integer2*.

```
(logtest x y) ≡ (not (zerop (logand x y)))
```

logbitp *index* *integer*   [*Function*]

logbitp is true if the bit in *integer* whose index is *index* (that is, its weight is 2^{index}) is a one-bit; otherwise it is false. For example:

```
(logbitp 2 6) is true
(logbitp 0 6) is false
(logbitp k n) ≡ (ldb-test (byte 1 k) n)
```

X3J13 voted in January 1989 ⟨7⟩ to clarify that the *index* must be a non-negative integer.

ash *integer* *count*   [*Function*]

This function shifts *integer* arithmetically left by *count* bit positions if *count* is positive, or right by −*count* bit positions if *count* is negative. The sign of the result is always the same as the sign of *integer*.

Mathematically speaking, this operation performs the computation *floor*(*integer* · 2^{count}).

Logically, this moves all of the bits in *integer* to the left, adding zero-bits at the bottom, or moves them to the right, discarding bits. (In this context the question of what gets shifted in on the left is irrelevant; integers, viewed as strings of bits, are "half-infinite," that is, conceptually extend infinitely far to the left.) For example:

(logbitp j (ash n k)) $\equiv$ (and (>= j k) (logbitp (- j k) n))

logcount *integer*   [*Function*]

The number of bits in *integer* is determined and returned. If *integer* is positive, the 1-bits in its binary representation are counted. If *integer* is negative, the 0-bits in its two's-complement binary representation are counted. The result is always a non-negative integer. For example:

(logcount 13) $\Rightarrow$ 3	;Binary representation is ...0001101
(logcount -13) $\Rightarrow$ 2	;Binary representation is ...1110011
(logcount 30) $\Rightarrow$ 4	;Binary representation is ...0011110
(logcount -30) $\Rightarrow$ 4	;Binary representation is ...1100010

The following identity always holds:

(logcount x) $\equiv$ (logcount (- (+ x 1)))
            $\equiv$ (logcount (lognot x))

integer-length *integer*   [*Function*]

This function performs the computation

$ceiling(\log_2(\textbf{if } integer < 0 \textbf{ then } - integer \textbf{ else } integer + 1))$

This is useful in two different ways. First, if *integer* is non-negative, then its value can be represented in unsigned binary form in a field whose width in bits is no smaller than (integer-length *integer*). Second, regardless of the sign of *integer*, its value can be represented in signed binary two's-complement form in a field whose width in bits is no smaller than (+ (integer-length *integer*) 1). For example:

(integer-length 0) $\Rightarrow$ 0
(integer-length 1) $\Rightarrow$ 1
(integer-length 3) $\Rightarrow$ 2
(integer-length 4) $\Rightarrow$ 3
(integer-length 7) $\Rightarrow$ 3
(integer-length -1) $\Rightarrow$ 0
(integer-length -4) $\Rightarrow$ 2
(integer-length -7) $\Rightarrow$ 3
(integer-length -8) $\Rightarrow$ 3

Compatibility note: This function is similar to the MacLisp function `haulong`. One may define `haulong` as

`(haulong x) ≡ (integer-length (abs x))`

12.8. Byte Manipulation Functions

Several functions are provided for dealing with an arbitrary-width field of contiguous bits appearing anywhere in an integer. Such a contiguous set of bits is called a *byte*. Here the term *byte* does not imply some fixed number of bits (such as eight), rather a field of arbitrary and user-specifiable width.

The byte-manipulation functions use objects called *byte specifiers* to designate a specific byte position within an integer. The representation of a byte specifier is implementation-dependent; in particular, it may or may not be a number. It is sufficient to know that the function `byte` will construct one, and that the byte-manipulation functions will accept them. The function `byte` accepts two integers representing the *position* and *size* of the byte and returns a byte specifier. Such a specifier designates a byte whose width is *size* and whose bits have weights $2^{position+size-1}$ through $2^{position}$.

byte *size position*   [*Function*]

`byte` takes two integers representing the size and position of a byte and returns a byte specifier suitable for use as an argument to byte-manipulation functions.

byte-size *bytespec*   [*Function*]
byte-position *bytespec*   [*Function*]

Given a byte specifier, `byte-size` returns the size specified as an integer; `byte-position` similarly returns the position. For example:

`(byte-size (byte j k)) ≡ j`
`(byte-position (byte j k)) ≡ k`

ldb *bytespec integer*   [*Function*]

bytespec specifies a byte of *integer* to be extracted. The result is returned as a non-negative integer. For example:

```
(logbitp j (ldb (byte s p) n)) ≡ (and (< j s) (logbitp (+ j p) n))
```

The name of the function ldb means "load byte."

Compatibility note: The MacLisp function haipart can be implemented in terms of ldb as follows:

```
(defun haipart (integer count)
  (let ((x (abs integer)))
    (if (minusp count)
        (ldb (byte (- count) 0) x)
        (ldb (byte count (max 0 (- (integer-length x) count)))
            x))))
```

If the argument *integer* is specified by a form that is a *place* form acceptable to setf, then setf may be used with ldb to modify a byte within the integer that is stored in that *place*. The effect is to perform a dpb operation and then store the result back into the *place*.

ldb-test *bytespec integer*   [*Function*]

ldb-test is a predicate that is true if any of the bits designated by the byte specifier *bytespec* are 1's in *integer*; that is, it is true if the designated field is non-zero.

```
(ldb-test bytespec n) ≡ (not (zerop (ldb bytespec n)))
```

mask-field *bytespec integer*   [*Function*]

This is similar to ldb; however, the result contains the specified byte of *integer* in the position specified by *bytespec*, rather than in position 0 as with ldb. The result therefore agrees with *integer* in the byte specified but has zero-bits everywhere else. For example:

```
(ldb bs (mask-field bs n)) ≡ (ldb bs n)

(logbitp j (mask-field (byte s p) n))
    ≡ (and (>= j p) (< j (+ p s)) (logbitp j n))

(mask-field bs n) ≡ (logand n (dpb -1 bs 0))
```

If the argument *integer* is specified by a form that is a *place* form acceptable to
setf, then setf may be used with mask-field to modify a byte within the integer
that is stored in that *place*. The effect is to perform a deposit-field operation
and then store the result back into the *place*.

---

dpb *newbyte bytespec integer*   [*Function*]

This returns a number that is the same as *integer* except in the bits specified by
bytespec. Let *s* be the size specified by *bytespec*; then the low *s* bits of *newbyte*
appear in the result in the byte specified by *bytespec*. The integer *newbyte* is
therefore interpreted as being right-justified, as if it were the result of ldb. For
example:

```
(logbitp j (dpb m (byte s p) n))
  ≡ (if (and (>= j p) (< j (+ p s)))
        (logbitp (- j p) m)
        (logbitp j n))
```

The name of the function dpb means "deposit byte."

---

deposit-field *newbyte bytespec integer*   [*Function*]

This function is to mask-field as dpb is to ldb. The result is an integer that
contains the bits of *newbyte* within the byte specified by *bytespec*, and elsewhere
contains the bits of *integer*. For example:

```
(logbitp j (deposit-field m (byte s p) n))
  ≡ (if (and (>= j p) (< j (+ p s)))
        (logbitp j m)
        (logbitp j n))
```

Implementation note: If the *bytespec* is a constant, one may of course construct, at compile
time, an equivalent mask *m*, for example by computing (deposit-field -1 *bytespec* 0).
Given this mask *m*, one may then compute

(deposit-field *newbyte bytespec integer*)

by computing

(logior (logand *newbyte* m) (logand *integer* (lognot m)))

where the result of (lognot m) can of course also be computed at compile time. However,
the following expression may also be used and may require fewer temporary registers in
some situations:

(logxor *integer* (logand *m* (logxor *integer newbyte*)))

A related, though possibly less useful, trick is that

```
(let ((z (logand (logxor x y) m)))
  (setq x (logxor z x))
  (setq y (logxor z y)))
```

interchanges those bits of x and y for which the mask m is 1, and leaves alone those bits of x and y for which m is 0.

12.9. Random Numbers

The Common Lisp facility for generating pseudo-random numbers has been carefully defined to make its use reasonably portable. While two implementations may produce different series of pseudo-random numbers, the distribution of values should be relatively independent of such machine-dependent aspects as word size.

random *number* &optional *state*   [*Function*]

(random *n*) accepts a positive number *n* and returns a number of the same kind between zero (inclusive) and *n* (exclusive). The number *n* may be an integer or a floating-point number. An approximately uniform choice distribution is used. If *n* is an integer, each of the possible results occurs with (approximate) probability $1/n$. (The qualifier "approximate" is used because of implementation considerations; in practice, the deviation from uniformity should be quite small.)

The argument *state* must be an object of type random-state; it defaults to the value of the variable *random-state*. This object is used to maintain the state of the pseudo-random-number generator and is altered as a side effect of the random operation.

Compatibility note: random of zero arguments as defined in MacLisp has been omitted because its value is too implementation-dependent (limited by fixnum range).

Implementation note: In general, even if random of zero arguments were defined as in MacLisp, it is not adequate to define (random *n*) for integral *n* to be simply (mod (random) *n*); this fails to be uniformly distributed if *n* is larger than the largest number produced by random, or even if *n* merely approaches this number. This is another reason for omitting random of zero arguments in Common Lisp. Assuming that the underlying mechanism produces "random bits" (possibly in chunks such as fixnums), the best approach is to produce enough random bits to construct an integer *k* some number *d* of bits larger than (integer-length n) (see integer-length), and then compute (mod k n). The quantity d should be at least 7, and preferably 10 or more.

To produce random floating-point numbers in the half-open range $[A, B)$, accepted practice (as determined by a look through the *Collected Algorithms from the ACM*, particularly algorithms 133, 266, 294, and 370) is to compute $X \cdot (B - A) + A$, where X is a floating-point number uniformly distributed over $[0.0, 1.0)$ and computed by calculating a random integer N in the range $[0, M)$ (typically by a multiplicative-congruential or linear-congruential method mod M) and then setting $X = N/M$. See also [27]. If one takes $M = 2^f$, where f is the length of the significand of a floating-point number (and it is in fact common to choose M to be a power of 2), then this method is equivalent to the following assembly-language-level procedure. Assume the representation has no hidden bit. Take a floating-point 0.5, and clobber its entire significand with random bits. Normalize the result if necessary.

For example, on the DEC PDP-10, assume that accumulator T is completely random (all 36 bits are random). Then the code sequence

```
LSH T,-9                  ;Clear high 9 bits; low 27 are random
FSC T,128.                ;Install exponent and normalize
```

will produce in T a random floating-point number uniformly distributed over $[0.0, 1.0)$. (Instead of the LSH instruction, one could do

```
TLZ T,777000              ;That's 777000 octal
```

but if the 36 random bits came from a congruential random-number generator, the high-order bits tend to be "more random" than the low-order ones, and so the LSH would be better for uniform distribution. Ideally all the bits would be the result of high-quality randomness.)

With a hidden-bit representation, normalization is not a problem, but dealing with the hidden bit is. The method can be adapted as follows. Take a floating-point 1.0 and clobber the explicit significand bits with random bits; this produces a random floating-point number in the range $[1.0, 2.0)$. Then simply subtract 1.0. In effect, we let the hidden bit creep in and then subtract it away again.

For example, on the DEC VAX, assume that register T is completely random (but a little less random than on the PDP-10, as it has only 32 random bits). Then the code sequence

```
INSV #^X81,#7,#9,T        ;Install correct sign bit and exponent
SUBF #^F1.0,T             ;Subtract 1.0
```

will produce in T a random floating-point number uniformly distributed over $[0.0, 1.0)$. Again, if the low-order bits are not random enough, then the instruction

```
ROTL #7,T
```

should be performed first.

Implementors may wish to consult reference [41] for a discussion of some efficient methods of generating pseudo-random numbers.

`*random-state*` [*Variable*]

This variable holds a data structure, an object of type `random-state`, that encodes the internal state of the random-number generator that `random` uses by default. The nature of this data structure is implementation-dependent. It may be printed out and successfully read back in, but may or may not function correctly as a random-number state object in another implementation. A call to `random` will perform a side effect on this data structure. Lambda-binding this variable to a different random-number state object will correctly save and restore the old state object.

`make-random-state &optional` *state* [*Function*]

This function returns a new object of type `random-state`, suitable for use as the value of the variable `*random-state*`. If *state* is `nil` or omitted, `make-random-state` returns a *copy* of the current random-number state object (the value of the variable `*random-state*`). If *state* is a state object, a copy of that state object is returned. If *state* is `t`, then a new state object is returned that has been "randomly" initialized by some means (such as by a time-of-day clock).

Rationale: Common Lisp purposely provides no way to initialize a `random-state` object from a user-specified "seed." The reason for this is that the number of bits of state information in a `random-state` object may vary widely from one implementation to another, and there is no simple way to guarantee that any user-specified seed value will be "random enough." Instead, the initialization of `random-state` objects is left to the implementor in the case where the argument `t` is given to `make-random-state`.

To handle the common situation of executing the same program many times in a reproducible manner, where that program uses `random`, the following procedure may be used:

1. Evaluate `(make-random-state t)` to create a `random-state` object.

2. Write that object to a file, using `print`, for later use.

3. Whenever the program is to be run, first use `read` to create a copy of the `random-state` object from the printed representation in the file. Then use the `random-state` object newly created by the `read` operation to initialize the random-number generator for the program.

It is for the sake of this procedure for reproducible execution that implementations are required to provide a read/print syntax for objects of type `random-state`.

It is also possible to make copies of a `random-state` object directly without going through the print/read process, simply by using the `make-random-state` function to copy the object; this allows the same sequence of random numbers to be generated many times within a single program.

Implementation note: A recommended way to implement the type random-state is effectively to use the machinery for defstruct. The usual structure syntax may then be used for printing random-state objects; one might look something like

```
#S(RANDOM-STATE DATA #(14 49 98436589 786345 8734658324 ...))
```

where the components are of course completely implementation-dependent.

random-state-p *object*   [*Function*]

random-state-p is true if its argument is a random-state object, and otherwise is false.

```
(random-state-p x) ≡ (typep x 'random-state)
```

12.10. Implementation Parameters

The values of the named constants defined in this section are implementation-dependent. They may be useful for parameterizing code in some situations.

most-positive-fixnum   [*Constant*]
most-negative-fixnum   [*Constant*]

The value of most-positive-fixnum is that fixnum closest in value to positive infinity provided by the implementation.

The value of most-negative-fixnum is that fixnum closest in value to negative infinity provided by the implementation.

X3J13 voted in January 1989 ⟨76⟩ to specify that fixnum must be a supertype of the type (signed-byte 16), and additionally that the value of array-dimension-limit must be a fixnum. This implies that the value of most-negative-fixnum must be less than or equal to -2^{15}, and the value of most-positive-fixnum must be greater than or equal to both $2^{15} - 1$ and the value of array-dimension-limit.

most-positive-short-float   [*Constant*]
least-positive-short-float   [*Constant*]
least-negative-short-float   [*Constant*]
most-negative-short-float   [*Constant*]

The value of most-positive-short-float is that short-format floating-point number closest in value to (but not equal to) positive infinity provided by the implementation.

The value of `least-positive-short-float` is that positive short-format floating-point number closest in value to (but not equal to) zero provided by the implementation.

The value of `least-negative-short-float` is that negative short-format floating-point number closest in value to (but not equal to) zero provided by the implementation. (Note that even if an implementation supports minus zero as a distinct short floating-point value, `least-negative-short-float` must not be minus zero.)

X3J13 voted in June 1989 ⟨79⟩ to clarify that these definitions are to be taken quite literally. In implementations that support denormalized numbers, the values of `least-positive-short-float` and `least-negative-short-float` may be denormalized.

The value of `most-negative-short-float` is that short-format floating-point number closest in value to (but not equal to) negative infinity provided by the implementation.

`most-positive-single-float`	[*Constant*]
`least-positive-single-float`	[*Constant*]
`least-negative-single-float`	[*Constant*]
`most-negative-single-float`	[*Constant*]
`most-positive-double-float`	[*Constant*]
`least-positive-double-float`	[*Constant*]
`least-negative-double-float`	[*Constant*]
`most-negative-double-float`	[*Constant*]
`most-positive-long-float`	[*Constant*]
`least-positive-long-float`	[*Constant*]
`least-negative-long-float`	[*Constant*]
`most-negative-long-float`	[*Constant*]

These are analogous to the constants defined above for short-format floating-point numbers.

`least-positive-normalized-short-float`	[*Constant*]
`least-negative-normalized-short-float`	[*Constant*]

X3J13 voted in June 1989 ⟨79⟩ to add these constants to the language.

The value of `least-positive-normalized-short-float` is that positive normalized short-format floating-point number closest in value to (but not equal to) zero provided by the implementation. In implementations that do not support denormalized numbers this may be the same as the value of least-positive-short-float.

The value of least-negative-normalized-short-float is that negative normalized short-format floating-point number closest in value to (but not equal to) zero provided by the implementation. (Note that even if an implementation supports minus zero as a distinct short floating-point value, least-negative-normalized-short-float must not be minus zero.) In implementations that do not support denormalized numbers this may be the same as the value of least-positive-short-float.

least-positive-normalized-single-float	[Constant]
least-negative-normalized-single-float	[Constant]
least-positive-normalized-double-float	[Constant]
least-negative-normalized-double-float	[Constant]
least-positive-normalized-long-float	[Constant]
least-negative-normalized-long-float	[Constant]

These are analogous to the constants defined above for short-format floating-point numbers.

short-float-epsilon	[Constant]
single-float-epsilon	[Constant]
double-float-epsilon	[Constant]
long-float-epsilon	[Constant]

These constants have as value, for each floating-point format, the smallest positive floating-point number e of that format such that the expression

```
(not (= (float 1 e) (+ (float 1 e) e)))
```

is true when actually evaluated.

short-float-negative-epsilon	[Constant]
single-float-negative-epsilon	[Constant]
double-float-negative-epsilon	[Constant]
long-float-negative-epsilon	[Constant]

These constants have as value, for each floating-point format, the smallest positive floating-point number e of that format such that the expression

```
(not (= (float 1 e) (- (float 1 e) e)))
```

is true when actually evaluated.

13

Characters

Common Lisp provides a character data type; objects of this type represent printed symbols such as letters.

In general, characters in Common Lisp are not true objects; eq cannot be counted upon to operate on them reliably. In particular, it is possible that the expression

```
(let ((x z) (y z)) (eq x y))
```

may be false rather than true, if the value of z is a character.

Rationale: This odd breakdown of eq in the case of characters allows the implementor enough design freedom to produce exceptionally efficient code on conventional architectures. In this respect the treatment of characters exactly parallels that of numbers, as described in chapter 12.

If two objects are to be compared for "identity," but either might be a character, then the predicate eql is probably appropriate.

X3J13 voted in March 1989 ⟨11⟩ to approve the following definitions and terminology for use in discussing character facilities in Common Lisp.

A *character repertoire* defines a collection of characters independent of their specific rendered image or font. (This corresponds to the mathematical notion of a set, but the term *character set* is avoided here because it has been used in the past to mean both what is here called a repertoire and what is here called a coded character set.) Character repertoires are specified independent of coding and their characters are identified only with a unique *character label*, a graphic symbol, and a character description. As an example, table 13-1 shows the character labels, graphic symbols, and character descriptions for all of the characters in the repertoire standard-char except for #\Space and #\Newline.

Every Common Lisp implementation must support the standard character repertoire as well as repertoires named base-character, extended-character, and

Table 13-1: Standard Character Labels, Glyphs, and Descriptions

			SM05	@	commercial at	SD13	`	grave accent
SP02	!	exclamation mark	LA02	A	capital A	LA01	a	small a
SP04	"	quotation mark	LB02	B	capital B	LB01	b	small b
SM01	#	number sign	LC02	C	capital C	LC01	c	small c
SC03	$	dollar sign	LD02	D	capital D	LD01	d	small d
SM02	%	percent sign	LE02	E	capital E	LE01	e	small e
SM03	&	ampersand	LF02	F	capital F	LF01	f	small f
SP05	´	apostrophe	LG02	G	capital G	LG01	g	small g
SP06	(	left parenthesis	LH02	H	capital H	LH01	h	small h
SP07	)	right parenthesis	LI02	I	capital I	LI01	i	small i
SM04	*	asterisk	LJ02	J	capital J	LJ01	j	small j
SA01	+	plus sign	LK02	K	capital K	LK01	k	small k
SP08	,	comma	LL02	L	capital L	LL01	l	small l
SP10	-	hyphen or minus sign	LM02	M	capital M	LM01	m	small m
SP11	.	period or full stop	LN02	N	capital N	LN01	n	small n
SP12	/	solidus	LO02	O	capital O	LO01	o	small o
ND10	0	digit 0	LP02	P	capital P	LP01	p	small p
ND01	1	digit 1	LQ02	Q	capital Q	LQ01	q	small q
ND02	2	digit 2	LR02	R	capital R	LR01	r	small r
ND03	3	digit 3	LS02	S	capital S	LS01	s	small s
ND04	4	digit 4	LT02	T	capital T	LT01	t	small t
ND05	5	digit 5	LU02	U	capital U	LU01	u	small u
ND06	6	digit 6	LV02	V	capital V	LV01	v	small v
ND07	7	digit 7	LW02	W	capital W	LW01	w	small w
ND08	8	digit 8	LX02	X	capital X	LX01	x	small x
ND09	9	digit 9	LY02	Y	capital Y	LY01	y	small y
SP13	:	colon	LZ02	Z	capital Z	LZ01	z	small z
SP14	;	semicolon	SM06	[	left square bracket	SM11	{	left curly bracket
SA03	<	less-than sign	SM07	\	reverse solidus	SM13	|	vertical bar
SA04	=	equals sign	SM08	]	right square bracket	SM14	}	right curly bracket
SA05	>	greater-than sign	SD15	^	circumflex accent	SD19	~	tilde
SP15	?	question mark	SP09	_	low line			

The characters in this table plus the space and newline characters make up the standard Common Lisp character repertoire (type standard-char). The character labels and character descriptions shown here are taken from ISO standard 6937/2 . The first character of the label categorizes the character as Latin, Numeric, or Special.

character. Other repertoires may be supported as well. X3J13 voted in June 1989 ⟨122⟩ to specify that names of repertoires may be used as type specifiers. Such types must be subtypes of `character`; that is, in a given implementation the repertoire named `character` must encompass all the character objects supported by that implementation.

A *coded character set* is a character repertoire plus an *encoding* that provides a bijective mapping between each character in the set and a number (typically a non-negative integer) that serves as the character representation. There are numerous internationally standardized coded character sets.

A character may be included in one or more character repertoires. Similarly, a character may be included in one or more coded character sets.

To ensure that each character is uniquely defined, we may use a universal registry of characters that incorporates a collection of distinguished repertoires called *character scripts* that form an exhaustive partition of all characters. That is, each character is included in exactly one character script. (Draft ISO 10646 Coded Character Set Standard, if eventually approved as a standard, may become the practical realization of this universal registry.)

(X3J13 voted in June 1989 ⟨122⟩ to specify that an implementation must document the character scripts it supports. For each script the documentation should discuss character labels, glyphs, and descriptions; any canonicalization processes performed by the reader that result in treating distinct characters as equivalent; any canonicalization performed by `format` in processing directives; the behavior of `char-upcase`, `char-downcase`, and the predicates `alpha-char-p`, `upper-case-p`, `lower-case-p`, `both-case-p`, `graphic-char-p`, `alphanumericp`, `char-equal`, `char-not-equal`, `char-lessp`, `char-greaterp`, `char-not-greaterp`, and `char-not-lessp` for characters in the script; and behavior with respect to input and output, including coded character sets and external coding schemes.)

In Common Lisp a *character* data object is identified by its *character code*, a unique numerical code. Each character code is composed from a character script and a character label. The convention by which a character script and character label compose a character code is implementation dependent. [X3J13 did not approve all parts of the proposal from its Subcommittee on Characters. As a result, some features that were approved appear to have no purpose. X3J13 wished to support the standardization by ISO of character scripts and coded character sets but declined to design facilities for use in Common Lisp until there has been more progress by ISO in this area. The approval of the terminology for scripts and labels gives a hint to implementors of likely directions for Common Lisp in the future.]

A character object that is classified as *graphic*, or displayable, has an associated *glpyh*. The glyph is the visual representation of the character. All other character data objects are classified as *non-graphic*.

This terminology assigns names to Common Lisp concepts in a manner consistent with related concepts discussed in various ISO standards for coded character sets and provides a demarcation between standardization activities. For example, facilities for manipulating characters, character scripts, and coded character sets are properly defined by a Common Lisp standard, but Common Lisp should not define standard character sets or standard character scripts.

13.1. Character Attributes

Every character has three attributes: code, bits, and font. The code attribute is intended to distinguish among the printed glyphs and formatting functions for characters. The bits attribute allows extra flags to be associated with a character. The font attribute permits a specification of the style of the glyphs (such as italics).

The treatment of character attributes in Common Lisp has not been entirely successful. The font attribute has not been widely used, for two reasons. First, a single integer, limited in most implementations to 255 at most, is not an adequate, convenient, or portable representation for a font. Second, in many applications where font information matters it is more convenient or more efficient to represent font information as shift codes that apply to many characters, rather than attaching font information separately to each character.

As for the bits attribute, it was intended to support character input from extended keyboards having extra "shift" keys. This, in turn, was imagined to support the programming of a portable EMACS-like editor in Common Lisp. (The EMACS command set is most convenient when the keyboard has separate "control" and "meta" keys.) The bits attribute has been used in the implementation of such editors and other interactive interfaces. However, software that relies crucially on these extended characters will not be portable to Common Lisp implementations that do not support them.

X3J13 voted in March 1989 ⟨11⟩ and in June 1989 ⟨122⟩ to revise considerably the treatment of characters in the language. The bits and font attributes are eliminated; instead a character may have *implementation-defined attributes*. The treatment of such attributes by existing character-handling functions is carefully constrained by certain rules.

Implementations are free to continue to support bits and font attributes, but they are formally regarded as implementation-defined attributes. The rules are generally consistent with the previous treatment of the bits and font attributes. My guess is that the font attribute as currently defined will wither away, but the bits attribute as defined by the first edition will continue to be supported as a *de facto* standard extension, because it fills a useful small purpose.

char-code-limit [*Constant*]

The value of char-code-limit is a non-negative integer that is the upper exclusive bound on values produced by the function char-code, which returns the *code* component of a given character; that is, the values returned by char-code are non-negative and strictly less than the value of char-code-limit.

Common Lisp does not at present explicitly guarantee that all integers between zero and the value of char-code-limit are valid character codes, and so it is wise in any case for the programmer to assume that the space of assigned character codes may be sparse.

char-font-limit [*Constant*]

The value of char-font-limit is a non-negative integer that is the upper exclusive bound on values produced by the function char-font, which returns the *font* component of a given character; that is, the values returned by char-font are non-negative and strictly less than the value of char-font-limit.

Implementation note: No Common Lisp implementation is required to support non-zero font attributes; if it does not, then char-font-limit should be 1.

X3J13 voted in March 1989 ⟨11⟩ to eliminate char-font-limit.

Experience has shown that numeric codes are not an especially convenient, let alone portable, representation for font information. A system based on typeface names, type styles, and point sizes would be much better. (Macintosh software developers made the same discovery and have recently converted to a new font identification scheme.)

char-bits-limit [*Constant*]

The value of char-bits-limit is a non-negative integer that is the upper exclusive bound on values produced by the function char-bits, which returns the *bits* component of a given character; that is, the values returned by char-bits are non-negative and strictly less than the value of char-bits-limit. Note that the value of char-bits-limit will be a power of 2.

Implementation note: No Common Lisp implementation is required to support non-zero bits attributes; if it does not, then char-bits-limit should be 1.

X3J13 voted in March 1989 ⟨11⟩ to eliminate char-bits-limit.

13.2. Predicates on Characters

The predicate `characterp` may be used to determine whether any Lisp object is a character object.

`standard-char-p` *char*   [*Function*]

The argument *char* must be a character object. `standard-char-p` is true if the argument is a "standard character," that is, an object of type `standard-char`.

Note that any character with a non-zero bits or font attribute is non-standard.

`graphic-char-p` *char*   [*Function*]

The argument *char* must be a character object. `graphic-char-p` is true if the argument is a "graphic" (printing) character, and false if it is a "non-graphic" (formatting or control) character. Graphic characters have a standard textual representation as a single glyph, such as A or * or =. By convention, the space character is considered to be graphic. Of the standard characters all but #\Newline are graphic. The semi-standard characters #\Backspace, #\Tab, #\Rubout, #\Linefeed, #\Return, and #\Page are not graphic.

Programs may assume that graphic characters of font 0 are all of the same width when printed, for example, for purposes of columnar formatting. (This does not prohibit the use of a variable-pitch font as font 0, but merely implies that every implementation of Common Lisp must provide *some* mode of operation in which font 0 is a fixed-pitch font.) Portable programs should assume that, in general, non-graphic characters and characters of other fonts may be of varying widths.

Any character with a non-zero bits attribute is non-graphic.

`string-char-p` *char*   [*Function*]

The argument *char* must be a character object. `string-char-p` is true if *char* can be stored into a string, and otherwise is false. Any character that satisfies `standard-char-p` also satisfies `string-char-p`; others may also.

X3J13 voted in March 1989 ⟨11⟩ to eliminate `string-char-p`.

`alpha-char-p` *char*   [*Function*]

The argument *char* must be a character object. `alpha-char-p` is true if the argument is an alphabetic character, and otherwise is false.

If a character is alphabetic, then it is perforce graphic. Therefore any character with a non-zero bits attribute cannot be alphabetic. Whether a character is alphabetic may depend on its font number.

Of the standard characters (as defined by standard-char-p), the letters A through Z and a through z are alphabetic.

upper-case-p *char*	[*Function*]
lower-case-p *char*	[*Function*]
both-case-p *char*	[*Function*]

The argument *char* must be a character object.

upper-case-p is true if the argument is an uppercase character, and otherwise is false.

lower-case-p is true if the argument is a lowercase character, and otherwise is false.

both-case-p is true if the argument is an uppercase character and there is a corresponding lowercase character (which can be obtained using char-downcase), or if the argument is a lowercase character and there is a corresponding uppercase character (which can be obtained using char-upcase).

If a character is either uppercase or lowercase, it is necessarily alphabetic (and therefore is graphic, and therefore has a zero bits attribute). However, it is permissible in theory for an alphabetic character to be neither uppercase nor lowercase (in a non-Roman font, for example).

Of the standard characters (as defined by standard-char-p), the letters A through Z are uppercase and a through z are lowercase.

digit-char-p *char* &optional (*radix* 10) [*Function*]

The argument *char* must be a character object, and *radix* must be a non-negative integer. If *char* is not a digit of the radix specified by *radix*, then digit-char-p is false; otherwise it returns a non-negative integer that is the "weight" of *char* in that radix.

Digits are necessarily graphic characters.

Of the standard characters (as defined by standard-char-p), the characters 0 through 9, A through Z, and a through z are digits. The weights of 0 through 9 are the integers 0 through 9, and of A through Z (and also a through z) are 10 through 35. digit-char-p returns the weight for one of these digits if and only if its weight is strictly less than *radix*. Thus, for example, the digits for radix 16 are

0 1 2 3 4 5 6 7 8 9 A B C D E F

Here is an example of the use of digit-char-p:

```
(defun convert-string-to-integer (str &optional (radix 10))
  "Given a digit string and optional radix, return an integer."
  (do ((j 0 (+ j 1))
       (n 0 (+ (* n radix)
               (or (digit-char-p (char str j) radix)
                   (error "Bad radix-~D digit: ~C"
                          radix
                          (char str j))))))
      ((= j (length str)) n)))
```

alphanumericp *char*   [*Function*]

The argument *char* must be a character object. alphanumericp is true if *char* is either alphabetic or numeric. By definition,

```
(alphanumericp x)
  ≡ (or (alpha-char-p x) (not (null (digit-char-p x))))
```

Alphanumeric characters are therefore necessarily graphic (as defined by the predicate graphic-char-p).

Of the standard characters (as defined by standard-char-p), the characters 0 through 9, A through Z, and a through z are alphanumeric.

char= *character* &rest *more-characters*   [*Function*]
char/= *character* &rest *more-characters*   [*Function*]
char< *character* &rest *more-characters*   [*Function*]
char> *character* &rest *more-characters*   [*Function*]
char<= *character* &rest *more-characters*   [*Function*]
char>= *character* &rest *more-characters*   [*Function*]

The arguments must all be character objects. These functions compare the objects using the implementation-dependent total ordering on characters, in a manner analogous to numeric comparisons by = and related functions.

The total ordering on characters is guaranteed to have the following properties:

- The standard alphanumeric characters obey the following partial ordering:

```
A<B<C<D<E<F<G<H<I<J<K<L<M<N<O<P<Q<R<S<T<U<V<W<X<Y<Z
a<b<c<d<e<f<g<h<i<j<k<l<m<n<o<p<q<r<s<t<u<v<w<x<y<z
0<1<2<3<4<5<6<7<8<9
```

either 9<A *or* Z<0
either 9<a *or* z<0

This implies that alphabetic ordering holds within each case (upper and lower), and that the digits as a group are not interleaved with letters. However, the ordering or possible interleaving of uppercase letters and lowercase letters is unspecified. (Note that both the ASCII and the EBCDIC character sets conform to this specification. As it happens, neither ordering interleaves uppercase and lowercase letters: in the ASCII ordering, 9<A and Z<a, whereas in the EBCDIC ordering z<A and Z<0.)

- If two characters have the same bits and font attributes, then their ordering by char< is consistent with the numerical ordering by the predicate < on their code attributes.

- If two characters differ in any attribute (code, bits, or font), then they are different.

X3J13 voted in March 1989 ⟨11⟩ to replace the notion of bits and font attributes with that of implementation-defined attributes.

- If two characters have identical implementation-defined attributes, then their ordering by char< is consistent with the numerical ordering by the predicate < on their codes, and similarly for char>, char<=, and char>=.

- If two characters differ in any implementation-defined attribute, then they are not char=.

The total ordering is not necessarily the same as the total ordering on the integers produced by applying char-int to the characters (although it is a reasonable implementation technique to use that ordering).

While alphabetic characters of a given case must be properly ordered, they need not be contiguous; thus (char<= #\a x #\z) is *not* a valid way of determining whether or not x is a lowercase letter. That is why a separate lower-case-p predicate is provided.

(char= #\d #\d) is true.
(char/= #\d #\d) is false.
(char= #\d #\x) is false.
(char/= #\d #\x) is true.
(char= #\d #\D) is false.
(char/= #\d #\D) is true.
(char= #\d #\d #\d #\d) is true.
(char/= #\d #\d #\d #\d) is false.

```
(char= #\d #\d #\x #\d) is false.
(char/= #\d #\d #\x #\d) is false.
(char= #\d #\y #\x #\c) is false.
(char/= #\d #\y #\x #\c) is true.
(char= #\d #\c #\d) is false.
(char/= #\d #\c #\d) is false.
(char< #\d #\x) is true.
(char<= #\d #\x) is true.
(char< #\d #\d) is false.
(char<= #\d #\d) is true.
(char< #\a #\e #\y #\z) is true.
(char<= #\a #\e #\y #\z) is true.
(char< #\a #\e #\e #\y) is false.
(char<= #\a #\e #\e #\y) is true.
(char> #\e #\d) is true.
(char>= #\e #\d) is true.
(char> #\d #\c #\b #\a) is true.
(char>= #\d #\c #\b #\a) is true.
(char> #\d #\d #\c #\a) is false.
(char>= #\d #\d #\c #\a) is true.
(char> #\e #\d #\b #\c #\a) is false.
(char>= #\e #\d #\b #\c #\a) is false.
(char> #\z #\A) may be true or false.
(char> #\Z #\a) may be true or false.
```

There is no requirement that (eq c1 c2) be true merely because (char= c1 c2) is true. While eq may distinguish two character objects that char= does not, it is distinguishing them not as *characters*, but in some sense on the basis of a lower-level implementation characteristic. (Of course, if (eq c1 c2) is true, then one may expect (char= c1 c2) to be true.) However, eql and equal compare character objects in the same way that char= does.

char-equal *character* &rest *more-characters*   [*Function*]
char-not-equal *character* &rest *more-characters*   [*Function*]
char-lessp *character* &rest *more-characters*   [*Function*]
char-greaterp *character* &rest *more-characters*   [*Function*]
char-not-greaterp *character* &rest *more-characters*   [*Function*]
char-not-lessp *character* &rest *more-characters*   [*Function*]

The predicate char-equal is like char=, and similarly for the others, except according to a different ordering such that differences of bits attributes and case are ignored, and font information is taken into account in an implementation-dependent manner.

X3J13 voted in March 1989 ⟨11⟩ to replace the notion of bits and font attributes with that of implementation-defined attributes. The effect, if any, of each such attribute on the behavior of `char-equal`, `char-not-equal`, `char-lessp`, `char-greaterp`, `char-not-greaterp`, and `char-not-lessp` must be specified as part of the definition of that attribute.

For the standard characters, the ordering is such that A=a, B=b, and so on, up to Z=z, and furthermore either 9<A or Z<0. For example:

```
(char-equal #\A #\a) is true.
(char= #\A #\a) is false.
(char-equal #\A #\Control-A) is true.
```

The ordering may depend on the font information. For example, an implementation might decree that (`char-equal` #\p #\p) be true, but that (`char-equal` #\p #\π) be false (where #\π is a lowercase p in some font). Assuming italics to be in font 1 and the Greek alphabet in font 2, this is the same as saying that (`char-equal` #0\p #1\p) may be true and at the same time (`char-equal` #0\p #2\p) may be false.

13.3. Character Construction and Selection

These functions may be used to extract attributes of a character and to construct new characters.

`char-code` *char*   [*Function*]

The argument *char* must be a character object. `char-code` returns the code attribute of the character object; this will be a non-negative integer less than the (normal) value of the variable `char-code-limit`.

This is usually what you need in order to treat a character as an index into a vector. The length of the vector should then be equal to `char-code-limit`. Be careful how you initialize this vector; remember that you cannot necessarily expect all non-negative integers less than `char-code-limit` to be valid character codes.

`char-bits` *char*   [*Function*]

The argument *char* must be a character object. `char-bits` returns the bits attribute of the character object; this will be a non-negative integer less than the (normal) value of the variable `char-bits-limit`.

| X3J13 voted in March 1989 ⟨11⟩ to eliminate char-bits.

char-font *char* [*Function*]

The argument *char* must be a character object. char-font returns the font attribute of the character object; this will be a non-negative integer less than the (normal) value of the variable char-font-limit.

| X3J13 voted in March 1989 ⟨11⟩ to eliminate char-font.

The references to the "normal" values of the "variables" char-code-limit, char-bits-limit, and char-font-limit in the descriptions of char-code, char-bits, and char-font were an oversight on my part. Early in the design of Common Lisp they were indeed variables, but they are at present defined to be constants, and their values therefore are always normal and should not change. But this point is now moot.

code-char *code* &optional (*bits* 0) (*font* 0) [*Function*]

All three arguments must be non-negative integers. If it is possible in the implementation to construct a character object whose code attribute is *code*, whose bits attribute is *bits*, and whose font attribute is *font*, then such an object is returned; otherwise nil is returned.

For any integers *c*, *b*, and *f*, if (code-char *c b f*) is not nil then

```
(char-code (code-char c b f)) ⇒ c
(char-bits (code-char c b f)) ⇒ b
(char-font (code-char c b f)) ⇒ f
```

If the font and bits attributes of a character object c are zero, then it is the case that

```
(char= (code-char (char-code c)) c)
```

is true.

X3J13 voted in March 1989 ⟨11⟩ to eliminate the *bits* and *font* arguments from the specification of code-char.

make-char *char* &optional (*bits* 0) (*font* 0) [*Function*]

The argument *char* must be a character, and *bits* and *font* must be non-negative integers. If it is possible in the implementation to construct a character object whose code attribute is the same as the code attribute of *char*, whose bits attribute

is *bits*, and whose font attribute is *font*, then such an object is returned; otherwise
nil is returned.

If *bits* and *font* are zero, then make-char cannot fail. This implies that for every
character object one can "turn off" its bits and font attributes.

X3J13 voted in March 1989 ⟨11⟩ to eliminate make-char.

13.4. Character Conversions

These functions perform various transformations on characters, including case conversions.

character *object*   [*Function*]

The function character coerces its argument to be a character if possible; see
coerce.

(character x) ≡ (coerce x ´character)

char-upcase *char*   [*Function*]
char-downcase *char*   [*Function*]

The argument *char* must be a character object. char-upcase attempts to convert
its argument to an uppercase equivalent; char-downcase attempts to convert its
argument to a lowercase equivalent.

char-upcase returns a character object with the same font and bits attributes
as *char*, but with possibly a different code attribute. If the code is different from
char's, then the predicate lower-case-p is true of *char*, and upper-case-p is
true of the result character. Moreover, if (char= (char-upcase x) x) is *not*
true, then it is true that

(char= (char-downcase (char-upcase x)) x)

Similarly, char-downcase returns a character object with the same font and bits
attributes as *char*, but with possibly a different code attribute. If the code is different
from *char*'s, then the predicate upper-case-p is true of *char*, and lower-case-p
is true of the result character. Moreover, if (char= (char-downcase x) x) is
not true, then it is true that

(char= (char-upcase (char-downcase x)) x)

Note that the action of char-upcase and char-downcase may depend on the bits and font attributes of the character. In particular, they have no effect on a character with a non-zero bits attribute, because such characters are by definition not alphabetic. See alpha-char-p.

X3J13 voted in March 1989 ⟨11⟩ to replace the notion of bits and font attributes with that of implementation-defined attributes. The effect of char-upcase and char-downcase is to preserve implementation-defined attributes.

---

digit-char *weight* &optional (*radix* 10) (*font* 0)   [*Function*]

All arguments must be integers. digit-char determines whether or not it is possible to construct a character object whose font attribute is *font*, and whose *code* is such that the result character has the weight *weight* when considered as a digit of the radix *radix* (see the predicate digit-char-p). It returns such a character if that is possible, and otherwise returns nil.

digit-char cannot return nil if *font* is zero, *radix* is between 2 and 36 inclusive, and *weight* is non-negative and less than *radix*.

If more than one character object can encode such a weight in the given radix, one will be chosen consistently by any given implementation; moreover, among the standard characters, uppercase letters are preferred to lowercase letters. For example:

```
(digit-char 7) ⇒ #\7
(digit-char 12) ⇒ nil
(digit-char 12 16) ⇒ #\C      ;not #\c
(digit-char 6 2) ⇒ nil
(digit-char 1 2) ⇒ #\1
```

Note that no argument is provided for specifying the *bits* component of the returned character, because a digit cannot have a non-zero *bits* component. The reasoning is that every digit is graphic (see digit-char-p) and no graphic character has a non-zero *bits* component (see graphic-char-p).

X3J13 voted in March 1989 ⟨11⟩ to eliminate the *font* argument from the specification of digit-char.

---

char-int *char*   [*Function*]

The argument *char* must be a character object. char-int returns a non-negative integer encoding the character object.

If the font and bits attributes of *char* are zero, then char-int returns the same integer char-code would. Also, `(char= c1 c2) ≡ (= (char-int c1) (char-int c2))`

for characters c1 and c2.

This function is provided primarily for the purpose of hashing characters.

int-char *integer*   [*Function*]

The argument must be a non-negative integer. int-char returns a character object c such that (char-int c) is equal to *integer*, if possible; otherwise int-char returns false.

X3J13 voted in March 1989 ⟨11⟩ to eliminate int-char.

char-name *char*   [*Function*]

The argument *char* must be a character object. If the character has a name, then that name (a string) is returned; otherwise nil is returned. All characters that have zero font and bits attributes and that are non-graphic (do not satisfy the predicate graphic-char-p) have names. Graphic characters may or may not have names.

The standard newline and space characters have the respective names Newline and Space. The semi-standard characters have the names Tab, Page, Rubout, Linefeed, Return, and Backspace.

Characters that have names can be notated as #\ followed by the name. (See section 22.1.4.) Although the name may be written in any case, it is stylish to capitalize it thus: #\Space.

char-name will only locate "simple" character names; it will not construct names such as Control-Space on the basis of the character's bits attribute.

The easiest way to get a name that includes the bits attribute of a character c is (format nil "~:C" c).

name-char *name*   [*Function*]

The argument name must be an object coerceable to a string as if by the function string. If the name is the same as the name of a character object (as determined by string-equal), that object is returned; otherwise nil is returned.

13.5. Character Control-Bit Functions

Common Lisp provides explicit names for four bits of the bits attribute: *Control*, *Meta*, *Hyper*, and *Super*. The following definitions are provided for manipulating these. Each Common Lisp implementation provides these functions for compatibility, even if it does not support any or all of the bits named below.

char-control-bit   [*Constant*]
char-meta-bit   [*Constant*]
char-super-bit   [*Constant*]
char-hyper-bit   [*Constant*]

The values of these named constants are the "weights" (as integers) for the four named control bits. The weight of the control bit is 1; of the meta bit, 2; of the super bit, 4; and of the hyper bit, 8.

If a given implementation of Common Lisp does not support a particular bit, then the corresponding constant is zero instead.

X3J13 voted in March 1989 ⟨11⟩ to eliminate all four of the constants char-control-bit, char-meta-bit, char-super-bit, and char-hyper-bit.

When Common Lisp was first designed, keyboards with "extra bits" were relatively rare. The bits attribute was originally designed to support input from keyboards in use at Stanford and M.I.T. circa 1981.

Since that time such extended keyboards have come into wider use. Notable here are the keyboards associated with certain personal computers and workstations. For example, in some specific applications the *command* and *option* keys of Apple Macintosh keyboards have had the connotations of *control* and *meta*. Macintosh II extended keyboards also have keys marked *control* whose use is analogous to that of *hyper* on the old M.I.T. keyboards. IBM PC personal computer keyboards have *alt* keys that function much like *meta* keys; similarly, keyboards on Sun workstations have keys very much like *meta* keys but labelled *left* and *right*.

char-bit *char name*   [*Function*]

char-bit takes a character object *char* and the name of a bit, and returns non-nil if the bit of that name is set in *char*, or nil if the bit is not set in *char*. For example:

(char-bit #\Control-X :control) ⇒ *true*

Valid values for *name* are implementation-dependent, but typically are :control, :meta, :hyper, and :super. It is an error to give char-bit the name of a bit not supported by the implementation.

If the argument *char* is specified by a form that is a *place* form acceptable to setf, then setf may be used with char-bit to modify a bit of the character stored in that *place*. The effect is to perform a `set-char-bit` operation and then store the result back into the *place*.

| X3J13 voted in March 1989 ⟨11⟩ to eliminate `char-bit`.

`set-char-bit` *char name newvalue*   [*Function*]

`char-bit` takes a character object *char*, the name of a bit, and a flag. A character is returned that is just like *char* except that the named bit is set or reset according to whether *newvalue* is non-`nil` or `nil`. Valid values for *name* are implementation-dependent, but typically are `:control`, `:meta`, `:hyper`, and `:super`. For example:

```
(set-char-bit #\X :control t) ⇒ #\Control-X
(set-char-bit #\Control-X :control t) ⇒ #\Control-X
(set-char-bit #\Control-X :control nil) ⇒ #\X
```

| X3J13 voted in March 1989 ⟨11⟩ to eliminate `set-char-bit`.

14

Sequences

The type sequence encompasses both lists and vectors (one-dimensional arrays). While these are different data structures with different structural properties leading to different algorithmic uses, they do have a common property: each contains an ordered set of elements. Note that nil is considered to be a sequence of length zero.

Some operations are useful on both lists and arrays because they deal with ordered sets of elements. One may ask the number of elements, reverse the ordering, extract a subsequence, and so on. For such purposes Common Lisp provides a set of generic functions on sequences.

Note that this remark, predating the design of the Common Lisp Object System, uses the term "generic" in a generic sense, and not necessarily in the technical sense used by CLOS (see chapter 2).

elt	reverse	map	remove
length	nreverse	some	remove-duplicates
subseq	concatenate	every	delete
copy-seq	position	notany	delete-duplicates
fill	find	notevery	substitute
replace	sort	reduce	nsubstitute
count	merge	search	mismatch

Some of these operations come in more than one version. Such versions are indicated by adding a suffix (or occasionally a prefix) to the basic name of the operation. In addition, many operations accept one or more optional keyword arguments that can modify the operation in various ways.

If the operation requires testing sequence elements according to some criterion, then the criterion may be specified in one of two ways. The basic operation accepts an item, and elements are tested for being eql to that item. (A test other than eql can be specified by the :test or :test-not keyword. It is an error

to use both of these keywords in the same call.) The variants formed by adding
-if and -if-not to the basic operation name do not take an item, but instead a
one-argument predicate, and elements are tested for satisfying or not satisfying the
predicate. As an example,

(remove *item sequence*)

returns a copy of *sequence* from which all elements eql to *item* have been removed;

(remove *item sequence* :test #'equal)

returns a copy of *sequence* from which all elements equal to *item* have been
removed;

(remove-if #'numberp *sequence*)

returns a copy of *sequence* from which all numbers have been removed.

If an operation tests elements of a sequence in any manner, the keyword argument
:key, if not nil, should be a function of one argument that will extract from an
element the part to be tested in place of the whole element. For example, the effect
of the MacLisp expression (assq item seq) could be obtained by

(find *item sequence* :test #'eq :key #'car)

This searches for the first element of *sequence* whose *car* is eq to *item*.

X3J13 voted in June 1988 ⟨90⟩ to allow the :key function to be only of type
symbol or function; a lambda-expression is no longer acceptable as a functional
argument. One must use the function special form or the abbreviation #' before
a lambda-expression that appears as an explicit argument form.

For some operations it can be useful to specify the direction in which the sequence is conceptually processed. In this case the basic operation normally processes the sequence in the forward direction, and processing in the reverse direction
is indicated by a non-nil value for the keyword argument :from-end. (The processing order specified by the :from-end is purely conceptual. Depending on the
object to be processed and on the implementation, the actual processing order may
be different. For this reason a user-supplied *test* function should be free of side
effects.)

Many operations allow the specification of a subsequence to be operated upon.
Such operations have keyword arguments called :start and :end. These arguments should be integer indices into the sequence, with *start* ≤ *end* (it is an error
if *start* > *end*). They indicate the subsequence starting with and *including* element
start and up to but *excluding* element *end*. The length of the subsequence is therefore *end* − *start*. If *start* is omitted, it defaults to zero; and if *end* is omitted or nil,

it defaults to the length of the sequence. Therefore if both *start* and *end* are omitted, the entire sequence is processed by default. For the most part, subsequence specification is permitted purely for the sake of efficiency; one could simply call subseq instead to extract the subsequence before operating on it. Note, however, that operations that calculate indices return indices into the original sequence, not into the subsequence:

```
(position #\b "foobar" :start 2 :end 5) ⇒ 3
(position #\b (subseq "foobar" 2 5)) ⇒ 1
```

If two sequences are involved, then the keyword arguments :start1, :end1, :start2, and :end2 are used to specify separate subsequences for each sequence.

X3J13 voted in June 1988 ⟨170⟩ (and further clarification was voted in January 1989 ⟨149⟩) to specify that these rules apply not only to all built-in functions that have keyword parameters named :start, :start1, :start2, :end, :end1, or :end2 but also to functions such as subseq that take required or optional parameters that are documented as being named *start* or *end*.

- A "start" argument must always be a non-negative integer and defaults to zero if not supplied; it is not permissible to pass nil as a "start" argument.

- An "end" argument must be either a non-negative integer or nil (which indicates the end of the sequence) and defaults to nil if not supplied; therefore supplying nil is equivalent to not supplying such an argument.

- If the "end" argument is an integer, it must be no greater than the active length of the corresponding sequence (as returned by the function length).

- The default value for the "end" argument is the active length of the corresponding sequence.

- The "start" value (after defaulting, if necessary) must not be greater than the corresponding "end" value (after defaulting, if necessary).

This may be summarized as follows. Let x be the sequence within which indices are to be considered. Let s be the "start" argument for that sequence of any standard function, whether explicitly specified or defaulted, through omission, to zero. Let e be the "end" argument for that sequence of any standard function, whether explicitly specified or defaulted, through omission or an explicitly passed nil value, to the active length of x, as returned by length. Then it is an error if the test (<= 0 s e (length x)) is not true.

For some functions, notably remove and delete, the keyword argument :count is used to specify how many occurrences of the item should be affected. If this is nil or is not supplied, all matching items are affected.

In the following function descriptions, an element *x* of a sequence "satisfies the test" if any of the following holds:

- A basic function was called, *testfn* was specified by the keyword :test, and (funcall *testfn item* (*keyfn x*)) is true.

- A basic function was called, *testfn* was specified by the keyword :test-not, and (funcall *testfn item* (*keyfn x*)) is false.

- An -if function was called, and (funcall *predicate* (*keyfn x*)) is true.

- An -if-not function was called, and (funcall *predicate* (*keyfn x*)) is false.

In each case *keyfn* is the value of the :key keyword argument (the default being the identity function). See, for example, remove.

In the following function descriptions, two elements *x* and *y* taken from sequences "match" if either of the following holds:

- *testfn* was specified by the keyword :test, and (funcall *testfn* (*keyfn x*) (*keyfn y*)) is true.

- *testfn* was specified by the keyword :test-not, and (funcall *testfn* (*keyfn x*) (*keyfn y*)) is false.

See, for example, search.

X3J13 voted in June 1988 ⟨90⟩ to allow the *testfn* or predicate to be only of type symbol or function; a lambda-expression is no longer acceptable as a functional argument. One must use the function special form or the abbreviation #´ before a lambda-expression that appears as an explicit argument form.

You may depend on the order in which arguments are given to *testfn*; this permits the use of non-commutative test functions in a predictable manner. The order of the arguments to *testfn* corresponds to the order in which those arguments (or the sequences containing those arguments) were given to the sequence function in question. If a sequence function gives two elements from the same sequence argument to *testfn*, they are given in the same order in which they appear in the sequence.

Whenever a sequence function must construct and return a new vector, it always returns a *simple* vector (see section 2.5). Similarly, any strings constructed will be simple strings.

X3J13 voted in January 1989 ⟨176⟩ to *deprecate* the use of :test-not keyword arguments and -if-not functions. This means that these features are very likely to be retained in the forthcoming standard but are regarded as candidates for removal in a future revision of the ANSI standard. X3J13 also voted in January 1989 ⟨87⟩ to add the complement function, intended to reduce or eliminate the need for these deprecated features. Time will tell. I note that many features in Fortran have been deprecated but very few indeed have actually been removed or altered incompatibly.

complement *fn*   [*Function*]

Returns a function whose value is the same as that of not applied to the result of applying the function *fn* to the same arguments. One could define complement as follows:

```
(defun complement (fn)
  #'(lambda (&rest arguments)
      (not (apply fn arguments))))
```

One intended use of complement is to supplant the use of :test-not arguments and -if-not functions.

```
(remove-if-not #'virtuous senators) ≡
  (remove-if (complement #'virtuous) senators)
```

```
(remove-duplicates telephone-book
                   :test-not #'mismatch) ≡
  (remove-duplicates telephone-book
                     :test (complement #'mismatch))
```

14.1. Simple Sequence Functions

Most of the following functions perform simple operations on a single sequence; make-sequence constructs a new sequence.

elt *sequence index*   [*Function*]

This returns the element of *sequence* specified by *index*, which must be a non-negative integer less than the length of the *sequence* as returned by length. The first element of a sequence has index 0.

(Note that elt observes the fill pointer in those vectors that have fill pointers. The array-specific function aref may be used to access vector elements that are beyond the vector's fill pointer.)

setf may be used with elt to destructively replace a sequence element with a new value.

subseq *sequence start* &optional *end*   [*Function*]

This returns the subsequence of *sequence* specified by *start* and *end*. subseq *always* allocates a new sequence for a result; it never shares storage with an old sequence. The result subsequence is always of the same type as the argument *sequence*.

  setf may be used with subseq to destructively replace a subsequence with a sequence of new values; see also replace.

copy-seq *sequence*   [*Function*]

A copy is made of the argument *sequence*; the result is equalp to the argument but not eq to it.

(copy-seq *x*) ≡ (subseq *x* 0)

but the name copy-seq is more perspicuous when applicable.

length *sequence*   [*Function*]

The number of elements in *sequence* is returned as a non-negative integer. If the sequence is a vector with a fill pointer, the "active length" as specified by the fill pointer is returned (see section 17.5).

reverse *sequence*   [*Function*]

The result is a new sequence of the same kind as *sequence*, containing the same elements but in reverse order. The argument is not modified.

nreverse *sequence*   [*Function*]

The result is a sequence containing the same elements as *sequence* but in reverse order. The argument may be destroyed and re-used to produce the result. The result may or may not be eq to the argument, so it is usually wise to say something like (setq x (nreverse x)), because simply (nreverse x) is not guaranteed to leave a reversed value in x.

  X3J13 voted in March 1989 ⟨153⟩ to clarify the permissible side effects of certain operations. When the *sequence* is a list, nreverse is permitted to perform a setf on any part, *car* or *cdr*, of the top-level list structure of that list. When the *sequence* is an array, nreverse is permitted to re-order the elements of the given array in order to produce the resulting array.

`make-sequence` *type size* `&key` `:initial-element`   [*Function*]

This returns a sequence of type *type* and of length *size*, each of whose elements has been initialized to the `:initial-element` argument. If specified, the `:initial-element` argument must be an object that can be an element of a sequence of type *type*. For example:

```
(make-sequence '(vector double-float)
               100
               :initial-element 1d0)
```

If an `:initial-element` argument is not specified, then the sequence will be initialized in an implementation-dependent way.

X3J13 voted in January 1989 ⟨7⟩ to clarify that the *type* argument must be a type specifier, and the *size* argument must be a non-negative integer less than the value of `array-dimension-limit`.

X3J13 voted in June 1989 ⟨158⟩ to specify that `make-sequence` should signal an error if the sequence *type* specifies the number of elements and the *size* argument is different.

X3J13 voted in March 1989 ⟨11⟩ to specify that if *type* is `string`, the result is the same as if `make-string` had been called with the same *size* and `:initial-element` arguments.

14.2. Concatenating, Mapping, and Reducing Sequences

The functions in this section each operate on an arbitrary number of sequences except for `reduce`, which is included here because of its conceptual relationship to the mapping functions.

`concatenate` *result-type* `&rest` *sequences*   [*Function*]

The result is a new sequence that contains all the elements of all the sequences in order. All of the sequences are copied from; the result does not share any structure with any of the argument sequences (in this `concatenate` differs from `append`). The type of the result is specified by *result-type*, which must be a subtype of `sequence`, as for the function `coerce`. It must be possible for every element of the argument sequences to be an element of a sequence of type *result-type*.

If only one *sequence* argument is provided and it has the type specified by *result-type*, `concatenate` is required to copy the argument rather than simply returning it. If a copy is not required, but only possibly type conversion, then the `coerce` function may be appropriate.

X3J13 voted in June 1989 ⟨158⟩ to specify that `concatenate` should signal an error if the sequence type specifies the number of elements and the sum of the argument lengths is different.

`map` *result-type function sequence* `&rest` *more-sequences*   [*Function*]

The *function* must take as many arguments as there are sequences provided; at least one sequence must be provided. The result of `map` is a sequence such that element *j* is the result of applying *function* to element *j* of each of the argument sequences. The result sequence is as long as the shortest of the input sequences.

If the *function* has side effects, it can count on being called first on all the elements numbered 0, then on all those numbered 1, and so on.

The type of the result sequence is specified by the argument *result-type* (which must be a subtype of the type `sequence`), as for the function `coerce`. In addition, one may specify `nil` for the result type, meaning that no result sequence is to be produced; in this case the *function* is invoked only for effect, and `map` returns `nil`. This gives an effect similar to that of `mapc`.

X3J13 voted in June 1989 ⟨158⟩ to specify that `map` should signal an error if the sequence type specifies the number of elements and the minimum of the argument lengths is different.

X3J13 voted in January 1989 ⟨121⟩ to restrict user side effects; see section 7.9.

Compatibility note: In MacLisp, Lisp Machine Lisp, Interlisp, and indeed even Lisp 1.5, the function `map` has always meant a non-value-returning version. However, standard computer science literature, including in particular the recent wave of papers on "functional programming," have come to use `map` to mean what in the past Lisp implementations have called `mapcar`. To simplify things henceforth, Common Lisp follows current usage, and what was formerly called `map` is named `mapl` in Common Lisp.

For example:

```
(map 'list #'- '(1 2 3 4)) ⇒ (-1 -2 -3 -4)
(map 'string
     #'(lambda (x) (if (oddp x) #\1 #\0))
     '(1 2 3 4))
  ⇒ "1010"
```

`map-into` *result-sequence function* `&rest` *sequences*   [*Function*]

X3J13 voted in June 1989 ⟨120⟩ to add the function `map-into`. It destructively modifies the *result-sequence* to contain the results of applying *function* to corresponding elements of the argument *sequences* in turn; it then returns *result-sequence*.

The arguments *result-sequence* and each element of *sequences* can each be either a list or a vector (one-dimensional array). The `function` must accept at least as many arguments as the number of argument *sequences* supplied to `map-into`. If *result-sequence* and the other argument *sequences* are not all the same length, the iteration terminates when the shortest sequence is exhausted. If *result-sequence* is a vector with a fill pointer, the fill pointer is ignored when deciding how many iterations to perform, and afterwards the fill pointer is set to the number of times the *function* was applied.

If the *function* has side effects, it can count on being called first on all the elements numbered 0, then on all those numbered 1, and so on.

If *result-sequence* is longer than the shortest element of *sequences*, extra elements at the end of *result-sequence* are unchanged.

The function `map-into` differs from `map` in that it modifies an existing sequence rather than creating a new one. In addition, `map-into` can be called with only two arguments (*result-sequence* and *function*), while `map` requires at least three arguments.

If *result-sequence* is `nil`, `map-into` immediately returns `nil`, because `nil` is a sequence of length zero.

`some` *predicate sequence* `&rest` *more-sequences*	[*Function*]
`every` *predicate sequence* `&rest` *more-sequences*	[*Function*]
`notany` *predicate sequence* `&rest` *more-sequences*	[*Function*]
`notevery` *predicate sequence* `&rest` *more-sequences*	[*Function*]

These are all predicates. The *predicate* must take as many arguments as there are sequences provided. The *predicate* is first applied to the elements with index 0 in each of the sequences, and possibly then to the elements with index 1, and so on, until a termination criterion is met or the end of the shortest of the *sequences* is reached.

If the *predicate* has side effects, it can count on being called first on all the elements numbered 0, then on all those numbered 1, and so on.

`some` returns as soon as any invocation of *predicate* returns a non-`nil` value; `some` returns that value. If the end of a sequence is reached, `some` returns `nil`. Thus, considered as a predicate, it is true if *some* invocation of *predicate* is true.

`every` returns `nil` as soon as any invocation of *predicate* returns `nil`. If the end of a sequence is reached, `every` returns a non-`nil` value. Thus, considered as a predicate, it is true if *every* invocation of *predicate* is true.

notany returns nil as soon as any invocation of *predicate* returns a non-nil value. If the end of a sequence is reached, notany returns a non-nil value. Thus, considered as a predicate, it is true if *no* invocation of *predicate* is true.

notevery returns a non-nil value as soon as any invocation of *predicate* returns nil. If the end of a sequence is reached, notevery returns nil. Thus, considered as a predicate, it is true if *not every* invocation of *predicate* is true.

| X3J13 voted in January 1989 ⟨121⟩ to restrict user side effects; see section 7.9.

Compatibility note: The order of the arguments here is not compatible with Interlisp and Lisp Machine Lisp. This is to stress the similarity of these functions to map. The functions are therefore extended here to functions of more than one argument, and to multiple sequences.

---

reduce *function sequence* &key :from-end :start :end   [*Function*]
   :initial-value

The reduce function combines all the elements of a sequence using a binary operation; for example, using + one can add up all the elements.

The specified subsequence of the *sequence* is combined or "reduced" using the *function*, which must accept two arguments. The reduction is left-associative, unless the :from-end argument is true (it defaults to nil), in which case it is right-associative. If an :initial-value argument is given, it is logically placed before the subsequence (after it if :from-end is true) and included in the reduction operation.

If the specified subsequence contains exactly one element and the keyword argument :initial-value is not given, then that element is returned and the *function* is not called. If the specified subsequence is empty and an :initial-value is given, then the :initial-value is returned and the *function* is not called.

If the specified subsequence is empty and no :initial-value is given, then the *function* is called with zero arguments, and reduce returns whatever the function does. (This is the only case where the *function* is called with other than two arguments.)

```
(reduce #'+ '(1 2 3 4)) ⇒ 10
(reduce #'- '(1 2 3 4)) ≡ (- (- (- 1 2) 3) 4) ⇒ -8
(reduce #'- '(1 2 3 4) :from-end t)        ;Alternating sum
   ≡ (- 1 (- 2 (- 3 4))) ⇒ -2
(reduce #'+ '()) ⇒ 0
(reduce #'+ '(3)) ⇒ 3
(reduce #'+ '(foo)) ⇒ foo
```

```
(reduce #'list '(1 2 3 4)) ⇒ (((1 2) 3) 4)
(reduce #'list '(1 2 3 4) :from-end t) ⇒ (1 (2 (3 4)))
(reduce #'list '(1 2 3 4) :initial-value 'foo)
   ⇒ ((((foo 1) 2) 3) 4)
(reduce #'list '(1 2 3 4)
        :from-end t :initial-value 'foo)
   ⇒ (1 (2 (3 (4 foo)))))
```

If the *function* produces side effects, the order of the calls to the *function* can be correctly predicted from the reduction ordering demonstrated above.

The name "reduce" for this function is borrowed from APL.

X3J13 voted in March 1988 ⟨152⟩ to extend the reduce function to take an additional keyword argument named :key. As usual, this argument defaults to the identity function. The value of this argument must be a function that accepts at least one argument. This function is applied once to each element of the sequence that is to participate in the reduction operation, in the order implied by the :from-end argument; the values returned by this function are combined by the reduction *function*. However, the :key function is *not* applied to the :initial-value argument (if any).

X3J13 voted in January 1989 ⟨121⟩ to restrict user side effects; see section 7.9.

14.3. Modifying Sequences

Each of these functions alters the contents of a sequence or produces an altered copy of a given sequence.

---

fill *sequence item* &key :start :end   [*Function*]

The *sequence* is destructively modified by replacing each element of the subsequence specified by the :start and :end parameters with the *item*. The *item* may be any Lisp object but must be a suitable element for the *sequence*. The *item* is stored into all specified components of the *sequence*, beginning at the one specified by the :start index (which defaults to zero), up to but not including the one specified by the :end index (which defaults to the length of the sequence). fill returns the modified *sequence*. For example:

```
(setq x (vector 'a 'b 'c 'd 'e)) ⇒ #(a b c d e)
(fill x 'z :start 1 :end 3) ⇒ #(a z z d e)
   and now x ⇒ #(a z z d e)
(fill x 'p) ⇒ #(p p p p p)
   and now x ⇒ #(p p p p p)
```

```
replace sequence1 sequence2 &key :start1 :end1              [Function]
        :start2 :end2
```

The sequence *sequence1* is destructively modified by copying successive elements into it from *sequence2*. The elements of *sequence2* must be of a type that may be stored into *sequence1*. The subsequence of *sequence2* specified by :start2 and :end2 is copied into the subsequence of *sequence1* specified by :start1 and :end1. (The arguments :start1 and :start2 default to zero. The arguments :end1 and :end2 default to nil, meaning the end of the appropriate sequence.) If these subsequences are not of the same length, then the shorter length determines how many elements are copied; the extra elements near the end of the longer subsequence are not involved in the operation. The number of elements copied may be expressed as:

(min (- *end1 start1*) (- *end2 start2*))

The value returned by replace is the modified *sequence1*.

If *sequence1* and *sequence2* are the same (eq) object and the region being modified overlaps the region being copied from, then it is as if the entire source region were copied to another place and only then copied back into the target region. However, if *sequence1* and *sequence2* are *not* the same, but the region being modified overlaps the region being copied from (perhaps because of shared list structure or displaced arrays), then after the replace operation the subsequence of *sequence1* being modified will have unpredictable contents.

```
remove item sequence &key :from-end :test :test-not         [Function]
        :start :end :count :key
remove-if predicate sequence &key :from-end :start :end      [Function]
          :count :key
remove-if-not predicate sequence &key :from-end :start       [Function]
              :end :count :key
```

The result is a sequence of the same kind as the argument *sequence* that has the same elements except that those in the subsequence delimited by :start and :end and satisfying the test (see above) have been removed. This is a non-destructive operation; the result is a copy of the input *sequence*, save that some elements are not copied. Elements not removed occur in the same order in the result as they did in the argument.

The :count argument, if supplied, limits the number of elements removed; if more than :count elements satisfy the test, then of these elements only the leftmost are removed, as many as specified by :count.

X3J13 voted in January 1989 ⟨148⟩ to clarify that the :count argument must be either nil or an integer, and that supplying a negative integer produces the same behavior as supplying zero.

A non-nil :from-end specification matters only when the :count argument is provided; in that case only the rightmost :count elements satisfying the test are removed. For example:

```
(remove 4 '(1 2 4 1 3 4 5)) ⇒ (1 2 1 3 5)
(remove 4 '(1 2 4 1 3 4 5) :count 1) ⇒ (1 2 1 3 4 5)
(remove 4 '(1 2 4 1 3 4 5) :count 1 :from-end t)
    ⇒ (1 2 4 1 3 5)
(remove 3 '(1 2 4 1 3 4 5) :test #'>) ⇒ (4 3 4 5)
(remove-if #'oddp '(1 2 4 1 3 4 5)) ⇒ (2 4 4)
(remove-if #'evenp '(1 2 4 1 3 4 5) :count 1 :from-end t)
    ⇒ (1 2 4 1 3 5)
```

The result of remove may share with the argument *sequence*; a list result may share a tail with an input list, and the result may be eq to the input *sequence* if no elements need to be removed.

X3J13 voted in January 1989 ⟨121⟩ to restrict user side effects; see section 7.9.

delete *item sequence* &key :from-end :test :test-not   [*Function*]
        :start :end :count :key
delete-if *predicate sequence* &key :from-end   [*Function*]
            :start :end :count :key
delete-if-not *predicate sequence* &key :from-end   [*Function*]
            :start :end :count :key

This is the destructive counterpart to remove. The result is a sequence of the same kind as the argument *sequence* that has the same elements except that those in the subsequence delimited by :start and :end and satisfying the test (see above) have been deleted. This is a destructive operation. The argument *sequence* may be destroyed and used to construct the result; however, the result may or may not be eq to *sequence*. Elements not deleted occur in the same order in the result as they did in the argument.

The :count argument, if supplied, limits the number of elements deleted; if more than :count elements satisfy the test, then of these elements only the leftmost are deleted, as many as specified by :count.

X3J13 voted in January 1989 ⟨148⟩ to clarify that the :count argument must be either nil or an integer, and that supplying a negative integer produces the same behavior as supplying zero.

A non-nil :from-end specification matters only when the :count argument is provided; in that case only the rightmost :count elements satisfying the test are deleted. For example:

```
(delete 4 '(1 2 4 1 3 4 5)) ⇒ (1 2 1 3 5)
(delete 4 '(1 2 4 1 3 4 5) :count 1) ⇒ (1 2 1 3 4 5)
(delete 4 '(1 2 4 1 3 4 5) :count 1 :from-end t)
    ⇒ (1 2 4 1 3 5)
(delete 3 '(1 2 4 1 3 4 5) :test #'>) ⇒ (4 3 4 5)
(delete-if #'oddp '(1 2 4 1 3 4 5)) ⇒ (2 4 4)
(delete-if #'evenp '(1 2 4 1 3 4 5) :count 1 :from-end t)
    ⇒ (1 2 4 1 3 5)
```

X3J13 voted in January 1989 ⟨121⟩ to restrict user side effects; see section 7.9.

X3J13 voted in March 1989 ⟨153⟩ to clarify the permissible side effects of certain operations. When the *sequence* is a list, delete is permitted to perform a setf on any part, *car* or *cdr*, of the top-level list structure of that list. When the *sequence* is an array, delete is permitted to alter the dimensions of the given array and to slide some of its elements into new positions without permuting them in order to produce the resulting array.

Furthermore, (delete-if *predicate sequence* ...) is required to behave exactly like

```
(delete nil sequence
        :test #'(lambda (unused item)
                   (declare (ignore unused))
                   (funcall predicate item))
        ...)
```

Compatibility note: In MacLisp, the delete function uses an equal comparison rather than eql, which is the default test for delete in Common Lisp. Where in MacLisp one would write (delete x y), one must in Common Lisp write (delete x y :test #'equal) to get the completely identical effect. Similarly, one can get the precise effect, and no more, of the MacLisp (delq x y) by writing in Common Lisp (delete x y :test #'eq).

---

remove-duplicates *sequence* &key :from-end :test   [*Function*]
                 :test-not :start :end :key
delete-duplicates *sequence* &key :from-end :test   [*Function*]
                 :test-not :start :end :key

The elements of *sequence* are compared pairwise, and if any two match, then the one occurring earlier in the sequence is discarded (but if the :from-end argument is true, then the one later in the sequence is discarded). The result is a sequence of the same kind as the argument sequence with enough elements removed so that no two of the remaining elements match. The order of the elements remaining in the result is the same as the order in which they appear in *sequence*.

remove-duplicates is the non-destructive version of this operation. The result of remove-duplicates may share with the argument *sequence*; a list result may share a tail with an input list, and the result may be eq to the input *sequence* if no elements need to be removed.

delete-duplicates may destroy the argument *sequence*.

Some examples:

```
(remove-duplicates '(a b c b d d e)) ⇒ (a c b d e)
(remove-duplicates '(a b c b d d e) :from-end t) ⇒ (a b c d e)
(remove-duplicates '((foo #\a) (bar #\%) (baz #\A))
                 :test #'char-equal :key #'cadr)
  ⇒ ((bar #\%) (baz #\A))
(remove-duplicates '((foo #\a) (bar #\%) (baz #\A))
                 :test #'char-equal :key #'cadr :from-end t)
  ⇒ ((foo #\a) (bar #\%))
```

These functions are useful for converting a sequence into a canonical form suitable for representing a set.

X3J13 voted in January 1989 ⟨121⟩ to restrict user side effects; see section 7.9.

X3J13 voted in March 1989 ⟨153⟩ to clarify the permissible side effects of certain operations. When the *sequence* is a list, delete-duplicates is permitted to perform a setf on any part, *car* or *cdr*, of the top-level list structure of that list. When the *sequence* is an array, delete-duplicates is permitted to alter the dimensions of the given array and to slide some of its elements into new positions without permuting them in order to produce the resulting array.

---

substitute *newitem olditem sequence* &key :from-end :test   [*Function*]
        :test-not :start :end :count :key
substitute-if *newitem test sequence* &key :from-end   [*Function*]
        :start :end :count :key
substitute-if-not *newitem test sequence* &key :from-end   [*Function*]
        :start :end :count :key

The result is a sequence of the same kind as the argument *sequence* that has the same elements except that those in the subsequence delimited by :start and :end and satisfying the test (see above) have been replaced by *newitem*. This is a non-destructive operation; the result is a copy of the input *sequence*, save that some elements are changed.

The :count argument, if supplied, limits the number of elements altered; if more than :count elements satisfy the test, then of these elements only the leftmost are replaced, as many as specified by :count.

X3J13 voted in January 1989 ⟨148⟩ to clarify that the :count argument must be either nil or an integer, and that supplying a negative integer produces the same behavior as supplying zero.

A non-nil :from-end specification matters only when the :count argument is provided; in that case only the rightmost :count elements satisfying the test are replaced. For example:

```
(substitute 9 4 '(1 2 4 1 3 4 5)) ⇒ (1 2 9 1 3 9 5)
(substitute 9 4 '(1 2 4 1 3 4 5) :count 1) ⇒ (1 2 9 1 3 4 5)
(substitute 9 4 '(1 2 4 1 3 4 5) :count 1 :from-end t)
   ⇒ (1 2 4 1 3 9 5)
(substitute 9 3 '(1 2 4 1 3 4 5) :test #'>) ⇒ (9 9 4 9 3 4 5)
(substitute-if 9 #'oddp '(1 2 4 1 3 4 5)) ⇒ (9 2 4 9 9 4 9)
(substitute-if 9 #'evenp '(1 2 4 1 3 4 5) :count 1 :from-end t)
   ⇒ (1 2 4 1 3 9 5)
```

The result of substitute may share with the argument *sequence*; a list result may share a tail with an input list, and the result may be eq to the input *sequence* if no elements need to be changed.

See also subst, which performs substitutions throughout a tree.

X3J13 voted in January 1989 ⟨121⟩ to restrict user side effects; see section 7.9.

nsubstitute *newitem olditem sequence* &key :from-end :test   [*Function*]
               :test-not :start :end :count :key
nsubstitute-if *newitem test sequence* &key :from-end   [*Function*]
                :start :end :count :key
nsubstitute-if-not *newitem test sequence* &key :from-end   [*Function*]
                :start :end :count :key

This is the destructive counterpart to substitute. The result is a sequence of the same kind as the argument *sequence* that has the same elements except that those in the subsequence delimited by :start and :end and satisfying the test (see above) have been replaced by *newitem*. This is a destructive operation. The argument *sequence* may be destroyed and used to construct the result; however, the result may or may not be eq to *sequence*.

See also nsubst, which performs destructive substitutions throughout a tree.

X3J13 voted in January 1989 ⟨121⟩ to restrict user side effects; see section 7.9.

X3J13 voted in March 1989 ⟨153⟩ to clarify the permissible side effects of certain operations. When the *sequence* is a list, nsubstitute or nsubstitute-if is required to perform a setf on any *car* of the top-level list structure of that list whose old contents must be replaced with *newitem* but is forbidden to perform a setf on any *cdr* of the list. When the *sequence* is an array, nsubstitute or nsubstitute-if is required to perform a setf on any element of the array whose old contents must be replaced with *newitem*. These functions, therefore, may successfully be used solely for effect, the caller discarding the returned value (though some programmers find this stylistically distasteful).

14.4. Searching Sequences for Items

Each of these functions searches a sequence to locate one or more elements satisfying some test.

```
find item sequence &key :from-end :test :test-not          [Function]
     :start :end :key
find-if predicate sequence &key :from-end :start :end :key  [Function]
find-if-not predicate sequence &key :from-end               [Function]
          :start :end :key
```

If the *sequence* contains an element satisfying the test, then the leftmost such element is returned; otherwise nil is returned.

If :start and :end keyword arguments are given, only the specified subsequence of *sequence* is searched.

If a non-nil :from-end keyword argument is specified, then the result is the *rightmost* element satisfying the test.

X3J13 voted in January 1989 ⟨121⟩ to restrict user side effects; see section 7.9.

```
position item sequence &key :from-end :test :test-not      [Function]
         :start :end :key
position-if predicate sequence &key :from-end              [Function]
          :start :end :key
position-if-not predicate sequence &key :from-end          [Function]
             :start :end :key
```

If the *sequence* contains an element satisfying the test, then the index within the sequence of the leftmost such element is returned as a non-negative integer; otherwise nil is returned.

If :start and :end keyword arguments are given, only the specified subsequence of *sequence* is searched. However, the index returned is relative to the entire sequence, not to the subsequence.

If a non-nil :from-end keyword argument is specified, then the result is the index of the *rightmost* element satisfying the test. (The index returned, however, is an index from the left-hand end, as usual.)

X3J13 voted in January 1989 ⟨121⟩ to restrict user side effects; see section 7.9.

Here is a simple piece of code that uses several of the sequence functions, notably position-if and find-if, to process strings. Note one use of loop as well.

```
(defun debug-palindrome (s)
  (flet ((match (x) (char-equal (first x) (third x))))
    (let* ((pairs (loop for c across s
                        for j from 0
                        when (alpha-char-p c)
                          collect (list c j)))
           (quads (mapcar #'append pairs (reverse pairs)))
           (diffpos (position-if (complement #'match) quads)))
      (when diffpos
        (let* ((diff (elt quads diffpos))
               (same (find-if #'match quads
                              :start (+ diffpos 1))))
          (if same
              (format nil
                      "/~A/ (at ~D) is not the reverse of /~A/"
                      (subseq s (second diff) (second same))
                      (second diff)
                      (subseq s (+ (fourth same) 1)
                              (+ (fourth diff) 1)))
              "This palindrome is completely messed up!"))))))
```

Here is an example of its behavior.

```
(setq panama        ;A putative palindrome?
      "A man, a plan, a canoe, pasta, heros, rajahs,
       a coloratura, maps, waste, percale, macaroni, a gag,
       a banana bag, a tan, a tag, a banana bag again
       (or a camel), a crepe, pins, Spam, a rut, a Rolo,
       cash, a jar, sore hats, a peon, a canal--Panama!")
```

```
(debug-palindrome panama)
  ⇒ "/wast/ (at 73) is not the reverse of /, pins/"

(replace panama "snipe" :start1 73)        ;Repair it
  ⇒ "A man, a plan, a canoe, pasta, heros, rajahs,
        a coloratura, maps, snipe, percale, macaroni, a gag,
        a banana bag, a tan, a tag, a banana bag again
        (or a camel), a crepe, pins, Spam, a rut, a Rolo,
        cash, a jar, sore hats, a peon, a canal--Panama!"

(debug-palindrome panama) ⇒ nil      ;Copacetic—a true palindrome

(debug-palindrome "Rubber baby buggy bumpers")
  ⇒ "/Rubber / (at 0) is not the reverse of /umpers/"

(debug-palindrome "Common Lisp: The Language")
  ⇒ "/Commo/ (at 0) is not the reverse of /guage/"

(debug-palindrome "Complete mismatches are hard to find")
  ⇒
  "/Complete mism/ (at 0) is not the reverse of /re hard to find/"

(debug-palindrome "Waltz, nymph, for quick jigs vex Bud")
  ⇒ "This palindrome is completely messed up!"

(debug-palindrome "Doc, note: I dissent.  A fast never
                    prevents a fatness.  I diet on cod.")
  ⇒nil        ;Another winner

(debug-palindrome "Top step's pup's pet spot") ⇒ nil
```

count *item sequence* &key :from-end :test :test-not   [*Function*]
  :start :end :key
count-if *predicate sequence* &key :from-end   [*Function*]
   :start :end :key
count-if-not *predicate sequence* &key :from-end   [*Function*]
   :start :end :key

The result is always a non-negative integer, the number of elements in the specified subsequence of *sequence* satisfying the test.

The :from-end argument does not affect the result returned; it is accepted purely for compatibility with other sequence functions.

| X3J13 voted in January 1989 ⟨121⟩ to restrict user side effects; see section 7.9.

mismatch *sequence1* *sequence2* &key :from-end :test   [*Function*]
   :test-not :key :start1 :start2 :end1 :end2

The specified subsequences of *sequence1* and *sequence2* are compared element-wise. If they are of equal length and match in every element, the result is nil. Otherwise, the result is a non-negative integer. This result is the index within *sequence1* of the leftmost position at which the two subsequences fail to match; or, if one subsequence is shorter than and a matching prefix of the other, the result is the index relative to *sequence1* beyond the last position tested.

If a non-nil :from-end keyword argument is given, then *one plus* the index of the *rightmost* position in which the sequences differ is returned. In effect, the (sub)sequences are aligned at their right-hand ends; then, the last elements are compared, the penultimate elements, and so on. The index returned is again an index relative to *sequence1*.

| X3J13 voted in January 1989 ⟨121⟩ to restrict user side effects; see section 7.9.

search *sequence1* *sequence2* &key :from-end :test :test-not   [*Function*]
  :key :start1 :start2 :end1 :end2

A search is conducted for a subsequence of *sequence2* that element-wise matches *sequence1*. If there is no such subsequence, the result is nil; if there is, the result is the index into *sequence2* of the leftmost element of the leftmost such matching subsequence.

If a non-nil :from-end keyword argument is given, the index of the leftmost element of the *rightmost* matching subsequence is returned.

The implementation may choose to search the sequence in any order; there is no guarantee on the number of times the test is made. For example, search with a non-nil :from-end argument might actually search a list from left to right instead of from right to left (but in either case would return the rightmost matching subsequence, of course). Therefore it is a good idea for a user-supplied predicate to be free of side effects.

| X3J13 voted in January 1989 ⟨121⟩ to restrict user side effects; see section 7.9.

14.5. Sorting and Merging

These functions may destructively modify argument sequences in order to put a sequence into sorted order or to merge two already sorted sequences.

sort *sequence predicate* &key :key   [*Function*]
stable-sort *sequence predicate* &key :key   [*Function*]

The *sequence* is destructively sorted according to an order determined by the *predicate*. The *predicate* should take two arguments, and return non-nil if and only if the first argument is strictly less than the second (in some appropriate sense). If the first argument is greater than or equal to the second (in the appropriate sense), then the *predicate* should return nil.

The sort function determines the relationship between two elements by giving keys extracted from the elements to the *predicate*. The :key argument, when applied to an element, should return the key for that element. The :key argument defaults to the identity function, thereby making the element itself be the key.

The :key function should not have any side effects. A useful example of a :key function would be a component selector function for a defstruct structure, used in sorting a sequence of structures.

(sort *a p* :key *s*) ≡ (sort *a* #´(lambda (x y) (*p* (*s* x) (*s* y))))

While the above two expressions are equivalent, the first may be more efficient in some implementations for certain types of arguments. For example, an implementation may choose to apply *s* to each item just once, putting the resulting keys into a separate table, and then sort the parallel tables, as opposed to applying *s* to an item every time just before applying the *predicate*.

If the :key and *predicate* functions always return, then the sorting operation will always terminate, producing a sequence containing the same elements as the original sequence (that is, the result is a permutation of *sequence*). This is guaranteed even if the *predicate* does not really consistently represent a total order (in which case the elements will be scrambled in some unpredictable way, but no element will be lost). If the :key function consistently returns meaningful keys, and the *predicate* does reflect some total ordering criterion on those keys, then the elements of the result sequence will be properly sorted according to that ordering.

The sorting operation performed by sort is not guaranteed *stable*. Elements considered equal by the *predicate* may or may not stay in their original order. (The *predicate* is assumed to consider two elements *x* and *y* to be equal if (funcall *predicate x y*) and (funcall *predicate y x*) are both false.) The function stable-sort guarantees stability but may be slower than sort in some situations.

The sorting operation may be destructive in all cases. In the case of an array argument, this is accomplished by permuting the elements in place. In the case of a list, the list is destructively reordered in the same manner as for nreverse. Thus if the argument should not be destroyed, the user must sort a copy of the argument.

Should execution of the :key function or the *predicate* cause an error, the state of the list or array being sorted is undefined. However, if the error is corrected, the sort will, of course, proceed correctly.

Note that since sorting requires many comparisons, and thus many calls to the *predicate*, sorting will be much faster if the *predicate* is a compiled function rather than interpreted.

An example:

```
(setq foovector (sort foovector #'string-lessp :key #'car))
```

If foovector contained these items before the sort

```
("Tokens" "The Lion Sleeps Tonight")
("Carpenters" "Close to You")
("Rolling Stones" "Brown Sugar")
("Beach Boys" "I Get Around")
("Mozart" "Eine Kleine Nachtmusik" (K 525))
("Beatles" "I Want to Hold Your Hand")
```

then after the sort foovector would contain

```
("Beach Boys" "I Get Around")
("Beatles" "I Want to Hold Your Hand")
("Carpenters" "Close to You")
("Mozart" "Eine Kleine Nachtmusik" (K 525))
("Rolling Stones" "Brown Sugar")
("Tokens" "The Lion Sleeps Tonight")
```

X3J13 voted in January 1989 ⟨121⟩ to restrict user side effects; see section 7.9.

merge *result-type* *sequence1* *sequence2* *predicate* &key :key   [*Function*]

The sequences *sequence1* and *sequence2* are destructively merged according to an order determined by the *predicate*. The result is a sequence of type *result-type*, which must be a subtype of sequence, as for the function coerce. The *predicate* should take two arguments and return non-nil if and only if the first argument is strictly less than the second (in some appropriate sense). If the first argument is greater than or equal to the second (in the appropriate sense), then the *predicate* should return nil.

The merge function determines the relationship between two elements by giving keys extracted from the elements to the *predicate*. The :key function, when applied to an element, should return the key for that element; the :key function defaults to the identity function, thereby making the element itself be the key.

The :key function should not have any side effects. A useful example of a :key function would be a component selector function for a defstruct structure, used to merge a sequence of structures.

If the :key and *predicate* functions always return, then the merging operation will always terminate. The result of merging two sequences x and y is a new sequence z, such that the length of z is the sum of the lengths of x and y, and z contains all the elements of x and y. If $x1$ and $x2$ are two elements of x, and $x1$ precedes $x2$ in x, then $x1$ precedes $x2$ in z, and similarly for elements of y. In short, z is an *interleaving* of x and y.

Moreover, if x and y were correctly sorted according to the *predicate*, then z will also be correctly sorted, as shown in this example.

```
(merge 'list '(1 3 4 6 7) '(2 5 8) #'<) ⇒ (1 2 3 4 5 6 7 8)
```

If x or y is not so sorted then z will not be sorted, but will nevertheless be an interleaving of x and y.

The merging operation is guaranteed *stable*; if two or more elements are considered equal by the *predicate*, then the elements from *sequence1* will precede those from *sequence2* in the result. (The *predicate* is assumed to consider two elements x and y to be equal if (funcall *predicate* x y) and (funcall *predicate* y x) are both false.) For example:

```
(merge 'string "BOY" "nosy" #'char-lessp) ⇒ "BnOosYy"
```

The result can *not* be "BnoOsYy", "BnOosyY", or "BnoOsyY". The function char-lessp ignores case, and so considers the characters Y and y to be equal, for example; the stability property then guarantees that the character from the first argument (Y) must precede the one from the second argument (y).

X3J13 voted in June 1989 ⟨158⟩ to specify that merge should signal an error if the sequence type specifies the number of elements and the sum of the lengths of the two sequence arguments is different.

X3J13 voted in January 1989 ⟨121⟩ to restrict user side effects; see section 7.9.

15

Lists

A *cons*, or dotted pair, is a compound data object having two components called the *car* and *cdr*. Each component may be any Lisp object. A *list* is a chain of conses linked by *cdr* fields; the chain is terminated by some atom (a non-cons object). An ordinary list is terminated by `nil`, the empty list (also written `()`). A list whose *cdr* chain is terminated by some non-`nil` atom is called a *dotted list*.

The recommended predicate for testing for the end of a list is `endp`.

15.1. Conses

These are the basic operations on conses viewed as pairs rather than as the constituents of a list.

---

car *list* [*Function*]

This returns the *car* of *list*, which must be a cons or `()`; that is, *list* must satisfy the predicate `listp`. By definition, the *car* of `()` is `()`. If the cons is regarded as the first cons of a list, then `car` returns the first element of the list. For example:

`(car '(a b c))` ⇒ a

See `first`. The *car* of a cons may be altered by using `rplaca` or `setf`.

---

cdr *list* [*Function*]

This returns the *cdr* of *list*, which must be a cons or `()`; that is, *list* must satisfy the predicate `listp`. By definition, the *cdr* of `()` is `()`. If the cons is regarded as the first cons of a list, then `cdr` returns the rest of the list, which is a list with all elements but the first of the original list. For example:

`(cdr '(a b c))` ⇒ (b c)

See rest. The *cdr* of a cons may be altered by using rplacd or setf.

caar *list*	[*Function*]
cadr *list*	[*Function*]
cdar *list*	[*Function*]
cddr *list*	[*Function*]
caaar *list*	[*Function*]
caadr *list*	[*Function*]
cadar *list*	[*Function*]
caddr *list*	[*Function*]
cdaar *list*	[*Function*]
cdadr *list*	[*Function*]
cddar *list*	[*Function*]
cdddr *list*	[*Function*]
caaaar *list*	[*Function*]
caaadr *list*	[*Function*]
caadar *list*	[*Function*]
caaddr *list*	[*Function*]
cadaar *list*	[*Function*]
cadadr *list*	[*Function*]
caddar *list*	[*Function*]
cadddr *list*	[*Function*]
cdaaar *list*	[*Function*]
cdaadr *list*	[*Function*]
cdadar *list*	[*Function*]
cdaddr *list*	[*Function*]
cddaar *list*	[*Function*]
cddadr *list*	[*Function*]
cdddar *list*	[*Function*]
cddddr *list*	[*Function*]

All of the compositions of up to four car and cdr operations are defined as separate Common Lisp functions. The names of these functions begin with c and end with r, and in between is a sequence of a and d letters corresponding to the composition performed by the function. For example:

(cddadr x) is the same as (cdr (cdr (car (cdr x))))

If the argument is regarded as a list, then cadr returns the second element of the list, caddr the third, and cadddr the fourth. If the first element of a list is a list, then `caar` is the first element of the sublist, `cdar` is the rest of that sublist, and `cadar` is the second element of the sublist, and so on.

As a matter of style, it is often preferable to define a function or macro to access part of a complicated data structure, rather than to use a long car/cdr string. For example, one might define a macro to extract the list of parameter variables from a lambda-expression:

```
(defmacro lambda-vars (lambda-exp) '(cadr ,lambda-exp))
```

and then use `lambda-vars` for this purpose instead of `cadr`. See also `defstruct`, which will automatically define new record data types and access functions for instances of them.

Any of these functions may be used to specify a *place* for `setf`.

cons *x y*   [*Function*]

cons is the primitive function to create a new *cons* whose *car* is *x* and whose *cdr* is *y*. For example:

```
(cons 'a 'b) ⇒ (a . b)
(cons 'a (cons 'b (cons 'c '())))) ⇒ (a b c)
(cons 'a '(b c d)) ⇒ (a b c d)
```

cons may be thought of as creating a *cons*, or as adding a new element to the front of a list.

tree-equal *x y* &key :test :test-not   [*Function*]

This is a predicate that is true if *x* and *y* are isomorphic trees with identical leaves, that is, if *x* and *y* are atoms that satisfy the test (by default `eql`), or if they are both conses and their *car*'s are `tree-equal` and their *cdr*'s are `tree-equal`. Thus `tree-equal` recursively compares conses (but not any other objects that have components). See `equal`, which does recursively compare certain other structured objects, such as strings.

X3J13 voted in January 1989 ⟨121⟩ to restrict user side effects; see section 7.9.

15.2. Lists

The following functions perform various operations on lists.

The list is one of the original Lisp data types. The very name "Lisp" is an abbreviation for "LISt Processing."

endp *object*   [*Function*]

The predicate endp is the recommended way to test for the end of a list. It is false
of conses, true of nil, and an error for all other arguments.

Implementation note: Implementations are encouraged to signal an error, especially in the
interpreter, for a non-list argument. The endp function is defined so as to allow compiled
code to perform simply an atom check or a null check if speed is more important than safety.

---

list-length *list*   [*Function*]

list-length returns, as an integer, the length of *list*. list-length differs from
length when the *list* is circular; length may fail to return, whereas list-length
will return nil. For example:

```
(list-length '()) ⇒ 0
(list-length '(a b c d)) ⇒ 4
(list-length '(a (b c) d)) ⇒ 3
(let ((x (list 'a b c)))
  (rplacd (last x) x)
  (list-length x)) ⇒ nil
```

list-length could be implemented as follows:

```
(defun list-length (x)
  (do ((n 0 (+ n 2))              ;Counter
       (fast x (cddr fast))       ;Fast pointer: leaps by 2
       (slow x (cdr slow)))       ;Slow pointer: leaps by 1
      (nil)
    ;; If fast pointer hits the end, return the count.
    (when (endp fast) (return n))
    (when (endp (cdr fast)) (return (+ n 1)))
    ;; If fast pointer eventually equals slow pointer,
    ;; then we must be stuck in a circular list.
    ;; (A deeper property is the converse: if we are
    ;; stuck in a circular list, then eventually the
    ;; fast pointer will equal the slow pointer.
    ;; That fact justifies this implementation.)
    (when (and (eq fast slow) (> n 0)) (return nil))))
```

See length, which will return the length of any sequence.

nth *n* *list*   [*Function*]

(nth *n* *list*) returns the *n*th element of *list*, where the *car* of the list is the "zeroth" element. The argument *n* must be a non-negative integer. If the length of the list is not greater than *n*, then the result is ( ), that is, nil. (This is consistent with the idea that the *car* and *cdr* of ( ) are each ( ).) For example:

```
(nth 0 '(foo bar gack)) ⇒ foo
(nth 1 '(foo bar gack)) ⇒ bar
(nth 3 '(foo bar gack)) ⇒ ()
```

Compatibility note: This is not the same as the Interlisp function called nth, which is similar to but not exactly the same as the Common Lisp function nthcdr. This definition of nth is compatible with Lisp Machine Lisp and NIL (New Implementation of Lisp). Also, some people have used macros and functions called nth of their own in their old MacLisp programs, which may not work the same way.

nth may be used to specify a *place* to setf; when nth is used in this way, the argument *n* must be less than the length of the *list*.

Note that the arguments to nth are reversed from the order used by most other sequence selector functions such as elt.

first *list*	[*Function*]
second *list*	[*Function*]
third *list*	[*Function*]
fourth *list*	[*Function*]
fifth *list*	[*Function*]
sixth *list*	[*Function*]
seventh *list*	[*Function*]
eighth *list*	[*Function*]
ninth *list*	[*Function*]
tenth *list*	[*Function*]

These functions are sometimes convenient for accessing particular elements of a list. first is the same as car, second is the same as cadr, third is the same as caddr, and so on. Note that the ordinal numbering used here is one-origin, as opposed to the zero-origin numbering used by nth:

```
(fifth x) ≡ (nth 4 x)
```

setf may be used with each of these functions to store into the indicated position of a list.

rest *list*   [*Function*]

rest means the same as cdr but mnemonically complements first. setf may
be used with rest to replace the *cdr* of a list with a new value.

nthcdr *n list*   [*Function*]

(nthcdr *n list*) performs the cdr operation *n* times on *list*, and returns the result.
For example:

```
(nthcdr 0 '(a b c)) ⇒ (a b c)
(nthcdr 2 '(a b c)) ⇒ (c)
(nthcdr 4 '(a b c)) ⇒ ()
```

In other words, it returns the *n*th *cdr* of the list.

Compatibility note: This is similar to the Interlisp function nth, except that the Interlisp
function is one-based instead of zero-based.

```
(car (nthcdr n x)) ≡ (nth n x)
```

X3J13 voted in January 1989 ⟨7⟩ to clarify that the argument *n* must be a non-
negative integer.

last *list*   [*Function*]

last returns the last cons (*not* the last element!) of *list*. If *list* is ( ), it returns ( ).
For example:

```
(setq x '(a b c d))
(last x) ⇒ (d)
(rplacd (last x) '(e f))
x ⇒ '(a b c d e f)
(last '(a b c . d)) ⇒ (c . d)
```

X3J13 voted in June 1988 ⟨106⟩ to extend the last function to accept an optional second argument. The effect is to make last complementary in operation
to butlast. The new description (with some additional examples) would be as
follows.

last *list* &optional (*n* 1)   [*Function*]

last returns the tail of the *list* consisting of the last *n* conses of *list*. The *list* may
be a dotted list. It is an error if the *list* is circular.

The argument *n* must be a non-negative integer. If *n* is zero, then the atom that terminates the *list* is returned. If *n* is not less than the number of cons cells making up the *list*, then the *list* itself is returned.

For example:

```
(setq x '(a b c d))
(last x) ⇒ (d)
(rplacd (last x) '(e f))
x ⇒ '(a b c d e f)
(last x 3) ⇒ (d e f)
(last '()) ⇒ ()
(last '(a b c . d)) ⇒ (c . d)
(last '(a b c . d) 0) ⇒ d
(last '(a b c . d) 2) ⇒ (b c . d)
(last '(a b c . d) 1729) ⇒ (a b c . d)
```

list &rest *args*   [*Function*]

list constructs and returns a list of its arguments. For example:

```
(list 3 4 'a (car '(b . c)) (+ 6 -2)) ⇒ (3 4 a b 4)
```

```
(list) ⇒ ()
(list (list 'a 'b) (list 'c 'd 'e)) ⇒ ((a b) (c d e))
```

list* *arg* &rest *others*   [*Function*]

list* is like list except that the last *cons* of the constructed list is "dotted." The last argument to list* is used as the *cdr* of the last cons constructed; this need not be an atom. If it is not an atom, then the effect is to add several new elements to the front of a list. For example:

```
(list* 'a 'b 'c 'd) ⇒ (a b c . d)
```

This is like

```
(cons 'a (cons 'b (cons 'c 'd)))
```

Also:

```
(list* 'a 'b 'c '(d e f)) ⇒ (a b c d e f)
(list* x) ≡ x
```

make-list *size* &key :initial-element   [*Function*]

This creates and returns a list containing *size* elements, each of which is initialized
to the :initial-element argument (which defaults to nil). *size* should be a
non-negative integer. For example:

```
(make-list 5) ⇒ (nil nil nil nil nil)
(make-list 3 :initial-element ´rah) ⇒ (rah rah rah)
```

append &rest *lists*   [*Function*]

The arguments to append are lists. The result is a list that is the concatenation of
the arguments. The arguments are not destroyed. For example:

```
(append ´(a b c) ´(d e f) ´() ´(g)) ⇒ (a b c d e f g)
```

Note that append copies the top-level list structure of each of its arguments *except*
the last. The function concatenate can perform a similar operation, but always
copies all its arguments. See also nconc, which is like append but destroys all
arguments but the last.

The last argument actually need not be a list but may be any Lisp object, which
becomes the tail end of the constructed list. For example, (append ´(a b c) ´d)
⇒ (a b c . d).

(append *x* ´()) is an idiom once frequently used to copy the list *x*, but the
copy-list function is more appropriate to this task.

copy-list *list*   [*Function*]

This returns a list that is equal to *list*, but not eq. Only the top level of list
structure is copied; that is, copy-list copies in the *cdr* direction but not in the
car direction. If the list is "dotted," that is, (cdr (last *list*)) is a non-nil atom,
this will be true of the returned list also. See also copy-seq and copy-tree.

copy-alist *list*   [*Function*]

copy-alist is for copying association lists. The top level of list structure of *list*
is copied, just as for copy-list. In addition, each element of *list* that is a cons is
replaced in the copy by a new cons with the same *car* and *cdr*.

copy-tree *object*   [*Function*]

copy-tree is for copying trees of conses. The argument *object* may be any Lisp
object. If it is not a cons, it is returned; otherwise the result is a new cons of the

results of calling copy-tree on the *car* and *cdr* of the argument. In other words, all conses in the tree are copied recursively, stopping only when non-conses are encountered. Circularities and the sharing of substructure are *not* preserved.

Compatibility note: This function is called copy in Interlisp.

revappend *x* *y*   [*Function*]

(revappend *x* *y*) is exactly the same as (append (reverse *x*) *y*) except that it is potentially more efficient. Both *x* and *y* should be lists. The argument *x* is copied, not destroyed. Compare this with nreconc, which destroys its first argument.

nconc &rest *lists*   [*Function*]

nconc takes lists as arguments. It returns a list that is the arguments concatenated together. The arguments are changed rather than copied. (Compare this with append, which copies arguments rather than destroying them.) For example:

```
(setq x '(a b c))
(setq y '(d e f))
(nconc x y) ⇒ (a b c d e f)
x ⇒ (a b c d e f)
```

Note, in the example, that the value of x is now different, since its last cons has been rplacd'd to the value of y. If one were then to evaluate (nconc x y) again, it would yield a piece of "circular" list structure, whose printed representation would be (a b c d e f d e f d e f ...), repeating forever; if the *print-circle* switch were non-nil, it would be printed as (a b c . #1=(d e f . #1#)).

   X3J13 voted in March 1989 ⟨153⟩ to clarify the permissible side effects of certain operations. The side-effect behavior of nconc is specified by a recursive relationship outlined in the following table, in which a call to nconc matching the earliest possible pattern on the left is required to have side-effect behavior equivalent to the corresponding expression on the right.

```
(nconc)                 nil        ; No side effects
(nconc nil . r)         (nconc . r)
(nconc x)               x
(nconc x y)             (let ((p x) (q y))
                          (rplacd (last p) q)
                          p)
(nconc x y . r)         (nconc (nconc x y) . r)
```

nreconc *x y*   [*Function*]

(nreconc *x y*) is exactly the same as (nconc (nreverse *x*) *y*) except that it
is potentially more efficient. Both *x* and *y* should be lists. The argument *x* is
destroyed. Compare this with revappend.

```
(setq planets '(jupiter mars earth venus mercury))
(setq more-planets '(saturn uranus pluto neptune))
(nreconc more-planets planets)
   ⇒ (neptune pluto uranus saturn jupiter mars earth venus mercury)
   and now the value of more-planets is not well defined
```

X3J13 voted in March 1989 ⟨153⟩ to clarify the permissible side effects of certain
operations; (nreconc *x y*) is permitted and required to have side-effect behavior
equivalent to that of (nconc (nreverse *x*) *y*).

push *item place*   [*Macro*]

The form *place* should be the name of a generalized variable containing a list; *item*
may refer to any Lisp object. The *item* is consed onto the front of the list, and
the augmented list is stored back into *place* and returned. The form *place* may be
any form acceptable as a generalized variable to setf. If the list held in *place* is
viewed as a push-down stack, then push pushes an element onto the top of the
stack. For example:

```
(setq x '(a (b c) d))
(push 5 (cadr x)) ⇒ (5 b c) and now x ⇒ (a (5 b c) d)
```

The effect of (push *item place*) is roughly equivalent to

(setf *place* (cons *item place*))

except that the latter would evaluate any subforms of *place* twice, while push takes
care to evaluate them only once. Moreover, for certain *place* forms push may be
significantly more efficient than the setf version.

X3J13 voted in March 1988 ⟨146⟩ to clarify order of evaluation (see section 7.2).
Note that *item* is fully evaluated before any part of *place* is evaluated.

pushnew *item place* &key :test :test-not :key   [*Macro*]

The form *place* should be the name of a generalized variable containing a list;
item may refer to any Lisp object. If the *item* is not already a member of the list
(as determined by comparisons using the :test predicate, which defaults to eql),

then the *item* is consed onto the front of the list, and the augmented list is stored back into *place* and returned; otherwise the unaugmented list is returned. The form *place* may be any form acceptable as a generalized variable to setf. If the list held in *place* is viewed as a set, then pushnew adjoins an element to the set; see adjoin.

The keyword arguments to pushnew follow the conventions for the generic sequence functions. See chapter 14. In effect, these keywords are simply passed on to the adjoin function.

pushnew returns the new contents of the *place*. For example:

```
(setq x '(a (b c) d))
(pushnew 5 (cadr x)) ⇒ (5 b c) and now x ⇒ (a (5 b c) d)
(pushnew 'b (cadr x)) ⇒ (5 b c) and x is unchanged
```

The effect of

```
(pushnew item place :test p)
```

is roughly equivalent to

```
(setf place (adjoin item place :test p))
```

except that the latter would evaluate any subforms of *place* twice, while pushnew takes care to evaluate them only once. Moreover, for certain *place* forms pushnew may be significantly more efficient than the setf version.

X3J13 voted in March 1988 ⟨146⟩ to clarify order of evaluation (see section 7.2). Note that *item* is fully evaluated before any part of *place* is evaluated.

pop *place* [*Macro*]

The form *place* should be the name of a generalized variable containing a list. The result of pop is the car of the contents of *place*, and as a side effect the cdr of the contents is stored back into *place*. The form *place* may be any form acceptable as a generalized variable to setf. If the list held in *place* is viewed as a push-down stack, then pop pops an element from the top of the stack and returns it. For example:

```
(setq stack '(a b c))
(pop stack) ⇒ a and now stack ⇒ (b c)
```

The effect of (pop *place*) is roughly equivalent to

```
(prog1 (car place) (setf place (cdr place)))
```

except that the latter would evaluate any subforms of *place* three times, while pop takes care to evaluate them only once. Moreover, for certain *place* forms pop may be significantly more efficient than the setf version.

| X3J13 voted in March 1988 ⟨146⟩ to clarify order of evaluation (see section 7.2).

butlast *list* &optional *n*   [*Function*]

This creates and returns a list with the same elements as *list*, excepting the last *n* elements. *n* defaults to 1. The argument is not destroyed. If the *list* has fewer than *n* elements, then () is returned. For example:

```
(butlast '(a b c d)) ⇒ (a b c)
(butlast '((a b) (c d))) ⇒ ((a b))
(butlast '(a)) ⇒ ()
(butlast nil) ⇒ ()
```

The name is from the phrase "all elements but the last."

nbutlast *list* &optional *n*   [*Function*]

This is the destructive version of butlast; it changes the *cdr* of the cons $n+1$ from the end of the *list* to nil. *n* defaults to 1. If the *list* has fewer than *n* elements, then nbutlast returns (), and the argument is not modified. (Therefore one normally writes (setq a (nbutlast a)) rather than simply (nbutlast a).) For example:

```
(setq foo '(a b c d))
(nbutlast foo) ⇒ (a b c)
foo ⇒ (a b c)
(nbutlast '(a)) ⇒ ()
(nbutlast 'nil) ⇒ ()
```

ldiff *list* *sublist*   [*Function*]

list should be a list, and *sublist* should be a sublist of *list*, that is, one of the conses that make up *list*. ldiff (meaning "list difference") will return a new (freshly consed) list, whose elements are those elements of *list* that appear before *sublist*. If *sublist* is not a tail of *list* (and in particular if *sublist* is nil), then a copy of the entire *list* is returned. The argument *list* is not destroyed. For example:

```
(setq x '(a b c d e))
(setq y (cdddr x)) ⇒ (d e)
(ldiff x y) ⇒ (a b c)
```

but (ldiff '(a b c d) '(c d)) ⇒ (a b c d)

since the sublist was not eq to any part of the list.

15.3. Alteration of List Structure

The functions rplaca and rplacd may be used to make alterations in already existing list structure, that is, to change the *car* or *cdr* of an existing cons. One may also use setf in conjunction with car and cdr.

The structure is not copied but is destructively altered; hence caution should be exercised when using these functions, as strange side effects can occur if portions of list structure become shared. The nconc, nreverse, nreconc, and nbutlast functions, already described, have the same property, as do certain of the generic sequence functions such as delete. However, they are normally not used for this side effect; rather, the list-structure modification is purely for efficiency, and compatible non-modifying functions are provided.

rplaca *x y*   [*Function*]

(rplaca *x y*) changes the *car* of *x* to *y* and returns (the modified) *x*. *x* must be a cons, but *y* may be any Lisp object. For example:

```
(setq g '(a b c))
(rplaca (cdr g) 'd) ⇒ (d c)
Now g ⇒ (a d c)
```

rplacd *x y*   [*Function*]

(rplacd *x y*) changes the *cdr* of *x* to *y* and returns (the modified) *x*. *x* must be a cons, but *y* may be any Lisp object. For example:

```
(setq x '(a b c))
(rplacd x 'd) ⇒ (a . d)
Now x ⇒ (a . d)
```

> The functions rplaca and rplacd go back to the earliest origins of Lisp, along with car, cdr, and cons. Nowadays, however, they seem to be falling by the way-side. More and more Common Lisp programmers use setf for nearly all structure modifications: (rplaca x y) is rendered as (setf (car x) y) or perhaps as (setf (first x) y). Even more likely is that a defstruct structure or a CLOS class is used in place of a list, if the data structure is at all complicated; in this case setf is used with a slot accessor.

15.4. Substitution of Expressions

A number of functions are provided for performing substitutions within a tree. All take a tree and a description of old subexpressions to be replaced by new ones. They come in non-destructive and destructive varieties and specify substitution either by two arguments or by an association list.

The naming conventions for these functions and for their keyword arguments generally follow the conventions for the generic sequence functions. See chapter 14.

subst *new old tree* &key :test :test-not :key   [*Function*]
subst-if *new test tree* &key :key   [*Function*]
subst-if-not *new test tree* &key :key   [*Function*]

(subst *new old tree*) makes a copy of *tree*, substituting *new* for every subtree or leaf of *tree* (whether the subtree or leaf is a *car* or a *cdr* of its parent) such that *old* and the subtree or leaf satisfy the test. It returns the modified copy of *tree*. The original *tree* is unchanged, but the result tree may share with parts of the argument *tree*.

Compatibility note: In MacLisp, subst is guaranteed *not* to share with the *tree* argument, and the idiom (subst nil nil x) was used to copy a tree x. In Common Lisp, the function copy-tree should be used to copy a tree, as the subst idiom will not work.

For example:

```
(subst 'tempest 'hurricane
       '(shakespeare wrote (the hurricane)))
   ⇒ (shakespeare wrote (the tempest))

(subst 'foo 'nil '(shakespeare wrote (twelfth night)))
   ⇒ (shakespeare wrote (twelfth night . foo) . foo)

(subst '(a . cons) '(old . pair)
          '((old . spice) ((old . shoes) old . pair) (old . pair))
       :test #'equal)
   ⇒ ((old . spice) ((old . shoes) a . cons) (a . cons))
```

This function is not destructive; that is, it does not change the *car* or *cdr* of any already existing list structure. One possible definition of subst:

```
(defun subst (old new tree &rest x &key test test-not key)
  (cond ((satisfies-the-test old tree :test test
                             :test-not test-not :key key)
         new)
        ((atom tree) tree)
        (t (let ((a (apply #'subst old new (car tree) x))
                 (d (apply #'subst old new (cdr tree) x)))
             (if (and (eql a (car tree))
                      (eql d (cdr tree)))
                 tree
                 (cons a d))))))
```

See also `substitute`, which substitutes for top-level elements of a sequence.

X3J13 voted in January 1989 ⟨121⟩ to restrict user side effects; see section 7.9.

nsubst *new old tree* &key :test :test-not :key	[*Function*]
nsubst-if *new test tree* &key :key	[*Function*]
nsubst-if-not *new test tree* &key :key	[*Function*]

`nsubst` is a destructive version of `subst`. The list structure of *tree* is altered by destructively replacing with *new* each leaf or subtree of the *tree* such that *old* and the leaf or subtree satisfy the test.

X3J13 voted in January 1989 ⟨121⟩ to restrict user side effects; see section 7.9.

sublis *alist tree* &key :test :test-not :key	[*Function*]

`sublis` makes substitutions for objects in a tree (a structure of conses). The first argument to `sublis` is an association list. The second argument is the tree in which substitutions are to be made, as for `subst`. `sublis` looks at all subtrees and leaves of the tree; if a subtree or leaf appears as a key in the association list (that is, the key and the subtree or leaf satisfy the test), it is replaced by the object with which it is associated. This operation is non-destructive. In effect, `sublis` can perform several `subst` operations simultaneously. For example:

```
(sublis '((x . 100) (z . zprime))
        '(plus x (minus g z x p) 4 . x))
  ⇒ (plus 100 (minus g zprime 100 p) 4 . 100)

(sublis '(((+ x y) . (- x y)) ((- x y) . (+ x y)))
        '(* (/ (+ x y) (+ x p)) (- x y))
        :test #'equal)
  ⇒ (* (/ (- x y) (+ x p)) (+ x y))
```

| X3J13 voted in January 1989 ⟨121⟩ to restrict user side effects; see section 7.9.

nsublis *alist tree* &key :test :test-not :key   [*Function*]

nsublis is like sublis but destructively modifies the relevant parts of the *tree*.
| X3J13 voted in January 1989 ⟨121⟩ to restrict user side effects; see section 7.9.

15.5. Using Lists as Sets

Common Lisp includes functions that allow a list of items to be treated as a *set*.
There are functions to add, remove, and search for items in a list, based on various
criteria. There are also set union, intersection, and difference functions.

The naming conventions for these functions and for their keyword arguments
generally follow the conventions that apply to the generic sequence functions. See
chapter 14.

member *item list* &key :test :test-not :key   [*Function*]
member-if *predicate list* &key :key   [*Function*]
member-if-not *predicate list* &key :key   [*Function*]

The *list* is searched for an element that satisfies the test. If none is found, nil is
returned; otherwise, the tail of *list* beginning with the first element that satisfied
the test is returned. The *list* is searched on the top level only. These functions are
suitable for use as predicates.

For example:

```
(member 'snerd '(a b c d)) ⇒ nil
(member-if #'numberp '(a #\Space 5/3 foo)) ⇒ (5/3 foo)
(member 'a '(g (a y) c a d e a f)) ⇒ (a d e a f)
```

Note, in the last example, that the value returned by member is eq to the portion
of the list beginning with a. Thus rplaca on the result of member may be used
to alter the found list element, if a check is first made that member did not return
nil.

See also find and position.
| X3J13 voted in January 1989 ⟨121⟩ to restrict user side effects; see section 7.9.

Compatibility note: In MacLisp, the member function uses an equal comparison rather than
eql, which is the default test for member in Common Lisp. Where in MacLisp one would
write (member x y), in Common Lisp one must write (member x y :test #'equal) to

get a completely identical effect. Similarly, one can get the precise effect, and no more, of the MacLisp (memq x y) by writing in Common Lisp (member x y :test #´eq).

---

tailp *sublist* *list*   [*Function*]

This predicate is true if *sublist* is a sublist of *list* (that is, one of the conses that makes up *list*); otherwise it is false. Another way to look at this is that tailp is true if (nthcdr *n* *list*) is *sublist*, for some value of *n*. See ldiff.

X3J13 voted in January 1989 ⟨175⟩ to strike the parenthetical remark that suggests that the *sublist* must be a cons, to clarify that tailp is true if and only if there exists an integer *n* such that

(eql *sublist* (nthcdr *n* *list*))

and to specify that *list* may be a dotted list (implying that implementations must use atom and not endp to check for the end of the *list*).

---

adjoin *item* *list* &key :test :test-not :key   [*Function*]

adjoin is used to add an element to a set, provided that it is not already a member. The equality test defaults to eql.

(adjoin *item* *list*) ≡ (if (member *item* *list*) *list* (cons *item* *list*))

In general, the test may be any predicate; the *item* is added to the list only if there is no element of the list that "satisfies the test."

adjoin deviates from the usual rules described in chapter 14 for the treatment of arguments named *item* and :key. If a :key function is specified, it is applied to *item* as well as to each element of the list. The rationale is that if the *item* is not yet in the list, it soon will be, and so the test is more properly viewed as being between two elements rather than between a separate *item* and an element.

(adjoin *item* *list* :key *fn*)
    ≡ (if (member (funcall *fn* *item*) *list* :key *fn*) *list* (cons *item* *list*))

See pushnew.

Notice of correction. In the first edition, the form (*fn* *item*) appeared in this example without the required funcall.

X3J13 voted in January 1989 ⟨121⟩ to restrict user side effects; see section 7.9.

union *list1* *list2* &key :test :test-not :key   [*Function*]
nunion *list1* *list2* &key :test :test-not :key   [*Function*]

union takes two lists and returns a new list containing everything that is an element of either of the *lists*. If there is a duplication between two lists, only one of the duplicate instances will be in the result. If either of the arguments has duplicate entries within it, the redundant entries may or may not appear in the result. For example:

```
(union '(a b c) '(f a d))
   ⇒ (a b c f d) or (b c f a d) or (d f a b c) or ...

(union '((x 5) (y 6)) '((z 2) (x 4)) :key #'car)
   ⇒ ((x 5) (y 6) (z 2)) or ((x 4) (y 6) (z 2)) or ...
```

There is no guarantee that the order of elements in the result will reflect the ordering of the arguments in any particular way. The implementation is therefore free to use any of a variety of strategies. The result list may share cells with, or be eq to, either of the arguments if appropriate.

In general, the test may be any predicate, and the union operation may be described as follows. For all possible ordered pairs consisting of one element from *list1* and one element from *list2*, the test is used to determine whether they "match." For every matching pair, at least one of the two elements of the pair will be in the result. Moreover, any element from either list that matches no element of the other will appear in the result. All this is very general, but probably not particularly useful unless the test is an equivalence relation.

The :test-not argument can be useful when the test function is the logical negation of an equivalence test. A good example of this is the function mismatch, which is logically inverted so that possibly useful information can be returned if the arguments do not match. This additional "useful information" is discarded in the following example; mismatch is used purely as a predicate.

```
(union '(#(a b) #(5 0 6) #(f 3))
       '(#(5 0 6) (a b) #(g h))
       :test-not
       #'mismatch)
   ⇒ (#(a b) #(5 0 6) #(f 3) #(g h))      ;One possible result
   ⇒ ((a b) #(f 3) #(5 0 6) #(g h))       ;Another possible result
```

Using :test-not #'mismatch differs from using :test #'equalp, for example, because mismatch will determine that #(a b) and (a b) are the same, while equalp would regard them as not the same.

nunion is the destructive version of union. It performs the same operation but may destroy the argument lists, perhaps in order to use their cells to construct the result.

X3J13 voted in January 1989 ⟨121⟩ to restrict user side effects; see section 7.9.

X3J13 voted in March 1989 ⟨153⟩ to clarify the permissible side effects of certain operations; nunion is permitted to perform a setf on any part, *car* or *cdr*, of the top-level list structure of any of the argument lists.

intersection *list1* *list2* &key :test :test-not :key   [*Function*]
nintersection *list1* *list2* &key :test :test-not :key   [*Function*]

intersection takes two lists and returns a new list containing everything that is an element of both argument lists. If either list has duplicate entries, the redundant entries may or may not appear in the result. For example:

(intersection '(a b c) '(f a d)) ⇒ (a)

There is no guarantee that the order of elements in the result will reflect the ordering of the arguments in any particular way. The implementation is therefore free to use any of a variety of strategies. The result list may share cells with, or be eq to, either of the arguments if appropriate.

In general, the test may be any predicate, and the intersection operation may be described as follows. For all possible ordered pairs consisting of one element from *list1* and one element from *list2*, the test is used to determine whether they "match." For every matching pair, exactly one of the two elements of the pair will be put in the result. No element from either list appears in the result that does not match an element from the other list. All this is very general, but probably not particularly useful unless the test is an equivalence relation.

nintersection is the destructive version of intersection. It performs the same operation, but may destroy *list1*, perhaps in order to use its cells to construct the result. (The argument *list2* is *not* destroyed.)

X3J13 voted in January 1989 ⟨121⟩ to restrict user side effects; see section 7.9.

X3J13 voted in March 1989 ⟨153⟩ to clarify the permissible side effects of certain operations; nintersection is permitted to perform a setf on any part, *car* or *cdr*, of the top-level list structure of any of the argument lists.

set-difference *list1* *list2* &key :test :test-not :key   [*Function*]
nset-difference *list1* *list2* &key :test :test-not :key   [*Function*]

set-difference returns a list of elements of *list1* that do not appear in *list2*. This operation is not destructive.

There is no guarantee that the order of elements in the result will reflect the ordering of the arguments in any particular way. The implementation is therefore free to use any of a variety of strategies. The result list may share cells with, or be eq to, either of the arguments if appropriate.

In general, the test may be any predicate, and the set difference operation may be described as follows. For all possible ordered pairs consisting of one element from *list1* and one element from *list2*, the test is used to determine whether they "match." An element of *list1* appears in the result if and only if it does not match any element of *list2*. This is very general and permits interesting applications. For example, one can remove from a list of strings all those strings containing one of a given list of characters:

```
;; Remove all flavor names that contain "c" or "w".
(set-difference '("strawberry" "chocolate" "banana"
                  "lemon" "pistachio" "rhubarb")
                '(#\c #\w)
                :test
                #'(lambda (s c) (find c s)))
⇒ ("banana" "rhubarb" "lemon")        ;One possible ordering
```

nset-difference is the destructive version of set-difference. This operation may destroy *list1*.

X3J13 voted in January 1989 ⟨121⟩ to restrict user side effects; see section 7.9.

Compatibility note: An approximately equivalent Interlisp function is ldifference.

---

set-exclusive-or *list1* *list2* &key :test :test-not :key   [*Function*]
nset-exclusive-or *list1* *list2* &key :test :test-not :key   [*Function*]

set-exclusive-or returns a list of elements that appear in exactly one of *list1* and *list2*. This operation is not destructive.

There is no guarantee that the order of elements in the result will reflect the ordering of the arguments in any particular way. The implementation is therefore free to use any of a variety of strategies. The result list may share cells with, or be eq to, either of the arguments if appropriate.

In general, the test may be any predicate, and the set-exclusive-or operation may be described as follows. For all possible ordered pairs consisting of one element from *list1* and one element from *list2*, the test is used to determine whether they "match." The result contains precisely those elements of *list1* and *list2* that appear in no matching pair.

nset-exclusive-or is the destructive version of set-exclusive-or. Both lists may be destroyed in producing the result.

X3J13 voted in January 1989 ⟨121⟩ to restrict user side effects; see section 7.9.

X3J13 voted in March 1989 ⟨153⟩ to clarify the permissible side effects of certain operations; nset-exclusive-or is permitted to perform a setf on any part, *car* or *cdr*, of the top-level list structure of any of the argument lists.

---

subsetp *list1* *list2* &key :test :test-not :key   [*Function*]

subsetp is a predicate that is true if every element of *list1* appears in ("matches" some element of) *list2*, and false otherwise.

X3J13 voted in January 1989 ⟨121⟩ to restrict user side effects; see section 7.9.

15.6. Association Lists

An *association list*, or *a-list*, is a data structure used very frequently in Lisp. An a-list is a list of pairs (conses); each pair is an association. The *car* of a pair is called the *key*, and the *cdr* is called the *datum*.

An advantage of the a-list representation is that an a-list can be incrementally augmented simply by adding new entries to the front. Moreover, because the searching function assoc searches the a-list in order, new entries can "shadow" old entries. If an a-list is viewed as a mapping from keys to data, then the mapping can be not only augmented but also altered in a non-destructive manner by adding new entries to the front of the a-list.

Sometimes an a-list represents a bijective mapping, and it is desirable to retrieve a key given a datum. For this purpose, the "reverse" searching function rassoc is provided. Other variants of a-list searches can be constructed using the function find or member.

It is permissible to let nil be an element of an a-list in place of a pair. Such an element is not considered to be a pair but is simply passed over when the a-list is searched by assoc.

---

acons *key datum a-list*   [*Function*]

acons constructs a new association list by adding the pair (*key* . *datum*) to the old *a-list*.

```
(acons x y a) ≡ (cons (cons x y) a)
```

This is a trivial convenience function, but I find I use it a lot.

pairlis *keys data* &optional *a-list*   [*Function*]

pairlis takes two lists and makes an association list that associates elements of the first list to corresponding elements of the second list. It is an error if the two lists *keys* and *data* are not of the same length. If the optional argument *a-list* is provided, then the new pairs are added to the front of it.

The new pairs may appear in the resulting a-list in any order; in particular, either forward or backward order is permitted. Therefore the result of the call

```
(pairlis '(one two) '(1 2) '((three . 3) (four . 19)))
```

might be

```
((one . 1) (two . 2) (three . 3) (four . 19))
```

but could equally well be

```
((two . 2) (one . 1) (three . 3) (four . 19))
```

assoc *item a-list* &key :test :test-not :key   [*Function*]
assoc-if *predicate a-list*   [*Function*]
assoc-if-not *predicate a-list*   [*Function*]

X3J13 voted in March 1988 ⟨9⟩ to allow assoc-if and assoc-if-not also to take a keyword argument named :key, to be used to determine whether a pair "satisfies the test" in the same manner as for sequence functions. The new function descriptions are therefore as follows:

assoc-if *predicate a-list* &key :key   [*Function*]
assoc-if-not *predicate a-list* &key :key   [*Function*]

The omission of :key arguments for these functions in the first edition was probably an oversight.

Each of these searches the association list *a-list*. The value is the first pair in the a-list such that the *car* of the pair satisfies the test, or nil if there is no such pair in the a-list. For example:

```
(assoc 'r '((a . b) (c . d) (r . x) (s . y) (r . z)))
        ⇒ (r . x)
(assoc 'goo '((foo . bar) (zoo . goo))) ⇒ nil
(assoc '2 '((1 a b c) (2 b c d) (-7 x y z))) ⇒ (2 b c d)
```

It is possible to rplacd the result of assoc *provided* that it is not nil, in order to "update" the "table" that was assoc's second argument. (However, it is often better to update an a-list by adding new pairs to the front, rather than altering old pairs.) For example:

```
(setq values '((x . 100) (y . 200) (z . 50)))
(assoc 'y values) ⇒ (y . 200)
(rplacd (assoc 'y values) 201)
(assoc 'y values) ⇒ (y . 201) now
```

A typical trick is to say (cdr (assoc x y)). Because the *cdr* of nil is guaranteed to be nil, this yields nil if no pair is found *or* if a pair is found whose *cdr* is nil. This is useful if nil serves its usual role as a "default value."

The two expressions

(assoc *item list* :test *fn*)

and

(find *item list* :test *fn* :key #'car)

are equivalent in meaning with one important exception: if nil appears in the a-list in place of a pair, and the *item* being searched for is nil, find will blithely compute the *car* of the nil in the a-list, find that it is equal to the *item*, and return nil, whereas assoc will ignore the nil in the a-list and continue to search for an actual pair (cons) whose *car* is nil. See find and position.

X3J13 voted in January 1989 ⟨121⟩ to restrict user side effects; see section 7.9.

Compatibility note: In MacLisp, the assoc function uses an equal comparison rather than eql, which is the default test for assoc in Common Lisp. Where in MacLisp one would write (assoc x y), in Common Lisp one must write (assoc x y :test #'equal) to get the completely identical effect. Similarly, one can get the precise effect, and no more, of the MacLisp (assq x y) by writing in Common Lisp (assoc x y :test #'eq).

In Interlisp, assoc uses an eq test, and sassoc uses an Interlisp equal test.

---

rassoc *item a-list* &key :test :test-not :key   [*Function*]
rassoc-if *predicate a-list*   [*Function*]
rassoc-if-not *predicate a-list*   [*Function*]

X3J13 voted in March 1988 ⟨9⟩ to allow rassoc-if and rassoc-if-not also to take a keyword argument named :key, to be used to determine whether a pair "satisfies the test" in the same manner as for sequence functions. The new function descriptions are therefore as follows:

rassoc-if *predicate a-list* &key :key   [*Function*]
rassoc-if-not *predicate a-list* &key :key   [*Function*]

The omission of :key arguments for these functions in the first edition was probably an oversight.

rassoc is the reverse form of assoc; it searches for a pair whose *cdr* satisfies the test, rather than the *car*. If the *a-list* is considered to be a mapping, then rassoc treats the *a-list* as representing the inverse mapping. For example:

(rassoc 'a '((a . b) (b . c) (c . a) (z . a))) ⇒ (c . a)

The expressions

(rassoc *item list* :test *fn*)

and

(find *item list* :test *fn* :key #'cdr)

are equivalent in meaning, except when the *item* is nil and nil appears in place of a pair in the a-list. See the discussion of the function assoc.

X3J13 voted in January 1989 ⟨121⟩ to restrict user side effects; see section 7.9.

16

Hash Tables

A hash table is a Lisp object that can efficiently map a given Lisp object to another Lisp object. Each hash table has a set of *entries*, each of which associates a particular *key* with a particular *value*. The basic functions that deal with hash tables can create entries, delete entries, and find the value that is associated with a given key. Finding the value is very fast, even if there are many entries, because hashing is used; this is an important advantage of hash tables over property lists.

A given hash table can associate only one *value* with a given *key*; if you try to add a second *value*, it will replace the first. Also, adding a value to a hash table is a destructive operation; the hash table is modified. By contrast, association lists can be augmented non-destructively.

Hash tables come in three kinds, the difference being whether the keys are compared with eq, eql, or equal. In other words, there are hash tables that hash on Lisp *objects* (using eq or eql) and there are hash tables that hash on *tree structure* (using equal).

Hash tables are created with the function make-hash-table, which takes various options, including which kind of hash table to make (the default being the eql kind). To look up a key and find the associated value, use gethash. New entries are added to hash tables using setf with gethash. To remove an entry, use remhash. Here is a simple example.

```
(setq a (make-hash-table))
(setf (gethash 'color a) 'brown)
(setf (gethash 'name a) 'fred)
(gethash 'color a) ⇒ brown
(gethash 'name a) ⇒ fred
(gethash 'pointy a) ⇒ nil
```

In this example, the symbols color and name are being used as keys, and the symbols brown and fred are being used as the associated values. The hash table

435

has two items in it, one of which associates from color to brown, and the other of which associates from name to fred.

Keys do not have to be symbols; they can be any Lisp object. Similarly, values can be any Lisp object.

When a hash table is first created, it has a *size*, which is the maximum number of entries it can hold. Usually the actual capacity of the table is somewhat less, since the hashing is not perfectly collision-free. With the maximum possible bad luck, the capacity could be very much less, but this rarely happens. If so many entries are added that the capacity is exceeded, the hash table will automatically grow, and the entries will be *rehashed* (new hash values will be recomputed, and everything will be rearranged so that the fast hash lookup still works). This is transparent to the caller; it all happens automatically.

There is a discrepancy between the preceding description of the size of a hash table and the description of the :size argument in the specification below of make-hash-table.

X3J13 voted in June 1989 ⟨99⟩ to regard the latter description as definitive: the :size argument is approximately the number of entries that can be inserted without having to enlarge the hash table. This definition is certainly more convenient for the user.

Compatibility note: This hash table facility is compatible with Lisp Machine Lisp. It is similar to the hasharray facility of Interlisp, and some of the function names are the same. However, it is *not* compatible with Interlisp. The exact details and the order of arguments are designed to be consistent with the rest of MacLisp rather than with Interlisp. For instance, the order of arguments to maphash is different, there is no "system hash table," and there is not the Interlisp restriction that keys and values may not be nil.

16.1. Hash Table Functions

This section documents the functions for hash tables, which use *objects* as keys and associate other objects with them.

make-hash-table &key :test :size :rehash-size   [*Function*]
                     :rehash-threshold

This function creates and returns a new hash table. The :test argument determines how keys are compared; it must be one of the three values #´eq, #´eql, or #´equal, or one of the three symbols eq, eql, or equal. If no test is specified, eql is assumed.

X3J13 voted in January 1989 ⟨100⟩ to add a fourth type of hash table: the value of #´equalp and the symbol equalp are to be additional valid possibilities for the :test argument.

Note that one consequence of the vote to change the rules of floating-point contagion ⟨37⟩ (described in section 12.1) is to require =, and therefore also equalp, to compare the values of numbers exactly and not approximately, making equalp a true equivalence relation on numbers.

Another valuable use of equalp hash tables is case-insensitive comparison of keys that are strings.

The :size argument sets the initial size of the hash table, in entries. (The actual size may be rounded up from the size you specify to the next "good" size, for example to make it a prime number.) You won't necessarily be able to store precisely this many entries into the table before it overflows and becomes bigger, but this argument does serve as a hint to the implementation of approximately how many entries you intend to store.

X3J13 voted in January 1989 ⟨7⟩ to clarify that the :size argument must be a non-negative integer.

X3J13 voted in June 1989 ⟨99⟩ to regard the preceding description of the :size argument as definitive: it is approximately the number of entries that can be inserted without having to enlarge the hash table.

The :rehash-size argument specifies how much to increase the size of the hash table when it becomes full. This can be an integer greater than zero, which is the number of entries to add, or it can be a floating-point number greater than 1, which is the ratio of the new size to the old size. The default value for this argument is implementation-dependent.

The :rehash-threshold argument specifies how full the hash table can get before it must grow. This can be an integer greater than zero and less than the :rehash-size (in which case it will be scaled whenever the table is grown), or it can be a floating-point number between zero and 1. The default value for this argument is implementation-dependent.

X3J13 voted in June 1989 ⟨99⟩ to replace the preceding specification of the :rehash-threshold argument with the following: The :rehash-threshold argument specifies how full the hash table can get before it must grow. It may be any real number between 0 and 1, inclusive. It indicates the maximum desired level of hash table occupancy. An implementation is permitted to ignore this argument. The default value for this argument is implementation-dependent.

An example of the use of make-hash-table:

```
(make-hash-table :rehash-size 1.5
                 :size (* number-of-widgets 43))
```

hash-table-p *object*   [*Function*]

hash-table-p is true if its argument is a hash table, and otherwise is false.

(hash-table-p x) ≡ (typep x ´hash-table)

gethash *key hash-table* &optional *default*   [*Function*]

gethash finds the entry in *hash-table* whose key is *key* and returns the associated
value. If there is no such entry, gethash returns *default*, which is nil if not
specified.

   gethash actually returns two values, the second being a predicate value that is
true if an entry was found, and false if no entry was found.

   setf may be used with gethash to make new entries in a hash table. If an entry
with the specified *key* already exists, it is removed before the new entry is added.
The *default* argument may be specified to gethash in this context; it is ignored by
setf but may be useful in such macros as incf that are related to setf:

(incf (gethash a-key table 0))

means approximately the same as

(setf (gethash a-key table 0)
      (+ (gethash a-key table 0) 1))

which in turn would be treated as simply

(setf (gethash a-key table)
      (+ (gethash a-key table 0) 1))

remhash *key hash-table*   [*Function*]

remhash removes any entry for *key* in *hash-table*. This is a predicate that is true
if there was an entry or false if there was not.

maphash *function hash-table*   [*Function*]

For each entry in *hash-table*, maphash calls *function* on two arguments: the key
of the entry and the value of the entry; maphash then returns nil. If entries are
added to or deleted from the hash table while a maphash is in progress, the results
are unpredictable, with one exception: if the *function* calls remhash to remove the
entry currently being processed by the *function*, or performs a setf of gethash
on that entry to change the associated value, then those operations will have the
intended effect. For example:

```
;;; Alter every entry in MY-HASH-TABLE, replacing the value with
;;; its square root. Entries with negative values are removed.
(maphash #'(lambda (key val)
             (if (minusp val)
                 (remhash key my-hash-table)
                 (setf (gethash key my-hash-table) (sqrt val))))
         my-hash-table)
```

X3J13 voted in January 1989 ⟨121⟩ to restrict user side effects; see section 7.9.

clrhash *hash-table* [*Function*]

This removes all the entries from *hash-table* and returns the hash table itself.

hash-table-count *hash-table* [*Function*]

This returns the number of entries in the *hash-table*. When a hash table is first created or has been cleared, the number of entries is zero.

with-hash-table-iterator (*mname hash-table*) {*form*}* [*Macro*]

X3J13 voted in January 1989 ⟨98⟩ to add the macro with-hash-table-iterator.

The name *mname* is bound and defined as if by macrolet, with the body *forms* as its lexical scope, to be a "generator macro" such that successive invocations (*mname*) will return entries, one by one, from the hash table that is the value of the expression *hash-table* (which is evaluated exactly once).

At each invocation of the generator macro, there are two possibilities. If there is yet another unprocessed entry in the hash table, then three values are returned: t, the key of the hash table entry, and the associated value of the hash table entry. On the other hand, if there are no more unprocessed entries in the hash table, then one value is returned: nil.

The implicit interior state of the iteration over the hash table entries has dynamic extent. While the name *mname* has lexical scope, it is an error to invoke the generator macro once the with-hash-table-iterator form has been exited.

Invocations of with-hash-table-iterator and related macros may be nested, and the generator macro of an outer invocation may be called from within an inner invocation (assuming that its name is visible or otherwise made available).

X3J13 voted in January 1989 ⟨121⟩ to restrict user side effects; see section 7.9.

Rationale: This facility is a bit more flexible than maphash. It makes possible a portable and efficient implementation of loop clauses for iterating over hash tables (see chapter 26).

```
(setq turtles (make-hash-table :size 9 :test 'eq))
(setf (gethash 'howard-kaylan turtles) '(musician lead-singer))
(setf (gethash 'john-barbata turtles) '(musician drummer))
(setf (gethash 'leonardo turtles) '(ninja leader blue))
(setf (gethash 'donatello turtles) '(ninja machines purple))
(setf (gethash 'al-nichol turtles) '(musician guitarist))
(setf (gethash 'mark-volman turtles) '(musician great-hair))
(setf (gethash 'raphael turtles) '(ninja cool rude red))
(setf (gethash 'michaelangelo turtles) '(ninja party-dude orange))
(setf (gethash 'jim-pons turtles) '(musician bassist))

(with-hash-table-iterator (get-turtle turtles)
  (labels ((try (got-one &optional key value)
             (when got-one      ;Remember, keys may show up in any order
               (when (eq (first value) 'ninja)
                 (format t "~%~:(~A~): ~{~A~^, ~}"
                      key (rest value)))
               (multiple-value-call #'try (get-turtle)))))
    (multiple-value-call #'try (get-turtle))))    ;Prints 4 lines
Michaelangelo: PARTY-DUDE, ORANGE
Leonardo: LEADER, BLUE
Raphael: COOL, RUDE, RED
Donatello: MACHINES, PURPLE
  ⇒ nil
```

hash-table-rehash-size *hash-table*	[*Function*]
hash-table-rehash-threshold *hash-table*	[*Function*]
hash-table-size *hash-table*	[*Function*]
hash-table-test *hash-table*	[*Function*]

X3J13 voted in March 1989 ⟨97⟩ to add four accessor functions that return values suitable for use in a call to make-hash-table in order to produce a new hash table with state corresponding to the current state of the argument hash table.

hash-table-rehash-size returns the current rehash size of a hash table.

hash-table-rehash-threshold returns the current rehash threshold.

hash-table-size returns the current size of a hash table.

hash-table-test returns the test used for comparing keys. If the test is one of the standard test functions, then the result will always be a symbol, even if the function itself was specified when the *hash-table* was created. For example:

```
(hash-table-test (make-hash-table :test #'equal)) ⇒ equal
```

Implementations that extend `make-hash-table` by providing additional possibilities for the `:test` argument may determine how the value returned by `hash-table-test` is related to such additional tests.

16.2. Primitive Hash Function

The function `sxhash` is a convenient tool for the user who needs to create more complicated hashed data structures than are provided by `hash-table` objects.

`sxhash` *object*   [*Function*]

`sxhash` computes a hash code for an object and returns the hash code as a nonnegative fixnum. A property of `sxhash` is that (`equal` *x* *y*) implies (= (`sxhash` *x*) (`sxhash` *y*)).

The manner in which the hash code is computed is implementation-dependent but independent of the particular "incarnation" or "core image." Hash values produced by `sxhash` may be written out to files, for example, and meaningfully read in again into an instance of the same implementation.

17

Arrays

An array is an object with components arranged according to a rectilinear coordinate system. In principle, an array in Common Lisp may have any number of dimensions, including zero. (A zero-dimensional array has exactly one element.) In practice, an implementation may limit the number of dimensions supported, but every Common Lisp implementation must support arrays of up to seven dimensions. Each dimension is a non-negative integer; if any dimension of an array is zero, the array has no elements.

An array may be a *general array*, meaning each element may be any Lisp object, or it may be a *specialized array*, meaning that each element must be of a given restricted type.

One-dimensional arrays are called vectors. General vectors may contain any Lisp object. Vectors whose elements are restricted to type string-char are called *strings*. Vectors whose elements are restricted to type bit are called *bit-vectors*.

X3J13 voted in March 1989 ⟨11⟩ to eliminate the type string-char and to redefine the type string to be the union of one or more specialized vector types, the types of whose elements are subtypes of the type character.

17.1. Array Creation

Do not be daunted by the many options of the function make-array. All that is required to construct an array is a list of the dimensions; most of the options are for relatively esoteric applications.

make-array *dimensions* &key :element-type :initial-element [*Function*]
          :initial-contents :adjustable :fill-pointer
          :displaced-to :displaced-index-offset

This is the primitive function for making arrays. The *dimensions* argument should be a list of non-negative integers that are to be the dimensions of the array; the length of the list will be the dimensionality of the array. Each dimension must be smaller than `array-dimension-limit`, and the product of all the dimensions must be smaller than `array-total-size-limit`. Note that if *dimensions* is `nil`, then a zero-dimensional array is created. For convenience when making a one-dimensional array, the single dimension may be provided as an integer rather than as a list of one integer.

An implementation of Common Lisp may impose a limit on the rank of an array, but this limit may not be smaller than 7. Therefore, any Common Lisp program may assume the use of arrays of rank 7 or less. The implementation-dependent limit on array rank is reflected in `array-rank-limit`.

The keyword arguments for `make-array` are as follows:

`:element-type`

This argument should be the name of the type of the elements of the array; an array is constructed of the most specialized type that can nevertheless accommodate elements of the given type. The type t specifies a general array, one whose elements may be any Lisp object; this is the default type.

X3J13 voted in January 1989 ⟨8⟩ to change `typep` and `subtypep` so that the specialized `array` type specifier means the same thing for discrimination purposes as for declaration purposes: it encompasses those arrays that can result by specifying *element-type* as the element type to the function `make-array`. Therefore we may say that if *type* is the `:element-type` argument, then the result will be an array of type (array *type*); put another way, for any type *A*,

```
(typep (make-array ... :element-type 'A ...)
       '(array A)))
```

is always true. See `upgraded-array-element-type`.

`:initial-element`

This argument may be used to initialize each element of the array. The value must be of the type specified by the `:element-type` argument. If the `:initial-element` option is omitted, the initial values of the array elements are undefined (unless the `:initial-contents` or `:displaced-to` option is used). The `:initial-element` option may not be used with the `:initial-contents` or `:displaced-to` option.

`:initial-contents`

This argument may be used to initialize the contents of the array. The value is a nested structure of sequences. If the array is zero-dimensional, then the value specifies the single element. Otherwise, the value must be a sequence whose length is equal to the first dimension; each element must be a nested structure for an array whose dimensions are the remaining dimensions, and so on. For example:

```
(make-array '(4 2 3)
            :initial-contents
            '(((a b c) (1 2 3))
              ((d e f) (3 1 2))
              ((g h i) (2 3 1))
              ((j k l) (0 0 0))))
```

The numbers of levels in the structure must equal the rank of the array. Each leaf of the nested structure must be of the type specified by the :type option. If the :initial-contents option is omitted, the initial values of the array elements are undefined (unless the :initial-element or :displaced-to option is used). The :initial-contents option may not be used with the :initial-element or :displaced-to option.

:adjustable

This argument, if specified and not nil, indicates that it must be possible to alter the array's size dynamically after it is created. This argument defaults to nil.

X3J13 voted in June 1989 ⟨3⟩ to clarify that if this argument is non-nil then the predicate adjustable-array-p will necessarily be true when applied to the resulting array; but if this argument is nil (or omitted) then the resulting array may or may not be adjustable, depending on the implementation, and therefore adjustable-array-p may be correspondingly true or false of the resulting array. Common Lisp provides no portable way to create a non-adjustable array, that is, an array for which adjustable-array-p is guaranteed to be false.

:fill-pointer

This argument specifies that the array should have a fill pointer. If this option is specified and not nil, the array must be one-dimensional. The value is used to initialize the fill pointer for the array. If the value t is specified, the length of the array is used; otherwise the value must be an integer between 0 (inclusive) and the length of the array (inclusive). This argument defaults to nil.

:displaced-to

This argument, if specified and not nil, specifies that the array will be a *displaced* array. The argument must then be an array; make-array will create an *indirect* or *shared* array that shares its contents with the specified array. In this case the

:displaced-index-offset option may be useful. It is an error if the array given as the :displaced-to argument does not have the same :element-type as the array being created. The :displaced-to option may not be used with the :initial-element or :initial-contents option. This argument defaults to nil.

:displaced-index-offset

This argument may be used only in conjunction with the displaced-to option. It must be a non-negative integer (it defaults to zero); it is made to be the index-offset of the created shared array.

When an array A is given as the :displaced-to argument to make-array when creating array B, then array B is said to be *displaced* to array A. Now the total number of elements in an array, called the *total size* of the array, is calculated as the product of all the dimensions (see array-total-size). It is required that the total size of A be no smaller than the sum of the total size of B plus the offset *n* specified by the :displaced-index-offset argument. The effect of displacing is that array B does not have any elements of its own but instead maps accesses to itself into accesses to array A. The mapping treats both arrays as if they were one-dimensional by taking the elements in row-major order, and then maps an access to element *k* of array B to an access to element *k+n* of array A.

If make-array is called with each of the :adjustable, :fill-pointer, and :displaced-to arguments either unspecified or nil, then the resulting array is guaranteed to be a *simple* array (see section 2.5).

X3J13 voted in June 1989 ⟨3⟩ to clarify that if one or more of the :adjustable, :fill-pointer, and :displaced-to arguments is true, then whether the resulting array is simple is unspecified.

Here are some examples of the use of make-array:

```
;;; Create a one-dimensional array of five elements.
(make-array 5)

;;; Create a two-dimensional array, 3 by 4, with four-bit elements.
(make-array '(3 4) :element-type '(mod 16))

;;; Create an array of single-floats.
(make-array 5 :element-type 'single-float))

;;; Making a shared array.
(setq a (make-array '(4 3)))
```

```
(setq b (make-array 8 :displaced-to a
                      :displaced-index-offset 2))
;;; Now it is the case that:
        (aref b 0) ≡ (aref a 0 2)
        (aref b 1) ≡ (aref a 1 0)
        (aref b 2) ≡ (aref a 1 1)
        (aref b 3) ≡ (aref a 1 2)
        (aref b 4) ≡ (aref a 2 0)
        (aref b 5) ≡ (aref a 2 1)
        (aref b 6) ≡ (aref a 2 2)
        (aref b 7) ≡ (aref a 3 0)
```

The last example depends on the fact that arrays are, in effect, stored in row-major order for purposes of sharing. Put another way, the indices for the elements of an array are ordered lexicographically.

Compatibility note: Both Lisp Machine Lisp, as described in reference [55], and Fortran [15, 3] store arrays in column-major order.

---

array-rank-limit   [*Constant*]

The value of array-rank-limit is a positive integer that is the upper exclusive bound on the rank of an array. This bound depends on the implementation but will not be smaller than 8; therefore every Common Lisp implementation supports arrays whose rank is between 0 and 7 (inclusive). (Implementors are encouraged to make this limit as large as practicable without sacrificing performance.)

array-dimension-limit   [*Constant*]

The value of array-dimension-limit is a positive integer that is the upper exclusive bound on each individual dimension of an array. This bound depends on the implementation but will not be smaller than 1024. (Implementors are encouraged to make this limit as large as practicable without sacrificing performance.)

X3J13 voted in January 1989 ⟨76⟩ to specify that the value of array-dimension-limit must be of type fixnum. This in turn implies that all valid array indices will be fixnums.

array-total-size-limit   [*Constant*]

The value of array-total-size-limit is a positive integer that is the upper exclusive bound on the total number of elements in an array. This bound depends on the implementation but will not be smaller than 1024. (Implementors are encouraged to make this limit as large as practicable without sacrificing performance.)

The actual limit on array size imposed by the implementation may vary according to the :element-type of the array; in this case the value of array-total-size-limit will be the smallest of these individual limits.

vector &rest *objects* [*Function*]

The function vector is a convenient means for creating a simple general vector with specified initial contents. It is analogous to the function list.

```
(vector a₁ a₂ ... aₙ)
  ≡ (make-array (list n) :element-type t
            :initial-contents (list a₁ a₂ ... aₙ))
```

17.2. Array Access

The function aref is normally used for accessing an element of an array. Other access functions, such as svref, char, and bit, may be more efficient in specialized circumstances.

aref *array* &rest *subscripts* [*Function*]

This accesses and returns the element of *array* specified by the *subscripts*. The number of subscripts must equal the rank of the array, and each subscript must be a non-negative integer less than the corresponding array dimension.

aref is unusual among the functions that operate on arrays in that it completely ignores fill pointers. aref can access without error any array element, whether active or not. The generic sequence function elt, however, observes the fill pointer; accessing an element beyond the fill pointer with elt is an error.

Note that this remark, predating the design of the Common Lisp Object System, uses the term "generic" in a generic sense and not necessarily in the technical sense used by CLOS (see chapter 2).

setf may be used with aref to destructively replace an array element with a new value.

Under some circumstances it is desirable to write code that will extract an element from an array a given a list z of the indices, in such a way that the code works regardless of the rank of the array. This is easy using apply:

```
(apply #'aref a z)
```

(The length of the list must of course equal the rank of the array.) This construction may be used with setf to alter the element so selected to some new value w:

```
(setf (apply #'aref a z) w)
```

svref *simple-vector index*   [*Function*]

The first argument must be a simple general vector, that is, an object of type simple-vector. The element of the *simple-vector* specified by the integer *index* is returned.

The *index* must be non-negative and less than the length of the vector.

setf may be used with svref to destructively replace a simple-vector element with a new value.

svref is identical to aref except that it requires its first argument to be a simple vector. In some implementations of Common Lisp, svref may be faster than aref in situations where it is applicable. See also schar and sbit.

17.3. Array Information

The following functions extract from an array interesting information other than the elements.

array-element-type *array*   [*Function*]

array-element-type returns a type specifier for the set of objects that can be stored in the *array*. This set may be larger than the set requested when the array was created; for example, the result of

```
(array-element-type (make-array 5 :element-type '(mod 5)))
```

could be (mod 5), (mod 8), fixnum, t, or any other type of which (mod 5) is a subtype. See subtypep.

array-rank *array*   [*Function*]

This returns the number of dimensions (axes) of *array*. This will be a non-negative integer. See array-rank-limit.

Compatibility note: In Lisp Machine Lisp, this is called array-#-dims. This name causes problems in other Lisp dialects because of the # character.

`array-dimension` *array axis-number*   [*Function*]

The length of dimension number *axis-number* of the *array* is returned. *array* may be any kind of array, and *axis-number* should be a non-negative integer less than the rank of *array*. If the *array* is a vector with a fill pointer, `array-dimension` returns the total size of the vector, including inactive elements, not the size indicated by the fill pointer. (The function `length` will return the size indicated by the fill pointer.)

Compatibility note: This is similar to the Lisp Machine Lisp function `array-dimension-n`, but takes its arguments in the other order, and is zero-origin for consistency instead of one-origin. In Lisp Machine Lisp (`array-dimension-n 0`) returns the length of the array leader.

`array-dimensions` *array*   [*Function*]

`array-dimensions` returns a list whose elements are the dimensions of *array*.

`array-total-size` *array*   [*Function*]

`array-total-size` returns the total number of elements in the *array*, calculated as the product of all the dimensions.

```
(array-total-size x)
   ≡ (apply #'* (array-dimensions x))
   ≡ (reduce #'* (array-dimensions x))
```

Note that the total size of a zero-dimensional array is 1. The total size of a one-dimensional array is calculated without regard for any fill pointer.

`array-in-bounds-p` *array* &rest *subscripts*   [*Function*]

This predicate checks whether the *subscripts* are all legal subscripts for *array*. The predicate is true if they are all legal; otherwise it is false. The *subscripts* must be integers. The number of *subscripts* supplied must equal the rank of the array. Like `aref`, `array-in-bounds-p` ignores fill pointers.

`array-row-major-index` *array* &rest *subscripts*   [*Function*]

This function takes an array and valid subscripts for the array and returns a single non-negative integer less than the total size of the array that identifies the accessed element in the row-major ordering of the elements. The number of *subscripts* supplied must equal the rank of the array. Each subscript must be a non-negative integer less than the corresponding array dimension. Like aref, array-row-major-index ignores fill pointers.

A possible definition of array-row-major-index, with no error checking, would be

```
(defun array-row-major-index (a &rest subscripts)
  (apply #'+ (maplist #'(lambda (x y)
                          (* (car x) (apply #'* (cdr y))))
                      subscripts
                      (array-dimensions a))))
```

For a one-dimensional array, the result of array-row-major-index always equals the supplied subscript.

---

row-major-aref *array index*   [*Function*]

X3J13 voted in March 1988 ⟨6⟩ to add the function row-major-aref. This allows any array element to be accessed as if the containing array were one-dimensional. The *index* must be a non-negative integer less than the total size of the *array*. It indexes into the array as if its elements were arranged one-dimensionally in row-major order. It may be understood in terms of aref as follows:

```
(row-major-aref array index) ≡
  (aref (make-array (array-total-size array))
                    :displaced-to array
                    :element-type (array-element-type array))
        index)
```

In other words, one may treat an array as one-dimensional by creating a new one-dimensional array that is displaced to the old one and then accessing the new array. Alternatively, aref may be understood in terms of row-major-aref:

```
(aref array i₀ i₁ ... i_{n-1}) ≡
  (row-major-aref array
                  (array-row-major-index array i₀ i₁ ... i_{n-1}))
```

That is, a multidimensional array access is equivalent to a row-major access using an equivalent row-major index.

Like aref, row-major-aref completely ignores fill pointers. A call to row-major-setf is suitable for use as a *place* for setf.

This operation makes it easier to write code that efficiently processes arrays of any rank. Suppose, for example, that one wishes to set every element of an array tennis-scores to zero. One might write

```
(fill (make-array (array-total-size tennis-scores)
                  :element-type (array-element-type tennis-scores)
                  :displaced-to tennis-scores)
      0)
```

Unfortunately, this incurs the overhead of creating a displaced array, and `fill` cannot be applied to multidimensional arrays. Another approach would be to handle each possible rank separately:

```
(ecase (array-rank tennis-scores)
  (0 (setf (aref tennis-scores) 0))
  (1 (dotimes (i0 (array-dimension tennis-scores 0))
       (setf (aref tennis-scores i0) 0)))
  (2 (dotimes (i0 (array-dimension tennis-scores 0))
       (dotimes (i1 (array-dimension tennis-scores 1))
         (setf (aref tennis-scores i0 i1) 0))))
  ...
  (7 (dotimes (i0 (array-dimension tennis-scores 0))
       (dotimes (i1 (array-dimension tennis-scores 1))
         (dotimes (i2 (array-dimension tennis-scores 1))
           (dotimes (i3 (array-dimension tennis-scores 1))
             (dotimes (i4 (array-dimension tennis-scores 1))
               (dotimes (i5 (array-dimension tennis-scores 1))
                 (dotimes (i6 (array-dimension tennis-scores 1))
                   (setf (aref tennis-scores i0 i1 i2 i3 i4 i5 i6)
                         0)))))))))
  )
```

It is easy to get tired of writing such code. Furthermore, this approach is undesirable because some implementations of Common Lisp will in fact correctly support arrays of rank greater than 7 (though no implementation is required to do so). A recursively nested loop does the job, but it is still pretty hairy:

```
(labels
  ((grok-any-rank (&rest indices)
     (let ((d (- (array-rank tennis-scores) (length indices))))
       (if (= d 0)
           (setf (apply #'row-major-aref indices) 0)
           (dotimes (i (array-dimension tennis-scores (- d 1)))
             (apply #'grok-any-rank i indices))))))
  (grok-any-rank))
```

Whether this code is particularly efficient depends on many implementation parameters, such as how &rest arguments are handled and how cleverly calls to apply are compiled. How much easier it is to use row-major-aref!

```
(dotimes (i (array-total-size tennis-scores))
  (setf (row-major-aref tennis-scores i) 0))
```

Surely this code is sweeter than the honeycomb.

---

adjustable-array-p *array*   [*Function*]

This predicate is true if the argument (which must be an array) is adjustable, and otherwise is false.

X3J13 voted in June 1989 ⟨3⟩ to clarify that adjustable-array-p is true of an array if and only if adjust-array, when applied to that array, will return the same array, that is, an array eq to the original array. If the :adjustable argument to make-array is non-nil when an array is created, then adjustable-array-p must be true of that array. If an array is created with the :adjustable argument nil (or omitted), then adjustable-array-p may be true or false of that array, depending on the implementation. X3J13 further voted to *define* the terminology "adjustable array" to mean precisely "an array of which adjustable-array-p is true." See make-array and adjust-array.

17.4. Functions on Arrays of Bits

The functions described in this section operate only on arrays of bits, that is, specialized arrays whose elements are all 0 or 1.

---

bit *bit-array* &rest *subscripts*   . [*Function*]
sbit *simple-bit-array* &rest *subscripts*   [*Function*]

bit is exactly like aref but requires an array of bits, that is, one of type (array bit). The result will always be 0 or 1. sbit is like bit but additionally requires that the first argument be a *simple* array (see section 2.5). Note that bit and sbit, unlike char and schar, allow the first argument to be an array of any rank.

setf may be used with bit or sbit to destructively replace a bit-array element with a new value.

bit and sbit are identical to aref except for the more specific type requirements on the first argument. In some implementations of Common Lisp, bit may be faster than aref in situations where it is applicable, and sbit may similarly be faster than bit.

bit-and *bit-array1* *bit-array2* &optional *result-bit-array*   [*Function*]
bit-ior *bit-array1* *bit-array2* &optional *result-bit-array*   [*Function*]
bit-xor *bit-array1* *bit-array2* &optional *result-bit-array*   [*Function*]
bit-eqv *bit-array1* *bit-array2* &optional *result-bit-array*   [*Function*]
bit-nand *bit-array1* *bit-array2* &optional *result-bit-array*   [*Function*]
bit-nor *bit-array1* *bit-array2* &optional *result-bit-array*   [*Function*]
bit-andc1 *bit-array1* *bit-array2* &optional *result-bit-array*   [*Function*]
bit-andc2 *bit-array1* *bit-array2* &optional *result-bit-array*   [*Function*]
bit-orc1 *bit-array1* *bit-array2* &optional *result-bit-array*   [*Function*]
bit-orc2 *bit-array1* *bit-array2* &optional *result-bit-array*   [*Function*]

These functions perform bit-wise logical operations on bit-arrays. All of the arguments to any of these functions must be bit-arrays of the same rank and dimensions. The result is a bit-array of matching rank and dimensions, such that any given bit of the result is produced by operating on corresponding bits from each of the arguments.

If the third argument is nil or omitted, a new array is created to contain the result. If the third argument is a bit-array, the result is destructively placed into that array. If the third argument is t, then the first argument is also used as the third argument; that is, the result is placed back in the first array.

The following table indicates what the result bit is for each operation as a function of the two corresponding argument bits.

argument1 0	0	1	1	
argument2 0	1	0	1	*Operation name*
bit-and 0	0	0	1	and
bit-ior 0	1	1	1	inclusive or
bit-xor 0	1	1	0	exclusive or
bit-eqv 1	0	0	1	equivalence (exclusive nor)
bit-nand 1	1	1	0	not-and
bit-nor 1	0	0	0	not-or
bit-andc1 0	1	0	0	and complement of *argument1* with *argument2*
bit-andc2 0	0	1	0	and *argument1* with complement of *argument2*
bit-orc1 1	1	0	1	or complement of *argument1* with *argument2*
bit-orc2 1	0	1	1	or *argument1* with complement of *argument2*

For example:

```
(bit-and #*1100 #*1010) ⇒ #*1000
(bit-xor #*1100 #*1010) ⇒ #*0110
(bit-andc1 #*1100 #*1010) ⇒ #*0100
```

See logand and related functions.

bit-not *bit-array* &optional *result-bit-array*   [*Function*]

The first argument must be an array of bits. A bit-array of matching rank and dimensions is returned that contains a copy of the argument with all the bits inverted. See lognot.

 .   If the second argument is nil or omitted, a new array is created to contain the result. If the second argument is a bit-array, the result is destructively placed into that array. If the second argument is t, then the first argument is also used as the second argument; that is, the result is placed back in the first array.

17.5. Fill Pointers

Several functions for manipulating a *fill pointer* are provided in Common Lisp to make it easy to incrementally fill in the contents of a vector and, more generally, to allow efficient varying of the length of a vector. For example, a string with a fill pointer has most of the characteristics of a PL/I varying string.

    The fill pointer is a non-negative integer no larger than the total number of elements in the vector (as returned by array-dimension); it is the number of "active" or "filled-in" elements in the vector. The fill pointer constitutes the "active length" of the vector; all vector elements whose index is less than the fill pointer are active, and the others are inactive. Nearly all functions that operate on the contents of a vector will operate only on the active elements. An important exception is aref, which can be used to access any vector element whether in the active region of the vector or not. It is important to note that vector elements not in the active region are still considered part of the vector.

Implementation note: An implication of this rule is that vector elements outside the active region may not be garbage-collected.

    Only vectors (one-dimensional arrays) may have fill pointers; multidimensional arrays may not. (Note, however, that one can create a multidimensional array that is *displaced* to a vector that has a fill pointer.)

array-has-fill-pointer-p *array*   [*Function*]

The argument must be an array. array-has-fill-pointer-p returns t if the array has a fill pointer, and otherwise returns nil. Note that array-has-fill-pointer-p always returns nil if the *array* is not one-dimensional.

`fill-pointer` *vector*   [*Function*]

The fill pointer of *vector* is returned. It is an error if the *vector* does not have a fill pointer.

    `setf` may be used with `fill-pointer` to change the fill pointer of a vector. The fill pointer of a vector must always be an integer between zero and the size of the vector (inclusive).

`vector-push` *new-element vector*   [*Function*]

vector must be a one-dimensional array that has a fill pointer, and *new-element* may be any object. `vector-push` attempts to store *new-element* in the element of the vector designated by the fill pointer, and to increase the fill pointer by 1. If the fill pointer does not designate an element of the vector (specifically, when it gets too big), it is unaffected and `vector-push` returns `nil`. Otherwise, the store and increment take place and `vector-push` returns the *former* value of the fill pointer (1 less than the one it leaves in the vector); thus the value of `vector-push` is the index of the new element pushed.

    It is instructive to compare `vector-push`, which is a function, with `push`, which is a macro that requires a *place* suitable for `setf`. A vector with a fill pointer effectively contains the place to be modified in its `fill-pointer` slot.

`vector-push-extend` *new-element vector* &optional *extension*   [*Function*]

`vector-push-extend` is just like `vector-push` except that if the fill pointer gets too large, the vector is extended (using `adjust-array`) so that it can contain more elements. If, however, the vector is not adjustable, then `vector-push-extend` signals an error.

    X3J13 voted in June 1989 ⟨3⟩ to clarify that `vector-push-extend` regards an array as not adjustable if and only if `adjustable-array-p` is false of that array.

    The optional argument *extension*, which must be a positive integer, is the minimum number of elements to be added to the vector if it must be extended; it defaults to a "reasonable" implementation-dependent value.

`vector-pop` *vector*   [*Function*]

vector must be a one-dimensional array that has a fill pointer. If the fill pointer is zero, `vector-pop` signals an error. Otherwise the fill pointer is decreased by 1, and the vector element designated by the new value of the fill pointer is returned.

17.6. Changing the Dimensions of an Array

This function may be used to resize or reshape an array. Its options are similar to those of `make-array`.

`adjust-array` *array new-dimensions* &key :element-type   [*Function*]
            :initial-element :initial-contents :fill-pointer
            :displaced-to :displaced-index-offset

`adjust-array` takes an array and a number of other arguments as for `make-array`. The number of dimensions specified by *new-dimensions* must equal the rank of *array*.

adjust-array returns an array of the same type and rank as *array*, with the specified *new-dimensions*. In effect, the *array* argument itself is modified to conform to the new specifications, but this may be achieved either by modifying the *array* or by creating a new array and modifying the *array* argument to be *displaced* to the new array.

In the simplest case, one specifies only the *new-dimensions* and possibly an `:initial-element` argument. Those elements of *array* that are still in bounds appear in the new array. The elements of the new array that are not in the bounds of *array* are initialized to the `:initial-element`; if this argument is not provided, then the initial contents of any new elements are undefined.

If `:element-type` is specified, then *array* must be such that it could have been originally created with that type; otherwise an error is signaled. Specifying `:element-type` to `adjust-array` serves only to require such an error check.

If `:initial-contents` or `:displaced-to` is specified, then it is treated as for `make-array`. In this case none of the original contents of *array* appears in the new array.

If `:fill-pointer` is specified, the fill pointer of the *array* is reset as specified. An error is signaled if *array* had no fill pointer already.

X3J13 voted in June 1988 ⟨2⟩ to clarify the treatment of the `:fill-pointer` argument as follows.

If the `:fill-pointer` argument is not supplied, then the fill pointer of the *array* is left alone. It is an error to try to adjust the *array* to a total size that is smaller than its fill pointer.

If the `:fill-pointer` argument is supplied, then its value must be either an integer, t, or `nil`. If it is an integer, then it is the new value for the fill pointer; it must be non-negative and no greater than the new size to which the *array* is being adjusted. If it is t, then the fill pointer is set equal to the new size for the *array*. If it is `nil`, then the fill pointer is left alone; it is as if the argument had not been supplied. Again, it is an error to try to adjust the *array* to a total size that is smaller than its fill pointer.

An error is signaled if a non-nil :fill-pointer value is supplied and the *array* to be adjusted does not already have a fill pointer.

This extended treatment of the :fill-pointer argument to adjust-array is consistent with the previously existing treatment of the :fill-pointer argument to make-array.

adjust-array may, depending on the implementation and the arguments, simply alter the given array or create and return a new one. In the latter case the given array will be altered so as to be displaced to the new array and have the given new dimensions.

It is not permitted to call adjust-array on an array that was not created with the :adjustable option. The predicate adjustable-array-p may be used to determine whether or not an array is adjustable.

X3J13 voted in January 1989 ⟨3⟩ to allow adjust-array to be applied to any array. If adjust-array is applied to an array that was originally created with :adjustable true, the array returned is eq to its first argument. It is not specified whether adjust-array returns an array eq to its first argument for any other arrays. If the array returned by adjust-array is not eq to its first argument, the original array is unchanged and does not share storage with the new array.

Under this new definition, it is wise to treat adjust-array in the same manner as delete and nconc: one should carefully retain the returned value, for example by writing

```
(setq my-array (adjust-array my-array ...))
```

rather than relying solely on a side effect.

If adjust-array is applied to an *array* that is displaced to another array *x*, then afterwards neither *array* nor the returned result is displaced to *x* unless such displacement is explicitly re-specified in the call to adjust-array.

For example, suppose that the 4-by-4 array m looks like this:

```
#2A( ( alpha      beta      gamma     delta )
     ( epsilon    zeta      eta       theta )
     ( iota       kappa     lambda    mu    )
     ( nu         xi        omicron   pi    ) )
```

Then the result of

```
(adjust-array m '(3 5) :initial-element 'baz)
```

is a 3-by-5 array with contents

```
#2A( ( alpha      beta       gamma      delta      baz )
     ( epsilon    zeta       eta        theta      baz )
     ( iota       kappa      lambda     mu         baz ) )
```

Note that if array a is created displaced to array b and subsequently array b is given to adjust-array, array a will still be displaced to array b; the effects of this displacement and the rule of row-major storage order must be taken into account.

X3J13 voted in June 1988 ⟨1⟩ to clarify the interaction of adjust-array with array displacement.

Suppose that an array *A* is to be adjusted. There are four cases according to whether or not *A* was displaced before adjustment and whether or not the result is displaced after adjustment.

- Suppose *A* is not displaced either before or after. The dimensions of *A* are altered, and the contents are rearranged as appropriate. Additional elements of *A* are taken from the :initial-element argument. However, the use of the :initial-contents argument causes all old contents to be discarded.

- Suppose *A* is not displaced before, but is displaced to array *C* after. None of the original contents of *A* appears in *A* afterwards; *A* now contains (some of) the contents of *C*, without any rearrangement of *C*.

- Suppose *A* is displaced to array *B* before the call, and is displaced to array *C* after the call. (Note that *B* and *C* may be the same array.) The contents of *B* do not appear in *A* afterwards (unless such contents also happen to be in *C*, as when *B* and *C* are the same, for example). If :displaced-index-offset is not specified in the call to adjust-array, it defaults to zero; the old offset (into *B*) is not retained.

- Suppose *A* is displaced to array *B* before the call, but is not displaced afterwards. In this case *A* gets a new "data region" and (some of) the contents of *B* are copied into it as appropriate to maintain the existing old contents. Additional elements of *A* are taken from the :initial-element argument. However, the use of the :initial-contents argument causes all old contents to be discarded.

If array *X* is displaced to array *Y*, and array *Y* is displaced to array *Z*, and array *Y* is altered by adjust-array, array *X* must now refer to the adjusted contents of *Y*. This means that an implementation may not collapse the chain to make *X* refer to *Z* directly and forget that the chain of reference passes through array *Y*. (Caching techniques are of course permitted, as long as they preserve the semantics specified here.)

If *X* is displaced to *Y*, it is an error to adjust *Y* in such a way that it no longer has enough elements to satisfy *X*. This error may be signaled at the time of the adjustment, but this is not required.

Note that omitting the `:displaced-to` argument to `adjust-array` is equivalent to specifying `:displaced-to nil`; in either case, the array is not displaced after the call regardless of whether it was displaced before the call.

18

Strings

A string is a specialized vector (one-dimensional array) whose elements are characters.

Specifically, the type `string` is identical to the type (`vector string-char`), which in turn is the same as (`array string-char (*)`).

X3J13 voted in March 1989 ⟨11⟩ to eliminate the type `string-char` and to redefine the type `string` to be the union of one or more specialized vector types, the types of whose elements are subtypes of the type `character`.

Any string-specific function defined in this chapter whose name begins with the prefix `string` will accept a symbol instead of a string as an argument *provided* that the operation never modifies that argument; the print name of the symbol is used. In this respect the string-specific sequence operations are not simply specializations of generic versions; the generic sequence operations described in chapter 14 never accept symbols as sequences. This slight inelegance is permitted in Common Lisp in the name of pragmatic utility. One may get the effect of having a generic sequence function operate on either symbols or strings by applying the coercion function `string` to any argument whose data type is in doubt.

Note that this remark, predating the design of the Common Lisp Object System, uses the term "generic" in a generic sense and not necessarily in the technical sense used by CLOS (see chapter 2).

Also, there is a slight non-parallelism in the names of string functions. Where the suffixes `equalp` and `eql` would be more appropriate, for historical compatibility the suffixes `equal` and `=` are used instead to indicate case-insensitive and case-sensitive character comparison, respectively.

Any Lisp object may be tested for being a string by the predicate `stringp`.

Note that strings, like all vectors, may have fill pointers (though such strings are not necessarily *simple*). String operations generally operate only on the active portion of the string (below the fill pointer). See `fill-pointer` and related functions.

460

18.1. String Access

The following functions access a single character element of a string.

char *string index*   [*Function*]
schar *simple-string index*   [*Function*]

The given *index* must be a non-negative integer less than the length of *string*, which must be a string. The character at position *index* of the string is returned as a character object.

    (This character will necessarily satisfy the predicate string-char-p.)

    X3J13 voted in March 1989 ⟨11⟩ to eliminate string-char-p.

    As with all sequences in Common Lisp, indexing is zero-origin. For example:

```
(char "Floob-Boober-Bab-Boober-Bubs" 0) ⇒ #\F
(char "Floob-Boober-Bab-Boober-Bubs" 1) ⇒ #\l
```

See aref and elt. In effect,

```
(char s j) ≡ (aref (the string s) j)
```

setf may be used with char to destructively replace a character within a string.

    For char, the string may be any string; for schar, it must be a simple string. In some implementations of Common Lisp, the function schar may be faster than char when it is applicable.

18.2. String Comparison

The naming conventions for these functions and for their keyword arguments generally follow the conventions for the generic sequence functions (see chapter 14).

    Note that this remark, predating the design of the Common Lisp Object System, uses the term "generic" in a generic sense and not necessarily in the technical sense used by CLOS (see chapter 2).

string= *string1 string2* &key :start1 :end1 :start2 :end2   [*Function*]

string= compares two strings and is true if they are the same (corresponding characters are identical) but is false if they are not. The function equal calls string= if applied to two strings.

    The keyword arguments :start1 and :start2 are the places in the strings to start the comparison. The arguments :end1 and :end2 are the places in the strings to stop comparing; comparison stops just *before* the position specified by a limit. The "start" arguments default to zero (beginning of string), and the "end" arguments (if either omitted or `nil`) default to the lengths of the strings (end of string), so that by default the entirety of each string is examined. These arguments are provided so that substrings can be compared efficiently.

`string=` is necessarily false if the (sub)strings being compared are of unequal length; that is, if

```
(not (= (- end1 start1) (- end2 start2)))
```

is true, then `string=` is false.

```
(string= "foo" "foo") is true
(string= "foo" "Foo") is false
(string= "foo" "bar") is false
(string= "together" "frog" :start1 1 :end1 3 :start2 2)
    is true
```

| X3J13 voted in June 1989 ⟨169⟩ to clarify string coercion (see `string`).

Compatibility note: `string=` is called `strequal` in Interlisp.

`string-equal` *string1 string2* &key :start1 :end1   [*Function*]
                :start2 :end2

`string-equal` is just like `string=` except that differences in case are ignored; two characters are considered to be the same if `char-equal` is true of them. For example:

```
(string-equal "foo" "Foo") is true
```

| X3J13 voted in June 1989 ⟨169⟩ to clarify string coercion (see `string`).

`string<` *string1 string2* &key :start1 :end1 :start2 :end2   [*Function*]
`string>` *string1 string2* &key :start1 :end1 :start2 :end2   [*Function*]
`string<=` *string1 string2* &key :start1 :end1 :start2 :end2   [*Function*]
`string>=` *string1 string2* &key :start1 :end1 :start2 :end2   [*Function*]
`string/=` *string1 string2* &key :start1 :end1 :start2 :end2   [*Function*]

These functions compare the two string arguments lexicographically, and the result is `nil` unless *string1* is respectively less than, greater than, less than or equal to, greater than or equal to, or not equal to *string2*. If the condition is satisfied, however, then the result is the index within the strings of the first character position at which the strings fail to match; put another way, the result is the length of the longest common prefix of the strings.

A string *a* is less than a string *b* if in the first position in which they differ the character of *a* is less than the corresponding character of *b* according to the function char<, or if string *a* is a proper prefix of string *b* (of shorter length and matching in all the characters of *a*).

The keyword arguments :start1 and :start2 are the places in the strings to start the comparison. The keyword arguments :end1 and :end2 are the places in the strings to stop comparing; comparison stops just *before* the position specified by a limit. The "start" arguments default to zero (beginning of string), and the "end" arguments (if either omitted or nil) default to the lengths of the strings (end of string), so that by default the entirety of each string is examined. These arguments are provided so that substrings can be compared efficiently. The index returned in case of a mismatch is an index into *string1*.

| X3J13 voted in June 1989 ⟨169⟩ to clarify string coercion (see string).

---

string-lessp *string1* *string2* &key :start1 :end1   [*Function*]
        :start2 :end2
string-greaterp *string1* *string2* &key :start1 :end1   [*Function*]
        :start2 :end2
string-not-greaterp *string1* *string2* &key :start1 :end1   [*Function*]
  :start2 :end2
string-not-lessp *string1* *string2* &key :start1 :end1   [*Function*]
        :start2 :end2
string-not-equal *string1* *string2* &key :start1 :end1   [*Function*]
        :start2 :end2

These are exactly like string<, string>, string<=, string>=, and string/=, respectively, except that distinctions between uppercase and lowercase letters are ignored. It is as if char-lessp were used instead of char< for comparing characters.

| X3J13 voted in June 1989 ⟨169⟩ to clarify string coercion (see string).

18.3. String Construction and Manipulation

Most of the interesting operations on strings may be performed with the generic sequence functions described in chapter 14. The following functions perform additional operations that are specific to strings.

Note that this remark, predating the design of the Common Lisp Object System, uses the term "generic" in a generic sense and not necessarily in the technical sense used by CLOS (see chapter 2).

`make-string` *size* &key :initial-element   [*Function*]

This returns a string (in fact a simple string) of length *size*, each of whose characters has been initialized to the `:initial-element` argument. If an `:initial-element` argument is not specified, then the string will be initialized in an implementation-dependent way.

Implementation note: It may be convenient to initialize the string to null characters, or to spaces, or to garbage ("whatever was there").

A string is really just a one-dimensional array of "string characters" (that is, those characters that are members of type `string-char`). More complex character arrays may be constructed using the function `make-array`.

X3J13 voted in March 1989 ⟨11⟩ to eliminate the type `string-char` and to add a keyword argument `:element-type` to `make-string`. The new function description is as follows.

`make-string` *size* &key :initial-element :element-type   [*Function*]

This returns a simple string of length *size*, each of whose characters has been initialized to the `:initial-element` argument. If an `:initial-element` argument is not specified, then the string will be initialized in an implementation-dependent way.

The `:element-type` argument names the type of the elements of the string; a string is constructed of the most specialized type that can accommodate elements of the given type. If `:element-type` is omitted, the type `character` is the default.

X3J13 voted in January 1989 ⟨7⟩ to clarify that the *size* argument must be a non-negative integer less than the value of `array-dimension-limit`.

`string-trim` *character-bag string*   [*Function*]
`string-left-trim` *character-bag string*   [*Function*]
`string-right-trim` *character-bag string*   [*Function*]

`string-trim` returns a substring of *string*, with all characters in *character-bag* stripped off the beginning and end. The function `string-left-trim` is similar but strips characters off only the beginning; `string-right-trim` strips off only

the end. The argument *character-bag* may be any sequence containing characters.
For example:

```
(string-trim '(#\Space #\Tab #\Newline) " garbanzo beans
        ") ⇒ "garbanzo beans"
(string-trim " (*)" " ( *three (silly) words* ) ")
   ⇒ "three (silly) words"
(string-left-trim " (*)" " ( *three (silly) words* ) ")
   ⇒ "three (silly) words* ) "
(string-right-trim " (*)" " ( *three (silly) words* ) ")
   ⇒ " ( *three (silly) words"
```

If no characters need to be trimmed from the *string*, then either the argument *string*
itself or a copy of it may be returned, at the discretion of the implementation.

X3J13 voted in June 1989 ⟨169⟩ to clarify string coercion (see string).

string-upcase *string* &key :start :end	[*Function*]
string-downcase *string* &key :start :end	[*Function*]
string-capitalize *string* &key :start :end	[*Function*]

string-upcase returns a string just like *string* with all lowercase characters replaced by the corresponding uppercase characters. More precisely, each character
of the result string is produced by applying the function char-upcase to the corresponding character of *string*.

string-downcase is similar, except that uppercase characters are converted to
lowercase characters (using char-downcase).

The keyword arguments :start and :end delimit the portion of the string to be
affected. The result is always of the same length as *string*, however.

The argument is not destroyed. However, if no characters in the argument
require conversion, the result may be either the argument or a copy of it, at the
implementation's discretion. For example:

```
(string-upcase "Dr. Livingstone, I presume?")
   ⇒ "DR. LIVINGSTONE, I PRESUME?"
(string-downcase "Dr. Livingstone, I presume?")
   ⇒ "dr. livingstone, i presume?"
(string-upcase "Dr. Livingstone, I presume?" :start 6 :end 10)
   ⇒ "Dr. LiVINGstone, I presume?"
```

string-capitalize produces a copy of *string* such that, for every word in
the copy, the first character of the word, if case-modifiable, is uppercase and any
other case-modifiable characters in the word are lowercase. For the purposes of

string-capitalize, a word is defined to be a consecutive subsequence consisting of alphanumeric characters or digits, delimited at each end either by a non-alphanumeric character or by an end of the string. For example:

```
(string-capitalize " hello ") ⇒ " Hello "
(string-capitalize
     "occlUDeD cASEmenTs FOreSTAll iNADVertent DEFenestraTION")
⇒ "Occluded Casements Forestall Inadvertent Defenestration"
(string-capitalize 'kludgy-hash-search) ⇒ "Kludgy-Hash-Search"
(string-capitalize "DON'T!") ⇒ "Don'T!"      ;not "Don't!"
(string-capitalize "pipe 13a, foo16c") ⇒ "Pipe 13a, Foo16c"
```

| X3J13 voted in June 1989 ⟨169⟩ to clarify string coercion (see string).

Compatibility note: Some very approximate Interlisp equivalents to string-upcase, string-downcase, and string-capitalize are u-case, l-case with second argument nil, and l-case with second argument t.

---

nstring-upcase *string* &key :start :end   [*Function*]
nstring-downcase *string* &key :start :end   [*Function*]
nstring-capitalize *string* &key :start :end   [*Function*]

These three functions are just like string-upcase, string-downcase, and string-capitalize but destructively modify the argument *string* by altering case-modifiable characters as necessary.

The keyword arguments :start and :end delimit the portion of the string to be affected. The argument *string* is returned as the result.

string *x*   [*Function*]

Most of the string functions effectively apply string to such of their arguments as are supposed to be strings. If *x* is a string, it is returned. If *x* is a symbol, its print name is returned.

If *x* is a string character (a character of type string-char), then a string containing that one character is returned.

X3J13 voted in March 1989 ⟨11⟩ to eliminate the type string-char and to redefine the type string to be the union of one or more specialized vector types, the types of whose elements are subtypes of the type character. Presumably converting a character to a string always works according to this vote.

In any other situation, an error is signaled.

To convert a sequence of characters to a string, use coerce. (Note that (coerce x 'string) will not succeed if x is a symbol. Conversely, string will not convert a list or other sequence to be a string.)

To get the string representation of a number or any other Lisp object, use prin1-to-string, princ-to-string, or format.

X3J13 voted in June 1989 ⟨169⟩ to specify that the following functions perform coercion on their *string* arguments identical to that performed by the function string.

string=	string-equal	string-trim
string<	string-lessp	string-left-trim
string>	string-greaterp	string-right-trim
string<=	string-not-greaterp	string-upcase
string>=	string-not-lessp	string-downcase
string/=	string-not-equal	string-capitalize

Note that nstring-upcase, nstring-downcase, and nstring-capitalize are absent from this list; because they modify destructively, the argument must be a string.

As part of the same vote X3J13 specified that string may perform additional implementation-dependent coercions but the returned value must be of type string. Only when no coercion is defined, whether standard or implementation-dependent, is string required to signal an error, in which case the error condition must be of type type-error.

19

Structures

Common Lisp provides a facility for creating named record structures with named components. In effect, the user can define a new data type; every data structure of that type has components with specified names. Constructor, access, and assignment constructs are automatically defined when the data type is defined.

This chapter is divided into two parts. The first part discusses the basics of the structure facility, which is very simple and allows the user to take advantage of the type-checking, modularity, and convenience of user-defined record data types. The second part, beginning with section 19.5, discusses a number of specialized features of the facility that have advanced applications. These features are completely optional, and you needn't even know they exist in order to take advantage of the basics.

19.1. Introduction to Structures

The structure facility is embodied in the defstruct macro, which allows the user to create and use aggregate data types with named elements. These are like "structures" in PL/I, or "records" in Pascal.

As an example, assume you are writing a Lisp program that deals with space ships in a two-dimensional plane. In your program, you need to represent a space ship by a Lisp object of some kind. The interesting things about a space ship, as far as your program is concerned, are its position (represented as x and y coordinates), velocity (represented as components along the x and y axes), and mass.

A ship might therefore be represented as a record structure with five components: x-position, y-position, x-velocity, y-velocity, and mass. This structure could in turn be implemented as a Lisp object in a number of ways. It could be a list of five elements; the x-position could be the *car*, the y-position the *cadr*, and so on. Equally well it could be a vector of five elements: the x-position could be element 0, the y-position element 1, and so on. The problem with either of these representations is that the components occupy places in the object that are quite arbitrary and hard to remember. Someone looking at (cadddr ship1) or (aref ship1 3) in a piece of code might find it difficult to determine that this is accessing the *y*-velocity component of ship1. Moreover, if the representation of a ship should have to be changed, it would be very difficult to find all the places in the code to be changed to match (not all occurrences of cadddr are intended to extract the *y*-velocity from a ship).

Ideally components of record structures should have names. One would like to write something like (ship-y-velocity ship1) instead of (cadddr ship1). One would also like a more mnemonic way to create a ship than this:

```
(list 0 0 0 0 0)
```

Indeed, one would like ship to be a new data type, just like other Lisp data types, that one could test with typep, for example. The defstruct facility provides all of this.

defstruct itself is a macro that defines a structure. For the space ship example, one might define the structure by saying:

```
(defstruct ship
   x-position
   y-position
   x-velocity
   y-velocity
   mass)
```

This declares that every ship is an object with five named components. The evaluation of this form does several things:

- It defines ship-x-position to be a function of one argument, a ship, that returns the *x*-position of the ship; ship-y-position and the other components are given similar function definitions. These functions are called the *access functions*, as they are used to access elements of the structure.

- The symbol ship becomes the name of a data type of which instances of ships are elements. This name becomes acceptable to typep, for example; (typep x 'ship) is true if x is a ship and false if x is any object other than a ship.

- A function named ship-p of one argument is defined; it is a predicate that is true if its argument is a ship and is false otherwise.

- A function called `make-ship` is defined that, when invoked, will create a data structure with five components, suitable for use with the access functions. Thus executing

```
(setq ship2 (make-ship))
```

sets `ship2` to a newly created `ship` object. One can specify the initial values of any desired component in the call to `make-ship` by using keyword arguments in this way:

```
(setq ship2 (make-ship :mass *default-ship-mass*
                       :x-position 0
                       :y-position 0))
```

This constructs a new ship and initializes three of its components. This function is called the *constructor function* because it constructs a new structure.

- The `#S` syntax can be used to read instances of `ship` structures, and a printer function is provided for printing out ship structures. For example, the value of the variable `ship2` shown above might be printed as

```
#S(ship x-position 0 y-position 0 x-velocity nil
        y-velocity nil mass 170000.0)
```

- A function called `copy-ship` of one argument is defined that, when given a `ship` object, will create a new `ship` object that is a copy of the given one. This function is called the *copier function*.

- One may use `setf` to alter the components of a `ship`:

```
(setf (ship-x-position ship2) 100)
```

This alters the *x*-position of *ship2* to be 100. This works because `defstruct` behaves as if it generates an appropriate `defsetf` form for each access function.

This simple example illustrates the power of `defstruct` to provide abstract record structures in a convenient manner. `defstruct` has many other features as well for specialized purposes.

19.2. How to Use Defstruct

All structures are defined through the `defstruct` construct. A call to `defstruct` defines a new data type whose instances have named slots.

defstruct *name-and-options* [*doc-string*] {*slot-description*}⁺   [*Macro*]

X3J13 voted in June 1988 ⟨58⟩ to allow a defstruct definition to have no *slot-description* at all; in other words, the occurrence of {*slot-description*}⁺ in the preceding header line would be replaced by {*slot-description*}* .

Such structure definitions are particularly useful if the :include option is used, perhaps with other options; for example, one can have two structures that are exactly alike except that they print differently (having different :print-function options).

Implementors are encouraged to permit this simple extension as soon as convenient. Users, however, may wish to maximize portability of their code by avoiding the use of this extension unless and until it is adopted as part of the ANSI standard.

This defines a record-structure data type. A general call to defstruct looks like the following example.

```
(defstruct (name option-1 option-2 ... option-m)
           doc-string
           slot-description-1
           slot-description-2
           ...
           slot-description-n)
```

The *name* must be a symbol; it becomes the name of a new data type consisting of all instances of the structure. The function typep will accept and use this name as appropriate. The *name* is returned as the value of the *defstruct* form.

Usually no options are needed at all. If no options are specified, then one may write simply *name* instead of (*name*) after the word defstruct. The syntax of options and the options provided are discussed in section 19.5.

If the optional documentation string *doc-string* is present, then it is attached to the *name* as a documentation string of type structure; see documentation.

Each *slot-description-j* is of the form

```
(slot-name default-init
           slot-option-name-1 slot-option-value-1
           slot-option-name-2 slot-option-value-2
           ...
           slot-option-name-kⱼ slot-option-value-kⱼ)
```

Each *slot-name* must be a symbol; an access function is defined for each slot. If no options and no *default-init* are specified, then one may write simply *slot-name* instead of (*slot-name*) as the slot description.

The *default-init* is a form that is evaluated *each time* a structure is to be constructed; the value is used as the initial value of the slot.

X3J13 voted in October 1988 ⟨54⟩ to clarify that a *default-init* form is evaluated only if the corresponding argument is not supplied to the constructor function. The preceding sentence should therefore read as follows:

The *default-init* is a form that is evaluated *each time* its value is to be used as the initial value of the slot.

If no *default-init* is specified, then the initial contents of the slot are undefined and implementation-dependent. The available slot-options are described in section 19.4.

Compatibility note: Slot-options are not currently provided in Lisp Machine Lisp, but this is an upward-compatible extension.

X3J13 voted in January 1989 ⟨57⟩ to specify that it is an error for two slots to have the same name; more precisely, no two slots may have names for whose print names string= would be true. Under this interpretation

```
(defstruct lotsa-slots slot slot)
```

obviously is incorrect but the following one is also in error, even assuming that the symbols coin:slot and blot:slot really are distinct (non-eql) symbols:

```
(defstruct no-dice coin:slot blot:slot)
```

To illustrate another case, the first defstruct form below is correct, but the second one is in error.

```
(defstruct one-slot slot)
(defstruct (two-slots (:include one-slot)) slot)
```

Rationale: Print names are the criterion for slot-names being the same, rather than the symbols themselves, because defstruct constructs names of accessor functions from the print names and interns the resulting new names in the current package.

X3J13 recommended that expanding a defstruct form violating this restriction should signal an error and noted, with an eye to the Common Lisp Object System ⟨12⟩, that the restriction applies only to the operation of the defstruct macro as such and not to the structure-class or structures defined with defclass.

X3J13 voted in March 1989 ⟨50⟩ to clarify that, while defining forms normally appear at top level, it is meaningful to place them in non-top-level contexts; defstruct must treat slot *default-init* forms and any initialization forms within the specification of a by-position constructor function as occurring within the enclosing lexical environment, not within the global environment.

defstruct not only defines an access function for each slot, but also arranges for setf to work properly on such access functions, defines a predicate named *name*-p, defines a constructor function named make-*name*, and defines a copier function named copy-*name*. All names of automatically created functions are interned in whatever package is current at the time the defstruct form is processed (see *package*). Also, all such functions may be declared inline at the discretion of the implementation to improve efficiency; if you do not want some function declared inline, follow the defstruct form with a notinline declaration to override any automatic inline declaration.

X3J13 voted in January 1989 ⟨56⟩ to specify that the results of redefining a defstruct structure (that is, evaluating more than one defstruct structure for the same name) are undefined.

The problem is that if instances have been created under the old definition and then remain accessible after the new definition has been evaluated, the accessors and other functions for the new definition may be incompatible with the old instances. Conversely, functions associated with the old definition may have been declared inline and compiled into code that remains accessible after the new definition has been evaluated; such code may be incompatible with the new instances.

In practice this restriction affects the development and debugging process rather than production runs of fully developed code. The defstruct feature is intended to provide "the most efficient" structure class. CLOS classes defined by defclass allow much more flexible structures to be defined and redefined.

Programming environments are allowed and encouraged to permit defstruct redefinition, perhaps with warning messages about possible interactions with other parts of the programming environment or memory state. It is beyond the scope of the Common Lisp language standard to define those interactions except to note that they are not portable.

19.3. Using the Automatically Defined Constructor Function

After you have defined a new structure with defstruct, you can create instances of this structure by using the constructor function. By default, defstruct defines this function automatically. For a structure named foo, the constructor function is normally named make-foo; you can specify a different name by giving it as the argument to the :constructor option, or specify that you don't want a normal constructor function at all by using nil as the argument (in which case one or more "by-position" constructors should be requested; see section 19.6).

A call to a constructor function, in general, has the form

(name-of-constructor-function
   slot-keyword-1 form-1
   slot-keyword-2 form-2
   . . .)

All arguments are keyword arguments. Each *slot-keyword* should be a keyword whose name matches the name of a slot of the structure (`defstruct` determines the possible keywords simply by interning each slot-name in the keyword package). All the *keywords* and *forms* are evaluated. In short, it is just as if the constructor function took all its arguments as `&key` parameters. For example, the `ship` structure shown in section 19.1 has a constructor function that takes arguments roughly as if its definition were

```
(defun make-ship (&key x-position y-position
                       x-velocity y-velocity mass)
   ...)
```

If *slot-keyword-j* names a slot, then that element of the created structure will be initialized to the value of *form-j*. If no pair *slot-keyword-j* and *form-j* is present for a given slot, then the slot will be initialized by evaluating the *default-init* form specified for that slot in the call to `defstruct`. (In other words, the initialization specified in the `defstruct` defers to any specified in a call to the constructor function.) If the default initialization form is used, it is evaluated at construction time, but in the lexical environment of the `defstruct` form in which it appeared. If the `defstruct` itself also did not specify any initialization, the element's initial value is undefined. You should always specify the initialization, either in the `defstruct` or in the call to the constructor function, if you care about the initial value of the slot.

Each initialization form specified for a `defstruct` component, when used by the constructor function for an otherwise unspecified component, is re-evaluated on every call to the constructor function. It is as if the initialization forms were used as *init* forms for the keyword parameters of the constructor function. For example, if the form (`gensym`) were used as an initialization form, either in the constructor-function call or as the default initialization form in the `defstruct` form, then every call to the constructor function would call `gensym` once to generate a new symbol.

X3J13 voted in October 1988 ⟨54⟩ to clarify that the default value in a defstruct slot is not evaluated unless it is needed in the creation of a particular structure instance. If it is never needed, there can be no type-mismatch error, even if the type of the slot is specified, and no warning should be issued.

For example, in the following sequence only the last form is in error.

```
(defstruct person (name .007 :type string))

(make-person :name "James")

(make-person)          ;Error to give name the value .007
```

19.4. Defstruct Slot-Options

Each *slot-description* in a defstruct form may specify one or more slot-options.
A slot-option consists of a pair of a keyword and a value (which is not a form to
be evaluated, but the value itself). For example:

```
(defstruct ship
   (x-position 0.0 :type short-float)
   (y-position 0.0 :type short-float)
   (x-velocity 0.0 :type short-float)
   (y-velocity 0.0 :type short-float)
   (mass *default-ship-mass* :type short-float :read-only t))
```

This specifies that each slot will always contain a short-format floating-point number, and that the last slot may not be altered once a ship is constructed.

The available slot-options are as follows.

:type

The option :type *type* specifies that the contents of the slot will always be of
the specified data type. This is entirely analogous to the declaration of a variable
or function; indeed, it effectively declares the result type of the access function.
An implementation may or may not choose to check the type of the new object
when initializing or assigning to a slot. Note that the argument form *type* is not
evaluated; it must be a valid type specifier.

:read-only

The option :read-only x, where x is not nil, specifies that this slot may not be
altered; it will always contain the value specified at construction time. setf will
not accept the access function for this slot. If x is nil, this slot-option has no
effect. Note that the argument form x is not evaluated.

Note that it is impossible to specify a slot-option unless a default value is specified first.

19.5. Defstruct Options

The preceding description of defstruct is all that the average user will need (or want) to know in order to use structures. The remainder of this chapter discusses more complex features of the defstruct facility.

This section explains each of the options that can be given to defstruct. A defstruct option may be either a keyword or a list of a keyword and arguments for that keyword. (Note that the syntax for defstruct options differs from the pair syntax used for slot-options. No part of any of these options is evaluated.)

:conc-name

This provides for automatic prefixing of names of access functions. It is conventional to begin the names of all the access functions of a structure with a specific prefix, the name of the structure followed by a hyphen. This is the default behavior.

The argument to the :conc-name option specifies an alternative prefix to be used. (If a hyphen is to be used as a separator, it must be specified as part of the prefix.) If nil is specified as an argument, then *no* prefix is used; then the names of the access functions are the same as the slot-names, and it is up to the user to name the slots reasonably.

Note that no matter what is specified for :conc-name, with a constructor function one uses slot keywords that match the slot-names, with no prefix attached. On the other hand, one uses the access-function name when using setf. Here is an example:

```
(defstruct door knob-color width material)
(setq my-door
      (make-door :knob-color 'red :width 5.0))
(door-width my-door) ⇒ 5.0
(setf (door-width my-door) 43.7)
(door-width my-door) ⇒ 43.7
(door-knob-color my-door) ⇒ red
```

:constructor

This option takes one argument, a symbol, which specifies the name of the constructor function. If the argument is not provided or if the option itself is not provided, the name of the constructor is produced by concatenating the string "MAKE-" and the name of the structure, putting the name in whatever package is current at the time the defstruct form is processed (see *package*). If the argument is provided and is nil, no constructor function is defined.

This option actually has a more general syntax that is explained in section 19.6.

:copier

This option takes one argument, a symbol, which specifies the name of the copier function. If the argument is not provided or if the option itself is not provided, the name of the copier is produced by concatenating the string "COPY-" and the name of the structure, putting the name in whatever package is current at the time the defstruct form is processed (see *package*). If the argument is provided and is nil, no copier function is defined.

The automatically defined copier function simply makes a new structure and transfers all components verbatim from the argument into the newly created structure. No attempt is made to make copies of the components. Corresponding components of the old and new structures will therefore be eql.

:predicate

This option takes one argument, which specifies the name of the type predicate. If the argument is not provided or if the option itself is not provided, the name of the predicate is made by concatenating the name of the structure to the string "-P", putting the name in whatever package is current at the time the defstruct form is processed (see *package*). If the argument is provided and is nil, no predicate is defined. A predicate can be defined only if the structure is "named"; if the :type option is specified and the :named option is not specified, then the :predicate option must either be unspecified or have the value nil.

:include

This option is used for building a new structure definition as an extension of an old structure definition. As an example, suppose you have a structure called person that looks like this:

```
(defstruct person name age sex)
```

Now suppose you want to make a new structure to represent an astronaut. Since astronauts are people too, you would like them also to have the attributes of name, age, and sex, and you would like Lisp functions that operate on person structures to operate just as well on astronaut structures. You can do this by defining astronaut with the :include option, as follows:

```
(defstruct (astronaut (:include person)
                      (:conc-name astro-))
   helmet-size
   (favorite-beverage 'tang))
```

The :include option causes the structure being defined to have the same slots as the included structure. This is done in such a way that the access functions for the included structure will also work on the structure being defined. In this example, an astronaut will therefore have five slots: the three defined in person and the two defined in astronaut itself. The access functions defined by the person structure can be applied to instances of the astronaut structure, and they will work correctly. Moreover, astronaut will have its own access functions for components defined by the person structure. The following examples illustrate how you can use astronaut structures:

```
(setq x (make-astronaut :name 'buzz
                        :age 45
                        :sex t
                        :helmet-size 17.5))
```

```
(person-name x) ⇒ buzz
(astro-name x) ⇒ buzz
```

```
(astro-favorite-beverage x) ⇒ tang
```

The difference between the access functions person-name and astro-name is that person-name may be correctly applied to any person, including an astronaut, while astro-name may be correctly applied only to an astronaut. (An implementation may or may not check for incorrect use of access functions.)

At most one :include option may be specified in a single defstruct form. The argument to the :include option is required and must be the name of some previously defined structure. If the structure being defined has no :type option, then the included structure must also have had no :type option specified for it. If the structure being defined has a :type option, then the included structure must have been declared with a :type option specifying the same representation type.

If no :type option is involved, then the structure name of the including structure definition becomes the name of a data type, of course, and therefore a valid type specifier recognizable by typep; moreover, it becomes a subtype of the included structure. In the above example, astronaut is a subtype of person; hence

```
(typep (make-astronaut) 'person)
```

is true, indicating that all operations on persons will also work on astronauts.

The following is an advanced feature of the :include option. Sometimes, when one structure includes another, the default values or slot-options for the slots that came from the included structure are not what you want. The new structure can specify default values or slot-options for the included slots different from those the included structure specifies, by giving the :include option as

```
(:include name slot-description-1 slot-description-2 ...)
```

Each *slot-description-j* must have a *slot-name* or *slot-keyword* that is the same as that of some slot in the included structure. If *slot-description-j* has no *default-init*, then in the new structure the slot will have no initial value. Otherwise its initial value form will be replaced by the *default-init* in *slot-description-j*. A normally writable slot may be made read-only. If a slot is read-only in the included structure, then it must also be so in the including structure. If a type is specified for a slot, it must be the same as, or a subtype of, the type specified in the included structure. If it is a strict subtype, the implementation may or may not choose to error-check assignments.

For example, if we had wanted to define astronaut so that the default age for an astronaut is 45, then we could have said:

```
(defstruct (astronaut (:include person (age 45)))
    helmet-size
    (favorite-beverage 'tang))
```

X3J13 voted in June 1988 ⟨41⟩ to require any structure type created by defstruct (or defclass) to be disjoint from any of the types cons, symbol, array, number, character, hash-table, readtable, package, pathname, stream, and random-state. A consequence of this requirement is that it is an error to specify any of these types, or any of their subtypes, to the defstruct :include option. (The first edition said nothing explicitly about this. Inasmuch as using such a type with the :include option was not defined to work, one might argue that such use was an error in Common Lisp as defined by the first edition.)

:print-function

This option may be used only if the :type option is not specified. The argument to the :print-function option should be a function of three arguments, in a form acceptable to the function special form, to be used to print structures of this type. When a structure of this type is to be printed, the function is called on three arguments: the structure to be printed, a stream to print to, and an integer indicating the current depth (to be compared against *print-level*). The printing function should observe the values of such printer-control variables as *print-escape* and *print-pretty*.

If the :print-function option is not specified and the :type option also not specified, then a default printing function is provided for the structure that will print out all its slots using #S syntax (see section 22.1.4).

X3J13 voted in January 1989 ⟨143⟩ to specify that user-defined printing functions for the defstruct :print-function option may print objects to the supplied stream using write, print1, princ, format, or print-object and expect circularities to be detected and printed using #n# syntax (when *print-circle* is non-nil, of course). See *print-circle*.

X3J13 voted in January 1989 ⟨55⟩ to clarify that if the :print-function option is not specified but the :include option *is* specified, then the print function is inherited from the included structure type. Thus, for example, an astronaut will be printed by the same printing function that is used for person.

X3J13 in the same vote extended the print-function option as follows: If the print-function option is specified but with no argument, then the standard default printing function (that uses #S syntax) will be used. This provides a means of overriding the inheritance rule. For example, if person and astronaut had been defined as

```
(defstruct (person
              (:print-function        ;Special print function
              (lambda (p s k)
                (format s "<~A, age ~D>"
                          (person-name p)
                          (person-age p)))))
    name age sex)

(defstruct (astronaut
              (:include person)
              (:conc-name astro-)
              (:print-function))        ;Use default print function
    helmet-size
    (favorite-beverage 'tang))
```

then an ordinary person would be printed as "<Joe Schmoe, age 27>" but an astronaut would be printed as, for example,

```
#S(ASTRONAUT NAME BUZZ AGE 45 SEX T
    HELMET-SIZE 17.5 FAVORITE-BEVERAGE TANG)
```

using the default #S syntax (yuk).

These changes make the behavior of defstruct with respect to the :include option a bit more like the behavior of classes in CLOS.

:type

The :type option explicitly specifies the representation to be used for the structure. It takes one argument, which must be one of the types enumerated below.

Specifying this option has the effect of forcing a specific representation and of forcing the components to be stored in the order specified in the defstruct form in corresponding successive elements of the specified representation. It also *prevents* the structure name from becoming a valid type specifier recognizable by typep (see section 19.7).

Normally this option is not specified, in which case the structure is represented in an implementation-dependent manner.

vector

This produces the same result as specifying (vector t). The structure is represented as a general vector, storing components as vector elements. The first component is vector element 1 if the structure is :named, and element 0 otherwise.

(vector *element-type*)

The structure is represented as a (possibly specialized) vector, storing components as vector elements. Every component must be of a type that can be stored in a vector of the type specified. The first component is vector element 1 if the structure is :named, and element 0 otherwise. The structure may be :named only if the type symbol is a subtype of the specified element-type.

list

The structure is represented as a list. The first component is the *cadr* if the structure is :named, and the *car* if it is :unnamed.

:named

The :named option specifies that the structure is "named"; this option takes no argument. If no :type option is specified, then the structure is always named; so this option is useful only in conjunction with the :type option. See section 19.7 for a further description of this option.

:initial-offset

This allows you to tell defstruct to skip over a certain number of slots before it starts allocating the slots described in the body. This option requires an argument, a non-negative integer, which is the number of slots you want defstruct to skip. The :initial-offset option may be used only if the :type option is also specified. See section 19.7.3 for a further description of this option.

19.6. By-Position Constructor Functions

If the :constructor option is given as (:constructor *name arglist*), then instead of making a keyword-driven constructor function, defstruct defines a "positional" constructor function, taking arguments whose meaning is determined by the argument's position rather than by a keyword. The *arglist* is used to describe what the arguments to the constructor will be. In the simplest case something like (:constructor make-foo (a b c)) defines make-foo to be a three-argument constructor function whose arguments are used to initialize the slots named a, b, and c.

In addition, the keywords &optional, &rest, and &aux are recognized in the argument list. They work in the way you might expect, but there are a few fine points worthy of explanation. Consider this example:

```
(:constructor create-foo
        (a &optional b (c 'sea) &rest d &aux e (f 'eff)))
```

This defines create-foo to be a constructor of one or more arguments. The first argument is used to initialize the a slot. The second argument is used to initialize the b slot. If there isn't any second argument, then the default value given in the body of the defstruct (if given) is used instead. The third argument is used to initialize the c slot. If there isn't any third argument, then the symbol sea is used instead. Any arguments following the third argument are collected into a list and used to initialize the d slot. If there are three or fewer arguments, then nil is placed in the d slot. The e slot *is not initialized*; its initial value is undefined. Finally, the f slot is initialized to contain the symbol eff.

The actions taken in the b and e cases were carefully chosen to allow the user to specify all possible behaviors. Note that the &aux "variables" can be used to completely override the default initializations given in the body.

With this definition, one can write

```
(create-foo 1 2)
```

instead of

```
(make-foo :a 1 :b 2)
```

and of course `create-foo` provides defaulting different from that of `make-foo`.

It is permissible to use the `:constructor` option more than once, so that you can define several different constructor functions, each taking different parameters.

Because a constructor of this type operates By Order of Arguments, it is sometimes known as a BOA constructor.

X3J13 voted in January 1989 ⟨53⟩ to allow `&key` and `&allow-other-keys` in the parameter list of a "positional" constructor. The initialization of slots corresponding to keyword parameters is performed in the same manner as for `&optional` parameters. A variant of the example shown above illustrates this:

```
(:constructor create-foo
        (a &optional b (c 'sea)
        &key p (q 'cue) ((:why y)) ((:you u) 'ewe)
        &aux e (f 'eff)))
```

The treatment of slots a, b, c, e, and f is the same as in the original example. In addition, if there is a `:p` keyword argument, it is used to initialize the p slot; if there isn't any `:p` keyword argument, then the default value given in the body of the `defstruct` (if given) is used instead. Similarly, if there is a `:q` keyword argument, it is used to initialize the q slot; if there isn't any `:q` keyword argument, then the symbol `cue` is used instead.

In order thoroughly to flog this presumably already dead horse, we further observe that if there is a `:why` keyword argument, it is used to initialize the y slot; otherwise the default value for slot y is used instead. Similarly, if there is a `:you` keyword argument, it is used to initialize the u slot; otherwise the symbol `ewe` is used instead.

If memory serves me correctly, `defstruct` was included in the original design for Common Lisp some time before keyword arguments were approved. The failure of positional constructors to accept keyword arguments may well have been an oversight on my part; there is no logical reason to exclude them. I am grateful to X3J13 for rectifying this.

A remaining difficulty is that the possibility of keyword arguments renders the term "positional constructor" a misnomer. Worse yet, it ruins the term "BOA constructor." I suggest that they continue to be called BOA constructors, as I refuse to abandon a good pun. (I regret appearing to have more compassion for puns than for horses.)

As part of the same vote X3J13 also changed `defstruct` to allow BOA constructors to have parameters (including supplied-p parameters) that do not correspond to any slot. Such parameters may be used in subsequent initialization forms in the parameter list. Consider this example:

```
(defstruct (ice-cream-factory
              (:constructor fabricate-factory
                (&key (capacity 5)
                      location
                      (local-flavors
                        (case location
                          ((hawaii) '(pineapple macadamia guava))
                          ((massachusetts) '(lobster baked-bean))
                          ((california) '(ginger lotus avocado
                                          bean-sprout garlic))
                          ((texas) '(jalapeno barbecue))))
                      (flavors (subseq (append local-flavors
                                               '(vanilla
                                                 chocolate
                                                 strawberry
                                                 pistachio
                                                 maple-walnut
                                                 peppermint))
                                0 capacity)))))
            (capacity 3)
            (flavors '(vanilla chocolate strawberry mango)))
```

The structure type ice-cream-factory has two constructors. The standard constructor, make-ice-cream-factory, takes two keyword arguments named :capacity and :flavors. For this constructor, the default for the capacity slot is 3 and the default list of flavors is America's favorite threesome and a dark horse (not a dead one). The BOA constructor fabricate-factory accepts four different keyword arguments. The :capacity argument defaults to 5, and the :flavors argument defaults in a complicated manner based on the other three. The :local-flavors argument may be specified directly, or may be allowed to default based on the :location of the factory. Here are examples of various factories:

```
(setq houston (fabricate-factory :capacity 4 :location 'texas))
(setq cambridge (fabricate-factory :location 'massachusetts))
(setq seattle (fabricate-factory :local-flavors '(salmon)))
(setq wheaton (fabricate-factory :capacity 4 :location 'illinois))
(setq pittsburgh (fabricate-factory :capacity 4))
(setq cleveland (make-factory :capacity 4))

(ice-cream-factory-flavors houston)
  ⇒ (jalapeno barbecue vanilla chocolate)
```

```
(ice-cream-factory-flavors cambridge)
 ⇒ (lobster baked-bean vanilla chocolate strawberry)

(ice-cream-factory-flavors seattle)
 ⇒ (salmon vanilla chocolate strawberry pistachio)

(ice-cream-factory-flavors wheaton)
 ⇒ (vanilla chocolate strawberry pistachio)

(ice-cream-factory-flavors pittsburgh)
 ⇒ (vanilla chocolate strawberry pistachio)

(ice-cream-factory-flavors cleveland)
 ⇒ (vanilla chocolate strawberry mango)
```

19.7. Structures of Explicitly Specified Representational Type

Sometimes it is important to have explicit control over the representation of a structure. The :type option allows one to specify that a structure must be implemented in a particular way, using a list or a specific kind of vector, and to specify the exact allocation of structure slots to components of the representation. A structure may also be "unnamed" or "named," according to whether the structure name is stored in (and thus recoverable from) the structure.

19.7.1. Unnamed Structures

Sometimes a particular data representation is imposed by external requirements, and yet it is desirable to document the data format as a defstruct-style structure. For example, consider expressions built up from numbers, symbols, and binary operations such as + and *. An operation might be represented as it is in Lisp, as a list of the operator and the two operands. This fact can be expressed succinctly with defstruct in this manner:

```
(defstruct (binop (:type list))
  (operator '? :type symbol)
  operand-1
  operand-2)
```

This will define a constructor function make-binop and three selector functions, namely binop-operator, binop-operand-1, and binop-operand-2. (It will *not*, however, define a predicate binop-p, for reasons explained below.)

The effect of make-binop is simply to construct a list of length 3:

```
(make-binop :operator '+ :operand-1 'x :operand-2 5)
   ⇒ (+ x 5)

(make-binop :operand-2 4 :operator '*)
   ⇒ (* nil 4)
```

It is just like the function list except that it takes keyword arguments and performs slot defaulting appropriate to the binop conceptual data type. Similarly, the selector functions binop-operator, binop-operand-1, and binop-operand-2 are essentially equivalent to car, cadr, and caddr, respectively. (They might not be completely equivalent because, for example, an implementation would be justified in adding error-checking code to ensure that the argument to each selector function is a length-3 list.)

We speak of binop as being a "conceptual" data type because binop is not made a part of the Common Lisp type system. The predicate typep will not recognize binop as a type specifier, and type-of will return list when given a binop structure. Indeed, there is no way to distinguish a data structure constructed by make-binop from any other list that happens to have the correct structure.

There is not even any way to recover the structure name binop from a structure created by make-binop. This can be done, however, if the structure is "named."

19.7.2. Named Structures

A "named" structure has the property that, given an instance of the structure, the structure name (that names the type) can be reliably recovered. For structures defined with no :type option, the structure name actually becomes part of the Common Lisp data-type system. The function type-of, when applied to such a structure, will return the structure name as the type of the object; the predicate typep will recognize the structure name as a valid type specifier.

For structures defined with a :type option, type-of will return a type specifier such as list or (vector t), depending on the type specified to the :type option. The structure name does not become a valid type specifier. However, if the :named option is also specified, then the first component of the structure (as created by a defstruct constructor function) will always contain the structure name. This allows the structure name to be recovered from an instance of the structure and allows a reasonable predicate for the conceptual type to be defined: the automatically defined *name*-p predicate for the structure operates by first checking that its argument is of the proper type (list, (vector t), or whatever) and then checking whether the first component contains the appropriate type name.

Consider the `binop` example shown above, modified only to include the `:named` option:

```
(defstruct (binop (:type list) :named)
  (operator '? :type symbol)
  operand-1
  operand-2)
```

As before, this will define a constructor function `make-binop` and three selector functions `binop-operator`, `binop-operand-1`, and `binop-operand-2`. It will also define a predicate `binop-p`.

The effect of `make-binop` is now to construct a list of length 4:

```
(make-binop :operator '+ :operand-1 'x :operand-2 5)
   ⇒ (binop + x 5)

(make-binop :operand-2 4 :operator '*)
   ⇒ (binop * nil 4)
```

The structure has the same layout as before except that the structure name `binop` is included as the first list element. The selector functions `binop-operator`, `binop-operand-1`, and `binop-operand-2` are essentially equivalent to `cadr`, `caddr`, and `cadddr`, respectively. The predicate `binop-p` is more or less equivalent to the following definition.

```
(defun binop-p (x)
  (and (consp x) (eq (car x) 'binop)))
```

The name `binop` is still not a valid type specifier recognizable to `typep`, but at least there is a way of distinguishing `binop` structures from other similarly defined structures.

19.7.3. Other Aspects of Explicitly Specified Structures

The `:initial-offset` option allows one to specify that slots be allocated beginning at a representational element other than the first. For example, the form

```
(defstruct (binop (:type list) (:initial-offset 2))
  (operator '? :type symbol)
  operand-1
  operand-2)
```

would result in the following behavior for `make-binop`:

```
(make-binop :operator '+ :operand-1 'x :operand-2 5)
    ⇒ (nil nil + x 5)

(make-binop :operand-2 4 :operator '*)
    ⇒ (nil nil * nil 4)
```

The selectors `binop-operator`, `binop-operand-1`, and `binop-operand-2` would
be essentially equivalent to `caddr`, `cadddr`, and `car` of `cddddr`, respectively. Similarly, the form

```
(defstruct (binop (:type list) :named (:initial-offset 2))
  (operator '? :type symbol)
  operand-1
  operand-2)
```

would result in the following behavior for `make-binop`:

```
(make-binop :operator '+ :operand-1 'x :operand-2 5)
    ⇒ (nil nil binop + x 5)

(make-binop :operand-2 4 :operator '*)
    ⇒ (nil nil binop * nil 4)
```

If the `:include` is used with the `:type` option, then the effect is first to skip over
as many representation elements as needed to represent the included structure, then
to skip over any additional elements specified by the `:initial-offset` option,
and then to begin allocation of elements from that point. For example:

```
(defstruct (binop (:type list) :named (:initial-offset 2))
  (operator '? :type symbol)
  operand-1
  operand-2)

(defstruct (annotated-binop (:type list)
                            (:initial-offset 3)
                            (:include binop))
  commutative associative identity)

(make-annotated-binop :operator '*
                      :operand-1 'x
                      :operand-2 5
                      :commutative t
```

```
                    :associative t
                    :identity 1)
 ⇒ (nil nil binop * x 5 nil nil nil t t 1)
```

The first two `nil` elements stem from the `:initial-offset` of 2 in the definition of `binop`. The next four elements contain the structure name and three slots for `binop`. The next three `nil` elements stem from the `:initial-offset` of 3 in the definition of `annotated-binop`. The last three list elements contain the additional slots for an `annotated-binop`.

20

The Evaluator

The mechanism that executes Lisp programs is called the evaluator. More precisely, the evaluator accepts a form and performs the computation specified by the form. This mechanism is made available to the user through the function `eval`.

The evaluator is typically implemented as an interpreter that traverses the given form recursively, performing each step of the computation as it goes. An interpretive implementation is not required, however. A permissible alternative approach is for the evaluator first to completely compile the form into machine-executable code and then invoke the resulting code. This technique virtually eliminates incompatibilities between interpreted and compiled code but also renders the `evalhook` mechanism relatively useless. Various mixed strategies are also possible. All of these approaches should produce the same results when executing a correct program but may produce different results for incorrect programs. For example, the approaches may differ as to when macro calls are expanded; macro definitions should not depend on the time at which they are expanded. Implementors should document the evaluation strategy for each implementation.

20.1. Run-Time Evaluation of Forms

The function `eval` is the main user interface to the evaluator. Hooks are provided for user-supplied debugging routines to obtain control during the execution of an interpretive evaluator. The functions `evalhook` and `applyhook` provide alternative interfaces to the evaluator mechanism for use by these debugging routines.

eval *form* [*Function*]

The *form* is evaluated in the current dynamic environment and a null lexical environment. Whatever results from the evaluation is returned from the call to `eval`.

Note that when you write a call to `eval` *two* levels of evaluation occur on the argument form you write. First the argument form is evaluated, as for arguments

490

to any function, by the usual argument evaluation mechanism (which involves an implicit use of eval). Then the argument is passed to the eval function, where another evaluation occurs. For example:

(eval (list ´cdr (car ´((quote (a . b)) c)))) ⇒ b

The argument form (list ´cdr (car ´((quote (a . b)) c))) is evaluated in the usual way to produce the argument (cdr (quote (a . b))); this is then given to eval because eval is being called explicitly, and eval evaluates its argument (cdr (quote (a . b))) to produce b.

If all that is required for some application is to obtain the current dynamic value of a given symbol, the function symbol-value may be more efficient than eval.

X3J13 voted in January 1989 〈121〉 to restrict user side effects; see section 7.9.

---

evalhook   [*Variable*]
applyhook   [*Variable*]

If the value of *evalhook* is not nil, then eval behaves in a special way. The non-nil value of *evalhook* should be a function that takes two arguments, a form and an environment; this is called the *eval hook function*. When a form is to be evaluated (any form at all, even a number or a symbol), whether implicitly or via an explicit call to eval, no attempt is made to evaluate the form. Instead, the hook function is invoked and is passed the form to be evaluated as its first argument. The hook function is then responsible for evaluating the form; whatever is returned by the hook function is assumed to be the result of evaluating the form.

The variable *applyhook* is similar to *evalhook* but is used when a function is about to be applied to arguments. If the value of *applyhook* is not nil, then eval behaves in a special way.

The non-nil value of *applyhook* should be a function that takes three arguments: a function, a list of arguments, and an environment; this is called the *apply hook function*.

X3J13 voted in January 1989 〈5〉 to revise the definition of *applyhook*. Its value should be a function of *two* arguments, a function and a list of arguments; no environment information is passed to an apply hook function.

This was simply a flaw in the first edition. Sorry about that.

When a function is about to be applied to a list of arguments, no attempt is made to apply the function. Instead, the hook function is invoked and is passed the function and the list of arguments as its first and second arguments. The hook function is then responsible for evaluating the form; whatever is returned by the hook function is assumed to be the result of evaluating the form. The apply hook function is used only for application of ordinary functions within eval. It is not used for applications via apply or funcall, for applications by such functions as map or reduce, or for invocation of macro-expansion functions by either eval or macroexpand.

X3J13 voted in June 1988 ⟨90⟩ to specify that the value of *macroexpand-hook* is first coerced to a function before being called as the expansion interface hook. This vote made no mention of *evalhook* or *applyhook*, but this may have been an oversight.

A proposal was submitted to X3J13 in September 1989 to specify that the value of *evalhook* or *applyhook* is first coerced to a function before being called. If this proposal is accepted, the value of either variable may be nil, any other symbol, a lambda-expression, or any object of type function.

The last argument passed to either kind of hook function contains information about the lexical environment in an implementation-dependent format. These arguments are suitable for the functions evalhook, applyhook, and macroexpand.

When either kind of hook function is invoked, both of the variables *evalhook* and *applyhook* are rebound to the value nil around the invocation of the hook function. This is so that the hook function will not be invoked recursively on evaluations and applications that occur in the course of executing the code of the hook function. The functions evalhook and applyhook are useful for performing recursive evaluations and applications within the hook function.

The hook feature is provided as an aid to debugging. The step facility is implemented using this hook.

If a non-local exit causes a throw back to the top level of Lisp, perhaps because an error could not be corrected, then *evalhook* and *applyhook* are automatically reset to nil as a safety feature.

---

evalhook *form evalhookfn applyhookfn* &optional *env*   [*Function*]
applyhook *function args evalhookfn applyhookfn* &optional *env* [*Function*]

The functions evalhook and applyhook are provided to make it easier to exploit the hook feature.

In the case of evalhook, the *form* is evaluated. In the case of applyhook, the *function* is applied to the list of arguments *args*. In either case, for the duration of the operation the variable *evalhook* is bound to *evalhookfn*, and *applyhook* is bound to *applyhookfn*. Furthermore, the *env* argument is used as the lexical environment for the operation; *env* defaults to the null environment. The check for a hook function is *bypassed* for the evaluation of the *form* itself (for evalhook) or for the application of the *function* to the *args* itself (for applyhook), but not for subsidiary evaluations and applications such as evaluations of subforms. It is this one-shot bypass that makes evalhook and applyhook so useful.

X3J13 voted in January 1989 ⟨5⟩ to eliminate the optional *env* parameter to applyhook, because it is not (and cannot) be useful. Any function that can be applied carries its own environment and does not need another environment to be specified separately. This was a flaw in the first edition.

Here is an example of a very simple tracing routine that uses just the evalhook feature.

```
(defvar *hooklevel* 0)

(defun hook (x)
  (let ((*evalhook* 'eval-hook-function))
    (eval x)))

(defun eval-hook-function (form &rest env)
  (let ((*hooklevel* (+ *hooklevel* 1)))
    (format *trace-output* "~%~V@TForm:   ~S"
            (* *hooklevel* 2) form)
    (let ((values (multiple-value-list
                    (evalhook form
                              #'eval-hook-function
                              nil
                              env))))
      (format *trace-output* "~%~V@TValue:~{ ~S~}"
              (* *hooklevel* 2) values)
      (values-list values))))
```

Using these routines, one might see the following interaction:

```
(hook '(cons (floor *print-base* 2) 'b))
  Form: (CONS (FLOOR *PRINT-BASE* 2) (QUOTE B))
    Form: (FLOOR *PRINT-BASE* 3)
      Form: *PRINT-BASE*
      Value: 10
      Form: 3
      Value: 3
    Value: 3 1
    Form: (QUOTE B)
    Value: B
  Value: (3 . B)
(3 . B)
```

constantp *object*   [*Function*]

If the predicate constantp is true of an object, then that object, when considered
as a form to be evaluated, always evaluates to the same thing; it is a constant. This
includes self-evaluating objects such as numbers, characters, strings, bit-vectors,
and keywords, as well as all constant symbols declared by defconstant, such as
nil, t, and pi. In addition, a list whose *car* is quote, such as (quote foo), is
considered to be a constant.

If constantp is false of an object, then that object, considered as a form, might
or might not always evaluate to the same thing.

20.2. The Top-Level Loop

Normally one interacts with Lisp through a "top-level read-eval-print loop," so
called because it is the highest level of control and consists of an endless loop that
reads an expression, evaluates it, and prints the results. One has an effect on the
state of the Lisp system only by invoking actions that have side effects.

The precise nature of the top-level loop for Common Lisp is purposely not rig-
orously specified here so that implementors can experiment to improve the user
interface. For example, an implementor may choose to require line-at-a-time input, or may provide a fancy editor or complex graphics-display interface. An
implementor may choose to provide explicit prompts for input, or may choose (as
MacLisp does) not to clutter up the transcript with prompts.

The top-level loop is required to trap all throws and recover gracefully. It is
also required to print all values resulting from evaluation of a form, perhaps on
separate lines. If a form returns zero values, as little as possible should be printed.

The following variables are maintained by the top-level loop as a limited safety
net, in case the user forgets to save an interesting input expression or output value.
(Note that the names of some of these variables violate the convention that names
of global variables begin and end with an asterisk.) These are intended primarily
for user interaction, which is why they have short names. Use of these variables
should be avoided in programs.

+   [*Variable*]
++   [*Variable*]
+++   [*Variable*]

While a form is being evaluated by the top-level loop, the variable + is bound to
the previous form read by the loop. The variable ++ holds the previous value of

+ (that is, the form evaluated two interactions ago), and +++ holds the previous value of ++.

- [*Variable*]

While a form is being evaluated by the top-level loop, the variable - is bound to the form itself; that is, it is the value about to be given to + once this interaction is done.

Notice of correction. In the first edition, the name of the variable - was inadvertently omitted.

*	[*Variable*]
**	[*Variable*]
***	[*Variable*]

While a form is being evaluated by the top-level loop, the variable * is bound to the result printed at the end of the last time through the loop; that is, it is the value produced by evaluating the form in +. If several values were produced, * contains the first value only; * contains nil if zero values were produced. The variable ** holds the previous value of * (that is, the result printed two interactions ago), and *** holds the previous value of **.

If the evaluation of + is aborted for some reason, then the values associated with *, **, and *** are not updated; they are updated only if the printing of values is at least begun (though not necessarily completed).

/	[*Variable*]
//	[*Variable*]
///	[*Variable*]

While a form is being evaluated by the top-level loop, the variable / is bound to a list of the results printed at the end of the last time through the loop; that is, it is a list of all values produced by evaluating the form in +. The value of * should always be the same as the *car* of the value of /. The variable // holds the previous value of / (that is, the results printed two interactions ago), and /// holds the previous value of //. Therefore the value of ** should always be the same as the *car* of //, and similarly for *** and ///.

If the evaluation of + is aborted for some reason, then the values associated with /, //, and /// are not updated; they are updated only if the printing of values is at least begun (though not necessarily completed).

As an example of the processing of these variables, consider the following possible transcript, where > is a prompt by the top-level loop for user input:

```
>(cons - -)                    ;Interaction 1
((CONS - -) CONS - -)          ;Cute, huh?

>(values)                      ;Interaction 2
                                    ;Nothing to print
>(cons 'a 'b)                  ;Interaction 3
(A . B)                        ;There is a single value

>(hairy-loop)^G                ;Interaction 4
### QUIT to top level.         ;(User aborts the computation.)

>(floor 13 4)                  ;Interaction 5
3                              ;There are two values
1
```

At this point we have:

```
+++ ⇒ (cons 'a 'b)      *** ⇒ NIL          /// ⇒ ()
++ ⇒ (hairy-loop)       ** ⇒ (A . B)       // ⇒ ((A . B))
+ ⇒ (floor 13 4)        * ⇒ 3              / ⇒ (3 1)
```

21

Streams

Streams are objects that serve as sources or sinks of data. Character streams produce or absorb characters; binary streams produce or absorb integers. The normal action of a Common Lisp system is to read characters from a character input stream, parse the characters as representations of Common Lisp data objects, evaluate each object (as a form) as it is read, and print representations of the results of evaluation to an output character stream.

Typically streams are connected to files or to an interactive terminal. Streams, being Lisp objects, serve as the ambassadors of external devices by which input/output is accomplished.

A stream, whether a character stream or a binary stream, may be input-only, output-only, or bidirectional. What operations may be performed on a stream depends on which of the six types of stream it is.

21.1. Standard Streams

There are several variables whose values are streams used by many functions in the Lisp system. These variables and their uses are listed here. By convention, variables that are expected to hold a stream capable of input have names ending with -input, and variables that are expected to hold a stream capable of output have names ending with -output. Variables expected to hold a bidirectional stream have names ending with -io.

standard-input   *[Variable]*

In the normal Lisp top-level loop, input is read from *standard-input* (that is, whatever stream is the value of the global variable *standard-input*). Many input functions, including read and read-char, take a stream argument that defaults to *standard-input*.

standard-output   [Variable]

In the normal Lisp top-level loop, output is sent to *standard-output* (that is, whatever stream is the value of the global variable *standard-output*). Many output functions, including print and write-char, take a stream argument that defaults to *standard-output*.

error-output   [Variable]

The value of *error-output* is a stream to which error messages should be sent. Normally this is the same as *standard-output*, but *standard-output* might be bound to a file and *error-output* left going to the terminal or to a separate file of error messages.

query-io   [Variable]

The value of *query-io* is a stream to be used when asking questions of the user. The question should be output to this stream, and the answer read from it. When the normal input to a program may be coming from a file, questions such as "Do you really want to delete all of the files in your directory?" should nevertheless be sent directly to the user; and the answer should come from the user, not from the data file. For such purposes *query-io* should be used instead of *standard-input* and *standard-output*. *query-io* is used by such functions as yes-or-no-p.

debug-io   [Variable]

The value of *debug-io* is a stream to be used for interactive debugging purposes. This is often the same as the value of *query-io*, but need not be.

terminal-io   [Variable]

The value of *terminal-io* is ordinarily the stream that connects to the user's console. Typically, writing to this stream would cause the output to appear on a display screen, for example, and reading from the stream would accept input from a keyboard.

It is intended that standard input functions such as read and read-char, when used with this stream, would cause "echoing" of the input into the output side of the stream. (The means by which this is accomplished are of course highly implementation-dependent.)

trace-output   [*Variable*]

The value of *trace-output* is the stream on which the trace function prints
its output.

The variables *standard-input*, *standard-output*, *error-output*,
trace-output, *query-io*, and *debug-io* are initially bound to synonym
streams that pass all operations on to the stream that is the value of *terminal-io*.
(See make-synonym-stream.) Thus any operations performed on those streams
will go to the terminal.

X3J13 voted in January 1989 ⟨165⟩ to replace the requirements of the preceding
paragraph with the following new requirements:

The seven standard stream variables, *standard-input*, *standard-output*,
query-io, *debug-io*, *terminal-io*, *error-output*, and *trace-output*, are initially bound to open streams. (These will be called *the standard initial streams*.)

The streams that are the initial values of *standard-input*, *query-io*,
debug-io, and *terminal-io* must support input.

The streams that are the initial values of *standard-output*, *error-output*, *trace-output*, *query-io*, *debug-io*, and *terminal-io* must
support output.

None of the standard initial streams (including the one to which *terminal-io*
is initially bound) may be a synonym, either directly or indirectly, for any of the
standard stream variables except *terminal-io*. For example, the initial value
of *trace-output* may be a synonym stream for *terminal-io* but not a
synonym stream for *standard-output* or *query-io*. (These are examples
of direct synonyms.) As another example, *query-io* may be a two-way stream
or echo stream whose input component is a synonym for *terminal-io*, but its
input component may not be a synonym for *standard-input* or *debug-io*.
(These are examples of indirect synonyms.)

Any or all of the standard initial streams may be direct or indirect synonyms
for one or more common implementation-dependent streams. For example, the
standard initial streams might all be synonym streams (or two-way or echo streams
whose components are synonym streams) to a pair of hidden terminal input and
output streams maintained by the implementation.

Part of the intent of these rules is to ensure that it is always safe to bind any
standard stream variable to the value of any other standard stream variable (that
is, unworkable circularities are avoided) without unduly restricting implementation
flexibility.

No user program should ever change the value of *terminal-io*. A program
that wants (for example) to divert output to a file should do so by binding the

value of *standard-output*; that way error messages sent to *error-output* can still get to the user by going through *terminal-io*, which is usually what is desired.

21.2. Creating New Streams

Perhaps the most important constructs for creating new streams are those that open files; see with-open-file and open. The following functions construct streams without reference to a file system.

---

make-synonym-stream *symbol*   [*Function*]

make-synonym-stream creates and returns a synonym stream. Any operations on the new stream will be performed on the stream that is then the value of the dynamic variable named by the *symbol*. If the value of the variable should change or be bound, then the synonym stream will operate on the new stream.

X3J13 voted in January 1989 ⟨167⟩ to specify that the result of make-synonym-stream is always a stream of type synonym-stream. Note that the type of a synonym stream is *always* synonym-stream, regardless of the type of the stream for which it is a synonym.

---

make-broadcast-stream &rest *streams*   [*Function*]

This returns a stream that works only in the output direction. Any output sent to this stream will be sent to all of the *streams* given. The set of operations that may be performed on the new stream is the intersection of those for the given streams. The results returned by a stream operation are the values resulting from performing the operation on the last stream in *streams*; the results of performing the operation on all preceding streams are discarded. If no *streams* are given as arguments, then the result is a "bit sink"; all output to the resulting stream is discarded.

X3J13 voted in January 1989 ⟨167⟩ to specify that the result of make-broadcast-stream is always a stream of type broadcast-stream.

---

make-concatenated-stream &rest *streams*   [*Function*]

This returns a stream that works only in the input direction. Input is taken from the first of the *streams* until it reaches end-of-file; then that stream is discarded, and input is taken from the next of the *streams*, and so on. If no arguments are given, the result is a stream with no content; any input attempt will result in end-of-file.

X3J13 voted in January 1989 ⟨167⟩ to specify that the result of make-concatenated-stream is always a stream of type concatenated-stream.

---

make-two-way-stream *input-stream output-stream*   [*Function*]

This returns a bidirectional stream that gets its input from *input-stream* and sends its output to *output-stream*.

   X3J13 voted in January 1989 ⟨167⟩ to specify that the result of make-two-way-stream is always a stream of type two-way-stream.

---

make-echo-stream *input-stream output-stream*   [*Function*]

This returns a bidirectional stream that gets its input from *input-stream* and sends its output to *output-stream*. In addition, all input taken from *input-stream* is echoed to *output-stream*.

   X3J13 voted in January 1989 ⟨167⟩ to specify that the result of make-echo-stream is always a stream of type echo-stream.

   X3J13 voted in January 1989 ⟨138⟩ to clarify the interaction of read-char, unread-char, and peek-char with echo streams. (See the descriptions of those functions for details.)

   X3J13 explicitly noted that the bidirectional streams that are the initial values of *query-io*, *debug-io*, and *terminal-io*, even though they may have some echoing behavior, conceptually are not necessarily the products of calls to make-echo-stream and therefore are not subject to the new rules about echoing on echo streams. Instead, these initial interactive streams may have implementation-dependent echoing behavior.

---

make-string-input-stream *string* &optional *start end*   [*Function*]

This returns an input stream. The input stream will supply, in order, the characters in the substring of *string* delimited by *start* and *end*; after the last character has been supplied, the stream will then be at end-of-file.

   X3J13 voted in January 1989 ⟨167⟩ to specify that the result of make-string-input-stream is always a stream of type string-stream.

---

make-string-output-stream   [*Function*]

This returns an output stream that will accumulate all output given it for the benefit of the function get-output-stream-string.

X3J13 voted in June 1989 ⟨122⟩ to let `make-string-output-stream` take an
`:element-type` argument.

`make-string-output-stream` &key `:element-type`   [*Function*]

This returns an output stream that will accumulate all output given it for the benefit
of the function `get-output-stream-string`.

The `:element-type` argument specifies what characters must be accepted by
the created stream. If the `:element-type` argument is omitted, the created stream
must accept all characters.

X3J13 voted in January 1989 ⟨167⟩ to specify that the result of `make-`
`string-output-stream` is always a stream of type `string-stream`.

`get-output-stream-string` *string-output-stream*   [*Function*]

Given a stream produced by `make-string-output-stream`, this returns a string
containing all the characters output to the stream so far. The stream is then reset;
thus each call to `get-output-stream-string` gets only the characters since the
last such call (or the creation of the stream, if no such previous call has been
made).

`with-open-stream` (*var stream*) {*declaration*}* {*form*}*   [*Macro*]

The form *stream* is evaluated and must produce a stream. The variable *var* is
bound with the stream as its value, and then the forms of the body are executed as
an implicit `progn`; the results of evaluating the last form are returned as the value
of the `with-open-stream` form. The stream is automatically closed on exit from
the `with-open-stream` form, no matter whether the exit is normal or abnormal;
see `close`. The stream should be regarded as having dynamic extent.

X3J13 voted in January 1989 ⟨167⟩ to specify that the stream created by
`with-open-stream` is always of type `file-stream`.

`with-input-from-string` (*var string* {*keyword value*}*)   [*Macro*]
                         {*declaration*}* {*form*}*

The body is executed as an implicit `progn` with the variable *var* bound to a character
input stream that supplies successive characters from the value of the form *string*.
`with-input-from-string` returns the results from the last *form* of the body.

The input stream is automatically closed on exit from the `with-input-`
`from-string` form, no matter whether the exit is normal or abnormal. The stream
should be regarded as having dynamic extent.

X3J13 voted in January 1989 ⟨167⟩ to specify that the stream created by with-input-from-string is always of type string-stream.

The following keyword options may be used:

:index

The form after the :index keyword should be a *place* acceptable to setf. If the with-input-from-string form is exited normally, then the *place* will have stored into it the index into the *string* indicating the first character not read (the length of the string if all characters were used). The *place* is not updated as reading progresses, but only at the end of the operation.

:start

The :start keyword takes an argument indicating, in the manner usual for sequence functions, the beginning of a substring of *string* to be used.

:end

The :end keyword takes an argument indicating, in the manner usual for sequence functions, the end of a substring of *string* to be used.

Here is an example of the use of with-input-from-string:

```
(with-input-from-string (s "Animal Crackers" :index j :start 6)
  (read s)) ⇒ crackers
```

As a side effect, the variable j is set to 15.

The :start and :index keywords may both specify the same variable, which is a pointer within the string to be advanced, perhaps repeatedly by some containing loop.

X3J13 voted in January 1989 ⟨121⟩ to restrict user side effects; see section 7.9.

with-output-to-string (*var* [*string*]) {*declaration*}* {*form*}*   [*Macro*]

The body is executed as an implicit progn with the variable *var* bound to a character output stream. All output to that stream is saved in a string. This may be done in one of two ways.

If no *string* argument is provided, then the value of with-output-from-string is a string containing all the collected output.

If *string* is specified, it must be a string with a fill pointer; the output is incrementally appended to the string, as if using vector-push-extend if the string is adjustable, and otherwise as if using vector-push. In this case with-output-to-string returns the results from the last *form* of the body.

In either case, the output stream is automatically closed on exit from the with-output-from-string form, no matter whether the exit is normal or abnormal. The stream should be regarded as having dynamic extent.

X3J13 voted in June 1989 ⟨122⟩ to let with-output-to-string take an :element-type argument.

with-output-to-string (*var* [*string* [:element-type *type*]])   [*Macro*]
{*declaration*}* {*form*}*

One may specify nil instead of a string as the *string* and use the :element-type argument to specify what characters must be accepted by the created stream. If no *string* argument is provided, or if it is nil and no :element-type is specified, the created stream must accept all characters.

X3J13 voted in October 1988 ⟨185⟩ to specify that if *string* is specified, it must be a string with a fill pointer; the output is incrementally appended to the string (as if by use of vector-push-extend).

In this way output cannot be accidentally lost. This change makes with-output-to-string behave in the same way that format does when given a string as its first argument.

X3J13 voted in January 1989 ⟨167⟩ to specify that the stream created by with-output-to-string is always of type string-stream.

X3J13 voted in January 1989 ⟨121⟩ to restrict user side effects; see section 7.9.

21.3. Operations on Streams

This section contains discussion of only those operations that are common to all streams. Input and output is rather complicated and is discussed separately in chapter 22. The interface between streams and the file system is discussed in chapter 23.

streamp *object*   [*Function*]

streamp is true if its argument is a stream, and otherwise is false.

(streamp x) ≡ (typep x 'stream)

X3J13 voted in January 1989 ⟨15⟩ to specify that streamp is unaffected by whether its argument, if a stream, is open or closed. In either case it returns true.

`open-stream-p` *stream*   [*Function*]

X3J13 voted in January 1989 ⟨167⟩ to add the predicate `open-stream-p`. It is true if its argument (which must be a stream) is open, and otherwise is false.

A stream is always created open; it remains open until closed with the `close` function. The macros `with-open-stream`, `with-input-from-string`, `with-output-to-string`, and `with-open-file` automatically close the created stream as control leaves their bodies, in effect imposing dynamic extent on the openness of the stream.

`input-stream-p` *stream*   [*Function*]

This predicate is true if its argument (which must be a stream) can handle input operations, and otherwise is false.

`output-stream-p` *stream*   [*Function*]

This predicate is true if its argument (which must be a stream) can handle output operations, and otherwise is false.

`stream-element-type` *stream*   [*Function*]

A type specifier is returned to indicate what objects may be read from or written to the argument *stream*, which must be a stream. Streams created by `open` will have an element type restricted to a subset of `character` or `integer`, but in principle a stream may conduct transactions using any Lisp objects.

`close` *stream* `&key` `:abort`   [*Function*]

The argument must be a stream. The stream is closed. No further input/output operations may be performed on it. However, certain inquiry operations may still be performed, and it is permissible to close an already closed stream.

X3J13 voted in January 1989 ⟨15⟩ and revised the vote in March 1989 to specify that if `close` is called on an open stream, the stream is closed and t is returned; but if `close` is called on a closed stream, it succeeds without error and returns an unspecified value. (The rationale for not specifying the value returned for a closed stream is that in some implementations closing certain streams does not really have an effect on them—for example, closing the `*terminal-io*` stream might not "really" close it—and it is not desirable to force such implementations to keep otherwise unnecessary state. Portable programs will of course not rely on such behavior.)

X3J13 also voted in January 1989 to specify exactly which inquiry functions may be applied to closed streams:

`streamp`	`pathname-host`	`namestring`
`pathname`	`pathname-device`	`file-namestring`
`truename`	`pathname-directory`	`directory-namestring`
`merge-pathnames`	`pathname-name`	`host-namestring`
`open`	`pathname-type`	`enough-namestring`
`probe-file`	`pathname-version`	`directory`

See the individual descriptions of these functions for more information on how they operate on closed streams.

X3J13 voted in January 1989 ⟨14⟩ to clarify the effect of closing various kinds of streams. First some terminology:

- A *composite* stream is one that was returned by a call to `make-synonym-stream`, `make-broadcast-stream`, `make-concatenated-stream`, `make-two-way-stream`, or `make-echo-stream`.

- The *constituents* of a composite stream are the streams that were given as arguments to the function that constructed it or, in the case of `make-synonym-stream`, the stream that is the `symbol-value` of the symbol that was given as an argument. (The constituent of a synonym stream may therefore vary over time.)

- A *constructed* stream is either a composite stream or one returned by a call to `make-string-input-stream`, `make-string-output-stream`, `with-input-from-string`, or `with-output-to-string`.

The effect of applying `close` to a constructed stream is to close that stream only. No input/output operations are permitted on the constructed stream once it has been closed (though certain inquiry functions are still permitted, as described above).

Closing a composite stream has no effect on its constituents; any constituents that are open remain open.

If a stream created by `make-string-output-stream` is closed, the result of then applying `get-output-stream-string` to the stream is unspecified.

If the `:abort` parameter is not `nil` (it defaults to `nil`), it indicates an abnormal termination of the use of the stream. An attempt is made to clean up any side effects of having created the stream in the first place. For example, if the stream performs output to a file that was newly created when the stream was created, then if possible the file is deleted and any previously existing file is not superseded.

X3J13 voted in January 1989 ⟨167⟩ to add the following accessor functions for obtaining information about streams.

broadcast-stream-streams *broadcast-stream*   [*Function*]

The argument must be of type broadcast-stream. A list of the constituent output streams (whether open or not) is returned.

concatenated-stream-streams *concatenated-stream*   [*Function*]

The argument must be of type concatenated-stream. A list of constituent streams (whether open or not) is returned. This list represents the ordered set of input streams from which the concatenated stream may yet read; the stream from which it is currently reading is first in the list. The list may be empty if no more streams remain to be read.

echo-stream-input-stream *echo-stream*   [*Function*]
echo-stream-output-stream *echo-stream*   [*Function*]

The argument must be of type echo-stream. The function echo-stream-input-stream returns the constituent input stream; echo-stream-output-stream returns the constituent output stream.

synonym-stream-symbol *synonym-stream*   [*Function*]

The argument must be of type synonym-stream. This function returns the symbol for whose value the *synonym-stream* is a synonym.

two-way-stream-input-stream *two-way-stream*   [*Function*]
two-way-stream-output-stream *two-way-stream*   [*Function*]

The argument must be of type two-way-stream. The function two-way-stream-input-stream returns the constituent input stream; two-way-stream-output-stream returns the constituent output stream.

interactive-stream-p *stream*   [*Function*]

X3J13 voted in June 1989 ⟨168⟩ to add the predicate interactive-stream-p, which returns t if the *stream* is interactive and otherwise returns nil. A type-error error is signalled if the argument is not of type stream.

The precise meaning of `interactive-stream-p` is implementation-dependent and may depend on the underlying operating system. The intent is to distinguish between interactive and batch (background, command-file) operations. Some characteristics that might distinguish a stream as interactive:

- The stream is connected to a person (or the equivalent) in such a way that the program can prompt for information and expect to receive input that might depend on the prompt.

- The program is expected to prompt for input and to support "normal input editing protocol" for that operating environment.

- A call to `read-char` might hang waiting for the user to type something rather than quickly returning a character or an end-of-file indication.

The value of `*terminal-io*` might or might not be interactive.

`stream-external-format` *stream*   [*Function*]

X3J13 voted in June 1989 ⟨122⟩ to add the function `stream-external-format`, which returns a specifier for the implementation-recognized scheme used for representing characters in the argument *stream*. See the `:external-format` argument to open.

22

Input/Output

Common Lisp provides a rich set of facilities for performing input/output. All input/output operations are performed on streams of various kinds. This chapter is devoted to stream data transfer operations. Streams are discussed in chapter 21, and ways of manipulating files through streams are discussed in chapter 23.

While there is provision for reading and writing binary data, most of the I/O operations in Common Lisp read or write characters. There are simple primitives for reading and writing single characters or lines of data. The format function can perform complex formatting of output data, directed by a control string in manner similar to a Fortran FORMAT statement or a PL/I PUT EDIT statement. The most useful I/O operations, however, read and write printed representations of arbitrary Lisp objects.

22.1. Printed Representation of Lisp Objects

Lisp objects in general are not text strings but complex data structures. They have very different properties from text strings as a consequence of their internal representation. However, to make it possible to get at and talk about Lisp objects, Lisp provides a representation of most objects in the form of printed text; this is called the *printed representation*, which is used for input/output purposes and in the examples throughout this book. Functions such as print take a Lisp object and send the characters of its printed representation to a stream. The collection of routines that does this is known as the (Lisp) *printer*. The read function takes characters from a stream, interprets them as a printed representation of a Lisp object, builds that object, and returns it; the collection of routines that does this is called the (Lisp) *reader*.

Ideally, one could print a Lisp object and then read the printed representation back in, and so obtain the same identical object. In practice this is difficult and for some purposes not even desirable. Instead, reading a printed representation produces an object that is (with obscure technical exceptions) `equal` to the originally printed object.

Most Lisp objects have more than one possible printed representation. For example, the integer twenty-seven can be written in any of these ways:

27   27.   #o33   #x1B   #b11011   #.(* 3 3 3)   81/3

A list of two symbols A and B can be printed in many ways:

```
    (A B)    (a b)    (  a  b  )    (\A |B|)
    (|\A|
  B
)
```

The last example, which is spread over three lines, may be ugly, but it is legitimate. In general, wherever whitespace is permissible in a printed representation, any number of spaces and newlines may appear.

When `print` produces a printed representation, it must choose arbitrarily from among many possible printed representations. It attempts to choose one that is readable. There are a number of global variables that can be used to control the actions of `print`, and a number of different printing functions.

This section describes in detail what is the standard printed representation for any Lisp object and also describes how `read` operates.

22.1.1. What the Read Function Accepts

The purpose of the Lisp reader is to accept characters, interpret them as the printed representation of a Lisp object, and construct and return such an object. The reader cannot accept everything that the printer produces; for example, the printed representations of compiled code objects cannot be read in. However, the reader has many features that are not used by the output of the printer at all, such as comments, alternative representations, and convenient abbreviations for frequently used but unwieldy constructs. The reader is also parameterized in such a way that it can be used as a lexical analyzer for a more general user-written parser.

The reader is organized as a recursive-descent parser. Broadly speaking, the reader operates by reading a character from the input stream and treating it in one of three ways. Whitespace characters serve as separators but are otherwise ignored. Constituent and escape characters are accumulated to make a *token*, which is then interpreted as a number or symbol. Macro characters trigger the invocation of functions (possibly user-supplied) that can perform arbitrary parsing actions, including recursive invocation of the reader.

More precisely, when the reader is invoked, it reads a single character from the input stream and dispatches according to the syntactic type of that character. Every character that can appear in the input stream must be of exactly one of the following kinds: *illegal, whitespace, constituent, single escape, multiple escape,* or *macro*. Macro characters are further divided into the types *terminating* and *non-terminating* (of tokens). (Note that macro characters have nothing whatever to do with macros in their operation. There is a superficial similarity in that macros allow the user to extend the syntax of Common Lisp at the level of forms, while macro characters allow the user to extend the syntax at the level of characters.) Constituents additionally have one or more attributes, the most important of which is *alphabetic*; these attributes are discussed further in section 22.1.2.

The parsing of Common Lisp expressions is discussed in terms of these syntactic character types because the types of individual characters are not fixed but may be altered by the user (see `set-syntax-from-char` and `set-macro-character`). The characters of the standard character set initially have the syntactic types shown in table 22-1. Note that the brackets, braces, question mark, and exclamation point (that is, [,], {, }, ?, and !) are normally defined to be constituents, but they are not used for any purpose in standard Common Lisp syntax and do not occur in the names of built-in Common Lisp functions or variables. These characters are explicitly reserved to the user. The primary intent is that they be used as macro characters; but a user might choose, for example, to make ! be a *single escape* character (as it is in Portable Standard Lisp).

The algorithm performed by the Common Lisp reader is roughly as follows:

1. If at end of file, perform end-of-file processing (as specified by the caller of the `read` function). Otherwise, read one character from the input stream, call it *x*, and dispatch according to the syntactic type of *x* to one of steps 2 to 7.

2. If *x* is an *illegal* character, signal an error.

3. If *x* is a *whitespace* character, then discard it and go back to step 1.

4. If *x* is a *macro* character (at this point the distinction between *terminating* and *non-terminating* macro characters does not matter), then execute the function associated with that character. The function may return zero values or one value (see `values`).

   The macro-character function may of course read characters from the input stream; if it does, it will see those characters following the macro character. The function may even invoke the reader recursively. This is how the macro character (constructs a list: by invoking the reader recursively to read the elements of the list.

Table 22-1: Standard Character Syntax Types

⟨tab⟩	*whitespace*	⟨page⟩	*whitespace*	⟨newline⟩	*whitespace*
⟨space⟩	*whitespace*	@	*constituent*	`	*terminating macro*
!	*constituent **	A	*constituent*	a	*constituent*
"	*terminating macro*	B	*constituent*	b	*constituent*
#	*non-terminating macro*	C	*constituent*	c	*constituent*
$	*constituent*	D	*constituent*	d	*constituent*
%	*constituent*	E	*constituent*	e	*constituent*
&	*constituent*	F	*constituent*	f	*constituent*
´	*terminating macro*	G	*constituent*	g	*constituent*
(	*terminating macro*	H	*constituent*	h	*constituent*
)	*terminating macro*	I	*constituent*	i	*constituent*
*	*constituent*	J	*constituent*	j	*constituent*
+	*constituent*	K	*constituent*	k	*constituent*
,	*terminating macro*	L	*constituent*	l	*constituent*
-	*constituent*	M	*constituent*	m	*constituent*
.	*constituent*	N	*constituent*	n	*constituent*
/	*constituent*	O	*constituent*	o	*constituent*
0	*constituent*	P	*constituent*	p	*constituent*
1	*constituent*	Q	*constituent*	q	*constituent*
2	*constituent*	R	*constituent*	r	*constituent*
3	*constituent*	S	*constituent*	s	*constituent*
4	*constituent*	T	*constituent*	t	*constituent*
5	*constituent*	U	*constituent*	u	*constituent*
6	*constituent*	V	*constituent*	v	*constituent*
7	*constituent*	W	*constituent*	w	*constituent*
8	*constituent*	X	*constituent*	x	*constituent*
9	*constituent*	Y	*constituent*	y	*constituent*
:	*constituent*	Z	*constituent*	z	*constituent*
;	*terminating macro*	[	*constituent **	{	*constituent **
<	*constituent*	\	*single escape*	|	*multiple escape*
=	*constituent*	]	*constituent **	}	*constituent **
>	*constituent*	^	*constituent*	~	*constituent*
?	*constituent **	_	*constituent*	⟨rubout⟩	*constituent*
⟨backspace⟩	*constituent*	⟨return⟩	*whitespace*	⟨linefeed⟩	*whitespace*

The characters marked with an asterisk are initially constituents but are reserved to the user for use as macro characters or for any other desired purpose.

If one value is returned, then return that value as the result of the read operation; the algorithm is done. If zero values are returned, then go back to step 1.

5. If *x* is a *single escape* character (normally \\), then read the next character and call it *y* (but if at end of file, signal an error instead). Ignore the usual syntax of *y* and pretend it is a *constituent* whose only attribute is *alphabetic*.

   (If *y* is a lowercase character, leave it alone; do not replace it with the corresponding uppercase character.)

   For the purposes of readtable-case, *y* is not replaceable.

   Use *y* to begin a token, and go to step 8.

6. If *x* is a *multiple escape* character (normally |), then begin a token (initially containing no characters) and go to step 9.

7. If *x* is a *constituent* character, then it begins an extended token. After the entire token is read in, it will be interpreted either as representing a Lisp object such as a symbol or number (in which case that object is returned as the result of the read operation), or as being of illegal syntax (in which case an error is signaled).

   If *x* is a lowercase character, replace it with the corresponding uppercase character.

   X3J13 voted in June 1989 ⟨150⟩ to introduce readtable-case. Consequently, the preceding sentence should be ignored. The case of *x* should not be altered; instead, *x* should be regarded as replaceable.

   Use *x* to begin a token, and go on to step 8.

8. (At this point a token is being accumulated, and an even number of *multiple escape* characters have been encountered.) If at end of file, go to step 10. Otherwise, read a character (call it *y*), and perform one of the following actions according to its syntactic type:

   • If *y* is a *constituent* or *non-terminating macro*, then do the following.

     If *y* is a lowercase character, replace it with the corresponding uppercase character.

     X3J13 voted in June 1989 ⟨150⟩ to introduce readtable-case. Consequently, the preceding sentence should be ignored. The case of *y* should not be altered; instead, *y* should be regarded as replaceable.

     Append *y* to the token being built, and repeat step 8.

- If *y* is a *single escape* character, then read the next character and call it *z* (but if at end of file, signal an error instead). Ignore the usual syntax of *z* and pretend it is a *constituent* whose only attribute is *alphabetic*.

  (If *z* is a lowercase character, leave it alone; do not replace it with the corresponding uppercase character.)

  For the purposes of `readtable-case`, *z* is not replaceable.

  Append *z* to the token being built, and repeat step 8.

- If *y* is a *multiple escape* character, then go to step 9.

- If *y* is an *illegal* character, signal an error.

- If *y* is a *terminating macro* character, it terminates the token. First "unread" the character *y* (see `unread-char`), then go to step 10.

- If *y* is a *whitespace* character, it terminates the token. First "unread" *y* if appropriate (see `read-preserving-whitespace`), then go to step 10.

9. (At this point a token is being accumulated, and an odd number of *multiple escape* characters have been encountered.) If at end of file, signal an error. Otherwise, read a character (call it *y*), and perform one of the following actions according to its syntactic type:

   - If *y* is a *constituent, macro,* or *whitespace* character, then ignore the usual syntax of that character and pretend it is a *constituent* whose only attribute is *alphabetic*.

     (If *y* is a lowercase character, leave it alone; do not replace it with the corresponding uppercase character.)

     For the purposes of `readtable-case`, *y* is not replaceable.

     Append *y* to the token being built, and repeat step 9.

   - If *y* is a *single escape* character, then read the next character and call it *z* (but if at end of file, signal an error instead). Ignore the usual syntax of *z* and pretend it is a *constituent* whose only attribute is *alphabetic*.

     (If *z* is a lowercase character, leave it alone; do not replace it with the corresponding uppercase character.)

     For the purposes of `readtable-case`, *z* is not replaceable.

     Append *z* to the token being built, and repeat step 9.

   - If *y* is a *multiple escape* character, then go to step 8.

   - If *y* is an *illegal* character, signal an error.

10. An entire token has been accumulated.

X3J13 voted in June 1989 ⟨150⟩ to introduce `readtable-case`. If the accumulated token is to be interpreted as a symbol, any case conversion of replaceable characters should be performed at this point according to the value of the `readtable-case` slot of the current readtable (the value of `*readtable*`).

Interpret the token as representing a Lisp object and return that object as the result of the read operation, or signal an error if the token is not of legal syntax.

X3J13 voted in March 1989 ⟨11⟩ to specify that implementation-defined attributes may be removed from the characters of a symbol token when constructing the print name. It is implementation-dependent which attributes are removed.

As a rule, a *single escape* character never stands for itself but always serves to cause the following character to be treated as a simple alphabetic character. A *single escape* character can be included in a token only if preceded by another *single escape* character.

A *multiple escape* character also never stands for itself. The characters between a pair of *multiple escape* characters are all treated as simple alphabetic characters, except that *single escape* and *multiple escape* characters must nevertheless be preceded by a *single escape* character to be included.

Compatibility note: In MacLisp, the | character is implemented as a macro character that reads characters up to the next unescaped | and then makes a token; no characters are ever read beyond the second | of a matching pair. In Common Lisp, the second | does not terminate the token being read but merely reverts to the ordinary (rather than multiple-escape) mode of token accumulation. This results in some differences in the way certain character sequences are interpreted. For example, the sequence |foo||bar| would be read in MacLisp as two distinct tokens, |foo| and |bar|, whereas in Common Lisp it would be treated as a single token equivalent to |foobar|. The sequence |foo|bar|baz| would be read in MacLisp as three distinct tokens, |foo|, bar, and |baz|, whereas in Common Lisp it would be treated as a single token equivalent to |fooBARbaz|; note that the middle three lowercase letters are converted to uppercase letters as they do not fall within a matching pair of vertical bars.

One reason for the different treatment of | in Common Lisp lies in the syntax for package-qualified symbol names. A sequence such as |foo:bar| ought to be interpreted as a symbol whose name is foo:bar; the colon should be treated as a simple alphabetic character because it lies within a pair of vertical bars. The symbol |bar| within the package |foo| can be notated not as |foo:bar| but as |foo|:|bar|; the colon can serve as a package marker because it falls outside the vertical bars, and yet the notation is treated as a single token thanks to the new rules adopted in Common Lisp.

In MacLisp, the parentheses are treated as additional character types. In Common Lisp they are simply *macro* characters, as described in section 22.1.3.

What MacLisp calls "single character objects" (tokens of type *single*) are not provided for explicitly in Common Lisp. They can be viewed as simply a kind of macro character. That is, the effect of

```
(setsyntax '$ 'single nil)
(setsyntax '% 'single nil)
```

in MacLisp can be achieved in Common Lisp by

```
(defun single-macro-character (stream char)
  (declare (ignore stream))
  (intern (string char)))
(set-macro-character '$ #'single-macro-character)
(set-macro-character '% #'single-macro-character)
```

22.1.2. Parsing of Numbers and Symbols

When an extended token is read, it is interpreted as a number or symbol. In general, the token is interpreted as a number if it satisfies the syntax for numbers specified in table 22-2; this is discussed in more detail below.

The characters of the extended token may serve various syntactic functions as shown in table 22-3, but it must be remembered that any character included in a token under the control of an escape character is treated as *alphabetic* rather than according to the attributes shown in the table. One consequence of this rule is that a whitespace, macro, or escape character will always be treated as alphabetic within an extended token because such a character cannot be included in an extended token except under the control of an escape character.

To allow for extensions to the syntax of numbers, a syntax for *potential numbers* is defined in Common Lisp that is more general than the actual syntax for numbers. Any token that is not a potential number and does not consist entirely of dots will always be taken to be a symbol, now and in the future; programs may rely on this fact. Any token that is a potential number but does not fit the actual number syntax defined below is a *reserved token* and has an implementation-dependent interpretation; an implementation may signal an error, quietly treat the token as a symbol, or take some other action. Programmers should avoid the use of such reserved tokens. (A symbol whose name looks like a reserved token can always be written using one or more escape characters.)

Just as *bignum* is the standard term used by Lisp implementors for very large integers, and *flonum* (rhymes with "low hum") refers to a floating-point number, the term *potnum* has been used widely as an abbreviation for "potential number." "Potnum" rhymes with "hot rum."

Table 22-2: Actual Syntax of Numbers

---

number ::= *integer* | *ratio* | *floating-point-number*
integer ::= [*sign*] {*digit*}⁺ [*decimal-point*]
ratio ::= [*sign*] {*digit*}⁺ / {*digit*}⁺
floating-point-number ::= [*sign*] {*digit*}* *decimal-point* {*digit*}⁺ [*exponent*]
                  | [*sign*] {*digit*}⁺ [*decimal-point* {*digit*}*] *exponent*
sign ::= + | -
decimal-point ::= .
digit ::= 0 | 1 | 2 | 3 | 4 | 5 | 6 | 7 | 8 | 9
exponent ::= *exponent-marker* [*sign*] {*digit*}⁺
exponent-marker ::= e | s | f | d | l | E | S | F | D | L

A token is a potential number if it satisfies the following requirements:

- It consists entirely of digits, signs (+ or -), ratio markers (/), decimal points
  (.), extension characters (^ or _), and number markers. (A number marker is a
  letter. Whether a letter may be treated as a number marker depends on context,
  but no letter that is adjacent to another letter may ever be treated as a number
  marker. Floating-point exponent markers are instances of number markers.)

- It contains at least one digit. (Letters may be considered to be digits, depending
  on the value of *read-base*, but only in tokens containing no decimal points.)

- It begins with a digit, sign, decimal point, or extension character.

- It does not end with a sign.

As examples, the following tokens are potential numbers, but they are *not* actually
numbers as defined below, and so are reserved tokens. (They do indicate some
interesting possibilities for future extensions.)

```
1b5000          777777q        1.7J        -3/4+6.7J      12/25/83
27^19           3^4/5          6//7        3.1.2.6        ^-43^
3.141_592_653_589_793_238_4                -3.7+2.6i-6.17j+19.6k
```

The following tokens are *not* potential numbers but are always treated as symbols:

```
/               /5             +           1+             1-
foo+            ab.cd          _           ^              ^/-
```

Table 22-3: Standard Constituent Character Attributes

!	*alphabetic*	⟨page⟩	*illegal*	⟨backspace⟩	*illegal*
"	*alphabetic* *	⟨return⟩	*illegal* *	⟨tab⟩	*illegal* *
#	*alphabetic* *	⟨space⟩	*illegal* *	⟨newline⟩	*illegal* *
$	*alphabetic*	⟨rubout⟩	*illegal*	⟨linefeed⟩	*illegal* *
%	*alphabetic*	.	*alphabetic, dot, decimal point*		
&	*alphabetic*	+	*alphabetic, plus sign*		
´	*alphabetic* *	–	*alphabetic, minus sign*		
(	*alphabetic* *	*	*alphabetic*		
)	*alphabetic* *	/	*alphabetic, ratio marker*		
,	*alphabetic* *	@	*alphabetic*		
0	*alphadigit*	A, a	*alphadigit*		
1	*alphadigit*	B, b	*alphadigit*		
2	*alphadigit*	C, c	*alphadigit*		
3	*alphadigit*	D, d	*alphadigit, double-float exponent marker*		
4	*alphadigit*	E, e	*alphadigit, float exponent marker*		
5	*alphadigit*	F, f	*alphadigit, single-float exponent marker*		
6	*alphadigit*	G, g	*alphadigit*		
7	*alphadigit*	H, h	*alphadigit*		
8	*alphadigit*	I, i	*alphadigit*		
9	*alphadigit*	J, j	*alphadigit*		
:	*package marker*	K, k	*alphadigit*		
;	*alphabetic* *	L, l	*alphadigit, long-float exponent marker*		
<	*alphabetic*	M, m	*alphadigit*		
=	*alphabetic*	N, n	*alphadigit*		
>	*alphabetic*	O, o	*alphadigit*		
?	*alphabetic*	P, p	*alphadigit*		
[	*alphabetic*	Q, q	*alphadigit*		
\	*alphabetic* *	R, r	*alphadigit*		
]	*alphabetic*	S, s	*alphadigit, short-float exponent marker*		
^	*alphabetic*	T, t	*alphadigit*		
_	*alphabetic*	U, u	*alphadigit*		
`	*alphabetic* *	V, v	*alphadigit*		
{	*alphabetic*	W, w	*alphadigit*		
|	*alphabetic* *	X, x	*alphadigit*		
}	*alphabetic*	Y, y	*alphadigit*		
~	*alphabetic*	Z, z	*alphadigit*		

These interpretations apply only to characters whose syntactic type is *constituent*. Entries marked with an asterisk are normally shadowed because the characters are of syntactic type *whitespace*, *macro*, *single escape*, or *multiple escape*. An *alphadigit* character is interpreted as a digit if it is a valid digit in the radix specified by `*read-base*`; otherwise it is alphabetic. Characters with an *illegal* attribute can never appear in a token except under the control of an escape character.

The following tokens are potential numbers if the value of *read-base* is 16 (an abnormal situation), but they are always treated as symbols if the value of *read-base* is 10 (the usual value):

```
bad-face      25-dec-83     a/b            fad_cafe       f^
```

It is possible for there to be an ambiguity as to whether a letter should be treated as a digit or as a number marker. In such a case, the letter is always treated as a digit rather than as a number marker.

   Note that the printed representation for a potential number may not contain any escape characters. An escape character robs the following character of all syntactic qualities, forcing it to be strictly alphabetic and therefore unsuitable for use in a potential number. For example, all of the following representations are interpreted as symbols, not numbers:

```
\256    25\64    1.0\E6    |100|    3\.14159    |3/4|    3\/4    5||
```

In each case, removing the escape character(s) would allow the token to be treated as a number.

   If a potential number can in fact be interpreted as a number according to the BNF syntax in table 22-2, then a number object of the appropriate type is constructed and returned. It should be noted that in a given implementation it may be that not all tokens conforming to the actual syntax for numbers can actually be converted into number objects. For example, specifying too large or too small an exponent for a floating-point number may make the number impossible to represent in the implementation. Similarly, a ratio with denominator zero (such as -35/000) cannot be represented in *any* implementation. In any such circumstance where a token with the syntax of a number cannot be converted to an internal number object, an error is signaled. (On the other hand, an error must not be signaled for specifying too many significant digits for a floating-point number; an appropriately truncated or rounded value should be produced.)

   There is an omission in the syntax of numbers as described in table 22-2, in that the syntax does not account for the possible use of letters as digits. The radix used for reading integers and ratios is normally decimal. However, this radix is actually determined by the value of the variable *read-base*, whose initial value is 10. *read-base* may take on any integral value between 2 and 36; let this value be n. Then a token x is interpreted as an integer or ratio in base n if it could be properly so interpreted in the syntax #nRx (see section 22.1.4). So, for example, if the value of *read-base* is 16, then the printed representation

```
(a small face in a bad place)
```

would be interpreted as if the following representation had been read with `*read-base*` set to 10:

```
(10 small 64206 in 10 2989 place)
```

because four of the seven tokens in the list can be interpreted as hexadecimal numbers. This facility is intended to be used in reading files of data that for some reason contain numbers not in decimal radix; it may also be used for reading programs written in Lisp dialects (such as MacLisp) whose default number radix is not decimal. Non-decimal constants in Common Lisp programs or portable Common Lisp data files should be written using #O, #X, #B, or #nR syntax.

When `*read-base*` has a value greater than 10, an ambiguity is introduced into the actual syntax for numbers because a letter can serve as either a digit or an exponent marker; a simple example is 1E0 when the value of `*read-base*` is 16. The ambiguity is resolved in accordance with the general principle that interpretation as a digit is preferred to interpretation as a number marker. The consequence in this case is that if a token can be interpreted as either an integer or a floating-point number, then it is taken to be an integer.

If a token consists solely of dots (with no escape characters), then an error is signaled, except in one circumstance: if the token is a single dot and occurs in a situation appropriate to "dotted list" syntax, then it is accepted as a part of such syntax. Signaling an error catches not only misplaced dots in dotted list syntax but also lists that were truncated by `*print-length*` cutoff, because such lists end with a three-dot sequence (...). Examples:

```
(a . b)          ;A dotted pair of a and b
(a.b)            ;A list of one element, the symbol named a.b
(a. b)           ;A list of two elements a. and b
(a .b)           ;A list of two elements a and .b
(a \. b)         ;A list of three elements a, ., and b
(a |.| b)        ;A list of three elements a, ., and b
(a \... b)       ;A list of three elements a, ..., and b
(a |...| b)      ;A list of three elements a, ..., and b
(a b . c)        ;A dotted list of a and b with c at the end
.iot             ;The symbol whose name is .iot
(. b)            ;Illegal; an error is signaled
(a .)            ;Illegal; an error is signaled
(a .. b)         ;Illegal; an error is signaled
(a . . b)        ;Illegal; an error is signaled
(a b c ...)      ;Illegal; an error is signaled
```

In all other cases, the token is construed to be the name of a symbol. If there are any package markers (colons) in the token, they divide the token into pieces used to control the lookup and creation of the symbol.

If there is a single package marker, and it occurs at the beginning of the token, then the token is interpreted as a keyword, that is, a symbol in the keyword package. The part of the token after the package marker must not have the syntax of a number.

If there is a single package marker not at the beginning or end of the token, then it divides the token into two parts. The first part specifies a package; the second part is the name of an external symbol available in that package. Neither of the two parts may have the syntax of a number.

If there are two adjacent package markers not at the beginning or end of the token, then they divide the token into two parts. The first part specifies a package; the second part is the name of a symbol within that package (possibly an internal symbol). Neither of the two parts may have the syntax of a number.

X3J13 voted in March 1988 ⟨16⟩ to clarify that, in the situations described in the preceding three paragraphs, the restriction on the syntax of the parts should be strengthened: none of the parts may have the syntax of even a *potential* number. Tokens such as :3600, :1/2, and editor:3.14159 were already ruled out; this clarification further declares that such tokens as :2^3, compiler:1.7J, and Christmas:12/25/83 are also in error and therefore should not be used in portable programs. Implementations may differ in their treatment of such package-marked potential numbers.

If a symbol token contains no package markers, then the entire token is the name of the symbol. The symbol is looked up in the default package, which is the value of the variable *package*.

All other patterns of package markers, including the cases where there are more than two package markers or where a package marker appears at the end of the token, at present do not mean anything in Common Lisp (see chapter 11). It is therefore currently an error to use such patterns in a Common Lisp program. The valid patterns for tokens may be summarized as follows:

nnnnn	a number
xxxxx	a symbol in the current package
:*xxxxx*	a symbol in the keyword package
ppppp:*xxxxx*	an external symbol in the *ppppp* package
ppppp::*xxxxx*	a (possibly internal) symbol in the *ppppp* package

where *nnnnn* has the syntax of a number, and *xxxxx* and *ppppp* do not have the syntax of a number.

In accordance with the X3J13 decision noted above ⟨16⟩, *xxxxx* and *ppppp* may not have the syntax of even a potential number.

---

read-base   [*Variable*]

The value of *read-base* controls the interpretation of tokens by read as being integers or ratios. Its value is the radix in which integers and ratios are to be read; the value may be any integer from 2 to 36 (inclusive) and is normally 10 (decimal radix). Its value affects only the reading of integers and ratios. In particular, floating-point numbers are always read in decimal radix. The value of *read-base* does not affect the radix for rational numbers whose radix is explicitly indicated by #O, #X, #B, or #nR syntax or by a trailing decimal point.

Care should be taken when setting *read-base* to a value larger than 10, because tokens that would normally be interpreted as symbols may be interpreted as numbers instead. For example, with *read-base* set to 16 (hexadecimal radix), variables with names such as a, b, f, bad, and face will be treated by the reader as numbers (with decimal values 10, 11, 15, 2989, and 64206, respectively). The ability to alter the input radix is provided in Common Lisp primarily for the purpose of reading data files in special formats, rather than for the purpose of altering the default radix in which to read programs. The user is strongly encouraged to use #O, #X, #B, or #nR syntax when notating non-decimal constants in programs.

Compatibility note: This variable corresponds to the variable called ibase in MacLisp and to the function called radix in Interlisp.

---

read-suppress   [*Variable*]

When the value of *read-suppress* is nil, the Lisp reader operates normally. When it is not nil, then most of the interesting operations of the reader are suppressed; input characters are parsed, but much of what is read is not interpreted.

The primary purpose of *read-suppress* is to support the operation of the read-time conditional constructs #+ and #- (see section 22.1.4). It is important for these constructs to be able to skip over the printed representation of a Lisp expression despite the possibility that the syntax of the skipped expression may not be entirely legal for the current implementation; this is because a primary application of #+ and #- is to allow the same program to be shared among several Lisp implementations despite small incompatibilities of syntax.

A non-nil value of *read-suppress* has the following specific effects on the Common Lisp reader:

- All extended tokens are completely uninterpreted. It matters not whether the token looks like a number, much less like a valid number; the pattern of package markers also does not matter. An extended token is simply discarded and treated as if it were nil; that is, reading an extended token when *read-suppress* is non-nil simply returns nil. (One consequence of this is that the error concerning improper dotted-list syntax will not be signaled.)

- Any standard # macro-character construction that requires, permits, or disallows an infix numerical argument, such as #nR, will not enforce any constraint on the presence, absence, or value of such an argument.

- The #\ construction always produces the value nil. It will not signal an error even if an unknown character name is seen.

- Each of the #B, #O, #X, and #R constructions always scans over a following token and produces the value nil. It will not signal an error even if the token does not have the syntax of a rational number.

- The #* construction always scans over a following token and produces the value nil. It will not signal an error even if the token does not consist solely of the characters 0 and 1.

- Each of the #. and #, constructions reads the following form (in suppressed mode, of course) but does not evaluate it. The form is discarded and nil is produced.

X3J13 voted in January 1989 ⟨162⟩ to remove #, from the language.

- Each of the #A, #S, and #: constructions reads the following form (in suppressed mode, of course) but does not interpret it in any way; it need not even be a list in the case of #S, or a symbol in the case of #:. The form is discarded and nil is produced.

- The #= construction is totally ignored. It does not read a following form. It produces no object, but is treated as whitespace.

- The ## construction always produces nil.

Note that, no matter what the value of *read-suppress*, parentheses still continue to delimit (and construct) lists; the #(construction continues to delimit vectors; and comments, strings, and the quote and backquote constructions continue to be interpreted properly. Furthermore, such situations as ´), #<, #), and #⟨space⟩ continue to signal errors.

In some cases, it may be appropriate for a user-written macro-character definition to check the value of *read-suppress* and to avoid certain computations or side effects if its value is not nil.

---

read-eval   [*Variable*]

X3J13 voted in June 1989 ⟨40⟩ to add a new reader control variable, *read-eval*, whose default value is t. If *read-eval* is false, the #. reader macro signals an error.

Printing is also affected. If *read-eval* is false and *print-readably* is true, any print-object method that would otherwise output a #. reader macro must either output something different or signal an error of type print-not-readable.

Binding *read-eval* to nil is useful when reading data that came from an untrusted source, such as a network or a user-supplied data file; it prevents the #. reader macro from being exploited as a "Trojan horse" to cause arbitrary forms to be evaluated.

22.1.3. Macro Characters

If the reader encounters a macro character, then the function associated with that macro character is invoked and may produce an object to be returned. This function may read following characters in the stream in whatever syntax it likes (it may even call read recursively) and return the object represented by that syntax. Macro characters may or may not be recognized, of course, when read as part of other special syntaxes (such as for strings).

The reader is therefore organized into two parts: the basic dispatch loop, which also distinguishes symbols and numbers, and the collection of macro characters. Any character can be reprogrammed as a macro character; this is a means by which the reader can be extended. The macro characters normally defined are as follows:

(

The left-parenthesis character initiates reading of a pair or list. The function read is called recursively to read successive objects until a right parenthesis is found to be next in the input stream. A list of the objects read is returned. Thus the input sequence

(a b c)

is read as a list of three objects (the symbols a, b, and c). The right parenthesis need not immediately follow the printed representation of the last object; whitespace characters and comments may precede it. This can be useful for putting one object on each line and making it easy to add new objects:

```
(defun traffic-light (color)
  (case color
    (green)
    (red (stop))
    (amber (accelerate))      ;Insert more colors after this line
    ))
```

It may be that *no* objects precede the right parenthesis, as in ( ) or ( ); this reads as a list of zero objects (the empty list).

If a token that is just a dot, not preceded by an escape character, is read after some object, then exactly one more object must follow the dot, possibly followed by whitespace, followed by the right parenthesis:

```
(a b c . d)
```

This means that the *cdr* of the last pair in the list is not nil, but rather the object whose representation followed the dot. The above example might have been the result of evaluating

```
(cons ´a (cons ´b (cons ´c ´d))) ⇒ (a b c . d)
```

Similarly, we have

```
(cons ´znets ´wolq-zorbitan) ⇒ (znets . wolq-zorbitan)
```

It is permissible for the object following the dot to be a list:

```
(a b c d . (e f . (g)))
```

is the same as

```
(a b c d e f g)
```

but a list following a dot is a non-standard form that print will never produce.

```
)
```

The right-parenthesis character is part of various constructs (such as the syntax for lists) using the left-parenthesis character and is invalid except when used in such a construct.

The single-quote (accent acute) character provides an abbreviation to make it easier to put constants in programs. The form ´*foo* reads the same as (quote *foo*): a list of the symbol quote and *foo*.

;

Semicolon is used to write comments.   The semicolon and all characters up to and including the next newline are ignored. Thus a comment can be put at the end of any line without affecting the reader. (A comment will terminate a token, but a newline would terminate the token anyway.)

There is no functional difference between using one semicolon and using more than one, but the conventions shown here are in common use.

```
;;;; COMMENT-EXAMPLE function.
;;; This function is useless except to demonstrate comments.
;;; (Actually, this example is much too cluttered with them.)

(defun comment-example (x y)       ;X is anything; Y is an a-list.
  (cond ((listp x) x)              ;If X is a list, use that.
        ;; X is now not a list. There are two other cases.
        ((symbolp x)
         ;; Look up a symbol in the a-list.
         (cdr (assoc x y)))        ;Remember, (cdr nil) is nil.
        ;; Do this when all else fails:
        (t (cons x                 ;Add x to a default list.
                 ´((lisp t)        ;LISP is okay.
                   (fortran nil)   ;FORTRAN is not.
                   (pl/i -500)     ;Note that you can put comments in
                   (ada .001)      ; "data" as well as in "programs".
                   ;; COBOL??
                   (teco -1.0e9))))))))
```

In this example, comments may begin with one to four semicolons.

• Single-semicolon comments are all aligned to the same column at the right; usually each comment concerns only the code it is next to. Occasionally a comment is long enough to occupy two or three lines; in this case, it is conventional to indent the continued lines of the comment one space (after the semicolon).

• Double-semicolon comments are aligned to the level of indentation of the code. A space conventionally follows the two semicolons. Such comments usually describe the state of the program at that point or the code section that follows the comment.

- Triple-semicolon comments are aligned to the left margin. They usually document whole programs or large code blocks.

- Quadruple-semicolon comments usually indicate titles of whole programs or large code blocks.

Compatibility note: These conventions arose among users of MacLisp and have been found to be very useful. The conventions are conveniently exploited by certain software tools, such as the EMACS editor and the ATSIGN listing program developed at MIT.

The ATSIGN listing program, alas, is no longer in use, but EMACS is widely available, especially the GNU EMACS implementation, which is available from the Free Software Foundation, 675 Massachusetts Avenue, Cambridge, Massachusetts 02139. Remember, GNU's Not UNIX.

"

The double quote character begins the printed representation of a string. Successive characters are read from the input stream and accumulated until another double quote is encountered. An exception to this occurs if a *single escape* character is seen; the escape character is discarded, the next character is accumulated, and accumulation continues. When a matching double quote is seen, all the accumulated characters up to but not including the matching double quote are made into a simple string and returned.

The backquote (accent grave) character makes it easier to write programs to construct complex data structures by using a template.

Notice of correction. In the first edition, the backquote character ⟨`⟩ appearing at the left margin above was inadvertently omitted.

As an example, writing

```
`(cond ((numberp ,x) ,@y) (t (print ,x) ,@y))
```

is roughly equivalent to writing

```
(list 'cond
      (cons (list 'numberp x) y)
      (list* 't (list 'print x) y))
```

The general idea is that the backquote is followed by a template, a picture of a data structure to be built. This template is copied, except that within the template commas can appear. Where a comma occurs, the form following the comma is to be evaluated to produce an object to be inserted at that point. Assume b has the value 3; then evaluating the form denoted by `(a b ,b ,(+ b 1) b) produces the result (a b 3 4 b).

If a comma is immediately followed by an at-sign (@), then the form following the at-sign is evaluated to produce a *list* of objects. These objects are then "spliced" into place in the template. For example, if x has the value (a b c), then

```
`(x ,x ,@x foo ,(cadr x) bar ,(cdr x) baz ,@(cdr x))
   ⇒ (x (a b c) a b c foo b bar (b c) baz b c)
```

The backquote syntax can be summarized formally as follows. For each of several situations in which backquote can be used, a possible interpretation of that situation as an equivalent form is given. Note that the form is equivalent only in the sense that when it is evaluated it will calculate the correct result. An implementation is quite free to interpret backquote in any way such that a backquoted form, when evaluated, will produce a result equal to that produced by the interpretation shown here.

- `*basic* is the same as ´*basic*, that is, (quote *basic*), for any form *basic* that is not a list or a general vector.

- `,*form* is the same as *form*, for any *form*, provided that the representation of *form* does not begin with "@" or ".". (A similar caveat holds for all occurrences of a form after a comma.)

- `,@*form* is an error.

- `(*x1* *x2* *x3* ... *xn* . *atom*) may be interpreted to mean

  (append [*x1*] [*x2*] [*x3*] ... [*xn*] (quote *atom*))

  where the brackets are used to indicate a transformation of an *xj* as follows:

  – [*form*] is interpreted as (list `*form*), which contains a backquoted form that must then be further interpreted.

  – [,*form*] is interpreted as (list *form*).

  – [,@*form*] is interpreted simply as *form*.

- `(*x1* *x2* *x3* ... *xn*) may be interpreted to mean the same as the backquoted form `(*x1* *x2* *x3* ... *xn* . nil), thereby reducing it to the previous case.

• `(*x1 x2 x3* ... *xn* . ,*form*) may be interpreted to mean

(append [*x1*] [*x2*] [*x3*] ... [*xn*] *form*)

where the brackets indicate a transformation of an *xj* as described above.

• `(*x1 x2 x3* ... *xn* . ,*@form*) is an error.

• `#(*x1 x2 x3* ... *xn*) may be interpreted to mean

(apply #´vector `(*x1 x2 x3* ... *xn*))

No other uses of comma are permitted; in particular, it may not appear within the #A or #S syntax.

Anywhere ",@" may be used, the syntax ",." may be used instead to indicate that it is permissible to destroy the list produced by the form following the ",."; this may permit more efficient code, using nconc instead of append, for example.

If the backquote syntax is nested, the innermost backquoted form should be expanded first. This means that if several commas occur in a row, the leftmost one belongs to the innermost backquote.

Once again, it is emphasized that an implementation is free to interpret a back-quoted form as any form that, when evaluated, will produce a result that is equal to the result implied by the above definition. In particular, no guarantees are made as to whether the constructed copy of the template will or will not share list structure with the template itself. As an example, the above definition implies that

`((,a b) ,c ,@d)

will be interpreted as if it were

(append (list (append (list a) (list ´b) ´nil)) (list c) d ´nil)

but it could also be legitimately interpreted to mean any of the following.

```
(append (list (append (list a) (list ´b))) (list c) d)
(append (list (append (list a) ´(b))) (list c) d)
(append (list (cons a ´(b))) (list c) d)
(list* (cons a ´(b)) c d)
(list* (cons a (list ´b)) c d)
(list* (cons a ´(b)) c (copy-list d))
```

(There is no good reason why copy-list should be performed, but it is not prohibited.)

Some users complain that backquote syntax is difficult to read, especially when it is nested. I agree that it can get complicated, but in some situations (such as writing macros that expand into definitions for other macros) such complexity is to be expected, and the alternative is much worse.

After I gained some experience in writing nested backquote forms, I found that I was not stopping to analyze the various patterns of nested backquotes and interleaved commas and quotes; instead, I was recognizing standard idioms wholesale, in the same manner that I recognize cadar as the primitive for "extract the lambda-list from the form ((lambda ...) ...))" without stopping to analyze it into "car of cdr of car." For example, ,x within a doubly-nested backquote form means "the value of x available during the second evaluation will appear here once the form has been twice evaluated," whereas ,´,x means "the value of x available during the first evaluation will appear here once the form has been twice evaluated" and ,,x means "the value of the value of x will appear here."

See appendix C for a systematic set of examples of the use of nested backquotes.

,

The comma character is part of the backquote syntax and is invalid if used other than inside the body of a backquote construction as described above.

#

This is a *dispatching* macro character. It reads an optional digit string and then one more character, and uses that character to select a function to run as a macro-character function.

The # character also happens to be a non-terminating macro character. This is completely independent of the fact that it is a dispatching macro character; it is a coincidence that the only standard dispatching macro character in Common Lisp is also the only standard non-terminating macro character.

See the next section for predefined # macro-character constructions.

22.1.4. Standard Dispatching Macro Character Syntax

The standard syntax includes forms introduced by the # character. These take the general form of a #, a second character that identifies the syntax, and following arguments in some form. If the second character is a letter, then case is not important; #O and #o are considered to be equivalent, for example.

Certain # forms allow an unsigned decimal number to appear between the # and the second character; some other forms even require it. Those forms that do not explicitly permit such a number to appear forbid it.

Table 22-4: Standard # Macro Character Syntax

#!	*undefined* *	#⟨backspace⟩	*signals error*
#"	*undefined*	#⟨tab⟩	*signals error*
##	*reference to* #= *label*	#⟨newline⟩	*signals error*
#$	*undefined*	#⟨linefeed⟩	*signals error*
#%	*undefined*	#⟨page⟩	*signals error*
#&	*undefined*	#⟨return⟩	*signals error*
#´	function *abbreviation*	#⟨space⟩	*signals error*
#(	*simple vector*	#+	*read-time conditional*
#)	*signals error*	#-	*read-time conditional*
#*	*bit-vector*	#.	*read-time evaluation*
#,	*load-time evaluation*	#/	*undefined*
#0	*used for infix arguments*	#A, #a	*array*
#1	*used for infix arguments*	#B, #b	*binary rational*
#2	*used for infix arguments*	#C, #c	*complex number*
#3	*used for infix arguments*	#D, #d	*undefined*
#4	*used for infix arguments*	#E, #e	*undefined*
#5	*used for infix arguments*	#F, #f	*undefined*
#6	*used for infix arguments*	#G, #g	*undefined*
#7	*used for infix arguments*	#H, #h	*undefined*
#8	*used for infix arguments*	#I, #i	*undefined*
#9	*used for infix arguments*	#J, #j	*undefined*
#:	*uninterned symbol*	#K, #k	*undefined*
#;	*undefined*	#L, #l	*undefined*
#<	*signals error*	#M, #m	*undefined*
#=	*label following object*	#N, #n	*undefined*
#>	*undefined*	#O, #o	*octal rational*
#?	*undefined* *	#P, #p	*pathname*
#@	*undefined*	#Q, #q	*undefined*
#[	*undefined* *	#R, #r	*radix-n rational*
#\	*character object*	#S, #s	*structure*
#]	*undefined* *	#T, #t	*undefined*
#^	*undefined*	#U, #u	*undefined*
#_	*undefined*	#V, #v	*undefined*
#`	*undefined*	#W, #w	*undefined*
#{	*undefined* *	#X, #x	*hexadecimal rational*
#|	*balanced comment*	#Y, #y	*undefined*
#}	*undefined* *	#Z, #z	*undefined*
#~	*undefined*	#⟨rubout⟩	*undefined*

The combinations marked by an asterisk are explicitly reserved to the user and will never be defined by Common Lisp.

X3J13 voted in June 1989 ⟨131⟩ to specify #P and #p (*undefined* in the first edition).

The currently defined # constructs are described below and summarized in table 22-4; more are likely to be added in the future. However, the constructs #!, #?, #[, #], #{, and #} are explicitly reserved for the user and will never be defined by the Common Lisp standard.

#\

#\x reads in as a character object that represents the character x. Also, #\name reads in as the character object whose name is name. Note that the backslash \ allows this construct to be parsed easily by EMACS-like editors.

In the single-character case, the character x must be followed by a non-constituent character, lest a name appear to follow the #\. A good model of what happens is that after #\ is read, the reader backs up over the \ and then reads an extended token, treating the initial \ as an escape character (whether it really is or not in the current readtable).

Uppercase and lowercase letters are distinguished after #\; #\A and #\a denote different character objects. Any character works after #\, even those that are normally special to read, such as parentheses. Non-printing characters may be used after #\, although for them names are generally preferred.

#\name reads in as a character object whose name is name (actually, whose name is (string-upcase name); therefore the syntax is case-insensitive). The name should have the syntax of a symbol. The following names are standard across all implementations:

newline   The character that represents the division between lines
space   The space or blank character

The following names are semi-standard; if an implementation supports them, they should be used for the described characters and no others.

rubout   The rubout or delete character.
page   The form-feed or page-separator character
tab   The tabulate character
backspace The backspace character
return   The carriage return character
linefeed   The line-feed character

In some implementations, one or more of these characters might be a synonym for a standard character; the #\Linefeed character might be the same as #\Newline, for example.

When the Lisp printer types out the name of a special character, it uses the same table as the #\ reader; therefore any character name you see typed out is acceptable as input (in that implementation). Standard names are always preferred over non-standard names for printing.

The following convention is used in implementations that support non-zero bits attributes for character objects. If a name after #\ is longer than one character and has a hyphen in it, then it may be split into the two parts preceding and following the first hyphen; the first part (actually, `string-upcase` of the first part) may then be interpreted as the name or initial of a bit, and the second part as the name of the character (which may in turn contain a hyphen and be subject to further splitting). For example:

```
#\Control-Space          #\Control-Meta-Tab
#\C-M-Return             #\H-S-M-C-Rubout
```

If the character name consists of a single character, then that character is used. Another \ may be necessary to quote the character.

```
#\Control-%              #\Control-Meta-\"
#\Control-\a             #\Meta->
```

If an unsigned decimal integer appears between the # and \, it is interpreted as a font number, to become the font attribute of the character object (see `char-font`).

X3J13 voted in March 1989 ⟨11⟩ to replace the notion of bits and font attributes with that of implementation-defined attributes. Presumably this eliminates the portable use of this syntax for font information, although the vote did not address this question directly.

#'

#'*foo* is an abbreviation for (`function` *foo*). *foo* may be the printed representation of any Lisp object. This abbreviation may be remembered by analogy with the ´ macro character, since the `function` and `quote` special forms are similar in form.

#(

A series of representations of objects enclosed by #(and) is read as a simple vector of those objects. This is analogous to the notation for lists.

If an unsigned decimal integer appears between the # and (, it specifies explicitly the length of the vector. In that case, it is an error if too many objects are specified before the closing), and if too few are specified, the last object (it is an error if there are none in this case) is used to fill all remaining elements of the vector. For example,

#(a b c c c c)   #6(a b c c c c)   #6(a b c)   #6(a b c c)

all mean the same thing: a vector of length 6 with elements a, b, and four instances of c. The notation #( ) denotes an empty vector, as does #0( ) (which is legitimate because it is not the case that too few elements are specified).

#*

A series of binary digits (0 and 1) preceded by #* is read as a simple bit-vector containing those bits, the leftmost bit in the series being bit 0 of the bit-vector.

If an unsigned decimal integer appears between the # and *, it specifies explicitly the length of the vector. In that case, it is an error if too many bits are specified, and if too few are specified the last one (it is an error if there are none in this case) is used to fill all remaining elements of the bit-vector. For example,

#*101111   #6*101111   #6*101   #6*1011

all mean the same thing: a vector of length 6 with elements 1, 0, 1, 1, 1, and 1. The notation #* denotes an empty bit-vector, as does #0* (which is legitimate because it is not the case that too few elements are specified).
| Compare this to #B, used for expressing integers in binary notation.

#:

#:*foo* requires *foo* to have the syntax of an unqualified symbol name (no embedded colons). It denotes an *uninterned* symbol whose name is *foo*. Every time this syntax is encountered, a different uninterned symbol is created. If it is necessary to refer to the same uninterned symbol more than once in the same expression, the #= syntax may be useful.

#.

#.*foo* is read as the object resulting from the evaluation of the Lisp object represented by *foo*, which may be the printed representation of any Lisp object. The evaluation is done during the read process, when the #. construct is encountered.
| X3J13 voted in June 1989 ⟨40⟩ to add a new reader control variable, *read-eval*. If it is true, the #. reader macro behaves as described above; if it is false, the #. reader macro signals an error.

The #. syntax therefore performs a read-time evaluation of *foo*. By contrast, #, (see below) performs a load-time evaluation.

Both #. and #, allow you to include, in an expression being read, an object that does not have a convenient printed representation; instead of writing a representation for the object, you write an expression that will *compute* the object.

#,

#.*foo* is read as the object resulting from the evaluation of the Lisp object represented by *foo*, which may be the printed representation of any Lisp object. The evaluation is done during the read process, unless the compiler is doing the reading, in which case it is arranged that *foo* will be evaluated when the file of compiled code is loaded. The #, syntax therefore performs a load-time evaluation of *foo*. By contrast, #. (see above) performs a read-time evaluation. In a sense, #, is like specifying (eval load) to eval-when, whereas #. is more like specifying (eval compile). It makes no difference when loading interpreted code; when code is to be compiled, however, #. specifies compile-time evaluation and #, specifies load-time evaluation.

X3J13 voted in January 1989 ⟨162⟩ to remove #, from the language. X3J13 noted that the first edition failed to make it clear that #, can be meaningful only within quoted forms. All sorts of anomalies can arise, including inconsistencies between the interpreter and compiler, if #, is not properly restricted. See load-time-eval.

#B

#b*rational* reads *rational* in binary (radix 2). For example, #B1101 ≡ 13, and #b101/11 ≡ 5/3.

Compare this to #*, used for expressing bit-vectors in binary notation.

#O

#o*rational* reads *rational* in octal (radix 8). For example, #o37/15 ≡ 31/13, and #o777 ≡ 511.

#X

#x*rational* reads *rational* in hexadecimal (radix 16). The digits above 9 are the letters A through F (the lowercase letters a through f are also acceptable). For example, #xF00 ≡ 3840.

#*n*R

#*radixr rational* reads *rational* in radix *radix*. *radix* must consist of only digits, and it is read in decimal; its value must be between 2 and 36 (inclusive).

For example, #3r102 is another way of writing 11, and #11R32 is another way of writing 35. For radices larger than 10, letters of the alphabet are used in order for the digits after 9.

#*n*A

The syntax #*n*A*object* constructs an *n*-dimensional array, using *object* as the value of the :initial-contents argument to make-array.

The value of *n* makes a difference: #2A((0 1 5) (foo 2 (hot dog))), for example, represents a 2-by-3 matrix:

```
0        1        5
foo      2        (hot dog)
```

In contrast, #1A((0 1 5) (foo 2 (hot dog))) represents a length-2 array whose elements are lists:

```
(0 1 5)     (foo 2 (hot dog))
```

Furthermore, #0A((0 1 5) (foo 2 (hot dog))) represents a zero-dimensional array whose sole element is a list:

```
((0 1 5) (foo 2 (hot dog)))
```

Similarly, #0Afoo (or, more readably, #0A foo) represents a zero-dimensional array whose sole element is the symbol foo. The expression #1Afoo would not be legal because foo is not a sequence.

#S

The syntax #s(*name slot1 value1 slot2 value2* ...) denotes a structure. This is legal only if *name* is the name of a structure already defined by defstruct and if the structure has a standard constructor macro, which it normally will. Let *cm* stand for the name of this constructor macro; then this syntax is equivalent to

#.(*cm keyword1* ´*value1 keyword2* ´*value2* ...)

where each *keywordj* is the result of computing

(intern (string *slotj*) ´keyword)

(This computation is made so that one need not write a colon in front of every slot name.) The net effect is that the constructor macro is called with the specified slots having the specified values (note that one does not write quote marks in the #S syntax). Whatever object the constructor macro returns is returned by the #S syntax.

#P

X3J13 voted in June 1989 ⟨131⟩ to define the reader syntax #p"..." to be equivalent to #.(parse-namestring "..."). Presumably this was meant to be taken descriptively and not literally. I would think, for example, that the committee did not wish to quibble over the package in which the name parse-namestring was to be read. Similarly, I would presume that the #p syntax operates normally rather than signaling an error when *read-eval* is false. I interpret the intent of the vote to be that #p reads a following form, which should be a string, that is then converted to a pathname as if by application of the standard function parse-namestring.

#*n*=

The syntax #*n*=*object* reads as whatever Lisp object has *object* as its printed representation. However, that object is labelled by *n*, a required unsigned decimal integer, for possible reference by the syntax #*n*# (below). The scope of the label is the expression being read by the outermost call to read. Within this expression the same label may not appear twice.

#*n*#

The syntax #*n*#, where *n* is a required unsigned decimal integer, serves as a reference to some object labelled by #*n*=; that is, #*n*# represents a pointer to the same identical (eq) object labelled by #*n*=. This permits notation of structures with shared or circular substructure. For example, a structure created in the variable y by this code:

```
(setq x (list 'p 'q))
(setq y (list (list 'a 'b) x 'foo x))
(rplacd (last y) (cdr y))
```

could be represented in this way:

```
((a b) . #1=(#2=(p q) foo #2# . #1#))
```

Without this notation, but with *print-length* set to 10, the structure would print in this way:

```
((a b) (p q) foo (p q) (p q) foo (p q) (p q) foo (p q) ...)
```

A reference #*n*# may occur only after a label #*n*=; forward references are not permitted. In addition, the reference may not appear as the labelled object itself (that is, one may not write #*n*= #*n*#), because the object labelled by #*n*= is not well defined in this case.

#+

The #+ syntax provides a read-time conditionalization facility; the syntax is

#+*feature form*

If *feature* is "true," then this syntax represents a Lisp object whose printed representation is *form*. If *feature* is "false," then this syntax is effectively whitespace; it is as if it did not appear.

The *feature* should be the printed representation of a symbol or list. If *feature* is a symbol, then it is true if and only if it is a member of the list that is the value of the global variable *features*.

Compatibility note: MacLisp uses the status special form for this purpose, and Lisp Machine Lisp duplicates status essentially only for the sake of (status features). The use of a variable allows one to bind the features list, when compiling, for example.

Otherwise, *feature* should be a Boolean expression composed of and, or, and not operators on (recursive) *feature* expressions.

For example, suppose that in implementation A the features spice and perq are true, and in implementation B the feature lispm is true. Then the expressions on the left below are read the same as those on the right in implementation A:

```
(cons #+spice "Spice" #+lispm "Lispm" x)      (cons "Spice" x)
(setq a '(1 2 #+perq 43 #+(not perq) 27))     (setq a '(1 2 43))
(let ((a 3) #+(or spice lispm) (b 3))         (let ((a 3) (b 3))
  (foo a))                                      (foo a))
(cons a #+perq #-perq b c)                    (cons a c)
```

In implementation B, however, they are read in this way:

```
(cons #+spice "Spice" #+lispm "Lispm" x)      (cons "Lispm" x)
(setq a '(1 2 #+perq 43 #+(not perq) 27))     (setq a '(1 2 27))
(let ((a 3) #+(or spice lispm) (b 3))         (let ((a 3) (b 3))
  (foo a))                                      (foo a))
(cons a #+perq #-perq b c)                    (cons a c)
```

The #+ construction must be used judiciously if unreadable code is not to result. The user should make a careful choice between read-time conditionalization and run-time conditionalization.

The #+ syntax operates by first reading the *feature* specification and then skipping over the *form* if the *feature* is "false." This skipping of a form is a bit tricky because of the possibility of user-defined macro characters and side effects caused by the #. and #, constructions. It is accomplished by binding the variable *read-suppress* to a non-nil value and then calling the read function. See the description of *read-suppress* for the details of this operation.

X3J13 voted in January 1989 ⟨162⟩ to remove #, from the language.

X3J13 voted in March 1988 ⟨163⟩ to specify that the keyword package is the default package during the reading of a feature specification. Thus #+spice means the same thing as #+:spice, and #+(or spice lispm) means the same thing as #+(or :spice :lispm). Symbols in other packages may be used as feature names, but one must use an explicit package prefix to cite one after #+.

#-

#-*feature form* is equivalent to #+(not *feature*) *form*.

#|

#|...|# is treated as a comment by the reader, just as everything from a semicolon to the next newline is treated as a comment. Anything may appear in the comment, except that it must be balanced with respect to other occurrences of #| and |#. Except for this nesting rule, the comment may contain any characters whatsoever.

The main purpose of this construct is to allow "commenting out" of blocks of code or data. The balancing rule allows such blocks to contain pieces already so commented out. In this respect the #|...|# syntax of Common Lisp differs from the /*...*/ comment syntax used by PL/I and C.

#<

This is not legal reader syntax. It is conventionally used in the printed representation of objects that cannot be read back in. Attempting to read a #< will cause an error. (More precisely, it *is* legal syntax, but the macro-character function for #< signals an error.)

The usual convention for printing unreadable data objects is to print some identifying information (the internal machine address of the object, if nothing else) preceded by #< and followed by >.

X3J13 voted in June 1989 ⟨40⟩ to add print-unreadable-object, a macro that prints an object using #<...> syntax and also takes care of checking the variable *print-readably*.

#⟨space⟩, #⟨tab⟩, #⟨newline⟩, #⟨page⟩, #⟨return⟩

A # followed by a whitespace character is not legal reader syntax. This prevents abbreviated forms produced via `*print-level*` cutoff from reading in again, as a safeguard against losing information. (More precisely, this *is* legal syntax, but the macro-character function for it signals an error.)

#)

This is not legal reader syntax. This prevents abbreviated forms produced via `*print-level*` cutoff from reading in again, as a safeguard against losing information. (More precisely, this *is* legal syntax, but the macro-character function for it signals an error.)

22.1.5. The Readtable

Previous sections describe the standard syntax accepted by the `read` function. This section discusses the advanced topic of altering the standard syntax either to provide extended syntax for Lisp objects or to aid the writing of other parsers.

There is a data structure called the *readtable* that is used to control the reader. It contains information about the syntax of each character equivalent to that in table 22-1. It is set up exactly as in table 22-1 to give the standard Common Lisp meanings to all the characters, but the user can change the meanings of characters to alter and customize the syntax of characters. It is also possible to have several readtables describing different syntaxes and to switch from one to another by binding the variable `*readtable*`.

Even if an implementation supports characters with non-zero bits and font attributes, it need not (but may) allow for such characters to have syntax descriptions in the readtable. However, every character of type `string-char` must be represented in the readtable.

X3J13 voted in March 1989 ⟨11⟩ to remove the type `string-char` and to replace the bits and font attributes with the notion of implementation-defined attributes. If any implementation-defined attributes are supported, an implementation may (but need not) allow for such characters to have syntax descriptions in the readtable. Characters that do not have non-standard values for any implementation-defined attribute must be represented in the readtable.

`*readtable*`   [*Variable*]

The value of `*readtable*` is the current readtable. The initial value of this is a readtable set up for standard Common Lisp syntax. You can bind this variable to temporarily change the readtable being used.

To program the reader for a different syntax, a set of functions are provided for manipulating readtables. Normally, you should begin with a copy of the standard Common Lisp readtable and then customize the individual characters within that copy.

copy-readtable &optional *from-readtable to-readtable*   [*Function*]

A copy is made of *from-readtable*, which defaults to the current readtable (the value of the global variable *readtable*). If *from-readtable* is nil, then a copy of a standard Common Lisp readtable is made. For example,

(setq *readtable* (copy-readtable nil))

will restore the input syntax to standard Common Lisp syntax, even if the original readtable has been clobbered (assuming it is not so badly clobbered that you cannot type in the above expression!). On the other hand,

(setq *readtable* (copy-readtable))

will merely replace the current readtable with a copy of itself.

   If *to-readtable* is unsupplied or nil, a fresh copy is made. Otherwise, *to-readtable* must be a readtable, which is destructively copied into.

readtablep *object*   [*Function*]

readtablep is true if its argument is a readtable, and otherwise is false.

(readtablep x) ≡ (typep x 'readtable)

set-syntax-from-char *to-char from-char* &optional   [*Function*]
   to-readtable from-readtable

This makes the syntax of *to-char* in *to-readtable* be the same as the syntax of *from-char* in *from-readtable*. The *to-readtable* defaults to the current readtable (the value of the global variable *readtable*), and *from-readtable* defaults to nil, meaning to use the syntaxes from the standard Lisp readtable.

   X3J13 voted in January 1989 ⟨7⟩ to clarify that the *to-char* and *from-char* must each be a character.

   Only attributes as shown in table 22-1 are copied; moreover, if a *macro character* is copied, the macro definition function is copied also. However, attributes as shown in table 22-3 are not copied; they are "hard-wired" into the extended-token parser. For example, if the definition of S is copied to *, then * will become a *constituent* that is *alphabetic* but cannot be used as an exponent indicator for short-format floating-point number syntax.

It works to copy a macro definition from a character such as " to another character; the standard definition for " looks for another character that is the same as the character that invoked it. It doesn't work to copy the definition of (to {, for example; it can be done, but it lets one write lists in the form {a b c), not {a b c}, because the definition always looks for a closing parenthesis, not a closing brace. See the function read-delimited-list, which is useful in this connection.

X3J13 voted in January 1989 ⟨156⟩ to specify that the set-syntax-from-char function returns t.

set-macro-character *char function* &optional	[*Function*]
non-terminating-p readtable	
get-macro-character *char* &optional *readtable*	[*Function*]

set-macro-character causes *char* to be a macro character that when seen by read causes *function* to be called. If *non-terminating-p* is not nil (it defaults to nil), then it will be a non-terminating macro character: it may be embedded within extended tokens. set-macro-character returns t.

get-macro-character returns the function associated with *char* and, as a second value, returns the *non-terminating-p* flag; it returns nil if *char* does not have macro-character syntax. In each case, *readtable* defaults to the current readtable.

X3J13 voted in January 1989 ⟨95⟩ to specify that if nil is explicitly passed as the second argument to get-macro-character, then the standard readtable is used. This is consistent with the behavior of copy-readtable.

The *function* is called with two arguments, *stream* and *char*. The *stream* is the input stream, and *char* is the macro character itself. In the simplest case, *function* may return a Lisp object. This object is taken to be that whose printed representation was the macro character and any following characters read by the *function*. As an example, a plausible definition of the standard single quote character is:

```
(defun single-quote-reader (stream char)
  (declare (ignore char))
  (list 'quote (read stream t nil t)))

(set-macro-character #\' #'single-quote-reader)
```

(Note that t is specified for the *recursive-p* argument to read; see section 22.2.1.) The function reads an object following the single-quote and returns a list of the symbol quote and that object. The *char* argument is ignored.

The function may choose instead to return *zero* values (for example, by using (values) as the return expression). In this case, the macro character and whatever it may have read contribute nothing to the object being read. As an example, here is a plausible definition for the standard semicolon (comment) character:

```
(defun semicolon-reader (stream char)
  (declare (ignore char))
  ;; First swallow the rest of the current input line.
  ;; End-of-file is acceptable for terminating the comment.
  (do () ((char= (read-char stream nil #\Newline t) #\Newline)))
  ;; Return zero values.
  (values))
```

```
(set-macro-character #\; #'semicolon-reader)
```

(Note that t is specified for the *recursive-p* argument to read-char; see section 22.2.1.)

The *function* should not have any side effects other than on the *stream*. Because of backtracking and restarting of the read operation, front ends (such as editors and rubout handlers) to the reader may cause *function* to be called repeatedly during the reading of a single expression in which the macro character only appears once.

Compatibility note: The ability to return either zero or one value is the closest Common Lisp macro characters come to the splicing macro characters of MacLisp or the splice macro characters of Interlisp. The Common Lisp definition does not allow the splicing of arbitrarily many values, but it does allow a macro-character function to decide after it is invoked whether or not to yield a value, an option not possible in MacLisp or Interlisp.

MacLisp has nothing equivalent to non-terminating macro characters. The Interlisp equivalents of terminating and non-terminating macro characters are macro characters with the ALWAYS or FIRST option, respectively. Common Lisp has nothing equivalent to the Interlisp ALONE macro-character option.

Here is an example of a more elaborate set of read-macro characters that I used in the implementation of the original simulator for Connection Machine Lisp [44, 57], a parallel dialect of Common Lisp. This simulator was used to gain experience with the language before freezing its design for full-scale implementation on a Connection Machine computer system. This example illustrates the typical manner in which a language designer can embed a new language within the syntactic and semantic framework of Lisp, saving the effort of designing an implementation from scratch.

Connection Machine Lisp introduces a new data type called a *xapping*, which is simply an unordered set of ordered pairs of Lisp objects. The first element of each pair is called the *index* and the second element the *value*. We say that the xapping maps each index to its corresponding value. No two pairs of the same xapping may have the same (that is, eql) index. Xappings may be finite or infinite sets of pairs; only certain kinds of infinite xappings are required, and special representations are used for them.

A finite xapping is notated by writing the pairs between braces, separated by whitespace. A pair is notated by writing the index and the value, separated by a right arrow (or an exclamation point if the host Common Lisp has no right-arrow character).

Remark: The original language design used the right arrow; the exclamation point was chosen to replace it on ASCII-only terminals because it is one of the six characters [ ] { } ! ? reserved by Common Lisp to the user.

While preparing the TEX manuscript for this book I made a mistake in font selection and discovered that by an absolutely incredible coincidence the right arrow has the same numerical code (octal 41) within TEX fonts as the ASCII exclamation point. The result was that although the manuscript called for right arrows, exclamation points came out in the printed copy. Imagine my astonishment!

Here is an example of a xapping that maps three symbols to strings:

```
{moe→"Oh, a wise guy, eh?" larry→"Hey, what's the idea?"
 curly→"Nyuk, nyuk, nyuk!"}
```

For convenience there are certain abbreviated notations. If the index and value for a pair are the same object *x*, then instead of having to write "$x{\to}x$" (or, worse yet, "#43=x→#43#") we may write simply *x* for the pair. If all pairs of a xapping are of this form, we call the xapping a *xet*. For example, the notation

```
{baseball chess cricket curling bocce 43-man-squamish}
```

is entirely equivalent in meaning to

```
{baseball→baseball curling→curling cricket→cricket
 chess→chess bocce→bocce 43-man-squamish→43-man-squamish}
```

namely a xet of symbols naming six sports.

Another useful abbreviation covers the situation where the *n* pairs of a finite xapping are integers, collectively covering a range from zero to $n - 1$. This kind of xapping is called a *xector* and may be notated by writing the values between brackets in ascending order of their indices. Thus

```
[tinker evers chance]
```

is merely an abbreviation for

```
{tinker→0 evers→1 chance→2}
```

There are two kinds of infinite xapping: constant and universal. A constant
xapping $\{→z\}$ maps every object to the same value z. The universal xapping $\{→\}$
maps every object to itself and is therefore the xet of all Lisp objects, sometimes
called simply the universe. Both kinds of infinite xet may be modified by explicitly
writing exceptions. One kind of exception is simply a pair, which specifies the value
for a particular index; the other kind of exception is simply $k→$ indicating that the
xapping does *not* have a pair with index k after all. Thus the notation

```
{sky→blue grass→green idea→ glass→ →red}
```

indicates a xapping that maps sky to blue, grass to green, and every other
object except idea and glass to red. Note well that the presence or absence of
whitespace on either side of an arrow is crucial to the correct interpretation of the
notation.

Here is the representation of a xapping as a structure:

```
(defstruct
  (xapping (:print-function print-xapping)
           (:constructor xap
              (domain range &optional
               (default ':unknown defaultp)
               (infinite (and defaultp :constant))
               (exceptions '()))))
  domain
  range
  default
  (infinite nil :type (member nil :constant :universal)
  exceptions)
```

The explicit pairs are represented as two parallel lists, one of indexes (domain)
and one of values (range). The default slot is the default value, relevant only
if the infinite slot is :constant. The exceptions slot is a list of indices for
which there are no values. (See the end of section 22.3.3 for the definition of
print-xapping.)

Here, then, is the code for reading xectors in bracket notation:

```
(defun open-bracket-macro-char (stream macro-char)
  (declare (ignore macro-char))
  (let ((range (read-delimited-list #\] stream t)))
    (xap (iota-list (length range)) range)))

(set-macro-character #\[ #'open-bracket-macro-char)
(set-macro-character #\] (get-macro-character #\) ))

(defun iota-list (n)        ;Return list of integers from 0 to n − 1
  (do ((j (- n 1) (- j 1))
       (z '() (cons j z)))
      ((< j 0) z)))
```

The code for reading xappings in the more general brace notation, with all the possibilities for xets (or individual xet pairs), infinite xappings, and exceptions, is a bit more complicated; it is shown in table 22-5. That code is used in conjunction with the initializations

```
(set-macro-character #\{ #'open-brace-macro-char)
(set-macro-character #\} (get-macro-character #\) ))
```

make-dispatch-macro-character *char*   [*Function*]
    &optional *non-terminating-p readtable*

This causes the character *char* to be a dispatching macro character in *readtable* (which defaults to the current readtable). If *non-terminating-p* is not nil (it defaults to nil), then it will be a non-terminating macro character: it may be embedded within extended tokens. make-dispatch-macro-character returns t.

Initially every character in the dispatch table has a character-macro function that signals an error. Use set-dispatch-macro-character to define entries in the dispatch table.

X3J13 voted in January 1989 ⟨7⟩ to clarify that *char* must be a character.

set-dispatch-macro-character *disp-char sub-char function*   [*Function*]
    &optional *readtable*
get-dispatch-macro-character *disp-char sub-char*   [*Function*]
    &optional *readtable*

set-dispatch-macro-character causes *function* to be called when the *disp-char* followed by *sub-char* is read. The *readtable* defaults to the current readtable.

Table 22-5: Macro Character Definition for Xapping Syntax

```
(defun open-brace-macro-char (s macro-char)
  (declare (ignore macro-char))
  (do ((ch (peek-char t s t nil t) (peek-char t s t nil t))
       (domain '()) (range '()) (exceptions '()))
      ((char= ch #\})
       (read-char s t nil t)
       (construct-xapping (reverse domain) (reverse range)))
    (cond ((char= ch #\→)
           (read-char s t nil t)
           (let ((nextch (peek-char nil s t nil t)))
             (cond ((char= nextch #\})
                    (read-char s t nil t)
                    (return (xap (reverse domain)
                                 (reverse range)
                                 nil :universal exceptions)))
                   (t (let ((item (read s t nil t)))
                        (cond ((char= (peek-char t s t nil t) #\})
                               (read-char s t nil t)
                               (return (xap (reverse domain)
                                            (reverse range)
                                            item :constant
                                            exceptions)))
                              (t (reader-error s
                                   "Default → item must be last")))))))
          (t (let ((item (read-preserving-whitespace s t nil t))
                   (nextch (peek-char nil s t nil t)))
               (cond ((char= nextch #\→)
                      (read-char s t nil t)
                      (cond ((member (peek-char nil s t nil t)
                                     '(#\Space #\Tab #\Newline))
                             (push item exceptions))
                            (t (push item domain)
                               (push (read s t nil t) range))))
                     ((char= nch #\})
                      (read-char s t nil t)
                      (push item domain)
                      (push item range)
                      (return (xap (reverse domain) (reverse range))))
                     (t (push item domain)
                        (push item range)))))))))
```

The arguments and return values for *function* are the same as for normal macro characters except that *function* gets *sub-char*, not *disp-char*, as its second argument and also receives a third argument that is the non-negative integer whose decimal representation appeared between *disp-char* and *sub-char*, or `nil` if no decimal integer appeared there.

The *sub-char* may not be one of the ten decimal digits; they are always reserved for specifying an infix integer argument. Moreover, if *sub-char* is a lowercase character (see `lower-case-p`), its uppercase equivalent is used instead. (This is how the rule is enforced that the case of a dispatch sub-character doesn't matter.)

`set-dispatch-macro-character` returns t.

`get-dispatch-macro-character` returns the macro-character function for *sub-char* under *disp-char*, or `nil` if there is no function associated with *sub-char*.

If the *sub-char* is one of the ten decimal digits 0 1 2 3 4 5 6 7 8 9, `get-dispatch-macro-character` always returns `nil`. If *sub-char* is a lowercase character, its uppercase equivalent is used instead.

X3J13 voted in January 1989 ⟨95⟩ to specify that if `nil` is explicitly passed as the second argument to `get-dispatch-macro-character`, then the standard readtable is used. This is consistent with the behavior of `copy-readtable`.

For either function, an error is signaled if the specified *disp-char* is not in fact a dispatch character in the specified readtable. It is necessary to use `make-dispatch-macro-character` to set up the dispatch character before specifying its sub-characters.

As an example, suppose one would like #$*foo* to be read as if it were (dollars *foo*). One might say:

```
(defun |#$-reader| (stream subchar arg)
  (declare (ignore subchar arg))
  (list 'dollars (read stream t nil t)))


(set-dispatch-macro-character #\# #\$ #'|#$-reader|)
```

Compatibility note: This macro-character mechanism is different from those in MacLisp, Interlisp, and Lisp Machine Lisp. Recently Lisp systems have implemented very general readers, even readers so programmable that they can parse arbitrary compiled BNF grammars. Unfortunately, these readers can be complicated to use. This design is an attempt to make the reader as simple as possible to understand, use, and implement. Splicing macros have been eliminated; a recent informal poll indicates that no one uses them to produce other than zero or one value. The ability to access parts of the object preceding the macro character has been eliminated. The MacLisp single-character-object feature has been eliminated because it is seldom used and trivially obtainable by defining a macro.

The user is encouraged to turn off most macro characters, turn others into single-character-object macros, and then use read purely as a lexical analyzer on top of which to build a parser. It is unnecessary, however, to cater to more complex lexical analysis or parsing than that needed for Common Lisp.

---

readtable-case *readtable*   [*Function*]

X3J13 voted in June 1989 ⟨150⟩ to introduce the function readtable-case to control the reader's interpretation of case. It provides access to a slot in a readtable, and may be used with setf to alter the state of that slot. The possible values for the slot are :upcase, :downcase, :preserve, and :invert; the readtable-case for the standard readtable is :upcase. Note that copy-readtable is required to copy the readtable-case slot along with all other readtable information.

Once the reader has accumulated a token as described in section 22.1.1, if the token is a symbol, "replaceable" characters (unescaped uppercase or lowercase constituent characters) may be modified under the control of the readtable-case of the current readtable:

- For :upcase, replaceable characters are converted to uppercase. (This was the behavior specified by the first edition.)

- For :downcase, replaceable characters are converted to lowercase.

- For :preserve, the cases of all characters remain unchanged.

- For :invert, if all of the replaceable letters in the extended token are of the same case, they are all converted to the opposite case; otherwise the cases of all characters in that token remain unchanged.

As an illustration, consider the following code.

```
(let ((*readtable* (copy-readtable nil)))
  (format t "READTABLE-CASE   Input    Symbol-name~
            ~%-----------------------------------~
            ~%")
  (dolist (readtable-case '(:upcase :downcase :preserve :invert))
    (setf (readtable-case *readtable*) readtable-case)
    (dolist (input '("ZEBRA" "Zebra" "zebra"))
      (format t ":~A~16T~A~24T~A~%"
                (string-upcase readtable-case)
                input
                (symbol-name (read-from-string input)))))))
```

The output from this test code should be

```
READTABLE-CASE  Input   Symbol-name
--------------------------------------
:UPCASE         ZEBRA   ZEBRA
:UPCASE         Zebra   ZEBRA
:UPCASE         zebra   ZEBRA
:DOWNCASE       ZEBRA   zebra
:DOWNCASE       Zebra   zebra
:DOWNCASE       zebra   zebra
:PRESERVE       ZEBRA   ZEBRA
:PRESERVE       Zebra   Zebra
:PRESERVE       zebra   zebra
:INVERT         ZEBRA   zebra
:INVERT         Zebra   Zebra
:INVERT         zebra   ZEBRA
```

The readtable-case of the current readtable also affects the printing of symbols (see *print-case* and *print-escape*).

22.1.6. What the Print Function Produces

The Common Lisp printer is controlled by a number of special variables. These are referred to in the following discussion and are fully documented at the end of this section.

How an expression is printed depends on its data type, as described in the following paragraphs.

Integers

If appropriate, a radix specifier may be printed; see the variable *print-radix*. If an integer is negative, a minus sign is printed and then the absolute value of the integer is printed. Integers are printed in the radix specified by the variable *print-base* in the usual positional notation, most significant digit first. The number zero is represented by the single digit 0 and never has a sign. A decimal point may then be printed, depending on the value of *print-radix*.

Ratios

If appropriate, a radix specifier may be printed; see the variable *print-radix*. If the ratio is negative, a minus sign is printed. Then the absolute value of the numerator is printed, as for an integer; then a /; then the denominator. The numerator and denominator are both printed in the radix specified by the variable *print-base*;

they are obtained as if by the `numerator` and `denominator` functions, and so ratios are always printed in reduced form (lowest terms).

Floating-point numbers

If the sign of the number (as determined by the function `float-sign`) is negative, then a minus sign is printed. Then the magnitude is printed in one of two ways. If the magnitude of the floating-point number is either zero or between 10^{-3} (inclusive) and 10^7 (exclusive), it may be printed as the integer part of the number, then a decimal point, followed by the fractional part of the number; there is always at least one digit on each side of the decimal point. If the format of the number does not match that specified by the variable `*read-default-float-format*`, then the exponent marker for that format and the digit 0 are also printed. For example, the base of the natural logarithms as a short-format floating-point number might be printed as `2.71828S0`.

For non-zero magnitudes outside of the range 10^{-3} to 10^7, a floating-point number will be printed in "computerized scientific notation." The representation of the number is scaled to be between 1 (inclusive) and 10 (exclusive) and then printed, with one digit before the decimal point and at least one digit after the decimal point. Next the exponent marker for the format is printed, except that if the format of the number matches that specified by the variable `*read-default-float-format*`, then the exponent marker E is used. Finally, the power of 10 by which the fraction must be multiplied to equal the original number is printed as a decimal integer. For example, Avogadro's number as a short-format floating-point number might be printed as `6.02S23`.

Complex numbers

A complex number is printed as `#C`, an open parenthesis, the printed representation of its real part, a space, the printed representation of its imaginary part, and finally a close parenthesis.

Characters

When `*print-escape*` is `nil`, a character prints as itself; it is sent directly to the output stream. When `*print-escape*` is not `nil`, then `#\` syntax is used. For example, the printed representation of the character `#\A` with control and meta bits on would be `#\CONTROL-META-A`, and that of `#\a` with control and meta bits on would be `#\CONTROL-META-\a`.

X3J13 voted in June 1989 ⟨40⟩ to specify that if `*print-readably*` is not `nil` then every object must be printed in a readable form, regardless of other printer control variables. For characters, the simplest approach is always to use `#\` syntax when `*print-readably*` is not `nil`, regardless of the value of `*print-escape*`.

Symbols

When *print-escape* is nil, only the characters of the print name of the symbol are output (but the case in which to print any uppercase characters in the print name is controlled by the variable *print-case*).

X3J13 voted in June 1989 ⟨150⟩ to specify that the new readtable-case slot of the current readtable also controls the case in which letters (whether uppercase or lowercase) in the print name of a symbol are output, no matter what the value of *print-escape*.

The remaining paragraphs describing the printing of symbols cover the situation when *print-escape* is not nil.

X3J13 voted in June 1989 ⟨40⟩ to specify that if *print-readably* is not nil then every object must be printed in a readable form, regardless of other printer control variables. For symbols, the simplest approach is to print them, when *print-readably* is not nil, as if *print-escape* were not nil, regardless of the actual value of *print-escape*.

Backslashes \ and vertical bars | are included as required. In particular, backslash or vertical-bar syntax is used when the name of the symbol would be otherwise treated by the reader as a potential number (see section 22.1.2). In making this decision, it is assumed that the value of *print-base* being used for printing would be used as the value of *read-base* used for reading; the value of *read-base* at the time of printing is irrelevant. For example, if the value of *print-base* were 16 when printing the symbol face, it would have to be printed as \FACE or \Face or |FACE|, because the token face would be read as a hexadecimal number (decimal value 64206) if *read-base* were 16.

The case in which to print any uppercase characters in the print name is controlled by the variable *print-case*.

X3J13 voted in June 1989 ⟨141⟩ to clarify the interaction of *print-case* with *print-escape*; see *print-case*.

As a special case [no pun intended], nil may sometimes be printed as ( ) instead, when *print-escape* and *print-pretty* are both not nil.

Package prefixes may be printed (using colon syntax) if necessary. The rules for package qualifiers are as follows. When the symbol is printed, if it is in the keyword package, then it is printed with a preceding colon; otherwise, if it is accessible in the current package, it is printed without any qualification; otherwise, it is printed with qualification. See chapter 11.

A symbol that is uninterned (has no home package) is printed preceded by #: if the variables *print-gensym* and *print-escape* are both non-nil; if either is nil, then the symbol is printed without a prefix, as if it were in the current package.

X3J13 voted in June 1989 ⟨40⟩ to specify that if `*print-readably*` is not `nil` then every object must be printed in a readable form, regardless of other printer control variables. For uninterned symbols, the simplest approach is to print them, when `*print-readably*` is not `nil`, as if `*print-escape*` and `*print-gensym*` were not `nil`, regardless of their actual values.

Implementation note: Because the `#:` syntax does not intern the following symbol, it is necessary to use circular-list syntax if `*print-circle*` is not `nil` and the same uninterned symbol appears several times in an expression to be printed. For example, the result of

```
(let ((x (make-symbol "FOO"))) (list x x))
```

would be printed as

```
(#:foo #:foo)
```

if `*print-circle*` were `nil`, but as

```
(#1=#:foo #1#)
```

if `*print-circle*` were not `nil`.

The case in which symbols are to be printed is controlled by the variable `*print-case*`.

It is also controlled by `*print-escape*` and the `readtable-case` slot of the current readtable (the value of `*readtable*`).

Strings

The characters of the string are output in order. If `*print-escape*` is not `nil`, a double quote is output before and after, and all double quotes and single escape characters are preceded by backslash. The printing of strings is not affected by `*print-array*`. If the string has a fill pointer, then only those characters below the fill pointer are printed.

X3J13 voted in June 1989 ⟨40⟩ to specify that if `*print-readably*` is not `nil` then every object must be printed in a readable form, regardless of other printer control variables. For strings, the simplest approach is to print them, when `*print-readably*` is not `nil`, as if `*print-escape*` were not `nil`, regardless of the actual value of `*print-escape*`.

Conses

Wherever possible, list notation is preferred over dot notation. Therefore the following algorithm is used:

1. Print an open parenthesis, (.

2. Print the *car* of the cons.

3. If the *cdr* is a cons, make it the current cons, print a space, and go to step 2.

4. If the *cdr* is not null, print a space, a dot, a space, and the *cdr*.

5. Print a close parenthesis,).

This form of printing is clearer than showing each individual cons cell. Although the two expressions below are equivalent, and the reader will accept either one and produce the same data structure, the printer will always print such a data structure in the second form.

```
(a . (b . ((c . (d . nil)) . (e . nil))))
```

```
(a b (c d) e)
```

The printing of conses is affected by the variables `*print-level*` and `*print-length*`.

X3J13 voted in June 1989 ⟨40⟩ to specify that if `*print-readably*` is not `nil` then every object must be printed in a readable form, regardless of other printer control variables. For conses, the simplest approach is to print them, when `*print-readably*` is not `nil`, as if `*print-level*` and `*print-length*` were `nil`, regardless of their actual values.

Bit-vectors

A bit-vector is printed as `#*` followed by the bits of the bit-vector in order. If `*print-array*` is `nil`, however, then the bit-vector is printed in a format (using `#<`) that is concise but not readable. If the bit-vector has a fill pointer, then only those bits below the fill pointer are printed.

X3J13 voted in June 1989 ⟨40⟩ to specify that if `*print-readably*` is not `nil` then every object must be printed in a readable form, regardless of other printer control variables. For bit-vectors, the simplest approach is to print them, when `*print-readably*` is not `nil`, as if `*print-array*` were not `nil`, regardless of the actual value of `*print-array*`.

Vectors

Any vector other than a string or bit-vector is printed using general-vector syntax; this means that information about specialized vector representations will be lost. The printed representation of a zero-length vector is `#()`. The printed representation of a non-zero-length vector begins with #(. Following that, the first element of the vector is printed. If there are any other elements, they are printed in turn, with a space printed before each additional element. A close parenthesis after the last element terminates the printed representation of the vector.

The printing of vectors is affected by the variables *print-level* and *print-length*. If the vector has a fill pointer, then only those elements below the fill pointer are printed.

If *print-array* is nil, however, then the vector is not printed as described above, but in a format (using #<) that is concise but not readable.

X3J13 voted in June 1989 ⟨40⟩ to specify that if *print-readably* is not nil then every object must be printed in a readable form, regardless of other printer control variables. For vectors, the simplest approach is to print them, when *print-readably* is not nil, as if *print-level* and *print-length* were nil and *print-array* were not nil, regardless of their actual values.

Arrays

Normally any array other than a vector is printed using #nA format. Let n be the rank of the array. Then # is printed, then n as a decimal integer, then A, then n open parentheses. Next the elements are scanned in row-major order. Imagine the array indices being enumerated in odometer fashion, recalling that the dimensions are numbered from 0 to $n-1$. Every time the index for dimension j is incremented, the following actions are taken:

1. If $j < n - 1$, then print a close parenthesis.

2. If incrementing the index for dimension j caused it to equal dimension j, reset that index to zero and increment dimension $j - 1$ (thereby performing these three steps recursively), unless $j = 0$, in which case simply terminate the entire algorithm. If incrementing the index for dimension j did not cause it to equal dimension j, then print a space.

3. If $j < n - 1$, then print an open parenthesis.

This causes the contents to be printed in a format suitable for use as the :initial-contents argument to make-array.

The lists effectively printed by this procedure are subject to truncation by *print-level* and *print-length*.

If the array is of a specialized type, containing bits or string-characters, then the innermost lists generated by the algorithm given above may instead be printed using bit-vector or string syntax, provided that these innermost lists would not be subject to truncation by *print-length*. For example, a 3-by-2-by-4 array of string-characters that would ordinarily be printed as

```
#3A(((#\s #\t #\o #\p) (#\s #\p #\o #\t))
    ((#\p #\o #\s #\t) (#\p #\o #\t #\s))
    ((#\t #\o #\p #\s) (#\o #\p #\t #\s)))
```

may instead be printed more concisely as

```
#3A(("stop" "spot") ("post" "pots") ("tops" "opts"))
```

If `*print-array*` is `nil`, then the array is printed in a format (using `#<`) that is concise but not readable.

X3J13 voted in June 1989 ⟨40⟩ to specify that if `*print-readably*` is not `nil` then every object must be printed in a readable form, regardless of other printer control variables. For arrays, the simplest approach is to print them, when `*print-readably*` is not `nil`, as if `*print-level*` and `*print-length*` were `nil` and `*print-array*` were not `nil`, regardless of their actual values.

Random-states

Common Lisp does not specify a specific syntax for printing objects of type `random-state`. However, every implementation must arrange to print a random-state object in such a way that, within the same implementation of Common Lisp, the function `read` can construct from the printed representation a copy of the random-state object as if the copy had been made by `make-random-state`.

Pathnames

Common Lisp does not specify a specific syntax for printing objects of type `pathname`. However, every implementation must arrange to print a pathname in such a way that, within the same implementation of Common Lisp, the function `read` can construct from the printed representation an equivalent instance of the pathname object.

X3J13 voted in June 1989 ⟨131⟩ to specify that if `*print-escape*` is true, a pathname should be printed by `write` as #P"..." where "..." is the namestring representation of the pathname. If `*print-escape*` is false, `write` prints a pathname by printing its namestring (presumably without escape characters or surrounding double quotes).

X3J13 voted in June 1989 ⟨40⟩ to specify that if `*print-readably*` is not `nil` then every object must be printed in a readable form, regardless of other printer control variables. For pathnames, the simplest approach is to print them, when `*print-readably*` is not `nil`, as if `*print-escape*` were `nil`, regardless of its actual value.

Structures defined by defstruct are printed under the control of the user-specified :print-function option to defstruct. If the user does not provide a printing function explicitly, then a default printing function is supplied that prints the structure using #S syntax (see section 22.1.4).

Any other types are printed in an implementation-dependent manner. It is recommended that printed representations of all such objects begin with the characters #< and end with > so that the reader will catch such objects and not permit them to be read under normal circumstances. It is specifically and purposely *not* required that a Common Lisp implementation be able to print an object of type hash-table, readtable, package, stream, or function in a way that can be read back in successfully by read; the use of #< syntax is especially recommended for the printing of such objects.

X3J13 voted in June 1989 ⟨40⟩ to specify that if *print-readably* is not nil then every object must be printed in a readable form, regardless of the values of other printer control variables; if this is not possible, then an error of type print-not-readable must be signaled to avoid printing an unreadable syntax such as #<...>.

X3J13 voted in June 1989 ⟨40⟩ to add print-unreadable-object, a macro that prints an object using #<...> syntax and also takes care of checking the variable *print-readably*.

When debugging or when frequently dealing with large or deep objects at top level, the user may wish to restrict the printer from printing large amounts of information. The variables *print-level* and *print-length* allow the user to control how deep the printer will print and how many elements at a given level the printer will print. Thus the user can see enough of the object to identify it without having to wade through the entire expression.

print-readably   [*Variable*]

The default value of *print-readably* is nil. If *print-readably* is true, then printing any object must either produce a printed representation that the reader will accept or signal an error. If printing is successful, the reader will, on reading the printed representation, produce an object that is "similar as a constant" (see section 25.1.4) to the object that was printed.

If *print-readably* is true and printing a readable printed representation is not possible, the printer signals an error of type print-not-readable rather than using an unreadable syntax such as #<. The printed representation produced when *print-readably* is true might or might not be the same as the printed representation produced when *print-readably* is false.

If *print-readably* is true and another printer control variable (such as *print-length*, *print-level*, *print-escape*, *print-gensym*, *print-array*, or an implementation-defined printer control variable) would cause the preceding requirements to be violated, that other printer control variable is ignored.

The printing of interned symbols is not affected by *print-readably*.

Note that the "similar as a constant" rule for readable printing implies that #A or #(syntax cannot be used for arrays of element-type other than t. An implementation will have to use another syntax or signal a print-not-readable error. A print-not-readable error will not be signaled for strings or bit-vectors.

All methods for print-object must obey *print-readably*. This rule applies to both user-defined methods and implementation-defined methods.

The reader control variable *read-eval* also affects printing. If *read-eval* is false and *print-readably* is true, any print-object method that would otherwise output a #. reader macro must either output something different or signal an error of type print-not-readable.

Readable printing of structures and objects of type standard-object is controlled by their print-object methods, not by their make-load-form methods. "Similarity as a constant" for these objects is application-dependent and hence is defined to be whatever these methods do.

print-readably allows errors involving data with no readable printed representation to be detected when writing the file rather than later on when the file is read.

print-readably is more rigorous than *print-escape*; output printed with escapes must be merely generally recognizable by humans, with a good chance of being recognizable by computers, whereas output printed readably must be reliably recognizable by computers.

---

print-escape   [Variable]

When this flag is nil, then escape characters are not output when an expression is printed. In particular, a symbol is printed by simply printing the characters of its print name. The function princ effectively binds *print-escape* to nil.

When this flag is not nil, then an attempt is made to print an expression in such a way that it can be read again to produce an equal structure. The function prin1 effectively binds *print-escape* to t. The initial value of this variable is t.

Compatibility note: *print-escape* controls what was called *slashification* in MacLisp.

---

print-pretty   [*Variable*]

When this flag is nil, then only a small amount of whitespace is output when
printing an expression.

    When this flag is not nil, then the printer will endeavor to insert extra whitespace
where appropriate to make the expression more readable. A few other simple
changes may be made, such as printing ´foo instead of (quote foo).

    The initial value of *print-pretty* is implementation-dependent.

    X3J13 voted in January 1989 ⟨139⟩ to adopt a facility for user-controlled pretty
printing in Common Lisp (see chapter 27).

print-circle   [*Variable*]

When this flag is nil (the default), then the printing process proceeds by recursive
descent; an attempt to print a circular structure may lead to looping behavior and
failure to terminate.

    When this flag is not nil, then the printer will endeavor to detect cycles in the
structure to be printed, and to use #n= and #n# syntax to indicate the circularities.

    X3J13 voted in June 1989 ⟨142⟩ to specify that if *print-circle* is true, the
printer is required to detect not only cycles but shared substructure, indicating both
through the use of #n= and #n# syntax. As an example, under the specification of
the first edition

(print ´(#1=(a #1#) #1#))

might legitimately print (#1=(A #1#) #1#) or (#1=(A #1#) #2=(A #2#)); the
vote specifies that the first form is required.

    X3J13 voted in January 1989 ⟨143⟩ to specify that user-defined printing functions
for the defstruct :print-function option, as well as user-defined methods for
the CLOS generic function print-object, may print objects to the supplied stream
using write, print1, princ, format, or print-object and expect circularities
to be detected and printed using #n# syntax (when *print-circle* is non-nil,
of course).

    It seems to me that the same ought to apply to abbreviation as controlled by
print-level and *print-length*, but that was not addressed by this vote.

print-base   [*Variable*]

The value of *print-base* determines in what radix the printer will print rationals.
This may be any integer from 2 to 36, inclusive; the default value is 10 (decimal
radix). For radices above 10, letters of the alphabet are used to represent digits
above 9.

Compatibility note: MacLisp calls this variable base, and its default value is 8, not 10.

In both MacLisp and Common Lisp, floating-point numbers are always printed in decimal, no matter what the value of *print-base*.

---

print-radix   [*Variable*]

If the variable *print-radix* is non-nil, the printer will print a radix specifier to indicate the radix in which it is printing a rational number. To prevent confusion of the letter O with the digit 0, and of the letter B with the digit 8, the radix specifier is always printed using lowercase letters. For example, if the current base is twenty-four (decimal), the decimal integer twenty-three would print as #24rN. If *print-base* is 2, 8, or 16, then the radix specifier used is #b, #o, or #x. For integers, base ten is indicated by a trailing decimal point instead of a leading radix specifier; for ratios, however, #10r is used. The default value of *print-radix* is nil.

print-case   [*Variable*]

The read function normally converts lowercase characters appearing in symbols to corresponding uppercase characters, so that internally print names normally contain only uppercase characters. However, users may prefer to see output using lowercase letters or letters of mixed case. This variable controls the case (upper, lower, or mixed) in which to print any uppercase characters in the names of symbols when vertical-bar syntax is not used. The value of *print-case* should be one of the keywords :upcase, :downcase, or :capitalize; the initial value is :upcase.

Lowercase characters in the internal print name are always printed in lowercase, and are preceded by a single escape character or enclosed by multiple escape characters. Uppercase characters in the internal print name are printed in uppercase, in lowercase, or in mixed case so as to capitalize words, according to the value of *print-case*. The convention for what constitutes a "word" is the same as for the function string-capitalize.

X3J13 voted in June 1989 ⟨141⟩ to clarify the interaction of *print-case* with *print-escape*. When *print-escape* is nil, *print-case* determines the case in which to print all uppercase characters in the print name of the symbol. When *print-escape* is not nil, the implementation has some freedom as to which characters will be printed so as to appear in an "escape context" (after an escape character, typically \, or between multiple escape characters, typically |); *print-case* determines the case in which to print all uppercase characters that will not appear in an escape context. For example, when the value of *print-case* is :upcase, an implementation might choose to print the symbol whose print name is "(S)HE" as \(S\)HE or as |(S)HE|, among other possibilities. When the value of *print-case* is :downcase, the corresponding output should be \(s\)he or |(S)HE|, respectively.

Consider the following test code. (For the sake of this example assume that readtable-case is :upcase in the current readtable; this is discussed further below.)

```
(let ((tabwidth 11))
  (dolist (sym '(|x| |FoObAr| |fOo|))
    (let ((tabstop -1))
      (format t "~&")
      (dolist (escape '(t nil))
        (dolist (case '(:upcase :downcase :capitalize))
          (format t "~VT" (* (incf tabstop) tabwidth))
          (write sym :escape escape :case case)))))
  (format t " %"))
```

An implementation that leans heavily on multiple-escape characters (vertical bars) might produce the following output:

|x|	|x|	|x|	x	x	x
|FoObAr|	|FoObAr|	|FoObAr|	FoObAr	foobar	Foobar
|fOo|	|fOo|	|fOo|	fOo	foo	foo

An implementation that leans heavily on single-escape characters (backslashes) might produce the following output:

\x	\x	\x	x	x	x
F\oO\bA\r	f\oo\ba\r	F\oo\ba\r	FoObAr	foobar	Foobar
\fO\o	\fo\o	\fo\o	fOo	foo	foo

These examples are not exhaustive; output using both kinds of escape characters (for example, |FoO|\bA\r) is permissible (though ugly).

X3J13 voted in June 1989 ⟨150⟩ to add a new readtable-case slot to readtables to control automatic case conversion during the reading of symbols. The value of readtable-case in the current readtable also affects the printing of unescaped letters (letters appearing in an escape context are always printed in their own case).

- If readtable-case is :upcase, unescaped uppercase letters are printed in the case specified by *print-case* and unescaped lowercase letters are printed in their own case. (If *print-escape* is non-nil, all lowercase letters will necessarily be escaped.)

- If readtable-case is :downcase, unescaped lowercase letters are printed in the case specified by *print-case* and unescaped uppercase letters are printed in their own case. (If *print-escape* is non-nil, all uppercase letters will necessarily be escaped.)

- If readtable-case is :preserve, all unescaped letters are printed in their own case, regardless of the value of *print-case*. There is no need to escape any letters, even if *print-escape* is non-nil, though the X3J13 vote did not prohibit escaping letters in this situation.

- If readtable-case is :invert, and if all unescaped letters are of the same case, then the case of all the unescaped letters is inverted; but if the unescaped letters are not all of the same case then each is printed in its own case. (Thus :invert does not always invert the case; the inversion is conditional.) There is no need to escape any letters, even if *print-escape* is non-nil, though the X3J13 vote did not prohibit escaping letters in this situation.

Consider the following code.

```
;;; Generate a table illustrating READTABLE-CASE and *PRINT-CASE*.

(let ((*readtable* (copy-readtable nil))
      (*print-case* *print-case*))
  (format t "READTABLE-CASE *PRINT-CASE*  Symbol-name  Output~
          ~%-----------------------------------------------------~
          ~%")
  (dolist (readtable-case '(:upcase :downcase :preserve :invert))
    (setf (readtable-case *readtable*) readtable-case)
    (dolist (print-case '(:upcase :downcase :capitalize))
      (dolist (sym '(|ZEBRA| |Zebra| |zebra|))
        (setq *print-case* print-case)
        (format t ":~A~15T:~A~29T~A~42T~A~%"
                  (string-upcase readtable-case)
                  (string-upcase print-case)
                  (symbol-name sym)
                  (prin1-to-string sym)))))))
```

Note that the call to prin1-to-string (the last argument in the call to format that is within the nested loops) effectively uses a non-nil value for *print-escape*.

Assuming an implementation that uses vertical bars around a symbol name if any characters need escaping, the output from this test code should be

```
| READTABLE-CASE *PRINT-CASE*   Symbol-name  Output
| -------------------------------------------------
| :UPCASE         :UPCASE       ZEBRA        ZEBRA
| :UPCASE         :UPCASE       Zebra        |Zebra|
| :UPCASE         :UPCASE       zebra        |zebra|
| :UPCASE         :DOWNCASE     ZEBRA        zebra
| :UPCASE         :DOWNCASE     Zebra        |Zebra|
| :UPCASE         :DOWNCASE     zebra        |zebra|
| :UPCASE         :CAPITALIZE   ZEBRA        Zebra
| :UPCASE         :CAPITALIZE   Zebra        |Zebra|
| :UPCASE         :CAPITALIZE   zebra        |zebra|
| :DOWNCASE       :UPCASE       ZEBRA        |ZEBRA|
| :DOWNCASE       :UPCASE       Zebra        |Zebra|
| :DOWNCASE       :UPCASE       zebra        ZEBRA
| :DOWNCASE       :DOWNCASE     ZEBRA        |ZEBRA|
| :DOWNCASE       :DOWNCASE     Zebra        |Zebra|
| :DOWNCASE       :DOWNCASE     zebra        zebra
| :DOWNCASE       :CAPITALIZE   ZEBRA        |ZEBRA|
| :DOWNCASE       :CAPITALIZE   Zebra        |Zebra|
| :DOWNCASE       :CAPITALIZE   zebra        Zebra
| :PRESERVE       :UPCASE       ZEBRA        ZEBRA
| :PRESERVE       :UPCASE       Zebra        Zebra
| :PRESERVE       :UPCASE       zebra        zebra
| :PRESERVE       :DOWNCASE     ZEBRA        ZEBRA
| :PRESERVE       :DOWNCASE     Zebra        Zebra
| :PRESERVE       :DOWNCASE     zebra        zebra
| :PRESERVE       :CAPITALIZE   ZEBRA        ZEBRA
| :PRESERVE       :CAPITALIZE   Zebra        Zebra
| :PRESERVE       :CAPITALIZE   zebra        zebra
| :INVERT         :UPCASE       ZEBRA        zebra
| :INVERT         :UPCASE       Zebra        Zebra
| :INVERT         :UPCASE       zebra        ZEBRA
| :INVERT         :DOWNCASE     ZEBRA        zebra
| :INVERT         :DOWNCASE     Zebra        Zebra
| :INVERT         :DOWNCASE     zebra        ZEBRA
| :INVERT         :CAPITALIZE   ZEBRA        zebra
| :INVERT         :CAPITALIZE   Zebra        Zebra
| :INVERT         :CAPITALIZE   zebra        ZEBRA
```

This illustrates all combinations for readtable-case and *print-case*.

Table 22-6: Examples of Print Level and Print Length Abbreviation

v	*n*	Output
0	1	#
1	1	(if ...)
1	2	(if # ...)
1	3	(if # # ...)
1	4	(if # # #)
2	1	(if ...)
2	2	(if (member x ...) ...)
2	3	(if (member x y) (+ # 3) ...)
3	2	(if (member x ...) ...)
3	3	(if (member x y) (+ (car x) 3) ...)
3	4	(if (member x y) (+ (car x) 3) '(foo . #(a b c d ...)))
3	5	(if (member x y) (+ (car x) 3) '(foo . #(a b c d "Baz")))

print-gensym   [*Variable*]

The *print-gensym* variable controls whether the prefix #: is printed before symbols that have no home package. The prefix is printed if the variable is not nil. The initial value of *print-gensym* is t.

print-level   [*Variable*]
print-length   [*Variable*]

The *print-level* variable controls how many levels deep a nested data object will print. If *print-level* is nil (the initial value), then no control is exercised. Otherwise, the value should be an integer, indicating the maximum level to be printed. An object to be printed is at level 0; its components (as of a list or vector) are at level 1; and so on. If an object to be recursively printed has components and is at a level equal to or greater than the value of *print-level*, then the object is printed as simply #.

The *print-length* variable controls how many elements at a given level are printed. A value of nil (the initial value) indicates that there be no limit to the number of components printed. Otherwise, the value of *print-length* should be an integer. Should the number of elements of a data object exceed the value *print-length*, the printer will print three dots, ..., in place of those elements beyond the number specified by *print-length*. (In the case of a dotted list, if the list contains exactly as many elements as the value of *print-length*, and in addition has the non-null atom terminating it, that terminating atom is printed rather than the three dots.)

print-level and *print-length* affect the printing not only of lists but also of vectors, arrays, and any other object printed with a list-like syntax. They do not affect the printing of symbols, strings, and bit-vectors.

The Lisp reader will normally signal an error when reading an expression that has been abbreviated because of level or length limits. This signal is given because the # dispatch character normally signals an error when followed by whitespace or), and because ... is defined to be an illegal token, as are all tokens consisting entirely of periods (other than the single dot used in dot notation).

As an example, table 22-6 shows the ways the object

```
(if (member x y) (+ (car x) 3) ´(foo . #(a b c d "Baz")))
```

would be printed for various values of *print-level* (in the column labeled *v*) and *print-length* (in the column labeled *n*).

print-array   [*Variable*]

If *print-array* is nil, then the contents of arrays other than strings are never printed. Instead, arrays are printed in a concise form (using #<) that gives enough information for the user to be able to identify the array but does not include the entire array contents. If *print-array* is not nil, non-string arrays are printed using #(, #*, or #*n*A syntax.

Notice of correction. In the first edition, the preceding paragraph mentioned the nonexistent variable print-array instead of *print-array*.

The initial value of *print-array* is implementation-dependent.

with-standard-io-syntax {*declaration*}* {*form*}*   [*Macro*]

X3J13 voted in June 1989 ⟨40⟩ to add the macro with-standard-io-syntax. Within the dynamic extent of the body, all reader/printer control variables, including any implementation-defined ones not specified by Common Lisp, are bound to values that produce standard read/print behavior. Table 22-7 shows the values to which standard Common Lisp variables are bound.

The values returned by with-standard-io-syntax are the values of the last body *form*, or nil if there are no body forms.

The intent is that a pair of executions, as shown in the following example, should provide reasonable reliable communication of data from one Lisp process to another:

Table 22-7: Standard Bindings for I/O Control Variables

Variable	Value
package	the common-lisp-user package
print-array	t
print-base	10
print-case	:upcase
print-circle	nil
print-escape	t
print-gensym	t
print-length	nil
print-level	nil
print-lines	nil *
print-miser-width	nil *
print-pprint-dispatch	nil *
print-pretty	nil
print-radix	nil
print-readably	t
print-right-margin	nil *
read-base	10
read-default-float-format	single-float
read-eval	t
read-suppress	nil
readtable	the standard readtable

* X3J13 voted in June 1989 ⟨139⟩ to introduce the printer control variables *print-right-margin*, *print-miser-width*, *print-lines*, and *print-pprint-dispatch* (see section 27.2) but did not specify the values to which with-standard-io-syntax should bind them. I recommend that all four should be bound to nil.

```
;;; Write DATA to a file.
(with-open-file (file pathname :direction :output)
  (with-standard-io-syntax
    (print data file)))

;;; ... Later, in another Lisp:
(with-open-file (file pathname :direction :input)
  (with-standard-io-syntax
    (setq data (read file))))
```

Using with-standard-io-syntax to bind all the variables, instead of using let and explicit bindings, ensures that nothing is overlooked and avoids problems with implementation-defined reader/printer control variables. If the user wishes to use a non-standard value for some variable, such as *package* or *read-eval*, it can be bound by let inside the body of with-standard-io-syntax. For example:

```
;;; Write DATA to a file. Forbid use of #. syntax.
(with-open-file (file pathname :direction :output)
  (let ((*read-eval* nil))
    (with-standard-io-syntax
      (print data file))))


;;; Read DATA from a file. Forbid use of #. syntax.
(with-open-file (file pathname :direction :input)
  (let ((*read-eval* nil))
    (with-standard-io-syntax
      (setq data (read file)))))
```

Similarly, a user who dislikes the arbitrary choice of values for *print-circle* and *print-pretty* can bind these variables to other values inside the body.

The X3J13 vote left it unclear whether with-standard-io-syntax permits declarations to appear before the body of the macro call. I believe that was the intent, and this is reflected in the syntax shown above; but this is only my interpretation.

22.2. Input Functions

The input functions are divided into two groups: those that operate on streams of characters and those that operate on streams of binary data.

22.2.1. Input from Character Streams

Many character input functions take optional arguments called *input-stream, eof-error-p*, and *eof-value*. The *input-stream* argument is the stream from which to obtain input; if unsupplied or nil it defaults to the value of the special variable *standard-input*. One may also specify t as a stream, meaning the value of the special variable *terminal-io*.

The *eof-error-p* argument controls what happens if input is from a file (or any other input source that has a definite end) and the end of the file is reached. If *eof-error-p* is true (the default), an error will be signaled at end of file. If it is false, then no error is signaled, and instead the function returns *eof-value*.

X3J13 voted in January 1989 ⟨7⟩ to clarify that an *eof-value* argument may be any Lisp datum whatsoever.

Functions such as read that read the representation of an object rather than a single character will always signal an error, regardless of *eof-error-p*, if the file ends in the middle of an object representation. For example, if a file does not contain enough right parentheses to balance the left parentheses in it, read will complain. If a file ends in a symbol or a number immediately followed by end-of-file, read will read the symbol or number successfully and when called again will see the end-of-file and only then act according to *eof-error-p*. Similarly, the function read-line will successfully read the last line of a file even if that line is terminated by end-of-file rather than the newline character. If a file contains ignorable text at the end, such as blank lines and comments, read will not consider it to end in the middle of an object. Thus an *eof-error-p* argument controls what happens when the file ends *between* objects.

Many input functions also take an argument called *recursive-p*. If specified and not nil, this argument specifies that this call is not a "top-level" call to read but an imbedded call, typically from the function for a macro character. It is important to distinguish such recursive calls for three reasons.

First, a top-level call establishes the context within which the #*n*= and #*n*# syntax is scoped. Consider, for example, the expression

```
(cons '#3=(p q r) '(x y . #3#))
```

If the single-quote macro character were defined in this way:

```
(set-macro-character #\'
                #'(lambda (stream char)
                   (declare (ignore char))
                   (list 'quote (read stream))))
```

then the expression could not be read properly, because there would be no way to know when read is called recursively by the first occurrence of ' that the label #3= would be referred to later in the containing expression. There would be no way to know because read could not determine that it was called by a macro-character function rather than from "top level." The correct way to define the single quote macro character uses the *recursive-p* argument:

```
(set-macro-character #\'
                #'(lambda (stream char)
                   (declare (ignore char))
                   (list 'quote (read stream t nil t))))
```

Second, a recursive call does not alter whether the reading process is to preserve whitespace or not (as determined by whether the top-level call was to read or read-preserving-whitespace). Suppose again that the single quote had the first, incorrect, macro-character definition shown above. Then a call to read-preserving-whitespace that read the expression ´foo would fail to preserve the space character following the symbol foo because the single-quote macro-character function calls read, not read-preserving-whitespace, to read the following expression (in this case foo). The correct definition, which passes the value t for the *recursive-p* argument to read, allows the top-level call to determine whether whitespace is preserved.

Third, when end-of-file is encountered and the *eof-error-p* argument is not nil, the kind of error that is signaled may depend on the value of *recursive-p*. If *recursive-p* is not nil, then the end-of-file is deemed to have occurred within the middle of a printed representation; if *recursive-p* is nil, then the end-of-file may be deemed to have occurred between objects rather than within the middle of one.

read &optional *input-stream eof-error-p eof-value recursive-p*   [*Function*]

read reads in the printed representation of a Lisp object from *input-stream*, builds a corresponding Lisp object, and returns the object.

Note that when the variable *read-suppress* is not nil, then read reads in a printed representation as best it can, but most of the work of interpreting the representation is avoided (the intent being that the result is to be discarded anyway). For example, all extended tokens produce the result nil regardless of their syntax.

read-default-float-format   [*Variable*]

The value of this variable must be a type specifier symbol for a specific floating-point format; these include short-float, single-float, double-float, and long-float and may include implementation-specific types as well. The default value is single-float.

read-default-float-format indicates the floating-point format to be used for reading floating-point numbers that have no exponent marker or have e or E for an exponent marker. (Other exponent markers explicitly prescribe the floating-point format to be used.) The printer also uses this variable to guide the choice of exponent markers when printing floating-point numbers.

read-preserving-whitespace &optional *in-stream eof-error-p*   [*Function*]
    eof-value recursive-p

Certain printed representations given to read, notably those of symbols and numbers, require a delimiting character after them. (Lists do not, because the close parenthesis marks the end of the list.) Normally read will throw away the delimiting character if it is a whitespace character; but read will preserve the character (using unread-char) if it is syntactically meaningful, because it may be the start of the next expression.

X3J13 voted in January 1989 ⟨138⟩ to clarify the interaction of unread-char with echo streams. These changes indirectly affect the echoing behavior of read-preserving-whitespace.

The function read-preserving-whitespace is provided for some specialized situations where it is desirable to determine precisely what character terminated the extended token.

As an example, consider this macro-character definition:

```
(defun slash-reader (stream char)
  (declare (ignore char))
  (do ((path (list (read-preserving-whitespace stream))
             (cons (progn (read-char stream nil nil t)
                          (read-preserving-whitespace
                            stream))
                   path)))
      ((not (char= (peek-char nil stream nil nil t) #\/))
       (cons 'path (nreverse path)))))
(set-macro-character #\/ #'slash-reader)
```

(This is actually a rather dangerous definition to make because expressions such as (/ x 3) will no longer be read properly. The ability to reprogram the reader syntax is very powerful and must be used with caution. This redefinition of / is shown here purely for the sake of example.)

Consider now calling read on this expression:

```
(zyedh /usr/games/zork /usr/games/boggle)
```

The / macro reads objects separated by more / characters; thus /usr/games/zork is intended to be read as (path usr games zork). The entire example expression should therefore be read as

```
(zyedh (path usr games zork) (path usr games boggle))
```

However, if read had been used instead of read-preserving-whitespace, then after the reading of the symbol zork, the following space would be discarded; the next call to peek-char would see the following /, and the loop would continue, producing this interpretation:

```
(zyedh (path usr games zork usr games boggle))
```

On the other hand, there are times when whitespace *should* be discarded. If a command interpreter takes single-character commands, but occasionally reads a Lisp object, then if the whitespace after a symbol is not discarded it might be interpreted as a command some time later after the symbol had been read.

Note that `read-preserving-whitespace` behaves *exactly* like `read` when the *recursive-p* argument is not `nil`. The distinction is established only by calls with *recursive-p* equal to `nil` or omitted.

`read-delimited-list` *char* &optional *input-stream recursive-p*   [*Function*]

This reads objects from *stream* until the next character after an object's representation (ignoring whitespace characters and comments) is *char*. (The *char* should not have whitespace syntax in the current readtable.) A list of the objects read is returned.

To be more precise, `read-delimited-list` looks ahead at each step for the next non-whitespace character and peeks at it as if with `peek-char`. If it is *char*, then the character is consumed and the list of objects is returned. If it is a constituent or escape character, then `read` is used to read an object, which is added to the end of the list. If it is a macro character, the associated macro function is called; if the function returns a value, that value is added to the list. The peek-ahead process is then repeated.

X3J13 voted in January 1989 ⟨138⟩ to clarify the interaction of `peek-char` with echo streams. These changes indirectly affect the echoing behavior of the function `read-delimited-list`.

This function is particularly useful for defining new macro characters. Usually it is desirable for the terminating character *char* to be a terminating macro character so that it may be used to delimit tokens; however, `read-delimited-list` makes no attempt to alter the syntax specified for *char* by the current readtable. The user must make any necessary changes to the readtable syntax explicitly. The following example illustrates this.

Suppose you wanted #{*a b c* ... *z*} to be read as a list of all pairs of the elements *a*, *b*, *c*, ..., *z*; for example:

`#{p q z a}` reads as `((p q) (p z) (p a) (q z) (q a) (z a))`

This can be done by specifying a macro-character definition for `#{` that does two things: read in all the items up to the `}`, and construct the pairs. `read-delimited-list` performs the first task.

Note that `mapcon` allows the mapped function to examine the items of the list after the current one, and that `mapcon` uses `nconc`, which is all right because `mapcar` will produce fresh lists.

```
(defun |#{-reader| (stream char arg)
  (declare (ignore char arg))
  (mapcon #'(lambda (x)
              (mapcar #'(lambda (y) (list (car x) y)) (cdr x)))
          (read-delimited-list #\} stream t)))
```

```
(set-dispatch-macro-character #\# #\{ #'|#{-reader|)
```

```
(set-macro-character #\} (get-macro-character #\) nil))
```

(Note that t is specified for the *recursive-p* argument.)

It is necessary here to give a definition to the character } as well to prevent it from being a constituent. If the line

```
(set-macro-character #\} (get-macro-character #\) nil))
```

shown above were not included, then the } in

```
#{p q z a}
```

would be considered a constituent character, part of the symbol named a}. One could correct for this by putting a space before the }, but it is better simply to use the call to set-macro-character.

Giving } the same definition as the standard definition of the character) has the twin benefit of making it terminate tokens for use with read-delimited-list and also making it illegal for use in any other context (that is, attempting to read a stray } will signal an error).

Note that read-delimited-list does not take an *eof-error-p* (or *eof-value*) argument. The reason is that it is always an error to hit end-of-file during the operation of read-delimited-list.

read-line &optional *input-stream eof-error-p eof-value*　　　　　[*Function*]
　　　　　　recursive-p

read-line reads in a line of text terminated by a newline. It returns the line as a character string (*without* the newline character). This function is usually used to get a line of input from the user. A second returned value is a flag that is false if the line was terminated normally, or true if end-of-file terminated the (non-empty) line. If end-of-file is encountered immediately (that is, appears to terminate an empty line), then end-of-file processing is controlled in the usual way by the *eof-error-p*, *eof-value*, and *recursive-p* arguments.

The corresponding output function is write-line.

read-char &optional *input-stream eof-error-p eof-value*   [*Function*]
            recursive-p

read-char inputs one character from *input-stream* and returns it as a character object.

The corresponding output function is write-char.

X3J13 voted in January 1989 ⟨138⟩ to clarify the interaction of read-char with echo streams (as created by make-echo-stream). A character is echoed from the input stream to the associated output stream the first time it is seen. If a character is read again because of an intervening unread-char operation, the character is not echoed again when read for the second time or any subsequent time.

unread-char *character* &optional *input-stream*   [*Function*]

unread-char puts the *character* onto the front of *input-stream*. The *character* must be the same character that was most recently read from the *input-stream*. The *input-stream* "backs up" over this character; when a character is next read from *input-stream*, it will be the specified character followed by the previous contents of *input-stream*. unread-char returns nil.

One may apply unread-char only to the character most recently read from *input-stream*. Moreover, one may not invoke unread-char twice consecutively without an intervening read-char operation. The result is that one may back up only by one character, and one may not insert any characters into the input stream that were not already there.

X3J13 voted in January 1989 ⟨181⟩ to clarify that one also may not invoke unread-char after invoking peek-char without an intervening read-char operation. This is consistent with the notion that peek-char behaves much like read-char followed by unread-char.

Rationale: This is not intended to be a general mechanism, but rather an efficient mechanism for allowing the Lisp reader and other parsers to perform one-character lookahead in the input stream. This protocol admits a wide variety of efficient implementations, such as simply decrementing a buffer pointer. To have to specify the character in the call to unread-char is admittedly redundant, since at any given time there is only one character that may be legally specified. The redundancy is intentional, again to give the implementation latitude.

X3J13 voted in January 1989 ⟨138⟩ to clarify the interaction of unread-char with echo streams (as created by make-echo-stream). When a character is "unread" from an echo stream, no attempt is made to "unecho" the character. However, a character placed back into an echo stream by unread-char will not be re-echoed when it is subsequently re-read by read-char.

`peek-char` &optional *peek-type input-stream eof-error-p*   [*Function*]
   eof-value recursive-p

What `peek-char` does depends on the *peek-type*, which defaults to `nil`. With a
peek-type of `nil`, `peek-char` returns the next character to be read from *input-
stream*, without actually removing it from the input stream. The next time input is
done from *input-stream*, the character will still be there. It is as if one had called
`read-char` and then `unread-char` in succession.

If *peek-type* is `t`, then `peek-char` skips over whitespace characters (but not
comments) and then performs the peeking operation on the next character. This
is useful for finding the (possible) beginning of the next printed representation of
a Lisp object. The last character examined (the one that starts an object) is not
removed from the input stream.

If *peek-type* is a character object, then `peek-char` skips over input characters
until a character that is `char=` to that object is found; that character is left in the
input stream.

X3J13 voted in January 1989 ⟨138⟩ to clarify the interaction of `peek-char`
with echo streams (as created by `make-echo-stream`). When a character from
an echo stream is only peeked at, it is not echoed at that time. The character
remains in the input stream and may be echoed when read by `read-char` at a later
time. Note, however, that if the *peek-type* is not `nil`, then characters skipped over
(and therefore consumed) by `peek-char` are treated as if they had been read by
`read-char`, and will be echoed if `read-char` would have echoed them.

`listen` &optional *input-stream*   [*Function*]

The predicate `listen` is true if there is a character immediately available from
input-stream, and is false if not. This is particularly useful when the stream obtains
characters from an interactive device such as a keyboard. A call to `read-char`
would simply wait until a character was available, but `listen` can sense whether
or not input is available and allow the program to decide whether or not to attempt
input. On a non-interactive stream, the general rule is that `listen` is true except
when at end-of-file.

`read-char-no-hang` &optional *input-stream eof-error-p*   [*Function*]
   eof-value recursive-p

This function is exactly like `read-char`, except that if it would be necessary to
wait in order to get a character (as from a keyboard), `nil` is immediately returned
without waiting. This allows one to efficiently check for input availability and get
the input if it is available. This is different from the `listen` operation in two ways.

First, read-char-no-hang potentially reads a character, whereas listen never inputs a character. Second, listen does not distinguish between end-of-file and no input being available, whereas read-char-no-hang does make that distinction, returning *eof-value* at end-of-file (or signaling an error if no *eof-error-p* is true) but always returning nil if no input is available.

clear-input &optional *input-stream*   [*Function*]

This clears any buffered input associated with *input-stream*. It is primarily useful for clearing type-ahead from keyboards when some kind of asynchronous error has occurred. If this operation doesn't make sense for the stream involved, then clear-input does nothing. clear-input returns nil.

read-from-string *string* &optional *eof-error-p eof-value* &key   [*Function*]
          :start :end :preserve-whitespace

The characters of *string* are given successively to the Lisp reader, and the Lisp object built by the reader is returned. Macro characters and so on will all take effect.

The arguments :start and :end delimit a substring of *string* beginning at the character indexed by :start and up to but not including the character indexed by :end. By default :start is 0 (the beginning of the string) and :end is (length *string*). This is the same as for other string functions.

The flag :preserve-whitespace, if provided and not nil, indicates that the operation should preserve whitespace as for read-preserving-whitespace. It defaults to nil.

As with other reading functions, the arguments *eof-error-p* and *eof-value* control the action if the end of the (sub)string is reached before the operation is completed; reaching the end of the string is treated as any other end-of-file event.

read-from-string returns two values: the first is the object read, and the second is the index of the first character in the string not read. If the entire string was read, the second result will be either the length of the string or one greater than the length of the string. The parameter :preserve-whitespace may affect this second value.

(read-from-string "(a b c)") $\Rightarrow$ (a b c) and 7

parse-integer *string* &key :start :end :radix   [*Function*]
          :junk-allowed

This function examines the substring of *string* delimited by :start and :end (which default to the beginning and end of the string). It skips over whitespace characters and then attempts to parse an integer. The :radix parameter defaults to 10 and must be an integer between 2 and 36.

If :junk-allowed is not nil, then the first value returned is the value of the number parsed as an integer or nil if no syntactically correct integer was seen.

If :junk-allowed is nil (the default), then the entire substring is scanned. The returned value is the value of the number parsed as an integer. An error is signaled if the substring does not consist entirely of the representation of an integer, possibly surrounded on either side by whitespace characters.

In either case, the second value is the index into the string of the delimiter that terminated the parse, or it is the index beyond the substring if the parse terminated at the end of the substring (as will always be the case if :junk-allowed is false).

Note that parse-integer does not recognize the syntactic radix-specifier prefixes #O, #B, #X, and #nR, nor does it recognize a trailing decimal point. It permits only an optional sign (+ or -) followed by a non-empty sequence of digits in the specified radix.

22.2.2. Input from Binary Streams

Common Lisp currently specifies only a very simple facility for binary input: the reading of a single byte as an integer.

read-byte *binary-input-stream* &optional *eof-error-p eof-value*   [Function]

read-byte reads one byte from the *binary-input-stream* and returns it in the form of an integer.

22.3. Output Functions

The output functions are divided into two groups: those that operate on streams of characters and those that operate on streams of binary data. The function format operates on streams of characters but is described in a section separate from the other character-output functions because of its great complexity.

22.3.1. Output to Character Streams

These functions all take an optional argument called *output-stream*, which is where to send the output. If unsupplied or nil, *output-stream* defaults to the value of the variable *standard-output*. If it is t, the value of the variable *terminal-io* is used.

write *object* &key :stream :escape :radix :base :circle   [*Function*]
    :pretty :level :length :case :gensym :array

The printed representation of *object* is written to the output stream specified by
:stream, which defaults to the value of *standard-output*.

    The other keyword arguments specify values used to control the generation of the
printed representation. Each defaults to the value of the corresponding global variable: see *print-escape*, *print-radix*, *print-base*, *print-circle*,
print-pretty, *print-level*, *print-length*, *print-case*, *print-
array*, and *print-gensym*. (This is the means by which these variables affect
printing operations: supplying default values for the write function.) Note that
the printing of symbols is also affected by the value of the variable *package*.
write returns *object*.

    X3J13 voted in June 1989 ⟨40⟩ to add the keyword argument :readably to
the function write, and voted in June 1989 ⟨139⟩ to add the keyword arguments
:right-margin, :miser-width, :lines, and :pprint-dispatch. The revised
description is as follows.

write *object* &key :stream :escape :radix :base :circle   [*Function*]
    :pretty :level :length :case :gensym :array :readably
    :right-margin :miser-width :lines :pprint-dispatch

The printed representation of *object* is written to the output stream specified by
:stream, which defaults to the value of *standard-output*.

    The other keyword arguments specify values used to control the generation of the
printed representation. Each defaults to the value of the corresponding global variable: see *print-escape*, *print-radix*, *print-base*, *print-circle*,
print-pretty, *print-level*, *print-length*, and *print-case*, in
addition to *print-array*, *print-gensym*, *print-readably*, *print-
right-margin*, *print-miser-width*, *print-lines*, and *print-pprint-
dispatch*. (This is the means by which these variables affect printing operations:
supplying default values for the write function.) Note that the printing of symbols
is also affected by the value of the variable *package*. write returns *object*.

prin1 *object* &optional *output-stream*   [*Function*]
print *object* &optional *output-stream*   [*Function*]
pprint *object* &optional *output-stream*   [*Function*]
princ *object* &optional *output-stream*   [*Function*]

prin1 outputs the printed representation of *object* to *output-stream*. Escape characters are used as appropriate. Roughly speaking, the output from prin1 is suitable

for input to the function read. prin1 returns the *object* as its value.

(prin1 *object* *output-stream*)
    ≡ (write *object* :stream *output-stream* :escape t)

print is just like prin1 except that the printed representation of *object* is preceded by a newline (see terpri) and followed by a space. print returns *object*.

pprint is just like print except that the trailing space is omitted and the *object* is printed with the *print-pretty* flag non-nil to produce "pretty" output. pprint returns no values (that is, what the expression (values) returns: zero values).

X3J13 voted in January 1989 ⟨139⟩ to adopt a facility for user-controlled pretty printing (see chapter 27).

princ is just like prin1 except that the output has no escape characters. A symbol is printed as simply the characters of its print name; a string is printed without surrounding double quotes; and there may be differences for other data types as well. The general rule is that output from princ is intended to look good to people, while output from prin1 is intended to be acceptable to the function read.

X3J13 voted in June 1987 ⟨140⟩ to clarify that princ prints a character in exactly the same manner as write-char: the character is simply sent to the output *stream*. This was implied by the specification in section 22.1.6 in the first edition, but is worth pointing out explicitly here.

princ returns the *object* as its value.

(princ *object* *output-stream*)
    ≡ (write *object* :stream *output-stream* :escape nil)

Compatibility note: In MacLisp, the functions prin1, print, and princ return t, not the argument *object*.

---

write-to-string *object* &key :escape :radix :base :circle   [*Function*]
                     :pretty :level :length :case :gensym :array
prin1-to-string *object*   [*Function*]
princ-to-string *object*   [*Function*]

The object is effectively printed as if by write, prin1, or princ, respectively, and the characters that would be output are made into a string, which is returned.

Compatibility note: The Interlisp function mkstring corresponds to the Common Lisp function princ-to-string.

> write-to-string *object* &key :escape :radix :base :circle [*Function*]
>   :pretty :level :length :case :gensym :array
>   :readably :right-margin :miser-width :lines
>   :pprint-dispatch

X3J13 voted in June 1989 (⟨40⟩ and ⟨139⟩) to add keyword arguments to write; presumably they should also be added to write-to-string.

> write-char *character* &optional *output-stream*   [*Function*]

write-char outputs the *character* to *output-stream*, and returns *character*.

> write-string *string* &optional *output-stream* &key :start   [*Function*]
>   :end
> write-line *string* &optional *output-stream* &key :start :end [*Function*]

write-string writes the characters of the specified substring of *string* to the *output-stream*. The :start and :end parameters delimit a substring of *string* in the usual manner (see chapter 14). write-line does the same thing but then outputs a newline afterwards. (See read-line.) In either case, the *string* is returned (*not* the substring delimited by :start and :end). In some implementations these may be much more efficient than an explicit loop using write-char.

> terpri &optional *output-stream*   [*Function*]
> fresh-line &optional *output-stream*   [*Function*]

The function terpri outputs a newline to *output-stream*. It is identical in effect to (write-char #\Newline *output-stream*); however, terpri always returns nil.

fresh-line is similar to terpri but outputs a newline only if the stream is not already at the start of a line. (If for some reason this cannot be determined, then a newline is output anyway.) This guarantees that the stream will be on a "fresh line" while consuming as little vertical distance as possible. fresh-line is a predicate that is true if it output a newline, and otherwise false.

> finish-output &optional *output-stream*   [*Function*]
> force-output &optional *output-stream*   [*Function*]
> clear-output &optional *output-stream*   [*Function*]

Some streams may be implemented in an asynchronous or buffered manner. The function finish-output attempts to ensure that all output sent to *output-stream* has reached its destination, and only then returns nil. force-output initiates the emptying of any internal buffers but returns `nil` without waiting for completion or acknowledgment.

The function `clear-output`, on the other hand, attempts to abort any outstanding output operation in progress in order to allow as little output as possible to continue to the destination. This is useful, for example, to abort a lengthy output to the terminal when an asynchronous error occurs. `clear-output` returns `nil`.

The precise actions of all three of these operations are implementation-dependent.

`print-unreadable-object` (*object stream*   [*Macro*]
                ⟦ `:type` *type* | `:identity` *id* ⟧)
                {*declaration*}* {*form*}*

X3J13 voted in June 1989 ⟨40⟩ to add `print-unreadable-object`, which will output a printed representation of *object* on *stream*, beginning with #< and ending with >. Everything output to the *stream* during execution of the body forms is enclosed in the angle brackets. If *type* is true, the body output is preceded by a brief description of the object's type and a space character. If *id* is true, the body output is followed by a space character and a representation of the object's identity, typically a storage address.

If `*print-readably*` is true, `print-unreadable-object` signals an error of type `print-not-readable` without printing anything.

The *object*, *stream*, *type*, and *id* arguments are all evaluated normally. The *type* and *id* default to false. It is valid to provide no body forms. If *type* and *id* are both true and there are no body forms, only one space character separates the printed type and the printed identity.

The value returned by `print-unreadable-object` is `nil`.

```
(defmethod print-object ((obj airplane) stream)
  (print-unreadable-object (obj stream :type t :identity t)
    (princ (tail-number obj) stream)))
(print my-airplane)   prints
#<Airplane NW0773 777500123135>        ;In implementation A
                    or perhaps
#<FAA:AIRPLANE NW0773 17>              ;In implementation B
```

The big advantage of `print-unreadable-object` is that it allows a user to write `print-object` methods that adhere to implementation-specific style without requiring the user to write implementation-dependent code.

The X3J13 vote left it unclear whether `print-unreadable-object` permits declarations to appear before the body of the macro call. I believe that was the intent, and this is reflected in the syntax shown above; but this is only my interpretation.

22.3.2. Output to Binary Streams

Common Lisp currently specifies only a very simple facility for binary output: the writing of a single byte as an integer.

`write-byte` *integer binary-output-stream*   [*Function*]

`write-byte` writes one byte, the value of *integer*. It is an error if *integer* is not of the type specified as the `:element-type` argument to `open` when the stream was created. The value *integer* is returned.

22.3.3. Formatted Output to Character Streams

The function `format` is very useful for producing nicely formatted text, producing good-looking messages, and so on. `format` can generate a string or output to a stream.

Formatted output is performed not only by the `format` function itself but by certain other functions that accept a control string "the way `format` does." For example, error-signaling functions such as `cerror` accept `format` control strings.

`format` *destination control-string* &rest *arguments*   [*Function*]

`format` is used to produce formatted output. `format` outputs the characters of *control-string*, except that a tilde (~) introduces a directive. The character after the tilde, possibly preceded by prefix parameters and modifiers, specifies what kind of formatting is desired. Most directives use one or more elements of *arguments* to create their output; the typical directive puts the next element of *arguments* into the output, formatted in some special way. It is an error if no argument remains for a directive requiring an argument, but it is not an error if one or more arguments remain unprocessed by a directive.

The output is sent to *destination*. If *destination* is `nil`, a string is created that contains the output; this string is returned as the value of the call to `format`.

X3J13 voted in January 1989 ⟨167⟩ to specify that when the first argument to `format` is `nil`, `format` creates a stream of type `string-stream` in much the same manner as `with-output-to-string`. (This stream may be visible to the user if, for example, the ~S directive is used to print a `defstruct` structure that has a user-supplied print function.)

In all other cases `format` returns `nil`, performing output to *destination* as a side effect. If *destination* is a stream, the output is sent to it. If *destination* is `t`, the output is sent to the stream that is the value of the variable `*standard-output*`.

If *destination* is a string with a fill pointer, then in effect the output characters are added to the end of the string (as if by use of vector-push-extend).

The format function includes some extremely complicated and specialized features. It is not necessary to understand all or even most of its features to use format effectively. The beginner should skip over anything in the following documentation that is not immediately useful or clear. The more sophisticated features (such as conditionals and iteration) are there for the convenience of programs with especially complicated formatting requirements.

A format directive consists of a tilde (~), optional prefix parameters separated by commas, optional colon (:) and at-sign (@) modifiers, and a single character indicating what kind of directive this is. The alphabetic case of the directive character is ignored. The prefix parameters are generally integers, notated as optionally signed decimal numbers.

X3J13 voted in June 1987 ⟨80⟩ to specify that if both colon and at-sign modifiers are present, they may appear in either order; thus ~:@R and ~@:R mean the same thing. However, it is traditional to put the colon first, and all the examples in this book put colons before at-signs.

Examples of control strings:

```
"~S"              ; An ~S directive with no parameters or modifiers
"~3,-4:@s"        ; An ~S directive with two parameters, 3 and −4,
                  ;  and both the colon and at-sign flags
"~,+4S"           ; First prefix parameter is omitted and takes
                  ;  on its default value; the second parameter is 4
```

Sometimes a prefix parameter is used to specify a character, for instance the padding character in a right- or left-justifying operation. In this case a single quote (´) followed by the desired character may be used as a prefix parameter, to mean the character object that is the character following the single quote. For example, you can use ~5,´0d to print an integer in decimal radix in five columns with leading zeros, or ~5,´*d to get leading asterisks.

In place of a prefix parameter to a directive, you can put the letter V (or v), which takes an argument from *arguments* for use as a parameter to the directive. Normally this should be an integer or character object, as appropriate. This feature allows variable-width fields and the like. If the argument used by a V parameter is nil, the effect is as if the parameter had been omitted. You may also use the character # in place of a parameter; it represents the number of arguments remaining to be processed.

It is an error to give a format directive more parameters than it is described here as accepting. It is also an error to give colon or at-sign modifiers to a directive in a combination not specifically described here as being meaningful.

X3J13 voted in January 1989 ⟨85⟩ to clarify the interaction between `format` and the various printer control variables (those named `*print-xxx*`). This is important because many `format` operations are defined, directly or indirectly, in terms of `prin1` or `princ`, which are affected by the printer control variables. The general rule is that `format` does not bind any of the standard printer control variables except as specified in the individual descriptions of directives. An implementation may not bind any standard printer control variable not specified in the description of a `format` directive, nor may an implementation fail to bind any standard printer control variables that is specified to be bound by such a description. (See these descriptions for specific changes voted by X3J13.)

One consequence of this change is that the user is guaranteed to be able to use the `format` ~A and ~S directives to do pretty printing, under control of the `*print-pretty*` variable. Implementations have differed on this point in their interpretations of the first edition. The new ~W directive may be more appropriate than either ~A and ~S for some purposes, whether for pretty printing or ordinary printing. See section 27.4 for a discussion of ~W and other new `format` directives related to pretty printing.

Here are some relatively simple examples to give you the general flavor of how `format` is used.

```
(format nil "foo") ⇒ "foo"

(setq x 5)

(format nil "The answer is ~D." x) ⇒ "The answer is 5."

(format nil "The answer is ~3D." x) ⇒ "The answer is   5."

(format nil "The answer is ~3,'0D." x) ⇒ "The answer is 005."

(format nil "The answer is ~:D." (expt 47 x))
                              ⇒ "The answer is 229,345,007."

(setq y "elephant")

(format nil "Look at the ~A!" y) ⇒ "Look at the elephant!"

(format nil "Type ~:C to ~A."
        (set-char-bit #\D :control t)
        "delete all your files")
    ⇒ "Type Control-D to delete all your files."
```

```
(setq n 3)

(format nil "~D item~:P found." n) ⇒ "3 items found."

(format nil "~R dog~:[s are~; is~] here." n (= n 1))
    ⇒ "three dogs are here."

(format nil "~R dog~:*~[s are~; is~:;s are~] here." n)
    ⇒ "three dogs are here."

(format nil "Here ~[are~;is~:;are~] ~:*~R pupp~:@P." n)
    ⇒ "Here are three puppies."
```

In the descriptions of the directives that follow, the term *arg* in general refers to the next item of the set of *arguments* to be processed. The word or phrase at the beginning of each description is a mnemonic (not necessarily an accurate one) for the directive.

~A

Ascii. An *arg*, any Lisp object, is printed without escape characters (as by princ). In particular, if *arg* is a string, its characters will be output verbatim. If *arg* is nil, it will be printed as nil; the colon modifier (~:A) will cause an *arg* of nil to be printed as (), but if *arg* is a composite structure, such as a list or vector, any contained occurrences of nil will still be printed as nil.

*~mincol*A inserts spaces on the right, if necessary, to make the width at least *mincol* columns. The @ modifier causes the spaces to be inserted on the left rather than the right.

*~mincol,colinc,minpad,padchar*A is the full form of ~A, which allows elaborate control of the padding. The string is padded on the right (or on the left if the @ modifier is used) with at least *minpad* copies of *padchar*; padding characters are then inserted *colinc* characters at a time until the total width is at least *mincol*. The defaults are 0 for *mincol* and *minpad*, 1 for *colinc*, and the space character for *padchar*.

X3J13 voted in January 1989 ⟨85⟩ to specify that format binds *print-escape* to nil during the processing of the ~A directive.

~S

S-expression. This is just like ~A, but *arg* is printed *with* escape characters (as by prin1 rather than princ). The output is therefore suitable for input to read. ~S accepts all the arguments and modifiers that ~A does.

X3J13 voted in January 1989 ⟨85⟩ to specify that format binds *print-escape* to t during the processing of the ~S directive.

~D

Decimal. An *arg*, which should be an integer, is printed in decimal radix. ~D will never put a decimal point after the number.

    *~mincol*D uses a column width of *mincol*; spaces are inserted on the left if the number requires fewer than *mincol* columns for its digits and sign. If the number doesn't fit in *mincol* columns, additional columns are used as needed.

    *~mincol,padchar*D uses *padchar* as the pad character instead of space.

    If *arg* is not an integer, it is printed in ~A format and decimal base.

    X3J13 voted in January 1989 ⟨85⟩ to specify that format binds *print-escape* to nil, *print-radix* to nil, and *print-base* to 10 during processing of ~D.

    The @ modifier causes the number's sign to be printed always; the default is to print it only if the number is negative. The : modifier causes commas to be printed between groups of three digits; the third prefix parameter may be used to change the character used as the comma. Thus the most general form of ~D is *~mincol,padchar,commachar*D.

    X3J13 voted in March 1988 ⟨82⟩ to add a fourth parameter, the *commainterval*. This must be an integer; if it is not provided, it defaults to 3. This parameter controls the number of digits in each group separated by the *commachar*.

    By extension, each of the ~B, ~O, and ~X directives accepts a *commainterval* as a fourth parameter, and the ~R directive accepts a *commainterval* as its fifth parameter. Examples:

```
(format nil "~,,´ ,4B" #xFACE) ⇒ "1111 1010 1100 1110"
(format nil "~,,´ ,4B" #x1CE) ⇒ "1 1100 1110"
(format nil "~19,,´ ,4B" #xFACE) ⇒ "1111 1010 1100 1110"
(format nil "~19,,´ ,4B" #x1CE) ⇒ "0000 0001 1100 1110"
```

This is one of those little improvements that probably don't matter much but aren't hard to implement either. It was pretty silly having the number 3 wired into the definition of comma separation when it is just as easy to make it a parameter.

~B

Binary. This is just like ~D but prints in binary radix (radix 2) instead of decimal. The full form is therefore *~mincol,padchar,commachar*B.

    X3J13 voted in January 1989 ⟨85⟩ to specify that format binds *print-escape* to nil, *print-radix* to nil, and *print-base* to 2 during processing of ~B.

~O

Octal. This is just like ~D but prints in octal radix (radix 8) instead of decimal. The full form is therefore *~mincol,padchar,commachar*O.

X3J13 voted in January 1989 ⟨85⟩ to specify that format binds *print-escape* to nil, *print-radix* to nil, and *print-base* to 8 during processing of ~O.

~X

Hexadecimal. This is just like ~D but prints in hexadecimal radix (radix 16) instead of decimal. The full form is therefore ~*mincol,padchar,commachar*X.

X3J13 voted in January 1989 ⟨85⟩ to specify that format binds *print-escape* to nil, *print-radix* to nil, and *print-base* to 16 during processing of ~X.

Compatibility note: In MacLisp and Lisp Machine Lisp the ~X directive outputs a space, and ~*n*X outputs *n* spaces, in a manner analogous to Fortran X format. In Common Lisp the directive ~@T is used for that purpose.

~R

Radix. ~*n*R prints *arg* in radix *n*. The modifier flags and any remaining parameters are used as for the ~D directive. Indeed, ~D is the same as ~10R. The full form here is therefore ~*radix,mincol,padchar,commachar*R.

X3J13 voted in January 1989 ⟨85⟩ to specify that format binds *print-escape* to nil, *print-radix* to nil, and *print-base* to the value of the first parameter during the processing of the ~R directive with a parameter.

If no parameters are given to ~R, then an entirely different interpretation is given.

Notice of correction. In the first edition, this sentence referred to "arguments" given to ~R. The correct term is "parameters."

The argument should be an integer; suppose it is 4. Then ~R prints *arg* as a cardinal English number: four; ~:R prints *arg* as an ordinal English number: fourth; ~@R prints *arg* as a Roman numeral: IV; and ~:@R prints *arg* as an old Roman numeral: IIII.

X3J13 voted in January 1989 ⟨85⟩ to specify that format binds *print-base* to 10 during the processing of the ~R directive with no parameter.

The first edition did not specify how ~R and its variants should handle arguments that are very large or not positive. Actual practice varies, and X3J13 has not yet addressed the topic. Here is a sampling of current practice.

For ~@R and ~:@R, nearly all implementations produce Roman numerals only for integers in the range 1 to 3999, inclusive. Some implementations will produce old-style Roman numerals for integers in the range 1 to 4999, inclusive. All other integers are printed in decimal notation, as if ~D had been used.

For zero, most implementations print zero for ~R and zeroth for ~:R.

For ~R with a negative argument, most implementations simply print the word minus followed by its absolute value as a cardinal in English.

For ~:R with a negative argument, some implementations also print the word minus followed by its absolute value as an ordinal in English; other implementations print the absolute value followed by the word previous. Thus the argument -4 might produce minus fourth or fourth previous. Each has its charm, but one is not always a suitable substitute for the other; users should be careful.

There is standard English nomenclature for fairly large integers (up to 10^{60}, at least), based on appending the suffix -illion to Latin names of integers. Thus we have the names *trillion, quadrillion, sextillion, septillion*, and so on. For extremely large integers, one may express powers of ten in English. One implementation gives 1606938044258990275541962092341162602522202993782792835301376 (which is 2^{200}, the result of (ash 1 200)) in this manner:

```
one times ten to the sixtieth power six hundred six times ten to the
fifty-seventh power nine hundred thirty-eight septdecillion forty-four
sexdecillion two hundred fifty-eight quindecillion nine hundred ninety
quattuordecillion two hundred seventy-five tredecillion five hundred
forty-one duodecillion nine hundred sixty-two undecillion ninety-two
decillion three hundred forty-one nonillion one hundred sixty-two
octillion six hundred two septillion five hundred twenty-two sextillion
two hundred two quintillion nine hundred ninety-three quadrillion seven
hundred eighty-two trillion seven hundred ninety-two billion eight hundred
thirty-five million three hundred one thousand three hundred seventy-six
```

Another implementation prints it this way (note the use of plus):

```
one times ten to the sixtieth power plus six hundred six times ten to the
fifty-seventh power plus ... plus two hundred seventy-five times ten to
the forty-second power plus five hundred forty-one duodecillion nine
hundred sixty-two undecillion ... three hundred seventy-six
```

(I have elided some of the text here to save space.)

Unfortunately, the meaning of this nomenclature differs between American English (in which k-illion means $10^{3(k+1)}$, so one trillion is 10^{12}) and British English (in which k-illion means 10^{6k}, so one trillion is 10^{18}). To avoid both confusion and prolixity, I recommend using decimal notation for all numbers above 999,999,999; this is similar to the escape hatch used for Roman numerals.

~P

Plural. If *arg* is not eql to the integer 1, a lowercase s is printed; if *arg* is eql to 1, nothing is printed. (Notice that if *arg* is a floating-point 1.0, the s *is* printed.) ~:P does the same thing, after doing a ~:* to back up one argument; that is, it prints a lowercase s if the *last* argument was not 1. This is useful after printing a number using ~D. ~@P prints y if the argument is 1, or ies if it is not. ~:@P does the same thing, but backs up first.

```
(format nil "~D tr~:@P/~D win~:P" 7 1) ⇒ "7 tries/1 win"
(format nil "~D tr~:@P/~D win~:P" 1 0) ⇒ "1 try/0 wins"
(format nil "~D tr~:@P/~D win~:P" 1 3) ⇒ "1 try/3 wins"
```

~C

Character. The next *arg* should be a character; it is printed according to the modifier flags.

~C prints the character in an implementation-dependent abbreviated format. This format should be culturally compatible with the host environment.

X3J13 voted in June 1987 ⟨84⟩ to specify that ~C performs exactly the same action as write-char if the character to be printed has zero for its bits attributes. X3J13 voted in March 1989 ⟨11⟩ to eliminate the bits and font attributes, replacing them with the notion of implementation-defined attributes. The net effect is that characters whose implementation-defined attributes all have the "standard" values should be printed by ~C in the same way that write-char would print them.

~:C spells out the names of the control bits and represents non-printing characters by their names: Control-Meta-F, Control-Return, Space. This is a "pretty" format for printing characters.

~:@C prints what ~:C would, and then if the character requires unusual shift keys on the keyboard to type it, this fact is mentioned: Control-∂ (Top-F). This is the format for telling the user about a key he or she is expected to type, in prompts, for instance. The precise output may depend not only on the implementation but on the particular I/O devices in use.

~@C prints the character so that the Lisp reader can read it, using #\ syntax.

X3J13 voted in January 1989 ⟨85⟩ to specify that format binds *print-escape* to t during the processing of the ~@C directive. Other variants of the ~C directive do not bind any printer control variables.

Rationale: In some implementations the ~S directive would do what ~C does, but ~C is compatible with Lisp dialects such as MacLisp that do not have a character data type.

~F

Fixed-format floating-point. The next *arg* is printed as a floating-point number.

The full form is ~*w*,*d*,*k*,*overflowchar*,*padchar*F. The parameter *w* is the width of the field to be printed; *d* is the number of digits to print after the decimal point; *k* is a scale factor that defaults to zero.

Exactly *w* characters will be output. First, leading copies of the character *padchar* (which defaults to a space) are printed, if necessary, to pad the field on the left. If the *arg* is negative, then a minus sign is printed; if the *arg* is not negative, then a plus sign is printed if and only if the @ modifier was specified. Then a sequence of digits, containing a single embedded decimal point, is printed; this represents the magnitude of the value of *arg* times 10^k, rounded to *d* fractional digits. (When rounding up and rounding down would produce printed values equidistant from the scaled value of *arg*, then the implementation is free to use either one. For example, printing the argument 6.375 using the format ~4,2F may correctly produce either 6.37 or 6.38.) Leading zeros are not permitted, except that a single zero digit is output before the decimal point if the printed value is less than 1, and this single zero digit is not output after all if $w = d + 1$.

If it is impossible to print the value in the required format in a field of width *w*, then one of two actions is taken. If the parameter *overflowchar* is specified, then *w* copies of that parameter are printed instead of the scaled value of *arg*. If the *overflowchar* parameter is omitted, then the scaled value is printed using more than *w* characters, as many more as may be needed.

If the *w* parameter is omitted, then the field is of variable width. In effect, a value is chosen for *w* in such a way that no leading pad characters need to be printed and exactly *d* characters will follow the decimal point. For example, the directive ~,2F will print exactly two digits after the decimal point and as many as necessary before the decimal point.

If the parameter *d* is omitted, then there is no constraint on the number of digits to appear after the decimal point. A value is chosen for *d* in such a way that as many digits as possible may be printed subject to the width constraint imposed by the parameter *w* and the constraint that no trailing zero digits may appear in the fraction, except that if the fraction to be printed is zero, then a single zero digit should appear after the decimal point if permitted by the width constraint.

If both *w* and *d* are omitted, then the effect is to print the value using ordinary free-format output; `prin1` uses this format for any number whose magnitude is either zero or between 10^{-3} (inclusive) and 10^7 (exclusive).

If *w* is omitted, then if the magnitude of *arg* is so large (or, if *d* is also omitted, so small) that more than 100 digits would have to be printed, then an implementation is free, at its discretion, to print the number using exponential notation instead, as if by the directive ~E (with all parameters to ~E defaulted, not taking their values from the ~F directive).

If *arg* is a rational number, then it is coerced to be a `single-float` and then printed. (Alternatively, an implementation is permitted to process a rational number by any other method that has essentially the same behavior but avoids such hazards as loss of precision or overflow because of the coercion. However, note that if *w* and *d* are unspecified and the number has no exact decimal representation, for example 1/3, some precision cutoff must be chosen by the implementation: only a finite number of digits may be printed.)

If *arg* is a complex number or some non-numeric object, then it is printed using the format directive ~*w*D, thereby printing it in decimal radix and a minimum field width of *w*. (If it is desired to print each of the real part and imaginary part of a complex number using a ~F directive, then this must be done explicitly with two ~F directives and code to extract the two parts of the complex number.)

X3J13 voted in January 1989 ⟨85⟩ to specify that format binds *print-escape* to nil during the processing of the ~F directive.

```
(defun foo (x)
    (format nil "~6,2F|~6,2,1,´*F|~6,2,,´?F|~6F|~,2F|~F"
            x x x x x x))
(foo 3.14159)   ⇒ "  3.14| 31.42|   3.14|3.1416|3.14|3.14159"
(foo -3.14159)  ⇒ " -3.14|-31.42|  -3.14|-3.142|-3.14|-3.14159"
(foo 100.0)     ⇒ "100.00|******|100.00| 100.0|100.00|100.0"
(foo 1234.0)    ⇒ "1234.00|******|??????|1234.0|1234.00|1234.0"
(foo 0.006)     ⇒ "  0.01|  0.06|  0.01| 0.006|0.01|0.006"
```

Compatibility note: The ~F directive is similar to the F*w*.*d* edit descriptor in Fortran.

The presence or absence of the @ modifier corresponds to the effect of the Fortran SS or SP edit descriptor; nothing in Common Lisp corresponds to the Fortran S edit descriptor.

The scale factor specified by the parameter *k* corresponds to the scale factor *k* specified by the Fortran *k*P edit descriptor.

In Fortran, the leading zero that precedes the decimal point when the printed value is less than 1 is optional; in Common Lisp, the implementation is required to print that zero digit.

In Common Lisp, the *w* and *d* parameters are optional; in Fortran, they are required.

In Common Lisp, the pad character and overflow character are user-specifiable; in Fortran, they are always space and asterisk, respectively.

A Fortran implementation is prohibited from printing a representation of negative zero; Common Lisp permits the printing of such a representation when appropriate.

In MacLisp and Lisp Machine Lisp, the ~F format directive takes a single parameter: the number of digits to use in the printed representation. This incompatibility between Common Lisp and MacLisp was introduced for the sake of cultural compatibility with Fortran.

~E

Exponential floating-point. The next *arg* is printed in exponential notation.

The full form is ~*w*,*d*,*e*,*k*,*overflowchar*,*padchar*,*exponentchar*E. The parameter *w* is the width of the field to be printed; *d* is the number of digits to print after the decimal point; e is the number of digits to use when printing the exponent; k is a scale factor that defaults to 1 (not zero).

Exactly w characters will be output. First, leading copies of the character *padchar* (which defaults to a space) are printed, if necessary, to pad the field on the left. If the *arg* is negative, then a minus sign is printed; if the *arg* is not negative, then a plus sign is printed if and only if the @ modifier was specified. Then a sequence of digits, containing a single embedded decimal point, is printed. The form of this sequence of digits depends on the scale factor k. If k is zero, then d digits are printed after the decimal point, and a single zero digit appears before the decimal point if the total field width will permit it. If k is positive, then it must be strictly less than $d+2$; k significant digits are printed before the decimal point, and $d-k+1$ digits are printed after the decimal point. If k is negative, then it must be strictly greater than $-d$; a single zero digit appears before the decimal point if the total field width will permit it, and after the decimal point are printed first $-k$ zeros and then $d + k$ significant digits. The printed fraction must be properly rounded. (When rounding up and rounding down would produce printed values equidistant from the scaled value of *arg*, then the implementation is free to use either one. For example, printing 637.5 using the format ~8.2E may correctly produce either 6.37E+02 or 6.38E+02.)

Following the digit sequence, the exponent is printed. First the character parameter *exponentchar* is printed; if this parameter is omitted, then the exponent marker that `prin1` would use is printed, as determined from the type of the floating-point number and the current value of `*read-default-float-format*`. Next, either a plus sign or a minus sign is printed, followed by e digits representing the power of 10 by which the printed fraction must be multiplied to properly represent the rounded value of *arg*.

If it is impossible to print the value in the required format in a field of width w, possibly because k is too large or too small or because the exponent cannot be printed in e character positions, then one of two actions is taken. If the parameter *overflowchar* is specified, then w copies of that parameter are printed instead of the scaled value of *arg*. If the *overflowchar* parameter is omitted, then the scaled value is printed using more than w characters, as many more as may be needed; if the problem is that d is too small for the specified k or that e is too small, then a larger value is used for d or e as may be needed.

If the w parameter is omitted, then the field is of variable width. In effect a value is chosen for w in such a way that no leading pad characters need to be printed.

If the parameter d is omitted, then there is no constraint on the number of digits to appear. A value is chosen for d in such a way that as many digits as possible may be printed subject to the width constraint imposed by the parameter w, the constraint of the scale factor k, and the constraint that no trailing zero digits may appear in the fraction, except that if the fraction to be printed is zero, then a single zero digit should appear after the decimal point if the width constraint allows it.

If the parameter e is omitted, then the exponent is printed using the smallest number of digits necessary to represent its value.

If all of w, d, and e are omitted, then the effect is to print the value using ordinary free-format exponential-notation output; prin1 uses this format for any non-zero number whose magnitude is less than 10^{-3} or greater than or equal to 10^7.

X3J13 voted in January 1989 ⟨83⟩ to amend the previous paragraph as follows:

If all of w, d, and e are omitted, then the effect is to print the value using ordinary free-format exponential-notation output; prin1 uses a similar format for any non-zero number whose magnitude is less than 10^{-3} or greater than or equal to 10^7. The only difference is that the ~E directive always prints a plus or minus sign before the exponent, while prin1 omits the plus sign if the exponent is non-negative.

(The amendment reconciles this paragraph with the specification several paragraphs above that ~E always prints a plus or minus sign before the exponent.)

If arg is a rational number, then it is coerced to be a single-float and then printed. (Alternatively, an implementation is permitted to process a rational number by any other method that has essentially the same behavior but avoids such hazards as loss of precision or overflow because of the coercion. However, note that if w and d are unspecified and the number has no exact decimal representation, for example 1/3, some precision cutoff must be chosen by the implementation: only a finite number of digits may be printed.)

If arg is a complex number or some non-numeric object, then it is printed using the format directive ~wD, thereby printing it in decimal radix and a minimum field width of w. (If it is desired to print each of the real part and imaginary part of a complex number using a ~E directive, then this must be done explicitly with two ~E directives and code to extract the two parts of the complex number.)

X3J13 voted in January 1989 ⟨85⟩ to specify that format binds *print-escape* to nil during the processing of the ~E directive.

```
(defun foo (x)
  (format nil
          "~9,2,1,,'*E|~10,3,2,2,'?,,'$E|~9,3,2,-2,'%@E|~9,2E"
          x x x x))
(foo 3.14159)   ⇒ "  3.14E+0| 31.42$-01|+.003E+03|  3.14E+0"
(foo -3.14159)  ⇒ " -3.14E+0|-31.42$-01|-.003E+03| -3.14E+0"
(foo 1100.0)    ⇒ "  1.10E+3| 11.00$+02|+.001E+06|  1.10E+3"
(foo 1100.0L0)  ⇒ "  1.10L+3| 11.00$+02|+.001L+06|  1.10L+3"
(foo 1.1E13)    ⇒ "*********| 11.00$+12|+.001E+16| 1.10E+13"
(foo 1.1L120)   ⇒ "*********|??????????|%%%%%%%%|1.10L+120"
```

```
(foo 1.1L1200) ⇒ "*********|??????????|%%%%%%%%|1.10L+1200"
```

Here is an example of the effects of varying the scale factor:

```
(dotimes (k 13)
  (format t " %Scale factor  2D: | 13,6,2,VE|"
          (- k 5) 3.14159))                              ;Prints 13 lines
Scale factor -5: | 0.000003E+06|
Scale factor -4: | 0.000031E+05|
Scale factor -3: | 0.000314E+04|
Scale factor -2: | 0.003142E+03|
Scale factor -1: | 0.031416E+02|
Scale factor  0: | 0.314159E+01|
Scale factor  1: | 3.141590E+00|
Scale factor  2: | 31.41590E-01|
Scale factor  3: | 314.1590E-02|
Scale factor  4: | 3141.590E-03|
Scale factor  5: | 31415.90E-04|
Scale factor  6: | 314159.0E-05|
Scale factor  7: | 3141590.E-06|
```

Compatibility note: The ~E directive is similar to the E$w.d$ and E$w.dEe$ edit descriptors in Fortran.

The presence or absence of the @ modifier corresponds to the effect of the Fortran SS or SP edit descriptor; nothing in Common Lisp corresponds to the Fortran S edit descriptor.

The scale factor specified by the parameter k corresponds to the scale factor k specified by the Fortran kP edit descriptor; note, however, that the default value for k is 1 in Common Lisp, as opposed to the default value of zero in Fortran. (On the other hand, note that a scale factor of 1 is used for Fortran list-directed output, which is roughly equivalent to using ~E with the w, d, e, and *overflowchar* parameters omitted.)

In Common Lisp, the w and d parameters are optional; in Fortran, they are required.

In Fortran, omitting e causes the exponent to be printed using either two or three digits; if three digits are required, then the exponent marker is omitted. In Common Lisp, omitting e causes the exponent to be printed using as few digits as possible; the exponent marker is never omitted.

In Common Lisp, the pad character and overflow character are user-specifiable; in Fortran they are always space and asterisk, respectively.

A Fortran implementation is prohibited from printing a representation of negative zero; Common Lisp permits the printing of such a representation when appropriate.

In MacLisp and Lisp Machine Lisp, the ~E format directive takes a single parameter: the number of digits to use in the printed representation. This incompatibility between Common Lisp and MacLisp was introduced for the sake of cultural compatibility with Fortran.

~G

General floating-point. The next *arg* is printed as a floating-point number in either fixed-format or exponential notation as appropriate.

The full form is ~*w*,*d*,*e*,*k*,*overflowchar*,*padchar*,*exponentchar*G. The format in which to print *arg* depends on the magnitude (absolute value) of the *arg*. Let *n* be an integer such that $10^{n-1} \le arg < 10^n$. (If *arg* is zero, let *n* be 0.) Let *ee* equal *e* + 2, or 4 if *e* is omitted. Let *ww* equal *w* − *ee*, or nil if *w* is omitted. If *d* is omitted, first let *q* be the number of digits needed to print *arg* with no loss of information and without leading or trailing zeros; then let *d* equal (max *q* (min *n* 7)). Let *dd* equal *d* − *n*.

If $0 \le dd \le d$, then *arg* is printed as if by the format directives

~*ww*,*dd*,,*overflowchar*,*padchar*F~*ee*@T

Note that the scale factor *k* is not passed to the ~F directive. For all other values of *dd*, *arg* is printed as if by the format directive

~*w*,*d*,*e*,*k*,*overflowchar*,*padchar*,*exponentchar*E

In either case, an @ modifier is specified to the ~F or ~E directive if and only if one was specified to the ~G directive.

X3J13 voted in January 1989 ⟨85⟩ to specify that format binds *print-escape* to nil during the processing of the ~G directive.

Examples:

```
(defun foo (x)
  (format nil
          "~9,2,1,,'*G|~9,3,2,3,'?,,'$G|~9,3,2,0,'%G|~9,2G"
          x x x))
```

```
(foo 0.0314159) ⇒ "   3.14E-2|314.2$-04|0.314E-01|   3.14E-2"
(foo 0.314159)  ⇒ "  0.31    |0.314    |0.314    | 0.31     "
(foo 3.14159)   ⇒ "   3.1    | 3.14    | 3.14    | 3.1      "
(foo 31.4159)   ⇒ "   31.    | 31.4    | 31.4    | 31.      "
(foo 314.159)   ⇒ " 3.14E+2| 314.    | 314.    |   3.14E+2"
(foo 3141.59)   ⇒ " 3.14E+3|314.2$+01.|0.314E+04|   3.14E+3"
(foo 3141.59L0) ⇒ " 3.14L+3|314.2$+01|0.314L+04|   3.14L+3"
(foo 3.14E12)   ⇒ "*********|314.0$+10|0.314E+13|   3.14E+12"
(foo 3.14L120)  ⇒ "*********|?????????|%%%%%%%%|3.14L+120"
(foo 3.14L1200) ⇒ "*********|?????????|%%%%%%%%|3.14L+1200"
```

Notice of correction. In the first edition, the example for the value 3.14E12 contained two typographical errors:

```
(foo 3.14E12)   ⇒  "*********|314.2$+10|0.314E+13| 3.14L+12"
                            ↑                        ↑
                       should be 0             should be E
```

These have been corrected above.

Compatibility note: The ˜G directive is similar to the G*w.d* edit descriptor in Fortran.

The Common Lisp rules for deciding between the use of ˜F and ˜E are compatible with the rules used by Fortran but have been extended to cover the cases where *w* or *d* is omitted or where *e* is specified.

In MacLisp and Lisp Machine Lisp, the ˜G format directive is equivalent to the Common Lisp ˜@* directive. This incompatibility between Common Lisp and MacLisp was introduced for the sake of cultural compatibility with Fortran.

˜$

Dollars floating-point. The next *arg* is printed as a floating-point number in fixed-format notation. This format is particularly convenient for printing a value as dollars and cents.

The full form is ˜*d,n,w,padchar*$. The parameter *d* is the number of digits to print after the decimal point (default value 2); *n* is the minimum number of digits to print before the decimal point (default value 1); *w* is the minimum total width of the field to be printed (default value 0).

First padding and the sign are output. If the *arg* is negative, then a minus sign is printed; if the *arg* is not negative, then a plus sign is printed if and only if the @ modifier was specified. If the : modifier is used, the sign appears before any padding, and otherwise after the padding. If *w* is specified and the number of other characters to be output is less than *w*, then copies of *padchar* (which defaults to a space) are output to make the total field width equal *w*. Then *n* digits are printed for the integer part of *arg*, with leading zeros if necessary; then a decimal point; then *d* digits of fraction, properly rounded.

If the magnitude of *arg* is so large that more than *m* digits would have to be printed, where *m* is the larger of *w* and 100, then an implementation is free, at its discretion, to print the number using exponential notation instead, as if by the directive ˜*w,q,,,,padchar*E, where *w* and *padchar* are present or omitted according to whether they were present or omitted in the ˜$ directive, and where $q = d + n - 1$, where *d* and *n* are the (possibly default) values given to the ˜$ directive.

If *arg* is a rational number, then it is coerced to be a single-float and then printed. (Alternatively, an implementation is permitted to process a rational number by any other method that has essentially the same behavior but avoids such hazards as loss of precision or overflow because of the coercion.)

If *arg* is a complex number or some non-numeric object, then it is printed using the format directive ~wD, thereby printing it in decimal radix and a minimum field width of *w*. (If it is desired to print each of the real part and imaginary part of a complex number using a ~$ directive, then this must be done explicitly with two ~$ directives and code to extract the two parts of the complex number.)

X3J13 voted in January 1989 ⟨85⟩ to specify that format binds *print-escape* to nil during the processing of the ~$ directive.

~%

This outputs a #\Newline character, thereby terminating the current output line and beginning a new one (see terpri).

~*n*% outputs *n* newlines.

No *arg* is used. Simply putting a newline in the control string would work, but ~% is often used because it makes the control string look nicer in the middle of a Lisp program.

~&

Unless it can be determined that the output stream is already at the beginning of a line, this outputs a newline (see fresh-line).

~*n*& calls fresh-line and then outputs *n* − 1 newlines. ~0& does nothing.

~|

This outputs a page separator character, if possible. ~*n*| does this *n* times. | is vertical bar, not capital I.

~~

Tilde. This outputs a tilde. ~*n*~ outputs *n* tildes.

~⟨newline⟩

Tilde immediately followed by a newline ignores the newline and any following non-newline whitespace characters. With a :, the newline is ignored, but any following whitespace is left in place. With an @, the newline is left in place, but any following whitespace is ignored. This directive is typically used when a format control string is too long to fit nicely into one line of the program:

```
(defun type-clash-error (fn nargs argnum right-type wrong-type)
  (format *error-output*
          "~&Function ~S requires its ~:[~:R~;~*~] ~
           argument to be of type ~S,~%but it was called ~
           with an argument of type ~S.~%"
          fn (eql nargs 1) argnum right-type wrong-type))
```

(type-clash-error 'aref nil 2 'integer 'vector) prints:
```
Function AREF requires its second argument to be of type INTEGER,
but it was called with an argument of type VECTOR.
```

(type-clash-error 'car 1 1 'list 'short-float) prints:
```
Function CAR requires its argument to be of type LIST,
but it was called with an argument of type SHORT-FLOAT.
```

Note that in this example newlines appear in the output only as specified by the ~&
and ~% directives; the actual newline characters in the control string are suppressed
because each is preceded by a tilde.

~T

Tabulate. This spaces over to a given column. *~colnum,colinc*T will output sufficient spaces to move the cursor to column *colnum*. If the cursor is already at or
beyond column *colnum*, it will output spaces to move it to column *colnum+k*colinc*
for the smallest positive integer *k* possible, unless *colinc* is zero, in which case no
spaces are output if the cursor is already at or beyond column *colnum*. *colnum* and
colinc default to 1.

Ideally, the current column position is determined by examination of the destination, whether a stream or string. (Although no user-level operation for determining
the column position of a stream is defined by Common Lisp, such a facility may
exist at the implementation level.) If for some reason the current absolute column
position cannot be determined by direct inquiry, format may be able to deduce the
current column position by noting that certain directives (such as ~%, or ~&, or ~A
with the argument being a string containing a newline) cause the column position
to be reset to zero, and counting the number of characters emitted since that point.
If that fails, format may attempt a similar deduction on the riskier assumption
that the destination was at column zero when format was invoked. If even this
heuristic fails or is implementationally inconvenient, at worst the ~T operation will
simply output two spaces. (All this implies that code that uses format is more
likely to be portable if all format control strings that use the ~T directive either
begin with ~% or ~& to force a newline or are designed to be used only when the

destination is known from other considerations to be at column zero.)

~@T performs *relative* tabulation. ~*colrel*,*colinc*@T outputs *colrel* spaces and then outputs the smallest non-negative number of additional spaces necessary to move the cursor to a column that is a multiple of *colinc*. For example, the directive ~3,8@T outputs three spaces and then moves the cursor to a "standard multiple-of-eight tab stop" if not at one already. If the current output column cannot be determined, however, then *colinc* is ignored, and exactly *colrel* spaces are output.

X3J13 voted in June 1989 ⟨139⟩ to define ~:T and ~:@T to perform tabulation relative to a point defined by the pretty printing process (see section 27.4).

~*

The next *arg* is ignored. ~*n** ignores the next *n* arguments.

~:* "ignores backwards"; that is, it backs up in the list of arguments so that the argument last processed will be processed again. ~*n*:* backs up *n* arguments.

When within a ~{ construct (see below), the ignoring (in either direction) is relative to the list of arguments being processed by the iteration.

~*n*@* is an "absolute goto" rather than a "relative goto": it goes to the *n*th *arg*, where 0 means the first one; *n* defaults to 0, so ~@* goes back to the first *arg*. Directives after a ~*n*@* will take arguments in sequence beginning with the one gone to. When within a ~{ construct, the "goto" is relative to the list of arguments being processed by the iteration.

~?

Indirection. The next *arg* must be a string, and the one after it a list; both are consumed by the ~? directive. The string is processed as a format control string, with the elements of the list as the arguments. Once the recursive processing of the control string has been finished, then processing of the control string containing the ~? directive is resumed. Example:

```
(format nil "~? ~D" "<~A ~D>" '("Foo" 5) 7) ⇒ "<Foo 5> 7"
(format nil "~? ~D" "<~A ~D>" '("Foo" 5 14) 7) ⇒ "<Foo 5> 7"
```

Note that in the second example three arguments are supplied to the control string "<~A ~D>", but only two are processed and the third is therefore ignored.

With the @ modifier, only one *arg* is directly consumed. The *arg* must be a string; it is processed as part of the control string as if it had appeared in place of the ~@? construct, and any directives in the recursively processed control string may consume arguments of the control string containing the ~@? directive. Example:

```
(format nil "~@? ~D" "<~A ~D>" "Foo" 5 7) ⇒ "<Foo 5> 7"
```

```
(format nil "~~@? ~D" "<~A ~D>" "Foo" 5 14 7) ⇒ "<Foo 5> 14"
```

Here is a rather sophisticated example. The format function itself, as implemented at one time in Lisp Machine Lisp, used a routine internal to the format package called format-error to signal error messages; format-error in turn used error, which used format recursively. Now format-error took a string and arguments, just like format, but also printed the control string to format (which at this point was available in the global variable *ctl-string*) and a little arrow showing where in the processing of the control string the error occurred. The variable *ctl-index* pointed one character after the place of the error.

```
(defun format-error (string &rest args)       ;Example
   (error nil "~~?~%~V@T↓~%~3@T\"~~A\"~~%"
          string args (+ *ctl-index* 3) *ctl-string*))
```

(The character set used in the Lisp Machine Lisp implementation contains a down-arrow character ↓, which is not a standard Common Lisp character.) This first processed the given string and arguments using ~?, then output a newline, tabbed a variable amount for printing the down-arrow, and printed the control string between double quotes (note the use of \" to include double quotes within the control string). The effect was something like this:

```
(format t "The item is a ~[Foo~;Bar~;Loser~]." 'quux)
>>ERROR: The argument to the FORMAT "~[" command
         must be a number.
                      ↓
   "The item is a ~[Foo~;Bar~;Loser~]."
```

Implementation note: Implementors may wish to report errors occurring within format control strings in the manner outlined here. It looks pretty flashy when done properly.

X3J13 voted in June 1989 ⟨139⟩ to introduce certain format directives to support the user interface to the pretty printer described in detail in chapter 27.

~
_

Conditional newline. Without any modifiers, the directive ~_ is equivalent to (pprint-newline :linear). The directive ~@_ is equivalent to (pprint-newline :miser). The directive ~:_ is equivalent to (pprint-newline :fill). The directive ~:@_ is equivalent to (pprint-newline :mandatory).

~W

Write. An *arg*, any Lisp object, is printed obeying *every* printer control variable (as by `write`). See section 27.4 for details.

~I

Indent. The directive `~nI` is equivalent to `(pprint-indent :block n)`. The directive `~:nI` is equivalent to `(pprint-indent :current n)`. In both cases, *n* defaults to zero, if it is omitted.

The format directives after this point are much more complicated than the foregoing; they constitute control structures that can perform case conversion, conditional selection, iteration, justification, and non-local exits. Used with restraint, they can perform powerful tasks. Used with abandon, they can produce completely unreadable and unmaintainable code.

The case-conversion, conditional, iteration, and justification constructs can contain other formatting constructs by bracketing them. These constructs must nest properly with respect to each other. For example, it is not legitimate to put the start of a case-conversion construct in each arm of a conditional and the end of the case-conversion construct outside the conditional:

```
(format nil "~:[abc~:@(def~;ghi~:@(jkl~]mno~)" x)      ;Illegal!
```

One might expect this to produce either `"abcDEFMNO"` or `"ghiJKLMNO"`, depending on whether x is false or true; but in fact the construction is illegal because the `~[...~;...~]` and `~(...~)` constructs are not properly nested.

The processing indirection caused by the `~?` directive is also a kind of nesting for the purposes of this rule of proper nesting. It is not permitted to start a bracketing construct within a string processed under control of a `~?` directive and end the construct at some point after the `~?` construct in the string containing that construct, or vice versa. For example, this situation is illegal:

```
(format nil "~?ghi~)" "abc~@(def")      ;Illegal!
```

One might expect it to produce `"abcDEFGHI"`, but in fact the construction is illegal because the `~?` and `~(...~)` constructs are not properly nested.

~(*str*~)

Case conversion. The contained control string *str* is processed, and what it produces is subject to case conversion: `~(` converts every uppercase character to the corresponding lowercase character; `~:(` capitalizes all words, as if by `string-capitalize`; `~@(` capitalizes just the first word and forces the rest to

lowercase; ~:@(converts every lowercase character to the corresponding uppercase character. In this example, ~@(is used to cause the first word produced by
~@R to be capitalized:

```
(format nil "~@R ~(~@R~)" 14 14) ⇒ "XIV xiv"
(defun f (n) (format nil "~@(~R~) error~:P detected." n))
(f 0) ⇒ "Zero errors detected."
(f 1) ⇒ "One error detected."
(f 23) ⇒ "Twenty-three errors detected."
```

~[str0~;str1~;...~;strn~]

Conditional expression. This is a set of control strings, called *clauses*, one of
which is chosen and used. The clauses are separated by ~; and the construct is
terminated by ~]. For example,

```
"~[Siamese~;Manx~;Persian~] Cat"
```

The *arg*th clause is selected, where the first clause is number 0. If a prefix parameter
is given (as ~n[), then the parameter is used instead of an argument. (This is useful
only if the parameter is specified by #, to dispatch on the number of arguments
remaining to be processed.) If *arg* is out of range, then no clause is selected (and
no error is signaled). After the selected alternative has been processed, the control
string continues after the ~].

~[str0~;str1~;...~;strn~:;default~] has a default case. If the *last* ~; used to
separate clauses is ~:; instead, then the last clause is an "else" clause that is
performed if no other clause is selected. For example:

```
"~[Siamese~;Manx~;Persian~:;Alley~] Cat"
```

~:[false~;true~] selects the *false* control string if *arg* is nil, and selects the
true control string otherwise.

~@[true~] tests the argument. If it is not nil, then the argument is not used
up by the ~@[command but remains as the next one to be processed, and the
one clause *true* is processed. If the *arg* is nil, then the argument is used up, and
the clause is not processed. The clause therefore should normally use exactly one
argument, and may expect it to be non-nil. For example:

```
(setq *print-level* nil *print-length* 5)
(format nil "~@[ print level = ~D~]~@[ print length = ~D~]"
            *print-level* *print-length*)
   ⇒ " print length = 5"
```

The combination of ~[and # is useful, for example, for dealing with English conventions for printing lists:

```
(setq foo "Items:~#[ none~; ~S~; ~S and ~S~
            ~:;~@{~#[~; and~] ~S~^,~}~].")
(format nil foo)
        ⇒ "Items: none."
(format nil foo 'foo)
        ⇒ "Items: FOO."
(format nil foo 'foo 'bar)
        ⇒ "Items: FOO and BAR."
(format nil foo 'foo 'bar 'baz)
        ⇒ "Items: FOO, BAR, and BAZ."
(format nil foo 'foo 'bar 'baz 'quux)
        ⇒ "Items: FOO, BAR, BAZ, and QUUX."
```

~;

This separates clauses in ~[and ~< constructions. It is an error elsewhere.

~]

This terminates a ~[. It is an error elsewhere.

~{*str*~}

Iteration. This is an iteration construct. The argument should be a list, which is used as a set of arguments as if for a recursive call to format. The string *str* is used repeatedly as the control string. Each iteration can absorb as many elements of the list as it likes as arguments; if *str* uses up two arguments by itself, then two elements of the list will get used up each time around the loop. If before any iteration step the list is empty, then the iteration is terminated. Also, if a prefix parameter *n* is given, then there will be at most *n* repetitions of processing of *str*. Finally, the ~^ directive can be used to terminate the iteration prematurely.

Here are some simple examples:

```
(format nil
        "The winners are:~{ ~S~}."
        '(fred harry jill))
    ⇒ "The winners are: FRED HARRY JILL."

(format nil "Pairs:~{ <~S,~S>~}." '(a 1 b 2 c 3))
    ⇒ "Pairs: <A,1> <B,2> <C,3>."
```

~:{*str*} is similar, but the argument should be a list of sublists. At each repetition step, one sublist is used as the set of arguments for processing *str*; on the next repetition, a new sublist is used, whether or not all of the last sublist had been processed. Example:

```
(format nil "Pairs:~:{ <~S,~S>~}."
            '((a 1) (b 2) (c 3)))
    ⇒ "Pairs: <A,1> <B,2> <C,3>."
```

~@{*str*} is similar to ~{*str*}, but instead of using one argument that is a list, all the remaining arguments are used as the list of arguments for the iteration. Example:

```
(format nil "Pairs:~@{ <~S,~S>~}."
            'a 1 'b 2 'c 3)
    ⇒ "Pairs: <A,1> <B,2> <C,3>."
```

If the iteration is terminated before all the remaining arguments are consumed, then any arguments not processed by the iteration remain to be processed by any directives following the iteration construct.

~:@{*str*} combines the features of ~:{*str*} and ~@{*str*}. All the remaining arguments are used, and each one must be a list. On each iteration, the next argument is used as a list of arguments to *str*. Example:

```
(format nil "Pairs:~:@{ <~S,~S>~}."
            '(a 1) '(b 2) '(c 3))
    ⇒ "Pairs: <A,1> <B,2> <C,3>."
```

Terminating the repetition construct with ~:} instead of ~} forces *str* to be processed at least once, even if the initial list of arguments is null (however, it will not override an explicit prefix parameter of zero).

If *str* is empty, then an argument is used as *str*. It must be a string and precede any arguments processed by the iteration. As an example, the following are equivalent:

```
(apply #'format stream string arguments)
(format stream "~1{~:}" string arguments)
```

This will use string as a formatting string. The ~1{ says it will be processed at most once, and the ~:} says it will be processed at least once. Therefore it is processed exactly once, using arguments as the arguments. This case may be handled more clearly by the ~? directive, but this general feature of ~{ is more powerful than ~?.

~}

This terminates a ~{. It is an error elsewhere.

~mincol,colinc,minpad,padchar<str~>

Justification. This justifies the text produced by processing *str* within a field at least *mincol* columns wide. *str* may be divided up into segments with ~;, in which case the spacing is evenly divided between the text segments.

With no modifiers, the leftmost text segment is left-justified in the field, and the rightmost text segment right-justified; if there is only one text element, as a special case, it is right-justified. The : modifier causes spacing to be introduced before the first text segment; the @ modifier causes spacing to be added after the last. The *minpad* parameter (default 0) is the minimum number of padding characters to be output between each segment. The padding character is specified by *padchar*, which defaults to the space character. If the total width needed to satisfy these constraints is greater than *mincol*, then the width used is *mincol+k*colinc* for the smallest possible non-negative integer value *k*; *colinc* defaults to 1, and *mincol* defaults to 0.

```
(format nil "~10<foo~;bar~>")      ⇒ "foo    bar"
(format nil "~10:<foo~;bar~>")     ⇒ "  foo   bar"
(format nil "~10:@<foo~;bar~>")    ⇒ "  foo bar "
(format nil "~10<foobar~>")        ⇒ "    foobar"
(format nil "~10:<foobar~>")       ⇒ "    foobar"
(format nil "~10@<foobar~>")       ⇒ "foobar    "
(format nil "~10:@<foobar~>")      ⇒ "  foobar  "
```

Note that *str* may include format directives. All the clauses in *str* are processed in order; it is the resulting pieces of text that are justified.

The ~^ directive may be used to terminate processing of the clauses prematurely, in which case only the completely processed clauses are justified.

If the first clause of a ~< is terminated with ~:; instead of ~;, then it is used in a special way. All of the clauses are processed (subject to ~^, of course), but the first one is not used in performing the spacing and padding. When the padded result has been determined, then if it will fit on the current line of output, it is output, and the text for the first clause is discarded. If, however, the padded text will not fit on the current line, then the text segment for the first clause is output before the padded text. The first clause ought to contain a newline (such as a ~%

directive). The first clause is always processed, and so any arguments it refers to will be used; the decision is whether to use the resulting segment of text, not whether to process the first clause. If the ~:; has a prefix parameter n, then the padded text must fit on the current line with n character positions to spare to avoid outputting the first clause's text. For example, the control string

```
"~%;; ~{~<~%;; ~1:; ~S~>~^,~}.~%"
```

can be used to print a list of items separated by commas without breaking items over line boundaries, beginning each line with ;; . The prefix parameter 1 in ~1:; accounts for the width of the comma that will follow the justified item if it is not the last element in the list, or the period if it is. If ~:; has a second prefix parameter, then it is used as the width of the line, thus overriding the natural line width of the output stream. To make the preceding example use a line width of 50, one would write

```
"~%;; ~{~<~%;; ~1,50:; ~S~>~^,~}.~%"
```

If the second argument is not specified, then format uses the line width of the output stream. If this cannot be determined (for example, when producing a string result), then format uses 72 as the line length.

~>

Terminates a ~<. It is an error elsewhere.

X3J13 voted in June 1989 ⟨139⟩ to introduce certain format directives to support the user interface to the pretty printer. If ~:> is used to terminate a ~<... directive, the directive is equivalent to a call on pprint-logical-block. See section 27.4 for details.

~^

Up and out. This is an escape construct. If there are no more arguments remaining to be processed, then the immediately enclosing ~{ or ~< construct is terminated. If there is no such enclosing construct, then the entire formatting operation is terminated. In the ~< case, the formatting *is* performed, but no more segments are processed before doing the justification. The ~^ should appear only at the *beginning* of a ~< clause, because it aborts the entire clause it appears in (as well as all following clauses). ~^ may appear anywhere in a ~{ construct.

```
(setq donestr "Done.~^ ~D warning~:P.~^ ~D error~:P.")
(format nil donestr) ⇒ "Done."
```

```
(format nil donestr 3) ⇒ "Done. 3 warnings."
(format nil donestr 1 5) ⇒ "Done. 1 warning. 5 errors."
```

If a prefix parameter is given, then termination occurs if the parameter is zero. (Hence ~^ is equivalent to ~#^.) If two parameters are given, termination occurs if they are equal. If three parameters are given, termination occurs if the first is less than or equal to the second and the second is less than or equal to the third. Of course, this is useless if all the prefix parameters are constants; at least one of them should be a # or a V parameter.

If ~^ is used within a ~:{ construct, then it merely terminates the current iteration step (because in the standard case it tests for remaining arguments of the current step only); the next iteration step commences immediately. To terminate the entire iteration process, use ~:^.

X3J13 voted in March 1988 ⟨81⟩ to clarify the behavior of ~:^ as follows. It may be used only if the command it would terminate is ~:{ or ~:@{. The entire iteration process is terminated if and only if the sublist that is supplying the arguments for the current iteration step is the last sublist (in the case of terminating a ~:{ command) or the last argument to that call to format (in the case of terminating a ~:@{ command). Note furthermore that while ~^ is equivalent to ~#^ in all circumstances, ~:^ is *not* equivalent to ~:#^ because the latter terminates the entire iteration if and only if no arguments remain for *the current iteration step* (as opposed to no arguments remaining for the entire iteration process).

Here are some examples of the differences in the behaviors of ~^, ~:^, and ~:#^.

```
(format nil
        "~:{/~S~^ ...~}"
        '((hot dog) (hamburger) (ice cream) (french fries)))
 ⇒ "/HOT .../HAMBURGER/ICE .../FRENCH ..."
```

For each sublist, " ..." appears after the first word unless there are no additional words.

```
(format nil
        "~:{/~S~:^ ...~}"
        '((hot dog) (hamburger) (ice cream) (french fries)))
 ⇒ "/HOT .../HAMBURGER .../ICE .../FRENCH"
```

For each sublist, " ..." always appears after the first word, unless it is the last sublist, in which case the entire iteration is terminated.

```
(format nil
       "~:{/~S~:#^ ...~}"
       '((hot dog) (hamburger) (ice cream) (french fries)))
   ⇒ "/HOT .../HAMBURGER"
```

For each sublist, " ..." appears after the first word, but if the sublist has only one word then the entire iteration is terminated.

If ~^ appears within a control string being processed under the control of a ~? directive, but not within any ~{ or ~< construct within that string, then the string being processed will be terminated, thereby ending processing of the ~? directive. Processing then continues within the string containing the ~? directive at the point following that directive.

If ~^ appears within a ~[or ~(construct, then all the commands up to the ~^ are properly selected or case-converted, the ~[or ~(processing is terminated, and the outward search continues for a ~{ or ~< construct to be terminated. For example:

```
(setq tellstr "~@(~@[~R~]~^ ~A.~)")
(format nil tellstr 23) ⇒ "Twenty-three."
(format nil tellstr nil "losers") ⇒ "Losers."
(format nil tellstr 23 "losers") ⇒ "Twenty-three losers."
```

Here are some examples of the use of ~^ within a ~< construct.

```
(format nil "~15<~S~;~^~S~;~^~S~>" 'foo)
       ⇒ "            FOO"
(format nil "~15<~S~;~^~S~;~^~S~>" 'foo 'bar)
       ⇒ "FOO        BAR"
(format nil "~15<~S~;~^~S~;~^~S~>" 'foo 'bar 'baz)
       ⇒ "FOO   BAR   BAZ"
```

Compatibility note: The ~Q directive and user-defined directives of Zetalisp have been omitted here, as well as control lists (as opposed to strings), which are rumored to be changing in meaning.

X3J13 voted in June 1989 ⟨139⟩ to introduce user-defined directives in the form of the ~/.../ directive. See section 27.4 for details.

The hairiest format control string I have ever seen in shown in table 22-8. It started innocently enough as part of the simulator for Connection Machine Lisp [44, 57]; the *xapping* data type, defined by defstruct, needed a :print-function

Table 22-8: Print Function for the Xapping Data Type

```
(defun print-xapping (xapping stream depth)
  (declare (ignore depth))
  (format stream
          ;; Are you ready for this one?
          "~:[{~;[~]~:{~S~:[→~S~;~*~]~:^ ~}~:[~; ~]~
           ~{~S→~^ ~}~:[~; ~]~[~*~;→~S~;→~*~]~:[}~;]~]"
          ;; Is that clear?
          (xectorp xapping)
          (do ((vp (xectorp xapping))
               (sp (finite-part-is-xetp xapping))
               (d (xapping-domain xapping) (cdr d))
               (r (xapping-range xapping) (cdr r))
               (z '() (cons (list (if vp (car r) (car d))
                                  (or vp sp)
                                  (car r))
                            z)))
              ((null d) (reverse z)))
          (and (xapping-domain xapping)
               (or (xapping-exceptions xapping)
                   (xapping-infinite xapping)))
          (xapping-exceptions xapping)
          (and (xapping-exceptions xapping)
               (xapping-infinite xapping))
          (ecase (xapping-infinite xapping)
            ((nil) 0)
            (:constant 1)
            (:universal 2))
          (xapping-default xapping)
          (xectorp xapping)))
```

See section 22.1.5 for the defstruct definition of the xapping data type, whose accessor functions are used in this code.

option so that xappings would print properly. As this data type became more complicated, step by step, so did the format control string.

See the description of set-macro-character for a discussion of xappings and the defstruct definition. Assume that the predicate xectorp is true of a xapping if it is a xector, and that the predicate finite-part-is-xetp is true if every value in the range is the same as its corresponding index.

Here is a blow-by-blow description of the parts of this format string:

`~:[{~;[~]`	Print "[" for a xector, and "{" otherwise.
`~:{~S~:[→~S~;~*~]~:^ ~}`	Given a list of lists, print the pairs. Each sublist has three elements: the index (or the value if we're printing a xector); a flag that is true for either a xector or xet (in which case no arrow is printed); and the value. Note the use of `~:{` to iterate, and the use of `~:^` to avoid printing a separating space after the final pair (or at all, if there are no pairs).
`~:[~; ~]`	If there were pairs and there are exceptions or an infinite part, print a separating space.
`~⟨newline⟩`	Do nothing. This merely allows the format control string to be broken across two lines.
`~{~S→~^ ~}`	Given a list of exception indices, print them. Note the use of `~{` to iterate, and the use of `~^` to avoid printing a separating space after the final exception (or at all, if there are no exceptions).
`~:[~; ~]`	If there were exceptions and there is an infinite part, print a separating space.
`~[~*~;→~S~;→~*~]`	Use `~[` to choose one of three cases for printing the infinite part.
`~:[}~;]~]`	Print "]" for a xector, and "}" otherwise.

22.4. Querying the User

The following functions provide a convenient and consistent interface for asking questions of the user. Questions are printed and the answers are read using the stream *query-io*, which normally is synonymous with *terminal-io* but can be rebound to another stream for special applications.

y-or-n-p &optional *format-string* &rest *arguments*   [*Function*]

This predicate is for asking the user a question whose answer is either "yes" or "no." It types out a message (if supplied), reads an answer in some implementation-dependent manner (intended to be short and simple, like reading a single character such as Y or N), and is true if the answer was "yes" or false if the answer was "no."

If the *format-string* argument is supplied and not nil, then a fresh-line operation is performed; then a message is printed as if the *format-string* and *arguments* were given to format. Otherwise it is assumed that any message has already been printed by other means. If you want a question mark at the end of the message, you must put it there yourself; y-or-n-p will not add it. However, the message should not contain an explanatory note such as (Y or N), because the nature of the interface provided for y-or-n-p by a given implementation might not involve typing a character on a keyboard; y-or-n-p will provide such a note if appropriate.

All input and output are performed using the stream in the global variable *query-io*.

Here are some examples of the use of y-or-n-p:

```
(y-or-n-p "Produce listing file?")
(y-or-n-p "Cannot connect to network host ~S. Retry?" host)
```

y-or-n-p should only be used for questions that the user knows are coming or in situations where the user is known to be waiting for a response of some kind. If the user is unlikely to anticipate the question, or if the consequences of the answer might be grave and irreparable, then y-or-n-p should not be used because the user might type ahead and thereby accidentally answer the question. For such questions as "Shall I delete all of your files?" it is better to use yes-or-no-p.

---

yes-or-no-p &optional *format-string* &rest *arguments*   [*Function*]

This predicate, like y-or-n-p, is for asking the user a question whose answer is either "yes" or "no." It types out a message (if supplied), attracts the user's attention (for example, by ringing the terminal's bell), and reads a reply in some implementation-dependent manner. It is intended that the reply require the user to take more action than just a single keystroke, such as typing the full word yes or no followed by a newline.

If the *format-string* argument is supplied and not nil, then a fresh-line operation is performed; then a message is printed as if the *format-string* and *arguments* were given to format. Otherwise it is assumed that any message has already been printed by other means. If you want a question mark at the end of the message, you must put it there yourself; yes-or-no-p will not add it. However, the message should not contain an explanatory note such as (Yes or No) because the nature of the interface provided for yes-or-no-p by a given implementation might not involve typing the reply on a keyboard; yes-or-no-p will provide such a note if appropriate.

All input and output are performed using the stream in the global variable *query-io*.

To allow the user to answer a yes-or-no question with a single character, use y-or-n-p. yes-or-no-p should be used for unanticipated or momentous questions; this is why it attracts attention and why it requires a multiple-action sequence to answer it.

23

File System Interface

A frequent use of streams is to communicate with a *file system* to which groups of data (files) can be written and from which files can be retrieved.

Common Lisp defines a standard interface for dealing with such a file system. This interface is designed to be simple and general enough to accommodate the facilities provided by "typical" operating system environments within which Common Lisp is likely to be implemented. The goal is to make Common Lisp programs that perform only simple operations on files reasonably portable.

To this end, Common Lisp assumes that files are named, that given a name one can construct a stream connected to a file of that name, and that the names can be fit into a certain canonical, implementation-independent form called a *pathname*.

Facilities are provided for manipulating pathnames, for creating streams connected to files, and for manipulating the file system through pathnames and streams.

23.1. File Names

Common Lisp programs need to use names to designate files. The main difficulty in dealing with names of files is that different file systems have different naming formats for files. For example, here is a table of several file systems (actually, operating systems that provide file systems) and what equivalent file names might look like for each one:

System	File Name
TOPS-20	`<LISPIO>FORMAT.FASL.13`
TOPS-10	`FORMAT.FAS[1,4]`
ITS	`LISPIO;FORMAT FASL`
MULTICS	`>udd>LispIO>format.fasl`
TENEX	`<LISPIO>FORMAT.FASL;13`
VAX/VMS	`[LISPIO]FORMAT.FAS;13`
UNIX	`/usr/lispio/format.fasl`

It would be impossible for each program that deals with file names to know about each different file name format that exists; a new Common Lisp implementation might use a format different from any of its predecessors. Therefore, Common Lisp provides *two* ways to represent file names: *namestrings*, which are strings in the implementation-dependent form customary for the file system, and *pathnames*, which are special abstract data objects that represent file names in an implementation-independent way. Functions are provided to convert between these two representations, and all manipulations of files can be expressed in machine-independent terms by using pathnames.

In order to allow Common Lisp programs to operate in a network environment that may have more than one kind of file system, the pathname facility allows a file name to specify which file system is to be used. In this context, each file system is called a *host*, in keeping with the usual networking terminology.

Different hosts may use different notations for file names. Common Lisp allows customary notation to be used for each host, but also supports a system of logical pathnames that provides a standard framework for naming files in a portable manner (see section 23.1.5).

23.1.1. Pathnames

All file systems dealt with by Common Lisp are forced into a common framework, in which files are named by a Lisp data object of type `pathname`.

A pathname always has six components, described below. These components are the common interface that allows programs to work the same way with different file systems; the mapping of the pathname components into the concepts peculiar to each file system is taken care of by the Common Lisp implementation.

host

The name of the file system on which the file resides.

device

Corresponds to the "device" or "file structure" concept in many host file systems: the name of a (logical or physical) device containing files.

directory

Corresponds to the "directory" concept in many host file systems: the name of a group of related files (typically those belonging to a single user or project).

name

The name of a group of files that can be thought of as the "same" file.

type

Corresponds to the "filetype" or "extension" concept in many host file systems; identifies the type of file. Files with the same names but different types are usually related in some specific way, for instance, one being a source file, another the compiled form of that source, and a third the listing of error messages from the compiler.

version

Corresponds to the "version number" concept in many host file systems. Typically this is a number that is incremented every time the file is modified.

Note that a pathname is not necessarily the name of a specific file. Rather, it is a specification (possibly only a partial specification) of how to access a file. A pathname need not correspond to any file that actually exists, and more than one pathname can refer to the same file. For example, the pathname with a version of "newest" may refer to the same file as a pathname with the same components except a certain number as the version. Indeed, a pathname with version "newest" may refer to different files as time passes, because the meaning of such a pathname depends on the state of the file system. In file systems with such facilities as "links," multiple file names, logical devices, and so on, two pathnames that look quite different may turn out to address the same file. To access a file given a pathname, one must do a file system operation such as open.

Two important operations involving pathnames are *parsing* and *merging*. Parsing is the conversion of a namestring (which might be something supplied interactively by the user when asked to supply the name of a file) into a pathname object. This operation is implementation-dependent, because the format of namestrings is implementation-dependent. Merging takes a pathname with missing components and supplies values for those components from a source of defaults.

Not all of the components of a pathname need to be specified. If a component of a pathname is missing, its value is nil. Before the file system interface can do anything interesting with a file, such as opening the file, all the missing components of a pathname must be filled in (typically from a set of defaults). Pathnames with missing components may be used internally for various purposes; in particular, parsing a namestring that does not specify certain components will result in a pathname with missing components.

X3J13 voted in January 1989 ⟨136⟩ to permit any component of a pathname to have the value :unspecific, meaning that the component simply does not exist, for file systems in which such a value makes sense. (For example, a UNIX file system usually does not support version numbers, so the version component of a pathname for a UNIX host might be :unspecific. Similarly, the file type is usually regarded in a UNIX file system as the part of a name after a period, but some file names contain no periods and therefore have no file types.)

When a pathname is converted to a namestring, the values nil and :unspecific have the same effect: they are treated as if the component were empty (that is, they each cause the component not to appear in the namestring). When merging, however, only a nil value for a component will be replaced with the default for that component; the value :unspecific will be left alone as if the field were filled.

The results are undefined if :unspecific is supplied to a file system in a component for which :unspecific does not make sense for that file system.

Programming hint: portable programs should be prepared to handle the value :unspecific in the device, directory, type, or version field in some implementations. Portable programs should not explicitly place :unspecific in any field because it might not be permitted in some situations, but portable programs may sometimes do so implicitly (by copying such a value from another pathname, for example).

A component of a pathname can also be the keyword :wild. This is only useful when the pathname is being used with a directory-manipulating operation, where it means that the pathname component matches anything. The printed representation of a pathname typically designates :wild by an asterisk; however, this is host-dependent.

See section 23.1.4 for a discussion of new wildcard pathname facilities.

What values are allowed for components of a pathname depends, in general, on the pathname's host. However, in order for pathnames to be usable in a system-independent way, certain global conventions are adhered to. These conventions are stronger for the type and version than for the other components, since the type and version are explicitly manipulated by many programs, while the other components are usually treated as something supplied by the user that just needs to be remembered and copied from place to place.

The type is always a string or nil or :wild. It is expected that most programs that deal with files will supply a default type for each file.

The version is either a positive integer or a special symbol. The meanings of nil and :wild have been explained above. The keyword :newest refers to the largest version number that already exists in the file system when reading a file, or to a version number greater than any already existing in the file system when writing a new file. Some Common Lisp implementors may choose to define other special version symbols. Some semi-standard names, suggested but not required to be supported by every Common Lisp implementation, are :oldest, to refer to the smallest version number that exists in the file system; :previous, to refer to the version previous to the newest version; and :installed, to refer to a version that is officially installed for users (as opposed to a working or development version). Some Common Lisp implementors may also choose to attach a meaning to non-positive version numbers (a typical convention is that 0 is synonymous with :newest and -1 with :previous), but such interpretations are implementation-dependent.

The host may be a string, indicating a file system, or a list of strings, of which the first names the file system and the rest may be used for such a purpose as inter-network routing.

The device, directory, and name can each be a string (with host-dependent rules on allowed characters and length) or possibly some other Common Lisp data structure (in which case such a component is said to be *structured* and has an implementation-dependent format). Structured components may be used to handle such file system features as hierarchical directories. Common Lisp programs do not need to know about structured components unless they do host-dependent operations. Specifying a string as a pathname component for a host that requires a structured component will cause conversion of the string to the appropriate form.

X3J13 voted in June 1989 ⟨133⟩ to define a specific format for structured directories (see section 23.1.3).

X3J13 voted in June 1989 ⟨129⟩ to approve the following clarifications and specifications of precisely what are valid values for the various components of a pathname.

Pathname component value strings never contain the punctuation characters that are used to separate fields in a namestring (for example, slashes and periods as used in UNIX file systems). Punctuation characters appear only in namestrings. Characters used as punctuation can appear in pathname component values with a non-punctuation meaning if the file system allows it (for example, UNIX file systems allow a file name to begin with a period).

When examining pathname components, conforming programs must be prepared to encounter any of the following siutations:

- Any component can be nil, which means the component has not been specified.

- Any component can be :unspecific, which means the component has no meaning in this particular pathname.

- The device, directory, name, and type can be strings.

- The host can be any object, at the discretion of the implementation.

- The directory can be a list of strings and symbols as described in section 23.1.3.

- The version can be any symbol or any integer. The symbol :newest refers to the largest version number that already exists in the file system when reading, overwriting, appending, superseding, or directory-listing an existing file; it refers to the smallest version number greater than any existing version number when creating a new file. Other symbols and integers have implementation-defined meaning. It is suggested, but not required, that implementations use positive integers starting at 1 as version numbers, recognize the symbol :oldest to designate the smallest existing version number, and use keyword symbols for other special versions.

When examining wildcard components of a wildcard pathname, conforming programs must be prepared to encounter any of the following additional values in any component or any element of a list that is the directory component:

- The symbol :wild, which matches anything.

- A string containing implementation-dependent special wildcard characters.

- Any object, representing an implementation-dependent wildcard pattern.

When constructing a pathname from components, conforming programs must follow these rules:

- Any component may be nil. Specifying nil for the host may, in some implementations, result in using a default host rather than an actual nil value.

- The host, device, directory, name, and type may be strings. There are implementation-dependent limits on the number and type of characters in these strings. A plausible assumption is that letters (of a single case) and digits are acceptable to most file systems.

- The directory may be a list of strings and symbols as described in section 23.1.3. There are implementation-dependent limits on the length and contents of the list.

- The version may be :newest.

- Any component may be taken from the corresponding component of another pathname. When the two pathnames are for different file systems (in implementations that support multiple file systems), an appropriate translation occurs. If no meaningful translation is possible, an error is signaled. The definitions of "appropriate" and "meaningful" are implementation-dependent.

- When constructing a wildcard pathname, the name, type, or version may be :wild, which matches anything.

- An implementation might support other values for some components, but a portable program should not use those values. A conforming program can use implementation-dependent values but this can make it non-portable; for example, it might work only with UNIX file systems.

The best way to compare two pathnames for equality is with `equal`, not `eql`. (On pathnames, `eql` is simply the same as `eq`.) Two pathname objects are `equal` if and only if all the corresponding components (host, device, and so on) are equivalent. (Whether or not uppercase and lowercase letters are considered equivalent in strings appearing in components depends on the file name conventions of the file system.) Pathnames that are `equal` should be functionally equivalent.

Some host file systems have features that do not fit into this pathname model. For instance, directories might be accessible as files; there might be complicated structure in the directories or names; or there might be a way to specify a directory relative to a "current" directory, such as the < syntax in MULTICS or the special ".." file name of UNIX. Such features are not allowed for by the standard Common Lisp file system interface. An implementation is free to accommodate such features in its pathname representation and provide a parser that can process such specifications in namestrings; such features are then likely to work within that single implementation. However, note that once a program depends explicitly on any such features, it will not be portable.

X3J13 voted in June 1989 ⟨133⟩ to define a specific format for structured directories (see section 23.1.3), so some of the specific examples in the previous paragraph no longer apply, but the principle is still correct.

23.1.2. Case Conventions

Issues of alphabetic case in pathnames are a major source of problems. In some file systems, the customary case is lowercase, in some uppercase, in some mixed. Some file systems are case-sensitive (that is, they treat `FOO` and `foo` as different file names) and others are not.

There are two kinds of pathname case portability problems: moving programs from one Common Lisp to another, and moving pathname component values from one file system to another. The solution to the first problem is the requirement that all Common Lisp implementations that support a particular file system must use compatible representations for pathname component values. The solution to the second problem is the use of a common representation for the least-common-denominator pathname component values that exist on all interesting file systems.

Requiring a common representation directly conflicts with the desire among programmers that use only one file system to work with the local conventions and to ignore issues of porting to other file systems. The common representation cannot be the same as local (varying) conventions.

X3J13 voted in June 1989 ⟨128⟩ to add a keyword argument `:case` to each of the functions `make-pathname`, `pathname-host`, `pathname-device`, `pathname-directory`, `pathname-name`, and `pathname-type`. The possible values for the argument are `:common` and `:local`. The default is `:local`.

The value `:local` means that strings given to `make-pathname` or returned by any of the pathname component accessors follow the local file system's conventions for alphabetic case. Strings given to `make-pathname` will be used exactly as written if the file system supports both cases. If the file system supports only one case, the strings will be translated to that case.

The value `:common` means that strings given to `make-pathname` or returned by any of the pathname component accessors follow this common convention:

• All uppercase means that a file system's customary case will be used.

• All lowercase means that the opposite of the customary case will be used.

• Mixed case represents itself.

Uppercase is used as the common case for no better reason than consistency with Lisp symbols. The second and third points allow translation from local representation to common and back to be information-preserving. (Note that translation from common to local representation and back may or may not be information-preserving, depending on the nature of the local representation.)

Namestrings always use `:local` file system case conventions.

Finally, `merge-pathnames` and `translate-pathname` map customary case in the input pathnames into customary case in the output pathname.

Examples of possible use of this convention:

• TOPS-20 is case-sensitive and prefers uppercase, translating lowercase to uppercase unless escaped with ^V; for a TOPS-20–based file system, a Common Lisp implementation should use identical representations for common and local.

• UNIX is case-sensitive and prefers lowercase; for a UNIX-based file system, a Common Lisp implementation should translate between common and local representations by inverting the case of non-mixed-case strings.

• VAX/VMS is uppercase-only (that is, the file system translates all file name arguments to uppercase); for a VAX/VMS-based file system, a Common Lisp implementation should translate common representation to local by converting to uppercase and should translate local representation to common with no change.

• The Macintosh operating system is case-insensitive and prefers lowercase, but remembers the cases of letters actually used to name a file; for a Macintosh-based file system, a Common Lisp implementation should translate between common and local representations by inverting the case of non-mixed-case strings and should ignore case when determining whether two pathnames are `equal`.

Here are some examples of this behavior. Assume that the host T runs TOPS-20,
U runs UNIX, V runs VAX/VMS, and M runs the Macintosh operating system.

```
;;; Returns two values: the PATHNAME-NAME from a namestring
;;; in :COMMON and :LOCAL representations (in that order).
(defun pathname-example (name)
  (let ((path (parse-namestring name))))
    (values (pathname-name path :case :common)
            (pathname-name path :case :local))))
```

```
                                                      ;Common  Local
(pathname-example "T:<ME>FOO.LISP")         ⇒ "FOO"  and "FOO"
(pathname-example "T:<ME>foo.LISP")         ⇒ "FOO"  and "FOO"
(pathname-example "T:<ME>^Vf^Vo^Vo.LISP")   ⇒ "foo"  and "foo"
(pathname-example "T:<ME>TeX.LISP")         ⇒ "TEX"  and "TEX"
(pathname-example "T:<ME>T^VeX.LISP")       ⇒ "TeX"  and "TeX"
(pathname-example "U:/me/FOO.lisp")         ⇒ "foo"  and "FOO"
(pathname-example "U:/me/foo.lisp")         ⇒ "FOO"  and "foo"
(pathname-example "U:/me/TeX.lisp")         ⇒ "TeX"  and "TeX"
(pathname-example "V:[me]FOO.LISP")         ⇒ "FOO"  and "FOO"
(pathname-example "V:[me]foo.LISP")         ⇒ "FOO"  and "FOO"
(pathname-example "V:[me]TeX.LISP")         ⇒ "TEX"  and "TEX"
(pathname-example "M:FOO.LISP")             ⇒ "foo"  and "FOO"
(pathname-example "M:foo.LISP")             ⇒ "FOO"  and "foo"
(pathname-example "M:TeX.LISP")             ⇒ "TeX"  and "TeX"
```

The following example illustrates the creation of new pathnames. The name is
converted from common representation to local because namestrings always use
local conventions.

```
(defun make-pathname-example (h n)
  (namestring (make-pathname :host h :name n :case :common))
```

```
(make-pathname-example "T" "FOO") ⇒ "T:FOO"
(make-pathname-example "T" "foo") ⇒ "T:^Vf^Vo^Vo"
(make-pathname-example "T" "TeX") ⇒ "T:T^VeX"
(make-pathname-example "U" "FOO") ⇒ "U:foo"
(make-pathname-example "U" "foo") ⇒ "U:FOO"
(make-pathname-example "U" "TeX") ⇒ "U:TeX"
(make-pathname-example "V" "FOO") ⇒ "V:FOO"
(make-pathname-example "V" "foo") ⇒ "V:FOO"
```

```
(make-pathname-example "V" "TeX") ⇒ "V:TeX"
(make-pathname-example "M" "FOO") ⇒ "M:foo"
(make-pathname-example "M" "foo") ⇒ "M:FOO"
(make-pathname-example "M" "TeX") ⇒ "M:TeX"
```

A big advantage of this set of conventions is that one can, for example, call make-pathname with :type "LISP" and :case :common, and the result will appear in a namestring as .LISP or .lisp, whichever is appropriate.

23.1.3. Structured Directories

X3J13 voted in June 1989 ⟨133⟩ to define a specific pathname component format for structured directories.

The value of a pathname's directory component may be a list. The *car* of the list should be a keyword, either :absolute or :relative. Each remaining element of the list should be a string or a symbol (see below). Each string names a single level of directory structure and should consist of only the directory name without any punctuation characters.

A list whose *car* is the symbol :absolute represents a directory path starting from the root directory. For example, the list (:absolute) represents the root directory itself; the list (:absolute "foo" "bar" "baz") represents the directory that in a UNIX file system would be called /foo/bar/baz.

A list whose *car* is the symbol :relative represents a directory path starting from a default directory. The list (:relative) has the same meaning as nil and hence normally is not used. The list (:relative "foo" "bar") represents the directory named bar in the directory named foo in the default directory.

In place of a string, at any point in the list, a symbol may occur to indicate a special file notation. The following symbols have standard meanings.

:wild   Wildcard match of one level of directory structure

:wild-inferiors Wildcard match of any number of directory levels

:up   Go upward in directory structure (semantic)

:back   Go upward in directory structure (syntactic)

(See section 23.1.4 for a discussion of wildcard pathnames.)

Implementations are permitted to add additional objects of any non-string type if necessary to represent features of their file systems that cannot be represented with the standard strings and symbols. Supplying any non-string, including any of the symbols listed below, to a file system for which it does not make sense signals an error of type `file-error`. For example, most implementations of the UNIX file system do not support `:wild-inferiors`. Any directory list in which `:absolute` or `:wild-inferiors` is immediately followed by `:up` or `:back` is illegal and when processed causes an error to be signaled.

The keyword `:back` has a "syntactic" meaning that depends only on the pathname and not on the contents of the file system. The keyword `:up` has a "semantic" meaning that depends on the contents of the file system; to resolve a pathname containing `:up` to a pathname whose directory component contains only `:absolute` and strings requires a search of the file system. Note that use of `:up` instead of `:back` can result in designating a different actual directory only in file systems that support multiple names for directories, perhaps via symbolic links. For example, suppose that there is a directory link such that

`(:absolute "X" "Y")`   is linked to   `(:absolute "A" "B")`

and there also exist directories

`(:absolute "A" "Q")`   and   `(:absolute "X" "Q")`

Then

`(:absolute "X" "Y" :up "Q")`   designates   `(:absolute "A" "Q")`

but

`(:absolute "X" "Y" :back "Q")`   designates   `(:absolute "X" "Q")`

If a string is used as the value of the `:directory` argument to `make-pathname`, it should be the name of a top-level directory and should not contain any punctuation characters. Specifying a string *s* is equivalent to specifying the list `(:absolute s)`. Specifying the symbol `:wild` is equivalent to specifying the list `(:absolute :wild-inferiors)` (or `(:absolute :wild)` in a file system that does not support `:wild-inferiors`).

The function `pathname-directory` always returns `nil`, `:unspecific`, or a list—never a string, never `:wild`. If a list is returned, it is not guaranteed to be freshly consed; the consequences of modifying this list are undefined.

In non-hierarchical file systems, the only valid list values for the directory component of a pathname are `(:absolute s)` (where *s* is a string) and `(:absolute :wild)`. The keywords `:relative`, `:wild-inferiors`, `:up`, and `:back` are not used in non-hierarchical file systems.

Pathname merging treats a relative directory specially. Let *pathname* and *defaults* be the first two arguments to `merge-pathnames`. If `(pathname-directory path-`

name) is a list whose *car* is :relative, and (pathname-directory *defaults*) is
a list, then the merged directory is the value of

```
(append (pathname-directory defaults)
        (cdr        ;Remove :relative from the front
          (pathname-directory pathname)))
```

except that if the resulting list contains a string or :wild immediately followed by
:back, both of them are removed. This removal of redundant occurrences of :back
is repeated as many times as possible. If (pathname-directory *defaults*) is not
a list or (pathname-directory *pathname*) is not a list whose *car* is :relative,
the merged directory is the value of

```
(or (pathname-directory pathname)
    (pathname-directory defaults))
```

A relative directory in the pathname argument to a function such as open is
merged with the value of *default-pathname-defaults* before the file system
is accessed.

Here are some examples of the use of structured directories. Suppose that host
L supports a Symbolics Lisp Machine file system, host U supports a UNIX file
system, and host V supports a VAX/VMS file system.

```
(pathname-directory (parse-namestring "V:[FOO.BAR]BAZ.LSP"))
   ⇒ (:ABSOLUTE "FOO" "BAR")

(pathname-directory (parse-namestring "U:/foo/bar/baz.lisp"))
   ⇒ (:ABSOLUTE "foo" "bar")

(pathname-directory (parse-namestring "U:../baz.lisp"))
   ⇒ (:RELATIVE :UP)

(pathname-directory (parse-namestring "U:/foo/bar/../mum/baz"))
   ⇒ (:ABSOLUTE "foo" "bar" :UP "mum")

(pathname-directory (parse-namestring "U:bar/../../ztesch/zip"))
   ⇒ (:RELATIVE "bar" :UP :UP "ztesch")

(pathname-directory (parse-namestring "L:>foo>**>bar>baz.lisp"))
   ⇒ (:ABSOLUTE "FOO" :WILD-INFERIORS "BAR")

(pathname-directory (parse-namestring "L:>foo>*>bar>baz.lisp"))
   ⇒ (:ABSOLUTE "FOO" :WILD "BAR")
```

23.1.4. Extended Wildcards

Some file systems provide more complex conventions for wildcards than simple component-wise wildcards representable by `:wild`. For example, the namestring `"F*O"` might mean a normal three-character name; a three-character name with the middle character wild; a name with at least two characters, beginning with `F` and ending with `O`; or perhaps a wild match spanning multiple directories. Similarly, the namestring `">foo>**>bar>"` might imply that the middle directory is named `"**"`; the middle directory is `:wild`; there are zero or more middle directories that are `:wild`; or perhaps that the middle directory name matches any two-letter name. Some file systems support even more complex wildcards, such as regular expressions.

X3J13 voted in June 1989 ⟨137⟩ to provide some facilities for dealing with more general wildcard pathnames in a fairly portable manner.

`wild-pathname-p` *pathname* &optional *field-key*   [*Function*]

Tests a pathname for the presence of wildcard components. If the first argument is not a pathname, string, or file stream, an error of type `type-error` is signaled.

If no *field-key* is provided, or the *field-key* is `nil`, the result is true if and only if *pathname* has any wildcard components.

If a non-null *field-key* is provided, it must be one of `:host`, `:device`, `:directory`, `:name`, `:type`, or `:version`. In this case, the result is true if and only if the indicated component of *pathname* is a wildcard.

Note that X3J13 voted in June 1989 ⟨129⟩ to specify that an implementation need not support wildcards in all fields; the only requirement is that the name, type, or version may be `:wild`. However, portable programs should be prepared to encounter either `:wild` or implementation-dependent wildcards in any pathname component. The function `wild-pathname-p` provides a portable way for testing the presence of wildcards.

`pathname-match-p` *pathname wildname*   [*Function*]

This predicate is true if and only if the *pathname* matches the *wildname*. The matching rules are implementation-defined but should be consistent with the behavior of the `directory` function. Missing components of *wildname* default to `:wild`.

If either argument is not a pathname, string, or file stream, an error of type `type-error` is signaled. It is valid for *pathname* to be a wild pathname; a wildcard field in *pathname* will match only a wildcard field in *wildname*; that is, `pathname-match-p` is not commutative. It is valid for *wildname* to be a non-wild pathname; I believe that in this case `pathname-match-p` will have the same behavior as `equal`, though the X3J13 specification did not say so.

`translate-pathname` *source from-wildname to-wildname* `&key`   [*Function*]

Translates the pathname *source*, which must match *from-wildname*, into a corresponding pathname (call it *result*), which is constructed so as to match *to-wildname*, and returns *result*.

The pathname *result* is a copy of *to-wildname* with each missing or wildcard field replaced by a portion of *source*; for this purpose a wildcard field is a pathname component with a value of `:wild`, a `:wild` element of a list-valued directory component, or an implementation-defined portion of a component, such as the `*` in the complex wildcard string `"foo*bar"` that some implementations support. An implementation that adds other wildcard features, such as regular expressions, must define how `translate-pathname` extends to those features. A missing field is a pathname component that is `nil`.

The portion of *source* that is copied into *result* is implementation-defined. Typically it is determined by the user interface conventions of the file systems involved. Usually it is the portion of *source* that matches a wildcard field of *from-wildname* that is in the same position as the missing or wildcard field of *to-wildname*. If there is no wildcard field in *from-wildname* at that position, then usually it is the entire corresponding pathname component of *source* or, in the case of a list-valued directory component, the entire corresponding list element. For example, if the name components of *source*, *from-wildname*, and *to-wildname* are `"gazonk"`, `"gaz*"`, and `"h*"` respectively, then in most file systems the wildcard fields of the name component of *from-wildname* and *to-wildname* are each `"*"`, the matching portion of *source* is `"onk"`, and the name component of *result* is `"honk"`; however, the exact behavior of `translate-pathname` is not dictated by the Common Lisp language and may vary according to the user interface conventions of the file systems involved.

During the copying of a portion of *source* into *result*, additional implementation-defined translations of alphabetic case or file naming conventions may occur, especially when *from-wildname* and *to-wildname* are for different hosts.

If any of the first three arguments is not a pathname, string, or file stream, an error of type `type-error` is signaled. It is valid for *source* to be a wild pathname; in general this will produce a wild *result* pathname. It is valid for *from-wildname* or *to-wildname* or both to be non-wild. An error is signaled if the *source* pathname does not match the *from-wildname*, that is, if (`pathname-match-p` *source from-wildname*) would not be true.

There are no specified keyword arguments for translate-pathname, but implementations are permitted to extend it by adding keyword arguments. There is one specified return value from translate-pathname; implementations are permitted to extend it by returning additional values.

Here is an implementation suggestion. One file system performs this operation by examining corresponding pieces of the three pathnames in turn, where a piece is a pathname component or a list element of a structured component such as a hierarchical directory. Hierarchical directory elements in *from-wildname* and *to-wildname* are matched by whether they are wildcards, not by depth in the directory hierarchy. If the piece in *to-wildname* is present and not wild, it is copied into the result. If the piece in *to-wildname* is :wild or nil, the corresponding piece in *source* is copied into the result. Otherwise, the piece in *to-wildname* might be a complex wildcard such as "foo*bar"; the portion of the piece in *source* that matches the wildcard portion of the corresponding piece in *from-wildname* (or the entire *source* piece, if the *from-wildname* piece is not wild and therefore equals the *source* piece) replaces the wildcard portion of the piece in *to-wildname* and the value produced is used in the result.

X3J13 voted in June 1989 ⟨128⟩ to require translate-pathname to map customary case in argument pathnames to the customary case in returned pathnames (see section 23.1.2).

Here are some examples of the use of the new wildcard pathname facilities. These examples are not portable. They are written to run with particular file systems and particular wildcard conventions and are intended to be illustrative, not prescriptive. Other implementations may behave differently.

```
(wild-pathname-p (make-pathname :name :wild)) ⇒ t
(wild-pathname-p (make-pathname :name :wild) :name) ⇒ t
(wild-pathname-p (make-pathname :name :wild) :type) ⇒ nil
(wild-pathname-p (pathname "S:>foo>**>")) ⇒ t          ;Maybe
(wild-pathname-p (make-pathname :name "F*O")) ⇒ t      ;Probably
```

One cannot rely on rename-file to handle wild pathnames in a predictable manner. However, one can use translate-pathname explicitly to control the process.

```
(defun rename-files (from to)
  "Rename all files that match the first argument by
   translating their names to the form of the second
   argument. Both arguments may be wild pathnames."
  (dolist (file (directory from))
    ;; DIRECTORY produces only pathnames that match from-wildname.
    (rename-file file (translate-pathname file from to))))
```

Assuming one particular set of popular wildcard conventions, this function might exhibit the following behavior. Not all file systems will run this example exactly as written.

```
(rename-files "/usr/me/*.lisp" "/dev/her/*.l")
   renames  /usr/me/init.lisp
       to   /dev/her/init.l
```

```
(rename-files "/usr/me/pcl*/*" "/sys/pcl/*/")
   renames  /usr/me/pcl-5-may/low.lisp
       to   /sys/pcl/pcl-5-may/low.lisp
   (in some file systems the result might be /sys/pcl/5-may/low.lisp)
```

```
(rename-files "/usr/me/pcl*/*" "/sys/library/*/")
   renames  /usr/me/pcl-5-may/low.lisp
       to   /sys/library/pcl-5-may/low.lisp
   (in some file systems the result might be /sys/library/5-may/low.lisp)
```

```
(rename-files "/usr/me/foo.bar" "/usr/me2/")
   renames  /usr/me/foo.bar
       to   /usr/me2/foo.bar
```

```
(rename-files "/usr/joe/*-recipes.text"
              "/usr/jim/personal/cookbook/joe´s-*-rec.text")
   renames  /usr/joe/lamb-recipes.text
       to   /usr/jim/personal/cookbook/joe´s-lamb-rec.text
   renames  /usr/joe/veg-recipes.text
       to   /usr/jim/personal/cookbook/joe´s-veg-rec.text
   renames  /usr/joe/cajun-recipes.text
       to   /usr/jim/personal/cookbook/joe´s-cajun-rec.text
   renames  /usr/joe/szechuan-recipes.text
       to   /usr/jim/personal/cookbook/joe´s-szechuan-rec.text
```

The following examples use UNIX syntax and the wildcard conventions of one particular version of UNIX.

```
(namestring
  (translate-pathname "/usr/dmr/hacks/frob.l"
                      "/usr/d*/hacks/*.l"
                      "/usr/d*/backup/hacks/backup-*.*"))
  ⇒ "/usr/dmr/backup/hacks/backup-frob.l"
```

```
(namestring
   (translate-pathname "/usr/dmr/hacks/frob.l"
                       "/usr/d*/hacks/fr*.l"
                       "/usr/d*/backup/hacks/backup-*.*"))
   ⇒ "/usr/dmr/backup/hacks/backup-ob.l"
```

The following examples are similar to the preceding examples but use two different hosts; host U supports a UNIX file system and host V supports a VAX/VMS file system. Note the translation of file type (from l to LSP) and the change of alphabetic case conventions.

```
(namestring
   (translate-pathname "U:/usr/dmr/hacks/frob.l"
                       "U:/usr/d*/hacks/*.l"
                       "V:SYS$DISK:[D*.BACKUP.HACKS]BACKUP-*.*"))
   ⇒ "V:SYS$DISK:[DMR.BACKUP.HACKS]BACKUP-FROB.LSP"
```

```
(namestring
   (translate-pathname "U:/usr/dmr/hacks/frob.l"
                       "U:/usr/d*/hacks/fr*.l"
                       "V:SYS$DISK:[D*.BACKUP.HACKS]BACKUP-*.*"))
   ⇒ "V:SYS$DISK:[DMR.BACKUP.HACKS]BACKUP-OB.LSP"
```

The next example is a version of the function translate-logical-pathname (simplified a bit) for a logical host named FOO. The points of interest are the use of pathname-match-p as a :test argument for assoc and the use of translate-pathname as a substrate for translate-logical-pathname.

```
(define-condition logical-translation-error (file-error))
```

```
(defun my-translate-logical-pathname (pathname &key rules)
   (let ((rule (assoc pathname rules :test #'pathname-match-p)))
     (unless rule
        (error 'logical-translation-error :pathname pathname))
     (translate-pathname pathname (first rule) (second rule))))
```

```
(my-translate-logical-pathname
   "FOO:CODE;BASIC.LISP"
   :rules '(("FOO:DOCUMENTATION;" "U:/doc/foo/")
            ("FOO:CODE;"          "U:/lib/foo/")
            ("FOO:PATCHES;*;"     "U:/lib/foo/patch/*/")))
   ⇒ #P"U:/lib/foo/basic.l"
```

23.1.5. Logical Pathnames

Pathname values are not portable, but sometimes they must be mentioned in a program (for example, the names of files containing the program and the data used by the program).

X3J13 voted in June 1989 ⟨130⟩ to provide some facilities for portable pathname values. The idea is to provide a portable framework for pathname values; these logical pathnames are then mapped to physical (that is, actual) pathnames by a set of implementation-dependent or site-dependent rules. The logical pathname facility therefore separates the concerns of program writing and user software architecture from the details of how a software system is embedded in a particular file system or operating environment.

Pathname values are not portable because not all Common Lisp implementations use the same operating system and file name syntax varies widely among operating systems. In addition, corresponding files at two different sites may have different names even when the operating system is the same; for example, they may be on different directories or different devices. The Common Lisp logical pathname system defines a particular pathname structure and namestring syntax that must be supported by all implementations.

`logical-pathname`   [*Class*]

This is a subclass of `pathname`.

23.1.5.1. Syntax of Logical Pathname Namestrings

The syntax of a logical pathname namestring is as follows:

logical-namestring ::= [*host* :] [;] {*directory* ;}* [*name*] [. *type* [. *version*]]

Note that a logical namestring has no *device* portion.

host ::= *word*
directory ::= *word* | *wildcard-word* | *wildcard-inferiors*
name ::= *word* | *wildcard-word*
type ::= *word* | *wildcard-word*
version ::= *word* | *wildcard-word*
word ::= {*letter* | *digit* | -}⁺
wildcard-word ::= [*word*] * {*word* *}* [*word*]
wildcard-inferiors ::= **

A *word* consists of one or more uppercase letters, digits, and hyphens.

A *wildcard word* consists of one or more asterisks, uppercase letters, digits, and hyphens, including at least one asterisk, with no two asterisks adjacent. Each asterisk matches a sequence of zero or more characters. The wildcard word * parses as :wild; all others parse as strings.

Lowercase letters may also appear in a word or wildcard word occurring in a namestring. Such letters are converted to uppercase when the namestring is converted to a pathname. The consequences of using other characters are unspecified.

The *host* is a word that has been defined as a logical pathname host by using setf with the function logical-pathname-translations.

There is no device, so the device component of a logical pathname is always :unspecific. No other component of a logical pathname can be :unspecific.

Each *directory* is a word, a wildcard word, or ** (which is parsed as :wild-inferiors). If a semicolon precedes the directories, the directory component is relative; otherwise it is absolute.

The *name* is a word or a wildcard word.

The *type* is a word or a wildcard word.

The *version* is a positive decimal integer or the word NEWEST (which is parsed as :newest) or * (which is parsed as :wild). The letters in NEWEST can be in either alphabetic case.

The consequences of using any value not specified here as a logical pathname component are unspecified. The null string "" is not a valid value for any component of a logical pathname, since the null string is not a word or a wildcard word.

23.1.5.2. Parsing of Logical Pathname Namestrings

Logical pathname namestrings are recognized by the functions logical-pathname and translate-logical-pathname. The host portion of the logical pathname namestring and its following colon must appear in the namestring arguments to these functions.

The function parse-namestring recognizes a logical pathname namestring when the *host* argument is logical or the *defaults* argument is a logical pathname. In this case the host portion of the logical pathname namestring and its following colon are optional. If the host portion of the namestring and the *host* argument are both present and do not match, an error is signaled. The host argument is logical if it is supplied and came from pathname-host of a logical pathname. Whether a host argument is logical if it is a string equal to a logical pathname host name is implementation-defined.

The function merge-pathnames recognizes a logical pathname namestring when the *defaults* argument is a logical pathname. In this case the host portion of the logical pathname namestring and its following colon are optional.

Whether the other functions that coerce strings to pathnames recognize logical pathname namestrings is implementation-defined. These functions include parse-namestring in circumstances other than those described above, merge-pathnames in circumstances other than those described above, the :defaults argument to make-pathname, and the following functions:

compile-file	file-write-date	pathname-name
compile-file-pathname	host-namestring	pathname-type
delete-file	load	pathname-version
directory	namestring	probe-file
directory-namestring	open	rename-file
dribble	pathname	translate-pathname
ed	pathname-device	truename
enough-namestring	pathname-directory	wild-pathname-p
file-author	pathname-host	with-open-file
file-namestring	pathname-match-p	

Note that many of these functions must accept logical pathnames even though they do not accept logical pathname namestrings.

23.1.5.3. Using Logical Pathnames

Some real file systems do not have versions. Logical pathname translation to such a file system ignores the version. This implies that a portable program cannot rely on being able to store in a file system more than one version of a file named by a logical pathname.

The type of a logical pathname for a Common Lisp source file is LISP. This should be translated into whatever implementation-defined type is appropriate in a physical pathname.

The logical pathname host name SYS is reserved for the implementation. The existence and meaning of logical pathnames for logical host SYS is implementation-defined.

File manipulation functions must operate with logical pathnames according to the following requirements:

- The following accept logical pathnames and translate them into physical pathnames as if by calling the function translate-logical-pathname:

`compile-file`	`ed`	`probe-file`
`compile-file-pathname`	`file-author`	`rename-file`
`delete-file`	`file-write-date`	`truename`
`directory`	`load`	`with-open-file`
`dribble`	`open`	

- Applying the function `pathname` to a stream created by the function `open` or the macro `with-open-file` using a logical pathname produces a logical pathname.

- The functions `truename`, `probe-file`, and `directory` never return logical pathnames.

- Calling `rename-file` with a logical pathname as the second argument returns a logical pathname as the first value.

- `make-pathname` returns a logical pathname if and only if the host is logical. If the `:host` argument to `make-pathname` is supplied, the host is logical if it came from the `pathname-host` of a logical pathname. Whether a `:host` argument is logical if it is a string equal to a logical pathname host name is implementation-defined.

`logical-pathname` *pathname*   [*Function*]

Converts the argument to a logical pathname and returns it. The argument can be a logical pathname, a logical pathname namestring containing a host component, or a stream for which the `pathname` function returns a logical pathname. For any other argument, `logical-pathname` signals an error of type `type-error`.

`translate-logical-pathname` *pathname* &key   [*Function*]

Translates a logical pathname to the corresponding physical pathname. The *pathname* argument is first coerced to a pathname. If it is not a pathname, string, or file stream, an error of type `type-error` is signaled.

If the coerced argument is a physical pathname, it is returned.

If the coerced argument is a logical pathname, the first matching translation (according to `pathname-match-p`) of the logical pathname host is applied, as if by calling `translate-pathname`. If the result is a logical pathname, this process is repeated. When the result is finally a physical pathname, it is returned.

If no translation matches a logical pathname, an error of type `file-error` is signaled.

`translate-logical-pathname` may perform additional translations, typically to provide translation of file types to local naming conventions, to accommodate physical file systems with names of limited length, or to deal with special character requirements such as translating hyphens to underscores or uppercase letters to lowercase. Any such additional translations are implementation-defined. Some implementations do no additional translations.

There are no specified keyword arguments for `translate-logical-pathname` but implementations are permitted to extend it by adding keyword arguments. There is one specified return value from `translate-logical-pathname`; implementations are permitted to extend it by returning additional values.

`logical-pathname-translations` *host*   [*Function*]

If the specified *host* is not the host component of a logical pathname and is not a string that has been defined as a logical pathname host name by `setf` of `logical-pathname-translations`, this function signals an error of type `type-error`; otherwise, it returns the list of translations for the specified *host*. Each translation is a list of at least two elements, from-wildname and to-wildname. Any additional elements are implementation-defined. A from-wildname is a logical pathname whose host is the specified *host*. A to-wildname is any pathname. Translations are searched in the order listed, so more specific from-wildnames must precede more general ones.

(`setf` (`logical-pathname-translations` *host*) *translations*) sets the list of translations for the logical pathname *host* to *translations*. If *host* is a string that has not previously been used as logical pathname host, a new logical pathname host is defined; otherwise an existing host's translations are replaced. Logical pathname host names are compared with `string-equal`.

When setting the translations list, each from-wildname can be a logical pathname whose host is *host* or a logical pathname namestring *s* parseable by (`parse-namestring` *s* *host-object*), where *host-object* is an appropriate object for representing the specified *host* to `parse-namestring`. (This circuitous specification dodges the fact that `parse-namestring` does not necessarily accept as its second argument any old string that names a logical host.) Each to-wildname can be anything coercible to a pathname by application of the function `pathname`. If to-wildname coerces to a logical pathname, `translate-logical-pathname` will retranslate the result, repeatedly if necessary.

Implementations may define additional functions that operate on logical pathname hosts (for example, to specify additional translation rules or options).

`load-logical-pathname-translations` *host*   [*Function*]

If a logical pathname host named *host* (a string) is already defined, this function returns `nil`. Otherwise, it searches for a logical pathname host definition in an implementation-defined manner. If none is found, it signals an error. If a definition is found, it installs the definition and returns t.

The search used by `load-logical-pathname-translations` should be documented, as logical pathname definitions will be created by users as well as by Lisp implementors. A typical search technique is to look in an implementation-defined directory for a file whose name is derived from the host name in an implementation-defined fashion.

`compile-file-pathname` *pathname* &key :output-file   [*Function*]

Returns the pathname that `compile-file` would write into, if given the same arguments. If the pathname argument is a logical pathname and the :output-file argument is unspecified, the result is a logical pathname. If an implementation supports additional keyword arguments to `compile-file`, `compile-file-pathname` must accept the same arguments.

23.1.5.4. Examples of the Use of Logical Pathnames

Here is a very simple example of setting up a logical pathname host named FOO. Suppose that no translations are necessary to get around file system restrictions, so all that is necessary is to specify the root of the physical directory tree that contains the logical file system. The namestring syntax in the to-wildname is implementation-specific.

```
(setf (logical-pathname-translations "foo")
      ´(("**;*.*.*"              "MY-LISPM:>library>foo>**>")))
```

The following is a sample use of that logical pathname. All return values are of course implementation-specific; all of the examples in this section are of course meant to be illustrative and not prescriptive.

```
(translate-logical-pathname "foo:bar;baz;mum.quux.3")
   ⇒ #P"MY-LISPM:>library>foo>bar>baz>mum.quux.3"
```

Next we have a more complex example, dividing the files among two file servers (U, supporting a UNIX file system, and V, supporting a VAX/VMS file system) and several different directories. This UNIX file system doesn't support :wild-inferiors in the directory, so each directory level must be translated individually. No file name or type translations are required except for .MAIL to .MBX. The namestring syntax used for the to-wildnames is implementation-specific.

```
(setf (logical-pathname-translations "prog")
      '(("RELEASED;*.*.*"    "U:/sys/bin/my-prog/")
        ("RELEASED;*;*.*.*"  "U:/sys/bin/my-prog/*/")
        ("EXPERIMENTAL;*.*.*"
                              "U:/usr/Joe/development/prog/")
        ("EXPERIMENTAL;DOCUMENTATION;*.*.*"
                              "V:SYS$DISK:[JOE.DOC]")
        ("EXPERIMENTAL;*;*.*.*"
                              "U:/usr/Joe/development/prog/*/")
        ("MAIL;**;*.MAIL"    "V:SYS$DISK:[JOE.MAIL.PROG...]*.MBX")
        ))
```

Here are sample uses of logical host PROG. All return values are of course implementation-specific.

```
(translate-logical-pathname "prog:mail;save;ideas.mail.3")
  ⇒ #P"V:SYS$DISK:[JOE.MAIL.PROG.SAVE]IDEAS.MBX.3"

(translate-logical-pathname "prog:experimental;spreadsheet.c")
  ⇒ #P"U:/usr/Joe/development/prog/spreadsheet.c"
```

Suppose now that we have a program that uses three files logically named MAIN.LISP, AUXILIARY.LISP, and DOCUMENTATION.LISP. The following translations might be provided by a software supplier as examples.

For a UNIX file system with long file names:

```
(setf (logical-pathname-translations "prog")
      '(("CODE;*.*.*"        "/lib/prog/")))

(translate-logical-pathname "prog:code;documentation.lisp")
  ⇒ #P"/lib/prog/documentation.lisp"
```

For a UNIX file system with 14-character file names, using .lisp as the type:

```
(setf (logical-pathname-translations "prog")
      '(("CODE;DOCUMENTATION.*.*" "/lib/prog/docum.*")
        ("CODE;*.*.*"             "/lib/prog/")))

(translate-logical-pathname "prog:code;documentation.lisp")
  ⇒ #P"/lib/prog/docum.lisp"
```

For a UNIX file system with 14-character file names, using .l as the type (the second translation shortens the compiled file type to .b):

```
(setf (logical-pathname-translations "prog")
      `(("**;*.LISP.*"          ,(logical-pathname "PROG:**;*.L.*"))
        (,(compile-file-pathname
            (logical-pathname "PROG:**;*.LISP.*"))
                              ,(logical-pathname "PROG:**;*.B.*"))
        ("CODE;DOCUMENTATION.*.*" "/lib/prog/documentatio.*")
        ("CODE;*.*.*"             "/lib/prog/")))

(translate-logical-pathname "prog:code;documentation.lisp")
   ⇒ #P"/lib/prog/documentatio.1"
```

23.1.5.5. Discussion of Logical Pathnames

Large programs can be moved between sites without changing any pathnames, provided all pathnames used are logical. A portable system construction tool can be created that operates on programs defined as sets of files named by logical pathnames.

Logical pathname syntax was chosen to be easily translated into the formats of most popular file systems, while still being powerful enough for storing large programs. Although they have hierarchical directories, extended wildcard matching, versions, and no limit on the length of names, logical pathnames can be mapped onto a less capable real file system by translating each directory that is used into a flat directory name, processing wildcards in the Lisp implementation rather than in the file system, treating all versions as :newest, and using translations to shorten long names.

Logical pathname words are restricted to non-case-sensitive letters, digits, and hyphens to avoid creating problems with real file systems that support limited character sets for file naming. (If logical pathnames were case-sensitive, it would be very difficult to map them into a file system that is not sensitive to case in its file names.)

It is not a goal of logical pathnames to be able to represent all possible file names. Their goal is rather to represent just enough file names to be useful for storing software. Real pathnames, in contrast, need to provide a uniform interface to all possible file names, including names and naming conventions that are not under the control of Common Lisp.

The choice of logical pathname syntax, using colon, semicolon, and period, was guided by the goals of being visually distinct from real file systems and minimizing the use of special characters.

The logical-pathname function is separate from the pathname function so that the syntax of logical pathname namestrings does not constrain the syntax of physical pathname namestrings in any way. Logical pathname syntax must be defined by Common Lisp so that logical pathnames can be conveniently exchanged between implementations, but physical pathname syntax is dictated by the operating environments.

The `compile-file-pathname` function and the specification of LISP as the type of a logical pathname for a Common Lisp source file together provide enough information about compilation to make possible a portable system construction tool. Suppose that it is desirable to call `compile-file` only if the source file is newer than the compiled file. For this to succeed, it must be possible to know the name of the compiled file without actually calling `compile-file`. In some implementations the compiler produces one of several file types, depending on a variety of implementation-dependent circumstances, so it is not sufficient simply to prescribe a standard logical file type for compiled files; `compile-file-pathname` provides access to the defaulting that is performed by `compile-file` "in a manner appropriate to the implementation's file system conventions."

The use of the logical pathname host name SYS for the implementation is current practice. Standardizing on this name helps users choose logical pathname host names that avoid conflicting with implementation-defined names.

Loading of logical pathname translations from a site-dependent file allows software to be distributed using logical pathnames. The assumed model of software distribution is a division of labor between the supplier of the software and the user installing it. The supplier chooses logical pathnames to name all the files used or created by the software, and supplies examples of logical pathname translations for a few popular file systems. Each example uses an assumed directory and/or device name, assumes local file naming conventions, and provides translations that will translate all the logical pathnames used or generated by the particular software into valid physical pathnames. For a powerful file system these translations can be quite simple. For a more restricted file system, it may be necessary to list an explicit translation for every logical pathname used (for example, when dealing with restrictions on the maximum length of a file name).

The user installing the software decides on which device and directory to store the files and edits the example logical pathname translations accordingly. If necessary, the user also adjusts the translations for local file naming conventions and any other special aspects of the user's local file system policy and local Common Lisp implementation. For example, the files might be divided among several file server hosts to share the load. The process of defining site-customized logical pathname translations is quite easy for a user of a popular file system for which the software supplier has provided an example. A user of a more unusual file system might have to take more time; the supplier can help by providing a list of all the logical pathnames used or generated by the software.

Once the user has created and executed a suitable `setf` form for setting the `logical-pathname-translations` of the relevant logical host, the software can be loaded and run. It may be necessary to use the translations again, or on another workstation at the same site, so it is best to save the `setf` form in the standard place where it can be found later by `load-logical-pathname-translations`. Often a software supplier will include a program for restoring software from the distribution medium to the file system and a program for loading the software from the file system into a Common Lisp; these programs will start by calling `load-logical-pathname-translations` to make sure that the logical pathname host is defined.

Note that the `setf` of `logical-pathname-translations` form isn't part of the program; it is separate and is written by the user, not by the software supplier. That separation and a uniform convention for doing the separation are the key aspects of logical pathnames. For small programs involving only a handful of files, it doesn't matter much. The real benefits come with large programs with hundreds or thousands of files and more complicated situations such as program-generated file names or porting a program developed on a system with long file names onto a system with a very restrictive limit on the length of file names.

23.1.6. Pathname Functions

These functions are what programs use to parse and default file names that have been typed in or otherwise supplied by the user.

Any argument called *pathname* in this book may actually be a pathname, a string or symbol, or a stream. Any argument called *defaults* may likewise be a pathname, a string or symbol, or a stream.

X3J13 voted in March 1988 ⟨134⟩ to change the language so that a symbol is *never* allowed as a pathname argument. More specifically, the following functions are changed to disallow a symbol as a *pathname* argument:

pathname	pathname-device	namestring
truename	pathname-directory	file-namestring
parse-namestring	pathname-name	directory-namestring
merge-pathnames	pathname-type	host-namestring
pathname-host	pathname-version	enough-namestring

(The function `require` was also changed by this vote but was deleted from the language by a vote in January 1989 ⟨154⟩.) Furthermore, the vote reaffirmed that the following functions do not accept symbols as *file*, *filename*, or *pathname* arguments:

open	rename-file	file-write-date
with-open-file	delete-file	file-author
load	probe-file	directory
compile-file		

In older implementations of Lisp that did not have strings, for example MacLisp, symbols were the only means for specifying pathnames. This was convenient only because the file systems of the time allowed only uppercase letters in file names. Typing (load 'foo) caused the function load to receive the symbol FOO (with uppercase letters because of the way symbols are parsed) and therefore to load the file named FOO. Now that many file systems, most notably UNIX, support case-sensitive file names, the use of symbols is less convenient and more error-prone.

X3J13 voted in March 1988 ⟨132⟩ to specify that a stream may be used as a pathname, file, or filename argument only if it was created by use of open or with-open-file, or if it is a synonym stream whose symbol is bound to a stream that may be used as a pathname.

If such a stream is used as a pathname, it is as if the pathname function were applied to the stream and the resulting pathname used in place of the stream. This represents the name used to open the file. This may be, but is not required to be, the actual name of the file.

It is an error to attempt to obtain a pathname from a stream created by any of the following:

make-two-way-stream	make-string-input-stream
make-echo-stream	make-string-output-stream
make-broadcast-stream	with-input-from-string
make-concatenated-stream	with-output-to-string

In the examples, it is assumed that the host named CMUC runs the TOPS-20 operating system, and therefore uses TOPS-20 file system syntax; furthermore, an explicit host name is indicated by following the host name with a double colon. Remember, however, that namestring syntax is implementation-dependent, and this syntax is used here purely for the sake of examples.

pathname *pathname*   [*Function*]

The pathname function converts its argument to be a pathname. The argument may be a pathname, a string or symbol, or a stream; the result is always a pathname.

X3J13 voted in March 1988 not to permit symbols as pathnames ⟨134⟩ and to specify exactly which streams may be used as pathnames ⟨132⟩.

X3J13 voted in January 1989 ⟨15⟩ to specify that pathname is unaffected by whether its argument, if a stream, is open or closed. X3J13 further commented that because some implementations cannot provide the "true name" of a file until the file is closed, in such an implementation pathname might, in principle, return a different (perhaps more specific) file name after the stream is closed. However, such behavior is prohibited; pathname must return the same pathname after a stream is closed as it would have while the stream was open. See truename.

truename *pathname*   [*Function*]

The truename function endeavors to discover the "true name" of the file associated with the *pathname* within the file system. If the *pathname* is an open stream already associated with a file in the file system, that file is used. The "true name" is returned as a pathname. An error is signaled if an appropriate file cannot be located within the file system for the given *pathname*.

The truename function may be used to account for any file name translations performed by the file system, for example.

For example, suppose that DOC: is a TOPS-20 logical device name that is translated by the TOPS-20 file system to be PS:<DOCUMENTATION>.

```
(setq file (open "CMUC::DOC:DUMPER.HLP"))
(namestring (pathname file)) ⇒ "CMUC::DOC:DUMPER.HLP"
(namestring (truename file))
    ⇒ "CMUC::PS:<DOCUMENTATION>DUMPER.HLP.13"
```

X3J13 voted in March 1988 not to permit symbols as pathnames ⟨134⟩ and to specify exactly which streams may be used as pathnames ⟨132⟩.

X3J13 voted in January 1989 ⟨15⟩ to specify that truename may be applied to a stream whether the stream is open or closed. X3J13 further commented that because some implementations cannot provide the "true name" of a file until the file is closed, in principle it would be possible in such an implementation for truename to return a different file name after the stream is closed. Such behavior is permitted; in this respect truename differs from pathname.

X3J13 voted in June 1989 ⟨137⟩ to clarify that truename accepts only non-wild pathnames; an error is signaled if wild-pathname-p would be true of the *pathname* argument.

X3J13 voted in June 1989 ⟨130⟩ to require truename to accept logical pathnames (see section 23.1.5). However, truename never returns a logical pathname.

parse-namestring *thing* &optional *host defaults* &key :start   [*Function*]
                              :end :junk-allowed

This turns *thing* into a pathname. The *thing* is usually a string (that is, a namestring), but it may be a symbol (in which case the print name is used) or a pathname or stream (in which case no parsing is needed, but an error check may be made for matching hosts).

X3J13 voted in March 1988 not to permit symbols as pathnames ⟨134⟩ and to specify exactly which streams may be used as pathnames ⟨132⟩. The *thing* argument may not be a symbol.

X3J13 voted in June 1989 ⟨130⟩ to require parse-namestring to accept logical pathname namestrings (see section 23.1.5).

This function does *not*, in general, do defaulting of pathname components, even though it has an argument named *defaults*; it only does parsing. The *host* and *defaults* arguments are present because in some implementations it may be that a namestring can only be parsed with reference to a particular file name syntax of several available in the implementation. If *host* is non-nil, it must be a host name that could appear in the host component of a pathname, or nil; if *host* is nil then the host name is extracted from the default pathname in *defaults* and used to determine the syntax convention. The *defaults* argument defaults to the value of *default-pathname-defaults*.

For a string (or symbol) argument, parse-namestring parses a file name within it in the range delimited by the :start and :end arguments (which are integer indices into *string*, defaulting to the beginning and end of the string).

See chapter 14 for a discussion of :start and :end arguments.

If :junk-allowed is not nil, then the first value returned is the pathname parsed, or nil if no syntactically correct pathname was seen.

If :junk-allowed is nil (the default), then the entire substring is scanned. The returned value is the pathname parsed. An error is signaled if the substring does not consist entirely of the representation of a pathname, possibly surrounded on either side by whitespace characters if that is appropriate to the cultural conventions of the implementation.

In either case, the second value is the index into the string of the delimiter that terminated the parse, or the index beyond the substring if the parse terminated at the end of the substring (as will always be the case if :junk-allowed is false).

If *thing* is not a string or symbol, then *start* (which defaults to zero in any case) is always returned as the second value.

Parsing an empty string always succeeds, producing a pathname with all components (except the host) equal to nil.

Note that if *host* is specified and not nil, and *thing* contains a manifest host name, an error is signaled if the hosts do not match.

If *thing* contains an explicit host name and no explicit device name, then it might be appropriate, depending on the implementation environment, for parse-namestring to supply the standard default device for that host as the device component of the resulting pathname.

`merge-pathnames` *pathname* &optional *defaults default-version*   [*Function*]

This is the function that most programs should call to process a file name supplied by the user. It fills in unspecified components of *pathname* from the *defaults*, and returns a new pathname. The *pathname* and *defaults* arguments may each be a pathname, stream, string, or symbol. The result is always a pathname.

X3J13 voted in March 1988 not to permit symbols as pathnames ⟨134⟩ and to specify exactly which streams may be used as pathnames ⟨132⟩.

X3J13 voted in June 1989 ⟨130⟩ to require `merge-namestrings` to recognize a logical pathname namestring as its first argument if its second argument is a logical pathname (see section 23.1.5).

X3J13 voted in January 1989 ⟨15⟩ to specify that `merge-pathname` is unaffected by whether the first argument, if a stream, is open or closed. If the first argument is a stream, `merge-pathname` behaves as if the function `pathname` were applied to the stream and the resulting pathname used instead.

X3J13 voted in June 1989 ⟨128⟩ to require `merge-pathnames` to map customary case in argument pathnames to the customary case in returned pathnames (see section 23.1.2).

defaults defaults to the value of `*default-pathname-defaults*`.

default-version defaults to `:newest`.

Here is an example of the use of `merge-pathnames`:

```
(merge-pathnames "CMUC::FORMAT"
                 "CMUC::PS:<LISPIO>.FASL")
```
⇒ a pathname object that re-expressed as a namestring would be
   `"CMUC::PS:<LISPIO>FORMAT.FASL.0"`

Defaulting of pathname components is done by filling in components taken from another pathname. This is especially useful for cases such as a program that has an input file and an output file, and asks the user for the name of both, letting the unsupplied components of one name default from the other. Unspecified components of the output pathname will come from the input pathname, except that the type should default not to the type of the input but to the appropriate default type for output from this program.

The pathname merging operation takes as input a given pathname, a defaults pathname, and a default version, and returns a new pathname. Basically, the missing components in the given pathname are filled in from the defaults pathname, except that if no version is specified the default version is used. The default version is usually `:newest`; if no version is specified the newest version in existence should be used. The default version can be `nil`, to preserve the information that it was missing in the input pathname.

If the given pathname explicitly specifies a host and does not supply a device, then if the host component of the defaults matches the host component of the given pathname, then the device is taken from the defaults; otherwise the device will be the default file device for that host. Next, if the given pathname does not specify a host, device, directory, name, or type, each such component is copied from the defaults. The merging rules for the version are more complicated and depend on whether the pathname specifies a name. If the pathname doesn't specify a name, then the version, if not provided, will come from the defaults, just like the other components. However, if the pathname does specify a name, then the version is not affected by the defaults. The reason is that the version "belongs to" some other file name and is unlikely to have anything to do with the new one. Finally, if this process leaves the version missing, the default version is used.

The net effect is that if the user supplies just a name, then the host, device, directory, and type will come from the defaults, but the version will come from the default version argument to the merging operation. If the user supplies nothing, or just a directory, the name, type, and version will come over from the defaults together. If the host's file name syntax provides a way to input a version without a name or type, the user can let the name and type default but supply a version different from the one in the defaults.

X3J13 voted in June 1989 ⟨135⟩ to agree to disagree: merge-pathname might or might not perform plausibility checking on its arguments to ensure that the resulting pathname can be converted a valid namestring. User beware: this could cause portability problems.

For example, suppose that host LOSER constrains file types to be three characters or fewer but host CMUC does not. Then "LOSER::FORMAT" is a valid namestring and "CMUC::PS:<LISPIO>.FASL" is a valid namestring, but

```
(merge-pathnames "LOSER::FORMAT" "CMUC::PS:<LISPIO>.FASL")
```

might signal an error in some implementations because the hypothetical result would be a pathname equivalent to the namestring "LOSER::FORMAT.FASL" which is illegal because the file type FASL has more than three characters. In other implementations merge-pathname might return a pathname but that pathname might cause namestring to signal an error.

---

default-pathname-defaults   [*Variable*]

This is the default pathname-defaults pathname; if any pathname primitive that needs a set of defaults is not given one, it uses this one. As a general rule, however, each program should have its own pathname defaults rather than using this one.

```
make-pathname &key :host :device :directory :name :type     [Function]
                  :version :defaults
```

Given some components, make-pathname constructs and returns a pathname. After the components specified explicitly by the :host, :device, :directory,
:name, :type, and :version arguments are filled in, the merging rules used by
merge-pathnames are used to fill in any missing components from the defaults
specified by the :defaults argument. The default value of the :defaults argument is a pathname whose host component is the same as the host component of
the value of *default-pathname-defaults*, and whose other components are
all nil.

   Whenever a pathname is constructed, whether by make-pathname or some other
function, the components may be canonicalized if appropriate. For example, if a
file system is insensitive to case, then alphabetic characters may be forced to be
all uppercase or all lowercase by the implementation.

   The following example assumes the use of UNIX syntax and conventions.

```
(make-pathname :host "technodrome"
               :directory '(:absolute "usr" "krang")
               :name "shredder")
 ⇒ #P"technodrome:/usr/krang/shredder"
```

X3J13 voted in June 1989 ⟨128⟩ to add a new keyword argument :case to
make-pathname. The new argument description is therefore as follows:

```
make-pathname &key :host :device :directory :name :type     [Function]
                  :version :defaults :case
```

See section 23.1.2 for a description of the :case argument.

   X3J13 voted in June 1989 ⟨135⟩ to agree to disagree: make-pathname might
or might not check on its arguments to ensure that the resulting pathname can be
converted to a valid namestring. If make-pathname does not check its arguments
and signal an error in problematical cases, namestring yet might or might not
signal an error when given the resulting pathname. User beware: this could cause
portability problems.

```
pathnamep object                                            [Function]
```

This predicate is true if *object* is a pathname, and otherwise is false.

```
(pathnamep x) ≡ (typep x 'pathname)
```

pathname-host *pathname*	[*Function*]
pathname-device *pathname*	[*Function*]
pathname-directory *pathname*	[*Function*]
pathname-name *pathname*	[*Function*]
pathname-type *pathname*	[*Function*]
pathname-version *pathname*	[*Function*]

These return the components of the argument *pathname*, which may be a pathname, string or symbol, or stream. The returned values can be strings, special symbols, or some other object in the case of structured components. The type will always be a string or a symbol. The version will always be a number or a symbol.

X3J13 voted in March 1988 not to permit symbols as pathnames ⟨134⟩ and to specify exactly which streams may be used as pathnames ⟨132⟩.

X3J13 voted in January 1989 ⟨15⟩ to specify that these operations are unaffected by whether the first argument, if a stream, is open or closed. If the first argument is a stream, each operation behaves as if the function pathname were applied to the stream and the resulting pathname used instead.

X3J13 voted in June 1989 ⟨128⟩ to add a keyword argument :case to all of the pathname accessor functions except pathname-version. The new argument descriptions are therefore as follows:

pathname-host *pathname* &key :case	[*Function*]
pathname-device *pathname* &key :case	[*Function*]
pathname-directory *pathname* &key :case	[*Function*]
pathname-name *pathname* &key :case	[*Function*]
pathname-type *pathname* &key :case	[*Function*]
pathname-version *pathname*	[*Function*]

See section 23.1.2 for a description of the :case argument.

X3J13 voted in June 1989 ⟨133⟩ to specify that pathname-directory always returns nil, :unspecific, or a list—never a string, never :wild (see section 23.1.3). If a list is returned, it is not guaranteed to be freshly consed; the consequences of modifying this list are undefined.

namestring *pathname*	[*Function*]
file-namestring *pathname*	[*Function*]
directory-namestring *pathname*	[*Function*]
host-namestring *pathname*	[*Function*]
enough-namestring *pathname* &optional *defaults*	[*Function*]

The *pathname* argument may be a pathname, a string or symbol, or a stream that is or was open to a file. The name represented by *pathname* is returned as a namelist in canonical form.

If *pathname* is a stream, the name returned represents the name used to *open* the file, which may not be the *actual* name of the file (see `truename`).

X3J13 voted in March 1988 not to permit symbols as pathnames ⟨134⟩ and to specify exactly which streams may be used as pathnames ⟨132⟩.

X3J13 voted in January 1989 ⟨15⟩ to specify that these operations are unaffected by whether the first argument, if a stream, is open or closed. If the first argument is a stream, each operation behaves as if the function `pathname` were applied to the stream and the resulting pathname used instead.

`namestring` returns the full form of the *pathname* as a string. `file-namestring` returns a string representing just the *name*, *type*, and *version* components of the *pathname*; the result of `directory-namestring` represents just the *directory-name* portion; and `host-namestring` returns a string for just the *host-name* portion. Note that a valid namestring cannot necessarily be constructed simply by concatenating some of the three shorter strings in some order.

`enough-namestring` takes another argument, *defaults*. It returns an abbreviated namestring that is just sufficient to identify the file named by *pathname* when considered relative to the *defaults* (which defaults to the value of `*default-pathname-defaults*`). That is, it is required that

```
(merge-pathnames (enough-namestring pathname defaults) defaults) ≡
 (merge-pathnames (parse-namestring pathname nil defaults) defaults)
```

in all cases; and the result of `enough-namestring` is, roughly speaking, the shortest reasonable string that will still satisfy this criterion.

X3J13 voted in June 1989 ⟨135⟩ to agree to disagree: `make-pathname` and `merge-pathnames` might or might not be able to produce pathnames that cannot be converted to valid namestrings. User beware: this could cause portability problems.

`user-homedir-pathname &optional` *host*   [*Function*]

Returns a pathname for the user's "home directory" on *host*. The *host* argument defaults in some appropriate implementation-dependent manner. The concept of "home directory" is itself somewhat implementation-dependent, but from the point of view of Common Lisp it is the directory where the user keeps personal files such as initialization files and mail. If it is impossible to determine this information, then `nil` is returned instead of a pathname; however, `user-homedir-pathname` never returns `nil` if the *host* argument is not specified. This function returns a pathname without any name, type, or version component (those components are all `nil`).

23.2. Opening and Closing Files

When a file is *opened*, a stream object is constructed to serve as the file system's ambassador to the Lisp environment; operations on the stream are reflected by operations on the file in the file system. The act of *closing* the file (actually, the stream) ends the association; the transaction with the file system is terminated, and input/output may no longer be performed on the stream. The stream function `close` may be used to close a file; the functions described below may be used to open them. The basic operation is `open`, but `with-open-file` is usually more convenient for most applications.

---

open *filename* &key :direction :element-type :if-exists   [*Function*]
    :if-does-not-exist :external-format

X3J13 voted in June 1989 ⟨122⟩ to add to the function `open` a new keyword argument `:external-format`. This argument did not appear in the preceding argument description in the first edition.

This returns a stream that is connected to the file specified by *filename*. The *filename* is the name of the file to be opened; it may be a string, a pathname, or a stream. (If the *filename* is a stream, then it is not closed first or otherwise affected; it is used merely to provide a file name for the opening of a new stream.)

X3J13 voted in January 1989 ⟨167⟩ to specify that the result of `open`, if it is a stream, is always a stream of type `file-stream`.

X3J13 voted in March 1988 ⟨132⟩ to specify exactly which streams may be used as pathnames. See section 23.1.6.

X3J13 voted in January 1989 ⟨15⟩ to specify that `open` is unaffected by whether the first argument, if a stream, is open or closed. If the first argument is a stream, `open` behaves as if the function `pathname` were applied to the stream and the resulting pathname used instead.

X3J13 voted in June 1989 ⟨137⟩ to clarify that `open` accepts only non-wild pathnames; an error is signaled if `wild-pathname-p` would be true of *filename*.

X3J13 voted in June 1989 ⟨130⟩ to require `open` to accept logical pathnames (see section 23.1.5).

The keyword arguments specify what kind of stream to produce and how to handle errors:

:direction

This argument specifies whether the stream should handle input, output, or both.

    :input

The result will be an input stream. This is the default.

:output

The result will be an output stream.

:io

The result will be a bidirectional stream.

:probe

The result will be a no-directional stream (in effect, the stream is created and then closed). This is useful for determining whether a file exists without actually setting up a complete stream.

:element-type

This argument specifies the type of the unit of transaction for the stream. Anything that can be recognized as being a finite subtype of character or integer is acceptable. In particular, the following types are recognized:

string-char

The unit of transaction is a string-character. The functions read-char and/or write-char may be used on the stream. This is the default.

character

The unit of transaction is any character, not just a string-character. The functions read-char and/or write-char may be used on the stream.

X3J13 voted in June 1989 ⟨122⟩ to eliminate the type string-char, add the type base-character, and redefine open to use the type character as the default :element-type.

The preceding two possibilities should therefore be replaced by the following.

character

The unit of transaction is any character, not just a string-character. The functions read-char and write-char (depending on the value of the :direction argument) may be used on the stream. This is the default.

base-character

The unit of transaction is a base character. The functions read-char and write-char (depending on the value of the :direction argument) may be used on the stream.

(unsigned-byte n)

The unit of transaction is an unsigned byte (a non-negative integer) of size n. The functions read-byte and/or write-byte may be used on the stream.

unsigned-byte

The unit of transaction is an unsigned byte (a non-negative integer); the size of the byte is determined by the file system. The functions read-byte and/or write-byte may be used on the stream.

(signed-byte *n*)

The unit of transaction is a signed byte of size *n*. The functions read-byte and/or write-byte may be used on the stream.

signed-byte

The unit of transaction is a signed byte; the size of the byte is determined by the file system. The functions read-byte and/or write-byte may be used on the stream.

bit

The unit of transaction is a bit (values 0 and 1). The functions read-byte and/or write-byte may be used on the stream.

(mod *n*)

The unit of transaction is a non-negative integer less than *n*. The functions read-byte and/or write-byte may be used on the stream.

:default

The unit of transaction is to be determined by the file system, based on the file it finds. The type can be determined by using the function stream-element-type.

:if-exists

This argument specifies the action to be taken if the :direction is :output or :io and a file of the specified name already exists. If the direction is :input or :probe, this argument is ignored.

:error

Signals an error. This is the default when the version component of the *filename* is not :newest.

:new-version

Creates a new file with the same file name but with a larger version number. This is the default when the version component of the *filename* is :newest.

`:rename`

Renames the existing file to some other name and then creates a new file with the specified name.

`:rename-and-delete`

Renames the existing file to some other name and then deletes it (but does not expunge it, on those systems that distinguish deletion from expunging). Then create a new file with the specified name.

`:overwrite`

Uses the existing file. Output operations on the stream will destructively modify the file. If the `:direction` is `:io`, the file is opened in a bidirectional mode that allows both reading and writing. The file pointer is initially positioned at the beginning of the file; however, the file is not truncated back to length zero when it is opened. This mode is most useful when the `file-position` function can be used on the stream.

`:append`

Uses the existing file. Output operations on the stream will destructively modify the file. The file pointer is initially positioned at the end of the file. If the `:direction` is `:io`, the file is opened in a bidirectional mode that allows both reading and writing.

`:supersede`

Supersedes the existing file. If possible, the implementation should arrange not to destroy the old file until the new stream is closed, against the possibility that the stream will be closed in "abort" mode (see `close`). This differs from `:new-version` in that `:supersede` creates a new file with the same name as the old one, rather than a file name with a higher version number.

`nil`

Does not create a file or even a stream, but instead simply returns `nil` to indicate failure.

If the `:direction` is `:output` or `:io` and the value of `:if-exists` is `:new-version`, then the version of the (newly created) file that is opened will be a version greater than that of any other file in the file system whose other pathname components are the same as those of *filename*.

If the `:direction` is `:input` or `:probe` or the value of `:if-exists` is not `:new-version`, *and* the version component of the *filename* is `:newest`, then the file opened is that file already existing in the file system that has a version greater than that of any other file in the file system whose other pathname components are the same as those of *filename*.

Some file systems permit yet other actions to be taken when a file already exists; therefore, some implementations provide implementation-specific :if-exist options.

Implementation note: The various file systems in existence today have widely differing capabilities. A given implementation may not be able to support all of these options in exactly the manner stated. An implementation is required to recognize all of these option keywords and to try to do something "reasonable" in the context of the host operating system. Implementors are encouraged to approximate the semantics specified here as closely as possible.

As an example, suppose that a file system does not support distinct file versions and does not distinguish the notions of deletion and expunging (in some file systems file deletion is reversible until an expunge operation is performed). Then :new-version might be treated the same as :rename or :supersede, and :rename-and-delete might be treated the same as :supersede.

If it is utterly impossible for an implementation to handle some option in a manner close to what is specified here, it may simply signal an error. The opening of files is an area where complete portability is too much to hope for; the intent here is simply to make things as portable as possible by providing specific names for a range of commonly supportable options.

:if-does-not-exist

This argument specifies the action to be taken if a file of the specified name does not already exist.

:error

Signals an error. This is the default if the :direction is :input, or if the :if-exists argument is :overwrite or :append.

:create

Creates an empty file with the specified name and then proceeds as if it had already existed (but do not perform any processing directed by the :if-exists argument). This is the default if the :direction is :output or :io, and the :if-exists argument is anything but :overwrite or :append.

nil

Does not create a file or even a stream, but instead simply returns nil to indicate failure. This is the default if the :direction is :probe.

X3J13 voted in June 1989 ⟨122⟩ to add to the function `open` a new keyword argument `:external-format`.

`:external-format`

This argument specifies an implementation-recognized scheme for representing characters in files. The default value is `:default` and is implementation-defined but must support the base characters. An error is signaled if the implementation does recognize the specified format.

This argument may be specified if the `:direction` argument is `:input`, `:output`, or `:io`. It is an error to write a character to the resulting stream that cannot be represented by the specified file format. (However, the `#\Newline` character cannot produce such an error; implementations must provide appropriate line division behavior for all character streams.)

See `stream-external-format`.

When the caller is finished with the stream, it should close the file by using the `close` function. The `with-open-file` form does this automatically, and so is preferred for most purposes. `open` should be used only when the control structure of the program necessitates opening and closing of a file in some way more complex than provided by `with-open-file`. It is suggested that any program that uses `open` directly should use the special form `unwind-protect` to close the file if an abnormal exit occurs.

`with-open-file` (*stream filename* {*options*}*)   [*Macro*]
              {*declaration*}* {*form*}*

`with-open-file` evaluates the *forms* of the body (an implicit `progn`) with the variable *stream* bound to a stream that reads or writes the file named by the value of *filename*. The *options* are evaluated and are used as keyword arguments to the function `open`.

When control leaves the body, either normally or abnormally (such as by use of `throw`), the file is automatically closed. If a new output file is being written, and control leaves abnormally, the file is aborted and the file system is left, so far as possible, as if the file had never been opened. Because `with-open-file` always closes the file, even when an error exit is taken, it is preferred over `open` for most applications.

filename is the name of the file to be opened; it may be a string, a pathname, or a stream.

X3J13 voted in March 1988 ⟨132⟩ to specify exactly which streams may be used as pathnames. See section 23.1.6.

X3J13 voted in June 1989 ⟨137⟩ to clarify that with-open-file accepts only non-wild pathnames; an error is signaled if wild-pathname-p would be true of the *filename* argument.

X3J13 voted in June 1989 ⟨130⟩ to require with-open-file to accept logical pathnames (see section 23.1.5).

For example:

```
(with-open-file (ifile name
                 :direction :input)
  (with-open-file (ofile (merge-pathname-defaults ifile
                                                  nil
                                                  "out")
                  :direction :output
                  :if-exists :supersede)
    (transduce-file ifile ofile)))
```

X3J13 voted in June 1989 ⟨184⟩ to specify that the variable *stream* is not always bound to a stream; rather it is bound to whatever would be returned by a call to open. For example, if the options include :if-does-not-exist nil, *stream* will be bound to nil if the file does not exist. In this case the value of *stream* should be tested within the body of the with-open-file form before it is used as a stream. For example:

```
(with-open-file (ifile name
                 :direction :input
                 :if-does-not-exist nil)
  ;; Process the file only if it actually exists.
  (when (streamp name)
    (compile-cobol-program ifile)))
```

Implementation note: While with-open-file tries to automatically close the stream on exit from the construct, for robustness it is helpful if the garbage collector can detect discarded streams and automatically close them.

23.3. Renaming, Deleting, and Other File Operations

These functions provide a standard interface to operations provided in some form by most file systems. It may be that some implementations of Common Lisp cannot support them all completely.

rename-file *file new-name*   [*Function*]

The specified *file* is renamed to *new-name* (which must be a file name). The *file*
may be a string, a pathname, or a stream. If it is an open stream associated with
a file, then the stream itself and the file associated with it are affected (if the file
system permits).

X3J13 voted in March 1988 ⟨132⟩ to specify exactly which streams may be used
as pathnames. See section 23.1.6.

rename-file returns three values if successful. The first value is the *new-*
name with any missing components filled in by performing a merge-pathnames
operation using *file* as the defaults. The second value is the truename of the file
before it was renamed. The third value is the truename of the file after it was
renamed.

If the renaming operation is not successful, an error is signaled.

It is an error to specify a file name containing a :wild component, for *file* to
contain a nil component where the file system does not permit a nil component,
or for the result of defaulting missing components of *new-name* from *file* to contain
a nil component where the file system does not permit a nil component.

X3J13 voted in June 1989 ⟨137⟩ to specify that supplying a wild pathname as
the *file* argument to rename-file has implementation-dependent consequences;
rename-file might signal an error, for example, or might rename all files that
match the wild pathname.

X3J13 voted in June 1989 ⟨130⟩ to require rename-file to accept logical pathnames (see section 23.1.5).

Compatibility note: This corresponds to the function called renamef in MacLisp and Lisp
Machine Lisp. The name renamef is not used in Common Lisp because the convention that
a trailing f means "file" conflicts with the use of a trailing f for forms related to setf.

---

delete-file *file*   [*Function*]

The specified *file* is deleted. The *file* may be a string, a pathname, or a stream.
If it is an open stream associated with a file, then the stream itself and the file
associated with it are affected (if the file system permits), in which case the stream
may or may not be closed immediately, and the deletion may be immediate or
delayed until the stream is explicitly closed, depending on the requirements of the
file system.

X3J13 voted in March 1988 ⟨132⟩ to specify exactly which streams may be used
as pathnames. See section 23.1.6.

`delete-file` returns a non-`nil` value if successful. It is left to the discretion of the implementation whether an attempt to delete a non-existent file is considered to be successful. If the deleting operation is not successful, an error is signaled.

It is an error to specify a file name that contains a `:wild` component or one that contains a `nil` component where the file system does not permit a `nil` component.

X3J13 voted in June 1989 ⟨137⟩ to clarify that supplying a wild pathname as the *file* argument to `delete-file` has implementation-dependent consequences; `delete-file` might signal an error, for example, or might delete all files that match the wild pathname.

X3J13 voted in June 1989 ⟨130⟩ to require `delete-file` to accept logical pathnames (see section 23.1.5).

Compatibility note: This corresponds to the function called `deletef` in MacLisp and Lisp Machine Lisp.

`probe-file` *file*   [*Function*]

This predicate is false if there is no file named *file*, and otherwise returns a pathname that is the true name of the file (which may be different from *file* because of file links, version numbers, or other artifacts of the file system). Note that if the *file* is an open stream associated with a file, then `probe-file` cannot return `nil` but will produce the true name of the associated file. See `truename` and the `:probe` value for the `:direction` argument to `open`.

Compatibility note: This corresponds to the function called `probef` in MacLisp and Lisp Machine Lisp.

X3J13 voted in March 1988 ⟨132⟩ to specify exactly which streams may be used as pathnames. See section 23.1.6.

X3J13 voted in June 1989 ⟨137⟩ to clarify that `probe-file` accepts only non-wild pathnames; an error is signaled if `wild-pathname-p` would be true of the *file* argument.

X3J13 voted in June 1989 ⟨130⟩ to require `probe-file` to accept logical pathnames (see section 23.1.5). However, `probe-file` never returns a logical pathname.

X3J13 voted in January 1989 ⟨15⟩ to specify that `probe-file` is unaffected by whether the first argument, if a stream, is open or closed. If the first argument is a stream, `probe-file` behaves as if the function `pathname` were applied to the stream and the resulting pathname used instead. However, X3J13 further commented that the treatment of open streams may differ considerably from one implementation to another; for example, in some operating systems open files are written under a temporary or invisible name and later renamed when closed. In general, programmers writing code intended to be portable should be very careful when using probe-file.

file-write-date *file*   [*Function*]

file can be a file name or a stream that is open to a file. This returns the time at which the file was created or last written as an integer in universal time format (see section 25.4.1), or nil if this cannot be determined.

X3J13 voted in March 1988 ⟨132⟩ to specify exactly which streams may be used as pathnames. See section 23.1.6.

X3J13 voted in June 1989 ⟨137⟩ to clarify that file-write-date accepts only non-wild pathnames; an error is signaled if wild-pathname-p would be true of the *file* argument.

X3J13 voted in June 1989 ⟨130⟩ to require file-write-date to accept logical pathnames (see section 23.1.5).

file-author *file*   [*Function*]

file can be a file name or a stream that is open to a file. This returns the name of the author of the file as a string, or nil if this cannot be determined.

X3J13 voted in March 1988 ⟨132⟩ to specify exactly which streams may be used as pathnames. See section 23.1.6.

X3J13 voted in June 1989 ⟨137⟩ to clarify that file-author accepts only non-wild pathnames; an error is signaled if wild-pathname-p would be true of the *file* argument.

X3J13 voted in June 1989 ⟨130⟩ to require file-author to accept logical pathnames (see section 23.1.5).

file-position *file-stream* &optional *position*   [*Function*]

file-position returns or sets the current position within a random-access file.

(file-position *file-stream*) returns a non-negative integer indicating the current position within the *file-stream*, or nil if this cannot be determined. The file position at the start of a file will be zero. The value returned by file-position increases monotonically as input or output operations are performed. For a character file, performing a single read-char or write-char operation may cause the file position to be increased by more than 1 because of character-set translations (such as translating between the Common Lisp #\Newline character and an external ASCII carriage-return/line-feed sequence) and other aspects of the implementation. For a binary file, every read-byte or write-byte operation increases the file position by 1.

(file-position *file-stream position*) sets the position within *file-stream* to be *position*. The *position* may be an integer, or :start for the beginning of the stream, or :end for the end of the stream. If the integer is too large or otherwise inappropriate, an error is signaled (the file-length function returns the length beyond which file-position may not access). An integer returned by file-position of one argument should, in general, be acceptable as a second argument for use with the same file. With two arguments, file-position returns t if the repositioning was performed successfully, or nil if it was not (for example, because the file was not random-access).

Implementation note: Implementations that have character files represented as a sequence of records of bounded size might choose to encode the file position as, for example, *record-number*256+character-within-record*. This is a valid encoding because it increases monotonically as each character is read or written, though not necessarily by 1 at each step. An integer might then be considered "inappropriate" as a second argument to file-position if, when decoded into record number and character number, it turned out that the specified record was too short for the specified character number.

Compatibility note: This corresponds to the function called filepos in MacLisp and Lisp Machine Lisp.

---

file-length *file-stream*   [*Function*]

file-stream must be a stream that is open to a file. The length of the file is returned as a non-negative integer, or nil if the length cannot be determined. For a binary file, the length is specifically measured in units of the :element-type specified when the file was opened (see open).

Compatibility note: This corresponds to the function called lengthf in MacLisp and Lisp Machine Lisp.

---

file-string-length *file-stream object*   [*Function*]

X3J13 voted in June 1989 ⟨122⟩ to add the function file-string-length. The *object* must be a string or a character. The function file-string-length returns a non-negative integer that is the difference between what the file-position of the *file-stream* would be after and before writing the *object* to the *file-stream*, or nil if this difference cannot be determined. The value returned may depend on the current state of the *file-stream*; that is, calling file-string-length on the same arguments twice may in certain circumstances produce two different integers.

23.4. Loading Files

To *load* a file is to read through the file, evaluating each form in it. Programs are typically stored in files containing calls to constructs such as defun, defmacro, and defvar, which define the functions and variables of the program.

Loading a compiled ("fasload") file is similar, except that the file does not contain text but rather pre-digested expressions created by the compiler that can be loaded more quickly.

load *filename* &key :verbose :print :if-does-not-exist   [*Function*]

This function loads the file named by *filename* into the Lisp environment. It is assumed that a text (character file) can be automatically distinguished from an object (binary) file by some appropriate implementation-dependent means, possibly by the file type. The defaults for *filename* are taken from the variable *default-pathname-defaults*. If the *filename* (after the merging in of the defaults) does not explicitly specify a type, and both text and object types of the file are available in the file system, load should try to select the more appropriate file by some implementation-dependent means.

If the first argument is a stream rather than a pathname, then load determines what kind of stream it is and loads directly from the stream.

The :verbose argument (which defaults to the value of *load-verbose*), if true, permits load to print a message in the form of a comment (that is, with a leading semicolon) to *standard-output* indicating what file is being loaded and other useful information.

The :print argument (default nil), if true, causes the value of each expression loaded to be printed to *standard-output*. If a binary file is being loaded, then what is printed may not reflect precisely the contents of the source file, but nevertheless some information will be printed.

X3J13 voted in March 1989 ⟨26⟩ to add the variable *load-print*; its value is used as the default for the :print argument to load.

The function load rebinds *package* to its current value. If some form in the file changes the value of *package* during loading, the old value will be restored when the loading is completed. (This was specified in the first edition under the description of *package*; for convenience I now mention it here as well.)

X3J13 voted in March 1988 ⟨132⟩ to specify exactly which streams may be used as pathnames. See section 23.1.6.

X3J13 voted in June 1989 ⟨137⟩ to clarify that supplying a wild pathname as the *filename* argument to load has implementation-dependent consequences; load might signal an error, for example, or might load all files that match the pathname.

X3J13 voted in June 1989 ⟨130⟩ to require load to accept logical pathnames (see section 23.1.5).

If a file is successfully loaded, load always returns a non-nil value. If :if-does-not-exist is specified and is nil, load just returns nil rather than signaling an error if the file does not exist.

X3J13 voted in March 1989 ⟨104⟩ to require that load bind *readtable* to its current value at the time load is called; the dynamic extent of the binding should encompass all of the file-loading activity. This allows a portable program to include forms such as

```
(in-package "FOO")

(eval-when (:execute :load-toplevel :compile-toplevel)
  (setq *readtable* foo:my-readtable))
```

without performing a net global side effect on the loading environment. Such statements allow the remainder of such a file to be read either as interpreted code or by compile-file in a syntax determined by an alternative readtable.

X3J13 voted in June 1989 ⟨112⟩ to require that load bind two new variables *load-pathname* and *load-truename*; the dynamic extent of the bindings should encompass all of the file-loading activity.

load-verbose   [*Variable*]

This variable provides the default for the :verbose argument to load. Its initial value is implementation-dependent.

load-print   [*Variable*]

X3J13 voted in March 1989 ⟨26⟩ to add *load-print*. This variable provides the default for the :print argument to load. Its initial value is nil.

load-pathname   [*Variable*]

X3J13 voted in June 1989 ⟨112⟩ to introduce *load-pathname*; it is initially nil but load binds it to a pathname that represents the file name given as the first argument to load merged with the defaults (see merge-pathname).

`*load-truename*`   [*Variable*]

X3J13 voted in June 1989 ⟨112⟩ to introduce `*load-truename*`; it is initially `nil`
but `load` binds it to the "true name" of the file being loaded. See `truename`.

X3J13 voted in March 1989 ⟨110⟩ to introduce a facility based on the Object
System whereby a user can specify how `compile-file` and `load` must cooperate
to reconstruct compile-time constant objects at load time. The protocol is simply
this: `compile-file` calls the generic function `make-load-form` on any object that
is referenced as a constant or as a self-evaluating form, if the object's metaclass is
`standard-class`, `structure-class`, any user-defined metaclass (not a subclass of
`built-in-class`), or any of a possibly empty implementation-defined list of other
metaclasses; `compile-file` will call `make-load-form` only once for any given
object (as determined by eq) within a single file. The user-programmability stems
from the possibility of user-defined methods for `make-load-form`. The helper
function `make-load-form-saving-slots` makes it easy to write commonly used
versions of such methods.

`make-load-form` *object*   [*Generic function*]

The argument is an object that is referenced as a constant or as a self-evaluating
form in a file being compiled by `compile-file`. The objective is to enable `load`
to construct an equivalent object.

The first value, called the *creation form*, is a form that, when evaluated at load
time, should return an object that is equivalent to the argument. The exact meaning
of "equivalent" depends on the type of object and is up to the programmer who
defines a method for `make-load-form`. This allows the user to program the notion
of "similar as a constant" (see section 25.1).

The second value, called the *initialization form*, is a form that, when evaluated
at load time, should perform further initialization of the object. The value returned
by the initialization form is ignored. If the `make-load-form` method returns only
one value, the initialization form is `nil`, which has no effect. If the object used as
the argument to `make-load-form` appears as a constant in the initialization form,
at load time it will be replaced by the equivalent object constructed by the creation
form; this is how the further initialization gains access to the object.

Two values are returned so that circular structures may be handled. The order of
evaluation rules discussed below for creation and initialization forms eliminates the
possibility of partially initialized objects in the absence of circular structures and
reduces the possibility to a minimum in the presence of circular structures. This
allows nodes in non-circular structures to be built out of fully initialized subparts.

Both the creation form and the initialization form can contain references to objects of user-defined types (defined precisely below). However, there must not be any circular dependencies in creation forms. An example of a circular dependency: the creation form for the object X contains a reference to the object Y, and the creation form for the object Y contains a reference to the object X. A simpler example: the creation form for the object X contains a reference to X itself. Initialization forms are not subject to any restriction against circular dependencies, which is the entire reason for having initialization forms. See the example of circular data structures below.

The creation form for an object is always evaluated before the initialization form for that object. When either the creation form or the initialization form refers to other objects of user-defined types that have not been referenced earlier in the compile-file, the compiler collects all of the creation and initialization forms. Each initialization form is evaluated as soon as possible after its creation form, as determined by data flow. If the initialization form for an object does not refer to any other objects of user-defined types that have not been referenced earlier in the compile-file, the initialization form is evaluated immediately after the creation form. If a creation or initialization form F references other objects of user-defined types that have not been referenced earlier in the compile-file, the creation forms for those other objects are evaluated before F and the initialization forms for those other objects are also evaluated before F whenever they do not depend on the object created or initialized by F. Where the above rules do not uniquely determine an order of evaluation, it is unspecified which of the possible orders of evaluation is chosen.

While these creation and initialization forms are being evaluated, the objects are possibly in an uninitialized state, analogous to the state of an object between the time it has been created by allocate-instance and it has been processed fully by initialize-instance. Programmers writing methods for make-load-form must take care in manipulating objects not to depend on slots that have not yet been initialized.

It is unspecified whether load calls eval on the forms or does some other operation that has an equivalent effect. For example, the forms might be translated into different but equivalent forms and then evaluated; they might be compiled and the resulting functions called by load (after they themselves have been loaded); or they might be interpreted by a special-purpose interpreter different from eval. All that is required is that the effect be equivalent to evaluating the forms.

It is valid for user programs to call make-load-form in circumstances other than compilation, providing the argument's metaclass is not built-in-class or a subclass of built-in-class.

Applying make-load-form to an object whose metaclass is standard-class or `structure-class` for which no user-defined method is applicable signals an error. It is valid to implement this either by defining default methods for the classes `standard-object` and `structure-object` that signal an error or by having no applicable method for those classes.

See `load-time-eval`.

In the following example, an equivalent instance of `my-class` is reconstructed by using the values of two of its slots. The value of the third slot is derived from those two values.

```
(defclass my-class ()    ((a :initarg :a :reader my-a)
   (b :initarg :b :reader my-b)
   (c :accessor my-c)))

(defmethod shared-initialize ((self my-class) slots &rest inits)
   (declare (ignore slots inits))
   (unless (slot-boundp self 'c)
     (setf (my-c self)
           (some-computation (my-a self) (my-b self)))))

(defmethod make-load-form ((self my-class))
   `(make-instance ',(class-name (class-of self))
                   :a ',(my-a self) :b ',(my-b self)))
```

This code will fail if either of the first two slots of some instance of `my-class` contains the instance itself. Another way to write the last form in the preceding example is

```
(defmethod make-load-form ((self my-class))
   (make-load-form-saving-slots self '(a b)))
```

This has the advantages of conciseness and handling circularities correctly.

In the next example, instances of class `my-frob` are "interned" in some way. An equivalent instance is reconstructed by using the value of the `name` slot as a key for searching for existing objects. In this case the programmer has chosen to create a new object if no existing object is found; an alternative possibility would be to signal an error in that case.

```
(defclass my-frob ()
   ((name :initarg :name :reader my-name)))

(defmethod make-load-form ((self my-frob))
   `(find-my-frob ',(my-name self) :if-does-not-exist :create))
```

In the following example, the data structure to be dumped is circular, because each node of a tree has a list of its children and each child has a reference back to its parent.

```
(defclass tree-with-parent () ((parent :accessor tree-parent)
                               (children :initarg :children)))

(defmethod make-load-form ((x tree-with-parent))
  (values
    `(make-instance ´,(class-of x)
                    :children ´,(slot-value x ´children))
    `(setf (tree-parent ´,x) ´,(slot-value x ´parent))))
```

Suppose `make-load-form` is called on one object in such a structure. The creation form creates an equivalent object and fills in the `children` slot, which forces creation of equivalent objects for all of its children, grandchildren, etc. At this point none of the parent slots have been filled in. The initialization form fills in the `parent` slot, which forces creation of an equivalent object for the parent if it was not already created. Thus the entire tree is recreated at load time. At compile time, `make-load-form` is called once for each object in the tree. All the creation forms are evaluated, in unspecified order, and then all the initialization forms are evaluated, also in unspecified order.

In this final example, the data structure to be dumped has no special properties and an equivalent structure can be reconstructed simply by reconstructing the slots' contents.

```
(defstruct my-struct a b c)
(defmethod make-load-form ((s my-struct))
  (make-load-form-saving-slots s))
```

This is easy to code using `make-load-form-saving-slots`.

`make-load-form-saving-slots` *object* &optional *slots*   [*Function*]

This returns two values suitable for return from a `make-load-form` method. The first argument is the object. The optional second argument is a list of the names of slots to preserve; it defaults to all of the local slots.

`make-load-form-saving-slots` returns forms that construct an equivalent object using `make-instance` and `setf` of `slot-value` for slots with values, or `slot-makunbound` for slots without values, or other functions of equivalent effect.

Because `make-load-form-saving-slots` returns two values, it can deal with circular structures; it works for any object of metaclass `standard-class` or structure-class. Whether the result is useful depends on whether the object's type and slot contents fully capture an application's idea of the object's state.

23.5. Accessing Directories

The following function is a very simple portable primitive for examining a directory. Most file systems can support much more powerful directory-searching primitives, but no two are alike. It is expected that most implementations of Common Lisp will extend the directory function or provide more powerful primitives.

directory *pathname* &key   [*Function*]

A list of pathnames is returned, one for each file in the file system that matches the given *pathname*. (The *pathname* argument may be a pathname, a string, or a stream associated with a file.) For a file that matches, the truename appears in the result list. If no file matches the *pathname*, it is not an error; directory simply returns nil, the list of no results. Keywords such as :wild and :newest may be used in *pathname* to indicate the search space.

X3J13 voted in March 1988 ⟨132⟩ to specify exactly which streams may be used as pathnames. See section 23.1.6.

X3J13 voted in January 1989 ⟨15⟩ to specify that directory is unaffected by whether the first argument, if a stream, is open or closed. If the first argument is a stream, directory behaves as if the function pathname were applied to the stream and the resulting pathname used instead. However, X3J13 commented that the treatment of open streams may differ considerably from one implementation to another; for example, in some operating systems open files are written under a temporary or invisible name and later renamed when closed. In general, programmers writing code intended to be portable should be careful when using directory.

X3J13 voted in June 1989 ⟨130⟩ to require directory to accept logical pathnames (see section 23.1.5). However, the result returned by directory never contains a logical pathname.

Implementation note: It is anticipated that an implementation may need to provide additional parameters to control the directory search. Therefore directory is specified to take additional keyword arguments so that implementations may experiment with extensions, even though no particular keywords are specified here.

As a simple example of such an extension, for a file system that supports the notion of cross-directory file links, a keyword argument :links might, if non-nil, specify that such links be included in the result list.

24

Errors

Errors may be signaled for a variety of reasons. Many built-in Common Lisp functions may signal an error when given incorrect arguments. Other functions, described in this chapter, may be called by user programs for the purpose of signaling an error.

When an error is signaled, it is handled in an implementation-dependent way. It is expected that each implementation of Common Lisp will provide an interactive debugger that prints the error message along with suitable contextual information such as which function detected the error. The user may interact with the debugger to examine or modify the state of the program in various ways, including abandoning the current computation ("aborting to top level") and continuing from the error. What "continuing" means depends on how the error is signaled; the details of this are specified below for each error-signaling function.

An implementation may also choose to provide means (such as the errset special form in MacLisp) for a program to trap all errors and prevent the debugger from stepping in for certain errors.

Rationale: Error handling of adequate flexibility and power for all systems written in Common Lisp appears to require a complex error classification system. Experience with several error-handling systems in such dialects as MacLisp and Lisp Machine Lisp indicates that further experimentation is needed in this area; it is too early to define a standard error-handling mechanism. Therefore Common Lisp provides standard ways to *signal* errors, but no standard ways to *handle* errors. Of course a complete Lisp system requires error-handling mechanisms, but many useful portable programs do not require them. It is expected that a future revision of Common Lisp will address the problem of portable error-handling mechanisms.

X3J13 voted in June 1988 ⟨30⟩ to adopt a proposal for a Common Lisp Condition System. This was the result of the research and experimentation alluded to in the preceding paragraph. Conditions subsume and generalize the notion of errors. The condition system also provides means for handling conditions (of which errors are a special case) and for restarting a computation after a condition has been signaled. See chapter 29.

Compatibility note: What is here called "continuing," Lisp Machine Lisp calls "proceeding" from an error.

In the new terminology introduced in chapter 29, what Lisp Machine Lisp called "proceeding" would be called "restarting," and "continuing" refers to the particular restart named `continue`.

24.1. General Error-Signaling Functions

The functions in this section provide various mechanisms for signaling warnings, breaks, continuable errors, and fatal errors.

In each case, the caller specifies an error message (a string) that may be processed (and perhaps displayed to the user) by the error-handling mechanism. All messages are constructed by applying the function `format` to the quantities `nil`, *format-string*, and all the *args* to produce a string.

An error message string should not contain a newline character at either the beginning or end, and should not contain any sort of herald indicating that it is an error. The system will take care of these according to whatever its preferred style may be.

Conventionally, error messages are complete English sentences ending with a period. Newlines in the middle of long messages are acceptable. There should be no indentation after a newline in the middle of an error message. The error message need not mention the name of the function that signals the error; it is assumed that the debugger will make this information available.

Implementation note: If the debugger in a particular implementation displays error messages indented from the prevailing left margin (for example, indented by seven spaces because they are prefixed by the seven-character herald "`Error: `"), then the debugger should take care of inserting the appropriate indentation into a multi-line error message. Similarly, a debugger that prefixes error messages with semicolons so that they appear to be comments should take care of inserting a semicolon at the beginning of each line in a multi-line error message. These rules are suggested because, even within a single implementation, there may be more than one program that presents error messages to the user, and they may use different styles of presentation. The caller of `error` cannot anticipate all such possible styles, and so it is incumbent upon the presenter of the message to make any necessary adjustments.

Common Lisp does not specify the manner in which error messages and other messages are displayed. For the purposes of exposition, a fairly simple style of textual presentation will be used in the examples in this chapter. The character > is used to represent the command prompt symbol for a debugger.

error *format-string* &rest *args*   [*Function*]

This function signals a fatal error. It is impossible to continue from this kind of error; thus error will never return to its caller.

The debugger printout in the following example is typical of what an implementation might print when error is called. Suppose that the (misspelled) symbol emergnecy-shutdown has no property named command (all too likely, as it is probably a typographical error for emergency-shutdown).

```
(defun command-dispatch (cmd)
  (let ((fn (get cmd 'command)))
    (if (not (null fn))
        (funcall fn))
        (error "The command ~S is unrecognized." cmd))))

(command-dispatch 'emergnecy-shutdown)
Error: The command EMERGNECY-SHUTDOWN is unrecognized.
Error signaled by function COMMAND-DISPATCH.
>
```

X3J13 voted in June 1988 ⟨30⟩ to adopt a proposal for a Common Lisp Condition System. This proposal modifies the definition of error to specify its interaction with the condition system. See section 29.4.1.

Compatibility note: Lisp Machine Lisp calls this function ferror. MacLisp has a function named error that takes different arguments and can signal either a fatal or a continuable error.

cerror *continue-format-string error-format-string* &rest *args*   [*Function*]

cerror is used to signal continuable errors. Like error, it signals an error and enters the debugger. However, cerror allows the program to be continued from the debugger after resolving the error.

If the program is continued after encountering the error, cerror returns nil. The code that follows the call to cerror will then be executed. This code should correct the problem, perhaps by accepting a new value from the user if a variable was invalid.

If the code that corrects the problem interacts with the program's use and might possibly be misled, it should make sure the error has really been corrected before continuing. One way to do this is to put the call to cerror and the correction code in a loop, checking each time to see if the error has been corrected before terminating the loop.

The *continue-format-string* argument, like the *error-format-string* argument, is given as a control string to format along with the *args* to construct a message string. The error message string is used in the same way that error uses it. The continue message string should describe the effect of continuing. The intent is that this message can be displayed as an aid to the user in deciding whether and how to continue. For example, it might be used by an interactive debugger as part of the documentation of its "continue" command.

The content of the continue message should adhere to the rules of style for error messages. It should not include any statement of how the "continue" command is given, since this may be different for each debugger. (It is up to the debugger to supply this information according to its own particular style of presentation and user interaction.)

X3J13 voted in June 1988 ⟨30⟩ to adopt a proposal for a Common Lisp Condition System. This proposal modifies the definition of cerror to specify its interaction with the condition system. See section 29.4.1.

Here is an example where the caller of cerror, if continued, fixes the problem without any further user interaction:

```
(let ((nvals (list-length vals)))
  (unless (= nvals 3)
    (cond ((< nvals 3)
           (cerror "Assume missing values are zero."
                   "Too few values in ~S;~%~
                    three are required, ~
                    but ~R ~:[were~;was~] supplied."
                   nvals (= nvals 1))
           (setq vals (append vals (subseq '(0 0 0) nvals))))
          (t (cerror "Ignore all values after the first three."
                     "Too many values in ~S;~%~
                      three are required, ~
                      but ~R were supplied."
                     nvals)
             (setq vals (subseq vals 0 3))))))
```

If vals were the list (-47), the interaction might look like this:

```
Error: Too few values in (-47);
       three are required, but one was supplied.
Error signaled by function EXAMPLE.
If continued: Assume missing values are zero.
>
```

In this example, a loop is used to ensure that a test is satisfied. (This example could be written more succinctly using assert or check-type, which indeed supply such loops.)

```
(do ()
    ((known-wordp word) word)
  (cerror "You will be prompted for a replacement word."
          "~S is an unknown word (possibly misspelled)."
          word)
  (format *query-io* "~&New word: ")
  (setq word (read *query-io*)))
```

In complex cases where the *error-format-string* uses some of the *args* and the *continue-format-string* uses others, it may be necessary to use the format directives ~* and ~@* to skip over unwanted arguments in one or both of the format control strings.

Compatibility note: The Lisp Machine Lisp function fsignal is similar to this, but returns :no-action rather than nil, and fails to distinguish between the error message and the continue message.

---

warn *format-string* &rest *args*   [*Function*]

warn prints an error message but normally doesn't go into the debugger. (However, this may be controlled by the variable *break-on-warnings*.)

X3J13 voted in March 1989 ⟨10⟩ to remove *break-on-warnings* from the language. See *break-on-signals*.

warn returns nil.

This function would be just the same as format with the output directed to the stream in error-output, except that warn may perform various implementation-dependent formatting and other actions. For example, an implementation of warn should take care of advancing to a fresh line before and after the error message and perhaps supplying the name of the function that called warn.

Compatibility note: The Lisp Machine Lisp function `compiler:warn` is an approximate equivalent to this.

X3J13 voted in June 1988 ⟨30⟩ to adopt a proposal for a Common Lisp Condition System. This proposal modifies the definition of `warn` to specify its interaction with the condition system. See section 29.4.9.

`*break-on-warnings*`   [*Variable*]

If `*break-on-warnings*` is not `nil`, then the function `warn` behaves like `break`. It prints its message and then goes to the debugger or break loop. Continuing causes `warn` to return `nil`. This flag is intended primarily for use when the user is debugging programs that issue warnings; in "production" use, the value of `*break-on-warnings*` should be `nil`.

X3J13 voted in March 1989 ⟨10⟩ to remove `*break-on-warnings*` from the language. See `*break-on-signals*`.

`break` &optional *format-string* &rest *args*   [*Function*]

`break` prints the message and goes directly into the debugger, without allowing any possibility of interception by programmed error-handling facilities. (Right now, there aren't any error-handling facilities defined in Common Lisp, but there might be in particular implementations, and there will be some defined by Common Lisp in the future.) When continued, `break` returns `nil`. It is permissible to call `break` with no arguments; a suitable default message will be provided.

`break` is presumed to be used as a way of inserting temporary debugging "break-points" in a program, not as a way of signaling errors; it is expected that continuing from a `break` will not trigger any unusual recovery action. For this reason, `break` does not take the additional `format` control string argument that `cerror` takes. This and the lack of any possibility of interception by programmed error handling are the only program-visible differences between `break` and `cerror`. The interactive debugger may choose to display them differently; for instance, a `cerror` message might be prefixed with the herald "`Error: `" and a `break` message with "`Break: `". This depends on the user-interface style of the particular implementation. A particular implementation may choose, according to its own style and needs, when `break` is called to go into a debugger different from the one used for handling errors. For example, it might go into an ordinary read-eval-print loop identical to the top-level one except for the provision of a "continue" command that causes `break` to return `nil`.

Compatibility note: In MacLisp, break is a special form (FEXPR) that takes two optional arguments. The first is a symbol (it would be a string if MacLisp had strings), which is not evaluated. The second is evaluated to produce a truth value specifying whether break should break (true) or return immediately (false). In Common Lisp one makes a call to break conditional by putting it inside a conditional form such as when or unless.

X3J13 voted in June 1988 ⟨30⟩ to adopt a proposal for a Common Lisp Condition System. This proposal modifies the definition of break to specify its interaction with the condition system. See section 29.4.11.

24.2. Specialized Error-Signaling Forms and Macros

These facilities are designed to make it convenient for the user to insert error checks into code.

check-type *place typespec* [*string*]   [*Macro*]

check-type signals an error if the contents of *place* are not of the desired type. Upon continuing from this error, the user will be asked for a new value; check-type will store the new value in *place* and start over, checking the type of the new value and signaling another error if it is still not of the desired type. Subforms of *place* may be evaluated multiple times because of the implicit loop generated. check-type returns nil.

The *place* must be a generalized variable reference acceptable to setf. The *typespec* must be a type specifier; it is not evaluated. The *string* should be an English description of the type, starting with an indefinite article ("a" or "an"); it is evaluated. If *string* is not supplied, it is computed automatically from *typespec*. (The optional *string* argument is allowed because some applications of check-type may require a more specific description of what is wanted than can be generated automatically from the type specifier.)

The error message will mention place, its contents, and the desired type.

The precise format and content of the error message is implementation-dependent. The example shown below is representative of current practice.

Implementation note: An implementation may choose to generate a somewhat differently worded error message if it recognizes that *place* is of a particular form, such as one of the arguments to the function that called check-type.

X3J13 voted in June 1988 ⟨30⟩ to adopt a proposal for a Common Lisp Condition System. This proposal modifies the definition of check-type to specify its interaction with the condition system. See section 29.4.2.

X3J13 voted in March 1988 ⟨146⟩ to clarify order of evaluation (see section 7.2).

Examples:

```
(setq aardvarks '(sam harry fred))
(check-type aardvarks (vector integer))
Error: The value of AARDVARKS, (SAM HARRY FRED),
       is not a vector of integers.


(setq naards 'foo)
(check-type naards (integer 0 *) "a positive integer")
Error: The value of NAARDS, FOO, is not a positive integer.
```

Compatibility note: In Lisp Machine Lisp the equivalent facility is called check-arg-type.

---

assert *test-form* [({*place*}*) [*string* {*arg*}*]]   [*Macro*]

assert signals an error if the value of *test-form* is nil. Continuing from this error will allow the user to alter the values of some variables, and assert will then start over, evaluating *test-form* again. assert returns nil.

test-form is any form. Each *place* (there may be any number of them, or none) must be a generalized-variable reference acceptable to setf. These should be variables on which *test-form* depends, whose values may sensibly be changed by the user in attempting to correct the error. Subforms of each *place* are only evaluated if an error is signaled, and may be re-evaluated if the error is re-signaled (after continuing without actually fixing the problem).

The *string* is an error message string, and the *args* are additional arguments; they are evaluated only if an error is signaled, and re-evaluated if the error is signaled again. The function format is applied in the usual way to *string* and *args* to produce the actual error message. If *string* is omitted (and therefore also the *args*), a default error message is used.

Implementation note: The debugger need not include the *test-form* in the error message, and the *places* should not be included in the message, but they should be made available for the user's perusal. If the user gives the "continue" command, he should be presented with the opportunity to alter the values of any or all of the references. The details of this depend on the implementation's style of user interface, of course.

X3J13 voted in June 1988 ⟨30⟩ to adopt a proposal for a Common Lisp Condition System. This proposal modifies the definition of assert to specify its interaction with the condition system. See section 29.4.2.

X3J13 voted in March 1988 ⟨146⟩ to clarify order of evaluation (see section 7.2).

X3J13 voted in June 1989 ⟨159⟩ to extend the specification of assert to allow a *place* whose setf method has more than one store variable (see define-setf-method).

Examples:

```
(assert (valve-closed-p v1))

(assert (valve-closed-p v1) ()
        "Live steam is escaping!")

(assert (valve-closed-p v1)
        ((valve-manual-control v1))
        "Live steam is escaping!")

;; Note here that the user is invited to change BASE,
;; but not the bounds MINBASE and MAXBASE.

(assert (<= minbase base maxbase)
        (base)
        "Base ~D is not in the range ~D, ~D"
        base minbase maxbase)

;; Note here that it is probably not desirable to include the
;; entire contents of the two matrices in the error message.
;; It is reasonable to assume that the debugger will give
;; the user access to the values of the places A and B.

(assert (= (array-dimension a 1)
           (array-dimension b 0))
        (a b)
        "Cannot multiply a ~D-by-~D matrix ~
         and a ~D-by-~D matrix."
        (array-dimension a 0)
        (array-dimension a 1)
        (array-dimension b 0)
        (array-dimension b 1))
```

24.3. Special Forms for Exhaustive Case Analysis

The syntax for etypecase and ctypecase is the same as for typecase, except that no otherwise clause is permitted. Similarly, the syntax for ecase and ccase is the same as for case except for the otherwise clause.

etypecase and ecase are similar to typecase and case, respectively, but signal a non-continuable error rather than returning nil if no clause is selected.

ctypecase and ccase are also similar to typecase and case, but signal a continuable error if no clause is selected.

---

etypecase *keyform* {(*type* {*form*}*)}*   [*Macro*]

This control construct is similar to typecase, but no explicit otherwise or t clause is permitted. If no clause is satisfied, etypecase signals an error with a message constructed from the clauses. It is not permissible to continue from this error. To supply an application-specific error message, the user should use typecase with an otherwise clause containing a call to error. The name of this function stands for "exhaustive type case" or "error-checking type case." For example:

```
(setq x 1/3)
(etypecase x
  (integer x)
  (symbol (symbol-value x)))
Error: The value of X, 1/3, is neither
       an integer nor a symbol.
>
```

X3J13 voted in June 1988 ⟨30⟩ to adopt a proposal for a Common Lisp Condition System. This proposal modifies the definition of etypecase to specify its interaction with the condition system. See section 29.4.3.

---

ctypecase *keyplace* {(*type* {*form*}*)}*   [*Macro*]

This control construct is similar to typecase, but no explicit otherwise or t clause is permitted. The *keyplace* must be a generalized variable reference acceptable to setf. If no clause is satisfied, ctypecase signals an error with a message constructed from the clauses. Continuing from this error causes ctypecase to accept a new value from the user, store it into *keyplace*, and start over, making the type tests again. Subforms of *keyplace* may be evaluated multiple times. The name of this function stands for "continuable exhaustive type case."

X3J13 voted in June 1988 ⟨30⟩ to adopt a proposal for a Common Lisp Condition System. This proposal modifies the definition of ctypecase to specify its interaction with the condition system. See section 29.4.3.

X3J13 voted in March 1988 ⟨146⟩ to clarify order of evaluation (see section 7.2).

ecase *keyform* {({({*key*}*) | *key*} {*form*}*)}*   [*Macro*]

This control construct is similar to case, but no explicit otherwise or t clause is permitted. If no clause is satisfied, ecase signals an error with a message constructed from the clauses. It is not permissible to continue from this error. To supply an error message, the user should use case with an otherwise clause containing a call to error. The name of this function stands for "exhaustive case" or "error-checking case." For example:

```
(setq x 1/3)
(ecase x
  (alpha (foo))
  (omega (bar))
  ((zeta phi) (baz)))
Error: The value of X, 1/3, is not
       ALPHA, OMEGA, ZETA, or PHI.
```

X3J13 voted in June 1988 ⟨30⟩ to adopt a proposal for a Common Lisp Condition System. This proposal modifies the definition of ecase to specify its interaction with the condition system. See section 29.4.3.

ccase *keyplace* {({({*key*}*) | *key*} {*form*}*)}*   [*Macro*]

This control construct is similar to case, but no explicit otherwise or t clause is permitted. The *keyplace* must be a generalized variable reference acceptable to setf. If no clause is satisfied, ccase signals an error with a message constructed from the clauses. Continuing from this error causes ccase to accept a new value from the user, store it into *keyplace*, and start over, making the clause tests again. Subforms of *keyplace* may be evaluated multiple times. The name of this function stands for "continuable exhaustive case."

X3J13 voted in June 1988 ⟨30⟩ to adopt a proposal for a Common Lisp Condition System. This proposal modifies the definition of ccase to specify its interaction with the condition system. See section 29.4.3.

X3J13 voted in March 1988 ⟨146⟩ to clarify order of evaluation (see section 7.2).

Rationale: The special forms `etypecase`, `ctypecase`, `ecase`, and `ccase` are included in Common Lisp, even though a user could write them himself using the other standard facilities provided, because it is likely that many users will want these. Common Lisp therefore provides a standard consistent set rather than allowing a variety of incompatible dialects to develop.

In addition, experience has shown that some Lisp programmers are too lazy to put an appropriate `otherwise` clause into every `case` statement to check for cases they didn't anticipate, even if they would agree that it will probably hurt them later. If an `otherwise` clause can be included very easily by adding one character to the name of the construct, it is perhaps more likely that programmers will take the trouble to do it.

The e versions do nothing more than supply automatically generated `otherwise` clauses, but correct implementation of the c versions requires some care. It is therefore especially important that the c versions be provided by the system so users don't have to puzzle them out on their own. Individual implementations may be able to do a better job of supporting these special forms, using their own idiosyncratic facilities, than can be done using the error-signaling facilities defined by Common Lisp.

25

Miscellaneous Features

In this chapter are described various things that don't seem to fit neatly anywhere else in this book: the compiler, the `documentation` function, debugging aids, environment inquiries (including facilities for calculating and measuring time), and the `identity` function.

25.1. The Compiler

The compiler is a program that may make code run faster by translating programs into an implementation-dependent form that can be executed more efficiently by the computer. Most of the time you can write programs without worrying about the compiler; compiling a file of code should produce an equivalent but more efficient program. When doing more esoteric things, you may need to think carefully about what happens at "compile time" and what happens at "load time." Then the difference between the syntaxes `#.` and `#,` becomes important, and the `eval-when` construct becomes particularly useful.

X3J13 voted in January 1989 ⟨162⟩ to remove `#,` from the language.

Most declarations are not used by the Common Lisp interpreter; they may be used to give advice to the compiler. The compiler may attempt to check your advice and warn you if it is inconsistent.

Unlike most other Lisp dialects, Common Lisp recognizes `special` declarations in interpreted code as well as compiled code. This potential source of incompatibility between interpreted and compiled code is thereby *eliminated* in Common Lisp.

The internal workings of a compiler will of course be highly implementation-dependent. The following functions provide a standard interface to the compiler, however.

676

compile *name* &optional *definition*   [*Function*]

If *definition* is supplied, it should be a lambda-expression, the interpreted function to be compiled. If it is not supplied, then *name* should be a symbol with a definition that is a lambda-expression; that definition is compiled and the resulting compiled code is put back into the symbol as its function definition.

X3J13 voted in October 1988 ⟨18⟩ to restate the preceding paragraph more precisely and to extend the capabilities of compile. If the optional *definition* argument is supplied, it may be either a lambda-expression (which is coerced to a function) or a function to be compiled; if no *definition* is supplied, the symbol-function of the symbol is extracted and compiled. It is permissible for the symbol to have a macro definition rather than a function definition; both macros and functions may be compiled.

It is an error if the function to be compiled was defined interpretively in a non-null lexical environment. (An implementation is free to extend the behavior of compile to compile such functions properly, but portable programs may not depend on this capability.) The consequences of calling compile on a function that is already compiled are unspecified.

The definition is compiled and a compiled-function object produced. If *name* is a non-nil symbol, then the compiled-function object is installed as the global function definition of the symbol and the symbol is returned. If *name* is nil, then the compiled-function object itself is returned. For example:

```
(defun foo ...) ⇒ foo        ;A function definition
(compile 'foo) ⇒ foo         ;Compile it
                             ;Now foo runs faster (maybe)

(compile nil
        '(lambda (a b c) (- (* b b) (* 4 a c))))
    ⇒ a compiled function of three arguments that computes b² − 4ac
```

X3J13 voted in June 1989 ⟨24⟩ to specify that compile returns two additional values indicating whether the compiler issued any diagnostics (see section 25.1.1).

X3J13 voted in March 1989 ⟨89⟩ to extend compile to accept as a *name* any function-name (a symbol or a list whose car is setf—see section 7.1). One may write (compile '(setf cadr)) to compile the setf expansion function for cadr.

compile-file *input-pathname* &key :output-file   [*Function*]

The *input-pathname* must be a valid file specifier, such as a pathname. The defaults for *input-filename* are taken from the variable *default-pathname-defaults*.

The file should be a Lisp source file; its contents are compiled and written as a binary object file.

X3J13 voted in March 1989 ⟨26⟩ to add two new keyword arguments `:verbose` and `:print` to `compile-file` by analogy with `load`. The new function definition is as follows.

`compile-file` *input-pathname* &key `:output-file` `:verbose`   [*Function*]
          `:print`

The `:verbose` argument (which defaults to the value of `*compile-verbose*`), if true, permits `compile-file` to print a message in the form of a comment to `*standard-output*` indicating what file is being compiled and other useful information.

The `:print` argument (which defaults to the value of `*compile-print*`), if true, causes information about top-level forms in the file being compiled to be printed to `*standard-output*`. Exactly what is printed is implementation-dependent; nevertheless something will be printed.

X3J13 voted in March 1988 ⟨132⟩ to specify exactly which streams may be used as pathnames (see section 23.1.6).

X3J13 voted in June 1989 ⟨137⟩ to clarify that supplying a wild pathname as the *input-pathname* argument to `compile-file` has implementation-dependent consequences; `compile-file` might signal an error, for example, or might compile all files that match the wild pathname.

X3J13 voted in June 1989 ⟨130⟩ to require `compile-file` to accept logical pathnames (see section 23.1.5).

The `:output-file` argument may be used to specify an output pathname; it defaults in a manner appropriate to the implementation's file system conventions.

X3J13 voted in June 1989 ⟨24⟩ to specify that `compile-file` returns three values: the `truename` of the output file (or `nil` if the file could not be created) and two values indicating whether the compiler issued any diagnostics (see section 25.1.1).

X3J13 voted in October 1988 ⟨21⟩ to specify that `compile-file`, like `load`, rebinds `*package*` to its current value. If some form in the file changes the value of `*package*`, the old value will be restored when compilation is completed.

X3J13 voted in June 1989 ⟨22⟩ to specify restrictions on conforming programs to ensure consistent handling of symbols and packages.

In order to guarantee that compiled files can be loaded correctly, the user must ensure that the packages referenced in the file are defined consistently at compile and load time. Conforming Common Lisp programs must satisfy the following requirements.

- The value of *package* when a top-level form in the file is processed by compile-file must be the same as the value of *package* when the code corresponding to that top-level form in the compiled file is executed by the loader. In particular, any top-level form in a file that alters the value of *package* must change it to a package of the same name at both compile and load time; moreover, if the first non-atomic top-level form in the file is not a call to in-package, then the value of *package* at the time load is called must be a package with the same name as the package that was the value of *package* at the time compile-file was called.

- For every symbol appearing lexically within a top-level form that was accessible in the package that was the value of *package* during processing of that top-level form at compile time, but whose home package was another package, at load time there must be a symbol with the same name that is accessible in both the load-time *package* and in the package with the same name as the compile-time home package.

- For every symbol in the compiled file that was an external symbol in its home package at compile time, there must be a symbol with the same name that is an external symbol in the package with the same name at load time.

If any of these conditions do not hold, the package in which load looks for the affected symbols is unspecified. Implementations are permitted to signal an error or otherwise define this behavior.

These requirements are merely an explicit statement of the status quo, namely that users cannot depend on any particular behavior if the package environment at load time is inconsistent with what existed at compile time.

X3J13 voted in March 1989 ⟨104⟩ to specify that compile-file must bind *readtable* to its current value at the time compile-file is called; the dynamic extent of the binding should encompass all of the file-loading activity. This allows a portable program to include forms such as

```
(in-package "FOO")

(eval-when (:execute :load-toplevel :compile-toplevel)
  (setq *readtable* foo:my-readtable))
```

without performing a net global side effect on the loading environment. Such statements allow the remainder of such a file to be read either as interpreted code or by compile-file in a syntax determined by an alternative readtable.

X3J13 voted in June 1989 ⟨112⟩ to require that compile-file bind two new variables *compile-file-pathname* and *compile-file-truename*; the dynamic extent of the bindings should encompass all of the file-compiling activity.

compile-verbose   [*Variable*]

X3J13 voted in March 1989 ⟨26⟩ to add *compile-verbose*. This variable provides the default for the :verbose argument to compile-file. Its initial value is implementation-dependent.

A proposal was submitted to X3J13 in October 1989 to rename this *compile-file-verbose* for consistency.

compile-print   [*Variable*]

X3J13 voted in March 1989 ⟨26⟩ to add *compile-print*. This variable provides the default for the :print argument to compile-file. Its initial value is implementation-dependent.

A proposal was submitted to X3J13 in October 1989 to rename this *compile-file-print* for consistency.

compile-file-pathname   [*Variable*]

X3J13 voted in June 1989 ⟨112⟩ to introduce *compile-file-pathname*; it is initially nil but compile-file binds it to a pathname that represents the file name given as the first argument to compile-file merged with the defaults (see merge-pathname).

compile-file-truename   [*Variable*]

X3J13 voted in June 1989 ⟨112⟩ to introduce *compile-file-truename*; it is initially nil but compile-file binds it to the "true name" of the pathname of the file being compiled. See truename.

load-time-value *form* [*read-only-p*]   [*Special form*]

X3J13 voted in March 1989 ⟨111⟩ to add a mechanism for delaying evaluation of a *form* until it can be done in the run-time environment.

If a load-time-value expression is seen by compile-file, the compiler performs its normal semantic processing (such as macro expansion and translation into machine code) on the form, but arranges for the execution of the *form* to occur at load time in a null lexical environment, with the result of this evaluation then being treated as an immediate quantity (that is, as if originally quoted) at run time. It is guaranteed that the evaluation of the *form* will take place only once when the file is loaded, but the order of evaluation with respect to the execution of top-level forms in the file is unspecified.

If a `load-time-value` expression appears within a function compiled with `compile`, the *form* is evaluated at compile time in a null lexical environment. The result of this compile-time evaluation is treated as an immediate quantity in the compiled code.

In interpreted code, *form* is evaluated (by `eval`) in a null lexical environment and one value is returned. Implementations that implicitly compile (or partially compile) expressions passed to `eval` may evaluate the *form* only once, at the time this compilation is performed. This is intentionally similar to the freedom that implementations are given for the time of expanding macros in interpreted code.

If the same (as determined by eq) list (`load-time-value` *form*) is evaluated or compiled more than once, it is unspecified whether the *form* is evaluated only once or is evaluated more than once. This can happen both when an expression being evaluated or compiled shares substructure and when the same expression is passed to `eval` or to `compile` multiple times. Since a `load-time-value` expression may be referenced in more than one place and may be evaluated multiple times by the interpreter, it is unspecified whether each execution returns a "fresh" object or returns the same object as some other execution. Users must use caution when destructively modifying the resulting object.

If two lists (`load-time-value` *form*) are `equal` but not `eq`, their values always come from distinct evaluations of *form*. Coalescing of these forms is not permitted.

The optional *read-only-p* argument designates whether the result may be considered a read-only constant. If `nil` (the default), the result must be considered ordinary, modifiable data. If `t`, the result is a read-only quantity that may, as appropriate, be copied into read-only space and may, as appropriate, be shared with other programs. The *read-only-p* argument is not evaluated and only the literal symbols `t` and `nil` are permitted.

This new feature addresses the same set of needs as the now-defunct #, reader syntax but in a cleaner and more general manner. Note that #, syntax was reliably useful only inside quoted structure (though this was not explicitly mentioned in the first edition), whereas a `load-time-value` form must appear outside quoted structure in a for-evaluation position.

See `make-load-form`.

`disassemble` *name-or-compiled-function*   [*Function*]

The argument should be a function object, a lambda-expression, or a symbol with a function definition. If the relevant function is not a compiled function, it is first compiled. In any case, the compiled code is then "reverse-assembled" and printed out in a symbolic format. This is primarily useful for debugging the compiler, but also often of use to the novice who wishes to understand the workings of compiled code.

Implementation note: Implementors are encouraged to make the output readable, preferably with helpful comments.

X3J13 voted in March 1988 ⟨65⟩ to clarify that when disassemble compiles a function, it never installs the resulting compiled-function object in the symbol-function of a symbol.

X3J13 voted in March 1989 ⟨89⟩ to extend disassemble to accept as a *name* any function-name (a symbol or a list whose car is setf—see section 7.1). Thus one may write (disassemble '(setf cadr)) to disassemble the setf expansion function for cadr.

function-lambda-expression *fn*   [*Function*]

X3J13 voted in January 1989 ⟨88⟩ to add a new function to allow the source code for a defined function to be recovered. (The committee noted that the first edition provided no portable way to recover a lambda-expression once it had been compiled or evaluated to produce a function.)

This function takes one argument, which must be a function, and returns three values.

The first value is the defining lambda-expression for the function, or nil if that information is not available. The lambda-expression may have been preprocessed in some ways but should nevertheless be of a form suitable as an argument to the function compile or for use in the function special form.

The second value is nil if the function was definitely produced by closing a lambda-expression in the null lexical environment; it is some non-nil value if the function might have been closed in some non-null lexical environment.

The third value is the "name" of the function; this is nil if the name is not available or if the function had no name. The name is intended for debugging purposes only and may be any Lisp object (not necessarily one that would be valid for use as a name in a defun or function special form, for example).

Implementation note: An implementation is always free to return the values nil, t, nil from this function but is encouraged to make more useful information available as appropriate. For example, it may not be desirable for files of compiled code to retain the source lambda-expressions for use after the file is loaded, but it is probably desirable for functions produced by "in-core" calls to `eval`, `compile`, or `defun` to retain the defining lambda-expression for debugging purposes. The function `function-lambda-expression` makes this information, if retained, accessible in a standard and portable manner.

`with-compilation-unit` ({*option-name option-value*}*) {*form*}*   *[Macro]*

X3J13 voted in March 1989 ⟨183⟩ to add `with-compilation-unit`, which exe- cutes the body forms as an implicit `progn`. Within the dynamic context of this form, warnings deferred by the compiler until "the end of compilation" will be de- ferred until the end of the outermost call to `with-compilation-unit`. The results are the same as those of the last of the forms (or `nil` if there is no *form*).

Each *option-name* is an unevaluated keyword; each *option-value* is evaluated. The set of keywords permitted may be extended by the implementation, but the only standard option keyword is `:override`; the default value for this option is `nil`. If `with-compilation-unit` forms are nested dynamically, only the outermost such call has any effect unless the `:override` value of an inner call is true.

The function `compile-file` should provide the effect of

```
(with-compilation-unit (:override nil) ...)
```

around its code.

Any implementation-dependent extensions to this behavior may be provided only as the result of an explicit programmer request by use of an implementation- dependent keyword. It is forbidden for an implementation to attach additional meaning to a conforming use of this macro.

Note that not all compiler warnings are deferred. In some implementations, it may be that none are deferred. This macro only creates an interface to the capability where it exists, it does not require the creation of the capability. An implementation that does not defer any compiler warnings may correctly implement this macro as an expansion into a simple `progn`.

25.1.1. Compiler Diagnostics

X3J13 voted in June 1987 ⟨27⟩ to specify that `compile` and `compile-file` may output warning messages; any such messages should go to the stream that is the value of `*error-output*`.

X3J13 voted in June 1989 ⟨24⟩ to specify the use of conditions to signal various erroneous situations during compilation. First, note that `error` and `warning` con- ditions may be signaled either by the compiler itself or by code being processed by the compiler (for example, arbitrary errors may occur during compile-time macro expansion or processing of `eval-when` forms). Considering only those conditions signaled *by the compiler* (as opposed to *during compilation*):

- Conditions of type `error` may be signaled by the compiler in situations where the compilation cannot proceed without intervention. Examples of such situations may include errors when opening a file or syntax errors.

- Conditions of type `warning` may be signaled by the compiler in situations where the standard explicitly states that a warning must, should, or may be signaled. They may also be signaled when the compiler can determine that a situation would result at runtime that would have undefined consequences or would cause an error to be signaled. Examples of such situations may include violations of type declarations, altering or rebinding a constant defined with `defconstant`, calls to built-in Lisp functions with too few or too many arguments or with malformed keyword argument lists, referring to a variable declared `ignore`, or unrecognized declaration specifiers.

- The compiler is permitted to signal diagnostics about matters of programming style as conditions of type `style-warning`, a subtype of `warning`. Although a `style-warning` condition *may* be signaled in these situations, no implementation is *required* to do so. However, if an implementation does choose to signal a condition, that condition will be of type `style-warning` and will be signaled by a call to the function `warn`. Examples of such situations may include redefinition of a function with an incompatible argument list, calls to functions (other than built-in functions) with too few or too many arguments or with malformed keyword argument lists, unreferenced local variables not declared `ignore`, or standard declaration specifiers that are ignored by the particular compiler in question.

Both `compile` and `compile-file` are permitted (but not required) to establish a handler for conditions of type `error`. Such a handler might, for example, issue a warning and restart compilation from some implementation-dependent point in order to let the compilation proceed without manual intervention.

The functions `compile` and `compile-file` each return three values. See the definitions of these functions for descriptions of the first value. The second value is `nil` if no compiler diagnostics were issued, and true otherwise. The third value is `nil` if no compiler diagnostics other than style warnings were issued; a non-`nil` value indicates that there were "serious" compiler diagnostics issued or that other conditions of type `error` or `warning` (but not `style-warning`) were signaled during compilation.

25.1.2. Compiled Functions

X3J13 voted in June 1989 ⟨23⟩ to impose certain requirements on the functions produced by the compilation process.

If a function is of type `compiled-function`, then all macro calls appearing lexically within the function have already been expanded and will not be expanded again when the function is called. The process of compilation effectively turns every `macrolet` or `symbol-macrolet` construct into a `progn` (or a `locally`) with all instances of the local macros in the body fully expanded.

If a function is of type `compiled-function`, then all `load-time-value` forms appearing lexically within the function have already been pre-evaluated and will not be evaluated again when the function is called.

Implementations are free to classify every function as a `compiled-function` provided that all functions satisfy the preceding requirements. Conversely, it is permissible for a function that is not a `compiled-function` to satisfy the preceding requirements.

If one or more functions are defined in a file that is compiled with `compile-file` and the compiled file is subsequently loaded by the function `load`, the resulting loaded function definitions must be of type `compiled-function`.

The function `compile` must produce an object of type `compiled-function` as the value that is either returned or stored into the `symbol-function` of a symbol argument.

Note that none of these restrictions addresses questions of the compilation technology or target instruction set. For example, a compiled function does not necessarily consist of native machine instructions. These requirements merely specify the behavior of the type system with respect to certain actions taken by `compile`, `compile-file`, and `load`.

25.1.3. Compilation Environment

X3J13 voted in June 1989 ⟨19⟩ to specify what information must be available at compile time for correct compilation and what need not be available until run time.

The following information must be present in the compile-time environment for a program to be compiled correctly. This information need not also be present in the run-time environment.

- In conforming code, macros referenced in the code being compiled must have been previously defined in the compile-time environment. The compiler must treat as a function call any form that is a list whose *car* is a symbol that does not name a macro or special form. (This implies that `setf` methods must also be available at compile time.)

- In conforming code, proclamations for `special` variables must be made in the compile-time environment before any bindings of those variables are processed by the compiler. The compiler must treat any binding of an undeclared variable as a lexical binding.

The compiler may incorporate the following kinds of information into the code it produces, if the information is present in the compile-time environment and is referenced within the code being compiled; however, the compiler is not required to do so. When compile-time and run-time definitions differ, it is unspecified which will prevail within the compiled code (unless some other behavior is explicitly specified below). It is also permissible for an implementation to signal an error at run time on detecting such a discrepancy. In all cases, the absence of the information at compile time is not an error, but its presence may enable the compiler to generate more efficient code.

- The compiler may assume that functions that are defined and declared `inline` in the compile-time environment will retain the same definitions at run time.

- The compiler may assume that, within a named function, a recursive call to a function of the same name refers to the same function, unless that function has been declared `notinline`. (This permits tail-recursive calls of a function to itself to be compiled as jumps, for example, thereby turning certain recursive schemas into efficient loops.)

- In the absence of `notinline` declarations to the contrary, `compile-file` may assume that a call within the file being compiled to a named function that is defined in that file refers to that function. (This rule permits *block compilation* of files.) The behavior of the program is unspecified if functions are redefined individually at run time.

- The compiler may assume that the signature (or "interface contract") of all built-in Common Lisp functions will not change. In addition, the compiler may treat all built-in Common Lisp functions as if they had been proclaimed `inline`.

- The compiler may assume that the signature (or "interface contract") of functions with `ftype` information available will not change.

- The compiler may "wire in" (that is, open-code or inline) the values of symbolic constants that have been defined with `defconstant` in the compile-time environment.

- The compiler may assume that any type definition made with `defstruct` or `deftype` in the compile-time environment will retain the same definition in the run-time environment. It may also assume that a class defined by `defclass` in the compile-time environment will be defined in the run-time environment in such a way as to have the same superclasses and metaclass. This implies that subtype/supertype relationships of type specifiers will not change between compile time and run time. (Note that it is not an error for an unknown type to appear in a declaration at compile time, although it is reasonable for the compiler to emit a warning in such a case.)

• The compiler may assume that if type declarations are present in the compile-time environment, the corresponding variables and functions present in the run-time environment will actually be of those types. If this assumption is violated, the run-time behavior of the program is undefined.

The compiler must not make any additional assumptions about consistency between the compile-time and run-time environments. In particular, the compiler may not assume that functions that are defined in the compile-time environment will retain either the same definition or the same signature at run time, except as described above. Similarly, the compiler may not signal an error if it sees a call to a function that is not defined at compile time, since that function may be provided at run time.

X3J13 voted in January 1989 ⟨20⟩ to specify the compile-time side effects of processing various macro forms.

Calls to defining macros such as `defmacro` or `defvar` appearing within a file being processed by `compile-file` normally have compile-time side effects that affect how subsequent forms in the same file are compiled. A convenient model for explaining how these side effects happen is that each defining macro expands into one or more `eval-when` forms and that compile-time side effects are caused by calls occurring in the body of an `(eval-when (:compile-toplevel) ...)` form.

The affected defining macros and their specific side effects are as follows. In each case, it is identified what a user must do to ensure that a program is conforming, and what a compiler must do in order to correctly process a conforming program.

deftype

The user must ensure that the body of a `deftype` form is evaluable at compile time if the type is referenced in subsequent type declarations. The compiler must ensure that a type specifier defined by `deftype` is recognized in subsequent type declarations. If the expansion of a type specifier is not defined fully at compile time (perhaps because it expands into an unknown type specifier or a `satisfies` of a named function that isn't defined in the compile-time environment), an implementation may ignore any references to this type in declarations and may signal a warning.

`defmacro` and `define-modify-macro`

The compiler must store macro definitions at compile time, so that occurrences of the macro later on in the file can be expanded correctly. The user must ensure that the body of the macro is evaluable at compile time if it is referenced within the file being compiled.

`defun`

No required compile-time side effects are associated with `defun` forms. In particular, `defun` does not make the function definition available at compile time. An implementation may choose to store information about the function for the purposes of compile-time error checking (such as checking the number of arguments on calls) or to permit later `inline` expansion of the function.

`defvar` and `defparameter`

The compiler must recognize that the variables named by these forms have been proclaimed `special`. However, it must not evaluate the *initial-value* form or `set` the variable at compile time.

`defconstant`

The compiler must recognize that the symbol names a constant. An implementation may choose to evaluate the *value-form* at compile time, load time, or both. Therefore the user must ensure that the *value-form* is evaluable at compile time (regardless of whether or not references to the constant appear in the file) and that it always evaluates to the same value. (There has been considerable variance among implementations on this point. The effect of this specification is to legitimize all of the implementation variants by requiring care of the user.)

`defsetf` and `define-setf-method`

The compiler must make `setf` methods available so that they may be used to expand calls to `setf` later on in the file. Users must ensure that the body of a call to `define-setf-method` or the complex form of `defsetf` is evaluable at compile time if the corresponding place is referred to in a subsequent `setf` in the same file. The compiler must make these `setf` methods available to compile-time calls to `get-setf-method` when its environment argument is a value received as the `&environment` parameter of a macro.

`defstruct`

The compiler must make the structure type name recognized as a valid type name in subsequent declarations (as described above for `deftype`) and make the structure slot accessors known to setf. In addition, the compiler must save enough information so that further defstruct definitions can include (with the :include option) a structure type defined earlier in the file being compiled. The functions that defstruct generates are not defined in the compile-time environment, although the compiler may save enough information about the functions to allow inline expansion of subsequent calls to these functions. The #S reader syntax may or may not be available for that structure type at compile time.

define-condition

The rules are essentially the same as those for defstruct. The compiler must make the condition type recognizable as a valid type name, and it must be possible to reference the condition type as the *parent-type* of another condition type in a subsequent define-condition form in the file being compiled.

defpackage

All of the actions normally performed by the defpackage macro at load time must also be performed at compile time.

Compile-time side effects may cause information about a definition to be stored in a different manner from information about definitions processed either interpretively or by loading a compiled file. In particular, the information stored by a defining macro at compile time may or may not be available to the interpreter (either during or after compilation) or during subsequent calls to compile or compile-file. For example, the following code is not portable because it assumes that the compiler stores the macro definition of foo where it is available to the interpreter.

```
(defmacro foo (x) `(car ,x))

(eval-when (:execute :compile-toplevel :load-toplevel)
  (print (foo '(a b c))))        ;Wrong
```

The goal may be accomplished portably by including the macro definition within the eval-when form:

```
(eval-when (eval compile load)
  (defmacro foo (x) `(car ,x))
  (print (foo '(a b c))))        ;Right
```

declaim

X3J13 voted in June 1989 ⟨144⟩ to add a new macro declaim for making proclamations recognizable at compile time. The declaration specifiers in the declaim form are effectively proclaimed at compile time so as to affect compilation of subsequent forms. (Note that compiler processing of a call to `proclaim` does not have any compile-time side effects, for `proclaim` is a function.)

in-package

X3J13 voted in March 1989 ⟨103⟩ to specify that all of the actions normally performed by the `in-package` macro at load time must also be performed at compile time.

X3J13 voted in June 1989 ⟨13⟩ to specify the compile-time side effects of processing various CLOS-related macro forms. Top-level calls to the CLOS defining macros have the following compile-time side effects; any other compile-time behavior is explicitly left unspecified.

defclass

The class name may appear in subsequent type declarations and can be used as a specializer in subsequent `defmethod` forms. Thus the compile-time behavior of `defclass` is similar to that of `deftype` or `defstruct`.

defgeneric

The generic function can be referenced in subsequent `defmethod` forms, but the compiler does not arrange for the generic function to be callable at compile time.

defmethod

The compiler does not arrange for the method to be callable at compile time. If there is a generic function with the same name defined at compile time, compiling a `defmethod` form does not add the method to that generic function; the method is added to the generic function only when the `defmethod` form is actually executed.

The error-signaling behavior described in the specification of `defmethod` in chapter 28 (if the function isn't a generic function or if the lambda-list is not congruent) occurs only when the defining form is executed, not at compile time.

The forms in `eql` parameter specializers are evaluated when the `defmethod` form is executed. The compiler is permitted to build in knowledge about what the form in an `eql` specializer will evaluate to in cases where the ultimate result can be syntactically inferred without actually evaluating it.

define-method-combination

The method combination can be used in subsequent `defgeneric` forms.

The body of a `define-method-combination` form is evaluated no earlier than when the defining macro is executed and possibly as late as generic function invocation time. The compiler may attempt to evaluate these forms at compile time but must not depend on being able to do so.

25.1.4. Similarity of Constants

X3J13 voted in March 1989 ⟨34⟩ to specify what objects can be in compiled constants and what relationship there must be between a constant passed to the compiler and the one that is established by compiling it and then loading its file.

The key is a definition of an equivalence relationship called "similarity as constants" between Lisp objects. Code passed through the file compiler and then loaded must behave as though quoted constants in it are similar in this sense to quoted constants in the corresponding source code. An object may be used as a quoted constant processed by `compile-file` if and only if the compiler can guarantee that the resulting constant established by loading the compiled file is "similar as a constant" to the original. Specific requirements are spelled out below.

Some types of objects, such as streams, are not supported in constants processed by the file compiler. Such objects may not portably appear as constants in code processed with `compile-file`. Conforming implementations are required to handle such objects either by having the compiler or loader reconstruct an equivalent copy of the object in some implementation-specific manner or by having the compiler signal an error.

Of the types supported in constants, some are treated as aggregate objects. For these types, being similar as constants is defined recursively. We say that an object of such a type has certain "basic attributes"; to be similar as a constant to another object, the values of the corresponding attributes of the two objects must also be similar as constants.

A definition of this recursive form has problems with any circular or infinitely recursive object such as a list that is an element of itself. We use the idea of depth-limited comparison and say that two objects are similar as constants if they are similar at all finite levels. This idea is implicit in the definitions below, and it applies in all the places where attributes of two objects are required to be similar as constants. The question of handling circular constants is the subject of a separate vote by X3J13 (see below).

The following terms are used throughout this section. The term *constant* refers to a quoted or self-evaluating constant, not a named constant defined by `defconstant`. The term *source code* is used to refer to the objects constructed when `compile-file` calls `read` (or the equivalent) and to additional objects constructed by macro expansion during file compilation. The term *compiled code* is used to refer to objects constructed by `load`.

Two objects are *similar as a constant* if and only if they are both of one of the types listed below and satisfy the additional requirements listed for that type.

number

Two numbers are similar as constants if they are of the same type and represent the same mathematical value.

character

Two characters are similar as constants if they both represent the same character. (The intent is that this be compatible with how eql is defined on characters.)

symbol

X3J13 voted in June 1989 ⟨22⟩ to define similarity as a constant for interned symbols. A symbol *S* appearing in the source code is similar as a constant to a symbol *S'* in the compiled code if their print names are similar as constants and either of the following conditions holds:

- *S* is accessible in *package* at compile time and *S'* is accessible in *package* at load time.

- *S'* is accessible in the package that is similar as a constant to the home package of symbol *S*.

The "similar as constants" relationship for interned symbols has nothing to do with *readtable* or how the function read would parse the characters in the print name of the symbol.

An uninterned symbol in the source code is similar as a constant to an uninterned symbol in the compiled code if their print names are similar as constants.

package

A package in the source code is similar as a constant to a package in the compiled code if their names are similar as constants. Note that the loader finds the corresponding package object as if by calling find-package with the package name as an argument. An error is signaled if no package of that name exists at load time.

random-state

We say that two random-state objects are *functionally equivalent* if applying random to them repeatedly always produces the same pseudo-random numbers in the same order.

Two random-states are similar as constants if and only if copies of them made via make-random-state are functionally equivalent. (Note that a constant random-state object cannot be used as the *state* argument to the function random because random performs a side effect on that argument.)

cons

Two conses are similar as constants if the values of their respective *car* and *cdr* attributes are similar as constants.

array

Two arrays are similar as constants if the corresponding values of each of the following attributes are similar as constants: for vectors (one-dimensional arrays), the length and element-type and the result of elt for all valid indices; for all other arrays, the array-rank, the result of array-dimension for all valid axis numbers, the array-element-type, and the result of aref for all valid indices. (The point of distinguishing vectors is to take any fill pointers into account.)

   If the array in the source code is a simple-array, then the corresponding array in the compiled code must also be a simple-array, but if the array in the source code is displaced, has a fill pointer, or is adjustable, the corresponding array in the compiled code is permitted to lack any or all of these qualities.

hash-table

Two hash tables are similar as constants if they meet three requirements. First, they must have the same test (for example, both are eql hash tables or both are equal hash tables). Second, there must be a unique bijective correspondence between the keys of the two tables, such that the corresponding keys are similar as constants. Third, for all keys, the values associated with two corresponding keys must be similar as constants.

   If there is more than one possible one-to-one correspondence between the keys of the two tables, it is unspecified whether the two tables are similar as constants. A conforming program cannot use such a table as a constant.

pathname

Two pathnames are similar as constants if all corresponding pathname components are similar as constants.

stream, readtable, and method

Objects of these types are not supported in compiled constants.

function

X3J13 voted in June 1989 ⟨35⟩ to specify that objects of type function are not supported in compiled constants.

`structure` and `standard-object`

X3J13 voted in March 1989 ⟨110⟩ to introduce a facility based on the Common Lisp Object System whereby a user can specify how `compile-file` and `load` must cooperate to reconstruct compile-time constant objects at load time (see `make-load-form`).

X3J13 voted in March 1989 ⟨33⟩ to specify the circumstances under which constants may be coalesced in compiled code.

Suppose A and B are two objects used as quoted constants in the source code, and that A' and B' are the corresponding objects in the compiled code. If A' and B' are `eql` but A and B were not `eql`, then we say that A and B have been *coalesced* by the compiler.

An implementation is permitted to coalesce constants appearing in code to be compiled if and only if they are similar as constants, except that objects of type `symbol`, `package`, `structure`, or `standard-object` obey their own rules and may not be coalesced by a separate mechanism.

Rationale: Objects of type `symbol` and `package` cannot be coalesced because the fact that they are named, interned objects means they are already as coalesced as it is useful for them to be. Uninterned symbols could perhaps be coalesced, but that was thought to be more dangerous than useful. Structures and objects could be coalesced if a "similar as a constant" predicate were defined for them; it would be a generic function. However, at present there is no such predicate. Currently `make-load-form` provides a protocol by which `compile-file` and `load` work together to construct an object in the compiled code that is equivalent to the object in the source code; a different mechanism would have to be added to permit coalescing.

Note that coalescing is possible only because it is forbidden to destructively modify constants ⟨36⟩ (see `quote`).

X3J13 voted in March 1989 ⟨32⟩ to specify that objects containing circular or infinitely recursive references may legitimately appear as constants to be compiled. The compiler is required to preserve `eql`-ness of substructures within a file compiled by `compile-file`.

25.2. Documentation

A simple facility is provided for attaching strings to symbols for the purpose of on-line documentation. Rather than using the property list of the symbol, a separate function `documentation` is provided so that implementations can optimize the storage of documentation strings.

documentation *symbol doc-type*   [*Function*]

This function returns the documentation string of type *doc-type* for the *symbol*, or nil if none exists. Both arguments must be symbols. Some kinds of documentation are provided automatically by certain Common Lisp constructs if the user writes an optional documentation string within them:

Construct	Documentation Type
defvar	variable
defparameter	variable
defconstant	variable
defun	function
defmacro	function
defstruct	structure
deftype	type
defsetf	setf

In addition, names of special forms may also have function documentation. (Macros and special forms are not really functions, of course, but it is convenient to group them with functions for documentation purposes.)

setf may be used with documentation to update documentation information.

X3J13 voted in June 1988 ⟨12⟩ to make documentation a CLOS generic function (see chapter 28).

X3J13 voted in March 1989 ⟨89⟩ to extend documentation to accept any function-name (a symbol or a list whose *car* is setf—see section 7.1). Thus one may write (documentation '(setf cadr) 'function) to determine whether there is any documentation for a setf expansion function for cadr.

25.3. Debugging Tools

The utilities described in this section are sufficiently complex and sufficiently dependent on the host environment that their complete definition is beyond the scope of this book. However, they are also sufficiently useful to warrant mention here. It is expected that every implementation will provide some version of these utilities, however clever or however simple.

trace {*function-name*}*   [*Macro*]
untrace {*function-name*}*   [*Macro*]

Invoking trace with one or more function-names (symbols) causes the functions named to be traced. Henceforth, whenever such a function is invoked, information about the call, the arguments passed, and the eventually returned values, if any, will be printed to the stream that is the value of *trace-output*. For example:

```
(trace fft gcd string-upcase)
```

If a function call is open-coded (possibly as a result of an inline declaration), then such a call may not produce trace output.

Invoking untrace with one or more function names will cause those functions not to be traced any more.

Tracing an already traced function, or untracing a function not currently being traced, should produce no harmful effects but may produce a warning message.

Calling trace with no argument forms will return a list of functions currently being traced.

Calling untrace with no argument forms will cause all currently traced functions to be no longer traced.

X3J13 voted in March 1989 ⟨89⟩ to extend trace and untrace to accept any function-name (a symbol or a list whose *car* is setf—see section 7.1). Thus one may write (trace (setf cadr)) to trace the setf expansion function for cadr.

X3J13 voted in January 1989 ⟨156⟩ to specify that the values returned by trace and untrace when given argument forms are implementation-dependent.

trace and untrace may also accept additional implementation-dependent argument formats. The format of the trace output is implementation-dependent.

step *form*   [*Macro*]

This evaluates *form* and returns what *form* returns. However, the user is allowed to interactively "single-step" through the evaluation of *form*, at least through those evaluation steps that are performed interpretively. The nature of the interaction is implementation-dependent. However, implementations are encouraged to respond to the typing of the character ? by providing help, including a list of commands.

X3J13 voted in January 1989 ⟨166⟩ to clarify that step evaluates its argument *form* in the current lexical environment (not simply a null environment), and that calls to step may be compiled, in which case an implementation may step through only those parts of the evaluation that are interpreted. (In other words, the *form* itself is unlikely to be stepped, but if executing it happens to invoke interpreted code, then that code may be stepped.)

time *form*   [*Macro*]

This evaluates *form* and returns what *form* returns. However, as a side effect, various timing data and other information are printed to the stream that is the value of *trace-output*. The nature and format of the printed information is implementation-dependent. However, implementations are encouraged to provide such information as elapsed real time, machine run time, storage management statistics, and so on.

Compatibility note: This facility is inspired by the Interlisp facility of the same name. Note that the MacLisp/Lisp Machine Lisp function time does something else entirely, namely return a quantity indicating relative elapsed real time.

X3J13 voted in January 1989 ⟨166⟩ to clarify that time evaluates its argument *form* in the current lexical environment (not simply a null environment), and that calls to time may be compiled.

describe *object*   [*Function*]

describe prints, to the stream in the variable *standard-output*, information about the *object*. Sometimes it will describe something that it finds inside something else; such recursive descriptions are indented appropriately. For instance, describe of a symbol will exhibit the symbol's value, its definition, and each of its properties. describe of a floating-point number will exhibit its internal representation in a way that is useful for tracking down round-off errors and the like. The nature and format of the output is implementation-dependent.

describe returns no values (that is, it returns what the expression (values) returns: zero values).

X3J13 voted in March 1989 ⟨63⟩ to let describe take an optional second argument:

describe *object* &optional *stream*   [*Function*]

The output is sent to the specified *stream*, which defaults to the value of *standard-output*; the *stream* may also be nil (meaning *standard-output*) or t (meaning *terminal-io*).

The behavior of describe depends on the generic function describe-object (see below).

X3J13 voted in January 1989 ⟨62⟩ to specify that describe is forbidden to prompt for or require user input when given exactly one argument; it also voted to permit implementations to extend describe to accept keyword arguments that may cause it to prompt for or to require user input.

describe-object *object stream*   [*Generic function*]
describe-object (*object* standard-object) *stream*   [*Primary method*]

X3J13 voted in March 1989 ⟨63⟩ to add the generic function describe-object, which writes a description of an object to a stream. The function describe-object is called by the describe function; it should not be called by the user.

Each implementation must provide a method on the class standard-object and methods on enough other classes to ensure that there is always an applicable method. Implementations are free to add methods for other classes. Users can write methods for describe-object for their own classes if they do not wish to inherit an implementation-supplied method.

The first argument may be any Lisp object. The second argument is a stream; it cannot be t or nil. The values returned by describe-object are unspecified.

Methods on describe-object may recursively call describe. Indentation, depth limits, and circularity detection are all taken care of automatically, provided that each method handles exactly one level of structure and calls describe recursively if there are more structural levels. If this rule is not obeyed, the results are undefined.

In some implementations the *stream* argument passed to a describe-object method is not the original stream but is an intermediate stream that implements parts of describe. Methods should therefore not depend on the identity of this stream.

Rationale: This proposal was closely modeled on the CLOS description of print-object, which was well thought out and provides a great deal of functionality and implementation freedom. Implementation techniques for print-object are applicable to describe-object.

The reason for making the return values for describe-object unspecified is to avoid forcing users to write (values) explicitly in all their methods; describe should take care of that.

---

inspect *object*   [*Function*]

inspect is an interactive version of describe. The nature of the interaction is implementation-dependent, but the purpose of inspect is to make it easy to wander through a data structure, examining and modifying parts of it. Implementations are encouraged to respond to the typing of the character ? by providing help, including a list of commands.

X3J13 voted in January 1989 ⟨156⟩ to specify that the values returned by inspect are implementation-dependent.

room &optional *x*   [*Function*]

room prints, to the stream in the variable *standard-output*, information about
the state of internal storage and its management. This might include descriptions
of the amount of memory in use and the degree of memory compaction, possibly
broken down by internal data type if that is appropriate. The nature and format
of the printed information is implementation-dependent. The intent is to provide
information that may help a user to tune a program to a particular implementation.

(room nil) prints out a minimal amount of information. (room t) prints out a
maximal amount of information. Simply (room) prints out an intermediate amount
of information that is likely to be useful.

X3J13 voted in January 1989 ⟨157⟩ to specify that the argument *x* may also be
the keyword :default, which has the same effect as passing no argument at all.

ed &optional *x*   [*Function*]

If the implementation provides a resident editor, this function should invoke it.

(ed) or (ed nil) simply enters the editor, leaving you in the same state as the
last time you were in the editor.

(ed *pathname*) edits the contents of the file specified by *pathname*. The *pathname* may be an actual pathname or a string.

X3J13 voted in June 1989 ⟨130⟩ to require ed to accept logical pathnames (see
section 23.1.5).

(ed *symbol*) tries to let you edit the text for the function named *symbol*. The
means by which the function text is obtained is implementation-dependent; it might
involve searching the file system, or pretty printing resident interpreted code, for
example.

X3J13 voted in March 1989 ⟨89⟩ to extend compile to accept as a *name* any
function-name (a symbol or a list whose *car* is setf—see section 7.1). Thus one
may write (ed '(setf cadr)) to edit the setf expansion function for cadr.

dribble &optional *pathname*   [*Function*]

(dribble *pathname*) may rebind *standard-input* and *standard-output*,
and may take other appropriate action, so as to send a record of the input/output
interaction to a file named by *pathname*. The primary purpose of this is to create
a readable record of an interactive session.

(dribble) terminates the recording of input and output and closes the dribble
file.

X3J13 voted in June 1989 ⟨130⟩ to require dribble to accept logical pathnames
(see section 23.1.5).

X3J13 voted in March 1988 ⟨68⟩ to clarify that dribble is intended primarily for interactive debugging and that its effect cannot be relied upon for use in portable programs.

Different implementations of Common Lisp have used radically different techniques for implementing dribble. All are reasonable interpretations of the original specification, and all behave in approximately the same way if dribble is called only from the interactive top level. However, they may have quite different behaviors if dribble is called from within compound forms.

Consider two models of the operation of dribble. In the "redirecting" model, a call to dribble with a pathname argument alters certain global variables such as *standard-output*, perhaps by constructing a broadcast stream directed to both the original value of *standard-output* and to the dribble file; other streams may be affected as well. A call to dribble with no arguments undoes these side effects.

In the "recursive" model, by contrast, a call to dribble with a pathname argument creates a new interactive command loop and calls it recursively. This new command loop is just like an ordinary read-eval-print loop except that it also echoes the interaction to the dribble file. A call to dribble with no arguments does a throw that exits the recursive command loop and returns to the original caller of dribble with an argument.

The two models may be distinguished by this test case:

```
(progn (dribble "basketball")
       (print "Larry")
       (dribble)
       (princ "Bird"))
```

If this form is input to the Lisp top level, in either model a newline (provided by the function print) and the words Larry Bird will be printed to the standard output. The redirecting dribble model will additionally print all but the word Bird to a file named basketball.

By contrast, the recursive dribble model will enter a recursive command loop and not print anything until (dribble) is executed from within the new interactive command loop. At that time the file named basketball will be closed, and then execution of the progn form will be resumed. A newline and "Larry " (note the trailing space) will be printed to the standard output, and then the call (dribble) may complain that there is no active dribble file. Once this error is resolved, the word Bird may be printed to the standard output.

Here is a slightly different test case:

```
(dribble "baby-food")
```

```
(progn (print "Mashed banana")
       (dribble)
       (princ "and cream of rice"))
```

If this form is input to the Lisp top level, in the redirecting model a newline and the words Mashed banana and cream of rice will be printed to the standard output and all but the words and cream of rice will be sent to a file named baby-food.

The recursive model will direct exactly the same output to the file named baby-food but will never print the words and cream of rice to the standard output because the call (dribble) does not return normally; it throws.

The redirecting model may be intuitively more appealing to some. The recursive model, however, may be more robust; it carefully limits the extent of the dribble operation and disables dribbling if a throw of any kind occurs. The vote by X3J13 was an explicit decision not to decide which model to use. Users are advised to call dribble only interactively, at top level.

apropos *string* &optional *package*   [*Function*]
apropos-list *string* &optional *package*   [*Function*]

(apropos *string*) tries to find all available symbols whose print names contain *string* as a substring. (A symbol may be supplied for the *string*, in which case the print name of the symbol is used.) Whenever apropos finds a symbol, it prints out the symbol's name; in addition, information about the function definition and dynamic value of the symbol, if any, is printed. If *package* is specified and not nil, then only symbols available in that package are examined; otherwise "all" packages are searched, as if by do-all-symbols. Because a symbol may be available by way of more than one inheritance path, apropos may print information about the same symbol more than once. The information is printed to the stream that is the value of *standard-output*. apropos returns no values (that is, it returns what the expression (values) returns: zero values).

apropos-list performs the same search that apropos does but prints nothing. It returns a list of the symbols whose print names contain *string* as a substring.

25.4. Environment Inquiries

Environment inquiry functions provide information about the environment in which a Common Lisp program is being executed. They are described here in two categories: first, those dealing with determination and measurement of time, and second, all the others, most of which deal with identification of the computer hardware and software.

25.4.1. Time Functions

Time is represented in three different ways in Common Lisp: Decoded Time, Universal Time, and Internal Time. The first two representations are used primarily to represent calendar time and are precise only to one second. Internal Time is used primarily to represent measurements of computer time (such as run time) and is precise to some implementation-dependent fraction of a second, as specified by `internal-time-units-per-second`. Decoded Time format is used only for absolute time indications. Universal Time and Internal Time formats are used for both absolute and relative times.

Decoded Time format represents calendar time as a number of components:

- *Second*: an integer between 0 and 59, inclusive.

- *Minute*: an integer between 0 and 59, inclusive.

- *Hour*: an integer between 0 and 23, inclusive.

- *Date*: an integer between 1 and 31, inclusive (the upper limit actually depends on the month and year, of course).

- *Month*: an integer between 1 and 12, inclusive; 1 means January, 12 means December.

- *Year*: an integer indicating the year A.D. However, if this integer is between 0 and 99, the "obvious" year is used; more precisely, that year is assumed that is equal to the integer modulo 100 and within fifty years of the current year (inclusive backwards and exclusive forwards). Thus, in the year 1978, year 28 is 1928 but year 27 is 2027. (Functions that return time in this format always return a full year number.)

Compatibility note: This is incompatible with the Lisp Machine Lisp definition in two ways. First, in Lisp Machine Lisp a year between 0 and 99 always has 1900 added to it. Second, in Lisp Machine Lisp time functions return the abbreviated year number between 0 and 99 rather than the full year number. The incompatibility is prompted by the imminent arrival of the twenty-first century. Note that (mod *year* 100) always reliably converts a year number to the abbreviated form, while the inverse conversion can be very difficult.

- *Day-of-week*: an integer between 0 and 6, inclusive; 0 means Monday, 1 means Tuesday, and so on; 6 means Sunday.

- *Daylight-saving-time-p*: a flag that, if not `nil`, indicates that daylight saving time is in effect.

- *Time-zone*: an integer specified as the number of hours west of GMT (Greenwich Mean Time). For example, in Massachusetts the time zone is 5, and in California it is 8. Any adjustment for daylight saving time is separate from this.

X3J13 voted in March 1989 ⟨178⟩ to specify that the time zone part of Decoded Time need not be an integer, but may be any rational number (either an integer or a ratio) in the range -24 to 24 (inclusive on both ends) that is an integral multiple of 1/3600.

Rationale: For all possible time designations to be accommodated, it is necessary to allow the time zone to be non-integral, for some places in the world have time standards offset from Greenwich Mean Time by a non-integral number of hours.

There appears to be no user demand for floating-point time zones. Since such zones would introduce inexact arithmetic, X3J13 did not consider adding them at this time.

This specification does require time zones to be represented as integral multiples of 1 second (rather than 1 hour). This prevents problems that could otherwise occur in converting Decoded Time to Universal Time.

Universal Time represents time as a single non-negative integer. For relative time purposes, this is a number of seconds. For absolute time, this is the number of seconds since midnight, January 1, 1900 GMT. Thus the time 1 is 00:00:01 (that is, 12:00:01 A.M.) on January 1, 1900 GMT. Similarly, the time 2398291201 corresponds to time 00:00:01 on January 1, 1976 GMT. Recall that the year 1900 was *not* a leap year; for the purposes of Common Lisp, a year is a leap year if and only if its number is divisible by 4, except that years divisible by 100 are *not* leap years, except that years divisible by 400 *are* leap years. Therefore the year 2000 will be a leap year. (Note that the "leap seconds" that are sporadically inserted by the world's official timekeepers as an additional correction are ignored; Common Lisp assumes that every day is exactly 86400 seconds long.) Universal Time format is used as a standard time representation within the ARPANET; see reference [22]. Because the Common Lisp Universal Time representation uses only non-negative integers, times before the base time of midnight, January 1, 1900 GMT cannot be processed by Common Lisp.

Internal Time also represents time as a single integer, but in terms of an implementation-dependent unit. Relative time is measured as a number of these units. Absolute time is relative to an arbitrary time base, typically the time at which the system began running.

get-decoded-time   [*Function*]

The current time is returned in Decoded Time format. Nine values are returned:

second, minute, hour, date, month, year, day-of-week, daylight-saving-time-p, and *time-zone.*

Compatibility note: In Lisp Machine Lisp *time-zone* is not currently returned. Consider, however, the use of Common Lisp in some mobile vehicle. It is entirely plausible that the time zone might change from time to time.

`get-universal-time`   [*Function*]

The current time of day is returned as a single integer in Universal Time format.

`decode-universal-time` *universal-time* &optional *time-zone*   [*Function*]

The time specified by *universal-time* in Universal Time format is converted to Decoded Time format. Nine values are returned: *second, minute, hour, date, month, year, day-of-week, daylight-saving-time-p,* and *time-zone.*

Compatibility note: In Lisp Machine Lisp *time-zone* is not currently returned. Consider, however, the use of Common Lisp in some mobile vehicle. It is entirely plausible that the time zone might change from time to time.

The *time-zone* argument defaults to the current time zone.

X3J13 voted in January 1989 ⟨47⟩ to specify that `decode-universal-time`, like `encode-universal-time`, ignores daylight saving time information if a *time-zone* is explicitly specified; in this case the returned *daylight-saving-time-p* value will necessarily be `nil` even if daylight saving time happens to be in effect in that time zone at the specified time.

`encode-universal-time` *second minute hour date month year*   [*Function*]
&optional *time-zone*

The time specified by the given components of Decoded Time format is encoded into Universal Time format and returned. If you do not specify *time-zone*, it defaults to the current time zone adjusted for daylight saving time. If you provide *time-zone* explicitly, no adjustment for daylight saving time is performed.

`internal-time-units-per-second`   [*Constant*]

This value is an integer, the implementation-dependent number of internal time units in a second. (The internal time unit must be chosen so that one second is an integral multiple of it.)

Rationale: The reason for allowing the internal time units to be implementation-dependent is so that `get-internal-run-time` and `get-internal-real-time` can execute with minimum overhead. The idea is that it should be very likely that a fixnum will suffice as the returned value from these functions. This probability can be tuned to the implementation by trading off the speed of the machine against the word size. Any particular unit will be inappropriate for some implementations: a microsecond is too long for a very fast machine, while a much smaller unit would force many implementations to return bignums for most calls to `get-internal-time`, rendering that function less useful for accurate timing measurements.

`get-internal-run-time` *[Function]*

The current run time is returned as a single integer in Internal Time format. The precise meaning of this quantity is implementation-dependent; it may measure real time, run time, CPU cycles, or some other quantity. The intent is that the difference between the values of two calls to this function be the amount of time between the two calls during which computational effort was expended on behalf of the executing program.

`get-internal-real-time` *[Function]*

The current time is returned as a single integer in Internal Time format. This time is relative to an arbitrary time base, but the difference between the values of two calls to this function will be the amount of elapsed real time between the two calls, measured in the units defined by `internal-time-units-per-second`.

`sleep` *seconds* *[Function]*

(`sleep` *n*) causes execution to cease and become dormant for approximately *n* seconds of real time, whereupon execution is resumed. The argument may be any non-negative non-complex number. `sleep` returns `nil`.

25.4.2. Other Environment Inquiries

For any of the following functions, if no appropriate and relevant result can be produced, `nil` is returned instead of a string.

Rationale: These inquiry facilities are functions rather than variables against the possibility that a Common Lisp process might migrate from machine to machine. This need not happen in a distributed environment; consider, for example, dumping a core image file containing a compiler and then shipping it to another site.

`lisp-implementation-type` *[Function]*

A string is returned that identifies the generic name of the particular Common Lisp implementation. Examples: `"Spice LISP"`, `"Zetalisp"`.

`lisp-implementation-version` *[Function]*

A string is returned that identifies the version of the particular Common Lisp implementation; this information should be of use to maintainers of the implementation. Examples: `"1192"`, `"53.7 with complex numbers"`, `"1746.9A, NEWIO 53, ETHER 5.3"`.

`machine-type` *[Function]*

A string is returned that identifies the generic name of the computer hardware on which Common Lisp is running. Examples: `"IMLAC"`, `"DEC PDP-10"`, `"DEC VAX-11/780"`.

`machine-version` *[Function]*

A string is returned that identifies the version of the computer hardware on which Common Lisp is running. Example: `"KL10, microcode 9"`.

`machine-instance` *[Function]*

A string is returned that identifies the particular instance of the computer hardware on which Common Lisp is running; this might be a local nickname, for example, or a serial number. Examples: `"MIT-MC"`, `"CMU GP-VAX"`.

`software-type` *[Function]*

A string is returned that identifies the generic name of any relevant supporting software. Examples: `"Spice"`, `"TOPS-20"`, `"ITS"`.

`software-version` *[Function]*

A string is returned that identifies the version of any relevant supporting software; this information should be of use to maintainers of the implementation.

short-site-name   [*Function*]
long-site-name   [*Function*]

A string is returned that identifies the physical location of the computer hardware.
Examples of short names: "MIT AI Lab", "CMU-CSD". Examples of long names:

"MIT Artificial Intelligence Laboratory"
"Massachusetts Institute of Technology
Artificial Intelligence Laboratory"
"Carnegie-Mellon University Computer Science Department"

See also user-homedir-pathname.

features   [*Variable*]

The value of the variable *features* should be a list of symbols that name "features" provided by the implementation. Most such names will be implementation-specific; typically a name for the implementation will be included.

One standard feature name is ieee-floating-point, which should be present if and only if full IEEE proposed floating-point arithmetic [23] is supported.

The value of this variable is used by the #+ and #- reader syntax.

X3J13 voted in March 1988 ⟨163⟩ to specify that feature names used with #+ and #- are read in the keyword package unless an explicit prefix designating some other package appears. The standard feature name ieee-floating-point is therefore actually the keyword :ieee-floating-point, though one need not write the colon when using it with #+ or #-; thus #+ieee-floating-point and #+:ieee-floating-point mean the same thing.

25.5. Identity Function

This function is occasionally useful as an argument to other functions that require functions as arguments. (Got that?)

identity *object*   [*Function*]

The *object* is returned as the value of identity.

The identity function is the default value for the :key argument to many sequence functions (see chapter 14).

Table 12-1 illustrates the behavior in the complex plane of the identity function regarded as a function of a complex numerical argument.

Many other constructs in Common Lisp have the behavior of identity when given a single argument. For example, one might well use values in place of identity. However, writing values of a single argument conventionally indicates that the argument form might deliver multiple values and that the intent is to pass on only the first of those values.

Compatibility note: In Maclisp, progn was a function of any number of arguments that returned its last argument, so progn could be used as an identity function. In Common Lisp, progn is a special form and therefore cannot be used for that purpose.

26

Loop

BY JON L WHITE

PREFACE: X3J13 voted in January 1989 ⟨115⟩ to adopt an extended definition of the loop macro as a part of the forthcoming draft Common Lisp standard.

This chapter presents the bulk of the Common Lisp Loop Facility proposal, written by Jon L White. I have edited it only very lightly to conform to the overall style of this book and have inserted a small number of bracketed remarks, identified by the initials GLS. (See the Acknowledgments to this second edition for acknowledgments to others who contributed to the Loop Facility proposal.)

—Guy L. Steele Jr.

26.1. Introduction

A *loop* is a series of expressions that are executed one or more times, a process known as *iteration*. The *Loop Facility* defines a variety of useful methods, indicated by *loop keywords*, to iterate and to accumulate values in a loop.

Loop keywords are not true Common Lisp keywords; they are symbols that are recognized by the Loop Facility and that provide such capabilities as controlling the direction of iteration, accumulating values inside the body of a loop, and evaluating expressions that precede or follow the loop body. If you do not use any loop keywords, the Loop Facility simply executes the loop body repeatedly.

26.2. How the Loop Facility Works

The driving element of the Loop Facility is the loop macro. When Lisp encounters a loop macro call form, it invokes the Loop Facility and passes to it the loop clauses as a list of unevaluated forms, as with any macro. The loop clauses contain Common Lisp forms and loop keywords. The loop keywords are recognized by their symbol name, regardless of the packages that contain them. The loop macro translates the given form into Common Lisp code and returns the expanded form.

The expanded loop form is one or more lambda-expressions for the local binding of loop variables and a block and a tagbody that express a looping control structure. The variables established in the loop construct are bound as if by using `let` or `lambda`. Implementations can interleave the setting of initial values with the bindings. However, the assignment of the initial values is always calculated in the order specified by the user. A variable is thus sometimes bound to a harmless value of the correct data type, and then later in the prologue it is set to the true initial value by using `setq`.

The expanded form consists of three basic parts in the tagbody:

- The *loop prologue* contains forms that are executed before iteration begins, such as initial settings of loop variables and possibly an initial termination test.

- The *loop body* contains those forms that are executed during iteration, including application-specific calculations, termination tests, and variable stepping. *Stepping* is the process of assigning a variable the next item in a series of items.

- The *loop epilogue* contains forms that are executed after iteration terminates, such as code to return values from the loop.

Expansion of the `loop` macro produces an implicit block (named `nil`). Thus, the Common Lisp macro `return` and the special form `return-from` can be used to return values from a loop or to exit a loop.

Within the executable parts of loop clauses and around the entire loop form, you can still bind variables by using the Common Lisp special form `let`.

26.3. Parsing Loop Clauses

The syntactic parts of a loop construct are called *clauses*; the scope of each clause is determined by the top-level parsing of that clause's keyword. The following example shows a loop construct with six clauses:

```
(loop for i from 1 to (compute-top-value)      ;First clause
      while (not (unacceptable i))              ;Second clause
      collect (square i)                        ;Third clause
      do (format t "Working on ~D now" i)       ;Fourth clause
      when (evenp i)                            ;Fifth clause
        do (format t "~D is a non-odd number" i)
      finally (format t "About to exit!"))      ;Sixth clause
```

Each loop keyword introduces either a compound loop clause or a simple loop clause that can consist of a loop keyword followed by a single Lisp form. The

number of forms in a clause is determined by the loop keyword that begins the
clause and by the auxiliary keywords in the clause. The keywords do, initially,
and finally are the only loop keywords that can take any number of Lisp forms
and group them as if in a single progn form.

Loop clauses can contain auxiliary keywords, which are sometimes called *prepositions*. For example, the first clause in the preceding code includes the prepositions
from and to, which mark the value from which stepping begins and the value at
which stepping ends.

26.3.1. Order of Execution

With the exceptions listed below, clauses are executed in the loop body in the order
in which they appear in the source. Execution is repeated until a clause terminates
the loop or until a Common Lisp return, go, or throw form is encountered. The
following actions are exceptions to the linear order of execution:

- All variables are initialized first, regardless of where the establishing clauses
  appear in the source. The order of initialization follows the order of these
  clauses.

- The code for any initially clauses is collected into one progn in the order in
  which the clauses appear in the source. The collected code is executed once in
  the loop prologue after any implicit variable initializations.

- The code for any finally clauses is collected into one progn in the order in
  which the clauses appear in the source. The collected code is executed once in
  the loop epilogue before any implicit values from the accumulation clauses are
  returned. Explicit returns anywhere in the source, however, will exit the loop
  without executing the epilogue code.

- A with clause introduces a variable binding and an optional initial value. The
  initial values are calculated in the order in which the with clauses occur.

- Iteration control clauses implicitly perform the following actions:

  - initializing variables

  - stepping variables, generally between each execution of the loop body

  - performing termination tests, generally just before the execution of the loop
    body

26.3.2. Kinds of Loop Clauses

Loop clauses fall into one of the following categories:

- variable initialization and stepping

    - The for and as constructs provide iteration control clauses that establish a variable to be initialized. You can combine for and as clauses with the loop keyword and to get parallel initialization and stepping.

    - The with construct is similar to a single let clause. You can combine with clauses using and to get parallel initialization.

    - The repeat construct causes iteration to terminate after a specified number of times. It uses an internal variable to keep track of the number of iterations.

    You can specify data types for loop variables (see section 26.12.1). It is an error to bind the same variable twice in any variable-binding clause of a single loop expression. Such variables include local variables, iteration control variables, and variables found by destructuring.

- value accumulation

    - The collect construct takes one form in its clause and adds the value of that form to the end of a list of values. By default, the list of values is returned when the loop finishes.

    - The append construct takes one form in its clause and appends the value of that form to the end of a list of values. By default, the list of values is returned when the loop finishes.

    - The nconc construct is similar to append, but its list values are concatenated as if by the Common Lisp function nconc. By default, the list of values is returned when the loop finishes.

    - The sum construct takes one form in its clause that must evaluate to a number and adds that number into a running total. By default, the cumulative sum is returned when the loop finishes.

    - The count construct takes one form in its clause and counts the number of times that the form evaluates to a non-nil value. By default, the count is returned when the loop finishes.

    - The minimize construct takes one form in its clause and determines the minimum value obtained by evaluating that form. By default, the minimum value is returned when the loop finishes.

— The maximize construct takes one form in its clause and determines the maximum value obtained by evaluating that form. By default, the maximum value is returned when the loop finishes.

- termination conditions

    — The loop-finish Lisp macro terminates iteration and returns any accumulated result. If specified, any finally clauses are evaluated.

    — The for and as constructs provide a termination test that is determined by the iteration control clause.

    — The repeat construct causes termination after a specified number of iterations.

    — The while construct takes one form, a condition, and terminates the iteration if the condition evaluates to nil. A while clause is equivalent to the expression (if (not *condition*) (loop-finish)).

    — The until construct is the inverse of while; it terminates the iteration if the condition evaluates to any non-nil value. An until clause is equivalent to the expression (if *condition* (loop-finish)).

    — The always construct takes one form and terminates the loop if the form ever evaluates to nil; in this case, it returns nil. Otherwise, it provides a default return value of t.

    — The never construct takes one form and terminates the loop if the form ever evaluates to non-nil; in this case, it returns nil. Otherwise, it provides a default return value of t.

    — The thereis construct takes one form and terminates the loop if the form ever evaluates to non-nil; in this case, it returns that value.

- unconditional execution

    — The do construct simply evaluates all forms in its clause.

    — The return construct takes one form and returns its value. It is equivalent to the clause do (return *value*).

- conditional execution

    — The if construct takes one form as a predicate and a clause that is executed when the predicate is true. The clause can be a value accumulation, unconditional, or another conditional clause; it can also be any combination of such clauses connected by the loop keyword and.

- The when construct is a synonym for if.

- The unless construct is similar to when except that it complements the predicate; it executes the following clause if the predicate is false.

- The else construct provides an optional component of if, when, and unless clauses that is executed when the predicate is false. The component is one of the clauses described under if.

- The end construct provides an optional component to mark the end of a conditional clause.

- miscellaneous operations

  - The named construct assigns a name to a loop construct.

  - The initially construct causes its forms to be evaluated in the loop prologue, which precedes all loop code except for initial settings specified by the constructs with, for, or as.

  - The finally construct causes its forms to be evaluated in the loop epilogue after normal iteration terminates. An unconditional clause can also follow the loop keyword finally.

26.3.3. Loop Syntax

The following syntax description provides an overview of the syntax for loop clauses. Detailed syntax descriptions of individual clauses appear in sections 26.6 through 26.12. A loop consists of the following types of clauses:

initial-final ::= *initially* | *finally*
variables ::= *with* | *initial-final* | *for-as* | *repeat*
main ::= *unconditional* | *accumulation* | *conditional* | *termination* | *initial-final*
loop ::= (loop [named *name*] {*variables*}* {*main*}*)

Note that a loop must have at least one clause; however, for backward compatibility, the following format is also supported:

(loop {*tag* | *expr*}*)

where *expr* is any Common Lisp expression that can be evaluated, and *tag* is any symbol not identifiable as a loop keyword. Such a format is roughly equivalent to the following one:

(loop do {*tag* | *expr*}*)

A loop prologue consists of any automatic variable initializations prescribed by the *variable* clauses, along with any *initially* clauses in the order they appear in the source.

A loop epilogue consists of *finally* clauses, if any, along with any implicit return value from an *accumulation* clause or an *end-test* clause.

26.4. User Extensibility

There is currently no specified portable method for users to add extensions to the Loop Facility. The names defloop and define-loop-method have been suggested as candidates for such a method.

26.5. Loop Constructs

The remaining sections of this chapter describe the constructs that the Loop Facility provides. The descriptions are organized according to the functionality of the constructs. Each section begins with a general discussion of a particular operation; it then presents the constructs that perform the operation.

- Section 26.6, "Iteration Control," describes iteration control clauses that allow directed loop iteration.

- Section 26.7, "End-Test Control," describes clauses that stop iteration by providing a conditional expression that can be tested after each execution of the loop body.

- Section 26.8, "Value Accumulation," describes constructs that accumulate values during iteration and return them from a loop. This section also discusses ways in which accumulation clauses can be combined within the Loop Facility.

- Section 26.9, "Variable Initializations," describes the with construct, which provides local variables for use within the loop body, and other constructs that provide local variables.

- Section 26.10, "Conditional Execution," describes how to execute loop clauses conditionally.

- Section 26.11, "Unconditional Execution," describes the do and return constructs. It also describes constructs that are used in the loop prologue and loop epilogue.

- Section 26.12, "Miscellaneous Features," discusses loop data types and destructuring. It also presents constructs for naming a loop and for specifying initial and final actions.

26.6. Iteration Control

Iteration control clauses allow you to direct loop iteration. The loop keywords as, for, and repeat designate iteration control clauses.

Iteration control clauses differ with respect to the specification of termination conditions and the initialization and stepping of loop variables. Iteration clauses by themselves do not cause the Loop Facility to return values, but they can be used in conjunction with value-accumulation clauses to return values (see section 26.8).

All variables are initialized in the loop prologue. The scope of the variable binding is *lexical* unless it is proclaimed special; thus, the variable can be accessed only by expressions that lie textually within the loop. Stepping assignments are made in the loop body before any other expressions are evaluated in the body.

The variable argument in iteration control clauses can be a *destructuring list*. A destructuring list is a tree whose non-null atoms are symbols that can be assigned a value (see section 26.12.2).

The iteration control clauses for, as, and repeat must precede any other loop clauses except initially, with, and named, since they establish variable bindings. When iteration control clauses are used in a loop, termination tests in the loop body are evaluated before any other loop body code is executed.

If you use multiple iteration clauses to control iteration, variable initialization and stepping occur sequentially by default. You can use the and construct to connect two or more iteration clauses when sequential binding and stepping are not necessary. The iteration behavior of clauses joined by and is analogous to the behavior of the Common Lisp macro do relative to do*.

[X3J13 voted in March 1989 ⟨114⟩ to correct a minor inconsistency in the original syntactic specification for loop. Only for and as clauses (not repeat clauses) may be joined by the and construct. The precise syntax is as follows.

for-as ::= {for | as} *for-as-subclause* {and *for-as-subclause*}*
for-as-subclause ::= *for-as-arithmetic* | *for-as-in-list*
       | *for-as-on-list* | *for-as-equals-then*
       | *for-as-across* | *for-as-hash* | *for-as-package*
for-as-arithmetic ::= *var* [*type-spec*] [{from | downfrom | upfrom} *expr1*]
            [{to | downto | upto | below | above} *expr2*]
            [by *expr3*]
for-as-in-list ::= *var* [*type-spec*] in *expr1* [by *step-fun*]

for-as-on-list ::= *var* [*type-spec*] on *expr1* [by *step-fun*]
for-as-equals-then ::= *var* [*type-spec*] = *expr1* [then *step-fun*]
for-as-across ::= *var* [*type-spec*] across *vector*
for-as-hash ::= *var* [*type-spec*] being {each | the}
                  {hash-key | hash-keys | hash-value | hash-values}
                  {in | of} *hash-table*
                  [using ({hash-value | hash-key} *other-var*)]
for-as-package ::= *var* [*type-spec*] being {each | the}
                  for-as-package-keyword
                  {in | of} *package*
for-as-package-keyword ::= symbol | present-symbol | external-symbol
                  | symbols | present-symbols | external-symbols

This correction made for and as clauses syntactically similar to with clauses. I
have changed all examples in this chapter to reflect the corrected syntax.—GLS]

In the following example, the variable x is stepped before y is stepped; thus, the
value of y reflects the updated value of x:

```
(loop for x from 1 to 9
      for y = nil then x
      collect (list x y))
  ⇒ ((1 NIL) (2 2) (3 3) (4 4) (5 5) (6 6) (7 7) (8 8) (9 9))
```

In the following example, x and y are stepped in parallel:

```
(loop for x from 1 to 9
      and y = nil then x
      collect (list x y))
  ⇒ ((1 NIL) (2 1) (3 2) (4 3) (5 4) (6 5) (7 6) (8 7) (9 8))
```

The for and as clauses iterate by using one or more local loop variables that are
initialized to some value and that can be modified or stepped after each iteration.
For these clauses, iteration terminates when a local variable reaches some specified
value or when some other loop clause terminates iteration. At each iteration,
variables can be stepped by an increment or a decrement or can be assigned a
new value by the evaluation of an expression. Destructuring can be used to assign
initial values to variables during iteration.

The for and as keywords are synonyms and may be used interchangeably.
There are seven syntactic representations for these constructs. In each syntactic
description, the data type of *var* can be specified by the optional *type-spec* argument.
If *var* is a destructuring list, the data type specified by the *type-spec* argument must
appropriately match the elements of the list (see sections 26.12.1 and 26.12.2).

> for *var* [*type-spec*] [{from | downfrom | upfrom} *expr1*]   [*Loop clause*]
>   [{to | downto | upto | below | above} *expr2*]
>   [by *expr3*]
> as *var* [*type-spec*] [{from | downfrom | upfrom} *expr1*]   [*Loop clause*]
>   [{to | downto | upto | below | above} *expr2*]
>   [by *expr3*]

[This is the first of seven for/as syntaxes.—GLS]

The for or as construct iterates from the value specified by *expr1* to the value specified by *expr2* in increments or decrements denoted by *expr3*. Each expression is evaluated only once and must evaluate to a number.

The variable *var* is bound to the value of *expr1* in the first iteration and is stepped by the value of *expr3* in each succeeding iteration, or by 1 if *expr3* is not provided.

The following loop keywords serve as valid prepositions within this syntax.

from

The loop keyword from marks the value from which stepping begins, as specified by *expr1*. Stepping is incremental by default. For decremental stepping, use above or downto with *expr2*. For incremental stepping, the default from value is 0.

downfrom, upfrom

The loop keyword downfrom indicates that the variable *var* is decreased in decrements specified by *expr3*; the loop keyword upfrom indicates that *var* is increased in increments specified by *expr3*.

to

The loop keyword to marks the end value for stepping specified in *expr2*. Stepping is incremental by default. For decremental stepping, use downto, downfrom, or above with *expr2*.

downto, upto

The loop keyword downto allows iteration to proceed from a larger number to a smaller number by the decrement *expr3*. The loop keyword upto allows iteration to proceed from a smaller number to a larger number by the increment *expr3*. Since there is no default for *expr1* in decremental stepping, you must supply a value with downto.

below, above

The loop keywords below and above are analogous to upto and downto, respectively. These keywords stop iteration just before the value of the variable *var* reaches the value specified by *expr2*; the end value of *expr2* is not included. Since there is no default for *expr1* in decremental stepping, you must supply a value with above.

by

The loop keyword by marks the increment or decrement specified by *expr3*. The value of *expr3* can be any positive number. The default value is 1.

At least one of these prepositions must be used with this syntax.

In an iteration control clause, the for or as construct causes termination when the specified limit is reached. That is, iteration continues until the value *var* is stepped to the exclusive or inclusive limit specified by *expr2*. The range is *exclusive* if *expr3* increases or decreases *var* to the value of *expr2* without reaching that value; the loop keywords below and above provide exclusive limits. An *inclusive* limit allows *var* to attain the value of *expr2*; to, downto, and upto provide inclusive limits.

A common convention is to use for to introduce new iterations and as to introduce iterations that depend on a previous iteration specification. [However, loop does not enforce this convention, and some of the examples below violate it. *De gustibus non disputandum est.*—GLS]

Examples:

```
;;; Print some numbers.
(loop as i from 1 to 5
      do (print i))                              ;Prints 5 lines
1
2
3
4
5
    ⇒ NIL


;;; Print every third number.
(loop for i from 10 downto 1 by 3
      do (print i))                              ;Prints 4 lines
10
7
4
1
    ⇒ NIL
```

```
;;; Step incrementally from the default starting value.
(loop as i below 5
      do (print i))                                    ;Prints 5 lines
0
1
2
3
4
      ⇒ NIL
```

for *var* [*type-spec*] in *expr1* [by *step-fun*]   [*Loop clause*]
as *var* [*type-spec*] in *expr1* [by *step-fun*]   [*Loop clause*]

[This is the second of seven for/as syntaxes.—GLS]

This construct iterates over the contents of a list. It checks for the end of the list as if using the Common Lisp function endp. The variable *var* is bound to the successive elements of the list *expr1* before each iteration. At the end of each iteration, the function *step-fun* is called on the list and is expected to produce a successor list; the default value for *step-fun* is the cdr function.

The for or as construct causes termination when the end of the list is reached. The loop keywords in and by serve as valid prepositions in this syntax.

Examples:

```
;;; Print every item in a list.
(loop for item in '(1 2 3 4 5) do (print item))       ;Prints 5 lines
1
2
3
4
5
      ⇒ NIL

;;; Print every other item in a list.
(loop for item in '(1 2 3 4 5) by #'cddr
      do (print item))                                 ;Prints 3 lines
1
3
5
      ⇒ NIL
```

```
;;; Destructure items of a list, and sum the x values
;;; using fixnum arithmetic.
(loop for (item . x) (t . fixnum)
          in '((A . 1) (B . 2) (C . 3))
       unless (eq item 'B) sum x)
   ⇒ 4
```

for *var* [*type-spec*] on *expr1* [by *step-fun*]   [*Loop clause*]
as *var* [*type-spec*] on *expr1* [by *step-fun*]   [*Loop clause*]

[This is the third of seven for/as syntaxes.—GLS]

This construct iterates over the contents of a list. It checks for the end of the list as if using the Common Lisp function endp. The variable *var* is bound to the successive tails of the list *expr1*. At the end of each iteration, the function *step-fun* is called on the list and is expected to produce a successor list; the default value for *step-fun* is the cdr function.

The loop keywords on and by serve as valid prepositions in this syntax. The for or as construct causes termination when the end of the list is reached.

Examples:

```
;;; Collect successive tails of a list.
(loop for sublist on '(a b c d)
         collect sublist)
   ⇒ ((A B C D) (B C D) (C D) (D))
```

```
;;; Print a list by using destructuring with the loop keyword ON.
(loop for (item) on '(1 2 3)
         do (print item))                          ;Prints 3 lines
1
2
3
      ⇒ NIL
```

```
;;; Print items in a list without using destructuring.
(loop for item in '(1 2 3)
         do (print item))                          ;Prints 3 lines
1
2
3
      ⇒ NIL
```

```
for var [type-spec] = expr1 [then expr2]          [Loop clause]
as var [type-spec] = expr1 [then expr2]           [Loop clause]
```

[This is the fourth of seven for/as syntaxes.—GLS]

This construct initializes the variable *var* by setting it to the result of evaluating *expr1* on the first iteration, then setting it to the result of evaluating *expr2* on the second and subsequent iterations. If *expr2* is omitted, the construct uses *expr1* on the second and subsequent iterations. When *expr2* is omitted, the expanded code shows the following optimization:

```
;;; Sample original code:
(loop for x = expr1 then expr2 do (print x))

;;; The usual expansion:
(tagbody
        (setq x expr1)
  tag (print x)
        (setq x expr2)
        (go tag))

;;; The optimized expansion:
(tagbody
  tag (setq x expr1)
        (print x)
        (go tag))
```

The loop keywords = and then serve as valid prepositions in this syntax. This construct does not provide any termination conditions.

Example:

```
;;; Collect some numbers.
(loop for item = 1 then (+ item 10)
      repeat 5
      collect item)
  ⇒ (1 11 21 31 41)
```

```
for var [type-spec] across vector          [Loop clause]
as var [type-spec] across vector           [Loop clause]
```

[This is the fifth of seven for/as syntaxes.—GLS]

This construct binds the variable *var* to the value of each element in the array *vector*.

The loop keyword across marks the array *vector*; across is used as a preposition in this syntax. Iteration stops when there are no more elements in the specified array that can be referenced.

Some implementations might use a [user-supplied—GLS] the special form in the *vector* form to produce more efficient code.

Example:

```
(loop for char across (the simple-string (find-message port))
         do (write-char char stream))
```

for *var* [*type-spec*] being {each | the}   [*Loop clause*]
    {hash-key | hash-keys | hash-value | hash-values}
    {in | of} *hash-table* [using ({hash-value | hash-key} *other-var*)]
as *var* [*type-spec*] being {each | the}   [*Loop clause*]
    {hash-key | hash-keys | hash-value | hash-values}
    {in | of} *hash-table* [using ({hash-value | hash-key} *other-var*)]

[This is the sixth of seven for/as syntaxes.—GLS]

This construct iterates over the elements, keys, and values of a hash table. The variable *var* takes on the value of each hash key or hash value in the specified hash table.

The following loop keywords serve as valid prepositions within this syntax.

being

The keyword being marks the loop method to be used, either hash-key or hash-value.

each, the

For purposes of readability, the loop keyword each should follow the loop keyword being when hash-key or hash-value is used. The loop keyword the is used with hash-keys and hash-values.

hash-key, hash-keys

These loop keywords access each key entry of the hash table. If the name hash-value is specified in a using construct with one of these loop methods, the iteration can optionally access the keyed value. The order in which the keys are accessed is undefined; empty slots in the hash table are ignored.

hash-value, hash-values

These loop keywords access each value entry of a hash table. If the name hash-key is specified in a `using` construct with one of these loop methods, the iteration can optionally access the key that corresponds to the value. The order in which the keys are accessed is undefined; empty slots in the hash table are ignored.

`using`

The loop keyword `using` marks the optional key or the keyed value to be accessed. It allows you to access the hash key if iterating over the hash values, and the hash value if iterating over the hash keys.

`in, of`

These loop prepositions mark the hash table *hash-table*.

   Iteration stops when there are no more hash keys or hash values to be referenced in the specified hash table.

```
for var [type-spec] being {each | the}                    [Loop clause]
    {symbol | present-symbol | external-symbol |
     symbols | present-symbols | external-symbols}
    {in | of} package
as var [type-spec] being {each | the}                     [Loop clause]
    {symbol | present-symbol | external-symbol |
     symbols | present-symbols | external-symbols}
    {in | of} package
```

[This is the last of seven `for`/`as` syntaxes.—GLS]
   This construct iterates over the symbols in a package. The variable *var* takes on the value of each symbol in the specified package.
   The following loop keywords serve as valid prepositions within this syntax.

`being`

The keyword `being` marks the loop method to be used: `symbol`, `present-symbol`, or `external-symbol`.

`each, the`

For purposes of readability, the loop keyword `each` should follow the loop keyword `being` when `symbol`, `present-symbol`, or `external-symbol` is used. The loop keyword `the` is used with `symbols`, `present-symbols`, and `external-symbols`.

`present-symbol, present-symbols`

These loop methods iterate over the symbols that are present but not external in a package. The package to be iterated over is specified in the same way that package arguments to the Common Lisp function find-package are specified. If you do not specify the package for the iteration, the current package is used. If you specify a package that does not exist, an error is signaled.

symbol, symbols

These loop methods iterate over symbols that are accessible from a given package. The package to be iterated over is specified in the same way that package arguments to the Common Lisp function find-package are specified. If you do not specify the package for the iteration, the current package is used. If you specify a package that does not exist, an error is signaled.

external-symbol, external-symbols

These loop methods iterate over the external symbols of a package. The package to be iterated over is specified in the same way that package arguments to the Common Lisp function find-package are specified. If you do not specify the package for the iteration, the current package is used. If you specify a package that does not exist, an error is signaled.

in, of

These loop prepositions mark the package *package*.

Iteration stops when there are no more symbols to be referenced in the specified package.
Example:

```
(loop for x being each present-symbol of "COMMON-LISP-USER"
       do (print x))                          ;Prints 7 lines in this example
COMMON-LISP-USER::IN
COMMON-LISP-USER::X
COMMON-LISP-USER::ALWAYS
COMMON-LISP-USER::FOO
COMMON-LISP-USER::Y
COMMON-LISP-USER::FOR
COMMON-LISP-USER::LUCID
   ⇒ NIL
```

repeat *expr*   [*Loop clause*]

The repeat construct causes iteration to terminate after a specified number of times. The loop body is executed *n* times, where *n* is the value of the expression *expr*.

The *expr* argument is evaluated one time in the loop prologue. If the expression evaluates to zero or to a negative number, the loop body is not evaluated.

The clause repeat *n* is roughly equivalent to a clause such as

```
for internal-variable downfrom (- n 1) to 0
```

but, in some implementations, the repeat construct might be more efficient.

Examples:

```
(loop repeat 3                                     ;Prints 3 lines
      do (format t "What I say three times is true~%"))
What I say three times is true
What I say three times is true
What I say three times is true
   ⇒ NIL


(loop repeat -15                                   ;Prints nothing
      do (format t "What you see is what you expect~%"))
   ⇒ NIL
```

26.7. End-Test Control

The loop keywords always, never, thereis, until, and while designate constructs that use a single test condition to determine when loop iteration should terminate.

The constructs always, never, and thereis provide specific values to be returned when a loop terminates. Using always, never, or thereis with value-returning accumulation clauses can produce unpredictable results. In all other respects these constructs behave like the while and until constructs.

The macro loop-finish can be used at any time to cause normal termination. In normal termination, finally clauses are executed and default return values are returned.

End-test control constructs can be used anywhere within the loop body. The termination conditions are tested in the order in which they appear.

while *expr*   [*Loop clause*]
until *expr*   [*Loop clause*]

The while construct allows iteration to continue until the specified expression *expr* evaluates to nil. The expression is re-evaluated at the location of the while clause.

The until construct is equivalent to while (not *expr*). If the value of the specified expression is non-nil, iteration terminates.

You can use while and until at any point in a loop. If a while or until clause causes termination, any clauses that precede it in the source are still evaluated.

Examples:

```
;;; A classic "while-loop".
(loop while (hungry-p) do (eat))


;;; UNTIL NOT is equivalent to WHILE.
(loop until (not (hungry-p)) do (eat))


;;; Collect the length and the items of STACK.
(let ((stack '(a b c d e f)))
  (loop while stack
        for item = (length stack) then (pop stack)
        collect item))
  ⇒ (6 A B C D E F)


;;; Use WHILE to terminate a loop that otherwise wouldn't
;;; terminate. Note that WHILE occurs after the WHEN.
(loop for i fixnum from 3
      when (oddp i) collect i
      while (< i 5))
  ⇒ (3 5)
```

always *expr*   [*Loop clause*]
never *expr*   [*Loop clause*]
thereis *expr*   [*Loop clause*]

The always construct takes one form and terminates the loop if the form ever evaluates to nil; in this case, it returns nil. Otherwise, it provides a default return value of t.

The never construct takes one form and terminates the loop if the form ever evaluates to non-nil; in this case, it returns nil. Otherwise, it provides a default return value of t.

The thereis construct takes one form and terminates the loop if the form ever evaluates to non-nil; in this case, it returns that value.

If the while or until construct causes termination, control is passed to the loop epilogue, where any finally clauses will be executed. Since always, never, and thereis use the Common Lisp macro return to terminate iteration, any finally clause that is specified is not evaluated.

Examples:

```
;;; Make sure I is always less than 11 (two ways).
;;; The FOR construct terminates these loops.

(loop for i from 0 to 10
      always (< i 11))
   ⇒ T

(loop for i from 0 to 10
      never (> i 11))
   ⇒ T

;;; If I exceeds 10, return I; otherwise, return NIL.
;;; The THEREIS construct terminates this loop.

(loop for i from 0
      thereis (when (> i 10) i) )
   ⇒ 11

;;; The FINALLY clause is not evaluated in these examples.

(loop for i from 0 to 10
      always (< i 9)
      finally (print "you won't see this"))
   ⇒ NIL

(loop never t
      finally (print "you won't see this"))
   ⇒ NIL

(loop thereis "Here is my value"
      finally (print "you won't see this"))
   ⇒ "Here is my value"

;;; The FOR construct terminates this loop,
;;;; so the FINALLY clause is evaluated.

(loop for i from 1 to 10
      thereis (> i 11)
      finally (print i))                        ;Prints 1 line
11
   ⇒ NIL
```

```
(defstruct mountain height difficulty (why "because it is there"))
(setq everest (make-mountain :height '(2.86e-13 parsecs)))
(setq chocorua (make-mountain :height '(1059180001 microns)))
(defstruct desert area (humidity 0))
(setq sahara (make-desert :area '(212480000 square furlongs)))
              ;First there is a mountain, then there is no mountain, then there is ...
(loop for x in (list everest sahara chocorua)          ; —GLS
      thereis (and (mountain-p x) (mountain-height x)))
   ⇒ (2.86E-13 PARSECS)
```

```
;;; If you could use this code to find a counterexample to
;;; Fermat's last theorem, it would still not return the value
;;; of the counterexample because all of the THEREIS clauses
;;; in this example return only T.   Of course, this code has
;;; never been observed to terminate.
```

```
(loop for z upfrom 2
      thereis
         (loop for n upfrom 3 below (log z 2)
               thereis
                  (loop for x below z
                        thereis
                           (loop for y below z
                                 thereis (= (+ (expt x n)
                                              (expt y n))
                                            (expt z n))))))
```

loop-finish   *[Macro]*

The macro loop-finish terminates iteration normally and returns any accumulated result. If specified, a finally clause is evaluated.

In most cases it is not necessary to use loop-finish because other loop control clauses terminate the loop. Use loop-finish to provide a normal exit from a nested condition inside a loop.

You can use loop-finish inside nested Lisp code to provide a normal exit from a loop. Since loop-finish transfers control to the loop epilogue, using loop-finish within a finally expression can cause infinite looping.

Implementations are allowed to provide this construct as a local macro by using macrolet.

Examples:

```
;;; Print a date in February, but exclude leap day.
;;; LOOP-FINISH exits from the nested condition.
(loop for date in date-list
      do (case date
           (29 (when (eq month 'february)
                 (loop-finish))
               (format t "~:@(~A~) ~A" month date)))))

;;; Terminate the loop, but return the accumulated count.
(loop for i in '(1 2 3 stop-here 4 5 6)
      when (symbolp i) do (loop-finish)
      count i)
  ⇒ 3

;;; This loop works just as well as the previous example.
(loop for i in '(1 2 3 stop-here 4 5 6)
      until (symbolp i)
      count i)
  ⇒ 3
```

26.8. Value Accumulation

Accumulating values during iteration and returning them from a loop is often useful. Some of these accumulations occur so frequently that special loop clauses have been developed to handle them.

The loop keywords append, appending, collect, collecting, nconc, and nconcing designate clauses that accumulate values in lists and return them.

The loop keywords count, counting, maximize, maximizing, minimize, minimizing, sum, and summing designate clauses that accumulate and return numerical values. [There is no semantic difference between the "ing" keywords and their non-"ing" counterparts. They are provided purely for the sake of stylistic diversity among users. I happen to prefer the non-"ing" forms—when I use loop at all.—GLS]

The loop preposition into can be used to name the variable used to hold partial accumulations. The variable is bound as if by the loop construct with (see section 26.9). If into is used, the construct does not provide a default return value; however, the variable is available for use in any finally clause.

You can combine value-returning accumulation clauses in a loop if all the clauses accumulate the same type of data object. By default, the Loop Facility returns only one value; thus, the data objects collected by multiple accumulation clauses as return values must have compatible types. For example, since both the `collect` and append constructs accumulate objects into a list that is returned from a loop, you can combine them safely.

```
;;; Collect every name and the kids in one list by using
;;; COLLECT and APPEND.
(loop for name in '(fred sue alice joe june)
      for kids in '((bob ken) () () (kris sunshine) ())
      collect name
      append kids)
   ⇒ (FRED BOB KEN SUE ALICE JOE KRIS SUNSHINE JUNE)
```

[In the preceding example, note that the items accumulated by the `collect` and append clauses are interleaved in the result list, according to the order in which the clauses were executed.—GLS]

Multiple clauses that do not accumulate the same type of data object can coexist in a loop only if each clause accumulates its values into a different user-specified variable. Any number of values can be returned from a loop if you use the Common Lisp function `values`, as the next example shows:

```
;;; Count and collect names and ages.
(loop for name in '(fred sue alice joe june)
      as age in '(22 26 19 20 10)
      append (list name age) into name-and-age-list
      count name into name-count
      sum age into total-age
      finally
         (return (values (round total-age name-count)
                         name-and-age-list)))
   ⇒ 19 and (FRED 22 SUE 26 ALICE 19 JOE 20 JUNE 10)
```

collect *expr* [into *var*]   [*Loop clause*]
collecting *expr* [into *var*]   [*Loop clause*]

During each iteration, these constructs collect the value of the specified expression into a list. When iteration terminates, the list is returned.

The argument *var* is set to the list of collected values; if *var* is specified, the loop does not return the final list automatically. If *var* is not specified, it is equivalent to specifying an internal name for *var* and returning its value in a `finally` clause. The *var* argument is bound as if by the construct `with`. You cannot specify a data type for *var*; it must be of type `list`.

Examples:

```
;;; Collect all the symbols in a list.
(loop for i in '(bird 3 4 turtle (1 . 4) horse cat)
      when (symbolp i) collect i)
   ⇒ (BIRD TURTLE HORSE CAT)


;;; Collect and return odd numbers.
(loop for i from 1 to 10
        if (oddp i) collect i)
   ⇒ (1 3 5 7 9)


;;; Collect items into local variable, but don't return them.
(loop for i in '(a b c d) by #'cddr
         collect i into my-list
         finally (print my-list))                 ;Prints 1 line
(A C)
     ⇒ NIL
```

append *expr* [into *var*]	[*Loop clause*]
appending *expr* [into *var*]	[*Loop clause*]
nconc *expr* [into *var*]	[*Loop clause*]
nconcing *expr* [into *var*]	[*Loop clause*]

These constructs are similar to collect except that the values of the specified expression must be lists.

The append keyword causes its list values to be concatenated into a single list, as if they were arguments to the Common Lisp function append.

The nconc keyword causes its list values to be concatenated into a single list, as if they were arguments to the Common Lisp function nconc. Note that the nconc keyword destructively modifies its argument lists.

The argument *var* is set to the list of concatenated values; if you specify *var*, the loop does not return the final list automatically. The *var* argument is bound as if by the construct with. You cannot specify a data type for *var*; it must be of type list.

Examples:

```
;;; Use APPEND to concatenate some sublists.
(loop for x in '((a) (b) ((c)))
        append x)
   ⇒ (A B (C))
```

```
;;; NCONC some sublists together. Note that only lists
;;; made by the call to LIST are modified.
(loop for i upfrom 0
      as x in '(a b (c))
      nconc (if (evenp i) (list x) '()))
   ⇒ (A (C))
```

count *expr* [into *var*] [*type-spec*]   [*Loop clause*]
counting *expr* [into *var*] [*type-spec*]   [*Loop clause*]

The count construct counts the number of times that the specified expression has a non-nil value.

The argument *var* accumulates the number of occurrences; if *var* is specified, the loop does not return the final count automatically. The *var* argument is bound as if by the construct with.

If into *var* is used, the optional *type-spec* argument specifies a data type for *var*. If there is no into variable, the optional *type-spec* argument applies to the internal variable that is keeping the count. In either case it is an error to specify a non-numeric data type. The default type is implementation-dependent, but it must be a subtype of (or integer float).

Example:

```
(loop for i in '(a b nil c nil d e)
      count i)
   ⇒ 5
```

sum *expr* [into *var*] [*type-spec*]   [*Loop clause*]
summing *expr* [into *var*] [*type-spec*]   [*Loop clause*]

The sum construct forms a cumulative sum of the values of the specified expression at each iteration.

The argument *var* is used to accumulate the sum; if *var* is specified, the loop does not return the final sum automatically. The *var* argument is bound as if by the construct with.

If into *var* is used, the optional *type-spec* argument specifies a data type for *var*. If there is no into variable, the optional *type-spec* argument applies to the internal variable that is keeping the sum. In either case it is an error to specify a non-numeric data type. The default type is implementation-dependent, but it must be a subtype of number.

Examples:

```
;;; Sum the elements of a list.

(loop for i fixnum in '(1 2 3 4 5)
      sum i)
   ⇒ 15


;;; Sum a function of elements of a list.

(setq series
      '(1.2 4.3 5.7))
   ⇒ (1.2 4.3 5.7)

(loop for v in series
      sum (* 2.0 v))
   ⇒ 22.4
```

maximize *expr* [into *var*] [*type-spec*]	[*Loop clause*]
maximizing *expr* [into *var*] [*type-spec*]	[*Loop clause*]
minimize *expr* [into *var*] [*type-spec*]	[*Loop clause*]
minimizing *expr* [into *var*] [*type-spec*]	[*Loop clause*]

The maximize construct compares the value of the specified expression obtained during the first iteration with values obtained in successive iterations. The maximum value encountered is determined and returned. If the loop never executes the body, the returned value is not meaningful.

The minimize construct is similar to maximize; it determines and returns the minimum value.

The argument *var* accumulates the maximum or minimum value; if *var* is specified, the loop does not return the maximum or minimum automatically. The *var* argument is bound as if by the construct with.

If into *var* is used, the optional *type-spec* argument specifies a data type for *var*. If there is no into variable, the optional *type-spec* argument applies to the internal variable that is keeping the intermediate result. In either case it is an error to specify a non-numeric data type. The default type is implementation-dependent, but it must be a subtype of (or integer float).

Examples:

```
(loop for i in '(2 1 5 3 4)
      maximize i)
   ⇒ 5
```

```
(loop for i in '(2 1 5 3 4)
      minimize i)
  ⇒ 1
```

```
;;; In this example, FIXNUM applies to the internal
;;; variable that holds the maximum value.
```

```
(setq series '(1.2 4.3 5.7))
  ⇒ (1.2 4.3 5.7)
```

```
(loop for v in series
      maximize (round v) fixnum)
  ⇒ 6
```

```
;;; In this example, FIXNUM applies to the variable RESULT.
```

```
(loop for v float in series
      minimize (round v) into result fixnum
      finally (return result))
  ⇒ 1
```

26.9. Variable Initializations

A local loop variable is one that exists only when the Loop Facility is invoked. At that time, the variables are declared and are initialized to some value. These local variables exist until loop iteration terminates, at which point they cease to exist. Implicitly variables are also established by iteration control clauses and the into preposition of accumulation clauses.

The loop keyword with designates a loop clause that allows you to declare and initialize variables that are local to a loop. The variables are initialized one time only; they can be initialized sequentially or in parallel.

By default, the with construct initializes variables sequentially; that is, one variable is assigned a value before the next expression is evaluated. However, by using the loop keyword and to join several with clauses, you can force initializations to occur in parallel; that is, all of the specified expressions are evaluated, and the results are bound to the respective variables simultaneously.

Use sequential binding for making the initialization of some variables depend on the values of previously bound variables. For example, suppose you want to bind the variables a, b, and c in sequence:

```
(loop with a = 1
      with b = (+ a 2)
      with c = (+ b 3)
      with d = (+ c 4)
      return (list a b c d))
  ⇒ (1 3 6 10)
```

The execution of the preceding loop is equivalent to the execution of the following code:

```
(let* ((a 1)
       (b (+ a 2))
       (c (+ b 3))
       (d (+ c 4)))
  (block nil
    (tagbody
      next-loop (return (list a b c d))
                (go next-loop)
      end-loop)))
```

If you are not depending on the value of previously bound variables for the initialization of other local variables, you can use parallel bindings as follows:

```
(loop with a = 1
      and b = 2
      and c = 3
      and d = 4
      return (list a b c d))
  ⇒ (1 2 3 4)
```

The execution of the preceding loop is equivalent to the execution of the following code:

```
(let ((a 1)
      (b 2)
      (c 3)
      (d 4))
  (block nil
    (tagbody
      next-loop (return (list a b c))
                (go next-loop)
      end-loop)))
```

with *var* [*type-spec*] [= *expr*] {and *var* [*type-spec*] [= *expr*]}*   [*Loop clause*]

The with construct initializes variables that are local to a loop. The variables are initialized one time only.

   If the optional *type-spec* argument is specified for any variable *var*, but there is no related expression *expr* to be evaluated, *var* is initialized to an appropriate default value for its data type. For example, for the data types t, number, and float, the default values are nil, 0, and 0.0, respectively. It is an error to specify a *type-spec* argument for *var* if the related expression returns a value that is not of the specified type. The optional and clause forces parallel rather than sequential initializations.

   Examples:

```
;;; These bindings occur in sequence.
(loop with a = 1
      with b = (+ a 2)
      with c = (+ b 3)
      with d = (+ c 4)
      return (list a b c d))
   ⇒ (1 3 6 10)


;;; These bindings occur in parallel.
(setq a 5 b 10 c 1729)
(loop with a = 1
      and b = (+ a 2)
      and c = (+ b 3)
      and d = (+ c 4)
      return (list a b c d))
   ⇒ (1 7 13 1733)


;;; This example shows a shorthand way to declare
;;; local variables that are of different types.
(loop with (a b c) (float integer float)
      return (format nil "~A ~A ~A" a b c))
   ⇒ "0.0 0 0.0"


;;; This example shows a shorthand way to declare
;;; local variables that are of the same type.
(loop with (a b c) float
      return (format nil "~A ~A ~A" a b c))
   ⇒ "0.0 0.0 0.0"
```

26.10. Conditional Execution

The loop keywords if, when, and unless designate constructs that are useful when you want some loop clauses to operate under a specified condition.

If the specified condition is true, the succeeding loop clause is executed. If the specified condition is not true, the succeeding clause is skipped, and program control moves to the clause that follows the loop keyword else. If the specified condition is not true and no else clause is specified, the entire conditional construct is skipped. Several clauses can be connected into one compound clause with the loop keyword and. The end of the conditional clause can be marked with the keyword end.

if *expr clause* {and *clause*}*   [*Loop clause*]
  [else *clause* {and *clause*}*] [end]
when *expr clause* {and *clause*}*   [*Loop clause*]
    [else *clause* {and *clause*}*] [end]
unless *expr clause* {and *clause*}*   [*Loop clause*]
    [else *clause* {and *clause*}*] [end]

The constructs when and if allow conditional execution of loop clauses. These constructs are synonyms and can be used interchangeably. [Compare this to the *macro* when, which does not allow an "else" part.—GLS]

If the value of the test expression *expr* is non-nil, the expression *clause1* is evaluated. If the test expression evaluates to nil and an else construct is specified, the statements that follow the else are evaluated; otherwise, control passes to the next clause.

The unless construct is equivalent to when (not *expr*) and if (not *expr*). If the value of the test expression *expr* is nil, the expression *clause1* is evaluated. If the test expression evaluates to non-nil and an else construct is specified, the statements that follow the else are evaluated; otherwise, control passes to the next clause. [Compare this to the *macro* unless, which does not allow an "else" part— or do I mean a "then" part?! Ugh. To prevent confusion, I strongly recommend as a matter of style that else not be used with unless loop clauses.—GLS]

The *clause* arguments must be either accumulation, unconditional, or conditional clauses (see section 26.3.2). Clauses that follow the test expression can be grouped by using the loop keyword and to produce a compound clause.

The loop keyword it can be used to refer to the result of the test expression in a clause. If multiple clauses are connected with and, the it construct must be used in the first clause in the block. Since it is a loop keyword, it may not be used as a local variable within a loop.

If when or if clauses are nested, each else is paired with the closest preceding when or if construct that has no associated else.

The optional loop keyword end marks the end of the clause. If this keyword is not specified, the next loop keyword marks the end. You can use end to distinguish the scoping of compound clauses.

```
;;; Group conditional clauses into a block.
(loop for i in numbers-list
      when (oddp i)
        do (print i)
        and collect i into odd-numbers
        and do (terpri)
      else      ;I is even
        collect i into even-numbers
      finally
        (return (values odd-numbers even-numbers)))

;;; Collect numbers larger than 3.
(loop for i in '(1 2 3 4 5 6)
      when (and (> i 3) i)
      collect it)      ;it refers to (and (> i 3) i)
  ⇒ (4 5 6)

;;; Find a number in a list.
(loop for i in '(1 2 3 4 5 6)
      when (and (> i 3) i)
      return it)
  ⇒ 4

;;; The preceding example is similar to the following one.
(loop for i in '(1 2 3 4 5 6)
      thereis (and (> i 3) i))
  ⇒ 4

;;; An example of using UNLESS with ELSE (yuk).          —GLS
(loop for turtle in teenage-mutant-ninja-turtles do
  (loop for x in '(joker brainiac shredder krazy-kat)
        unless (evil x)
          do (eat (make-pizza :anchovies t))
        else unless (and (eq x 'shredder) (attacking-p x))
                do (cut turtle slack);When the evil Shredder attacks,
              else (fight turtle x)));those turtle boys don't cut no slack
```

```
;;; Nest conditional clauses.
(loop for i in list
      when (numberp i)
        when (bignump i)
          collect i into big-numbers
        else      ;Not (bignump i)
          collect i into other-numbers
      else      ;Not (numberp i)
        when (symbolp i)
          collect i into symbol-list
        else      ;Not (symbolp i)
          (error "found a funny value in list ~S, value ~S~%"
                 "list i))

;;; Without the END marker, the last AND would apply to the
;;; inner IF rather than the outer one.
(loop for x from 0 to 3
      do (print x)
      if (zerop (mod x 2))
        do (princ " a")
        and if (zerop (floor x 2))
              do (princ " b")
            end
        and do (princ " c")))
```

26.11. Unconditional Execution

The loop construct do (or doing) takes one or more expressions and simply evaluates them in order.

The loop construct return takes one expression and returns its value. It is equivalent to the clause do (return *value*).

do {*expr*}*   [*Loop clause*]
doing {*expr*}*   [*Loop clause*]

The do construct simply evaluates the specified expressions wherever they occur in the expanded form of loop.

The *expr* argument can be any non-atomic Common Lisp form. Each *expr* is evaluated in every iteration.

The constructs do, `initially`, and `finally` are the only loop keywords that take an arbitrary number of forms and group them as if using an implicit progn. Because every loop clause must begin with a loop keyword, you would use the keyword do when no control action other than execution is required.

Examples:

```
;;; Print some numbers.
(loop for i from 1 to 5
      do (print i))                                              ;Prints 5 lines
1
2
3
4
5
    ⇒ NIL

;;; Print numbers and their squares.
;;; The DO construct applies to multiple forms.
(loop for i from 1 to 4
      do (print i)
         (print (* i i)))                                        ;Prints 8 lines
1
1
2
4
3
9
4
16
    ⇒ NIL
```

return *expr*   [*Loop clause*]

The return construct terminates a loop and returns the value of the specified expression as the value of the loop. This construct is similar to the Common Lisp special form return-from and the Common Lisp macro return.

The Loop Facility supports the return construct for backward compatibility with older loop implementations. The return construct returns immediately and does not execute any finally clause that is given.

Examples:

```
;;; Signal an exceptional condition.
(loop for item in '(1 2 3 a 4 5)
      when (not (numberp item))
      return (cerror "enter new value"
                     "non-numeric value: ~s"
                     item))                              ;Signals an error
>>Error: non-numeric value: A


;;; The previous example is equivalent to the following one.
(loop for item in '(1 2 3 a 4 5)
     when (not (numberp item))
     do (return
           (cerror "enter new value"
                   "non-numeric value: ~s"
                   item)))                               ;Signals an error
>>Error: non-numeric value: A
```

26.12. Miscellaneous Features

The Loop Facility provides the named construct to name a loop so that the Common Lisp special form return-from can be used.

The loop keywords initially and finally designate loop constructs that cause expressions to be evaluated before and after the loop body, respectively.

The code for any initially clauses is collected into one progn in the order in which the clauses appeared in the loop. The collected code is executed once in the loop prologue after any implicit variable initializations.

The code for any finally clauses is collected into one progn in the order in which the clauses appeared in the loop. The collected code is executed once in the loop epilogue before any implicit values are returned from the accumulation clauses. Explicit returns in the loop body, however, will exit the loop without executing the epilogue code.

26.12.1. Data Types

Many loop constructs take a *type-spec* argument that allows you to specify certain data types for loop variables. While it is not necessary to specify a data type for any variable, by doing so you ensure that the variable has a correctly typed initial value. The type declaration is made available to the compiler for more efficient loop expansion. In some implementations, fixnum and float declarations are especially useful; the compiler notices them and emits more efficient code.

The *type-spec* argument has the following syntax:

type-spec ::= of-type *d-type-spec*
d-type-spec ::= *type-specifier* | (*d-type-spec* . *d-type-spec*)

A *type-specifier* in this syntax can be any Common Lisp type specifier. The *d-type-spec* argument is used for destructuring, as described in section 26.12.2. If the *d-type-spec* argument consists solely of the types fixnum, float, t, or nil, the of-type keyword is optional. The of-type construct is optional in these cases to provide backward compatibility; thus the following two expressions are the same:

```
;;; This expression uses the old syntax for type specifiers.
(loop for i fixnum upfrom 3 ...)

;;; This expression uses the new syntax for type specifiers.
(loop for i of-type fixnum upfrom 3 ...)
```

26.12.2. Destructuring

Destructuring allows you to bind a set of variables to a corresponding set of values anywhere that you can normally bind a value to a single variable. During loop expansion, each variable in the variable list is matched with the values in the values list. If there are more variables in the variable list than there are values in the values list, the remaining variables are given a value of nil. If there are more values than variables listed, the extra values are discarded.

Suppose you want to assign values from a list to the variables a, b, and c. You could use one for clause to bind the variable numlist to the *car* of the specified expression, and then you could use another for clause to bind the variables a, b, and c sequentially.

```
;;; Collect values by using FOR constructs.
(loop for numlist in '((1 2 4.0) (5 6 8.3) (8 9 10.4))
      for a integer = (first numlist)
      and for b integer = (second numlist)
      and for c float = (third numlist)
      collect (list c b a))
   ⇒ ((4.0 2 1) (8.3 6 5) (10.4 9 8))
```

Destructuring makes this process easier by allowing the variables to be bound in parallel in each loop iteration. You can declare data types by using a list of *type-spec* arguments. If all the types are the same, you can use a shorthand destructuring syntax, as the second example following illustrates.

```
;;; Destructuring simplifies the process.
(loop for (a b c) (integer integer float) in
        '((1 2 4.0) (5 6 8.3) (8 9 10.4))
        collect (list c b a)))
    ⇒ ((4.0 2 1) (8.3 6 5) (10.4 9 8))

;;; If all the types are the same, this way is even simpler.
(loop for (a b c) float in
        '((1.0 2.0 4.0) (5.0 6.0 8.3) (8.0 9.0 10.4))
        collect (list c b a))
    ⇒ ((4.0 2.0 1.0) (8.3 6.0 5.0) (10.4 9.0 8.0))
```

If you use destructuring to declare or initialize a number of groups of variables into types, you can use the loop keyword and to simplify the process further.

```
;;; Initialize and declare variables in parallel
;;; by using the AND construct.
(loop with (a b) float = '(1.0 2.0)
        and (c d) integer = '(3 4)
        and (e f)
        return (list a b c d e f))
    ⇒ (1.0 2.0 3 4 NIL NIL)
```

A data type specifier for a destructuring pattern is a tree of type specifiers with the same shape as the tree of variables, with the following exceptions:

- When aligning the trees, an atom in the type specifier tree that matches a cons in the variable tree declares the same type for each variable.

- A cons in the type specifier tree that matches an atom in the variable tree is a non-atomic type specifer.

```
;;; Declare X and Y to be of type VECTOR and FIXNUM, respectively.
(loop for (x y) of-type (vector fixnum) in my-list do ...)
```

If nil is used in a destructuring list, no variable is provided for its place.

```
(loop for (a nil b) = '(1 2 3)
      do (return (list a b)))
  ⇒ (1 3)
```

Note that nonstandard lists can specify destructuring.

```
(loop for (x . y) = '(1 . 2)
      do (return y))
  ⇒ 2
```

```
(loop for ((a . b) (c . d))
         of-type ((float . float) (integer . integer))
         in '(((1.2 . 2.4) (3 . 4)) ((3.4 . 4.6) (5 . 6)))
      collect (list a b c d))
  ⇒ ((1.2 2.4 3 4) (3.4 4.6 5 6))
```

[It is worth noting that the destructuring facility of loop predates, and differs in some details from, that of destructuring-bind, an extension that has been provided by many implementors of Common Lisp.—GLS]

initially {*expr*}*	[*Loop clause*]
finally [do | doing] {*expr*}*	[*Loop clause*]
finally return *expr*	[*Loop clause*]

The initially construct causes the specified expression to be evaluated in the loop prologue, which precedes all loop code except for initial settings specified by constructs with, for, or as. The finally construct causes the specified expression to be evaluated in the loop epilogue after normal iteration terminates.

The *expr* argument can be any non-atomic Common Lisp form.

Clauses such as return, always, never, and thereis can bypass the finally clause.

The Common Lisp macro return (or the return loop construct) can be used after finally to return values from a loop. The evaluation of the return form inside the finally clause takes precedence over returning the accumulation from clauses specified by such keywords as collect, nconc, append, sum, count, maximize, and minimize; the accumulation values for these pre-empted clauses are not returned by the loop if return is used.

The constructs do, initially, and finally are the only loop keywords that take an arbitrary number of (non-atomic) forms and group them as if by using an implicit progn.

Examples:

```
;;; This example parses a simple printed string representation
;;; from BUFFER (which is itself a string) and returns the
;;; index of the closing double-quote character.

(loop initially (unless (char= (char buffer 0) #\")
                  (loop-finish))
      for i fixnum from 1 below (string-length buffer)
      when (char= (char buffer i) #\")
        return i)

;;; The FINALLY clause prints the last value of I.
;;; The collected value is returned.

(loop for i from 1 to 10
      when (> i 5)
        collect i
        finally (print i))                              ;Prints 1 line
11
   ⇒ (6 7 8 9 10)


;;; Return both the count of collected numbers
;;; as well as the numbers themselves.

(loop for i from 1 to 10
      when (> i 5)
        collect i into number-list
        and count i into number-count
        finally (return (values number-count number-list)))
   ⇒ 5 and (6 7 8 9 10)
```

named *name*   [*Loop clause*]

The named construct allows you to assign a name to a loop construct so that you can use the Common Lisp special form return-from to exit the named loop.

Only one name may be assigned per loop; the specified name becomes the name of the implicit block for the loop.

If used, the named construct must be the first clause in the loop expression, coming right after the word loop.

Example:

```
;;; Just name and return.
(loop named max
      for i from 1 to 10
      do (print i)
      do (return-from max 'done))                    ;Prints 1 line
1
   ⇒ DONE
```

27

Pretty Printing

BY RICHARD C. WATERS

PREFACE: X3J13 voted in January 1989 ⟨139⟩ to adopt a facility for user-controlled pretty printing as a part of the forthcoming draft Common Lisp standard. This facility is the culmination of thirteen years of design, testing, revision, and use of this approach.

This chapter presents the bulk of the Common Lisp pretty printing specification, written by Richard C. Waters. I have edited it only very lightly to conform to the overall style of this book.

—Guy L. Steele Jr.

27.1. Introduction

Pretty printing has traditionally been a black box process, displaying program code using a set of fixed layout rules. Its utility can be greatly enhanced by opening it up to user control. The facilities described in this chapter provide general and powerful means for specifying pretty-printing behavior.

By providing direct access to the mechanisms within the pretty printer that make dynamic decisions about layout, the macros and functions `pprint-logical-block`, `pprint-newline`, and `pprint-indent` make it possible to specify pretty printing layout rules as a part of any function that produces output. They also make it very easy for the function to support detection of circularity and sharing and abbreviation based on length and nesting depth. Using the function `set-pprint-dispatch`, one can associate a user-defined pretty printing function with any type of object. A small set of new `format` directives allows concise implementation of user-defined pretty-printing functions. Together, these facilities enable users to redefine the way code is displayed and allow the full power of pretty printing to be applied to complex combinations of data structures.

748

Implementation note: This chapter describes the interface of the XP pretty printer. XP is described fully in [54], which also explains how to obtain a portable implementation. XP uses a highly efficient linear-time algorithm. When properly integrated into a Common Lisp, this algorithm supports pretty printing that is only fractionally slower than ordinary printing.

27.2. Pretty Printing Control Variables

The function `write` accepts keyword arguments named `:pprint-dispatch`, `:miser-width`, `:right-margin`, and `:lines`, corresponding to these variables.

`*print-pprint-dispatch*`   [*Variable*]

When `*print-pretty*` is not `nil`, printing is controlled by the 'pprint dispatch table' stored in the variable `*print-pprint-dispatch*`. The initial value of `*print-pprint-dispatch*` is implementation-dependent and causes traditional pretty printing of Lisp code. The last section of this chapter explains how the contents of this table can be changed.

`*print-right-margin*`   [*Variable*]

A primary goal of pretty printing is to keep the output between a pair of margins. The left margin is set at the column where the output begins. If this cannot be determined, the left margin is set to zero.

When `*print-right-margin*` is not `nil`, it specifies the right margin to use when making layout decisions. When `*print-right-margin*` is `nil` (the initial value), the right margin is set at the maximum line length that can be displayed by the output stream without wraparound or truncation. If this cannot be determined, the right margin is set to an implementation-dependent value.

To allow for the possibility of variable-width fonts, `*print-right-margin*` is in units of ems—the width of an "m" in the font being used to display characters on the relevant output stream at the moment when the variables are consulted.

`*print-miser-width*`   [*Variable*]

If `*print-miser-width*` is not `nil`, the pretty printer switches to a compact style of output (called miser style) whenever the width available for printing a substructure is less than or equal to `*print-miser-width*` ems. The initial value of `*print-miser-width*` is implementation-dependent.

print-lines   [Variable]

When given a value other than its initial value of nil, *print-lines* limits the
number of output lines produced when something is pretty printed. If an attempt
is made to go beyond *print-lines* lines, " .." (a space and two periods) is
printed at the end of the last line followed by all of the suffixes (closing delimiters)
that are pending to be printed.

```
(let ((*print-right-margin* 25) (*print-lines* 3))
  (pprint '(progn (setq a 1 b 2 c 3 d 4))))

(PROGN (SETQ A 1
             B 2
             C 3 ..))
```

(The symbol ".." is printed out to ensure that a reader error will occur if the
output is later read. A symbol different from "..." is used to indicate that a
different kind of abbreviation has occurred.)

27.3. Dynamic Control of the Arrangement of Output

The following functions and macros support precise control of what should be done
when a piece of output is too large to fit in the space available. Three concepts
underlie the way these operations work: *logical blocks*, *conditional newlines*, and
sections. Before proceeding further, it is important to define these terms.

The first line of figure 27-1 shows a schematic piece of output. The characters
in the output are represented by hyphens. The positions of conditional newlines
are indicated by digits. The beginnings and ends of logical blocks are indicated in
the figure by "<" and ">" respectively.

The output as a whole is a logical block and the outermost section. This section
is indicated by the 0's on the second line of figure 27-1. Logical blocks nested
within the output are specified by the macro pprint-logical-block. Conditional
newline positions are specified by calls on pprint-newline. Each conditional
newline defines two sections (one before it and one after it) and is associated with
a third (the section immediately containing it).

The section after a conditional newline consists of all the output up to, but
not including, (a) the next conditional newline immediately contained in the same
logical block; or if (a) is not applicable, (b) the next newline that is at a lesser level
of nesting in logical blocks; or if (b) is not applicable, (c) the end of the output.

The section before a conditional newline consists of all the output back to, but
not including, (a) the previous conditional newline that is immediately contained

Figure 27-1: Example of Logical Blocks, Conditional Newlines, and Sections

```
<-1---<--<--2---3->--4-->->
0000000000000000000000000000
11 11111111111111111111111111
       22 222
          333 3333
       44444444444444 44444
```

in the same logical block; or if (a) is not applicable, (b) the beginning of the immediately containing logical block. The last four lines in figure 27-1 indicate the sections before and after the four conditional newlines.

The section immediately containing a conditional newline is the shortest section that contains the conditional newline in question. In figure 27-1, the first conditional newline is immediately contained in the section marked with 0's, the second and third conditional newlines are immediately contained in the section before the fourth conditional newline, and the fourth conditional newline is immediately contained in the section after the first conditional newline.

Whenever possible, the pretty printer displays the entire contents of a section on a single line. However, if the section is too long to fit in the space available, line breaks are inserted at conditional newline positions within the section.

`pprint-newline` *kind* &optional *stream*   [*Function*]

The *stream* (which defaults to `*standard-output*`) follows the standard conventions for stream arguments to printing functions (that is, `nil` stands for `*standard-output*` and t stands for `*terminal-io*`). The *kind* argument specifies the style of conditional newline. It must be one of `:linear`, `:fill`, `:miser`, or `:mandatory`. An error is signaled if any other value is supplied. If *stream* is a pretty printing stream created by `pprint-logical-block`, a line break is inserted in the output when the appropriate condition below is satisfied. Otherwise, `pprint-newline` has no effect. The value `nil` is always returned.

If *kind* is `:linear`, it specifies a 'linear-style' conditional newline. A line break is inserted if and only if the immediately containing section cannot be printed on one line. The effect of this is that line breaks are either inserted at every linear-style conditional newline in a logical block or at none of them.

If *kind* is `:miser`, it specifies a 'miser-style' conditional newline. A line break is inserted if and only if the immediately containing section cannot be printed on one line and miser style is in effect in the immediately containing logical block. The effect of this is that miser-style conditional newlines act like linear-style conditional newlines, but only when miser style is in effect. Miser style is in effect for a logical block if and only if the starting position of the logical block is less than or equal to `*print-miser-width*` from the right margin.

If *kind* is `:fill`, it specifies a 'fill-style' conditional newline. A line break is inserted if and only if either (a) the following section cannot be printed on the end of the current line, (b) the preceding section was not printed on a single line, or (c) the immediately containing section cannot be printed on one line and miser style is in effect in the immediately containing logical block. If a logical block is broken up into a number of subsections by fill-style conditional newlines, the basic effect is that the logical block is printed with as many subsections as possible on each line. However, if miser style is in effect, fill-style conditional newlines act like linear-style conditional newlines.

If *kind* is `:mandatory`, it specifies a 'mandatory-style' conditional newline. A line break is always inserted. This implies that none of the containing sections can be printed on a single line and will therefore trigger the insertion of line breaks at linear-style conditional newlines in these sections.

When a line break is inserted by any type of conditional newline, any blanks that immediately precede the conditional newline are omitted from the output and indentation is introduced at the beginning of the next line. By default, the indentation causes the following line to begin in the same horizontal position as the first character in the immediately containing logical block. (The indentation can be changed via `pprint-indent`.)

There are a variety of ways *un*conditional newlines can be introduced into the output (for example, via `terpri` or by printing a string containing a newline character). As with mandatory conditional newlines, this prevents any of the containing sections from being printed on one line. In general, when an unconditional newline is encountered, it is printed out without suppression of the preceding blanks and without any indentation following it. However, if a per-line prefix has been specified (see `pprint-logical-block`), that prefix will always be printed no matter how a newline originates.

---

pprint-logical-block (*stream-symbol list*   [*Macro*]
           ⟦ {:prefix | :per-line-prefix} *p* | :suffix *s* ⟧)
    {*form*}*

This macro causes printing to be grouped into a logical block. It returns `nil`.

The *stream-symbol* must be a symbol. If it is `nil`, it is treated the same as if it were `*standard-output*`. If it is `t`, it is treated the same as if it were *terminal-io*. The run-time value of *stream-symbol* must be a stream (or nil standing for *standard-output* or t standing for *terminal-io*). The logical block is printed into this destination stream.

The body (which consists of the *forms*) can contain any arbitrary Lisp forms. Within the body, *stream-symbol* (or *standard-output* if *stream-symbol* is nil, or *terminal-io* if *stream-symbol* is t) is bound to a "pretty printing" stream that supports decisions about the arrangement of output and then forwards the output to the destination stream. All the standard printing functions (for example, write, princ, terpri) can be used to send output to the pretty printing stream created by pprint-logical-block. All and only the output sent to this pretty printing stream is treated as being in the logical block.

pprint-logical-block and the pretty printing stream it creates have dynamic extent. It is undefined what happens if output is attempted outside of this extent to the pretty printing stream created. It is unspecified what happens if, within this extent, any output is sent directly to the underlying destination stream (by calling write-char, for example).

The :suffix, :prefix, and :per-line-prefix arguments must all be expressions that (at run time) evaluate to strings. The :suffix argument *s* (which defaults to the null string) specifies a suffix that is printed just after the logical block. The :prefix and :per-line-prefix arguments are mutually exclusive. If neither :prefix nor :per-line-prefix is specified, a :prefix of the null string is assumed. The :prefix argument specifies a prefix *p* that is printed before the beginning of the logical block. The :per-line-prefix specifies a prefix *p* that is printed before the block and at the beginning of each subsequent line in the block. An error is signaled if :prefix and :per-line-prefix are both used or if a :suffix, :prefix, or :pre-line-prefix argument does not evaluate to a string.

The *list* is interpreted as being a list that the body is responsible for printing. (See pprint-exit-if-list-exhausted and pprint-pop.) If *list* does not (at run time) evaluate to a list, it is printed using write. (This makes it easier to write printing functions that are robust in the face of malformed arguments.) If *print-circle* (and possibly also *print-shared*) is not nil and *list* is a circular (or shared) reference to a cons, then an appropriate "#*n*#" marker is printed. (This makes it easy to write printing functions that provide full support for circularity and sharing abbreviation.) If *print-level* is not nil and the logical block is at a dynamic nesting depth of greater than *print-level* in logical blocks, "#" is printed. (This makes it easy to write printing functions that provide full support for depth abbreviation.)

If any of the three preceding conditions occurs, the indicated output is printed on *stream-symbol* and the *body* is skipped along with the printing of the prefix and suffix. (If the body is not responsible for printing a list, then the first two tests above can be turned off by supplying `nil` for the *list* argument.)

In addition to the *list* argument of `pprint-logical-block`, the arguments of the standard printing functions such as `write`, `print`, `pprint`, `print1`, and `pprint`, as well as the arguments of the standard `format` directives such as `~A`, `~S`, (and `~W`) are all checked (when necessary) for circularity and sharing. However, such checking is not applied to the arguments of the functions `write-line`, `write-string`, and `write-char` or to the literal text output by `format`. A consequence of this is that you must use one of the latter functions if you want to print some literal text in the output that is not supposed to be checked for circularity or sharing. (See the examples below.)

Implementation note: Detection of circularity and sharing is supported by the pretty printer by in essence performing the requested output twice. On the first pass, circularities and sharing are detected and the actual outputting of characters is suppressed. On the second pass, the appropriate "#*n*=" and "#*n*#" markers are inserted and characters are output.

A consequence of this two-pass approach to the detection of circularity and sharing is that the body of a `pprint-logical-block` must not perform any side-effects on the surrounding environment. This includes not modifying any variables that are bound outside of its scope. Obeying this restriction is facilitated by using `pprint-pop`, instead of an ordinary `pop` when traversing a list being printed by the body of a `pprint-logical-block`.)

`pprint-exit-if-list-exhausted`   [*Macro*]

`pprint-exit-if-list-exhausted` tests whether or not the *list* argument of `pprint-logical-block` has been exhausted (see `pprint-pop`). If this list has been reduced to `nil`, `pprint-exit-if-list-exhausted` terminates the execution of the immediately containing `pprint-logical-block` except for the printing of the suffix. Otherwise `pprint-exit-if-list-exhausted` returns `nil`. An error message is issued if `pprint-exit-if-list-exhausted` is used anywhere other than syntactically nested within a call on `pprint-logical-block`. It is undefined what happens if `pprint-pop` is executed outside of the dynamic extent of this `pprint-logical-block`.

`pprint-pop`   [*Macro*]

`pprint-pop` pops elements one at a time off the *list* argument of `pprint-logical-block`, taking care to obey `*print-length*`, `*print-circle*`, and `*print-shared*`. An error message is issued if it is used anywhere other than syntactically nested within a call on `pprint-logical-block`. It is undefined what

happens if pprint-pop is executed outside of the dynamic extent of this call on
pprint-logical-block.

Each time pprint-pop is called, it pops the next value off the *list* argument of
pprint-logical-block and returns it. However, before doing this, it performs
three tests. If the remaining list is not a list (neither a cons nor nil), ". " is
printed followed by the remaining list. (This makes it easier to write printing
functions that are robust in the face of malformed arguments.) If *print-length*
is nil and pprint-pop has already been called *print-length* times within the
immediately containing logical block, "..." is printed. (This makes it easy to write
printing functions that properly handle *print-length*.) If *print-circle*
(and possibly also *print-shared*) is not nil, and the remaining list is a circular
(or shared) reference, then ". " is printed followed by an appropriate "#*n*#" marker.
(This catches instances of cdr circularity and sharing in lists.)

If any of the three preceding conditions occurs, the indicated output is printed on
the pretty printing stream created by the immediately containing pprint-logical-
block and the execution of the immediately containing pprint-logical-block
is terminated except for the printing of the suffix.

If pprint-logical-block is given a *list* argument of nil—because it is not processing a list—pprint-pop can still be used to obtain support for *print-length*
(see the example function pprint-vector below). In this situation, the first and
third tests above are disabled and pprint-pop always returns nil.

pprint-indent *relative-to n* &optional *stream*   [*Function*]

pprint-indent specifies the indentation to use in a logical block. *Stream* (which
defaults to *standard-output*) follows the standard conventions for stream arguments to printing functions. The argument *n* specifies the indentation in ems. If
relative-to is :block, the indentation is set to the horizontal position of the first
character in the block plus *n* ems. If *relative-to* is :current, the indentation is set
to the current output position plus *n* ems.

The argument *n* can be negative; however, the total indentation cannot be moved
left of the beginning of the line or left of the end of the rightmost per-line prefix.
Changes in indentation caused by pprint-indent do not take effect until after
the next line break. In addition, in miser mode all calls on pprint-indent are
ignored, forcing the lines corresponding to the logical block to line up under the
first character in the block.

An error is signaled if a value other than :block or :current is supplied
for *relative-to*. If *stream* is a pretty printing stream created by pprint-logical-
block, pprint-indent sets the indentation in the innermost dynamically enclosing

logical block. Otherwise, pprint-indent has no effect. The value nil is always returned.

---

pprint-tab *kind colnum colinc* &optional *stream*   [*Function*]

pprint-tab specifies tabbing as performed by the standard format directive ~T. *Stream* (which defaults to *standard-output*) follows the standard conventions for stream arguments to printing functions. The arguments *colnum* and *colinc* correspond to the two parameters to ~T and are in terms of ems. The *kind* argument specifies the style of tabbing. It must be one of :line (tab as by ~T) :section (tab as by ~T, but measuring horizontal positions relative to the start of the dynamically enclosing section), :line-relative (tab as by ~@T), or :section-relative (tab as by ~@T, but measuring horizontal positions relative to the start of the dynamically enclosing section). An error is signaled if any other value is supplied for *kind*. If *stream* is a pretty printing stream created by pprint-logical-block, tabbing is performed. Otherwise, pprint-tab has no effect. The value nil is always returned.

---

pprint-fill *stream list* &optional *colon? atsign?*   [*Function*]
pprint-linear *stream list* &optional *colon? atsign?*   [*Function*]
pprint-tabular *stream list* &optional *colon? atsign? tabsize*   [*Function*]

These three functions specify particular ways of pretty printing lists. *Stream* follows the standard conventions for stream arguments to printing functions. Each function prints parentheses around the output if and only if *colon?* (default t) is not nil. Each function ignores its *atsign?* argument and returns nil. (These two arguments are included in this way so that these functions can be used via ~/.../ and as set-pprint-dispatch functions as well as directly.) Each function handles abbreviation and the detection of circularity and sharing correctly and uses write to print *list* when given a non-list argument.

The function pprint-linear prints a list either all on one line or with each element on a separate line. The function pprint-fill prints a list with as many elements as possible on each line. The function pprint-tabular is the same as pprint-fill except that it prints the elements so that they line up in columns. This function takes an additional argument tabsize (default 16) that specifies the column spacing in ems.

As an example of the interaction of logical blocks, conditional newlines, and indentation, consider the function pprint-defun below. This function pretty prints a list whose *car* is defun in the standard way assuming that the length of the list is exactly 4.

```
;;; Pretty printer function for DEFUN forms.

(defun pprint-defun (list)
  (pprint-logical-block (nil list :prefix "(" :suffix ")")
    (write (first list))
    (write-char #\space)
    (pprint-newline :miser)
    (pprint-indent :current 0)
    (write (second list))
    (write-char #\space)
    (pprint-newline :fill)
    (write (third list))
    (pprint-indent :block 1)
    (write-char #\space)
    (pprint-newline :linear)
    (write (fourth list))))
```

Suppose that one evaluates the following:

```
(pprint-defun '(defun prod (x y) (* x y)))
```

If the line width available is greater than or equal to 26, all of the output appears on one line. If the width is reduced to 25, a line break is inserted at the linear-style conditional newline before (* X Y), producing the output shown below. The (pprint-indent :block 1) causes (* X Y) to be printed at a relative indentation of 1 in the logical block.

```
(DEFUN PROD (X Y)
  (* X Y))
```

If the width is 15, a line break is also inserted at the fill-style conditional newline before the argument list. The argument list lines up under the function name because of the call on (pprint-indent :current 0) before the printing of the function name.

```
(DEFUN PROD
       (X Y)
  (* X Y))
```

If *print-miser-width* were greater than or equal to 14, the output would have been entirely in miser mode. All indentation changes are ignored in miser mode and line breaks are inserted at miser-style conditional newlines. The result would have been as follows:

```
(DEFUN
 PROD
 (X Y)
 (* X Y))
```

As an example of the use of a per-line prefix, consider that evaluating the expression

```
(pprint-logical-block (nil nil :per-line-prefix ";;; ")
  (pprint-defun '(defun prod (x y) (* x y))))
```

produces the output

```
;;; (DEFUN PROD
;;;        (X Y)
;;;   (* X Y))
```

with a line width of 20 and `nil` as the value of the printer control variable `*print-miser-width*`.

(If `*print-miser-width*` were not `nil` the output

```
;;; (DEFUN
;;;  PROD
;;;  (X Y)
;;;  (* X Y))
```

might appear instead.)

As a more complex (and realistic) example, consider the function `pprint-let` below. This specifies how to pretty print a `let` in the standard style. It is more complex than `pprint-defun` because it has to deal with nested structure. Also, unlike `pprint-defun`, it contains complete code to print readably any possible list that begins with the symbol `let`. The outermost `pprint-logical-block` handles the printing of the input list as a whole and specifies that parentheses should be printed in the output. The second `pprint-logical-block` handles the list of binding pairs. Each pair in the list is itself printed by the innermost `pprint-logical-block`. (A `loop` is used instead of merely decomposing the pair into two elements so that readable output will be produced no matter whether the list corresponding to the pair has one element, two elements, or (being malformed) has more than two elements.) A space and a fill-style conditional newline are placed after each pair except the last. The loop at the end of the topmost `pprint-logical-block` prints out the forms in the body of the `let` separated by spaces and linear-style conditional newlines.

```
;;; Pretty printer function for LET forms,
;;; carefully coded to handle malformed binding pairs.

(defun pprint-let (list)
  (pprint-logical-block (nil list :prefix "(" :suffix ")")
    (write (pprint-pop))
    (pprint-exit-if-list-exhausted)
    (write-char #\space)
    (pprint-logical-block
        (nil (pprint-pop) :prefix "(" :suffix ")")
      (pprint-exit-if-list-exhausted)
      (loop (pprint-logical-block
                (nil (pprint-pop) :prefix "(" :suffix ")")
              (pprint-exit-if-list-exhausted)
              (loop (write (pprint-pop))
                    (pprint-exit-if-list-exhausted)
                    (write-char #\space)
                    (pprint-newline :linear)))
            (pprint-exit-if-list-exhausted)
            (write-char #\space)
            (pprint-newline :fill)))
    (pprint-indent :block 1)
    (loop (pprint-exit-if-list-exhausted)
          (write-char #\space)
          (pprint-newline :linear)
          (write (pprint-pop)))))
```

Suppose that the following is evaluated with *print-level* having the value 4 and *print-circle* having the value t.

```
(pprint-let '#1=(let (x (*print-length* (f (g 3)))
                      (z . 2) (k (car y)))
                  (setq x (sqrt z)) #1#))
```

If the line length is greater than or equal to 77, the output produced appears on one line. However, if the line length is 76, line breaks are inserted at the linear-style conditional newlines separating the forms in the body and the output below is produced. Note that the degenerate binding pair X is printed readably even though it fails to be a list; a depth abbreviation marker is printed in place of (G 3); the binding pair (Z . 2) is printed readably even though it is not a proper list; and appropriate circularity markers are printed.

```
#1=(LET (X (*PRINT-LENGTH* (F #)) (Z . 2) (K (CAR Y)))
       (SETQ X (SQRT Z))
       #1#)
```

If the line length is reduced to 35, a line break is inserted at one of the fill-style conditional newlines separating the binding pairs.

```
#1=(LET (X (*PRINT-PRETTY* (F #))
           (Z . 2) (K (CAR Y)))
       (SETQ X (SQRT Z))
       #1#)
```

Suppose that the line length is further reduced to 22 and *print-length* is set to 3. In this situation, line breaks are inserted after both the first and second binding pairs. In addition, the second binding pair is itself broken across two lines. Clause (b) of the description of fill-style conditional newlines prevents the binding pair (Z . 2) from being printed at the end of the third line. Note that the length abbreviation hides the circularity from view and therefore the printing of circularity markers disappears.

```
(LET (X
      (*PRINT-LENGTH*
       (F #))
      (Z . 2) ...)
  (SETQ X (SQRT Z))
  ...)
```

The function pprint-tabular could be defined as follows:

```
(defun pprint-tabular (s list &optional (c? t) a? (size 16))
  (declare (ignore a?))
  (pprint-logical-block
      (s list :prefix (if c? "(" "") :suffix (if c? ")" ""))
    (pprint-exit-if-list-exhausted)
    (loop (write (pprint-pop) :stream s)
          (pprint-exit-if-list-exhausted)
          (write-char #\space s)
          (pprint-tab :section-relative 0 size s)
          (pprint-newline :fill s))))
```

Evaluating the following with a line length of 25 produces the output shown.

```
(princ "Roads ")
(pprint-tabular nil '(elm main maple center) nil nil 8)

Roads ELM     MAIN
      MAPLE   CENTER
```

The function below prints a vector using #(. . .) notation.

```
(defun pprint-vector (v)
  (pprint-logical-block (nil nil :prefix "#(" :suffix ")")
    (let ((end (length v)) (i 0))
      (when (plusp end)
        (loop (pprint-pop)
              (write (aref v i))
              (if (= (incf i) end) (return nil))
              (write-char #\space)
              (pprint-newline :fill))))))
```

Evaluating the following with a line length of 15 produces the output shown.

```
(pprint-vector '#(12 34 567 8 9012 34 567 89 0 1 23))

#(12 34 567 8
  9012 34 567
  89 0 1 23)
```

27.4. Format Directive Interface

The primary interface to operations for dynamically determining the arrangement of output is provided through the functions above. However, an additional interface is provided via a set of format directives because, as shown by the examples in this section and the next, format strings are typically a much more compact way to specify pretty printing. In addition, without such an interface, one would have to abandon the use of format when interacting with the pretty printer.

~W

Write. An *arg*, any Lisp object, is printed obeying *every* printer control variable (as by write). In addition, ~W interacts correctly with depth abbreviation by not resetting the depth counter to zero. ~W does not accept parameters. If given the colon modifier, ~W binds *print-pretty* to t. If given the atsign modifier, ~W binds *print-level* and *print-length* to nil.

~W provides automatic support for circularity detection. If *print-circle* (and possibly also *print-shared*) is not nil and ~W is applied to an argument that is a circular (or shared) reference, an appropriate "#n#" marker is inserted in the output instead of printing the argument.

~
_

Conditional newline. Without any modifiers, ~_ is equivalent to (pprint-newline :linear). The directive ~@_ is equivalent to (pprint-newline :miser). The directive ~:_ is equivalent to (pprint-newline :fill). The directive ~:@_ is equivalent to (pprint-newline :mandatory).

~<*str*~:>

Logical block. If ~:> is used to terminate a ~<... directive, the directive is equivalent to a call on pprint-logical-block. The format argument corresponding to the ~<...~:> directive is treated in the same way as the *list* argument to pprint-logical-block, thereby providing automatic support for non-list arguments and the detection of circularity, sharing, and depth abbreviation. The portion of the format control string nested within the ~<...~:> specifies the :prefix (or :per-line-prefix), :suffix, and body of the pprint-logical-block.

The format string portion enclosed by ~<...~:> can be divided into segments ~<*prefix*~;*body*~;*suffix*~:> by ~; directives. If the first section is terminated by ~@;, it specifies a per-line prefix rather than a simple prefix. The prefix and suffix cannot contain format directives. An error is signaled if either the prefix or suffix fails to be a constant string or if the enclosed portion is divided into more than three segments.

If the enclosed portion is divided into only two segments, the suffix defaults to the null string. If the enclosed portion consists of only a single segment, both the prefix and the suffix default to the null string. If the colon modifier is used (that is, ~:<...~:>), the prefix and suffix default to "(" and ")", respectively, instead of the null string.

The body segment can be any arbitrary format control string. This format control string is applied to the elements of the list corresponding to the ~<...~:> directive as a whole. Elements are extracted from this list using pprint-pop, thereby providing automatic support for malformed lists and the detection of circularity, sharing, and length abbreviation. Within the body segment, ~^ acts like pprint-exit-if-list-exhausted.

~<...~:> supports a feature not supported by pprint-logical-block. If ~:@> is used to terminate the directive (that is, ~<...~:@>), then a fill-style conditional newline is automatically inserted after each group of blanks immediately contained in the body (except for blanks after a ~<newline> directive). This makes it easy to achieve the equivalent of paragraph filling.

If the atsign modifier is used with ~<...~:>, the entire remaining argument list is passed to the directive as its argument. All of the remaining arguments are always consumed by ~@<...~:>, even if they are not all used by the format string nested in the directive. Other than the difference in its argument, ~@<...~:> is exactly the same as ~<...~:>, except that circularity (and sharing) detection is not applied if the ~@<...~:> is at top level in a format string. This ensures that circularity detection is applied only to data lists and not to format argument lists.

To a considerable extent, the basic form of the directive ~<...~> is incompatible with the dynamic control of the arrangement of output by ~W, ~_, ~<...~:>, ~I, and ~:T. As a result, an error is signaled if any of these directives is nested within ~<...~>. Beyond this, an error is also signaled if the ~<...~:;...~> form of ~<...~> is used in the same format string with ~W, ~_, ~<...~:>, ~I, or ~:T.

~I

Indent. ~*n*I is equivalent to (pprint-indent :block *n*). ~:*n*I is equivalent to (pprint-indent :current *n*). In both cases, *n* defaults to zero if it is omitted.

~:T

Tabulate. If the colon modifier is used with the ~T directive, the tabbing computation is done relative to the column where the section immediately containing the directive begins, rather than with respect to column zero. ~*n,m*:T is equivalent to (pprint-tab :section *n m*). ~*n,m*:@T is equivalent to (pprint-tab :section-relative *n m*). The numerical parameters are both interpreted as being in units of ems and both default to 1.

~/*name*/

Call function. User-defined functions can be called from within a format string by using the directive ~/*name*/. The colon modifier, the atsign modifier, and arbitrarily many parameters can be specified with the ~/*name*/ directive. The *name* can be any string that does not contain "/". All of the characters in *name* are treated as if they were upper case. If *name* contains a ":" or "::", then everything up to but not including the first ":" or "::" is taken to be a string that names a package. Everything after the first ":" or "::" (if any) is taken to be a string that names a symbol. The function corresponding to a ~/*name*/ directive is obtained by looking up the symbol that has the indicated name in the indicated package. If *name* does not contain a ":" or "::", then the whole name string is looked up in the user package.

When a ~/*name*/ directive is encountered, the indicated function is called with four or more arguments. The first four arguments are the output stream, the format argument corresponding to the directive, the value t if the colon modifier was used (nil otherwise), and the value t if the atsign modifier was used (nil otherwise). The remaining arguments consist of any parameters specified with the directive. The function should print the argument appropriately. Any values returned by the function are ignored.

The three functions pprint-linear, pprint-fill, and pprint-tabular are designed so that they can be called by ~/.../ (that is, ~/pprint-linear/, ~/pprint-fill/, and ~/pprint-tabular/. In particular they take colon and atsign arguments.

As examples of the convenience of specifying pretty printing with format strings, consider the functions pprint-defun and pprint-let used as examples in the last section. They can be more compactly defined as follows. The function pprint-vector cannot be defined using format, because the data structure it traverses is not a list. The function pprint-tabular is inconvenient to define using format, because of the need to pass its tabsize argument through to a ~:T directive nested within an iteration over a list.

```
(defun pprint-defun (list)
  (format t "~:<~W ~@_~:I~W ~:_~W~1I ~_~W~:>" list))

(defun pprint-let (list)
  (format t "~:<~W~^ ~:<~@{~:<~@{~W~^ ~_~}~:>~^ ~:_~}~:>~1I~
             ~@{~^ ~_~W~}~:>"
          list))
```

27.5. Compiling Format Control Strings

The control strings used by format are essentially programs that perform printing. The macro formatter provides the efficiency of using a compiled function for printing without losing the visual compactness of format strings.

formatter *control-string*   [*Macro*]

The *control-string* must be a literal string. An error is signaled if *control-string* is not a valid format control string. The macro formatter expands into an expression of the form (function (lambda (stream &rest args) ...)) that does the printing specified by *control-string*. The lambda created accepts an output stream as its first argument and zero or more data values as its remaining arguments. The value returned by the lambda is the tail (if any) of the data values that are not printed out by *control-string*. (For example, if the *control-string* is `"~A~A"`, the cddr (if any) of the data values is returned.) The form (formatter `"~%~2@{~S, ~}"`) is equivalent to the following:

```
#'(lambda (stream &rest args)
     (terpri stream)
     (dotimes (n 2)
       (if (null args) (return nil))
       (prin1 (pop args) stream)
       (write-string ", " stream))
     args)
```

In support of the above mechanism, format is extended so that it accepts functions as its second argument as well as strings. When a function is provided, it must be a function of the form created by formatter. The function is called with the appropriate output stream as its first argument and the data arguments to format as its remaining arguments. The function should perform whatever output is necessary and return the unused tail of the arguments (if any). The directives ~? and ~{~} with no body are also extended so that they accept functions as well as control strings. Every other standard function that takes a format string as an argument (for example, error and warn) is also extended so that it can accept functions of the form above instead.

27.6. Pretty Printing Dispatch Tables

When *print-pretty* is not nil, the pprint dispatch table in the variable *print-pprint-dispatch* controls how objects are printed. The information in this table takes precedence over all other mechanisms for specifying how to print objects. In particular, it overrides user-defined print-object methods and print functions for structures. However, if there is no specification for how to pretty print a particular kind of object, it is then printed using the standard mechanisms as if *print-pretty* were nil.

A pprint dispatch table is a mapping from keys to pairs of values. The keys are type specifiers. The values are functions and numerical priorities. Basic insertion and retrieval is done based on the keys with the equality of keys being tested by equal. The function to use when pretty printing an object is chosen by finding the highest priority function in *print-pprint-dispatch* that is associated with a type specifier that matches the object.

copy-pprint-dispatch &optional *table*   [*Function*]

A copy is made of *table*, which defaults to the current pprint dispatch table. If *table* is nil, a copy is returned of the initial value of *print-pprint-dispatch*.

pprint-dispatch *object* &optional *table*   [*Function*]

This retrieves the highest priority function from a pprint table that is associated with a type specifier in the table that matches *object*. The function is chosen by finding all the type specifiers in *table* that match the object and selecting the highest priority function associated with any of these type specifiers. If there is more than one highest priority function, an arbitrary choice is made. If no type specifiers match the object, a function is returned that prints object with *print-pretty* bound to nil.

As a second return value, pprint-dispatch returns a flag that is t if a matching type specifier was found in *table* and nil if not.

Table (which defaults to *print-pprint-dispatch*) must be a pprint dispatch table. *Table* can be nil, in which case retrieval is done in the initial value of *print-pprint-dispatch*.

When *print-pretty* is t, (write object :stream s) is equivalent to (funcall (pprint-dispatch object) s object).

set-pprint-dispatch *type function* &optional *priority table*   [*Function*]

This puts an entry into a pprint dispatch table and returns nil. The *type* must be a valid type specifier and is the key of the entry. The first action of set-pprint-dispatch is to remove any pre-existing entry associated with *type*. This guarantees that there will never be two entries associated with the same type specifier in a given pprint dispatch table. Equality of type specifiers is tested by equal.

Two values are associated with each type specifier in a pprint dispatch table: a function and a priority. The *function* must accept two arguments: the stream to send output to and the object to be printed. The *function* should pretty print the object on the stream. The *function* can assume that object satisfies *type*. The *function* should obey *print-readably*. Any values returned by the *function* are ignored.

The *priority* (which defaults to 0) must be a non-complex number. This number is used as a priority to resolve conflicts when an object matches more than one entry. An error is signaled if priority fails to be a non-complex number.

The *table* (which defaults to the value of *print-pprint-dispatch*) must be a pprint dispatch table. The specified entry is placed in this table.

It is permissible for *function* to be `nil`. In this situation, there will be no *type* entry in *table* after `set-pprint-dispatch` is evaluated.

To facilitate the use of pprint dispatch tables for controlling the pretty printing of Lisp code, the *type-specifier* argument of the function `set-pprint-dispatch` is allowed to contain the form (`cons` *car-type cdr-type*). This form indicates that the corresponding object must be a cons whose *car* satisfies the type specifier *car-type* and whose *cdr* satisfies the type specifier *cdr-type*. The *cdr-type* can be omitted, in which case it defaults to t.

The initial value of `*print-pprint-dispatch*` is implementation-dependent. However, the initial entries all use a special class of priorities that are less than every priority that can be specified using `set-pprint-dispatch`. This guarantees that pretty printing functions specified by users will override everything in the initial value of `*print-pprint-dispatch*`.

Consider the following examples. The first form restores `*print-pprint-dispatch*` to its initial value. The next two forms then specify a special way of pretty printing ratios. Note that the more specific type specifier has to be associated with a higher priority.

```
(setq *print-pprint-dispatch*
      (copy-pprint-dispatch nil))

(defun div-print (s r colon? atsign?)
  (declare (ignore colon? atsign?))
  (format s "(/ ~D ~D)" (numerator (abs r)) (denominator r)))

(set-pprint-dispatch 'ratio (formatter "#.~/div-print/"))

(set-pprint-dispatch '(and ratio (satisfies minusp))
  (formatter "#.(- ~/div-print/)")
  5)

(pprint '(1/3 -2/3)) prints: (#.(/ 1 3) #.(- (/ 2 3)))
```

The following two forms illustrate the specification of pretty printing functions for particular types of Lisp code. The first form illustrates how to specify the traditional method for printing quoted objects using "'" syntax. Note the care taken to ensure that data lists that happen to begin with `quote` will be printed readably. The second form specifies that lists beginning with the symbol `my-let` should print the same way that lists beginning with `let` print when the initial pprint dispatch table is in effect.

```
(set-pprint-dispatch '(cons (member quote))
  #'(lambda (s list)
       (if (and (consp (cdr list)) (null (cddr list)))
            (funcall (formatter "'~W") s (cadr list))
            (pprint-fill s list)))))

(set-pprint-dispatch '(cons (member my-let))
  (pprint-dispatch '(let) nil))
```

The next example specifies a default method for printing lists that do not correspond to function calls. Note that, as shown in the definition of pprint-tabular
above, pprint-linear, pprint-fill, and pprint-tabular are defined with optional colon and atsign arguments so that they can be used as pprint dispatch
functions as well as ~/.../ functions.

```
(set-pprint-dispatch
   '(cons (not (and symbol (satisfies fboundp))))
   #'pprint-fill
   -5)
```

With a line length of 9, (pprint '(0 b c d e f g h i j k)) prints:

```
(0 b c d
 e f g h
 i j k)
```

This final example shows how to define a pretty printing function for a user
defined data structure.

```
(defstruct family mom kids)

(set-pprint-dispatch 'family
  #'(lambda (s f)
       (format s "~@<#<~;~W and ~2I~_~/pprint-fill/~;>~:>"
                 (family-mom f) (family-kids f))))
```

The pretty printing function for the structure family specifies how to adjust the
layout of the output so that it can fit aesthetically into a variety of line widths. In
addition, it obeys the printer control variables *print-level*, *print-length*,
print-lines, *print-circle*, *print-shared*, and *print-escape*, and
can tolerate several different kinds of malformity in the data structure. The output

below shows what is printed out with a right margin of 25, *print-pretty* t,
print-escape nil, and a malformed kids list.

```
(write (list 'principal-family
             (make-family :mom "Lucy"
                          :kids '("Mark" "Bob" . "Dan")))
       :right-margin 25 :pretty T :escape nil :miser-width nil)
```

```
(PRINCIPAL-FAMILY
 #<Lucy and
     Mark Bob . Dan>)
```

Note that a pretty printing function for a structure is different from the structure's
print function. While print functions are permanently associated with a structure,
pretty printing functions are stored in pprint dispatch tables and can be rapidly
changed to reflect different printing needs. If there is no pretty printing function
for a structure in the current print dispatch table, the print function (if any) is used
instead.

28

Common Lisp Object System

BY DANIEL G. BOBROW, LINDA G. DEMICHIEL, RICHARD P. GABRIEL,
SONYA E. KEENE, GREGOR KICZALES, AND DAVID A. MOON

PREFACE: X3J13 voted in June 1988 ⟨12⟩ to adopt the first two chapters (of three) of the Common Lisp Object System specification as a part of the forthcoming draft Common Lisp standard.

This chapter presents the bulk of the first two chapters of the Common Lisp Object System specification; it is substantially identical to these two specification chapters as previously published elsewhere [5, 6, 7]. I have edited the material only very lightly to conform to the overall style of this book and to save a substantial number of pages by using a typographically condensed presentation. I have inserted a small number of bracketed remarks, identified by the initials GLS. The chapter divisions of the original specification have become section divisions in this chapter; references to the three chapters of the original specification now refer to the three "parts" of the specification. (See the Acknowledgments to this second edition for acknowledgments to others who contributed to the Common Lisp Object System specification.) This is not the last word on CLOS; X3J13 may well refine this material further. Keene has written a good tutorial introduction to CLOS [26].

—Guy L. Steele Jr.

28.1. Programmer Interface Concepts

The Common Lisp Object System (CLOS) is an object-oriented extension to Common Lisp. It is based on generic functions, multiple inheritance, declarative method combination, and a meta-object protocol.

The first two parts of this specification describe the standard Programmer Interface for the Common Lisp Object System. The first part, Programmer Interface Concepts, contains a description of the concepts of the Common Lisp Object System, and the second part, Functions in the Programmer Interface, contains a description of the functions and macros in the Common Lisp Object System Programmer Interface. The third part, The Common Lisp Object System Meta-Object

Protocol, explains how the Common Lisp Object System can be customized. [The third part has not yet been approved by X3J13 for inclusion in the forthcoming Common Lisp standard and is not included in this book.—GLS]

The fundamental objects of the Common Lisp Object System are classes, instances, generic functions, and methods.

A *class* object determines the structure and behavior of a set of other objects, which are called its *instances*. Every Common Lisp object is an *instance* of a class. The class of an object determines the set of operations that can be performed on the object.

A *generic function* is a function whose behavior depends on the classes or identities of the arguments supplied to it. A generic function object contains a set of methods, a lambda-list, a method combination type, and other information. The *methods* define the class-specific behavior and operations of the generic function; a method is said to *specialize* a generic function. When invoked, a generic function executes a subset of its methods based on the classes of its arguments.

A generic function can be used in the same ways as an ordinary function in Common Lisp; in particular, a generic function can be used as an argument to funcall and apply and can be given a global or a local name.

A *method* is an object that contains a method function, a sequence of *parameter specializers* that specify when the given method is applicable, and a sequence of *qualifiers* that is used by the *method combination* facility to distinguish among methods. Each required formal parameter of each method has an associated parameter specializer, and the method will be invoked only on arguments that satisfy its parameter specializers.

The method combination facility controls the selection of methods, the order in which they are run, and the values that are returned by the generic function. The Common Lisp Object System offers a default method combination type and provides a facility for declaring new types of method combination.

28.1.1. Error Terminology

The terminology used in this chapter to describe erroneous situations differs from the terminology used in the first edition. The new terminology involves *situations*; a situation is the evaluation of an expression in some specific context. For example, a situation might be the invocation of a function on arguments that fail to satisfy some specified constraints.

In the specification of the Common Lisp Object System, the behavior of programs in all situations is described, and the options available to the implementor are defined. No implementation is allowed to extend the syntax or semantics of the Object System except as explicitly defined in the Object System specification. In particular, no implementation is allowed to extend the syntax of the Object System in such a way that ambiguity between the specified syntax of the Object System and those extensions is possible.

"When situation S occurs, an error is signaled."

This terminology has the following meaning:

- If this situation occurs, an error will be signaled in the interpreter and in code compiled under all compiler safety optimization levels.

- Valid programs may rely on the fact that an error will be signaled in the interpreter and in code compiled under all compiler safety optimization levels.

- Every implementation is required to detect such an error in the interpreter and in code compiled under all compiler safety optimization levels.

"When situation S occurs, an error should be signaled."

This terminology has the following meaning:

- If this situation occurs, an error will be signaled at least in the interpreter and in code compiled under the safest compiler safety optimization level.

- Valid programs may not rely on the fact that an error will be signaled.

- Every implementation is required to detect such an error at least in the interpreter and in code compiled under the safest compiler safety optimization level.

- When an error is not signaled, the results are undefined (see below).

"When situation S occurs, the results are undefined."

This terminology has the following meaning:

- If this situation occurs, the results are unpredictable. The results may range from harmless to fatal.

- Implementations are allowed to detect this situation and signal an error, but no implementation is required to detect the situation.

- No valid program may depend on the effects of this situation, and all valid programs are required to treat the effects of this situation as unpredictable.

"When situation S occurs, the results are unspecified."

This terminology has the following meaning:

- The effects of this situation are not specified in the Object System, but the effects are harmless.

- Implementations are allowed to specify the effects of this situation.

- No portable program can depend on the effects of this situation, and all portable programs are required to treat the situation as unpredictable but harmless.

"The Common Lisp Object System may be extended to cover situation S."

The meaning of this terminology is that an implementation is free to treat situation S in one of three ways:

- When situation S occurs, an error is signaled at least in the interpreter and in code compiled under the safest compiler safety optimization level.

- When situation S occurs, the results are undefined.

- When situation S occurs, the results are defined and specified.

In addition, this terminology has the following meaning:

- No portable program can depend on the effects of this situation, and all portable programs are required to treat the situation as undefined.

"Implementations are free to extend the syntax S."

This terminology has the following meaning:

- Implementations are allowed to define unambiguous extensions to syntax S.

- No portable program can depend on this extension, and all portable programs are required to treat the syntax as meaningless.

The Common Lisp Object System specification may disallow certain extensions while allowing others.

28.1.2. Classes

A *class* is an object that determines the structure and behavior of a set of other objects, which are called its *instances*.

A class can inherit structure and behavior from other classes. A class whose definition refers to other classes for the purpose of inheriting from them is said to be a *subclass* of each of those classes. The classes that are designated for purposes of inheritance are said to be *superclasses* of the inheriting class.

A class can have a *name*. The function `class-name` takes a class object and returns its name. The name of an anonymous class is `nil`. A symbol can *name* a class. The function `find-class` takes a symbol and returns the class that the symbol names. A class has a *proper name* if the name is a symbol and if the name of the class names that class. That is, a class C has the *proper name S* if $S = $ (`class-name` C) and $C = $ (`find-class` S). Notice that it is possible for (`find-class` S_1) = (`find-class` S_2) and $S_1 \neq S_2$. If $C = $ (`find-class` S), we say that C is the *class named S*.

A class C_1 is a *direct superclass* of a class C_2 if C_2 explicitly designates C_1 as a superclass in its definition. In this case, C_2 is a *direct subclass* of C_1. A class C_n is a *superclass* of a class C_1 if there exists a series of classes $C_2, \ldots, C_{n-1}$ such that C_{i+1} is a direct superclass of C_i for $1 \leq i < n$. In this case, C_1 is a *subclass* of C_n. A class is considered neither a superclass nor a subclass of itself. That is, if C_1 is a superclass of C_2, then $C_1 \neq C_2$. The set of classes consisting of some given class C along with all of its superclasses is called "C and its superclasses."

Each class has a *class precedence list*, which is a total ordering on the set of the given class and its superclasses. The total ordering is expressed as a list ordered from most specific to least specific. The class precedence list is used in several ways. In general, more specific classes can *shadow*, or override, features that would otherwise be inherited from less specific classes. The method selection and combination process uses the class precedence list to order methods from most specific to least specific.

When a class is defined, the order in which its direct superclasses are mentioned in the defining form is important. Each class has a *local precedence order*, which is a list consisting of the class followed by its direct superclasses in the order mentioned in the defining form.

A class precedence list is always consistent with the local precedence order of each class in the list. The classes in each local precedence order appear within the class precedence list in the same order. If the local precedence orders are inconsistent with each other, no class precedence list can be constructed, and an error is signaled. The class precedence list and its computation is discussed in section 28.1.5.

Classes are organized into a *directed acyclic graph*. There are two distinguished classes, named t and `standard-object`. The class named t has no superclasses. It is a superclass of every class except itself. The class named `standard-object` is an instance of the class `standard-class` and is a superclass of every class that is an instance of `standard-class` except itself.

There is a mapping from the Common Lisp Object System class space into the Common Lisp type space. Many of the standard Common Lisp types have a corresponding class that has the same name as the type. Some Common Lisp types do not have a corresponding class. The integration of the type and class systems is discussed in section 28.1.4.

Classes are represented by objects that are themselves instances of classes. The class of the class of an object is termed the *metaclass* of that object. When no misinterpretation is possible, the term *metaclass* will be used to refer to a class that has instances that are themselves classes. The metaclass determines the form of inheritance used by the classes that are its instances and the representation of the instances of those classes. The Common Lisp Object System provides a default metaclass, standard-class, that is appropriate for most programs. The meta-object protocol provides mechanisms for defining and using new metaclasses.

Except where otherwise specified, all classes mentioned in this chapter are instances of the class standard-class, all generic functions are instances of the class standard-generic-function, and all methods are instances of the class standard-method.

28.1.2.1. Defining Classes

The macro defclass is used to define a new named class. The definition of a class includes the following:

- The name of the new class. For newly defined classes this is a proper name.

- The list of the direct superclasses of the new class.

- A set of *slot specifiers*. Each slot specifier includes the name of the slot and zero or more *slot options*. A slot option pertains only to a single slot. If a class definition contains two slot specifiers with the same name, an error is signaled.

- A set of *class options*. Each class option pertains to the class as a whole.

The slot options and class options of the defclass form provide mechanisms for the following:

- Supplying a default initial value form for a given slot.

- Requesting that methods for generic functions be automatically generated for reading or writing slots.

- Controlling whether a given slot is shared by instances of the class or whether each instance of the class has its own slot.

- Supplying a set of initialization arguments and initialization argument defaults to be used in instance creation.

- Indicating that the metaclass is to be other than the default.

- Indicating the expected type for the value stored in the slot.

- Indicating the documentation string for the slot.

28.1.2.2. Creating Instances of Classes

The generic function `make-instance` creates and returns a new instance of a class. The Object System provides several mechanisms for specifying how a new instance is to be initialized. For example, it is possible to specify the initial values for slots in newly created instances either by giving arguments to `make-instance` or by providing default initial values.

Further initialization activities can be performed by methods written for generic functions that are part of the initialization protocol. The complete initialization protocol is described in section 28.1.9.

28.1.2.3. Slots

An object that has `standard-class` as its metaclass has zero or more named slots. The slots of an object are determined by the class of the object. Each slot can hold one value. The name of a slot is a symbol that is syntactically valid for use as a variable name.

When a slot does not have a value, the slot is said to be *unbound*. When an unbound slot is read, the generic function `slot-unbound` is invoked. The system-supplied primary method for `slot-unbound` signals an error.

The default initial value form for a slot is defined by the `:initform` slot option. When the `:initform` form is used to supply a value, it is evaluated in the lexical environment in which the `defclass` form was evaluated. The `:initform` along with the lexical environment in which the `defclass` form was evaluated is called a *captured* `:initform`. See section 28.1.9.

A *local slot* is defined to be a slot that is visible to exactly one instance, namely the one in which the slot is allocated. A *shared slot* is defined to be a slot that is visible to more than one instance of a given class and its subclasses.

A class is said to *define* a slot with a given name when the `defclass` form for that class contains a slot specifier with that name. Defining a local slot does not immediately create a slot; it causes a slot to be created each time an instance of the class is created. Defining a shared slot immediately creates a slot.

The `:allocation` slot option to `defclass` controls the kind of slot that is defined. If the value of the `:allocation` slot option is `:instance`, a local slot is created. If the value of `:allocation` is `:class`, a shared slot is created.

A slot is said to be *accessible* in an instance of a class if the slot is defined by the class of the instance or is inherited from a superclass of that class. At most one slot of a given name can be accessible in an instance. A shared slot defined by a class is accessible in all instances of that class. A detailed explanation of the inheritance of slots is given in section 28.1.3.2.

28.1.2.4. Accessing Slots

Slots can be accessed in two ways: by use of the primitive function `slot-value` and by use of generic functions generated by the `defclass` form.

The function `slot-value` can be used with any slot name specified in the `defclass` form to access a specific slot accessible in an instance of the given class.

The macro `defclass` provides syntax for generating methods to read and write slots. If a *reader* is requested, a method is automatically generated for reading the value of the slot, but no method for storing a value into it is generated. If a *writer* is requested, a method is automatically generated for storing a value into the slot, but no method for reading its value is generated. If an *accessor* is requested, a method for reading the value of the slot and a method for storing a value into the slot are automatically generated. Reader and writer methods are implemented using `slot-value`.

When a reader or writer is specified for a slot, the name of the generic function to which the generated method belongs is directly specified. If the name specified for the writer option is the symbol *name*, the name of the generic function for writing the slot is the symbol *name*, and the generic function takes two arguments: the new value and the instance, in that order. If the name specified for the accessor option is the symbol *name*, the name of the generic function for reading the slot is the symbol *name*, and the name of the generic function for writing the slot is the list (`setf` *name*).

A generic function created or modified by supplying reader, writer, or accessor slot options can be treated exactly as an ordinary generic function.

Note that `slot-value` can be used to read or write the value of a slot whether or not reader or writer methods exist for that slot. When `slot-value` is used, no reader or writer methods are invoked.

The macro `with-slots` can be used to establish a lexical environment in which specified slots are lexically available as if they were variables. The macro `with-slots` invokes the function `slot-value` to access the specified slots.

The macro `with-accessors` can be used to establish a lexical environment in which specified slots are lexically available through their accessors as if they were variables. The macro `with-accessors` invokes the appropriate accessors to access the specified slots. Any accessors specified by `with-accessors` must already have been defined before they are used.

28.1.3. Inheritance

A class can inherit methods, slots, and some `defclass` options from its super-classes. The following sections describe the inheritance of methods, the inheritance of slots and slot options, and the inheritance of class options.

28.1.3.1. Inheritance of Methods

A subclass inherits methods in the sense that any method applicable to all instances of a class is also applicable to all instances of any subclass of that class.

The inheritance of methods acts the same way regardless of whether the method was created by using one of the method-defining forms or by using one of the `defclass` options that causes methods to be generated automatically.

The inheritance of methods is described in detail in section 28.1.7.

28.1.3.2. Inheritance of Slots and Slot Options

The set of names of all slots accessible in an instance of a class C is the union of the sets of names of slots defined by C and its superclasses. The *structure* of an instance is the set of names of local slots in that instance.

In the simplest case, only one class among C and its superclasses defines a slot with a given slot name. If a slot is defined by a superclass of C, the slot is said to be *inherited*. The characteristics of the slot are determined by the slot specifier of the defining class. Consider the defining class for a slot S. If the value of the `:allocation` slot option is `:instance`, then S is a local slot and each instance of C has its own slot named S that stores its own value. If the value of the `:allocation` slot option is `:class`, then S is a shared slot, the class that defined S stores the value, and all instances of C can access that single slot. If the `:allocation` slot option is omitted, `:instance` is used.

In general, more than one class among C and its superclasses can define a slot with a given name. In such cases, only one slot with the given name is accessible in an instance of C, and the characteristics of that slot are a combination of the several slot specifiers, computed as follows:

• All the slot specifiers for a given slot name are ordered from most specific to least specific, according to the order in C's class precedence list of the classes that define them. All references to the specificity of slot specifiers immediately following refer to this ordering.

- The allocation of a slot is controlled by the most specific slot specifier. If the most specific slot specifier does not contain an :allocation slot option, :instance is used. Less specific slot specifiers do not affect the allocation.

- The default initial value form for a slot is the value of the :initform slot option in the most specific slot specifier that contains one. If no slot specifier contains an :initform slot option, the slot has no default initial value form.

- The contents of a slot will always be of type (and T_1 ... T_n) where $T_1, \ldots, T_n$ are the values of the :type slot options contained in all of the slot specifiers. If no slot specifier contains the :type slot option, the contents of the slot will always be of type t. The result of attempting to store in a slot a value that does not satisfy the type of the slot is undefined.

- The set of initialization arguments that initialize a given slot is the union of the initialization arguments declared in the :initarg slot options in all the slot specifiers.

- The documentation string for a slot is the value of the :documentation slot option in the most specific slot specifier that contains one. If no slot specifier contains a :documentation slot option, the slot has no documentation string.

A consequence of the allocation rule is that a shared slot can be shadowed. For example, if a class C_1 defines a slot named S whose value for the :allocation slot option is :class, that slot is accessible in instances of C_1 and all of its subclasses. However, if C_2 is a subclass of C_1 and also defines a slot named S, C_1's slot is not shared by instances of C_2 and its subclasses. When a class C_1 defines a shared slot, any subclass C_2 of C_1 will share this single slot unless the defclass form for C_2 specifies a slot of the same name or there is a superclass of C_2 that precedes C_1 in the class precedence list of C_2 that defines a slot of the same name.

A consequence of the type rule is that the value of a slot satisfies the type constraint of each slot specifier that contributes to that slot. Because the result of attempting to store in a slot a value that does not satisfy the type constraint for the slot is undefined, the value in a slot might fail to satisfy its type constraint.

The :reader, :writer, and :accessor slot options create methods rather than define the characteristics of a slot. Reader and writer methods are inherited in the sense described in section 28.1.3.1.

Methods that access slots use only the name of the slot and the type of the slot's value. Suppose a superclass provides a method that expects to access a shared slot of a given name, and a subclass defines a local slot with the same name. If the method provided by the superclass is used on an instance of the subclass, the method accesses the local slot.

28.1.3.3. Inheritance of Class Options

The :default-initargs class option is inherited. The set of defaulted initialization arguments for a class is the union of the sets of initialization arguments
specified in the :default-initargs class options of the class and its superclasses.
When more than one default initial value form is supplied for a given initialization
argument, the default initial value form that is used is the one supplied by the class
that is most specific according to the class precedence list.

If a given :default-initargs class option specifies an initialization argument
of the same name more than once, an error is signaled.

28.1.3.4. Examples

```
(defclass C1 ()
  ((S1 :initform 5.4 :type number)
   (S2 :allocation :class)))

(defclass C2 (C1)
  ((S1 :initform 5 :type integer)
   (S2 :allocation :instance)
   (S3 :accessor C2-S3)))
```

Instances of the class C1 have a local slot named S1, whose default initial value
is 5.4 and whose value should always be a number. The class C1 also has a shared
slot named S2.

There is a local slot named S1 in instances of C2. The default initial value of
S1 is 5. The value of S1 will be of type (and integer number). There are also
local slots named S2 and S3 in instances of C2. The class C2 has a method for
C2-S3 for reading the value of slot S3; there is also a method for (setf C2-S3)
that writes the value of S3.

28.1.4. Integrating Types and Classes

The Common Lisp Object System maps the space of classes into the Common Lisp
type space. Every class that has a proper name has a corresponding type with the
same name.

The proper name of every class is a valid type specifier. In addition, every class
object is a valid type specifier. Thus the expression (typep *object class*) evaluates
to true if the class of *object* is *class* itself or a subclass of *class*. The evaluation
of the expression (subtypep *class1 class2*) returns the values t and t if *class1*

is a subclass of *class2* or if they are the same class; otherwise it returns the values `nil` and `t`. If *I* is an instance of some class *C* named *S* and *C* is an instance of `standard-class`, the evaluation of the expression (`type-of` *I*) will return *S* if *S* is the proper name of *C*; if *S* is not the proper name of *C*, the expression (`type-of` *I*) will return *C*.

Because the names of classes and class objects are type specifiers, they may be used in the special form `the` and in type declarations.

Many but not all of the predefined Common Lisp type specifiers have a corresponding class with the same proper name as the type. These type specifiers are listed in table 28-1. For example, the type `array` has a corresponding class named `array`. No type specifier that is a list, such as (`vector double-float 100`), has a corresponding class. The form `deftype` does not create any classes.

Each class that corresponds to a predefined Common Lisp type specifier can be implemented in one of three ways, at the discretion of each implementation. It can be a *standard class* (of the kind defined by `defclass`), a *structure class* (defined by `defstruct`), or a *built-in class* (implemented in a special, non-extensible way).

A built-in class is one whose instances have restricted capabilities or special representations. Attempting to use `defclass` to define subclasses of a built-in class signals an error. Calling `make-instance` to create an instance of a built-in class signals an error. Calling `slot-value` on an instance of a built-in class signals an error. Redefining a built-in class or using `change-class` to change the class of an instance to or from a built-in class signals an error. However, built-in classes can be used as parameter specializers in methods.

It is possible to determine whether a class is a built-in class by checking the metaclass. A standard class is an instance of `standard-class`, a built-in class is an instance of `built-in-class`, and a structure class is an instance of `structure-class`.

Each structure type created by `defstruct` without using the `:type` option has a corresponding class. This class is an instance of `structure-class`. The `:include` option of `defstruct` creates a direct subclass of the class that corresponds to the included structure.

The purpose of specifying that many of the standard Common Lisp type specifiers have a corresponding class is to enable users to write methods that discriminate on these types. Method selection requires that a class precedence list can be determined for each class.

The hierarchical relationships among the Common Lisp type specifiers are mirrored by relationships among the classes corresponding to those types. The existing type hierarchy is used for determining the class precedence list for each class that corresponds to a predefined Common Lisp type. In some cases, the first edition did not specify a local precedence order for two supertypes of a given type specifier.

For example, `null` is a subtype of both `symbol` and `list`, but the first edition did not specify whether `symbol` is more specific or less specific than `list`. The CLOS specification defines those relationships for all such classes.

Table 28-1 lists the set of classes required by the Object System that correspond to predefined Common Lisp type specifiers. The superclasses of each such class are presented in order from most specific to most general, thereby defining the class precedence list for the class. The local precedence order for each class that corresponds to a Common Lisp type specifier can be derived from this table.

Individual implementations may be extended to define other type specifiers to have a corresponding class. Individual implementations can be extended to add other subclass relationships and to add other elements to the class precedence lists in the above table as long as they do not violate the type relationships and disjointness requirements specified in section 2.15. A standard class defined with no direct superclasses is guaranteed to be disjoint from all of the classes in the table, except for the class named `t`.

[At this point the original CLOS report specified that certain Common Lisp types were to appear in table 28-1 if and only if X3J13 voted to make them disjoint from `cons`, `symbol`, `array`, `number`, and `character`. X3J13 voted to do so in June 1988 ⟨41⟩. I have added these types and their class precedence lists to the table; the new types are indicated by asterisks.—GLS]

28.1.5. Determining the Class Precedence List

The `defclass` form for a class provides a total ordering on that class and its direct superclasses. This ordering is called the *local precedence order*. It is an ordered list of the class and its direct superclasses. The *class precedence list* for a class C is a total ordering on C and its superclasses that is consistent with the local precedence orders for C and its superclasses.

A class precedes its direct superclasses, and a direct superclass precedes all other direct superclasses specified to its right in the superclasses list of the `defclass` form. For every class C, define

$$R_C = \{(C, C_1), (C_1, C_2), \ldots, (C_{n-1}, C_n)\}$$

where $C_1, \ldots, C_n$ are the direct superclasses of C in the order in which they are mentioned in the `defclass` form. These ordered pairs generate the total ordering on the class C and its direct superclasses.

Let S_C be the set of C and its superclasses. Let R be

$$R = \bigcup_{c \in S_C} R_c$$

Table 28-1: Class Precedence Lists for Predefined Types

Predefined Common Lisp Type	Class Precedence List for Corresponding Class
array	(array t)
bit-vector	(bit-vector vector array sequence t)
character	(character t)
complex	(complex number t)
cons	(cons list sequence t)
float	(float number t)
function *	(function t)
hash-table *	(hash-table t)
integer	(integer rational number t)
list	(list sequence t)
null	(null symbol list sequence t)
number	(number t)
package *	(package t)
pathname *	(pathname t)
random-state *	(random-state t)
ratio	(ratio rational number t)
rational	(rational number t)
readtable *	(readtable t)
sequence	(sequence t)
stream *	(stream t)
string	(string vector array sequence t)
symbol	(symbol t)
t	(t)
vector	(vector array sequence t)

[An asterisk indicates a type added to this table as a consequence of a portion of the CLOS specification that was conditional on X3J13 voting to make that type disjoint from certain other built-in types ⟨41⟩.—GLS]

The set R may or may not generate a partial ordering, depending on whether the R_c, $c \in S_C$, are consistent; it is assumed that they are consistent and that R generates a partial ordering. When the R_c are not consistent, it is said that R is inconsistent.

To compute the class precedence list for C, topologically sort the elements of S_C with respect to the partial ordering generated by R. When the topological sort must select a class from a set of two or more classes, none of which are preceded by other classes with respect to R, the class selected is chosen deterministically, as described below. If R is inconsistent, an error is signaled.

28.1.5.1. Topological Sorting

Topological sorting proceeds by finding a class C in S_C such that no other class precedes that element according to the elements in R. The class C is placed first in the result. Remove C from S_C, and remove all pairs of the form (C, D), $D \in S_C$, from R. Repeat the process, adding classes with no predecessors to the end of the result. Stop when no element can be found that has no predecessor.

If S_C is not empty and the process has stopped, the set R is inconsistent. If every class in the finite set of classes is preceded by another, then R contains a loop. That is, there is a chain of classes $C_1, \ldots, C_n$ such that C_i precedes C_{i+1}, $1 \leq i < n$, and C_n precedes C_1.

Sometimes there are several classes from S_C with no predecessors. In this case select the one that has a direct subclass rightmost in the class precedence list computed so far. If there is no such candidate class, R does not generate a partial ordering—the R_c, $c \in S_C$, are inconsistent.

In more precise terms, let $\{N_1, \ldots, N_m\}$, $m \geq 2$, be the classes from S_C with no predecessors. Let $(C_1 \ldots C_n)$, $n \geq 1$, be the class precedence list constructed so far. C_1 is the most specific class, and C_n is the least specific. Let $1 \leq j \leq n$ be the largest number such that there exists an i where $1 \leq i \leq m$ and N_i is a direct superclass of C_j; N_i is placed next.

The effect of this rule for selecting from a set of classes with no predecessors is that classes in a simple superclass chain are adjacent in the class precedence list and that classes in each relatively separated subgraph are adjacent in the class precedence list. For example, let T_1 and T_2 be subgraphs whose only element in common is the class J. Suppose that no superclass of J appears in either T_1 or T_2. Let C_1 be the bottom of T_1; and let C_2 be the bottom of T_2. Suppose C is a class whose direct superclasses are C_1 and C_2 in that order; then the class precedence list for C will start with C and will be followed by all classes in T_1 except J. All the classes of T_2 will be next. The class J and its superclasses will appear last.

28.1.5.2. Examples

This example determines a class precedence list for the class pie. The following classes are defined:

```
(defclass pie (apple cinnamon) ())
(defclass apple (fruit) ())
(defclass cinnamon (spice) ())
(defclass fruit (food) ())
(defclass spice (food) ())
(defclass food () ())
```

The set $S = \{$pie, apple, cinnamon, fruit, spice, food, standard-object, t$\}$. The set $R = \{$(pie, apple), (apple, cinnamon), (cinnamon, standard-object), (apple, fruit), (fruit, standard-object), (cinnamon, spice), (spice, standard-object), (fruit, food), (food, standard-object), (spice, food), (standard-object, t)$\}$.

[The original CLOS specification [5, 6] contained a minor error in this example: the pairs (cinnamon, standard-object), (fruit, standard-object), and (spice, standard-object) were inadvertently omitted from R in the preceding paragraph. It is important to understand that defclass implicitly appends the class standard-object to the list of superclasses when the metaclass is standard-class (the normal situation), in order to insure that standard-object will be a superclass of every instance of standard-class except standard-object itself (see section 28.1.2). R_c is then generated from this augmented list of superclasses; this is where the extra pairs come from. I have corrected the example by adding these pairs as appropriate throughout the example. The final result, the class precedence list for pie, is unchanged.—GLS]

The class pie is not preceded by anything, so it comes first; the result so far is (pie). Remove pie from S and pairs mentioning pie from R to get $S = \{$apple, cinnamon, fruit, spice, food, standard-object, t$\}$ and $R = \{$(apple, cinnamon), (cinnamon, standard-object), (apple, fruit), (fruit, standard-object), (cinnamon, spice), (spice, standard-object), (fruit, food), (food, standard-object), (spice, food), (standard-object, t)$\}$.

The class apple is not preceded by anything, so it is next; the result is (pie apple). Removing apple and the relevant pairs results in $S = \{$cinnamon, fruit, spice, food, standard-object, t$\}$ and $R = \{$(cinnamon, standard-object), (fruit, standard-object), (cinnamon, spice), (spice, standard-object), (fruit, food), (food, standard-object), (spice, food), (standard-object, t)$\}$.

The classes cinnamon and fruit are not preceded by anything, so the one with a direct subclass rightmost in the class precedence list computed so far goes next. The class apple is a direct subclass of fruit, and the class pie is a direct subclass of cinnamon. Because apple appears to the right of pie in the precedence list, fruit goes next, and the result so far is (pie apple fruit). $S = \{$cinnamon, spice, food, standard-object, t$\}$; $R = \{$(cinnamon, standard-object), (cinnamon, spice), (spice, standard-object), (food, standard-object), (spice, food), (standard-object, t)$\}$.

The class cinnamon is next, giving the result so far as (pie apple fruit cinnamon). At this point $S = \{$spice, food, standard-object, t$\}$; $R = \{$(spice, standard-object), (food, standard-object), (spice, food), (standard-object, t)$\}$.

The classes spice, food, standard-object, and t are then added in that order, and the final class precedence list for pie is

```
(pie apple fruit cinnamon spice food standard-object t)
```

It is possible to write a set of class definitions that cannot be ordered. For example:

```
(defclass new-class (fruit apple) ())
(defclass apple (fruit) ())
```

The class fruit must precede apple because the local ordering of superclasses must be preserved. The class apple must precede fruit because a class always precedes its own superclasses. When this situation occurs, an error is signaled when the system tries to compute the class precedence list.

The following might appear to be a conflicting set of definitions:

```
(defclass pie (apple cinnamon) ())
(defclass pastry (cinnamon apple) ())
(defclass apple () ())
(defclass cinnamon () ())
```

The class precedence list for pie is

```
(pie apple cinnamon standard-object t)
```

The class precedence list for pastry is

```
(pastry cinnamon apple standard-object t)
```

It is not a problem for apple to precede cinnamon in the ordering of the super-classes of pie but not in the ordering for pastry. However, it is not possible to build a new class that has both pie and pastry as superclasses.

28.1.6. Generic Functions and Methods

A *generic function* is a function whose behavior depends on the classes or identities of the arguments supplied to it. The *methods* define the class-specific behavior and operations of the generic function. The following sections describe generic functions and methods.

28.1.6.1. Introduction to Generic Functions

A generic function object contains a set of methods, a lambda-list, a method combination type, and other information.

Like an ordinary Lisp function, a generic function takes arguments, performs a series of operations, and perhaps returns useful values. An ordinary function has a single body of code that is always executed when the function is called. A generic function has a set of bodies of code of which a subset is selected for execution. The selected bodies of code and the manner of their combination are determined by the classes or identities of one or more of the arguments to the generic function and by its method combination type.

Ordinary functions and generic functions are called with identical function-call syntax.

Generic functions are true functions that can be passed as arguments, returned as values, used as the first argument to `funcall` and `apply`, and otherwise used in all the ways an ordinary function may be used.

A name can be given to an ordinary function in one of two ways: a *global* name can be given to a function using the `defun` construct; a *local* name can be given using the `flet` or `labels` special forms. A generic function can be given a global name using the `defmethod` or `defgeneric` construct. A generic function can be given a local name using the `generic-flet`, `generic-labels`, or `with-added-methods` special forms. The name of a generic function, like the name of an ordinary function, can be either a symbol or a two-element list whose first element is `setf` and whose second element is a symbol. This is true for both local and global names.

The `generic-flet` special form creates new local generic functions using the set of methods specified by the method definitions in the `generic-flet` form. The scoping of generic function names within a `generic-flet` form is the same as for `flet`.

The `generic-labels` special form creates a set of new mutually recursive local generic functions using the set of methods specified by the method definitions in the `generic-labels` form. The scoping of generic function names within a `generic-labels` form is the same as for `labels`.

The `with-added-methods` special form creates new local generic functions by adding the set of methods specified by the method definitions with a given name in the `with-added-methods` form to copies of the methods of the lexically visible generic function of the same name. If there is a lexically visible ordinary function of the same name as one of the specified generic functions, that function becomes the method function of the default method for the new generic function of that name.

The generic-function macro creates an anonymous generic function with the set of methods specified by the method definitions that appear in the generic-function form.

When a defgeneric form is evaluated, one of three actions is taken:

- If a generic function of the given name already exists, the existing generic function object is modified. Methods specified by the current defgeneric form are added, and any methods in the existing generic function that were defined by a previous defgeneric form are removed. Methods added by the current defgeneric form might replace methods defined by defmethod or defclass. No other methods in the generic function are affected or replaced.

- If the given name names a non-generic function, a macro, or a special form, an error is signaled.

- Otherwise a generic function is created with the methods specified by the method definitions in the defgeneric form.

Some forms specify the options of a generic function, such as the type of method combination it uses or its argument precedence order. They will be referred to as "forms that specify generic function options." These forms are defgeneric, generic-function, generic-flet, generic-labels, and with-added-methods.

Some forms define methods for a generic function. They will be referred to as "method-defining forms." These forms are defgeneric, defmethod, generic-function, generic-flet, generic-labels, with-added-methods, and defclass. Note that all the method-defining forms except defclass and defmethod are also forms that specify generic function options.

28.1.6.2. Introduction to Methods

A method object contains a method function, a sequence of *parameter specializers* that specify when the given method is applicable, a lambda-list, and a sequence of *qualifiers* that are used by the method combination facility to distinguish among methods.

A method object is not a function and cannot be invoked as a function. Various mechanisms in the Object System take a method object and invoke its method function, as is the case when a generic function is invoked. When this occurs it is said that the method is invoked or called.

A method-defining form contains the code that is to be run when the arguments to the generic function cause the method that it defines to be invoked. When a method-defining form is evaluated, a method object is created and one of four actions is taken:

- If a generic function of the given name already exists and if a method object already exists that agrees with the new one on parameter specializers and qualifiers, the new method object replaces the old one. For a definition of one method agreeing with another on parameter specializers and qualifiers, see section 28.1.6.3.

- If a generic function of the given name already exists and if there is no method object that agrees with the new one on parameter specializers and qualifiers, the existing generic function object is modified to contain the new method object.

- If the given name names a non-generic function, a macro, or a special form, an error is signaled.

- Otherwise a generic function is created with the methods specified by the method-defining form.

If the lambda-list of a new method is not congruent with the lambda-list of the generic function, an error is signaled. If a method-defining form that cannot specify generic function options creates a new generic function, a lambda-list for that generic function is derived from the lambda-lists of the methods in the method-defining form in such a way as to be congruent with them. For a discussion of *congruence*, see section 28.1.6.4.

Each method has a *specialized lambda-list*, which determines when that method can be applied. A specialized lambda-list is like an ordinary lambda-list except that a *specialized parameter* may occur instead of the name of a required parameter. A specialized parameter is a list (*variable-name parameter-specializer-name*), where *parameter-specializer-name* is either a name that names a class or a list (eql *form*). A parameter specializer name denotes a parameter specializer as follows:

- A name that names a class denotes that class.

- The list (eql *form*) denotes the type specifier (eql *object*), where *object* is the result of evaluating *form*. The form *form* is evaluated in the lexical environment in which the method-defining form is evaluated. Note that *form* is evaluated only once, at the time the method is defined, not each time the generic function is called.

Parameter specializer names are used in macros intended as the user-level interface (defmethod), while parameter specializers are used in the functional interface.

[It is very important to understand clearly the distinction made in the preceding paragraph. A parameter specializer name has the form of a type specifier but is semantically quite different from a type specifier: a parameter specializer name of the form (eql *form*) is not a type specifier, for it contains a *form* to be evaluated. Type specifiers never contain forms to be evaluated. All parameter specializers (as opposed to parameter specializer names) are valid type specifiers, but not all type specifiers are valid parameter specializers. Macros such as defmethod take parameter specializer names and treat them as specifications for constructing certain type specifiers (parameter specializers) that may then be used with such functions as find-method.—GLS]

Only required parameters may be specialized, and there must be a parameter specializer for each required parameter. For notational simplicity, if some required parameter in a specialized lambda-list in a method-defining form is simply a variable name, its parameter specializer defaults to the class named t.

Given a generic function and a set of arguments, an *applicable method* is a method for that generic function whose parameter specializers are satisfied by their corresponding arguments. The following definition specifies what it means for a method to be applicable and for an argument to satisfy a parameter specializer.

Let $\langle A_1, \ldots, A_n \rangle$ be the required arguments to a generic function in order. Let $\langle P_1, \ldots, P_n \rangle$ be the parameter specializers corresponding to the required parameters of the method *M* in order. The method *M* is *applicable* when each A_i *satisfies* P_i. If P_i is a class, and if A_i is an instance of a class *C*, then it is said that A_i *satisfies* P_i when $C = P_i$ or when *C* is a subclass of P_i. If P_i is of the form (eql *object*), then it is said that A_i satisfies P_i when the function eql applied to A_i and *object* is true.

Because a parameter specializer is a type specifier, the function typep can be used during method selection to determine whether an argument satisfies a parameter specializer. In general a parameter specializer cannot be a type specifier list, such as (vector single-float). The only parameter specializer that can be a list is (eql *object*). This requires that Common Lisp define the type specifier eql as if the following were evaluated:

```
(deftype eql (object) `(member ,object))
```

[See section 4.3.—GLS]

A method all of whose parameter specializers are the class named t is called a *default method*; it is always applicable but may be shadowed by a more specific method.

Methods can have *qualifiers*, which give the method combination procedure a way to distinguish among methods. A method that has one or more qualifiers is called a *qualified* method. A method with no qualifiers is called an *unqualified method*. A qualifier is any object other than a list, that is, any non-nil atom. The qualifiers defined by standard method combination and by the built-in method combination types are symbols.

In this specification, the terms *primary method* and *auxiliary method* are used to partition methods within a method combination type according to their intended use. In standard method combination, primary methods are unqualified methods, and auxiliary methods are methods with a single qualifier that is one of :around, :before, or :after. When a method combination type is defined using the short form of define-method-combination, primary methods are methods qualified with the name of the type of method combination, and auxiliary methods have the qualifier :around. Thus the terms *primary method* and *auxiliary method* have only a relative definition within a given method combination type.

28.1.6.3. Agreement on Parameter Specializers and Qualifiers

Two methods are said to agree with each other on parameter specializers and qualifiers if the following conditions hold:

- Both methods have the same number of required parameters. Suppose the parameter specializers of the two methods are $P_{1,1} \ldots P_{1,n}$ and $P_{2,1} \ldots P_{2,n}$.

- For each $1 \leq i \leq n$, $P_{1,i}$ agrees with $P_{2,i}$. The parameter specializer $P_{1,i}$ agrees with $P_{2,i}$ if $P_{1,i}$ and $P_{2,i}$ are the same class or if $P_{1,i} = (\text{eql } object_1)$, $P_{2,i} = (\text{eql } object_2)$, and $(\text{eql } object_1 \ object_2)$. Otherwise $P_{1,i}$ and $P_{2,i}$ do not agree.

- The lists of qualifiers of both methods contain the same non-nil atoms in the same order. That is, the lists are equal.

28.1.6.4. Congruent Lambda-Lists for All Methods of a Generic Function

These rules define the congruence of a set of lambda-lists, including the lambda-list of each method for a given generic function and the lambda-list specified for the generic function itself, if given.

- Each lambda-list must have the same number of required parameters.

- Each lambda-list must have the same number of optional parameters. Each method can supply its own default for an optional parameter.

- If any lambda-list mentions &rest or &key, each lambda-list must mention one or both of them.

- If the generic function lambda-list mentions &key, each method must accept all of the keyword names mentioned after &key, either by accepting them explicitly, by specifying &allow-other-keys, or by specifying &rest but not &key. Each method can accept additional keyword arguments of its own. The checking of the validity of keyword names is done in the generic function, not in each method. A method is invoked as if the keyword argument pair whose keyword is :allow-other-keys and whose value is t were supplied, though no such argument pair will be passed.

- The use of &allow-other-keys need not be consistent across lambda-lists. If &allow-other-keys is mentioned in the lambda-list of any applicable method or of the generic function, any keyword arguments may be mentioned in the call to the generic function.

- The use of &aux need not be consistent across methods.

If a method-defining form that cannot specify generic function options creates a generic function, and if the lambda-list for the method mentions keyword arguments, the lambda-list of the generic function will mention &key (but no keyword arguments).

28.1.6.5. Keyword Arguments in Generic Functions and Methods

When a generic function or any of its methods mentions &key in a lambda-list, the specific set of keyword arguments accepted by the generic function varies according to the applicable methods. The set of keyword arguments accepted by the generic function for a particular call is the union of the keyword arguments accepted by all applicable methods and the keyword arguments mentioned after &key in the generic function definition, if any. A method that has &rest but not &key does not affect the set of acceptable keyword arguments. If the lambda-list of any applicable method or of the generic function definition contains &allow-other-keys, all keyword arguments are accepted by the generic function.

The lambda-list congruence rules require that each method accept all of the keyword arguments mentioned after &key in the generic function definition, by accepting them explicitly, by specifying &allow-other-keys, or by specifying &rest but not &key. Each method can accept additional keyword arguments of its own, in addition to the keyword arguments mentioned in the generic function definition.

If a generic function is passed a keyword argument that no applicable method accepts, an error is signaled.

For example, suppose there are two methods defined for `width` as follows:

```
(defmethod width ((c character-class) &key font) ...)

(defmethod width ((p picture-class) &key pixel-size) ...)
```

Assume that there are no other methods and no generic function definition for `width`. The evaluation of the following form will signal an error because the keyword argument `:pixel-size` is not accepted by the applicable method.

```
(width (make-instance 'character-class :char #\Q)
       :font 'baskerville :pixel-size 10)
```

The evaluation of the following form will signal an error.

```
(width (make-instance 'picture-class :glyph (glyph #\Q))
       :font 'baskerville :pixel-size 10)
```

The evaluation of the following form will not signal an error if the class named `character-picture-class` is a subclass of both `picture-class` and `character-class`.

```
(width (make-instance 'character-picture-class :char #\Q)
       :font 'baskerville :pixel-size 10)
```

28.1.7. Method Selection and Combination

When a generic function is called with particular arguments, it must determine the code to execute. This code is called the *effective method* for those arguments. The effective method is a *combination* of the applicable methods in the generic function. A combination of methods is a Lisp expression that contains calls to some or all of the methods. If a generic function is called and no methods apply, the generic function `no-applicable-method` is invoked.

When the effective method has been determined, it is invoked with the same arguments that were passed to the generic function. Whatever values it returns are returned as the values of the generic function.

28.1.7.1. Determining the Effective Method

The effective method for a set of arguments is determined by the following three-step procedure:

1. Select the applicable methods.

2. Sort the applicable methods by precedence order, putting the most specific method first.

3. Apply method combination to the sorted list of applicable methods, producing the effective method.

Selecting the Applicable Methods. This step is described in section 28.1.6.2.

Sorting the Applicable Methods by Precedence Order. To compare the precedence of two methods, their parameter specializers are examined in order. The default examination order is from left to right, but an alternative order may be specified by the `:argument-precedence-order` option to `defgeneric` or to any of the other forms that specify generic function options.

The corresponding parameter specializers from each method are compared. When a pair of parameter specializers are equal, the next pair are compared for equality. If all corresponding parameter specializers are equal, the two methods must have different qualifiers; in this case, either method can be selected to precede the other.

If some corresponding parameter specializers are not equal, the first pair of parameter specializers that are not equal determines the precedence. If both parameter specializers are classes, the more specific of the two methods is the method whose parameter specializer appears earlier in the class precedence list of the corresponding argument. Because of the way in which the set of applicable methods is chosen, the parameter specializers are guaranteed to be present in the class precedence list of the class of the argument.

If just one parameter specializer is (`eql` *object*), the method with that parameter specializer precedes the other method. If both parameter specializers are `eql` forms, the specializers must be the same (otherwise the two methods would not both have been applicable to this argument).

The resulting list of applicable methods has the most specific method first and the least specific method last.

Applying Method Combination to the Sorted List of Applicable Methods. In the simple case—if standard method combination is used and all applicable methods are primary methods—the effective method is the most specific method. That method can call the next most specific method by using the function `call-next-method`. The method that `call-next-method` will call is referred to as the *next method*. The predicate `next-method-p` tests whether a next method exists. If `call-next-method` is called and there is no next most specific method, the generic function `no-next-method` is invoked.

In general, the effective method is some combination of the applicable methods. It is defined by a Lisp form that contains calls to some or all of the applicable methods, returns the value or values that will be returned as the value or values of the generic function, and optionally makes some of the methods accessible by means of call-next-method. This Lisp form is the body of the effective method; it is augmented with an appropriate lambda-list to make it a function.

The role of each method in the effective method is determined by its method qualifiers and the specificity of the method. A qualifier serves to mark a method, and the meaning of a qualifier is determined by the way that these marks are used by this step of the procedure. If an applicable method has an unrecognized qualifier, this step signals an error and does not include that method in the effective method.

When standard method combination is used together with qualified methods, the effective method is produced as described in section 28.1.7.2.

Another type of method combination can be specified by using the :method-combination option of defgeneric or of any of the other forms that specify generic function options. In this way this step of the procedure can be customized.

New types of method combination can be defined by using the define-method-combination macro.

The meta-object level also offers a mechanism for defining new types of method combination. The generic function compute-effective-method receives as arguments the generic function, the method combination object, and the sorted list of applicable methods. It returns the Lisp form that defines the effective method. A method for compute-effective-method can be defined directly by using defmethod or indirectly by using define-method-combination. A *method combination object* is an object that encapsulates the method combination type and options specified by the :method-combination option to forms that specify generic function options.

Implementation note: In the simplest implementation, the generic function would compute the effective method each time it was called. In practice, this will be too inefficient for some implementations. Instead, these implementations might employ a variety of optimizations of the three-step procedure. Some illustrative examples of such optimizations are the following:

- Use a hash table keyed by the class of the arguments to store the effective method.

- Compile the effective method and save the resulting compiled function in a table.

- Recognize the Lisp form as an instance of a pattern of control structure and substitute a closure that implements that structure.

- Examine the parameter specializers of all methods for the generic function and enumerate all possible effective methods. Combine the effective methods, together with code to select from among them, into a single function and compile that function. Call that function whenever the generic function is called.

28.1.7.2. Standard Method Combination

Standard method combination is supported by the class standard-generic-function. It is used if no other type of method combination is specified or if the built-in method combination type standard is specified.

Primary methods define the main action of the effective method, while *auxiliary methods* modify that action in one of three ways. A primary method has no method qualifiers.

An auxiliary method is a method whose method qualifier is :before, :after, or :around. Standard method combination allows no more than one qualifier per method; if a method definition specifies more than one qualifier per method, an error is signaled.

- A :before method has the keyword :before as its only qualifier. A :before method specifies code that is to be run before any primary method.

- An :after method has the keyword :after as its only qualifier. An :after method specifies code that is to be run after primary methods.

- An :around method has the keyword :around as its only qualifier. An :around method specifies code that is to be run instead of other applicable methods but that is able to cause some of them to be run.

The semantics of standard method combination are as follows:

- If there are any :around methods, the most specific :around method is called. It supplies the value or values of the generic function.

- Inside the body of an :around method, call-next-method can be used to call the next method. When the next method returns, the :around method can execute more code, perhaps based on the returned value or values. The generic function no-next-method is invoked if call-next-method is used and there is no applicable method to call. The function next-method-p may be used to determine whether a next method exists.

- If an :around method invokes call-next-method, the next most specific :around method is called, if one is applicable. If there are no :around methods or if call-next-method is called by the least specific :around method, the other methods are called as follows:

– All the :before methods are called, in most-specific-first order. Their values are ignored. An error is signaled if call-next-method is used in a :before method.

– The most specific primary method is called. Inside the body of a primary method, call-next-method may be used to call the next most specific primary method. When that method returns, the previous primary method can execute more code, perhaps based on the returned value or values. The generic function no-next-method is invoked if call-next-method is used and there are no more applicable primary methods. The function next-method-p may be used to determine whether a next method exists. If call-next-method is not used, only the most specific primary method is called.

– All the :after methods are called in most-specific-last order. Their values are ignored. An error is signaled if call-next-method is used in an :after method.

• If no :around methods were invoked, the most specific primary method supplies the value or values returned by the generic function. The value or values returned by the invocation of call-next-method in the least specific :around method are those returned by the most specific primary method.

In standard method combination, if there is an applicable method but no applicable primary method, an error is signaled.

The :before methods are run in most-specific-first order and the :after methods are run in least-specific-first order. The design rationale for this difference can be illustrated with an example. Suppose class C_1 modifies the behavior of its superclass, C_2, by adding :before and :after methods. Whether the behavior of the class C_2 is defined directly by methods on C_2 or is inherited from its superclasses does not affect the relative order of invocation of methods on instances of the class C_1. Class C_1's :before method runs before all of class C_2's methods. Class C_1's :after method runs after all of class C_2's methods.

By contrast, all :around methods run before any other methods run. Thus a less specific :around method runs before a more specific primary method.

If only primary methods are used and if call-next-method is not used, only the most specific method is invoked; that is, more specific methods shadow more general ones.

28.1.7.3. Declarative Method Combination

The macro define-method-combination defines new forms of method combination. It provides a mechanism for customizing the production of the effective method. The default procedure for producing an effective method is described in section 28.1.7.1. There are two forms of define-method-combination. The short form is a simple facility; the long form is more powerful and more verbose. The long form resembles defmacro in that the body is an expression that computes a Lisp form; it provides mechanisms for implementing arbitrary control structures within method combination and for arbitrary processing of method qualifiers. The syntax and use of both forms of define-method-combination are explained in section 28.2.

28.1.7.4. Built-in Method Combination Types

The Common Lisp Object System provides a set of built-in method combination types. To specify that a generic function is to use one of these method combination types, the name of the method combination type is given as the argument to the :method-combination option to defgeneric or to the :method-combination option to any of the other forms that specify generic function options.

The names of the built-in method combination types are +, and, append, list, max, min, nconc, or, progn, and standard.

The semantics of the standard built-in method combination type were described in section 28.1.7.2. The other built-in method combination types are called *simple built-in method combination types*.

The simple built-in method combination types act as though they were defined by the short form of define-method-combination. They recognize two roles for methods:

- An :around method has the keyword symbol :around as its sole qualifier. The meaning of :around methods is the same as in standard method combination. Use of the functions call-next-method and next-method-p is supported in :around methods.

- A primary method has the name of the method combination type as its sole qualifier. For example, the built-in method combination type and recognizes methods whose sole qualifier is and; these are primary methods. Use of the functions call-next-method and next-method-p is not supported in primary methods.

The semantics of the simple built-in method combination types are as follows:

- If there are any :around methods, the most specific :around method is called. It supplies the value or values of the generic function.

- Inside the body of an :around method, the function call-next-method can be used to call the next method. The generic function no-next-method is invoked if `call-next-method` is used and there is no applicable method to call. The function `next-method-p` may be used to determine whether a next method exists. When the next method returns, the `:around` method can execute more code, perhaps based on the returned value or values.

- If an `:around` method invokes `call-next-method`, the next most specific `:around` method is called, if one is applicable. If there are no `:around` methods or if `call-next-method` is called by the least specific `:around` method, a Lisp form derived from the name of the built-in method combination type and from the list of applicable primary methods is evaluated to produce the value of the generic function. Suppose the name of the method combination type is *operator* and the call to the generic function is of the form

    (*generic-function* a_1 ... a_n)

    Let $M_1, \ldots, M_k$ be the applicable primary methods in order; then the derived Lisp form is

    (*operator* $\langle M_1\ a_1 \ldots a_n \rangle$ ... $\langle M_k\ a_1 \ldots a_n \rangle$)

    If the expression $\langle M_i\ a_1 \ldots a_n \rangle$ is evaluated, the method M_i will be applied to the arguments $a_1 \ldots a_n$. For example, if *operator* is `or`, the expression $\langle M_i\ a_1 \ldots a_n \rangle$ is evaluated only if $\langle M_j\ a_1 \ldots a_n \rangle$, $1 \leq j < i$, returned `nil`.

    The default order for the primary methods is `:most-specific-first`. However, the order can be reversed by supplying `:most-specific-last` as the second argument to the `:method-combination` option.

    The simple built-in method combination types require exactly one qualifier per method. An error is signaled if there are applicable methods with no qualifiers or with qualifiers that are not supported by the method combination type. An error is signaled if there are applicable `:around` methods and no applicable primary methods.

28.1.8. Meta-objects

The implementation of the Object System manipulates classes, methods, and generic functions. The meta-object protocol specifies a set of generic functions defined by methods on classes; the behavior of those generic functions defines the behavior of the Object System. The instances of the classes on which those methods are defined are called *meta-objects*. Programming at the meta-object protocol level involves defining new classes of meta-objects along with methods specialized on these classes.

28.1.8.1. Metaclasses

The *metaclass* of an object is the class of its class. The metaclass determines the representation of instances of its instances and the forms of inheritance used by its instances for slot descriptions and method inheritance. The metaclass mechanism can be used to provide particular forms of optimization or to tailor the Common Lisp Object System for particular uses. The protocol for defining metaclasses is discussed in the third part of the CLOS specification, The Common Lisp Object System Meta-Object Protocol. [The third part has not yet been approved by X3J13 for inclusion in the forthcoming Common Lisp standard and is not included in this book.—GLS]

28.1.8.2. Standard Metaclasses

The Common Lisp Object System provides a number of predefined meta-classes. These include the classes `standard-class`, `built-in-class`, and `structure-class`:

• The class `standard-class` is the default class of classes defined by `defclass`.

• The class `built-in-class` is the class whose instances are classes that have special implementations with restricted capabilities. Any class that corresponds to a standard Common Lisp type might be an instance of `built-in-class`. The predefined Common Lisp type specifiers that are required to have corresponding classes are listed in table 28-1. It is implementation-dependent whether each of these classes is implemented as a built-in class.

• All classes defined by means of `defstruct` are instances of `structure-class`.

28.1.8.3. Standard Meta-objects

The Object System supplies a standard set of meta-objects, called *standard meta-objects*. These include the class `standard-object` and instances of the classes `standard-method`, `standard-generic-function`, and `method-combination`.

• The class `standard-method` is the default class of methods that are defined by the forms `defmethod`, `defgeneric`, `generic-function`, `generic-flet`, `generic-labels`, and `with-added-methods`.

• The class `standard-generic-function` is the default class of generic functions defined by the forms `defmethod`, `defgeneric`, `generic-function`, `generic-flet`, `generic-labels`, `with-added-methods`, and `defclass`.

- The class named standard-object is an instance of the class standard-class and is a superclass of every class that is an instance of standard-class except itself.

- Every method combination object is an instance of a subclass of the class method-combination.

28.1.9. Object Creation and Initialization

The generic function make-instance creates and returns a new instance of a class. The first argument is a class or the name of a class, and the remaining arguments form an *initialization argument* list.

The initialization of a new instance consists of several distinct steps, including the following: combining the explicitly supplied initialization arguments with default values for the unsupplied initialization arguments, checking the validity of the initialization arguments, allocating storage for the instance, filling slots with values, and executing user-supplied methods that perform additional initialization. Each step of make-instance is implemented by a generic function to provide a mechanism for customizing that step. In addition, make-instance is itself a generic function and thus also can be customized.

The Object System specifies system-supplied primary methods for each step and thus specifies a well-defined standard behavior for the entire initialization process. The standard behavior provides four simple mechanisms for controlling initialization:

- Declaring a symbol to be an initialization argument for a slot. An initialization argument is declared by using the :initarg slot option to defclass. This provides a mechanism for supplying a value for a slot in a call to make-instance.

- Supplying a default value form for an initialization argument. Default value forms for initialization arguments are defined by using the :default-initargs class option to defclass. If an initialization argument is not explicitly provided as an argument to make-instance, the default value form is evaluated in the lexical environment of the defclass form that defined it, and the resulting value is used as the value of the initialization argument.

- Supplying a default initial value form for a slot. A default initial value form for a slot is defined by using the :initform slot option to defclass. If no initialization argument associated with that slot is given as an argument to make-instance or is defaulted by :default-initargs, this default initial value form is evaluated in the lexical environment of the defclass form that defined it, and the resulting value is stored in the slot. The :initform form for a local slot may be used when creating an instance, when updating an instance to conform to a redefined class, or when updating an instance to conform to the definition of a different class. The :initform form for a shared slot may be used when defining or re-defining the class.

• Defining methods for initialize-instance and shared-initialize. The slot-filling behavior described above is implemented by a system-supplied primary method for initialize-instance which invokes shared-initialize. The generic function shared-initialize implements the parts of initialization shared by these four situations: when making an instance, when re-initializing an instance, when updating an instance to conform to a redefined class, and when updating an instance to conform to the definition of a different class. The system-supplied primary method for shared-initialize directly implements the slot-filling behavior described above, and initialize-instance simply invokes shared-initialize.

28.1.9.1. Initialization Arguments

An initialization argument controls object creation and initialization. It is often convenient to use keyword symbols to name initialization arguments, but the name of an initialization argument can be any symbol, including nil. An initialization argument can be used in two ways: to fill a slot with a value or to provide an argument for an initialization method. A single initialization argument can be used for both purposes.

An *initialization argument list* is a list of alternating initialization argument names and values. Its structure is identical to a property list and also to the portion of an argument list processed for &key parameters. As in those lists, if an initialization argument name appears more than once in an initialization argument list, the leftmost occurrence supplies the value and the remaining occurrences are ignored. The arguments to make-instance (after the first argument) form an initialization argument list. Error checking of initialization argument names is disabled if the keyword argument pair whose keyword is :allow-other-keys and whose value is non-nil appears in the initialization argument list.

An initialization argument can be associated with a slot. If the initialization argument has a value in the initialization argument list, the value is stored into the slot of the newly created object, overriding any :initform form associated with the slot. A single initialization argument can initialize more than one slot. An initialization argument that initializes a shared slot stores its value into the shared slot, replacing any previous value.

An initialization argument can be associated with a method. When an object is created and a particular initialization argument is supplied, the generic functions `initialize-instance`, `shared-initialize`, and `allocate-instance` are called with that initialization argument's name and value as a keyword argument pair. If a value for the initialization argument is not supplied in the initialization argument list, the method's lambda-list supplies a default value.

Initialization arguments are used in four situations: when making an instance, when re-initializing an instance, when updating an instance to conform to a re-defined class, and when updating an instance to conform to the definition of a different class.

Because initialization arguments are used to control the creation and initialization of an instance of some particular class, we say that an initialization argument is "an initialization argument for" that class.

28.1.9.2. Declaring the Validity of Initialization Arguments

Initialization arguments are checked for validity in each of the four situations that use them. An initialization argument may be valid in one situation and not another. For example, the system-supplied primary method for `make-instance` defined for the class `standard-class` checks the validity of its initialization arguments and signals an error if an initialization argument is supplied that is not declared valid in that situation.

There are two means of declaring initialization arguments valid.

- Initialization arguments that fill slots are declared valid by the `:initarg` slot option to `defclass`. The `:initarg` slot option is inherited from superclasses. Thus the set of valid initialization arguments that fill slots for a class is the union of the initialization arguments that fill slots declared valid by that class and its superclasses. Initialization arguments that fill slots are valid in all four contexts.

- Initialization arguments that supply arguments to methods are declared valid by defining those methods. The keyword name of each keyword parameter specified in the method's lambda-list becomes an initialization argument for all classes for which the method is applicable. Thus method inheritance controls the set of valid initialization arguments that supply arguments to methods. The generic functions for which method definitions serve to declare initialization arguments valid are as follows:

  - Making an instance of a class: `allocate-instance`, `initialize-instance`, and `shared-initialize`. Initialization arguments declared valid by these methods are valid when making an instance of a class.

— Re-initializing an instance: the functions `reinitialize-instance` and `shared-initialize`. Initialization arguments declared valid by these methods are valid when re-initializing an instance.

— Updating an instance to conform to a redefined class: `update-instance-for-redefined-class` and `shared-initialize`. Initialization arguments declared valid by these methods are valid when updating an instance to conform to a redefined class.

— Updating an instance to conform to the definition of a different class: `update-instance-for-different-class` and `shared-initialize`. Initialization arguments declared valid by these methods are valid when updating an instance to conform to the definition of a different class.

The set of valid initialization arguments for a class is the set of valid initialization arguments that either fill slots or supply arguments to methods, along with the predefined initialization argument `:allow-other-keys`. The default value for `:allow-other-keys` is `nil`. The meaning of `:allow-other-keys` is the same here as when it is passed to an ordinary function.

28.1.9.3. Defaulting of Initialization Arguments

A *default value form* can be supplied for an initialization argument by using the `:default-initargs` class option. If an initialization argument is declared valid by some particular class, its default value form might be specified by a different class. In this case `:default-initargs` is used to supply a default value for an inherited initialization argument.

The `:default-initargs` option is used only to provide default values for initialization arguments; it does not declare a symbol as a valid initialization argument name. Furthermore, the `:default-initargs` option is used only to provide default values for initialization arguments when making an instance.

The argument to the `:default-initargs` class option is a list of alternating initialization argument names and forms. Each form is the default value form for the corresponding initialization argument. The default value form of an initialization argument is used and evaluated only if that initialization argument does not appear in the arguments to `make-instance` and is not defaulted by a more specific class. The default value form is evaluated in the lexical environment of the `defclass` form that supplied it; the result is used as the initialization argument's value.

The initialization arguments supplied to `make-instance` are combined with defaulted initialization arguments to produce a *defaulted initialization argument list*.

A defaulted initialization argument list is a list of alternating initialization argument names and values in which unsupplied initialization arguments are defaulted and in which the explicitly supplied initialization arguments appear earlier in the list than the defaulted initialization arguments. Defaulted initialization arguments are ordered according to the order in the class precedence list of the classes that supplied the default values.

There is a distinction between the purposes of the :default-initargs and the :initform options with respect to the initialization of slots. The :default-initargs class option provides a mechanism for the user to give a default value form for an initialization argument without knowing whether the initialization argument initializes a slot or is passed to a method. If that initialization argument is not explicitly supplied in a call to make-instance, the default value form is used, just as if it had been supplied in the call. In contrast, the :initform slot option provides a mechanism for the user to give a default initial value form for a slot. An :initform form is used to initialize a slot only if no initialization argument associated with that slot is given as an argument to make-instance or is defaulted by :default-initargs.

The order of evaluation of default value forms for initialization arguments and the order of evaluation of :initform forms are undefined. If the order of evaluation matters, use initialize-instance or shared-initialize methods.

28.1.9.4. Rules for Initialization Arguments

The :initarg slot option may be specified more than once for a given slot. The following rules specify when initialization arguments may be multiply defined:

- A given initialization argument can be used to initialize more than one slot if the same initialization argument name appears in more than one :initarg slot option.

- A given initialization argument name can appear in the lambda-list of more than one initialization method.

- A given initialization argument name can appear both in an :initarg slot option and in the lambda-list of an initialization method.

If two or more initialization arguments that initialize the same slot are given in the arguments to make-instance, the leftmost of these initialization arguments in the initialization argument list supplies the value, even if the initialization arguments have different names.

If two or more different initialization arguments that initialize the same slot have default values and none is given explicitly in the arguments to make-instance, the initialization argument that appears in a :default-initargs class option in the most specific of the classes supplies the value. If a single :default-initargs class option specifies two or more initialization arguments that initialize the same slot and none is given explicitly in the arguments to make-instance, the leftmost argument in the :default-initargs class option supplies the value, and the values of the remaining default value forms are ignored.

Initialization arguments given explicitly in the arguments to make-instance appear to the left of defaulted initialization arguments. Suppose that the classes C_1 and C_2 supply the values of defaulted initialization arguments for different slots, and suppose that C_1 is more specific than C_2; then the defaulted initialization argument whose value is supplied by C_1 is to the left of the defaulted initialization argument whose value is supplied by C_2 in the defaulted initialization argument list. If a single :default-initargs class option supplies the values of initialization arguments for two different slots, the initialization argument whose value is specified farther to the left in the default-initargs class option appears farther to the left in the defaulted initialization argument list.

If a slot has both an :initform form and an :initarg slot option, and the initialization argument is defaulted using :default-initargs or is supplied to make-instance, the captured :initform form is neither used nor evaluated.

The following is an example of the preceding rules:

```
(defclass q () ((x :initarg a)))

(defclass r (q) ((x :initarg b))
  (:default-initargs a 1 b 2))
```

Form	Defaulted Initialization Argument List	Contents of Slot
(make-instance 'r)	(a 1 b 2)	1
(make-instance 'r 'a 3)	(a 3 b 2)	3
(make-instance 'r 'b 4)	(b 4 a 1)	4
(make-instance 'r 'a 1 'a 2)	(a 1 a 2 b 2)	1

28.1.9.5. Shared-Initialize

The generic function shared-initialize is used to fill the slots of an instance using initialization arguments and :initform forms when an instance is created, when an instance is re-initialized, when an instance is updated to conform to a redefined class, and when an instance is updated to conform to a different class. It uses standard method combination. It takes the following arguments: the instance to be initialized, a specification of a set of names of slots accessible in that instance, and any number of initialization arguments. The arguments after the first two must form an initialization argument list.

The second argument to `shared-initialize` may be one of the following:

- It can be a list of slot names, which specifies the set of those slot names.

- It can be `nil`, which specifies the empty set of slot names.

- It can be the symbol t, which specifies the set of all of the slots.

There is a system-supplied primary method for `shared-initialize` whose first parameter specializer is the class `standard-object`. This method behaves as follows on each slot, whether shared or local:

- If an initialization argument in the initialization argument list specifies a value for that slot, that value is stored into the slot, even if a value has already been stored in the slot before the method is run. The affected slots are independent of which slots are indicated by the second argument to `shared-initialize`.

- Any slots indicated by the second argument that are still unbound at this point are initialized according to their `:initform` forms. For any such slot that has an `:initform` form, that form is evaluated in the lexical environment of its defining `defclass` form and the result is stored into the slot. For example, if a `:before` method stores a value in the slot, the `:initform` form will not be used to supply a value for the slot. If the second argument specifies a name that does not correspond to any slots accessible in the instance, the results are unspecified.

- The rules mentioned in section 28.1.9.4 are obeyed.

The generic function `shared-initialize` is called by the system-supplied primary methods for the generic functions `initialize-instance`, `reinitialize-instance`, `update-instance-for-different-class`, and `update-instance-for-redefined-class`. Thus methods can be written for `shared-initialize` to specify actions that should be taken in all of these contexts.

28.1.9.6. Initialize-Instance

The generic function `initialize-instance` is called by `make-instance` to initialize a newly created instance. It uses standard method combination. Methods for `initialize-instance` can be defined in order to perform any initialization that cannot be achieved with the simple slot-filling mechanisms.

During initialization, initialize-instance is invoked after the following actions have been taken:

- The defaulted initialization argument list has been computed by combining the supplied initialization argument list with any default initialization arguments for the class.

- The validity of the defaulted initialization argument list has been checked. If any of the initialization arguments has not been declared valid, an error is signaled.

- A new instance whose slots are unbound has been created.

The generic function initialize-instance is called with the new instance and the defaulted initialization arguments. There is a system-supplied primary method for initialize-instance whose parameter specializer is the class standard-object. This method calls the generic function shared-initialize to fill in the slots according to the initialization arguments and the :initform forms for the slots; the generic function shared-initialize is called with the following arguments: the instance, t, and the defaulted initialization arguments.

Note that initialize-instance provides the defaulted initialization argument list in its call to shared-initialize, so the first step performed by the system-supplied primary method for shared-initialize takes into account both the initialization arguments provided in the call to make-instance and the defaulted initialization argument list.

Methods for initialize-instance can be defined to specify actions to be taken when an instance is initialized. If only :after methods for initialize-instance are defined, they will be run after the system-supplied primary method for initialization and therefore they will not interfere with the default behavior of initialize-instance.

The Object System provides two functions that are useful in the bodies of initialize-instance methods. The function slot-boundp returns a boolean value that indicates whether a specified slot has a value; this provides a mechanism for writing :after methods for initialize-instance that initialize slots only if they have not already been initialized. The function slot-makunbound causes the slot to have no value.

28.1.9.7. Definitions of Make-Instance and Initialize-Instance

The generic function make-instance behaves as if it were defined as follows, except that certain optimizations are permitted:

```
(defmethod make-instance ((class standard-class) &rest initargs)
  (setq initargs (default-initargs class initargs))
  ...
  (let ((instance (apply #'allocate-instance class initargs)))
    (apply #'initialize-instance instance initargs)
    instance))

(defmethod make-instance ((class-name symbol) &rest initargs)
  (apply #'make-instance (find-class class-name) initargs))
```

The elided code in the definition of make-instance checks the supplied initialization arguments to determine whether an initialization argument was supplied that neither filled a slot nor supplied an argument to an applicable method. This check could be implemented using the generic functions class-prototype, compute-applicable-methods, function-keywords, and class-slot-initargs. See the third part of the Common Lisp Object System specification for a description of this initialization argument check. [The third part has not yet been approved by X3J13 for inclusion in the forthcoming Common Lisp standard and is not included in this book.—GLS]

The generic function initialize-instance behaves as if it were defined as follows, except that certain optimizations are permitted:

```
(defmethod initialize-instance
          ((instance standard-object) &rest initargs)
  (apply #'shared-initialize instance t initargs)))
```

These procedures can be customized at either the Programmer Interface level, the meta-object level, or both.

Customizing at the Programmer Interface level includes using the :initform, :initarg, and :default-initargs options to defclass, as well as defining methods for make-instance and initialize-instance. It is also possible to define methods for shared-initialize, which would be invoked by the generic functions reinitialize-instance, update-instance-for-redefined-class, update-instance-for-different-class, and initialize-instance. The meta-object level supports additional customization by allowing methods to be defined on make-instance, default-initargs, and allocate-instance. Parts 2 and 3 of the Common Lisp Object System specification document each of these generic functions and the system-supplied primary methods. [The third part has not yet been approved by X3J13 for inclusion in the forthcoming Common Lisp standard and is not included in this book.—GLS]

Implementations are permitted to make certain optimizations to initialize-instance and shared-initialize. The description of shared-initialize in section 28.2 mentions the possible optimizations.

Because of optimization, the check for valid initialization arguments might not be implemented using the generic functions class-prototype, compute-applicable-methods, function-keywords, and class-slot-initargs. In addition, methods for the generic function default-initargs and the system-supplied primary methods for allocate-instance, initialize-instance, and shared-initialize might not be called on every call to make-instance or might not receive exactly the arguments that would be expected.

28.1.10. Redefining Classes

A class that is an instance of standard-class can be redefined if the new class will also be an instance of standard-class. Redefining a class modifies the existing class object to reflect the new class definition; it does not create a new class object for the class. Any method object created by a :reader, :writer, or :accessor option specified by the old defclass form is removed from the corresponding generic function. Methods specified by the new defclass form are added.

When the class C is redefined, changes are propagated to its instances and to instances of any of its subclasses. Updating such an instance occurs at an implementation-dependent time, but no later than the next time a slot of that instance is read or written. Updating an instance does not change its identity as defined by the eq function. The updating process may change the slots of that particular instance, but it does not create a new instance. Whether updating an instance consumes storage is implementation-dependent.

Note that redefining a class may cause slots to be added or deleted. If a class is redefined in a way that changes the set of local slots accessible in instances, the instances will be updated. It is implementation-dependent whether instances are updated if a class is redefined in a way that does not change the set of local slots accessible in instances.

The value of a slot that is specified as shared both in the old class and in the new class is retained. If such a shared slot was unbound in the old class, it will be unbound in the new class. Slots that were local in the old class and that are shared in the new class are initialized. Newly added shared slots are initialized.

Each newly added shared slot is set to the result of evaluating the captured :initform form for the slot that was specified in the defclass form for the new class. If there is no :initform form, the slot is unbound.

If a class is redefined in such a way that the set of local slots accessible in an instance of the class is changed, a two-step process of updating the instances of the class takes place. The process may be explicitly started by invoking the generic function `make-instances-obsolete`. This two-step process can happen in other circumstances in some implementations. For example, in some implementations this two-step process will be triggered if the order of slots in storage is changed.

The first step modifies the structure of the instance by adding new local slots and discarding local slots that are not defined in the new version of the class. The second step initializes the newly added local slots and performs any other user-defined actions. These steps are further specified in the next two sections.

28.1.10.1. Modifying the Structure of Instances

The first step modifies the structure of instances of the redefined class to conform to its new class definition. Local slots specified by the new class definition that are not specified as either local or shared by the old class are added, and slots not specified as either local or shared by the new class definition that are specified as local by the old class are discarded. The names of these added and discarded slots are passed as arguments to `update-instance-for-redefined-class` as described in the next section.

The values of local slots specified by both the new and old classes are retained. If such a local slot was unbound, it remains unbound.

The value of a slot that is specified as shared in the old class and as local in the new class is retained. If such a shared slot was unbound, the local slot will be unbound.

28.1.10.2. Initializing Newly Added Local Slots

The second step initializes the newly added local slots and performs any other user-defined actions. This step is implemented by the generic function `update-instance-for-redefined-class`, which is called after completion of the first step of modifying the structure of the instance.

The generic function `update-instance-for-redefined-class` takes four required arguments: the instance being updated after it has undergone the first step, a list of the names of local slots that were added, a list of the names of local slots that were discarded, and a property list containing the slot names and values of slots that were discarded and had values. Included among the discarded slots are slots that were local in the old class and that are shared in the new class.

The generic function `update-instance-for-redefined-class` also takes any number of initialization arguments. When it is called by the system to update an instance whose class has been redefined, no initialization arguments are provided.

There is a system-supplied primary method for the generic function `update-instance-for-redefined-class` whose parameter specializer for its instance argument is the class `standard-object`. First this method checks the validity of initialization arguments and signals an error if an initialization argument is supplied that is not declared valid (see section 28.1.9.2.) Then it calls the generic function `shared-initialize` with the following arguments: the instance, the list of names of the newly added slots, and the initialization arguments it received.

28.1.10.3. Customizing Class Redefinition

Methods for `update-instance-for-redefined-class` may be defined to specify actions to be taken when an instance is updated. If only `:after` methods for `update-instance-for-redefined-class` are defined, they will be run after the system-supplied primary method for initialization and therefore will not interfere with the default behavior of `update-instance-for-redefined-class`. Because no initialization arguments are passed to `update-instance-for-redefined-class` when it is called by the system, the `:initform` forms for slots that are filled by `:before` methods for `update-instance-for-redefined-class` will not be evaluated by `shared-initialize`.

Methods for `shared-initialize` may be defined to customize class redefinition (see section 28.1.9.5).

28.1.10.4. Extensions

There are two allowed extensions to class redefinition:

- The Object System may be extended to permit the new class to be an instance of a metaclass other than the metaclass of the old class.

- The Object System may be extended to support an updating process when either the old or the new class is an instance of a class other than `standard-class` that is not a built-in class.

28.1.11. Changing the Class of an Instance

The function `change-class` can be used to change the class of an instance from its current class, C_{from}, to a different class, C_{to}; it changes the structure of the instance to conform to the definition of the class C_{to}.

Note that changing the class of an instance may cause slots to be added or deleted.

When change-class is invoked on an instance, a two-step updating process takes place. The first step modifies the structure of the instance by adding new local slots and discarding local slots that are not specified in the new version of the instance. The second step initializes the newly added local slots and performs any other user-defined actions. These steps are further described in the following two sections.

28.1.11.1. Modifying the Structure of an Instance

In order to make an instance conform to the class C_{to}, local slots specified by the class C_{to} that are not specified by the class C_{from} are added, and local slots not specified by the class C_{to} that are specified by the class C_{from} are discarded.

The values of local slots specified by both the class C_{to} and the class C_{from} are retained. If such a local slot was unbound, it remains unbound.

The values of slots specified as shared in the class C_{from} and as local in the class C_{to} are retained.

This first step of the update does not affect the values of any shared slots.

28.1.11.2. Initializing Newly Added Local Slots

The second step of the update initializes the newly added slots and performs any other user-defined actions. This step is implemented by the generic function update-instance-for-different-class. The generic function update-instance-for-different-class is invoked by change-class after the first step of the update has been completed.

The generic function update-instance-for-different-class is invoked on two arguments computed by change-class. The first argument passed is a copy of the instance being updated and is an instance of the class C_{from}; this copy has dynamic extent within the generic function change-class. The second argument is the instance as updated so far by change-class and is an instance of the class C_{to}.

The generic function update-instance-for-different-class also takes any number of initialization arguments. When it is called by change-class, no initialization arguments are provided.

There is a system-supplied primary method for the generic function update-instance-for-different-class that has two parameter specializers, each of which is the class standard-object. First this method checks the validity of initialization arguments and signals an error if an initialization argument is supplied that is not declared valid (see section 28.1.9.2). Then it calls the generic function `shared-initialize` with the following arguments: the instance, a list of names of the newly added slots, and the initialization arguments it received.

28.1.11.3. Customizing the Change of Class of an Instance

Methods for `update-instance-for-different-class` may be defined to specify actions to be taken when an instance is updated. If only `:after` methods for `update-instance-for-different-class` are defined, they will be run after the system-supplied primary method for initialization and will not interfere with the default behavior of `update-instance-for-different-class`. Because no initialization arguments are passed to `update-instance-for-different-class` when it is called by `change-class`, the `:initform` forms for slots that are filled by `:before` methods for `update-instance-for-different-class` will not be evaluated by `shared-initialize`.

Methods for `shared-initialize` may be defined to customize class redefinition (see section 28.1.9.5).

28.1.12. Reinitializing an Instance

The generic function `reinitialize-instance` may be used to change the values of slots according to initialization arguments.

The process of reinitialization changes the values of some slots and performs any user-defined actions.

Reinitialization does not modify the structure of an instance to add or delete slots, and it does not use any `:initform` forms to initialize slots.

The generic function `reinitialize-instance` may be called directly. It takes one required argument, the instance. It also takes any number of initialization arguments to be used by methods for `reinitialize-instance` or for `shared-initialize`. The arguments after the required instance must form an initialization argument list.

There is a system-supplied primary method for `reinitialize-instance` whose parameter specializer is the class `standard-object`. First this method checks the validity of initialization arguments and signals an error if an initialization argument is supplied that is not declared valid (see section 28.1.9.2). Then it calls the generic function `shared-initialize` with the following arguments: the instance, `nil`, and the initialization arguments it received.

28.1.12.1. Customizing Reinitialization

Methods for the generic function reinitialize-instance may be defined to specify actions to be taken when an instance is updated. If only :after methods for reinitialize-instance are defined, they will be run after the system-supplied primary method for initialization and therefore will not interfere with the default behavior of reinitialize-instance.

Methods for shared-initialize may be defined to customize class redefinition (see section 28.1.9.5).

28.2. Functions in the Programmer Interface

This section describes the functions, macros, special forms, and generic functions provided by the Common Lisp Object System Programmer Interface. The Programmer Interface comprises the functions and macros that are sufficient for writing most object-oriented programs.

This section is reference material that requires an understanding of the basic concepts of the Common Lisp Object System. The functions are arranged in alphabetical order for convenient reference.

The description of each function, macro, special form, and generic function includes its purpose, its syntax, the semantics of its arguments and returned values, and often an example and cross-references to related functions.

The syntax description for a function, macro, or special form describes its parameters. The description of a generic function includes descriptions of the methods that are defined on that generic function by the Common Lisp Object System. A *method signature* is used to describe the parameters and parameter specializers for each method.

The following is an example of the format for the syntax description of a generic function with the method signature for one primary method:

```
f x y &optional z &key :k                              [Generic function]
f (x class) (y t) &optional z &key :k                  [Primary method]
```

This description indicates that the generic function f has two required parameters, x and y. In addition, there is an optional parameter z and a keyword parameter :k.

The method signature indicates that this method on the generic function f has two required parameters, x, which must be an instance of the class class, and y, which can be any object. In addition, there is an optional parameter z and a keyword parameter :k. The signature also indicates that this method on f is a primary method and has no qualifiers.

The syntax description for a generic function describes the lambda-list of the generic function itself, while the method signatures describe the lambda-lists of the defined methods.

The generic functions described in this book are all standard generic functions. They all use standard method combination.

Any implementation of the Common Lisp Object System is allowed to provide additional methods on the generic functions described here.

It is useful to categorize the functions and macros according to their role in this standard:

• *Tools used for simple object-oriented programming*

These tools allow for defining new classes, methods, and generic functions and for making instances. Some tools used within method bodies are also listed here. Some of the macros listed here have a corresponding function that performs the same task at a lower level of abstraction.

```
call-next-method              initialize-instance
change-class                  make-instance
defclass                      next-method-p
defgeneric                    slot-boundp
defmethod                     slot-value
generic-flet                  with-accessors
generic-function              with-added-methods
generic-labels                with-slots
```

• *Functions underlying the commonly used macros*

```
add-method                    reinitialize-instance
class-name                    remove-method
compute-applicable-methods    shared-initialize
ensure-generic-function       slot-exists-p
find-class                    slot-makunbound
find-method                   slot-missing
function-keywords             slot-unbound
make-instances-obsolete       update-instance-for-different-class
no-applicable-method          update-instance-for-redefined-class
no-next-method
```

• *Tools for declarative method combination*

```
call-method                   method-combination-error
define-method-combination     method-qualifiers
invalid-method-error
```

• *General Common Lisp support tools*

class-of   print-object
documentation   symbol-macrolet

[Note that describe appeared in this list in the original CLOS proposal [5, 7], but X3J13 voted in March 1989 ⟨63⟩ not to make describe a generic function after all (see describe-object).—GLS]

[At this point the original CLOS report contained a description of the ⟦ ⟧ and ↓ notation; that description is omitted here. I have adopted the notation for use throughout this book. It is described in section 1.2.5.—GLS]

add-method *generic-function method*   [*Generic function*]
add-method   [*Primary method*]
  (*generic-function* standard-generic-function) (*method* method)

The generic function add-method adds a method to a generic function. It destructively modifies the generic function and returns the modified generic function as its result.

The *generic-function* argument is a generic function object.

The *method* argument is a method object. The lambda-list of the method function must be congruent with the lambda-list of the generic function, or an error is signaled.

The modified generic function is returned. The result of add-method is eq to the *generic-function* argument.

If the given method agrees with an existing method of the generic function on parameter specializers and qualifiers, the existing method is replaced. See section 28.1.6.3 for a definition of agreement in this context.

If the method object is a method object of another generic function, an error is signaled.

See section 28.1.6.3 as well as defmethod, defgeneric, find-method, and remove-method.

call-method *method next-method-list*   [*Macro*]

The macro call-method is used in method combination. This macro hides the implementation-dependent details of how methods are called. It can be used only within an effective method form, for the name call-method is defined only within the lexical scope of such a form.

The macro `call-method` invokes the specified method, supplying it with arguments and with definitions for `call-next-method` and for `next-method-p`. The arguments are the arguments that were supplied to the effective method form containing the invocation of `call-method`. The definitions of `call-next-method` and `next-method-p` rely on the list of method objects given as the second argument to `call-method`.

The `call-next-method` function available to the method that is the first subform will call the first method in the list that is the second subform. The `call-next-method` function available in that method, in turn, will call the second method in the list that is the second subform, and so on, until the list of next methods is exhausted.

The *method* argument is a method object; the *next-method-list* argument is a list of method objects.

A list whose first element is the symbol `make-method` and whose second element is a Lisp form can be used instead of a method object as the first subform of `call-method` or as an element of the second subform of `call-method`. Such a list specifies a method object whose method function has a body that is the given form.

The result of `call-method` is the value or values returned by the method invocation.

See `call-next-method`, `define-method-combination`, and `next-method-p`.

`call-next-method &rest` *args*   [*Function*]

The function `call-next-method` can be used within the body of a method defined by a method-defining form to call the next method.

The function `call-next-method` returns the value or values returned by the method it calls. If there is no next method, the generic function `no-next-method` is called.

The type of method combination used determines which methods can invoke `call-next-method`. The standard method combination type allows `call-next-method` to be used within primary methods and `:around` methods.

The standard method combination type defines the next method according to the following rules:

- If `call-next-method` is used in an `:around` method, the next method is the next most specific `:around` method, if one is applicable.

- If there are no `:around` methods at all or if `call-next-method` is called by the least specific `:around` method, other methods are called as follows:

- All the :before methods are called, in most-specific-first order. The function call-next-method cannot be used in :before methods.

- The most specific primary method is called. Inside the body of a primary method, call-next-method may be used to pass control to the next most specific primary method. The generic function no-next-method is called if call-next-method is used and there are no more primary methods.

- All the :after methods are called in most-specific-last order. The function call-next-method cannot be used in :after methods.

For further discussion of the use of call-next-method, see sections 28.1.7.2 and 28.1.7.4.

When call-next-method is called with no arguments, it passes the current method's original arguments to the next method. Neither argument defaulting, nor using setq, nor rebinding variables with the same names as parameters of the method affects the values call-next-method passes to the method it calls.

When call-next-method is called with arguments, the next method is called with those arguments. When providing arguments to call-next-method, the following rule must be satisfied or an error is signaled: The ordered set of methods applicable for a changed set of arguments for call-next-method must be the same as the ordered set of applicable methods for the original arguments to the generic function. Optimizations of the error checking are possible, but they must not change the semantics of call-next-method.

If call-next-method is called with arguments but omits optional arguments, the next method called defaults those arguments.

The function call-next-method returns the value or values returned by the method it calls.

Further computation is possible after call-next-method returns.

The definition of the function call-next-method has lexical scope (for it is defined only within the body of a method defined by a method-defining form) and indefinite extent.

For generic functions using a type of method combination defined by the short form of define-method-combination, call-next-method can be used in :around methods only.

The function next-method-p can be used to test whether or not there is a next method.

If call-next-method is used in methods that do not support it, an error is signaled.

See sections 28.1.7, 28.1.7.2, and 28.1.7.4 as well as the functions define-method-combination, next-method-p, and no-next-method.

change-class *instance new-class*   [*Generic function*]
change-class (*instance* standard-object)   [*Primary method*]
             (*new-class* standard-class)
change-class (*instance* t) (*new-class* symbol)   [*Primary method*]

The generic function change-class changes the class of an instance to a new class. It destructively modifies and returns the instance.

If in the old class there is any slot of the same name as a local slot in the new class, the value of that slot is retained. This means that if the slot has a value, the value returned by slot-value after change-class is invoked is eql to the value returned by slot-value before change-class is invoked. Similarly, if the slot was unbound, it remains unbound. The other slots are initialized as described in section 28.1.11.

The *instance* argument is a Lisp object.

The *new-class* argument is a class object or a symbol that names a class.

If the second of the preceding methods is selected, that method invokes change-class on *instance* and (find-class *new-class*).

The modified instance is returned. The result of change-class is eq to the *instance* argument.

Examples:

```
(defclass position () ())

(defclass x-y-position (position)
  ((x :initform 0 :initarg :x)
   (y :initform 0 :initarg :y)))

(defclass rho-theta-position (position)
  ((rho :initform 0)
   (theta :initform 0)))

(defmethod update-instance-for-different-class :before
          ((old x-y-position)
           (new rho-theta-position)
           &key)
  ;; Copy the position information from old to new to make new
  ;; be a rho-theta-position at the same position as old.
  (let ((x (slot-value old 'x))
        (y (slot-value old 'y)))
    (setf (slot-value new 'rho) (sqrt (+ (* x x) (* y y)))
          (slot-value new 'theta) (atan y x))))
```

```
;;; At this point an instance of the class x-y-position can be
;;; changed to be an instance of the class rho-theta-position
;;; using change-class:

(setq p1 (make-instance 'x-y-position :x 2 :y 0))

(change-class p1 'rho-theta-position)

;;; The result is that the instance bound to p1 is now
;;; an instance of the class rho-theta-position.
;;; The update-instance-for-different-class method
;;; performed the initialization of the rho and theta
;;; slots based on the values of the x and y slots,
;;; which were maintained by the old instance.
```

After completing all other actions, change-class invokes the generic function update-instance-for-different-class. The generic function update-instance-for-different-class can be used to assign values to slots in the transformed instance.

The generic function change-class has several semantic difficulties. First, it performs a destructive operation that can be invoked within a method on an instance that was used to select that method. When multiple methods are involved because methods are being combined, the methods currently executing or about to be executed may no longer be applicable. Second, some implementations might use compiler optimizations of slot access, and when the class of an instance is changed the assumptions the compiler made might be violated. This implies that a programmer must not use change-class inside a method if any methods for that generic function access any slots, or the results are undefined.

See section 28.1.11 as well as update-instance-for-different-class.

class-name *class*	*[Generic function]*
class-name (*class* class)	*[Primary method]*

The generic function class-name takes a class object and returns its name. The *class* argument is a class object. The *new-value* argument is any object. The name of the given class is returned.

The name of an anonymous class is nil.

If *S* is a symbol such that *S* =(class-name *C*) and *C* = (find-class *S*), then *S* is the proper name of *C* (see section 28.1.2).

See also section 28.1.2 and find-class.

(setf class-name) *new-value class*   *[Generic function]*
(setf class-name) *new-value* (*class* class)   *[Primary method]*

The generic function (setf class-name) takes a class object and sets its name.
The *class* argument is a class object. The *new-value* argument is any object.

class-of *object*   *[Function]*

The function class-of returns the class of which the given object is an instance.
The argument to class-of may be any Common Lisp object. The function
class-of returns the class of which the argument is an instance.

compute-applicable-methods *generic-function*   *[Function]*
   function-arguments

Given a generic function and a set of arguments, the function compute-
applicable-methods returns the set of methods that are applicable for those
arguments.
   The methods are sorted according to precedence order. See section 28.1.7.
   The *generic-function* argument must be a generic function object. The *function-
arguments* argument is a list of the arguments to that generic function. The result
is a list of the applicable methods in order of precedence. See section 28.1.7.

defclass *class-name* ({*superclass-name*}*)   *[Macro]*
        ({*slot-specifier*}*) ⟦↓*class-option*⟧

class-name ::= *symbol*
superclass-name ::= *symbol*
slot-specifier ::= *slot-name* | (*slot-name* ⟦↓ *slot-option* ⟧)
slot-name ::= *symbol*
slot-option ::= {:reader *reader-function-name*}*
               | {:writer *writer-function-name*}*
               | {:accessor *reader-function-name*}*
               | {:allocation *allocation-type*}
               | {:initarg *initarg-name*}*
               | {:initform *form*}
               | {:type *type-specifier*}
               | {:documentation *string*}

reader-function-name ::= *symbol*
writer-function-name ::= *function-name/*
function-name ::= {*symbol* | (setf *symbol*)}
initarg-name ::= *symbol*
allocation-type ::= :instance | :class
class-option ::= (:default-initargs *initarg-list*)
                 | (:documentation *string*)
                 | (:metaclass *class-name*)
initarg-list ::= {*initarg-name default-initial-value-form*}*

The macro defclass defines a new named class. It returns the new class object
as its result.

The syntax of defclass provides options for specifying initialization arguments
for slots, for specifying default initialization values for slots, and for requesting that
methods on specified generic functions be automatically generated for reading and
writing the values of slots. No reader or writer functions are defined by default;
their generation must be explicitly requested.

Defining a new class also causes a type of the same name to be defined. The
predicate (typep *object class-name*) returns true if the class of the given object
is *class-name* itself or a subclass of the class *class-name*. A class object can be
used as a type specifier. Thus (typep *object class*) returns true if the class of the
object is *class* itself or a subclass of *class*.

The *class-name* argument is a non-nil symbol. It becomes the proper name of
the new class. If a class with the same proper name already exists and that class
is an instance of standard-class, and if the defclass form for the definition
of the new class specifies a class of class standard-class, the definition of the
existing class is replaced.

Each *superclass-name* argument is a non-nil symbol that specifies a direct superclass of the new class. The new class will inherit slots and methods from each of
its direct superclasses, from their direct superclasses, and so on. See section 28.1.3
for a discussion of how slots and methods are inherited.

Each *slot-specifier* argument is the name of the slot or a list consisting of the slot
name followed by zero or more slot options. The *slot-name* argument is a symbol
that is syntactically valid for use as a variable name. If there are any duplicate slot
names, an error is signaled.

The following slot options are available:

- The :reader slot option specifies that an unqualified method is to be defined on
  the generic function named *reader-function-name* to read the value of the given
  slot. The *reader-function-name* argument is a non-nil symbol. The :reader
  slot option may be specified more than once for a given slot.

- The :writer slot option specifies that an unqualified method is to be defined on the generic function named *writer-function-name* to write the value of the slot. The *writer-function-name* argument is a function-name. The :writer slot option may be specified more than once for a given slot.

- The :accessor slot option specifies that an unqualified method is to be defined on the generic function named *reader-function-name* to read the value of the given slot and that an unqualified method is to be defined on the generic function named (setf *reader-function-name*) to be used with setf to modify the value of the slot. The *reader-function-name* argument is a non-nil symbol. The :accessor slot option may be specified more than once for a given slot.

- The :allocation slot option is used to specify where storage is to be allocated for the given slot. Storage for a slot may be located in each instance or in the class object itself, for example. The value of the *allocation-type* argument can be either the keyword :instance or the keyword :class. The :allocation slot option may be specified at most once for a given slot. If the :allocation slot option is not specified, the effect is the same as specifying :allocation :instance.

  - If *allocation-type* is :instance, a local slot of the given name is allocated in each instance of the class.

  - If *allocation-type* is :class, a shared slot of the given name is allocated. The value of the slot is shared by all instances of the class. If a class C_1 defines such a shared slot, any subclass C_2 of C_1 will share this single slot unless the defclass form for C_2 specifies a slot of the same name or there is a superclass of C_2 that precedes C_1 in the class precedence list of C_2 and that defines a slot of the same name.

- The :initform slot option is used to provide a default initial value form to be used in the initialization of the slot. The :initform slot option may be specified at most once for a given slot. This form is evaluated every time it is used to initialize the slot. The lexical environment in which this form is evaluated is the lexical environment in which the defclass form was evaluated. Note that the lexical environment refers both to variables and to functions. For local slots, the dynamic environment is the dynamic environment in which make-instance was called; for shared slots, the dynamic environment is the dynamic environment in which the defclass form was evaluated. See section 28.1.9.

  No implementation is permitted to extend the syntax of defclass to allow (*slot-name form*) as an abbreviation for (*slot-name* :initform *form*).

- The `:initarg` slot option declares an initialization argument named *initarg-name* and specifies that this initialization argument initializes the given slot. If the initialization argument has a value in the call to `initialize-instance`, the value will be stored into the given slot, and the slot's `:initform` slot option, if any, is not evaluated. If none of the initialization arguments specified for a given slot has a value, the slot is initialized according to the `:initform` slot option, if specified. The `:initarg` slot option can be specified more than once for a given slot. The *initarg-name* argument can be any symbol.

- The `:type` slot option specifies that the contents of the slot will always be of the specified data type. It effectively declares the result type of the reader generic function when applied to an object of this class. The result of attempting to store in a slot a value that does not satisfy the type of the slot is undefined. The `:type` slot option may be specified at most once for a given slot. The `:type` slot option is further discussed in section 28.1.3.2.

- The `:documentation` slot option provides a documentation string for the slot.

Each class option is an option that refers to the class as a whole or to all class slots. The following class options are available:

- The `:default-initargs` class option is followed by a list of alternating initialization argument names and default initial value forms. If any of these initialization arguments does not appear in the initialization argument list supplied to `make-instance`, the corresponding default initial value form is evaluated, and the initialization argument name and the form's value are added to the end of the initialization argument list before the instance is created (see section 28.1.9). The default initial value form is evaluated each time it is used. The lexical environment in which this form is evaluated is the lexical environment in which the `defclass` form was evaluated. The dynamic environment is the dynamic environment in which `make-instance` was called. If an initialization argument name appears more than once in a `:default-initargs` class option, an error is signaled. The `:default-initargs` class option may be specified at most once.

- The `:documentation` class option causes a documentation string to be attached to the class name. The documentation type for this string is `type`. The form (`documentation` *class-name* `'type`) may be used to retrieve the documentation string. The `:documentation` class option may be specified at most once.

- The `:metaclass` class option is used to specify that instances of the class being defined are to have a different metaclass than the default provided by the system (the class `standard-class`). The *class-name* argument is the name of the desired metaclass. The `:metaclass` class option may be specified at most once.

The new class object is returned as the result.

If a class with the same proper name already exists and that class is an instance of standard-class, and if the defclass form for the definition of the new class specifies a class of class standard-class, the existing class is redefined, and instances of it (and its subclasses) are updated to the new definition at the time that they are next accessed (see section 28.1.10).

Note the following rules of defclass for standard classes:

- It is not required that the superclasses of a class be defined before the defclass form for that class is evaluated.

- All the superclasses of a class must be defined before an instance of the class can be made.

- A class must be defined before it can be used as a parameter specializer in a defmethod form.

The Object System may be extended to cover situations where these rules are not obeyed.

Some slot options are inherited by a class from its superclasses, and some can be shadowed or altered by providing a local slot description. No class options except :default-initargs are inherited. For a detailed description of how slots and slot options are inherited, see section 28.1.3.2.

The options to defclass can be extended. An implementation must signal an error if it observes a class option or a slot option that is not implemented locally.

It is valid to specify more than one reader, writer, accessor, or initialization argument for a slot. No other slot option may appear more than once in a single slot description, or an error is signaled.

If no reader, writer, or accessor is specified for a slot, the slot can be accessed only by the function slot-value.

See sections 28.1.2, 28.1.3, 28.1.10, 28.1.5, 28.1.9 as well as slot-value, make-instance, and initialize-instance.

---

defgeneric *function-name lambda-list*   [*Macro*]
              ⟦ ↓*option* | {*method-description*}* ⟧

function-name ::= {*symbol* | (setf *symbol*)}
lambda-list ::= ({*var*}*
                  [&optional {*var* | (*var*)}*]
                  [&rest *var*]
                  [&key {*keyword-parameter*}* [&allow-other-keys]])

keyword-parameter ::= *var* | ({*var* | (*keyword var*)})

option ::= (`:argument-precedence-order` {*parameter-name*}⁺)

      | (`declare` {*declaration*}⁺)

      | (`:documentation` *string*)

      | (`:method-combination` *symbol* {*arg*}*)

      | (`:generic-function-class` *class-name*)

      | (`:method-class` *class-name*)

method-description ::= (`:method` {*method-qualifier*}*

                      specialized-lambda-list

                      ⟦ {*declaration*}* | *documentation* ⟧

                      {*form*}*)

method-qualifier ::= *non-nil-atom*

specialized-lambda-list ::=

    ({*var* | (*var parameter-specializer-name*)}*

    [`&optional` {*var* | (*var* [*initform* [*supplied-p-parameter*]])}*]

    [`&rest` *var*]

    [`&key` {*specialized-keyword-parameter*}* [`&allow-other-keys`]]

    [`&aux` {*var* | (*var* [*initform*])}*])

specialized-keyword-parameter ::=

    var | ({*var* | (*keyword var*)} [*initform* [*supplied-p-parameter*]])

parameter-specializer-name ::= *symbol* | (`eql` *eql-specializer-form*)

The macro `defgeneric` is used to define a generic function or to specify options and declarations that pertain to a generic function as a whole.

If (`fboundp` *function-name*) is `nil`, a new generic function is created. If (`fdefinition` *function-specifier*) is a generic function, that generic function is modified. If *function-name*/ names a non-generic function, a macro, or a special form, an error is signaled.

[X3J13 voted in March 1989 ⟨89⟩ to use `fdefinition` in the previous paragraph, as shown, rather than `symbol-function`, as it appeared in the original report on CLOS [5, 7]. The vote also changed all occurrences of *function-specifier* in the original report to *function-name*; this change is reflected here.—GLS]

Each *method-description* defines a method on the generic function. The lambda-list of each method must be congruent with the lambda-list specified by the *lambda-list* option. If this condition does not hold, an error is signaled. See section 28.1.6.4 for a definition of congruence in this context.

The macro `defgeneric` returns the generic function object as its result.

The *function-name* argument is a non-`nil` symbol or a list of the form (`setf` *symbol*).

The *lambda-list* argument is an ordinary function lambda-list with the following exceptions:

- The use of &aux is not allowed.

- Optional and keyword arguments may not have default initial value forms nor use supplied-p parameters. The generic function passes to the method all the argument values passed to it, and only those; default values are not supported. Note that optional and keyword arguments in method definitions, however, can have default initial value forms and can use supplied-p parameters.

The following options are provided. A given option may occur only once, or an error is signaled.

- The :argument-precedence-order option is used to specify the order in which the required arguments in a call to the generic function are tested for specificity when selecting a particular method. Each required argument, as specified in the *lambda-list* argument, must be included exactly once as a *parameter-name* so that the full and unambiguous precedence order is supplied. If this condition is not met, an error is signaled.

- The declare option is used to specify declarations that pertain to the generic function. The following standard Common Lisp declaration is allowed:

  - An optimize declaration specifies whether method selection should be optimized for speed or space, but it has no effect on methods. To control how a method is optimized, an optimize declaration must be placed directly in the defmethod form or method description. The optimization qualities speed and space are the only qualities this standard requires, but an implementation can extend the Common Lisp Object System to recognize other qualities. A simple implementation that has only one method selection technique and ignores the optimize declaration is valid.

  The special, ftype, function, inline, notinline, and declaration declarations are not permitted. Individual implementations can extend the declare option to support additional declarations. If an implementation notices a declaration that it does not support and that has not been proclaimed as a non-standard declaration name in a declaration proclamation, it should issue a warning.

- The :documentation argument associates a documentation string with the generic function. The documentation type for this string is function. The form (documentation *function-name* 'function) may be used to retrieve this string.

- The :generic-function-class option may be used to specify that the generic function is to have a different class than the default provided by the system (the class standard-generic-function). The *class-name* argument is the name of a class that can be the class of a generic function. If *function-name* specifies an existing generic function that has a different value for the :generic-function-class argument and the new generic function class is compatible with the old, change-class is called to change the class of the generic function; otherwise an error is signaled.

- The :method-class option is used to specify that all methods on this generic function are to have a different class from the default provided by the system (the class standard-method). The *class-name* argument is the name of a class that is capable of being the class of a method.

- The :method-combination option is followed by a symbol that names a type of method combination. The arguments (if any) that follow that symbol depend on the type of method combination. Note that the standard method combination type does not support any arguments. However, all types of method combination defined by the short form of define-method-combination accept an optional argument named *order*, defaulting to :most-specific-first, where a value of :most-specific-last reverses the order of the primary methods without affecting the order of the auxiliary methods.

The *method-description* arguments define methods that will be associated with the generic function. The *method-qualifier* and *specialized-lambda-list* arguments in a method description are the same as for defmethod.

The *form* arguments specify the method body. The body of the method is enclosed in an implicit block. If *function-name* is a symbol, this block bears the same name as the generic function. If *function-name* is a list of the form (setf *symbol*), the name of the block is *symbol*.

The generic function object is returned as the result.

The effect of the defgeneric macro is as if the following three steps were performed: first, methods defined by previous defgeneric forms are removed; second, ensure-generic-function is called; and finally, methods specified by the current defgeneric form are added to the generic function.

If no method descriptions are specified and a generic function of the same name does not already exist, a generic function with no methods is created.

The *lambda-list* argument of defgeneric specifies the shape of lambda-lists for the methods on this generic function. All methods on the resulting generic function must have lambda-lists that are congruent with this shape. If a defgeneric form is evaluated and some methods for that generic function have lambda-lists that are not congruent with that given in the defgeneric form, an error is signaled. For further details on method congruence, see section 28.1.6.4.

Implementations can extend defgeneric to include other options. It is required that an implementation signal an error if it observes an option that is not implemented locally.

See section 28.1.6.4 as well as defmethod, ensure-generic-function, and generic-function.

---

define-method-combination *name* ⟦ ↓*short-form-option* ⟧   [*Macro*]
define-method-combination *name lambda-list*   [*Macro*]
       ({*method-group-specifier*}*)
       [(:arguments . *lambda-list*)]
       [(:generic-function *generic-fn-symbol*)]
       ⟦ {*declaration*}* | *doc-string* ⟧
       {*form*}*

short-form-option ::= :documentation *string*
     | :identity-with-one-argument *boolean*
     | :operator *operator*
method-group-specifier ::= (*variable* { {*qualifier-pattern*}+ | *predicate*}
      ⟦ ↓*long-form-option* ⟧)
long-form-option ::= :description *format-string*
     | :order *order*
     | :required *boolean*

The macro define-method-combination is used to define new types of method combination.

There are two forms of define-method-combination. The short form is a simple facility for the cases that are expected to be most commonly needed. The long form is more powerful but more verbose. It resembles defmacro in that the body is an expression, usually using backquote, that computes a Lisp form. Thus arbitrary control structures can be implemented. The long form also allows arbitrary processing of method qualifiers.

In both the short and long forms, *name* is a symbol. By convention, non-keyword, non-nil symbols are usually used.

The short-form syntax of define-method-combination is recognized when the second subform is a non-nil symbol or is not present. When the short form is used, *name* is defined as a type of method combination that produces a Lisp form (*operator method-call method-call* ...). The *operator* is a symbol that can be the name of a function, macro, or special form. The *operator* can be specified by a keyword option; it defaults to *name*.

Keyword options for the short form are the following:

- The :documentation option is used to document the method-combination type.

- The :identity-with-one-argument option enables an optimization when *boolean* is true (the default is false). If there is exactly one applicable method and it is a primary method, that method serves as the effective method and *operator* is not called. This optimization avoids the need to create a new effective method and avoids the overhead of a function call. This option is designed to be used with operators such as progn, and, +, and max.

- The :operator option specifies the name of the operator. The *operator* argument is a symbol that can be the name of a function, macro, or special form. By convention, *name* and *operator* are often the same symbol. This is the default, but it is not required.

None of the subforms is evaluated.

These types of method combination require exactly one qualifier per method. An error is signaled if there are applicable methods with no qualifiers or with qualifiers that are not supported by the method combination type.

A method combination procedure defined in this way recognizes two roles for methods. A method whose one qualifier is the symbol naming this type of method combination is defined to be a primary method. At least one primary method must be applicable or an error is signaled. A method with :around as its one qualifier is an auxiliary method that behaves the same as an :around method in standard method combination. The function call-next-method can be used only in :around methods; it cannot be used in primary methods defined by the short form of the define-method-combination macro.

A method combination procedure defined in this way accepts an optional argument named *order*, which defaults to :most-specific-first. A value of :most-specific-last reverses the order of the primary methods without affecting the order of the auxiliary methods.

The short form automatically includes error checking and support for :around methods.

For a discussion of built-in method combination types, see section 28.1.7.4.

The long-form syntax of define-method-combination is recognized when the second subform is a list.

The *lambda-list* argument is an ordinary lambda-list. It receives any arguments provided after the name of the method combination type in the :method-combination option to defgeneric.

A list of method group specifiers follows. Each specifier selects a subset of the applicable methods to play a particular role, either by matching their qualifiers against some patterns or by testing their qualifiers with a predicate. These method group specifiers define all method qualifiers that can be used with this type of method combination. If an applicable method does not fall into any method group, the system signals the error that the method is invalid for the kind of method combination in use.

Each method group specifier names a variable. During the execution of the forms in the body of define-method-combination, this variable is bound to a list of the methods in the method group. The methods in this list occur in most-specific-first order.

A qualifier pattern is a list or the symbol *. A method matches a qualifier pattern if the method's list of qualifiers is equal to the qualifier pattern (except that the symbol * in a qualifier pattern matches anything). Thus a qualifier pattern can be one of the following: the empty list (), which matches unqualified methods; the symbol *, which matches all methods; a true list, which matches methods with the same number of qualifiers as the length of the list when each qualifier matches the corresponding list element; or a dotted list that ends in the symbol * (the * matches any number of additional qualifiers).

Each applicable method is tested against the qualifier patterns and predicates in left-to-right order. As soon as a qualifier pattern matches or a predicate returns true, the method becomes a member of the corresponding method group and no further tests are made. Thus if a method could be a member of more than one method group, it joins only the first such group. If a method group has more than one qualifier pattern, a method need only satisfy one of the qualifier patterns to be a member of the group.

The name of a predicate function can appear instead of qualifier patterns in a method group specifier. The predicate is called for each method that has not been assigned to an earlier method group; it is called with one argument, the method's qualifier list. The predicate should return true if the method is to be a member of the method group. A predicate can be distinguished from a qualifier pattern because it is a symbol other than nil or *.

If there is an applicable method whose qualifiers are not valid for the method combination type, the function invalid-method-error is called.

Method group specifiers can have keyword options following the qualifier patterns or predicate. Keyword options can be distinguished from additional qualifier patterns because they are neither lists nor the symbol *. The keyword options are:

- The :description option is used to provide a description of the role of methods in the method group. Programming environment tools use (apply #'format stream *format-string* (method-qualifiers *method*)) to print this description, which is expected to be concise. This keyword option allows the description of a method qualifier to be defined in the same module that defines the meaning of the method qualifier. In most cases, *format-string* will not contain any format directives, but they are available for generality. If :description is not specified, a default description is generated based on the variable name and the qualifier patterns and on whether this method group includes the unqualified methods. The argument *format-string* is not evaluated.

- The :order option specifies the order of methods. The *order* argument is a form that evaluates to :most-specific-first or :most-specific-last. If it evaluates to any other value, an error is signaled. This keyword option is a convenience and does not add any expressive power. If :order is not specified, it defaults to :most-specific-first.

- The :required option specifies whether at least one method in this method group is required. If the *boolean* argument is non-nil and the method group is empty (that is, no applicable methods match the qualifier patterns or satisfy the predicate), an error is signaled. This keyword option is a convenience and does not add any expressive power. If :required is not specified, it defaults to nil. The *boolean* argument is not evaluated.

The use of method group specifiers provides a convenient syntax to select methods, to divide them among the possible roles, and to perform the necessary error checking. It is possible to perform further filtering of methods in the body forms by using normal list-processing operations and the functions method-qualifiers and invalid-method-error. It is permissible to use setq on the variables named in the method group specifiers and to bind additional variables. It is also possible to bypass the method group specifier mechanism and do everything in the body forms. This is accomplished by writing a single method group with * as its only qualifier pattern; the variable is then bound to a list of all of the applicable methods, in most-specific-first order.

The body *forms* compute and return the Lisp form that specifies how the methods are combined, that is, the effective method. The effective method uses the macro call-method. The definition of this macro has lexical scope and is available only in an effective method form. Given a method object in one of the lists produced by the method group specifiers and a list of next methods, the macro call-method will invoke the method so that call-next-method will have available the next methods.

When an effective method has no effect other than to call a single method, some implementations employ an optimization that uses the single method directly as the effective method, thus avoiding the need to create a new effective method. This optimization is active when the effective method form consists entirely of an invo-cation of the call-method macro whose first subform is a method object and whose second subform is nil. Each define-method-combination body is responsible for stripping off redundant invocations of progn, and, multiple-value-prog1, and the like, if this optimization is desired.

The list (:arguments . *lambda-list*) can appear before any declaration or doc-umentation string. This form is useful when the method combination type performs some specific behavior as part of the combined method and that behavior needs access to the arguments to the generic function. Each parameter variable defined by *lambda-list* is bound to a form that can be inserted into the effective method. When this form is evaluated during execution of the effective method, its value is the corresponding argument to the generic function. If *lambda-list* is not congruent to the generic function's lambda-list, additional ignored parameters are automatic-ally inserted until it is congruent. Thus it is permissible for *lambda-list* to receive fewer arguments than the number that the generic function expects.

Erroneous conditions detected by the body should be reported with method-combination-error or invalid-method-error; these functions add any neces-sary contextual information to the error message and will signal the appropriate error.

The body *forms* are evaluated inside the bindings created by the lambda-list and method group specifiers. Declarations at the head of the body are positioned directly inside bindings created by the lambda-list and outside the bindings of the method group variables. Thus method group variables cannot be declared.

Within the body *forms*, *generic-function-symbol* is bound to the generic function object.

If a *doc-string* argument is present, it provides the documentation for the method combination type.

The functions method-combination-error and invalid-method-error can be called from the body *forms* or from functions called by the body *forms*. The actions of these two functions can depend on implementation-dependent dynamic variables automatically bound before the generic function compute-effective-method is called.

Note that two methods with identical specializers, but with different qualifiers, are not ordered by the algorithm described in step 2 of the method selection and combination process described in section 28.1.7. Normally the two meth-ods play different roles in the effective method because they have different qual-ifiers, and no matter how they are ordered in the result of step 2 the effective method is the same. If the two methods play the same role and their order mat-ters, an error is signaled. This happens as part of the qualifier pattern matching in define-method-combination.

The value returned by the define-method-combination macro is the new method combination object.

Most examples of the long form of define-method-combination also illustrate the use of the related functions that are provided as part of the declarative method combination facility.

```
;;; Examples of the short form of define-method-combination

(define-method-combination and :identity-with-one-argument t)

(defmethod func and ((x class1) y)
  ...)

;;; The equivalent of this example in the long form is:

(define-method-combination and
        (&optional (order ':most-specific-first))
        ((around (:around))
         (primary (and) :order order :required t))
  (let ((form (if (rest primary)
                  `(and ,@(mapcar #'(lambda (method)
                                      `(call-method ,method ()))
                                  primary))
                  `(call-method ,(first primary) ()))))
    (if around
        `(call-method ,(first around)
                      (,@(rest around)
                       (make-method ,form)))
        form)))


;;; Examples of the long form of define-method-combination

;;; The default method-combination technique

(define-method-combination standard ()
        ((around (:around))
         (before (:before))
         (primary () :required t)
         (after (:after)))
```

```
    (flet ((call-methods (methods)
             (mapcar #'(lambda (method)
                         `(call-method ,method ()))
                     methods)))
      (let ((form (if (or before after (rest primary))
                      `(multiple-value-prog1
                         (progn ,@(call-methods before)
                                (call-method ,(first primary)
                                             ,(rest primary)))
                       ,@(call-methods (reverse after)))
                      `(call-method ,(first primary) ()))))
        (if around
            `(call-method ,(first around)
                          (,@(rest around)
                           (make-method ,form)))
            form)))))

;;; A simple way to try several methods until one returns non-nil

(define-method-combination or ()
        ((methods (or)))
  `(or ,@(mapcar #'(lambda (method)
                     `(call-method ,method ()))
                 methods)))

;;; A more complete version of the preceding

(define-method-combination or
        (&optional (order ':most-specific-first))
        ((around (:around))
         (primary (or)))
  ;; Process the order argument
  (case order
    (:most-specific-first)
    (:most-specific-last (setq primary (reverse primary)))
    (otherwise (method-combination-error
                "~S is an invalid order.~@
                 :most-specific-first and :most-specific-last ~
                 are the possible values."
                                        order)))
```

```
  ;; Must have a primary method
  (unless primary
    (method-combination-error "A primary method is required."))
  ;; Construct the form that calls the primary methods
  (let ((form (if (rest primary)
                  `(or ,@(mapcar #'(lambda (method)
                                     `(call-method ,method ())))
                              primary))
                  `(call-method ,(first primary) ()))))
    ;; Wrap the around methods around that form
    (if around
        `(call-method ,(first around)
                      (,@(rest around)
                       (make-method ,form)))
        form)))

;;; The same thing, using the :order and :required keyword options
(define-method-combination or
        (&optional (order ':most-specific-first))
        ((around (:around))
         (primary (or) :order order :required t))
  (let ((form (if (rest primary)
                  `(or ,@(mapcar #'(lambda (method)
                                     `(call-method ,method ())))
                              primary))
                  `(call-method ,(first primary) ()))))
    (if around
        `(call-method ,(first around)
                      (,@(rest around)
                       (make-method ,form)))
        form)))

;;; This short-form call is behaviorally identical to the preceding.
(define-method-combination or :identity-with-one-argument t)

;;; Order methods by positive integer qualifiers; note that :around
;;; methods are disallowed here in order to keep the example small.

(define-method-combination example-method-combination ()
        ((methods positive-integer-qualifier-p))
```

```
`(progn ,@(mapcar #'(lambda (method)
                      `(call-method ,method ()))
                  (stable-sort methods #'<
                    :key #'(lambda (method)
                             (first (method-qualifiers
                                      method)))))))))

(defun positive-integer-qualifier-p (method-qualifiers)
  (and (= (length method-qualifiers) 1)
       (typep (first method-qualifiers) '(integer 0 *))))

;;; Example of the use of :arguments
(define-method-combination progn-with-lock ()
        ((methods ()))
        (:arguments object)
  `(unwind-protect
       (progn (lock (object-lock ,object))
              ,@(mapcar #'(lambda (method)
                            `(call-method ,method ()))
                        methods))
     (unlock (object-lock ,object)))))
```

The :method-combination option of defgeneric is used to specify that a generic function should use a particular method combination type. The argument to the :method-combination option is the name of a method combination type.

See sections 28.1.7 and 28.1.7.4 as well as call-method, method-qualifiers, method-combination-error, invalid-method-error, and defgeneric.

---

defmethod *function-name* {*method-qualifier*}*   [*Macro*]
            specialized-lambda-list
            ⟦ {*declaration*}* | *doc-string* ⟧ {*form*}*

function-name ::= {*symbol* | (setf *symbol*)}
method-qualifier ::= *non-nil-atom*
parameter-specializer-name ::= *symbol* | (eql *eql-specializer-form*)

The macro defmethod defines a method on a generic function.

If (fboundp *function-name*) is nil, a generic function is created with default values for the argument precedence order (each argument is more specific than the arguments to its right in the argument list), for the generic function class (the class `standard-generic-function`), for the method class (the class `standard-method`), and for the method combination type (the standard method combination type). The lambda-list of the generic function is congruent with the lambda-list of the method being defined; if the `defmethod` form mentions keyword arguments, the lambda-list of the generic function will mention `&key` (but no keyword arguments). If *function-name* names a non-generic function, a macro, or a special form, an error is signaled.

If a generic function is currently named by *function-name*, where *function-name* is a symbol or a list of the form (`setf` *symbol*), the lambda-list of the method must be congruent with the lambda-list of the generic function. If this condition does not hold, an error is signaled. See section 28.1.6.4 for a definition of congruence in this context.

The *function-name* argument is a non-`nil` symbol or a list of the form (`setf` *symbol*). It names the generic function on which the method is defined.

Each *method-qualifier* argument is an object that is used by method combination to identify the given method. A method qualifier is a non-`nil` atom. The method combination type may further restrict what a method qualifier may be. The standard method combination type allows for unqualified methods or methods whose sole qualifier is the keyword `:before`, the keyword `:after`, or the keyword `:around`.

A *specialized-lambda-list* is like an ordinary function lambda-list except that the name of a required parameter can be replaced by a specialized parameter, a list of the form (*variable-name parameter-specializer-name*). Only required parameters may be specialized. A parameter specializer name is a symbol that names a class or (`eql` *eql-specializer-form*). The parameter specializer name (`eql` *eql-specializer-form*) indicates that the corresponding argument must be `eql` to the object that is the value of *eql-specializer-form* for the method to be applicable. If no parameter specializer name is specified for a given required parameter, the parameter specializer defaults to the class named `t`. See section 28.1.6.2.

The *form* arguments specify the method body. The body of the method is enclosed in an implicit block. If *function-name* is a symbol, this block bears the same name as the generic function. If *function-name* is a list of the form (`setf` *symbol*), the name of the block is *symbol*.

The result of `defmethod` is the method object.

The class of the method object that is created is that given by the method class option of the generic function on which the method is defined.

If the generic function already has a method that agrees with the method being defined on parameter specializers and qualifiers, `defmethod` replaces the existing method with the one now being defined. See section 28.1.6.3 for a definition of agreement in this context.

The parameter specializers are derived from the parameter specializer names as described in section 28.1.6.2.

The expansion of the `defmethod` macro refers to each specialized parameter (see the `ignore` declaration specifier), including parameters that have an explicit parameter specializer name of t. This means that a compiler warning does not occur if the body of the method does not refer to a specialized parameter. Note that a parameter that specializes on t is not synonymous with an unspecialized parameter in this context.

See sections 28.1.6.2, 28.1.6.4, and 28.1.6.3.

[At this point the original CLOS report [5, 7] contained a specification for `describe` as a generitc function. This specification is omitted here because X3J13 voted in March 1989 ⟨63⟩ not to make `describe` a generic function after all (see `describe-object`).—GLS]

`documentation` *x* `&optional` *doc-type*	[*Generic function*]
`documentation`	[*Primary method*]
`(`*method* `standard-method) &optional` *doc-type*	
`documentation`	[*Primary method*]
`(`*generic-function* `standard-generic-function) &optional` *doc-type*	
`documentation (`*class* `standard-class) &optional` *doc-type*	[*Primary method*]
`documentation`	[*Primary method*]
`(`*method-combination* `method-combination) &optional` *doc-type*	
`documentation`	[*Primary method*]
`(`*slot-description* `standard-slot-description) &optional` *doc-type*	
`documentation (`*symbol* `symbol) &optional` *doc-type*	[*Primary method*]
`documentation (`*list* `list) &optional` *doc-type*	[*Primary method*]

The ordinary function `documentation` (see section 25.2) is replaced by a generic function. The generic function `documentation` returns the documentation string associated with the given object if it is available; otherwise `documentation` returns `nil`.

The first argument of `documentation` is a symbol, a function-name list of the form (`setf` *symbol*), a method object, a class object, a generic function object, a method combination object, or a slot description object. Whether a second argument should be supplied depends on the type of the first argument.

- If the first argument is a method object, a class object, a generic function object, a method combination object, or a slot description object, the second argument must not be supplied, or an error is signaled.

- If the first argument is a symbol or a list of the form (setf *symbol*), the second argument must be supplied.

  – The forms

    (documentation *symbol* ´function)

    and

    (documentation ´(setf *symbol*) ´function)

    return the documentation string of the function, generic function, special form, or macro named by the symbol or list.

  – The form (documentation *symbol* ´variable) returns the documentation string of the special variable or constant named by the symbol.

  – The form (documentation *symbol* ´structure) returns the documentation string of the defstruct structure named by the symbol.

  – The form (documentation *symbol* ´type) returns the documentation string of the class object named by the symbol, if there is such a class. If there is no such class, it returns the documentation string of the type specifier named by the symbol.

  – The form (documentation *symbol* ´setf) returns the documentation string of the defsetf or define-setf-method definition associated with the symbol.

  – The form (documentation *symbol* ´method-combination) returns the documentation string of the method combination type named by the symbol.

An implementation may extend the set of symbols that are acceptable as the second argument. If a symbol is not recognized as an acceptable argument by the implementation, an error must be signaled.

The documentation string associated with the given object is returned unless none is available, in which case documentation returns nil.

(setf documentation) *new-value* *x* &optional *doc-type*   [*Generic function*]
(setf documentation) *new-value*   [*Primary method*]
  (*method* standard-method) &optional *doc-type*
(setf documentation) *new-value*   [*Primary method*]
  (*generic-function* standard-generic-function) &optional *doc-type*
(setf documentation) *new-value*   [*Primary method*]
  (*class* standard-class) &optional *doc-type*
(setf documentation) *new-value*   [*Primary method*]
  (*method-combination* method-combination) &optional *doc-type*
(setf documentation) *new-value*   [*Primary method*]
  (*slot-description* standard-slot-description) &optional *doc-type*
(setf documentation) *new-value*   [*Primary method*]
  (*symbol* symbol) &optional *doc-type*
(setf documentation) *new-value*   [*Primary method*]
  (*list* list) &optional *doc-type*

The generic function (setf documentation) is used to update the documentation. The first argument of (setf documentation) is the new documentation.

The second argument of documentation is a symbol, a function-name list of the form (setf *symbol*), a method object, a class object, a generic function object, a method combination object, or a slot description object. Whether a third argument should be supplied depends on the type of the second argument. See documentation.

ensure-generic-function *function-name* &key :lambda-list   [*Function*]
  :argument-precedence-order :declare :documentation
  :generic-function-class :method-combination :method-class
  :environment

function-name ::= {*symbol* | (setf *symbol*)}

The function ensure-generic-function is used to define a globally named generic function with no methods or to specify or modify options and declarations that pertain to a globally named generic function as a whole.

If (fboundp *function-name*) is nil, a new generic function is created. If (fdefinition *function-name*) is a non-generic function, a macro, or a special form, an error is signaled.

[X3J13 voted in March 1989 ⟨89⟩ to use fdefinition in the previous paragraph, as shown, rather than symbol-function, as it appeared in the original report on CLOS [5, 7]. The vote also changed all occurrences of *function-specifier* in the original report to *function-name*; this change is reflected here.—GLS]

If *function-name* specifies a generic function that has a different value for any of the following arguments, the generic function is modified to have the new value: :argument-precedence-order, :declare, :documentation, :method-combination.

If *function-name* specifies a generic function that has a different value for the :lambda-list argument, and the new value is congruent with the lambda-lists of all existing methods or there are no methods, the value is changed; otherwise an error is signaled.

If *function-name* specifies a generic function that has a different value for the :generic-function-class argument and if the new generic function class is compatible with the old, change-class is called to change the class of the generic function; otherwise an error is signaled.

If *function-name* specifies a generic function that has a different :method-class value, the value is changed but any existing methods are not changed.

The *function-name* argument is a symbol or a list of the form (setf *symbol*).

The keyword arguments correspond to the *option* arguments of defgeneric, except that the :method-class and :generic-function-class arguments can be class objects as well as names.

The :environment argument is the same as the &environment argument to macro expansion functions. It is typically used to distinguish between compile-time and run-time environments.

The :method-combination argument is a method combination object.

The generic function object is returned. See defgeneric.

find-class *symbol* &optional *errorp environment* [*Function*]

The function find-class returns the class object named by the given symbol in the given environment.

The first argument to find-class is a symbol.

If there is no such class and the *errorp* argument is not supplied or is non-nil, find-class signals an error. If there is no such class and the *errorp* argument is nil, find-class returns nil. The default value of *errorp* is t.

The optional *environment* argument is the same as the &environment argument to macro expansion functions. It is typically used to distinguish between compile-time and run-time environments.

The result of find-class is the class object named by the given symbol.

The class associated with a particular symbol can be changed by using setf with find-class. The results are undefined if the user attempts to change the class associated with a symbol that is defined as a type specifier in chapter 4. See section 28.1.4.

find-method *generic-function method-qualifiers*   *[Generic function]*
            specializers &optional *errorp*

find-method   *[Primary method]*
  (*generic-function* standard-generic-function) *method-qualifiers*
  specializers &optional *errorp*

The generic function find-method takes a generic function and returns the method
object that agrees on method qualifiers and parameter specializers with the *method-
qualifiers* and *specializers* arguments of find-method. See section 28.1.6.3 for a
definition of agreement in this context.

The *generic-function* argument is a generic function.

The *method-qualifiers* argument is a list of the method qualifiers for the method.
The order of the method qualifiers is significant.

The *specializers* argument is a list of the parameter specializers for the method.
It must correspond in length to the number of required arguments of the generic
function, or an error is signaled. This means that to obtain the default method on a
given generic function, a list whose elements are the class named t must be given.

If there is no such method and the *errorp* argument is not supplied or is non-nil,
find-method signals an error. If there is no such method and the *errorp* argument
is nil, find-method returns nil. The default value of *errorp* is t.

The result of find-method is the method object with the given method qualifiers
and parameter specializers.

See section 28.1.6.3.

function-keywords *method*   *[Generic function]*
function-keywords (*method* standard-method)   *[Primary method]*

The generic function function-keywords is used to return the keyword parameter
specifiers for a given method.

The *method* argument is a method object.

The generic function function-keywords returns two values: a list of the
explicitly named keywords and a boolean that states whether &allow-other-keys
had been specified in the method definition.

generic-flet ({ (*function-name lambda-list*   *[Special form]*
                  ⟦ ↓*option* | {*method-description*}* ⟧)}*)
                {*form*}*

The generic-flet special form is analogous to the flet special form. It produces
new generic functions and establishes new lexical function definition bindings.

Each generic function is created with the set of methods specified by its method descriptions.

The special form generic-flet is used to define generic functions whose names are meaningful only locally and to execute a series of forms with these function definition bindings. Any number of such local generic functions may be defined.

The names of functions defined by generic-flet have lexical scope; they retain their local definitions only within the body of the generic-flet. Any references within the body of the generic-flet to functions whose names are the same as those defined within the generic-flet are thus references to the local functions instead of to any global functions of the same names. The scope of these generic function definition bindings, however, includes only the body of generic-flet, not the definitions themselves. Within the method bodies, local function names that match those being defined refer to global functions defined outside the generic-flet. It is thus not possible to define recursive functions with generic-flet.

The *function-name*, *lambda-list*, *option*, *method-qualifier*, and *specialized-lambda-list* arguments are the same as for defgeneric.

A generic-flet local method definition is identical in form to the method definition part of a defmethod.

The body of each method is enclosed in an implicit block. If *function-name* is a symbol, this block bears the same name as the generic function. If *function-name* is a list of the form (setf *symbol*), the name of the block is *symbol*.

The result returned by generic-flet is the value or values returned by the last form executed. If no forms are specified, generic-flet returns nil.

See generic-labels, defmethod, defgeneric, and generic-function.

generic-function *lambda-list* [[↓*option* | {*method-description*}*]]   [*Macro*]

option ::= (:argument-precedence-order {*parameter-name*}⁺)
        | (declare {*declaration*}⁺)
        | (:documentation *string*)
        | (:method-combination *symbol* {*arg*}*)
        | (:generic-function-class *class-name*)
        | (:method-class *class-name*)
method-description ::= (:method {*method-qualifier*}*
                          specialized-lambda-list
                          {*declaration* | *documentation*}*
                          {*form*}*)

The `generic-function` macro creates an anonymous generic function. The generic function is created with the set of methods specified by its method descriptions.

The *option, method-qualifier,* and *specialized-lambda-list* arguments are the same as for `defgeneric`.

The generic function object is returned as the result.

If no method descriptions are specified, an anonymous generic function with no methods is created.

See `defgeneric`, `generic-flet`, `generic-labels`, and `defmethod`.

`generic-labels` ({(*function-name lambda-list*   [*Special form*]
                 ⟦ ↓*option* | {*method-description*}* ⟧)}*)
              {*form*}*

The `generic-labels` special form is analogous to the `labels` special form. It produces new generic functions and establishes new lexical function definition bindings. Each generic function is created with the set of methods specified by its method descriptions.

The special form `generic-labels` is used to define generic functions whose names are meaningful only locally and to execute a series of forms with these function definition bindings. Any number of such local generic functions may be defined.

The names of functions defined by `generic-labels` have lexical scope; they retain their local definitions only within the body of the `generic-labels` construct. Any references within the body of the `generic-labels` construct to functions whose names are the same as those defined within the `generic-labels` form are thus references to the local functions instead of to any global functions of the same names. The scope of these generic function definition bindings includes the method bodies themselves as well as the body of the `generic-labels` construct.

The *function-name, lambda-list, option, method-qualifier,* and *specialized-lambda-list* arguments are the same as for `defgeneric`.

A `generic-labels` local method definition is identical in form to the method definition part of a `defmethod`.

The body of each method is enclosed in an implicit block. If *function-name* is a symbol, this block bears the same name as the generic function. If *function-name* is a list of the form (`setf` *symbol*), the name of the block is *symbol*.

The result returned by `generic-labels` is the value or values returned by the last form executed. If no forms are specified, `generic-labels` returns `nil`.

See `generic-flet`, `defmethod`, `defgeneric`, `generic-function`.

initialize-instance *instance* &rest *initargs*   [*Generic function*]
initialize-instance (*instance* standard-object)   [*Primary method*]
  &rest *initargs*

The generic function initialize-instance is called by make-instance to initialize a newly created instance. The generic function initialize-instance is called with the new instance and the defaulted initialization arguments.

The system-supplied primary method on initialize-instance initializes the slots of the instance with values according to the initialization arguments and the :initform forms of the slots. It does this by calling the generic function shared-initialize with the following arguments: the instance, t (this indicates that all slots for which no initialization arguments are provided should be initialized according to their :initform forms) and the defaulted initialization arguments.

The *instance* argument is the object to be initialized.

The *initargs* argument consists of alternating initialization argument names and values.

The modified instance is returned as the result.

Programmers can define methods for initialize-instance to specify actions to be taken when an instance is initialized. If only :after methods are defined, they will be run after the system-supplied primary method for initialization and therefore will not interfere with the default behavior of initialize-instance.

See sections 28.1.9, 28.1.9.4, and 28.1.9.2 as well as shared-initialize, make-instance, slot-boundp, and slot-makunbound.

invalid-method-error *method format-string* &rest *args*   [*Function*]

The function invalid-method-error is used to signal an error when there is an applicable method whose qualifiers are not valid for the method combination type. The error message is constructed by using a format string and any arguments to it. Because an implementation may need to add additional contextual information to the error message, invalid-method-error should be called only within the dynamic extent of a method combination function.

The function invalid-method-error is called automatically when a method fails to satisfy every qualifier pattern and predicate in a define-method-combination form. A method combination function that imposes additional restrictions should call invalid-method-error explicitly if it encounters a method it cannot accept.

The *method* argument is the invalid method object.

The *format-string* argument is a control string that can be given to format, and *args* are any arguments required by that string.

Whether `invalid-method-error` returns to its caller or exits via `throw` is implementation-dependent.

See `define-method-combination`.

make-instance *class* &rest *initargs*	[*Generic function*]
make-instance (*class* standard-class) &rest *initargs*	[*Primary method*]
make-instance (*class* symbol) &rest *initargs*	[*Primary method*]

The generic function `make-instance` creates a new instance of the given class.

The generic function `make-instance` may be used as described in section 28.1.9.

The *class* argument is a class object or a symbol that names a class. The remaining arguments form a list of alternating initialization argument names and values.

If the second of the preceding methods is selected, that method invokes `make-instance` on the arguments (`find-class` *class*) and *initargs*.

The initialization arguments are checked within `make-instance` (see section 28.1.9).

The new instance is returned.

The meta-object protocol can be used to define new methods on `make-instance` to replace the object-creation protocol.

See section 28.1.9 as well as `defclass`, `initialize-instance`, and `class-of`.

make-instances-obsolete *class*	[*Generic function*]
make-instances-obsolete (*class* standard-class)	[*Primary method*]
make-instances-obsolete (*class* symbol)	[*Primary method*]

The generic function `make-instances-obsolete` is invoked automatically by the system when `defclass` has been used to redefine an existing standard class and the set of local slots accessible in an instance is changed or the order of slots in storage is changed. It can also be explicitly invoked by the user.

The function `make-instances-obsolete` has the effect of initiating the process of updating the instances of the class. During updating, the generic function `update-instance-for-redefined-class` will be invoked.

The *class* argument is a class object symbol that names the class whose instances are to be made obsolete.

If the second of the preceding methods is selected, that method invokes `make-instances-obsolete` on (`find-class` *class*).

The modified class is returned. The result of `make-instances-obsolete` is eq to the *class* argument supplied to the first of the preceding methods.

See section 28.1.10 as well as `update-instance-for-redefined-class`.

`method-combination-error` *format-string* &rest *args*   [*Function*]

The function `method-combination-error` is used to signal an error in method combination. The error message is constructed by using a `format` string and any arguments to it. Because an implementation may need to add additional contextual information to the error message, `method-combination-error` should be called only within the dynamic extent of a method combination function.

The *format-string* argument is a control string that can be given to `format`, and *args* are any arguments required by that string.

Whether `method-combination-error` returns to its caller or exits via `throw` is implementation-dependent.

See `define-method-combination`.

`method-qualifiers` *method*   [*Generic function*]
`method-qualifiers` (*method* `standard-method`)   [*Primary method*]

The generic function `method-qualifiers` returns a list of the qualifiers of the given method.

The *method* argument is a method object.

A list of the qualifiers of the given method is returned.

Example:

```
(setq methods (remove-duplicates methods
                          :from-end t
                          :key #'method-qualifiers
                          :test #'equal))
```

See `define-method-combination`.

`next-method-p`   [*Function*]

The locally defined function `next-method-p` can be used within the body of a method defined by a method-defining form to determine whether a next method exists.

The function `next-method-p` takes no arguments.

The function `next-method-p` returns true or false.

Like `call-next-method`, the function `next-method-p` has lexical scope (for it is defined only within the body of a method defined by a method-defining form) and indefinite extent.

See `call-next-method`.

no-applicable-method *generic-function*   [*Generic function*]
&rest *function-arguments*
no-applicable-method (*generic-function* t)   [*Primary method*]
&rest *function-arguments*

The generic function no-applicable-method is called when a generic function of the class standard-generic-function is invoked and no method on that generic function is applicable. The default method signals an error.

The generic function no-applicable-method is not intended to be called by programmers. Programmers may write methods for it.

The *generic-function* argument of no-applicable-method is the generic function object on which no applicable method was found.

The *function-arguments* argument is a list of the arguments to that generic function.

no-next-method *generic-function method* &rest *args*   [*Generic function*]
no-next-method   [*Primary method*]
(*generic-function* standard-generic-function)
(*method* standard-method) &rest *args*

The generic function no-next-method is called by call-next-method when there is no next method. The system-supplied method on no-next-method signals an error.

The generic function no-next-method is not intended to be called by programmers. Programmers may write methods for it.

The *generic-function* argument is the generic function object to which the method that is the second argument belongs.

The *method* argument is the method that contains the call to call-next-method for which there is no next method.

The *args* argument is a list of the arguments to call-next-method.

See call-next-method.

print-object *object stream*   [*Generic function*]
print-object (*object* standard-object) *stream*   [*Primary method*]

The generic function print-object writes the printed representation of an object to a stream. The function print-object is called by the print system; it should not be called by the user.

Each implementation must provide a method on the class standard-object and methods on enough other classes so as to ensure that there is always an applicable method. Implementations are free to add methods for other classes. Users can write methods for print-object for their own classes if they do not wish to inherit an implementation-supplied method.

The first argument is any Lisp object. The second argument is a stream; it cannot be t or nil.

The function print-object returns its first argument, the object.

Methods on print-object must obey the print control special variables named *print-xxx* for various xxx. The specific details are the following:

- Each method must implement *print-escape*.

- The *print-pretty* control variable can be ignored by most methods other than the one for lists.

- The *print-circle* control variable is handled by the printer and can be ignored by methods.

- The printer takes care of *print-level* automatically, provided that each method handles exactly one level of structure and calls write (or an equivalent function) recursively if there are more structural levels. The printer's decision of whether an object has components (and therefore should not be printed when the printing depth is not less than *print-level*) is implementation-dependent. In some implementations its print-object method is not called; in others the method is called, and the determination that the object has components is based on what it tries to write to the stream.

- Methods that produce output of indefinite length must obey *print-length*, but most methods other than the one for lists can ignore it.

- The *print-base*, *print-radix*, *print-case*, *print-gensym*, and *print-array* control variables apply to specific types of objects and are handled by the methods for those objects.

- X3J13 voted in June 1989 ⟨40⟩ to add the following point. All methods for print-object must obey *print-readably*, which takes precedence over all other printer control variables. This includes both user-defined methods and implementation-defined methods.

If these rules are not obeyed, the results are undefined.

In general, the printer and the print-object methods should not rebind the print control variables as they operate recursively through the structure, but this is implementation-dependent.

In some implementations the stream argument passed to a print-object method is not the original stream but is an intermediate stream that implements part of the printer. Methods should therefore not depend on the identity of this stream.

All of the existing printing functions (write, prinl, print, princ, pprint, write-to-string, prin1-to-string, princ-to-string, the ~S and ~A format operations, and the ~B, ~D, ~E, ~F, ~G, ~$, ~O, ~R, and ~X format operations when they encounter a non-numeric value) are required to be changed to go through the print-object generic function. Each implementation is required to replace its former implementation of printing with one or more print-object methods. Exactly which classes have methods for print-object is not specified; it would be valid for an implementation to have one default method that is inherited by all system-defined classes.

---

reinitialize-instance *instance* &rest *initargs*   [*Generic function*]
reinitialize-instance (*instance* standard-object)   [*Primary method*]
    &rest *initargs*

The generic function reinitialize-instance can be used to change the values of local slots according to initialization arguments. This generic function is called by the Meta-Object Protocol. It can also be called by users.

The system-supplied primary method for reinitialize-instance checks the validity of initialization arguments and signals an error if an initialization argument is supplied that is not declared valid. The method then calls the generic function shared-initialize with the following arguments: the instance, nil (which means no slots should be initialized according to their :initform forms) and the initialization arguments it received.

The *instance* argument is the object to be initialized.

The *initargs* argument consists of alternating initialization argument names and values.

The modified instance is returned as the result.

Initialization arguments are declared valid by using the :initarg option to defclass, or by defining methods for reinitialize-instance or shared-initialize. The keyword name of each keyword parameter specifier in the lambda-list of any method defined on reinitialize-instance or shared-initialize is declared a valid initialization argument name for all classes for which that method is applicable.

See sections 28.1.12, 28.1.9.4, 28.1.9.2 as well as initialize-instance, slot-boundp, update-instance-for-redefined-class, update-instance-for-different-class, slot-makunbound, and shared-initialize.

remove-method *generic-function method*   [*Generic function*]
remove-method   [*Primary method*]
   (*generic-function* standard-generic-function) *method*

The generic function remove-method removes a method from a generic function.
It destructively modifies the specified generic function and returns the modified
generic function as its result.

   The *generic-function* argument is a generic function object.

   The *method* argument is a method object. The function remove-method does
not signal an error if the method is not one of the methods on the generic function.

   The modified generic function is returned. The result of remove-method is eq
to the *generic-function* argument.

   See find-method.

shared-initialize *instance slot-names* &rest *initargs*   [*Generic function*]
shared-initialize (*instance* standard-object)   [*Primary method*]
                   slot-names &rest *initargs*

The generic function shared-initialize is used to fill the slots of an instance
using initialization arguments and :initform forms. It is called when an instance is created, when an instance is re-initialized, when an instance is updated to conform to a redefined class, and when an instance is updated to conform to a different class. The generic function shared-initialize is called by
the system-supplied primary method for initialize-instance, reinitialize-
instance, update-instance-for-redefined-class, and update-instance-
for-different-class.

   The generic function shared-initialize takes the following arguments: the
instance to be initialized, a specification of a set of names of slots accessible in
that instance, and any number of initialization arguments. The arguments after the
first two must form an initialization argument list. The system-supplied primary
method on shared-initialize initializes the slots with values according to the
initialization arguments and specified :initform forms. The second argument
indicates which slots should be initialized according to their :initform forms if
no initialization arguments are provided for those slots.

   The system-supplied primary method behaves as follows, regardless of whether
the slots are local or shared:

• If an initialization argument in the initialization argument list specifies a value
   for that slot, that value is stored into the slot, even if a value has already been
   stored in the slot before the method is run.

- Any slots indicated by the second argument that are still unbound at this point are initialized according to their `:initform` forms. For any such slot that has an `:initform` form, that form is evaluated in the lexical environment of its defining `defclass` form and the result is stored into the slot. For example, if a `:before` method stores a value in the slot, the `:initform` form will not be used to supply a value for the slot.

- The rules mentioned in section 28.1.9.4 are obeyed.

The *instance* argument is the object to be initialized.

The *slot-names* argument specifies the slots that are to be initialized according to their `:initform` forms if no initialization arguments apply. It is supplied in one of three forms as follows:

- It can be a list of slot names, which specifies the set of those slot names.

- It can be `nil`, which specifies the empty set of slot names.

- It can be the symbol t, which specifies the set of all of the slots.

The *initargs* argument consists of alternating initialization argument names and values.

The modified instance is returned as the result.

Initialization arguments are declared valid by using the `:initarg` option to `defclass`, or by defining methods for `shared-initialize`. The keyword name of each keyword parameter specifier in the lambda-list of any method defined on `shared-initialize` is declared a valid initialization argument name for all classes for which that method is applicable.

Implementations are permitted to optimize `:initform` forms that neither produce nor depend on side effects by evaluating these forms and storing them into slots before running any `initialize-instance` methods, rather than by handling them in the primary `initialize-instance` method. (This optimization might be implemented by having the `allocate-instance` method copy a prototype instance.)

Implementations are permitted to optimize default initial value forms for initialization arguments associated with slots by not actually creating the complete initialization argument list when the only method that would receive the complete list is the method on `standard-object`. In this case, default initial value forms can be treated like `:initform` forms. This optimization has no visible effects other than a performance improvement.

See sections 28.1.9, 28.1.9.4, 28.1.9.2 as well as `initialize-instance`, `reinitialize-instance`, `update-instance-for-redefined-class`, `update-instance-for-different-class`, `slot-boundp`, and `slot-makunbound`.

`slot-boundp` *instance slot-name*   *[Function]*

The function `slot-boundp` tests whether a specific slot in an instance is bound.

   The arguments are the instance and the name of the slot.

   The function `slot-boundp` returns true or false.

   This function allows for writing `:after` methods on `initialize-instance` in order to initialize only those slots that have not already been bound.

   If no slot of the given name exists in the instance, `slot-missing` is called as follows:

```
(slot-missing (class-of instance)
              instance
              slot-name
              'slot-boundp)
```

   The function `slot-boundp` is implemented using `slot-boundp-using-class`. See `slot-missing`.

`slot-exists-p` *object slot-name*   *[Function]*

The function `slot-exists-p` tests whether the specified object has a slot of the given name.

   The *object* argument is any object. The *slot-name* argument is a symbol.

   The function `slot-exists-p` returns true or false.

   The function `slot-exists-p` is implemented using `slot-exists-p-using-class`.

`slot-makunbound` *instance slot-name*   *[Function]*

The function `slot-makunbound` restores a slot in an instance to the unbound state.

   The arguments to `slot-makunbound` are the instance and the name of the slot.

   The instance is returned as the result.

   If no slot of the given name exists in the instance, `slot-missing` is called as follows:

```
(slot-missing (class-of instance)
              instance
              slot-name
              'slot-makunbound)
```

   The function `slot-makunbound` is implemented using `slot-makunbound-using-class`. See `slot-missing`.

slot-missing *class object slot-name operation*   [*Generic function*]
        &optional *new-value*
slot-missing (*class* t) *object slot-name operation*   [*Primary method*]
        &optional *new-value*

The generic function slot-missing is invoked when an attempt is made to access a slot in an object whose metaclass is standard-class and the name of the slot provided is not a name of a slot in that class. The default method signals an error.

The generic function slot-missing is not intended to be called by programmers. Programmers may write methods for it.

The required arguments to slot-missing are the class of the object that is being accessed, the object, the slot name, and a symbol that indicates the operation that caused slot-missing to be invoked. The optional argument to slot-missing is used when the operation is attempting to set the value of the slot.

If a method written for slot-missing returns values, these values get returned as the values of the original function invocation.

The generic function slot-missing may be called during evaluation of slot-value, (setf slot-value), slot-boundp, and slot-makunbound. For each of these operations the corresponding symbol for the *operation* argument is slot-value, setf, slot-boundp, and slot-makunbound, respectively.

The set of arguments (including the class of the instance) facilitates defining methods on the metaclass for slot-missing.

slot-unbound *class instance slot-name*   [*Generic function*]
slot-unbound (*class* t) *instance slot-name*   [*Primary method*]

The generic function slot-unbound is called when an unbound slot is read in an instance whose metaclass is standard-class. The default method signals an error.

The generic function slot-unbound is not intended to be called by programmers. Programmers may write methods for it. The function slot-unbound is called only by the function slot-value-using-class and thus indirectly by slot-value.

The arguments to slot-unbound are the class of the instance whose slot was accessed, the instance itself, and the name of the slot.

If a method written for slot-unbound returns values, these values get returned as the values of the original function invocation.

An unbound slot may occur if no :initform form was specified for the slot and the slot value has not been set, or if slot-makunbound has been called on the slot.

See slot-makunbound.

`slot-value` *object slot-name* [*Function*]

The function `slot-value` returns the value contained in the slot *slot-name* of the given object. If there is no slot with that name, `slot-missing` is called. If the slot is unbound, `slot-unbound` is called.

The macro `setf` can be used with `slot-value` to change the value of a slot.

The arguments are the object and the name of the given slot.

The result is the value contained in the given slot.

If an attempt is made to read a slot and no slot of the given name exists in the instance, `slot-missing` is called as follows:

```
(slot-missing (class-of instance)
              instance
              slot-name
              'slot-value)
```

If an attempt is made to write a slot and no slot of the given name exists in the instance, `slot-missing` is called as follows:

```
(slot-missing (class-of instance)
              instance
              slot-name
              'setf
              new-value)
```

The function `slot-value` is implemented using `slot-value-using-class`.

Implementations may optimize `slot-value` by compiling it in-line.

See `slot-missing` and `slot-unbound`.

[At this point the original CLOS report [5, 7] contained a specification for `symbol-macrolet`. This specification is omitted here. Instead, a description of `symbol-macrolet` appears with those of related constructs in chapter 7.—GLS]

`update-instance-for-different-class` [*Generic function*]
   previous current &rest *initargs*
`update-instance-for-different-class` [*Primary method*]
   (*previous* `standard-object`) (*current* `standard-object`) &rest *initargs*

The generic function `update-instance-for-different-class` is not intended to be called by programmers. Programmers may write methods for it. This function is called only by the function `change-class`.

The system-supplied primary method on `update-instance-for-different-class` checks the validity of initialization arguments and signals an error if an initialization argument is supplied that is not declared valid. This method then initializes slots with values according to the initialization arguments and initializes the newly added slots with values according to their :initform forms. It does this by calling the generic function shared-initialize with the following arguments: the instance, a list of names of the newly added slots, and the initialization arguments it received. Newly added slots are those local slots for which no slot of the same name exists in the previous class.

Methods for update-instance-for-different-class can be defined to specify actions to be taken when an instance is updated. If only :after methods for update-instance-for-different-class are defined, they will be run after the system-supplied primary method for initialization and therefore will not interfere with the default behavior of update-instance-for-different-class.

The arguments to update-instance-for-different-class are computed by change-class. When change-class is invoked on an instance, a copy of that instance is made; change-class then destructively alters the original instance. The first argument to update-instance-for-different-class, *previous*, is that copy; it holds the old slot values temporarily. This argument has dynamic extent within change-class; if it is referenced in any way once update-instance-for-different-class returns, the results are undefined. The second argument to update-instance-for-different-class, *current*, is the altered original instance.

The intended use of *previous* is to extract old slot values by using slot-value or with-slots or by invoking a reader generic function, or to run other methods that were applicable to instances of the original class.

The *initargs* argument consists of alternating initialization argument names and values.

The value returned by update-instance-for-different-class is ignored by change-class.

See the example for the function change-class.

Initialization arguments are declared valid by using the :initarg option to defclass, or by defining methods for update-instance-for-different-class or shared-initialize. The keyword name of each keyword parameter specifier in the lambda-list of any method defined on update-instance-for-different-class or shared-initialize is declared a valid initialization argument name for all classes for which that method is applicable.

Methods on update-instance-for-different-class can be defined to initialize slots differently from change-class. The default behavior of change-class is described in section 28.1.11.

See sections 28.1.11, 28.1.9.4, and 28.1.9.2 as well as change-class and shared-initialize.

```
update-instance-for-redefined-class                    [Generic function]
```
   instance added-slots discarded-slots property-list &rest *initargs*
```
update-instance-for-redefined-class                    [Primary method]
```
   (*instance* `standard-object`) *added-slots discarded-slots property-list*
   &rest *initargs*

The generic function `update-instance-for-redefined-class` is not intended to be called by programmers. Programmers may write methods for it. The generic function `update-instance-for-redefined-class` is called by the mechanism activated by `make-instances-obsolete`.

The system-supplied primary method on `update-instance-for-different-class` checks the validity of initialization arguments and signals an error if an initialization argument is supplied that is not declared valid. This method then initializes slots with values according to the initialization arguments and initializes the newly added slots with values according to their `:initform` forms. It does this by calling the generic function `shared-initialize` with the following arguments: the instance, a list of names of the newly added slots, and the initialization arguments it received. Newly added slots are those local slots for which no slot of the same name exists in the old version of the class.

When `make-instances-obsolete` is invoked or when a class has been redefined and an instance is being updated, a property list is created that captures the slot names and values of all the discarded slots with values in the original instance. The structure of the instance is transformed so that it conforms to the current class definition. The arguments to `update-instance-for-redefined-class` are this transformed instance, a list of the names of the new slots added to the instance, a list of the names of the old slots discarded from the instance, and the property list containing the slot names and values for slots that were discarded and had values. Included in this list of discarded slots are slots that were local in the old class and are shared in the new class.

The *initargs* argument consists of alternating initialization argument names and values.

The value returned by `update-instance-for-redefined-class` is ignored.

Initialization arguments are declared valid by using the `:initarg` option to `defclass` or by defining methods for `update-instance-for-redefined-class` or `shared-initialize`. The keyword name of each keyword parameter specifier in the lambda-list of any method defined on `update-instance-for-redefined-class` or `shared-initialize` is declared a valid initialization argument name for all classes for which that method is applicable.

See sections 28.1.10, 28.1.9.4, and 28.1.9.2 as well as `shared-initialize` and `make-instances-obsolete`.

```
(defclass position () ())

(defclass x-y-position (position)
  ((x :initform 0 :accessor position-x)
   (y :initform 0 :accessor position-y)))

;;; It turns out polar coordinates are used more than Cartesian
;;; coordinates, so the representation is altered and some new
;;; accessor methods are added.

(defmethod update-instance-for-redefined-class :before
           ((pos x-y-position) added deleted plist &key)
  ;; Transform the x-y coordinates to polar coordinates
  ;; and store into the new slots.
  (let ((x (getf plist 'x))
        (y (getf plist 'y)))
    (setf (position-rho pos) (sqrt (+ (* x x) (* y y)))
          (position-theta pos) (atan y x))))

(defclass x-y-position (position)
    ((rho :initform 0 :accessor position-rho)
     (theta :initform 0 :accessor position-theta)))

;;; All instances of the old x-y-position class will be updated
;;; automatically.

;;; The new representation is given the look and feel of the old one.

(defmethod position-x ((pos x-y-position))
  (with-slots (rho theta) pos (* rho (cos theta))))

(defmethod (setf position-x) (new-x (pos x-y-position))
    (with-slots (rho theta) pos
      (let ((y (position-y pos)))
        (setq rho (sqrt (+ (* new-x new-x) (* y y)))
              theta (atan y new-x))
        new-x)))

(defmethod position-y ((pos x-y-position))
  (with-slots (rho theta) pos (* rho (sin theta))))
```

```
(defmethod (setf position-y) (new-y (pos x-y-position))
   (with-slots (rho theta) pos
      (let ((x (position-x pos)))
         (setq rho (sqrt (+ (* x x) (* new-y new-y)))
               theta (atan new-y x))
         new-y)))
```

with-accessors ({*slot-entry*}*) *instance-form*   [*Macro*]
        {*declaration*}* {*form*}*

The macro with-accessors creates a lexical environment in which specified slots
are lexically available through their accessors as if they were variables. The macro
with-accessors invokes the appropriate accessors to access the specified slots.
Both setf and setq can be used to set the value of the slot.

    The result returned is that obtained by executing the forms specified by the *body*
argument.

    Example:

```
(with-accessors ((x position-x) (y position-y)) p1
   (setq x y))
```

    A with-accessors expression of the form

(with-accessors (*slot-entry*₁ ... *slot-entry*ₙ) *instance*
    *declaration*₁ ... *declaration*ₘ)
    *form*₁ ... *form*ₖ)

expands into the equivalent of

(let ((*in instance*))
    (symbol-macrolet ((*variable-name*₁ (*accessor-name*₁ *in*))
                         ...
                     (*variable-name*ₙ (*accessor-name*ₙ *in*))))
    *declaration*₁ ... *declaration*ₘ)
    *form*₁ ... *form*ₖ)

    [X3J13 voted in March 1989 ⟨173⟩ to modify the definition of symbol-macrolet
substantially and also voted ⟨172⟩ to allow declarations before the body of
symbol-macrolet but with peculiar treatment of special and type declarations.
The syntactic changes are reflected in this definition of with-accessors.—GLS]

    See with-slots and symbol-macrolet.

with-added-methods (*function-name lambda-list*   [*Special form*]
                     [[↓*option* | {*method-description*}*]])
                    {*form*}*

The with-added-methods special form produces new generic functions and establishes new lexical function definition bindings. Each generic function is created
by adding the set of methods specified by its method definitions to a copy of the
lexically visible generic function of the same name and its methods. If such a
generic function does not already exist, a new generic function is created; this
generic function has lexical scope.

The special form with-added-methods is used to define functions whose names
are meaningful only locally and to execute a series of forms with these function
definition bindings.

The names of functions defined by with-added-methods have lexical scope;
they retain their local definitions only within the body of the with-added-methods
construct. Any references within the body of the with-added-methods construct to functions whose names are the same as those defined within the
with-added-methods form are thus references to the local functions instead of
to any global functions of the same names. The scope of these generic function
definition bindings includes the method bodies themselves as well as the body of
the with-added-methods construct.

The *function-name, option, method-qualifier,* and *specialized-lambda-list* arguments are the same as for defgeneric.

The body of each method is enclosed in an implicit block. If *function-name* is a
symbol, this block bears the same name as the generic function. If *function-name*
is a list of the form (setf *symbol*), the name of the block is *symbol*.

The result returned by with-added-methods is the value or values of the last
form executed. If no forms are specified, with-added-methods returns nil.

If a generic function with the given name already exists, the lambda-list specified
in the with-added-methods form must be congruent with the lambda-lists of all
existing methods on that function as well as with the lambda-lists of all methods
defined by the with-added-methods form; otherwise an error is signaled.

If *function-name* specifies an existing generic function that has a different value
for any of the following *option* arguments, the copy of that generic function
is modified to have the new value: :argument-precedence-order, declare,
:documentation, :generic-function-class, :method-combination.

If *function-name* specifies an existing generic function that has a different value
for the :method-class *option* argument, that value is changed in the copy of that
generic function, but any methods copied from the existing generic function are
not changed.

If a function of the given name already exists, that function is copied into the default method for a generic function of the given name. Note that this behavior differs from that of defgeneric.

If a macro or special form of the given name already exists, an error is signaled.

If there is no existing generic function, the *option* arguments have the same default values as the *option* arguments to defgeneric.

See generic-labels, generic-flet, defmethod, defgeneric, and ensure-generic-function.

---

with-slots ({*slot-entry*}*) *instance-form* {*declaration*}* {*form*}*   [*Macro*]

slot-entry ::= *slot-name* | (*variable-name slot-name*)

The macro with-slots creates a lexical context for referring to specified slots as though they were variables. Within such a context the value of the slot can be specified by using its slot name, as if it were a lexically bound variable. Both setf and setq can be used to set the value of the slot.

The macro with-slots translates an appearance of the slot name as a variable into a call to slot-value.

The result returned is that obtained by executing the forms specified by the *body* argument.

Example:

```
(with-slots (x y) position-1
  (sqrt (+ (* x x) (* y y))))

(with-slots ((x1 x) (y1 y)) position-1
  (with-slots ((x2 x) (y2 y)) position-2
    (psetf x1 x2
           y1 y2))))

(with-slots (x y) position
  (setq x (1+ x)
        y (1+ y)))
```

A with-slots expression of the form:

```
(with-slots (slot-entry₁ ... slot-entryₙ) instance
  declaration₁ ... declarationₘ)
  form₁ ... formₖ)
```

expands into the equivalent of

```
(let ((in instance))
  (symbol-macrolet (Q₁ ... Qₙ)
    declaration₁ ... declarationₘ)
    form₁ ... formₖ)
```

where Q_j is

(*slot-entry$_j$* (slot-value *in* '*slot-entry$_j$*))

if *slot-entry$_j$* is a symbol and is

(*variable-name$_j$* (slot-value *in* '*slot-name$_j$*))

if *slot-entry$_j$* is of the form (*variable-name$_j$* *slot-name$_j$*).

   [X3J13 voted in March 1989 ⟨173⟩ to modify the definition of symbol-macrolet substantially and also voted ⟨172⟩ to allow declarations before the body of symbol-macrolet but with peculiar treatment of special and type declarations. The syntactic changes are reflected in this definition of with-slots.—GLS]

   See with-accessors and symbol-macrolet.

29

Conditions

BY KENT M. PITMAN

PREFACE: The language defined by the first edition contained an enormous lacuna: although facilities were specified for signaling errors, no means was defined for handling errors. This occurred not through neglect of the issue, but because this part of the Lisp language generally was in a state of flux. There were several proposals at the time. The committee, finding that it could not agree on any one proposal, agreed to disagree and omit error handling from Common Lisp for the time being. This defect has now been addressed.

X3J13 voted in June 1988 ⟨30⟩ to adopt the Common Lisp Condition System as a part of the forthcoming draft Common Lisp standard. X3J13 voted in March 1989 ⟨186⟩ to amend the specification of conditions to integrate them with the Common Lisp Object System (see chapter 28). X3J13 voted in June 1989 ⟨31⟩ to amend the specification of restarts in certain ways. These amendments have been incorporated here with little further comment.

This chapter presents the bulk of the Common Lisp Condition System proposal, written by Kent M. Pitman and amended by X3J13. I have edited it only very lightly to conform to the overall style of this book and have inserted a small number of bracketed remarks identified by the initials GLS. Please see the Acknowledgments to this second edition for the author's acknowledgments to others who contributed to the Condition System proposal.

—Guy L. Steele Jr.

29.1. Introduction

Often we find it useful to describe a function in terms of its behavior in "normal situations." For example, we may say informally that the function + returns the sum of its arguments or that the function read-char returns the next available character on a given input stream.

Sometimes, however, an "exceptional situation" will arise that does not fit neatly into such descriptions. For example, + might receive an argument that is not a number, or read-char might receive as a single argument a stream that has no more available characters. This distinction between normal and exceptional situations is in some sense arbitrary but is often very useful in practice.

For example, suppose a function f were defined to allow only integer arguments but also guaranteed to detect and signal an error for non-integer arguments. Such a description is in fact internally inconsistent (that is, paradoxical) because the function's behavior is well-defined for non-integers. Yet we would not want this annoying paradox to force description of f as a function that accepts any kind of argument (just in case f is being called only as a quick way to signal an error, for example). Using the normal/exceptional distinction, we can say clearly that f accepts integers in the normal situation and signals an error in exceptional situations. Moreover, we can say that when we refer to the definition of a function informally, it is acceptable to speak only of its normal behavior. For example, we can speak informally about f as a function that accepts only integers without feeling that we are committing some awful fraud.

Not all exceptional situations are errors. For example, a program that is directing the typing of a long line of text may come to an end-of-line. It is possible that no real harm will result from failing to signal end-of-line to its caller because the operating system will simply force a carriage return on the output device, which will continue typing on the next line. However, it may still be interesting to establish a protocol whereby the printing program can inform its caller of end-of-line exceptions. The caller could then opt to deal with these situations in interesting ways at certain times. For example, a caller might choose to terminate printing, obtaining an end-of-line truncation. The important thing, however, is that the failure of the caller to provide advice about the situation need not prevent the printer program from operating correctly.

Mechanisms for dealing with exceptional situations vary widely. When an exceptional situation is encountered, a program may attempt to handle it by returning a distinguished value, returning an additional value, setting a variable, calling a function, performing a special transfer of control, or stopping the program altogether and entering the debugger.

For the most part, the facilities described in this chapter do not introduce any fundamentally new way of dealing with exceptional situations. Rather, they encapsulate and formalize useful patterns of data and control flow that have been seen to be useful in dealing with exceptional situations.

A proper conceptual approach to errors should perhaps begin from first principles, with a discussion of *conditions* in general, and eventually work up to the concept of an *error* as just one of the many kinds of conditions. However, given the primitive state of error-handling technology, a proper buildup may be as inappropriate as requiring that a beggar learn to cook a gourmet meal before being allowed to eat. Thus, we deal first with the essentials—error handling—and then go back later to fill in the missing details.

29.2. Changes in Terminology

In this section, we introduce changes to the terminology defined in section 1.2.4.

A *condition* is an interesting situation in a program that has been detected and announced. Later we allow this term also to refer to objects that programs use to represent such situations.

An *error* is a condition in which normal program execution may not continue without some form of intervention (either interactively by the user or under some sort of program control, as described below).

The process by which a condition is formally announced by a program is called *signaling*. The function `signal` is the primitive mechanism by which such announcement is done. Other abstractions, such as `error` and `cerror`, are built using `signal`.

The first edition is ambiguous about the reason why a particular program action "is an error." There are two principal reasons why an action may be an error without being required to signal an error:

- Detecting the error might be prohibitively expensive.

  For example, `(+ nil 3)` is an error. It is likely that the designers of Common Lisp believed this would be an error in all implementations but felt it might be excessively expensive to detect the problem in compiled code on stock hardware, so they did not require that it signal an error.

- Some implementations might implement the behavior as an extension.

  For example, `(loop for x from 1 to 3 do (print x))` is an error because `loop` is not defined to take atoms in its body. In fact, however, some implementations offer an extension that makes this well-defined. In order to leave room for such extensions, the first edition used the "is an error" terminology to keep implementors from being forced to signal an error in the extended implementations.

  [This example was written well before the vote by X3J13 in January 1989 to add exactly this extension to the forthcoming draft standard (see chapter 26).—GLS]

In this chapter, we use the following terminology. [Compare this to the terminology presented in section 28.1.1.—GLS]

- If the signaling of a condition or error is part of a function's contract in all situations, we say that it "signals" or "must signal" that condition or error.

- If the signaling of a condition or error is optional for some important reason (such as performance), we say that the program "might signal" that condition or error. In this case, we are defining the operation to be illegal in all implementations, but allowing some implementations to fail to detect the error.

- If an action is left undefined for the sake of implementation-dependent extension, we say that it "is undefined" or "has undefined effect." This means that it is not possible to depend portably upon the effects of that action. A program that has undefined effect may enter the debugger, transfer control, or modify data in unpredictable ways.

- In the special case where only the return value of an operation is not well defined but any side effect and transfer-of-control behavior is well defined, we say that it has "undefined value." In this case, the number and nature of the return values is not defined, but the function can reasonably be expected to return. It is worth noting that under this description, there are some (though not many) legitimate ways in which such return value(s) can be used. For example, if the function foo has no side effects and undefined value, the expression (length (list (foo))) is completely well defined even for portable code. However, the effect of (print (list (foo))) is not well defined.

29.3. Survey of Concepts

This section discusses various aspects of the condition system by topic, illustrating them with extensive examples. The next section contains definitions of specific functions, macros, and other facilities.

29.3.1. Signaling Errors

Conceptually, signaling an error in a program is an admission by that program that it does not know how to continue and requires external intervention. Once an error is signaled, any decision about how to continue must come from the "outside."

The simplest way to signal an error is to use the error function with format-style arguments describing the error for the sake of the user interface. If error is called and there are no active handlers (described in sections 29.3.2 and 29.3.3), the debugger will be entered and the error message will be typed out. For example:

```
Lisp> (defun factorial (x)
         (cond ((or (not (typep x 'integer)) (minusp x))
                (error "~S is not a valid argument to FACTORIAL."
                       x))
               ((zerop x) 1)
               (t (* x (factorial (- x 1)))))))
  ⇒ FACTORIAL
Lisp> (factorial 20)
  ⇒ 2432902008176640000
Lisp> (factorial -1)
Error: -1 is not a valid argument to FACTORIAL.
To continue, type :CONTINUE followed by an option number:
 1: Return to Lisp Toplevel.
Debug>
```

In general, a call to error cannot directly return. Unless special work has been done to override this behavior, the debugger will be entered and there will be no option to simply continue.

The only exception may be that some implementations may provide debugger commands for interactively returning from individual stack frames; even then, however, such commands should never be used except by someone who has read the erring code and understands the consequences of continuing from that point. In particular, the programmer should feel confident about writing code like this:

```
(defun wargames:no-win-scenario ()
   (when (true) (error "Pushing the button would be stupid."))
   (push-the-button))
```

In this scenario, there should be no chance that the function error will return and the button will be pushed.

Remark: It should be noted that the notion of "no chance" that the button will be pushed is relative only to the language model; it assumes that the language is accurately implemented. In practice, compilers have bugs, computers have glitches, and users have been known to interrupt at inopportune moments and use the debugger to return from arbitrary stack frames. Such violations of the language model are beyond the scope of the condition system but not necessarily beyond the scope of potential failures that the programmer should consider and defend against. The possibility of such unusual failures may of course also influence the design of code meant to handle less drastic situations, such as maintaining a database uncorrupted.—KMP and GLS

In some cases, the programmer may have a single, well-defined idea of a reasonable recovery strategy for this particular error. In that case, he can use the function cerror, which specifies information about what would happen if the user did simply continue from the call to cerror. For example:

```
Lisp> (defun factorial (x)
         (cond ((not (typep x 'integer))
                (error "~S is not a valid argument to FACTORIAL."
                       x))
               ((minusp x)
                (let ((x-magnitude (- x)))
                  (cerror "Compute -(~D!) instead."
                          "(-~D)! is not defined." x-magnitude)
                  (- (factorial x-magnitude))))
               ((zerop x) 1)
               (t (* x (factorial (- x 1)))))))
 ⇒ FACTORIAL
Lisp> (factorial -3)
Error: (-3)! is not defined.
To continue, type :CONTINUE followed by an option number:
 1: Compute -(3!) instead.
 2: Return to Lisp Toplevel.
Debug> :continue 1
 ⇒ -6
```

29.3.2. Trapping Errors

By default, a call to error will force entry into the debugger. You can override that behavior in a variety of ways. The simplest (and most blunt) tool for inhibiting entry to the debugger on an error is to use ignore-errors. In the normal situation, forms in the body of ignore-errors are evaluated sequentially and the last value is returned. If a condition of type error is signaled, ignore-errors immediately returns two values, namely nil and the condition that was signaled; the debugger is not entered and no error message is printed. For example:

```
Lisp> (setq filename "nosuchfile")
 ⇒ "nosuchfile"
Lisp> (ignore-errors (open filename :direction :input))
 ⇒ NIL and #<FILE-ERROR 3437523>
```

The second return value is an object that represents the kind of error. This is explained in greater detail in section 29.3.4.

In many cases, however, ignore-errors is not desirable because it deals with too many kinds of errors. Contrary to the belief of some, a program that does not enter the debugger is not necessarily better than one that does. Excessive use of ignore-errors may keep the program out of the debugger, but it may not increase the program's reliability, because the program may continue to run after encountering errors other than those you meant to work past. In general, it is better to attempt to deal only with the particular kinds of errors that you believe could legitimately happen. That way, if an unexpected error comes along, you will still find out about it.

ignore-errors is a useful special case built from a more general facility, handler-case, that allows the programmer to deal with particular kinds of conditions (including non-error conditions) without affecting what happens when other kinds of conditions are signaled. For example, an effect equivalent to that of ignore-errors above is achieved in the following example:

```
Lisp> (setq filename "nosuchfile")
 ⇒ "nosuchfile"
Lisp> (handler-case (open filename :direction :input)
        (error (condition)
          (values nil condition)))
 ⇒ NIL and #<FILE-ERROR 3437525>
```

However, using handler-case, one can indicate a more specific condition type than just "error." Condition types are explained in detail later, but the syntax looks roughly like the following:

```
Lisp> (makunbound 'filename)
 ⇒ FILENAME
Lisp> (handler-case (open filename :direction :input)
        (file-error (condition)
          (values nil condition)))
Error: The variable FILENAME is unbound.
To continue, type :CONTINUE followed by an option number:
  1: Retry getting the value of FILENAME.
  2: Specify a value of FILENAME to use this time.
  3: Specify a value of FILENAME to store and use.
  4: Return to Lisp Toplevel.
Debug>
```

29.3.3. Handling Conditions

Blind transfer of control to a handler-case is only one possible kind of recovery action that can be taken when a condition is signaled. The low-level mechanism offers great flexibility in how to continue once a condition has been signaled.

The basic idea behind condition handling is that a piece of code called the *signaler* recognizes and announces the existence of an exceptional situation using signal or some function built on signal (such as error).

The process of signaling involves the search for and invocation of a *handler*, a piece of code that will attempt to deal appropriately with the situation.

If a handler is found, it may either *handle* the situation, by performing some non-local transfer of control, or *decline* to handle it, by failing to perform a non-local transfer of control. If it declines, other handlers are sought.

Since the lexical environment of the signaler might not be available to handlers, a data structure called a *condition* is created to represent explicitly the relevant state of the situation. A condition either is created explicitly using make-condition and then passed to a function such as signal, or is created implicitly by a function such as signal when given appropriate non-condition arguments.

In order to handle the error, a handler is permitted to use any non-local transfer of control such as go to a tag in a tagbody, return from a block, or throw to a catch. In addition, structured abstractions of these primitives are provided for convenience in exception handling.

A handler can be made dynamically accessible to a program by use of handler-bind. For example, to create a handler for a condition of type arithmetic-error, one might write:

```
(handler-bind ((arithmetic-error handler))body)
```

The handler is a function of one argument, the condition. If a condition of the designated type is signaled while the *body* is executing (and there are no intervening handlers), the handler would be invoked on the given condition, allowing it the option of transferring control. For example, one might write a macro that executes a body, returning either its value(s) or the two values nil and the condition:

```
(defmacro without-arithmetic-errors (&body forms)
  (let ((tag (gensym)))
    '(block ,tag
       (handler-bind ((arithmetic-error
                        #'(lambda (c)          ;Argument c is a condition
                            (return-from ,tag (values nil c)))))
         ,@body)))))
```

The handler is executed in the dynamic context of the signaler, except that the set of available condition handlers will have been rebound to the value that was active at the time the condition handler was made active. If a handler declines (that is, it does not transfer control), other handlers are sought. If no handler is found and the condition was signaled by `error` or `cerror` (or some function such as `assert` that behaves like these functions), the debugger is entered, still in the dynamic context of the signaler.

29.3.4. Object-Oriented Basis of Condition Handling

Of course, the ability of the handler to usefully handle an exceptional situation is related to the quality of the information it is provided. For example, if all errors were signaled by

(error "*some format string*")

then the only piece of information that would be accessible to the handler would be an object of type `simple-error` that had a slot containing the format string.

If this were done, `string-equal` would be the preferred way to tell one error from another, and it would be very hard to allow flexibility in the presentation of error messages because existing handlers would tend to be broken by even tiny variations in the wording of an error message. This phenomenon has been the major failing of most error systems previously available in Lisp. It is fundamentally important to decouple the error message string (the human interface) from the objects that formally represent the error state (the program interface). We therefore have the notion of typed conditions, and of formal operations on those conditions that make them inspectable in a structured way.

This object-oriented approach to condition handling has the following important advantages over a text-based approach:

• Conditions are classified according to subtype relationships, making it easy to test for categories of conditions.

• Conditions have named slot values through which parameters are conveyed from the program that signals the condition to the program that handles it.

• Inheritance of methods and slots reduces the amount of explicit specification necessary to achieve various interesting effects.

Some condition types are defined by this document, but the set of condition types is extensible using `define-condition`. Common Lisp condition types are in fact CLOS classes, and condition objects are ordinary CLOS objects;

define-condition merely provides an abstract interface that is a bit more convenient than defclass for defining conditions.

Here, as an example, we define a two-argument function called divide that is patterned after the / function but does some stylized error checking:

```
(defun divide (numerator denominator)
  (cond ((or (not (numberp numerator))
             (not (numberp denominator)))
         (error "(DIVIDE ´~S ´~S) - Bad arguments."
                numerator denominator))
        ((zerop denominator)
         (error 'division-by-zero
                :operator 'divide
                :operands (list numerator denominator)))
        (t ...)))
```

Note that in the first clause we have used error with a string argument and in the second clause we have named a particular condition type, division-by-zero. In the case of a string argument, the condition type that will be signaled is simple-error.

The particular kind of error that is signaled may be important in cases where handlers are active. For example, simple-error inherits from type error, which in turn inherits from type condition. On the other hand, division-by-zero inherits from arithmetic-error, which inherits from error, which inherits from condition. So if a handler existed for arithmetic-error while a division-by-zero condition was signaled, that handler would be tried; however, if a simple-error condition were signaled in the same context, the handler for type arithmetic-error would not be tried.

29.3.5. Restarts

In older Lisp dialects (such as MacLisp), an attempt to signal an error of a given type often carried with it an implicit promise to support the standard recovery strategy for that type of error. If the signaler knew the type of error but for whatever reason was unable to deal with the standard recovery strategy for that kind of error, it was necessary to signal an untyped error (for which there was no defined recovery strategy). This sometimes led to confusion when people signaled typed errors without realizing the full implications of having done so, but more often than not it meant that users simply avoided typed errors altogether.

The Common Lisp Condition System, which is modeled after the Zetalisp condition system, corrects this troublesome aspect of previous Lisp dialects by creating a clear separation between the act of signaling an error of a particular type and the act of saying that a particular way of recovery is appropriate. In the divide example above, simply signaling an error does not imply a willingness on the part of the signaler to cooperate in any corrective action. For example, the following sample interaction illustrates that the only recovery action offered for this error is "Return to Lisp Toplevel":

```
Lisp> (+ (divide 3 0) 7)
Error: Attempt to divide 3 by 0.
To continue, type :CONTINUE followed by an option number:
 1: Return to Lisp Toplevel.
Debug> :continue 1
Returned to Lisp Toplevel.
Lisp>
```

When an error is detected and the function error is called, execution cannot continue normally because error will not directly return. Control can be transferred to other points in the program, however, by means of specially established "restarts."

29.3.6. Anonymous Restarts

The simplest kind of restart involves structured transfer of control using a macro called restart-case. The restart-case form allows execution of a piece of code in a context where zero or more restarts are active, and where if one of those restarts is "invoked," control will be transferred to the corresponding clause in the restart-case form. For example, we could rewrite the previous divide example as follows.

```
(defun divide (numerator denominator)
  (loop
    (restart-case
        (return
          (cond ((or (not (numberp numerator))
                     (not (numberp denominator)))
                 (error "(DIVIDE ´~S ´~S) - Bad arguments."
                        numerator denominator))
                ((zerop denominator)
                 (error 'division-by-zero
                        :operator 'divide
                        :operands (list numerator denominator)))
                (t ...)))
```

```
(nil (arg1 arg2)
    :report "Provide new arguments for use by DIVIDE."
    :interactive
        (lambda ()
            (list (prompt-for 'number "Numerator: ")
                  (prompt-for 'number "Denominator: ")))
    (setq numerator arg1 denominator arg2))
(nil (result)
    :report "Provide a value to return from DIVIDE."
    :interactive
        (lambda () (list (prompt-for 'number "Result: ")))
    (return result)))))
```

Remark: The function prompt-for used in this chapter in a number of places is not a part of Common Lisp. It is used in the examples in this chapter only to keep the presentation simple. It is assumed to accept a type specifier and optionally a format string and associated arguments. It uses the format string and associated arguments as part of an interactive prompt, and uses read to read a Lisp object; however, only an object of the type indicated by the type specifier is accepted.

The question of whether or not prompt-for (or something like it) would be a useful addition to Common Lisp is under consideration by X3J13, but as of January 1989 no action has been taken. In spite of its use in a number of examples, nothing in the Common Lisp Condition System depends on this function.

In the example, the nil at the head of each clause means that it is an "anonymous" restart. Anonymous restarts are typically invoked only from within the debugger. As we shall see later, it is possible to have "named restarts" that may be invoked from code without the need for user intervention.

If the arguments to anonymous restarts are not optional, then special information must be provided about what the debugger should use as arguments. Here the :interactive keyword is used to specify that information.

The :report keyword introduces information to be used when presenting the restart option to the user (by the debugger, for example).

Here is a sample interaction that takes advantage of the restarts provided by the revised definition of divide:

```
Lisp> (+ (divide 3 0) 7)
Error: Attempt to divide 3 by 0.
To continue, type :CONTINUE followed by an option number:
 1: Provide new arguments for use by the DIVIDE function.
 2: Provide a value to return from the DIVIDE function.
```

```
 3: Return to Lisp Toplevel.
Debug> :continue 1
1
Numerator: 4
Denominator: 2
 ⇒ 9
```

29.3.7. Named Restarts

In addition to anonymous restarts, one can have named restarts, which can be invoked by name from within code. As a trivial example, one could write

```
(restart-case (invoke-restart 'foo 3)
  (foo (x) (+ x 1)))
```

to add 3 to 1, returning 4. This trivial example is conceptually analogous to writing:

```
(+ (catch 'something (throw 'something 3)) 1)
```

For a more realistic example, the code for the function symbol-value might signal an unbound variable error as follows:

```
(restart-case (error "The variable ~S is unbound." variable)
  (continue ()
     :report
        (lambda (s)       ;Argument s is a stream
           (format s "Retry getting the value of ~S." variable))
    (symbol-value variable))
  (use-value (value)
     :report
        (lambda (s)       ;Argument s is a stream
           (format s "Specify a value of ~S to use this time."
                   variable))
    value)
  (store-value (value)
     :report
        (lambda (s)       ;Argument s is a stream
           (format s "Specify a value of ~S to store and use."
                   variable))
    (setf (symbol-value variable) value)
   value))
```

If this were part of the implementation of `symbol-value`, then it would be possible for users to write a variety of automatic handlers for unbound variable errors. For example, to make unbound variables evaluate to themselves, one might write

```
(handler-bind ((unbound-variable
                #'(lambda (c)       ;Argument c is a condition
                    (when (find-restart 'use-value)
                      (invoke-restart 'use-value
                                      (cell-error-name c))))))
  body)
```

29.3.8. Restart Functions

For commonly used restarts, it is conventional to define a program interface that hides the use of `invoke-restart`. Such program interfaces to restarts are called *restart functions*.

The normal convention is for the function to share the name of the restart. The pre-defined functions `abort`, `continue`, `muffle-warning`, `store-value`, and `use-value` are restart functions. With `use-value` the above example of `handler-bind` could have been written more concisely as

```
(handler-bind ((unbound-variable
                #'(lambda (c)       ;Argument c is a condition
                    (use-value (cell-error-name c)))))
  body)
```

29.3.9. Comparison of Restarts and Catch/Throw

One important feature that `restart-case` (or `restart-bind`) offers that `catch` does not is the ability to reason about the available points to which control might be transferred without actually attempting the transfer. One could, for example, write

```
(ignore-errors (throw ...))
```

which is a sort of poor man's variation of

```
(when (find-restart 'something)
  (invoke-restart 'something))
```

but there is no way to use `ignore-errors` and `throw` to simulate something like

```
(when (and (find-restart 'something)
           (find-restart 'something-else))
  (invoke-restart 'something))
```

or even just

```
(when (and (find-restart 'something)
           (yes-or-no-p "Do something? "))
  (invoke-restart 'something))
```

because the degree of inspectability that comes with simply writing

```
(ignore-errors (throw ...))
```

is too primitive—getting the desired information also forces transfer of control, perhaps at a time when it is not desirable.

Many programmers have previously evolved strategies like the following on a case-by-case basis:

```
(defvar *foo-tag-is-available* nil)

(defun fn-1 ()
  (catch 'foo
    (let ((*foo-tag-is-available* t))
      ... (fn-2) ...)))

(defun fn-2 ()
  ...
  (if *foo-tag-is-available* (throw 'foo t))
  ...)
```

The facility provided by restart-case and find-restart is intended to provide a standardized protocol for this sort of information to be communicated between programs that were developed independently so that individual variations from program to program do not thwart the overall modularity and debuggability of programs.

Another difference between the restart facility and the catch/throw facility is that a catch with any given tag completely shadows any outer pending catch that uses the same tag. Because of the presence of compute-restarts, however, it is possible to see shadowed restarts, which may be very useful in some situations (particularly in an interactive debugger).

29.3.10. Generalized Restarts

restart-case is a mechanism that allows only imperative transfer of control for its associated restarts. restart-case is built on a lower-level mechanism called restart-bind, which does not force transfer of control.

restart-bind is to restart-case as handler-bind is to handler-case. The syntax is

(restart-bind ((*name function . options*)) . *body*)

The *body* is executed in a dynamic context within which the *function* will be called whenever (invoke-restart '*name*) is executed. The *options* are keyword-style and are used to pass information such as that provided with the :report keyword in restart-case.

A restart-case expands into a call to restart-bind where the function simply does an unconditional transfer of control to a particular body of code, passing along "argument" information in a structured way.

It is also possible to write restarts that do not transfer control. Such restarts may be useful in implementing various special commands for the debugger that are of interest only in certain situations. For example, one might imagine a situation where file space was exhausted and the following was done in an attempt to free space in directory dir:

```
(restart-bind ((nil #'(lambda () (expunge-directory dir))
                    :report-function
                    #'(lambda (stream)
                        (format stream "Expunge ~A."
                                (directory-namestring dir)))))
   (cerror "Try this file operation again."
           'directory-full :directory dir))
```

In this case, the debugger might be entered and the user could first perform the expunge (which would not transfer control from the debugger context) and then retry the file operation:

```
Lisp> (open "FOO" :direction :output)
Error: The directory PS:<JDOE> is full.
To continue, type :CONTINUE followed by an option number:
 1: Try this file operation again.
 2: Expunge PS:<JDOE>.
 3: Return to Lisp Toplevel.
Debug> :continue 2
```

```
Expunging PS:<JDOE> ... 3 records freed.
Debug> :continue 1
  ⇒ #<OUTPUT-STREAM "PS:<JDOE>FOO.LSP" 2323473>
```

29.3.11. Interactive Condition Handling

When a program does not know how to continue, and no active handler is able to advise it, the "interactive condition handler," or "debugger," can be entered. This happens implicitly through the use of functions such as error and cerror, or explicitly through the use of the function invoke-debugger.

The interactive condition handler never returns directly; it returns only through structured non-local transfer of control to specially defined restart points that can be set up either by the system or by user code. The mechanisms that support the establishment of such structured restart points for portable code are outlined in sections 29.3.5 through 29.3.10.

Actually, implementations may also provide extended debugging facilities that allow return from arbitrary stack frames. Although such commands are frequently useful in practice, their effects are implementation-dependent because they violate the Common Lisp program abstraction. The effect of using such commands is undefined with respect to Common Lisp.

29.3.12. Serious Conditions

The ignore-errors macro will trap conditions of type error. There are, however, conditions that are not of type error.

Some conditions are not considered errors but are still very serious, so we call them *serious conditions* and we use the type serious-condition to represent them. Conditions such as those that might be signaled for "stack overflow" or "storage exhausted" are in this category.

The type error is a subtype of serious-condition, and it would technically be correct to use the term "serious condition" to refer to all serious conditions whether errors or not. However, normally we use the term "serious condition" to refer to things of type serious-condition but not of type error.

The point of the distinction between errors and other serious conditions is that some conditions are known to occur for reasons that are beyond the scope of Common Lisp to specify clearly. For example, we know that a stack will generally be used to implement function calling, and we know that stacks tend to be of finite size and are prone to overflow. Since the available stack size may vary from implementation to implementation, from session to session, or from function call to function call, it would be confusing to have expressions such as (ignore-errors (+ a b)) return a number sometimes and nil other times if a and b were always bound to numbers and the stack just happened to overflow on a particular call. For this reason, only conditions of type error and not all conditions of type serious-condition are trapped by ignore-errors. To trap other conditions, a lower-level facility must be used (such as handler-bind or handler-case).

By convention, the function error is preferred over signal to signal conditions of type serious-condition (including those of type error). It is the use of the function error, and not the type of the condition being signaled, that actually causes the debugger to be entered.

Compatibility note: The Common Lisp Condition System differs from that of Zetalisp in this respect. In Zetalisp the debugger is entered for an unhandled signal if the error function is used *or* if the condition is of type error.

29.3.13. Non-Serious Conditions

Some conditions are neither errors nor serious conditions. They are signaled to give other programs a chance to intervene, but if no action is taken, computation simply continues normally.

For example, an implementation might choose to signal a non-serious (and implementation-dependent) condition called end-of-line when output reaches the last character position on a line of character output. In such an implementation, the signaling of this condition might allow a convenient way for other programs to intervene, producing output that is truncated at the end of a line.

By convention, the function signal is used to signal conditions that are not serious. It would be possible to signal serious conditions using signal, and the debugger would not be entered if the condition went unhandled. However, by convention, handlers will generally tend to assume that serious conditions and errors were signaled by calling the error function (and will therefore force entry to the interactive condition handler) and that they should work to avoid this.

29.3.14. Condition Types

Some types of conditions are predefined by the system. All types of conditions are subtypes of condition. That is, (typep *x* ´condition) is true if and only if the value of *x* is a condition.

Implementations supporting multiple (or non-hierarchical) type inheritance are expressly permitted to exploit multiple inheritance in the tree of condition types as implementation-dependent extensions, as long as such extensions are compatible with the specifications in this chapter. [X3J13 voted in March 1989 ⟨186⟩ to integrate the Condition System and the Object System, so multiple inheritance is always available for condition types.—GLS]

In order to avoid problems in portable code that runs both in systems with multiple type inheritance and in systems without it, programmers are explicitly warned that while all correct Common Lisp implementations will ensure that (typep c ´condition) is true for all conditions *c* (and all subtype relationships indicated in this chapter will also be true), it should *not* be assumed that two condition types specified to be subtypes of the same third type are disjoint. (In some cases, disjoint subtypes are identified explicitly, but such disjointness is not to be assumed by default.) For example, it follows from the subtype descriptions contained in this chapter that in all implementations (typep c ´control-error) implies (typep c ´error), but note that (typep c ´control-error) does *not* imply (not (typep c ´cell-error)).

29.3.15. Signaling Conditions

When a condition is signaled, the system tries to locate the most appropriate handler for the condition and to invoke that handler.

Handlers are established dynamically using handler-bind or abstractions built on handler-bind.

If an appropriate handler is found, it is called. In some circumstances, the handler may *decline* simply by returning without performing a non-local transfer of control. In such cases, the search for an appropriate handler is picked up where it left off, as if the called handler had never been present.

If no handler is found, or if all handlers that were found decline, signal returns nil.

Although it follows from the description above, it is perhaps worth noting explicitly that the lookup procedure described here will prefer a general but more (dynamically) local handler over a specific but less (dynamically) local handler. Experience with existing condition systems suggests that this is a reasonable approach and works adequately in most situations. Some care should be taken when binding handlers for very general kinds of conditions, such as is done in ignore-errors. Often, binding for a more specific condition type than error is more appropriate.

29.3.16. Resignaling Conditions

[The contents of this section are still a subject of some debate within X3J13. The reader may wish to take this section with a grain of salt.—GLS]

Note that signaling a condition has no side effect on that condition, and that there is no dynamic state contained in a condition object. As such, it may at times be reasonable and appropriate to consider caching condition objects for repeated use, re-signaling conditions from within handlers, or saving conditions away somewhere and re-signaling them later.

For example, it may be desirable for the system to pre-allocate objects of type storage-condition so that they can be signaled when needed without attempting to allocate more storage.

29.3.17. Condition Handlers

A *handler* is a function of one argument, the condition to be handled. The handler may inspect the object to be sure it is "interested" in handling the condition.

A handler is executed in the dynamic context of the signaler, except that the set of available condition handlers will have been rebound to the value that was active at the time the condition handler was made active. The intent of this is to prevent infinite recursion because of errors in a condition handler.

After inspecting the condition, the handler should take one of the following actions:

- It might *decline* to handle the condition (by simply returning). When this happens, the returned values are ignored and the effect is the same as if the handler had been invisible to the mechanism seeking to find a handler. The next handler in line will be tried, or if no such handler exists, the condition will go unhandled.

- It might *handle* the condition (by performing some non-local transfer of control). This may be done either primitively using go, return, or throw, or more abstractly using a function such as abort or invoke-restart.

- It might signal another condition.

- It might invoke the interactive debugger.

In fact, the latter two actions (signaling another condition or entering the debugger) are really just ways of putting off the decision to either handle or decline, or trying to get someone else to make such a decision. Ultimately, all a handler can do is to handle or decline to handle.

29.3.18. Printing Conditions

When *print-escape* is nil (for example, when the princ function or the ~A directive is used with format), the report method for the condition will be invoked. This will be done automatically by functions such as `invoke-debugger`, `break`, and `warn`, but there may still be situations in which it is desirable to have a condition report under explicit user control. For example,

```
(let ((form '(open "nosuchfile")))
  (handler-case (eval form)
    (serious-condition (c)
      (format t "~&Evaluation of ~S failed:~%~A" form c))))
```

might print something like

```
Evaluation of (OPEN "nosuchfile") failed:
The file "nosuchfile" was not found.
```

Some suggestions about the form of text typed by report methods:

- The message should generally be a complete sentence, beginning with a capital letter and ending with appropriate punctuation (usually a period).

- The message should *not* include any introductory text such as "`Error:`" or "`Warning:`" and should not be followed by a trailing newline. Such text will be added as may be appropriate to context by the routine invoking the report method.

- Except where unavoidable, the tab character (which is only semi-standard any- way) should not be used in error messages. Its effect may vary from one imple- mentation to another and may cause problems even within an implementation because it may do different things depending on the column at which the error report begins.

- Single-line messages are preferred, but newlines in the middle of long messages are acceptable.

- If any program (for example, the debugger) displays messages indented from the prevailing left margin (for example, indented seven spaces because they are prefixed by the seven-character herald "`Error: `"), then that program will take care of inserting the appropriate indentation into the extra lines of a multi-line error message. Similarly, a program that prefixes error messages with semicolons so that they appear to be comments should take care of inserting a semicolon at the beginning of each line in a multi-line error message. (These rules are important because, even within a single implementation, there may be more than one program that presents error messages to the user, and they may use different styles of presentation. The caller of `error` cannot anticipate all such possible styles, and so it is incumbent upon the presenter of the message to make any necessary adjustments.)

[Note: These recommendations expand upon those in section 24.1.—GLS]

When *print-escape* is not nil, the object should print in some useful (but usually fairly abbreviated) fashion according to the style of the implementation. It is not expected that a condition will be printed in a form suitable for read. Something like #<ARITHMETIC-ERROR 1734> is fine.

X3J13 voted in March 1989 ⟨186⟩ to integrate the Condition System and the Object System. In the original Condition System proposal, no function was provided for directly accessing or setting the printer for a condition type, or for invoking it; the techniques described above were the sole interface to reporting. The vote specified that, in CLOS terms, condition reporting is mediated through the print-object method for the condition type (that is, class) in question, with *print-escape* bound to nil. Specifying (:report *fn*) to define-condition when defining condition type *C* is equivalent to a separate method definition:

```
(defmethod print-object ((x C) stream)
  (if *print-escape*
      (call-next-method)
      (funcall #'fn x stream)))
```

Note that the method uses *fn* to print the condition only when *print-escape* has the value nil.

29.4. Program Interface to the Condition System

This section describes functions, macros, variables, and condition types associated with the Common Lisp Condition System.

29.4.1. Signaling Conditions

The functions in this section provide various mechanisms for signaling warnings, breaks, continuable errors, and fatal errors.

error *datum* &rest *arguments*   [*Function*]

[This supersedes the description of error given in section 24.1.—GLS]

Invokes the signal facility on a condition. If the condition is not handled, (invoke-debugger *condition*) is executed. As a consequence of calling invoke-debugger, error never directly returns to its caller; the only exit from this function can come by non-local transfer of control in a handler or by use of an interactive debugging command.

If *datum* is a condition, then that condition is used directly. In this case, it is an error for the list of *arguments* to be non-empty; that is, error must have been called with exactly one argument, the condition.

If *datum* is a condition type (a class or class name), then the condition used is effectively the result of (apply #'make-condition *datum* *arguments*).

If *datum* is a string, then the condition used is effectively the result of

```
(make-condition 'simple-error
                :format-string datum
                :format-arguments arguments)
```

cerror *continue-format-string datum* &rest *arguments*   [*Function*]

[This supersedes the description of cerror given in section 24.1.—GLS]

The function cerror invokes the error facility on a condition. If the condition is not handled, (invoke-debugger *condition*) is executed. While signaling is going on, and while control is in the debugger (if it is reached), it is possible to continue program execution (thereby returning from the call to cerror) using the continue restart.

If *datum* is a condition, then that condition is used directly. In this case, the list of *arguments* need not be empty, but will be used only with the *continue-format-string* and will not be used to initialize *datum*.

If *datum* is a condition type (a class or class name), then the condition used is effectively the result of (apply #'make-condition *datum* *arguments*).

If *datum* is a string, then the condition used is effectively the result of

```
(make-condition 'simple-error
                :format-string datum
                :format-arguments arguments)
```

The *continue-format-string* must be a string. Note that if *datum* is not a string, then the format arguments used by the *continue-format-string* will still be the list of *arguments* (which is in keyword format if *datum* is a condition type). In this case, some care may be necessary to set up the *continue-format-string* correctly. The format directive ~*, which ignores and skips over format arguments, may be particularly useful in this situation.

The value returned by cerror is nil.

signal *datum* &rest *arguments*   [*Function*]

Invokes the signal facility on a condition. If the condition is not handled, signal returns nil.

If *datum* is a condition, then that condition is used directly. In this case, it is an error for the list of *arguments* to be non-empty; that is, error must have been called with exactly one argument, the condition.

If *datum* is a condition type (a class or class name), then the condition used is effectively the result of (apply #'make-condition *datum* *arguments*).

If *datum* is a string, then the condition used is effectively the result of

```
(make-condition 'simple-error
                :format-string datum
                :format-arguments arguments)
```

Note that if (typep *condition* *break-on-signals*) is true, then the debugger will be entered prior to beginning the process of signaling. The continue restart function may be used to continue with the signaling process; the restart is associated with the signaled condition as if by use of with-condition-restarts. This is true also for all other functions and macros that signal conditions, such as warn, error, cerror, assert, and check-type.

During the dynamic extent of a call to signal with a particular condition, the effect of calling signal again on that condition object for a distinct abstract event is not defined. For example, although a handler *may* resignal a condition in order to allow outer handlers first shot at handling the condition, two distinct asynchronous keyboard events must not signal an the same (eq) condition object at the same time.

For further details about signaling and handling, see the discussion of condition handlers in section 29.3.17.

break-on-signals   [*Variable*]

This variable is intended primarily for use when the user is debugging programs that do signaling. The value of *break-on-signals* should be suitable as a second argument to typep, that is, a type or type specifier.

When (typep *condition* *break-on-signals*) is true, then calls to signal (and to other advertised functions such as error that implicitly call signal) will enter the debugger prior to signaling that *condition*. The continue restart may be used to continue with the normal signaling process; the restart is associated with the signaled condition as if by use of with-condition-restarts.

Note that nil is a valid type specifier. If the value of *break-on-signals* is nil, then signal will never enter the debugger in this implicit manner.

When setting this variable, the user is encouraged to choose the most restrictive specification that suffices. Setting this flag effectively violates the modular handling of condition signaling that this chapter seeks to establish. Its complete effect may be unpredictable in some cases, since the user may not be aware of the variety or number of calls to `signal` that are used in programs called only incidentally.

By default—and certainly in any "production" use—the value of this variable should be `nil`, both for reasons of performance and for reasons of modularity and abstraction.

X3J13 voted in March 1989 ⟨10⟩ to remove `*break-on-warnings*` from the language; `*break-on-signals*` offers all the power of `*break-on-warnings*` and more.

Compatibility note: This variable is similar to the Zetalisp variable `trace-conditions` except for the obvious difference that `zl:trace-conditions` takes a type or list of types while `*break-on-signals*` takes a single type specifier.

[There is no loss of generality in Common Lisp because the `or` type specifier may be used to indicate that any of a set of conditions should enter the debugger.—GLS]

29.4.2. Assertions

These facilities are designed to make it convenient for the user to insert error checks into code.

`check-type` *place typespec* [*string*]   [*Macro*]

[This supersedes the description of `check-type` given in section 24.2.—GLS]

A `check-type` form signals an error of type `type-error` if the contents of *place* are not of the desired type.

If a condition is signaled, handlers of this condition can use the functions `type-error-datum` and `type-error-expected-type` to access the contents of *place* and the *typespec*, respectively.

This function can return only if the `store-value` restart is invoked, either explicitly from a handler or implicitly as one of the options offered by the debugger. The restart is associated with the signaled condition as if by use of `with-condition-restarts`.

If `store-value` is called, `check-type` will store the new value that is the argument to `store-value` (or that is prompted for interactively by the debugger) in *place* and start over, checking the type of the new value and signaling another error if it is still not the desired type. Subforms of *place* may be evaluated multiple times because of the implicit loop generated. `check-type` returns `nil`.

The *place* must be a generalized variable reference acceptable to setf. The *typespec* must be a type specifier; it is not evaluated. The string should be an English description of the type, starting with an indefinite article ("a" or "an"); it is evaluated. If the *string* is not supplied, it is computed automatically from the *typespec*. (The optional *string* argument is allowed because some applications of check-type may require a more specific description of what is wanted than can be generated automatically from the type specifier.)

The error message will mention the *place*, its contents, and the desired type.

Implementation note: An implementation may choose to generate a somewhat differently worded error message if it recognizes that *place* is of a particular form, such as one of the arguments to the function that called check-type.

```
Lisp> (setq aardvarks '(sam harry fred))
 ⇒ (SAM HARRY FRED)
Lisp> (check-type aardvarks (array * (3)))
Error: The value of AARDVARKS, (SAM HARRY FRED),
       is not a 3-long array.
To continue, type :CONTINUE followed by an option number:
 1: Specify a value to use instead.
 2: Return to Lisp Toplevel.
Debug> :continue 1
Use Value: #(sam fred harry)
 ⇒ NIL
Lisp> aardvarks
 ⇒ #<ARRAY-3 13571>
Lisp> (map 'list #'identity aardvarks)
 ⇒ (SAM FRED HARRY)
Lisp> (setq aacount 'foo)
 ⇒ FOO
Lisp> (check-type aacount (integer 0 *) "a non-negative integer")
Error: The value of AACOUNT, FOO, is not a non-negative integer.
To continue, type :CONTINUE followed by an option number:
 1: Specify a value to use instead.
 2: Return to Lisp Toplevel.
Debug> :continue 2
Lisp>
```

Compatibility note: In Zetalisp, the equivalent facility is called check-arg-type.

assert *test-form* [({*place*}*) [*datum* {*argument*}*]]   [*Macro*]

[This supersedes the description of assert given in section 24.2.—GLS]

An assert form signals an error if the value of the *test-form* is nil. Continuing from this error using the continue restart will allow the user to alter the values of some variables, and assert will then start over, evaluating the *test-form* again. (The restart is associated with the signaled condition as if by use of with-condition-restarts.) assert returns nil.

The *test-form* may be any form. Each *place* (there may be any number of them, or none) must be a generalized variable reference acceptable to setf. These should be variables on which *test-form* depends, whose values may sensibly be changed by the user in attempting to correct the error. Subforms of each *place* are evaluated only if an error is signaled, and may be re-evaluated if the error is re-signaled (after continuing without actually fixing the problem).

The *datum* and *argument*s are evaluated only if an error is to be signaled, and re-evaluated if the error is to be signaled again.

If *datum* is a condition, then that condition is used directly. In this case, it is an error to specify any *argument*s.

If *datum* is a condition type (a class or class name), then the condition used is effectively the result of (apply #'make-condition *datum* (list {*argument*}*)).

If *datum* is a string, then the condition used is effectively the result of

```
(make-condition 'simple-error
                :format-string datum
                :format-arguments (list {argument}* ))
```

If *datum* is omitted, then a condition of type simple-error is constructed using the *test-form* as data. For example, the following might be used:

```
(make-condition 'simple-error
  :format-string "The assertion ~S failed."
  :format-arguments '(test-form))
```

Note that the *test-form* itself, and not its value, is used as the format argument.

Implementation note: The debugger need not include the *test-form* in the error message, and any *places* should not be included in the message, but they should be made available for the user's perusal. If the user gives the "continue" command, an opportunity should be presented to alter the values of any or all of the references. The details of this depend on the implementation's style of user interface, of course.

Here is an example of the use of assert:

```
(setq x (make-array '(3 5) :initial-element 3))
(setq y (make-array '(3 5) :initial-element 7))

(defun matrix-multiply (a b)
  (let ((*print-array* nil))
    (assert (and (= (array-rank a) (array-rank b) 2)
                 (= (array-dimension a 1)
                    (array-dimension b 0)))
            (a b)
            "Cannot multiply ~S by ~S." a b)
    (really-matrix-multiply a b)))

(matrix-multiply x y)
Error: Cannot multiply #<ARRAY-3-5 12345> by #<ARRAY-3-5 12364>.
To continue, type :CONTINUE followed by an option number:
 1: Specify new values.
 2: Return to Lisp Toplevel.
Debug> :continue 1
Value for A: x
Value for B: (make-array '(5 3) :initial-element 6)
 ⇒#2A((54 54 54 54 54)
      (54 54 54 54 54)
      (54 54 54 54 54)
      (54 54 54 54 54)
      (54 54 54 54 54))
```

29.4.3. Exhaustive Case Analysis

The syntax for etypecase and ctypecase is the same as for typecase, except that no otherwise clause is permitted. Similarly, the syntax for ecase and ccase is the same as for case except for the otherwise clause.

etypecase and ecase are similar to typecase and case, respectively, but signal a non-continuable error rather than returning nil if no clause is selected.

ctypecase and ccase are also similar to typecase and case, respectively, but signal a continuable error if no clause is selected.

etypecase *keyform* {(*type* {*form*}*)}*   [*Macro*]

[This supersedes the description of etypecase given in section 24.3.—GLS]

This control construct is similar to typecase, but no explicit otherwise or t clause is permitted. If no clause is satisfied, etypecase signals an error (of type type-error) with a message constructed from the clauses. It is not permissible to continue from this error. To supply an error message, the user should use typecase with an otherwise clause containing a call to error. The name of this function stands for "exhaustive type case" or "error-checking type case."

Example:

```
Lisp> (setq x 1/3)
 ⇒ 1/3
Lisp> (etypecase x
        (integer (* x 4))
        (symbol (symbol-value x)))
Error: The value of X, 1/3, is neither an integer nor a symbol.
To continue, type :CONTINUE followed by an option number:
 1: Return to Lisp Toplevel.
Debug>
```

ctypecase *keyplace* {(*type* {*form*}*)}*   [*Macro*]

[This supersedes the description of ctypecase given in section 24.3.—GLS]

This control construct is similar to typecase, but no explicit otherwise or t clause is permitted.

The *keyplace* must be a generalized variable reference acceptable to setf. If no clause is satisfied, ctypecase signals an error (of type type-error) with a message constructed from the clauses. This error may be continued using the store-value restart. The argument to store-value is stored in *keyplace* and then ctypecase starts over, making the type tests again. Subforms of *keyplace* may be evaluated multiple times. If the store-value restart is invoked interactively, the user will be prompted for the value to be used.

The name of this function is mnemonic for "continuable (exhaustive) type case."

Example:

```
Lisp> (setq x 1/3)
 ⇒ 1/3
Lisp> (ctypecase x
        (integer (* x 4))
        (symbol (symbol-value x)))
Error: The value of X, 1/3, is neither an integer nor a symbol.
To continue, type :CONTINUE followed by an option number:
```

```
  1: Specify a value to use instead.
  2: Return to Lisp Toplevel.
Debug> :continue 1
Use value: 3.7
Error: The value of X, 3.7, is neither an integer nor a symbol.
To continue, type :CONTINUE followed by an option number:
  1: Specify a value to use instead.
  2: Return to Lisp Toplevel.
Debug> :continue 1
Use value: 12
  ⇒ 48
```

ecase *keyform* {({({*key*}*) | *key*} {*form*}*)}*   [*Macro*]

[This supersedes the description of ecase given in section 24.3.—GLS]

This control construct is similar to case, but no explicit otherwise or t clause
is permitted. If no clause is satisfied, ecase signals an error (of type type-error)
with a message constructed from the clauses. It is not permissible to continue
from this error. To supply an error message, the user should use case with an
otherwise clause containing a call to error. The name of this function stands
for "exhaustive case" or "error-checking case."

Example:

```
Lisp> (setq x 1/3)
  ⇒ 1/3
Lisp> (ecase x
         (alpha (foo))
         (omega (bar))
         ((zeta phi) (baz)))
Error: The value of X, 1/3, is not ALPHA, OMEGA, ZETA, or PHI.
To continue, type :CONTINUE followed by an option number:
  1: Return to Lisp Toplevel.
Debug>
```

ccase *keyplace* {({({*key*}*) | *key*} {*form*}*)}*   [*Macro*]

[This supersedes the description of ccase given in section 24.3.—GLS]

This control construct is similar to case, but no explicit otherwise or t clause
is permitted.

The *keyplace* must be a generalized variable reference acceptable to setf. If no
clause is satisfied, ccase signals an error (of type type-error) with a message

constructed from the clauses. This error may be continued using the `store-value` restart. The argument to `store-value` is stored in *keyplace* and then `ccase` starts over, making the type tests again. Subforms of *keyplace* may be evaluated multiple times. If the `store-value` restart is invoked interactively, the user will be prompted for the value to be used.

The name of this function is mnemonic for "continuable (exhaustive) case."

Implementation note: The `type-error` signaled by `ccase` and `ecase` is free to choose any representation of the acceptable argument type that it wishes for placement in the expected-type slot. It will always work to use type `(member . keys)`, but in some cases it may be more efficient, for example, to use a type that represents an integer subrange or a type composed using the `or` type specifier.

29.4.4. Handling Conditions

These macros allow a program to gain control when a condition is signaled.

`handler-case` *expression* {(*typespec* ([*var*]) {*form*}*)}*   [*Macro*]

Executes the given *expression* in a context where various specified handlers are active.

Each *typespec* may be any type specifier. If during the execution of the `expression` a condition is signaled for which there is an appropriate clause—that is, one for which `(typep condition 'typespec)` is true—and if there is no intervening handler for conditions of that type, then control is transferred to the body of the relevant clause (unwinding the dynamic state appropriately in the process) and the given variable `var` is bound to the condition that was signaled. If no such condition is signaled and the computation runs to completion, then the values resulting from the `expression` are returned by the `handler-case` form.

If more than one case is provided, those cases are made accessible in parallel. That is, in

```
(handler-case expression
  (type₁ (var₁) form₁)
  (type₂ (var₂) form₂))
```

if the first clause (containing *form₁*) has been selected, the handler for the second is no longer visible (and vice versa).

The cases are searched sequentially from top to bottom. If a signaled condition matches more than one case (possible if there is type overlap) the earlier of the two cases will be selected.

If the variable *var* is not needed, it may be omitted. That is, a clause such as

(*type* (*var*) (declare (ignore *var*)) *form*)

may be written using the following shorthand notation:

(*type* () *form*)

If there are no forms in a selected case, the case returns nil. Note that

```
(handler-case expression
  (type₁ (var₁) . body₁)
  (type₂ (var₂) . body₂)
  ...)
```

is approximately equivalent to

```
(block #1=#:block-1
  (let (#2=#:var-2)
    (tagbody
      (handler-bind ((type₁ #´(lambda (temp)
                                (setq #2# temp)
                                (go #3=#;tag-3)))
                     (type₂ #´(lambda (temp)
                                (setq #2# temp)
                                (go #4=#:tag-4)))
                     ...)
        (return-from #1# expression))
      #3# (return-from #1# (let ((var₁ #2#)) . body₁))
      #4# (return-from #1# (let ((var₂ #2#)) . body₂))
      ...)))
```

[Note the use of "gensyms" such as #:block-1 as block names, variables, and tagbody tags in this example, and the use of #*n*= and #*n*# read-macro syntax to indicate that the very same gensym appears in multiple places.—GLS]

As a special case, the *typespec* can also be the symbol :no-error in the last clause. If it is, it designates a clause that will take control if the *expression* returns normally. In that case, a completely general lambda-list may follow the symbol :no-error, and the arguments to which the lambda-list parameters are bound are like those for multiple-value-call on the return value of the *expression*. For example,

```
(handler-case expression
  (type₁ (var₁) . body₁)
  (type₂ (var₂) . body₂)
  ...
  (typeₙ (varₙ) . bodyₙ)
  (:no-error (nvar₁ nvar₂ ... nvarₘ) . nbody))
```

is approximately equivalent to

```
(block #1=#:error-return
  (multiple-value-call #'(lambda (nvar₁ nvar₂ ... nvarₘ) . nbody)
    (block #2=#:normal-return
      (return-from #1#
        (handler-case (return-from #2# expression)
          (type₁ (var₁) . body₁)
          (type₂ (var₂) . body₂)
          ...
          (typeₙ (varₙ) . bodyₙ))))))
```

Examples of the use of handler-case:

```
(handler-case (/ x y)
  (division-by-zero () nil))

(handler-case (open *the-file* :direction :input)
  (file-error (condition) (format t "~&Fooey: ~A~%" condition)))

(handler-case (some-user-function)
  (file-error (condition) condition)
  (division-by-zero () 0)
  ((or unbound-variable undefined-function) () 'unbound))

(handler-case (intern x y)
  (error (condition) condition)
  (:no-error (symbol status)
    (declare (ignore symbol))
    status))
```

ignore-errors {*form*}*   [*Macro*]

Executes its body in a context that handles conditions of type error by returning
control to this form. If no such condition is signaled, any values returned by the

last form are returned by ignore-errors. Otherwise, two values are returned: nil and the error condition that was signaled.

ignore-errors could be defined by

```
(defmacro ignore-errors (&body forms)
  `(handler-case (progn ,@forms)
     (error (c) (values nil c))))
```

handler-bind ({(*typespec handler*)}*) {*form*}*   [*Macro*]

Executes body in a dynamic context where the given handler bindings are in effect. Each *typespec* may be any type specifier. Each *handler* form should evaluate to a function to be used to handle conditions of the given type(s) during execution of the *forms*. This function should take a single argument, the condition being signaled.

If more than one binding is specified, the bindings are searched sequentially from top to bottom in search of a match (by visual analogy with typecase). If an appropriate *typespec* is found, the associated handler is run in a context where none of the handler bindings are visible (to avoid recursive errors). For example, in the case of

```
(handler-bind ((unbound-variable #'(lambda ...))
               (error #'(lambda ...)))
  ...)
```

if an unbound variable error is signaled in the body (and not handled by an intervening handler), the first function will be called. If any other kind of error is signaled, the second function will be called. In either case, neither handler will be active while executing the code in the associated function.

29.4.5. Defining Conditions

[The contents of this section are still a subject of some debate within X3J13. The reader may wish to take this section with a grain of salt, two aspirin tablets, and call a hacker in the morning.—GLS]

define-condition *name* ({*parent-type*}*)   [*Macro*]
               [({*slot-specifier*}*) {*option*}*]

Defines a new condition type called *name*, which is a subtype of each given *parent-type*. Except as otherwise noted, the arguments are not evaluated.

Objects of this condition type will have all of the indicated *slots*, plus any additional slots inherited from the parent types (its superclasses). If the *slots* list is omitted, the empty list is assumed.

A *slot* must have the form

slot-specifier ::= *slot-name* | (*slot-name* [[↓ *slot-option*]])

For the syntax of a *slot-option*, see defclass. The slots of a condition object are normal CLOS slots. Note that with-slots may be used instead of accessor functions to access slots of a condition object.

make-condition will accept keywords (in the keyword package) with the print name of any of the designated slots, and will initialize the corresponding slots in conditions it creates.

Accessors are created according to the same rules as used by defclass.

The valid *options* are as follows:

(:documentation *doc-string*)

The *doc-string* should be either nil or a string that describes the purpose of the condition type. If this option is omitted, nil is assumed. Calling (documentation ´*name* ´type) will retrieve this information.

(:report *exp*)

If *exp* is not a literal string, it must be a suitable argument to the function special form. The expression (function *exp*) will be evaluated in the current lexical environment. It should produce a function of two arguments, a condition and a stream, that prints on the stream a description of the condition. This function is called whenever the condition is printed while *print-escape* is nil.

If *exp* is a literal string, it is shorthand for

```
(lambda (c s)
  (declare (ignore c))
  (write-string exp s))
```

[That is, a function is provided that will simply write the given string literally to the stream, regardless of the particular condition object supplied.—GLS]

The :report option is processed *after* the new condition type has been defined, so use of the slot accessors within the report function is permitted. If this option is not specified, information about how to report this type of condition will be inherited from the *parent-type*.

[X3J13 voted in March 1989 ⟨186⟩ to integrate the Condition System and the Object System. In the original Condition System proposal, define-condition allowed only one *parent-type* (the inheritance structure was a simple hierarchy). Slot descriptions were much simpler, even simpler than those for defstruct:

slot ::= *slot-name* | (*slot-name*) | (*slot-name default-value*)

Similarly, define-condition allowed a :conc-name option similar to that of defstruct:

(:conc-name *symbol-or-string*)

Not now part of Common Lisp. As with defstruct, this sets up automatic prefixing of the names of slot accessors. Also as in defstruct, the default behavior is to use the name of the new type, *name*, followed by a hyphen. (Generated names are interned in the package that is current at the time that the define-condition is processed).

One consequence of the vote was to make define-condition slot descriptions like those of defclass.—GLS]

Here are some examples of the use of define-condition.

The following form defines a condition of type peg/hole-mismatch that inherits from a condition type called blocks-world-error:

```
(define-condition peg/hole-mismatch (blocks-world-error)
                  (peg-shape hole-shape)
   (:report
     (lambda (condition stream)
       (with-slots (peg-shape hole-shape) condition
         (format stream "A ~A peg cannot go in a ~A hole."
                 peg-shape hole-shape)))))
```

The new type has slots peg-shape and hole-shape, so make-condition will accept :peg-shape and :hole-shape keywords. The with-slots macro may be used to access the peg-shape and hole-shape slots, as illustrated in the :report information.

Here is another example. This defines a condition called machine-error that inherits from error:

```
(define-condition machine-error (error)
                  ((machine-name
                     :reader machine-error-machine-name))
```

```
(:report (lambda (condition stream)
          (format stream "There is a problem with ~A."
                  (machine-error-machine-name condition)))))
```

Building on this definition, we can define a new error condition that is a subtype of `machine-error` for use when machines are not available:

```
(define-condition machine-not-available-error (machine-error) ()
  (:report (lambda (condition stream)
            (format stream "The machine ~A is not available."
                    (machine-error-machine-name condition)))))
```

We may now define a still more specific condition, built upon `machine-not-available-error`, that provides a default for `machine-name` but does not provide any new slots or report information. It just gives the `machine-name` slot a default initialization:

```
(define-condition my-favorite-machine-not-available-error
                  (machine-not-available-error)
                  ((machine-name :initform "MC.LCS.MIT.EDU")))
```

Note that since no `:report` clause was given, the information inherited from `machine-not-available-error` will be used to report this type of condition.

29.4.6. Creating Conditions

The function `make-condition` is the basic means for creating condition objects.

`make-condition` *type* &rest *slot-initializations*   [*Function*]

Constructs a condition object of the given *type* using *slot-initializations* as a specification of the initial value of the slots. The newly created condition is returned.

The *slot-initializations* are alternating keyword/value pairs. For example:

```
(make-condition 'peg/hole-mismatch
                :peg-shape 'square :hole-shape 'round)
```

29.4.7. Establishing Restarts

The lowest-level form that creates restart points is called `restart-bind`. The `restart-case` macro is an abstraction that addresses many common needs for `restart-bind` while offering a more palatable syntax. See also `with-simple-`

restart. The function that transfers control to a restart point established by one of these macros is called invoke-restart.

All restarts have dynamic extent; a restart does not survive execution of the form that establishes it.

with-simple-restart (*name format-string* {*format-argument*}*)   [*Macro*]
                    {*form*}*

This is shorthand for one of the most common uses of restart-case.

If the restart designated by *name* is not invoked while executing the *forms*, all values returned by the last *form* are returned. If that restart is invoked, control is transferred to the with-simple-restart form, which immediately returns the two values nil and t.

The *name* may be nil, in which case an anonymous restart is established. with-simple-restart could be defined by

```
(defmacro with-simple-restart ((restart-name format-string
                                &rest format-arguments)
                               &body forms)
  `(restart-case (progn ,@forms)
     (,restart-name ()
       :report
         (lambda (stream)
           (format stream ,format-string ,@format-arguments))
       (values nil t))))
```

Here is an example of the use of with-simple-restart.

```
Lisp> (defun read-eval-print-loop (level)
        (with-simple-restart
            (abort "Exit command level ~D." level)
          (loop
            (with-simple-restart
                (abort "Return to command level ~D." level)
              (let ((form (prog2 (fresh-line)
                                 (read)
                                 (fresh-line))))
                (prin1 (eval form)))))))
  ⇒ READ-EVAL-PRINT-LOOP
Lisp> (read-eval-print-loop 1)
(+ 'a 3)
```

```
Error: The argument, A, to the function + was of the wrong type.
       The function expected a number.
To continue, type :CONTINUE followed by an option number:
 1: Specify a value to use this time.
 2: Return to command level 1.
 3: Exit command level 1.
 4: Return to Lisp Toplevel.
Debug>
```

Compatibility note: In contrast to the way that Zetalisp has traditionally defined `abort` as a kind of condition to be handled, the Common Lisp Condition System defines `abort` as a way to restart ("proceed" in Zetalisp terms).

Remark: Some readers may wonder what ought to be done by the "abort" key (or whatever the implementation's interrupt key is—Control-C or Control-G, for example). Such interrupts, whether synchronous or asynchronous in nature, are beyond the scope of this chapter and indeed are not currently addressed by Common Lisp at all. This may be a topic worth standardizing under separate cover. Here is some speculation about some possible things that might happen.

An implementation might simply call `abort` or `break` directly without signaling any condition.

Another implementation might signal some condition related to the fact that a key had been pressed rather than to the action that should be taken. This is one way to allow user customization. Perhaps there would be an implementation-dependent `keyboard-interrupt` condition type with a slot containing the key that was pressed—or perhaps there would be such a condition type, but rather than its having slots, different subtypes of that type with names like `keyboard-abort`, `keyboard-break`, and so on might be signaled. That implementation would then document the action it would take if user programs failed to handle the condition, and perhaps ways for user programs to usefully dismiss the interrupt.

Implementation note: Implementors are encouraged to make sure that there is always a restart named `abort` around any user code so that user code can call `abort` at any time and expect something reasonable to happen; exactly what the reasonable thing is may vary somewhat. Typically, in an interactive program, invoking `abort` should return the user to top level, though in some batch or multi-processing situations killing the running process might be more appropriate.

restart-case *expression* {(*case-name arglist*   [*Macro*]
                           {*keyword value*}*
                           {*form*}*)}*

The *expression* is evaluated in a dynamic context where the clauses have special meanings as points to which control may be transferred. If the *expression* finishes executing and returns any values, all such values are simply returned by the restart-case form. While the *expression* is running, any code may transfer control to one of the clauses (see invoke-restart). If a transfer occurs, the *forms* in the body of that clause will be evaluated and any values returned by the last such *form* will be returned by the restart-case form.

As a special case, if the *expression* is a list whose *car* is signal, error, cerror, or warn, then with-condition-restarts is implicitly used to associate the restarts with the condition to be signaled. For example,

```
(restart-case (signal weird-error)
  (become-confused ...)
  (rewind-line-printer ...)
  (halt-and-catch-fire ...))
```

is equivalent to

```
(restart-case (with-condition-restarts
                weird-error
                (list (find-restart 'become-confused)
                      (find-restart 'rewind-line-printer)
                      (find-restart 'halt-and-catch-fire))
                (signal weird-error))
  (become-confused ...)
  (rewind-line-printer ...)
  (halt-and-catch-fire ...))
```

If there are no *forms* in a selected clause, restart-case returns nil.

The *case-name* may be nil or a symbol naming this restart.

It is possible to have more than one clause use the same *case-name*. In this case, the first clause with that name will be found by find-restart. The other clauses are accessible using compute-restarts. [In this respect, restart-case is rather different from case!—GLS]

Each *arglist* is a normal lambda-list containing parameters to be bound during the execution of its corresponding *forms*. These parameters are used to pass any necessary data from a call to invoke-restart to the restart-case clause.

By default, invoke-restart-interactively will pass no arguments and all parameters must be optional in order to accommodate interactive restarting. However, the parameters need not be optional if the :interactive keyword has been used to inform invoke-restart-interactively about how to compute a proper argument list.

The valid *keyword value* pairs are the following:

:test *fn*
The *fn* must be a suitable argument for the function special form. The expression
(function *fn*) will be evaluated in the current lexical environment. It should
produce a function of one argument, a condition. If this function returns nil
when given some condition, functions such as find-restart, compute-restart,
and invoke-restart will not consider this restart when searching for restarts
associated with that condition. If this pair is not supplied, it is as if

```
(lambda (c) (declare (ignore c)) t)
```

were used for the *fn*.

:interactive *fn*
The *fn* must be a suitable argument for the function special form. The expression (function *fn*) will be evaluated in the current lexical environment. It
should produce a function of no arguments that returns arguments to be used by
invoke-restart-interactively when invoking this function. This function will
be called in the dynamic environment available prior to any restart attempt. It may
interact with the user on the stream in *query-io*.
    If a restart is invoked interactively but no :interactive option was supplied,
the argument list used in the invocation is the empty list.

:report *exp*
If *exp* is not a literal string, it must be a suitable argument to the function special
form. The expression (function *exp*) will be evaluated in the current lexical
environment. It should produce a function of one argument, a stream, that prints
on the stream a description of the restart. This function is called whenever the
restart is printed while *print-escape* is nil.
    If *exp* is a literal string, it is shorthand for

```
(lambda (s) (write-string exp s))
```

[That is, a function is provided that will simply write the given string literally to
the stream.—GLS]
    If a named restart is asked to report but no report information has been supplied,
the name of the restart is used in generating default report text.
    When *print-escape* is nil, the printer will use the report information for a
restart. For example, a debugger might announce the action of typing ":continue"
by executing the equivalent of

```
(format *debug-io* "~&~S -- ~A~%" ':continue some-restart)
```

which might then display as something like

```
:CONTINUE -- Return to command level.
```

It is an error if an unnamed restart is used and no report information is provided.

Rationale: Unnamed restarts are required to have report information on the grounds that they are generally only useful interactively, and an interactive option that has no description is of little value.

Implementation note: Implementations are encouraged to warn about this error at compilation time.

At run time, this error might be noticed when entering the debugger. Since signaling an error would probably cause recursive entry into the debugger (causing yet another recursive error, and so on), it is suggested that the debugger print some indication of such problems when they occur, but not actually signal errors.

Note that

```
(restart-case expression
    (name₁ arglist₁ options₁ . body₁)
    (name₂ arglist₂ options₂ . body₂)
    ...)
```

is essentially equivalent to

```
(block #1=#:block-1
  (let ((#2=#:var-2 nil))
    (tagbody
      (restart-bind ((name₁ #'(lambda (&rest temp)
                                (setq #2# temp)
                                (go #3=#:tag-3))
                             ⟨slightly transformed options₁⟩)
                     (name₂ #'(lambda (&rest temp)
                                (setq #2# temp)
                                (go #4=#:tag-4))
                             ⟨slightly transformed options₂⟩)
                     ...)
        (return-from #1# expression))
```

```
      #3# (return-from #1#
                 (apply #´(lambda arglist₁ . body₁) #2#))
      #4# (return-from #1#
                 (apply #´(lambda arglist₂ . body₂) #2#))
     ...)))
```

[Note the use of "gensyms" such as #:block-1 as block names, variables, and tagbody tags in this example, and the use of #*n*= and #*n*# read-macro syntax to indicate that the very same gensym appears in multiple places.—GLS]

Here are some examples of the use of restart-case.

```
(loop
  (restart-case (return (apply function some-args))
    (new-function (new-function)
        :report "Use a different function."
        :interactive
          (lambda ()
              (list (prompt-for ´function "Function: ")))
        (setq function new-function))))
```

```
(loop
  (restart-case (return (apply function some-args))
    (nil (new-function)
        :report "Use a different function."
        :interactive
          (lambda ()
              (list (prompt-for ´function "Function: ")))
        (setq function new-function))))
```

```
(restart-case (a-command-loop)
  (return-from-command-level ()
      :report
        (lambda (s)      ;Argument s is a stream
          (format s "Return from command level ~D." level))
    nil))
```

```
(loop
  (restart-case (another-random-computation)
    (continue () nil)))
```

The first and second examples are equivalent from the point of view of someone using the interactive debugger, but they differ in one important aspect for non-interactive handling. If a handler "knows about" named restarts, as in, for example,

```
(when (find-restart 'new-function)
  (invoke-restart 'new-function the-replacement))
```

then only the first example, and not the second, will have control transferred to its correction clause, since only the first example uses a restart named new-function.

Here is a more complete example:

```
(let ((my-food 'milk)
      (my-color 'greenish-blue))
  (do ()
      ((not (bad-food-color-p my-food my-color)))
    (restart-case (error 'bad-food-color
                         :food my-food :color my-color)
      (use-food (new-food)
          :report "Use another food."
        (setq my-food new-food))
      (use-color (new-color)
          :report "Use another color."
        (setq my-color new-color))))
  ;; We won't get to here until MY-FOOD
  ;; and MY-COLOR are compatible.
  (list my-food my-color))
```

Assuming that use-food and use-color have been defined as

```
(defun use-food (new-food)
  (invoke-restart 'use-food new-food))

(defun use-color (new-color)
  (invoke-restart 'use-color new-color))
```

a handler can then restart from the error in either of two ways. It may correct the color or correct the food. For example:

```
#'(lambda (c) ... (use-color 'white) ...)     ;Corrects color

#'(lambda (c) ... (use-food 'cheese) ...)     ;Corrects food
```

Here is an example using handler-bind and restart-case that refers to a condition type foo-error, presumably defined elsewhere:

```
(handler-bind ((foo-error #´(lambda (ignore) (use-value 7))))
  (restart-case (error ´foo-error)
    (use-value (x) (* x x))))
  ⇒ 49
```

restart-bind ({(*name function* {*keyword value*}*)}*) {*form*}*   [*Macro*]

Executes a body of forms in a dynamic context where the given restart bindings
are in effect.

Each *name* may be nil to indicate an anonymous restart, or some other symbol
to indicate a named restart.

Each *function* is a form that should evaluate to a function to be used to perform
the restart. If invoked, this function may either perform a non-local transfer of
control or it may return normally. The function may take whatever arguments the
programmer feels are appropriate; it will be invoked only if invoke-restart is
used from a program, or if a user interactively asks the debugger to invoke it. In
the case of interactive invocation, the :interactive-function option is used.

The valid *keyword value* pairs are as follows:

:test-function *form*

The *form* will be evaluated in the current lexical environment and should return a function of one argument, a condition. If this function returns nil when
given some condition, functions such as find-restart, compute-restart, and
invoke-restart will not consider this restart when searching for restarts associated with that condition. If this pair is not supplied, it is as if

```
#´(lambda (c) (declare (ignore c)) t)
```

were used for the *form*.

:interactive-function *form*

The *form* will be evaluated in the current lexical environment and should return a function of no arguments that constructs a list of arguments to be used
by invoke-restart-interactively when invoking this restart. The function
may prompt interactively using *query-io* if necessary.

:report-function *form*

The *form* will be evaluated in the current lexical environment and should return
a function of one argument, a stream, that prints on the stream a summary of the

action this restart will take. This function is called whenever the restart is printed while *print-escape* is nil.

---

with-condition-restarts *condition-form restarts-form*   [*Macro*]
          {declaration}* {form}*

The value of *condition-form* should be a condition *C* and the value of *restarts-form* should be a list of restarts (*R1 R2* ...). The *form*s of the body are evaluated as an implicit progn. While in the dynamic context of the body, an attempt to find a restart associated with a particular condition *C'* will consider the restarts *R1, R2,* ... if *C'* is eq to *C*.

Usually this macro is not used explicitly in code, because restart-case handles most of the common uses in a way that is syntactically more concise.

[The X3J13 vote ⟨31⟩ left it unclear whether with-condition-restarts permits declarations to appear at the heads of its body. I believe that was the intent, but this is only my interpretation.—GLS]

29.4.8. Finding and Manipulating Restarts

The following functions determine what restarts are active and invoke restarts.

---

compute-restarts &optional *condition*   [*Function*]

Uses the dynamic state of the program to compute a list of the restarts that are currently active. See restart-bind.

If *condition* is nil or not supplied, all outstanding restarts are returned. If *condition* is not nil, only restarts associated with that condition are returned.

Each restart represents a function that can be called to perform some form of recovery action, usually a transfer of control to an outer point in the running program. Implementations are free to implement these objects in whatever manner is most convenient; the objects need have only dynamic extent (relative to the scope of the binding form that instantiates them).

The list that results from a call to compute-restarts is ordered so that the inner (that is, more recently established) restarts are nearer the head of the list.

Note, too, that compute-restarts returns all valid restarts, including anonymous ones, even if some of them have the same name as others and would therefore not be found by find-restart when given a symbol argument.

Implementations are permitted, but not required, to return different (that is, non-eq) lists from repeated calls to compute-restarts while in the same dynamic environment. It is an error to modify the list that is returned by compute-restarts.

`restart-name` *restart*   [*Function*]

Returns the name of the given *restart*, or `nil` if it is not named.

`find-restart` *restart-identifier* `&optional` *condition*   [*Function*]

Searches for a particular restart in the current dynamic environment.

If *condition* is `nil` or not supplied, all outstanding restarts are considered. If *condition* is not `nil`, only restarts associated with that condition are considered.

If the *restart-identifier* is a non-`nil` symbol, then the innermost (that is, most recently established) restart with that name is returned; `nil` is returned if no such restart is found.

If *restart-identifier* is a restart object, then it is simply returned, unless it is not currently active, in which case `nil` is returned.

Although anonymous restarts have a name of `nil`, it is an error for the symbol `nil` to be given as the *restart-identifier*. Applications that would seem to require this should be rewritten to make appropriate use of `compute-restarts` instead.

`invoke-restart` *restart-identifier* `&rest` *arguments*   [*Function*]

Calls the function associated with the given *restart-identifier*, passing any given *arguments*. The *restart-identifier* must be a restart or the non-null name of a restart that is valid in the current dynamic context. If the argument is not valid, an error of type `control-error` will be signaled.

Implementation note: Restart functions call this function, not vice versa.

`invoke-restart-interactively` *restart-identifier*   [*Function*]

Calls the function associated with the given *restart-identifier*, prompting for any necessary arguments. The *restart-identifier* must be a restart or the non-null name of a restart that is valid in the current dynamic context. If the argument is not valid, an error of type `control-error` will be signaled.

The function `invoke-restart-interactively` will prompt for arguments by executing the code provided in the `:interactive` keyword to `restart-case` or `:interactive-function` keyword to `restart-bind`.

If no `:interactive` or `:interactive-function` option has been supplied in the corresponding `restart-case` or `restart-bind`, then it is an error if the restart takes required arguments. If the arguments are optional, an empty argument list will be used in this case.

Once `invoke-restart-interactively` has calculated the arguments, it simply performs (`apply #´invoke-restart` *restart-identifier arguments*).

`invoke-restart-interactively` is used internally by the debugger and may also be useful in implementing other portable, interactive debugging tools.

29.4.9. Warnings

Warnings are a subclass of errors that are conventionally regarded as "mild."

`warn` *datum* &rest *arguments*   [*Function*]

[This supersedes the description of `warn` given in section 24.1.—GLS]

Warns about a situation, by signaling a condition of type `warning`.

If *datum* is a condition, then that condition is used directly. In this case, if the condition is not of type `warning` or arguments is non-`nil`, an error of type `type-error` is signaled.

If *datum* is a condition type (a class or class name), then the condition used is effectively the result of (`apply #´make-condition` *datum arguments*). This result must be of type `warning` or an error of type `type-error` is signaled.

If *datum* is a string, then the condition used is effectively the result of

```
(make-condition ´simple-error
                :format-string datum
                :format-arguments arguments)
```

The precise mechanism for warning is as follows.

1. The warning condition is signaled.

   While the `warning` condition is being signaled, the `muffle-warning` restart is established for use by a handler to bypass further action by `warn` (that is, to cause `warn` to immediately return `nil`).

   As part of the signaling process, if (`typep` *condition* `*break-on-signals*`) is true, then a `break` will occur prior to beginning the signaling process.

2. If no handlers for the warning condition are found, or if all such handlers decline, then the condition will be reported to `*error-output*` by the `warn` function (with possible implementation-specific extra output such as motion to a fresh line before or after the display of the warning, or supplying some introductory text mentioning the name of the function that called `warn` or the fact that this is a warning).

3. The value returned by `warn` (if it returns) is `nil`.

29.4.10. Restart Functions

Common Lisp has the following restart functions built in.

abort &optional *condition*   [*Function*]

This function transfers control to the restart named abort. If no such restart exists, abort signals an error of type control-error.

If *condition* is nil or not supplied, all outstanding restarts are considered. If *condition* is not nil, only restarts associated with that condition are considered.

The purpose of the abort restart is generally to allow control to return to the innermost "command level."

continue &optional *condition*   [*Function*]

This function transfers control to the restart named continue. If no such restart exists, continue returns nil.

If *condition* is nil or not supplied, all outstanding restarts are considered. If *condition* is not nil, only restarts associated with that condition are considered.

The continue restart is generally part of simple protocols where there is a single "obvious" way to continue, as with break and cerror. Some user-defined protocols may also wish to incorporate it for similar reasons. In general, however, it is more reliable to design a special-purpose restart with a name that better suits the particular application.

muffle-warning &optional *condition*   [*Function*]

This function transfers control to the restart named muffle-warning. If no such restart exists, muffle-warning signals an error of type control-error.

If *condition* is nil or not supplied, all outstanding restarts are considered. If *condition* is not nil, only restarts associated with that condition are considered.

warn sets up this restart so that handlers of warning conditions have a way to tell warn that a warning has already been dealt with and that no further action is warranted.

store-value *value* &optional *condition*   [*Function*]

This function transfers control (and one value) to the restart named store-value. If no such restart exists, store-value returns nil.

If *condition* is nil or not supplied, all outstanding restarts are considered. If *condition* is not nil, only restarts associated with that condition are considered.

The store-value restart is generally used by handlers trying to recover from errors of types such as cell-error or type-error, where the handler may wish to supply a replacement datum to be stored permanently.

---

use-value *value* &optional *condition*   [*Function*]

This function transfers control (and one value) to the restart named use-value. If no such restart exists, use-value returns nil.

If *condition* is nil or not supplied, all outstanding restarts are considered. If *condition* is not nil, only restarts associated with that condition are considered.

The use-value restart is generally used by handlers trying to recover from errors of types such as cell-error, where the handler may wish to supply a replacement datum for one-time use.

29.4.11. Debugging Utilities

Common Lisp does not specify exactly what a debugger is or does, but it does provide certain means for indicating intent to transfer control to a supervisory or debugging facility.

---

break &optional *format-string* &rest *format-arguments*   [*Function*]

[This supersedes the description of break given in section 24.1.—GLS]

The function break prints the message described by the *format-string* and *format-arguments* and then goes directly into the debugger without allowing any possibility of interception by programmed error-handling facilities.

If no *format-string* is supplied, a suitable default will be generated.

If continued, break returns nil.

Note that break is presumed to be used as a way of inserting temporary debugging "breakpoints" in a program, not as a way of signaling errors; it is expected that continuing from a break will not trigger any unusual recovery action. For this reason, break does not take the additional format control string that cerror takes as its first argument. This and the lack of any possibility of interception by programmed error handling are the only program-visible differences between break and cerror. The user interface aspects of these functions are permitted to vary more widely; for example, it is permissible for a read-eval-print loop to be entered by break rather than by the conventional debugger.

break could be defined by

```
(defun break (&optional (format-string "Break")
              &rest format-arguments)
  (with-simple-restart (continue "Return from BREAK.")
    (invoke-debugger
      (make-condition 'simple-condition
                      :format-string format-string
                      :format-arguments format-arguments)))
  nil)
```

invoke-debugger *condition*   [*Function*]

Attempts interactive handling of its argument, which must be a condition.

If the variable *debugger-hook* is not nil, it will be called as a function on two arguments: the *condition* being handled and the value of *debugger-hook*. If a hook function returns normally, the standard debugger will be tried.

The standard debugger will never directly return. Return can occur only by a special transfer of control, such as the use of a restart.

Remark: The exact way in which the debugger interacts with users is expected to vary considerably from system to system. For example, some systems may use a keyboard interface, while others may use a mouse interface. Of those systems using keyboard commands, some may use single-character commands and others may use parsed line-at-a-time commands. The exact set of commands will vary as well. The important properties of a debugger are that it makes information about the error accessible and that it makes the set of apparent restarts easily accessible.

It is desirable to have a mode where the debugger allows other features, such as the ability to inspect data, stacks, etc. However, it may sometimes be appropriate to have this kind of information hidden from users. Experience on the Lisp Machines has shown that some users who are not programmers develop a terrible phobia of debuggers. The reason for this usually may be traced to the fact that the debugger is very foreign to them and provides an overwhelming amount of information of interest only to programmers. With the advent of restarts, there is a clear mechanism for the construction of "friendly" debuggers. Programmers can be taught how to get to the information they need for debugging, but it should be possible to construct user interfaces to the debugger that are natural, convenient, intelligible, and friendly even to non-programmers.

---

debugger-hook   [*Variable*]

This variable should hold either nil or a function of two arguments, a condition and the value of *debugger-hook*. This function may either handle the condition (transfer control) or return normally (allowing the standard debugger to run).

Note that, to minimize recursive errors while debugging, *debugger-hook* is bound to nil when calling this function. When evaluating code typed in by the user interactively, the hook function may want to bind *debugger-hook* to the function that was its second argument so that recursive errors can be handled using the same interactive facility.

29.5. Predefined Condition Types

[The proposal for the Common Lisp Condition System introduced a new notation for documenting types, treating them in the same syntactic manner as functions and variables. This notation is used in this section but is not reflected throughout the entire book.—GLS]

X3J13 voted in March 1989 ⟨186⟩ to integrate the Condition System and the Object System. All condition types are CLOS classes and all condition objects are ordinary CLOS objects.

restart   [*Type*]

This is the data type used to represent a restart.

The Common Lisp condition type hierarchy is illustrated in table 29-1.

The types that are not leaves in the hierarchy (that is, condition, warning, storage-condition, error, arithmetic-error, control-error, and so on) are provided primarily for type inclusion purposes. Normally they would not be directly instantiated.

Implementations are permitted to support non-portable synonyms for these types, as well as to introduce other types that are above, below, or between the types shown in this tree as long as the indicated subtype relationships are not violated.

The types simple-condition, serious-condition, and warning are pairwise disjoint. The type error is also disjoint from types simple-condition and warning.

condition   [*Type*]

All types of conditions, whether error or non-error, must inherit from this type.

warning   [*Type*]

All types of warnings should inherit from this type. This is a subtype of condition.

Table 29-1: Condition Type Hierarchy

```
condition
    simple-condition
    serious-condition
        error
                simple-error
                arithmetic-error
                    division-by-zero
                    floating-point-overflow
                    floating-point-underflow
                    ...
                cell-error
                    unbound-variable
                    undefined-function
                    ...
                control-error
                file-error
                package-error
                program-error
                stream-error
                    end-of-file
                    ...
                type-error
                    simple-type-error
                    ...
            ...
        storage-condition
        ...
    warning
        simple-warning
        ...
    ...
```

serious-condition   *[Type]*

All serious conditions (conditions serious enough to require interactive intervention
if not handled) should inherit from this type. This is a subtype of condition.

   This condition type is provided primarily for terminological convenience. In
fact, signaling a condition that inherits from serious-condition does not force
entry into the debugger. Rather, it is conventional to use error (or something built

on error) to signal conditions that are of this type, and to use signal to signal conditions that are not of this type.

error   [*Type*]

All types of error conditions inherit from this condition. This is a subtype of serious-condition.

The default condition type for signal and warn is simple-condition. The default condition type for error and cerror is simple-error.

simple-condition   [*Type*]

Conditions signaled by signal when given a format string as a first argument are of this type. This is a subtype of condition. The initialization keywords :format-string and :format-arguments are supported to initialize the slots, which can be accessed using simple-condition-format-string and simple-condition-format-arguments. If :format-arguments is not supplied to make-condition, the format-arguments slot defaults to nil.

simple-warning   [*Type*]

Conditions signaled by warn when given a format string as a first argument are of this type. This is a subtype of warning. The initialization keywords :format-string and :format-arguments are supported to initialize the slots, which can be accessed using simple-condition-format-string and simple-condition-format-arguments. If :format-arguments is not supplied to make-condition, the format-arguments slot defaults to nil.

In implementations supporting multiple inheritance, this type will also be a subtype of simple-condition.

simple-error   [*Type*]

Conditions signaled by error and cerror when given a format string as a first argument are of this type. This is a subtype of error. The initialization keywords :format-string and :format-arguments are supported to initialize the slots, which can be accessed using simple-condition-format-string and simple-condition-format-arguments. If :format-arguments is not supplied to make-condition, the format-arguments slot defaults to nil.

In implementations supporting multiple inheritance, this type will also be a subtype of simple-condition.

`simple-condition-format-string` *condition*   [*Function*]

Accesses the format-string slot of a given *condition*, which must be of type `simple-condition`, `simple-warning`, `simple-error`, or `simple-type-error`.

`simple-condition-format-arguments` *condition*   [*Function*]

Accesses the format-arguments slot of a given *condition*, which must be of type `simple-condition`, `simple-warning`, `simple-error`, or `simple-type-error`.

`storage-condition`   [*Type*]

Conditions that relate to storage overflow should inherit from this type. This is a subtype of `serious-condition`.

`type-error`   [*Type*]

Errors in the transfer of data in a program should inherit from this type. This is a subtype of `error`. For example, conditions to be signaled by `check-type` should inherit from this type. The initialization keywords `:datum` and `:expected-type` are supported to initialize the slots, which can be accessed using `type-error-datum` and `type-error-expected-type`.

`type-error-datum` *condition*   [*Function*]

Accesses the datum slot of a given *condition*, which must be of type `type-error`.

`type-error-expected-type` *condition*   [*Function*]

Accesses the expected-type slot of a given *condition*, which must be of type `type-error`. Users of `type-error` conditions are expected to fill this slot with an object that is a valid Common Lisp type specifier.

`simple-type-error`   [*Type*]

Conditions signaled by facilities similar to `check-type` may want to use this type. The initialization keywords `:format-string` and `:format-arguments` are supported to initialize the slots, which can be accessed using `simple-condition-format-string` and `simple-condition-format-arguments`. If `:format-arguments` is not supplied to `make-condition`, the format-arguments slot defaults to `nil`.

In implementations supporting multiple inheritance, this type will also be a sub-type of simple-condition.

program-error   [*Type*]

Errors relating to incorrect program syntax that are statically detectable should inherit from this type (regardless of whether they are in fact statically detected). This is a subtype of error. This is *not* a subtype of control-error.

control-error   [*Type*]

Errors in the dynamic transfer of control in a program should inherit from this type. This is a subtype of error. This is *not* a subtype of program-error.

The errors that result from giving throw a tag that is not active or from giving go or return-from a tag that is no longer dynamically available are control errors.

On the other hand, the errors that result from naming a go tag or return-from tag that is not lexically apparent are not control errors. They are program errors. See program-error.

package-error   [*Type*]

Errors that occur during operations on packages should inherit from this type. This is a subtype of error. The initialization keyword :package is supported to initialize the slot, which can be accessed using package-error-package.

package-error-package *condition*   [*Function*]

Accesses the package (or package name) that was being modified or manipulated in a *condition* of type package-error.

stream-error   [*Type*]

Errors that occur during input from, output to, or closing a stream should inherit from this type. This is a subtype of error. The initialization key-word :stream is supported to initialize the slot, which can be accessed using stream-error-stream.

stream-error-stream *condition*   [*Function*]

Accesses the offending stream of a *condition* of type stream-error.

`end-of-file`   *[Type]*

The error that results when a read operation is done on a stream that has no more tokens or characters should inherit from this type. This is a subtype of `stream-error`.

`file-error`   *[Type]*

Errors that occur during an attempt to open a file, or during some low-level transaction with a file system, should inherit from this type. This is a subtype of `error`. The initialization keyword `:pathname` is supported to initialize the slot, which can be accessed using `file-error-pathname`.

`file-error-pathname` *condition*   *[Function]*

Accesses the offending pathname of a *condition* of type `file-error`.

`cell-error`   *[Type]*

Errors that occur while accessing a location should inherit from this type. This is a subtype of `error`. The initialization keyword `:name` is supported to initialize the slot, which can be accessed using `cell-error-name`.

`cell-error-name` *condition*   *[Function]*

Accesses the offending cell name of a *condition* of type `cell-error`.

`unbound-variable`   *[Type]*

The error that results from trying to access the value of an unbound variable should inherit from this type. This is a subtype of `cell-error`.

`undefined-function`   *[Type]*

The error that results from trying to access the value of an undefined function should inherit from this type. This is a subtype of `cell-error`.

Remark: [Note: This remark was written well before the vote by X3J13 in June 1988 ⟨12⟩ to add the Common Lisp Object System to the forthcoming draft standard (see chapter 28) and the vote to integrate the Condition System and the Object System. I have retained the remark here for reasons of historical interest.—GLS]

Some readers may wonder why undefined-function is not defined to inherit from some condition such as control-error. The answer is that any such arrangement would require the presence of multiple inheritance—a luxury we do not currently have (without resorting to deftype, which we are currently avoiding). When the Common Lisp Object System comes into being, we might want to consider issues like this. Multiple inheritance makes a lot of things in a condition system much more flexible to deal with.

---

arithmetic-error   [*Type*]

Errors that occur while doing arithmetic type operations should inherit from this type. This is a subtype of error. The initialization keywords :operation and :operands are supported to initialize the slots, which can be accessed using arithmetic-error-operation and arithmetic-error-operands.

arithmetic-error-operation *condition*   [*Function*]

Accesses the offending operation of a condition of type arithmetic-error.

arithmetic-error-operands *condition*   [*Function*]

Accesses a list of the offending operands in a condition of type arithmetic-error.

division-by-zero   [*Type*]

Errors that occur because of division by zero should inherit from this type. This is a subtype of arithmetic-error.

floating-point-overflow   [*Type*]

Errors that occur because of floating-point overflow should inherit from this type. This is a subtype of arithmetic-error.

floating-point-underflow   [*Type*]

Errors that occur because of floating-point underflow should inherit from this type. This is a subtype of arithmetic-error.

Appendix A

Series

BY RICHARD C. WATERS

PREFACE: A series is a data structure much like a sequence, with similar kinds of operations. The difference is that in many situations, operations on series may be composed functionally and yet execute iteratively, without the need to construct intermediate series values explicitly. In this manner, series provide both the clarity of a functional programming style and the efficiency of an iterative programming style.

The remainder of this chapter consists of a description by Richard C. Waters of his work on an existing implementation of series. This is the culmination of many years of design and use of this approach, during which some 100,000 lines of application code have been written (by about half a dozen people over the course of seven years) using the series facility in nearly all iteration situations. This includes one large system (KBEmacs) of over 40,000 lines of code.

I have edited the chapter only very lightly to conform to the overall style of this book. Please see the Preface to this book for more information about the genesis of the series approach and its relationship to the work of X3J13.

—Guy L. Steele Jr.

A.1. Introduction

Series combine aspects of sequences, streams, and loops. Like sequences, series represent totally ordered multi-sets. In addition, the series functions have the same flavor as the sequence functions—namely, they operate on whole series, rather than extracting elements to be processed by other functions. For instance, the series expression below computes the sum of the positive elements in a list.

```
(collect-sum (choose-if #'plusp (scan '(1 -2 3 -4)))) ⇒ 4
```

Like streams, series can represent unbounded sets of elements and are supported by lazy evaluation: each element of a series is not computed until it is needed.

For instance, the series expression below returns a list of the first five even natural numbers and their sum. The call on scan-range returns a series of all the even natural numbers. However, since no elements beyond the first five are ever used, no elements beyond the first five are ever computed.

```
(let ((x (subseries (scan-range :from 0 :by 2) 0 5)))
  (values (collect x) (collect-sum x)))
  ⇒ (0 2 4 6 8) and 20
```

Like sequences and unlike streams, a series is not altered when its elements are accessed. For instance, both users of x above receive the same elements.

A totally ordered multi-set of elements can be represented in a loop by the successive values of a variable. This is extremely efficient, because it avoids the need to store the elements as a group in any kind of data structure. In most situations, series expressions achieve this same high level of efficiency, because they are automatically transformed into loops before being evaluated or compiled. For instance, the first expression above is transformed into a loop like the following.

```
(let ((sum 0))
  (dolist (i '(1 -2 3 -4) sum)
    (when (plusp i) (setq sum (+ sum i))))) ⇒ 4
```

A wide variety of algorithms can be expressed clearly and succinctly with series expressions. In particular, at least 90 percent of the loops programmers typically write can be replaced by series expressions that are much easier to understand and modify, and just as efficient. From this perspective, the key feature of series is that they are supported by a rich set of functions. These functions more or less correspond to the union of the operations provided by the sequence functions, the loop clauses, and the vector operations of APL.

Some series expressions cannot be transformed into loops. This is unfortunate, because while transformable series expressions are much more efficient than equivalent expressions involving sequences or streams, non-transformable series expressions are much less efficient. Whenever a problem comes up that blocks the transformation of a series expression, a warning message is issued. On the basis of information in the message, it is usually easy to provide an efficient fix for the problem (see section A.3).

Fortunately, most series expressions can be transformed into loops. In particular, pure expressions (ones that do not store series in variables) can always be transformed. As a result, the best approach for programmers to take is simply to write series expressions without worrying about transformability. When problems come up, they can be ignored (since they cannot lead to the computation of incorrect results) or dealt with on an individual basis.

Implementation note: The series functions and the theory underlying them are described in greater detail in [52, 53]. These reports also discuss the algorithms required to transform series expressions into loops and explain how to obtain a portable implementation.

A.2. Series Functions

Throughout this chapter the notation S_j is used to denote the jth element of the series S. As in a list or vector, the first element of a series has the subscript zero.

The # macro character syntax #Z*list* denotes a series that contains the elements of *list*. This syntax is also used when series are printed.

```
(choose-if #´symbolp #Z(a 2 b)) ⇒ #Z(a b)
```

Series are self-evaluating objects and the series data type is disjoint from all other types.

series *element-type*   [*Type specifier*]

The type specifier (series *element-type*) denotes the set of series whose elements are all members of the type *element-type*.

series *arg* &rest *args*   [*Function*]

The function series returns an unbounded series that endlessly repeats the values of the arguments. The second example below shows the preferred method for constructing a bounded series.

```
(series ´b ´c) ⇒ #Z(b c b c b c ...)
(scan (list ´a ´b ´c)) ⇒ #Z(a b c)
```

A.2.1. Scanners

Scanners create series outputs based on non-series inputs. Either they operate based on some formula (for example, scanning a range of integers) or they enumerate the elements in an aggregate data structure (for example, scanning the elements in a list or array).

scan-range &key (:start 0) (:by 1) (:type 'number)   [*Function*]
    :upto :below :downto :above :length

The function scan-range returns a series of numbers starting with the :start
argument (default integer 0) and counting up by the :by argument (default integer
1). The :type argument (default number) is a type specifier indicating the type of
numbers in the series produced. The :type argument must be a (not necessarily
proper) subtype of number. The :start and :by arguments must be of that type.

One of the last five arguments may be used to specify the kind of end test to
be used; these are called *termination arguments*. If :upto is specified, counting
continues only so long as the numbers generated are less than or equal to :upto. If
:below is specified, counting continues only so long as the numbers generated are
less than :below. If :downto is specified, counting continues only so long as the
numbers generated are greater than or equal to :downto. If :above is specified,
counting continues only so long as the numbers generated are greater than :above.
If :length is specified, it must be a non-negative integer and the output series has
this length.

If none of the termination arguments are specified, the output has unbounded
length. If more than one termination argument is specified, it is an error.

```
(scan-range :upto 4) ⇒ #Z(0 1 2 3 4)
(scan-range :from 1 :by -1 :above -4) ⇒ #Z(1 0 -1 -2 -3)
(scan-range :from .5 :by .1 :type 'float) ⇒ #Z(.5 .6 .7 ...)
(scan-range) ⇒ #Z(0 1 2 3 4 5 6 ...)
```

scan *sequence*   [*Function*]
scan *type sequence*   [*Function*]

scan returns a series containing the elements of *sequence* in order. The *type*
argument is a type specifier indicating the type of sequence to be scanned; it must
be a (not necessarily proper) subtype of sequence. If *type* is omitted, it defaults
to list. (This function exhibits an argument pattern that is unusual for Common
Lisp: an "optional" argument preceding a required argument. This pattern cannot
be expressed in the usual manner with &optional. It is indicated above by two
definition lines, showing the two possible argument patterns.)

If the *sequence* is a list, it must be a proper list ending in nil. Scanning is
significantly more efficient if it can be determined at compile time whether *type* is
a subtype of list or vector and for vectors what the length of the vector is.

```
(scan '(a b c)) ⇒ #Z(a b c)
(scan 'string "BAR") ⇒ #Z(#\B #\A #\R)
```

`scan-sublists` *list*   [*Function*]

`scan-sublists` returns a series containing the successive sublists of *list*. The *list* must be a proper list ending in `nil`.

`(scan-sublists '(a b c))` $\Rightarrow$ `#Z((a b c) (b c) (c))`

`scan-multiple` *type first-sequence* `&rest` *more-sequences*   [*Function*]

Several sequences can be scanned at once by using several calls on `scan`. Each call on `scan` will test to see when its sequence runs out of elements and execution will stop as soon as any of the sequences are exhausted. Although very robust, this approach to scanning can be inefficient. In situations where it is known in advance which sequence is the shortest, `scan-multiple` can be used to obtain the same results more rapidly.

  `scan-multiple` is similar to `scan` except that several sequences can be scanned at once. If there are *n* sequence inputs, `scan-multiple` returns *n* series containing the elements of these sequences. It must be the case that none of the sequence inputs is shorter than the first sequence. All of the output series are the same length as the first input sequence. Extra elements in the other input sequences are ignored. Using `scan-multiple` is more efficient than using multiple instances of `scan`, because `scan-multiple` only has to check for the first input running out of elements.

  If *type* is of the form (`values` t_1 ... tx_m), then there must be *m* sequence inputs and the *i*th sequence must have type t_i. Otherwise there can be any number of sequence inputs, each of which must have type *type*.

```
(multiple-value-bind (data weights)
    (scan-multiple 'list '(1 6 3 2 8) '(2 3 3 3 2))
  (collect (map-fn t #'* data weights)))
  ⇒ (2 18 9 6 16)
```

`scan-lists-of-lists` *lists-of-lists* `&optional` *leaf-test*   [*Function*]
`scan-lists-of-lists-fringe` *lists-of-lists* `&optional` *leaf-test* [*Function*]

The argument *lists-of-lists* is viewed as a tree where each internal node is a non-empty list and the elements of the list are the children of the node. `scan-lists-of-lists` and `scan-lists-of-lists-fringe` each scan *lists-of-lists* in preorder and return a series of its nodes. `scan-lists-of-lists` returns every node in the tree. `scan-lists-of-lists-fringe` returns only the leaf nodes.

  The scan proceeds as follows. The argument *lists-of-lists* can be any Lisp object. If *lists-of-lists* is an atom or satisfies the predicate *leaf-test* (if present), it is a leaf node. (The predicate can count on being applied only to conses.) Otherwise, *lists-of-lists* is a (not necessarily proper) list. The first element of *lists-of-lists* is recursively scanned in full, followed by the second and so on until a non-cons *cdr* is encountered. Whether or not this final *cdr* is nil, it is ignored.

```
(scan-lists-of-lists '((2) (nil)))
  ⇒ #Z(((2) (nil)) (2) 2 (nil) nil)
(scan-lists-of-lists-fringe '((2) (nil))) ⇒ #Z(2 nil)
(scan-lists-of-lists-fringe '((2) (nil))
                          #'(lambda (e) (numberp (car e))))
  ⇒ #Z((2) nil)
```

scan-alist *a-list* &optional (*test* #'eql)   [*Function*]
scan-plist *plist*   [*Function*]
scan-hash *table*   [*Function*]

When given an association list, a property list, or a hash table (respectively), each of these functions produces two outputs: a series of keys *K* and a series of the corresponding values *V*. Each key in the input appears exactly once in the output, even if it appears more than once in the input. (The *test* argument of scan-alist specifies the equality test between keys; it defaults to eql.) The two outputs have the same length. Each V_j is the value returned by the appropriate accessing function (cdr of assoc, getf, or gethash, respectively) when given K_j. scan-alist and scan-plist scan keys in the order they appear in the underlying structure. scan-hash scans keys in no particular order.

```
(scan-plist '(a 1 b 3)) ⇒ #Z(a b) and #Z(1 3)
(scan-alist '((a . 1) nil (a . 3) (b . 2)))
  ⇒ #Z(a b) and #Z(1 2)
```

scan-symbols &optional (*package* *package*)   [*Function*]

scan-symbols returns a series, in no particular order, and possibly containing duplicates, of the symbols accessible in *package* (which defaults to the current package).

scan-file *file-name* &optional (*reader* #'read)   [*Function*]

scan-file opens the file named by the string *file-name* and applies the function *reader* to it repeatedly until the end of the file is reached. *Reader* must accept the standard input function arguments *input-stream*, *eof-error-p*, and *eof-value* as its arguments. (For instance, *reader* can be read, read-preserving-white-space, read-line, or read-char.) If omitted, *reader* defaults to read. scan-file returns a series of the values returned by *reader*, up to but not including the value returned when the end of the file is reached. The file is correctly closed, even if an abort occurs.

scan-fn *type init step* &optional *test*   [*Function*]

The higher-order function scan-fn supports the general concept of scanning. The *type* argument is a type specifier indicating the type of values returned by *init* and *step*. The values type specifier can be used for this argument to indicate multiple types; however, *type* cannot indicate zero values. If *type* indicates m types $t_1, \ldots, t_m$, then scan-fn returns m series $T1, \ldots, Tm$, where Ti has the type (series t_i). The arguments *init*, *step*, and *test* are functions.

The *init* must be of type (function () (values $t_1 \ldots t_m$)).
The *step* must be of type (function ($t_1 \ldots t_m$) (values $t_1 \ldots t_m$)).
The *test* (if present) must be of type (function ($t_1 \ldots t_m$) t).
The elements of the Ti are computed as follows:

(values $T1_0 \ldots Tm_0$) = (funcall *init*)
(values $T1_j \ldots Tm_j$) = (funcall *step* $T1_{(j-1)} \ldots Tm_{(j-1)}$)

The outputs all have the same length. If there is no *test*, the outputs have unbounded length. If there is a *test*, the outputs consist of the elements up to, but not including, the first elements (with index j, say) for which the following termination test is not nil.

(funcall *test* $T1_j \ldots Tm_j$)

It is guaranteed that *step* will not be applied to the elements that pass this termination test.

If *init*, *step*, or *test* has side effects when invoked, it can count on being called in the order indicated by the equations above, with *test* called just before *step* on each cycle. However, given the lazy evaluation nature of series, these functions will not be called until their outputs are actually used (if ever). In addition, no assumptions can be made about the relative order of evaluation of these calls with regard to execution in other parts of a given series expression. The first example below scans down a list stepping two elements at a time. The second example generates two unbounded series: the integers counting up from 1 and the sequence of partial sums of the first i integers.

```
(scan-fn t #'(lambda () '(a b c d)) #'cddr #'null)
  ⇒ #Z((a b c d) (c d))

(scan-fn '(values integer integer)
         #'(lambda () (values 1 0))
         #'(lambda (i sum) (values (+ i 1) (+ sum i))))
  ⇒ #Z(1 2 3 4 ...) and #Z(0 1 3 6 ...)
```

scan-fn-inclusive *type init step test*   [*Function*]

The higher-order function scan-fn-inclusive is the same as scan-fn except
that the first set of elements for which *test* returns a non-null value is included in
the output. As with scan-fn, it is guaranteed that *step* will not be applied to the
elements for which *test* is non-null.

A.2.2. Mapping

By far the most common kind of series operation is mapping. In cognizance of this
fact, four different ways are provided for specifying mapping: one fundamental
form (map-fn) and three shorthand forms that are more convenient in particular
common situations.

map-fn *type function* &rest *series-inputs*   [*Function*]

The higher-order function map-fn supports the general concept of mapping. The
type argument is a type specifier indicating the type of values returned by *function*.
The values construct can be used to indicate multiple types; however, *type* cannot
indicate zero values. If *type* indicates m types $t_1, \ldots, t_m$, then map-fn returns m
series $T1, \ldots, Tm$, where Ti has the type (series t_i). The argument *function* is
a function. The remaining arguments (if any) are all series. Let these series be
$S1, \ldots, Sn$ and suppose that Si has the type (series s_i).
    The *function* must be of type

```
(function (s₁ ... sₙ) (values t₁ ... tₘ))
```
$$\text{(function } (s_1 \ \ldots \ s_n) \text{ (values } t_1 \ \ldots \ t_m))$$

    The length of each output is the same as the length of the shortest input. If
there are no bounded series inputs, the outputs are unbounded. The elements of
the Ti are the results of applying *function* to the corresponding elements of the
series inputs.

$$(\text{values } T1_j \ \ldots \ Tm_j) \equiv (\text{funcall } function \ S1_j \ \ldots \ Sn_j)$$

If *function* has side effects, it can count on being called first on the Si_0, then on the Si_1, and so on. However, given the lazy evaluation nature of series, *function* will not be called on any group of input elements until the result is actually used (if ever). In addition, no assumptions can be made about the relative order of evaluation of the calls on *function* with regard to execution in other parts of a given series expression.

```
(map-fn 'integer #'+ #Z(1 2 3) #Z(4 5)) ⇒ #Z(5 7)
(map-fn t #'gensym) ⇒ #Z(#:G3 #:G4 #:G5 ...)
(map-fn '(values integer rational) #'floor #Z(1/4 9/5 12/3))
   ⇒ #Z(0 1 4) and #Z(1/4 4/5 0)
```

The # macro character syntax #M makes it easy to specify uses of map-fn where *type* is t and the *function* is a named function. The notation (#M*function* ...) is an abbreviation for (map-fn t #'*function* ...). The form *function* can be the printed representation of any Lisp object. The notation #M*function* can appear only in the function position of a list.

```
(collect (#M1+ (scan '(1 2 3)))) ⇒ (2 3 4)
```

mapping ({({*var* | ({*var*}*)} *value*)}*) {*declaration*}* {*form*}*   [*Macro*]

The macro mapping makes it easy to specify uses of map-fn where *type* is t and the *function* is a literal lambda. The syntax of mapping is analogous to that of let. The binding list specifies zero or more variables that are bound in parallel to successive values of series. The *value* part of each pair is an expression that must produce a series. The *declarations* and *forms* are treated as the body of a lambda expression that is mapped over the series values. A series of the first values returned by this lambda expression is returned as the result of mapping.

```
(mapping ((x r) (y s)) ...) ≡
   (map-fn t #'(lambda (x y) ...) r s)


(mapping ((x (scan '(2 -2 3))))
   (expt (abs x) 3))
   ⇒ #Z(8 8 27)
```

The form mapping supports a special syntax that facilitates the use of series functions returning multiple values. Instead of being a single variable, the variable part of a *var-value* pair can be a list of variables. This list is treated the same way as the first argument to multiple-value-bind and can be used to access the elements of multiple series returned by a series function.

```
(mapping (((i v) (scan-plist '(a 1 b 2))))
   (list i v))
   ⇒ #Z((a 1) (b 2))
```

iterate ({({*var* | ({*var*}*)} *value*)}*) {*declaration*}* {*form*}*   [*Macro*]

The form iterate is the same as mapping, except that after mapping the *forms* over the *values*, the results are discarded and nil is returned.

```
(let ((item (scan '((1) (-2) (3)))))
   (iterate ((x (#Mcar item)))
     (if (plusp x) (prin1 x))))
   ⇒ nil (after printing "13")
```

To a first approximation, iterate and mapping differ in the same way as mapc and mapcar. In particular, like mapc, iterate is intended to be used in situations where the *forms* are being evaluated for side effects rather than for their results. However, given the lazy evaluation semantics of series, the difference between iterate and mapping is more than just a question of efficiency.

If mapcar is used in a situation where the output is not used, time is wasted unnecessarily creating the output list. However, if mapping is used in a situation where the output is not used, no computation is performed, because series elements are not computed until they are used. Thus iterate can be thought of as a declaration that the indicated computation is to be performed even though the output is not used for anything.

A.2.3. Truncation and Other Simple Transducers

Transducers compute series from series and form the heart of most series expressions. Mapping is by far the most common transducer. This section presents a number of additional simple transducers.

cotruncate &rest *series-inputs*   [*Function*]
until *bools* &rest *series-inputs*   [*Function*]
until-if *pred* &rest *series-inputs*   [*Function*]

Each of these functions accepts one or more series inputs $S1, \ldots, Sn$ as its &rest argument and returns n series outputs $T1, \ldots, Tn$ that contain the same elements in the same order—that is, $Ti_j=Si_j$. Let k be the length of the shortest input Si. cotruncate truncates the series so that each output has length k. Let k' be the position of the first element in the boolean series *bools* that is not nil or, if every element is nil, the length of *bools*. until truncates the series so that each output has length (min k k'). Let itk'' be the position of the first element in *S1* such that (*pred* $S1_{k''}$) is not nil or, if there is no such element, the length of *S1*. until-if truncates the series so that each output has length (min k k'').

```
(cotruncate #Z(1 2 -3 4) #Z(a b c))
  ⇒ #Z(1 2 -3) and #Z(a b c)
(until #Z(nil nil t nil) #Z(1 2 -3 4) #Z(a b c))
  ⇒ #Z(1 2) and #Z(a b)
(until-if #´minusp #Z(1 2 -3 4) #Z(a b c))
  ⇒ #Z(1 2) and #Z(a b)
```

previous *items* &optional (*default* nil) (*amount* 1)   [*Function*]

The series returned by previous is the same as the input series *items* except that it is shifted to the right by the positive integer *amount*. The shifting is done by inserting *amount* copies of *default* before *items* and discarding *amount* elements from the end of *items*.

```
(previous #Z(10 11 12) 0) ⇒ #Z(0 10 11)
```

latch *items* &key :after :before :pre :post   [*Function*]

The series returned by latch is the same as the input series *items* except that some of the elements are replaced by other values. latch acts like a *latch* electronic circuit component. Each input element causes the creation of a corresponding output element. After a specified number of non-null input elements have been encountered, the latch is triggered and the output mode is permanently changed.

The :after and :before arguments specify the latch point. The latch point is just after the :after-th non-null element in *items* or just before the :before-th non-null element. If neither :after nor :before is specified, an :after of 1 is assumed. If both are specified, it is an error.

If a :pre is specified, every element prior to the latch point is replaced by this value. If a :post is specified, every element after the latch point is replaced by this value. If neither is specified, a :post of nil is assumed.

```
(latch #Z(nil c nil d e)) ⇒ #Z(nil c nil nil nil)
(latch #Z(nil c nil d e) :before 2 :post t) ⇒ #Z(nil c nil t t)
```

collecting-fn *type init function* &rest *series-inputs*   [*Function*]

The higher-order function `collecting-fn` supports the general concept of a simple transducer with internal state. The *type* argument is a type specifier indicating the type of values returned by *function*. The `values` construct can be used to indicate multiple types; however, *type* cannot indicate zero values. If *type* indicates m types $t_1, \ldots, t_m$, then `collecting-fn` returns m series $T1, \ldots, Tm$, where Ti has the type (`series` t_i). The arguments *init* and *function* are functions. The remaining arguments (if any) are all series. Let these series be $S1, \ldots, Sn$ and suppose that Si has the type (`series` s_i).

The *init* must be of type (`function` () (`values` $t_1 \ldots t_m$)).

The *function* must be of type

(`function` ($t_1 \ldots t_m\ s_1 \ldots s_n$) (`values` $t_1 \ldots t_m$))

The length of each output is the same as the length of the shortest input. If there are no bounded series inputs, the outputs are unbounded. The elements of the Ti are computed as follows:

(`values` $T1_0 \ldots Tm_0$) $\equiv$
  (`multiple-value-call` *function* (`funcall` *init*) $S1_0 \ldots Sn_0$)

(`values` $T1_j \ldots Tm_j$) $\equiv$
  (`funcall` *function* $T1_{(j-1)} \ldots Tm_{(j-1)}\ S1_j \ldots Sn_j$)

If *init* or *function* has side effects, it can count on being called in the order indicated by the equations above. However, given the lazy evaluation nature of series, these functions will not be called until their outputs are actually used (if ever). In addition, no assumptions can be made about the relative order of evaluation of these calls with regard to execution in other parts of a given series expression. The second example below computes a series of partial sums of the numbers in an input series. The third example computes two output series: the partial sums of its first input and the partial products of its second input.

```
(defun running-averages (float-list)
  (multiple-value-call #'map-fn
    'float #'/
    (collecting-fn '(values float integer)
                   #'(lambda () (values 0.0 0))
                   #'(lambda (s n x) (values (+ s x) (+ n 1))))
                   float-list)))
```

```
(collecting-fn 'integer #'(lambda () 0) #'+ #Z(1 2 3))
  ⇒ #Z(1 3 6)

(collecting-fn '(values integer integer)
               #'(lambda () (values 0 1))
               #'(lambda (sum prod x y)
                   (values (+ sum x) (* prod y)))
               #Z(4 6 8)
               #Z(1 2 3))
  ⇒ #Z(4 10 18) and #Z(1 2 6)
```

A.2.4. Conditional and Other Complex Transducers

This section presents a number of complex transducers, including ones that support conditional computation.

choose *bools* &optional (*items bools*)   [*Function*]
choose-if *pred items*   [*Function*]

Each of these functions takes in a series of elements (*items*) and returns a series containing the same elements in the same order, but with some elements removed. choose removes *items$_j$* if *bools$_j$* is nil or *j* is beyond the end of *bools*. If *items* is omitted, choose returns the non-null elements of *bools*. choose-if removes *items$_j$* if (*pred items$_j$*) is nil.

```
(choose #Z(t nil t nil) #Z(a b c d)) ⇒ #Z(a c)
(collect-sum (choose-if #'plusp #Z(-1 2 -3 4))) ⇒ 6
```

expand *bools items* &optional (*default* nil)   [*Function*]

expand is a quasi-inverse of choose. The output contains the elements of the input series *items* spread out into the positions specified by the non-null elements in *bools*—that is, *items$_j$* is in the position occupied by the *j*th non-null element in *bools*. The other positions in the output are occupied by *default*. The output stops as soon as *bools* runs out of elements or a non-null element in *bools* is encountered for which there is no corresponding element in *items*.

```
(expand #Z(nil t nil t t) #Z(a b c)) ⇒ #Z(nil a nil b c)
(expand #Z(nil t nil t t) #Z(a)) ⇒ #Z(nil a nil)
```

split *items* &rest *test-series-inputs*   [*Function*]
split-if *items* &rest *test-predicates*   [*Function*]

These functions are like choose and choose-if except that instead of producing
one restricted output, they partition the input series *items* between several outputs.
If there are *n* test inputs following *items*, then there are $n + 1$ outputs. Each input
element is placed in exactly one output series, depending on the outcome of a
sequence of tests. If the element *items*$_j$ fails the first $k - 1$ tests and passes the
*k*h test, it is put in the *k*th output. If *items*$_j$ fails every test, it is placed in the
last output. In addition, all output stops as soon as any series input runs out of
elements. The test inputs to split are series of values; *items*$_j$ passes the *k*th test
if the *j*th element of the *k*th test series is not nil. The test inputs to split-if are
predicates; *items*$_j$ passes the *k*th test if the *k*th test predicate returns non-null when
applied to *items*$_j$.

```
(split #Z(-1 2 3 -4) #Z(t nil nil t))
  ⇒ #Z(-1 -4) and #Z(2 3)
(multiple-value-bind (+x -x) (split-if #Z(-1 2 3 -4) #´plusp)
  (values (collect-sum +x) (collect-sum -x)))
  ⇒ 5 and -5
```

catenate &rest *series-inputs*   [*Function*]

catenate combines two or more series into one long series by appending them
end to end. The length of the output is the sum of the lengths of the inputs.

```
(catenate #Z(b c) #Z() #Z(d)) ⇒ #Z(b c d)
```

subseries *items* *start* &optional *below*   [*Function*]

subseries returns a series containing the elements of the input series *items* indexed
by the non-negative integers from *start* up to, but not including, *below*. If *below*
is omitted or greater than the length of *items*, the output goes all the way to the
end of *items*.

```
(subseries #Z(a b c d) 1) ⇒ #Z(b c d)
(subseries #Z(a b c d) 1 3) ⇒ #Z(b c)
```

positions *bools*   [*Function*]

positions returns a series of the indices of the non-null elements in the series
input *bools*.

```
(positions #Z(t nil t 44)) ⇒ #Z(0 2 3)
```

mask *monotonic-indices*   [*Function*]

mask is a quasi-inverse of positions. The series input *monotonic-indices* must be
a strictly increasing series of non-negative integers. The output, which is always
unbounded, contains t in the positions specified by *monotonic-indices* and nil
everywhere else.

```
(mask #Z(0 2 3)) ⇒ #Z(t nil t t nil nil ...)
(mask #Z()) ⇒ #Z(nil nil ...)
(mask (positions #Z(nil a nil b nil)))
   ⇒ #Z(nil t nil t nil ...)
```

mingle *items1 items2 comparator*   [*Function*]

The series returned by mingle contains all and only the elements of the two
input series. The length of the output is the sum of the lengths of the inputs and
is unbounded if either input is unbounded. The order of the elements remains
unchanged; however, the elements from the two inputs are stably intermixed under
the control of the *comparator*.

The *comparator* must accept two arguments and return non-null if and only if its
first argument is strictly less than its second argument (in some appropriate sense).
At each step, the *comparator* is used to compare the current elements in the two
series. If the current element from *items2* is strictly less than the current element
from *items1*, the current element is removed from *items2* and transferred to the
output. Otherwise, the next output element comes from *items1*.

```
(mingle #Z(1 3 7 9) #Z(4 5 8) #'<) ⇒ #Z(1 3 4 5 7 8 9)
(mingle #Z(1 7 3 9) #Z(4 5 8) #'<) ⇒ #Z(1 4 5 7 3 8 9)
```

chunk *m n items*   [*Function*]

This function has the effect of breaking up the input series *items* into (possibly
overlapping) chunks of length *m*. The starting positions of successive chunks
differ by *n*. The inputs *m* and *n* must both be positive integers.

chunk produces *m* output series. The *i*th chunk provides the *i*th element for each
of the *m* outputs. Suppose that the length of *items* is *l*. The length of each output
is $\lfloor 1 + (l - m)/n \rfloor$. The *i*th element of the *k*th output is the $(i * n + k)$th element of
items (*i* and *k* counting from zero).

Note that if $l < m$, there will be no output elements, and if $l - m$ is not a multiple of n, the last few input elements will not appear in the output. If $m \geq n$, one can guarantee that the last chunk will contain the last element of *items* by catenating $n - 1$ copies of an appropriate padding value to the end of *items*.

The first example below shows chunk being used to compute a moving average. The second example shows chunk being used to convert a property list into an association list.

```
(mapping (((xi xi+1 xi+2) (chunk 3 1 #Z(1 5 3 4 5 6))))
  (/ (+ xi xi+1 xi+2) 3))
  ⇒ #Z(3 4 4 5)
(collect
  (mapping (((prop val) (chunk 2 2 (scan '(a 2 b 5 c 8)))))
    (cons prop val)))
  ⇒ ((a . 2) (b . 5) (c . 8))
```

A.2.5. Collectors

Collectors produce non-series outputs based on series inputs. They either create a summary value based on some formula (the sum, for example) or collect the elements of a series in an aggregate data structure (such as a list).

collect-first *items* &optional (*default* nil)   [*Function*]
collect-last *items* &optional (*default* nil)   [*Function*]
collect-nth *n items* &optional (*default* nil)   [*Function*]

Given a series *items*, these functions return the first element, the last element, and the nth element, respectively. If *items* has no elements (or no nth element), *default* is returned. If *default* is not specified, then nil is used for *default*.

```
(collect-first #Z() 'z) ⇒ z
(collect-last #Z(a b c)) ⇒ c
(collect-nth 1 #Z(a b c)) ⇒ b
```

collect-length *items*   [*Function*]

collect-length returns the number of elements in a series.

```
(collect-length #Z(a b c)) ⇒ 3
```

collect-sum *numbers* &optional (*type* ´number)   [*Function*]

collect-sum returns the sum of the elements in a series of numbers. The *type* is a
type specifier that indicates the type of sum to be created. If *type* is not specified,
then number is used for the *type*. If there are no elements in the input, a zero (of
the appropriate type) is returned.

(collect-sum #Z(1.1 1.2 1.3)) ⇒ 3.6
(collect-sum #Z() ´complex) ⇒ #C(0 0)

collect-max *numbers*   [*Function*]
collect-min *numbers*   [*Function*]

Given a series of non-complex numbers, these functions compute the maximum
element and the minimum element, respectively. If there are no elements in the
input, nil is returned.

(collect-max #Z(2 1 4 3)) ⇒ 4
(collect-min #Z(1.2 1.1 1.4 1.3)) ⇒ 1.1
(collect-min #Z()) ⇒ nil

collect-and *bools*   [*Function*]

collect-and returns the and of the elements in a series. As with the macro and,
nil is returned if any element of *bools* is nil. Otherwise, the last element of *bools*
is returned. The value t is returned if there are no elements in *bools*.

(collect-and #Z(a b c)) ⇒ c
(collect-and #Z(a nil c)) ⇒ nil

collect-or *bools*   [*Function*]

collect-or returns the or of the elements in a series. As with the macro or, nil
is returned if every element of *bools* is nil. Otherwise, the first non-null element
of *bools* is returned. The value nil is returned if there are no elements in *bools*.

(collect-or #Z(nil b c)) ⇒ b
(collect-or #Z()) ⇒ nil

collect *items*   [*Function*]
collect *type items*   [*Function*]

collect returns a sequence containing the elements of the series *items*. The *type*
is a type specifier indicating the type of sequence to be created. It must be either

a proper subtype of sequence or the symbol bag. If *type* is omitted, it defaults to list. (This function exhibits an argument pattern that is unusual for Common Lisp: an "optional" argument preceding a required argument. This pattern cannot be expressed in the usual manner with &optional. It is indicated above by two definition lines, showing the two possible argument patterns.)

If the *type* is bag, a list is created with the elements in whatever order can be most efficiently obtained. Otherwise, the order of the elements in the sequence is the same as the order in *items*. If *type* specifies a length (that is, of a vector) this length must be greater than or equal to the length of *items*.

The *n*th element of *items* is placed in the *n*th slot of the sequence produced. Any unneeded slots are left in their initial state. Collecting is significantly more efficient if it can be determined at compile time whether *type* is a subtype of list or vector and for vectors what the length of the vector is.

```
(collect #Z(a b c)) ⇒ (a b c)
(collect 'bag #Z(a b c)) ⇒ (c a b) or (b a c) or ...
(collect '(vector integer 3) #Z(1 2 3)) ⇒ #(1 2 3)
```

collect-append *sequences*   [*Function*]
collect-append *type sequences*   [*Function*]

Given a series of sequences, collect-append returns a new sequence by concatenating these sequences together in order. The *type* is a type specifier indicating the type of sequence created and must be a proper subtype of sequence. If *type* is omitted, it defaults to list. (This function exhibits an argument pattern that is unusual for Common Lisp: an "optional" argument preceding a required argument. This pattern cannot be expressed in the usual manner with &optional. It is indicated above by two definition lines, showing the two possible argument patterns.)

It must be possible for every element of every sequence in the input series to be an element of a sequence of type *type*. The result does not share any structure with the sequences in the input.

```
(collect-append #Z((a b) nil (c d))) ⇒ (a b c d)
(collect-append 'string #Z("a " "big " "cat")) ⇒ "a big cat"
```

collect-nconc *lists*   [*Function*]

collect-nconc nconcs the elements of the series *lists* together in order and returns the result. This is the same as collect-append except that the input must be a series of lists, the output is always a list, the concatenation is done rapidly by destructively modifying the input elements, and therefore the output shares all of its structure with the input elements.

collect-alist *keys values*   [*Function*]
collect-plist *keys values*   [*Function*]
collect-hash *keys values* &key :test :size :rehash-size   [*Function*]
             :rehash-threshold

Given a series of keys and a series of corresponding values, these functions return an association list, a property list, and a hash table, respectively. Following the order of the input, each *keys_j-values_j* pair is entered into the output so that it overrides all earlier associations. If one of the input series is longer than the other, the extra elements are ignored. The keyword arguments of collect-hash specify attributes of the hash table produced and have the same meanings as the arguments to make-hash-table.

```
(collect-alist #Z(a b c) #Z(1 2)) ⇒ ((b . 2) (a . 1))
(collect-plist #Z(a b c) #Z(1 2)) ⇒ (b 2 a 1)
(collect-hash #Z() #Z(1 2) :test #´eq) ⇒ ⟨an empty hash table⟩
```

collect-file *file-name items* &optional (*printer* #´print)   [*Function*]

This creates a file named *file-name* and writes the elements of the series *items* into it using the function *printer*. *Printer* must accept two inputs: an object and an output stream. (For instance, *printer* can be print, prin1, princ, pprint, write-char, write-string, or write-line.) If omitted, *printer* defaults to print. The value t is returned. The file is correctly closed, even if an abort occurs.

collect-fn *type init function* &rest *series-inputs*   [*Function*]

The higher-order function collect-fn supports the general concept of collecting. It is identical to collecting-fn except that it returns only the last element of each series computed. If there are no elements in these series, the values returned by *init* are passed on directly as the output of collect-fn.

```
(collect-fn ´integer #´(lambda () 0) #´+ #Z(1 2 3)) ⇒ 6
(collect-fn ´integer #´(lambda () 0) #´+ #Z()) ⇒ 0
(collect-fn ´integer #´(lambda () 1) #´* #Z(1 2 3 4 5)) ⇒ 120
```

A.2.6. Alteration of Series

Series that come from scanning data structures such as lists and vectors are closely linked to these structures. The function `alter` can be used to modify the underlying data structure with reference to the series derived from it. (Conversely, it is possible to modify a series by destructively modifying the data structure it is derived from. However, given the lazy evaluation nature of series, the effects of such modifications can be very hard to predict. As a result, this kind of modification is inadvisable.)

`alter` *destinations items*   [*Function*]

`alter` changes the series *destinations* so that it contains the elements in the series *items*. More importantly, in the manner of `setf`, the data structure that underlies *destinations* is changed so that if the series *destinations* were to be regenerated, the new values would be obtained. The alteration process stops as soon as either input runs out of elements. The value `nil` is always returned. In the example below each negative element in a list is replaced with its square.

```
(let* ((data (list 1 -2 3 4 -5 6))
       (x (choose-if #'minusp (scan data))))
  (alter x (#M* x x))
  data)
  ⇒ (1 4 3 4 25 6)
```

`alter` can be applied only to series that are *alterable*. `scan`, `scan-alist`, `scan-multiple`, `scan-plist`, and `scan-lists-of-lists-fringe` produce alterable series. However, the alterability of the output of `scan-lists-of-lists-fringe` is incomplete. If `scan-lists-of-lists-fringe` is applied to an object that is a leaf, altering the output series does not change the object.

In general, the output of a transducer is alterable as long as the elements of the output come directly from the elements of an input that is alterable. In particular, the outputs of `choose`, `choose-if`, `split`, `split-if`, `cotruncate`, `until`, `until-if`, and `subseries` are alterable as long as the corresponding inputs are alterable.

`to-alter` *items alter-fn* `&rest` *args*   [*Function*]

Given a series *items*, `to-alter` returns an alterable series *A* containing the same elements. The argument *alter-fn* is a function. The remaining arguments are all series. Let these series be *S1*, . . . , *Sn*. If there are *n* arguments after *alter-fn*, *alter-fn* must accept *n* + 1 inputs. If (`alter` *A B*) is later encountered, the expression (map-fn t *alter-fn B S1* ... *Sn*) is implicitly evaluated. For each element in *B*, *alter-fn* should make appropriate changes in the data structure underlying *A*.

As an example, consider the following definition of a series function that scans the elements of a list. Alteration is performed by changing cons cells in the list being scanned.

```
(defun scan-list (list)
  (declare (optimizable-series-function))
  (let ((sublists (scan-sublists list)))
    (to-alter (#Mcar sublists)
              #'(lambda (new parent) (setf (car parent) new))
              sublists)))
```

A.3. Optimization

Series expressions are transformed into loops by pipelining them—the computation is converted from a form where entire series are computed one after the other to a form where the series are incrementally computed in parallel. In the resulting loop, each individual element is computed just once, used, and then discarded before the next element is computed. For this pipelining to be possible, a number of restrictions have to be satisfied. Before these restrictions are explained, it will be useful to consider a related issue.

The composition of two series functions cannot be pipelined unless the destination function consumes series elements in the same order that the source function produces them. Taken together, the series functions guarantee that this will always be true, because they all follow the same fixed processing order. In particular, they are all *preorder* functions—they process the elements of their series inputs and outputs in ascending order starting with the first element. Further, while it is easy for users to define new series functions, it is impossible to define one that is not a preorder function.

It turns out that most series operations can easily be implemented in a preorder fashion, the most notable exceptions being reversal and sorting. As a result, little is lost by outlawing non-preorder series functions. If some non-preorder operation has to be applied to a series, the series can be collected into a list or vector and the operation applied to this new data structure. (This is inefficient, but no less efficient than what would be required if non-preorder series functions were supported.)

A.3.1. Basic Restrictions

The transformation of series expressions into loops is required to occur at some time before compiled code is actually run. Optimization may or may not be applied to interpreted code. If any of the restrictions described below are violated, optimization is not possible. In this situation, a warning message is issued at the time optimization is attempted and the code is left unoptimized. This is not a fatal error and does not prevent the correct results from being computed. However, given the large improvements in efficiency to be gained, it is well worth fixing any violations that occur. This is usually easy to do.

`*suppress-series-warnings*`   [*Variable*]

If this variable is set (or bound) to anything other than its default value of `nil`, warnings about conditions that block the optimization of series expressions are suppressed.

Before the restrictions on series expressions are discussed, it will be useful to define precisely what is meant by the term *series expression*. This term is semantic rather than syntactic in nature. Imagine a program converted from Lisp code into a data flow graph. In a data flow graph, functions are represented as boxes, and both control flow and data flow are represented as arrows between the boxes. Constructs such as `let` and `setq` are converted into patterns of data flow arcs. Control constructs such as `if` and `loop` are converted into patterns of control flow arcs. Suppose further that all loops have been converted into tail recursions so that the graph is acyclic.

A series expression is a subgraph of the data flow graph for a program that contains a group of interacting series functions. More specifically, given a call f on a series function, the series expression E containing it is defined as follows. E contains f. Every function using a series created by a function in E is in E. Every function computing a series used by a function in E is in E. Finally, suppose that two functions g and h are in E and that there is a data flow path consisting of series and/or non-series data flow arcs from g to h. Every function touched by this path (be it a series function or not) is in E.

For optimization to be possible, series expressions have to be statically analyzable. As with most other optimization processes, a series expression cannot be transformed into a loop at compile time, unless it can be determined at compile time exactly what computation is being performed. This places a number of relatively minor limits on what can be written. For example, for optimization to be possible the type arguments to higher-order functions such as `map-fn` and `collecting-fn` have to be quoted constants. Similarly, the numeric arguments to `chunk` have to be constants. In addition, if `funcall` is used to call a series function, the function called has to be of the form (`function` ...).

For optimization to be possible, every series created within a series expression must be used solely inside the expression. If a series is transmitted outside of the expression that creates it, it has to be physically represented as a whole. This is incompatible with the transformations required to pipeline the creating expression. To avoid this problem, a series must not be returned as a result of a series expression as a whole, assigned to a free variable, assigned to a special variable, or stored in a data structure. A corollary of the last point is that when defining new optimizable series functions, series cannot be passed into &rest arguments. Further, optimization is blocked if a series is passed as an argument to an ordinary Lisp function. Series can be passed only to the series functions in section A.2 and to new series functions defined using the declaration optimizable-series-function.

For optimization to be possible, series expressions must correspond to straight-line computations. That is to say, the data flow graph corresponding to a series expression cannot contain any conditional branches. (Complex control flow is incompatible with pipelining.) Optimization is possible in the presence of standard straight-line forms such as progn, funcall, setq, lambda, let, let*, and multiple-value-bind as long as none of the variables bound are special. There is also no problem with macros as long as they expand into series functions and straight-line forms. However, optimization is blocked by forms that specify complex control flow (i.e., conditionals if, cond, etc., looping constructs loop, do, etc., or branching constructs tagbody, go, catch, etc.).

In the first example below, optimization is blocked, because the if form is inside the series expression. In the second example, however, optimization is possible, because although the if feeds data to the series expression, it is not inside the corresponding subgraph. Both of the expressions below produce the same value, but the second one is much more efficient.

```
(collect (if flag (scan x) (scan y)))   ;Warning message issued
(collect (scan (if flag x y)))
```

A.3.2. Constraint Cycles

Even if a series expression satisfies all of the restrictions above, it still may not be possible to transform the expression into a loop. The sole remaining problem is that if a series is used in two places, the two uses may place incompatible constraints on the times at which series elements should be produced.

The series expression below shows a situation where this problem arises. The expression creates a series x of the elements in a list. It then creates a normalized series by dividing each element of x by the sum of the elements in x. Finally, the expression returns the maximum of the normalized elements.

```
(let ((x (scan '(1 2 5 2))))              ;Warning message issued
   (collect-max (#M/ x (series (collect-sum x)))))) ⇒ 1/2
```

Figure A-1: A Constraint Cycle in a Series Expression

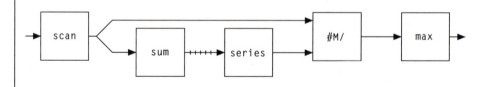

The two uses of x in the expression place contradictory constraints on the way pipelined evaluation must proceed; collect-sum requires that all of the elements of x be produced before the sum can be returned, and series requires that its input be available before it can start to produce its output. However, #M/ requires that the first element of x be available at the same time as the first element of the output of series. For pipelining to work, the first element of the output of series (and therefore the output of collect-sum) must be available before the second element of x is produced. Unfortunately, this is impossible.

The essence of the inconsistency above is the cycle of constraints used in the argument. This in turn stems from a cycle in the data flow graph underlying the expression. In figure A-1 function calls are represented by boxes and data flow is represented by arrows. Simple arrows indicate the flow of series values and cross-hatched arrows indicate the flow of non-series values.

Given a data flow graph corresponding to a series expression, a *constraint cycle* is a closed oriented loop of data flow arcs such that each arc is traversed exactly once and no non-series arc is traversed backward. (Series data flow arcs can be traversed in either direction.) A constraint cycle is said to *pass through* an input or output port when exactly one of the arcs in the cycle touches the port. In figure A-1 the data flow arcs touching scan, sum, series, and #M/ form a constraint cycle. Note that if the output of scan were not a series, this loop would not be a constraint cycle, because there would be no valid way to traverse it. Also note that while the constraint cycle passes through all the other ports it touches, it does not pass through the output of scan.

Whenever a constraint cycle passes through a non-series output, an argument analogous to the one above can be constructed and therefore pipelining will be impossible. When this situation arises, a warning message is issued identifying the problematical port and the cycle passing through it. For instance, the warning triggered by the example above states that the constraint cycle associated with scan, collect-sum, series, and #M/ passes through the non-series output of collect-sum.

Given this kind of detailed information, it is easy to alleviate the problem. To start with, every cycle must contain at least one function that has two series data flows leaving it. At worst, the cycle can be broken by duplicating this function (and any functions computing series used by it). For instance, the example above can be rewritten as shown below.

```
(let ((x (scan '(1 2 5 2)))
      (sum (collect-sum (scan '(1 2 5 2)))))
  (collect-max (#M/ x (series sum))))
  ⇒ 1/2
```

It would be easy enough to automatically apply code copying to break problematical constraint cycles. However, this is not done for two reasons. First, there is considerable virtue in maintaining the property that each function in a series expression turns into one piece of computation in the loop produced. Users can be confident that series expressions that look simple and efficient actually are simple and efficient. Second, with a little creativity, constraint problems can often be resolved in ways that are much more efficient than copying code. In the example above, the conflict can be eliminated efficiently by interchanging the operation of computing the maximum with the operation of normalizing an element.

```
(let ((x (scan '(1 2 5 2))))
  (/ (collect-max x) (collect-sum x))) ⇒ 1/2
```

The restriction that optimizable series expressions cannot contain constraint cycles that pass through non-series outputs places limitations on the qualitative character of optimizable series expressions. In particular, they all must have the general form of creating some number of series using scanners, computing various intermediate series using transducers, and then computing one or more summary results using collectors. The output of a collector cannot be used in the intermediate computation unless it is the output of a separate subexpression.

It is worthy of note that the last expression above fixes the constraint conflict by moving the non-series output out of the cycle, rather than by breaking the cycle. This illustrates the fact that constraint cycles that do not pass through non-series outputs do not necessarily cause problems. They cause problems only if they pass through *off-line* ports.

A series input port or series output port of a series function is *on-line* if and only if it is processed in lockstep with all the other on-line ports as follows: the initial element of each on-line input is read, then the initial element of each on-line output is written, then the second element of each on-line input is read, then the second element of each on-line output is written, and so on. Ports that are not on-line are off-line. If all of the series ports of a function are on-line, the function is said to be on-line; otherwise, it is off-line. (The above extends the standard definition of the term *on-line* so that it applies to individual ports as well as whole functions.)

If all of the ports a cycle passes through are on-line, the lockstep processing of these ports guarantees that there cannot be any conflicts between the constraints associated with the cycle. However, passing through an off-line port leads to the same kinds of problems as passing through a non-series output.

Most of the series functions are on-line. In particular, scanners and collectors are all on-line as are many transducers. However, the transducers in section A.2.4 are off-line. In particular, the series inputs of catenate, choose-if, chunk, expand, mask, mingle, positions, and subseries along with the series outputs of choose, split, and split-if are off-line.

In summary, the fourth and final restriction is that **for optimization to be possible, a series expression cannot contain a constraint cycle that passes through a non-series output or an off-line port**. Whenever this restriction is violated a warning message is issued. Violations can be fixed either by breaking the cycle or restructuring the computation so that the offending port is removed from the cycle.

A.3.3. Defining New Series Functions

New functions operating on series can be defined just as easily as new functions operating on any other data type. However, expressions containing these new functions cannot be transformed into loops unless a complete analysis of the functions is available. Among other things, this implies that the definition of a new series function must appear before its first use.

optimizable-series-function   [*Declaration specifier*]

The declaration specifier (optimizable-series-function *integer*) indicates that the function being defined is a series function that needs to be analyzed so that it can be optimized when it appears in series expressions. (A warning is issued if the function being defined neither takes a series as input nor produces a series as output.) *Integer* (default 1) specifies the number of values returned by the function being defined. (This cannot necessarily be determined by local analysis.) The only place optimizable-series-function is allowed to appear is in a declaration immediately inside a defun. As an example, the following shows how a simplified version of collect-sum could be defined.

```
(defun simple-collect-sum (numbers)
  (declare (optimizable-series-function 1))
  (collect-fn 'number #'(lambda () 0) #'+ numbers))
```

`off-line-port`   *[Declaration specifier]*

The declaration specifier (`off-line-port` *port-spec1 port-spec2* ...) specifies
that the indicated inputs and outputs are off-line. This declaration specifier is only
allowed in a `defun` that contains the declaration `optimizable-series-function`.
Each *port-spec* must either be a symbol that is one of the inputs of the function or an integer *j* indicating the *j*th output (counting from zero). For example,
(`off-line-port` x 1) indicates that the input x and the second output are off-
line. Every port that is not mentioned in an `off-line-port` declaration is assumed
to be on-line. A warning is issued whenever a port's actual on-line/off-line status
does not agree with its declared status. This makes it easier to keep track of which
ports are off-line and which are not. Note that off-line ports virtually never arise
when defining scanners or reducers.

A.3.4. Declarations

A key feature of Lisp is that variable declarations are strictly optional. Nevertheless,
it is often the case that they are necessary in situations where efficiency matters.
Therefore, it is important that it be *possible* for programmers to provide declarations
for every variable in a program. The transformation of series expressions into loops
presents certain problems in this regard, because the loops created contain variables
not evident in the original code. However, if the information described below is
supplied by the user, appropriate declarations can be generated for all of the loop
variables created.

All the explicit variables that are bound in a series expression (for example, by a
`let` that is part of the expression) should be given informative declarations making
use of the type specifier (`series` *element-type*) where appropriate.

Informative types should be supplied to series functions (such as `scan` and
`map-fn`) that have type arguments. When using `scan` it is important to specify
the type of element in the sequence as well as the sequence itself (for example, by
using (`vector * integer`) as opposed to merely `vector`). The form (`list` *element-type*) can be used to specify the type of elements in a list.

If it is appropriate to have a type more specific than (`series t`) associated with the output of `#M`, `#Z`, `scan-alist`, `scan-file`, `scan-hash`,
`scan-lists-of-lists-fringe`, `scan-lists-of-lists`, `scan-plist`, `series`,
`latch`, or `catenate`, then the form `the` must be used to specify this type.

Finally, if the expression computing a non-series argument to a series variable is
neither a variable nor a constant, `the` must be used to specify the type of its result.

For example, the declarations in the series expressions below are sufficient to
ensure that every loop variable will have an accurate declaration.

```
(collect-last (choose-if #´plusp (scan ´(list integer) data)))

(collect ´(vector * float)
         (map-fn ´float #´/
                (series (the integer (car data)))
                (the (series integer) (scan-file f)))))
```

The amount of information the user has to provide is reduced by the fact that this information can be propagated from place to place. For instance, the variable holding the output of choose-if holds a subset of the elements held by the input variable. As a result, it is appropriate for it to have the same type. When defining a new series function, the type specifier series-element-type can be used to indicate where type propagation should occur.

series-element-type   [*Type specifier*]

The type specifier (series-element-type *variable*) denotes the type of elements in the series held in *variable*. *Variable* must be a variable carrying a series value (for example, a series argument of a series function). series-element-type can be used only in three places: in a declaration in a let, mapping, producing, or other binding form in a series expression; in a declaration in a defun being used to define a series function; or in a type argument to a series function. As an example, consider that collect-last could have been defined as follows. The use of series-element-type ensures that the internal variable keeping track of the most recent item has the correct type.

```
(defun collect-last (items &optional (default nil))
  (declare (optimizable-series-function))
  (collect-fn ´(series-element-type items)
              #´(lambda () default)
              #´(lambda (old new) new)
              items))
```

A.4. Primitives

A large number of series functions are provided, because there are a large number of useful operations that can be performed on series. However, this functionality can be boiled down to a small number of primitive constructs.

collecting-fn embodies the fundamental idea of series computations that utilize internal state. It can be used as the basis for defining any on-line transducer.

until embodies the fundamental idea of producing a series that is shorter than the shortest input series. In particular, it embodies the idea of computing a bounded series from non-series inputs. Together with collecting-fn, until can be used to define scan-fn, which can be used as the basis for defining all the other scanners.

collect-last embodies the fundamental idea of producing a non-series value from a series. Together with collecting-fn, it can be used to define collect-fn, which (with the occasional assistance of until) can be used as the basis for defining all the other collectors.

producing embodies the fundamental idea of preorder computation. It can be used as the basis for defining all the other series functions, including the off-line transducers.

In addition to the above, four primitives support various specialized aspects of series functions. Alterability is supported by the function to-alter and the declaration propagate-alterability. The propagation of type information is supported by the type specifier series-element-type. The best implementation of certain series functions requires the form encapsulated.

producing *output-list input-list* {*declaration*}* {*form*}*   [*Macro*]

producing computes and returns a group of series and non-series outputs given a group of series and non-series inputs. The key feature of producing is that some or all of the series inputs and outputs can be processed in an off-line way. To support this, the processing in the body (consisting of the *forms*) is performed from the perspective of generators and gatherers (see appendix B). Each series input is converted to a generator before being used in the body. Each series output is associated with a gatherer in the body.

The *output-list* has the same syntax as the binding list of a let. The names of the variables must be distinct from each other and from the names of the variables in the input-list. If there are *n* variables in the *output-list*, producing computes *n* outputs. There must be at least one output variable. The variables act as the names for the outputs and can be used in either of two ways. First, if an output variable has a value associated with it in the *output-list*, then the variable is treated as holding a non-series value. The variable is initialized to the indicated value and can be used in any way desired in the body. The eventual output value is whatever value is in the variable when the execution of the body terminates. Second, if an output variable does not have a value associated with it in the *output-list*, the variable is given as its value a gatherer that collects elements. The only valid way to use the variable in the body is in a call on next-out. The output returned is a series containing these elements. If the body never terminates, this series is unbounded.

The *input-list* also has the same syntax as the binding list of a let. The names of the variables must be distinct from each other and the names of the variables in the *output-list*. The values can be series or non-series. If the value is not explicitly specified, it defaults to nil. The variables act logically both as inputs and state variables and can be used in one of two ways. First, if an input variable is associated with a non-series value, then it is given this value before the evaluation of the body begins and can be used in any way desired in the body. Second, if an input variable is associated with a series, then the variable is given a generator corresponding to this series as its initial value. The only valid way to use the variable in the body is in a call on next-in.

There can be declarations at the start of the body. However, the only declarations allowed are ignore declarations, type declarations, and propagate-alterability declarations (see below). In particular, it is an error for any of the input or output variables to be special.

In conception, the body can contain arbitrary Lisp expressions. After the appropriate generators and gatherers have been set up, the body is executed until it terminates. If the body never terminates, the series outputs (if any) are unbounded in length and the non-series outputs (if any) are never produced.

Although easy to understand, this view of what can happen in the body presents severe difficulties when optimizing (and even when evaluating) series expressions that contain calls on producing. As a result, several limitations are imposed on the form of the body to simplify the processing required.

The first limitation is that, exclusive of any declarations, the body must have the form (loop (tagbody ...)). The following example shows how producing could be used to implement a scanner creating an unbounded series of integers.

```
(producing (nums) ((num 0))
  (declare (integer num) (type (series integer) nums))
  (loop
    (tagbody
      (setq num (1+ num))
      (next-out nums num))))
  ⇒ #Z(1 2 3 4 ...)
```

The second limitation is that the form terminate-producing must be used to terminate the execution of the body. Any other method of terminating the body (with return, for example) is an error. The following example shows how producing could be used to implement the operation of summing a series. The function terminate-producing is used to stop the computation when numbers runs out of elements.

```
(producing ((sum 0)) ((numbers #Z(1 2 3)) num)
  (loop
    (tagbody
      (setq num (next-in numbers (terminate-producing)))
      (setq sum (+ sum num)))))
  ⇒ 6
```

The third limitation is that calls on next-out associated with output variables must appear at top level in the tagbody in the body. They cannot be nested in other forms. In addition, an output variable can be the destination of at most one call on next-out and if it is the destination of a next-out, it cannot be used in any other way.

If the call on next-out for a given output appears in the final part of the tagbody in the body, after everything other than other calls on next-out, then the output is an on-line output—a new value is written on every cycle of the body. Otherwise the output is off-line.

The following example shows how producing could be used to split a series into two parts. Items are read in one at a time and tested. Depending on the test, they are written to one of two outputs. Note the use of labels and branches to keep the calls on next-out at top level. Both outputs are off-line. The first example above shows an on-line output.

```
(producing (items-1 items-2) ((items #Z(1 -2 3 -4)) item)
  (loop
    (tagbody (setq item (next-in items (terminate-producing)))
             (if (not (plusp item)) (go D))
             (next-out items-1 item)
             (go F)
      D      (next-out items-2 item)
      F      )))
  ⇒ #Z(1 3) and #Z(-2 -4)
```

The fourth limitation is that the calls on next-in associated with an input variable v must appear at top level in the tagbody in the body, nested in assignments of the form (setq *var* (next-in v ...)). They cannot be nested in other forms. In addition, an input variable can be the source for at most one call on next-in and if it is the source for a next-in, it cannot be used in any other way.

If the call on next-in for a given input has as its sole termination action (terminate-producing) and appears in the initial part of the tagbody in the body, before anything other than similar calls on next-in, then the input is an on-line input—a new value is read on every cycle of the body. Otherwise the input is off-line.

The example below shows how producing could be used to concatenate two series. To start with, elements are read from the first input series. When this runs out, a flag is set and reading begins from the second input. Both inputs are off-line. (Compare this to the example above, which shows an on-line input.)

```
(producing (items) ((item-1 #Z(1 2))
                    (item-2 #Z(3 4))
                    (in-2 nil)
                    item)
  (loop
    (tagbody (if in-2 (go D))
             (setq item (next-in item-1 (setq in-2 t) (go D)))
             (go F)
       D     (setq item (next-in item-2 (terminate-producing)))
       F     (next-out items item)))))
 ⇒ #Z(1 2 3 4)
```

terminate-producing   [*Macro*]

This form (which takes no arguments) is used to terminate execution of (the expansion of) the producing macro.

As with the form go, terminate-producing does not return any values; rather, control immediately leaves the current context.

The form terminate-producing is allowed to appear only in a producing body and causes the termination of the enclosing call on producing.

propagate-alterability   [*Declaration specifier*]

The declaration specifier (propagate-alterability *input output*) indicates that attempts to alter an element of *output* should be satisfied by altering the corresponding element of *input*. (The corresponding element of *input* is the one most recently read at the moment when the output element is written.)

This declaration may appear only in a call on producing. The *input* and *output* arguments must be an input and an output, respectively, of the producing macro. The example below shows how the propagation of alterability could be supported in a simplified version of until.

```
(defun simple-until (bools items)
  (declare (optimizable-series-function))
  (producing (z) ((x bools) (y items) bool item)
    (declare (propagate-alterability y z))
    (loop
      (tagbody
        (setq bool (next-in x (terminate-producing)))
        (setq item (next-in y (terminate-producing)))
        (if bool (terminate-producing))
        (next-out z item)))))
```

encapsulated *encapsulating-fn scanner-or-collector*   [*Macro*]

Some of the features provided by Common Lisp are supported solely by encapsulating forms. For example, there is no way to specify a cleanup expression that will always be run, even when an abort occurs, without using
unwind-protect. encapsulated makes it possible to take advantage of forms
such as unwind-protect when defining a series function.

  encapsulated specifies a function that places an encapsulating form around
the computation performed by its second argument. The first argument must be a
quoted function that takes a Lisp expression and wraps the appropriate encapsulating form around it, returning the resulting code. The second input must be a literal
call on scan-fn, scan-fn-inclusive, or collect-fn. The second argument can
count on being evaluated in the scope of the encapsulating form. The values returned by the second argument are returned as the values of encapsulated. The
following shows how encapsulated could be used to define a simplified version
of collect-file.

```
(defun collect-file-wrap (file name body)
  `(with-open-file (,file ,name :direction :output) ,body))

(defmacro simple-collect-file (name items)
  (let ((file (gensym)))
    `(encapsulated #'(lambda (body)
                       (collect-file-wrap ',file ',name body))
                   (collect-fn t #'(lambda () t)
                               #'(lambda (state item)
                                   (print item ,file)
                                   state)
                               ,items))))
```

Appendix B

Generators and Gatherers

BY CRISPIN PERDUE AND RICHARD C. WATERS

PREFACE: Generators and gatherers are yet another approach, closely related to series, to providing iteration in a functional style.

The remainder of this chapter consists of a description by Crispin Perdue and Richard C. Waters of their work on an existing implementation of generators and gatherers. I have edited the chapter only very lightly to conform to the overall style of this book. Please see the Preface to this book for more information about the genesis of the generators/gatherers approach and its relationship to the work of X3J13.

—Guy L. Steele Jr.

B.1. Introduction

Generators are generalized input streams in the sense of Smalltalk [20]. A generator can produce a potentially unbounded number of elements of any type. Individual elements are not computed until requested by next-in. When an element is taken from a generator, it is removed by side effect. Subsequent uses of next-in obtain later elements.

There is a close relationship between a generator and a series of the elements it produces. In particular, any series can be converted into a generator. As a result, all the scanner functions used for creating series (see appendix A) can be used to create generators as well. There is no need to have a separate set of functions for creating generators.

Gatherers are generalized output streams. Elements of any type can be entered into a gatherer using next-out. The gatherer combines the elements together in time-sequence order into a net result. This result can be retrieved using result-of.

There is a close relationship between a gatherer and a collector function that combines elements in the same way. In particular, any one-input one-output collector can be converted into a gatherer. As a result, all the collectors used for computing summary results from series can be used to create gatherers. There is no need to have a separate set of functions for creating gatherers.

B.2. Generators

These functions create and process generators.

generator *series*   [*Function*]

Given a series, generator returns a generator containing the same elements.

next-in *generator* {*action*}*   [*Macro*]

next-in returns the next element in the generator *generator*. The *actions* can be any Lisp expressions. They are evaluated if and only if no more elements can be retrieved from *generator*. If there are no more elements and no actions, it is an error. It is also an error to apply next-in to a generator a second time after the generator has run out of elements. As an example of generators, consider the following.

```
(let ((x (generator (scan '(1 2 3 4)))))
   (with-output-to-string (s)
      (loop (prin1 (next-in x (return)) s)
            (prin1 (next-in x (return)) s)
            (princ "," s))))
⇒ "12,34,"
```

B.3. Gatherers

These functions create and process gatherers.

gatherer *collector*   [*Function*]

The *collector* must be a function of type (function ((series t_1)) t_2). Given this function, gatherer returns a gatherer that accepts elements of type t_1 and returns a final result of type t_2. The method for combining elements used by the gatherer is the same as the one used by the *collector*.

next-out *gatherer item*   [*Function*]

Given a gatherer and a value, next-out enters the value into the gatherer.

result-of *gatherer*   [*Function*]

result-of retrieves the net result from a gatherer. result-of can be applied at any time. However, it is an error to apply result-of twice to the same gatherer or to apply next-out to a gatherer once result-of has been applied.

```
(let ((g (gatherer #'collect-sum)))
  (dolist (i '(1 2 3 4))
    (next-out g i)
    (if (evenp i) (next-out g (* 10 i))))
  (result-of g))
⇒ 70
```

gathering ({(*var fn*)}*) {*form*}*   [*Macro*]

The first subform must be a list of pairs. The first element of each pair, *var*, must be a variable name. The second element of each pair, *fn*, must be a form that when wrapped in (function ...) is acceptable as an argument to gatherer. Each symbol is bound to a gatherer constructed from the corresponding collector. The body (consisting of the *forms*) is evaluated in the scope of these bindings. When this evaluation is complete, gathering returns the result-of each gatherer. If there are *n* pairs in the binding list, gathering returns *n* values. For example:

```
(defun examp (data)
  (gathering ((x collect) (y collect-sum))
    (iterate ((i (scan data)))
      (case (first i)
        (:slot (next-out x (second i)))
        (:part (dolist (j (second i)) (next-out x j))))
      (next-out y (third i)))))
```

(examp '((:slot a 10) (:part (c d) 40))) ⇒ (a c d) and 50

As a further illustration of gatherers, consider the following definition for a simplified version of gathering that handles only one binding pair.

```
(defmacro simple-gathering (((var collector)) &body body)
  `(let ((,var (gatherer (function ,collector))))
     ,@body
     (result-of ,var)))
```

The full capabilities of gathering can be supported in much the same way.

B.4. Discussion

The idea of generators and gatherers was first proposed by Pavel Curtis. A key aspect of his proposal was the realization that generators and gatherers can be implemented simply and elegantly as closures and that these closures can be compiled very efficiently if certain conditions are met.

First, the compiler must support an optimization Curtis calls "let eversion" in addition to the optimization methods presented in [45]. If a closure is created and used entirely within a limited lexical scope, the scopes of any bound variables nested in the closure can be enlarged (everted) to enclose all the uses of the closure. This allows the variables to be allocated on the stack rather than the heap.

Second, for a generator/gatherer closure to be compiled efficiently, it must be possible to determine at compile time exactly what closure is involved and exactly what the scope of use of the closure is. There are several aspects to this. The expression creating the generator/gatherer cannot refer to a free series variable. The generator/gatherer must be stored in a local variable. This variable must be used only in calls of next-in, next-out, and result-of, and not inside a closure. In particular the generator/gatherer cannot be stored in a data structure, stored in a special variable, or returned as a result value.

All of the examples above satisfy these restrictions. For instance, once the uses of gathering and iterate have been optimized, the body of examp is as efficient as any loop performing the same computation.

The implementation discussed in [52] includes a portable Common Lisp implementation of generators and gatherers. Although the implementation does not support optimizations of the kind discussed in [45], it fully optimizes uses of gathering.

Appendix C

Backquote

Here is the code for an implementation of backquote syntax (see section 22.1.3) that I have found quite useful in explaining to myself the behavior of nested backquotes. It implements the formal rules for backquote processing and optionally applies a code simplifier to the result. One must be very careful in choosing the simplification rules; the rules given here work, but some Common Lisp implementations have run into trouble at one time or another by using a simplification rule that does not work in all cases. Code transformations that are plausible when single forms are involved are likely to fail in the presence of splicing.

At the end of this appendix are some samples of nested backquote syntax with commentary.

```
;;; Common Lisp backquote implementation, written in Common Lisp.
;;; Author: Guy L. Steele Jr.     Date: 27 December 1985
;;; Tested under Symbolics Common Lisp and Lucid Common Lisp.
;;; This software is in the public domain.

;;; $ is pseudo-backquote and % is pseudo-comma.  This makes it
;;; possible to test this code without interfering with normal
;;; Common Lisp syntax.

;;; The following are unique tokens used during processing.
;;; They need not be symbols; they need not even be atoms.

(defvar *comma* (make-symbol "COMMA"))
(defvar *comma-atsign* (make-symbol "COMMA-ATSIGN"))
(defvar *comma-dot* (make-symbol "COMMA-DOT"))
(defvar *bq-list* (make-symbol "BQ-LIST"))
(defvar *bq-append* (make-symbol "BQ-APPEND"))
(defvar *bq-list** (make-symbol "BQ-LIST*"))
(defvar *bq-nconc* (make-symbol "BQ-NCONC"))
```

960

```
(defvar *bq-clobberable* (make-symbol "BQ-CLOBBERABLE"))
(defvar *bq-quote* (make-symbol "BQ-QUOTE"))
(defvar *bq-quote-nil* (list *bq-quote* nil))

;;; Reader macro characters:
;;;     $foo is read in as (BACKQUOTE foo)
;;;     %foo is read in as (#:COMMA foo)
;;;     %@foo is read in as (#:COMMA-ATSIGN foo)
;;;     %.foo is read in as (#:COMMA-DOT foo)
;;; where #:COMMA is the value of the variable *COMMA*, etc.

;;; BACKQUOTE is an ordinary macro (not a read-macro) that
;;; processes the expression foo, looking for occurrences of
;;; #:COMMA, #:COMMA-ATSIGN, and #:COMMA-DOT.  It constructs code
;;; in strict accordance with the rules on pages 349-350 of
;;; the first edition (pages 528-529 of this second edition).
;;; It then optionally applies a code simplifier.
(set-macro-character #\$
  #'(lambda (stream char)
      (declare (ignore char))
      (list 'backquote (read stream t nil t))))

(set-macro-character #\%
  #'(lambda (stream char)
      (declare (ignore char))
        (case (peek-char nil stream t nil t)
          (#\@ (read-char stream t nil t)
               (list *comma-atsign* (read stream t nil t)))
          (#\. (read-char stream t nil t)
               (list *comma-dot* (read stream t nil t)))
          (otherwise (list *comma* (read stream t nil t))))))


;;; If the value of *BQ-SIMPLIFY* is non-NIL, then BACKQUOTE
;;; processing applies the code simplifier.  If the value is NIL,
;;; then the code resulting from BACKQUOTE is exactly that
;;; specified by the official rules.

(defparameter *bq-simplify* t)

(defmacro backquote (x)
  (bq-completely-process x))
```

```
;;; Backquote processing proceeds in three stages:
;;;
;;; (1) BQ-PROCESS applies the rules to remove occurrences of
;;; #:COMMA, #:COMMA-ATSIGN, and #:COMMA-DOT corresponding to
;;; this level of BACKQUOTE.  (It also causes embedded calls to
;;; BACKQUOTE to be expanded so that nesting is properly handled.)
;;; Code is produced that is expressed in terms of functions
;;; #:BQ-LIST, #:BQ-APPEND, and #:BQ-CLOBBERABLE.  This is done
;;; so that the simplifier will simplify only list construction
;;; functions actually generated by BACKQUOTE and will not involve
;;; any user code in the simplification.  #:BQ-LIST means LIST,
;;; #:BQ-APPEND means APPEND, and #:BQ-CLOBBERABLE means IDENTITY
;;; but indicates places where "%." was used and where NCONC may
;;; therefore be introduced by the simplifier for efficiency.
;;;
;;; (2) BQ-SIMPLIFY, if used, rewrites the code produced by
;;; BQ-PROCESS to produce equivalent but faster code.  The
;;; additional functions #:BQ-LIST* and #:BQ-NCONC may be
;;; introduced into the code.
;;;
;;; (3) BQ-REMOVE-TOKENS goes through the code and replaces
;;; #:BQ-LIST with LIST, #:BQ-APPEND with APPEND, and so on.
;;; #:BQ-CLOBBERABLE is simply eliminated (a call to it being
;;; replaced by its argument).  #:BQ-LIST* is replaced by either
;;; LIST* or CONS (the latter is used in the two-argument case,
;;; purely to make the resulting code a tad more readable).

(defun bq-completely-process (x)
  (let ((raw-result (bq-process x)))
    (bq-remove-tokens (if *bq-simplify*
                          (bq-simplify raw-result)
                          raw-result))))

(defun bq-process (x)
  (cond ((atom x)
         (list *bq-quote* x))
        ((eq (car x) 'backquote)
         (bq-process (bq-completely-process (cadr x))))
        ((eq (car x) *comma*) (cadr x))
        ((eq (car x) *comma-atsign*)
         (error ",@~S after `" (cadr x)))
```

```
          ((eq (car x) *comma-dot*)
           (error ",.~S after `" (cadr x)))
          (t (do ((p x (cdr p))
                  (q '() (cons (bracket (car p)) q)))
                 ((atom p)
                  (cons *bq-append*
                        (nreconc q (list (list *bq-quote* p)))))
               (when (eq (car p) *comma*)
                 (unless (null (cddr p)) (error "Malformed ,~S" p))
                 (return (cons *bq-append*
                               (nreconc q (list (cadr p))))))
               (when (eq (car p) *comma-atsign*)
                 (error "Dotted ,@~S" p))
               (when (eq (car p) *comma-dot*)
                 (error "Dotted ,.~S" p))))))
```

```
;;; This implements the bracket operator of the formal rules.

(defun bracket (x)
  (cond ((atom x)
         (list *bq-list* (bq-process x)))
        ((eq (car x) *comma*)
         (list *bq-list* (cadr x)))
        ((eq (car x) *comma-atsign*)
         (cadr x))
        ((eq (car x) *comma-dot*)
         (list *bq-clobberable* (cadr x)))
        (t (list *bq-list* (bq-process x)))))
```

```
;;; This auxiliary function is like MAPCAR but has two extra
;;; purposes: (1) it handles dotted lists; (2) it tries to make
;;; the result share with the argument x as much as possible.

(defun maptree (fn x)
  (if (atom x)
      (funcall fn x)
      (let ((a (funcall fn (car x)))
            (d (maptree fn (cdr x))))
        (if (and (eql a (car x)) (eql d (cdr x)))
            x
            (cons a d)))))
```

```
;;; This predicate is true of a form that when read looked
;;; like %@foo or %.foo.

(defun bq-splicing-frob (x)
  (and (consp x)
       (or (eq (car x) *comma-atsign*)
           (eq (car x) *comma-dot*)))))


;;; This predicate is true of a form that when read
;;; looked like %@foo or %.foo or just plain %foo.

(defun bq-frob (x)
  (and (consp x)
       (or (eq (car x) *comma*)
           (eq (car x) *comma-atsign*)
           (eq (car x) *comma-dot*)))))

;;; The simplifier essentially looks for calls to #:BQ-APPEND and
;;; tries to simplify them.  The arguments to #:BQ-APPEND are
;;; processed from right to left, building up a replacement form.
;;; At each step a number of special cases are handled that,
;;; loosely speaking, look like this:
;;;
;;;   (APPEND (LIST a b c) foo) => (LIST* a b c foo)
;;;         provided a, b, c are not splicing frobs
;;;   (APPEND (LIST* a b c) foo) => (LIST* a b (APPEND c foo))
;;;         provided a, b, c are not splicing frobs
;;;   (APPEND (QUOTE (x)) foo) => (LIST* (QUOTE x) foo)
;;;   (APPEND (CLOBBERABLE x) foo) => (NCONC x foo)

(defun bq-simplify (x)
  (if (atom x)
      x
      (let ((x (if (eq (car x) *bq-quote*)
                   x
                   (maptree #'bq-simplify x))))
        (if (not (eq (car x) *bq-append*))
            x
            (bq-simplify-args x)))))
```

```
(defun bq-simplify-args (x)
  (do ((args (reverse (cdr x)) (cdr args))
       (result
         nil
         (cond ((atom (car args))
                (bq-attach-append *bq-append* (car args) result))
               ((and (eq (caar args) *bq-list*)
                     (notany #'bq-splicing-frob (cdar args)))
                (bq-attach-conses (cdar args) result))
               ((and (eq (caar args) *bq-list**)
                     (notany #'bq-splicing-frob (cdar args)))
                (bq-attach-conses
                  (reverse (cdr (reverse (cdar args))))
                  (bq-attach-append *bq-append*
                                    (car (last (car args)))
                                    result)))
               ((and (eq (caar args) *bq-quote*)
                     (consp (cadar args))
                     (not (bq-frob (cadar args)))
                     (null (cddar args)))
                (bq-attach-conses (list (list *bq-quote*
                                              (caadar args)))
                                  result))
               ((eq (caar args) *bq-clobberable*)
                (bq-attach-append *bq-nconc* (cadar args) result))
               (t (bq-attach-append *bq-append*
                                    (car args)
                                    result)))))
      ((null args) result)))

(defun null-or-quoted (x)
  (or (null x) (and (consp x) (eq (car x) *bq-quote*))))

;;; When BQ-ATTACH-APPEND is called, the OP should be #:BQ-APPEND
;;; or #:BQ-NCONC.  This produces a form (op item result) but
;;; some simplifications are done on the fly:
;;;
;;;   (op '(a b c) '(d e f g)) => '(a b c d e f g)
;;;   (op item 'nil) => item, provided item is not a splicable frob
;;;   (op item 'nil) => (op item), if item is a splicable frob
;;;   (op item (op a b c)) => (op item a b c)
```

```
(defun bq-attach-append (op item result)
  (cond ((and (null-or-quoted item) (null-or-quoted result))
         (list *bq-quote* (append (cadr item) (cadr result))))
        ((or (null result) (equal result *bq-quote-nil*))
         (if (bq-splicing-frob item) (list op item) item))
        ((and (consp result) (eq (car result) op))
         (list* (car result) item (cdr result)))
        (t (list op item result))))
```

```
;;; The effect of BQ-ATTACH-CONSES is to produce a form as if by
;;; `(LIST* ,@items ,result) but some simplifications are done
;;; on the fly.
;;;
;;; (LIST* 'a 'b 'c 'd) => '(a b c . d)
;;; (LIST* a b c 'nil) => (LIST a b c)
;;; (LIST* a b c (LIST* d e f g)) => (LIST* a b c d e f g)
;;; (LIST* a b c (LIST d e f g)) => (LIST a b c d e f g)
```

```
(defun bq-attach-conses (items result)
  (cond ((and (every #'null-or-quoted items)
              (null-or-quoted result))
         (list *bq-quote*
               (append (mapcar #'cadr items) (cadr result))))
        ((or (null result) (equal result *bq-quote-nil*))
         (cons *bq-list* items))
        ((and (consp result)
              (or (eq (car result) *bq-list*)
                  (eq (car result) *bq-list**)))
         (cons (car result) (append items (cdr result))))
        (t (cons *bq-list** (append items (list result))))))
```

```
;;; Removes funny tokens and changes (#:BQ-LIST* a b) into
;;; (CONS a b) instead of (LIST* a b), purely for readability.
```

```
(defun bq-remove-tokens (x)
  (cond ((eq x *bq-list*) 'list)
        ((eq x *bq-append*) 'append)
        ((eq x *bq-nconc*) 'nconc)
        ((eq x *bq-list**) 'list*)
        ((eq x *bq-quote*) 'quote)
        ((atom x) x)
```

```
((eq (car x) *bq-clobberable*)
 (bq-remove-tokens (cadr x)))
((and (eq (car x) *bq-list**)
      (consp (cddr x))
      (null (cdddr x)))
 (cons 'cons (maptree #'bq-remove-tokens (cdr x))))
(t (maptree #'bq-remove-tokens x))))
```

Suppose that we first make the following definitions:

```
(setq q '(r s))
(defun r (x) (reduce #'* x))
(setq r '(3 5))
(setq s '(4 6))
```

Without simplification, the notation `$$(%%q)` (which stands for `` `(,,q)``) is read as the expression

```
(APPEND (LIST 'APPEND) (LIST (APPEND (LIST 'LIST) (LIST Q))))
```

The value of this expression is

```
(APPEND (LIST (R S)))
```

and the value of this value is (24). We conclude that the net effect of twice-evaluating `` `(,,q)`` is to take the value 24 of the value (r s) of q and plug it into the template ( ) to produce (24).

With simplification, the notation `$$(%%q)` is read as the expression

```
(LIST 'LIST Q)
```

The value of this expression is

```
(LIST (R S))
```

and the value of this value is (24). Thus the two ways of reading `$$(%%q)` do not produce the same expression—this we expected—but the values of the two ways are different as well. Only the values of the values are the same. In general, Common Lisp guarantees the result of an expression with backquotes nested to depth k only after k successive evaluations have been performed; the results after fewer than k evaluations are implementation-dependent.

(Note that in the expression `'(foo ,(process '(bar ,x)))` the backquotes are *not* doubly nested. The inner backquoted expression occurs within the textual scope of a comma belonging to the outer backquote. The correct way to determine the backquote nesting level of any subexpression is to start a count at zero and proceed up the S-expression tree, adding one for each backquote and subtracting one for each comma. This is similar to the rule for determining nesting level with respect to parentheses by scanning a character string linearly, adding or subtracting one as parentheses are passed.)

It is convenient to extend the "$\equiv$" notation to handle multiple evaluation: $x \equiv\equiv y$ means that the expressions x and y may have different results but they have the same results when twice evaluated. Similarly, $x \equiv\equiv\equiv y$ means that the values of the values of the values of x and y are the same, and so on.

We can illustrate the differences between non-splicing and splicing backquote inclusions quite concisely:

```
$$(%%q)  ≡
  (APPEND (LIST 'APPEND) (LIST (APPEND (LIST 'LIST) (LIST Q))))
  ≡≡ (LIST 'LIST Q) ⇒ (LIST (R S)) ⇒ (24)

$$(%@%q) ≡
  (APPEND (LIST 'APPEND) (LIST Q))
  ≡≡ Q ⇒ (R S) ⇒ 24

$$(%%@q) ≡
  (APPEND (LIST 'APPEND) (LIST (APPEND (LIST 'LIST) Q)))
  ≡≡ (CONS 'LIST Q) ⇒ (LIST R S) ⇒ ((3 5) (4 6))

$$(%@%@q) ≡
  (APPEND (LIST 'APPEND) Q)
  ≡≡ (CONS 'APPEND Q) ⇒ (APPEND R S) ⇒ (3 5 4 6)
```

In each case I have shown both the unsimplified and simplified forms and then traced the intermediate evaluations of the simplified form. (Actually, the unsimplified forms do contain one simplification without which they would be unreadable: the nil that terminates each list has been systematically suppressed, so that one sees (append x y) rather than (append x y 'nil).)

The following driver function is useful for tracing the behavior of nested backquote syntax through multiple evaluations. The argument ls is a list of strings; each string will be processed by the reader (read-from-string). The argument n is the number of evaluations desired.

```
(defun try (ls &optional (n 0))
  (dolist (x ls)
    (format t "~&~A"
            (substitute #\` #\$ (substitute #\, #\% x)))
```

```
     (do ((form (macroexpand (read-from-string x))) (eval form))
          (str " = " "~% => ")
          (j 0 (+ j 1)))
        ((>= j n)
          (format t str)
          (write form :pretty t))
       (format t str)
       (write form :pretty t)))
  (format t "~&"))
```

This driver routine makes it easy to explore a large number of cases systematically. Here is a list of examples that illustrate not only the differences between , and ,@ but also their interaction with ´.

```
(setq fools2 ´(
"$$(foo %%p)"
"$$(foo %%@q)"
"$$(foo %´%r)"
"$$(foo %´%@s)"
"$$(foo %@%p)"
"$$(foo %@%@q)"
"$$(foo %@´%r)"
"$$(foo %@´%@s)"
))
```

Consider this set of sample values:

```
(setq p ´(union x y))
(setq q ´((union x y) (list ´sqrt 9)))
(setq r ´(union x y))
(setq s ´((union x y)))
```

Here is what happened when I executed (try fools2 2) with a non-nil value for the variable *bq-simplify* (to see simplified forms). I have interpolated some remarks.

```
``(foo ,,p) = (LIST ´LIST ´´FOO P)
=> (LIST ´FOO (UNION X Y))
=> (FOO (A B C))
```

So ,,p means "the value of p is a form; use the value of the value of p."

```
``(foo ,,@q) = (LIST* ´LIST ´´FOO Q)
=> (LIST ´FOO (UNION X Y) (LIST ´SQRT 9))
=> (FOO (A B C) (SQRT 9))
```

So `,,@q` means "the value of q is a list of forms; splice the list of values of the elements of the value of q."

```
``(foo ,´,r) = (LIST ´LIST ´´FOO (LIST ´QUOTE R))
=> (LIST ´FOO ´(UNION X Y))
=> (FOO (UNION X Y))
```

So `,´,r` means "the value of r may be any object; use the value of r that is available at the time of first evaluation, that is, when the outer backquote is evaluated." (To use the value of r that is available at the time of second evaluation, that is, when the inner backquote is evaluated, just use `,r`.)

```
``(foo ,´,@s) = (LIST ´LIST ´´FOO (CONS ´QUOTE S))
=> (LIST ´FOO ´(UNION X Y))
=> (FOO (UNION X Y))
```

So `,´,@s` means "the value of s must be a singleton list of any object; use the element of the value of s that is available at the time of first evaluation, that is, when the outer backquote is evaluated." Note that s must be a singleton list because it will be spliced into a form `(quote )`, and the `quote` special form requires exactly one subform to appear; this is generally true of the sequence `´,@`. (To use the value of s that is available at the time of second evaluation, that is, when the inner backquote is evaluated, just use `,@s`, in which case the list s is not restricted to be singleton, or `,(car s)`.)

```
``(foo ,@,p) = (LIST ´CONS ´´FOO P)
=> (CONS ´FOO (UNION X Y))
=> (FOO A B C)
```

So `,@,p` means "the value of p is a form; splice in the value of the value of p."

```
``(foo ,@,@q) = (LIST ´CONS ´´FOO (CONS ´APPEND Q))
=> (CONS ´FOO (APPEND (UNION X Y) (LIST ´SQRT 9)))
=> (FOO A B C SQRT 9)
```

So `,@,@q` means "the value of q is a list of forms; splice each of the values of the elements of the value of q, so that many splicings occur."

```
``(foo ,@´,r) = (LIST ´CONS ´´FOO (LIST ´QUOTE R))
=> (CONS ´FOO ´(UNION X Y))
=> (FOO UNION X Y)
```

So ,@´,r means "the value of r must be a list; splice in the value of r that is available at the time of first evaluation, that is, when the outer backquote is evaluated." (To splice the value of r that is available at the time of second evaluation, that is, when the inner backquote is evaluated, just use ,@r.)

```
``(foo ,@´,@s) = (LIST ´CONS ´´FOO (CONS ´QUOTE S))
=> (CONS ´FOO ´(UNION X Y))
=> (FOO UNION X Y)
```

So ,@´,@s means "the value of s must be a singleton list whose element is a list; splice in the list that is the element of the value of s that is available at the time of first evaluation, that is, when the outer backquote is evaluated." (To splice the element of the value of s that is available at the time of second evaluation, that is, when the inner backquote is evaluated, just use ,@(car s).)

I leave it to the reader to explore the possibilities of triply nested backquotes.

```
(setq fools3 ´(
"$$$(foo %%%p)"       "$$$(foo %%%@q)"
"$$$(foo %%´%r)"      "$$$(foo %%´%@s)"
"$$$(foo %%@%p)"      "$$$(foo %%@%@q)"
"$$$(foo %%@´%r)"     "$$$(foo %%@´%@s)"
"$$$(foo %´%%p)"      "$$$(foo %´%%@q)"
"$$$(foo %´%´%r)"     "$$$(foo %´%´%@s)"
"$$$(foo %´%@%p)"     "$$$(foo %´%@%@q)"
"$$$(foo %´%@´%r)"    "$$$(foo %´%@´%@s)"
"$$$(foo %@%%p)"      "$$$(foo %@%%@q)"
"$$$(foo %@%´%r)"     "$$$(foo %@%´%@s)"
"$$$(foo %@%@%p)"     "$$$(foo %@%@%@q)"
"$$$(foo %@%@´%r)"    "$$$(foo %@%@´%@s)"
"$$$(foo %@´%%p)"     "$$$(foo %@´%%@q)"
"$$$(foo %@´%´%r)"    "$$$(foo %@´%´%@s)"
"$$$(foo %@´%@%p)"    "$$$(foo %@´%@%@q)"
"$$$(foo %@´%@´%r)" "$$$(foo %@´%@´%@s)"
))
```

It is a pleasant exercise to construct values for p, q, r, and s that will allow execution of (try fools3 3) without error.

References

[1]   Adobe Systems Incorporated. *PostScript Language Reference Manual*. Addison-Wesley (Reading, Massachusetts, 1985).

[2]   Alberga, Cyril N., Bosman-Clark, Chris, Mikelsons, Martin, Van Deusen, Mary S., and Padget, Julian. Experience with an uncommon Lisp. In *Proc. 1986 ACM Conference on Lisp and Functional Programming*. ACM SIGPLAN/SIGACT/SIGART (Cambridge, Massachusetts, August 1986), 39–53.

[3]   *American National Standard Programming Language FORTRAN*, ANSI X3.9-1978 edition. American National Standards Institute, Inc. (New York, 1978).

[4]   Bates, Raymond L., Dyer, David, and Feber, Mark. Recent developments in ISI-Interlisp. In *Proc. 1984 ACM Symposium on Lisp and Functional Programming*. ACM SIGPLAN/SIGACT/SIGART (Austin, Texas, August 1984), 129–139.

[5]   Bobrow, Daniel G., DiMichiel, Linda G., Gabriel, Richard P., Keene, Sonya E., Kiczales, Gregor, and Moon, David A. Common Lisp Object System Specification: X3J13 Document 88-002R. *SIGPLAN Notices 23* (September 1988).

[6]   Bobrow, Daniel G., DiMichiel, Linda G., Gabriel, Richard P., Keene, Sonya E., Kiczales, Gregor, and Moon, David A. Common Lisp Object System specification: 1. Programmer interface concepts. *Lisp and Symbolic Computation 1*, 3/4 (January 1989), 245–298.

[7]   Bobrow, Daniel G., DiMichiel, Linda G., Gabriel, Richard P., Keene, Sonya E., Kiczales, Gregor, and Moon, David A. Common Lisp Object System specification: 2. Functions in the programmer interface. *Lisp and Symbolic Computation 1*, 3/4 (January 1989), 299–394.

[8]   Bobrow, Daniel G., and Kiczales, Gregor. The Common Lisp Object System metaobject kernel: A status report. In *Proc. 1988 ACM Conference on Lisp and Functional Programming*. ACM SIGPLAN/SIGACT/SIGART (Snowbird, Utah, July 1988), 309–315.

[9]   Brooks, Rodney A., and Gabriel, Richard P. A critique of Common Lisp. In *Proc. 1984 ACM Symposium on Lisp and Functional Programming*. ACM SIGPLAN/SIGACT/SIGART (Austin, Texas, August 1984), 1–8.

[10] Brooks, Rodney A., Gabriel, Richard P., and Steele, Guy L., Jr. S-1 Common Lisp implementation. In *Proc. 1982 ACM Symposium on Lisp and Functional Program-*

ming. ACM SIGPLAN/SIGACT/SIGART (Pittsburgh, Pennsylvania, August 1982), 108–113.

[11] Brooks, Rodney A., Gabriel, Richard P., and Steele, Guy L., Jr. An optimizing compiler for lexically scoped lisp. In *Proc. 1982 Symposium on Compiler Construction.* ACM SIGPLAN (Boston, June 1982), 261–275. Proceedings published as *ACM SIGPLAN Notices 17*, 6 (June 1982).

[12] Clinger, William (ed.) *The Revised Revised Report on Scheme; or, An Uncommon Lisp.* AI Memo 848. MIT Artificial Intelligence Laboratory (Cambridge, Massachusetts, August 1985).

[13] Clinger, William (ed.) *The Revised Revised Report on Scheme; or, An Uncommon Lisp.* Computer Science Department Technical Report 174. Indiana University (Bloomington, Indiana, June 1985).

[14] Cody, William J., Jr., and Waite, William. *Software Manual for the Elementary Functions.* Prentice-Hall (Englewood Cliffs, New Jersey, 1980).

[15] Committee, ANSI X3J3. Draft proposed American National Standard Fortran. *ACM SIGPLAN Notices 11*, 3 (March 1976).

[16] Coonen, Jerome T. Errata for "An implementation guide to a proposed standard for floating-point arithmetic." *Computer 14*, 3 (March 1981), 62. These are errata for [17].

[17] Coonen, Jerome T. An implementation guide to a proposed standard for floating-point arithmetic. *Computer 13*, 1 (January 1980), 68–79. Errata for this paper appeared as [16].

[18] DiMichiel, Linda G. Overview: The Common Lisp Object System. *Lisp and Symbolic Computation 1*, 3/4 (January 1989), 227–244.

[19] Fateman, Richard J. Reply to an editorial. *ACM SIGSAM Bulletin 25* (March 1973), 9–11.

[20] Goldberg, Adele, and Robson, David. *Smalltalk-80: The Language and Its Implementation.* Addison-Wesley (Reading, Massachusetts, 1983).

[21] Griss, Martin L., Benson, Eric, and Hearn, Anthony C. Current status of a portable LISP compiler. In *Proc. 1982 Symposium on Compiler Construction.* ACM SIGPLAN (Boston, June 1982), 276–283. Proceedings published as *ACM SIGPLAN Notices 17*, 6 (June 1982).

[22] Harrenstien, Kenneth L. *Time Server.* Request for Comments (RFC) 738 (NIC 42218). ARPANET Network Working Group (October 1977). Available from the ARPANET Network Information Center.

[23] IEEE Computer Society Standard Committee, Floating-Point Working Group, Microprocessor Standards Subcommittee. A proposed standard for binary floating-point arithmetic. *Computer 14*, 3 (March 1981), 51–62.

[24] ISO. *Information Processing—Coded Character Sets for Text Communication, Part 2: Latin Alphabetic and Non-alphabetic Graphic Characters.* ISO (1983).

[25] Kahan, W. Branch cuts for complex elementary functions; or, Much ado about nothing's sign bit. In Iserles, A., and Powell, M. (eds.), *The State of the Art in Numerical Analysis.* Clarendon Press (1987), 165–211.

[26] Keene, Sonya E. *Object-Oriented Programming in Common Lisp: A Programmer's Guide to CLOS.* Addison-Wesley (Reading, Massachusetts, 1989).

[27]   Knuth, Donald E. *Seminumerical Algorithms*. Volume 2 of *The Art of Computer Programming*. Addison-Wesley (Reading, Massachusetts, 1969).

[28]   Knuth, Donald E. *The TEXbook*. Volume A of *Computers and Typesetting*. Addison-Wesley (Reading, Massachusetts, 1986).

[29]   Knuth, Donald E. *TEX: The Program*. Volume B of *Computers and Typesetting*. Addison-Wesley (Reading, Massachusetts, 1986).

[30]   Lamport, Leslie. *LATEX: A Document Preparation System*. Addison-Wesley (Reading, Massachusetts, 1986).

[31]   Marti, J., Hearn, A. C., Griss, M. L., and Griss, C. Standard Lisp report. *ACM SIGPLAN Notices 14*, 10 (October 1979), 48–68.

[32]   McDonnell, E. E. The story of o. *APL Quote Quad 8*, 2 (December 1977), 48–54.

[33]   Moon, David. *MacLISP Reference Manual, Revision 0*. MIT Project MAC (Cambridge, Massachusetts, April 1974).

[34]   Moon, David, Stallman, Richard, and Weinreb, Daniel. *LISP Machine Manual, Fifth Edition*. MIT Artificial Intelligence Laboratory (Cambridge, Massachusetts, January 1983).

[35]   Padget, Julian, et al. Desiderata for the standardisation of Lisp. In *Proc. 1986 ACM Conference on Lisp and Functional Programming*. ACM SIGPLAN/SIGACT/SIGART (Cambridge, Massachusetts, August 1986), 54–66.

[36]   Penfield, Paul, Jr. Principal values and branch cuts in complex APL. In *APL 81 Conference Proceedings*. ACM SIGAPL (San Francisco, September 1981), 248–256. Proceedings published as *APL Quote Quad 12*, 1 (September 1981).

[37]   Pitman, Kent M. *The Revised MacLISP Manual*. MIT/LCS/TR 295. MIT Laboratory for Computer Science (Cambridge, Massachusetts, May 1983).

[38]   Pitman, Kent M. *Exceptional Situations in Lisp*. Working paper 268. MIT Artificial Intelligence Laboratory (Cambridge, Massachusetts).

[39]   Queinnec, Christian, and Cointe, Pierre. An open-ended data representation model for EU_LISP. In *Proc. 1988 ACM Conference on Lisp and Functional Programming*. ACM SIGPLAN/SIGACT/SIGART (Snowbird, Utah, July 1988), 298–308.

[40]   Rees, Jonathan, Clinger, William, et al. Revised[3] report on the algorithmic language Scheme. *ACM SIGPLAN Notices 21*, 12 (December 1986), 37–79.

[41]   Reiser, John F. *Analysis of Additive Random Number Generators*. Technical Report STAN-CS-77-601. Stanford University Computer Science Department (Palo Alto, California, March 1977).

[42]   Roylance, Gerald. Expressing mathematical subroutines constructively. In *Proc. 1988 ACM Conference on Lisp and Functional Programming*. ACM SIGPLAN/SIGACT/SIGART (Snowbird, Utah, July 1988), 8–13.

[43]   Steele, Guy L., Jr. An overview of Common Lisp. In *Proc. 1982 ACM Symposium on Lisp and Functional Programming*. ACM SIGPLAN/SIGACT/SIGART (Pittsburgh, Pennsylvania, August 1982), 98–107.

[44]   Steele, Guy L., Jr., and Hillis, W. Daniel. Connection Machine Lisp: Fine-grained parallel symbolic processing. In *Proc. 1986 ACM Conference on Lisp and Functional Programming*. ACM SIGPLAN/SIGACT/SIGART (Cambridge, Massachusetts, August 1986), 279–297.

[45]   Steele, Guy Lewis, Jr. *RABBIT: A Compiler for SCHEME (A Study in Compiler Optimization)*. Technical Report 474. MIT Artificial Intelligence Laboratory (Cambridge, Massachusetts, May 1978).

[46]   Steele, Guy Lewis, Jr., and Sussman, Gerald Jay. *The Revised Report on SCHEME: A Dialect of LISP*. AI Memo 452. MIT Artificial Intelligence Laboratory (Cambridge, Massachusetts, January 1978).

[47]   Suzuki, Norihisa. Analysis of pointer "rotation". *Communications of the ACM 25*, 5 (May 1982), 330–335.

[48]   Swanson, Mark, Kessler, Robert, and Lindstrom, Gary.   An implementation of Portable Standard Lisp on the BBN Butterfly. In *Proc. 1988 ACM Conference on Lisp and Functional Programming*. ACM SIGPLAN/SIGACT/SIGART (Snowbird, Utah, July 1988), 132–142.

[49]   Symbolics, Inc. *Signalling and Handling Conditions*. (Cambridge, Massachusetts, 1983).

[50]   Teitelman, Warren, et al. *InterLISP Reference Manual*. Xerox Palo Alto Research Center (Palo Alto, California, 1978). Third revision.

[51]   The Utah Symbolic Computation Group. *The Portable Standard LISP Users Manual*. Technical Report TR-10. Department of Computer Science, University of Utah (Salt Lake City, Utah, January 1982).

[52]   Waters, Richard C. *Optimization of Series Expressions, Part I: User's Manual for the Series Macro Package*. AI Memo 1082. MIT Artificial Intelligence Laboratory (Cambridge, Massachusetts, January 1989).

[53]   Waters, Richard C. *Optimization of Series Expressions, Part II: Overview of the Theory and Implementation*. AI Memo 1083. MIT Artificial Intelligence Laboratory (Cambridge, Massachusetts, January 1989).

[54]   Waters, Richard C. *XP: A Common Lisp Pretty Printing System*. AI Memo 1102. MIT Artificial Intelligence Laboratory (Cambridge, Massachusetts, March 1989).

[55]   Weinreb, Daniel, and Moon, David. *LISP Machine Manual, Fourth Edition*. MIT Artificial Intelligence Laboratory (Cambridge, Massachusetts, July 1981).

[56]   Wholey, Skef, and Fahlman, Scott E. The design of an instruction set for Common Lisp. In *Proc. 1984 ACM Symposium on Lisp and Functional Programming*. ACM SIGPLAN/SIGACT/SIGART (Austin, Texas, August 1984), 150–158.

[57]   Wholey, Skef, and Steele, Guy L., Jr. Connection Machine Lisp: A dialect of Common Lisp for data parallel programming. In Kartashev, Lana P., and Kartashev, Steven I. (eds.), *Proc. Second International Conference on Supercomputing*. Volume III. International Supercomputing Institute (Santa Clara, California, May 1987), 45–54.

Index of X3J13 Votes

This is an index of issues voted upon by X3J13. For the benefit of those readers who may wish to cross-reference to the X3J13 working documents or to the minutes of the X3J13 meetings, each vote is identified below by the (sometimes whimsical) descriptive label used in X3J13 discussions. Each label consists of the name of an issue and the name of the solution that was approved (many issues had more than one proposed solution) separated by a colon. A few solutions had no explicit name. Page numbers indicate where each issue is cited in the text; a following number in parentheses indicates that the issue is cited that many times on the page.

Index

aardvarks, 671, 890
abbreviating data type
    specifiers, 60–62
abort function, 913
    implementation notes, 903
above, iteration control and,
    719
abs function, 303; 309
absolute time, 702, 703. *See
    also* internal time
absolute value, obtaining, 303
access forms, setf method for,
    140–145
access functions
    automatic prefixing of
        names of, 476
    defstruct and, 469, 473
    :include and, 478
access operations, 123
accessible slots, 776
accessing directories, 663
accessing form, 140
accessor functions
    for hash tables, 440
    for streams, 507–508
    See also object-oriented
        programming
accessor method, 777
:accessor slot option, 779, 824
    redefining classes and, 810
accumulation of values. *See*
    value accumulation
accuracy, 288–289
    transitivity and, 290
acons function, 431
acos function, 305
    branch cuts for, 311–312
acosh function, 308
    branch cuts for, 313–314
acute accent ('). *See* single quote
Ada, 17, 111, 231–232, 526
    and and, 111
    integer compatibility notes,
        17

addition (+), 295. *See also*
    numbers
add-method generic function,
    817
add-method primary method,
    817
adjoin function, 427
adjustable array, 452
adjustable-array-p function,
    452
    vector-push-extend and, 455
:adjustable keyword
    in arrays, 444, 445, 452, 457
adjust-array function,
    456– 459
:after method, 796–797
agreement, on parameter
    specializers and qualifiers,
        791
Algol, 43–44
a-list. *See* association lists
allocate-instance, 803
allocation, of slots, 778–779
:allocation keyword slot
    option, 776, 778, 779, 824
:allow-other-keys keyword
    82–83
    initialization argument
        validity and, 804
&allow-other-keys lambda-
    list keyword, 77, 80, 83
    apply and, 146
    defmacro and, 196
    destructuring and, 205
    in function type specifier, 57
    in generic functions and
        methods, 792
    positional constructors and, 483
alphabetic
    characters, in tokens, 517
    ordering, 378–379
alpha-char-p function, 376,
    377
alphanumeric characters, 378

alphanumericp function, 378
alter function, 942
alteration, of a series, 942–943
always construct
    end-test control and, 726
    loop clause, 727–728
    termination conditions and,
        713
amber, meaning of, 525
ampersand (&), for lambda-list
    keywords, 76
anagrams, 556
and macro, 110–111
    multiple iteration and, 716
    multiple values and, 185
    type specifier, 52
    See also conditionals; if; when;
        unless; until
Andrews, Julie, 226
anonymous restarts, 875–877
ANSI Common Lisp system, in
    common-lisp package, 258, 278
antimony, 281, 285
APL, 29, 31, 34, 308, 309, 314,
    924
apostrophe ('). *See* single quote
apples, 178
apples, compared with oranges,
    225–226
append function, 418; 12
    loop clause, 732
    loop keyword, 730
    See also concatenate
:append keyword, in open, 649
appending, 730
    loop clause, 732
Apple Macintosh, 618
    extended keyboards, 386
applicable methods, 790, 832
    applying method combination
        to sorted list of, 794–795
    keyword arguments, 792–793
    lack of, 850
    selecting, 794

Index of Constants

Index of Functions

Index of Generic Functions

Index of Loop Clauses

Index of Macros

Index of Special Forms

Index of Variables